Baseball
Prospectus

1999 Edition

Baseball
Prospectus

1999 Edition

Clay Davenport
Rany Jazayerli
Chris Kahrl
Keith Law
Dave Pease
Steven Rubio
Joseph S. Sheehan
Mike Wolverton
Keith Woolner

Brassey's Sports

Brassey's

An Imprint of Batsford Brassey, Inc.
WASHINGTON • LONDON

Editorial Offices:
22883 Quicksilver Drive
Dulles, VA 20166

Order Department:
P.O. Box 960
Herndon, VA 20172

Batsford Brassey books are available at special discounts for bulk purchases for sales promotions, premiums, fund-raising, or educational use.

Designed by Pen & Palette Unlimited

First Edition
10 9 8 7 6 5 4 3 2 1
Printed in the United States of America

Dedications

Rany Jazayerli: I dedicate this one to my best friend, Belsam, who by the most fortunate coincidence is also my wife.

Chris Kahrl: I'd like to dedicate this year's effort to my favorite travelling companion and drinking buddy, my wife, Stephanie. I'd also like to dedicate this book to my late great-grandfather, whose stories about Mel Ott and the Polo Grounds thrilled one young historically minded baseball fan.

Keith Law: To Christa, for love, support, and encouragement; to my family, for the same; to friends, classmates, faculty, and co-workers for the support you've given me over the past two years: thank you all.

Steven Rubio: Having noticed that every dedication in last year's book except his own included hosannas to significant others, Steven Rubio would like to dedicate his contributions to his wife, Robin Smith, without whom there would be no season tickets.

Joseph S. Sheehan: I dedicate my work on this book to my wife's parents, Henry and Angie Gonzalez. Over the four years of my involvement in this project, their support has been overwhelming and underappreciated. Thank you from the bottom of my heart. And to the 1,215 people I'm not mentioning here, know that you're not forgotten.

Mike Wolverton: I want to thank my wife Cindy for putting up with my baseball obsession over the past decade, and both her and my son Scott for putting up with my baseball obsession in the decades to come.

Keith Woolner: This year's MVP goes to my wife Kathy for suffering through deadline-induced widowhood, especially when she thought she was all done with all that silliness after the World Series. Posthumous thanks to Freddy Parent, the shortstop on the 1903 World Champion Boston Red Sox, for employing my grandfather at his gas station as a boy. Thanks to Nate C. and Tom F. (my Stathead co-conspirators), and to the readership of Red Sox list (there is life after Mo, I promise). A big thanks to Craig Wright for his pioneering work on evaluating catcher's defense, which inspired my article digging deeper into the topic. Lastly, thanks to every ball player I've had the privilege of seeing play in person, except for Joe Rudi.

Contents

Fungoes

Introduction

Welcome to *Baseball Prospectus 1999*, and thanks for either picking it up for a peek on a bookstore shelf, or for ordering or buying the book. We hope you'll end up agreeing with us that what you have here is the best baseball annual in the world. Whether you're a baseball fan or a serious rotogeek or a big-time stathead, we have the book for you.

Why do you need this book? We want to give you the kind of information that lets you draw your own conclusions about players and player talent. As much information as is being generated and made available in today's sports world for consumption by fans, useful interpretation of that information seems pretty rare, and rarer still is the stuff that's fun to read. My old man gripes about "baseball numerology," and he has a point. The *Baseball Prospectus* is supposed to give you a blend of opinion, fact, and some educated guesses that will hopefully be only the beginning in terms of your own journey into learning how to separate fact from a happily reported Joe Randa signing in a neighborhood near you.

Why is it important for you to come to your own conclusions? Baseball, like any organization or institution, has its share of cherished myths that need to be reevaluated to see whether they're telling us any kind of objective truth. Through the research reflected in this book, we hope you'll reevaluate both how you think about the game and how you come to form your opinions about some players. Just as we're willing to take some good-natured potshots at popular interpretations of anything related to baseball, we're also committed to evaluating the statistical tools that have been created over the years, to see if they really convey information we can use to draw useful conclusions. Statistical research of baseball isn't new anymore, and fortunately or not, some of the concepts and new statistics that were revolutionary or exciting fifteen or twenty years ago have gone without being checked up on in the meantime to see if they were true in the first place. One of our first projects on this score is Keith Woolner's evaluation of whether or not a statistic like Catcher ERA (CERA) reflects a catcher's game-calling skills or not.

You'll find that we have some format changes between this year's edition and previous ones. First off, the "extra guys" have been taken out of the end of each team chapter, and put together as an alphabetical appendix in the back. Readers said that finding the more obscure minor league players alphabetically would be more useful, and we aim to please. You may also notice some changes in our basic tool for player evaluation, the Davenport Translations. First off, we've made room to include secondary defensive positions for players who played more than one position. Although we're not forecasting pitcher performance this year, in his explanatory essay about the Davenport Translations, Clay gives you some tips about how to use a pitcher's recent statistics in categories like KWH and Peripheral ERA (PERA) to make some educated guesses about a pitcher's future. We're also introducing our new hitter projection tool, Wilton (following in the footsteps of our old tool, Vlad II). Early performance reviews indicate that Wilton does a slightly better job of forecasting than Vlad II did, while retaining a similar willingness to take some risks and project breakouts for younger players. Keep in mind that our projections for '99 are park-adjusted, so what you see is what we expect if offensive levels stay at the same level they've been at for the past three years.

You'll also find that we've added two boxes to the end of each major league team chapter: Mike Wolverton's Support-Neutral Won-Loss Report for that team, and Rany Jazayerli's Pitcher Abuse Points Report. In terms of giving you the tools you should have to interpret major league pitching performance, we think these are handier to have within their teams' chapters. You can kick around some of the ideas these sections convey after reading through the initial chapters where Mike and Rany explain what they're doing. I think you'll enjoy using them to form your own opinions about what you can expect from a team's major league pitchers in the coming season.

Finally, I'd like to waste some of your valuable time by offering a word of thanks to some very special people who have helped to make *Baseball Prospectus 1999* possible. To Gary Huckabay, we owe a debt of gratitude for creating this project in the first place. I'd like to thank Greg Spira for his constant suggestions on how to improve our web site and for his willingness to fill a special niche within the BP family as a sort of special projects coordinator. He's the brains behind the constantly growing Internet Baseball Awards, and has also helped to put together a projection tools survey that we hope you'll check out on our web page. I'd like to also thank Joe Sheehan for his layout and editing expertise.

Beyond the immediate BP family, I'd like to also thank the good folks at Brassey's, especially Ron Davis and Don McKeon. I'd like to offer special praise to Don Rodgers of Pen & Palette for his slaving away on the layout of this year's book. Finally, for their contributions to the Baseball Prospectus web site, we'd like to thank the following people: Steven Carter, Jeff Bower, Andres Phippard, Tony Soltero, James Kushner, Gregg Pearlman, Brian Jenkins, John Mayne, King Banaian, Felix Wisgo, and Jeff Pease. We don't pretend to have all the good ideas, and we're grateful that our readers are willing and able to contribute interesting content to our web site. I strongly recommend you check our site out: www.baseballprospectus.com. Lastly, we'd like to acknowledge Craig Wright, a baseball research pioneer whose work helped to inspire some of the BP crew in their own research efforts.

We appreciate your feedback on what you want to see in future editions of the *Prospectus*, what you think is interesting, and what we can do to continue to provide you with a good book. Our goal all along is to write the kind of book we'd like to read, and when I say "we," I mean you and me and every baseball fan. Enjoy yourself, and let us know what you think.

Chris Kahrl
Chicago

Davenport Translations

by Clay Davenport

The statistics used here at the BP are the structural framework of the book, the starting point from which most discussions follow. As such, it is very important for you to understand what these tools are and have at least some idea of how they work.

Translations

One of the most difficult tasks in analyzing statistics, major or minor, is comparing numbers from different leagues. That is why Davenport Translations (DTs), are the single most important tool in this book. The DTs allow us to take any player, regardless of what league he played in, and estimate what his stats would have been had he had displayed the same level of skill in some other league. This is similar to the Major League Equivalencies (MLEs) developed by Bill James in the 1980s. There are several significant differences between the two, however.

The MLE process usually converts the statistics of a Triple-A or Double-A player to the home park of the parent club. While useful for making a prediction of a rookie player's statistics for next year, it makes it difficult to compare a Boston farmhand's MLE to that of a Houston player. In order to compare the same player's MLE in two different seasons, you have the same problem, plus a sample size problem: STATS Inc., which now publishes the MLEs, only presents one MLE season at a time. There is no MLE for a player like Deivi Cruz, who came from A ball directly to the majors; MLEs don't cover A-ball. And there is nothing for pitchers at all.

The DTs have a different underlying philosophy. We're not very worried about the actual player numbers, preferring instead to focus on their value. To make player comparisons as easy as possible, the DTs convert the statistics of all players to a single, unified scale: not just Triple-A and Double-A players, but every player and pitcher, from the majors all the way down to the Pioneer and Appalachian Leagues. And not just for last year; you need to see a sequence of at least three years, so that you can see progress, regress, and the fluke years that stick out like dislocated pinkies.

For every player in the book, **the printed lines are his Translated statistics, not his real statistics.** All batter statistics are translated to a league that resembles the major leagues of the mid-1990s: one with a .260 batting average, .330 on-base average, and .420 slugging average. Pitcher statistics are converted to a similar round number scale, albeit a bit more favorable than real life: a league with a 4.00 ERA,

giving up exactly 9 hits, 3 walks, and 6 strikeouts per nine innings. Doing this makes it as easy as possible to tell how the player compares to the average.

The real statistics of a player can be misleading. A player's statistical line is the product of many factors, and the internal rating scheme each of us carries around in our heads to make snap judgments that this line is "good" and that line is "bad" is not very good at taking all of those other forces into account or at giving them the proper weight. People make judgments based on what we consider "normal," which for the majority of us means the majors, in the first five years or so we were seriously interested in baseball. The standards we use—a .300 average, a 20-win season, a 3.00 ERA, 40 home runs—were the product of a place and time, and make as little sense for evaluating a 1998 Carolina League player as trying to use a single dime in a pay phone.

Of the forces that control a player's statistics, the only one we really care about is the player's performance. The others, which we need to eliminate, include:

- League offense. Being a good hitter doesn't depend on having a high batting average, slugging average, or on-base average, but on having *better* statistics than the other players in the league. The single most important thing to do when analyzing player statistics is to compare his performance to the average player in his league—in short, to normalize it.
- Park. The player's home park can seriously distort his apparent value. This is usually not as important as the league adjustment, although in an extreme park, like Coors Field, it can change a player's value by up to 30%. The factor works both ways. While Coors inflates a player's value, a park like Vancouver's in the PCL makes a 15-20% dent in a hitter's statistics. But what's good for the hitter is bad for the pitcher... and the other way around.
- The level of competition. Other things being equal, hitting against better pitchers and better fielders results in worse batting statistics. League quality runs downhill from the major leagues, through Triple-A and Double-A, into the high-A leagues (Florida, California, and Carolina), to slow-A (Midwest and South Atlantic), to short-season A and rookie leagues. Each step tends to knock off about 15% of the player's relative value.
- His age, especially compared to his peers. The mixture of knowledge, skill, and physical ability that makes a

ballplayer typically peaks in the late 20s. Younger than that and physical tools rule; older than that, and aging starts to cut into their speed, eyesight, and strength, leaving them unable to use their knowledge of the game to the fullest extent. The younger they are when they start to achieve, the longer they'll have to develop their talent to its fullest. In the minors, an older player has an extra something that can set him apart from his teammates: an edge in experience or physical development or something else that leads to better performance, but usually disappears when he moves into a more appropriate league for his age.

The Translations' job is to eliminate those surrounding biases to reveal only the core performance. How?

The first step is to compare the statistics of a player to the league in which he played and to the statistics of a destination league—the league to which you'll convert the statistics. For instance, let's look at Paul Konerko's 1997 season, and convert it to our standard season:

	AB	H	DB	TP	HR	BB	SB	CS	BA	OBA	SA
Konerko, 1997	483	156	31	1	37	64	2	3	.323	.402	.621
PCL, 1997	494	145	31	4	15	53	10	5	.293	.362	.465
Standard	495	129	26	3	16	52	9	5	.260	.330	.420

Konerko was *Baseball America*'s Minor League Player of the Year in 1997, on the basis of an impressive batting season... but look at how high the offense was in the PCL in 1997! The standardized season matches up reasonably well with the high-offense 1990s, but the PCL blows it away. In fact, the 1997 PCL had a higher OBA and a higher SA than the 1930 National League (.358/.458), the highest-offense major league season in the twentieth century (the 1890s had some higher ones, peaking in 1894). It was, in fact, the highest offense league in Organized Baseball in at least twenty years.

As if that weren't enough, he's playing in an extreme hitter's park. Playing half of your games in Albuquerque inflates offense by about 10%. The first thing we do is calculate his park- and league-adjusted Equivalent Average (see below), which tells us how his total offense compares to his league. Paul gets a .302 (based on Albuquerque's 1.094 park factor and the PCL values shown in the appendix). The difficulty adjustment (.9089, from the appendix) is a measure of how much the average player would lose in EqA between this league and the standard league; that brings Paul's EqA down to a less unimpressive .275 (don't get me wrong; few 21-year-olds are capable of hitting that well). We are deceived by the impressiveness of his raw numbers; those same numbers, in the 1998 National League, would have produced a .336 EqA, roughly equal to Jim Thome.

The first rule in translating is that the resulting numbers have to produce the identical EqA in the destination league—

in this case, .275. Batting outs (AB-H, 327) provide the starting point. A first guess OBA, essentially the relative OBA (OBA1/OBA2 × OBA3, where 1 refers to the player, 2 to his actual league, 3 to the destination league) is made, which would be .366; other adjustments, for the difficulty rating and park factors, bring that down further, to .354. That allows you to set plate appearances at (outs/(1-OBA)), or 506.

Walk rates (BB/AB) come from a simple normalizing procedure (BBR1/BBR2 × BBR3), which yields us .1300. That gets multiplied by the difficulty rating to give us .118. Now we can split our 506 PA into (506/(1+.118)) = 453 at-bats and 53 walks.

The remaining elements don't come so easily. A first guess at each of singles, doubles, triples, and home runs is made through simple normalization plus the difficulty adjustment, in much the same way as the walks. For Konerko, that first guess looks like

	AB	H	DB	TP	HR	BB	SB	CS
Konerko 1st guess	453	123	22	1	34	53	—	—

Trouble is, this line produces a .298 EqA. To get that down to .275, the program looks at a number of other variables, such as the double:home run ratio for the player and both leagues. These ratios are crucial to the next step: an iterative procedure that must produce an EqA of .275, while balancing the relative contribution of each element to their genuine values. For instance, the double:homer ratios of Konerko (.838), the PCL (2.067), and the standard (1.600) suggests that Konerko's db:hr ratio in the standard sleague should be about .649. The program starts adding or subtracting hits, doubles, and so forth, always testing it against the desired EqA and the various ratios (not all of which are equally important; the batting average as a percentage of total offense, for instance, is more important than triples), until it finds one that has the right EqA and minimizes the error in the various ratios. The final line...

	AB	H	DB	TP	HR	BB	SB	CS	BA	OBA	SA	EQA
Konerko DT	453	118	15	1	26	53	2	2	.260	.338	.470	.275

... reflects the multiple balancing act. Most of the cuts needed to pare the EqA down to .275 from the first guess were taken from power; the needs of the BA ratios kept it from dropping any further than .260.

Pitcher DTs are made by converting the pitching lines into batting lines and proceeding from there. Some things are different. The difficulty ratings for leagues are not quite as sharp for pitchers as for hitters, since the improvement in fielding mitigates the improvement in opposing hitters. Team defense is an important consideration, and not simply for unearned runs; a wide-ranging shortstop who turns singles into outs saves a pitcher earned runs as well.

Equivalent Average and Equivalent Runs (EqA and EqR)

The DTs may be the primary tool of the book, but EqA is close behind. EqA is not a part of the DTs, but a stand-alone tool to rate a player's total offensive contribution, adjusted for league and park. EqR measures the total contribution, in terms of runs; EqA measures the rate, in terms proportional to the familiar batting average scale.

EqA developed, in numerous steps over a period of years, from a combination of batting average and the Bill James statistic secondary average. That combination was inherently close to the scale of batting average, although my refinements carried it away from that. The basic, starting formula, the "Raw EqA" or "REQA" or "Raw", is

$$\text{Raw EqA} = \frac{H + TB + SB + 1.5\,BB}{AB + BB + CS + \dfrac{SB}{3}}$$

For example, the raw EqA for Mark McGwire in 1998 is

$$\frac{(152\,H + 383\,TB + 1\,SB + 162 \times 1.5\,BB)}{(509\,AB + 162\,BB + 0\,CS + \tfrac{1}{3}\,SB)}$$

or

779/671.333,

or

1.160.

Sharp-eyed readers may note that I have made a small change in the formula, switching from a ⅔ BB in the denominator to ½ BB in the numerator. That simplifies the formula a bit, as well as gaining a small, albeit insignificant, edge in accuracy.

Raw EqA is very strongly related to run scoring; more so than OPS, which it resembles. Ignoring the stolen base terms for a moment, we see that
Raw EqA looks like:

$$\frac{H + 1.5\,BB + TB}{AB + BB}$$

while OPS looks like:

$$\frac{H + BB}{AB + BB} + \frac{TB}{AB}$$

Those who have taken a close look at OPS have found that the two "pieces" are not exactly equal. Because the slugging average of a league is typically about 25% higher than the league on-base average (see the 1998 NL: .410 slugging, .328 on-base, +25%), a point of on-base is worth about 1.25 points of slugging.

The raw EqA formula can be broken up into an "on-base component" (H + 1.5 BB) and a "slugging component" (TB), each divided by AB+BB. EqA effectively equalizes the two

components; compared to OPS, it raises the on-base side (by counting walks higher), and reduces the slugging side (by dividing by plate appearances). For the 1998 NL, the on-base component would be .372, the slugging component .374, less than a 1% difference.

The whole point of developing the equation is to be able to relate it to run scoring . . . which brings up a second question that needs to be answered before continuing.

There is a difference between runs produced by a team and runs produced by a player who is part of a team. Actions leading to run scoring are cumulative; a double produces no runs unless it was preceded by or followed by more hits and walks. When you are looking at the entire team, or at pitchers, there's no problem; the stats reflect a full sequence, even if you don't know what the spacing was. But when you look at one player you don't see a full sequence; by the time Ken Griffey bats again, the effects of Ken Griffey's previous appearance have long since been resolved.

This second type of run value, being part of a greater whole, has been called the marginal value of a player's runs by other analysts. I'm going to refer to the first type as the absolute value; it represents the number of runs a team with these statistics would score (or, alternatively, what a team of nine Ken Griffeys would score). Runs Created, the best-known formula for estimating runs, calculates the absolute run value. And the absolute type of the equivalent run formula looks like

$$EqR_{(absolute)} = \left(\frac{REQA}{LgREQA}\right)^2 \times PA \times \frac{LgR}{LgPA}$$

Anything that starts with "Lg" means use the league value of that statistic; PA is at-bats plus walks.

In words, a team's run production rate, per plate appearance, goes up as the square of his relative REQA. The 1998 Yankees had a team REQA of .8355, compared to a league REQA of .7824; combine that information with 6296 plate appearances and a league average of .1319 runs per plate appearance, and you get an EqR of 947 runs. The Yankees actually scored 965 runs, so the EqR was a little short; however, the estimates from other equations was worse (Linear weights produces a 934 estimate, Runs Created 935).

If you look at the entire 1990s, the Equivalent Runs formula given above has been off by an average of 22.72 runs. Linear weights, modified to produce runs scored instead of runs above or below average, has been off by 23.08 runs over that time. Runs created, modified to allow it to use league runs scored as a known variable (as EqR and LW both do) has an average error of 23.71 runs; without the modification it would miss by 25.16. OPS actually does better than RC; using the proper formula for OPS (OBA/LgOBA + SA/LgSA -1), it has an average error of 23.62. Done improperly, though, the way it is normally done (comparing OPS to the league OPS, instead of each component separately), and the accuracy drops to 24.15. Try to estimate runs from batting average, though, and the best you can do is an error of 43.05 runs.

The best way to figure out the marginal value of a player is to calculate EqR, using the absolute formula, for the larger whole—his team, or even his league. Then subtract out the individual's at-bats, hits, and so forth, to get a league without Player X. Calculate that EqR. The difference between the EqRs with the player and the EqR without the player is his marginal value. And that is too much work. Fortunately, in EqR, we can approximate that result with the following formula:

$$EqR_{(marginal)} = 2 \times \frac{REQA}{LgREQA} - 1 \times PA \times \frac{LgR}{LgPA}$$

The 1998 NL REQA was .7525, and its runs per plate appearance was .1225, as can be found in the appendix. McGwire's EqR is $2 \times (1.160/.7525) - 1$, or 2.083 times his 671 PA times .1225, for a total of 171 equivalent runs.

Instead of going up as the square of the relative REQA, an exponential function, it goes up as the linear $2x - 1$. Had we used the team formula on McGwire's statistics, we would have gotten 195 runs.

Basic EqR is important—it's what I use to verify the accuracy of the formula, for instance—but we are primarily interested in park and league adjusted values. We cannot say with any certainty how an individual player will react to a different park or league. We can be a lot more confident about how an average player sent to that park would do, though, and the adjustment technique relies on that. In the EqA system, adjustments are applied to the league, not the individual. The adjusted league raw EqA is

$$ALgREQA = \left(\frac{PF \times LgRPO \times DH}{.17235} + 1 \right) \times \frac{1}{2} \times LgREQA$$

PF is the park factor. For St. Louis last year, it was 1.023. LgRPO is league runs per out, .1801. DH is an adjustment for whether the league has a DH or not; it's 1.00 in the NL, and .95 in every other 1998 league. The ".17235" is close to the long-term average of major league runs per out. For McGwire and the rest of the Cardinals, the ALgREQA is .7785.

And then EPER, which is adjusted EqR, comes the same way as EQR did; for individuals,

$$EPER_{(marginal)} = \left(2 \times \frac{REQA}{ALgREQA} - 1 \right) \times PA \times \frac{LgR}{LgPA}$$

or for teams,

$$EPER_{(absolute)} = \left(\frac{REQA}{ALgREQA} \right)^2 \times PA \times \frac{LgR}{LgPA}$$

McGwire's EPER is $2 \times 1.160/.7785 - 1$, or 1.9801, times 671 times .1225, or 163. That is tied for 21st on the all-time single-season list.

EPER are as good a measure of a player's total offensive contribution as you will find anywhere, but a total statistic is only part of the package. We also need to know the rate. The person with the best batting average, for instance, gets far more acclaim than the man with the most hits, to take the best-known rate and total pair. I believe that the person who should be acclaimed the best hitter is the one who produces the most EPER per out made—outs being baseball's clock. But the rate statistic I use is not the nice, simple EPER divided by outs. There's a reason for this.

While batting average has many flaws as a primary evaluation tool, it does have one enormous advantage: familiarity. I don't mean how to calculate it—I mean that anybody who is any kind of baseball fan has an intuitive sense of how good or bad a number is if it is a batting average. Just say "Three thirty-seven"; you probably have a good idea of where that stands on the all-time leader board, or where that place in the race for a batting title within a season. You know that its awfully good, possibly good enough to win a batting title, but nowhere near a record.

Even though batting average should be retired from its perch of measuring how good a "hitter" someone is, it would be a shame to lose that intuitive feel for a number that the batting average scale provides us. So I copied it.

The formula for Equivalent Average that follows is complicated because I'm forcing it into a scale that doesn't fit it, like the Greek myth of Procrustes (an innkeeper who made sure his one bed fit all his guests perfectly, by subjecting them to an ax or a rack). As a result, I've got a rating that is based on a player's total offensive performance per out made, yet is immediately comprehensible as "good," "bad," "record-setting," or "back to the minors." Lifetime goals like a career .300 average have almost the exact same meaning with EqA that they do with batting average, because in either case, about 150 players have done it.

Single-season and career records for adjusted EqA are also similar to batting average. The best EqA in major league history—using official baseball's definition of major league—belongs to Fred Dunlap, who put up a .433 EqA in the 1884 Union Association, a joke as far as major leagues go. A more rational definition would say that Babe Ruth's .425 in 1920 was the best. That is right in the neighborhood of the batting average record, whether you look at Hornsby in '24 (.424), or Lajoie '01 (.426), or Hugh Duffy (.440 in 1894). Career, Ruth's .380 EqA is a little higher than Cobb's .366.

Getting the EqA to come out like that wasn't easy, though; like Procrustes, we have to torture the numbers to do it. The final step of the puzzle, the adjusted EqA or "EPEqA," is:

$$EPEQA = \left(\frac{EPER}{5 \times (AB - H + CS)} \right)^{0.4}$$

For McGwire, 163 EPER, divided by 5, divided by 357 outs, is .0913; raise that to the ⅖ power, and you get .384. McGwire's .384 EPEQA is the 26th best in major league history.

That last bit means "raised to the two-fifths power," which your calculator may not be able to handle with ease. The world doesn't always conform to simpler relationships. This also explains why the value of .17235 was used in the EPER equation as a standard value of runs per out: because it makes the average team come out to .260, on the nose to the fifth decimal place. And that's good for not other reason than because .260 is the round number closest to Major League Baseball's all-time batting average. Using .260, then, is the mean Equivalent Average of every league in history, after league adjustments have been applied. Pretty much everywhere in the book, when we say EqA or EqR, we are talking about EPEqA or EPER.

Fielding

Defense can be a substantial part of a player's game, and is too easily ignored by statistical analysts. No one else makes the same effort to make sense of minor league defensive statistics as we do at BP.

Our defensive measures are similar in approach to the Fielding Runs (FR) developed by Pete Palmer and Total Baseball: the key to a good rating is to make more plays per opportunity than an average player. It is not simply avoiding errors; in fact, range is more important.

For all players, we break down the total games played into an estimate of innings played. Infielders are rated on assists and errors per inning; outfielders, on putouts, assists, and errors per game. We do have catcher defense rated this year, albeit only for 1998: caught stealing and pickoffs are good, stolen bases, passed balls, and errors are bad. Admittedly, crucial parts of player defense are overlooked because the data is either totally unavailable or blurred beyond recognition: the ability of a catcher to handle a pitching staff, of infielders to catch line drives, first basemen who go to the bag for unassisted putouts, outfielders whose reputation makes runners come to a halt.

A major difference between our unnamed ratings and FR is that ours are based on the idea of a replacement level fielder, not league average. A replacement fielder is, roughly, the worst in the league at a given position who still gets to play it. Doing this automatically scales the position towards its value: an average shortstop, for instance, will be worth about 33 runs more than a replacement-level shortstop, while an average first baseman is only about 12 runs better than his replacement counterpart. That difference, 21 runs, is about the same as the offensive difference between the two positions.

Furthermore, we have attempted to correct for certain biases that afflict the fielding statistics. Balls in play depends on more than just strikeouts, for instance; the failure to account for hits causes FR to overestimate the value of players on a poor-fielding team, and underestimate those on a good-fielding team. The ground/fly ratio and left/right breakdown of the staff affect where batted balls go into play, and can be adjusted for; these can lead to drastic differences from FR.

Reading the Hitter DT

Bubba Trammell		OF						Age 27											
YEAR	TEAM	LGE	AB	H	DB	TP	HR	BB	R	RBI	SB	CS	OUT	BA	OBA	SA	EQA	EQR	DEFENSE
1996	Jacksnvl	Sou	309	93	13	1	19	23	40	55	2	1	217	.301	.349	.534	.295	51	66-OF 88
1996	Toledo	Int	178	48	10	1	5	21	25	22	4	1	131	.270	.347	.421	.269	25	45-OF 97
1997	Toledo	Int	322	79	9	1	22	31	36	50	2	2	245	.245	.312	.484	.266	45	74-OF 82
1997	Detroit	AL	121	27	5	0	4	15	14	12	3	1	95	.223	.309	.364	.238	13	19-OF 108
1998	Durham	Int	216	56	7	0	11	30	29	32	4	1	161	.259	.350	.444	.276	32	55-OF 94
1998	TampaBay	AL	195	54	16	1	12	17	26	34	0	2	143	.277	.335	.554	.290	32	31-OF 93
1999	*TampaBay*	*AL*	*475*	*128*	*20*	*1*	*29*	*49*	*64*	*81*	*5*	*3*	*350*	*.269*	*.338*	*.499*	*.278*	*72*	

The first line consists of the player's name, his primary position, and his age on June 30, 1999.

Year, team, and league are self-explanatory. For most players, their translated 1996-98 statistics are shown. Trivial appearances, such as a player's rehab assignment, cups of coffee, or other lines with fewer than 50 plate appearances are usually dropped. 1995 data is included for players who missed all of one of one of the last three seasons.

The 1999 line is different. It is a projection, made to the expected standards of the 1999 season and the indicated park. It is not a translation, but our best guess at what his actual 1999 statistics would look like if he spent 1999 in the majors. Almost every hitter in the book has a projection line; that does not mean we expect every hitter to play in the majors next season. Playing time is primarily based on his playing time in recent seasons, at whatever level he was in; it is not meant to be a serious estimate of his actual playing time.

At-Bats, Hits, Doubles, Triples, Home Runs, Bases on Balls, Stolen Bases, Caught Stealing, Outs (AB–H+CS), Batting Average, On-Base Average, Slugging Average, Equivalent Average, and Equivalent Runs are all produced from the translation process; that process, along with EqA and EqR, are were previously discussed in some detail. A perfectly average player would have the following statistics:

BA – Batting average	.260
OBA – On-base average	.330
SA – Slugging average	.420
AB – At-bats	500
H – Hits	130
DB – Doubles	26
TP – Triples	3
HR – Home runs	16
BB – Walks	52
SB – Steals	9

CS – Caught stealing	5	(rounded off; actually an exact 2:1 sb:cs ratio).
EQA – Equivalent average	.260	
EQR – Equivalent runs	65	

Runs and RBIs are estimated from the batter's style. Style—by which I mean how much of his production comes from singles, from home runs, and so on—strongly determines whether the player's run production will be expressed more in the scoring of runs or the driving in of runs: see Rickey Henderson for an example of the former, Juan Gonzalez for an example of the latter. The estimated R and RBI values do not take into account batting order position or quality of teammates, both of which are important variables.

Defense shows the player's performance rate at the position, or top two positions, at which he played at least 15 games. The number-hyphen-position combination indicates full games played; Trammell is rated as having played in 66 games in the outfield in 1996 for Jacksonville. The number afterwards is a rating; 100 is average, 85 is replacement level, 110 is solid Gold-Glove material. The system becomes more reliable as the games played increases; Trammell, a poor fielder (average rating, 91) was able to get a 108 rating for 19 games at Detroit in 1997, but that has to be regarded as a fluke due to the small sample size. I'm not really comfortable with the ratings for anything under 50 games.

The Pitcher DT

Mike Mussina			RHP					Age 30								
YEAR	TEAM	LGE	IP	H	ER	HR	BB	K	ERA	W	L	H/9	HR/9	BB/9	K/9	KWH	PERA
1996	Baltimor	AL	244.0	258	110	27	55	201	4.06	13	14	9.52	1.00	2.03	7.41	2.14	3.95
1997	Baltimor	AL	227.0	199	76	25	47	211	3.01	16	9	7.89	0.99	1.86	8.37	3.57	2.97
1998	Baltimor	AL	208.7	185	70	21	37	169	3.02	15	8	7.98	0.91	1.60	7.29	3.13	2.93

Pitcher Translations are translated to a different league from the hitters, with the idea being to make the table as easy to follow as we can. Towards that end, the standard pitching league has the following characteristics:

An Earned Run Average (**ERA**) of exactly	4.00
Hits per nine innings (**H/9**)	9.00
Homers per nine innings (**HR/9**)	1.00
Walks per nine innings (**BB/9**)	3.00
Strikeouts per nine (**K/9**)	6.00

As for hitters, the age is for June 30, 1999. Innings, hits, earned runs, walks, and strikeouts, and the various per nine inning ratios that go with them, are directly produced from the translation.

Wins and losses are apportioned by assuming the pitcher is backed by an average offense and that he gets one decision per nine innings of work. Actual wins and losses will track the number of decisions closely, but will depend very much on actual run support. Any pitcher with a translated ERA under 4.00 will be shown as having a winning record; any ERA over 4.00 will show a losing record.

The two unfamiliar elements in the line are KWH and PERA. KWH is a measure of the pitcher's "stuff." It is defined as

$$KWH = \frac{K \times K}{H \times BB} \times 0.75$$

The "× 0.75" is there to make the league average KWH come out to 1.00. Looked at another way, it is the K:W ratio times the K:H ratio. What we have found is that, given two pitchers who have the same ERA this season, the one with the better KWH is about twice as likely to be a better pitcher during the following season. Pitchers with KWH above 1.00 are 50% more likely than their sub-1.00 counterparts to still be pitching four years from now, and more than twice as likely to still be pitching effectively, even though they had the same ERA and age in the original season. Minor leaguers who can get their KWH above 1.00 are three times as likely to get promoted to the majors. In fact, KWH has a better correlation with getting promoted than does their DT-ERA in the minors.

PERA is "peripheral ERA": it is the ERA that one would expect from the pitcher's innings, hits, home runs, and walks. It is usually quite close to the actual ERA, although for some pitchers (check out Kerry Wood) the difference can be extreme. In most cases, PERA functions as a sort of luck indicator: PERA is actually a better indicator of next year's ERA than this year's ERA is. There is a 70% chance that next year's ERA will move in the direction of this year's PERA.

Support-Neutral Records

by Michael Wolverton

Measuring the value of individual starts is an idea that's gained acceptance over the past couple of decades, both among serious baseball analysts and even among the mainstream baseball media. By looking at a pitcher's performance start by start, the reasoning goes, we can learn something about his consistency throughout the year and how that impacted his team—something we can't get by looking at average or cumulative run prevention.

However, the two most prominent tools developed for evaluating individual starts, Quality Starts and Bill James's Game Score, each have serious limitations as measures of pitching performance. The arguments against Quality Starts are well known. Detractors point out that the worst qualifying outing—6 innings and 3 earned runs—is not "quality" at all. Furthermore, Quality Starts makes no attempt to quantify the degree of quality a start has—6 innings, 3 runs is the same as 8 innings, 2 runs which is the same as a 9-inning shutout. In short, it's too crude a measure. Partly in response to this crudeness problem, Bill James developed the Game Score, which is a weighted sum of the numbers associated with a start in a box score (IP, H, R, ER, BB, K). Game Score is acknowledged as an interesting measure of "game domination" by a starter, but it has weaknesses as a total measure of starter quality (i.e., his contribution to team victories): the weights on the terms are more or less arbitrary, it's too dependent on strikeouts, and it isn't park-adjusted.

Despite the weaknesses of these two measures, looking at a pitcher's starts game-by-game is still a good idea. Evaluating each start's contribution to winning, rather than cumulative run-prevention over the course of a year (ERA or Pitching Runs), can help us answer questions like: Given equal ERAs, do some pitchers pitch in a way that will tend to win more games than other pitchers? In particular, is it better for a starter to be flaky—either very good or very bad on a given day—or consistently average? Does the park have a smaller influence on the value of the start when the start is very good or very bad? The key, of course, is developing statistics that measure the start's impact on winning the game.

A collection of measures I've been working with does just that. I've given the measures the heading "Support-Neutral," because they measure a starter's contribution to winning and losing irrespective of the support he receives from his team's offense and bullpen. A starter's Support-Neutral W/L record (SNW/SNL) is his expected (in the statistical sense) W/L record—how many games he would be expected to win and lose given his pitching performances,

assuming he had a league average offense and bullpen behind him. A starter's Support-Neutral Value Added (SNVA) measures the total number of extra games his team would be expected to win with his pitching performances instead of an average pitcher. The game-by-game perspective of the SN stats removes distortions that can be introduced in cumulative run prevention stats like ERA and Thorn and Palmer's Adjusted Pitching Wins (APW). As a result, I think the SN stats give a more accurate pitcher of a starter's value than APW.

How They're Calculated

The basic idea behind the calculation of the SN stats is pretty simple. I'll use SN Wins (SNW) to illustrate. A starter's SNW total is calculated by determining, for each individual start he makes over the season, the probability that he would get the win given the way he pitched in that game, and then summing up the individual probabilities over all of his starts. The sum gives you the number of wins a pitcher could expect to get for an average team, given his performances. A "performance" here consists only of the number of innings pitched, the number of runs (not earned runs) given up while the starter was in the game, the number of outs and locations of the runners when the starter left the game, the park in which the game was played, and whether the pitcher was at home or on the road—SNW assumes that these are the only things that influence whether the pitcher wins or loses.

Getting these probabilities is a little complicated. The starter gets a W when two things happen: (1) he leaves the game with the lead, and (2) his team holds it without ever giving it up. To get the probability of a pitcher getting a W for an average team, I look at all the different possible sequences of innings that could lead to a W. For example, consider David Cone's start in the famous "Knoblauch's Boner" game 2 of the ALCS (8 IP, 1 R at home). Such a start would result in a W if...

- his team scored 2 in the first 8 innings and his relievers gave up 0 in the 9th, or
- his team scored 3 in the first 8 innings and his relievers gave up 0 in the 9th, or
- his team scored 3 in the first 8 innings and his relievers gave up 1 in the 9th, or
- etc., etc., etc....

I figure out each of the individual probabilities above, except I substitute "league average" for "his," and then combine them using the simplest laws of probability. The individual inning probabilities (e.g., the probability of "average relievers gave up 1 in the 9th") just come from the league single-inning scoring distribution for that year. For example, in 1997 major league teams scored 0 runs in about 71% of the innings, 1 run in 15% of the innings, 2 runs in 7% of the innings, etc. Park effects are figured in by changing the definition of "average team." For example, an average team will score more runs in Coors and fewer in Dodger Stadium, and the run scoring distribution is altered to reflect that.

The end results of all the calculations are three probabilities: the start resulting in a W for the pitcher (SNW), the start resulting in an L for the pitcher (SNL), and the start resulting in a win for an average team (SNVA). Cone's start—8 IP, 1 R at home in Yankee Stadium—calculates to a 0.74 SNW and a 0.05 SNL. This start will result in a *team* win 84% of the time; since SNVA is concerned with comparing a starter to a league average pitcher, and since an average pitcher's starts will presumably result in 50% wins, Cone's start gets an SNVA rating of 0.84—0.5 = 0.34 games above average.

The only major aspect of the SN stats left to explain is how they remove bullpen support from a starter's numbers. The input used to calculate SNW, SNL, and SNVA includes the state of the bases when he leaves the game. So, for example, if a starter gets yanked with 2 outs in the 7th after 3 runs have scored with runners on first and third, and his reliever allows both runners to score, the SN stats will be calculated based on 6 full innings, 3 runs in, and runners on 1st and 3rd with 2 outs, rather than what that game's box score would tell you: 6 full innings, 2 outs, 5 runs allowed.

Why They're Good Measures of Pitcher Value

That's a lot of calculation to go through to get a measure of pitching value. Is it worth it? In particular, do the SN stats tell us anything that Thorn and Palmer's Adjusted Pitching Wins (APW) weren't already telling us? In fact, they do. Consider the following two pitchers:

Pitcher A			Pitcher B		
Start	IP	R	Start	IP	R
Game 1	4	8	Game 1	0	14
Game 2	4	8	Game 2	8	2
TOTAL	8	16	TOTAL	8	16

Any stat based on measuring cumulative run prevention (e.g., ERA and APW) will rate these two pitchers even. But baseball intuition tells us that Pitcher B has helped his team more. An average team is very likely to go 0-2 behind Pitcher A's two starts, but that same average team has a pretty good shot at winning Pitcher B's second game. And the SN stats accurately measure what our intuition tells us: Pitcher A's SNW/L record is right around 0-2 (more accurately, 0.0-1.8) while Pitcher B's SNW/L record is closer to 1-1 (more accu-

rately, 0.6-1.1). Pitcher A's SNVA mark shows him 0.86 games below average, while Pitcher B's SNVA is a much more tolerable 0.27 games below average.

The key insight that causes SN stats to work in this case is: All runs are not created equal.

Pitcher B's Game 1 isn't a whole lot worse than Pitcher A's Game 1, even though he gave up a lot more runs in fewer innings. Cumulative run prevention stats (ERA, APW) treat run number 14 in that game as equal to run number 1, and that's where they go wrong. In fact, APW concludes that Pitcher B's start in Game 1 cost his team well over a full game in the standings—an absolute impossibility. SNVA's conclusion is a much more reasonable .5 game cost—he guaranteed them a single loss, and that's all.

That's easy to show with hypothetical examples, but do SN stats and APW tell us anything different about the value of real pitchers? Yes, quite often. Here's a pronounced example—the 1992 records of Charlie Leibrandt and Melido Perez:

	APW	SNVA
Leibrandt	0.85	1.55
Perez,M	2.46	1.78

APW (when calculated using runs instead of earned runs) evaluates Perez as being over 1½ wins better than Leibrandt. However, SNVA shows that, when the pitchers' performance is evaluated game by game, Leibrandt and Perez were virtually tied. The key here again is how the runs fell start by start. Perez was Mr. Steady during 1992, never getting bombed, but also rarely dominating. Leibrandt, on the other hand, had his share of disastrous outings, but pitched exceptionally most of the rest of the time. Those awful starts showed up disproportionately in Leibrandt's ERA and APW, but the SN measurements give a more balanced and accurate view of Leibrandt's contribution to the Braves that year.

Quick Guide to the SN Numbers in This Book

The tables and discussions of Support Neutral stats in this book deal with the following measures:

- a pitcher's Support-Neutral W/L record (SNW, SNL),
- his Support-Neutral Winning Percentage (SNPct): SNW/(SNW+SNL)—this is the Support-Neutral rate statistic, analogous to RA, and I refer to it extensively in the team discussions,
- his actual W/L record (W, L),
- his runs allowed per 9 innings (RA—that is, ERA without the "E"),
- his Adjusted Pitching Wins (APW): a measure of the number of wins a pitcher is worth, computed from the number of runs he prevented that a league average pitcher would have allowed. Same as the Total Baseball

measure except using runs rather than earned runs. It is included in the tables for comparison with SNVA.

- his Support-Neutral Value Added (SNVA)
- his Support-Neutral Wins Above Replacement (SNWAR)—the number of SNWs a pitcher has above what a .425 pitcher would get in the same number of (Support-Neutral) decisions.

A word about park effects: The park effect numbers appearing with the Support-Neutral team sections are 2-year averages of one-year park factors from 1997 and 1998. The exceptions, for which one-year factors were used, are the new ballparks, and one which have undergone significant

renovation between 1997 and 1998—Tampa Bay, Arizona, Montreal, and Anaheim. The DH is accounted for by treating it as a "ground rule" of the park and incorporating it into the park effect, so I'm combining the effect of the park itself with the effect of the rules played in that park (DH or no DH). As a result, the park effects used for the calculation of the SN numbers are adjusted so that the difference between AL and NL scoring in 1998 was added to or subtracted from each park, depending on which league it came from: AL parks inflated run scoring by an additional 6% over the raw park factor, and NL parks deflated run scoring by an additional 6%.

1998 SNW/L Leader Boards

Top 20 ML Starters, ranked by SNWs over a .425 pitcher:

Pitcher	Team	SNW	SNL	SNPct	W	L	RA	APW	SNVA	SNWAR
Maddux, G.	ATL	18.7	7.7	.710	18	9	2.69	5.37	5.37	7.52
Glavine, T.	ATL	17.6	6.8	.722	20	6	2.63	5.05	5.12	7.24
Clemens, R.	TOR	17.5	7.6	.697	20	6	2.99	4.92	4.86	6.85
Martinez, P.	BOS	16.9	8.3	.670	19	7	3.16	4.58	3.99	6.18
Brown, K.	SDP	17.5	9.1	.657	18	7	2.71	4.32	3.88	6.18
Rogers, Ken	OAK	16.6	8.5	.662	16	8	3.62	3.79	3.83	5.95
Leiter, A.	NYM	14.4	5.5	.722	17	6	2.56	4.27	4.16	5.92
Schilling, C.	PHI	17.6	10.1	.634	15	14	3.38	3.99	3.45	5.80
Johnson, R.	S/H	16.7	10.1	.624	19	11	3.76	2.84	3.08	5.32
Moyer, J.	SEA	16.1	9.5	.627	15	9	3.80	3.04	3.08	5.18
Harnisch, P.	CIN	14.3	7.6	.653	13	7	3.40	3.08	3.11	4.99
Arrojo, R.	TAM	14.5	8.2	.638	14	12	3.74	3.06	3.06	4.83
Wells, D.	NYY	14.1	8.6	.622	18	4	3.61	2.92	2.77	4.47
Cone, D.	NYY	13.9	8.5	.620	20	7	3.86	2.29	2.55	4.36
Colon, B.	CLE	13.7	8.6	.614	14	9	4.01	2.51	2.62	4.23
Reed, R.	NYM	13.9	8.9	.610	16	11	3.56	2.37	2.35	4.22
Smoltz, J.	ATL	11.8	6.3	.653	17	3	3.11	2.81	2.60	4.14
Cordova, F.	PIT	14.4	9.8	.596	13	14	3.72	2.40	2.29	4.13
Daal, O.	ARI	10.9	5.2	.677	8	10	3.38	2.25	2.66	4.07
Hernandez, O.	NYY	10.8	5.1	.680	12	4	3.38	2.27	2.72	4.04

For the fifth time in the seven years of the existence of the Support-Neutral stats, Greg Maddux has finished on top of the National League rankings. In those seven years, a total of only three NL pitchers have finished above him in a season—Jose Rijo (in 1993), Kevin Brown (in 1996), and John Smoltz (also in 1996). Nearly as boring is Roger Clemens, who, like Maddux, won his second consecutive league SNW/L crown in 1998. Clemens has also finished second (1992), third (1994), and fourth (1996) in the AL. Two pitchers who rank high on this list but got little attention during the season are Francisco Cordova and Omar Daal.

Bottom 10 ML Starters, ranked by SNWs over a .425 pitcher:

Pitcher	Team	SNW	SNL	SNPct	W	L	RA	APW	SNVA	SNWAR
Dickson, J.	ANA	3.6	9.8	.267	7	10	7.73	-3.00	-2.96	-2.11
Vazquez, J.	MON	7.3	14.4	.334	5	15	6.30	-4.13	-3.50	-1.97
Castillo, F.	DET	3.5	9.4	.274	3	9	8.61	-3.42	-2.82	-1.95
Larkin, A.	FLA	2.8	8.0	.262	3	8	9.08	-3.75	-2.52	-1.77
Witt, B.	T/S	3.6	9.0	.286	6	8	8.06	-2.88	-2.61	-1.76
Navarro, J.	CHW	7.0	13.0	.349	8	15	6.91	-3.16	-2.85	-1.51
Drabek, D.	BAL	4.7	9.6	.328	6	11	7.37	-2.70	-2.25	-1.39
Cloude, K.	SEA	7.4	12.9	.363	8	10	6.72	-2.74	-2.56	-1.26
Watson, A.	ANA	2.8	6.8	.295	5	7	7.57	-1.99	-1.92	-1.25
Haney, C.	KCR	2.3	5.7	.284	4	6	7.92	-1.70	-1.62	-1.13

Last year I wrote in the Angels comment that Jason Dickson's 1997 pitch counts "look a little ominous." Ominous turned out to be an understatement, as Dickson went from being the AL's best rookie pitcher in 1997 to the ML's worst pitcher in 1998. The Angels were the only team to boast two representatives on the worst list—Alan Watson joined the party at #9—but last year's White Sox partners in crime, Jaime Navarro and Doug Drabek, stepped their games up a notch to be recognized a year after Drabek left Chicago. The Expos' Javier Vazquez was an impressive mix of durability and ineptitude; Felipe Alou gave him 32 starts, though nearly every one was wretched.

Luckiest 10 ML Starters, ranked by
[W − E(W)] + [E(L) − L)]:

Pitcher	Team	E(W)	E(L)	W	L	Diff.
Helling, R.	TEX	13.2	10.8	20	7	10.6
Wakefield, T.	BOS	11.4	11.9	17	8	9.5
Tapani, K.	CHC	12.7	12.0	19	9	9.3
Smoltz, J.	ATL	11.6	6.3	17	3	8.7
Wells, D.	NYY	14.1	8.6	18	4	8.5
Reynolds, S.	HOU	13.9	11.3	19	8	8.4
Rueter, K.	SFG	10.2	11.4	16	9	8.1
Millwood, K.	ATL	10.8	9.7	17	8	7.9
Cone, D.	NYY	13.8	8.5	20	7	7.7
Baldwin, J.	CHW	7.7	8.2	13	6	7.5

The race for luckiest starter went down to the wire in 1998, with Kevin Tapani leading Rick Helling as late as September 17. Helling's last two starts resulted in a very lucky no-decision followed by his 20th win, while Tapani lost his final two starts, and that was enough to give Helling the coveted luck title. Tim Wakefield actually snuck into second place with a pair of wins in his last three starts. Some of the pitchers on the list show that it's better to be lucky than good, but others, like John Smoltz and David Wells, show that it's really nice to be good and lucky.

Unluckiest 10 ML Starters, ranked by
[W − E(W)] + [E(L) − L)]:

Pitcher	Team	E(W)	E(L)	W	L	Diff.
Saunders, T.	TAM	11.6	8.9	6	15	-11.7
Blair, W.	A/N	7.6	10.1	5	16	-8.5
Alvarez, W.	TAM	8.8	9.0	6	14	-7.8
Daal, O.	ARI	10.8	5.2	8	10	-7.6
Thompson, J.	DET	13.9	10.6	11	15	-7.3
Thomson, J.	COL	10.6	7.9	7	11	-6.8
Schilling, C.	PHI	17.6	10.1	15	14	-6.4
Guzman, J.	T/B	12.1	11.8	10	16	-6.2
Bohanon, B.	N/L	7.6	4.8	5	8	-5.8
Lieber, J.	PIT	9.9	10.2	8	14	-5.7

No one should be surprised to see the top of this list dominated by expansion teams. Saunders was especially unlucky, not only ranking first in 1998, but also ranking second among all seasons since 1992. The only season with less luck was Jim Abbott's 1992, when he went 7-15 despite pitch-

ing well enough to go about 14-8. The top non-expansion finisher was Detroit's Justin Thompson, making his second appearance on one of these lists in his three-year career. He might be taking lessons from Curt Schilling; this is Schilling's fourth appearance on the list in the past seven years.

Team Totals, teams ranked by
SNW − SNL:

Team	SNW	SNL	SNPct.	E(W)	W	L	RA	AdjRA	SNVA
ATL	75.3	43.5	.634	74.7	90	40	3.40	3.46	14.94
NYY	69.6	49.6	.584	69.3	86	39	4.10	4.13	9.59
NYM	64.7	48.5	.572	63.1	62	48	3.91	4.03	7.47
HOU	64.0	51.8	.553	62.7	76	39	3.89	4.09	5.57
TOR	63.9	55.2	.536	63.4	67	51	4.00	4.50	3.90
CLE	60.7	52.0	.538	59.4	66	51	4.84	4.59	4.24
BOS	57.9	52.0	.527	56.1	64	50	4.71	4.64	2.66
LAD	60.7	55.9	.521	58.8	58	56	4.19	4.62	2.11
CHC	59.6	55.5	.518	58.1	61	67	4.78	4.71	2.09
SDP	59.0	56.1	.512	57.3	67	45	4.01	4.48	1.00
TAM	56.3	53.5	.513	53.8	39	79	4.96	4.70	1.32
PIT	58.2	56.1	.509	56.2	53	68	4.59	4.58	0.88
CIN	54.2	56.5	.490	52.1	52	60	4.87	4.82	-1.11
BAL	55.2	59.0	.483	52.7	56	64	5.16	5.22	-1.77
STL	54.1	58.4	.481	52.1	58	57	4.91	5.11	-2.56
OAK	54.6	60.0	.477	53.2	52	60	5.48	5.25	-2.58
SEA	55.4	61.0	.476	53.9	60	56	5.29	5.18	-2.85
ARI	54.9	60.7	.475	52.9	46	75	5.02	5.00	-2.79
PHI	55.3	61.8	.472	54.4	50	60	5.06	5.02	-3.44
COL	54.3	61.0	.471	52.7	51	69	6.01	4.86	-3.08
ANA	53.0	60.6	.467	51.3	60	53	5.23	5.23	-3.45
KCR	53.1	60.9	.465	52.1	55	71	5.67	5.33	-4.07
SFG	52.5	61.0	.463	50.6	59	51	5.03	5.26	-4.21
MIN	51.7	60.2	.462	49.4	46	67	5.29	5.37	-4.11
DET	52.0	61.3	.459	49.5	45	78	5.74	5.61	-4.42
TEX	53.3	64.1	.454	51.6	68	57	5.94	5.52	-4.98
MIL	49.4	60.9	.448	46.9	45	64	5.46	5.40	-5.74
MON	45.9	64.8	.415	43.4	42	69	5.11	5.68	-9.29
CHW	47.0	66.5	.414	44.9	60	60	5.92	5.89	-9.40
FLA	42.9	72.5	.372	40.1	37	72	6.01	6.37	-14.37
ML	1688.5	1740.9	.492	1636.7	1737	1757	4.95	4.95	-28.38

Yes, Maddux and Clemens's dominance of the top starter lists is getting fairly old, but at least those two don't win every single year. The Braves do. This is the seventh consecutive year they have led the majors in SNVA, and none of those years has been particularly close. It just keeps getting better for the Braves: 1998 saw their second highest SNVA of the past seven years, second only to 1997. Another interesting thing about this list is that major league starters as a whole were worth 28 games below the average major league pitcher. That's not a typo or a bug—starters' ERAs were quite a bit higher than relievers' last year.

Bullpen Support

In the May 6 Rockie-Phillies game at the Vet, Phillies starter Matt Beech was throwing a shutout through 5 but ran into a bit of trouble in the sixth. He got the first out to start the inning, and another one later, before he was yanked, but in between he gave up a HBP, a walk, and a couple of singles to load the bases with one run in. Needing only one out to get out of the inning, Beech's reliever (Jerry Spradlin) served up a gopher ball to Larry Walker, and watched as all three of Beech's runners trotted in to score. Suddenly what looked like an excellent start for Beech turned into a 5⅔ IP, 4 run bad day.

On the other end of the spectrum, consider Francisco Cordova's start on July 15 in Fenway. He also was throwing a shutout, but completely collapsed in the seventh, giving up four consecutive singles before getting pulled, leaving the game with the bases loaded and nobody out. Jason Christiansen and Elmer Dessens came in and completely bailed Cordova out, getting a K followed by a double play, and not allowing any of Cordova's runners to cross the plate. What could have easily been a 6 IP, 3 or 4 run generic start for Cordova turned into a 6 IP 1 run near-gem.

Almost every baseball fan recognizes that there's some unfairness in situations like those. Even the most innumerate TV color man will remark that Beech was unlucky to be charged with those extra three runs, or that Cordova was lucky to be spared any more damage to his ERA after he left his game. What we're interested in as analysts is quantifying this unfairness—seeing how severe it can be over the course of a year or career, and coming up with statistics that remove it.

The clear way to do this is to measure the expected outcome given the state of the bases and number of outs when the starter left the game, and compare that to the actual outcome that occured after the reliever(s) came in. The difference between the two will measure the bullpen support the starter received. I've deliberately used the ambiguous word "outcome," because there are many possible specific measurements you could plug in there.

One possibility for outcome is the number of the starters' runners left on base—I'll call these "inherited runners" from now on—that score. The expected number of inherited runners scoring can be determined by counting up the number of on-base runners that scored in each bases/outs configuration over a large number of games. I did this for most games of the 1997 season. Subtract this expectation from the actual number of inherited runners that the relievers let in, and you get the number of runs the relievers subtracted from or added to the starter's totals. Another notion of outcome, closely related to the one above, is the starter's RA. Use the expected number of inherited runners scoring to calculate an expected RA for the starter, subtract it from his actual RA, and you get the extra runs added to or subtracted from the starters' RA by his relievers.

A third possible measurement to use for outcome is the expected probability of winning the game, i.e., SNVA. Here we compare the starter's SNVA using the new method of cal-

culation—which takes into account the state of the runners on base when the starter leaves the game—to the SNVA using the old method of calculation. I called the latter SNVAn (n is for "no state"), and it is calculated assuming that the starter leaves the bases empty after all the runs charged to him in a box score have scored. This is the method I used to rank starters below. It has the advantage of giving prominence to those situations where the inherited runners are likely to make a difference—where they make a big difference in the probability of winning the game. I called this measure "Bullpen Support", and I abbreviated it "BSup" (to distinguish it from Blown Saves, and any other term that "BS" might bring to mind).

Below are the starters who are best- and worst- supported by their bullpens. Each table includes:

- IR—Inherited Runs: Runners left on base by the starter that eventually scored.
- E(IR)—Expected Inherited Runs: the number of runners left on base by the starter that would be expected to score, given the bases they occupied and the number of outs.
- RA/A—Run Average, Adjusted
- E(RA)/A—Expected Run Average, Adjusted: RA calculated by subtracting out IR and adding in E(IR)
- SNVA_n, SNVA, BSup—described above

10 ML Starters most hurt by their relievers, ranked by Bullpen Support:

Pitcher	Team	IR	E(IR)	RA/A	E(RA)/A	SNVA_n	SNVA	BSup
Clark, M.	CHC	18	11.6	4.81	4.54	-0.53	0.21	-0.74
Burkett, J.	TEX	23	18.1	5.63	5.42	-1.38	-0.72	-0.66
Aybar, M.	STL	12	7.4	7.15	6.53	-1.48	-0.89	-0.59
Vazquez, J.	MON	13	7.4	7.01	6.68	-4.09	-3.50	-0.59
Thompson, J.	DET	11	7.0	4.51	4.35	1.05	1.64	-0.59
Ortiz, R.	SFG	8	3.2	6.22	5.63	-1.56	-1.06	-0.50
Gardner, M.	SFG	9	5.5	4.71	4.55	0.04	0.49	-0.44
Drabek, D.	BAL	13	9.0	7.46	7.10	-2.66	-2.25	-0.41
Sanchez, J.	FLA	13	9.5	5.46	5.26	-0.99	-0.59	-0.40
Park, C.	LAD	11	7.5	4.54	4.38	0.16	0.54	-0.38

Mark Clark ran away with the "honor" of being most hurt by his bullpen. Of the runners Clark left on base when he was yanked, we would expect 11.6 to score, but 18 scored, adding an undeserved 6.4 runs to Clark's total runs allowed, and about a quarter of a run to his RA. Justin Thompson was let down by his teammates on two fronts. He received the fifth-worst bullpen support in the majors, and received bad enough overall support to have the fifth-unluckiest W/L record in the majors. So no matter which of the big traditional pitching statistics (ERA or W/L) you looked at in 1998, you were getting a significantly deflated view of Thompson's real value.

10 ML Starters most helped by their relievers, ranked by Bullpen Support:

Pitcher	Team	IR	E(IR)	RA/A	E(RA)/A	SNVA_n	SNVA	BSup
Stottlemyre, T.	S/T	1	5.7	4.39	4.58	0.77	0.30	0.47
Swift, B.	SEA	3	7.8	6.03	6.34	-1.60	-2.03	0.43
Martinez, P.	BOS	1	5.4	3.11	3.27	4.42	3.99	0.43
Alvarez, W.	TAM	6	12.0	4.65	5.01	0.40	-0.02	0.43
Irabu, H.	NYY	3	8.4	4.09	4.38	1.83	1.43	0.41
Burba, D.	CLE	2	6.6	4.22	4.42	1.58	1.23	0.35
Cordova, F.	PIT	4	7.8	3.72	3.87	2.62	2.29	0.34
Erickson, S.	BAL	5	8.2	4.53	4.64	1.25	0.93	0.32
Fassero, J.	SEA	1	5.0	4.51	4.67	0.65	0.33	0.32
Springer, D.	TAM	5	9.0	6.23	6.59	-1.54	-1.83	0.29

Todd Stottlemyre managed to get good bullpen support from two teams in 1998. None of the 8 runners he turned over to Cardinal relievers, and only 1 of 7 turned over to the Ranger bullpen, ended up scoring—good enough to make him the easy winner of the bullpen support trophy. Without looking, guess which was the only team to have two representatives on the best-bullpen-support list. If you said Seattle Mariners, you're a lot smarter than I am. Having two on the above list doesn't mean the Mariners had a good bullpen in 1998. It just means that Swift and Fassero happened to catch them on their (rare) good innings.

Top 5 Teams, ranked by Bullpen Support of starters:

Team	IR	E(IR)	RA/A	E(RA)/A	SNVA_n	SNVA	BSup
BOS	25	34.2	4.64	4.72	3.34	2.66	0.68
TAM	41	51.1	4.70	4.79	1.92	1.32	0.60
PIT	30	39.0	4.58	4.66	1.48	0.88	0.60
CHW	34	43.4	5.89	5.98	-8.88	-9.40	0.53
ATL	14	20.1	3.46	3.51	15.36	14.94	0.42

Bottom 5 Teams, ranked by Bullpen Support of starters:

Team	IR	E(IR)	RA/A	E(RA)/A	SNVA_n	SNVA	BSup
LAD	45	30.2	4.62	4.48	0.70	2.11	-1.41
DET	65	53.3	5.61	5.50	-5.82	-4.42	-1.39
SFG	49	41.3	5.26	5.19	-5.34	-4.21	-1.12
NYM	41	31.2	4.03	3.95	6.49	7.47	-0.98
CHC	52	43.3	4.71	4.63	1.17	2.09	-0.93

These lists are not measuring bullpen quality as a whole, only bullpen support of starting pitchers. The Red Sox top ranking, for example, doesn't have much to do with the terrific season of closer Tom Gordon. Instead, it largely reflects the work of middle guys like Jim Corsi, Derek Lowe, and Greg Swindell, who often took the game from the starter to Gordon. By contrast, another team with an excellent closer, the Giants, had some rough appearances by middle relievers like Rich Rodriguez, John Johnstone, and Julian Tavarez when they relieved starters. They cost the starters almost 8 runs, with Russ Ortiz and Mark Gardner bearing the brunt of the damage.

Pitcher Abuse Points

by Rany Jazayerli

Kerry Wood needs no introduction. The most compelling arm to hit baseball since Dwight Gooden's entry 14 years ago was hailed as the Cubs' savior from the moment Derek Bell swung and missed for strikeout #20. The uncanny timing that found Wood in the middle of the first pennant race for the Cubs this decade put manager Jim Riggleman in a squeeze. The Cubs were obligated, both for the sake of Wood and the long-term future of the franchise, to coddle his arm and do everything in their power to prevent injury. But the Cubs were faced with the ravings of fans nationwide who expected Wood to carry them to a glorious postseason, and columnists who should have known better, but persisted in calling on Wood to throw nine innings and "learn to finish what he starts."

The Cubs didn't go that far; Wood's one-hit shutout of the Astros remains the only complete game of his pro career. But Riggleman tried to let Wood pitch into the 8th inning often, and Wood developed some mild arm "soreness" after the All-Star break. The Cubs did their best after that to treat him with caution, but on August 26, with his bullpen worn out, Riggleman let Wood throw a career-high 132 pitches. One start later, Wood's elbow had had enough: he was out for the rest of the regular season.

The topic of pitcher abuse is one we follow closely. The injury rate of pitchers, in particular young pitchers, is astonishing—several times higher than that for hitters. For every prospect that runs the gauntlet and becomes a successful major league pitcher, a dozen more have their careers stalled or ended by injury. This is a reality that has persisted since the game was invented; the act of throwing overhand is inherently unnatural, and the repetition of throwing, even with excellent mechanics, can lead to inflammation or injury to the muscles of the rotator cuff, or in the ligaments that hold the elbow in place.

For a century it has been an accepted part of the game that pitchers get hurt all the time, yet no systematic effort was ever made to figure out why, or how to prevent the guilty factors as much as possible. There has certainly been a constant, unyielding evolution in the game to lower the total number of innings thrown by any one pitcher; this has occurred hand-in-hand with the continuing maturation of bullpen use. But pitchers certainly don't seem to get injured any less now than they have historically. Cy Young threw over 320 innings for fifteen straight seasons, and pitched until he was 44. No one has hit 300 innings even once since 1980—yet we see that pitchers still get hurt all the time.

This duality—that despite throwing fewer innings with each passing decade, pitchers do not appear to suffer any fewer injuries—has not surprisingly given each generation of veteran players and sportswriters the opportunity to belittle the current crop of pitchers and deride their "manhood" and talk about how great pitchers used to "gut it out" and "pitch through the pain." When Jaret Wright and Bartolo Colon were going through a dead-arm period late last season, Bob Feller was quoted as saying their difficulties were all psychological—an obvious insinuation that their complaints of pain were somehow not genuine.

That's Bob Feller for you—everyone told him he was God's gift to baseball when he was 17, and sixty years later no one has managed to convince him to the contrary. The reality is this: arm injuries aren't a mirage, they're a medical fact, and their persistence isn't a criticism of the modern athlete, but a reflection of the game's mechanisms. Pitchers throw fewer innings than they used to—but to compare 260 innings thrown by Roger Clemens with 260 innings thrown by Christy Mathewson is a gross oversimplification. Mathewson faced fewer batters and threw far fewer pitches in the deadball era, and in his own autobiography talked about not throwing with maximum effort on each pitch. Even comparing starters from the 1960s with those of today fails to consider the enormous strike zone and higher mound that guys like Juan Marichal and Bob Gibson were throwing 300 innings a year from.

But the manner by which innings totals have come down over the last 25 years—in 1974, Catfish Hunter threw 318 innings, good for fifth in the AL—hasn't really addressed the problems. You see, it is not the total number of innings thrown but the number thrown per outing, that is the major culprit. A certain amount of exertion is needed by a pitcher to maintain arm strength and hold on to the muscle memory that forms from constant practice. That's why pitchers throw between starts—it certainly doesn't increase their risk of injury, as long as they don't throw for too long. In Atlanta, Leo Mazzone has the Braves' starters throw twice between starts instead of once, and he has a track record of pitcher health unrivaled in modern history.

So what is the main element in the drop-off in starters' innings? It's the switch to the five-man rotation—which limits the number of outings in which a pitcher throws, but does nothing to protect how much he throws during each outing. When Hunter threw 318 innings, he made 41 starts—no one has come within three of that number since 1987. And right there is the first problem that needs to be addressed—organizations look carefully at the total amount of work a pitcher has received, while ignoring the more germane issue of the pace at which he is worked. You'll see an organization voice concern because Joe Rookie threw a career-high 180 innings, oblivious to the fact that the year before he threw 160 innings in a compressed minor league season.

Another problem—in reality, the greater problem—is that not all pitchers are equally susceptible to injury. Young pitchers are far, far more likely to show long-term effects to overuse; it takes until a pitcher is at least 25 or 26 before his rotator cuff has completely matured and he can take on a full workload. In Craig Wright's excellent book *The Diamond Appraised*, he used the number of batters faced per start (BFP) as a measure of how overworked a starter might be. In particular, he found that pitchers with more than 30 BFP a start before they turned 25 were far more likely to crash and burn than those pitchers who reached that workload at a later age. Look at the Mets: Dallas Green slagged David Cone's arm when Cone was in his late 20s, and while his durability has suffered, Cone has continued to pitch effectively. But the Mets abused the Young Guns—Bill Pulsipher, Jason Isringhausen, and Paul Wilson—when they were in their early 20s, and right now the three are trying to make it back with peashooters.

But given enough abuse, even a veteran pitcher can suffer major injuries from overuse. When Orel Hershiser led the NL in innings pitched three straight years from 1987-1989, then blew out his arm in 1990, it was graphic evidence that being overworked at any age can lead to injury. So when Greg Maddux led the NL innings from 1991–93, there was a widespread assumption that he, like Hershiser, was a surgery case waiting to happen. It didn't. Maddux went on to lead the NL in innings the next two seasons, throwing 202 innings in just 25 starts in the strike-shortened 1994, and has continued to be the best pitcher in baseball. More than anyone, Maddux has made the convincing argument that it's the pitches, stupid.

Maddux isn't just the best pitcher of our time: he's the most efficient pitcher of our time. He not only faces fewer batters per inning, but his impeccable control and penchant for groundball outs has helped him to throw fewer pitches per batter than anyone in the game. We've all marveled at his 89-pitch complete games, and that, as much as the amazing Cox/Mazzone tandem in Atlanta, has made Maddux the picture of health at 250 innings a year.

Partly because of Maddux's impact on the game, and largely because of the exponential growth of statistics available today, pitch counts are routinely reported in box scores. Ten years ago, even five years ago, you could watch your favorite pitcher labor through the 7th and 8th innings of a game and have no idea the next morning if he threw 110 or 150 pitches. Today, that information is readily available—and a manager cannot expect to let his starter throw 140 pitches without being noticed. In the 1997 World Series, the whole nation watched as Jim Leyland let Kevin Brown and rookie Livan Hernandez rack up enormous pitch counts, sometimes in games that were already in the bag.

And yet, no one has systematically looked at the pitch counts of each starter and attempted to make sense of the data. What we have are anecdotes—Bartolo Colon threw 136 pitches yesterday—but we don't have any way of putting that into context. How dangerous is a 130-pitch game? Is it worse to throw 140 pitches in one game or throw 120 pitches in three straight starts? What's a reasonable workload for a 22-year-old pitcher?

I don't claim to have the answers; I'm not sure anyone does. But for the first time, we have the data to try to find out. When Dwight Gooden threw 16 complete games and 276 innings at the age of 20, it was generally appreciated that he was probably overused. But by how much? What would have been an appropriate limit for him? No one could make heads or tails of the question because they didn't have the information to study it. But last year, every time Kerry Wood took the mound, everyone kept one eye on the radar gun and another on his pitch count. In itself, that's a huge step.

We still need a universal measure to compare pitchers with each other, however. Average pitch count per start is a useful tool, but it has a major limitation: a pitcher who throws 130 pitches one start, then gets bombed in his next start and throws 70 pitches, is indistinguishable from the pitcher that throws 100 pitches in each start. Yet it's not the total number of pitches thrown that are dangerous, it's the number thrown when tired—when mechanics fall off, muscles are sore, and the body is unable to handle the stress of each pitch as well. So we need a way to measure, on a start-by-start basis, how much abuse a pitcher is subject to.

So I designed a system to do just that. It's not perfect, and we still need several seasons' worth of data to check its accuracy—but it's a start. Any system created for the purposes of evaluating a pitcher's workload should:

1. Examine each start individually. Any method that adds together separate outings is bound to smooth out the variations from one start to the next and lose important information.

2. Assume that the pitcher can handle a certain workload without any danger, and only penalize him for working beyond that level.

3. Beyond the pitcher's "safe level," each additional pitch thrown should draw a greater penalty than the one before, since the more fatigued a pitcher becomes, the greater the risk of injury from additional work. In other words, the 147th pitch thrown should cost more than the 106th pitch thrown.

The system I created is called Pitcher Abuse Points, or "PAP" for short. The system works by awarding pitchers PAPs based on the number of pitches they throw in each start. For all pitchers, the "safe level" is set at 100 pitches—in other words, if Brad Radke threw exactly 100 pitches in every start, he would have 0 PAPs to his name. But beyond that:

Situation	PAP/pitch
1–100	0
101–110	1
111–120	2
121–130	3
131–140	4
141–150	5
151–160	6

And so on. An ideal system would increase the penalty for each pitch more consistently: 1.3 PAPs for pitch 113, 1.4 PAPs for pitch 114, etc. As designed, the system loses only a little detail in its scoring, but it's a lot easier to use. With a little experience, you can calculate a PAP score in your head by knowing the pitch count.

This is an arbitrary, empirical system. We simply don't have the data available to test how valid or accurate it is—not yet. We hope to be able to do so as near in the future as possible. The system can't delineate from pitcher to pitcher, so it treats knuckleballers like Tim Wakefield the same as porcelain-arms like Steve Ontiveros. In other words, the results need to be interpreted from their context—just like any other statistic. But it allows us to draw some pretty strong conclusions nevertheless.

What represents a "normal" or "healthy" PAP score? Well, 181 pitchers made at least 10 starts in the major leagues last year. Here is a table of where they scored in terms of average PAP score per start:

PAP/Start	# of Pitchers	Cumulative %
30+	4	2.2
25–30	5	5.0
20–25	6	8.3
15–20	13	15.5
10–15	33	33.7
5–10	49	60.8
0–5	71	100.0

A good rule of thumb is the Rule of 15: about 15 percent of starting pitchers will average over 15 PAPs per start.

Anything over 15 PAPs a start is high; anything over 20 PAPs a start is too high.

Before we get to the whole point of this essay—who's being abused and who isn't—I want to stress again how important age is to this whole equation. It really is not that big a deal for Roger Clemens or Rick Reed or Mike Morgan to go out and throw 110 or 115 pitches a start. But that kind of load on a Kevin Millwood or a Jose Rosado or Kerry Wood is a truly dangerous thing. Their arms are simply not physically mature yet, and repeated poundings are not only more likely to damage them, but they may cause a more subtle deterioration of the muscles from a long history of small traumas, and when that pitcher is 30 years old he may not have a defined "injury" but simply can't bring it the way he once did. Remember Bob Feller? He won 107 games before he turned 23, and was generally healthy throughout his career. Yet his strikeouts consistently dropped off throughout his career: he led the AL in K's seven times before he was 30, but not once afterwards. His last good season was at age 32. By comparison, Warren Spahn, whose career was delayed until he was 25 by World War II, managed to throw 290 innings or more seven times and threw no less than 246 innings every season in a 17-year stretch—and still went 23-7 at the age of 42.

So age matters. With that in mind, I've split the leader lists into three groups, separated by age. Here's the first group, the veterans (ages 30 and older):

Team	Pitcher	Age	PAP	GS	PAP/S
SEA/HOU	Johnson, Randy	34	1687	34	49.62
PHI	Schilling, Curt	31	1331	35	38.03
TOR	Clemens, Roger	35	1206	33	36.55
ANA	Finley, Chuck	35	907	34	26.68
SEA	Fassero, Jeff	35	787	32	24.59
NYM	Leiter, Al	32	752	28	26.86
BAL	Erickson, Scott	30	733	36	20.36
STL/TEX	Stottlemyre, Todd	33	624	33	18.91
TOR	Williams, Woody	31	584	32	18.25
ARZ	Benes, Andy	30	537	34	15.79

No major surprises on this list; the top three names are three of the most respected workhorses in the game. Only one other pitcher in baseball approaches their workload (we'll get to him later). Of the three of them, the one I'm most concerned about is Schilling, who has already suffered arm troubles that cost him nearly two years of effectiveness. Finley had his best season in five years, and was ridden hard with the Angels in the race all season despite a thin rotation. Names like Leiter, Erickson, Stottlemyre, and Benes are understandable—they're called upon to be the aces of their staff (okay, not Erickson). The interesting names on the list are Jeff Fassero, who wasn't put in the rotation until he was 30 but has handled increasingly heavy workloads with ease, and Woody Williams, who got off to a great start with the Blue Jays (6-2, 2.60 ERA through May), but was worked into the ground by Tim Johnson, going 2-6 with a 5.46 ERA after the All-Star Break.

The next list is that of the tweener group, with some experience but still not carte blanche to throw as much as they want (ages 25-29):

Team	Pitcher	Age	PAP	GS	PAP/S
BOS	Martinez, Pedro	26	957	33	29.00
PIT	Schmidt, Jason	25	648	33	19.64
NYY	Pettite, Andy	26	641	32	20.03
COL	Kile, Darryl	29	619	35	17.69
TEX	Helling, Rick	27	585	33	17.73
MIN	Radke, Brad	25	554	32	17.31
NYY	Hernandez, Orlando	28	537	21	25.57
BAL	Mussina, Mike	29	520	29	17.93
LA	Park, Chan Ho	25	500	34	14.71
TEX	Sele, Aaron	28	426	33	12.91

This list isn't fundamentally different than the first one. Almost all the pitchers on this list are #1 or #2 starters, they're just younger. Pedro Martinez, who leads the list by a long margin, has finished first and second in Cy Young balloting the last two years, and Kile, Radke, Mussina, and Park are the aces of their staffs. Helling and Sele were the Rangers' co-aces last year, at least until Stottlemyre was picked up. Two interesting names are Pettite and Hernandez, who were the Yankees' #3 and #4 starters, and while they both pitched well—these are the Yankees, remember—with a deep and talented bullpen, you'd think Joe Torre could have used some restraint. Pettite had a 6.14 ERA in August and September and after getting blown out by the Indians in the ALCS, the specter of his turn in the rotation seemed to be the greatest impediment to the Yankees' World Championship. Hernandez racked up his PAPs in just 21 starts, though it must be said that if he's really 28, I'm 15. My facial hair just grew in early. Jason Schmidt is the biggest surprise on the list; he's not really the Pirates' ace (Francisco Cordova is) and didn't throw a complete game, but worked deep into the count against most hitters and needs to be more aggressive and get more one-pitch outs to cut down his workload.

Finally, the real meat of this article, the youngsters (ages 24 and less):

Team	Pitcher	Age	PAP	GS	PAP/S
FLA	Hernandez, Livan	23	1520	33	46.06
CLE	Colon, Bartolo	23	606	31	19.55
CHC	Wood, Kerry	21	532	26	20.46
TB	Saunders, Tony	24	496	31	16.00
CLE	Wright, Jaret	22	444	32	13.88

Team	Pitcher	Age	PAP	GS	PAP/S
FLA	Sanchez, Jesus	23	389	29	13.41
TOR	Carpenter, Chris	23	357	24	14.88
ATL	Millwood, Kevin	23	325	29	11.21
LA	Valdes, Ismael	24	305	27	11.30
TOR	Escobar, Kelvim	22	274	10	27.40

Those of you who originally read about the PAP system when it debuted on our web site (www.baseballprospectus.com) last summer, remember the insults we poured on Jim Leyland for his handling of Livan Hernandez. As hard as it is to believe, the abuse actually got worse after the All-Star Break; before the break Hernandez and Bartolo Colon were both in the running for the title of Most Abused Pitcher, but Livan pulled away and lapped the field in the second half. Jim Leyland has been hailed by all of baseball as a genius and a player's manager, and as recently as 18 months ago we generally agreed with that sentiment. Leyland simply had no track record of sending young pitchers to the guillotine like he did last year. I can understand the frustration of managing a gutted-down team, but this was inexcusable. You know you're not trying to win, so why not use the opportunity to let the young pitchers in the bullpen get some experience, rather than forcing your "ace," who had all of 9 career wins coming into the season, to average over 7 innings a start? And it wasn't just Hernandez; Jesus Sanchez ranks sixth on the list, and just missing the list in 11th place is Rafael Medina, who in just 12 starts recorded 240 PAPs. The question is why, Jim, why? I don't have the answers, in part because no one in the media bothered to notice what was going on and ask Leyland if he had lost his marbles. No one seemed to notice that Hernandez, obviously feeling the strain of an incomprehensible workload, nearly pulled off an ugly trifecta: he led the NL in hits allowed, was second in walks, and third in homers. If Hernandez goes down with a career-threatening rotator cuff tear in May and the media blames John Boles for not having Leyland's "touch," I'm going to be ill.

On a radio show last summer, I was asked what pitcher on a contending team I was most concerned would lose his effectiveness for the postseason. I answered Bartolo Colon, who was worked with complete lack of restraint by Mike Hargrove at the beginning of the year, and it showed: Colon, 9-4 with a terrific 2.46 ERA at the Break, was just 5-5 with a 5.65 ERA after, though he did bounce back to pitch well in the playoffs. Teammate Jaret Wright was handled the same way by Hargrove, pitching less only because he was less effective. Chris Carpenter, despite being the #4 starter in Toronto, was shown little mercy by Tim Johnson, and teammate Kelvim Escobar made a late move to the rotation and was used cruelly for 10 starts. Tony Saunders was a favorite of Larry Rothschild in Florida, and Rothschild showed that affection by letting Saunders throw an average of 6.5 innings a start, a high workload for a young pitcher who led all of baseball with 111 walks. Kevin Millwood makes the list, a surprise for a Braves' starter, though he's toward the bottom, and certainly didn't show any signs of abuse. It's hard to believe Ismael Valdes was still just 24, and last year's workload was nothing compared to his mistreatment by Tommy Lasorda in 1995 and 1996. He's already showed warning signs, as he made just 27 starts last year and his strikeout rate has slipped a notch. The Dodgers need to be extra vigilant with him this year.

And then there is Kerry Wood, who ranks third on the list and was the youngest starter in all of baseball last season. I don't think he's in any imminent danger of collapse; the Cubs shut him down immediately at the first signs of elbow pain and stubbornly refused to take a chance on his return, despite the tightest of pennant races, until they were 100% certain he was healthy. He's a big guy, has good mechanics, and doesn't rely on a splitter. But the Cubs need to turn their back on public opinion for once and be absolutely paranoid when it comes to protecting the most prized arm of the decade.

A complete listing of the PAP scores for every pitcher who started a single game this season is broken up by team, and I guess I should explain some of the terminology I use:

PAP: If you don't know what this is by now, you're flipping through the book at Barnes & Noble or somewhere instead of reading the essay straight through. Read this article from the beginning, after buying the book. Trust us. It's a great read.

PAP/S: PAP score per start.

MAX: The highest pitch count reached in a single start all season.

115+: The number of starts that pitcher threw at least 115 pitches.

130+: The number of starts that pitcher threw at least 130 pitches.

Each team is also ranked within their league, so you can see, for example, where the Braves (and therefore Bobby Cox) lie in relation to the NL, and see just how outstanding Felipe Alou really is.

There's one more category I need to tell you about. Age is such an important factor in evaluating pitchers that I felt compelled to try to come up with a formula to adjust PAP scores for age. I have even less data to suggest what the age adjustment should be than I do for the PAP system in general, but the system is only going to be refined by trial and error. The resulting number could be called the Age-Adjusted Pitcher Abuse Points, or AAPAP for short, but we're not getting paid for long acronyms. So I called it simply the Age-Adjusted Workload, or AAW. I made AAW a rate stat, not measuring the total amount of abuse, but the amount of abuse

per start—that is, it's dependent on PAP/S, not total PAP. Here's the formula:

$$AAW = PAP/S \times X$$

where X depends on age.

Age 32 and older: X = 1. In other words, no adjustment is made.
Age 31 and younger: X = (38 − age)/6.

If a starter is 31, X = 1.17, so a slight upward adjustment is made. A 26-year-old starter would have his PAPs doubled, and a 20-year-old starter (there were none last year) would have his PAPs tripled. That seems fair to start off with. It's easy to look at Randy Johnson and Livan Hernandez and say that Hernandez was put more directly in harm's way, despite a slightly lower PAP score. But how about Johnson vs. Kerry Wood? Or Curt Schilling vs. Pedro Martinez? This formula gives us some way of making that comparison across age lines.

What's a reasonable AAW? Here, I'll run the same kind of list I did for PAP/S earlier:

AAW	# of SP	Cum. %
50+	5	2.8
40–50	6	6.1
30–40	8	10.5
25–30	12	17.1
20–25	13	24.3
15–20	21	35.9
10–15	29	51.9
5–10	37	72.4
0–5	50	100.0

Whereas in looking at PAP/S a score of 15 begins to push the envelope and 20 starts to get dangerous, the cutoffs for AAW are probably 25 to be concerned and 30 to be worried.

If you've come this far, we might as well run the mother of all lists. Here, according to their AAW, were the 10 most senselessly used pitchers of 1998 (min: 10 starts):

Team	Pitcher	Age	PAP	GS	PAP/S	AAW
FLA	Hernandez, Livan	23	1520	33	46.06	115.15
TOR	Escobar, Kelvim	22	274	10	27.40	73.07
BOS	Martinez, Pedro	26	957	33	29.00	58.00
CHC	Wood, Kerry	21	532	26	20.46	57.97
FLA	Medina, Rafael	23	240	12	20.00	50.00
SEA/HOU	Johnson, Randy	34	1687	34	49.62	49.62
CLE	Colon, Bartolo	23	606	31	19.55	48.87
PHI	Schilling, Curt	31	1331	35	38.03	44.34
NYY	Hernandez, Orlando	"28"	537	21	25.57	42.62
PIT	Schmidt, Jason	25	648	33	19.64	42.55

Congratulations to Livan Hernandez, who in a landslide wins the 1998 Most Abused Pitcher award. Feel free to take a bow, Livan. Just don't raise your arms in triumph. You might hurt yourself.

Atlanta Braves

As the decade nears its end, the Team of the Decade nears a crossroads. A run of success unparalleled by any non-Yankee team ever continued unabated last year, as the Braves set a franchise high with 106 wins and were the first team since the 1902 Pirates to have five 16-game winners. But another early exit from the playoffs has raised the level of anxiety in Atlanta another notch, and it is now a fair question whether the Braves will find a way to jump through all the hoops and win a second World Series before their dynasty gets dispersed to the four winds. For seven years the Braves gallantly fought the inertia that dooms most successful teams—the tendency to stick with the personnel that achieved the success to begin with, sticking with marginal veterans while blocking promising youngsters, all the while moving closer and closer to a complete breakdown. But last year, for the first time, the Braves began to crack.

There is an enormous amount of literature on the subject of player aging, all of which suggests that the average player improves up to the age of 27, begins to decline slowly after that, and then degenerates steeply after reaching his early 30s. And while there is tremendous variability between players, anytime a large set of players are grouped together, that variability cancels out and the general trend becomes meaningful—and so small differences in a team's overall age has a profound impact on the team's outlook. The difference between youth and experience is not that great when measured on a team-wide scale; a team with an average age of 26 is quite raw, whereas any team over the age of 29 is primed for a steep decline. And one of the most underappreciated factors in the Braves' run has been their ability to constantly re-tool pieces of their team, replacing worn-out parts with new ones and keeping pace with the treadmill of aging that has doomed so many teams before them.

The chart at right summarizes the average age of the Braves' eight regulars (and part-timers with at least 250 PA), as well as their top five starters and closer, since their rise to greatness.

> ## Braves Prospectus
>
> **1998 record:** 106-56; First place, NL East
> Lost to San Diego Padres in NLCS, 4-2
>
> **Pythagorean W/L:** 108-54
>
> **Runs scored:** 826 (t-4th in NL)
>
> **Runs allowed:** 581 (1st in NL)
>
> **Team EQA:** .275 (3rd in NL)
>
> **Park:** Turner Field (slight pitchers')
>
> **1998:** More of the same, as an excellent rotation supported one of the league's better offenses.
>
> **1999:** Questionable signings could bring them back to the pack, as the team is aging.

Eight years ago, the "Miracle" Braves won with a pitching staff that was incredibly young despite the presence of 34-year-old Charlie Leibrandt and veterans Alejandro Pena and Juan Berenguer as closers. Tom Glavine, the second-oldest starting pitcher, was just 25. The offense, however, featured no regulars under the age of 25, and it was clear that for the Braves to sustain their new-found place at the top, replenishing the lineup with an infusion of young hitters was a top priority. To the Braves' everlasting credit, they were able to do just that, and do it spectacularly well: 23-year-olds Javy Lopez and Ryan Klesko entered the starting lineup in 1994, and 23-year-old Chipper Jones stepped right in the following season. All three performed wonderfully from the outset, and remain an integral part of the Braves' lineup to this day. Coupled with the rejuvenation of the pitching staff in 1993—marked by the replacement of Leibrandt with Greg Maddux, and the end of a reliance on thirtysomething closers—the Braves were able to maintain their dynasty into the mid-90s without feeling the irresistible tide of age pulling at the franchise.

But high tide has come. Since their World Championship in 1995, the Braves have hopped aboard the veteran train, and it's accelerating. The pitching staff has consistently aged since 1993, which is what happens when the same three pitchers (Maddux, Glavine, Smoltz) have combined to miss barely a dozen starts in that span. The historic greatness of the rotation is reason enough to forgive the Braves for their complacency. The Big Three will in all likelihood still be among the top pitchers in baseball when they're all 36 or 37.

Year	Offense	Pitching	Total
1991	28.2	26.5	27.4
1992	28.1	28.3	28.2
1993	29.3	26.0	27.7
1994	27.6	26.7	27.2
1995	27.1	27.2	27.1
1996	27.1	27.5	27.3
1997	27.6	28.5	28.0
1998	29.1	29.0	29.1

But look at the offense; in particular, look at the year-and-a-half jump between 1997 and 1998. The aging process met a big roadblock named Andruw Jones in 1997, but last year the Braves, for the first time, approached the off-season not as an opportunity for renewal, but as an opportunity to add veterans.

They replaced Fred McGriff, who at 35 was in obvious decline, with Andres Galarraga, who was even older at 37 and dropping about 4,000 feet of altitude. Jeff Blauser, who was 33, was let go and 35-year-old Walt Weiss was brought in; when Weiss proved fragile, Ozzie Guillen, at the very edge of retiring at 34, was picked up to be his caddy. Since the Braves' fabulous run began, not once had they brought in a new regular player who was older than 30. In 1998, that policy went out with the dishwater. When Tony Graffanino struggled, 33-year-old Keith Lockhart was entrusted with the lion's share of playing time at second, and the Braves' lineup had suddenly become overpopulated with hitters on the downside of their careers.

What has happened is eerily similar to what GM John Schuerholz did with the Royals in the early 80s: he got desperate. The Royals had built their own dynasty in the mid-70s on the shoulders of a young core, and when holes formed they were filled by players from within, like Willie Wilson and Dan Quisenberry. But the franchise's inability to win a title frustrated Schuerholz, and starting in 1982 he traded for veterans like Vida Blue, Gaylord Perry, and Jim Sundberg. Unable to accept that great teams sometimes don't win championships because the better team doesn't always win a short playoff series, Schuerholz tried to isolate a missing ingredient—veteran leadership—and doused the team with it.

In an attempt to seal the Braves' place in history with a second championship, he's at it again. In 1996, he showed the first sign by trading for Terry Pendleton—even though the team's once-heroic veteran was 36 and his skills had eroded beyond detectability, and even with Chipper Jones entrenched at third. That same year he traded Jason Schmidt, the Braves' top young pitcher, and once-great prospect Ron Wright to Pittsburgh for Denny Neagle. Schuerholz had gained insight over the years, possibly the result of working alongside Bobby Cox, and had the wisdom to pick the right "veteran" to acquire—a 27-year-old pitcher just then coming into his own. But the Neagle trade was a harbinger of a changing relationship with the farm system. Whereas before it was regarded as a source of future players, now it was being used to produce trading chips for veteran players from other organizations.

The disappointment of another early exit from the playoffs in 1997 made the desperation more acute. The Braves' lineup had, for years, leaned a little toward the left side, and the growing sentiment that what was missing was a right-handed power hitter finally came to a stunning resolution, when the Braves signed Galarraga to a gargantuan contract, ignoring not only his age but the massive park effects that were on his side for five years. To the credit of a franchise whose controversial moves always seem to turn up roses, Galarraga has so far proven to be exactly what the Braves thought they needed, and what they expected from him: tremendous right-handed power sandwiched between Jones and Klesko, protecting the team's perceived Achilles's heel, weakness against left-handed pitching.

What happened then? The Braves had another excellent regular season—their best yet, with the most wins by a National League team in 12 years—and lost in the NLCS again. Why? Because anything can happen in a short series. The Astros, top to bottom, looked like the most balanced team in the NL going into the playoffs—and they were bounced in the first round. The Padres had a banged-up line-up and above-average hitters at only four positions—but their pitchers got hot at the right time, and sent the Braves back to square one.

The Braves remain convinced that if they patch up the holes that remain, they can somehow force the luck factor to disappear from the postseason, the way the Yankees appeared to do last year. Galarraga had a great year and we still couldn't win, goes the thinking, so we need to add more right-handed bats. They traded Neagle, their second-youngest starting pitcher, for Bret Boone, who is 30, coming off a career year, and has a career OBP of .311. They replaced Michael Tucker, who turns 28 in June, with Brian Jordan, who is 32, coming off a career year, and has a career OBP of .339. Suddenly the Braves' lineup is leaning again, but in the other direction: five of the eight starters bat right-handed, and 23-year-old George Lombard, the Braves' best hitting prospect, is without a job.

What the Braves are trying certainly could work. Not mentioned above is that the Royals did win a World Championship under Schuerholz, and they did so with only two regulars in the lineup younger than 28. But they didn't win it with their offense. They won with a rotation featuring three pitchers (Saberhagen, Gubicza, and Danny Jackson) no older than 23, and nobody older than 28—a rotation which in the last quarter century has been exceeded only by these same Braves in both youth and talent. The Royals also won with the sort of cosmic breaks that every team hopes for, but none can count on. The Braves could win a title again this year, simply because they're a great team and no one in the NL East looks strong enough to challenge them—and once they make the playoffs, the karma they've been trying to capture for years may suddenly show up.

But it's a risky game they're playing. The Braves do have a very strong farm system—but that strength is almost entirely counted on the pitching side of the ledger, and while Bruce Chen looks to inherit Neagle's spot, the Big Three are tied up in long-term contracts and another spot in the rotation doesn't look to open up for years. If the Braves want to sustain their dynasty for another eight years, they need to find a way to convert that talent into a useful commodity—say, by trading two of their good young pitchers to the Yankees for D'Angelo Jimenez, or by finding a way to pluck Calvin Pickering away from the Orioles. The Braves are still the prohibitive favorite to win the NL East, and even at their present course it may be two or three years before their line-up drifts back to mediocrity and the rotation becomes too old and too fragile to sustain the team's success on its own. The telling irony is that the Braves' two best hitting prospects—Lombard and Marcus Giles—play the two positions blocked by the acquisitions of Jordan and Boone. Throwing Rob Bell, one of the best pitching prospects in the game, into the Neagle-for-Boone deal suggests that the Braves may simply not know what to do with a reservoir of pitching talent that is the envy of baseball, and may not have forged a plan for turning over that talent into the rejuvenation of a franchise that is headed towards the precipice faster than they realize.

HITTERS (Averages: BA .260/ OBA .330/ SA .420, EQA .260)

Danny Bautista — OF — Bats R — Age 27

YEAR	TEAM	LGE	AB	H	DB	TP	HR	BB	R	RBI	SB	CS	OUT	BA	OBA	SA	EQA	EQR	DEFENSE
1996	Detroit	AL	63	15	2	0	2	8	6	7	1	2	50	.238	.324	.365	.236	7	15-OF 100
1997	Richmond	Int	169	42	6	2	2	16	16	16	1	0	127	.249	.314	.343	.231	16	37-OF 115
1997	Atlanta	NL	103	25	4	2	3	5	10	11	2	0	78	.243	.278	.408	.236	11	34-OF 90
1998	Atlanta	NL	143	36	8	0	4	8	13	15	1	0	107	.252	.291	.392	.235	14	33-OF 86
1999	Atlanta	NL	175	46	9	1	4	13	18	20	1	0	129	.263	.314	.394	.249	20	

He does few things well and nothing great, but his two finest talents—defense and hitting left-handers—perfectly complement Klesko's two main weaknesses, and Cox knows how to use him. His crucial muff that sealed the Braves' NLCS loss could punch his ticket out of town; while Cox doesn't have a history of burying a player over one play, Bautista had a tenuous grip on a roster spot to begin with.

Greg Colbrunn — 1B — Bats R — Age 29

YEAR	TEAM	LGE	AB	H	DB	TP	HR	BB	R	RBI	SB	CS	OUT	BA	OBA	SA	EQA	EQR	DEFENSE
1996	Florida	NL	512	148	25	2	17	29	55	69	3	5	369	.289	.327	.445	.262	65	126-1B 110
1997	Minnesot	AL	214	60	11	0	6	8	20	25	1	2	156	.280	.306	.416	.244	23	51-1B 99
1998	Colorado	NL	118	33	6	2	2	8	14	13	3	3	88	.280	.325	.415	.252	14	22-1B 112
1998	Atlanta	NL	44	13	1	0	2	2	5	6	1	0	31	.295	.326	.455	.270	6	
1999	Arizona	NL	227	64	11	1	7	12	24	29	3	2	165	.282	.318	.432	.257	28	

For the second straight year, the Braves picked him up late, as his ability to hit left-handers and right-handers equally well and play a couple of positions clumsily is valuable for a team which wastes a couple of roster spots on Rafael Belliard and outfielders who don't hit. Signed by Arizona, where Showalter is claiming he'll play first, third, the outfield corners, and catch.

Mark DeRosa — SS — Bats R — Age 24

YEAR	TEAM	LGE	AB	H	DB	TP	HR	BB	R	RBI	SB	CS	OUT	BA	OBA	SA	EQA	EQR	DEFENSE
1996	Eugene	Nwn	260	47	5	1	1	25	11	9	1	2	215	.181	.253	.219	.148	9	69-SS 95
1997	Durham	Car	347	82	6	1	7	19	22	27	3	5	270	.236	.276	.320	.200	24	90-SS 96
1998	Greenvil	Sou	455	100	16	1	7	43	35	33	4	8	363	.220	.287	.305	.202	33	126-SS 88
1999	Atlanta	NL	407	97	14	1	8	32	34	36	4	4	314	.238	.294	.337	.221	36	

In a great position to be a valuable role player as soon as this year, working himself into a starting job soon after that. He was the starting QB at Penn and has made huge strides since entering pro ball. His glove gets good marks, and Walt Weiss needs frequent days off. Weiss is also slightly better hitting left-handed, and DeRosa hit nearly .350 against lefties last year. You don't usually see platoons at shortstop and I don't expect one here, but DeRosa could be a Mark Loretta-like utility man, getting on base and playing four positions.

Andres Galarraga   1B   Bats R   Age 38

YEAR	TEAM	LGE	AB	H	DB	TP	HR	BB	R	RBI	SB	CS	OUT	BA	OBA	SA	EQA	EQR	DEFENSE
1996	Colorado	NL	601	155	31	2	39	43	72	93	13	8	454	.258	.307	.511	.271	87	158-1B 95
1997	Colorado	NL	586	173	26	2	39	56	83	107	11	8	421	.295	.357	.546	.299	102	152-1B 93
1998	Atlanta	NL	554	169	24	1	47	66	87	119	7	7	392	.305	.379	.606	.319	113	145-1B 89
1999	Atlanta	NL	554	151	22	2	37	59	73	97	9	5	408	.273	.343	.520	.291	94	

Okay, we blew it. We insulted, mocked, derided, jeered, and ridiculed the Braves for signing an overrated product of thin air. So then Galarraga, who had hit .281/331/.510 on the road in his five years in Colorado, hits .296/.375/.615 on the road in 1998, putting up his highest unadjusted OPS since 1993. Lost in his move to lower elevation is the fact that he was also 37, and could have easily collapsed even if he had remained in Denver. He didn't, and we salute the Big Cat for making us eat crow. That's why baseball is such a great game: even the greatest truths can be wrong from time to time. Despite his immense power, he's not an extreme flyball hitter, which may partly explain his ability to make the transition. Frankly, we're grasping at straws here. Will he sustain it? I wouldn't bet against him, but he is 38. I don't expect a sudden collapse. He earned his salary last year, but by 2000 he may be a very expensive platoon player.

Marcus Giles   2B   Bats R   Age 21

YEAR	TEAM	LGE	AB	H	DB	TP	HR	BB	R	RBI	SB	CS	OUT	BA	OBA	SA	EQA	EQR	DEFENSE
1997	Danville	App	204	49	5	0	4	22	19	18	2	1	156	.240	.314	.324	.226	19	42-2B 91
1998	Macon	SAL	505	145	19	1	26	70	74	84	6	3	363	.287	.374	.483	.294	85	126-2B 98
1999	Atlanta	NL	382	122	16	1	20	46	58	71	5	2	262	.319	.393	.524	.314	73	

Brian Giles's little brother registered on the prospect radar screen like a squadron of B-52s last year, doing everything right offensively: good average, plate discipline, and as much power as you will ever see from a 20-year-old. And he's a second baseman. The Braves let him beat up on Sally league pitching all summer, which seems curious. Then again, the last Braves' phenom to spend a whole summer in Macon was Andruw Jones, who played at four levels the next year on his way to the World Series. Giles is new to second and may not be able to handle the position in the long run, and the trade for Bret Boone is going to have him waiting anyways. But even if he has to move to left, his bat should carry him to the majors.

Tony Graffanino   2B   Bats R   Age 27

YEAR	TEAM	LGE	AB	H	DB	TP	HR	BB	R	RBI	SB	CS	OUT	BA	OBA	SA	EQA	EQR	DEFENSE
1996	Richmond	Int	352	93	21	1	7	33	43	37	8	5	264	.264	.327	.389	.250	41	93-2B 95
1997	Atlanta	NL	186	48	9	0	9	27	26	27	5	4	142	.258	.352	.452	.275	28	50-2B 129
1998	Atlanta	NL	288	61	12	1	6	26	21	22	1	5	232	.212	.277	.323	.201	21	72-2B 117
1999	Atlanta	NL	247	57	13	1	5	25	25	23	4	3	193	.231	.301	.352	.231	25	

A much better defensive second baseman than Lockhart, he could have won the second base job outright with a remotely useful season. But his struggles contributed to the desperation to fill that hole from outside the organization, dooming him. He now joins the endless pool of players who regard spring training at-bats as life-and-death situations.

Ozzie Guillen   SS   Bats L   Age 35

YEAR	TEAM	LGE	AB	H	DB	TP	HR	BB	R	RBI	SB	CS	OUT	BA	OBA	SA	EQA	EQR	DEFENSE
1996	ChiSox	AL	495	129	23	8	4	8	38	41	6	6	372	.261	.272	.364	.213	39	131-SS 96
1997	ChiSox	AL	485	119	22	6	4	23	39	38	5	3	369	.245	.280	.340	.211	38	137-SS 100
1998	Atlanta	NL	263	73	16	1	1	26	29	26	1	5	195	.278	.343	.357	.242	28	63-SS 94
1999	Atlanta	NL	343	85	17	3	2	17	26	27	3	4	262	.248	.283	.332	.212	27	

Guillen's OPS with the Braves was the highest of his career. If I'm the Sox, I sue for breach of contract. Even doing this well, Ozzie's a marginal shortstop, but Rafael Belliard's eight-year term as occupant of the Wasted Roster Spot™ is up.

Wes Helms   3B   Bats R   Age 23

YEAR	TEAM	LGE	AB	H	DB	TP	HR	BB	R	RBI	SB	CS	OUT	BA	OBA	SA	EQA	EQR	DEFENSE
1996	Durham	Car	254	71	7	1	10	10	23	33	1	1	184	.280	.307	.433	.251	29	65-3B 87
1996	Greenvil	Sou	230	53	10	1	4	9	15	17	1	1	178	.230	.259	.335	.198	16	62-3B 81
1997	Greenvil	Sou	303	70	8	0	8	26	25	27	2	2	235	.231	.292	.337	.217	26	83-3B 85
1997	Richmond	Int	110	20	2	0	3	9	6	6	1	1	91	.182	.244	.282	.172	6	31-3B 97
1998	Richmond	Int	442	108	18	0	12	31	39	43	4	2	336	.244	.294	.367	.228	42	122-3B 92
1999	*Atlanta*	*NL*	*441*	*114*	*16*	*1*	*14*	*25*	*39*	*50*	*4*	*2*	*329*	*.259*	*.298*	*.395*	*.241*	*47*	

In his second stab at Triple-A pitching, he got it right, reviving his prospect status. He still doesn't bring anything special to the table, and his plate discipline has never been good, but his defense is considered exceptional and he has the sort of medium power that many teams expect at the hot corner. He's got no future in this organization, but after the Devil Rays' success with Bobby Smith last year, expect some team to trade for Helms in the hope that he can do the same.

Adam Johnson   OF   Bats L   Age 23

YEAR	TEAM	LGE	AB	H	DB	TP	HR	BB	R	RBI	SB	CS	OUT	BA	OBA	SA	EQA	EQR	DEFENSE
1996	Eugene	Nwn	317	81	11	4	5	13	25	29	2	1	237	.256	.285	.363	.221	27	76-OF 97
1997	Durham	Car	504	133	22	2	22	40	58	67	11	6	377	.264	.318	.446	.261	65	122-OF 102
1998	Greenvil	Sou	406	90	13	1	16	30	33	41	5	5	321	.222	.275	.377	.221	37	86-OF 99
1999	*Atlanta*	*NL*	*419*	*107*	*20*	*2*	*16*	*28*	*43*	*52*	*7*	*4*	*316*	*.255*	*.302*	*.427*	*.252*	*50*	

A late draft pick battling uphill, but he'll have one more chance to establish himself as a legitimate prospect with a big year. He has a broad range of skills, although they all took a hit as he made the jump to Double-A. Small and not thought of as a power hitter, but if he breaks through this year, he can be dominant—and he's young enough to do just that. A gamble, but a good one.

Andruw Jones   CF   Bats R   Age 22

YEAR	TEAM	LGE	AB	H	DB	TP	HR	BB	R	RBI	SB	CS	OUT	BA	OBA	SA	EQA	EQR	DEFENSE
1996	Durham	Car	242	66	5	2	12	35	36	37	8	3	179	.273	.365	.459	.286	39	65-OF 114
1996	Greenvil	Sou	154	53	6	1	10	13	27	30	8	3	104	.344	.395	.591	.326	32	37-OF 128
1996	Atlanta	NL	105	22	5	1	5	8	10	12	3	0	83	.210	.265	.419	.236	11	23-OF 130
1997	Atlanta	NL	399	93	17	1	19	58	54	50	16	12	318	.233	.330	.424	.259	54	126-OF 104
1998	Atlanta	NL	580	157	33	7	33	44	85	90	29	5	428	.271	.322	.522	.286	94	156-OF 121
1999	*Atlanta*	*NL*	*535*	*152*	*29*	*3*	*33*	*53*	*84*	*90*	*28*	*8*	*391*	*.284*	*.349*	*.535*	*.300*	*97*	

We projected him to hit .271 with 31 homers, 92 RBI, and 27 steals, and he hit .271 with 31 homers, 90 RBI, and 27 steals. But we were way off in the walks department—78, compared to the 40 he drew—which illustrates the remaining hurdle for Jones to clear. If he learns to command the strike zone, and he's shown flickers of it in the past, he will be unstoppable. Probably the best defensive outfielder in the game, and the manner Cox dealt with his loafing early in the year—pulling him from a game mid-inning, but putting him back in the lineup after that—was the perfect way to help him grow out of his immaturity without wounding him. I can't shake the perception that his career is going to resemble Hank Aaron's. Expect a major breakout this year, as he begins a long run aboard MVP ballots.

Chipper Jones   3B   Bats B   Age 27

YEAR	TEAM	LGE	AB	H	DB	TP	HR	BB	R	RBI	SB	CS	OUT	BA	OBA	SA	EQA	EQR	DEFENSE	
1996	Atlanta	NL	595	179	31	4	30	88	102	105	12	1	417	.301	.391	.518	.311	113	113-3B 81	33-SS 96
1997	Atlanta	NL	598	176	40	2	23	79	99	91	17	5	427	.294	.377	.483	.297	102	141-3B 89	
1998	Atlanta	NL	601	189	28	5	36	99	112	118	17	7	419	.314	.411	.557	.326	127	159-3B 96	
1999	*Atlanta*	*NL*	*615*	*189*	*33*	*5*	*31*	*90*	*107*	*111*	*19*	*5*	*431*	*.307*	*.396*	*.528*	*.318*	*123*		

Another great year—his best yet—but he continues to struggle against left-handers, hitting .298/.380/.403, compared to .319/.413/.610 against RHPs. That vulnerability alters the Braves' perception of their own team; despite having good right-handed bats in Lopez, Galarraga, and Andruw, they look at Chipper, Klesko, and Weiss and see three regulars who can be taken out of the game by a good bullpen. Thats was a big factor in the trade for Bret Boone, the signing of Brian Jordan, and the departure of Michael Tucker. It also hurts the lineup, because with Weiss leading off and Chipper batting third, they have to bat a right-hander second, which is why Bret Boone, low OBP and all, is rumored to be batting at the top of the lineup.

Ryan Klesko   LF   Bats L   Age 28

YEAR	TEAM	LGE	AB	H	DB	TP	HR	BB	R	RBI	SB	CS	OUT	BA	OBA	SA	EQA	EQR	DEFENSE	
1996	Atlanta	NL	525	144	19	4	33	70	75	93	5	3	384	.274	.360	.514	.294	90	131-OF 87	
1997	Atlanta	NL	467	122	23	5	25	50	58	74	3	4	349	.261	.333	.493	.276	70	107-OF 89	10-1B 83
1998	Atlanta	NL	426	117	25	1	20	59	63	67	5	3	312	.275	.363	.479	.288	69	104-OF 90	
1999	Atlanta	NL	439	120	23	2	24	57	61	74	5	3	322	.273	.357	.499	.293	75		

His slugging dropped for the third straight year, and he constantly has to deal with the perception that he hasn't developed the way Chipper Jones and Javy Lopez did. Playing out of position appears to be grinding him down, and he's had snippy episodes with management over his contract. He may not be with the Braves much longer, but they can't afford to give up his power at this point. He never learned to hit lefties, mustering just a .614 OPS the last three years.

Keith Lockhart   2B   Bats L   Age 34

YEAR	TEAM	LGE	AB	H	DB	TP	HR	BB	R	RBI	SB	CS	OUT	BA	OBA	SA	EQA	EQR	DEFENSE	
1996	KansasCy	AL	425	111	30	3	7	28	48	42	11	7	321	.261	.307	.395	.242	46	69-2B 101	42-3B 90
1997	Atlanta	NL	147	41	5	3	6	15	18	23	0	0	106	.279	.346	.476	.280	22	12-2B 118	
1998	Atlanta	NL	365	94	17	0	11	31	37	42	2	2	273	.258	.316	.395	.245	41	83-2B 116	
1999	Atlanta	NL	311	81	16	1	10	28	35	38	4	2	232	.260	.322	.415	.258	39		

An excellent bench player, but Graffanino's struggles forced him into a starting role, and the Braves found that Lockhart is . . . an excellent bench player. The acquisition of Boone allows him to ease back into a less-demanding role while giving his defensive versatility more value. I wouldn't write him off; he can still contribute to a winning team.

George Lombard   OF   Bats L   Age 23

YEAR	TEAM	LGE	AB	H	DB	TP	HR	BB	R	RBI	SB	CS	OUT	BA	OBA	SA	EQA	EQR	DEFENSE
1996	Macon	SAL	450	96	8	3	12	27	30	33	10	8	362	.213	.258	.324	.196	31	107-OF 100
1997	Durham	Car	466	115	16	4	13	54	61	49	20	5	356	.247	.325	.382	.252	57	125-OF 101
1998	Greenvil	Sou	412	114	15	2	19	55	68	59	22	4	302	.277	.362	.461	.289	68	113-OF 84
1999	Atlanta	NL	438	116	14	4	14	44	59	52	22	6	328	.265	.332	.411	.266	60	

He's that most sought-after of men: the tools player made good. The Braves have an aggressive draft philosophy, picking high school athletes, and one of the most impressive characteristics about the organization is that they have had a lot of success with what has historically been a shaky strategy. In the last two years Lombard doubled his walk rate and raised his power output while advancing to Double-A. The Red Sox had a prospect like this last year, Michael Coleman, who fell flat on his face in 1998. Braves' prospects have an excellent history of sustaining the gains they make. The signing of Brian Jordan closes a window of opportunity for Lombard, at least until Jordan gets hurt. In the meantime, Lombard's left-handed power, speed, and defense could make him a handy bench player.

Javy Lopez   C   Bats R   Age 28

YEAR	TEAM	LGE	AB	H	DB	TP	HR	BB	R	RBI	SB	CS	OUT	BA	OBA	SA	EQA	EQR	DEFENSE
1996	Atlanta	NL	485	132	17	1	23	31	47	69	0	6	359	.272	.316	.454	.257	60	
1997	Atlanta	NL	414	122	24	0	25	42	57	75	1	1	293	.295	.360	.534	.299	71	
1998	Atlanta	NL	488	139	18	1	36	33	60	88	5	3	352	.285	.330	.547	.289	79	126-C 102
1999	Atlanta	NL	474	138	18	0	33	37	58	87	3	2	338	.291	.342	.538	.296	80	

He gets almost no attention in the Braves' constellation of stars, but after Mike Piazza, there isn't a better-hitting catcher in the game. He started to develop a reputation as a clutch hitter last season, and his game-tying homer against the Cubs in the Division Series added to it. As we've said a million times, there's no evidence that clutch-hitting exists, but there's no harm if it gets Lopez some much-deserved accolades. His defense is actually good, and despite Eddie Perez's fluky season, the Braves need to convince Greg Maddux to work with Lopez more, because they're handing playoff opponents an advantage every time Lopez sits.

Ricky Magdaleno   SS   Bats R   Age 24

YEAR	TEAM	LGE	AB	H	DB	TP	HR	BB	R	RBI	SB	CS	OUT	BA	OBA	SA	EQA	EQR	DEFENSE
1996	Chattang	Sou	428	90	13	1	15	53	39	42	2	4	342	.210	.297	.350	.224	41	127-SS 90
1997	Chattang	Sou	184	41	7	1	6	34	24	21	1	1	144	.223	.344	.370	.254	23	58-SS 88
1997	Indianap	AA	156	32	8	0	4	15	12	13	0	1	125	.205	.275	.333	.207	12	51-SS 91
1998	Richmond	Int	244	63	8	1	4	20	22	24	1	2	183	.258	.314	.348	.230	23	53-SS 96
1999	*Atlanta*	*NL*	*280*	*68*	*9*	*0*	*9*	*29*	*27*	*31*	*1*	*2*	*214*	*.243*	*.314*	*.371*	*.241*	*30*	

He's most famous for being one of the few real prospects to cave in to the owners and play in the replacement spring training in 1995. Magdaleno still has to live that indiscretion down, but he has a wide range of offensive skills and can play several positions. He left the Reds organization, where they weren't about to give up on Pokey Reese, but the Braves are also well stocked with middle infielders. He needs to find the right circumstances soon if he wants a career.

Marty Malloy   2B   Bats L   Age 26

YEAR	TEAM	LGE	AB	H	DB	TP	HR	BB	R	RBI	SB	CS	OUT	BA	OBA	SA	EQA	EQR	DEFENSE
1996	Greenvil	Sou	424	115	17	1	4	43	48	40	7	6	315	.271	.338	.344	.241	45	104-2B 97
1997	Richmond	Int	412	109	14	4	2	35	46	34	13	6	309	.265	.322	.333	.233	40	100-2B 95
1998	Richmond	Int	473	112	16	1	5	41	44	34	12	5	366	.237	.298	.307	.213	39	122-2B 104
1999	*Atlanta*	*NL*	*432*	*114*	*17*	*2*	*5*	*35*	*46*	*40*	*11*	*5*	*323*	*.264*	*.319*	*.347*	*.239*	*45*	

Buried for years, but the Braves' second base woes opened an opportunity and Malloy squeezed onto the postseason roster. He represents the greatest challenge to Keith Lockhart's roster spot, being cheaper and younger, but with less power and little experience playing anywhere other than second base.

Pascual Matos   C   Bats R   Age 24

YEAR	TEAM	LGE	AB	H	DB	TP	HR	BB	R	RBI	SB	CS	OUT	BA	OBA	SA	EQA	EQR	DEFENSE
1996	Durham	Car	217	41	4	1	5	6	8	10	3	0	176	.189	.211	.286	.155	8	
1997	Durham	Car	430	94	11	1	14	9	22	33	2	3	339	.219	.235	.347	.189	26	
1998	Greenvil	Sou	335	72	7	1	10	6	16	23	2	1	264	.215	.229	.331	.181	18	94-C 101
1999	*Atlanta*	*NL*	*324*	*71*	*8*	*1*	*10*	*6*	*16*	*25*	*2*	*1*	*254*	*.219*	*.233*	*.343*	*.192*	*21*	

This is why Eddie Perez has job security. Matos has some power and evidently plays good defense, as he'd be out of a job if he didn't. This is what an average hitter does facing a healthy Bret Saberhagen. The Braves have another catching "prospect," Fernando Lunar, who hit .220 with a K/BB ratio greater than 8 while being named one of the ten best prospects in the Carolina League because he plays defense like a more agile Charles Johnson. Neither guy has a future.

Tyrone Pendergrass   OF   Bats B   Age 22

YEAR	TEAM	LGE	AB	H	DB	TP	HR	BB	R	RBI	SB	CS	OUT	BA	OBA	SA	EQA	EQR	DEFENSE
1996	Danville	App	222	55	4	2	3	14	22	17	13	4	171	.248	.292	.324	.221	20	54-OF 108
1997	Macon	SAL	495	117	12	2	6	53	58	35	31	10	387	.236	.310	.305	.226	47	127-OF 103
1998	Danville	Car	525	139	20	6	5	43	61	47	21	10	396	.265	.320	.354	.239	55	128-OF 103
1999	*Atlanta*	*NL*	*478*	*121*	*15*	*4*	*5*	*39*	*55*	*39*	*26*	*8*	*365*	*.253*	*.309*	*.333*	*.235*	*49*	

Another guy with more tools than Jeff Gordon's pit crew, but not much of a hitter. The Braves have an impressive track record with these guys, but he needs to make a successful jump to AA before he gets too excited. No relation to Teddy, apparently, even if he does have a deep voice.

Eddie Perez   C   Bats R   Age 31

YEAR	TEAM	LGE	AB	H	DB	TP	HR	BB	R	RBI	SB	CS	OUT	BA	OBA	SA	EQA	EQR	DEFENSE
1996	Atlanta	NL	155	38	8	1	4	9	13	16	0	0	117	.245	.287	.387	.230	15	
1997	Atlanta	NL	190	40	5	0	6	12	11	15	0	1	151	.211	.257	.332	.196	13	
1998	Atlanta	NL	149	50	10	0	7	16	24	28	1	1	100	.336	.400	.544	.317	28	37-C 99
1999	*Atlanta*	*NL*	*166*	*46*	*6*	*0*	*7*	*13*	*17*	*24*	*0*	*1*	*121*	*.277*	*.330*	*.440*	*.265*	*22*	

The poster boy for Jazayerli's Rule of Backup Catchers: he got into a lucky groove for 150 at-bats, and the ".336" in his batting line is going to be paying off five years from now, as he continues to get chances from teams who think he'll recapture the magic. It's debatable whether he needed the boost after earning the job as the personal catcher to the Smartest Pitcher Who Ever Lived. He's in no danger of losing his job, but he's also no threat to take playing time away from Lopez.

Curtis Pride		OF				Bats L		Age 30									
YEAR	TEAM	LGE	AB	H	DB	TP	HR	BB	R	RBI	SB	CS	OUT	BA	OBA	SA	EQA	EQR	DEFENSE
1996	Detroit	AL	260	76	17	5	9	30	42	39	11	7	191	.292	.366	.500	.291	44	37-OF 98
1997	Detroit	AL	160	33	4	4	2	24	18	13	6	4	131	.206	.310	.319	.224	16	26-OF 90
1998	Richmond	Int	77	15	1	1	1	12	9	5	5	0	62	.195	.303	.273	.222	7	
1998	Atlanta	NL	107	27	8	1	3	9	14	12	4	0	80	.252	.310	.430	.260	14	
1999	*Atlanta*	*NL*	*198*	*49*	*9*	*3*	*6*	*25*	*29*	*23*	*10*	*3*	*152*	*.247*	*.332*	*.414*	*.267*	*28*	

A valuable fifth outfielder because he can play defense and pinch-run, and because he understood his role as a bench player without generating controversy asking for more playing time. Depending on whether the Braves give Lombard a bench job or send him to Triple-A, he could be handed a larger role or downsized. In that sense, he's not much different than you or me.

Randall Simon		1B				Bats L		Age 24									
YEAR	TEAM	LGE	AB	H	DB	TP	HR	BB	R	RBI	SB	CS	OUT	BA	OBA	SA	EQA	EQR	DEFENSE	
1996	Greenvil	Sou	494	124	16	1	16	28	40	53	3	5	375	.251	.291	.385	.229	47	80-1B 93	33-OF 88
1997	Richmond	Int	515	152	31	1	15	13	50	66	1	5	368	.295	.312	.447	.254	60	125-1B 87	
1998	Richmond	Int	476	107	14	1	11	20	29	35	3	3	372	.225	.256	.328	.194	31	116-1B 85	
1999	*Atlanta*	*NL*	*483*	*127*	*22*	*1*	*12*	*16*	*39*	*50*	*3*	*4*	*360*	*.263*	*.287*	*.387*	*.231*	*46*		

Briefly the heir apparent at first, Simon has sabotaged his own career by refusing to learn the strike zone, and last year even his modest power disappeared. First basemen with Hal Morris power, Ricky Jordan discipline, and Cecil Fielder batting average aren't from the world of prospects. Young enough to revive his career, but it would be almost unprecedented for him to improve as much as he needs to.

Mike Tucker		RF				Bats L		Age 28									
YEAR	TEAM	LGE	AB	H	DB	TP	HR	BB	R	RBI	SB	CS	OUT	BA	OBA	SA	EQA	EQR	DEFENSE
1996	KansasCy	AL	332	84	19	4	11	38	45	41	10	5	253	.253	.330	.434	.263	45	86-OF 96
1997	Atlanta	NL	499	141	26	6	15	47	65	68	10	7	365	.283	.344	.449	.272	70	106-OF 102
1998	Atlanta	NL	413	101	27	3	14	51	54	51	8	3	315	.245	.328	.426	.261	55	108-OF 98
1999	*Cincnnti*	*NL*	*417*	*112*	*25*	*3*	*15*	*47*	*56*	*58*	*10*	*5*	*310*	*.269*	*.343*	*.451*	*.275*	*62*	

A good player, but his minor league record, a pretty swing, and two consecutive hot starts have created expectations he was unable to meet, and he leaves Atlanta as a disappointment. He's an introverted guy and may have not adapted to the national attention the Braves get, so getting away to Cincinnati may be good for him. He's going to be fighting with about eight other candidates for three spots in the lineup.

Walt Weiss		SS				Bats B		Age 35									
YEAR	TEAM	LGE	AB	H	DB	TP	HR	BB	R	RBI	SB	CS	OUT	BA	OBA	SA	EQA	EQR	DEFENSE
1996	Colorado	NL	496	115	16	2	6	78	59	42	7	2	383	.232	.336	.308	.235	51	146-SS 86
1997	Colorado	NL	385	94	21	4	4	66	54	38	4	2	293	.244	.355	.351	.255	48	114-SS 97
1998	Atlanta	NL	347	98	16	2	1	61	58	35	8	1	250	.282	.390	.349	.273	49	90-SS 99
1999	*Atlanta*	*NL*	*338*	*85*	*15*	*1*	*3*	*60*	*47*	*33*	*4*	*1*	*254*	*.251*	*.364*	*.328*	*.258*	*43*	

Weiss had a hot April, after which he wasn't very helpful. After hitting just .227 with a .318 OBP after the All-Star break, it's a legitimate question whether he has enough left for even one more season. Even if he does, his total lack of power and weakness against left-handers makes him an easy target in the lineup.

Gerald Williams		OF				Bats R		Age 32									
YEAR	TEAM	LGE	AB	H	DB	TP	HR	BB	R	RBI	SB	CS	OUT	BA	OBA	SA	EQA	EQR	DEFENSE
1996	NYYanks	AL	228	60	13	4	5	14	24	25	7	10	177	.263	.306	.421	.241	25	81-OF 87
1996	Milwauke	AL	91	17	4	0	0	3	3	3	3	1	75	.187	.213	.231	.131	2	22-OF 122
1997	Milwauke	AL	559	140	33	2	10	21	54	47	23	9	428	.250	.278	.370	.224	51	152-OF 108
1998	Atlanta	NL	265	81	18	2	11	19	41	40	12	6	190	.306	.352	.513	.290	43	67-OF 110
1999	*Atlanta*	*NL*	*336*	*87*	*21*	*2*	*8*	*16*	*35*	*35*	*12*	*7*	*256*	*.259*	*.293*	*.405*	*.242*	*37*	

Had a fabulous season as a part-timer, playing all over the outfield and hitting .363 with an extra-base hit every 6 at-bats against left-handers. It would be an upset if his encore performance was as good, and signing Brian Jordan leaves only one left-handed outfielder in the starting lineup. Williams brings more offense and better defense to the table than Bautista does, so his job security shouldn't be threatened.

Glenn Williams — 2B — Bats R — Age 21

YEAR	TEAM	LGE	AB	H	DB	TP	HR	BB	R	RBI	SB	CS	OUT	BA	OBA	SA	EQA	EQR	DEFENSE
1996	Macon	SAL	184	30	3	1	3	14	7	6	2	1	155	.163	.222	.239	.140	6	47-SS 90
1997	Macon	SAL	298	71	10	1	11	22	27	32	4	4	231	.238	.291	.389	.231	30	73-SS 88
1998	Danville	Car	474	96	14	1	10	38	29	32	1	2	380	.203	.262	.300	.188	29	125-2B 89
1999	*Atlanta*	*NL*	*385*	*86*	*14*	*1*	*11*	*27*	*30*	*35*	*4*	*2*	*301*	*.223*	*.274*	*.351*	*.218*	*33*	

Williams was signed out of Australia when he was 16, and scouts gushed about his talents to the point where some suggested he was ready to handle AA pitching. Four years later, he's still overmatched at A-ball. He's still young enough where he can't be written off entirely, but he took a step back last year and his strikeout-to-walk data is terrible. The Josh Booty of second baseman.

PITCHERS (Averages: 4.00 ERA, 9.00 H/9, 1.00 HR/9, 3.00 BB/9, 6.00 K/9, 1.00 KWH)

Jamie Arnold — Throws R — Age 25

YEAR	TEAM	LGE	IP	H	ER	HR	BB	K	ERA	W	L	H/9	HR/9	BB/9	K/9	KWH	PERA
1996	Greenvil	Sou	126.0	170	75	19	40	50	5.36	5	9	12.14	1.36	2.86	3.57	0.28	5.71
1997	Durham	Car	23.0	33	23	2	14	14	9.00	0	3	12.91	0.78	5.48	5.48	0.32	5.87
1998	Greenvil	Sou	80.0	110	49	13	42	36	5.51	3	6	12.38	1.46	4.73	4.05	0.21	6.19
1998	Richmond	Int	21.3	33	20	1	16	9	8.44	0	2	13.92	0.42	6.75	3.80	0.12	6.33

Former first-round draft pick who illustrates the difficult road high school pitchers follow. He was advertised as "polished" for an 18-year-old, which is a kiss of death, because it means he doesn't have a fastball. He has bounced around from level to level, finally reaching AAA this year, but his K/BB ratios are uniformly abysmal. Not a prospect.

Rob Bell — Throws R — Age 22

YEAR	TEAM	LGE	IP	H	ER	HR	BB	K	ERA	W	L	H/9	HR/9	BB/9	K/9	KWH	PERA
1996	Eugene	Nwn	76.3	124	58	7	33	44	6.84	2	6	14.62	0.83	3.89	5.19	0.35	6.48
1997	Macon	SAL	142.7	188	81	19	51	93	5.11	6	10	11.86	1.20	3.22	5.87	0.68	5.49
1998	DanvillC	Car	173.0	211	89	11	54	136	4.63	8	11	10.98	0.57	2.81	7.08	1.22	4.53

Here's the first of an amazing crop of pitching prospects who are beginning to emerge for the Braves. Bell has always had a good fastball, but he perfected an outstanding curve last season, leading the Braves' minor league system in strikeouts while maintaining remarkable control for someone so young. The Reds did well to get him in the Neagle deal, as he may be their best prospect now. He averaged a tad over 26 batters per start, which is a little higher than you'd like to see from a 21 year old, but that's not the Braves' problem now.

Pedro Borbon — Throws L — Age 31

YEAR	TEAM	LGE	IP	H	ER	HR	BB	K	ERA	W	L	H/9	HR/9	BB/9	K/9	KWH	PERA
1995	Atlanta	NL	33.0	31	11	2	16	31	3.00	3	1	8.45	0.55	4.36	8.45	1.45	3.55
1996	Atlanta	NL	36.0	28	11	1	6	28	2.75	3	1	7.00	0.25	1.50	7.00	3.50	2.00
1998	Greenvil	Sou	18.3	25	14	2	14	7	6.87	1	1	12.27	0.98	6.87	3.44	0.10	5.89
1998	Richmond	Int	23.3	33	17	1	8	12	6.56	1	2	12.73	0.39	3.09	4.63	0.41	5.01

Was just establishing himself as one of the best left-handed relievers in baseball when his shoulder collapsed, and the road back has proven to be longer and more treacherous than anyone expected. It's hard to predict what he's going to do after rotator cuff surgery; some pitchers show nothing for two or three years and then suddenly regain their stuff. I'd be surprised if he's one of them.

Micah Bowie — Throws L — Age 24

YEAR	TEAM	LGE	IP	H	ER	HR	BB	K	ERA	W	L	H/9	HR/9	BB/9	K/9	KWH	PERA
1996	Durham	Car	65.3	67	31	5	36	49	4.27	3	4	9.23	0.69	4.96	6.75	0.75	3.99
1997	Durham	Car	38.0	40	18	3	27	31	4.26	2	2	9.47	0.71	6.39	7.34	0.67	4.50
1997	Greenvil	Sou	44.0	38	17	3	25	33	3.48	3	2	7.77	0.61	5.11	6.75	0.86	3.27
1998	Greenvil	Sou	161.3	148	64	13	55	124	3.57	10	8	8.26	0.73	3.07	6.92	1.42	3.24

Bowie had made steady progress through the system, pitching well but never bowling anyone over until last year. He developed a changeup while pitching in Australia last winter, and came back a new man. He was especially hot during second half, allowing just one run over a 41-inning stretch. He's already had an injury setback, but rehabbed an elbow ligament tear without surgery. He needs to be handled with care, but he's a fine prospect. While the Braves don't really need him, as a lefty he should have no problem finding an organization who does.

Adam Butler — Throws L — Age 25

YEAR	TEAM	LGE	IP	H	ER	HR	BB	K	ERA	W	L	H/9	HR/9	BB/9	K/9	KWH	PERA
1996	Greenvil	Sou	34.7	42	21	7	15	24	5.45	1	3	10.90	1.82	3.89	6.23	0.69	5.71
1997	Greenvil	Sou	49.0	45	15	3	14	43	2.76	3	2	8.27	0.55	2.57	7.90	2.20	3.12
1998	Richmond	Int	100.3	103	37	8	27	77	3.32	7	4	9.24	0.72	2.42	6.91	1.60	3.68

He's been overlooked in an organization bursting at the seams with pitchers, and despite a second excellent season in relief, he got barely five innings in his brief callups. The emergence of Odalis Perez and John Rocker may leave him stuck once again, but if the Braves stop screwing around with guys like Norm Charlton, Butler can be an asset.

Mike Cather — Throws R — Age 28

YEAR	TEAM	LGE	IP	H	ER	HR	BB	K	ERA	W	L	H/9	HR/9	BB/9	K/9	KWH	PERA
1996	Greenvil	Sou	82.3	113	48	2	30	42	5.25	3	6	12.35	0.22	3.28	4.59	0.39	4.92
1997	Greenvil	Sou	36.0	44	19	2	8	20	4.75	2	2	11.00	0.50	2.00	5.00	0.85	4.25
1997	Richmond	Int	25.0	21	7	1	9	16	2.52	2	1	7.56	0.36	3.24	5.76	1.02	2.52
1997	Atlanta	NL	37.3	27	12	1	17	26	2.89	3	1	6.51	0.24	4.10	6.27	1.10	2.17
1998	Atlanta	NL	41.3	42	19	7	11	30	4.14	2	3	9.15	1.52	2.40	6.53	1.46	4.14

Very quietly had another fine season as a middle reliever before missing most of the second half with an injury. At his best his sinker overwhelms hitters and kills rallies with groundball double plays, and having a pitcher like Cather in middle relief is what separates good bullpens from bad ones. If he's healthy, I see no reason why he can't continue to be successful.

Norm Charlton — Throws L — Age 36

YEAR	TEAM	LGE	IP	H	ER	HR	BB	K	ERA	W	L	H/9	HR/9	BB/9	K/9	KWH	PERA
1996	Seattle	AL	78.0	64	27	6	31	72	3.12	6	3	7.38	0.69	3.58	8.31	1.96	2.77
1997	Seattle	AL	73.7	86	47	7	42	54	5.74	3	5	10.51	0.86	5.13	6.60	0.61	4.89
1998	Baltimor	AL	36.0	47	23	5	23	40	5.75	1	3	11.75	1.25	5.75	10.00	1.11	5.75
1998	Atlanta	NL	13.3	7	2	0	8	6	1.35	1	0	4.73	0.00	5.40	4.05	0.48	1.35

I suppose Cox and Mazzone deserve credit for getting anything out of him, but the real question is why were they screwing with him in the first place? You have two dozen young pitchers ready to step into a relief role, and you dig up this fossil who's been getting pasted for the last two years? It's not like Charlton was going after an ethnic record like El Presidente, although he may very well hold the saves record for guys with dyed blond hair and a prominent jaw.

Bruce Chen — Throws L — Age 22

YEAR	TEAM	LGE	IP	H	ER	HR	BB	K	ERA	W	L	H/9	HR/9	BB/9	K/9	KWH	PERA
1996	Eugene	Nwn	34.3	33	16	2	16	32	4.19	2	2	8.65	0.52	4.19	8.39	1.45	3.41
1997	Macon	SAL	143.3	156	73	23	54	120	4.58	7	9	9.80	1.44	3.39	7.53	1.28	4.65
1998	Greenvil	Sou	139.3	115	48	13	40	130	3.10	9	6	7.43	0.84	2.58	8.40	2.76	2.71
1998	Richmond	Int	24.7	19	5	1	18	25	1.82	2	1	6.93	0.36	6.57	9.12	1.37	2.92
1998	Atlanta	NL	20.3	25	8	3	9	16	3.54	1	1	11.07	1.33	3.98	7.08	0.85	5.31

The Braves' other prospects, great as they are, are just pretenders to the throne. Chen is the Prince. When those around him discuss his success, one aspect towers over all: mound presence. He throws hard, has excellent command of four pitches, but what distinguishes him is that he sets up hitters with uncanny ease for a 21-year-old. The Neagle trade was made with him in mind. Chen certainly looks ready, he has an opportunity waiting for him, and he has the best crew in baseball to help him develop. He may be the best pitching prospect in the game.

Derrin Ebert		Throws L				Age 22										
YEAR	TEAM	LGE	IP	H	ER	HR	BB	K	ERA	W	L	H/9	HR/9	BB/9	K/9	KWH	PERA
1996	Durham	Car	162.3	227	109	16	40	74	6.04	5	13	12.59	0.89	2.22	4.10	0.45	5.49
1997	Greenvil	Sou	175.7	208	82	23	45	81	4.20	10	10	10.66	1.18	2.31	4.15	0.53	4.76
1998	Richmond	Int	166.0	205	83	13	45	76	4.50	8	10	11.11	0.70	2.44	4.12	0.47	4.61

There are prospects, and then there is Derrin Ebert, staff filler. That's not entirely fair; if he were in the Angels' organization, he'd be one of their three best minor league pitchers. He's young, left-handed, and held his own in Triple-A last year. But his strikeout rate is not nearly high enough to sustain success in the majors, and he has been worked very hard, averaging 172 innings the last four years, starting at age 18. It will be enough of a surprise if he avoids injury the next two years; if he somehow turns in a Jeff Ballard-like season for someone, it will be a miracle.

Tom Glavine		Throws L				Age 33										
YEAR	TEAM	LGE	IP	H	ER	HR	BB	K	ERA	W	L	H/9	HR/9	BB/9	K/9	KWH	PERA
1996	Atlanta	NL	240.0	237	83	14	81	164	3.11	17	10	8.89	0.52	3.04	6.15	1.05	3.45
1997	Atlanta	NL	237.0	218	86	21	71	136	3.27	16	10	8.28	0.80	2.70	5.16	0.90	3.23
1998	Atlanta	NL	231.7	215	63	13	67	144	2.45	19	7	8.35	0.51	2.60	5.59	1.08	3.07

Everyone whines about all the help he gets from the umpires, and it's certainly a valid point. But Glavine is a wonderful pitcher, and what seems to be missed is that he underwent a career transition—a mid-life crisis of sorts—from 1993 to 1995, as his K/BB ratios dropped ominously and his ERA spiked upwards. But he altered his style, becoming more of a groundball pitcher, and he's pitching as well as he ever has. He wasn't the best pitcher in the NL—his slight advantage over Maddux in win-loss record is a reflection of better run support—but he was clearly second-best, and there's no reason to think he won't continue to be one of the best pitchers in baseball. With 173 wins, four 20-win seasons and 2 Cys, he's well on target for the Hall of Fame.

Kerry Ligtenberg		Throws R				Age 28										
YEAR	TEAM	LGE	IP	H	ER	HR	BB	K	ERA	W	L	H/9	HR/9	BB/9	K/9	KWH	PERA
1996	Durham	Car	55.7	79	26	4	20	49	4.20	3	3	12.77	0.65	3.23	7.92	1.14	5.50
1997	Greenvil	Sou	34.3	25	8	3	15	30	2.10	3	1	6.55	0.79	3.93	7.86	1.80	2.36
1997	Richmond	Int	23.7	26	14	3	2	26	5.32	1	2	9.89	1.14	0.76	9.89	9.75	4.18
1997	Atlanta	NL	15.0	13	5	4	4	17	3.00	1	1	7.80	2.40	2.40	10.20	4.17	3.60
1998	Atlanta	NL	73.7	55	22	6	21	72	2.69	6	2	6.72	0.73	2.57	8.80	3.37	2.20

The great thing about the radar gun is that it can trump even a scout's evaluation: Ligtenberg, as everyone knows, was a Northern League find, but once he started popping 91 or 92 with control and got turned over to the Braves, he was on the fast track. A hitter who got signed out of an independent league would never advance that fast. Ligtenberg was no fluke; he has a great reliever's arsenal, and had a 1.13 ERA after the Break, holding batters to a .153 average.

Greg Maddux		Throws R				Age 33										
YEAR	TEAM	LGE	IP	H	ER	HR	BB	K	ERA	W	L	H/9	HR/9	BB/9	K/9	KWH	PERA
1996	Atlanta	NL	247.0	236	78	10	27	155	2.84	18	9	8.60	0.36	0.98	5.65	2.83	2.81
1997	Atlanta	NL	228.7	215	59	9	18	157	2.32	19	6	8.46	0.35	0.71	6.18	4.78	2.64
1998	Atlanta	NL	251.7	212	70	13	40	186	2.50	20	8	7.58	0.46	1.43	6.65	3.06	2.36

Don Sutton, the Braves' announcer, has gone on record to say there will never be another 300-game winner. Sutton is an intelligent man and he has first-hand knowledge of how difficult that feat is, but that's an incredibly short-sighted comment. I mean, he's an announcer for the Braves, meaning he sees Greg Maddux every day—and he thinks 300 wins is unreachable? Maddux already has 202 wins, and was 32 when last season ended. At the same age, Sutton had 190 wins. Of the nine 300-game winners in the live-ball era, you know how many had more wins at the same age? One—Tom Seaver, with 203. Of course, the pitchers who rack up wins early in their career are usually overworked and burn out, and Bob Feller and Catfish Hunter did just that. But Maddux ain't being overworked. It's a wild prediction, but I'll make it anyway: before he retires, Maddux is going to pass Sutton himself with his 325th win, becoming the winningest righthander since Grover Cleveland Alexander.

Jason Marquis Throws R Age 20

YEAR	TEAM	LGE	IP	H	ER	HR	BB	K	ERA	W	L	H/9	HR/9	BB/9	K/9	KWH	PERA
1996	Danville	App	21.0	44	22	0	7	13	9.43	0	2	18.86	0.00	3.00	5.57	0.41	7.29
1997	Macon	SAL	138.7	203	88	14	68	81	5.71	5	10	13.18	0.91	4.41	5.26	0.36	6.04
1998	DanvillC	Car	111.3	151	73	4	49	94	5.90	4	8	12.21	0.32	3.96	7.60	0.90	5.01

Marquis went just 2-12 with a 4.87 ERA, but no one in the organization is buying those numbers, and with good reason. He throws 95 and made great strides with his curveball last year, while striking out 135 men in just 115 innings. When you pitch like that in the Carolina League as a teenager, you're a prospect. He was working on a changeup in the instructional league, and if he masters it, he could force the Braves' hand as early as this year.

Dennis Martinez Throws R Age 44

YEAR	TEAM	LGE	IP	H	ER	HR	BB	K	ERA	W	L	H/9	HR/9	BB/9	K/9	KWH	PERA
1996	Clevelnd	AL	115.3	114	47	10	30	48	3.67	7	6	8.90	0.78	2.34	3.75	0.51	3.51
1997	Seattle	AL	52.0	63	37	8	25	17	6.40	2	4	10.90	1.38	4.33	2.94	0.14	5.37
1998	Atlanta	NL	92.3	114	49	8	18	57	4.78	4	6	11.11	0.78	1.75	5.56	1.19	4.58

Maybe if the Braves hadn't spent so much time getting Martinez his record for wins by a Latin pitcher, and had spent more of their resources on, say, finding a middle infielder who could hit, they wouldn't have been so punchless in October. Martinez had a very servicable year as a middle reliever, but if your touch is so magic you can restore a 43-year-old who had a 7.71 ERA the year before, don't you think you could turn one of your 22-year-old fireballers into something more special? Martinez has had a wonderful career and made a remarkable comeback from his days as an alcoholic. He has 245 wins while never winning more than 16 games in a season, which will almost certainly cost him Hall of Fame consideration.

Kevin McGlinchy Throws R Age 22

YEAR	TEAM	LGE	IP	H	ER	HR	BB	K	ERA	W	L	H/9	HR/9	BB/9	K/9	KWH	PERA
1996	Danville	App	66.3	80	29	3	12	40	3.93	4	3	10.85	0.41	1.63	5.43	1.25	4.07
1997	Durham	Car	137.3	172	78	16	38	80	5.11	6	9	11.27	1.05	2.49	5.24	0.73	4.98
1998	DanvillC	Car	138.7	149	61	10	34	89	3.96	8	7	9.67	0.65	2.21	5.78	1.17	3.83
1998	Greenvil	Sou	32.3	39	17	6	13	16	4.73	2	2	10.86	1.67	3.62	4.45	0.38	5.57

McGlinchy is nine days younger than Chen and about that far behind him as a pitcher. A classic power pitcher, he made big strides from 1997 and could emerge this year. The Braves are asking him to work as a reliever in winter ball, a move they're hinting could be for good. Given that the one thing the major league staff is missing is a couple of hard-throwing right-handed relievers (who can throw strikes, Mr. Wohlers), it's a good idea for both McGlinchy and the organization.

Kevin Millwood Throws R Age 24

YEAR	TEAM	LGE	IP	H	ER	HR	BB	K	ERA	W	L	H/9	HR/9	BB/9	K/9	KWH	PERA
1996	Durham	Car	146.3	168	81	20	63	104	4.98	6	10	10.33	1.23	3.87	6.40	0.77	4.86
1997	Greenvil	Sou	61.3	65	32	7	23	49	4.70	3	4	9.54	1.03	3.38	7.19	1.20	4.26
1997	Richmond	Int	59.7	43	13	2	15	38	1.96	6	1	6.49	0.30	2.26	5.73	1.68	1.81
1997	Atlanta	NL	51.0	61	25	1	19	38	4.41	3	3	10.76	0.18	3.35	6.71	0.93	4.24
1998	Atlanta	NL	177.0	186	79	18	51	150	4.02	10	10	9.46	0.92	2.59	7.63	1.78	3.97

The injury to John Smoltz in the spring moved him to the #4 spot in the rotation, meaning he didn't have to go nine days between starts, and the regular work allowed him to break through where Jason Schmidt and Brad Woodall had failed. He's not really a 17-8 pitcher, and while I expect him to move up some this year, I don't think he has the upside that Chen has. At his peak he should have one or two seasons that look like they were pulled from Smoltz's record, but for most of his career he should be the quintessential #2 or #3 starter.

Denny Neagle Throws L Age 30

YEAR	TEAM	LGE	IP	H	ER	HR	BB	K	ERA	W	L	H/9	HR/9	BB/9	K/9	KWH	PERA
1996	Pittsbrg	NL	187.0	190	58	21	32	118	2.79	14	7	9.14	1.01	1.54	5.68	1.72	3.66
1996	Atlanta	NL	39.3	44	24	5	13	16	5.49	1	3	10.07	1.14	2.97	3.66	0.34	4.58
1997	Atlanta	NL	229.7	223	87	19	44	153	3.41	15	11	8.74	0.74	1.72	6.00	1.79	3.29
1998	Atlanta	NL	213.0	207	84	26	54	151	3.55	13	11	8.75	1.10	2.28	6.38	1.53	3.63

Probably sitting on a ledge after the trade; after all, he grew up as a Pirate in the mid-90s, so he's already tasted the second division. He was already coming into his own before the Braves acquired him, and while they polished him up a bit, I don't think he's going to have a difficult transition to pitching as a Red. His win-loss record may drop, but he's good for 210 innings with a 3.40 ERA. He was the only flyball pitcher in the Braves' rotation, a piece of information the Reds would do well to consider when deciding which of their 49 outfielders to start on the days he pitches.

Odalis Perez   Throws L   Age 21

YEAR	TEAM	LGE	IP	H	ER	HR	BB	K	ERA	W	L	H/9	HR/9	BB/9	K/9	KWH	PERA
1996	Eugene	Nwn	22.3	36	19	3	13	23	7.66	0	2	14.51	1.21	5.24	9.27	0.85	6.85
1997	Macon	SAL	86.3	85	34	5	33	66	3.54	6	4	8.86	0.52	3.44	6.88	1.16	3.54
1998	Greenvil	Sou	131.7	139	57	16	44	114	3.90	8	7	9.50	1.09	3.01	7.79	1.59	4.17
1998	Richmond	Int	24.7	27	9	4	7	19	3.28	2	1	9.85	1.46	2.55	6.93	1.43	4.74
1998	Atlanta	NL	11.0	11	5	1	3	5	4.09	0	1	9.00	0.82	2.45	4.09	0.57	3.27

We're not done with pitching prospects yet. Perez was the youngest pitcher to appear in the major leagues last year, and was very impressive in September as well as the postseason. The Braves liked him in that role so much that he's probably won a spot in their bullpen this year, and as a left-handed reliever who keeps the ball down and doesn't beat himself with wildness, he could be amazingly valuable.

Ruben Quevedo   Throws R   Age 22

YEAR	TEAM	LGE	IP	H	ER	HR	BB	K	ERA	W	L	H/9	HR/9	BB/9	K/9	KWH	PERA
1997	Danville	App	64.3	62	42	6	35	37	5.88	2	5	8.67	0.84	4.90	5.18	0.47	3.92
1998	Macon	SAL	108.3	144	52	15	38	71	4.32	6	6	11.96	1.25	3.16	5.90	0.69	5.57
1998	DanvillC	Car	32.0	35	25	3	15	24	7.03	1	3	9.84	0.84	4.22	6.75	0.82	4.50

Another outstanding pitching prospect. Quevedo is a very young Venezuelan who has a good sinking fastball and command of four pitches. He's tasted nothing but success as a pro. Prospects like Quevedo are the ones the Braves should be dealing to restock their arsenal with young hitters; alternatively, they could go after Barry Larkin and try, for one year at least, to copy the Yankees' formula: build a team so utterly without weakness that they're invulnerable. But having a dozen Grade A or B pitching prospects and an enormous hole developing at shortstop is not an efficient way to build a team.

Jon Ratliff   Throws R   Age 27

YEAR	TEAM	LGE	IP	H	ER	HR	BB	K	ERA	W	L	H/9	HR/9	BB/9	K/9	KWH	PERA
1996	Iowa	AmA	92.3	125	66	10	34	51	6.43	3	7	12.18	0.97	3.31	4.97	0.46	5.46
1997	Orlando	Sou	90.7	142	68	10	35	47	6.75	3	7	14.10	0.99	3.47	4.67	0.33	6.35
1997	Iowa	AmA	30.3	38	23	6	7	20	6.82	1	2	11.27	1.78	2.08	5.93	1.13	5.64
1998	Richmond	Int	148.3	195	91	17	66	111	5.52	6	10	11.83	1.03	4.00	6.73	0.72	5.46

A Cubs first-rounder in 1993, Ratliff had gone nowhere before signing with the Braves as a six-year minor league free agent. He's still not a viable candidate for a major league job, but he added a knuckle-curve last year and his strikeout rate was easily the best of his career. A reliable Triple-A starter; it must be incredibly frustrating to know that you're 90% the pitcher Mark Clark is, but you'll be lucky to earn 5% of his career income.

John Rocker   Throws L   Age 24

YEAR	TEAM	LGE	IP	H	ER	HR	BB	K	ERA	W	L	H/9	HR/9	BB/9	K/9	KWH	PERA
1996	Macon	SAL	102.0	127	76	10	76	65	6.71	3	8	11.21	0.88	6.71	5.74	0.33	5.38
1996	Durham	Car	57.7	76	25	5	27	32	3.90	3	3	11.86	0.78	4.21	4.99	0.37	5.31
1997	Durham	Car	34.7	42	22	4	22	27	5.71	1	3	10.90	1.04	5.71	7.01	0.59	5.19
1997	Greenvil	Sou	114.7	131	60	12	58	77	4.71	5	8	10.28	0.94	4.55	6.04	0.59	4.71
1998	Atlanta	NL	38.3	25	9	4	20	38	2.11	3	1	5.87	0.94	4.70	8.92	2.17	2.35

The Braves already have more pitching prospects than the entire AL West, and then they get lucky. Rocker was plodding along with an undistinguished minor league career just a year ago, but the Braves moved him to the pen, something clicked (probably his 97-mph fastball), and he was suddenly holding major league hitters to a .172 average. I'm not as optimistic about his short-term future as you'd think; his fastball doesn't move as much as you'd like, and when he can't get his breaking ball over for strikes, hitters can sit and wait for a pitch to drive. Long-term, he's a stud.

Rudy Seanez   Throws R   Age 30

YEAR	TEAM	LGE	IP	H	ER	HR	BB	K	ERA	W	L	H/9	HR/9	BB/9	K/9	KWH	PERA
1996	Albuquer	PCL	19.7	29	17	0	13	16	7.78	0	2	13.27	0.00	5.95	7.32	0.51	5.49
1997	Omaha	AmA	48.7	60	40	12	28	37	7.40	1	4	11.10	2.22	5.18	6.84	0.61	6.10
1998	Richmond	Int	21.0	15	9	1	7	25	3.86	1	1	6.43	0.43	3.00	10.71	4.46	2.14
1998	Atlanta	NL	36.3	27	12	2	15	46	2.97	3	1	6.69	0.50	3.72	11.39	3.92	2.23

The man Bill James once described as "the worst pitching prospect in the history of the world" proved to be another feather in the cap for Cox and Mazzone. He commanded unconditional surrender from right-handed batters, who hit .125 with nary an extra-base hit all season. I wouldn't count on him to repeat that, due to a health record that can only be seen if you're over 18 and have a major credit card.

Jacob Shumate   Throws R   Age 23

YEAR	TEAM	LGE	IP	H	ER	HR	BB	K	ERA	W	L	H/9	HR/9	BB/9	K/9	KWH	PERA
1995	Macon	SAL	52.0	71	77	11	106	39	13.33	0	6	12.29	1.90	18.35	6.75	0.15	7.79
1997	Eugene	Nwn	15.7	36	43	2	49	12	24.70	0	2	20.68	1.15	28.15	6.89	0.06	10.34
1998	Macon	SAL	47.7	63	65	6	98	40	12.27	0	5	11.90	1.13	18.50	7.55	0.19	6.99

Not really a prospect, but he is remarkable. The Braves took him in the first round in 1994, and professed to be mildly concerned when he walked 52 batters in just 32 innings. So the next year he walked 119 terrified souls in just 69 innings, and his career has progressed from there. The Braves have doggedly pushed him up the chain, finally landing him in Double-A for a brief stint last year. He might be making some progress—he had a career-low 6.75 ERA last year—but he also threw 40 wild pitches in 53 innings, so maybe not.

John Smoltz   Throws R   Age 32

YEAR	TEAM	LGE	IP	H	ER	HR	BB	K	ERA	W	L	H/9	HR/9	BB/9	K/9	KWH	PERA
1996	Atlanta	NL	257.0	211	84	19	51	248	2.94	19	10	7.39	0.67	1.79	8.68	4.29	2.45
1997	Atlanta	NL	253.3	257	96	22	56	215	3.41	16	12	9.13	0.78	1.99	7.64	2.41	3.59
1998	Atlanta	NL	169.7	153	54	10	40	158	2.86	13	6	8.12	0.53	2.12	8.38	3.06	2.86

His career is a set of conflicting images: for the first eight years of his career he was regarded as an underachiever, because he regularly went 15-12 despite good ERAs on a great team, while also being considered one of the premier postseason pitchers of our time. Now he's gone 45-17 the last three years. The true picture is actually easy to see: the improvement in his control in 1996 transformed him from a very good pitcher to one of baseball's elite. He got stronger as he continued to rehab from his injury, going 12-1 with a 2.29 ERA after the All-Star Break, and is as good a bet as any to win 20 games this year.

Russ Springer   Throws R   Age 30

YEAR	TEAM	LGE	IP	H	ER	HR	BB	K	ERA	W	L	H/9	HR/9	BB/9	K/9	KWH	PERA
1996	Philadel	NL	98.0	112	55	12	37	85	5.05	4	7	10.29	1.10	3.40	7.81	1.31	4.68
1997	Houston	NL	55.3	53	27	5	24	66	4.39	3	3	8.62	0.81	3.90	10.73	2.57	3.58
1998	Arizona	NL	33.7	31	14	4	13	34	3.74	2	2	8.29	1.07	3.48	9.09	2.15	3.48
1998	Atlanta	NL	20.7	24	9	0	15	18	3.92	1	1	10.45	0.00	6.53	7.84	0.67	4.35

The Braves raised some eyebrows when they traded Alan Embree for Springer, who's certainly no one's idea of a top reliever. The emergence of Rocker and Perez helps take away the sting of losing Embree, but Springer is an unremarkable pitcher who was all but forgotten in October. He is more than capable of pitching middle relief, but there are approximately 29 teams who need a middle reliever more than the Braves do.

Mark Wohlers   Throws R   Age 29

YEAR	TEAM	LGE	IP	H	ER	HR	BB	K	ERA	W	L	H/9	HR/9	BB/9	K/9	KWH	PERA
1996	Atlanta	NL	79.0	75	27	8	20	90	3.08	6	3	8.54	0.91	2.28	10.25	4.05	3.42
1997	Atlanta	NL	69.7	64	28	4	35	82	3.62	4	4	8.27	0.52	4.52	10.59	2.25	3.36
1998	Richmond	Int	12.7	27	28	5	40	14	19.89	0	1	19.18	3.55	28.42	9.95	0.14	12.08
1998	Atlanta	NL	21.0	22	22	2	32	21	9.43	0	2	9.43	0.86	13.71	9.00	0.47	5.57

There are two possibilities here: if his complete inability to throw strikes is the byproduct of an injury, he could return to form. If it's a psychological hangup, he's probably done. Steve Blass disease, as Steve Blass proved, is all but incurable. One thin strand of silver lining: he was 8-for-8 in save situations. Don't tell us we don't try to be positive.

SNWLP				ATLANTA BRAVES								Park Effect: -3.4%
PITCHER	GS	IP	R	SNW	SNL	SNPCT	W	L	RA	APW	SNVA	SNWAR
Chen, B.	4	20.3	9	1.3	1.3	.510	2	0	3.98	0.15	0.05	0.22
Glavine, T.	33	229.3	67	17.6	6.8	.722	20	6	2.63	5.05	5.12	7.24
Maddux, G.	34	251.0	75	18.7	7.7	.710	18	9	2.69	5.37	5.37	7.52
Martinez, D.	5	26.3	20	1.6	2.2	.416	1	3	6.84	-0.63	-0.30	-0.03
Millwood, K.	29	171.7	86	10.9	9.7	.529	17	8	4.51	0.25	0.47	2.13
Neagle, D.	31	208.3	91	13.3	9.6	.581	15	11	3.93	1.62	1.62	3.59
Smoltz, J.	26	167.7	58	11.8	6.3	.653	17	3	3.11	2.81	2.60	4.14
TOTALS	162	1074.7	406	75.3	43.5	.634	90	40	3.40	14.61	14.94	24.79

The Best Starting Rotation of All Time™ rolls along. When scanning the SNW/L numbers for the past seven years, you can't help but stumble across trivia about the Braves' dominance that makes your jaw drop. In each of the past seven years the Braves have had three starters among the NL's top 15, and it's not the same three guys every time. Seven different Braves starters have cracked the top 15 during that stretch—Maddux, Glavine, Smoltz, Avery, Neagle, Mercker, and Leibrandt. Here's my favorite: during the past seven years, the average SN record of the Braves' fourth-best starter is 12.2-9.6, for a .559 SNPct. That's as good as Rick Helling pitched as the Rangers' ace last year. Think about having that sort of performance, reliably over seven years, from the #4 man in the rotation. During the three seasons Neagle pitched for the Braves (I'm counting 1996), he finished 6th, 8th, and 12th among NL starters. He never finished higher than fourth on the Braves. No wonder they traded him. Every year, those who predict an implosion from Tom Glavine have gotten egg on their faces. To add insult to injury, 1998 marked the fourth consecutive year that Glavine improved his SNPct from his previous season. He's not only not collapsing, he's getting better.

Pitcher Abuse Points

PITCHER	AGE	GS	PAP	PAP/S	AAW	MAX	115+	130+
Glavine, Tom*	32	34	525	15.44	15.44	126	14	0
Maddux, Greg	32	34	109	3.21	3.21	120	2	0
Martinez, Dennis	43	5	6	1.20	1.20	106	0	0
Millwood, Kevin	23	29	325	11.21	28.02	131	6	1
Neagle, Denny	29	31	226	7.29	10.94	127	4	0
Smoltz, John	31	26	146	5.62	6.55	125	2	0
TOTAL		163	1351	8.29	12.28	131	28	1
RANKING (NL)			7	7	8		6	11-T

*includes rainout start

You might expect the Braves to rank near the bottom of the league in pitcher workload, given their outstanding ability to keep their starters healthy over the years. But not everyone can be as efficient as Maddux is. The Braves still rank in the middle of the pack, which still isn't bad for a veteran staff where none of the starters are likely to get pulled early because of ineffectiveness. The success of Mazzone and Cox at keeping everyone healthy is partly attributable to limiting their pitch counts, but I can't stress it enough: Mazzone's regimen of throwing twice between starts really seems to work. I am a little concerned about Kevin Millwood, who was worked harder than anyone but Glavine despite being the junior member of the staff. But otherwise, I see no reason why the Braves can't keep doing what they've been doing all decade.

Florida Marlins

The 1997 Marlins won the World Series, and this surprised some folks. As we argued last year, the fundamental reason for their success was not their various free agent pickups or Wayne Huizenga's checkbook. The Marlins won because of the previous four years of hard work from the front office, coaching staff, and scouting network assembled by general manager Dave Dombrowski. It was the hard work of that player development posse that produced Edgar Renteria, Charles Johnson, Livan Hernandez, and Felix Heredia. That player development effort put them in a position to trade for Gary Sheffield, Robb Nen, and Jay Powell long before they were either adding or dumping salary. Even before the Huizenga diktat to dump salary was handed down, they had talent in the farm system that reflected the wisdom of their development scheme: Julio Ramirez, Aaron Cames, Alex Gonzalez, Nate Rolison, Amaury Garcia, and Brett Billingsley all come to mind. Dombrowski's management team had done one of the most difficult things to do in baseball: to make a team that was making progress into a team good to win enough games during the regular season to clinch the wild-card, and with good enough top-notch talent to win a short series against postseason regulars like the Braves, Indians, or Yankees. That wasn't just luck. Most of the talent was already in place, and all of their work and having Kevin Brown was enough to make the Braves mortal.

But the salary dump was commanded, and salary dump they did. What ensued was one of the most creative player acquisition strategies ever seen, crammed into less than nine months, and to accompanying howls from the media. As Dombrowski put it, "it might be good for the Marlins, but it's not good for baseball." No less an authority than George Will fulminated that, "for the first time ever, there would in no meaningful sense be a defending champion." In evaluating the Marlins and where they're going, Dombrowski is right in one sense and wrong in another, while George Will is just being silly.

Lets tackle Will's statement first. Although what he said in terms of a world series winner dismantling itself is true, the spirit of the comment from his baseball anthology *Bunts* doesn't jibe with baseball history. The great game has one storied franchise that has enjoyed periods of greatness, only to peddle away the players it relied upon to reach its titles; its various dismantlings were all financially motivated. I'm talking about the A's, first in their Philadelphia incarnation, and later in Oakland. First, there's the 1914-1915 first-to-worst Philadelphia A's. American League champs in 1914 (and World Series winners in 1911 and 1913), the A's lost pitchers Eddie Plank and Chief Bender to do-it-yourself free agency when both men jumped to the Federal League. They traded second baseman Eddie Collins for financial reasons to the White Sox, and Home Run Baker retired, apparently for salary-related complaints. After the season started, when it became clear the A's weren't going to compete, owner/manager Connie Mack traded two more rotation regulars (Bob Shawkey and Herb Pennock), his starting shortstop (Jack Barry) and starting rightfielder (Eddie Murphy). That's four starting pitchers and four starting players gone by July of 1915. Mack would turn the trick again, tearing down his team to try to start over after a good run where the A's won the World Series in '29 and '30, lost it in '31, finished second in '32, and started dismantling from there . The A's would go through the same cycle under owner Charlie Finley in the 70s: three straight World Series wins from '72–'74, a division title in '75, and then a free agency wipeout and some commissioner's interference that left them with only Billy North and Vida Blue by '77. Although they provide the most dramatic examples, A's teams through the ages aren't the only winning teams being dismantled for economic reasons: nobody wept when the '83 NL champion Phillies dumped half of their starting lineup after losing the World Series to the Orioles, and the evisceration of three-time NL East champion Pirates after '92 was dictated by bean-counters while being made worse by a misguided preference for Andy Van Slyke over Barry Bonds.

Marlins Prospectus

1998 record: 54-108; Fifth place, NL East

Pythagorean W/L: 56-106

Runs scored: 667 (13th in NL)

Runs allowed: 923 (16th in NL)

Team EQA: .248 (14th in NL)

Park: Pro Player Stadium (good pitchers')

1998: Frustrating exercise as a succession of ill-prepared pitchers were thrown to the wolves.

1999: Development of core young players boost the Marlins towards .500.

There are further reasons to be reluctant to invest Will's comment with much significance. The '97 Marlins were a fortunate team, but there were no guarantees that the '97 champs were going to be that competitive going into '98. The players they traded away were almost universally old players; the average age of the position players they traded when they traded them was 32, and of the group, only Gary Sheffield and Moises Alou look like they'll be productive major leaguers for any length of time. The average age of the pitchers they traded was 31, and although it meant losing the coveted Brown, remember that Al Leiter has yet to meet a surgery his left arm isn't willing to try out. That the Marlins didn't keep the old gang together, just to watch them not win was not a bad decision. The recent history of winning teams bitterly clinging to the players who got them there, especially older players, is pretty bad. In the 90s alone, the bitter, slow collapses of first the A's and then the Blue Jays as they slowly retreated from their multi-year runs only deepened their organizational slumps as they over committed to the veterans who helped them win. The Tigers' long struggle to remain mediocre after their brief moment of glory in '84 and their stunning disappointment in '87 left them one of the worst organizations in major league baseball, putting them in a hole they still haven't really climbed out of.

So what about Dombrowski's statement? He's right in terms of what happened being good for the Marlins. The talent they've acquired is better than what they got coming out of the Expansion Draft, and puts to shame the '97 drafts of the Devil Rays and Diamondbacks. The comparison isn't completely fair, in that the Marlins managed to acquire players who weren't eligible for the Expansion Draft. The Marlins wanted their meat fresh; there were no minor league veterans, and few players with any experience at Triple-A. Notable exceptions, like Derrek Lee and Raffy Medina, went directly onto the major league team. The subsequent acquisition of one of the most in-demand players in the majors, Mike Piazza, was a masterstroke on two counts. It simultaneously created the opportunity to dump huge, dubious financial commitments to Gary Sheffield and Bobby Bonilla (and a potential arbitration loss to Charles Johnson) while creating the opportunity to subsequently turn Piazza into something more useful for the Marlins' future. Although this sort of dramatic change was disorienting for fans and sportswriters, in terms of pursuing a goal (to make the Marlins' organization stronger for the future), it was brilliant. If it disappointed litigious season ticket holders, tough. If those people wanted to watch a World Series winner, they had their chance in '97. In life, there are no guarantees.

That's not to say mistakes weren't made. In leveling their team after the World Series victory, the team really could have used an appropriate sendoff for Jim Leyland. However

valuable his skills may or may not be in managing a veteran team or in finding ways to use almost any collection of relievers, Jim Leyland was not the man to have running a team looking to hit bottom fast so that it could start anew. If the motivation for the decision was loyalty or a desire to let Leyland manage the National League in the '99 All-Star game, that loyalty ended up being horribly misplaced. He placed unacceptable burdens on his young rotation, and it's an open question whether or not Livan Hernandez or Jesus Sanchez will be healthy when the next good Marlins teams come around.

Dombrowski's observation is also correct, in that something bad happened to baseball as a direct product of the dismantling of the '97 Marlins. The tremendous amount of whining in the media that what the Marlins were doing was wrong or proof of something fundamentally wrong in baseball was a definite misfortune for an industry that has had its share of bad news, much of it self-inflicted. What the complaining made clear is that as wonderful as the season was for the industry as a whole, the media is a fickle friend indeed. It probably started with a baseball-themed screed, Dave Rosenbaum's *If They Don't Win, It's a Shame*, a baseball book that didn't actually have much baseball in it, but which did give fans a one-sided view into the prickly relationship between the media and the '97 Marlins. Commentary along these lines did nothing to address what the Marlins had done well or badly, instead being used to reinforce preconceived notions about what's happening in baseball today. How intractable the problem with reactionary baseball commentary is remains to be seen; perhaps no amount of progress would satisfy some sportswriters. Bashing baseball is one of the sportswriting profession's favorite pastimes, and that isn't going to change.

Where is Dombrowski wrong, then? He's wrong in that the Marlins were free to do what they needed, and that's good for baseball and baseball teams. As "bad" as it was perceived to be for the great game, it was good for baseball when Bud Selig studied the issue to see if there was something that could have been done to stop the dismantling, and concluded there was not. There would not be an autocratic decision to screw the Marlins and stick them with players they no longer valued, as Bowie Kuhn did to Charlie Finley in the '70s. There would be no intervention. The Marlins would get to run their business as they saw fit, and since it was their money all along, bully for them. In the wake of the dive of '98, the Marlins have been bought by financier John Henry, who has promised to nearly triple the team's salary budget. In the wake of Dombrowski's massive talent-acquisition campaign, the Marlins are not going to be a perennial weak sister. Just as the Marlins' rise to greatness and collapse into misery symbolizes shortening cycles of competitive to crummy in today's game, the sale to Henry reinforces the lesson: the Marlins are building again. Three years from now, when the Braves are running out of steam and the Mets are burned out from their determined campaign to clinch second place, Dave Dombrowski is going to have a team loaded with talent,

and he'll be backed by a wealthy owner. That's how organizations build winners: intelligence, hard work, and cash. If you want a story about the first-to-worst Marlins, and not some broken record about industry ills, remember that it takes all three, and that the Fish will be fine.

HITTERS (Averages: BA .260/ OBA .330/ SA .420, EQA .260)

Fletcher Bates · OF · Bats B · Age 25

YEAR	TEAM	LGE	AB	H	DB	TP	HR	BB	R	RBI	SB	CS	OUT	BA	OBA	SA	EQA	EQR	DEFENSE
1996	Columbia	SAL	506	111	9	4	12	45	40	42	6	3	398	.219	.283	.324	.210	40	132-OF 91
1997	St Lucie	Fla	253	66	10	4	9	27	31	34	4	3	190	.261	.332	.439	.264	34	62-OF 86
1997	Binghmtn	Eas	242	53	8	1	9	21	23	24	7	2	191	.219	.281	.372	.228	24	57-OF 98
1998	Portland	Eas	534	127	16	2	9	38	46	42	12	5	412	.238	.288	.326	.214	44	139-OF 96
1999	*Florida*	*NL*	*503*	*121*	*18*	*3*	*12*	*36*	*47*	*48*	*13*	*4*	*386*	*.241*	*.291*	*.360*	*.234*	*51*	

Bates is considered a great athlete, and he's got that great arm ("Best in the Eastern League") that seems to be the feature of every dubious outfield prospect. He's big, he's fast, he's strong, he was a high school teammate of Trot Nixon's, but he's also not a great hitter.

David Berg · INF · Bats R · Age 28

YEAR	TEAM	LGE	AB	H	DB	TP	HR	BB	R	RBI	SB	CS	OUT	BA	OBA	SA	EQA	EQR	DEFENSE	
1995	Brevard	Fla	400	102	9	1	3	50	43	34	5	2	300	.255	.338	.305	.233	39	55-SS 81	51-3B 101
1996	Portland	Eas	409	98	15	2	6	31	38	33	11	4	315	.240	.293	.330	.219	35	91-SS 97	
1997	Charlott	Int	419	104	16	3	7	44	47	39	11	5	320	.248	.320	.351	.238	44	108-SS 94	
1998	Florida	NL	183	59	6	0	4	27	30	26	3	0	124	.322	.410	.421	.299	30		
1999	*Florida*	*NL*	*281*	*76*	*12*	*1*	*6*	*30*	*34*	*32*	*6*	*2*	*207*	*.270*	*.341*	*.384*	*.264*	*37*		

Won his version of the lottery, which is that he earned the utility infield job over a stack of candidates, getting playing time as a platoon mate for Craig Counsell. As his career should show, he wouldn't be the worst guy in the world to have play regularly pending the arrival or development of a prospect.

Josh Booty · 3B · Bats R · Age 24

YEAR	TEAM	LGE	AB	H	DB	TP	HR	BB	R	RBI	SB	CS	OUT	BA	OBA	SA	EQA	EQR	DEFENSE
1996	KaneCnty	Mid	481	88	9	1	16	32	23	31	1	2	395	.183	.234	.306	.175	25	124-3B 90
1997	Portland	Eas	443	78	13	1	14	21	18	24	2	1	366	.176	.213	.305	.163	20	112-3B 104
1998	Florida	NL	19	3	1	0	0	3	1	1	0	0	16	.158	.273	.211	.165	1	
1998	Charlott	Int	126	15	1	0	3	6	3	3	0	1	112	.119	.159	.198	—	-1	34-3B 112
1999	*Florida*	*NL*	*419*	*78*	*9*	*1*	*14*	*23*	*20*	*28*	*1*	*1*	*342*	*.186*	*.229*	*.313*	*.183*	*24*	

During the year, prospect maven Dave Rawnsley made a dubious claim that a ripple effect from the major league turnover was affecting the performance of minor league players. They were pushing too hard to achieve the suddenly attainable goal of reaching the major leagues, you see. This is pretty silly: you might as well argue that we know Richard Nixon was evil because he was a Quaker. The problem is that one set of facts (some players played badly) has no proven relationship with another (they want to play in the majors). Even if for the sake of argument you wanted to pretend that we could know that Josh Booty's performance was affected because he was pressing, there's the nagging little problem that he's been a consistently terrible ballplayer for his entire professional career, and whether or not he's pressing or dying his hair teal or wearing his lucky underwear has very little impact on that. The man hasn't hit well at A-ball yet. He is not, nor has he ever been, a legitimate prospect. Finally designated for assignment in late November.

John Cangelosi · OF · Bats B · Age 36

YEAR	TEAM	LGE	AB	H	DB	TP	HR	BB	R	RBI	SB	CS	OUT	BA	OBA	SA	EQA	EQR	DEFENSE	
1996	Houston	NL	265	73	13	4	1	45	45	26	14	10	202	.275	.381	.366	.267	37	62-OF	95
1997	Florida	NL	192	47	3	0	3	20	19	16	5	1	146	.245	.316	.307	.225	18	44-OF	99
1998	Florida	NL	172	45	6	0	2	31	24	17	2	4	131	.262	.374	.331	.253	21	26-OF	100
1999	*Florida*	*NL*	*176*	*44*	*5*	*1*	*2*	*29*	*22*	*17*	*4*	*4*	*136*	*.250*	*.356*	*.324*	*.252*	*22*		

One of the ones that didn't get away, Cangelosi did his usual work as a pinch-hitter and fill-in. He's good for his niche as a sixth outfielder, but he's hardly singular in his abilities. He just has the good fortune to know people like his GM and manager from his days with the White Sox.

Luis Castillo   2B   Bats B   Age 23

YEAR	TEAM	LGE	AB	H	DB	TP	HR	BB	R	RBI	SB	CS	OUT	BA	OBA	SA	EQA	EQR	DEFENSE
1996	Portland	Eas	415	112	13	4	1	56	68	31	36	16	319	.270	.357	.328	.252	51	108-2B 101
1996	Florida	NL	165	45	2	1	1	15	23	12	15	4	124	.273	.333	.315	.243	18	38-2B 97
1997	Florida	NL	263	64	5	0	1	29	27	16	13	11	210	.243	.318	.274	.211	21	63-2B 102
1997	Charlott	Int	127	41	4	0	0	14	20	12	6	4	90	.323	.390	.354	.268	17	35-2B 88
1998	Charlott	Int	374	95	7	1	1	67	62	25	28	12	291	.254	.367	.286	.248	45	100-2B 86
1998	Florida	NL	153	32	4	2	1	23	17	10	3	0	121	.209	.312	.281	.218	13	42-2B 94
1999	*Florida*	*NL*	*474*	*126*	*11*	*3*	*2*	*64*	*69*	*37*	*32*	*12*	*361*	*.264*	*.351*	*.312*	*.254*	*58*	

I'm more skeptical of Castillo than most of the rest of the BP team, but there's little reason to exult about it. He hasn't come around yet, and until he can start lining a couple of balls over infielders' heads, he isn't a major league ball player.

Ramon Castro   C   Bats R   Age 23

YEAR	TEAM	LGE	AB	H	DB	TP	HR	BB	R	RBI	SB	CS	OUT	BA	OBA	SA	EQA	EQR	DEFENSE
1996	Quad Cit	Mid	318	70	7	0	7	22	20	24	1	0	248	.220	.271	.308	.197	21	
1997	Kissimme	Fla	415	108	13	0	9	47	44	45	0	0	307	.260	.335	.357	.245	46	
1998	Jackson	Tex	166	36	3	0	6	11	10	15	0	1	131	.217	.266	.343	.204	12	46-C 103
1998	Portland	Eas	88	21	1	0	3	7	7	9	0	0	67	.239	.295	.352	.223	8	
1999	*Florida*	*NL*	*306*	*76*	*8*	*0*	*10*	*25*	*27*	*34*	*0*	*0*	*230*	*.248*	*.305*	*.373*	*.241*	*33*	

The prize for trading Jay Powell to the Astros, Castro is a top-notch defensive catcher: he was gunning almost half of opposing thieves at Jackson, and his gamecalling has improved since he learned to "habla." He's got a Bo Diaz-sized case of the slows on the bases, which for a player this young is surprising. Only an elbow injury kept him from a September callup in '98, but he's expected to be 100% in camp. He should be the Marlins' starting catcher by '00.

Chris Clapinski   UT   Bats B   Age 27

YEAR	TEAM	LGE	AB	H	DB	TP	HR	BB	R	RBI	SB	CS	OUT	BA	OBA	SA	EQA	EQR	DEFENSE	
1996	Portland	Eas	73	16	2	0	3	10	8	8	2	1	58	.219	.313	.370	.241	8	22-SS 96	
1996	Charlott	Int	354	85	12	1	8	43	40	34	8	4	273	.240	.322	.347	.238	38	85-SS 90	
1997	Charlott	Int	337	77	16	1	9	40	39	33	10	2	262	.228	.310	.362	.240	37	39-2B 80	32-SS 96
1998	Charlott	Int	308	68	9	1	6	31	28	24	7	2	242	.221	.292	.315	.215	26	26-OF 91	24-3B 112
1999	*Florida*	*NL*	*334*	*78*	*13*	*1*	*10*	*39*	*38*	*35*	*9*	*2*	*258*	*.234*	*.314*	*.368*	*.249*	*40*		

Clapinski has to wish he had Dave Berg's good luck. A minor league free agent, he could end up anywhere. He'll be a very handy utilityman for any team that wants to keep him around.

Craig Counsell   2B   Bats L   Age 28

YEAR	TEAM	LGE	AB	H	DB	TP	HR	BB	R	RBI	SB	CS	OUT	BA	OBA	SA	EQA	EQR	DEFENSE
1997	ColSprin	PCL	353	83	15	3	3	34	36	27	8	2	272	.235	.302	.320	.221	31	91-2B 90
1997	Florida	NL	164	49	10	2	1	19	23	20	1	1	116	.299	.372	.402	.273	23	47-2B 110
1998	Florida	NL	336	86	19	5	5	53	48	39	3	0	250	.256	.357	.387	.266	46	101-2B 100
1999	*Florida*	*NL*	*365*	*98*	*21*	*3*	*7*	*48*	*50*	*44*	*7*	*2*	*269*	*.268*	*.354*	*.400*	*.274*	*53*	

Fully healed from his ugly beaning…physically. You have to hope he doesn't become a latter-day Dickie Thon. it's cold-hearted to mention, but he's replaceable. He's worth keeping and playing if you aren't paying top dollar for him, and worth dumping once he gets expensive. Second is a position where almost every organization has someone like Counsell or Jason Hardtke or Jeff Patzke or Frankie Menechino. If you absolutely need somebody, you just have to remember to sign one of these guys in December as a minor league free agent.

Brandon Cromer   UT   Bats L   Age 25

YEAR	TEAM	LGE	AB	H	DB	TP	HR	BB	R	RBI	SB	CS	OUT	BA	OBA	SA	EQA	EQR	DEFENSE	
1996	Knoxvill	Sou	311	71	11	4	6	48	36	31	2	3	243	.228	.331	.347	.240	34	64-SS 85	24-3B 124
1997	Carolina	Sou	191	35	7	2	3	24	14	12	1	3	159	.183	.274	.288	.191	13	45-SS 87	
1997	Calgary	PCL	219	38	10	1	5	16	12	12	2	1	182	.174	.230	.297	.172	11	33-SS 101	27-2B 100
1998	Portland	Eas	391	77	8	3	11	36	27	30	2	1	315	.197	.265	.317	.198	28	63-OF 90	38-3B 92
1999	*Florida*	*NL*	*362*	*75*	*10*	*2*	*10*	*36*	*29*	*31*	*3*	*2*	*289*	*.207*	*.279*	*.329*	*.217*	*32*		

A worthwhile gamble to snag on waivers at the time, Cromer's now a minor league free agent. His lack of development should be particularly frightening to both Andy Thompson and Kevin Witt, in that like them, Cromer's a guy who was supposed to be a power-hitter on the left side of the infield when the Jays picked him, and he's turned out to be a positionless flop.

Brian Daubach   OF/1B   Bats L   Age 27

YEAR	TEAM	LGE	AB	H	DB	TP	HR	BB	R	RBI	SB	CS	OUT	BA	OBA	SA	EQA	EQR	DEFENSE	
1996	Binghmtn	Eas	435	109	12	1	15	59	51	53	6	5	331	.251	.340	.386	.255	54	120-1B 107	
1997	Charlott	Int	456	110	21	2	16	54	49	55	1	6	352	.241	.322	.401	.247	53	97-1B 92	
1998	Charlott	Int	488	134	28	2	23	64	70	77	6	3	357	.275	.359	.482	.287	79	96-OF 81	21-1B 98
1999	*Florida*	*NL*	*460*	*121*	*24*	*1*	*23*	*54*	*59*	*70*	*5*	*3*	*342*	*.263*	*.340*	*.470*	*.283*	*73*		

The Marlins' Minor League Player of the Year, Daubach is a minor league vet with a proven power stroke. The Marlins have tried moving him to the outfield, where he might stand a chance as a pinch-hitter and part-timer. Released after the season, expected to sign in Japan.

Todd Dunwoody   CF   Bats L   Age 24

YEAR	TEAM	LGE	AB	H	DB	TP	HR	BB	R	RBI	SB	CS	OUT	BA	OBA	SA	EQA	EQR	DEFENSE
1996	Portland	Eas	546	134	20	4	19	38	57	58	20	12	424	.245	.295	.401	.238	59	138-OF 102
1997	Charlott	Int	397	98	12	4	21	34	51	53	20	3	302	.247	.306	.456	.265	54	104-OF 108
1998	Charlott	Int	100	28	5	2	5	11	15	16	3	2	74	.280	.351	.520	.290	17	26-OF 123
1998	Florida	NL	434	111	27	7	6	24	44	43	6	1	324	.256	.295	.392	.237	44	99-OF 111
1999	*Florida*	*NL*	*506*	*135*	*23*	*7*	*18*	*33*	*59*	*65*	*16*	*5*	*376*	*.267*	*.312*	*.447*	*.267*	*69*	

He's got Devon White's skills set. He's fast, has good power, and can play an excellent centerfield. He's still struggling with breaking stuff, but if he learns to lay off, he can be a major asset. He didn't do it in his rookie season, which means that he's still going to have to improve. He may not be a middle-of-the-order type, but good teams are willing to stick a player like Dunwoody in the lineup, whether it's burying him in the seventh slot, or getting creative and batting him second instead of some bat-control out-maker, er, "artist."

Matt Erickson   3B   Bats L   Age 23

YEAR	TEAM	LGE	AB	H	DB	TP	HR	BB	R	RBI	SB	CS	OUT	BA	OBA	SA	EQA	EQR	DEFENSE
1997	Utica	NYP	243	58	3	0	3	33	25	19	3	2	187	.239	.330	.288	.223	22	62-3B 109
1998	KaneCnty	Mid	450	122	17	1	4	55	56	43	7	4	332	.271	.350	.340	.248	51	102-3B 91
1999	*Florida*	*NL*	*334*	*92*	*9*	*0*	*5*	*40*	*39*	*36*	*5*	*3*	*245*	*.275*	*.353*	*.347*	*.258*	*41*	

The future at third for the Fish. Erickson was named the best glove at third in the Midwestern League, and he's showing a great line-drive stroke and a great ability to get on base. He probably needs to push his way out of or past the Florida State League quickly if he's going to end up having a solid career; moving up a level per year wouldn't get him to the majors until he's 26.

Cliff Floyd   LF/1B   Bats L   Age 26

YEAR	TEAM	LGE	AB	H	DB	TP	HR	BB	R	RBI	SB	CS	OUT	BA	OBA	SA	EQA	EQR	DEFENSE
1996	Montreal	NL	225	52	13	4	6	30	30	25	6	1	174	.231	.322	.404	.256	29	67-OF 84
1997	Charlott	Int	128	44	5	0	8	8	21	24	6	2	86	.344	.382	.570	.318	24	30-OF 92
1997	Florida	NL	137	32	9	1	6	25	22	19	5	2	107	.234	.352	.445	.277	22	28-OF 107
1998	Florida	NL	589	170	46	3	24	51	91	84	29	16	435	.289	.345	.499	.284	93	144-OF 88
1999	*Florida*	*NL*	*465*	*130*	*35*	*3*	*20*	*43*	*71*	*67*	*23*	*9*	*344*	*.280*	*.341*	*.497*	*.291*	*78*	

He was finally healthy and had the kind of year prospect hounds knew he had in him. It isn't a good sign that just about every defensive measure available consistently says Floyd's awful; he's been moved around so many times and been hurt so many different times that improvement is hopefully possible. Floyd was roundly criticized for calling Bubba "Bill" when some left-overs from the world champion Marlins visited the White House. Sounds like a good way to get audited to me.

Amaury Garcia   2B   Bats R   Age 24

YEAR	TEAM	LGE	AB	H	DB	TP	HR	BB	R	RBI	SB	CS	OUT	BA	OBA	SA	EQA	EQR	DEFENSE
1996	KaneCnty	Mid	401	90	12	3	6	45	43	30	19	11	322	.224	.303	.314	.220	36	108-2B 95
1997	Brevard	Fla	483	128	20	1	7	43	59	44	22	7	362	.265	.325	.354	.244	53	123-2B 88
1998	Portland	Eas	541	133	14	3	12	39	50	49	16	11	419	.246	.297	.349	.224	50	135-2B 86
1999	*Florida*	*NL*	*497*	*120*	*18*	*2*	*8*	*36*	*48*	*41*	*20*	*9*	*386*	*.241*	*.293*	*.334*	*.228*	*48*	

After an All-Star season, Garcia is nearing the point where he can pass by Luis Castillo. He has reasonable command of the strikezone, some actual sock in his bat, and the front office doesn't seem too concerned about his glovework.

Alex Gonzalez   SS   Bats R   Age 22

YEAR	TEAM	LGE	AB	H	DB	TP	HR	BB	R	RBI	SB	CS	OUT	BA	OBA	SA	EQA	EQR	DEFENSE
1997	Portland	Eas	442	95	11	3	13	20	26	35	3	4	351	.215	.249	.342	.195	30	130-SS 94
1998	Charlott	Int	415	104	17	6	9	25	36	43	3	5	316	.251	.293	.386	.230	40	106-SS 93
1998	Florida	NL	86	14	2	0	3	9	5	5	0	0	72	.163	.242	.291	.177	5	22-SS 93
1999	*Florida*	*NL*	*437*	*108*	*19*	*4*	*13*	*24*	*38*	*48*	*4*	*4*	*333*	*.247*	*.286*	*.398*	*.239*	*46*	

After missing '96 with a dislocated shoulder, Gonzalez has come very far very fast. In the field, he's considered outstanding despite a weak arm (he makes up for it with a quick release). He was named the best prospect in the International League for 1998. Take a gander at the Tejada comment about what you should know in terms of 22-year-old shortstops who become regulars; just about all of them were good prospects, and just about all of them flopped, and consider Gonzalez's poor on-base ability. I don't think the Marlins should go out of their way to move Renteria aside.

Brandon Harper   C   Bats R   Age 23

YEAR	TEAM	LGE	AB	H	DB	TP	HR	BB	R	RBI	SB	CS	OUT	BA	OBA	SA	EQA	EQR	DEFENSE
1997	Utica	NYP	154	27	3	1	1	13	6	5	0	0	127	.175	.240	.227	.143	5	
1998	KaneCnty	Mid	417	76	12	0	4	33	17	16	0	1	342	.182	.242	.240	.150	15	110-C 90
1999	*Florida*	*NL*	*299*	*58*	*7*	*0*	*4*	*22*	*15*	*15*	*0*	*0*	*241*	*.194*	*.249*	*.258*	*.172*	*15*	

Probably the long-term inheritor of Charles Johnson's job, Harper is considered a primo glove behind the plate. He'll need to learn how to hit first.

Ryan Jackson   1B/OF   Bats L   Age 27

YEAR	TEAM	LGE	AB	H	DB	TP	HR	BB	R	RBI	SB	CS	OUT	BA	OBA	SA	EQA	EQR	DEFENSE	
1997	Portland	Eas	479	114	15	1	14	35	39	47	2	3	368	.238	.290	.361	.223	43	96-OF 94	
1998	Charlott	Int	48	15	1	0	2	4	7	7	1	0	33	.312	.365	.458	.288	7		
1998	Florida	NL	260	66	14	1	6	22	26	28	1	1	195	.254	.312	.385	.241	28	35-1B 89	20-OF 94
1999	*Florida*	*NL*	*312*	*82*	*11*	*1*	*11*	*24*	*31*	*39*	*2*	*1*	*231*	*.263*	*.315*	*.410*	*.257*	*39*		

A Duke product, Jackson was almost washed up after missing '96 with a knee injury. However, he bounced back with a good year at Portland in '97, and impressed Leyland in camp enough to force Derrek Lee into a part-time role. He isn't a prospect, but he can do almost everything Jim Eisenreich was going to do for considerably less money.

Jaime Jones   OF   Bats L   Age 22

YEAR	TEAM	LGE	AB	H	DB	TP	HR	BB	R	RBI	SB	CS	OUT	BA	OBA	SA	EQA	EQR	DEFENSE
1996	KaneCnty	Mid	239	54	7	1	7	13	18	21	4	1	186	.226	.266	.351	.212	19	59-OF 80
1997	Brevard	Fla	377	96	18	1	11	39	42	44	3	1	282	.255	.325	.395	.251	45	59-OF 86
1998	Portland	Eas	436	115	16	0	11	49	49	50	3	1	322	.264	.338	.376	.252	51	105-OF 83
1999	*Florida*	*NL*	*376*	*101*	*10*	*0*	*13*	*39*	*42*	*48*	*5*	*1*	*276*	*.269*	*.337*	*.399*	*.266*	*50*	

A big-time tools player, Jones has also happily been a pretty good ballplayer so far. He's missed considerable time to injuries since being drafted in '95, but didn't really make progress at Portland as much as he proved he could make the jump between A-ball and Double-A. There have been some criticisms that he's indolent in the field, so you can add that to the list of things he needs to get better at.

Randy Knorr   C   Bats R   Age 30

YEAR	TEAM	LGE	AB	H	DB	TP	HR	BB	R	RBI	SB	CS	OUT	BA	OBA	SA	EQA	EQR	DEFENSE
1996	Houston	NL	87	17	2	0	2	6	4	5	0	1	71	.195	.247	.287	.172	4	
1997	New Orln	AA	247	53	6	0	4	19	15	16	0	0	194	.215	.271	.287	.189	15	
1998	Charlott	Int	197	54	8	0	5	27	25	25	1	1	144	.274	.362	.391	.266	26	58-C 90
1998	Florida	NL	49	10	5	1	2	1	4	5	0	0	39	.204	.220	.469	.225	5	
1999	*Florida*	*NL*	*218*	*55*	*6*	*0*	*8*	*22*	*21*	*27*	*0*	*0*	*163*	*.252*	*.321*	*.390*	*.254*	*27*	

A courtesy mention, since Knorr is a catcher, every team carries at least two, he has major league experience, and there are no warrants for his arrest in most states or Canada as far as I know.

Mark Kotsay   RF   Bats L   Age 23

YEAR	TEAM	LGE	AB	H	DB	TP	HR	BB	R	RBI	SB	CS	OUT	BA	OBA	SA	EQA	EQR	DEFENSE
1996	KaneCnty	Mid	61	15	1	0	2	13	10	7	2	0	46	.246	.378	.361	.275	9	
1997	Portland	Eas	428	112	19	0	15	61	61	54	12	4	320	.262	.354	.411	.270	61	110-OF 104
1997	Florida	NL	52	10	1	1	0	4	4	2	3	0	42	.192	.250	.250	.182	3	
1998	Florida	NL	579	165	26	6	13	38	66	70	11	6	420	.285	.329	.418	.258	71	139-OF 106
1999	*Florida*	*NL*	*471*	*132*	*22*	*3*	*13*	*42*	*60*	*59*	*13*	*4*	*343*	*.280*	*.339*	*.423*	*.273*	*67*	

He does everything well: he fields well, he throws well, he hits for some power, he runs well, gets good marks for his good work ethic. Although some folks are saying his rookie season was a disappointment, he's the kind of player who only needs to get slightly better in each phase of the game to become a superstar. He's young enough to make those broad improvements, and should have a good sophomore year.

Derrek Lee   1B   Bats R   Age 23

YEAR	TEAM	LGE	AB	H	DB	TP	HR	BB	R	RBI	SB	CS	OUT	BA	OBA	SA	EQA	EQR	DEFENSE
1996	Memphis	Sou	500	134	22	1	31	52	67	81	10	4	370	.268	.337	.502	.283	79	133-1B 88
1997	LasVegas	PCL	446	117	17	0	11	51	57	48	13	3	332	.262	.338	.374	.255	54	124-1B 112
1997	San Dieg	NL	54	14	3	0	1	10	8	6	0	0	40	.259	.375	.370	.269	8	14-1B 107
1998	Florida	NL	455	108	25	1	20	50	53	58	6	2	349	.237	.313	.429	.255	57	119-1B 110
1999	*Florida*	*NL*	*432*	*113*	*22*	*1*	*18*	*45*	*54*	*59*	*10*	*2*	*321*	*.262*	*.331*	*.442*	*.275*	*64*	

Battling to become the most famous graduate of El Camino High School. He's clearly ahead of the member of BP's authorship team, and just needs to catch up to Larry Linville of *M*A*S*H* fame. The playing time in the projection isn't a misprint; I can certainly see the Marlins keeping Jackson around for some part-time and pinch-hitting work. Definitely one of the big prizes of the trading frenzy, and more valuable than Wally Joyner for the rest of their adult lives.

Kevin Millar   1B/3B   Bats R   Age 27

YEAR	TEAM	LGE	AB	H	DB	TP	HR	BB	R	RBI	SB	CS	OUT	BA	OBA	SA	EQA	EQR	DEFENSE	
1996	Portland	Eas	464	123	13	0	14	29	43	51	5	3	344	.265	.308	.384	.239	48	80-1B 80	25-3B 115
1997	Portland	Eas	496	133	16	1	17	46	52	63	1	2	365	.268	.330	.407	.255	60	122-1B 94	
1998	Charlott	Int	45	13	3	0	2	7	8	7	1	0	32	.289	.385	.489	.304	8		
1999	*Florida*	*NL*	*224*	*60*	*7*	*0*	*10*	*20*	*24*	*31*	*1*	*1*	*165*	*.268*	*.328*	*.433*	*.268*	*31*		

There's very little he can't do as a hitter, but he's already been saddled with the dreaded "minor league hitter" label. This year's injuries didn't help. Because he's right-handed and so are Derrek Lee and Kevin Orie, he's a longshot even if he has healed up.

Kevin Orie   3B   Bats R   Age 26

YEAR	TEAM	LGE	AB	H	DB	TP	HR	BB	R	RBI	SB	CS	OUT	BA	OBA	SA	EQA	EQR	DEFENSE
1996	Orlando	Sou	298	88	14	0	9	38	41	43	1	0	210	.295	.375	.433	.283	45	79-3B 90
1997	ChiCubs	NL	360	94	22	3	9	41	44	44	1	2	268	.261	.337	.414	.260	46	99-3B 115
1998	ChiCubs	NL	203	37	11	0	3	19	12	11	1	1	167	.182	.252	.281	.178	11	54-3B 106
1998	Iowa	PCL	89	30	5	0	6	10	15	19	1	0	59	.337	.404	.596	.333	19	19-3B 109
1998	Florida	NL	175	47	7	1	7	15	20	24	1	0	128	.269	.326	.440	.264	23	47-3B 103
1999	*Florida*	*NL*	*412*	*105*	*19*	*1*	*15*	*43*	*45*	*53*	*2*	*1*	*308*	*.255*	*.325*	*.415*	*.263*	*55*	

With all the talk about how Jeff Pentland was as a great hitting coach because of what he's done for Sammy Sosa, why didn't anybody mention that his tinkering with Kevin Orie's swing to get more power was a major screwup? Batting coaches are at their best when you don't notice them, but this year's orgy of congratulations shouldn't go unpunished. By going .500 in terms of pupils, Pentland is really no better or worse off than Walt Hriniak, who over a long career really only seemed to have helped one player (Ron Karkovice) and ruined another (Rich Gedman). Orie's a useful guy to have around, but his constant injury problems will keep him from ever being a star. Think Vance Law, and you won't be disappointed.

Julio Ramirez — CF — Bats R — Age 21

YEAR	TEAM	LGE	AB	H	DB	TP	HR	BB	R	RBI	SB	CS	OUT	BA	OBA	SA	EQA	EQR	DEFENSE
1996	Brevard	Fla	61	14	1	0	0	4	3	3	1	2	49	.230	.277	.246	.169	3	
1997	KaneCnty	Mid	378	89	11	3	12	28	43	36	23	5	294	.235	.288	.376	.237	40	97-OF 100
1998	Brevard	Fla	556	138	12	6	13	39	60	50	34	17	435	.248	.297	.362	.231	56	134-OF 110
1999	Florida	NL	425	109	13	4	10	27	50	41	28	9	325	.256	.301	.370	.247	49	

Finally had an injury-free season in '98, and named the fifth-best prospect of the Florida State League. A briliant defensive player, he can casually spear almost any baserunner. He's extremely fast (71 steals in '98), and offensively he's considered to have the highest potential ceiling of any hitter in the organization. Already being compared to Vlad Guerrero, even with the knowledge of what Vlad did this year at the major league level.

Mike Redmond — C — Bats R — Age 28

YEAR	TEAM	LGE	AB	H	DB	TP	HR	BB	R	RBI	SB	CS	OUT	BA	OBA	SA	EQA	EQR	DEFENSE
1996	Portland	Eas	388	85	7	0	4	19	19	20	2	2	305	.219	.256	.268	.170	18	
1997	Charlott	Int	60	11	3	0	1	1	2	2	0	1	50	.183	.197	.283	.131	2	
1998	Charlott	Int	57	11	2	0	1	0	2	2	0	0	46	.193	.193	.281	.131	1	
1998	Florida	NL	118	40	6	0	3	6	15	18	0	0	78	.339	.371	.466	.288	17	35-C 108
1999	Florida	NL	187	47	3	0	5	6	12	17	0	1	141	.251	.275	.348	.216	15	

The Marlins seem unnaturally fond of him, and they plan on letting him platoon at catcher with the recently-acquired Jorge Fabregas if his knee is healed up. The trade for Guillermo Garcia from the Reds may mean his recovery isn't moving along fast enough.

Edgar Renteria — SS — Bats R — Age 23

YEAR	TEAM	LGE	AB	H	DB	TP	HR	BB	R	RBI	SB	CS	OUT	BA	OBA	SA	EQA	EQR	DEFENSE
1996	Charlott	Int	129	30	4	0	2	9	12	9	7	3	102	.233	.283	.310	.210	10	35-SS 98
1996	Florida	NL	433	136	19	3	5	36	62	51	14	2	299	.314	.367	.406	.276	60	105-SS 101
1997	Florida	NL	617	173	20	3	5	49	73	55	27	16	460	.280	.333	.347	.241	65	149-SS 97
1998	Florida	NL	518	151	17	2	4	52	79	44	45	26	393	.292	.356	.355	.254	64	129-SS 97
1999	Florida	NL	527	156	18	3	3	46	76	48	39	18	389	.296	.353	.359	.263	69	

As I've pointed out, I wouldn't move him to around the infield or out of town to make room for Alex Gonzalez. He is not going to become a free agent early because of the questions about his actual birth date. The Marlins signed him at 15 while claiming to not know it (wink, wink).

Victor Rodriguez — SS/2B — Bats R — Age 22

YEAR	TEAM	LGE	AB	H	DB	TP	HR	BB	R	RBI	SB	CS	OUT	BA	OBA	SA	EQA	EQR	DEFENSE
1996	Brevard	Fla	441	114	13	2	1	28	39	31	11	5	332	.259	.303	.304	.213	35	110-SS 84
1997	Portland	Eas	393	90	12	3	2	23	29	23	9	4	307	.229	.272	.290	.193	25	84-2B 86
1998	Portland	Eas	220	57	6	1	4	17	21	21	4	3	166	.259	.312	.350	.231	21	56-SS 89
1999	Florida	NL	294	77	9	1	3	19	28	25	7	3	220	.262	.307	.330	.231	28	

Semi-prospect making slow progress at the plate and in the field. Kind of tall and storky for a shortstop, he may be having trouble with adjusting as he fills out physically. With the other middle infielders in the organization, Rodriguez gets little notice, but he may sneak past them all.

Nate Rolison   1B   Bats L   Age 22

YEAR	TEAM	LGE	AB	H	DB	TP	HR	BB	R	RBI	SB	CS	OUT	BA	OBA	SA	EQA	EQR	DEFENSE
1996	KaneCnty	Mid	481	102	12	0	13	49	37	40	2	2	381	.212	.285	.318	.208	38	133-1B 103
1997	Brevard	Fla	476	113	12	0	15	34	37	47	2	1	364	.237	.288	.357	.222	42	114-1B 86
1998	Portland	Eas	482	125	25	2	15	58	60	61	4	0	357	.259	.339	.413	.263	63	132-1B 93
1999	Florida	NL	482	121	18	1	16	47	48	58	2	1	362	.251	.318	.392	.253	58	

The best power-hitting prospect in the organization, before they acquired Derrek Lee. There's almost no chance that Rolison can be moved to another position (like the outfield) and play it in the majors, so the Marlins will have to let Rolison tear up the PCL for a year or two before deciding what to do about having the two of them.

John Roskos   1B   Bats R   Age 24

YEAR	TEAM	LGE	AB	H	DB	TP	HR	BB	R	RBI	SB	CS	OUT	BA	OBA	SA	EQA	EQR	DEFENSE
1996	Portland	Eas	393	95	19	1	8	57	47	41	3	2	300	.242	.338	.356	.247	45	60-1B 83
1997	Portland	Eas	440	117	17	1	18	40	48	59	3	4	327	.266	.327	.432	.259	56	
1998	Charlott	Int	409	104	16	1	9	38	39	43	0	3	308	.254	.318	.364	.236	42	72-1B 88
1999	Florida	NL	409	108	17	1	12	38	42	50	1	2	303	.264	.327	.399	.258	51	

He gets mentioned as a catcher from time to time, except he couldn't really catch very well when his right elbow was sound, and now after surgery, they think he still has a few chips floating around. He isn't really a good enough offensive player to live with at first, at which point you have to shelve any ambitions to make him the new Johnny Wockenfuss. Designated for assignment after the year.

Preston Wilson   OF   Bats R   Age 24

YEAR	TEAM	LGE	AB	H	DB	TP	HR	BB	R	RBI	SB	CS	OUT	BA	OBA	SA	EQA	EQR	DEFENSE
1996	St Lucie	Fla	85	13	0	0	2	7	3	2	1	1	73	.153	.217	.224	.126	2	19-OF 114
1997	St Lucie	Fla	243	52	6	1	8	7	14	18	2	2	193	.214	.236	.346	.190	15	60-OF 92
1997	Binghmtn	Eas	255	66	8	1	14	16	27	36	5	1	190	.259	.303	.463	.260	33	62-OF 101
1998	Norfolk	Int	72	16	3	1	1	2	4	5	1	1	57	.222	.243	.333	.189	4	
1998	Charlott	Int	350	91	18	2	21	30	45	54	10	5	264	.260	.318	.503	.275	52	86-OF 102
1999	Florida	NL	416	103	19	2	20	28	44	54	11	4	317	.248	.295	.447	.259	54	

Although he's not nearly as good as he's made out to be, he is turning out better than most of us statheads thought he would. Still terrible when it comes to waiting for his pitch, and easily embarassed by a good pitcher. He's a good fielder and he can run, but right now, he's a significantly worse prospect than Kotsay, and not that really close to Dunwoody either.

Gregg Zaun   C   Bats B   Age 28

YEAR	TEAM	LGE	AB	H	DB	TP	HR	BB	R	RBI	SB	CS	OUT	BA	OBA	SA	EQA	EQR	DEFENSE
1996	Baltimor	AL	107	24	8	1	1	10	10	9	0	0	83	.224	.291	.346	.220	9	
1997	Florida	NL	144	44	11	2	2	26	27	21	1	0	100	.306	.412	.451	.306	26	
1998	Florida	NL	298	57	11	2	6	37	26	21	5	2	243	.191	.281	.302	.205	23	83-C 100
1999	Texas	AL	237	56	12	1	5	32	30	24	3	1	182	.236	.327	.359	.237	25	

Blew his opportunity and traded to Texas after the acquisition of Jorge Fabregas. He'll never have a year like '97 again, but he's someone Melvin and Oates know. Good enough to watch Charles Johnson, and good enough to watch Pudge. That, and wuss out on reviewing horror flicks.

PITCHERS (Averages: 4.00 ERA, 9.00 H/9, 1.00 HR/9, 3.00 BB/9, 6.00 K/9, 1.00 KWH)

Antonio Alfonseca   Throws R   Age 27

YEAR	TEAM	LGE	IP	H	ER	HR	BB	K	ERA	W	L	H/9	HR/9	BB/9	K/9	KWH	PERA
1996	Charlott	Int	74.3	89	40	6	23	44	4.84	3	5	10.78	0.73	2.78	5.33	0.71	4.48
1997	Charlott	Int	58.0	66	32	7	19	34	4.97	2	4	10.24	1.09	2.95	5.28	0.69	4.50
1997	Florida	NL	26.0	38	14	3	9	17	4.85	1	2	13.15	1.04	3.12	5.88	0.63	5.88
1998	Florida	NL	71.7	79	33	11	31	42	4.14	4	4	9.92	1.38	3.89	5.27	0.54	4.77

The Six-Fingered Menace, "Pulpo" isn't really a great prospect. He's sort of been Leyland's newfangled Vicente Palacios guy, doing anything he's asked to do. That can be handy, and to Leyland's credit he's never been overly obsessive about roles for his relievers.

Manny Barrios   Throws R   Age 24

YEAR	TEAM	LGE	IP	H	ER	HR	BB	K	ERA	W	L	H/9	HR/9	BB/9	K/9	KWH	PERA
1996	Jackson	Tex	65.0	71	30	4	30	60	4.15	3	4	9.83	0.55	4.15	8.31	1.27	4.15
1997	New Orln	AmA	79.3	84	36	5	33	65	4.08	4	5	9.53	0.57	3.74	7.37	1.14	3.97
1998	Charlott	Int	24.7	19	8	3	9	19	2.92	2	1	6.93	1.09	3.28	6.93	1.58	2.55
1998	Albuquer	PCL	37.7	46	20	7	15	28	4.78	2	2	10.99	1.67	3.58	6.69	0.85	5.50

A hard-throwing reliever, Barrios was sent to the Dodgers in the Piazza trade, then reclaimed on waivers when the Pastaman made one of his many screwups in his brief, inglorious tenure as the Dodgers' GM. Traded to the Reds for minor league veteran catcher Guillermo García.

Brent Billingsley   Throws L   Age 24

YEAR	TEAM	LGE	IP	H	ER	HR	BB	K	ERA	W	L	H/9	HR/9	BB/9	K/9	KWH	PERA
1996	Utica	NYP	82.0	126	63	10	34	47	6.91	2	7	13.83	1.10	3.73	5.16	0.39	6.37
1997	KaneCnty	Mid	158.0	202	84	12	56	108	4.78	7	11	11.51	0.68	3.19	6.15	0.77	4.90
1998	Portland	Eas	172.3	191	84	26	70	140	4.39	9	10	9.97	1.36	3.66	7.31	1.10	4.75

Already termed a crafty lefty at the age of 24, Billingsley mixes an adequate fastball and curve with a devastating changeup. A sleeper candidate for the rotation, and better equipped to succeed at the major league level than Fontenot or Dempster or Larkin.

Travis Burgus   Throws L   Age 26

YEAR	TEAM	LGE	IP	H	ER	HR	BB	K	ERA	W	L	H/9	HR/9	BB/9	K/9	KWH	PERA
1996	KaneCnty	Mid	86.3	122	41	1	46	66	4.27	5	5	12.72	0.10	4.80	6.88	0.58	5.21
1997	Portland	Eas	49.7	79	48	11	26	21	8.70	1	5	14.32	1.99	4.71	3.81	0.16	7.61
1998	Portland	Eas	55.7	54	16	4	32	39	2.59	4	2	8.73	0.65	5.17	6.31	0.66	3.88

One of the greatest pitchers in University of San Diego history, an anecdote he can use for minutes to charm and amuse friends and guests. An arm injury in '97 forced him to move to the pen, and he flashed a good power/groundball assortment.

A.J. Burnett   Throws R   Age 22

YEAR	TEAM	LGE	IP	H	ER	HR	BB	K	ERA	W	L	H/9	HR/9	BB/9	K/9	KWH	PERA
1996	Kingsprt	App	52.7	58	36	0	61	37	6.15	2	4	9.91	0.00	10.42	6.32	0.29	4.78
1997	Pittsfld	NYP	38.7	46	37	5	46	28	8.61	1	3	10.71	1.16	10.71	6.52	0.28	5.82
1998	KaneCnty	Mid	114.0	102	33	5	51	119	2.61	9	4	8.05	0.39	4.03	9.39	2.04	3.08

A big Arkansas kid, and possibly the best thing they got from the Mets in their various deals. Yes, potentially better than Yarnall. Burnett had a very slow start, missing April and most of May with a broken hand. Coming back on strict pitch counts, he completely dominated the Midwest League. The translation should give you an idea: it's extremely difficult to pitch well enough in a low A-league to get something that ends up looking this good. He has good mechanics and a deceptive delivery, throwing hard and mixing in a knuckle-curve and a good change. The future doesn't get any brighter for a low A-ball pitcher than this.

Aaron Cames   Throws R   Age 23

YEAR	TEAM	LGE	IP	H	ER	HR	BB	K	ERA	W	L	H/9	HR/9	BB/9	K/9	KWH	PERA
1996	Utica	NYP	70.0	85	35	4	21	46	4.50	4	4	10.93	0.51	2.70	5.91	0.89	4.37
1997	KaneCnty	Mid	140.7	188	77	15	46	103	4.93	6	10	12.03	0.96	2.94	6.59	0.92	5.37
1998	Brevard	Fla	143.0	174	85	14	67	116	5.35	6	10	10.95	0.88	4.22	7.30	0.87	4.97

When you aren't Kerry Wood, how do you get to be a pitching prospect? You could try what Cames has done: be consistently healthy and okay when you pitch. He had a decent '97 at Kane County, a decent year in the Florida State League, and followed that up with a decent campaign in the Maryland Fall League. He doesn't throw blazing heat or a jaw-dropping breaking pitch. He just gets people out, and he's been consistently solid so far.

Scott Comer — Throws L — Age 22

YEAR	TEAM	LGE	IP	H	ER	HR	BB	K	ERA	W	L	H/9	HR/9	BB/9	K/9	KWH	PERA
1997	Pittsfld	NYP	84.0	109	38	7	16	56	4.07	4	5	11.68	0.75	1.71	6.00	1.35	4.82
1998	KaneCnty	Mid	90.7	123	51	17	11	55	5.06	4	6	12.21	1.69	1.09	5.46	1.68	5.86

A huge lefty out of Oregon, Comer's control has been excellent for a pitcher this young. Almost too good, considering that he allowed 13 homeruns in the Midwest League in 14 starts. He's essentially what the Marlins got for Dennis Cook, since Fletcher Bates looks like a non-prospect.

Vic Darensbourg — Throws L — Age 28

YEAR	TEAM	LGE	IP	H	ER	HR	BB	K	ERA	W	L	H/9	HR/9	BB/9	K/9	KWH	PERA
1996	Charlott	Int	64.7	66	26	6	35	54	3.62	4	3	9.19	0.84	4.87	7.52	0.95	4.18
1997	Charlott	Int	24.3	26	11	4	15	16	4.07	1	2	9.62	1.48	5.55	5.92	0.49	4.81
1998	Florida	NL	72.0	55	26	5	27	67	3.25	5	3	6.88	0.62	3.38	8.38	2.27	2.37

Broke his pitching hand in '97, which led to his dropping off some people's radar screens, including ours. After a month or two, Leyland figured out that this short lefty's better off piching an inning or two, instead of being used as a strict lefty-getter. An experiment with starting him in '94 led to surgery on his elbow to remove bone chips that cost him all of '95. Left in relief, he should be the new Dennis Cook: a strikeout/flyout lefty, good for 70 innings from the pen.

Ryan Dempster — Throws R — Age 22

YEAR	TEAM	LGE	IP	H	ER	HR	BB	K	ERA	W	L	H/9	HR/9	BB/9	K/9	KWH	PERA
1996	Charl-SC	SAL	131.3	184	97	19	66	86	6.65	4	11	12.61	1.30	4.52	5.89	0.46	6.10
1997	Brevard	Fla	156.3	239	113	25	52	99	6.51	5	12	13.76	1.44	2.99	5.70	0.59	6.62
1998	Portland	Eas	45.0	36	18	9	15	26	3.60	3	2	7.20	1.80	3.00	5.20	0.94	3.20
1998	Charlott	Int	33.3	34	12	4	11	20	3.24	2	2	9.18	1.08	2.97	5.40	0.80	4.05
1998	Florida	NL	56.7	77	43	6	35	32	6.83	2	4	12.23	0.95	5.56	5.08	0.28	5.72

Clearly wasn't ready, and rushing him up was one of the most unfortunate of the various live sacrifices made in '98. What's strange about it is that his assortment isn't even that good. It doesn't look like he throws that hard, and tossing him into the fire at the first sign of success was thoughtless.

Scott DeWitt — Throws L — Age 24

YEAR	TEAM	LGE	IP	H	ER	HR	BB	K	ERA	W	L	H/9	HR/9	BB/9	K/9	KWH	PERA
1996	KaneCnty	Mid	138.3	206	115	12	62	81	7.48	3	12	13.40	0.78	4.03	5.27	0.39	5.99
1997	Brevard	Fla	123.7	187	93	18	59	89	6.77	4	10	13.61	1.31	4.29	6.48	0.54	6.55
1998	Portland	Eas	60.3	69	33	7	36	49	4.92	3	4	10.29	1.04	5.37	7.31	0.72	4.92

Another one of those big, hulking guys from Oregon that seem to come out of the forests and throw heat. DeWitt has been moved to the pen, and although the results weren't initially happy, lefties who throw hard are roughly as valuable as two seconds of Bill Cosby's time, so there's a good chance you'll be hearing about him.

Geoff Duncan — Throws R — Age 24

YEAR	TEAM	LGE	IP	H	ER	HR	BB	K	ERA	W	L	H/9	HR/9	BB/9	K/9	KWH	PERA
1996	Utica	NYP	36.3	70	31	5	24	31	7.68	1	3	17.34	1.24	5.94	7.68	0.43	8.17
1997	KaneCnty	Mid	79.3	118	57	9	34	60	6.47	2	7	13.39	1.02	3.86	6.81	0.67	6.13
1998	Brevard	Fla	29.3	47	19	2	10	21	5.83	1	2	14.42	0.61	3.07	6.44	0.70	6.14
1998	Portland	Eas	58.0	43	19	3	31	56	2.95	4	2	6.67	0.47	4.81	8.69	1.76	2.48

A 69th round draft pick in '96 after a college career at Georgia Tech where he essentially pitched garbage time. He's been completely dominating as a reliever since then, so he's somebody who will get a long look in camp.

Brian Edmondson   Throws R   Age 26

YEAR	TEAM	LGE	IP	H	ER	HR	BB	K	ERA	W	L	H/9	HR/9	BB/9	K/9	KWH	PERA
1996	Binghmtn	Eas	110.7	161	75	17	39	65	6.10	4	8	13.09	1.38	3.17	5.29	0.50	6.26
1997	Norfolk	Int	68.0	71	25	5	34	52	3.31	5	3	9.40	0.66	4.50	6.88	0.84	4.10
1998	Atlanta	NL	16.7	15	9	2	8	7	4.86	1	1	8.10	1.08	4.32	3.78	0.31	3.78
1998	Florida	NL	60.3	65	25	8	27	29	3.73	4	3	9.70	1.19	4.03	4.33	0.36	4.48

Snagged from the Braves on waivers after they were returning him to the Mets (he was a Rule V pick from the previous December). He looked good for a brief moment, but his season rapidly went down the tubes once the league figured him out.

Alex Fernandez   Throws R   Age 29

YEAR	TEAM	LGE	IP	H	ER	HR	BB	K	ERA	W	L	H/9	HR/9	BB/9	K/9	KWH	PERA
1995	ChiSox	AL	210.0	188	73	18	52	162	3.13	14	9	8.06	0.77	2.23	6.94	2.01	3.00
1996	ChiSox	AL	256.7	244	90	30	57	196	3.16	18	11	8.56	1.05	2.00	6.87	2.07	3.44
1997	Florida	NL	223.7	196	81	26	62	163	3.26	15	10	7.89	1.05	2.49	6.56	1.64	3.14

After missing '98 after having a torn rotator cuff repaired, the big man is tentatively pencilled in as the Opening Day starter for '99. Reports on his health are good, and with the sale of the team, it's unlikely that he'll be shipped off. Overall, I'm not that optimistic that he'll be back to where he was; Fernandez's conditioning has always been dubious, but we'll have to see what kind of shape he shows up in.

Joe Fontenot   Throws R   Age 22

YEAR	TEAM	LGE	IP	H	ER	HR	BB	K	ERA	W	L	H/9	HR/9	BB/9	K/9	KWH	PERA
1996	San Jose	Cal	127.7	178	95	8	67	82	6.70	4	10	12.55	0.56	4.72	5.78	0.42	5.50
1997	Shrevprt	Tex	139.3	200	106	14	64	85	6.85	4	11	12.92	0.90	4.13	5.49	0.42	5.88
1998	Portland	Eas	38.3	40	15	1	13	24	3.52	2	2	9.39	0.23	3.05	5.63	0.83	3.52
1998	Florida	NL	43.7	59	31	5	18	22	6.39	1	4	12.16	1.03	3.71	4.53	0.34	5.56

Fontenot is actually closer to being a good major league pitcher than these numbers would lead you to believe. He's got very inconsistent mechanics, but throws four good pitches (fastball, a sharp curve, change, cut fastball), although he tends to lose one or two of them at once. A good pitching coach is going to help him iron that sort of thing out. He's exactly the sort of pitcher you put in middle relief to work on his command and keep him healthy until he has some success.

Geoff Goetz   Throws L   Age 20

YEAR	TEAM	LGE	IP	H	ER	HR	BB	K	ERA	W	L	H/9	HR/9	BB/9	K/9	KWH	PERA
1998	Columbia	SAL	73.7	88	50	4	44	42	6.11	2	6	10.75	0.49	5.38	5.13	0.34	4.76
1998	KaneCnty	Mid	40.0	60	26	6	27	24	5.85	1	3	13.50	1.35	6.08	5.40	0.27	6.75

The other part of what the Marlins got for Piazza, Goetz was the Mets' top choice in the '97 draft. He's a great athlete (he used to play center field in high school on the days he didn't pitch), and he throws hard with a good curve. He's a good two or three years away, but Dombrowski should be around to brag if/when he makes it.

Oscar Henriquez   Throws R   Age 25

YEAR	TEAM	LGE	IP	H	ER	HR	BB	K	ERA	W	L	H/9	HR/9	BB/9	K/9	KWH	PERA
1995	Kissimme	Fla	41.7	56	36	4	33	28	7.78	1	4	12.10	0.86	7.13	6.05	0.32	5.83
1996	Kissimme	Fla	32.0	39	22	0	32	31	6.19	1	3	10.97	0.00	9.00	8.72	0.58	5.06
1997	New Orln	AmA	71.3	77	31	4	26	68	3.91	4	4	9.71	0.50	3.28	8.58	1.73	3.91
1998	Charlott	Int	32.0	31	11	3	11	31	3.09	3	1	8.72	0.84	3.09	8.72	2.11	3.66
1998	Florida	NL	20.3	28	20	4	11	18	8.85	0	2	12.39	1.77	4.87	7.97	0.79	6.64

Part of the package received for Moises Alou, Henriquez still pumps gas at 96-98. Traded to the Mets for Jorge Fabregas, he should be given a crack at the major league pen.

Livan Hernandez — Throws R — Age 24

YEAR	TEAM	LGE	IP	H	ER	HR	BB	K	ERA	W	L	H/9	HR/9	BB/9	K/9	KWH	PERA
1996	Portland	Eas	93.3	95	47	15	34	76	4.53	4	6	9.16	1.45	3.28	7.33	1.34	4.24
1996	Charlott	Int	52.3	61	26	3	35	40	4.47	3	3	10.49	0.52	6.02	6.88	0.56	4.64
1997	Charlott	Int	83.3	81	34	5	34	48	3.67	5	4	8.75	0.54	3.67	5.18	0.63	3.46
1997	Florida	NL	97.7	83	34	5	35	64	3.13	7	4	7.65	0.46	3.23	5.90	1.06	2.76
1998	Florida	NL	239.3	277	120	38	95	149	4.51	12	15	10.42	1.43	3.57	5.60	0.63	5.00

He doesn't look like the horse from *Animal Farm*, but he may just as well be. At least it's only the joints in his right arm will be made into glue or gelatin. Not even having an Eric Gregg in every umpiring crew can save him from blowing out his arm. Maybe accepting the power of prayer and lighting a candle for St. Jobe (patron saint of successful surgeries) will let him have a career. If Boles is creative, he could put Hernandez in the pen, but that may just be delaying the inevitable.

Mark Johnson — Throws R — Age 24

YEAR	TEAM	LGE	IP	H	ER	HR	BB	K	ERA	W	L	H/9	HR/9	BB/9	K/9	KWH	PERA
1997	Kissimme	Fla	144.0	201	85	11	45	93	5.31	6	10	12.56	0.69	2.81	5.81	0.72	5.37
1998	Portland	Eas	143.7	161	84	13	61	92	5.26	6	10	10.09	0.81	3.82	5.76	0.65	4.39

The best pitcher of the three acquired in exchange for Moises Alou, Johnson had a good year in Double-A. It was initially feared that he'd been overworked in college, but he's been solid so far. He mixes a low 90s fastball with a great slider and a handy change. A power-groundball pitcher, and you know we like those. A much better prospect now than Brian Meadows was a year ago.

Andy Larkin — Throws R — Age 25

YEAR	TEAM	LGE	IP	H	ER	HR	BB	K	ERA	W	L	H/9	HR/9	BB/9	K/9	KWH	PERA
1996	Brevard	Fla	25.3	45	25	1	8	14	8.88	1	2	15.99	0.36	2.84	4.97	0.41	6.39
1996	Portland	Eas	48.7	53	18	6	9	32	3.33	3	2	9.80	1.11	1.66	5.92	1.61	4.07
1997	Charlott	Int	148.3	179	95	23	69	86	5.76	5	11	10.86	1.40	4.19	5.22	0.45	5.28
1998	Charlott	Int	54.3	59	34	8	30	34	5.63	2	4	9.77	1.33	4.97	5.63	0.49	4.80
1998	Florida	NL	77.0	108	80	13	51	40	9.35	1	8	12.62	1.52	5.96	4.68	0.22	6.43

Another body tossed into the fire in the great rotation blowout of '98. He's had shoulder surgery to add to the elbow troubles that had plagued him for the last three years, so his chances of having a career at all are up to modern medicine, and then he can work on figuring out how to pitch.

Eric Ludwick — Throws R — Age 27

YEAR	TEAM	LGE	IP	H	ER	HR	BB	K	ERA	W	L	H/9	HR/9	BB/9	K/9	KWH	PERA
1996	Louisvil	AmA	60.7	62	24	4	27	62	3.56	4	3	9.20	0.59	4.01	9.20	1.72	3.86
1997	Louisvil	AmA	78.7	78	32	7	28	68	3.66	5	4	8.92	0.80	3.20	7.78	1.59	3.66
1997	Oakland	AL	25.3	31	19	6	15	14	6.75	1	2	11.01	2.13	5.33	4.97	0.32	6.04
1998	Charlott	Int	26.0	29	17	1	13	20	5.88	1	2	10.04	0.35	4.50	6.92	0.80	4.15
1998	Florida	NL	34.0	47	28	8	16	25	7.41	1	3	12.44	2.12	4.24	6.62	0.62	6.62

Just about the unluckiest guy in the major leagues last year. He endured three separate injuries, none of them to his arm, which ended up costing him the place in the Marlins' rotation he'd earned in camp. He still has his four good pitches, so he's still a prospect of sorts, just an unlucky one. Designated for assignment at season's end.

Matt Mantei — Throws R — Age 25

YEAR	TEAM	LGE	IP	H	ER	HR	BB	K	ERA	W	L	H/9	HR/9	BB/9	K/9	KWH	PERA
1996	Florida	NL	18.7	15	12	2	20	22	5.79	1	1	7.23	0.96	9.64	10.61	1.21	3.86
1998	Charlott	Int	16.7	13	9	2	17	21	4.86	1	1	7.02	1.08	9.18	11.34	1.50	3.78
1998	Florida	NL	55.3	41	17	1	20	57	2.77	4	2	6.67	0.16	3.25	9.27	2.97	1.95

Its amazing that Mantei still throws hard. Drafted Rule 5 out of the Mariners organization before '95, but went down with a herniated disk. Almost as soon as he came back, he had shoulder trouble for almost two years before having rotator cuff surgery. Throws hard heat with movement, and works high. In Florida's humid air, that spells success. I don't like his chances of staying healthy, but if he can, he'll be a great closer, and he won't need years of preparation to do it.

Brian Meadows   Throws R   Age 23

YEAR	TEAM	LGE	IP	H	ER	HR	BB	K	ERA	W	L	H/9	HR/9	BB/9	K/9	KWH	PERA
1996	Brevard	Fla	137.3	167	89	20	26	54	5.83	5	10	10.94	1.31	1.70	3.54	0.50	4.92
1996	Portland	Eas	26.7	30	15	1	4	10	5.06	1	2	10.13	0.34	1.35	3.38	0.62	3.71
1997	Portland	Eas	174.3	229	92	21	46	91	4.75	8	11	11.82	1.08	2.37	4.70	0.59	5.27
1998	Florida	NL	177.3	229	96	20	42	81	4.87	8	12	11.62	1.02	2.13	4.11	0.51	5.08

Mixes a decent fastball with a one-knuckle curve that he throws as a waste pitch; it's rarely a strike. Britt Burns has been credited with turning him around in the second half of '97, and that was what basically got him into a major league rotation in '98. Meadows should not be confused with any of the Marlins' good prospects, but there are worse guys to goof off with as your fifth starter.

Rafael Medina   Throws R   Age 24

YEAR	TEAM	LGE	IP	H	ER	HR	BB	K	ERA	W	L	H/9	HR/9	BB/9	K/9	KWH	PERA
1996	Norwich	Eas	101.3	92	48	8	54	88	4.26	5	6	8.17	0.71	4.80	7.82	1.17	3.46
1997	LasVegas	PCL	67.3	85	46	11	35	42	6.15	2	5	11.36	1.47	4.68	5.61	0.44	5.61
1998	Charlott	Int	59.0	54	22	8	24	35	3.36	4	3	8.24	1.22	3.66	5.34	0.71	3.66
1998	Florida	NL	69.7	81	45	9	48	45	5.81	3	5	10.46	1.16	6.20	5.81	0.39	5.17

It surprised no one when Medina got hurt again (shoulder this time), but he can still get his fastball up to 96 once in awhile, and he complements it with a good curve. He's battled weight problems as well as injuries, so I'm not going to predict success. When he's been 100%, which is rare, he's looked good. If he can avoid being the new Bobby Munoz, he can end up having a career.

Blaine Mull   Throws R   Age 22

YEAR	TEAM	LGE	IP	H	ER	HR	BB	K	ERA	W	L	H/9	HR/9	BB/9	K/9	KWH	PERA
1996	Lansing	Mid	166.7	243	103	13	41	80	5.56	6	13	13.12	0.70	2.21	4.32	0.48	5.56
1997	Wichita	Tex	43.3	70	36	4	23	13	7.48	1	4	14.54	0.83	4.78	2.70	0.08	6.65
1997	Wilmngtn	Car	106.3	153	57	7	32	45	4.82	5	7	12.95	0.59	2.71	3.81	0.31	5.42
1998	Brevard	Fla	93.7	143	60	8	36	48	5.77	3	7	13.74	0.77	3.46	4.61	0.34	6.05
1998	Portland	Eas	32.3	44	33	8	16	19	9.19	1	3	12.25	2.23	4.45	5.29	0.38	6.68

The payment for sending away Mr. Marlin, Jeff Conine. His assortment of stuff is solid but unspectacular, so the hope is that he'll actually get to be good once he fills out and physically matures. Already being touted for being a "bulldog" because he gets tougher with men on. Don't listen to the Kansas sabermetric mafia: not a great prospect, yet.

Todd Noel   Throws R   Age 20

YEAR	TEAM	LGE	IP	H	ER	HR	BB	K	ERA	W	L	H/9	HR/9	BB/9	K/9	KWH	PERA
1998	Rockford	Mid	82.7	117	57	2	42	47	6.21	3	6	12.74	0.22	4.57	5.12	0.34	5.23
1998	KaneCnty	Mid	35.3	59	30	2	20	18	7.64	1	3	15.03	0.51	5.09	4.58	0.21	6.37

An flamethrower with the Cubs' organization who racks up nagging injuries (tendinitis last year), but he's managed to avoid any major surgeries so far. The Marlins want him to refine his slider and develop a changeup; he has a tendency to overthrow when he gets into trouble.

Kirt Ojala   Throws L   Age 30

YEAR	TEAM	LGE	IP	H	ER	HR	BB	K	ERA	W	L	H/9	HR/9	BB/9	K/9	KWH	PERA
1996	Indianap	AmA	128.3	175	76	15	38	73	5.33	5	9	12.27	1.05	2.66	5.12	0.60	5.54
1997	Charlott	Int	147.0	171	73	13	55	89	4.47	7	9	10.47	0.80	3.37	5.45	0.63	4.53
1997	Florida	NL	29.3	29	9	5	17	17	2.76	2	1	8.90	1.53	5.22	5.22	0.44	4.60
1998	Florida	NL	127.3	134	64	15	54	69	4.52	6	8	9.47	1.06	3.82	4.88	0.49	4.24

Your basic lefty junkballer, currently toying with throwing a knuckleball. Even without that, he's always been one of my favorites, for no particularly good reason. In '92, he was a staff workhorse for a Prince William team that also had Sterling Hitchcock. Brad Ausmus caught, Andy Fox played third, and you've probably heard of some of the extra bodies on that team: Mike Figga, Robert Eenhorn, and Sherman Obando. Who were considered the prospects on that team? Blass-disease victim Sam Millitello, and a speedy centerfielder named Jason Robertson. The race doesn't always go to the swift or to the strong, and being left-handed doesn't hurt.

Jesus Sanchez   **Throws L**   **Age 24**

YEAR	TEAM	LGE	IP	H	ER	HR	BB	K	ERA	W	L	H/9	HR/9	BB/9	K/9	KWH	PERA
1996	St Lucie	Fla	90.0	65	23	9	25	63	2.30	8	2	6.50	0.90	2.50	6.30	1.83	2.20
1997	Binghmtn	Eas	164.7	163	78	23	57	137	4.26	8	10	8.91	1.26	3.12	7.49	1.51	3.99
1998	Florida	NL	176.7	188	88	18	83	126	4.48	9	11	9.58	0.92	4.23	6.42	0.76	4.28

After missing half of the '96 season because of shoulder surgery, you'd think Sanchez was exactly the kind of pitcher that the Fish would have been careful with after snagging him from the Mets. He's a fun pitcher to watch when he's going good: he's agressive, throws hard for a lefty, and has a pretty deceptive delivery. We'll see if he's survived Leyland's rough use.

Justin Speier   **Throws R**   **Age 25**

YEAR	TEAM	LGE	IP	H	ER	HR	BB	K	ERA	W	L	H/9	HR/9	BB/9	K/9	KWH	PERA
1996	Daytona	Fla	38.3	39	20	5	22	27	4.70	2	2	9.16	1.17	5.17	6.34	0.64	4.46
1996	Orlando	Sou	25.7	26	7	3	4	11	2.45	2	1	9.12	1.05	1.40	3.86	0.87	3.51
1997	Orlando	Sou	73.7	90	46	8	22	48	5.62	3	5	11.00	0.98	2.69	5.86	0.87	4.89
1998	Iowa	PCL	50.0	57	29	10	19	39	5.22	2	4	10.26	1.80	3.42	7.02	1.05	5.22
1998	Florida	NL	19.7	27	17	8	11	14	7.78	0	2	12.36	3.66	5.03	6.41	0.49	8.24

A non-prospect, but a legacy and a "battler," so he got an opportunity. All sorts of people end up being useful relievers, so it isn't beyond the realm of possibility that Speier could succeed in the majors. But his talent isn't what got him there, and even nepotism can go only so far.

Rob Stanifer   **Throws R**   **Age 27**

YEAR	TEAM	LGE	IP	H	ER	HR	BB	K	ERA	W	L	H/9	HR/9	BB/9	K/9	KWH	PERA
1996	Brevard	Fla	43.0	79	25	5	11	22	5.23	2	3	16.53	1.05	2.30	4.60	0.42	7.33
1996	Portland	Eas	33.0	35	18	4	9	24	4.91	2	2	9.55	1.09	2.45	6.55	1.37	4.09
1997	Charlott	Int	27.3	38	15	3	7	19	4.94	1	2	12.51	0.99	2.30	6.26	1.02	5.60
1997	Florida	NL	45.7	44	20	10	14	25	3.94	3	2	8.67	1.97	2.76	4.93	0.76	4.34
1998	Charlott	Int	39.3	43	19	1	13	22	4.35	2	2	9.84	0.23	2.97	5.03	0.65	3.66
1998	Florida	NL	48.7	57	30	5	20	28	5.55	2	3	10.54	0.92	3.70	5.18	0.52	4.62

Designated for assignment, so the fun is whether or not he's going to be menacing your neighborhood. A one-man mortar team, good for starting high-velocity souvenir showers.

Mike Tejera   **Throws L**   **Age 22**

YEAR	TEAM	LGE	IP	H	ER	HR	BB	K	ERA	W	L	H/9	HR/9	BB/9	K/9	KWH	PERA
1997	Utica	NYP	64.3	93	45	11	15	39	6.30	2	5	13.01	1.54	2.10	5.46	0.82	6.30
1998	KaneCnty	Mid	52.0	60	25	5	15	30	4.33	3	3	10.38	0.87	2.60	5.19	0.75	4.50
1998	Portland	Eas	109.0	121	49	16	35	76	4.05	6	6	9.99	1.32	2.89	6.28	1.02	4.62

A short lefty picked out of a nearby Miami high school in the '95 draft, Tejera was actually a member of the Cuban junior national team who defected. More advanced than much of this year's rotation fodder, he may sneak in once the repercussions of Leyland's abuses come into full bloom.

Ed Yarnall   **Throws L**   **Age 23**

YEAR	TEAM	LGE	IP	H	ER	HR	BB	K	ERA	W	L	H/9	HR/9	BB/9	K/9	KWH	PERA
1997	St Lucie	Fla	103.7	112	34	7	34	86	2.95	8	4	9.72	0.61	2.95	7.47	1.46	3.91
1997	Binghmtn	Eas	32.3	22	10	2	10	25	2.78	3	1	6.12	0.56	2.78	6.96	2.13	1.67
1998	Binghmtn	Eas	46.3	23	5	0	17	40	0.97	5	0	4.47	0.00	3.30	7.77	3.07	0.58
1998	Portland	Eas	15.3	10	4	2	4	12	2.35	1	1	5.87	1.17	2.35	7.04	2.70	1.76
1998	Charlott	Int	71.7	82	51	10	36	40	6.40	2	6	10.30	1.26	4.52	5.02	0.41	4.90

Half of the bounty for four months' of Mike Piazza's time. That's a heavy burden, but Yarnall should deliver. The top pitching prospect in the Eastern League, he's got a fastball with plenty of movement, a good curve, slider, and change, a deceptive three-quarters delivery, and he's working on an over-the-top delivery to change his look from time to time. He'll be given every opportunity to win a rotation spot in camp.

SNWLP				FLORIDA MARLINS							Park Effect: -11.9%	
PITCHER	GS	IP	R	SNW	SNL	SNPCT	W	L	RA	APW	SNVA	SNWAR
Dempster, R.	11	48.7	38	2.0	5.0	.289	1	5	7.03	-1.40	-1.40	-0.96
Fontenot, J.	8	42.7	34	1.4	4.2	.245	0	7	7.17	-1.30	-1.37	-1.01
Hammond, C.	3	13.7	11	0.5	1.4	.276	0	2	7.24	-0.43	-0.40	-0.28
Heredia, F.	2	9.7	12	0.1	1.5	.050	0	2	11.17	-0.73	-0.65	-0.58
Hernandez, L.	33	234.3	133	10.7	15.0	.415	11	11	5.11	-1.73	-2.23	-0.26
Larkin, A.	14	72.3	73	2.8	8.0	.262	3	8	9.08	-3.75	-2.52	-1.77
Ludwick, E.	6	22.3	17	0.9	2.4	.281	1	3	6.85	-0.60	-0.61	-0.48
Meadows, B.	31	174.3	106	9.0	13.0	.409	11	13	5.47	-2.00	-1.97	-0.36
Medina, R.	12	67.3	50	2.8	5.5	.341	2	6	6.68	-1.68	-1.29	-0.69
Ojala, K.	13	73.0	48	3.2	5.9	.352	1	7	5.92	-1.20	-1.34	-0.67
Sanchez, J.	29	166.0	95	9.4	10.5	.471	7	8	5.15	-1.31	-0.59	0.91
TOTALS	162	924.3	617	42.9	72.5	.372	37	72	6.01	-16.13	-14.37	-6.16

If I followed my mother's advice—if you can't say something nice don't say anything at all—I would leave this space blank. The 1998 Marlins had arguably the worst pitching staff of the past seven years. I say arguably because the 1995 Twins actually had a worse SNPct (.358 to the Marlins' .372), but the Marlins sustained their incompetence over a full 162-game season. I can't decide which is more impressive. At any rate, the -14.37 SNVA is easily the worst recorded since the SN numbers were developed. Livan Hernandez completely lost the ability to pitch effectively in 1998, but that didn't stop Leyland from sending him out inning after inning. The result is that Hernandez had the most SN losses in the league. His total was the third-most since 1992, behind heroes Mike Moore (15.9 in 1993) and Jaime Navarro (15.7 in 1997). Besides Hernandez, only one pitcher who made a start for Florida in 1998 also made a start for them in 1997. That was Kirt Ojala, who like Hernandez went into the tank in 1998. He made five effective starts for the World Champion version of the Marlins, but 13 dubious ones for the economy aisle version. It's hard to find a bright spot in the Marlins' 1998, but the closest thing would be Jesus Sanchez, the only Marlins pitcher whose performance rated above replacement level. Sanchez also showed some signs of development during the year, recording an SN record of 4.1-5.5 (428) before the All-Star break, and 5.3-5.1 (.510) after.

Pitcher Abuse Points

PITCHER	AGE	GS	PAP	PAP/S	AAW	MAX	115+	130+
Dempster, Ryan	21	11	9	0.82	2.32	106	0	0
Fontenot, Joe	21	8	47	5.88	16.65	125	1	0
Hernandez, Livan	23	33	1520	46.06	115.15	153	19	9
Larkin, Andy	24	14	115	8.21	19.17	132	2	1
Ludwick, Eric	26	6	13	2.17	4.33	108	0	0
Meadows, Brian	22	31	49	1.58	4.22	115	1	0
Medina, Rafael	23	12	240	20.00	50.00	138	4	2
Ojala, Kirt	29	13	44	3.38	5.08	114	0	0
Sanchez, Jesus	23	29	389	13.41	33.53	146	6	2
TOTAL		162	2433	15.02	37.29	153	33	14
RANKING (NL)			1	1	1		4	1

What more can I say? Jim Leyland is the reason I invented the PAP system in the first place, so I guess I owe him a debt of gratitude. Only twice all last year did a major league pitcher reach the dreaded 150-pitch barrier: Livan Hernandez with 153 pitches on June 14, and Livan again with 150 just 11 days later. It wasn't just Hernandez, Sanchez, and Medina—Joe Fontenot and Andy Larkin were handled harshly, and Dempster was saved only by how badly he pitched. Give Brian Meadows a gold star: he never threw more than 115 pitches in a game. Now if only he had a fastball. Marlins fans, just thank God that Ed Yarnall struggled in Triple-A and wasn't brought up to face the firing squad.

Montreal Expos

The saga of the Montreal Expos—in many respects, baseball's longest-running active soap opera, now that Cal has taken a day off—is approaching a climax and, in all likelihood, a conclusion. Unless there's a massive turnaround in the government's position on public funding for a private-enterprise baseball stadium, the Expos will go on the block as a whole, instead of in parts. Barring another unusual turn of events—emergence of a local buyer or group thereof—baseball's presence in Montreal will end, and the team will head south in the general direction of northern Virginia. While the general consensus is that the consortium that purchases the team will be getting one heck of a bargain financially, the state of the team that they purchase is up in the air. The farm system has thinned, and the major-league team has major holes in key functional areas.

The frustrated but loyal group of Expo fans that will be left behind have been witness to one of the greatest fountains of talent in the last two or three decades of Major League Base-ball. The club has survived and occasionally contended on the foundation of a steady stream of talent from the farm system and as bounty received from the dumping of more highly-paid veterans. From 1992 to 1996, the team scarcely had a hole created by a departure that wasn't immediately filled from within.

The problem now is that the talent pool has thinned out considerably, and most of the promising players in the system came in by way of dump trades in the last twelve months. While Jim Beattie has been successful in convincing other teams to part with their top prospects in exchange for Expo stars, often of questionable talent (e.g., Grudzielanek) or of questionable health (e.g., Lansing, Carlos Perez), the team's ability to continue this is now hampered. The Expos have perhaps three or four major players who would fetch top prospects in trade, and the team won't be in any position to move them if it wishes to remain respectable in the standings. While this bust in the inevitable cycle of team competitiveness may not seem problematic—if the system has prospects now, why would they need to dump—recall that the Expos haven't had this type of scarcity in their farm sys-

tem since the mid-80s. That malaise only ended when Dave Dombrowski arrived and changed the organization's entire player development philosophy.

At the same time, the major-league team is moving toward the situation the 1997 Pirates found themselves in: a strong, young pitching staff matched by a weak offense and questionable defense. While contention in 1999 is neither a goal for the current Expo regime nor a relevant or desirable outcome for the team's next set of owners, the team is not well set up for contention post-move (or, potentially, when a new ballpark opens in Montreal). Most distressingly, the de-emphasis of plate discipline among hitters at all levels in the organization is a change from the somewhat more walk-centric philosophy espoused by Dombrowski and his successor, Dan Duquette, earlier this decade.

The Expos drew just 439 walks this year, ahead only of the aforementioned Pirates in free-pass futility. That, coupled with the lowest batting average in the majors, led the Expos to the lowest OBA in the majors and, not surprisingly, the fewest runs scored of any team not employing Quinton McCracken. The dismal parade of ineptitude was most damaging at the top of the order, where Wilton (10 walks) Guerrero, Orlando (18) Cabrera, and the since-traded Mark (21) Grudzielanek combined for fewer than 50 walks in nearly 950 trips to the plate. With so little to work with, it is a wonder Vlad (44) Guerrero found as many as 109 baserunners to drive in.

The removal of the eyesore roof of the O this season produced a dampening effect on offense, and while it's tempting to use that as the scapegoat for the team's offensive woes, the inability to reach base consistently is not limited to the major-league club. At AAA Ottawa, only one player, 29-year-old Allen Battle, drew more than 50 walks, and no player under age 27 drew as many as 30 walks. At AA Harrisburg, the situation was no different: the team leader in walks had 42, the team's most important prospects failed to get on base consistently, and only two part-timers (Geoff Blum and Trace Coquillette) posted respectable OBAs. The organizational leader in walks, Talmadge Nunnari, was a 23-year-old first

> ## Expos Prospectus
>
> **1998 record:** 65-97; Fourth place, NL East
>
> **Pythagorean W/L:** 65-97
>
> **Runs scored:** 644 (16th in NL)
>
> **Runs allowed:** 783 (10th in NL)
>
> **Team EQA:** .256 (9th in NL)
>
> **Park:** Olympic Stadium (extreme pitchers' in 1998 after roof removal)
>
> **1998:** Despite poor record, the Expos developed their top three starters.
>
> **1999:** As much upside as any team in the league; the Expos could challenge for the wild card.

baseman who spent most of the year in the low-A Sally League and who has little power to show for his plate discipline.

This isn't to say that all is lost for the Expos' offense, merely that their outlook is clouded by a consistently lacking feature. Peter Bergeron, acquired from the Dodgers in the Perez/Grudzielanek trade in July, drew nearly 80 walks this year and projects to post OBAs in the upper .300s when he reaches the majors, giving the Expos their first true leadoff hitter since the team traded Delino DeShields. Rondell White was enjoying a superb season at the plate, and set career highs in on-base and slugging percentages before a freak injury ended his season. And Vladimir Guerrero showed himself to be an anchor for the team's lineup for the next five seasons.

The issue is that these three players need to be grouped with other hitters who show something offensively if they're going to put a winning team on the field, wherever that field may lie. The team gets virtually no production from its middle infield or from behind the plate, and while its corner infield spots are not so vacant, production there will likely be below average. Given the paucity of high-level offensive talent in the system, the situation isn't likely to improve enough in the next few years to take this team over .500.

As inept as the Expos have been at putting players on the field who can get on base, they have been equally "ept" at assembling a pitching staff that keeps opposing players off base. Since coming over from Florida last spring, Dustin Hermanson has made two quantum leaps forward in his control despite the challenge of a move to the rotation. Javier Vazquez's record and ERA weren't pretty, but his peripherals, including his walk rate, were quite good for someone who effectively skipped two levels this spring. Even seemingly lost causes like Miguel Batista showed newfound control under the tutelage of Felipe Alou's staff.

Beattie and company have obviously focused on control as a high priority in many of their transactions involving pitchers. They coaxed a few last good months out of Carlos Perez, then trading him before he slumped for Ted Lilly, a hard-throwing lefthander with good control. They acquired the best pitching prospect in baseball, Carl Pavano, and another strong control prospect, Tony Armas, for Pedro Martinez. Two of the three pitchers acquired for Mike Lansing have at least shown the potential for good control.

However, the assembly of this pitching staff is indicative of a general problem with the Expos' strategy of late, and is the final cause for concern among any potential Expo suitors: the team's cycle of pump-and-dump player development is running out of steam. Aside from White and Guerrero, the team's key players and prospects—in fact, all of its top prospects above A-ball except Jose Fernandez—came to the team through trades, almost all of which were salary dumps. While that's a reasonable and even a strong strategy for a team that is rebuilding, it is not sustainable over a period of a decade or more, which is why the system's architect, Dombrowski, left for a greener pasture.

In their self-proclaimed penury, the Expos did more than just slash their major-league salary budget to seven figures: they took their eye off the player-development ball. The club's first-round pick in '98, Josh McKinley, wasn't projected as a first-rounder by many (if any) scouts, and rumors were rampant that the team chose him for his signability. Last year's top pick, Donnie Bridges, had arm problems two months before the draft. The team lost its top pick in '96, John Patterson, because they didn't send him a contract offer immediately. Their top remaining pick from that year, Milton Bradley, is a tools guy who hasn't shown many prospect skills yet. Aside from Michael Barrett, the top Expo prospects among players drafted by the team is Matt Blank, a crafty lefthander who faces tough odds in making the majors, and Nunnari.

As a result, whoever chooses to buy the team can expect a significant lag between the date of purchase and contention, if not respectability. If the climate should change to the point where a downtown Montreal stadium becomes a reality, the fans who hopelessly watched Pedro Martinez and Larry Walker leave town will be left with a much less appealing on-field product than the lost opportunity of 1994. That type of liability may not show up in American Baseball Capital's financial projections, but its impact on the team's future bottom line is unquestionably serious.

HITTERS (Averages: BA .260/ OBA .330/ SA .420, EQA .260)

Shane Andrews   3B   Bats R   Age 27

YEAR	TEAM	LGE	AB	H	DB	TP	HR	BB	R	RBI	SB	CS	OUT	BA	OBA	SA	EQA	EQR	DEFENSE
1996	Montreal	NL	372	81	14	2	18	37	36	44	2	1	292	.218	.289	.411	.239	41	115-3B 115
1997	Montreal	NL	64	13	2	0	4	3	4	7	0	0	51	.203	.239	.422	.219	6	
1998	Montreal	NL	497	125	28	0	30	62	62	79	1	7	379	.252	.335	.489	.274	74	139-3B 120
1999	*Montreal*	*NL*	*374*	*91*	*16*	*1*	*20*	*41*	*41*	*54*	*2*	*4*	*287*	*.243*	*.318*	*.452*	*.266*	*53*	

A running theme with Expo players is that "you can put up with this guy's bat if you're getting extra offense elsewhere." Except that the Expos aren't getting extra offense from any positions on the defensive end of the spectrum (2b, ss, c). Andrews did recover nicely from major shoulder surgery and led the team in walks, but the Expos need more offense from the hot corner.

Michael Barrett   C/3B   Bats R   Age 22

YEAR	TEAM	LGE	AB	H	DB	TP	HR	BB	R	RBI	SB	CS	OUT	BA	OBA	SA	EQA	EQR	DEFENSE	
1996	Delmarva	SAL	482	103	19	2	4	12	20	23	2	5	384	.214	.233	.286	.161	20		
1997	WPalmB	Fla	424	109	14	0	10	33	40	43	4	2	317	.257	.311	.361	.234	42		
1998	Harrisbg	Eas	453	141	24	2	18	24	56	70	6	5	317	.311	.346	.492	.282	67	80-C 101	32-3B 100
1998	Montreal	NL	23	7	2	0	1	4	4	4	0	0	16	.304	.407	.522	.317	5		
1999	*Montreal*	*NL*	*462*	*131*	*22*	*1*	*16*	*25*	*48*	*61*	*5*	*4*	*335*	*.284*	*.320*	*.439*	*.265*	*61*		

The phenom, as the Montreal press is fond of calling him, took a nice step forward this year by crushing Eastern League pitching. He just switched to catching in '96, so his solid defense there is quite impressive. Still, mentioning him in the same breath as Sir Vlad is premature; Barrett's OPS of .883 pales next to Vlad's Harrisburg OPS of 1.050, and Vlad was only 20 at that time. Like nearly all Expo farmhands, needs to get on base more often.

Peter Bergeron   CF   Bats L   Age 21

YEAR	TEAM	LGE	AB	H	DB	TP	HR	BB	R	RBI	SB	CS	OUT	BA	OBA	SA	EQA	EQR	DEFENSE
1996	Yakima	Nwn	238	52	2	1	4	20	16	16	6	6	192	.218	.279	.286	.193	16	53-OF 100
1997	Savannah	SAL	508	133	14	3	5	60	59	46	14	12	387	.262	.340	.331	.238	53	131-OF 98
1998	SanAnton	Tex	413	117	13	4	7	51	63	45	20	6	302	.283	.362	.385	.269	57	107-OF 108
1998	Harrisbg	Eas	135	32	8	3	0	15	18	10	6	2	105	.237	.313	.341	.235	14	29-OF 115
1999	*Montreal*	*NL*	*519*	*142*	*18*	*4*	*6*	*55*	*70*	*50*	*25*	*9*	*386*	*.274*	*.343*	*.358*	*.260*	*66*	

Here's why I said, "nearly all." Stolen in the Perez/Grudz dump, Bergeron is potentially the leadoff hitter the Expos desperately need in front of Vlad and Rondell. He should eventually post .400 OBAs in the majors, and his glovework is strong enough to push White to left (where he's less likely to hurt himself). Brett Butler comparisons are not out of line, although some prefer to use Steve Finley's name. ETA: mid-99.

Milton Bradley   OF   Bats B   Age 21

YEAR	TEAM	LGE	AB	H	DB	TP	HR	BB	R	RBI	SB	CS	OUT	BA	OBA	SA	EQA	EQR	DEFENSE
1997	Vermont	NYP	201	48	5	1	3	14	15	16	3	4	157	.239	.288	.318	.206	15	49-OF 99
1998	CapeFear	SAL	281	73	13	2	5	20	28	28	6	5	213	.260	.309	.374	.235	29	49-OF 96
1998	Jupiter	Fla	260	64	9	1	4	25	27	22	8	5	201	.246	.312	.335	.228	25	60-OF 110
1999	*Montreal*	*NL*	*392*	*107*	*15*	*2*	*8*	*31*	*44*	*42*	*14*	*10*	*295*	*.273*	*.326*	*.383*	*.253*	*47*	

The Expos' #2 pick in '96 didn't quite rip through the Sally League (.825 OPS in 281 AB), but the team promoted him anyway. He scuffled in a tough park in Jupiter, although his walk rate improved and his defense remained a plus. The team was pleased with his development this year; I still want to see the plate discipline carried through a full season. He looks like he's at least three years away. Ages 4 and Up.

Orlando Cabrera   SS   Bats R   Age 25

YEAR	TEAM	LGE	AB	H	DB	TP	HR	BB	R	RBI	SB	CS	OUT	BA	OBA	SA	EQA	EQR	DEFENSE	
1996	Delmarva	SAL	529	117	13	2	10	38	43	37	21	10	422	.221	.273	.310	.203	39	66-SS 91	62-2B 103
1997	WPalmB	Fla	281	67	11	0	5	22	30	21	15	7	221	.238	.294	.331	.221	25	62-SS 81	
1997	Harrisbg	Eas	131	36	10	0	4	12	19	16	5	2	97	.275	.336	.443	.269	18	33-SS 87	
1997	Ottawa	Int	122	31	3	2	2	5	13	10	7	1	92	.254	.283	.361	.230	12	19-SS 106	
1998	Ottawa	Int	269	53	7	3	0	24	19	11	12	7	223	.197	.263	.245	.175	14	44-SS 97	20-2B 100
1998	Montreal	NL	264	77	16	5	4	20	36	32	7	2	189	.292	.342	.436	.270	36	47-SS 97	23-2B 101
1999	*Montreal*	*NL*	*518*	*128*	*21*	*4*	*8*	*37*	*54*	*45*	*23*	*9*	*399*	*.247*	*.297*	*.349*	*.235*	*54*		

Good wheels and an above-average glove, but no walks and no power. He's cheap, Felipe is comfortable with him, and it's good to have someone like him to compensate for Wilton's poor glove behind the young pitchers.

Trace Coquillette   2B/3B   Bats R   Age 25

YEAR	TEAM	LGE	AB	H	DB	TP	HR	BB	R	RBI	SB	CS	OUT	BA	OBA	SA	EQA	EQR	DEFENSE	
1996	WPalmB	Fla	270	63	14	2	2	23	25	20	5	4	211	.233	.294	.322	.213	22	34-2B 93	33-3B 70
1997	WPalmB	Fla	190	53	9	0	7	22	25	26	4	4	141	.279	.354	.437	.271	27	44-2B 85	
1997	Harrisbg	Eas	290	65	11	2	7	19	24	24	7	3	228	.224	.272	.348	.214	24	55-2B 101	
1998	Harrisbg	Eas	187	57	6	0	7	12	24	26	7	2	132	.305	.347	.449	.276	27	44-2B 97	
1998	Ottawa	Int	248	55	8	0	6	15	17	19	2	2	195	.222	.266	.327	.200	17	45-2B 86	19-3B 95
1999	*Montreal*	*NL*	*405*	*104*	*16*	*1*	*12*	*27*	*41*	*44*	*11*	*4*	*305*	*.257*	*.303*	*.390*	*.248*	*47*		

Good-glove, mediocre-stick second baseman who, like many Expo prospects, has struggled with midseason promotions. Left his glove and his bat in Harrisburg, apparently. Another potential Mordecai impersonator.

Jose Fernandez   3B   Bats L   Age 24

YEAR	TEAM	LGE	AB	H	DB	TP	HR	BB	R	RBI	SB	CS	OUT	BA	OBA	SA	EQA	EQR	DEFENSE
1996	Delmarva	SAL	436	108	14	2	10	37	43	42	10	7	335	.248	.307	.358	.231	43	124-3B 96
1997	WPalmB	Fla	352	96	13	2	8	32	42	39	11	7	263	.273	.333	.389	.252	42	95-3B 104
1997	Harrisbg	Eas	95	19	2	1	3	9	7	8	1	0	76	.200	.269	.337	.210	8	18-3B 82
1998	Harrisbg	Eas	370	105	16	1	16	32	50	52	13	5	270	.284	.341	.462	.276	54	85-3B 96
1998	Ottawa	Int	59	14	2	1	0	4	5	4	2	1	46	.237	.286	.305	.206	4	
1999	*Montreal*	*NL*	*425*	*115*	*19*	*2*	*12*	*34*	*50*	*50*	*13*	*7*	*317*	*.271*	*.325*	*.409*	*.261*	*55*	

If the improvement is real, he'll present the Expos with an interesting problem in 2000: who to deal between him, Widger, and Barrett. Actually, the answer is simple—Widger—but the organization's commitment to the worst of the troika worries me. Fernandez is still filling out and earns kudos for his arm; like other Expo prospects, he's been jerked around the field (3b, 1b, of) and has struggled with midseason promotions.

Brad Fullmer   1B   Bats L   Age 24

YEAR	TEAM	LGE	AB	H	DB	TP	HR	BB	R	RBI	SB	CS	OUT	BA	OBA	SA	EQA	EQR	DEFENSE
1996	WPalmB	Fla	385	110	18	0	8	28	40	45	2	4	279	.286	.334	.395	.251	44	78-OF 85
1996	Harrisbg	Eas	97	25	3	1	3	3	7	11	0	0	72	.258	.280	.402	.230	9	
1997	Harrisbg	Eas	351	98	16	2	14	24	40	49	5	3	256	.279	.325	.456	.266	47	67-1B 116
1997	Montreal	NL	40	12	1	0	3	2	4	8	0	0	28	.300	.333	.550	.292	6	
1998	Montreal	NL	510	146	44	2	16	43	69	71	7	7	371	.286	.342	.475	.275	74	123-1B 89
1999	*Montreal*	*NL*	*491*	*140*	*30*	*2*	*16*	*32*	*56*	*67*	*6*	*4*	*355*	*.285*	*.329*	*.452*	*.273*	*69*	

On the one hand, he didn't fare too badly compared to the more touted rookie first basemen in the NL, Todd Helton and Travis Lee. On the other hand, none of them were exceptional, and Fullmer's .773 OPS isn't pretty. He's young and held his walk rate despite skipping Triple-A and leaving a hitter's park, so there is cause for optimism, but he'll probably fall behind Helton and both Lees in '99.

Vladimir Guerrero   RF   Bats R   Age 23

YEAR	TEAM	LGE	AB	H	DB	TP	HR	BB	R	RBI	SB	CS	OUT	BA	OBA	SA	EQA	EQR	DEFENSE
1996	Harrisbg	Eas	414	138	25	5	16	43	71	72	14	6	282	.333	.396	.534	.314	78	103-OF 92
1997	Montreal	NL	323	95	22	2	11	21	39	47	2	4	232	.294	.337	.477	.273	45	66-OF 103
1998	Montreal	NL	631	214	38	7	43	47	100	134	12	11	428	.339	.385	.626	.325	129	155-OF 95
1999	*Montreal*	*NL*	*526*	*176*	*34*	*4*	*31*	*38*	*80*	*104*	*12*	*7*	*357*	*.335*	*.379*	*.591*	*.325*	*107*	

Getting his due, although you wonder where his star would be if he were in New York or LA. Turns 23 in February, and already holds the club records for homers, RBI, and extra-base hits in a season. He's still prone to the boneheaded play in the field, and I'd like to see him walk more, but those nits are not worth picking. Signed a five-year deal in August.

Wilton Guerrero — 2B — Bats R — Age 24

YEAR	TEAM	LGE	AB	H	DB	TP	HR	BB	R	RBI	SB	CS	OUT	BA	OBA	SA	EQA	EQR	DEFENSE	
1996	Albuquer	PCL	402	111	16	6	2	23	46	35	19	9	301	.276	.315	.361	.238	41	62-2B 96	28-SS 112
1997	LosAngls	NL	358	106	10	9	5	11	35	42	5	5	257	.296	.317	.416	.249	40	89-2B 99	
1998	LosAngls	NL	181	54	5	3	0	5	19	16	6	2	129	.298	.317	.359	.238	18	26-2B 89	
1998	Albuquer	PCL	117	29	2	1	1	8	13	8	8	2	90	.248	.296	.308	.221	10	19-2B 88	
1998	Montreal	NL	224	67	12	6	2	12	28	27	3	0	157	.299	.335	.433	.267	29	51-2B 92	
1999	*Montreal*	*NL*	*448*	*133*	*19*	*9*	*3*	*17*	*51*	*48*	*16*	*6*	*321*	*.297*	*.323*	*.400*	*.259*	*55*		

Imported to make Vlad happy? Perhaps, but the Expos had no viable middle infield alternatives in the upper levels, so he's not as useless in Montreal as he would be to other clubs. The cost of the long-term contract he will eventually get will be brushed aside as the cost of doing business with his brother. The Expos are considering moving him to centerfield, which makes almost as little sense as the rumored Womack shift from second to center in Pittsburgh.

Bob Henley — C — Bats R — Age 26

YEAR	TEAM	LGE	AB	H	DB	TP	HR	BB	R	RBI	SB	CS	OUT	BA	OBA	SA	EQA	EQR	DEFENSE
1996	Harrisbg	Eas	292	58	9	1	2	60	33	20	1	1	235	.199	.335	.257	.220	27	
1997	Harrisbg	Eas	276	70	9	0	8	24	27	30	3	1	207	.254	.313	.373	.240	29	
1998	Ottawa	Int	124	25	3	1	3	10	8	9	1	1	100	.202	.261	.315	.194	8	28-C 101
1998	Montreal	NL	117	38	7	1	4	11	19	19	3	0	79	.325	.383	.504	.307	21	30-C 101
1999	*Montreal*	*NL*	*274*	*67*	*10*	*1*	*7*	*28*	*28*	*29*	*3*	*1*	*208*	*.245*	*.315*	*.365*	*.245*	*31*	

Will be Widger's caddy, playing twice a week or so for the next year or two, or until the club decides Barrett is a catcher after all. Don't be fooled by Henley's hot cup of coffee; that's an iced latte in disguise.

Terry Jones — OF — Bats B — Age 28

YEAR	TEAM	LGE	AB	H	DB	TP	HR	BB	R	RBI	SB	CS	OUT	BA	OBA	SA	EQA	EQR	DEFENSE
1996	ColSprin	PCL	480	103	4	1	1	31	28	20	17	9	386	.215	.262	.233	.166	22	123-OF 100
1997	ColSprin	PCL	347	61	5	2	1	19	16	12	22	5	291	.176	.219	.210	.140	11	84-OF 94
1998	Ottawa	Int	275	51	3	2	0	26	21	10	20	5	229	.185	.256	.211	.170	14	78-OF 104
1998	Montreal	NL	214	51	9	2	1	22	29	14	18	5	168	.238	.309	.313	.231	22	56-OF 115
1999	*Montreal*	*NL*	*436*	*96*	*10*	*3*	*1*	*33*	*44*	*21*	*35*	*8*	*348*	*.220*	*.275*	*.264*	*.207*	*34*	

Jones is a track star who unfortunately chose a career in baseball. Felipe said Jones would be the fourth or fifth outfielder next year, which is good news if you were worried he'd play everyday.

Scott Livingstone — UT — Bats L — Age 33

YEAR	TEAM	LGE	AB	H	DB	TP	HR	BB	R	RBI	SB	CS	OUT	BA	OBA	SA	EQA	EQR	DEFENSE
1996	SanDieg	NL	172	51	5	1	2	10	16	19	0	1	122	.297	.335	.372	.245	18	14-1B 98
1997	StLouis	NL	41	7	1	0	0	1	1	1	1	0	34	.171	.190	.195	.073	0	
1998	Montreal	NL	110	24	7	0	0	6	7	5	1	1	87	.218	.259	.282	.178	6	
1999	*Montreal*	*NL*	*106*	*26*	*5*	*0*	*0*	*6*	*8*	*7*	*1*	*1*	*81*	*.245*	*.286*	*.292*	*.204*	*8*	

On June 4th, the Expos had to use a DH against Tampa Bay. This was the best they could muster.

Derrick May — OF — Bats L — Age 30

YEAR	TEAM	LGE	AB	H	DB	TP	HR	BB	R	RBI	SB	CS	OUT	BA	OBA	SA	EQA	EQR	DEFENSE
1996	Houston	NL	261	67	11	3	6	31	31	30	2	2	196	.257	.336	.391	.253	32	56-OF 104
1997	Philadel	NL	149	34	5	1	1	9	11	9	3	1	116	.228	.272	.295	.195	10	42-OF 88
1998	Montreal	NL	181	45	7	0	6	13	16	20	0	0	136	.249	.299	.387	.236	18	35-OF 88
1999	*Montreal*	*NL*	*205*	*54*	*7*	*0*	*8*	*20*	*22*	*27*	*1*	*1*	*152*	*.263*	*.329*	*.415*	*.263*	*27*	

The great Nepotista, and a great example of the kind of player you don't get excited about. Aside from Seguignol, who only had 42 AB, May led Expos leftfielders in OPS at .648.

Ryan McGuire — 1B/LF — Bats L — Age 27

YEAR	TEAM	LGE	AB	H	DB	TP	HR	BB	R	RBI	SB	CS	OUT	BA	OBA	SA	EQA	EQR	DEFENSE	
1996	Ottawa	Int	451	108	16	0	11	55	50	44	8	3	346	.239	.322	.348	.238	48	117-1B 92	
1997	Ottawa	Int	184	49	8	1	2	30	27	19	4	2	137	.266	.369	.353	.262	24	50-1B 117	
1997	Montreal	NL	198	49	15	2	3	20	21	21	0	4	153	.247	.317	.389	.238	21	29-OF 108	19-1B 108
1998	Montreal	NL	212	43	8	0	2	33	20	14	0	0	169	.203	.310	.269	.208	17	33-1B 92	28-OF 91
1999	*Montreal*	*NL*	*289*	*68*	*9*	*0*	*7*	*37*	*30*	*29*	*3*	*2*	*223*	*.235*	*.322*	*.339*	*.241*	*32*		

Even I have my limits when it comes to guys who walk. McGuire gets his uniform dirty (with Astroturf dye) and has a good eye, but he's never hit for any power, and this season he couldn't even get on base 30% of the time. Better options are available on waivers.

Mike Mordecai — UT — Bats R — Age 31

YEAR	TEAM	LGE	AB	H	DB	TP	HR	BB	R	RBI	SB	CS	OUT	BA	OBA	SA	EQA	EQR	DEFENSE
1996	Atlanta	NL	107	25	4	0	2	10	10	9	1	0	82	.234	.299	.327	.220	9	12-2B 116
1997	Richmond	Int	121	33	4	0	3	7	11	13	0	1	89	.273	.312	.380	.236	12	
1997	Atlanta	NL	81	14	2	1	0	6	2	2	0	1	68	.173	.230	.222	.127	2	
1998	Montreal	NL	120	26	3	2	4	9	10	12	1	0	94	.217	.271	.375	.222	11	
1999	*Montreal*	*NL*	*149*	*32*	*6*	*1*	*4*	*11*	*11*	*13*	*0*	*0*	*117*	*.215*	*.269*	*.349*	*.217*	*13*	

Spent the year about 30 seconds away from losing his job, but folks like Jose Vidro couldn't string together two hits to take the utility slot away. If Felipe goes for a glove in the middle like Coquillette, Mordecai should finally hit the road this spring.

Talmadge Nunnari — 1B — Bats L — Age 24

YEAR	TEAM	LGE	AB	H	DB	TP	HR	BB	R	RBI	SB	CS	OUT	BA	OBA	SA	EQA	EQR	DEFENSE
1997	Vermont	NYP	240	52	4	0	3	20	15	15	2	2	190	.217	.277	.271	.186	14	60-1B 86
1998	CapeFear	SAL	293	62	6	0	2	29	18	16	1	2	233	.212	.283	.253	.182	16	74-1B 105
1998	Jupiter	Fla	201	46	7	0	2	23	17	15	0	1	156	.229	.308	.294	.211	16	53-1B 107
1999	*Montreal*	*NL*	*376*	*91*	*5*	*0*	*6*	*34*	*29*	*32*	*1*	*2*	*287*	*.242*	*.305*	*.303*	*.219*	*32*	

After starring in the Sun Belt Conference at Jacksonville U., Talmadge has continued to flash the Hal Morris skill set: good eye, no power, old for his leagues. Not a prospect.

F.P. Santangelo — UT — Bats B — Age 31

YEAR	TEAM	LGE	AB	H	DB	TP	HR	BB	R	RBI	SB	CS	OUT	BA	OBA	SA	EQA	EQR	DEFENSE	
1996	Montreal	NL	390	104	18	5	7	50	51	46	4	2	288	.267	.350	.392	.262	51	108-OF 104	16-3B 111
1997	Montreal	NL	348	83	20	4	5	52	45	35	6	5	270	.239	.338	.362	.247	41	79-OF 98	22-3B 105
1998	Montreal	NL	386	88	13	0	7	47	39	32	8	4	302	.228	.312	.316	.224	36	74-OF 100	27-2B 94
1999	*Montreal*	*NL*	*367*	*88*	*15*	*3*	*5*	*50*	*43*	*35*	*7*	*3*	*282*	*.240*	*.331*	*.338*	*.247*	*43*		

A dismal year, and it can't all be blamed on the creaky knees. The epitome of the "super-sub," Santangelo is overtaxed in an everyday role, especially on a team that needs help creating runs. If he takes time to heal up, he could return to useful form for about 350-400 PA.

Brian Schneider — C — Bats L — Age 22

YEAR	TEAM	LGE	AB	H	DB	TP	HR	BB	R	RBI	SB	CS	OUT	BA	OBA	SA	EQA	EQR	DEFENSE	
1997	CapeFear	SAL	390	87	12	0	5	47	34	29	1	3	306	.223	.307	.292	.210	31		
1998	CapeFear	SAL	135	35	3	1	5	13	15	17	3	2	102	.259	.324	.407	.253	16	35-C 101	
1998	Jupiter	Fla	300	68	6	1	3	19	18	19	2	2	234	.227	.273	.283	.187	18	76-C	104

An unusual developmental strategy the Expos have is the midseason promotion, followed by a non-promotion the next spring. Schneider began '98 where he ended '97, in Cape Fear, and he crushed the ball for about a month before he was promoted to Jupiter, where he struggled across the board. Karl Chatman and Carlos Adolfo had similar seasons, and I just don't see any evidence that this is helping anyone's development.

Fernando Seguignol   1B   Bats B   Age 24

YEAR	TEAM	LGE	AB	H	DB	TP	HR	BB	R	RBI	SB	CS	OUT	BA	OBA	SA	EQA	EQR	DEFENSE
1996	Delmarva	SAL	424	88	8	2	7	36	27	27	5	6	342	.208	.270	.285	.187	26	98-OF 89
1997	WPalmB	Fla	456	105	14	2	16	27	35	45	3	3	354	.230	.273	.375	.219	40	117-1B 113
1998	Harrisbg	Eas	282	79	8	0	21	26	37	51	5	1	204	.280	.341	.532	.292	47	58-1B 104
1998	Ottawa	Int	107	25	6	0	5	11	11	14	0	0	82	.234	.305	.430	.251	13	23-OF 82
1998	Montreal	NL	42	11	5	0	2	4	5	7	0	0	31	.262	.326	.524	.283	7	
1999	*Montreal*	*NL*	*429*	*107*	*17*	*1*	*20*	*35*	*45*	*56*	*5*	*2*	*324*	*.249*	*.306*	*.434*	*.259*	*56*	

I think this guy will be better than Fullmer by 2000. Seguignol tightened up his plate discipline substantially at Harrisburg this year, and his numbers shot up in the key scouting categories. His voluminous whiffs say he needs a year in Triple-A to consolidate his gains, but if he can hold on to them, he could easily become the power-hitting first baseman this team needs.

Darond Stovall   OF   Bats B   Age 26

YEAR	TEAM	LGE	AB	H	DB	TP	HR	BB	R	RBI	SB	CS	OUT	BA	OBA	SA	EQA	EQR	DEFENSE
1996	Harrisbg	Eas	273	54	4	1	8	26	21	20	7	3	222	.198	.268	.308	.200	20	71-OF 106
1997	Harrisbg	Eas	167	39	3	1	5	18	17	17	3	0	128	.234	.308	.353	.235	17	41-OF 106
1997	Ottawa	Int	341	76	18	1	4	27	28	23	8	10	275	.223	.280	.317	.202	25	94-OF 98
1998	Ottawa	Int	149	29	4	0	6	17	14	13	4	2	122	.195	.277	.342	.216	13	36-OF 94
1998	Montreal	NL	78	17	3	1	2	7	7	7	1	0	61	.218	.282	.359	.223	7	
1999	*Florida*	*NL*	*317*	*70*	*12*	*1*	*8*	*29*	*30*	*27*	*10*	*6*	*253*	*.221*	*.286*	*.341*	*.225*	*30*	

The organizational obsession with the toolsy Stovall cooled when he was pushed off the 40-man roster in June . . . and 29 other teams ignored him. Could be Florida's fifth outfielder this year after they signed him to a minor-league deal in November.

Andrew Tracy   1B   Bats L   Age 25

YEAR	TEAM	LGE	AB	H	DB	TP	HR	BB	R	RBI	SB	CS	OUT	BA	OBA	SA	EQA	EQR	DEFENSE
1996	Vermont	NYP	181	36	4	0	3	21	12	12	0	0	146	.199	.282	.271	.191	12	53-1B 94
1997	CapeFear	SAL	213	51	3	1	5	17	17	19	2	1	163	.239	.296	.333	.219	18	52-1B 95
1998	Jupiter	Fla	253	51	5	1	6	28	19	19	2	2	204	.202	.281	.300	.201	18	67-1B 97
1998	Harrisbg	Eas	213	45	7	2	8	20	18	22	1	1	169	.211	.279	.376	.224	20	51-1B 97
1999	*Montreal*	*NL*	*338*	*77*	*9*	*0*	*11*	*33*	*28*	*35*	*1*	*1*	*262*	*.228*	*.296*	*.352*	*.232*	*34*	

College player who hasn't moved up as quickly as the Expos hoped. His power has increased slightly as he's moved up, but at his current rate of advancement, he'll be 26 or 27 when he makes the majors.

Jon Tucker   1B   Bats L   Age 22

YEAR	TEAM	LGE	AB	H	DB	TP	HR	BB	R	RBI	SB	CS	OUT	BA	OBA	SA	EQA	EQR	DEFENSE
1996	GreatFls	Pio	165	38	3	0	6	7	11	15	4	3	130	.230	.262	.358	.209	13	35-1B 100
1997	VeroBch	Fla	420	109	12	0	13	31	39	47	3	2	313	.260	.310	.381	.239	44	110-1B 108
1998	SanAnton	Tex	357	94	20	1	9	35	40	42	2	3	266	.263	.329	.401	.252	42	73-1B 110
1998	Harrisbg	Eas	80	22	5	0	3	16	14	12	0	0	58	.275	.396	.450	.297	14	
1999	*Montreal*	*NL*	*405*	*115*	*19*	*1*	*13*	*36*	*48*	*55*	*4*	*2*	*292*	*.284*	*.342*	*.432*	*.275*	*58*	

Throw-in on the Perez/Grudz dump with a good glove, a good eye, and a hill to climb with the popular Fullmer and powerful Seguignol ahead of him. At 21, Tucker held his own in the Texas League and briefly mashed the Eastern League; he'll spend the year at Ottawa but may move to the outfield with Seguignol in the way.

Jose Vidro   2B/3B   Bats B   Age 24

YEAR	TEAM	LGE	AB	H	DB	TP	HR	BB	R	RBI	SB	CS	OUT	BA	OBA	SA	EQA	EQR	DEFENSE	
1996	Harrisbg	Eas	450	108	18	1	16	25	37	47	2	1	343	.240	.280	.391	.228	43	76-3B 111	30-2B 95
1997	Ottawa	Int	277	86	11	0	13	19	35	45	2	0	191	.310	.355	.491	.289	43	44-3B 116	19-2B 82
1997	Montreal	NL	168	40	12	1	2	12	16	14	1	0	128	.238	.289	.357	.223	15	25-3B 103	
1998	Ottawa	Int	231	60	12	1	2	21	24	21	3	2	173	.260	.321	.346	.235	23	29-2B 95	22-3B 102
1998	Montreal	NL	207	49	13	0	0	28	23	15	2	2	160	.237	.328	.300	.225	19	46-2B	94
1999	*Montreal*	*NL*	*430*	*117*	*23*	*1*	*12*	*35*	*48*	*53*	*4*	*1*	*314*	*.272*	*.327*	*.414*	*.264*	*56*		

I don't see what the fuss is about, and there's no room for him at second or at third. His glovework at second is woefully inadequate, bordering on inattentive; he'll do things like forget to come in with the pitcher up.

Rondell White — CF — Bats R — Age 27

YEAR	TEAM	LGE	AB	H	DB	TP	HR	BB	R	RBI	SB	CS	OUT	BA	OBA	SA	EQA	EQR	DEFENSE
1996	Montreal	NL	331	93	18	4	6	24	42	37	11	6	244	.281	.330	.414	.257	41	75-OF 113
1997	Montreal	NL	588	155	27	4	29	35	66	81	13	8	441	.264	.305	.471	.261	76	145-OF 113
1998	Montreal	NL	361	113	22	2	19	33	60	61	18	8	256	.313	.371	.543	.305	66	95-OF 113
1999	*Montreal*	*NL*	*402*	*116*	*22*	*3*	*19*	*28*	*54*	*61*	*15*	*6*	*292*	*.289*	*.335*	*.500*	*.289*	*65*	

Was quietly on his way to his best season when disaster struck in a Little League catch attempt. He has tightened his plate discipline and started generating more power. Should move to left when Bergeron arrives, if only for his own protection.

Chris Widger — C — Bats R — Age 28

YEAR	TEAM	LGE	AB	H	DB	TP	HR	BB	R	RBI	SB	CS	OUT	BA	OBA	SA	EQA	EQR	DEFENSE
1996	Tacoma	PCL	348	96	12	1	11	24	38	42	6	1	253	.276	.323	.411	.255	42	
1997	Montreal	NL	276	62	19	3	7	24	28	28	2	0	214	.225	.287	.391	.233	28	
1998	Montreal	NL	420	103	18	1	17	32	43	50	7	1	318	.245	.299	.414	.246	48	118-C 101
1999	*Montreal*	*NL*	*357*	*89*	*16*	*1*	*14*	*26*	*37*	*43*	*6*	*1*	*269*	*.249*	*.300*	*.417*	*.254*	*44*	

Signed to a four-year deal before the season in a feel-good frenzy of deal-signing. The Expos apparently forgot that Widger isn't anything worth holding onto for four years.

PITCHERS (Averages: 4.00 ERA, 9.00 H/9, 1.00 HR/9, 3.00 BB/9, 6.00 K/9, 1.00 KWH)

Tony Armas — Throws R — Age 21

YEAR	TEAM	LGE	IP	H	ER	HR	BB	K	ERA	W	L	H/9	HR/9	BB/9	K/9	KWH	PERA
1997	Greensbr	SAL	50.0	47	14	4	15	41	2.52	4	2	8.46	0.72	2.70	7.38	1.79	3.24
1997	Tampa	Fla	44.0	55	27	2	18	20	5.52	2	3	11.25	0.41	3.68	4.09	0.30	4.70
1998	Jupiter	Fla	144.0	182	73	14	65	101	4.56	7	9	11.38	0.88	4.06	6.31	0.65	5.12

Pitched well in his first full season of high-A, adding some velocity this year. He's the furthest along of the Jupiter troika between him, Nicholson, and Westbrook, but probably won't make the major league rotation until mid-2000.

Miguel Batista — Throws R — Age 28

YEAR	TEAM	LGE	IP	H	ER	HR	BB	K	ERA	W	L	H/9	HR/9	BB/9	K/9	KWH	PERA
1996	Charlott	Int	80.0	98	51	4	43	46	5.74	3	6	11.03	0.45	4.84	5.18	0.38	4.72
1997	Iowa	AmA	115.0	148	71	18	41	74	5.56	4	9	11.58	1.41	3.21	5.79	0.68	5.56
1997	ChiCubs	NL	38.3	37	20	4	22	25	4.70	2	2	8.69	0.94	5.17	5.87	0.58	3.99
1998	Montreal	NL	134.3	152	63	13	59	84	4.22	7	8	10.18	0.87	3.95	5.63	0.59	4.49

Pitched 135 innings for Montreal, a few of them good. Alou loves his fastball, and may try to turn him into a short reliever. In terms of anything other than a salary dump, the Oh! Henry deal looks like a dud for the Expos.

Shayne Bennett — Throws R — Age 27

YEAR	TEAM	LGE	IP	H	ER	HR	BB	K	ERA	W	L	H/9	HR/9	BB/9	K/9	KWH	PERA
1996	Harrisbg	Eas	89.0	105	36	6	37	65	3.64	5	5	10.62	0.61	3.74	6.57	0.82	4.55
1997	Harrisbg	Eas	44.3	59	31	6	21	26	6.29	1	4	11.98	1.22	4.26	5.28	0.41	5.68
1997	Ottawa	Int	33.7	27	8	0	21	22	2.14	3	1	7.22	0.00	5.61	5.88	0.64	2.67
1997	Montreal	NL	22.7	23	8	2	8	7	3.18	2	1	9.13	0.79	3.18	2.78	0.20	3.97
1998	Montreal	NL	90.7	107	60	9	40	54	5.96	3	7	10.62	0.89	3.97	5.36	0.51	4.76

"Roo" has yet to do anything impressive above Double-A. The Expos would probably be better served breaking a starter in Earl-Weaver style as a middle reliever, and sending Bennett back to Triple-A next year.

Matt Blank · Throws L · Age 23

YEAR	TEAM	LGE	IP	H	ER	HR	BB	K	ERA	W	L	H/9	HR/9	BB/9	K/9	KWH	PERA
1997	Vermont	NYP	84.7	119	42	3	20	46	4.46	4	5	12.65	0.32	2.13	4.89	0.67	5.00
1998	CapeFear	SAL	121.7	175	63	7	31	65	4.66	6	8	12.95	0.52	2.29	4.81	0.58	5.33
1998	Jupiter	Fla	38.7	46	19	3	11	19	4.42	2	2	10.71	0.70	2.56	4.42	0.54	4.42

The organization's pitcher of the year, going 14-3 with an ERA under 2.60 at Cape Fear and Jupiter. He only throws in the mid-80s, relying on control and offspeed stuff to survive. Needless to say, that becomes tougher to live on as you go up the ladder. Could benefit from working more quickly to keep hitters off balance.

Shawn Boskie · Throws R · Age 32

YEAR	TEAM	LGE	IP	H	ER	HR	BB	K	ERA	W	L	H/9	HR/9	BB/9	K/9	KWH	PERA
1996	Calfrnia	AL	194.3	213	96	35	54	131	4.45	10	12	9.86	1.62	2.50	6.07	1.12	4.68
1997	Baltimor	AL	77.3	95	49	13	22	49	5.70	3	6	11.06	1.51	2.56	5.70	0.86	5.24
1998	Ottawa	Int	85.0	113	48	7	21	39	5.08	3	6	11.96	0.74	2.22	4.13	0.48	5.08
1998	Montreal	NL	17.3	36	21	6	4	9	10.90	0	2	18.69	3.12	2.08	4.67	0.42	10.38

The team decided that pulling rookies out of Double-A in the hopes that one of them would work out was preferable to Boskie's 2 hits per 3 outs shtick.

Mel Bunch · Throws R · Age 27

YEAR	TEAM	LGE	IP	H	ER	HR	BB	K	ERA	W	L	H/9	HR/9	BB/9	K/9	KWH	PERA
1996	Omaha	AmA	148.3	210	107	32	66	82	6.49	4	12	12.74	1.94	4.00	4.98	0.36	6.67
1997	Harrisbg	Eas	46.7	57	29	7	23	34	5.59	2	3	10.99	1.35	4.44	6.56	0.66	5.40
1997	Ottawa	Int	75.7	120	63	13	44	45	7.49	2	6	14.27	1.55	5.23	5.35	0.29	7.14
1998	Ottawa	Int	101.3	118	58	16	49	77	5.15	4	7	10.48	1.42	4.35	6.84	0.77	5.15

After a dismal 1997, Bunch recovered somewhat. He still has tremendous stuff, with a 90-plus fastball and good curve, but his command isn't great and his background doesn't scream success. He's a guy Felipe Alou can turn into something very valuable, either at the back of a rotation or in the pen.

Ronald Chiavacci · Throws R · Age 21

YEAR	TEAM	LGE	IP	H	ER	HR	BB	K	ERA	W	L	H/9	HR/9	BB/9	K/9	KWH	PERA
1998	Jupiter	Fla	7.3	6	2	0	3	4	2.45	1	0	7.36	0.00	3.68	4.91	0.67	2.45

Slipped all the way to the 42nd round in this year's draft, as most teams thought he'd return to school for his senior year. He's strong, with an average fastball but great command and control. He could move up quickly if he picks up some velocity.

Rick DeHart · Throws L · Age 29

YEAR	TEAM	LGE	IP	H	ER	HR	BB	K	ERA	W	L	H/9	HR/9	BB/9	K/9	KWH	PERA
1996	Harrisbg	Eas	41.3	60	22	4	21	21	4.79	2	3	13.06	0.87	4.57	4.57	0.26	5.88
1997	Ottawa	Int	61.0	71	34	6	22	42	5.02	3	4	10.48	0.89	3.25	6.20	0.85	4.57
1997	Montreal	NL	30.3	35	19	8	13	26	5.64	1	2	10.38	2.37	3.86	7.71	1.11	5.64
1998	Ottawa	Int	52.3	52	19	5	17	37	3.27	4	2	8.94	0.86	2.92	6.36	1.16	3.61
1998	Montreal	NL	27.7	37	21	3	12	13	6.83	1	2	12.04	0.98	3.90	4.23	0.29	5.53

Organizational soldier who seems sufficiently up to the challenge of International League hitters.

Ben Fleetham · Throws R · Age 26

YEAR	TEAM	LGE	IP	H	ER	HR	BB	K	ERA	W	L	H/9	HR/9	BB/9	K/9	KWH	PERA
1996	Delmarva	SAL	17.7	17	7	3	9	17	3.57	1	1	8.66	1.53	4.58	8.66	1.42	4.08
1996	WPalmB	Fla	29.0	22	11	0	17	34	3.41	2	1	6.83	0.00	5.28	10.55	2.32	2.48
1997	Harrisbg	Eas	49.3	35	21	4	33	50	3.83	3	2	6.39	0.73	6.02	9.12	1.62	2.74
1998	Ottawa	Int	56.3	57	25	3	41	52	3.99	3	3	9.11	0.48	6.55	8.31	0.87	4.15

Widely expected to go in the Rule 5 draft last December, but teams were busy taking guys like Luis Saturria. Fleetham throws hard but had control problems on his way up, culminating in a poor 1998 showing, with 42 walks and 5 wild pitches in 55.2 innings. Relievers who put 15 guys on every 9 innings don't last long. At this point, Fleetham looks like a Snackwell's Brad Pennington.

Dustin Hermanson — Throws R — Age 26

YEAR	TEAM	LGE	IP	H	ER	HR	BB	K	ERA	W	L	H/9	HR/9	BB/9	K/9	KWH	PERA
1996	LasVegas	PCL	46.3	42	17	4	27	47	3.30	3	2	8.16	0.78	5.24	9.13	1.46	3.69
1997	Montreal	NL	161.7	140	61	16	60	122	3.40	10	8	7.79	0.89	3.34	6.79	1.33	3.12
1998	Montreal	NL	186.0	173	75	22	50	139	3.63	12	9	8.37	1.06	2.42	6.73	1.68	3.39

The ace, and unlike Carlos Perez, not overworked. Hermanson is the next target of Beattie/Brochu's long-term deal machine, and rightly so, as he could anchor their rotation when they either get a new stadium or move to Virginia. Should be one of the top ten right-handed starters in the NL this year.

Mike Johnson — Throws R — Age 23

YEAR	TEAM	LGE	IP	H	ER	HR	BB	K	ERA	W	L	H/9	HR/9	BB/9	K/9	KWH	PERA
1996	Hagerstn	SAL	152.7	229	98	9	45	95	5.78	6	11	13.50	0.53	2.65	5.60	0.66	5.60
1997	Baltimor	AL	40.3	54	31	11	13	28	6.92	1	3	12.05	2.45	2.90	6.25	0.84	6.69
1997	Montreal	NL	51.0	57	30	8	19	25	5.29	2	4	10.06	1.41	3.35	4.41	0.43	4.76
1998	Harrisbg	Eas	32.0	43	28	10	10	29	7.88	1	3	12.09	2.81	2.81	8.16	1.47	7.03
1998	Ottawa	Int	110.3	110	54	19	34	75	4.40	5	7	8.97	1.55	2.77	6.12	1.13	4.16

A Rule V pick out of the Jays' organization, traded from Baltimore last year. Like many Expo pitching prospects, Johnson has decent stuff and no real clue what to do with it. He pitched poorly at three levels this year, surrendering 31 homers in 145 innings, including nine in 33.2 innings at Harrisburg. If the shelling hasn't demoralized him, he could be a solid reliever by 2000.

Steve Kline — Throws L — Age 26

YEAR	TEAM	LGE	IP	H	ER	HR	BB	K	ERA	W	L	H/9	HR/9	BB/9	K/9	KWH	PERA
1996	Canton	Eas	142.3	203	104	17	56	83	6.58	4	12	12.84	1.07	3.54	5.25	0.45	5.94
1997	Buffalo	AmA	48.3	65	29	3	12	34	5.40	2	3	12.10	0.56	2.23	6.33	1.11	5.03
1997	Clevelnd	AL	27.0	43	16	6	11	16	5.33	1	2	14.33	2.00	3.67	5.33	0.41	7.33
1997	Montreal	NL	27.0	32	16	5	9	18	5.33	1	2	10.67	1.67	3.00	6.00	0.84	5.33
1998	Montreal	NL	71.7	68	24	4	37	69	3.01	5	3	8.54	0.50	4.65	8.67	1.42	3.52

Felipe works his magic again, taking a borderline lefty who seemed destined to a career of cups of coffee and getting about 72 useful innings out of him. He goes into '99 as the #1 LH setup man.

Ted Lilly — Throws L — Age 23

YEAR	TEAM	LGE	IP	H	ER	HR	BB	K	ERA	W	L	H/9	HR/9	BB/9	K/9	KWH	PERA
1996	Yakima	Nwn	51.0	38	13	0	16	42	2.29	5	1	6.71	0.00	2.82	7.41	2.18	1.94
1997	SanBern	Cal	130.0	138	53	10	31	109	3.67	8	6	9.55	0.69	2.15	7.55	2.08	3.74
1998	SanAnton	Tex	104.7	132	50	8	36	75	4.30	6	6	11.35	0.69	3.10	6.45	0.89	4.82
1998	Albuquer	PCL	32.0	38	16	3	9	21	4.50	2	2	10.69	0.84	2.53	5.91	0.97	4.50
1998	Ottawa	Int	40.0	47	24	8	18	42	5.40	1	3	10.58	1.80	4.05	9.45	1.56	5.40

Boasts a 93-mph fastball, a solid breaking ball, and a nice resume for a 22-year-old. The Perez/Grudzielanek deal could turn out to be grand theft Lasorda. One warning sign: his fastball dropped to around 89 after he arrived in Ottawa, and the Expos were considering sending him to winter ball. If his arm isn't damaged goods, he's a potential star.

Mike Maddux — Throws R — Age 37

YEAR	TEAM	LGE	IP	H	ER	HR	BB	K	ERA	W	L	H/9	HR/9	BB/9	K/9	KWH	PERA
1996	Boston	AL	68.0	69	26	10	22	32	3.44	5	3	9.13	1.32	2.91	4.24	0.51	4.10
1997	Seattle	AL	11.7	20	10	1	7	7	7.71	0	1	15.43	0.77	5.40	5.40	0.26	6.94
1998	Montreal	NL	55.0	53	23	3	14	30	3.76	3	3	8.67	0.49	2.29	4.91	0.91	3.11

If you're considering hiring Kevin Kennedy as your manager, allow me to present Exhibit A for the opposition. Maddux was superb in 1995 in a swing role, and blew out so badly that he just barely started recovering in 1998. He pitched well enough to return, and is capable of providing about 60 innings of quality relief.

Trey Moore   **Throws L**   **Age 26**

YEAR	TEAM	LGE	IP	H	ER	HR	BB	K	ERA	W	L	H/9	HR/9	BB/9	K/9	KWH	PERA
1996	Lancastr	Cal	91.3	122	52	10	31	49	5.12	4	6	12.02	0.99	3.05	4.83	0.48	5.42
1996	PortCity	Sou	49.0	94	60	7	30	32	11.02	1	4	17.27	1.29	5.51	5.88	0.27	8.08
1997	Harrisbg	Eas	157.0	181	92	14	66	99	5.27	6	11	10.38	0.80	3.78	5.68	0.62	4.53
1998	Ottawa	Int	13.0	20	8	1	4	6	5.54	0	1	13.85	0.69	2.77	4.15	0.34	6.23
1998	Montreal	NL	60.3	83	35	5	15	32	5.22	3	4	12.38	0.75	2.24	4.77	0.62	5.22

Finesse lefty acquired in the Fassero dump (which looks worse by the minute) who was rushed to the majors and then went down for the year with shoulder woes. Out until mid-99; even if he recovers fully, he's not a long-term solution in the rotation.

Guillermo Mota   **Throws R**   **Age 25**

YEAR	TEAM	LGE	IP	H	ER	HR	BB	K	ERA	W	L	H/9	HR/9	BB/9	K/9	KWH	PERA
1997	CapeFear	SAL	110.7	208	98	11	48	64	7.97	2	10	16.92	0.89	3.90	5.20	0.31	7.48
1998	Jupiter	Fla	38.0	27	10	0	8	17	2.37	3	1	6.39	0.00	1.89	4.03	1.00	1.42
1998	Harrisbg	Eas	16.3	12	3	0	3	14	1.65	2	0	6.61	0.00	1.65	7.71	4.08	1.65

Here's a story: Mota was a shortstop in the Mets organization who hit like Rey Ordonez. Realizing they already had Rey Ordonez, the Mets left him eligible for the Rule 5 draft after '96. The Expos took him, made him a pitcher, and voila! he's throwing gas with great control. He missed some time this year after surgery, and moved to the bullpen to reduce the strain on his arm. The Expos see him moving up as a reliever, but hope he might return to the rotation a few years down the road. A great sleeper.

John Nicholson   **Throws R**   **Age 21**

YEAR	TEAM	LGE	IP	H	ER	HR	BB	K	ERA	W	L	H/9	HR/9	BB/9	K/9	KWH	PERA
1997	Asheville	SAL	134.0	163	76	16	45	76	5.10	6	9	10.95	1.07	3.02	5.10	0.59	4.90
1998	Jupiter	Fla	144.0	195	93	6	65	91	5.81	5	11	12.19	0.38	4.06	5.69	0.49	5.06

His heat already runs into the low-to-mid 90s with good tailing movement. Considered very mature for his age. He was quite hittable in a friendly park, and needs to gain experience. He showed clear signs of fatigue down the stretch.

Carl Pavano   **Throws R**   **Age 23**

YEAR	TEAM	LGE	IP	H	ER	HR	BB	K	ERA	W	L	H/9	HR/9	BB/9	K/9	KWH	PERA
1996	Trenton	Eas	176.7	190	73	17	45	114	3.72	11	9	9.68	0.87	2.29	5.81	1.14	3.97
1997	Pawtuckt	Int	161.0	162	58	13	30	121	3.24	11	7	9.06	0.73	1.68	6.76	2.26	3.41
1998	Ottawa	Int	18.7	13	4	1	6	12	1.93	2	0	6.27	0.48	2.89	5.79	1.38	1.93
1998	Montreal	NL	134.0	137	66	19	39	75	4.43	7	8	9.20	1.28	2.62	5.04	0.79	4.10

A future ace, despite the rocky introduction to the majors. He showed the incredible poise that was his hallmark throughout his minor-league tenure, and didn't show any ill effects from the tendinitis that kept him off the Opening Day roster. May not break out until 2000, but when he does, look out.

Jeremy Powell   **Throws R**   **Age 23**

YEAR	TEAM	LGE	IP	H	ER	HR	BB	K	ERA	W	L	H/9	HR/9	BB/9	K/9	KWH	PERA
1996	Delmarva	SAL	141.7	205	101	13	76	67	6.42	4	12	13.02	0.83	4.83	4.26	0.22	5.91
1997	WPalmB	Fla	149.0	201	82	5	70	92	4.95	7	10	12.14	0.30	4.23	5.56	0.45	5.01
1998	Harrisbg	Eas	125.3	140	61	14	36	60	4.38	6	8	10.05	1.01	2.59	4.31	0.54	4.31
1998	Montreal	NL	24.7	29	24	6	10	13	8.76	1	2	10.58	2.19	3.65	4.74	0.44	5.84

Didn't belong in the majors, and it showed. Powell relies on control to survive, as his fastball hasn't fooled anyone above A-ball. At 22, he could easily find more velocity in the next year or two, but he's outclassed by the prospects behind him.

J.D. Smart		Throws R				Age 25											
YEAR	TEAM	LGE	IP	H	ER	HR	BB	K	ERA	W	L	H/9	HR/9	BB/9	K/9	KWH	PERA
1996	Delmarva	SAL	135.7	252	119	20	38	62	7.89	3	12	16.72	1.33	2.52	4.11	0.30	7.76
1997	WPalmB	Fla	95.0	138	54	13	26	45	5.12	4	7	13.07	1.23	2.46	4.26	0.42	6.06
1997	Harrisbg	Eas	69.3	85	31	6	23	33	4.02	4	4	11.03	0.78	2.99	4.28	0.42	4.67
1998	Harrisbg	Eas	71.7	86	30	2	19	34	3.77	4	4	10.80	0.25	2.39	4.27	0.53	4.14
1998	Ottawa	Int	35.0	36	19	3	10	13	4.89	2	2	9.26	0.77	2.57	3.34	0.35	3.86

Blew through Harrisburg after flirting with retirement, but hit a wall at Ottawa, where he was inconsistent with a merely adequate fastball. Could be a surprise relief star in Felipe's care, but I don't see him starting for this organization.

Anthony Telford		Throws R				Age 33											
YEAR	TEAM	LGE	IP	H	ER	HR	BB	K	ERA	W	L	H/9	HR/9	BB/9	K/9	KWH	PERA
1996	Ottawa	Int	111.0	154	67	12	37	54	5.43	4	8	12.49	0.97	3.00	4.38	0.38	5.59
1997	Montreal	NL	90.7	80	30	12	30	55	2.98	6	4	7.94	1.19	2.98	5.46	0.95	3.37
1998	Montreal	NL	90.7	91	42	10	32	53	4.17	5	5	9.03	0.99	3.18	5.26	0.72	3.87

From despair to where? Felipe's bullpen of magic beans, apparently. Telford toiled in the minors for about ten years, racking up just 70.1 major-league innings in that time with Baltimore. Now, despite mediocre minor-league numbers, Telford has put up two solid seasons as a regular right-handed setup man, thus adding to Felipe's reputation for taking beer vendors and getting good relief innings out of them.

Mike Thurman		Throws R				Age 25											
YEAR	TEAM	LGE	IP	H	ER	HR	BB	K	ERA	W	L	H/9	HR/9	BB/9	K/9	KWH	PERA
1996	WPalmB	Fla	105.0	159	66	6	26	52	5.66	4	8	13.63	0.51	2.23	4.46	0.49	5.57
1996	Harrisbg	Eas	23.3	31	15	7	5	11	5.79	1	2	11.96	2.70	1.93	4.24	0.59	6.56
1997	Harrisbg	Eas	113.0	115	50	14	29	64	3.98	7	6	9.16	1.12	2.31	5.10	0.92	3.90
1998	Ottawa	Int	106.7	115	44	12	46	63	3.71	6	6	9.70	1.01	3.88	5.32	0.56	4.39
1998	Montreal	NL	66.3	64	36	7	24	29	4.88	3	4	8.68	0.95	3.26	3.93	0.41	3.66

Great control will get you through Double-A, maybe Triple-A, but rare is the bird who can make it through the majors without great stuff. Thurman's "rapide" can touch the low 90s, but without great movement, it's not a pitch to bank on. He has about a year and a half to establish himself at the back of the Expos' rotation before the Jupiter boys arrive. I'm not confident he can pull it off.

Ugueth Urbina		Throws R				Age 25											
YEAR	TEAM	LGE	IP	H	ER	HR	BB	K	ERA	W	L	H/9	HR/9	BB/9	K/9	KWH	PERA
1996	Montreal	NL	117.7	107	48	18	42	98	3.67	7	6	8.18	1.38	3.21	7.50	1.60	3.67
1997	Montreal	NL	66.0	55	26	10	26	75	3.55	4	3	7.50	1.36	3.55	10.23	2.95	3.27
1998	Montreal	NL	69.0	42	10	2	30	85	1.30	7	1	5.48	0.26	3.91	11.09	4.30	1.57

The second-best closer in baseball this year, and a deserving All-Star, now and for years to come. He's locked in at super-low prices for the next three years, and Alou has remained careful not to overuse him. I still think the injury worries were overblown, and that he could have been a great starter.

Marc Valdes		Throws R				Age 27											
YEAR	TEAM	LGE	IP	H	ER	HR	BB	K	ERA	W	L	H/9	HR/9	BB/9	K/9	KWH	PERA
1996	Portland	Eas	62.3	74	27	5	12	36	3.90	4	3	10.68	0.72	1.73	5.20	1.09	4.33
1996	Charlott	Int	53.3	67	26	10	16	21	4.39	3	3	11.31	1.69	2.70	3.54	0.31	5.57
1996	Florida	NL	49.3	66	29	5	22	12	5.29	2	3	12.04	0.91	4.01	2.19	0.07	5.47
1997	Montreal	NL	96.3	89	32	2	35	49	2.99	7	4	8.31	0.19	3.27	4.58	0.58	2.99
1998	Montreal	NL	36.7	44	32	7	19	26	7.85	1	3	10.80	1.72	4.66	6.38	0.61	5.65

First the magic disappeared, when Valdes was shelled out of the rotation. Then he sprained a ligament in his pitching elbow, underwent surgery, and missed the rest of the season. Not a great bet for a comeback this year.

Javier Vazquez   Throws R   Age 23

YEAR	TEAM	LGE	IP	H	ER	HR	BB	K	ERA	W	L	H/9	HR/9	BB/9	K/9	KWH	PERA
1996	Delmarva	SAL	149.3	216	93	18	66	106	5.60	6	11	13.02	1.08	3.98	6.39	0.59	6.09
1997	WPalmB	Fla	109.0	121	43	11	31	75	3.55	7	5	9.99	0.91	2.56	6.19	1.12	4.21
1997	Harrisbg	Eas	41.7	17	4	2	11	36	0.86	5	0	3.67	0.43	2.38	7.78	5.20	0.00
1998	Montreal	NL	171.7	209	115	33	62	126	6.03	6	13	10.96	1.73	3.25	6.61	0.92	5.50

Don't let the won-lost record fool you; Vazquez was barely 40 innings out of A-ball when he made the rotation out of spring training. Under the circumstances, he held his own, showing remarkable maturity and poise. Ninety-nine percent of pitching prospects would have wilted in the same situation. Vazquez is a keeper, and gives the Expos the chance three potential aces at the start of their rotation.

Jake Westbrook   Throws R   Age 21

YEAR	TEAM	LGE	IP	H	ER	HR	BB	K	ERA	W	L	H/9	HR/9	BB/9	K/9	KWH	PERA
1996	Portland	Nwn	22.3	32	11	2	6	11	4.43	1	1	12.90	0.81	2.42	4.43	0.47	5.64
1997	Asheville	SAL	166.3	229	104	21	69	62	5.63	6	12	12.39	1.14	3.73	3.35	0.18	5.79
1998	Jupiter	Fla	159.0	220	83	14	67	59	4.70	8	10	12.45	0.79	3.79	3.34	0.18	5.55

Great stuff, but he's busy trying to thread the needle rather than just airing it out. Better that than to have no stuff, of course. He's clearly not on track for the majors with that dropping strikeout rate. Could come alive with good coaching, or he could be a Triple-A All-Star in 2007.

Tim Young   Throws L   Age 25

YEAR	TEAM	LGE	IP	H	ER	HR	BB	K	ERA	W	L	H/9	HR/9	BB/9	K/9	KWH	PERA
1997	CapeFear	SAL	49.3	51	19	0	21	37	3.47	3	2	9.30	0.00	3.83	6.75	0.96	3.47
1997	WPalmB	Fla	15.0	11	1	0	4	9	0.60	2	0	6.60	0.00	2.40	5.40	1.38	1.80
1998	Harrisbg	Eas	34.0	36	21	4	11	37	5.56	1	3	9.53	1.06	2.91	9.79	2.59	4.24
1998	Ottawa	Int	27.0	28	12	1	11	28	4.00	2	1	9.33	0.33	3.67	9.33	1.91	3.67
1998	Montreal	NL	6.3	6	4	0	4	6	5.68	0	1	8.53	0.00	5.68	8.53	1.12	2.84

Lefty Crimson Tide alum who ripped through the Expos' system in two years, posting an ERA over 2.10 at just one level (Harrisburg). He came down with a slight tear in his left labrum in mid-September, but continued pitching, so it's unclear if he'll miss time in '99. If he's healthy, he could supplant Kline as the primary LH setup man.

SNWLP						MONTREAL EXPOS					Park Effect: -22.3%	
PITCHER	GS	IP	R	SNW	SNL	SNPCT	W	L	RA	APW	SNVA	SNWAR
Batista, M.	13	71.3	26	4.7	3.1	.604	2	2	3.28	0.76	0.74	1.38
Boskie, S.	5	17.7	21	0.7	3.1	.175	1	3	10.70	-1.32	-1.14	-0.94
Hermanson, D.	30	184.0	80	10.9	10.0	.522	14	11	3.91	0.62	0.42	2.03
Johnson, M.	2	7.3	12	0.1	1.5	.056	0	2	14.73	-0.89	-0.68	-0.57
Moore, T.	11	56.0	33	2.6	4.5	.370	2	5	5.30	-0.71	-0.85	-0.39
Pavano, C.	23	132.7	67	6.9	8.4	.451	6	8	4.55	-0.52	-0.79	0.39
Perez, C.	23	163.3	79	7.9	9.6	.452	7	10	4.35	-0.28	-0.82	0.47
Powell, J.	6	24.0	24	1.2	3.0	.288	1	5	9.00	-1.32	-0.91	-0.57
Thurman, M.	13	66.0	38	3.1	5.1	.376	4	5	5.18	-0.74	-1.01	-0.41
Valdes, M.	4	13.0	15	0.6	2.2	.223	0	3	10.38	-0.92	-0.75	-0.56
Vazquez, J.	32	171.3	120	7.3	14.4	.334	5	15	6.30	-4.13	-3.50	-1.97
TOTALS	162	906.7	515	45.9	64.8	.415	42	69	5.11	-9.44	-9.29	-1.14

Last year we said: "With Pedro Martinez, the Expos' starting staff was third-best in the NL. With a replacement-level starter in his place, they would have been third-worst." The Expos replaced Martinez with a combination of Trey Moore and Carl Pavano, and what happened? OK, we were off by one: they were second-worst in the NL. One positive note that the Expos can take out of 1998 is the in-season development of pitching überprospect Pavano. Pavano struggled through the end of July, going 2.9-6.0 (.327) in 13 starts. Starting in August, though, he showed some of his potential by going 4.0-2.4 (.622) in 10 starts.

Pitcher Abuse Points

PITCHER	AGE	GS	PAP	PAP/S	AAW	MAX	115+	130+
Batista, Miguel	27	13	35	2.69	4.94	117	1	0
Boskie, Shawn	31	5	0	0.00	0.00	87	0	0
Hermanson, Dustin	25	31	107	3.45	7.48	127	1	0
Moore, Trey	25	11	0	0.00	0.00	98	0	0
Pavano, Carl	22	23	31	1.35	3.59	117	1	0
Perez, Carlos	27	23	188	8.17	14.99	125	4	0
Powell, Jeremy	22	6	0	0.00	0.00	90	0	0
Thurman, Mike	24	13	5	0.38	0.90	105	0	0
Vazquez, Javier	21	32	80	2.50	7.08	115	1	0
TOTAL		163	446	2.75	4.54	127	8	0
RANKING (NL)			16	16	16		16	14-T

Felipe Alou is the anti-Leyland. I've loved what he's done for years, and now we have some evidence to back it up. Only twice all year did an Expo starter throw more than 117 pitches in a game. Alou has turned a struggling reliever (Dustin Hermanson) into a terrific starter, he's already made Pedro Martinez into the best young starter in the game, and the Expos are now using a couple of solid prospects—Javier Vazquez and Jeremy Powell—and Carl Pavano, the best 23-and-younger pitcher in baseball not named Kerry Wood. Keeping Alou to nurture this talent was worth every penny they'll pay him. Now if they can only find some more pennies to keep their players…

New York Mets

Met fans are understandably unhappy this October, what with the Yankees winning their second World Series in three years and a three-ring circus worthy of P.T. Barnum (and his cigar) breaking out in their front office. Instead of appreciating the players' efforts on their behalf—the Mets worked extremely hard to give their fans the month of October off—fans are getting bad flashbacks to the Kool-Aid Acid Test that was the Met universe in the late 80s and early 90s. With the November move to bring back Bobby Bonilla—a disappointment, if not an outright failure, in his previous NY tenure—who can blame a Met fan who kidnaps Vince Coleman or Juan Samuel to keep them away from Frank Cashen?

The Mets' current rebuilding plan is, to be kind, no plan. The team resembles a naïve tourist ambling through the bustling markets of Florence, buying items almost at random, negotiating himself to worse and worse transactions, and having his pockets picked by prepubescent urchins whose English vocabluaries comprise two or three choice expletives. The Mets have raised their profile and their budget, but being active and extravagant doesn't make you a champion; it makes you the '98 Orioles or Dodgers: fodder for back-page headlines mocking your incompetence.

To be fair, the team is in a difficult spot. In addition to sharing Gotham with a team on a tremendous run of success (with an insane mayor backing them), the Mets have to contend with baseball's team of the '90s. Sharing a division with the Braves hasn't been kind to any team this decade, particularly those with weak—or, in the Mets' case, nonexistent—farm systems. Everyone but Atlanta is out of the divisional race from the day the season opens, which puts them in the semi-random tumbler that determines the wild-card spot. Competing against teams that get to play the Diamondbacks or Reds or 12–15 times a year is clearly a competitive disadvantage.

The Mets can look in other directions besides north-northeast to find a successful strategy for contending. Two teams this decade have competed successfully in the Braves'

shadow: the 1994 Expos and the 1997 Marlins, both of whom might have enjoyed more protracted runs were it not for various exogenous events that ended their runs prematurely. In both cases, the teams used their farm systems to build a core, and then supplement it with shrewd pickups in trades (both), via waivers (Expos), or via the free-agent market (Marlins):

- The '94 Expos, whose destiny we will unfortunately never know, featured one of the best examples of inexpensive talent collection since the creation of the late-80s A's. Their top three starters included two minor-league free agents (Jeff Fassero and Butch Henry) and a prospect obtained in a dump trade (Pedro Martinez). Their offense included homegrown hitting stars like Larry Walker or brilliant trade pickups like Moises Alou. Their bullpen featured a one-two punch of Rojas and Wetteland that was comparable to that of Rivera and . . . well, Wetteland. Yet the team had no major free agents.

- The '97 Marlins relied more heavily on the free agent route, and while many of the signings were of mediocre ex-good players (Bonilla, Devon White) or severely overpriced good players (Alou), the Kevin Brown and Alex Fernandez acquisitions were clearly additive. The Marlins used their farm system to trade for Gary Sheffield and to fill key holes at catcher and shortstop. They swiped Robb Nen and Jay Powell in lopsided trades to create another devastating one-two bullpen punch.

There are drawbacks to these examples: two data points do not a trend make (unless you're a consultant), and the unstated tie between these two franchises is the presence of Dave Dombrowski, one of the game's premier talent evaluators among GMs. Despite these caveats, it's no leap to say that trying to build a team through free agency to match the Braves is both prohibitively expensive and incredibly difficult. The Mets, in particular, have shown themselves to be poor judges of talent—both their own and that of outside

> ## Mets Prospectus
>
> **1998 record:** 88-74; Second place, NL East
> **Pythagorean W/L:** 88-74
> **Runs scored:** 706 (11th in NL)
> **Runs allowed:** 645 (4th in NL)
> **Team EQA:** .260 (8th in NL)
> **Park:** Shea Stadium (moderate pitchers')
> **1998:** Wild-card run torpedoed by a complete lack of offense from half the lineup.
> **1999:** Committed to a push, but the lineup is old and the pitching is likely to regress.

players—and to have minimal willpower when it comes to choosing between a quick-fix free agent and developing a player internally.

The 1998 Mets' cast wasn't even good enough for the wild card, even with a few players exceeding expectations. Even having imported Bobby Bonilla and Robin Ventura, the team isn't going to catch Atlanta. The difference between the two clubs is not one to be closed via free agency: the difference is more than the value of one or two free agents, no matter how good they might be. For a player to propel the Mets to parity or near-parity with the Braves, he'd have to hit, pitch, and then play shortstop on days when he's not pitching—and excel at all three.

The team's offense is clearly its Achilles's heel. Despite two-thirds of a Piazza season, a superb year from Olerud, and a career year from Brian McRae, the Mets scored just 706 runs, good for tenth in the league (roughly the same after park adjustments). If that's as well as they did with only one player (Alfonzo) really failing to live up to expectations, how will they do when Olerud comes back to earth or if Piazza loses two months to a knee problem? By the time this book hits stores, they may have added more, but the problem is more widespread than these additions can fix. They're well below average offensively in both outfield corners, and below replacement level at short. In the league where pitchers hit, a second automatic out puts tremendous pressure on the other seven guys.

Defensively, the team isn't all that much better off. Saint Rey didn't help the team finish in the top half of the league in either double-plays or in converting them. While Alfonzo will be a huge improvement at second over Baerga, and Ventura and McRae will be assets, they're hardly enough to prop up an otherwise subpar defensive unit. Bringing Bonilla back to play any position other than bench coach only exacerbates the situation.

The one area in which the '98 Mets excelled was pitching. The Mets finished fourth in the NL in team ERA, behind Houston, San Diego (in extreme pitchers' parks), and the Braves. Al Leiter's best season yet anchored a rotation bolstered by Rick Reed and Masato Yoshii, all of whom met or exceeded expectations for the season. Bobby Jones continued to frustrate the team, which has never fully acknowledged that he can't throw 200 innings or make more than 30 starts, and the back of the rotation was a revolving door, with Hideo Nomo and Willie Blair giving scoreboard operators a good workout. It's likely we'll see Octavio Dotel take over the fifth slot, but even so, the team is extremely dependent on Yoshii, who was 2-7 with an ERA around 4.5 after June 1, and

Leiter, who is just one year removed from a 4.34 ERA and a 5.4 BB/9 IP ratio. The rotation could be very good, but it could just as easily be awful.

The bullpen offered a similar study in contrasts and reliance upon a few key performers. While Dennis Cook and Turk Wendell each turned in his best season, Greg McMichael was inconsistent, Mel Rojas was a disaster, and John Franco continued his gradual decline. Bringing in Armando Benitez and Oscar Henriquez, and sending Mel Rojas away should help, but hardly convert the bullpen into an overwhelming strength.

Basically, this isn't a team that has a clear plan of where it's going or a well-grounded sense of its relative position in the NL hierarchy. The Mets could ill afford any return to power or input by Frank Cashen, the architect of the disastrous '91–'93 teams, but Steve Phillips legal problems seem to disappeared for the time being. They also can't afford continued farm system strip-mining, as injuries and trades have completely the gutted the organization's upper levels, leaving the team with little choice but to turn to the expensive end of the free agent market if they wish to fill short-term needs.

Lurking in the background was the team's one remaining trump card—Hundley. He represented both an opportunity to inject some life into the farm system and/or rebuilding process and an opportunity to demonstrate to the fans that the Mets have a concrete plan. In a move that didn't fill either need, Hundley was converted into Benitez and Roger Cedeno, which is good except that the Mets don't seem to want to use Cedeno.

The upper levels of the Mets' minor-league system resembles those of the Mariners of a year or two ago. The Mets have one major impact prospect above A-ball (Dotel), a pair of players with potential (raw Scott Hunter and surprising Dan Murray), and a whole lot of Ruben Sierras. In this kind of situation, Jim Bowden or John Hart or Cam Bonifay would be looking for underappreciated players to acquire as throw-ins to the deal. The Mets' player-evaluation skills don't give the team's fans hope for similar swindles.

What they've done should tell fans exactly how out of touch with reality the team is. Do they believe a quick fix will launch this team to competitiveness? Do they see a grand push for the wild card in the next two to three seasons as a valid goal? Do they even realize a second-place finish is their best possibility? Are they prepared for—or even envisioning—a '92-'93-style meltdown? Most of all, have they learned a thing from watching the hated Yankees this decade?

HITTERS (Averages: BA .260/ OBA .330/ SA .420, EQA .260)

Benny Agbayani   OF   Bats R   Age 27

YEAR	TEAM	LGE	AB	H	DB	TP	HR	BB	R	RBI	SB	CS	OUT	BA	OBA	SA	EQA	EQR	DEFENSE
1996	Norfolk	Int	329	85	11	5	7	29	38	35	10	4	248	.258	.318	.386	.247	38	77-OF 97
1997	Norfolk	Int	465	128	16	1	9	55	64	49	21	11	348	.275	.352	.372	.258	59	115-OF 97
1998	Norfolk	Int	318	75	13	3	7	40	39	31	10	5	248	.236	.321	.362	.242	36	75-OF 86
1999	*NYMets*	*NL*	*366*	*92*	*14*	*3*	*9*	*43*	*47*	*39*	*16*	*8*	*282*	*.251*	*.330*	*.380*	*.257*	*47*	

From his native Hawaiian, the name translates roughly as "cannon fodder."

Edgardo Alfonzo   2B/3B   Bats R   Age 25

YEAR	TEAM	LGE	AB	H	DB	TP	HR	BB	R	RBI	SB	CS	OUT	BA	OBA	SA	EQA	EQR	DEFENSE	
1996	NY Mets	NL	371	100	16	2	4	27	37	36	2	0	271	.270	.319	.356	.237	37	57-2B 101	23-3B 104
1997	NY Mets	NL	518	162	26	2	11	66	80	72	9	6	362	.313	.390	.434	.289	81	123-3B 107	
1998	NY Mets	NL	559	159	28	2	19	69	80	79	9	3	403	.284	.363	.444	.281	84	140-3B 92	
1999	*NYMets*	*NL*	*522*	*153*	*27*	*2*	*16*	*58*	*72*	*74*	*9*	*3*	*372*	*.293*	*.364*	*.444*	*.288*	*83*		

Expected to take a huge step forward this year, but didn't; if anything, he lost ground at the plate and in the field. The Mets desperately need to get him back on track. Much more valuable at second, or <heresy> shortstop </heresy>. Now that they've signed Robin Ventura, Alfonzo's plugged in for second, and the lineup is significantly stronger.

Jermaine Allensworth OF   Bats R   Age 27

YEAR	TEAM	LGE	AB	H	DB	TP	HR	BB	R	RBI	SB	CS	OUT	BA	OBA	SA	EQA	EQR	DEFENSE
1996	Calgary	PCL	340	97	15	3	8	35	53	40	20	4	247	.285	.352	.418	.275	49	86-OF 100
1996	Pittsbrg	NL	228	58	9	3	4	24	28	23	9	6	176	.254	.325	.373	.244	26	54-OF 114
1997	Pittsbrg	NL	367	92	18	2	3	46	46	31	11	7	282	.251	.334	.335	.239	39	95-OF 107
1998	Pittsbrg	NL	232	71	14	3	3	19	34	28	8	4	166	.306	.359	.431	.274	33	62-OF 106
1998	KansasCy	AL	72	14	4	0	0	9	9	3	7	0	58	.194	.284	.250	.212	6	19-OF 110
1998	NY Mets	NL	54	11	3	0	2	2	3	4	0	2	45	.204	.232	.370	.187	3	
1999	*NYMets*	*NL*	*389*	*102*	*20*	*4*	*6*	*37*	*51*	*39*	*19*	*6*	*293*	*.262*	*.326*	*.380*	*.258*	*50*	

Potentially one of the best fourth outfielders in baseball. He's a superior fielder in center, isn't a zero with the bat, and doesn't show much of a platoon split. However, he has neither the on-base ability nor the power required to play everyday. As with hundreds of other not-quite-good-enough players, Allensworth can be very valuable if he's used correctly. Won't get 434 AB on this team.

Carlos Baerga   2B   Bats B   Age 30

YEAR	TEAM	LGE	AB	H	DB	TP	HR	BB	R	RBI	SB	CS	OUT	BA	OBA	SA	EQA	EQR	DEFENSE
1996	Clevelnd	AL	416	105	18	0	11	14	31	40	1	1	312	.252	.277	.375	.220	36	100-2B 99
1996	NY Mets	NL	83	16	1	0	3	6	4	6	0	0	67	.193	.247	.313	.186	5	
1997	NY Mets	NL	465	129	23	1	10	24	42	52	1	6	342	.277	.313	.396	.240	48	115-2B 96
1998	NY Mets	NL	512	140	28	1	8	27	47	53	0	1	373	.273	.310	.379	.237	51	130-2B 93
1999	*NYMets*	*NL*	*438*	*116*	*14*	*0*	*12*	*20*	*34*	*48*	*0*	*2*	*324*	*.265*	*.297*	*.379*	*.237*	*44*	

Remember all the writers who reported this spring that Baerga had found his swing again and solved his problems at the plate? I think the Mets would like to have a word with them. Peaked early, should be headed for a NRI somewhere in '99.

Maurice Bruce   2B   Bats R   Age 24

YEAR	TEAM	LGE	AB	H	DB	TP	HR	BB	R	RBI	SB	CS	OUT	BA	OBA	SA	EQA	EQR	DEFENSE
1997	Kingsprt	App	125	24	2	0	1	8	6	4	3	2	103	.192	.241	.232	.149	4	22-OF 92
1997	Pittsfld	NYP	116	31	3	1	2	8	13	11	5	2	87	.267	.315	.362	.239	12	24-2B 88
1998	Columbia	SAL	511	128	10	1	8	30	43	40	16	8	391	.250	.292	.321	.214	41	93-3B 94
1999	*NYMets*	*NL*	*369*	*97*	*7*	*1*	*8*	*21*	*37*	*34*	*16*	*6*	*278*	*.263*	*.303*	*.352*	*.238*	*38*	

Nice season at the plate, but he was very old for his league. Like some other guys named Mo, has his problems in the field; they're moving him back to second, where his bat should be much more valuable. Won the MVP as a second baseman in the Maryland Fall League. Should jump to Double-A this year, which is what he needs if he's going to have a career.

Alberto Castillo   C   Bats R   Age 23

YEAR	TEAM	LGE	AB	H	DB	TP	HR	BB	R	RBI	SB	CS	OUT	BA	OBA	SA	EQA	EQR	DEFENSE
1997	Norfolk	Int	83	17	0	0	1	15	9	5	1	0	66	.205	.327	.241	.212	7	
1997	NY Mets	NL	59	12	1	0	0	9	4	3	0	1	48	.203	.309	.220	.184	4	
1998	Norfolk	Int	49	8	0	0	1	10	4	3	0	0	41	.163	.305	.224	.194	3	
1999	*NY Mets*	*NL*	*75*	*15*	*0*	*0*	*1*	*14*	*7*	*5*	*0*	*0*	*60*	*.200*	*.326*	*.240*	*.216*	*7*	

Popular gloveman who has to hope the pitcher's wild when he bats. A nice third catcher on a team that doesn't need one.

Alex Escobar   OF   Bats R   Age 20

YEAR	TEAM	LGE	AB	H	DB	TP	HR	BB	R	RBI	SB	CS	OUT	BA	OBA	SA	EQA	EQR	DEFENSE
1998	Columbia	SAL	418	118	13	2	20	45	64	60	24	6	306	.282	.352	.467	.285	66	99-OF 101
1999	*NYMets*	*NL*	*294*	*90*	*13*	*1*	*14*	*27*	*44*	*47*	*13*	*3*	*207*	*.306*	*.364*	*.500*	*.304*	*53*	

Tremendous talent who is in the process of putting his tools to good use on the diamond. I say "in the process" because he still has room for improvement, despite his great season. While his walk rate is adequate and improving, he still struggles with pitch selection. He's also missed time in the last few years with leg injuries. All that aside, he's already the best hitting prospect in the system and one of the best in baseball, and he could get even better before he reaches the majors.

Jorge Fabregas   C   Bats L   Age 29

YEAR	TEAM	LGE	AB	H	DB	TP	HR	BB	R	RBI	SB	CS	OUT	BA	OBA	SA	EQA	EQR	DEFENSE
1996	Calfrnia	AL	249	69	2	0	3	16	20	23	0	1	181	.277	.321	.321	.224	21	
1997	ChiSox	AL	318	89	11	1	7	12	27	35	1	1	230	.280	.306	.387	.237	32	
1998	Arizona	NL	150	30	1	0	2	14	8	8	0	0	120	.200	.268	.247	.172	7	38-C 118
1998	NY Mets	NL	32	6	1	0	1	1	1	2	0	0	26	.188	.212	.312	.164	1	
1999	*Florida*	*NL*	*238*	*59*	*5*	*0*	*6*	*15*	*18*	*23*	*0*	*0*	*179*	*.248*	*.292*	*.345*	*.226*	*22*	

Colangelo's Folly briefly became the Mets' problem. Teams should have now learned what we all knew last winter: Fabregas can't hit. The only pitch he can hammer is a chest-high fastball, and if you know that on the mound, Fabregas is an out. The Mets paid the Marlins to take him, getting a potentially good reliever (Oscar Henriquez) in return.

Matt Franco   PH   Bats L   Age 29

YEAR	TEAM	LGE	AB	H	DB	TP	HR	BB	R	RBI	SB	CS	OUT	BA	OBA	SA	EQA	EQR	DEFENSE	
1996	Norfolk	Int	503	140	24	1	6	32	50	50	3	2	365	.278	.321	.366	.239	51	84-3B 86	37-1B 97
1997	NY Mets	NL	163	45	5	0	5	14	18	20	1	0	118	.276	.333	.399	.256	20	20-3B 112	
1998	NY Mets	NL	162	46	8	2	1	24	22	19	0	1	117	.284	.376	.377	.268	22		
1999	*NYMets*	*NL*	*215*	*59*	*11*	*2*	*3*	*20*	*25*	*24*	*1*	*1*	*157*	*.274*	*.336*	*.386*	*.259*	*27*		

When you have two pitchers in your lineup every day, you need to keep plenty of pinch-hitters around.

Lenny Harris   UT   Bats L   Age 34

YEAR	TEAM	LGE	AB	H	DB	TP	HR	BB	R	RBI	SB	CS	OUT	BA	OBA	SA	EQA	EQR	DEFENSE	
1996	Cincnnti	NL	301	85	17	2	5	22	38	32	11	6	222	.282	.331	.402	.255	36	27-OF 92	20-3B 98
1997	Cincnnti	NL	236	63	12	1	3	19	25	23	3	3	176	.267	.322	.364	.238	24	31-OF 82	13-2B 99
1998	Cincnnti	NL	122	37	8	0	0	8	13	12	1	3	88	.303	.346	.369	.245	13		
1998	NY Mets	NL	168	40	6	0	7	10	16	18	6	2	130	.238	.281	.399	.235	17	37-OF 100	
1999	*Colorado*	*NL*	*271*	*78*	*15*	*1*	*6*	*20*	*33*	*32*	*8*	*4*	*197*	*.288*	*.337*	*.417*	*.238*	*27*		

Endlessly overrated utility player; there are a hundred guys like him in Triple-A right now who will play for the major-league minimum and no guaranteed money. Signed a two-year deal with Colorado; maybe they're hoping to use him in short relief as well.

Todd Hundley   C   Bats B   Age 30

YEAR	TEAM	LGE	AB	H	DB	TP	HR	BB	R	RBI	SB	CS	OUT	BA	OBA	SA	EQA	EQR	DEFENSE
1996	NY Mets	NL	547	147	27	1	45	82	82	110	0	3	403	.269	.364	.569	.306	104	
1997	NY Mets	NL	418	114	19	2	31	84	71	85	1	3	307	.273	.394	.550	.315	85	
1998	NY Mets	NL	124	21	4	0	3	17	8	8	1	1	104	.169	.270	.274	.188	8	23-OF 87
1999	*LosAngls*	*NL*	*297*	*73*	*11*	*0*	*19*	*53*	*40*	*50*	*1*	*1*	*225*	*.246*	*.360*	*.475*	*.298*	*55*	

(Todd Hundley *continued*)

Even if he can't catch anymore, Hundley's bat is more than sufficient for first base, and the odds are that he will catch in some capacity. The Dodgers have taken a risk by acquiring before they're sure he can catch, but it isn't like Eric Karros is a great player, so Hundley can take over at first if he can't throw in March.

Scott Hunter   OF   Bats R Age 23

YEAR	TEAM	LGE	AB	H	DB	TP	HR	BB	R	RBI	SB	CS	OUT	BA	OBA	SA	EQA	EQR	DEFENSE
1996	St Lucie	Fla	476	114	13	1	3	33	47	28	27	8	370	.239	.289	.290	.209	37	120-OF 91
1997	Binghmtn	Eas	286	64	9	2	7	19	28	22	17	6	228	.224	.272	.343	.217	25	72-OF 95
1998	Binghmtn	Eas	484	143	20	2	13	42	71	58	28	11	352	.295	.352	.426	.273	68	116-OF 102
1999	NYMets	NL	424	112	17	1	9	32	54	40	28	8	320	.264	.316	.373	.254	52	

Toolsy semi-prospect who tightened his plate discipline in repeating Double-A. The Mets are high on him for his speed, defense, and raw power; I'll withhold judgment until I see him control the strike zone at Triple-A.

Butch Huskey   OF   Bats R Age 27

YEAR	TEAM	LGE	AB	H	DB	TP	HR	BB	R	RBI	SB	CS	OUT	BA	OBA	SA	EQA	EQR	DEFENSE	
1996	NY Mets	NL	417	119	16	2	16	30	46	59	1	2	300	.285	.333	.448	.266	55	61-1B 90	26-OF 103
1997	NY Mets	NL	469	133	25	1	25	29	56	73	7	5	341	.284	.325	.501	.276	68	77-OF 104	14-1B 93
1998	NY Mets	NL	370	96	16	0	15	28	40	45	8	7	281	.259	.312	.424	.250	44	89-OF 93	
1999	NYMets	NL	390	104	15	1	18	25	41	53	7	4	290	.267	.311	.449	.265	52		

More in line with expectations. Huskey may have played himself right out of the Mets' plans, which isn't necessarily a problem: even in '97, he didn't hit enough to play a corner outfield role, and his glove is questionable at best. Would be fun to watch in Colorado.

Mike Kinkade   "3B"   Bats R Age 26

YEAR	TEAM	LGE	AB	H	DB	TP	HR	BB	R	RBI	SB	CS	OUT	BA	OBA	SA	EQA	EQR	DEFENSE
1996	Beloit	Mid	499	118	13	1	10	27	37	39	11	7	388	.236	.276	.327	.206	37	127-3B 105
1997	El Paso	Tex	441	131	19	4	9	39	58	56	10	3	313	.297	.354	.420	.271	60	106-3B 87
1998	Louisvil	Int	288	79	16	3	6	30	39	34	7	2	211	.274	.343	.413	.265	38	52-3B 86
1998	Norfolk	Int	123	29	2	0	1	2	7	6	4	1	95	.236	.248	.276	.175	6	27-3B 84
1999	NYMets	NL	404	112	21	3	7	30	47	45	11	4	296	.277	.327	.396	.260	51	

His defense is awful but he looks like he'll hit in the majors, but if he isn't playing third he only hits well enough to be a good pinch-hitter. Why the Mets acquired him is anyone's guess, unless they wanted someone on the roster to make Bonilla's glovework look good.

Terrence Long   CF   Bats L Age 23

YEAR	TEAM	LGE	AB	H	DB	TP	HR	BB	R	RBI	SB	CS	OUT	BA	OBA	SA	EQA	EQR	DEFENSE
1995	Columbia	SAL	186	35	1	0	3	22	12	10	4	3	154	.188	.274	.242	.178	10	46-OF 86
1996	Columbia	SAL	482	127	15	3	12	26	49	49	14	4	359	.263	.301	.382	.238	50	120-OF 102
1997	St Lucie	Fla	469	105	19	3	9	36	41	37	12	5	369	.224	.279	.335	.213	39	118-OF 98
1998	Binghmtn	Eas	454	127	16	7	15	56	68	62	17	8	335	.280	.359	.445	.279	69	123-OF 98
1999	NYMets	NL	459	124	19	4	14	44	60	56	19	7	342	.270	.334	.420	.270	65	

Converted his tools into skills while moving up a level to Double-A, which is very impressive. Improved his plate discipline and used his strength to drive more balls, resulting in across-the-board offensive improvements. I'd like to see a repeat at Triple-A before I get too excited, but the Mets may have their replacement for Brian McRae already.

Luis Lopez   2B   Bats B Age 28

YEAR	TEAM	LGE	AB	H	DB	TP	HR	BB	R	RBI	SB	CS	OUT	BA	OBA	SA	EQA	EQR	DEFENSE	
1996	San Dieg	NL	139	25	3	0	2	10	6	5	0	0	114	.180	.235	.245	.148	5	25-SS 92	11-2B 97
1997	Norfolk	Int	200	56	7	1	3	7	16	20	2	4	148	.280	.304	.370	.227	18	37-SS 83	
1997	NY Mets	NL	177	47	12	1	1	14	18	16	1	4	134	.266	.319	.362	.231	17	27-SS 109	13-2B 92
1998	NY Mets	NL	266	69	14	2	2	22	27	24	2	2	199	.259	.316	.350	.232	26	31-2B 95	
1999	NYMets	NL	290	78	18	1	3	20	29	29	3	3	215	.269	.316	.369	.244	32		

A great hitter compared to Rey Ordonez. Alfonzo's move to second makes Lopez a defensive sub at second and an offensive sub at short.

Brian McRae   CF   Bats B   Age 31

YEAR	TEAM	LGE	AB	H	DB	TP	HR	BB	R	RBI	SB	CS	OUT	BA	OBA	SA	EQA	EQR	DEFENSE
1996	ChiCubs	NL	621	168	31	5	17	76	95	74	31	10	463	.271	.350	.419	.272	89	145-OF 103
1997	ChiCubs	NL	413	95	27	4	6	53	51	37	11	6	324	.230	.318	.358	.239	45	102-OF 105
1997	NY Mets	NL	145	36	5	2	5	14	15	18	2	4	113	.248	.314	.414	.245	17	28-OF 103
1998	NY Mets	NL	554	151	38	5	23	84	92	83	21	13	416	.273	.368	.484	.290	94	148-OF 97
1999	*NYMets*	*NL*	*568*	*153*	*35*	*4*	*19*	*79*	*86*	*77*	*21*	*11*	*426*	*.269*	*.359*	*.445*	*.285*	*92*	

A career year, mostly from an extremely hot summer where he showed the best power of his career. It probably won't last. He's much better suited to bat second than leadoff, and that's his preference. Not a great player, but a fun one to have around for his constant Cub-bashing.

Ralph Milliard   2B   Bats R   Age 25

YEAR	TEAM	LGE	AB	H	DB	TP	HR	BB	R	RBI	SB	CS	OUT	BA	OBA	SA	EQA	EQR	DEFENSE
1996	Charlott	Int	245	59	11	1	5	35	30	25	5	3	189	.241	.336	.355	.246	28	67-2B 100
1996	Florida	NL	62	10	2	0	0	15	8	2	2	0	52	.161	.325	.194	.205	5	19-2B 100
1997	Charlott	Int	131	32	4	0	4	7	12	12	4	2	101	.244	.283	.366	.224	12	31-2B 92
1998	Norfolk	Int	412	95	16	3	12	68	56	45	12	5	322	.231	.340	.371	.254	52	125-2B 103
1999	*NYMets*	*NL*	*346*	*82*	*12*	*2*	*10*	*46*	*43*	*37*	*12*	*4*	*268*	*.237*	*.327*	*.370*	*.255*	*44*	

Milliard/Alfonzo at second and short would be much more appetizing than Alfonzo/Ordonez, because Milliard can field and put runs on the board, you know, play baseball. Deserves a shot at a starting spot as long as guys like Joey Cora and Mike Benjamin have jobs.

John Olerud   1B   Bats L   Age 30

YEAR	TEAM	LGE	AB	H	DB	TP	HR	BB	R	RBI	SB	CS	OUT	BA	OBA	SA	EQA	EQR	DEFENSE
1996	Toronto	AL	387	101	20	0	18	57	53	58	1	0	286	.261	.356	.452	.280	59	98-1B 92
1997	NY Mets	NL	524	153	29	1	24	88	85	90	0	0	371	.292	.394	.489	.304	95	139-1B 100
1998	NY Mets	NL	562	203	38	4	24	100	114	118	2	2	361	.361	.458	.571	.349	130	152-1B 104
1999	*NYMets*	*NL*	*528*	*166*	*29*	*1*	*23*	*88*	*87*	*96*	*1*	*1*	*363*	*.314*	*.412*	*.504*	*.322*	*107*	

An excellent season for the man Cito Gaston's venom can't touch any more. The Mets are probably expecting him to stay at this level, so when he drops back to his normal ('97) level, they'll wonder what went wrong.

Rey Ordonez   SS   Bats when the rules insist   Age 27

YEAR	TEAM	LGE	AB	H	DB	TP	HR	BB	R	RBI	SB	CS	OUT	BA	OBA	SA	EQA	EQR	DEFENSE
1996	NY Mets	NL	504	133	13	4	1	26	36	39	0	3	374	.264	.300	.312	.209	37	143-SS 103
1997	NY Mets	NL	354	76	5	3	1	21	20	16	9	5	283	.215	.259	.254	.171	17	108-SS 103
1998	NY Mets	NL	505	127	22	2	1	27	37	35	3	7	385	.251	.289	.309	.202	35	144-SS 94
1999	*NYMets*	*NL*	*439*	*109*	*14*	*2*	*1*	*22*	*31*	*30*	*5*	*5*	*335*	*.248*	*.284*	*.296*	*.204*	*32*	

What can I say that you don't already know? He isn't getting better at the plate, and his defense is still overrated because of the highlight-reel plays. You knew that. The Mets would be better off putting Alfonzo at short and signing anyone other than Baerga to play second. You knew that too.

Jay Payton   LF   Bats R   Age 26

YEAR	TEAM	LGE	AB	H	DB	TP	HR	BB	R	RBI	SB	CS	OUT	BA	OBA	SA	EQA	EQR	DEFENSE	
1995	Binghmtn	Eas	355	114	13	2	14	24	49	55	11	5	246	.321	.364	.487	.291	56	82-OF 112	
1995	Norfolk	Int	196	46	10	3	4	12	21	17	9	2	152	.235	.279	.378	.231	19	48-OF 105	
1996	Norfolk	Int	152	46	4	2	6	11	22	22	8	1	107	.303	.350	.474	.288	24		
1998	Norfolk	Int	318	70	9	2	6	21	24	23	8	5	253	.220	.268	.318	.200	23	46-OF 98	23-1B 93
1998	NY Mets	NL	22	7	2	0	0	1	3	2	0	0	15	.318	.348	.409	.263	3		
1999	*NYMets*	*NL*	*218*	*53*	*7*	*2*	*5*	*17*	*22*	*21*	*7*	*3*	*168*	*.243*	*.298*	*.362*	*.238*	*23*		

(Jay Payton *continued*)

I would love to be wrong, but I don't believe Payton is ever going to be truly healthy. He rips his elbow up on basic things like hard swings or routine throws, and his offensive performance this year indicates he hadn't really recovered. The Mets should take anything they get from Payton at this point as a bonus.

Tony Phillips | UT | **Bats B Age 40**

YEAR	TEAM	LGE	AB	H	DB	TP	HR	BB	R	RBI	SB	CS	OUT	BA	OBA	SA	EQA	EQR	DEFENSE	
1996	ChiSox	AL	570	159	29	3	12	121	103	74	14	10	421	.279	.405	.404	.289	95	132-OF 103	
1997	ChiSox	AL	127	40	3	0	3	29	26	18	4	1	88	.315	.442	.409	.312	24	19-OF 119	
1997	Anaheim	AL	397	103	28	2	6	72	63	44	9	9	303	.259	.373	.385	.268	56	37-2B 100	29-OF 93
1998	Toronto	AL	47	16	2	0	2	9	9	9	0	0	31	.340	.446	.511	.333	10		
1998	NY Mets	NL	189	44	10	0	4	39	28	20	1	1	146	.233	.364	.349	.259	25	48-OF 90	
1999	*Oakland_*	*AL*	*325*	*76*	*16*	*1*	*5*	*74*	*54*	*34*	*5*	*4*	*253*	*.234*	*.376*	*.335*	*.262*	*44*		

Not a bad stretch-run pickup, but he played pretty poorly for the Mets. Yes, he's 40, but he still gets on base more reliably than 90% of major-league leadoff hitters, and someone should be able to find a role for him. The problem is that he's a menace at almost every position, and that's more dangerous to his future than anything else.

Mike Piazza | C | **Bats R Age 30**

YEAR	TEAM	LGE	AB	H	DB	TP	HR	BB	R	RBI	SB	CS	OUT	BA	OBA	SA	EQA	EQR	DEFENSE
1996	LosAngls	NL	557	193	14	0	39	85	94	126	0	3	367	.346	.433	.582	.339	123	
1997	LosAngls	NL	564	208	26	1	45	73	104	141	4	1	357	.369	.441	.658	.360	139	
1998	LosAngls	NL	150	44	5	0	10	12	18	27	0	0	106	.293	.346	.527	.292	24	35-C 94
1998	NY Mets	NL	397	141	27	0	27	50	72	91	1	0	256	.355	.427	.627	.348	91	99-C 97
1999	*NYMets*	*NL*	*522*	*181*	*20*	*0*	*36*	*67*	*83*	*117*	*1*	*1*	*342*	*.347*	*.421*	*.592*	*.344*	*119*	

Despite the booing and the unfair criticism, Piazza was huge for the Mets. Whether he's worth the contract isn't really a relevant factor; he's a bona fide superstar, and the Mets want that more than they want the best team they can assemble. The fact that he's the best-hitting catcher in history is just a bonus. Will be a first baseman by the halfway point of the contract.

Todd Pratt | C | **Bats R Age 32**

YEAR	TEAM	LGE	AB	H	DB	TP	HR	BB	R	RBI	SB	CS	OUT	BA	OBA	SA	EQA	EQR	DEFENSE
1997	Norfolk	Int	205	54	5	1	7	21	22	26	1	1	152	.263	.332	.400	.254	25	
1997	NY Mets	NL	106	30	3	0	3	13	12	14	0	1	77	.283	.361	.396	.264	14	
1998	Norfolk	Int	115	35	2	0	5	12	15	18	1	0	80	.304	.370	.452	.287	18	
1998	NY Mets	NL	69	19	10	1	2	3	9	10	0	0	50	.275	.306	.536	.278	10	
1999	*NYMets*	*NL*	*213*	*62*	*10*	*1*	*10*	*20*	*26*	*35*	*1*	*1*	*152*	*.291*	*.352*	*.488*	*.291*	*35*	

Pratt could clearly help a number of teams that are instead relying on "solutions" like Matt Walbeck. Could surprise a lot of people who had given up on him if he gets the chance.

Vance Wilson | C | **Bats R Age 26**

YEAR	TEAM	LGE	AB	H	DB	TP	HR	BB	R	RBI	SB	CS	OUT	BA	OBA	SA	EQA	EQR	DEFENSE
1996	St Lucie	Fla	313	65	7	0	6	24	18	20	1	2	250	.208	.264	.288	.184	18	
1997	Binghmtn	Eas	317	71	7	0	10	14	19	26	2	3	249	.224	.257	.341	.198	22	
1998	Norfolk	Int	152	32	1	0	3	7	6	8	0	2	122	.211	.245	.276	.163	7	45-C 93
1999	*NYMets*	*NL*	*218*	*48*	*2*	*0*	*6*	*10*	*12*	*16*	*1*	*2*	*172*	*.220*	*.254*	*.312*	*.194*	*14*	

Broke his arm in a home plate collision in June, but he was already seventh or eighth on the Mets' depth chart at catcher at that point. Still relying on a now-ancient hot AFL campaign to boost his rep. No better than a backup catcher, and he may not even be that good.

PITCHERS (Averages: 4.00 ERA, 9.00 H/9, 1.00 HR/9, 3.00 BB/9, 6.00 K/9, 1.00 KWH)

Juan (JD) Arteaga   Throws L   Age 24

YEAR	TEAM	LGE	IP	H	ER	HR	BB	K	ERA	W	L	H/9	HR/9	BB/9	K/9	KWH	PERA
1997	Pittsfld	NYP	25.0	53	26	1	6	15	9.36	0	3	19.08	0.36	2.16	5.40	0.53	7.56
1998	St Lucie	Fla	35.0	48	18	2	9	19	4.63	2	2	12.34	0.51	2.31	4.89	0.63	5.14
1998	Binghmtn	Eas	116.3	141	50	9	25	74	3.87	7	6	10.91	0.70	1.93	5.72	1.16	4.41

The winningest pitcher in the University of Miami's history, Arteaga slipped to the 26th round because he doesn't throw all that hard. However, he's left-handed, throws strikes, and he gets people out; I don't see any reason to question it. While with Miami, he was named one of the top two pitchers in the 1996 CWS, along with ex-Met prospect Ed Yarnall.

Rigo Beltran   Throws L Age 29

YEAR	TEAM	LGE	IP	H	ER	HR	BB	K	ERA	W	L	H/9	HR/9	BB/9	K/9	KWH	PERA
1996	Louisvil	AmA	125.7	163	76	16	29	104	5.44	5	9	11.67	1.15	2.08	7.45	1.72	5.23
1997	Louisvil	AmA	53.0	54	18	7	23	36	3.06	4	2	9.17	1.19	3.91	6.11	0.78	4.25
1997	St Louis	NL	54.3	49	23	3	16	45	3.81	3	3	8.12	0.50	2.65	7.45	1.94	2.98
1998	Norfolk	Int	92.7	118	49	15	41	76	4.76	4	6	11.46	1.46	3.98	7.38	0.90	5.63

Tweener who makes the book because he is all the Mets have to show for handing Juan Acevedo to the Cardinals on a silver platter.

Willie Blair   Throws R   Age 33

YEAR	TEAM	LGE	IP	H	ER	HR	BB	K	ERA	W	L	H/9	HR/9	BB/9	K/9	KWH	PERA
1996	San Dieg	NL	87.0	90	51	14	27	60	5.28	4	6	9.31	1.45	2.79	6.21	1.11	4.24
1997	Detroit	AL	177.7	187	73	16	40	88	3.70	11	9	9.47	0.81	2.03	4.46	0.78	3.80
1998	Arizona	NL	150.0	173	83	28	47	66	4.98	7	10	10.38	1.68	2.82	3.96	0.40	5.10
1998	NY Mets	NL	29.3	23	8	4	9	19	2.45	2	1	7.06	1.23	2.76	5.83	1.31	2.76

Blair is fine to have around as a fifth or sixth starter, and he was moderately successful in long relief before his 1997. Traded to the Tigers for Joe Randa, he's probably overjoyed to be reunited with Deivi Cruz. Expectations that he'll get to where he was is would be unrealistic, but he'll be useful.

Eric Cammack   Throws R   Age 23

YEAR	TEAM	LGE	IP	H	ER	HR	BB	K	ERA	W	L	H/9	HR/9	BB/9	K/9	KWH	PERA
1997	Pittsfld	NYP	28.7	16	7	2	19	17	2.20	2	1	5.02	0.63	5.97	5.34	0.71	1.88
1998	Columbia	SAL	30.0	24	16	2	17	28	4.80	1	2	7.20	0.60	5.10	8.40	1.44	3.00
1998	St Lucie	Fla	34.7	28	14	3	16	38	3.63	2	2	7.27	0.78	4.15	9.87	2.42	2.86

Hard-throwing relief prospect whose mentality draws comparisons to Randy Myers and Wes Gardner. Working on developing a second pitch, which is all that's limiting his upward mobility right now.

Brad Clontz   Throws R   Age 28

YEAR	TEAM	LGE	IP	H	ER	HR	BB	K	ERA	W	L	H/9	HR/9	BB/9	K/9	KWH	PERA
1996	Atlanta	NL	82.3	84	48	11	31	45	5.25	3	6	9.18	1.20	3.39	4.92	0.58	4.15
1997	Atlanta	NL	48.0	57	23	3	16	38	4.31	2	3	10.69	0.56	3.00	7.12	1.19	4.31
1998	LosAngls	NL	20.7	17	12	3	9	13	5.23	1	1	7.40	1.31	3.92	5.66	0.83	3.05
1998	Norfolk	Int	41.0	50	27	4	16	38	5.93	2	3	10.98	0.88	3.51	8.34	1.35	4.83

Sidearmer who completely bottomed out in 1997, only to stage a partial comeback this year. He still shouldn't be allowed to face lefties, but would thrive in a LaRussian specialist situation.

Dennis Cook   Throws L   Age 36

YEAR	TEAM	LGE	IP	H	ER	HR	BB	K	ERA	W	L	H/9	HR/9	BB/9	K/9	KWH	PERA
1996	Texas	AL	73.7	49	24	2	29	64	2.93	5	3	5.99	0.24	3.54	7.82	2.16	1.71
1997	Florida	NL	63.7	66	24	4	25	56	3.39	4	3	9.33	0.57	3.53	7.92	1.43	3.82
1998	NYMets	NL	70.0	61	17	5	24	72	2.19	6	2	7.84	0.64	3.09	9.26	2.66	2.96

Signed for three more years, until he's 39. Thirty-nine! It was a good season, but the Mets are overreacting to his ERA, and they're doing what they generally do—buying high. More likely to get hurt than to repeat.

Octavio Dotel   Throws R   Age 25

YEAR	TEAM	LGE	IP	H	ER	HR	BB	K	ERA	W	L	H/9	HR/9	BB/9	K/9	KWH	PERA
1996	Columbia	SAL	103.7	150	76	10	61	81	6.60	3	9	13.02	0.87	5.30	7.03	0.54	5.99
1997	St Lucie	Fla	47.7	57	21	3	28	28	3.97	3	2	10.76	0.57	5.29	5.29	0.37	4.72
1997	Binghmtn	Eas	55.3	76	47	5	37	31	7.64	1	5	12.36	0.81	6.02	5.04	0.26	5.86
1998	Binghmtn	Eas	66.7	52	21	4	25	59	2.84	5	2	7.02	0.54	3.38	7.97	2.01	2.43
1998	Norfolk	Int	100.0	88	42	9	40	98	3.78	6	5	7.92	0.81	3.60	8.82	2.05	3.24

Dotel improved his command and changed speeds more effectively in '98, leading to a breakout season that put him in the Mets' plans for '99. Has not been overworked, a rarity in this system. One of the best pitching prospects in the NL.

James Dougherty   Throws L Age 21

YEAR	TEAM	LGE	IP	H	ER	HR	BB	K	ERA	W	L	H/9	HR/9	BB/9	K/9	KWH	PERA
1998	Columbia	SAL	128.3	144	56	10	60	66	3.93	7	7	10.10	0.70	4.21	4.63	0.38	4.42

Goes by his middle name, Kevin, but appears in print as James, Kevin, or occasionally as Mufasa. Missed the first six weeks of the season after getting hit in the face with a Yohanny Valera throw, then proceeded to go 15-2 the rest of the way. Confuses hitters with his delivery; you expect a hard fastball, but he doesn't hit 90 on the gun and throws a lot of breaking stuff. His peripherals weren't great, so unless he can pull this off at Double-A, he's a borderline prospect at best.

John Franco   Throws L   Age 38

YEAR	TEAM	LGE	IP	H	ER	HR	BB	K	ERA	W	L	H/9	HR/9	BB/9	K/9	KWH	PERA
1996	NY Mets	NL	53.3	59	14	2	20	43	2.36	4	2	9.96	0.34	3.38	7.26	1.18	3.88
1997	NY Mets	NL	59.7	54	18	3	18	47	2.72	5	2	8.15	0.45	2.72	7.09	1.70	2.87
1998	NY Mets	NL	66.7	67	23	4	26	54	3.11	4	3	9.05	0.54	3.51	7.29	1.26	3.64

Looks like he's starting to slow down, although he was hardly to blame for the Mets' failure to win the wild card. He wasn't quite as sharp this year as he has been in the past five seasons, and hitters hit him harder. Should survive his two-year extension, but he'll probably have to hang it up after that.

Dickey Gonzalez   Throws R   Age 20

YEAR	TEAM	LGE	IP	H	ER	HR	BB	K	ERA	W	L	H/9	HR/9	BB/9	K/9	KWH	PERA
1997	Kingsprt	App	61.0	95	41	7	12	39	6.05	2	5	14.02	1.03	1.77	5.75	1.00	6.20
1997	Columbia	SAL	44.3	69	33	10	18	33	6.70	1	4	14.01	2.03	3.65	6.70	0.66	7.31
1998	Columbia	SAL	106.7	132	63	11	16	66	5.32	4	8	11.14	0.93	1.35	5.57	1.55	4.64
1998	St Lucie	Fla	44.0	59	24	9	14	17	4.91	2	3	12.07	1.84	2.86	3.48	0.26	6.14

Came out of nowhere to surprise the Mets, who had considered returning him to Kingsport this year. Has good stuff, but doesn't have total command of all his pitches yet, leading to a lot of hits and a lot of groundballs. Warning: faced over 24 batters per start, covering 158 innings, both high for a 19-year-old, but his mechanics don't appear to put a great strain on his elbow.

Arnold Gooch   Throws R   Age 22

YEAR	TEAM	LGE	IP	H	ER	HR	BB	K	ERA	W	L	H/9	HR/9	BB/9	K/9	KWH	PERA
1996	St Lucie	Fla	164.0	160	82	12	56	111	4.50	8	10	8.78	0.66	3.07	6.09	1.03	3.51
1997	Binghmtn	Eas	160.7	198	96	11	72	77	5.38	6	12	11.09	0.62	4.03	4.31	0.31	4.76
1998	Binghmtn	Eas	160.7	191	93	16	58	91	5.21	7	11	10.70	0.90	3.25	5.10	0.56	4.71

Improved, but not enough to restore hope, especially since it was his second time around the league. In '96, when he was the toast of the Florida State League, he had a hard fastball and a plus breaking pitch, but he's lost command of the latter and hasn't gotten it back. Even if he finds what he lost, all the innings he's thrown in the last three years might catch up to him.

Bobby Jones   Throws R   Age 29

YEAR	TEAM	LGE	IP	H	ER	HR	BB	K	ERA	W	L	H/9	HR/9	BB/9	K/9	KWH	PERA
1996	NY Mets	NL	193.0	236	98	27	43	104	4.57	9	12	11.01	1.26	2.01	4.85	0.80	4.94
1997	NY Mets	NL	192.3	192	85	25	57	112	3.98	11	10	8.98	1.17	2.67	5.24	0.86	3.88
1998	NY Mets	NL	200.0	189	78	23	48	105	3.51	12	10	8.51	1.03	2.16	4.72	0.91	3.42

A victim of high expectations: Jones is still trying to live up to the promise of his 1994 season, which was characterized by a lot of luck and relief support, and to the Mets' insistence that he throw about 200 innings a year. The Mets should either acknowledge that Jones is a 175-inning, #4 starter, or just trade him to someone else who knows how to use him.

Kyle Kessel — Throws L — Age 23

YEAR	TEAM	LGE	IP	H	ER	HR	BB	K	ERA	W	L	H/9	HR/9	BB/9	K/9	KWH	PERA
1996	Pittsfld	NYP	70.7	122	62	10	22	40	7.90	2	6	15.54	1.27	2.80	5.09	0.45	7.26
1997	Columbia	SAL	159.7	181	79	11	67	96	4.45	8	10	10.20	0.62	3.78	5.41	0.57	4.34
1998	St Lucie	Fla	83.7	130	66	13	31	45	7.10	2	7	13.98	1.40	3.33	4.84	0.38	6.67

Exhibit #835 of how the Mets still haven't learned their lesson about overworking young pitchers. Kessel has great mound presence and good enough stuff that he should have blown past the FSL, but injuries restricted him to 20 mediocre starts. When healthy, his fastball tops 90 with movement, but he needs to work on his curveball to be a major-league starter.

Al Leiter — Throws L — Age 33

YEAR	TEAM	LGE	IP	H	ER	HR	BB	K	ERA	W	L	H/9	HR/9	BB/9	K/9	KWH	PERA
1996	Florida	NL	218.0	163	65	15	112	179	2.68	17	7	6.73	0.62	4.62	7.39	1.32	2.60
1997	Florida	NL	154.7	139	69	14	83	118	4.02	8	9	8.09	0.81	4.83	6.87	0.91	3.49
1998	NY Mets	NL	197.7	150	44	8	65	158	2.00	18	4	6.83	0.36	2.96	7.19	1.92	2.19

The only question is whether the newfound consistency is real. If his walk rate remains at the new level, the 4-year, $32 million deal could be a bargain. Still, I'm skeptical, because we're talking about a survivor of multiple surgeries.

Greg McMichael — Throws R — Age 32

YEAR	TEAM	LGE	IP	H	ER	HR	BB	K	ERA	W	L	H/9	HR/9	BB/9	K/9	KWH	PERA
1996	Atlanta	NL	88.7	89	34	4	26	71	3.45	6	4	9.03	0.41	2.64	7.21	1.63	3.35
1997	NY Mets	NL	87.3	79	32	8	25	72	3.30	6	4	8.14	0.82	2.58	7.42	1.97	3.19
1998	LosAngls	NL	14.7	17	7	1	6	10	4.30	1	1	10.43	0.61	3.68	6.14	0.74	4.30
1998	NY Mets	NL	56.0	65	26	8	26	40	4.18	3	3	10.45	1.29	4.18	6.43	0.71	4.98

Boomeranged from the Mets to LA to the Mets again this year. Despite similar first/second half ERAs, McMichael was a lot more hittable after the break, giving up a .318 average with much more power (7 HR, versus 2 before the break). Can help a team, but not in the setup role where he's most needed.

Mark Mimbs — Throws L — Age 30

YEAR	TEAM	LGE	IP	H	ER	HR	BB	K	ERA	W	L	H/9	HR/9	BB/9	K/9	KWH	PERA
1995	Albuquer	PCL	102.0	116	38	8	24	84	3.35	6	5	10.24	0.71	2.12	7.41	1.90	4.15
1996	Albuquer	PCL	151.7	179	86	15	48	108	5.10	6	11	10.62	0.89	2.85	6.41	1.02	4.57
1997	New Orln	AmA	30.3	46	24	2	10	20	7.12	1	2	13.65	0.59	2.97	5.93	0.65	5.64
1997	Pawtuckt	Int	80.7	119	62	11	35	61	6.92	2	7	13.28	1.23	3.90	6.81	0.67	6.25
1998	Norfolk	Int	102.7	81	28	8	26	70	2.45	8	3	7.10	0.70	2.28	6.14	1.74	2.37

Deserves a chance, regardless of his status in '95. He's been getting Triple-A hitters out consistently for the last four years, with a short blip in Pawtucket in 1997 the only stain on his record. He was outstanding in 14 starts for Norfolk.

Dan Murray — Throws R — Age 25

YEAR	TEAM	LGE	IP	H	ER	HR	BB	K	ERA	W	L	H/9	HR/9	BB/9	K/9	KWH	PERA
1996	St Lucie	Fla	98.0	146	69	4	60	44	6.34	3	8	13.41	0.37	5.51	4.04	0.17	5.79
1997	St Lucie	Fla	149.3	192	88	6	67	64	5.30	6	11	11.57	0.36	4.04	3.86	0.24	4.82
1998	Binghmtn	Eas	158.3	188	72	14	57	115	4.09	9	9	10.69	0.80	3.24	6.54	0.93	4.60

At 24, coming off back-to-back middling years with St. Lucie, Murray faced a crucial test in Double-A . . . and passed, pushing himself at least to Norfolk in '99. Great mound presence makes up for stuff that's merely above-average, and he obviously learned how to fool Double-A hitters. The one sign of a trouble is the much higher home run rate.

Hideo Nomo   **Throws R**   **Age 30**

YEAR	TEAM	LGE	IP	H	ER	HR	BB	K	ERA	W	L	H/9	HR/9	BB/9	K/9	KWH	PERA
1996	LosAngls	NL	226.3	198	89	24	79	208	3.54	14	11	7.87	0.95	3.14	8.27	2.07	3.18
1997	LosAngls	NL	205.3	213	101	25	83	207	4.43	10	13	9.34	1.10	3.64	9.07	1.82	4.21
1998	LosAngls	NL	69.0	60	35	9	34	66	4.57	3	5	7.83	1.17	4.43	8.61	1.60	3.52
1998	NY Mets	NL	93.0	74	42	12	52	86	4.06	5	5	7.16	1.16	5.03	8.32	1.44	3.19

Deteriorated to the point where the Mets felt he wasn't worth using for most of their September stretch run. His mechanics are officially a toxic Superfund site, leading to a loss of control that explains much of his ineffectiveness. He'll never get his '95–96 form back, but he can easily be an above-average starter given the right pitching coach.

Rick Reed   **Throws R**   **Age 34**

YEAR	TEAM	LGE	IP	H	ER	HR	BB	K	ERA	W	L	H/9	HR/9	BB/9	K/9	KWH	PERA
1996	Norfolk	Int	169.7	206	85	13	36	99	4.51	8	11	10.93	0.69	1.91	5.25	0.99	4.46
1997	NY Mets	NL	205.0	201	75	19	27	101	3.29	14	9	8.82	0.83	1.19	4.43	1.41	3.29
1998	NY Mets	NL	217.0	202	69	31	26	139	2.86	16	8	8.38	1.29	1.08	5.76	2.76	3.32

No reason that he can't stay at this level—he's been pitching about this well for the last six years. As an aside, think about how Jim Bowden must feel about letting Reed get away.

Armando Reynoso   **Throws R**   **Age 33**

YEAR	TEAM	LGE	IP	H	ER	HR	BB	K	ERA	W	L	H/9	HR/9	BB/9	K/9	KWH	PERA
1996	Colorado	NL	191.7	175	66	25	49	83	3.10	13	8	8.22	1.17	2.30	3.90	0.60	3.38
1997	NY Mets	NL	91.0	103	45	7	26	42	4.45	4	6	10.19	0.69	2.57	4.15	0.49	4.15
1998	NY Mets	NL	70.0	64	26	4	30	37	3.34	5	3	8.23	0.51	3.86	4.76	0.53	3.21

Came off the DL to reel off a string of good starts that pushed the Mets briefly into a six-man rotation. Not a great bet for protracted health, which won't matter if his walk rate doesn't come down. Signed by the Diamondbacks for their rotation.

Grant Roberts   **Throws R**   **Age 21**

YEAR	TEAM	LGE	IP	H	ER	HR	BB	K	ERA	W	L	H/9	HR/9	BB/9	K/9	KWH	PERA
1996	Kingsprt	App	63.0	72	25	4	41	50	3.57	4	3	10.29	0.57	5.86	7.14	0.64	4.57
1997	Columbia	SAL	124.3	132	45	2	54	80	3.26	8	6	9.55	0.14	3.91	5.79	0.67	3.69
1998	St Lucie	Fla	69.7	90	39	12	42	52	5.04	3	5	11.63	1.55	5.43	6.72	0.54	5.94

Considered one of the best, if not the best, pitching prospect in the Mets' system coming into this year, but surgery took him out for half the season, after which he was effectively rehabbing at St. Lucie. Pitched well in the Maryland Fall League, so the Mets hope to move him up to Double-A and see him resume his progress.

Mel Rojas   **Throws R**   **Age 32**

YEAR	TEAM	LGE	IP	H	ER	HR	BB	K	ERA	W	L	H/9	HR/9	BB/9	K/9	KWH	PERA
1996	Montreal	NL	83.0	58	26	5	27	83	2.82	6	3	6.29	0.54	2.93	9.00	3.30	1.95
1997	ChiCubs	NL	62.0	54	25	12	27	55	3.63	4	3	7.84	1.74	3.92	7.98	1.56	3.77
1997	NY Mets	NL	26.0	27	16	4	5	28	5.54	1	2	9.35	1.38	1.73	9.69	4.36	4.15
1998	NY Mets	NL	60.0	70	35	10	27	38	5.25	3	4	10.50	1.50	4.05	5.70	0.57	5.10

Can be fixed by a team with patience. His mechanics have been a wreck since he left Montreal, which isn't the first time that's happened to an ex-Expo hurler. Now a Dodger; the unrealistic expectations in LA may inhibit his recovery.

Jae Weong Seo   **Throws R**   **Age 22**

YEAR	TEAM	LGE	IP	H	ER	HR	BB	K	ERA	W	L	H/9	HR/9	BB/9	K/9	KWH	PERA
1998	St Lucie	Fla	34.7	32	14	3	11	28	3.63	2	2	8.31	0.78	2.86	7.27	1.67	3.37

Hard-throwing Korean import who was shut down for much of the season with a strained and stretched medial collateral ligament. He came back as good as new, and took a no-hitter into the 8th inning of the final game of the FSL championship series. Also pitched well in the Instructional League. The elbow is a serious concern, but if he can stay healthy he should advance quickly.

Scott Stewart — Throws L — Age 23

YEAR	TEAM	LGE	IP	H	ER	HR	BB	K	ERA	W	L	H/9	HR/9	BB/9	K/9	KWH	PERA
1995	Charl-SC	SAL	70.3	106	48	9	16	30	6.14	2	6	13.56	1.15	2.05	3.84	0.40	6.14
1997	St Lucie	Fla	121.3	134	65	11	21	48	4.82	5	8	9.94	0.82	1.56	3.56	0.61	4.01
1998	Norfolk	Int	52.7	62	37	12	20	27	6.32	2	4	10.59	2.05	3.42	4.61	0.44	5.64
1998	Binghmtn	Eas	88.7	105	45	13	28	51	4.57	4	6	10.66	1.32	2.84	5.18	0.66	4.97

Skipped Double-A, receiving severe head trauma in Triple-A before his demotion to Binghamton. He reestablished himself there, becoming the team's top starter in the second half. His fastball doesn't burn the radar guns, but he gets good reviews for its movement. Faces an uphill battle, but the Mets don't have to rush him.

Jeff Tam — Throws R — Age 28

YEAR	TEAM	LGE	IP	H	ER	HR	BB	K	ERA	W	L	H/9	HR/9	BB/9	K/9	KWH	PERA
1996	Binghmtn	Eas	59.0	68	24	6	18	34	3.66	4	3	10.37	0.92	2.75	5.19	0.71	4.42
1997	Norfolk	Int	107.3	159	75	9	13	50	6.29	3	9	13.33	0.75	1.09	4.19	0.91	5.53
1998	Norfolk	Int	63.0	46	13	3	6	41	1.86	6	1	6.57	0.43	0.86	5.86	4.57	1.57
1998	NY Mets	NL	14.3	14	9	2	3	7	5.65	1	1	8.79	1.26	1.88	4.40	0.87	3.77

Lifer with mediocre stuff, impeccable control: he has 40 walks in the past three years, spanning 252.2 innings. As good—or bad—as many other RH relievers with full pensions. Known as "Qui" to his lawyer friends.

Derek Wallace — Throws R — Age 27

Has nearly completed his recovery from an aneurysm that nearly ended his career. He was originally a favorite to take over from Franco after the latter's contract expired, but Wallace's injury forced the Mets to sign Franco for two more years. Wallace should be an effective major-league reliever soon, but his shot at closing in New York has dimmed considerably.

Turk Wendell — Throws R — Age 32

YEAR	TEAM	LGE	IP	H	ER	HR	BB	K	ERA	W	L	H/9	HR/9	BB/9	K/9	KWH	PERA
1996	ChiCubs	NL	80.3	65	25	8	42	68	2.80	6	3	7.28	0.90	4.71	7.62	1.27	3.14
1997	ChiCubs	NL	63.3	54	27	4	36	49	3.84	4	3	7.67	0.57	5.12	6.96	0.93	3.13
1997	NY Mets	NL	16.3	17	9	3	13	9	4.96	1	1	9.37	1.65	7.16	4.96	0.27	4.96
1998	NY Mets	NL	78.3	63	21	4	30	53	2.41	7	2	7.24	0.46	3.45	6.09	1.11	2.53

I think he finally stopped the whole licorice/teeth-brushing bit when Fox didn't pick up "That Great Big Pitching Freak Show" for its fall schedule. Concentrating on baseball full-time, Wendell had one of his best seasons, establishing himself as Franco's setup man. Could easily step into the closer role if Franco scuffles.

Paul Wilson — Throws R — Age 26

YEAR	TEAM	LGE	IP	H	ER	HR	BB	K	ERA	W	L	H/9	HR/9	BB/9	K/9	KWH	PERA
1995	Binghmtn	Eas	116.3	114	40	6	23	104	3.09	8	5	8.82	0.46	1.78	8.05	3.09	3.17
1995	Norfolk	Int	62.3	75	30	4	21	59	4.33	3	4	10.83	0.58	3.03	8.52	1.66	4.48
1996	NY Mets	NL	147.7	173	98	16	67	98	5.97	5	11	10.54	0.98	4.08	5.97	0.62	4.81
1998	St Lucie	Fla	16.0	33	18	3	5	10	10.12	0	2	18.56	1.69	2.81	5.62	0.45	9.00
1998	Norfolk	Int	38.7	45	18	2	9	24	4.19	2	2	10.47	0.47	2.09	5.59	1.07	3.96

Could be good again, but will he ever be healthy? He was shut down once in March, again in April for a month...you get the idea. The Norfolk time was encouraging, but he's still trying to get his old mechanics back, and that could take another year even if he stays healthy.

Masato Yoshii — Throws R — Age 34

YEAR	TEAM	LGE	IP	H	ER	HR	BB	K	ERA	W	L	H/9	HR/9	BB/9	K/9	KWH	PERA
1998	NY Mets	NL	176.3	164	66	23	47	107	3.37	12	8	8.37	1.17	2.40	5.46	1.11	3.47

The Mets deserve credit for increasing their international scouting presence, with Yoshii as the first fruit of their labors. Hitters adjusted to his delivery the second time around, so his final numbers paint a slightly rosy picture, but he should still be more than adequate for the back of the rotation.

SNWLP					NEW YORK METS						Park Effect: -6.5%	
PITCHER	GS	IP	R	SNW	SNL	SNPCT	W	L	RA	APW	SNVA	SNWAR
Blair, W.	2	14.3	2	1.2	0.2	.832	1	1	1.26	0.52	0.45	0.57
Bohanon, B.	4	21.0	7	1.5	0.8	.660	1	1	3.00	0.36	0.29	0.54
Jones, B.	30	195.3	94	10.6	10.6	.501	9	9	4.33	0.52	0.03	1.61
Leiter, A.	28	193.0	55	14.4	5.5	.722	17	6	2.56	4.27	4.16	5.92
Mlicki, D.	10	57.0	38	2.6	4.5	.365	1	4	6.00	-0.90	-0.88	-0.42
Nomo, H.	16	85.7	49	5.1	5.4	.485	4	5	5.15	-0.54	-0.11	0.63
Pulsipher, B.	1	4.0	5	0.1	0.6	.101	0	0	11.25	-0.29	-0.27	-0.22
Reed, R.	31	212.3	84	13.9	8.9	.610	16	11	3.56	2.37	2.35	4.22
Reynoso, A.	11	68.3	31	5.0	3.1	.612	7	3	4.08	0.37	0.78	1.51
Yoshii, M.	29	171.7	79	10.4	8.8	.542	6	8	4.14	0.81	0.69	2.23
TOTALS	162	1022.7	444	64.7	48.5	.572	62	48	3.91	7.49	7.47	16.60

Sometimes you have to give major league GMs credit. The rumors that circulated in June that the Mariners were actually willing to trade Randy Johnson for Hideo Nomo were amazing. It was hard to believe that a major league GM would really equate the value of Nomo, whose career had been in freefall ever since his splashy debut in 1995, to a superstar like Johnson (free agent or not). It was hard to believe that GMs would be unable to look past the W/L records and the Dodger uniform, and realize that Nomo's value was little more than a three-year-old memory. Well, it wasn't really that hard to believe, and that was the problem. But when the real Nomo trade was announced, it became clear that GMs were much more baseball-savvy than the gossip columnists made them appear. They had not rated Nomo as equivalent in value to a Randy Johnson. In fact, two major league GMs had gotten Nomo's just about right: after you throw in Brad Clontz, he was worth a couple of journeymen like Dave Mlicki and Greg McMichael. How did the Mets starters react to the Piazza trade? Not too well. Jones had a .622 SNPct pre-Piazza, .461 with Piazza. Leiter was .758 pre-Piazza, .708 with Piazza. Reed was .725 pre-Piazza, .564 with Piazza. Yoshii was .744 pre-Piazza, .461 with Piazza. I'll leave it up to the reader to decide how seriously to take those numbers.

Pitcher Abuse Points

PITCHER	AGE	GS	PAP	PAP/S	AAW	MAX	115+	130+
Jones, Bobby	28	30	308	10.27	17.11	138	4	1
Leiter, Al	32	28	752	26.86	26.86	139	14	3
Mlicki, Dave	30	10	70	7.00	9.33	130	1	1
Nomo, Hideo	29	16	39	2.44	3.66	117	1	0
Reed, Rick	32	31	229	7.39	7.39	127	5	0
Reynoso, Armando	32	11	130	11.82	11.82	119	4	0
Yoshii, Masato	33	29	160	5.52	5.52	133	2	1
TOTAL		162	1688	10.42	11.95	139	31	6
RANKING (NL)			4	4	9		5	5

The importance of looking at workloads in light of age: the Mets finished fouth in the NL in PAPs, but Bobby Jones, the youngster in the rotation, was 28—and their overall AAW is rather impressive. Al Leiter was hit pretty hard, and doesn't exactly have a track record as a workhorse, so I'd be concerned about a drop-off this year. No one else on the roster is in much danger, so give Bobby Valentine some credit. He's done some weird things with pitchers in his time with the Rangers, and watched Edwin Correa's arm disintegrate into molten slag, but his handling of the pitching staff was not one of the reasons for the Mets' late collapse. His handling of the shortstop position, on the other hand...

Philadelphia Phillies

The Phillies have apparently hired an assistant general manager, following in a great tradition of baseball's early years by bringing in a current player for the position. Curt Schilling's intentions are understandable; after making a long-term commitment to the team, he wanted the Phils to take advantage of their late-July proximity to the wild-card leaders. However, he did not take into account the numerous teams between the Phils and the Cubs/Mets, who were leading the race at the time, nor did he consider the possibility that the Phillies' record was in no way indicative of the team's talent level. The Phillies' success to that date had come from a fair amount of luck and health, neither of which last long in Philly. Discarding thoughts of long-term strategy to make a grab for a prize as elusive as the wild-card slot does nothing to perpetuate the Phillies' reputation as a team floundering in the purgatory between contention and rebuilding.

The Phillies' indecision is exemplified by their failure to make any sort of move to capitalize on their bullpen strength at the trading deadline. By not moving, the Phillies not only squandered a golden opportunity to capitalize on a talent surplus that may have been quite temporary, but also sent a strong signal to their fans that management's commitment to the long-term rebuilding program is weak and malleable. Fur-thermore, the inaction may have led players to believe that they can influence the team's policies by talking or complaining to the media—a procedure that can only damage the team's reputation and increase fan dissatisfaction.

The team's situation in late July was quite simple: they were about seven games behind the wild card leaders, with two other teams in front of them to boot. Taking command of the race seemed possible, but far from likely. The Phils made it to that point on the strength of strong first-half performances from guys like Doug Glanville and Desi Relaford, both of whom were playing well above their minor-league numbers would have indicated, and a strong bullpen thriving despite the absence of the team's star closer. Ricky Bottalico went down in April and had elbow surgery that was expected to keep him out six weeks; in July, he had returned

from his rehab, but was having problems with his velocity and hittability. In his absence, Mark Leiter had taken up the slack as the closer, pitching better than he had at any point in his career, and he continued to close as Bottalico continued to "rehab" in the majors. Wayne Gomes came up from the minors and pitched with a level of control he had never shown in the minors. Jerry Spradlin and Yorkis Perez underwent similar transformations.

So on July 29, the team was 55-50 and faced with a dilemma. The fans and the Philly media were fully prepared all through May and June to see the team trade away Leiter or Bottalico in July, expecting that the Phils would be partially or completely buried at that point. When the team appeared to be in the wild-card race and Schilling began a mild public campaign to prevent a dump trade, public opinion turned against making such a deal.

In fact, the team was in a very good position to make such a deal, reduce salary, and still improve its chances in the wild-card race. The bullpen was clearly a point of strength, but the rotation was a point of weakness and the lineup's strength wasn't likely to remain so. The rotation at that point comprised Schilling, Mark Portugal, struggling rookie Carlton Loewer, and two question marks: Matt Beech and Tyler Green, both of whom appeared to be possible injury victims. Green, of course, has been injured for most of his pro career, and Beech's struggles after a good June stretch was a major cause for concern.

The lineup's dubious nature did not stop with Glanville and Relaford. Mark Lewis hit under .200 for the first two months of the season before starting to produce in June and July. Mike Lieberthal was struggling through a very disappointing season, and Gregg Jefferies was, as usual, a zero in left. Scranton could provide little ammo for reloading beyond catcher Bobby Estalella.

Trading one of the three could-be closers (Leiter, Gomes, Bottalico) could have brought in a starting pitcher or a rookie hitter who would have improved the Phillies overall. In particular, Leiter's sudden emergence should have made trading him not only desirable, but urgent. He had already

Phillies Prospectus

1998 record: 75-87; Third place, NL East

Pythagorean W/L: 71-91

Runs scored: 713 (9th in NL)

Runs allowed: 808 (12th in NL)

Team EQA: .249 (13th in NL)

Park: Veterans Stadium (moderate hitters')

1998: Another treadmill season, as the team surrounds Rolen and Schilling with 23 mediocrities.

1999: No reason to believe the improvement in 1998 was real; a slide to the cellar is likely.

begun to struggle with his control in July, while Gomes had become the team's most reliable reliever. Although the general consensus seemed to be that trading Leiter would weaken the team, there was little reason to believe the team would be worse off with Gomes closing, Leiter on another team, and the bounty of a Leiter deal in the rotation or in left. The going assumption that Bottalico would be ready before the end of the season only bolstered the case for making a deal.

In the end, of course, the Phils didn't make the play-offs—or even remain above the .500 mark. The team lost its last two July contests, then went 11-20 in August and 9-15 in September to finish 14 games behind the Cubs. It is easy for any observer to now comment that the Phillies should have moved Leiter in July, but it should have been quite clear to them then: trading Leiter would have had a minimal impact on the bullpen, but could have brought the team needed help in another area. In fact, Leiter and Gomes were both awful in August, two starting pitchers (Green and Beech) went down with injuries, and several expected offensive producers (e.g., Lewis, Estalella, Brogna, Glanville) didn't down the stretch.

This organizational overreliance on veterans—or, conversely, a chronic mistrust of rookies or "unproven" talents—is hardly new. In the spring of '98, the team decided to make Desi Relaford their starting shortstop, but there was concern about his ability to adjust to fielding in the majors. To make him feel more comfortable, they chose to import a veteran second baseman to serve as Relaford's double-play partner and as a fielding mentor of sorts to the rookie. However, Relaford would probably have been most comfortable with continuity: the team could easily have promoted his 1997 double-play partner, 2B David Doster, who would clearly be an adequate offensive solution at the position as well. Instead, they signed Mark Lewis, a poor-hitting, mediocre-fielding utility infielder with whom Relaford had never played. Lewis's salary proved wasted money, and rather than unlocking value in Doster, the team left him to rot as Scranton's third baseman.

The November trade with the Cardinals represents the latest manifestation of the Phils' infatuation with all things tried and true. The Phillies traded Bottalico at the absolute bottom of his value, unless the team believes he'll never return to his dominant '96-97 self, which seems a rather pessimistic and unlikely scenario. In exchange, they acquired an older reliever coming off a much more serious injury (Jeff Brantley), a 33-year-old left fielder who has played more than 122 games once since 1993 (Ron Gant), and a good starting pitching prospect (Cliff Politte) who struggled in his first exposure to baseball above Double-A. Given the ease with which a team could find an adequate, $250,000 left fielder on waivers, the Phils would have been significantly better off trying to obtain a second prospect from the Cards, such as one of their multiple young shortstops.

The Phillies have even continued to rely on old friends to fill front office and player-development positions. Of greatest concern is the August appointment of Dallas Green as the team's interim director of player development. Green may or may not have his valid uses, but if there is one job he is not fit for, it is player development, not after his experiences with a Mets organization that has spent the better part of this decade dismembering its once-numerous pitching prospects by working them to death. Even this year, despite the appointment of Ed Wade, who has regularly stated his concern for the way the Phils have ruined pitching prospects in the past, both Evan Thomas and Randy Wolf were subjected to punishing workloads that will likely show their effects this season.

Four months after the July trading deadline, the Phillies find themselves no better off than they were before then, and perhaps significantly worse off. By allowing players, the media, and other outside sources to convince them that they were legitimate wild-card contenders, the Phils failed to capitalize on Leiter's success before he collapsed and thus add more long-term value to the organization. Instead, they had to deal him to Seattle for Paul Spoljaric, another of Lou Piniella's scapegoats, but not exactly the kind of player who will help make things get better. The front office's attention has begun to turn to the embryonic attempts to bring state funding to Philadelphia to construct a replacement for the Vet. One wonders when they will start assembling a contending team to fill it.

HITTERS (Averages: BA .260/ OBA .330/ SA .420, EQA .260)

Bob Abreu   RF   Bats L   Age 25

YEAR	TEAM	LGE	AB	H	DB	TP	HR	BB	R	RBI	SB	CS	OUT	BA	OBA	SA	EQA	EQR	DEFENSE
1996	Tucson	PCL	472	117	12	8	13	74	68	54	20	13	368	.248	.350	.390	.260	64	122-OF 96
1997	New Orln	AA	196	53	8	4	2	20	26	20	7	3	146	.270	.338	.383	.255	24	43-OF 108
1997	Houston	NL	188	47	11	2	3	23	25	19	6	2	143	.250	.332	.378	.252	23	44-OF 101
1998	Philadel	NL	493	151	28	6	18	86	94	80	20	11	353	.306	.409	.497	.311	95	141-OF 101
1999	*Philadel*	*NL*	*465*	*131*	*22*	*6*	*13*	*66*	*74*	*63*	*20*	*10*	*344*	*.282*	*.371*	*.439*	*.285*	*74*	

I'm sure the Devil Rays are happy with the way this one turned out. Of course, they do have the great Mike Kelly, so I'm sure they don't miss Abreu and his .400 OBA one bit. Given the Phils' current roster, Abreu should be leading off or hitting second, so that he could be on base for Rolen and Estalella. Very good and likely to get better.

Marlon Anderson   2B   Bats L   Age 25

YEAR	TEAM	LGE	AB	H	DB	TP	HR	BB	R	RBI	SB	CS	OUT	BA	OBA	SA	EQA	EQR	DEFENSE
1996	Clearwtr	Fla	257	65	8	1	3	12	26	19	14	1	193	.253	.286	.327	.222	22	60-2B 109
1996	Reading	Eas	311	75	11	1	3	21	28	22	12	5	241	.241	.289	.312	.212	25	75-2B 115
1997	Reading	Eas	543	115	12	3	7	31	35	30	18	9	437	.212	.254	.284	.182	31	136-2B 99
1998	Scran-WB	Int	571	166	28	9	14	23	65	71	17	10	415	.291	.318	.445	.259	71	135-2B 95
1998	Philadel	NL	43	14	3	0	1	1	6	6	2	0	29	.326	.341	.465	.283	6	
1999	*Philadel*	*NL*	*582*	*160*	*24*	*6*	*11*	*26*	*64*	*60*	*25*	*9*	*431*	*.275*	*.306*	*.393*	*.246*	*65*	

Had a nice little season after years of totally unwarranted hype. Of course, he drew only 28 walks in over 600 plate appearances, so the hype still exceeds the reality. He'll start the year as the Phils' second baseman and spend the next several years as one of the game's more overrated players.

Alex Arias   IF   Bats R   Age 31

YEAR	TEAM	LGE	AB	H	DB	TP	HR	BB	R	RBI	SB	CS	OUT	BA	OBA	SA	EQA	EQR	DEFENSE	
1996	Florida	NL	225	63	12	2	3	18	26	25	2	0	162	.280	.333	.391	.254	26	35-3B 91	16-SS 108
1997	Florida	NL	93	23	2	0	1	13	10	8	0	1	71	.247	.340	.301	.228	9	18-3B 69	
1998	Philadel	NL	132	38	5	0	2	14	16	15	2	0	94	.288	.356	.371	.261	16	29-SS 98	
1999	*Philadel*	*NL*	*128*	*35*	*2*	*0*	*3*	*13*	*13*	*15*	*1*	*0*	*93*	*.273*	*.340*	*.359*	*.252*	*15*		

To their credit, the Phils hung with their slumping future (Relaford) even as they crept into the wild-card race. Arias had a fine season in a role he can handle, but is overtaxed in anything more. Signed a two-year, $1 million deal in October.

Rico Brogna   1B   Bats L   Age 29

YEAR	TEAM	LGE	AB	H	DB	TP	HR	BB	R	RBI	SB	CS	OUT	BA	OBA	SA	EQA	EQR	DEFENSE
1996	NY Mets	NL	190	50	9	1	8	20	22	27	0	0	140	.263	.333	.447	.268	26	42-1B 96
1997	Philadel	NL	542	136	31	1	22	36	58	66	11	3	409	.251	.298	.434	.250	64	142-1B 111
1998	Philadel	NL	560	146	34	3	21	52	67	73	7	8	422	.261	.324	.445	.260	73	144-1B 114
1999	*Philadel*	*NL*	*518*	*134*	*27*	*1*	*22*	*44*	*59*	*69*	*8*	*4*	*388*	*.259*	*.317*	*.442*	*.262*	*68*	

One of the countless players who had 100 RBI this season without doing anything particularly special. Brogna's trick? He hit behind Scott (.391 OBA) Rolen. His OPS was lower than Brad Fullmer's, Travis Lee's, and Sean Casey's, and only 30 points above Derrek Lee's; you could make an argument he was the worst everyday 1b in the NL. With Burrell on the bullet train to the Vet, now is the time to trade Brogna before people realize he's a pumpkin.

Pat Burrell   1B   Bats R   Age 22

YEAR	TEAM	LGE	AB	H	DB	TP	HR	BB	R	RBI	SB	CS	OUT	BA	OBA	SA	EQA	EQR	DEFENSE
1998	Clearwtr	Fla	132	36	4	0	6	22	20	20	1	0	96	.273	.377	.439	.287	21	20-1B 97
1999	*Philadel*	*NL*	*106*	*34*	*4*	*1*	*6*	*19*	*19*	*22*	*1*	*0*	*72*	*.321*	*.424*	*.547*	*.333*	*23*	

Could not have had a better debut. Obviously, 159 PA is a small sample, but he posted a .952 OPS in a pitcher's league, with lots of walks and power. Signed quickly, showed a great work ethic than won raves from his coaches. Should start '99 in Double-A, ticketed for the Show in 2000.

Shayne Carnes   1B   Bats L   Age 22

YEAR	TEAM	LGE	AB	H	DB	TP	HR	BB	R	RBI	SB	CS	OUT	BA	OBA	SA	EQA	EQR	DEFENSE
1998	Batavia	NYP	241	64	4	0	5	20	21	25	1	0	177	.266	.322	.344	.235	24	58-1B 104
1999	*Philadel*	*NL*	*189*	*59*	*5*	*0*	*5*	*16*	*22*	*27*	*1*	*0*	*130*	*.312*	*.366*	*.418*	*.278*	*26*	

A '98 draft pick, 24th round out of Alabama-Birmingham, where he holds the single-season and career HR records. Wins points for intensity, quickness, intelligence, and power. A projection at this point, but the team thinks he could advance quickly.

Andy Dominique   3B   Bats R   Age 23

YEAR	TEAM	LGE	AB	H	DB	TP	HR	BB	R	RBI	SB	CS	OUT	BA	OBA	SA	EQA	EQR	DEFENSE
1997	Batavia	NYP	279	61	5	0	8	19	19	22	2	1	219	.219	.268	.323	.201	20	63-1B 91
1998	Piedmont	SAL	518	119	13	0	16	47	42	50	0	1	400	.230	.294	.347	.221	46	42-3B 82 33-1B 103
1999	*Philadel*	*NL*	*405*	*101*	*9*	*0*	*13*	*32*	*34*	*45*	*1*	*1*	*305*	*.249*	*.304*	*.368*	*.235*	*41*	

A man without a position until the end of the season, when he started playing his old college position, third base. Sent to the Instructional League to learn to catch, which makes his bat significantly more interesting.

Nate Espy   1B   Bats R   Age 21

YEAR	TEAM	LGE	AB	H	DB	TP	HR	BB	R	RBI	SB	CS	OUT	BA	OBA	SA	EQA	EQR	DEFENSE
1998	Martnsvl	App	225	59	6	0	7	33	28	28	1	1	167	.262	.357	.382	.262	29	56-1B 94
1999	*Philadel*	*NL*	*180*	*56*	*7*	*0*	*8*	*28*	*28*	*32*	*1*	*1*	*125*	*.311*	*.404*	*.483*	*.309*	*33*	

Eighteenth-rounder out of Lurleen High School in Pensacola, Espy was apparently a bit older than his classmates—20, to be exact. His debut was very promising: good plate discipline, has a solid swing, good power and projects to improve. Needs to do it again in A-ball before the Phils start playing musical positions.

Bobby Estalella   C   Bats R   Age 24

YEAR	TEAM	LGE	AB	H	DB	TP	HR	BB	R	RBI	SB	CS	OUT	BA	OBA	SA	EQA	EQR	DEFENSE
1996	Reading	Eas	364	80	9	1	18	57	41	47	2	2	286	.220	.325	.398	.252	46	
1997	Scran-WB	Int	434	99	20	0	17	50	46	50	3	0	335	.228	.308	.392	.244	49	
1997	Philadel	NL	29	10	1	0	4	7	7	9	0	0	19	.345	.472	.793	.394	9	
1998	Scran-WB	Int	242	67	11	1	15	60	46	48	0	0	175	.277	.421	.517	.322	51	68-C 99
1998	Philadel	NL	164	30	6	1	8	14	11	16	0	0	134	.183	.247	.378	.210	14	44-C 89
1999	*Philadel*	*NL*	*419*	*104*	*20*	*1*	*22*	*64*	*56*	*65*	*1*	*0*	*315*	*.248*	*.348*	*.458*	*.280*	*65*	

Really struggled in the majors, but that's an anomaly. He may not ever hit .300, but he'll draw walks, hit for power, and provide above-average defense. Went down over the winter with a torn rotator cuff, requiring major surgery. The best guess is that he'll be able to play by late May, which at best means he could be ready for the majors by August.

Doug Glanville   OF   Bats R   Age 28

YEAR	TEAM	LGE	AB	H	DB	TP	HR	BB	R	RBI	SB	CS	OUT	BA	OBA	SA	EQA	EQR	DEFENSE
1996	Iowa	AA	371	102	17	2	2	15	36	30	13	9	278	.275	.303	.348	.225	33	86-OF 102
1996	ChiCubs	NL	82	19	4	1	1	4	7	6	2	0	63	.232	.267	.341	.212	7	22-OF 85
1997	ChiCubs	NL	468	135	22	4	4	27	53	46	15	11	344	.288	.327	.378	.244	51	129-OF 92
1998	Philadel	NL	672	183	26	7	9	46	78	65	24	7	496	.272	.319	.372	.244	73	159-OF 111
1999	*Philadel*	*NL*	*569*	*159*	*26*	*4*	*8*	*31*	*64*	*57*	*22*	*9*	*419*	*.279*	*.317*	*.381*	*.247*	*63*	

Once he faded from his hot start, it became readily apparent that Glanville was not and will not be any sort of solution at the top of the lineup. On a team with a strong offense, he's a great cog to plug in at #8 and throw in center every day for stellar defense; on the Phils, he's an out machine in a lineup full of them. He'll drop to the 2-hole this year.

Kevin Jordan   UT   Bats R   Age 29

YEAR	TEAM	LGE	AB	H	DB	TP	HR	BB	R	RBI	SB	CS	OUT	BA	OBA	SA	EQA	EQR	DEFENSE
1996	Philadel	NL	131	37	7	0	4	6	14	16	2	1	95	.282	.314	.427	.254	15	28-1B 89
1997	Philadel	NL	176	46	5	0	7	5	13	20	0	1	131	.261	.282	.409	.231	17	15-1B 99
1998	Philadel	NL	248	67	7	0	4	9	18	23	0	0	181	.270	.296	.347	.220	21	
1999	*Philadel*	*NL*	*302*	*71*	*10*	*1*	*5*	*9*	*18*	*22*	*1*	*1*	*232*	*.235*	*.257*	*.325*	*.196*	*20*	

Moderately useful spare part who could get needlessly expensive by hitting arbitration.

Harry Kiil   OF   Bats R   Age 25

YEAR	TEAM	LGE	AB	H	DB	TP	HR	BB	R	RBI	SB	CS	OUT	BA	OBA	SA	EQA	EQR	DEFENSE
1997	Piedmont	SAL	268	49	5	1	5	27	17	14	5	2	221	.183	.258	.265	.178	15	77-OF 92
1998	Clearwtr	Fla	400	83	13	1	8	50	38	30	9	4	321	.207	.296	.305	.213	34	100-OF 84
1999	*Philadel*	*NL*	*350*	*76*	*12*	*1*	*8*	*40*	*35*	*30*	*10*	*3*	*277*	*.217*	*.297*	*.326*	*.225*	*33*	

Signed as an amateur free agent in May '97, Kiil had a strong sophomore season, drawing 70 walks and showing good power and speed. He's 24 this year, so he needs to keep racing up the ladder, but he should have a good future as at least a fourth outfielder in the majors.

Mark Lewis — 2B — Bats R — Age 29

YEAR	TEAM	LGE	AB	H	DB	TP	HR	BB	R	RBI	SB	CS	OUT	BA	OBA	SA	EQA	EQR	DEFENSE	
1996	Detroit	AL	535	139	30	3	10	39	56	55	6	1	397	.260	.310	.383	.241	57	143-2B 94	
1997	San Fran	NL	341	91	15	5	11	25	37	44	2	2	252	.267	.317	.437	.257	42	50-3B 98	17-2B 97
1998	Philadel	NL	514	125	19	2	10	51	49	49	3	3	392	.243	.312	.346	.230	50	139-2B 102	
1999	*Philadel*	*NL*	*455*	*116*	*18*	*2*	*11*	*40*	*45*	*50*	*4*	*2*	*341*	*.255*	*.315*	*.376*	*.243*	*50*		

A disastrous signing, not to mention a superfluous one with David Doster and Kevin Jordan around. The team wanted Desi Relaford to partner with a veteran so he could learn from him in the field; unfortunately, it looks like he learned from Lewis at the plate as well.

Mike Lieberthal — C — Bats R — Age 27

YEAR	TEAM	LGE	AB	H	DB	TP	HR	BB	R	RBI	SB	CS	OUT	BA	OBA	SA	EQA	EQR	DEFENSE
1996	Philadel	NL	166	42	5	0	8	11	15	22	0	0	124	.253	.299	.428	.247	19	
1997	Philadel	NL	454	111	21	1	22	47	50	61	2	4	347	.244	.315	.441	.256	58	
1998	Philadel	NL	310	77	15	3	8	19	28	33	2	1	234	.248	.292	.394	.234	31	82-C 102
1999	*Philadel*	*NL*	*320*	*81*	*15*	*1*	*12*	*24*	*32*	*39*	*3*	*2*	*241*	*.253*	*.305*	*.419*	*.250*	*38*	

Felled by a strange pelvic injury that wiped out nearly two months of his season, and threw the Phils' grand plans for a trade into flux. He wasn't having much of a season to begin with, and at this point, the team should give Estalella the everyday job. With Estalella's injury, the Phillies are saying Lieberthal will be fine by spring training, so it looks like he'll be the starter.

Wendell Magee — OF — Bats R — Age 26

YEAR	TEAM	LGE	AB	H	DB	TP	HR	BB	R	RBI	SB	CS	OUT	BA	OBA	SA	EQA	EQR	DEFENSE
1997	Scran-WB	Int	294	68	14	1	9	26	27	30	4	6	232	.231	.294	.378	.228	29	79-OF 104
1997	Philadel	NL	115	23	2	0	2	9	5	6	0	4	96	.200	.258	.270	.164	5	32-OF 115
1998	Scran-WB	Int	505	134	22	4	18	38	53	65	5	6	377	.265	.317	.432	.254	61	124-OF 102
1998	Philadel	NL	74	21	6	1	1	8	11	9	0	0	53	.284	.354	.432	.273	10	
1999	*Philadel*	*NL*	*509*	*136*	*26*	*2*	*17*	*40*	*56*	*65*	*7*	*5*	*378*	*.267*	*.321*	*.426*	*.258*	*64*	

Wasn't awful in a September trial, but wasn't good enough to convince the team he's the solution in left for '99. The Phils acquired Ron Gant, which would relegate Magee to a bench role he can handle, or put him on the trading block. Punished lefties in Triple-A this year (.630 SLG).

Billy McMillon — OF — Bats L — Age 27

YEAR	TEAM	LGE	AB	H	DB	TP	HR	BB	R	RBI	SB	CS	OUT	BA	OBA	SA	EQA	EQR	DEFENSE
1996	Charlott	Int	336	104	19	1	14	34	49	55	4	2	234	.310	.373	.497	.296	56	89-OF 88
1997	Charlott	Int	202	49	9	0	7	26	27	23	6	0	153	.243	.329	.391	.258	26	51-OF 91
1997	Scran-WB	Int	92	25	5	1	3	10	13	12	2	0	67	.272	.343	.446	.275	13	22-OF 108
1997	Philadel	NL	72	21	4	1	2	6	10	10	2	1	52	.292	.346	.458	.276	10	16-OF 107
1998	Scran-WB	Int	267	61	10	1	9	28	27	28	4	2	208	.228	.302	.375	.235	28	68-OF 94
1999	*Philadel*	*NL*	*309*	*81*	*17*	*1*	*11*	*33*	*38*	*41*	*6*	*2*	*230*	*.262*	*.333*	*.430*	*.267*	*42*	

Never got a chance, and at this point, never will. Could still help about a dozen teams in the majors currently floundering for left field help, like Montreal. He and Magee would have made a cheap, adequate platoon in left if the Phils hadn't traded for Ron Gant.

Jason Michaels — OF — Bats R — Age 23

YEAR	TEAM	LGE	AB	H	DB	TP	HR	BB	R	RBI	SB	CS	OUT	BA	OBA	SA	EQA	EQR	DEFENSE
1998	Batavia	NYP	242	49	4	1	6	27	18	19	2	1	194	.202	.283	.302	.203	18	62-OF 88
1999	*Philadel*	*NL*	*187*	*44*	*3*	*0*	*7*	*19*	*16*	*21*	*1*	*1*	*144*	*.235*	*.306*	*.364*	*.235*	*19*	

Exploded in August, hitting all of his 11 homers and raising his average over 100 points after tightening his swing and adjusting to the wooden bat. His arm doesn't look like it's enough to work in right, so he'll have to hit to be a major league LF. Could be a breakout prospect in '99.

Desi Relaford   SS   Bats B   Age 25

YEAR	TEAM	LGE	AB	H	DB	TP	HR	BB	R	RBI	SB	CS	OUT	BA	OBA	SA	EQA	EQR	DEFENSE
1996	Tacoma	PCL	315	59	6	0	5	22	16	14	9	5	261	.187	.240	.254	.162	14	74-2B 113
1996	Scran-WB	Int	84	18	2	1	1	8	9	5	5	1	67	.214	.283	.298	.212	7	19-SS 105
1997	Scran-WB	Int	517	135	29	3	9	37	63	49	24	7	389	.261	.310	.381	.245	58	130-SS 102
1998	Philadel	NL	490	118	25	3	5	36	44	39	9	6	378	.241	.293	.335	.217	42	133-SS 93
1999	*Philadel*	*NL*	*483*	*120*	*28*	*2*	*6*	*34*	*51*	*41*	*17*	*6*	*369*	*.248*	*.298*	*.352*	*.231*	*47*	

In April, he was a star; after that, he was Desi Relaford. Okay, that's disingenuous; his slump reached epic proportions and clearly destroyed his confidence. I think he could be an adequate all-around solution at short on a team with offense in the right places.

Scott Rolen   3B   Bats R   Age 24

YEAR	TEAM	LGE	AB	H	DB	TP	HR	BB	R	RBI	SB	CS	OUT	BA	OBA	SA	EQA	EQR	DEFENSE
1996	Reading	Eas	226	74	16	0	8	29	40	37	6	2	154	.327	.404	.504	.313	42	60-3B 95
1996	Scran-WB	Int	166	41	9	0	3	26	21	17	3	4	129	.247	.349	.355	.248	20	42-3B 102
1996	Philadel	NL	130	33	4	0	5	14	13	16	0	2	99	.254	.326	.400	.247	15	37-3B 81
1997	Philadel	NL	562	159	35	3	22	79	89	85	13	6	409	.283	.371	.473	.291	93	154-3B 108
1998	Philadel	NL	596	169	42	4	32	96	104	104	15	8	435	.284	.383	.529	.307	113	159-3B 102
1999	*Philadel*	*NL*	*575*	*170*	*39*	*3*	*29*	*86*	*99*	*101*	*18*	*8*	*413*	*.296*	*.387*	*.525*	*.311*	*111*	

The player you build around. Advanced across the board this year, and is now just slightly behind Chipper Jones among NL third basemen. He, Abreu, and Estalella could form a nice lineup core for the next half-dozen years if the Phils play the rest of their cards right.

Jimmy Rollins   SS   Bats B   Age 20

YEAR	TEAM	LGE	AB	H	DB	TP	HR	BB	R	RBI	SB	CS	OUT	BA	OBA	SA	EQA	EQR	DEFENSE
1996	Martnsvl	App	176	30	1	0	1	19	7	6	3	2	148	.170	.251	.193	.140	5	49-SS 87
1997	Piedmont	SAL	568	142	16	4	7	48	61	46	21	5	431	.250	.308	.329	.229	54	136-SS 96
1998	Clearwtr	Fla	492	102	11	5	6	35	33	29	11	5	395	.207	.260	.287	.186	30	118-SS 96
1999	*Philadel*	*NL*	*463*	*116*	*12*	*3*	*7*	*33*	*45*	*40*	*16*	*5*	*352*	*.251*	*.300*	*.335*	*.228*	*44*	

Has his defenders, and to be fair, he was battling a pair of injuries while being among the FSL's youngest. Still, the year was completely miserable with the bat, and Rollins's glove, while good, will not make him a major-league regular. Except perhaps with the Mets.

Kevin Sefcik   IF   Bats R   Age 28

YEAR	TEAM	LGE	AB	H	DB	TP	HR	BB	R	RBI	SB	CS	OUT	BA	OBA	SA	EQA	EQR	DEFENSE	
1996	Scran-WB	Int	176	49	6	3	0	14	22	15	7	2	129	.278	.332	.347	.244	19	43-SS 99	
1996	Philadel	NL	116	33	5	3	0	10	15	12	3	0	83	.284	.341	.379	.258	14	19-3B 84	14-SS 116
1997	Scran-WB	Int	122	36	8	1	1	7	15	13	4	1	87	.295	.333	.402	.259	15		
1997	Philadel	NL	119	32	1	0	3	4	8	12	1	2	89	.269	.293	.353	.217	10	16-2B 98	
1998	Philadel	NL	168	52	7	2	3	25	28	23	4	2	118	.310	.399	.429	.293	27	38-OF 109	
1999	*Philadel*	*NL*	*207*	*59*	*10*	*2*	*3*	*19*	*26*	*24*	*6*	*2*	*150*	*.285*	*.345*	*.396*	*.264*	*27*		

Can't ask for much more from your 25th man. Don't expect a repeat, although if he hangs on to most of the OBA, he's still helping the team.

Reggie Taylor   OF   Bats L   Age 22

YEAR	TEAM	LGE	AB	H	DB	TP	HR	BB	R	RBI	SB	CS	OUT	BA	OBA	SA	EQA	EQR	DEFENSE
1996	Piedmont	SAL	512	124	15	3	1	22	37	29	15	9	397	.242	.273	.289	.192	32	130-OF 96
1997	Clearwtr	Fla	543	118	12	2	12	28	38	36	20	12	437	.217	.256	.313	.193	36	131-OF 111
1998	Reading	Eas	334	85	12	4	5	11	32	27	16	7	256	.254	.278	.359	.221	29	77-OF 97
1999	*Philadel*	*NL*	*415*	*105*	*12*	*4*	*8*	*15*	*38*	*36*	*19*	*8*	*318*	*.253*	*.279*	*.359*	*.224*	*38*	

Would make a great wide receiver or track star, but is an all-around lousy ballplayer: no power, no plate discipline, poor baserunning skills. Burrell and Valent should bury him quickly.

Eric Valent   RF   Bats L   Age 22

YEAR	TEAM	LGE	AB	H	DB	TP	HR	BB	R	RBI	SB	CS	OUT	BA	OBA	SA	EQA	EQR	DEFENSE
1998	Piedmont	SAL	89	34	5	0	6	12	17	22	0	0	55	.382	.455	.640	.363	22	19-OF 97
1998	Clearwtr	Fla	125	29	3	1	4	13	12	13	0	1	97	.232	.304	.368	.231	12	30-OF 96
1999	*Philadel*	*NL*	*171*	*59*	*7*	*0*	*11*	*19*	*26*	*37*	*0*	*1*	*113*	*.345*	*.411*	*.579*	*.331*	*36*	

A great start, to say the least. Gets good reviews for his glove and arm, which distinguishes him from Burrell and Espy. Kept his plate discipline in a short stint at Clearwater, and projects to hit the majors by late 2000.

PITCHERS (Averages: 4.00 ERA, 9.00 H/9, 1.00 HR/9, 3.00 BB/9, 6.00 K/9, 1.00 KWH)

Matt Beech   Throws L   Age 27

YEAR	TEAM	LGE	IP	H	ER	HR	BB	K	ERA	W	L	H/9	HR/9	BB/9	K/9	KWH	PERA
1996	Reading	Eas	129.0	137	63	16	34	97	4.40	6	8	9.56	1.12	2.37	6.77	1.51	4.12
1996	Philadel	NL	41.7	52	29	9	10	30	6.26	1	4	11.23	1.94	2.16	6.48	1.30	5.62
1997	Philadel	NL	138.7	155	74	26	52	108	4.80	6	9	10.06	1.69	3.38	7.01	1.09	5.00
1998	Philadel	NL	122.7	132	69	20	58	105	5.06	5	9	9.68	1.47	4.26	7.70	1.08	4.77

Was turning into quite a pitcher when his arm fell off. Back-to-back 170-inning seasons didn't help, but he was 24 in the first of those two, and doesn't throw a lot of pitches, so I wouldn't blame it all on arm abuse. Didn't rely on velocity before Tommy John surgery, so his chances of returning to form are relatively high.

Joel Bennett   Throws R   Age 29

YEAR	TEAM	LGE	IP	H	ER	HR	BB	K	ERA	W	L	H/9	HR/9	BB/9	K/9	KWH	PERA
1996	Bowie	Eas	51.3	49	26	6	18	33	4.56	3	3	8.59	1.05	3.16	5.79	0.93	3.68
1997	Bowie	Eas	104.0	120	55	12	42	99	4.76	5	7	10.38	1.04	3.63	8.57	1.46	4.67
1998	Rochestr	Int	95.0	121	51	8	37	76	4.83	4	7	11.46	0.76	3.51	7.20	0.97	5.02
1998	Scran-WB	Int	44.7	62	31	6	25	27	6.25	1	4	12.49	1.21	5.04	5.44	0.35	6.04

Could obviously help a team that needs a fifth starter to soak up innings, a category which included at least the post-August 1 Phillies.

Brett Black   Throws R   Age 24

YEAR	TEAM	LGE	IP	H	ER	HR	BB	K	ERA	W	L	H/9	HR/9	BB/9	K/9	KWH	PERA
1997	Batavia	NYP	36.7	41	13	3	3	33	3.19	2	2	10.06	0.74	0.74	8.10	6.64	3.93
1998	Piedmont	SAL	59.0	84	28	6	11	46	4.27	3	4	12.81	0.92	1.68	7.02	1.72	5.49

Control-artist closer who has now walked 10 batters in 107 innings as a professional, with 154 strikeouts. The Phils need to promote pitchers more aggressively. Black still hasn't hit the FSL because Kyle Kawabata was Clearwater's closer, and there's no value to developing "closers."

Ricky Bottalico   Throws R   Age 29

YEAR	TEAM	LGE	IP	H	ER	HR	BB	K	ERA	W	L	H/9	HR/9	BB/9	K/9	KWH	PERA
1996	Philadel	NL	68.3	50	22	7	22	66	2.90	5	3	6.59	0.92	2.90	8.69	2.97	2.37
1997	Philadel	NL	75.3	73	28	7	38	80	3.35	5	3	8.72	0.84	4.54	9.56	1.73	3.82
1998	Philadel	NL	45.3	58	28	7	23	25	5.56	2	3	11.51	1.39	4.57	4.96	0.35	5.76

A disaster of a season for Bottalico and the Phillies, who had an opportunity to trade a closer in the midst of a pennant race and wound up keeping all three (Leiter, Bottalico, Gomes) and winning nothing. Bottalico is allegedly 100%, although he never showed it in September. He's now the Cardinals' problem.

Ryan Brannan — Throws R — Age 24

YEAR	TEAM	LGE	IP	H	ER	HR	BB	K	ERA	W	L	H/9	HR/9	BB/9	K/9	KWH	PERA
1997	Clearwtr	Fla	26.0	26	3	0	10	18	1.04	3	0	9.00	0.00	3.46	6.23	0.93	3.12
1997	Reading	Eas	51.7	61	18	2	18	31	3.14	4	2	10.63	0.35	3.14	5.40	0.66	4.18
1998	Reading	Eas	55.3	63	31	6	29	32	5.04	2	4	10.25	0.98	4.72	5.20	0.42	4.72
1998	Scran-WB	Int	16.3	23	17	0	12	10	9.37	0	2	12.67	0.00	6.61	5.51	0.27	5.51

Took two huge steps back, as Brannan was smacked out of Triple-A and struggled with his control and command at Double-A. Also awful in the AFL, walking nearly a batter per inning. He's pitching like he's hiding an injury, which is not terribly surprising in this organization.

Rob Burger — Throws R — Age 23

YEAR	TEAM	LGE	IP	H	ER	HR	BB	K	ERA	W	L	H/9	HR/9	BB/9	K/9	KWH	PERA
1996	Piedmont	SAL	143.3	207	109	14	69	104	6.84	4	12	13.00	0.88	4.33	6.53	0.57	5.90
1997	Clearwtr	Fla	155.0	171	90	11	105	117	5.23	6	11	9.93	0.64	6.10	6.79	0.57	4.53
1998	Reading	Eas	116.0	135	85	23	68	80	6.59	3	10	10.47	1.78	5.28	6.21	0.52	5.51

When it comes to young arms, the Phils are serial killers. Burger threw over 320 innings at ages 20 and 21, and he positively imploded at Reading, losing his rotation spot in the process. The reduced workload might do him some good, but at this point, I'm not optimistic about him ever fulfilling his once-great potential.

Paul Byrd — Throws R — Age 28

YEAR	TEAM	LGE	IP	H	ER	HR	BB	K	ERA	W	L	H/9	HR/9	BB/9	K/9	KWH	PERA
1996	NY Mets	NL	46.0	53	21	8	20	28	4.11	2	3	10.37	1.57	3.91	5.48	0.55	5.09
1997	Richmond	Int	16.0	17	7	2	1	10	3.94	1	1	9.56	1.12	0.56	5.62	4.41	3.94
1997	Atlanta	NL	52.7	53	33	7	26	33	5.64	2	4	9.06	1.20	4.44	5.64	0.59	4.27
1998	Richmond	Int	100.0	108	45	8	36	65	4.05	5	6	9.72	0.72	3.24	5.85	0.81	4.05
1998	Philadel	NL	56.3	42	14	7	15	35	2.24	5	1	6.71	1.12	2.40	5.59	1.46	2.40

So Terry Francona keeps claiming that you "can't find a 20-game winner" on waivers, which is only true if your offense is incapable of creating a 20-game winner. Byrd may not be an ace, but he is and has always been a capable pitcher who can be a #4 starter for the Phils next year. They can use one of those. Terry: You'd be amazed what you can find on waivers. Just ask Omar Daal.

David Coggin — Throws R — Age 22

YEAR	TEAM	LGE	IP	H	ER	HR	BB	K	ERA	W	L	H/9	HR/9	BB/9	K/9	KWH	PERA
1996	Piedmont	SAL	150.0	244	128	18	52	78	7.68	4	13	14.64	1.08	3.12	4.68	0.36	6.66
1997	Clearwtr	Fla	148.7	207	110	17	98	84	6.66	5	12	12.53	1.03	5.93	5.09	0.26	5.99
1998	Reading	Eas	109.3	119	55	9	61	51	4.53	5	7	9.80	0.74	5.02	4.20	0.27	4.36

Missed May with an inflamed right shoulder, which is probably the result of abuse worse than that of Burger: 325 innings at ages 20 and 21. Like Burger, Coggin pitched like he was hurt this year. He was less advanced than Burger to begin with, so his outlook is much more dim. The Phils really have too many of these guys, and not enough healthy starter prospects.

Robert Dodd — Throws L — Age 26

YEAR	TEAM	LGE	IP	H	ER	HR	BB	K	ERA	W	L	H/9	HR/9	BB/9	K/9	KWH	PERA
1996	Reading	Eas	42.7	50	21	4	25	28	4.43	2	3	10.55	0.84	5.27	5.91	0.47	4.85
1996	Scran-WB	Int	20.0	36	19	4	9	11	8.55	0	2	16.20	1.80	4.05	4.95	0.28	8.10
1997	Reading	Eas	78.0	75	30	7	21	68	3.46	5	4	8.65	0.81	2.42	7.85	2.20	3.35
1998	Scran-WB	Int	40.0	44	16	5	18	32	3.60	2	2	9.90	1.12	4.05	7.20	0.97	4.50

Flourished on a move to the pen in '97 at Reading, should be ready for a major-league short relief role later this year.

Geoff Geary   Throws R   Age 22

YEAR	TEAM	LGE	IP	H	ER	HR	BB	K	ERA	W	L	H/9	HR/9	BB/9	K/9	KWH	PERA
1998	Batavia	NYP	87.0	117	28	9	18	55	2.90	7	3	12.10	0.93	1.86	5.69	1.08	5.28

Coaches rave about this kid, who slipped to the fifth round because of his size and a fastball that tops out around 91. Extremely poised and confident, with a work ethic the Phils love. Threw over 200 innings this year between college and the pros; that's a Phillie prospect if I ever saw one.

Wayne Gomes   Throws R   Age 26

YEAR	TEAM	LGE	IP	H	ER	HR	BB	K	ERA	W	L	H/9	HR/9	BB/9	K/9	KWH	PERA
1996	Reading	Eas	64.3	67	36	7	49	62	5.04	3	4	9.37	0.98	6.85	8.67	0.88	4.62
1997	Scran-WB	Int	37.7	36	10	2	22	29	2.39	3	1	8.60	0.48	5.26	6.93	0.80	3.58
1997	Philadel	NL	43.3	48	24	4	22	22	4.98	2	3	9.97	0.83	4.57	4.57	0.34	4.57
1998	Philadel	NL	96.3	98	43	9	33	80	4.02	5	6	9.16	0.84	3.08	7.47	1.48	3.83

Had a season I didn't think he had in him. Scuffled at the end, possibly a result of his highest-ever relief workload; if he's not hiding an injury and the Phils are willing to be patient, he should steal Brantley's closer job by midsummer.

Mike Grace   Throws R   Age 29

YEAR	TEAM	LGE	IP	H	ER	HR	BB	K	ERA	W	L	H/9	HR/9	BB/9	K/9	KWH	PERA
1996	Philadel	NL	80.3	75	30	9	15	44	3.36	5	4	8.40	1.01	1.68	4.93	1.29	3.25
1997	Scran-WB	Int	72.0	99	46	1	27	41	5.75	3	5	12.38	0.12	3.38	5.12	0.47	4.87
1997	Philadel	NL	39.0	33	15	4	9	23	3.46	2	2	7.62	0.92	2.08	5.31	1.34	2.77
1998	Scran-WB	Int	69.7	109	47	7	18	30	6.07	2	6	14.08	0.90	2.33	3.88	0.34	6.20
1998	Philadel	NL	93.7	121	54	10	28	43	5.19	4	6	11.63	0.96	2.69	4.13	0.41	5.09

When the two moons of Deneb IV are in perfect alignment with Charon, and Jupiter is in the second quadrant of Sagittarius, Grace will be healthy for about 200 pitches. I didn't say he'd be "good," only that he'd be healthy.

Tyler Green   Throws R   Age 29

YEAR	TEAM	LGE	IP	H	ER	HR	BB	K	ERA	W	L	H/9	HR/9	BB/9	K/9	KWH	PERA
1995	Philadel	NL	148.0	164	75	15	63	80	4.56	7	9	9.97	0.91	3.83	4.86	0.46	4.44
1997	Scran-WB	Int	68.7	96	57	13	29	30	7.47	2	6	12.58	1.70	3.80	3.93	0.24	6.42
1997	Philadel	NL	78.0	77	46	9	41	52	5.31	3	6	8.88	1.04	4.73	6.00	0.64	4.04
1998	Philadel	NL	165.3	149	86	23	79	105	4.68	8	10	8.11	1.25	4.30	5.72	0.70	3.70

Ruined before he even turned pro, slagged like so many other Wichita State alums. He's missed time with elbow or shoulder woes in five of his eight pro seasons, and all that the surgery and rehab have done is destroyed any trace of the pitcher the Phils drafted. Like Grace, the Phils can't—and shouldn't—include him in their plans.

Jason Kershner   Throws L   Age 22

YEAR	TEAM	LGE	IP	H	ER	HR	BB	K	ERA	W	L	H/9	HR/9	BB/9	K/9	KWH	PERA
1996	Piedmont	SAL	149.3	242	118	18	68	95	7.11	4	13	14.58	1.08	4.10	5.73	0.41	6.75
1997	Clearwtr	Fla	94.3	144	56	12	24	39	5.34	4	6	13.74	1.14	2.29	3.72	0.33	6.30
1998	Clearwtr	Fla	90.0	133	62	10	28	48	6.20	3	7	13.30	1.00	2.80	4.80	0.46	6.00

Cause: Pitched 168 innings in 1996 at age 20. Effect: has missed time with elbow woes in each of the last two seasons. He also hasn't been the same pitcher, allowing over a hit an inning with a drastic falloff in his strikeout rate. Must be a coincidence.

Randy Knoll   Throws R   Age 22

YEAR	TEAM	LGE	IP	H	ER	HR	BB	K	ERA	W	L	H/9	HR/9	BB/9	K/9	KWH	PERA
1996	Piedmont	SAL	136.3	175	74	11	35	86	4.89	6	9	11.55	0.73	2.31	5.68	0.91	4.82
1996	Clearwtr	Fla	19.7	22	10	3	2	15	4.58	1	1	10.07	1.37	0.92	6.86	3.83	4.58
1997	Clearwtr	Fla	29.0	42	21	0	8	15	6.52	1	2	13.03	0.00	2.48	4.66	0.50	4.97
1998	Clearwtr	Fla	19.7	38	17	7	12	11	7.78	0	2	17.39	3.20	5.49	5.03	0.20	10.07

Pitched 171.2 innings in 1996 at age 19; has pitched 50.2 innings in two years since. Must be a coincidence.

Mark Leiter　　　　Throws R　　　Age 36

YEAR	TEAM	LGE	IP	H	ER	HR	BB	K	ERA	W	L	H/9	HR/9	BB/9	K/9	KWH	PERA
1996	Montreal	NL	71.3	71	31	12	18	42	3.91	4	4	8.96	1.51	2.27	5.30	1.04	4.04
1996	San Fran	NL	139.7	155	81	25	48	107	5.22	6	10	9.99	1.61	3.09	6.89	1.15	4.83
1997	Philadel	NL	185.3	226	120	26	58	133	5.83	7	14	10.97	1.26	2.82	6.46	1.01	5.05
1998	Philadel	NL	92.0	70	32	8	44	78	3.13	6	4	6.85	0.78	4.30	7.63	1.48	2.64

They should have traded him during the season. Yes, they were almost in the wild-card race, but there were four teams ahead of them, their pitching staff was a mess, and the payoff of winning the wild card was certain obliteration by Atlanta or Houston. Of course, hindsight tells us the Phils folded with Leiter's help, so it's all very easy to say now. I see no reason Leiter couldn't serve as a setup man or righty-killing specialist for Seattle in '99 now that he's been traded for Paul Spoljaric.

Carlton Loewer　　　　Throws R　　　Age 25

YEAR	TEAM	LGE	IP	H	ER	HR	BB	K	ERA	W	L	H/9	HR/9	BB/9	K/9	KWH	PERA
1996	Reading	Eas	170.3	225	115	25	57	96	6.08	6	13	11.89	1.32	3.01	5.07	0.54	5.60
1997	Scran-WB	Int	182.3	214	110	20	44	124	5.43	7	13	10.56	0.99	2.17	6.12	1.22	4.54
1998	Scran-WB	Int	91.0	99	33	5	20	57	3.26	6	4	9.79	0.49	1.98	5.64	1.23	3.76
1998	Philadel	NL	127.3	160	77	18	36	54	5.44	5	9	11.31	1.27	2.54	3.82	0.38	5.23

Developed a two-seam fastball this year, and used it to finally get over the Triple-A hump. Not a potential ace, but a #3 or #4 innings eater, with three or four very good years in him. Great command and poise, and poor taste in representation.

Calvin Maduro　　　　Throws R　　　Age 24

YEAR	TEAM	LGE	IP	H	ER	HR	BB	K	ERA	W	L	H/9	HR/9	BB/9	K/9	KWH	PERA
1996	Bowie	Eas	120.3	137	52	8	35	68	3.89	7	6	10.25	0.60	2.62	5.09	0.72	4.11
1996	Rochestr	Int	43.7	53	22	8	18	35	4.53	2	3	10.92	1.65	3.71	7.21	0.96	5.56
1996	Philadel	NL	15.3	14	6	1	2	10	3.52	1	1	8.22	0.59	1.17	5.87	2.68	2.93
1997	Scran-WB	Int	79.3	80	44	11	52	43	4.99	4	5	9.08	1.25	5.90	4.88	0.33	4.54
1997	Philadel	NL	72.0	89	55	13	37	28	6.88	2	6	11.13	1.62	4.63	3.50	0.18	5.62
1998	Scran-WB	Int	172.3	233	117	27	61	101	6.11	6	13	12.17	1.41	3.19	5.27	0.54	5.85

Slagged in '96, and he's never been the same, although his workload has remained too high. The premature stint in Philly in '97 didn't help. I still think he could take a half-year off and come back as a very good, if not dominating, reliever. Released.

Ryan Nye　　　　Throws R　　　Age 26

YEAR	TEAM	LGE	IP	H	ER	HR	BB	K	ERA	W	L	H/9	HR/9	BB/9	K/9	KWH	PERA
1996	Reading	Eas	85.7	92	42	9	30	70	4.41	5	5	9.67	0.95	3.15	7.35	1.33	4.20
1996	Scran-WB	Int	80.7	107	48	10	30	45	5.36	3	6	11.94	1.12	3.35	5.02	0.47	5.47
1997	Scran-WB	Int	107.3	130	66	20	29	68	5.53	4	8	10.90	1.68	2.43	5.70	0.92	5.28
1998	Scran-WB	Int	133.0	163	77	8	48	92	5.21	6	9	11.03	0.54	3.25	6.23	0.81	4.60

A hittable one-pitch pony. Should be converted to relief at this point, since the slider isn't enough to get him through five or six innings.

Yorkis Perez　　　　Throws L　　　Age 31

YEAR	TEAM	LGE	IP	H	ER	HR	BB	K	ERA	W	L	H/9	HR/9	BB/9	K/9	KWH	PERA
1996	Florida	NL	48.7	55	25	2	29	42	4.62	2	3	10.17	0.37	5.36	7.77	0.83	4.44
1997	Binghmtn	Eas	26.7	19	4	1	12	27	1.35	3	0	6.41	0.34	4.05	9.11	2.40	2.02
1997	Norfolk	Int	20.0	26	9	2	7	18	4.05	1	1	11.70	0.90	3.15	8.10	1.34	5.40
1997	NY Mets	NL	8.7	17	8	2	3	6	8.31	0	1	17.65	2.08	3.12	6.23	0.53	9.35
1998	Philadel	NL	53.3	43	21	3	23	39	3.54	3	3	7.26	0.51	3.88	6.58	1.15	2.70

He and Spradlin were probably the best day-in, day-out relievers the Phils had. Didn't just murder lefties (.602 OPS) this year, but was pretty effective against righties as well (.663), and to Francona's credit, he used Perez against both instead of playing LaRussa games.

Mark Portugal   **Throws R**   **Age 36**

YEAR	TEAM	LGE	IP	H	ER	HR	BB	K	ERA	W	L	H/9	HR/9	BB/9	K/9	KWH	PERA
1996	Cincnnti	NL	158.7	151	68	20	40	84	3.86	9	9	8.57	1.13	2.27	4.76	0.88	3.52
1997	Philadel	NL	13.7	18	7	0	5	2	4.61	1	1	11.85	0.00	3.29	1.32	0.03	4.61
1998	Philadel	NL	171.0	191	78	26	29	96	4.11	9	10	10.05	1.37	1.53	5.05	1.25	4.47

Another body the Phils might have traded, although it would probably have sent Schilling completely postal. Better pitchers are available on the waiver wire, and at this point, Portugal's knees should be a major cause for concern for any suitor.

Mark Rutherford   **Throws R**   **Age 24**

YEAR	TEAM	LGE	IP	H	ER	HR	BB	K	ERA	W	L	H/9	HR/9	BB/9	K/9	KWH	PERA
1997	Batavia	NYP	10.0	17	9	0	5	6	8.10	0	1	15.30	0.00	4.50	5.40	0.32	6.30
1997	Piedmont	SAL	53.0	64	25	5	12	28	4.25	3	3	10.87	0.85	2.04	4.75	0.77	4.58
1998	Clearwtr	Fla	111.0	126	49	13	23	48	3.97	6	6	10.22	1.05	1.86	3.89	0.60	4.38

A '97 12th rounder who's had three things as a pro: good success, low strikeout rates, and arm troubles. Shut down for the fall and winter with a twinge in his arm, whatever that means.

Ken Ryan   **Throws R**   **Age 30**

YEAR	TEAM	LGE	IP	H	ER	HR	BB	K	ERA	W	L	H/9	HR/9	BB/9	K/9	KWH	PERA
1996	Philadel	NL	89.7	77	29	4	43	64	2.91	7	3	7.73	0.40	4.32	6.42	0.93	3.01
1997	Philadel	NL	21.0	34	22	6	12	9	9.43	0	2	14.57	2.57	5.14	3.86	0.15	8.14
1998	Philadel	NL	23.7	23	11	1	19	15	4.18	1	2	8.75	0.38	7.23	5.70	0.39	3.80

If he's truly 100%, he could turn into a very nice surprise for the Phils this year, and to their credit, they have been extremely patient. Control was an issue pre-surgery, and still is, but he has solved it once before.

Curt Schilling   **Throws R**   **Age 32**

YEAR	TEAM	LGE	IP	H	ER	HR	BB	K	ERA	W	L	H/9	HR/9	BB/9	K/9	KWH	PERA
1996	Philadel	NL	184.3	157	62	16	47	163	3.03	13	7	7.67	0.78	2.29	7.96	2.70	2.78
1997	Philadel	NL	256.7	215	86	26	52	284	3.02	18	11	7.54	0.91	1.82	9.96	5.41	2.70
1998	Philadel	NL	275.7	242	88	22	56	276	2.87	20	11	7.90	0.72	1.83	9.01	4.22	2.78

Worth twice what they pay him, as he's now thrown over 700 innings of sub-3 DT-ERA ball over the last three years. Signing one more established starter may have the ripple effect of reducing Schilling's innings if the bullpen's workload drops on the days he isn't pitching, and given Schilling's history, that should be at the front of Wade's mind this winter.

Anthony Shumaker   **Throws L**   **Age 26**

YEAR	TEAM	LGE	IP	H	ER	HR	BB	K	ERA	W	L	H/9	HR/9	BB/9	K/9	KWH	PERA
1996	Piedmont	SAL	28.7	31	13	3	13	26	4.08	1	2	9.73	0.94	4.08	8.16	1.26	4.40
1996	Clearwtr	Fla	27.0	55	23	2	14	18	7.67	1	2	18.33	0.67	4.67	6.00	0.32	7.67
1997	Clearwtr	Fla	65.7	92	32	1	23	50	4.39	3	4	12.61	0.14	3.15	6.85	0.89	4.93
1998	Reading	Eas	159.0	188	84	21	49	89	4.75	7	11	10.64	1.19	2.77	5.04	0.64	4.81

Moved into Reading's rotation this year, and didn't really miss a beat, posting a sub-3 ERA as a starter. If he keeps it up at Triple-A, you'll start reading about this crafty lefty the Phils have in the minors. Not as good as the Wolf/Burger types, but his arm is in significantly better shape.

Jerry Spradlin   **Throws R**   **Age 32**

YEAR	TEAM	LGE	IP	H	ER	HR	BB	K	ERA	W	L	H/9	HR/9	BB/9	K/9	KWH	PERA
1996	Indianap	AmA	96.0	116	56	14	27	62	5.25	4	7	10.88	1.31	2.53	5.81	0.92	4.97
1997	Philadel	NL	82.7	89	40	10	25	60	4.35	4	5	9.69	1.09	2.72	6.53	1.21	4.25
1998	Philadel	NL	83.3	65	30	9	18	70	3.24	5	4	7.02	0.97	1.94	7.56	3.14	2.38

A revelation, and still one of the more unheralded setup men in the NL. Guys like this really do grow on trees. Traded to Cleveland for Chad Ogea, where he should be in middle relief.

Garrett Stephenson   Throws R   Age 27

YEAR	TEAM	LGE	IP	H	ER	HR	BB	K	ERA	W	L	H/9	HR/9	BB/9	K/9	KWH	PERA
1996	Rochestr	Int	121.0	133	60	13	45	72	4.46	6	7	9.89	0.97	3.35	5.36	0.65	4.31
1997	Scran-WB	Int	27.7	33	19	6	11	20	6.18	1	2	10.73	1.95	3.58	6.51	0.83	5.53
1997	Philadel	NL	117.3	109	41	11	35	72	3.14	8	5	8.36	0.84	2.68	5.52	1.02	3.30
1998	Scran-WB	Int	68.0	98	53	14	16	37	7.01	2	6	12.97	1.85	2.12	4.90	0.65	6.49
1998	Philadel	NL	24.3	34	21	3	18	16	7.77	1	2	12.58	1.11	6.66	5.92	0.31	6.29

His big mouth strikes again. Thrown into the Bottalico fiasco, so he's the Cardinals' headache now. Not a good bet to ever do anything like his '97 again.

Evan Thomas   Throws R   Age 25

YEAR	TEAM	LGE	IP	H	ER	HR	BB	K	ERA	W	L	H/9	HR/9	BB/9	K/9	KWH	PERA
1996	Batavia	NYP	70.7	103	49	6	30	40	6.24	2	6	13.12	0.76	3.82	5.09	0.39	5.86
1997	Clearwtr	Fla	80.0	92	37	9	28	62	4.16	4	5	10.35	1.01	3.15	6.97	1.12	4.61
1997	Reading	Eas	82.0	115	49	9	31	64	5.38	3	6	12.62	0.99	3.40	7.02	0.86	5.71
1998	Reading	Eas	154.3	211	68	13	47	97	3.97	9	8	12.30	0.76	2.74	5.66	0.71	5.31

As you can see, had problems with hittability in Reading. Still worth watching, but his stock has dropped. Severely overused in August, Thomas left the Arizona Fall League early with arm soreness, but supposedly was pain-free when he reported to the Instructional League.

Tomoyuki Uchiyama   Throws R   Age 30

YEAR	TEAM	LGE	IP	H	ER	HR	BB	K	ERA	W	L	H/9	HR/9	BB/9	K/9	KWH	PERA
1998	Reading	Eas	113.3	160	62	13	54	67	4.92	5	8	12.71	1.03	4.29	5.32	0.39	5.88

So, is it in the Japanese rule book that you have to have a contortionist windup to pitch in their majors? He twists himself around far enough to put his right hand in his left front pocket, which doesn't seem healthy. Of more immediate relevance is his age (29) and the fact that he fared poorly against Double-A hitters.

Adam Walker   Throws L   Age 23

YEAR	TEAM	LGE	IP	H	ER	HR	BB	K	ERA	W	L	H/9	HR/9	BB/9	K/9	KWH	PERA
1997	Martnsvl	App	23.3	52	40	1	16	14	15.43	0	3	20.06	0.39	6.17	5.40	0.18	8.10
1998	Piedmont	SAL	77.7	86	28	2	27	65	3.24	5	4	9.97	0.23	3.13	7.53	1.36	3.82

Winless in his first season as a pro, Walker went 9-0 this year around a three-month DL stint with an inflamed left elbow. If the injury isn't serious, it may have saved him from being worked to death. Here's hoping he gets past the Clearwater graveyard quickly, as his low-90s fastball and great control mark him a prospect.

Mike Welch   Throws R   Age 26

YEAR	TEAM	LGE	IP	H	ER	HR	BB	K	ERA	W	L	H/9	HR/9	BB/9	K/9	KWH	PERA
1996	Binghmtn	Eas	49.7	67	31	4	10	41	5.62	2	4	12.14	0.72	1.81	7.43	1.88	5.07
1997	Norfolk	Int	51.3	58	19	6	15	28	3.33	4	2	10.17	1.05	2.63	4.91	0.68	4.38
1998	Scran-WB	Int	70.3	114	59	5	16	25	7.55	2	6	14.59	0.64	2.05	3.20	0.26	6.14
1998	Philadel	NL	21.3	28	17	7	6	14	7.17	0	2	11.81	2.95	2.53	5.91	0.87	6.75

Tweener who may be sacrificed for a few weeks if the bullpen is swamped with work again next year.

Ken Westmoreland   Throws R   Age 24

YEAR	TEAM	LGE	IP	H	ER	HR	BB	K	ERA	W	L	H/9	HR/9	BB/9	K/9	KWH	PERA
1998	Batavia	NYP	32.7	54	17	1	8	19	4.68	2	2	14.88	0.28	2.20	5.23	0.63	5.79
1998	Piedmont	SAL	28.3	42	16	4	23	22	5.08	1	2	13.34	1.27	7.31	6.99	0.38	6.67

University of Alabama star who signed late, but pitched well in five starts at Piedmont, despite a worrisome walk rate. Just a name to add to the "watch him" list.

Darrin Winston   Throws L   Age 32

YEAR	TEAM	LGE	IP	H	ER	HR	BB	K	ERA	W	L	H/9	HR/9	BB/9	K/9	KWH	PERA
1995	Calgary	PCL	49.7	62	29	9	19	35	5.26	2	4	11.23	1.63	3.44	6.34	0.78	5.62
1997	Scran-WB	Int	85.3	90	40	9	35	49	4.22	4	5	9.49	0.95	3.69	5.17	0.57	4.22
1997	Philadel	NL	12.0	9	7	4	2	7	5.25	0	1	6.75	3.00	1.50	5.25	2.04	3.00
1998	Scran-WB	Int	21.7	48	29	6	10	14	12.05	0	2	19.94	2.49	4.15	5.82	0.31	10.38
1998	Philadel	NL	25.7	33	16	7	5	10	5.61	1	2	11.57	2.45	1.75	3.51	0.45	6.31

A great story, but lefties posted an OPS over 1.000 against him in 46 plate appearances this year, and the Phils are not at a point where a situational righty-getting lefty is a pressing need.

Randy Wolf   Throws L   Age 22

YEAR	TEAM	LGE	IP	H	ER	HR	BB	K	ERA	W	L	H/9	HR/9	BB/9	K/9	KWH	PERA
1997	Batavia	NYP	36.3	45	12	2	10	31	2.97	3	1	11.15	0.50	2.48	7.68	1.60	4.46
1998	Reading	Eas	25.0	17	4	0	3	25	1.44	3	0	6.12	0.00	1.08	9.00	9.19	1.08
1998	Scran-WB	Int	143.7	183	84	16	43	99	5.26	6	10	11.46	1.00	2.69	6.20	0.93	5.07

Überprospect who faced a dangerously high workload at SWB this year. He reached Triple-A after just 11 pro starts, and should be a very good pitcher if the Phils haven't ruined him; if they have, the entire organization should be canned, because they just wasted their best pitching prospect this decade. Wolf sports a good fastball and great change-up, works quickly, and throws strikes.

SNWLP	PHILADELPHIA PHILLIES											Park Effect: +1.6%
PITCHER	GS	IP	R	SNW	SNL	SNPCT	W	L	RA	APW	SNVA	SNWAR
Beech, M.	21	117.0	78	5.7	8.8	.391	3	9	6.00	-1.57	-1.46	-0.49
Byrd, P.	8	55.0	16	4.2	1.6	.719	5	2	2.62	1.27	1.30	1.72
Grace, M.	15	82.7	58	3.5	6.8	.337	4	7	6.31	-1.39	-1.59	-0.91
Green, T.	27	159.3	97	8.0	10.8	.425	6	11	5.48	-1.24	-1.55	-0.01
Loewer, C.	21	122.7	86	5.8	9.1	.388	7	8	6.31	-2.06	-1.64	-0.56
Portugal, M.	26	166.3	88	9.6	9.6	.500	10	5	4.76	-0.00	-0.13	1.44
Ryan, K.	1	3.0	1	0.2	0.1	.611	0	0	3.00	0.06	0.06	0.06
Schilling, C.	35	268.7	101	17.6	10.1	.634	15	14	3.38	3.99	3.45	5.80
Stephenson, G.	6	23.0	24	0.8	3.0	.206	0	2	9.39	-1.15	-1.03	-0.83
Welch, M.	2	6.3	16	0.0	1.7	.007	0	2	22.74	-1.23	-0.84	-0.73
TOTALS	162	1004.0	565	55.3	61.8	.472	50	60	5.06	-3.32	-3.44	5.49

Déjà vu. Not much has changed with the Phillies starting staff over the past year. The only difference is who played the role of token Non-Schilling-Phillie-With-Value. In 1997, it was Garrett Stephenson. In 1998, it was a Mark Portugal/Paul Byrd amalgam. Other than that, you're pretty much seeing the same thing: Schilling, surrounded by a bunch of injuries, disappointments, and stiffs. The end results were the same, too: 1997's staff ranked 20th in the majors, 1998's ranked 19th. In no way is Curt Schilling a lock for the Hall of Fame, or even likely at this point, but it is at least conceivable that he will be a candidate by the time he retires. If so, it's likely that he'll be a marginal candidate, only because right now he's running behind a bunch of other contemporary pitchers (Clemens, Maddux, Cone, Glavine, Johnson, Smoltz, and Brown). Schilling would need all the help he can get, especially with those wins and losses. As you can see above, he didn't get that help last year, and in fact he hasn't gotten it throughout his entire Phillies career. According to the Support-Neutral numbers, he's been the majors' tenth-best starting pitcher over the past seven years, but he's also the sixth unluckiest. I suppose it was nice to see Schilling show loyalty to the Phillies by re-signing with them last year, but he may eventually regret voluntarily spending the prime of his career with a bad team.

Pitchers Abuse Points

PITCHER	AGE	GS	PAP	PAP/S	AAW	MAX	115+	130+
Beech, Matt	26	21	137	6.52	13.05	124	3	0
Byrd, Paul	27	8	52	6.50	11.92	118	1	0
Grace, Mike	28	15	12	0.80	1.33	105	0	0
Green, Tyler	28	27	115	4.26	7.10	120	2	0
Loewer, Carlton	24	21	71	3.38	7.89	117	2	0
Portugal, Mark	35	26	59	2.27	2.27	123	1	0
Schilling, Curt	31	35	1331	38.03	44.37	147	26	7
Stephenson, Garrett	26	6	4	0.67	1.33	102	0	0
TOTAL		162	1781	10.99	14.61	147	35	7
RANKING (NL)			3	3	5		3	2-T

The Phillies rank at the top of the league in Pitcher Abuse Points, but you can pin that solely on Curt Schilling. He picked up 75% of the team's PAPs on his own; only Pedro Martinez garnered a higher percentage of his team's PAPs. Terry Francona did an excellent job handling everyone else on the staff, so I'll just focus on Schilling. In my opinion, Schilling is a serious injury risk, and Francona should have used more restraint the last two seasons. I know it must be difficult, given how well he has pitched and how Schilling himself looks like he wants to kill somebody if he's asked to come out of a game. But Schilling has been down this road before: he was one of the best pitchers in the league in 1992, but threw ten complete games despite not getting into the rotation until late May. After another hard season of labor in 1993, Schilling missed a whole year to injury and took two more years getting back to his current form. I would be very surprised if he gets 300 K's again this season. If the Phillies want to build their staff around him, they can't wear him out in the process.

Chicago Cubs

As TV networks and programming shift and blend into a bodacious mélange that give cultural critics like Robert Bork sweaty nightmares, the Cubs entered the '98 season needing to mix things up. They needed to make people remember they existed for more than just suds, sun and fun. TribCorp was so unexcited about its baseball programming that it transferred a third of the schedule to cable to make way for such teen angst-and-gore classics as "Dawson's Creek" and "Buffy the Vampire Slayer." For the Cubs, mediocrity was tolerable as long as Harry was singing and Ryno was waving at fans and groundballs. But in 1997, the Cubs couldn't even accomplish these middle-of-the-road goals. The '97 team had unmasked the previous seasons to be little better than the irrelevant bad teams that Brian McRae had said they were. Desperate to avoid further public relations disasters, the Cubs dug up the lost city of gold and handed Sammy Sosa the keys, while Ryno rode into the sunset, again, with greater ceremony. The management troika of Andy MacPhail, Ed Lynch, and Jim Riggleman was on the spot. They'd put in four years on a signature piece of WGN programming, but ratings were sinking, their jobs were on the line, and all they really had to show for their troubles was the introduction of Beanie Baby days.

Its times like this that great leaders set their jaws, grit their teeth, and tell their team that nothing less than greatness will do. The men, tired of the years of humiliating defeat, rally 'round and mount an epic campaign that sets the world on ear and inspires generations as they prove that underdogs have their days. This being real life and not a script, the Cubs mumbled a prayer, ginned up the car for a run down to Sears, and caught wildcard fever. If I were Oliver Stone, I'd film a grainy scene of Lynch, Riggleman, and MacPhail masterminding one of the most cynical seasons ever foisted on baseball fans in Chicago. To say they put one over on the Windy City would be an understatement. In response to their instincts for self-preservation, the troika

would contend on the cheap, opening up the purse strings just enough to build a better today, just enough that they'd be around to see tomorrow.

Is that worth it? I can understand any management team making sacrifices to preserve themselves and their plans for the future. But then you have to ask whether the Cubs have a plan. If they do, it's either more secret than the plot to frame O.J., or it just possibly doesn't technically actually exist. There is very little doubt that MacPhail, Lynch, and Riggleman are baseball men of the highest pedigree, and fairly or not, well-regarded professionals. Where they've foundered is on what George Bush called "the vision thing."

Isn't trying to win a plan? What's wrong with trying to win? Absolutely nothing. There are two pretty well-proven methods to build a winning team. You can build a winner to win right now; the Marlins and the Padres are good recent examples of teams going for broke with veteran-laden teams. If that doesn't appeal to you, you can take a few years to build a team to win year after year; the Braves and Yankees are obviously the reigning examples nowadays, but the Astros have muscled into their company pretty quickly. The Indians have had good success so far by combining elements of both approaches, starting off with a great pair of hitters in their prime, adding a new group of veterans every year, and taking their chances.

Even in the Cubs' limited tradition of victory, they have one example of each of these kinds of teams. The division-winning '84 Cubs were an old, veteran team built to win that year, and Dallas Green spared nothing to make it happen. As we know, fortune didn't smile on them. The average age of the lineup was over 30, and the average age of the rotation was just under 30. A team depending on Ron Cey and Keith Moreland and Gary Matthews at the same time isn't a team built for tomorrow. It's to Green's credit that he seized the Cubs' narrow window of opportunity and added Rick Sutcliffe and Dennis Eckersley, because he was in a division with two

Cubs Prospectus

1998 record: 90-73; Second place, NL Central; National League wild card; Lost to Atlanta Braves in Division Series, 3-0

Pythagorean W/L: 85-77

Runs scored: 831 (3rd in NL)

Runs allowed: 792 (11th in NL)

Team EQA: .267 (6th in NL)

Park: Wrigley Field (good hitters')

1998: Some unexpected performances and some luck carried an average team to the post-season.

1999: The Cubs are facing a steep offensive falloff, making them unlikely to contend.

teams with more staying power: Whitey Herzog's Cardinals and Davey Johnson's then-precocious Mets, the teams that would split the division title for the next four years.

By contrast, the division-winning '89 Cubs were an interesting mix of promising young players and good veterans, and after '89, they looked like they still had some of the pieces of a team that could compete into the future. The only old regulars in the lineup were Andre Dawson and Vance Law, and they had four regulars who were 25 or younger: Jerome Walton, Dwight Smith, Mark Grace, and Damon Berryhill (yes, not all of them turned out too well, but that's another story). The average age was just a sliver over 27. The rotation was older (almost 29), but the ace was some 23-year-old named Maddux. That team was good enough to take advantage of Davey Johnson's first season where his Mets didn't win 90 games. The next year, the Pirates started taking advantage of their long-term planning to put together a three-year division title run, while the '89 Cubs squandered their opportunity.

But if you can state that there are two very general patterns in terms of the contenders you build, what about this year's Cubs? The '98 Cubs don't fit into either group of winners. They don't have a good young core of talent to start building something to last, and they didn't go for broke to make a push with what they did have. Ed Lynch made some thoughtful additions in the off-season, adding Jeff Blauser, Mickey Morandini, and Henry Rodriguez, which makes them look like an old, go-for-broke team. But as the summer wore on, it became clear they weren't going for broke in terms of trying to win. They'd been built to compete with the Mets and the Giants, and designed to be around the fourth- or sixth-best National League team. In a league where the distance between the top three and the rest of the league is a yawning chasm, the goal was the wild card. The Cubs didn't have to study the standings or the rosters of the Padres, Astros, and Braves particularly hard to know that if they wanted to compete with those teams, they'd have to do something dramatic if they wanted to be competitive if they actually reached the postseason.

Instead, as the wild card chase "heated up," they focused on beating the Mets, fueled by such inspired acquisitions as Matt Karchner, Mike Morgan, and Gary Gaetti. The Cubs correctly identified what they had to trade (high draft-pick pitching, almost entirely at A-ball), and sort of identified what they needed (relief pitching, starting pitching, a bat at third and/or catcher). They could have helped themselves become a team that could play with the big boys, and if there's a way to do it without subsequently looking terrible, trading young pitchers is a great way to do it. Mostly that's because young pitchers as a group endure casualty rates

similar to those National Geographic videos about baby sea turtles hatching and trying to make it to the sea. Trade them, and a good number are going to get killed off on somebody else's watch. But the Cubs took their asset (young minor league pitchers), and got . . . Matt Karchner? You wouldn't pick Matt Karchner or Felix Heredia in the first round, yet that's effectively what the Cubs did by sending off Jon Garland and Todd Noel. At best, they were sensible enough to claim Glenallen Hill on waivers, and cheap enough to spite themselves and wait eleven days between Gary Gaetti's designation for assignment and the point he was a free agent. They may have made moves that served notice that they knew they had problems, but they'd done nothing in terms of actually solving any of them.

I'm not arguing against aiming for the wild card spot in general; the key is making sure that it isn't your end destination. Although the Marlins took advantage of the existence of the wild card to win the World Series in '97, what was important was that they had also gone out of their way to build a team that could go toe-to-toe with the Braves in a short series. The '98 Cubs weren't that kind of team. They were a team built to save their leadership by being just barely good enough to say they'd won a booby prize, the right to be squashed by one of the three good teams in the league. Of course, it was a lucrative booby prize, with fans flocking and ratings soaring and jobs saved, but a booby prize nonetheless.

Having invested so much effort into saving themselves, the management trio is going to have to demonstrate that there was a reason to keep them around. It's that "vision thing" again. At least by his public pronouncements, Jim Riggleman doesn't seem to get it. He's saying the Cubs should re-sign Gaetti and keep the current team together, but what happens to that lineup when Sammy Sosa doesn't hit 66 home runs, or Mickey Morandini isn't having the best year he's going to ever have? Does a team good enough to be a speed bump for the great teams in '98 fall as far as fifth or sixth in the NL Central? It's tougher to judge MacPhail and Lynch; in terms of major league personnel decisions, they're generally frugal, cautious, and easily satisfied. In terms of minor league player development, although the Cubs don't have much more than Kerry Wood to point to with pride, the system is much better off than it was five years ago. Much credit here needs to go to Jim Hendry and David Wilder, but it also reflects well on Lynch and MacPhail. What we need to take away from '98 is that the Cubs made a play at contention without building a team that could contend, and that they didn't capitalize on their opportunity. With this group of players, that opportunity isn't going to come again, which means disappointment in 1999.

HITTERS (Averages: BA .260/ OBA .330/ SA .420, EQA .260)

Dennis Abreu   SS   Bats R   Age 21

YEAR	TEAM	LGE	AB	H	DB	TP	HR	BB	R	RBI	SB	CS	OUT	BA	OBA	SA	EQA	EQR	DEFENSE	
1997	Rockford	Mid	482	132	13	2	1	35	49	37	18	14	364	.274	.323	.315	.224	43	96-SS 90	30-2B 86
1998	Daytona	Fla	525	108	15	2	2	27	26	21	10	7	424	.206	.245	.253	.160	22	124-SS 94	
1999	*ChiCubs*	*NL*	*482*	*123*	*14*	*2*	*1*	*27*	*42*	*32*	*18*	*10*	*369*	*.255*	*.295*	*.299*	*.207*	*36*		

Bobby Abreu's kid brother, Dennis is still very raw. He's especially erratic in the field. Nevertheless, he's fast and makes contact, so the Venezuelan is the best shortstop prospect in the organization. A good year and a half away from being rumored for the major league job.

Manny Alexander   SS/2B   Bats R   Age 28

YEAR	TEAM	LGE	AB	H	DB	TP	HR	BB	R	RBI	SB	CS	OUT	BA	OBA	SA	EQA	EQR	DEFENSE	
1995	Baltimor	AL	239	56	9	1	3	19	24	17	11	5	188	.234	.291	.318	.215	20	67-2B 87	
1997	NY Mets	NL	148	36	9	3	2	10	20	13	10	0	112	.243	.291	.385	.246	17	17-SS 112	17-2B 103
1997	ChiCubs	NL	98	27	3	1	1	8	10	10	2	1	72	.276	.330	.357	.243	10	22-SS 110	
1998	ChiCubs	NL	263	60	8	1	6	19	21	22	4	1	204	.228	.280	.335	.213	21	28-SS 93	
1999	*ChiCubs*	*NL*	*231*	*55*	*10*	*2*	*4*	*15*	*21*	*20*	*7*	*2*	*178*	*.238*	*.285*	*.351*	*.221*	*21*		

No longer bitching about not playing every day, which shows that even Manny learns his limitations. The decision to have him DH on June 27 against Jose Rosado is exactly the sort of thing that makes interleague play pathetic, but on a smaller scale, just another reason why more Cubs fans should wonder why they carried two left-handed-hitting backup catchers.

Jeff Blauser   SS   Bats R   Age 33

YEAR	TEAM	LGE	AB	H	DB	TP	HR	BB	R	RBI	SB	CS	OUT	BA	OBA	SA	EQA	EQR	DEFENSE
1995	Atlanta	NL	427	87	15	2	12	59	42	38	6	5	345	.204	.300	.333	.222	40	112-SS 100
1996	Atlanta	NL	264	63	13	1	10	40	36	33	5	0	201	.239	.339	.409	.265	36	67-SS 93
1997	Atlanta	NL	520	160	30	4	18	73	84	85	4	1	361	.308	.393	.485	.303	92	133-SS 95
1998	ChiCubs	NL	360	79	9	3	5	62	41	31	2	2	283	.219	.334	.303	.231	36	100-SS 94
1999	*ChiCubs*	*NL*	*382*	*100*	*17*	*2*	*9*	*62*	*53*	*48*	*4*	*1*	*283*	*.262*	*.365*	*.387*	*.268*	*53*	

I admired Blauser for his unwillingness just to blame the elbow injury he struggled with all season, but things got so bad Riggleman considered replacing Blauser with His Mannyness in June. Riggleman failed to use Blauser to best advantage by not using him for what he was able contribute, getting on base. His defensive limitations will never go away, so while I like his chances of matching his projection, it's just as well that '99 is the last year he's under contract.

Brant Brown   OF/1B   Bats L   Age 28

YEAR	TEAM	LGE	AB	H	DB	TP	HR	BB	R	RBI	SB	CS	OUT	BA	OBA	SA	EQA	EQR	DEFENSE
1996	Iowa	AA	342	95	19	2	7	20	37	38	6	5	252	.278	.318	.406	.248	39	92-1B 101
1997	Iowa	AA	257	71	13	2	11	27	34	38	6	5	191	.276	.345	.471	.276	38	45-OF 84
1997	ChiCubs	NL	135	30	6	1	5	8	12	13	2	1	106	.222	.266	.393	.223	12	19-OF 106
1998	ChiCubs	NL	346	101	16	7	15	32	46	57	4	6	251	.292	.352	.509	.286	55	79-OF 100
1999	*ChiCubs*	*NL*	*377*	*108*	*18*	*5*	*17*	*30*	*47*	*60*	*7*	*6*	*275*	*.286*	*.339*	*.496*	*.278*	*56*	

Not really a center fielder, he lines up deeper than even the ill-fated Jerome Walton, with a tendency to forget to call people off. It was a nice season, but few things were more disgraceful than Riggleman's failure to take responsibility for using a bad outfielder (Brown) as a defensive replacement for a worse one (Glenallen Hill) on that fateful afternoon in Milwaukee. The manager made the decision, and after Brown failed to make the play, Riggs subsequently went out of his way to play anyone else other than Brant Brown, including using Orlando Merced as a defensive replacement in the playoff game against the Giants. I hope Brown can shrug it off and play.

Roosevelt Brown   OF   Bats L   Age 23

YEAR	TEAM	LGE	AB	H	DB	TP	HR	BB	R	RBI	SB	CS	OUT	BA	OBA	SA	EQA	EQR	DEFENSE
1996	Macon	SAL	418	103	10	0	15	24	36	43	9	6	321	.246	.287	.378	.228	40	81-OF 93
1997	KaneCnty	Mid	212	42	4	0	3	17	11	11	2	2	172	.198	.258	.259	.170	10	56-OF 83
1997	Brevard	Fla	114	25	4	1	1	7	7	7	0	2	91	.219	.264	.298	.183	7	29-OF 88
1998	Daytona	Fla	238	68	8	2	7	18	26	31	1	1	171	.286	.336	.424	.262	30	58-OF 90
1998	WestTenn	Sou	158	37	4	0	6	9	12	16	2	1	122	.234	.275	.373	.221	14	33-OF 91
1999	*ChiCubs*	*NL*	*386*	*106*	*14*	*1*	*14*	*23*	*38*	*50*	*5*	*3*	*283*	*.275*	*.315*	*.425*	*.252*	*45*	

Snagged from the Marlins in the minor league portion of the Rule 5 draft (he was the prize from the Braves in the Pendleton deal). Brown has been a minor steal, and dominated the '98 Arizona Fall League. Lacks great speed or defensive skills, so he'll go as far as his bat speed can take him.

Pat Cline   C   Bats R   Age 24

YEAR	TEAM	LGE	AB	H	DB	TP	HR	BB	R	RBI	SB	CS	OUT	BA	OBA	SA	EQA	EQR	DEFENSE
1996	Daytona	Fla	432	107	13	1	17	46	47	53	6	1	326	.248	.320	.400	.252	52	
1997	Orlando	Sou	269	60	9	0	7	22	21	23	2	1	210	.223	.282	.335	.212	22	
1997	Iowa	AA	95	20	1	0	3	10	7	8	0	1	76	.211	.286	.316	.205	7	
1998	Iowa	PCL	415	105	16	1	11	34	40	44	2	2	312	.253	.310	.376	.237	43	124-C 89
1999	*ChiCubs*	*NL*	*371*	*94*	*11*	*0*	*12*	*30*	*35*	*42*	*3*	*1*	*278*	*.253*	*.309*	*.380*	*.239*	*39*	

The expectation was that working with Terry Kennedy at Iowa would make Cline better behind the plate. Although he improved, he's still not a good catcher, and at the plate, he gets overly pull-conscious. Despite these shortcomings, the Cubs need to turn to Cline over Servais.

Micah Franklin   Bats B   OF   Age 27

YEAR	TEAM	LGE	AB	H	DB	TP	HR	BB	R	RBI	SB	CS	OUT	BA	OBA	SA	EQA	EQR	DEFENSE
1996	Toledo	Int	178	39	6	1	6	25	19	19	2	1	140	.219	.315	.365	.240	20	50-OF 103
1996	Louisvil	AA	292	66	14	2	13	38	33	37	2	3	229	.226	.315	.421	.252	36	81-OF 101
1997	Louisvil	AA	328	65	8	1	9	44	29	27	2	0	263	.198	.293	.311	.214	28	88-OF 85
1998	Iowa	PCL	351	101	14	1	19	49	52	60	4	3	253	.288	.375	.496	.296	60	87-OF 89
1999	*ChiCubs*	*NL*	*385*	*102*	*18*	*1*	*19*	*51*	*51*	*60*	*4*	*2*	*285*	*.265*	*.351*	*.465*	*.279*	*59*	

Another year, another organization, another good season for Franklin. If a team's desperately in need of power from the left side, it can help itself quickly, easily, and cheaply by signing Franklin.

Gary Gaetti   3B   Bats R   Age 40

YEAR	TEAM	LGE	AB	H	DB	TP	HR	BB	R	RBI	SB	CS	OUT	BA	OBA	SA	EQA	EQR	DEFENSE	
1996	St Louis	NL	521	141	26	4	23	39	59	75	1	2	382	.271	.321	.468	.267	70	118-3B 101	
1997	St Louis	NL	501	125	20	1	19	40	50	59	6	3	379	.250	.305	.407	.245	56	120-3B 109	11-1B 89
1998	St Louis	NL	304	80	21	1	12	33	38	43	1	1	225	.263	.335	.457	.271	43	76-3B 98	
1998	ChiCubs	NL	124	40	9	0	8	12	20	25	0	0	84	.323	.382	.589	.321	24	32-3B 112	
1999	*ChiCubs*	*NL*	*443*	*108*	*23*	*1*	*15*	*40*	*44*	*52*	*1*	*1*	*336*	*.244*	*.306*	*.402*	*.243*	*49*		

Watching him play for the Cubs down the stretch was amazing, because it was almost like he was still the same player who shook the world in the '87 World Series. As much as it was fun to see him do what he did, I thinks it's hard to expect him to keep being productive at his age.

Mark Grace   1B   Bats L   Age 35

YEAR	TEAM	LGE	AB	H	DB	TP	HR	BB	R	RBI	SB	CS	OUT	BA	OBA	SA	EQA	EQR	DEFENSE
1996	ChiCubs	NL	544	175	34	2	10	65	82	79	1	3	372	.322	.394	.447	.293	86	138-1B 103
1997	ChiCubs	NL	548	167	31	4	13	90	89	83	1	4	385	.305	.403	.447	.297	92	148-1B 110
1998	ChiCubs	NL	591	182	39	3	18	95	98	95	4	8	417	.308	.404	.475	.302	105	156-1B 104
1999	*ChiCubs*	*NL*	*532*	*162*	*29*	*2*	*12*	*84*	*83*	*79*	*2*	*4*	*374*	*.305*	*.399*	*.434*	*.292*	*86*	

If he lasts around this level for another three years, he'll be in Keith Hernandez territory in terms of career numbers, and at that point, will belong in Keith Hernandez territory in terms of belonging in the Hall of Fame. In my opinion, neither of them belong, but the differences between the support for Hernandez and the potential support for Grace will be interesting to follow.

Jose Hernandez   INF   Bats R   Age 29

YEAR	TEAM	LGE	AB	H	DB	TP	HR	BB	R	RBI	SB	CS	OUT	BA	OBA	SA	EQA	EQR	DEFENSE	
1996	ChiCubs	NL	329	77	13	1	10	26	30	33	4	0	252	.234	.290	.371	.230	32	75-SS 95	22-3B 83
1997	ChiCubs	NL	181	47	9	4	7	15	20	25	1	5	139	.260	.316	.470	.258	23	25-3B 83	13-2B 88
1998	ChiCubs	NL	484	122	22	7	24	42	54	70	3	7	369	.252	.312	.475	.262	65	57-3B 109	35-SS 99
1999	*ChiCubs*	*NL*	*357*	*96*	*17*	*4*	*17*	*30*	*43*	*54*	*4*	*3*	*264*	*.269*	*.326*	*.482*	*.271*	*50*		

Finally given a chance to play everyday. He should probably play second against most lefties, and then split the rest of his time between third and short. My favorite Cub, and that's not just because his multi-positional lifestyle makes him a score-card inkspot waiting to happen.

Glenallen Hill   DH   Bats R   Age 34

YEAR	TEAM	LGE	AB	H	DB	TP	HR	BB	R	RBI	SB	CS	OUT	BA	OBA	SA	EQA	EQR	DEFENSE
1996	San Fran	NL	378	104	20	0	21	35	48	60	5	3	277	.275	.337	.495	.280	57	87-OF 91
1997	San Fran	NL	397	104	28	3	12	22	43	47	6	4	297	.262	.301	.438	.250	47	80-OF 94
1998	Seattle	AL	255	73	20	2	12	15	31	41	1	1	183	.286	.326	.522	.282	39	60-OF 88
1998	ChiCubs	NL	131	46	3	0	9	14	20	29	0	0	85	.351	.414	.580	.333	27	26-OF 104
1999	*ChiCubs*	*NL*	*385*	*110*	*24*	*1*	*18*	*27*	*47*	*60*	*4*	*2*	*277*	*.286*	*.333*	*.494*	*.277*	*56*	

Woody Woodward was flogged for waiving him, but how much value do corner outfielders with Hill's track record really have? He's not exactly a commodity. His skills, mashing lefties and popping an occasional homerun, aren't rare. He's fun to watch, sort of an anorexic Kevin Mitchell in terms of production and fielding adventures.

Tyler Houston   C/UT   Bats L   Age 28

YEAR	TEAM	LGE	AB	H	DB	TP	HR	BB	R	RBI	SB	CS	OUT	BA	OBA	SA	EQA	EQR	DEFENSE
1996	ChiCubs	NL	114	38	4	0	3	9	15	17	2	2	78	.333	.382	.447	.286	17	
1997	ChiCubs	NL	194	48	7	0	3	10	14	16	1	0	146	.247	.284	.330	.211	15	
1998	ChiCubs	NL	251	65	8	1	9	14	23	29	2	2	188	.259	.298	.406	.240	26	52-C 95
1999	*ChiCubs*	*NL*	*211*	*59*	*6*	*0*	*8*	*12*	*20*	*28*	*1*	*1*	*153*	*.280*	*.318*	*.422*	*.252*	*24*	

Houston isn't much of a catcher, but he's a handy bench player. Had a run-in with Craig Biggio during the season, where Houston had clearly had enough of Biggio's tedious stepping-in ceremony. Biggio didn't like getting lip from a scrub, and that sort of thing helps brew things up between two teams. This is how great rivalries get started, assuming the Cubs were a threat.

Robin Jennings   OF   Bats L   Age 27

YEAR	TEAM	LGE	AB	H	DB	TP	HR	BB	R	RBI	SB	CS	OUT	BA	OBA	SA	EQA	EQR	DEFENSE
1996	Iowa	AA	333	92	12	5	15	32	41	52	2	0	241	.276	.340	.477	.279	49	76-OF 94
1996	ChiCubs	NL	58	13	4	0	0	3	4	3	1	0	45	.224	.262	.293	.190	4	
1997	Iowa	AA	467	119	17	3	16	49	52	58	4	2	350	.255	.326	.407	.254	57	117-OF 87
1998	Iowa	PCL	294	61	14	1	10	28	26	27	3	3	236	.207	.276	.364	.218	26	72-OF 90
1999	*ChiCubs*	*NL*	*347*	*88*	*16*	*1*	*13*	*34*	*39*	*44*	*4*	*2*	*261*	*.254*	*.320*	*.418*	*.254*	*42*	

He's never going to get an opportunity. Although Jennings does several things well, he keeps getting hurt. He'd still make a good fourth or fifth outfielder: he has some power, get on base a little, and handle either outfield corner.

Lance Johnson   CF   Bats L   Age 35

YEAR	TEAM	LGE	AB	H	DB	TP	HR	BB	R	RBI	SB	CS	OUT	BA	OBA	SA	EQA	EQR	DEFENSE
1996	NY Mets	NL	689	237	33	20	11	38	117	98	45	14	465	.344	.378	.498	.302	117	151-OF 108
1997	NY Mets	NL	265	82	11	6	1	34	43	31	12	10	193	.309	.388	.408	.277	39	55-OF 116
1997	ChiCubs	NL	143	42	5	2	4	10	18	19	4	2	103	.294	.340	.441	.269	19	31-OF 105
1998	ChiCubs	NL	299	84	8	4	2	28	37	28	11	7	222	.281	.343	.355	.247	34	69-OF 100
1999	*ChiCubs*	*NL*	*353*	*105*	*11*	*7*	*4*	*30*	*48*	*41*	*15*	*7*	*255*	*.297*	*.352*	*.402*	*.265*	*46*	

He's definitely beginning to lose it in the field. Speed players tend to age well, so I can see him hanging around in the same way Willie McGee has. He just won't be as good at it as McGee has been, which considering McGee was the one who won an MVP award, makes sense.

Terrell Lowery   **CF**   **Bats R**   **Age 28**

YEAR	TEAM	LGE	AB	H	DB	TP	HR	BB	R	RBI	SB	CS	OUT	BA	OBA	SA	EQA	EQR	DEFENSE
1996	Binghmtn	Eas	212	46	7	2	4	34	25	19	4	3	169	.217	.325	.325	.233	22	49-OF 95
1996	Norfolk	Int	193	39	4	1	3	20	15	12	4	2	156	.202	.277	.280	.194	13	53-OF 98
1997	Iowa	AA	390	106	20	2	12	55	56	52	8	6	290	.272	.362	.426	.274	57	104-OF 102
1998	Iowa	PCL	241	60	7	1	8	23	25	27	4	2	183	.249	.314	.386	.244	27	60-OF 113
1999	*TampaBay*	*AL*	*325*	*84*	*12*	*1*	*12*	*42*	*43*	*43*	*6*	*4*	*245*	*.258*	*.343*	*.412*	*.260*	*42*	

Lowery is an excellent spare part. He can paste lefties, play a great center field, and pinch-run. Basically, the same skill set that Gerald Williams parlayed into millions. Signed by the Devil Rays, he'd be an improvement on Mike Kelly.

Sandy Martinez   **C**   **Bats L**   **Age 26**

YEAR	TEAM	LGE	AB	H	DB	TP	HR	BB	R	RBI	SB	CS	OUT	BA	OBA	SA	EQA	EQR	DEFENSE
1996	Toronto	AL	225	47	7	3	3	15	14	15	0	0	178	.209	.258	.307	.189	14	
1997	Syracuse	Int	322	67	10	0	4	23	20	18	5	2	257	.208	.261	.276	.182	18	
1998	ChiCubs	NL	87	23	10	1	0	13	14	9	1	0	64	.264	.360	.402	.271	12	20-C 95
1999	*ChiCubs*	*NL*	*181*	*44*	*12*	*1*	*2*	*14*	*18*	*16*	*2*	*0*	*137*	*.243*	*.297*	*.354*	*.227*	*17*	

The Cubs consider him a project player. Maybe they're right, and we can call him the Uwe Blab of baseball. For whatever reason he got something going as far as being Kerry Wood's personal catcher, so he may hang around for years.

Jason Maxwell   **2B/SS**   **Bats R**   **Age 27**

YEAR	TEAM	LGE	AB	H	DB	TP	HR	BB	R	RBI	SB	CS	OUT	BA	OBA	SA	EQA	EQR	DEFENSE	
1996	Orlando	Sou	437	104	11	0	8	42	42	36	12	3	336	.238	.305	.318	.223	39	95-SS 94	21-2B 104
1997	Orlando	Sou	409	89	11	3	8	61	45	35	8	6	326	.218	.319	.318	.227	40	114-SS 100	
1998	Iowa	PCL	473	117	22	2	10	44	50	47	6	1	357	.247	.311	.366	.238	49	102-2B 90	16-SS 97
1999	*ChiCubs*	*NL*	*419*	*107*	*17*	*1*	*12*	*46*	*49*	*48*	*8*	*2*	*314*	*.255*	*.329*	*.387*	*.252*	*50*		

A much better player than Manny Alexander any way you want to add it up. Maxwell's even the better defensive player: Alexander has the great arm, but poor judgment, range, and double-play skills. If we want to talk about what's wrong with baseball, it's that Maxwell hasn't been given the same opportunites. A great platoon partner for Morandini: hit over .300 with good power and more than half his season's total for walks against lefties.

Rod McCall   **1B**   **Bats L**   **Age 27**

YEAR	TEAM	LGE	AB	H	DB	TP	HR	BB	R	RBI	SB	CS	OUT	BA	OBA	SA	EQA	EQR	DEFENSE
1996	Canton	Eas	440	118	17	1	19	41	49	62	1	0	322	.268	.331	.441	.265	58	30-1B 95
1997	Buffalo	AA	108	24	3	0	5	8	8	12	0	0	84	.222	.276	.389	.226	10	
1997	Iowa	AA	149	40	2	0	11	19	19	27	0	0	109	.268	.351	.503	.289	24	19-1B 84
1998	Iowa	PCL	357	77	10	0	19	54	39	46	0	2	282	.216	.319	.403	.249	44	80-1B 92
1999	*ChiCubs*	*NL*	*362*	*92*	*13*	*0*	*22*	*47*	*44*	*59*	*0*	*1*	*271*	*.254*	*.340*	*.472*	*.275*	*54*	

Potentially one of the best pinch-hitters in baseball today, if he were given an opportunity to stick. He's got tremendous power, reasonable strike zone judgment, and tremendous power. Did I mention he can hit the ball a long ways? Deserves a shot to be Phil Stephenson.

Orlando Merced   **OF/1B**   **Bats L**   **Age 32**

YEAR	TEAM	LGE	AB	H	DB	TP	HR	BB	R	RBI	SB	CS	OUT	BA	OBA	SA	EQA	EQR	DEFENSE
1996	Pittsbrg	NL	451	126	20	1	18	53	60	65	6	4	329	.279	.355	.448	.277	66	106-OF 108
1997	Toronto	AL	364	98	23	2	10	47	52	46	7	3	269	.269	.353	.426	.272	52	91-OF 99
1998	Minnesot	AL	200	57	8	0	6	18	22	26	1	4	147	.285	.344	.415	.258	25	33-1B 95
1999	*ChiCubs*	*NL*	*271*	*73*	*10*	*0*	*10*	*32*	*32*	*37*	*3*	*3*	*201*	*.269*	*.347*	*.417*	*.264*	*36*	

Merced has never been a star, no matter how charitably some people felt about him when the Pirates traded him to Toronto. He's a nice spare part and bench player, but he should never see regular playing time again, and his unwillingness to accept that got him cut by the Twins.

Chad Meyers   2B   Bats R   Age 23

YEAR	TEAM	LGE	AB	H	DB	TP	HR	BB	R	RBI	SB	CS	OUT	BA	OBA	SA	EQA	EQR	DEFENSE	
1996	Willmspt	NYP	241	57	6	0	3	25	27	17	13	4	188	.237	.308	.299	.222	22	54-2B 97	
1997	Rockford	Mid	443	114	17	2	4	57	64	36	27	10	339	.257	.342	.332	.247	51	97-2B 86	20-OF 87
1998	Daytona	Fla	183	48	4	1	3	26	27	17	10	4	139	.262	.354	.344	.255	23	45-2B 80	
1998	WestTenn	Sou	288	67	8	0	1	47	44	16	23	6	227	.233	.340	.271	.236	31	72-2B 85	
1999	*ChiCubs*	*NL*	*426*	*114*	*14*	*1*	*5*	*58*	*68*	*37*	*33*	*9*	*321*	*.268*	*.355*	*.340*	*.258*	*54*		

The new and improved Bobby Morris. Meyers was a center fielder at Creighton (Jim Hendry's old program), but the Cubs have converted him to second. He's still rough in the field, and even his defenders say he'll never be smooth. He's worked hard to make himself better on his footwork when turning the deuce, and he's good enough offensively to make the experiment worthwhile.

Matt Mieske   OF   Bats R   Age 31

YEAR	TEAM	LGE	AB	H	DB	TP	HR	BB	R	RBI	SB	CS	OUT	BA	OBA	SA	EQA	EQR	DEFENSE
1996	Milwauke	AL	366	97	24	3	13	24	38	48	1	6	275	.265	.310	.454	.254	45	105-OF 101
1997	Milwauke	AL	250	62	16	3	5	19	26	26	1	0	188	.248	.301	.396	.240	27	67-OF 94
1998	Iowa	PCL	104	22	1	0	5	9	7	11	0	0	82	.212	.274	.365	.218	9	22-OF 90
1998	ChiCubs	NL	96	28	5	0	2	11	13	12	0	0	68	.292	.364	.406	.271	13	22-OF 88
1999	*ChiCubs*	*NL*	*222*	*59*	*13*	*1*	*7*	*18*	*23*	*29*	*0*	*1*	*164*	*.266*	*.321*	*.428*	*.255*	*27*	

Should have been on the roster instead of Sandy Martinez. Should have been on the field on a Wednesday in September instead of Brant Brown. At least he owns the last highlight of the Cubs' season: his RBI single against Rich Rodriguez in the wild-card-clinching game. An adequate fifth outfielder.

Mickey Morandini   2B   Bats L   Age 33

YEAR	TEAM	LGE	AB	H	DB	TP	HR	BB	R	RBI	SB	CS	OUT	BA	OBA	SA	EQA	EQR	DEFENSE
1996	Philadel	NL	540	136	25	6	3	52	67	43	23	5	409	.252	.318	.337	.237	56	133-2B 100
1997	Philadel	NL	553	164	38	2	2	65	80	58	13	14	403	.297	.371	.383	.264	72	139-2B 94
1998	ChiCubs	NL	576	170	19	4	9	76	86	69	14	1	407	.295	.377	.389	.277	82	144-2B 103
1999	*ChiCubs*	*NL*	*532*	*151*	*25*	*4*	*5*	*66*	*75*	*58*	*15*	*5*	*386*	*.284*	*.363*	*.374*	*.264*	*69*	

There's his career year, so don't blink. He came to the right town in terms of finding a constituency for his Gold Glove campaign: only in Chicago is a second baseman who doesn't turn the pivot that well but has very good hands get taken seriously in terms of his defensive value.

Jose Nieves   SS   Bats R   Age 24

YEAR	TEAM	LGE	AB	H	DB	TP	HR	BB	R	RBI	SB	CS	OUT	BA	OBA	SA	EQA	EQR	DEFENSE
1996	Rockford	Mid	399	82	13	1	5	23	23	21	9	5	322	.206	.249	.281	.176	21	91-SS 98
1997	Daytona	Fla	326	75	10	1	4	16	23	21	8	3	254	.230	.266	.304	.195	21	64-SS 92
1998	WestTenn	Sou	309	78	18	2	7	11	29	29	11	7	238	.252	.278	.392	.227	29	79-SS 85
1998	Iowa	PCL	74	16	3	0	0	2	3	3	1	1	59	.216	.237	.257	.151	3	
1999	*ChiCubs*	*NL*	*371*	*94*	*18*	*3*	*6*	*12*	*33*	*32*	*12*	*6*	*283*	*.253*	*.277*	*.367*	*.220*	*32*	

With soft hands and good range, he was named the best defensive shortstop of the Southern League, but that doesn't completely jibe with the numbers. At the plate, he isn't a complete zero, able to smack a ball to the power alleys once in awhile. I'm not really high on him, but there's a pretty good chance that he'll be given a crack at the shortstop job by '00.

Bo Porter   OF   Bats R   Age 26

YEAR	TEAM	LGE	AB	H	DB	TP	HR	BB	R	RBI	SB	CS	OUT	BA	OBA	SA	EQA	EQR	DEFENSE
1996	Rockford	Mid	388	69	9	0	5	48	27	18	13	8	327	.178	.268	.240	.177	22	100-OF 92
1997	Daytona	Fla	438	100	8	2	10	45	39	38	9	6	344	.228	.300	.324	.219	39	114-OF 100
1998	WestTenn	Sou	458	102	15	4	7	56	55	34	26	11	367	.223	.307	.319	.227	45	122-OF 95
1999	*ChiCubs*	*NL*	*471*	*110*	*15*	*3*	*9*	*52*	*54*	*40*	*24*	*11*	*372*	*.234*	*.310*	*.335*	*.230*	*47*	

Porter's been old for his leagues, but he could be a good fourth outfielder. He's a rare combination of patience at the plate and speed on the bases.

Brad Ramsey   C   Bats R   Age 22

YEAR	TEAM	LGE	AB	H	DB	TP	HR	BB	R	RBI	SB	CS	OUT	BA	OBA	SA	EQA	EQR	DEFENSE
1998	Daytona	Fla	306	72	14	1	5	27	28	26	2	1	235	.235	.297	.337	.221	27	64-C 81
1999	*ChiCubs*	*NL*	*241*	*71*	*9*	*0*	*7*	*19*	*26*	*33*	*1*	*1*	*171*	*.295*	*.346*	*.419*	*.264*	*31*	

Already considered a good catch-and-throw type, Ramsey has also shown some offensive skills. A bit of a free-swinger, and struck by the usual assortment of nagging injuries that hit all catchers.

Henry Rodriguez   LF/1B   Bats L   Age 31

YEAR	TEAM	LGE	AB	H	DB	TP	HR	BB	R	RBI	SB	CS	OUT	BA	OBA	SA	EQA	EQR	DEFENSE	
1996	Montreal	NL	527	140	31	1	37	40	64	91	2	0	387	.266	.317	.539	.283	83	71-OF 86	48-1B 94
1997	Montreal	NL	473	112	26	3	26	45	52	67	2	3	364	.237	.303	.469	.259	62	106-OF 95	
1998	ChiCubs	NL	412	102	18	1	33	56	55	75	1	3	313	.248	.338	.536	.288	70	97-OF 101	
1999	*ChiCubs*	*NL*	*417*	*106*	*21*	*1*	*27*	*46*	*50*	*70*	*1*	*2*	*313*	*.254*	*.328*	*.504*	*.277*	*63*		

Henry is one of the major reasons that you have to hope the Cubs figured things out as far as how you build a Wrigley winner: with power, and not by playing both Lance Johnson and Doug Glanville. His defense was surehanded in an immobile sort of way, but that was expected. My theory on his walks? We're talking about 47 that he drew under his own power, and a career-high .334 OBP. If he isn't poking home runs, that isn't enough to make you want him in the lineup.

Scott Servais   C   Bats R   Age 32

YEAR	TEAM	LGE	AB	H	DB	TP	HR	BB	R	RBI	SB	CS	OUT	BA	OBA	SA	EQA	EQR	DEFENSE
1996	ChiCubs	NL	442	114	12	0	13	33	39	48	0	2	330	.258	.309	.373	.235	44	
1997	ChiCubs	NL	381	94	14	0	8	26	31	35	0	1	288	.247	.295	.346	.220	33	
1998	ChiCubs	NL	324	72	13	1	8	28	26	29	1	0	252	.222	.284	.343	.216	27	91-C 99
1999	*ChiCubs*	*NL*	*330*	*80*	*10*	*0*	*10*	*25*	*27*	*34*	*0*	*1*	*251*	*.242*	*.296*	*.364*	*.225*	*30*	

There's no good reason to explain why any team would stick with Servais as stolidly, helplessly, and hopelessly as the Cubs. At least he gives good interview. He can beat the snot out of especially weak lefty junk, so he has some value as a platoon partner with a baseball player.

Sammy Sosa   RF   Bats R   Age 30

YEAR	TEAM	LGE	AB	H	DB	TP	HR	BB	R	RBI	SB	CS	OUT	BA	OBA	SA	EQA	EQR	DEFENSE
1996	ChiCubs	NL	495	133	20	2	39	37	66	87	15	5	367	.269	.320	.554	.288	82	111-OF 104
1997	ChiCubs	NL	635	153	30	3	35	49	71	84	18	12	494	.241	.295	.463	.254	81	152-OF 100
1998	ChiCubs	NL	637	195	22	0	67	77	107	149	19	10	452	.306	.381	.656	.331	142	158-OF 98
1999	*ChiCubs*	*NL*	*581*	*169*	*23*	*1*	*49*	*57*	*85*	*118*	*16*	*7*	*419*	*.291*	*.354*	*.587*	*.307*	*109*	

Rollicking good times, with the sunbaked thousands salaaming the great Sammy as he put on the best single season Wrigley has probably ever seen. I honestly believe that learning to relax and not trying to do everything on his own, as he says he felt he had to do previously, actually made a difference. No, I wouldn't say Sosa was being protected by having Grace and Rodriguez hit behind him. I'd say that when he says he felt more comfortable, we should pay attention, because we're talking about a player with an almost religious work ethic, and when he's wanted to do things like get more selective, he's done it. Starting to slip in the field, but it isn't a problem yet.

Pedro Valdes   OF   Bats L   Age 26

YEAR	TEAM	LGE	AB	H	DB	TP	HR	BB	R	RBI	SB	CS	OUT	BA	OBA	SA	EQA	EQR	DEFENSE
1996	Iowa	AA	398	114	15	0	15	33	45	56	2	0	284	.286	.341	.437	.269	53	87-OF 95
1997	Iowa	AA	465	127	21	1	13	45	57	56	8	2	340	.273	.337	.406	.261	59	115-OF 102
1998	Iowa	PCL	224	62	5	0	12	23	26	35	2	1	163	.277	.344	.460	.275	32	53-OF 98
1999	*ChiCubs*	*NL*	*325*	*91*	*12*	*0*	*15*	*27*	*38*	*48*	*4*	*1*	*235*	*.280*	*.335*	*.455*	*.271*	*45*	

Teams can use players who play the field well, players who hit for average, players who do a solid job of getting on base. Teams can use Pedro Valdes. The Cubs have avoided him, but he can play.

Ron Walker   3B   Bats R   Age 23

YEAR	TEAM	LGE	AB	H	DB	TP	HR	BB	R	RBI	SB	CS	OUT	BA	OBA	SA	EQA	EQR	DEFENSE
1997	Willmspt	NYP	190	52	2	0	6	12	16	22	0	0	138	.274	.317	.379	.241	20	42-3B 80
1998	Daytona	Fla	352	84	8	1	16	37	35	44	2	1	269	.239	.311	.403	.247	41	71-3B 76
1999	ChiCubs	NL	267	74	7	0	13	24	30	40	1	0	193	.277	.337	.449	.269	36	

Already looking like the Cubs' future third baseman. Walker has a strong arm and great power; a good comp might be Dean Palmer. He missed time in '98 with a strained elbow, but the organization has been impressed with his work ethic so far. More than a year away.

Alan Zinter   1B/C   Bats B   Age 31

YEAR	TEAM	LGE	AB	H	DB	TP	HR	BB	R	RBI	SB	CS	OUT	BA	OBA	SA	EQA	EQR	DEFENSE	
1996	Pawtuckt	Int	354	82	11	2	17	49	42	47	3	1	273	.232	.325	.418	.258	46	45-1B 85	
1997	Tacoma	PCL	394	92	9	2	13	51	41	44	2	1	303	.234	.321	.365	.242	44	72-1B 93	
1998	Iowa	PCL	412	107	12	1	15	62	52	55	2	4	309	.260	.357	.403	.265	56	53-1B 84	38-C 91
1999	ChiCubs	NL	373	97	12	1	18	57	50	57	3	2	278	.260	.358	.442	.277	56		

Remember when Zinter was traded by the Mets to the Tigers for Rico Brogna? There still isn't much to separate them except for dumb luck. Probably a better hitter than Brogna is right now, but he's never going to get a shot at a job.

Julio Zuleta   1B   Bats R   Age 24

YEAR	TEAM	LGE	AB	H	DB	TP	HR	BB	R	RBI	SB	CS	OUT	BA	OBA	SA	EQA	EQR	DEFENSE
1996	Willmspt	NYP	228	51	8	1	1	14	15	13	3	2	179	.224	.269	.281	.185	13	41-1B 104
1997	Rockford	Mid	429	99	18	1	5	25	29	30	2	3	333	.231	.273	.312	.197	29	103-1B 94
1998	Daytona	Fla	356	96	8	1	11	27	35	42	3	2	262	.270	.321	.390	.247	40	76-1B 93
1998	WestTenn	Sou	137	35	4	0	2	6	9	11	0	1	103	.255	.287	.328	.207	10	26-1B 100
1999	ChiCubs	NL	425	112	12	0	12	24	36	46	3	2	315	.264	.303	.376	.233	41	

Once a sore-armed catcher, Zuleta was a non-prospect, but he finished up as the Cubs' Minor League Player of the Year. He learned to stop upper-cutting everything, and he may end up getting a shot as a pinch-hitter if the Cubs stop carrying three catchers or twelve pitchers.

PITCHERS (Averages: 4.00 ERA, 9.00 H/9 1.00 HR/9, 3.00 BB/9,, 6.00 K/9, 1.00 KWH)

Terry Adams   Throws R   Age 26

YEAR	TEAM	LGE	IP	H	ER	HR	BB	K	ERA	W	L	H/9	HR/9	BB/9	K/9	KWH	PERA
1996	ChiCubs	NL	102.3	93	35	6	47	71	3.08	7	4	8.18	0.53	4.13	6.24	0.86	3.25
1997	ChiCubs	NL	78.7	92	36	3	37	58	4.12	4	5	10.53	0.34	4.23	6.64	0.74	4.35
1998	ChiCubs	NL	75.3	76	35	7	38	67	4.18	4	4	9.08	0.84	4.54	8.00	1.17	4.06

Adams has serious mechanical problems, constantly flying open in his delivery. For a guy who throws as hard as he does, it also doesn't help that he almost never works the inside corner. Adams's failure to develop has been mentioned as one of the reasons the Cubs let pitching coach Phil Regan walk away.

Rod Beck   Throws R   Age 30

YEAR	TEAM	LGE	IP	H	ER	HR	BB	K	ERA	W	L	H/9	HR/9	BB/9	K/9	KWH	PERA
1996	San Fran	NL	63.3	56	19	9	9	43	2.70	5	2	7.96	1.28	1.28	6.11	2.75	3.13
1997	San Fran	NL	70.0	69	28	7	7	47	3.60	4	4	8.87	0.90	0.90	6.04	3.43	3.34
1998	ChiCubs	NL	82.0	89	30	11	18	74	3.29	5	4	9.77	1.21	1.98	8.12	2.56	4.28

I had no idea he could be this much fun to watch on a daily basis. He'll consistently refute almost anything Riggleman says, play catch with the fans, and do everything you'd ever want from a ballplayer in terms of entertaining people. What is it with the moustache? I grew a Fu Manchu in college during Goose Gossage's year with the Cubs, and not only did I seem to win my barstool arguments much more easily, nobody argued with me in class. Looking at the Shooter, I can't help but feel that if he shaved it off, he'd bear an uncanny resemblance to Rick Reuschel, and although it shouldn't make a bit of difference, it wouldn't be the same. Is he a great closer? Not really. We're talking about a fat guy who gives up too many long flyballs in Wrigley Field. He's neither a strength nor a problem, but he does make for good drama.

Mark Clark · Throws R · Age 31

YEAR	TEAM	LGE	IP	H	ER	HR	BB	K	ERA	W	L	H/9	HR/9	BB/9	K/9	KWH	PERA
1996	NY Mets	NL	209.0	235	94	20	44	126	4.05	11	12	10.12	0.86	1.89	5.43	1.15	4.18
1997	NY Mets	NL	141.7	171	72	19	43	65	4.57	7	9	10.86	1.21	2.73	4.13	0.43	4.96
1997	ChiCubs	NL	65.0	53	18	6	11	46	2.49	5	2	7.34	0.83	1.52	6.37	2.72	2.49
1998	ChiCubs	NL	218.0	245	104	23	43	148	4.29	11	13	10.11	0.95	1.78	6.11	1.56	4.21

As you know from reading Mike Wolverton's SNWLP stuff, he was baseball's unluckiest pitcher. When things are going well, Clark is changing speeds well, and since coming over from the AL, he's been a solid fourth starter. Two good months with the Cubs in '97, and suddenly they were talking as if he was a guaranteed ace down the stretch. A few bad outings shut that up quickly.

Courtney Duncan · Throws R · Age 24

Year	Team	Lge	IP	H	ER	HR	BB	K	ERA	W	L	H/9	HR/9	BB/9	K/9	KWH	PERA
1996	Willmspt	NYP	78.0	103	47	10	40	51	5.42	3	6	11.88	1.15	4.62	5.88	0.47	5.65
1997	Daytona	Fla	122.7	102	32	4	40	88	2.35	10	4	7.48	0.29	2.93	6.46	1.42	2.49
1997	Orlando	Sou	43.3	43	26	2	27	35	5.40	2	3	8.93	0.42	5.61	7.27	0.79	3.74
1998	WestTenn	Sou	163.3	157	75	8	93	122	4.13	9	9	8.65	0.44	5.12	6.72	0.76	3.64

Initially expected to be a good control pitcher, but walking 103 men this year squelched that. His fastball has average veloc- ity but nasty movement, but he has good control of his other three pitches. I still like him, but short righthanded pitchers aren't a great bunch to bet on, either in terms of long-term success or in terms of their organizations appreciating them when they look good.

Kyle Farnsworth · Throws R · Age 23

YEAR	TEAM	LGE	IP	H	ER	HR	BB	K	ERA	W	L	H/9	HR/9	BB/9	K/9	KWH	PERA
1996	Rockford	Mid	107.7	152	65	10	35	57	5.43	4	8	12.71	0.84	2.93	4.76	0.46	5.60
1997	Daytona	Fla	159.0	203	87	17	54	81	4.92	7	11	11.49	0.96	3.06	4.58	0.45	5.09
1998	WestTenn	Sou	82.0	70	25	7	18	58	2.74	6	3	7.68	0.77	1.98	6.37	2.00	2.74
1998	Iowa	PCL	99.3	140	81	17	35	65	7.34	3	8	12.68	1.54	3.17	5.89	0.65	6.25

The man the Cubs are calling their best pitching prospect now that Wood is a major leaguer and Garland is pitching for the Southside Reinserfs. The big jump forward at this year came from adding a split-fingered fastball to go with a fastball, slider, and change. I don't think the big flop at Iowa will hold him back too much.

Chris Gissell · Throws R · Age 21

YEAR	TEAM	LGE	IP	H	ER	HR	BB	K	ERA	W	L	H/9	HR/9	BB/9	K/9	KWH	PERA
1997	Rockford	Mid	138.0	193	94	9	65	71	6.13	4	11	12.59	0.59	4.24	4.63	0.30	5.48
1998	Rockford	Mid	31.3	38	11	0	17	15	3.16	2	1	10.91	0.00	4.88	4.31	0.26	4.31
1998	Daytona	Fla	136.0	171	76	14	42	92	5.03	6	9	11.32	0.93	2.78	6.09	0.88	4.96

A skinny righthander drafted out of high school; the Cubs are one of the more agressive teams when it comes to drafting high school pitching. He's got three good pitches (fastball, curve, circle change), but he has the bad habit of overusing whichever one seems to work the best on any given day. Once he starts being more consistent, he'll get a shot at the Cubs' rotation.

Jeremi Gonzalez · Throws R · Age 24

YEAR	TEAM	LGE	IP	H	ER	HR	BB	K	ERA	W	L	H/9	HR/9	BB/9	K/9	KWH	PERA
1996	Orlando	Sou	93.7	110	38	7	25	65	3.65	5	5	10.57	0.67	2.40	6.25	1.15	4.32
1997	Iowa	AmA	60.3	56	28	8	20	49	4.18	3	4	8.35	1.19	2.98	7.31	1.61	3.58
1997	ChiCubs	NL	150.3	125	60	17	63	84	3.59	9	8	7.48	1.02	3.77	5.03	0.67	3.11
1998	ChiCubs	NL	112.7	130	65	13	38	65	5.19	5	8	10.38	1.04	3.04	5.19	0.64	4.63

Lost for the season in July when his elbow went "ping," he managed to avoid Tommy John surgery, and the timetable for his return has been optimistically set for June. His reputation went south almost instantly: whereas the Cubs were raving about his instincts and savvy on the mound in '97, they were complaining about his poor focus and inability to concentrate in '98. I think he was just pitching worse, and started calling him names when it happened.

Chris Haney   Throws L   Age 30

YEAR	TEAM	LGE	IP	H	ER	HR	BB	K	ERA	W	L	H/9	HR/9	BB/9	K/9	KWH	PERA
1996	KansasCy	AL	230.7	254	105	24	41	114	4.10	13	13	9.91	0.94	1.60	4.45	0.94	4.06
1997	KansasCy	AL	25.3	29	13	1	4	16	4.62	1	2	10.30	0.36	1.42	5.68	1.65	3.91
1998	KansasCy	AL	103.0	120	61	16	33	50	5.33	4	7	10.49	1.40	2.88	4.37	0.47	4.89

Damn your eyes, Jazayerli. Your team would stick me with having to write the Haney comment this year. He's a free agent, he's injury prone, and he sucks. Next!

Felix Heredia   Throws L   Age 23

YEAR	TEAM	LGE	IP	H	ER	HR	BB	K	ERA	W	L	H/9	HR/9	BB/9	K/9	KWH	PERA
1996	Portland	Eas	59.3	56	11	3	15	33	1.67	6	1	8.49	0.46	2.28	5.01	0.97	3.03
1997	Florida	NL	58.0	55	26	3	27	48	4.03	3	3	8.53	0.47	4.19	7.45	1.16	3.41
1998	Florida	NL	42.0	42	27	1	29	35	5.79	2	3	9.00	0.21	6.21	7.50	0.75	3.06
1998	ChiCubs	NL	18.0	20	8	1	6	15	4.00	1	1	10.00	0.50	3.00	7.50	1.41	4.00

The only pitcher the Cubs acquired who has a future. Even so, his future would be much, much better if Jim Riggleman would take a deep breath or two and leave him on the mound. He throws hard and wild, and he's 22. Using him like Tony Fossas isn't going to make him any better, and if the alternative is bringing in Matt Karchner, it's better to just see if Heredia can make progress.

Steve Hoff   Throws L   Age 21

YEAR	TEAM	LGE	IP	H	ER	HR	BB	K	ERA	W	L	H/9	HR/9	BB/9	K/9	KWH	PERA
1997	Clinton	Mid	74.0	87	28	5	19	52	3.41	5	3	10.58	0.61	2.31	6.32	1.23	4.26
1997	R Cucmng	Cal	64.7	86	53	7	47	41	7.38	2	5	11.97	0.97	6.54	5.71	0.31	5.85
1998	Brevard	Fla	79.3	118	56	8	30	33	6.35	3	6	13.39	0.91	3.40	3.74	0.23	6.01
1998	Daytona	Fla	27.3	44	24	5	14	20	7.90	1	2	14.49	1.65	4.61	6.59	0.49	7.24

A lefty who gets people out with good breaking stuff? Hold the phone . . . can I get a gross of those? Made in Taiwan? Are those cheaper? Nah, thanks, I'll take domestic. Despite bouncing to his third organization in two years, he's a decent prospect.

Matt Karchner   Throws R   Age 32

YEAR	TEAM	LGE	IP	H	ER	HR	BB	K	ERA	W	L	H/9	HR/9	BB/9	K/9	KWH	PERA
1996	ChiSox	AL	59.3	62	34	9	33	45	5.16	3	4	9.40	1.37	5.01	6.83	0.74	4.55
1997	ChiSox	AL	54.0	49	14	4	23	29	2.33	4	2	8.17	0.67	3.83	4.83	0.56	3.33
1998	ChiSox	AL	37.7	34	18	2	17	29	4.30	2	2	8.12	0.48	4.06	6.93	1.09	3.11
1998	ChiCubs	NL	29.0	32	16	6	13	20	4.97	1	2	9.93	1.86	4.03	6.21	0.72	5.28

How to get snookered: start believing that saving games is a skill. Pitching is a skill. A pitcher's command of his pitches is a skill. A pitcher's ability to play professional baseball and stay healthy doing it is a skill. Saves may be a drama-laden stat for the boxscore, the beat writer, or the accountant, but recording them isn't a skill. But the Cubs saw that Karchner had logged 25 saves in six months as a closer, and they figured he was somebody they could use. What they got was a tender-armed, homer-prone accident. Can Karchner help a team? Sure, but so can about fifty guys in Triple-A, if you just want them for relief work.

Brian McNichol   Throws L   Age 25

YEAR	TEAM	LGE	IP	H	ER	HR	BB	K	ERA	W	L	H/9	HR/9	BB/9	K/9	KWH	PERA
1996	Daytona	Fla	34.7	48	26	6	16	17	6.75	1	3	12.46	1.56	4.15	4.41	0.28	6.23
1997	Daytona	Fla	38.3	39	15	2	13	28	3.52	2	2	9.16	0.47	3.05	6.57	1.16	3.52
1997	Orlando	Sou	110.7	179	88	18	40	74	7.16	3	9	14.56	1.46	3.25	6.02	0.57	6.99
1998	WestTenn	Sou	175.3	190	79	15	56	124	4.06	9	10	9.75	0.77	2.87	6.37	1.08	4.06

A good-looking prospect. He's a huge lefty (6'6") with good velocity who can throw four pitches for strikes. The current thinking is that he's turned the corner now that he has confidence in himself. Named the Cubs' Minor League Pitcher of the Year, but a longshot for the rotation in '99.

Kurt Miller — Throws R — Age 26

YEAR	TEAM	LGE	IP	H	ER	HR	BB	K	ERA	W	L	H/9	HR/9	BB/9	K/9	KWH	PERA
1996	Charlott	Int	69.7	76	30	7	26	33	3.88	4	4	9.82	0.90	3.36	4.26	0.41	4.26
1996	Florida	NL	47.0	62	38	6	31	27	7.28	1	4	11.87	1.15	5.94	5.17	0.28	5.74
1997	Charlott	Int	28.3	28	11	2	21	25	3.49	2	1	8.89	0.64	6.67	7.94	0.80	4.13
1998	Iowa	PCL	159.0	178	79	12	80	110	4.47	8	10	10.08	0.68	4.53	6.23	0.64	4.42

Miller is a good example of what can happen to a young pitcher who gets pushed hard before he's 20, but who manages to avoid a major blowout. The Rangers abused him before the Marlins rescued him. The damage was done, and it's taken a good four years for Miller to recover well enough to get to the point that he's useful again. He ended up garnering All-Star honors in the PCL in '98, and why the Cubs chose Don Wengert over him in July defies explanation.

Mike Morgan — Throws R — Age 39

YEAR	TEAM	LGE	IP	H	ER	HR	BB	K	ERA	W	L	H/9	HR/9	BB/9	K/9	KWH	PERA
1996	St Louis	NL	102.7	131	61	14	38	50	5.35	4	7	11.48	1.23	3.33	4.38	0.38	5.35
1996	Cincnnti	NL	28.0	29	8	2	7	17	2.57	2	1	9.32	0.64	2.25	5.46	1.07	3.54
1997	Cincnnti	NL	166.7	166	77	13	44	93	4.16	9	10	8.96	0.70	2.38	5.02	0.89	3.51
1998	Minnesot	AL	101.3	104	33	12	21	49	2.93	7	4	9.24	1.07	1.87	4.35	0.82	3.82
1998	ChiCubs	NL	23.3	33	19	8	14	9	7.33	1	2	12.73	3.09	5.40	3.47	0.13	7.71

The grand old man keeps rolling along. Still has value as a five-inning fifth starter, although he's getting to the point that he may not be able to even sustain that role.

Terry Mulholland — Throws L — Age 36

YEAR	TEAM	LGE	IP	H	ER	HR	BB	K	ERA	W	L	H/9	HR/9	BB/9	K/9	KWH	PERA
1996	Philadel	NL	133.7	164	68	17	20	47	4.58	6	9	11.04	1.14	1.35	3.16	0.51	4.78
1996	Seattle	AL	71.3	70	28	4	22	34	3.53	4	4	8.83	0.50	2.78	4.29	0.56	3.41
1997	ChiCubs	NL	163.3	159	65	20	41	67	3.58	10	8	8.76	1.10	2.26	3.69	0.52	3.64
1997	San Fran	NL	30.0	29	19	5	5	22	5.70	1	2	8.70	1.50	1.50	6.60	2.50	3.60
1998	ChiCubs	NL	113.7	106	45	7	35	66	3.56	7	6	8.39	0.55	2.77	5.23	0.88	3.17

One of the great might-have-beens is if the Cubs had just put Mulholland in the rotation as soon as Gonzalez went down: would consistent innings every five days turn out to be more valuable than a "clutch" relief appearance or three every week? Within a season, I'd take the starts. Despite his new two-year contract, the Cubs are saying he isn't guaranteed a rotation spot; it will depend on whether or not they acquire another left-handed reliever. The best pickoff artist in baseball today.

Rodney Myers — Throws R — Age 30

YEAR	TEAM	LGE	IP	H	ER	HR	BB	K	ERA	W	L	H/9	HR/9	BB/9	K/9	KWH	PERA
1996	ChiCubs	NL	68.7	67	36	6	37	46	4.72	3	5	8.78	0.79	4.85	6.03	0.64	3.93
1997	Iowa	AmA	131.0	179	92	17	41	61	6.32	4	11	12.30	1.17	2.82	4.19	0.38	5.63
1998	Iowa	PCL	95.3	100	50	9	48	64	4.72	5	6	9.44	0.85	4.53	6.04	0.64	4.25
1998	ChiCubs	NL	18.3	28	12	3	5	14	5.89	1	1	13.75	1.47	2.45	6.87	1.05	6.38

Well, if they figured they could use Matt Karchner, sure, why not put Rodney Myers on the postseason roster too? Roster scrappie with extra snouts.

Phillip Norton — Throws L — Age 23

YEAR	TEAM	LGE	IP	H	ER	HR	BB	K	ERA	W	L	H/9	HR/9	BB/9	K/9	KWH	PERA
1996	Willmspt	NYP	73.7	113	52	2	38	46	6.35	2	6	13.81	0.24	4.64	5.62	0.37	5.74
1997	Rockford	Mid	104.3	118	55	5	47	74	4.74	5	7	10.18	0.43	4.05	6.38	0.74	4.23
1997	Daytona	Fla	42.7	46	9	6	14	34	1.90	4	1	9.70	1.27	2.95	7.17	1.35	4.43
1998	Daytona	Fla	66.0	65	30	5	30	39	4.09	3	4	8.86	0.68	4.09	5.32	0.58	3.68
1998	WestTenn	Sou	121.3	124	48	12	42	95	3.56	7	6	9.20	0.89	3.12	7.05	1.30	3.86

Owner of the best portside curve in the organization, Norton used it to rack up 173 strikeouts in '98. He's still a relatively unheralded prospect. He's got a decent fastball, and he isn't afraid to claim the inside corner. In terms of Cubs' pitching prospects, he's looking better than Duncan or Farnsworth, and about even with McNichol.

Marc Pisciotta   **Throws R**   **Age 28**

YEAR	TEAM	LGE	IP	H	ER	HR	BB	K	ERA	W	L	H/9	HR/9	BB/9	K/9	KWH	PERA
1996	Calgary	PCL	64.3	77	36	3	49	37	5.04	3	4	10.77	0.42	6.85	5.18	0.27	4.90
1997	Iowa	AmA	43.7	38	15	2	24	37	3.09	3	2	7.83	0.41	4.95	7.63	1.13	3.09
1997	ChiCubs	NL	29.3	21	8	1	14	19	2.45	2	1	6.44	0.31	4.30	5.83	0.92	2.15
1998	ChiCubs	NL	45.7	47	19	5	30	29	3.74	3	2	9.26	0.99	5.91	5.72	0.45	4.34
1998	Iowa	PCL	29.0	40	25	4	17	22	7.76	1	2	12.41	1.24	5.28	6.83	0.53	6.21

The Sandy Martinez of the pitching staff, in that for some reason the Cubs came into the year talking about "Cookies" as a prospect, when he was your run-of-the-mill minor league reliever with an adequate fastball and control problems. That kind of player can be useful, if you pick your spots and have some patience, but Riggleman got antsy, and Pisciotta was whacked. As far as major leaguers who played in the Little League World Series, he's got nothing on Lloyd McClendon.

Steve Rain   **Throws R**   **Age 24**

YEAR	TEAM	LGE	IP	H	ER	HR	BB	K	ERA	W	L	H/9	HR/9	BB/9	K/9	KWH	PERA
1996	Orlando	Sou	37.7	37	15	5	11	37	3.58	2	2	8.84	1.19	2.63	8.84	2.52	3.82
1996	Iowa	AmA	25.7	20	9	3	8	20	3.16	2	1	7.01	1.05	2.81	7.01	1.87	2.81
1997	Iowa	AmA	43.7	61	31	8	34	43	6.39	1	4	12.57	1.65	7.01	8.86	0.67	6.60
1998	Iowa	PCL	101.3	128	75	13	62	68	6.66	3	8	11.37	1.15	5.51	6.04	0.44	5.51

On alternate days, it seems like he has control of one of his three pitches (fastball, forkball, and slider), so Rain spent the season getting smacked around. He's physically huge at 6'6", but he's also had problems keeping his weight down. Rain is one of those guys who may suddenly get everything working right all at once, or he could just be Charlie Kerfeld without the good year.

Jay Ryan   **Throws R**   **Age 23**

YEAR	TEAM	LGE	IP	H	ER	HR	BB	K	ERA	W	L	H/9	HR/9	BB/9	K/9	KWH	PERA
1996	Daytona	Fla	67.3	88	44	12	37	40	5.88	2	5	11.76	1.60	4.95	5.35	0.37	6.01
1996	Orlando	Sou	33.3	47	30	7	21	19	8.10	1	3	12.69	1.89	5.67	5.13	0.27	6.75
1997	Daytona	Fla	172.0	193	101	27	62	107	5.28	7	12	10.10	1.41	3.24	5.60	0.72	4.76
1998	WestTenn	Sou	148.7	179	78	21	48	96	4.72	7	10	10.84	1.27	2.91	5.81	0.80	5.02

After arm injuries in '96, he probably won't ever throw as hard as when he was drafted out of high school. He still has a solid heater and a good curve, but he doesn't have particularly good command. A disappointment so far.

Kennie Steenstra   **Throws R**   **Age 28**

YEAR	TEAM	LGE	IP	H	ER	HR	BB	K	ERA	W	L	H/9	HR/9	BB/9	K/9	KWH	PERA
1996	Iowa	AmA	152.0	209	108	24	55	82	6.39	5	12	12.38	1.42	3.26	4.86	0.44	5.98
1997	Iowa	AmA	150.3	205	104	14	44	86	6.23	5	12	12.27	0.84	2.63	5.15	0.61	5.33
1998	Iowa	PCL	138.0	200	89	15	39	77	5.80	5	10	13.04	0.98	2.54	5.02	0.57	5.80

Its being claimed that Steenstra has rebuilt his approach. Velocity-impaired, he used to aggressively challenge batters and work the inside corner, but now he's looking to nibble and work hitters on location. It didn't really yield different or better results, but the experience will probably make him a better pitching coach ten years from now. Signed by the Royals.

Dave Stevens   **Throws R**   **Age 29**

YEAR	TEAM	LGE	IP	H	ER	HR	BB	K	ERA	W	L	H/9	HR/9	BB/9	K/9	KWH	PERA
1996	Minnesot	AL	60.0	55	24	11	20	29	3.60	4	3	8.25	1.65	3.00	4.35	0.57	3.75
1997	SaltLake	PCL	86.0	99	47	9	30	54	4.92	4	6	10.36	0.94	3.14	5.65	0.74	4.50
1997	Minnesot	AL	24.3	42	19	8	15	16	7.03	1	2	15.53	2.96	5.55	5.92	0.30	9.25
1998	Iowa	PCL	47.0	48	20	2	17	29	3.83	3	2	9.19	0.38	3.26	5.55	0.77	3.64
1998	ChiCubs	NL	39.0	45	18	6	15	29	4.15	2	2	10.38	1.38	3.46	6.69	0.93	4.85

Possibly the league leader in warmups before the sixth inning as a result of Jim Riggleman's itchy, twitchy, Pepto management style. More than once, he'd warm up twice for games he'd subsequently never enter. He's lost some velocity, but his slider has a bit more bite now. Another ex-Twin working for Andy MacPhail, not that you want to collect too many of those.

Kevin Tapani								Throws R		Age 35						
YEAR	TEAM	LGE	IP	H	ER	HR	BB	K	ERA	W	L	H/9	HR/9	BB/9	K/9	KWH	PERA
1996	ChiSox	AL	224.3	233	101	30	60	147	4.05	12	13	9.35	1.20	2.41	5.90	1.16	4.05
1997	ChiCubs	NL	88.0	75	27	7	21	49	2.76	7	3	7.67	0.72	2.15	5.01	1.14	2.76
1998	ChiCubs	NL	224.0	253	108	30	57	125	4.34	11	14	10.17	1.21	2.29	5.02	0.81	4.50

It was not a good year for Tapani; it was a Pete Vuckovich or Lamarr Hoyt type of year, where he got good run support and pitched badly most of the time. He has adapted relatively well to life without his forkball, but his chances of blowing out his arm this year are pretty good.

Steve Trachsel								Throws R		Age 28						
YEAR	TEAM	LGE	IP	H	ER	HR	BB	K	ERA	W	L	H/9	HR/9	BB/9	K/9	KWH	PERA
1996	ChiCubs	NL	206.0	197	78	30	59	119	3.41	13	10	8.61	1.31	2.58	5.20	0.91	3.76
1997	ChiCubs	NL	211.3	223	91	33	63	145	3.88	12	11	9.50	1.41	2.68	6.18	1.12	4.34
1998	ChiCubs	NL	213.7	213	96	28	77	137	4.04	12	12	8.97	1.18	3.24	5.77	0.86	3.96

Kevin Brown Lite? Trachsel will happily blast his critics or interleague play, then turn around and bitch about scratch hits, bullpen betrayals, and wind-aided shots. In an age of mealy-mouthed agent-scripted "I thank God, Mom, and country for everything I am today" soundbites, Trachsel is a breath of fresh angry air. I doubt that he's ever going to suddenly become a much better pitcher than he's been, but he's the most reliable veteran starter the Cubs have. His game against the Giants in the wild-card clincher looked like a masterpiece of wildness by design. I'm concerned about his health, in that he wasn't durable or consistent after the All-Star break.

Don Wengert								Throws R		Age 29						
YEAR	TEAM	LGE	IP	H	ER	HR	BB	K	ERA	W	L	H/9	HR/9	BB/9	K/9	KWH	PERA
1996	Oakland	AL	165.3	192	79	25	48	74	4.30	8	10	10.45	1.36	2.61	4.03	0.45	4.84
1997	Oakland	AL	142.0	165	74	19	36	66	4.69	7	9	10.46	1.20	2.28	4.18	0.55	4.69
1998	Iowa	PCL	50.0	67	32	2	15	36	5.76	2	4	12.06	0.36	2.70	6.48	0.97	4.86
1998	ChiCubs	NL	51.0	58	26	8	22	38	4.59	3	3	10.24	1.41	3.88	6.71	0.85	4.94

He's everything Tanyon Sturtze ever hoped to grow up to be and more. He had no business being in the rotation for a month, and letting him try when you knew what his track record was qualifies as one of the worst decisions any team made on the season. If you want a symbol for the Cubs' season, pick Don Wengert's furrowed unibrow.

Kerry Wood								Throws R		Age 22						
YEAR	TEAM	LGE	IP	H	ER	HR	BB	K	ERA	W	L	H/9	HR/9	BB/9	K/9	KWH	PERA
1996	Daytona	Fla	115.0	89	52	9	77	108	4.07	6	7	6.97	0.70	6.03	8.45	1.28	3.05
1997	Orlando	Sou	90.3	72	48	2	75	83	4.78	4	6	7.17	0.20	7.47	8.27	0.96	3.19
1997	Iowa	AmA	57.3	45	36	2	50	69	5.65	2	4	7.06	0.31	7.85	10.83	1.59	3.14
1998	ChiCubs	NL	171.7	123	61	15	78	214	3.20	12	7	6.45	0.79	4.09	11.22	3.58	2.41

Was he overused? At 21, he pitched fewer innings (counting his Iowa start and his postseason start) and faced fewer batters per start than famous flameouts like Mark Fidrych or famous greats like Tom Seaver. Neither of them threw as hard as Wood. It isn't guaranteed either way in terms of him going on to have a long career or blowing out early, and under the circumstances, the Cubs were neither overly cautious or aggressive as far as his workload. As far as comparing his career to Nolan Ryan's, the key difference is that Ryan never threw 200 innings in the majors before he was 25, while the Cubs will have to be remarkably cautious to avoid doing that with Wood over the next three years.

SNWLP						CHICAGO CUBS						Park Effect: +3.2%	
PITCHER	GS	IP	R	SNW	SNL	SNPCT	W	L	RA	APW	SNVA	SNWAR
Clark, M.	33	213.7	116	12.0	11.6	.508	9	14	4.89	-0.21	0.21	1.97
Gonzalez, J.	20	110.0	72	5.6	7.9	.415	7	6	5.89	-1.30	-0.98	-0.14
Morgan, M.	5	22.7	21	0.9	2.3	.281	0	1	8.34	-0.86	-0.73	-0.47
Mulholland, T.	6	39.7	11	2.9	1.2	.706	3	0	2.50	0.98	0.74	1.14
Tapani, K.	34	218.0	118	12.8	12.0	.516	19	9	4.87	-0.18	0.32	2.25
Trachsel, S.	33	208.0	107	12.1	11.1	.520	15	8	4.63	0.37	0.58	2.21
Wengert, D.	6	28.3	21	1.3	2.4	.357	1	4	6.67	-0.57	-0.46	-0.26
Wood, K.	26	166.7	69	12.0	6.9	.636	13	6	3.73	1.92	2.42	3.97
TOTALS	163	1007.0	535	59.6	55.5	.510	67	48	4.78	0.16	2.09	10.67

The Cubs repeated their starting pitching success of 1997 by again having an unspectacular but deep rotation. As in 1997, the 1998 Cubs had #2, #3, and #4 guys who finished right around the .500 SNPct mark. The biggest difference: in 1997, the #1 starter was also right around the .500 mark, while in 1998 the #1 starter was some guy named Kerry Wood. Wood promises to be an elite major league starter, something that's been missing from Wrigley Field since Greg Maddux was around. Despite his limited number of starts, Wood had the best season of a Cubs starter (in SNWAR) since Maddux in 1992. Wood's season represented the best by a rookie since Hideo Nomo's debut in 1995, although Nomo's season was better. He beat Wood in SNPct (.660 to .636), SNVA (3.17 to 2.42), and SNWAR (4.93 to 3.97). I'm sure it'll be fine with Wood to rank below Nomo on the rookie season scale, provided he ends up ahead of Nomo on his career. Steve Trachsel has taken over in the 90's where Bret Saberhagen left off. His SNPcts over the last three even years were .624, .602, and .520. Over the last three odd years: .470, .411, .485. If you're superstitious, maybe Steve will "forget" to change that 1998 calendar.

Pitcher Abuse Points								
PITCHER	AGE	GS	PAP	PAP/S	AAW	MAX	115+	130+
Clark, Mark	30	33	321	9.73	12.97	126	8	0
Gonzalez, Jeremi	23	20	154	7.70	19.25	136	2	1
Morgan, Mike	38	5	5	1.00	1.00	105	0	0
Mulholland, Terry	35	6	64	10.67	10.67	121	2	0
Tapani, Kevin	34	34	310	9.12	9.12	123	7	0
Trachsel, Steve	27	33	270	8.18	15.00	122	4	0
Wengert, Don	28	6	22	3.67	6.11	116	1	0
Wood, Kerry	21	26	532	20.46	57.97	132	13	1
TOTAL		163	1678	10.29	19.82	136	37	2
RANKING (NL)			5	5	3		1	7-T

We've already talked about Wood at length, but as you can see here, he easily led the Cubs' staff in PAPs, even without adjusting for age. Be careful, Mr. Riggleman. Jeremi Gonzalez had the second-highest AAW on the staff and went out for the year with arm miseries, which is why the names "Wengert" and "Morgan" are up there at all. The rest of the staff was treated with more kindness, but Cubs fans probably aren't all that concerned about Mark Clark's shoulder. Prediction: if Wood averages over 20 PAPs a start this year, he won't win more than 50 games after he turns 32. (This may be the most frivolous prediction I've ever made, since it'll be at least 2015 before I'm proved wrong.)

Cincinnati Reds

Over time, the Reds have consistently managed to pull off move after move where the team has turned nothing into something of value. Jim Bowden has exploited the inefficiencies of the major-league trade, waiver, and free agent markets to usually obtain more value than he gives up. His tenure has included the successful signings of washouts like the Petes (Schourek and Harnisch) and the Jeffs (Brantley and Shaw), all of whom flourished in Cincinnati given an opportunity and some adroit handling. He has taken players whom he bought at their lowest value and sold them at market peaks, including the Shaw trade this year and the Smiley trade last year. And he has rescued stranded players like Gabe White or Roberto Petagine from the farm systems in which they were languishing. As a result, the Reds have remained respectable in the past three seasons despite their inability to compensate players on par with their better-heeled brethren in Cleveland.

However, "respectable" is not a respectable goal for a team. The Reds have continued to struggle to develop their own talent, and one might argue the situation has worsened in the past few years. Coupling a solid player-acquisition history like Bowden's with a farm system that regularly churns out players capable of contributing at the major-league level would produce a team able to contend in the NL Central. Instead, the Reds face a situation where just one major roster member who has come up since 1992 is a product of the farm system, leaving holes in the team's lineup, defense, bullpen, and rotation that Bowden's strategy is unable to fill.

The team's woes are twofold: they have drafted poorly in recent years, and they haven't been able to develop many of the talented players who come into the system. The draft woes are exemplified by their 1997 selections. While it is clearly early to close to the book on these players, most of whom have slightly over one professional season under their belts, at this juncture, they collectively look like one of the worst collections of drafted players by any team in recent memory.

The first problem is an organizational overemphasis on drafting two risky player types: high-workload pitchers and toolsy hitters. The Reds have drafted a large number of high school pitchers, the riskiest type of player in any draft, in recent years, and have had little success in this regard. Their 1997 draft is no exception:

- Their top pitching selection, Monte Roundtree (#4 overall), pitched 37 ineffective innings last year, then missed this season with an injury.
- Their #10 pick, David Runk, has pitched 19.1 innings for Billings since he was drafted, surrendering 28 walks and 22 runs.
- Their #11 pick, Clint Brewer, was 0-7 as a reliever for Charles-ton this year, with a 6.66 ERA and 90 hits and 49 walks allowed in 73 innings.

At the same time, the team has drafted a number of hitters who possess good or even excellent tools, but who don't show the particular skills necessary to play baseball:

- #3 pick Thad Markray has hit .181/.258/.236 since his selection, barely cracking .100 in his first exposure to A-ball.
- #5 pick DeWayne Wise, a star quarterback in high school who turned down Clemson and South Carolina, has great speed but has shown neither plate discipline nor power as a pro.
- #6 pick Toby Sanchez, an extremely raw college first baseman, has now struck out in 239 of his 586 professional at bats.

In fact, the '97 draft may turn out to be one of the best in the Reds' recent attempts, with #7 pick Mike Frank and #9 pick Scott Williamson both on track to play in the majors in 1999. Since they drafted Trevor Hoffman in 1989, the Reds have only produced two players who spent 1998 in prominent major-league roles (Dan Wilson and Brett Tomko), and haven't produced anyone else more valuable than Scott Sullivan.

Compounding the problem is the mishandling of the players the Reds bring into the system in the first place. They've promoted a number of promising hitting prospects during the past few seasons, only to see them scuffle badly enough to return them to their original levels. They've drafted a number

---

Reds Prospectus

1998 record: 77-85; Fourth place, NL Central

Pythagorean W/L: 80-82

Runs scored: 750 (7th in NL)

Runs allowed: 760 (8th in NL)

Team EQA: .261 (7th in NL)

Park: Cinergy Field (slight hitters')

1998: Caught between rebuilding and contending, the Reds split the difference.

1999: Plenty of talent; they will be in the wild-card mix deep into September.

of pitchers who have been injured when they entered the system, or who were injured shortly after turning pro. They've even overworked their own prospects a number of times, including Curt Lyons and Scott Sullivan, or acquired overworked pitchers in trade, such as Jim Crowell and possibly Dennis Reyes.

As a result, the team isn't producing the players they need to just fill out the ballclub, assuming Bowden can keep his external talent pipeline flowing. The club has only four major homegrown players on its roster—Tomko and Sullivan are joined there by Reggie Sanders ('87) and Barry Larkin ('85).

In fact, Bowden has populated most of the 25-man roster with either retreads or players acquired in retread trades. The Reds scored hugely with Brantley, getting several good years out of him before trading him for Dmitri Young, now their everyday left fielder and their top young hitter. Shaw brought them Paul Konerko (since dealt for Mike Cameron) and Dennis Reyes, with Reyes and Cameron both projected to play major roles with the Reds in '99. Sean Casey came as the return on Dave Burba, a throw-in on a large trade with the Giants in '95. And now, the Reds have thrown Mike Remlinger in with Bret Boone in the deal that brought them Denny Neagle, Michael Tucker, and Rob Bell.

At the same time, Bowden has filled several holes with new veteran imports. Pete Harnisch, given up for dead by most other teams after a season of injuries, depression, and bad pitching, had the best year of his career. Gabe White, jerked around by an Expo team that, perplexingly, couldn't find a way to use him, came over for a non-prospect and has pitched well in relief. Jason Bere and Steve Parris have shots at rotation spots for 1999.

While many of these players have exceeded expectations, it should be clear that this is not a championship team, or even a wild-card contender (assuming that is even a goal worth pursuing). Bowden may indeed have a superior ability to pick out other teams' underperforming veterans, scraping the goop off, and turning them into valuable commodities. However, these players are generally unpredictable, often come with significant baggage (or without it, in the case of Bere's fastball), and most importantly no one has ever built a contending team solely around that level of talent and that type of acquisition.

Furthermore, Bowden may have miscalculated when he dealt Brantley and Shaw this year. In both situations, Bowden signed the veterans to contracts for salaries well below what they might have received in the free agent market, because both wanted to play in Cincinnati. (Brantley, for one, was jokingly called an "assistant GM" for his efforts to convince other players to sign with the Reds.) Today's financial climate makes those players extremely attractive in trade, to the point where Bowden would find himself trading players just weeks or months after he swore that such moves were out of the question. After the Shaw deal made it clear that a long-term contract was no guarantee that the player would stay a Red, Pete Harnisch included a short-term no-trade clause in the long-term deal he signed shortly before the July 1998 trading deadline. If other players make this demand, or demand full no-trade clauses, Bowden will find himself unable to execute on his polish-and-dump strategy in the future.

With that avenue closed and the return on retread investments highly uncertain, the Reds should be able to turn to their farm system . . . which they can't, because the necessary talent pool isn't there. While the system is producing a few valuable players, with Jason LaRue and Williamson on the rise, there is minimal margin for error and no excess talent for trading purposes, and recent drafts look even less promising than those of the early 90s. Without the farm system as a reliable, controlled generator of talent, the Reds face a less certain future.

Bowden is also forgoing a potentially attractive talent-acquisition strategy that would tie closely to his forte (and his favorite activity): trading. Some teams, such as Atlanta and Los Angeles, have a "prospect credibility" with other teams, allowing them to reap a higher return when trading prospects than other teams do. If the Reds' system was churning out talent more regularly, he would find he'd have greatly increased flexibility in the trade market.

Of course, Bowden has signed on for four more years, so it is entirely possible that, more invested in the team's future, he'll shift his focus toward developing the farm system. Instead of continuing to outsource player development and acquire developed players when they reach Triple-A, Bowden will likely find it cheaper to develop the players internally.

HITTERS (Averages: BA .260/ OBA .330/ SA .420, EQA .260)

Aaron Boone   **3B**   **Bats R   Age 26**

YEAR	TEAM	LGE	AB	H	DB	TP	HR	BB	R	RBI	SB	CS	OUT	BA	OBA	SA	EQA	EQR	DEFENSE
1996	Chattang	Sou	548	148	30	3	16	28	60	63	15	7	407	.270	.306	.423	.250	63	125-3B 95
1997	Indianap	AA	477	134	24	3	19	38	61	67	11	4	347	.281	.334	.463	.273	68	118-3B 105
1997	Cincnnti	NL	49	12	0	0	0	2	3	2	1	0	37	.245	.275	.245	.177	2	
1998	Indianap	Int	330	68	12	1	5	25	25	20	11	4	266	.206	.262	.294	.193	22	76-3B 112
1998	Cincnnti	NL	180	50	14	2	2	17	26	19	6	1	131	.278	.340	.411	.266	24	48-3B 107
1999	*Cincnnti*	*NL*	*490*	*128*	*25*	*2*	*13*	*33*	*54*	*54*	*16*	*5*	*367*	*.261*	*.308*	*.400*	*.249*	*57*	

Did not hit at all in Triple-A this year, but the Reds are apparently prepared to hand him the job at third and cross their fingers. Should be a step up from Greene in the field, but with three steps down in offense, the Reds didn't help themselves.

Bret Boone   **2B**   **Bats R   Age 30**

YEAR	TEAM	LGE	AB	H	DB	TP	HR	BB	R	RBI	SB	CS	OUT	BA	OBA	SA	EQA	EQR	DEFENSE
1996	Cincnnti	NL	517	117	20	3	12	35	40	44	2	2	402	.226	.275	.346	.212	41	137-2B 96
1997	Cincnnti	NL	440	95	21	1	8	47	38	35	4	5	350	.216	.292	.323	.212	36	133-2B 99
1998	Cincnnti	NL	581	154	32	1	27	52	69	83	6	5	432	.265	.325	.463	.267	80	154-2B 102
1999	*Atlanta*	*NL*	*484*	*117*	*26*	*1*	*16*	*43*	*49*	*55*	*5*	*3*	*370*	*.242*	*.304*	*.399*	*.245*	*55*	

Now, of course, you trade him. Yes, the 24 dingers were nice, but that .782 OPS is the second-highest of his career, he's 29, and he's signed for two more years of decent money. Trade him they did, to Atlanta in the deal that landed Denny Neagle, Michael Tucker, and Rob Bell. Did the Reds get the three-best players in the deal?

Andy Burress   **OF**   **Bats R   Age 21**

YEAR	TEAM	LGE	AB	H	DB	TP	HR	BB	R	RBI	SB	CS	OUT	BA	OBA	SA	EQA	EQR	DEFENSE
1996	Billings	Pio	102	21	2	0	3	3	5	6	1	1	82	.206	.229	.314	.174	5	
1997	Billings	Pio	98	19	3	0	2	4	4	5	0	0	79	.194	.225	.286	.160	4	
1997	Charl-WV	SAL	87	16	1	0	1	5	3	3	0	0	71	.184	.228	.230	.132	2	
1998	Burlingt	Mid	452	112	16	4	10	51	54	46	12	3	343	.248	.324	.367	.246	52	118-OF 79
1999	*Cincnnti*	*NL*	*328*	*87*	*11*	*2*	*10*	*30*	*37*	*40*	*7*	*2*	*243*	*.265*	*.327*	*.402*	*.258*	*41*	

In a curious decision, the Reds decided to promote Burress all the way to the Midwest League, even though he had never really shown much of anything in three seasons in the Pioneer League. Burress responded with a true breakthrough season. He had 23 walks as a pro before '98, and drew 62 this year. He also began to assert himself on the base paths. It's just one year, but that kind of progress after a big promotion is a great sign of an emerging prospect.

Sean Casey   **1B**   **Bats L   Age 24**

YEAR	TEAM	LGE	AB	H	DB	TP	HR	BB	R	RBI	SB	CS	OUT	BA	OBA	SA	EQA	EQR	DEFENSE
1996	Kinston	Car	348	107	15	2	11	30	44	52	1	1	242	.307	.362	.457	.282	51	70-1B 75
1997	Akron	Eas	237	85	13	1	8	18	35	43	0	1	153	.359	.404	.523	.315	43	49-1B 87
1997	Buffalo	AA	73	27	5	0	5	9	14	17	0	0	46	.370	.439	.644	.356	17	
1998	Indianap	Int	94	29	6	1	1	12	14	13	0	0	65	.309	.387	.426	.286	14	20-1B 91
1998	Cincnnti	NL	301	82	19	1	8	45	44	40	1	1	220	.272	.367	.422	.276	44	78-1B 91
1999	*Cincnnti*	*NL*	*368*	*117*	*23*	*1*	*13*	*40*	*53*	*62*	*1*	*1*	*252*	*.318*	*.385*	*.492*	*.302*	*63*	

A handy pickup, although one wonders what Bowden could have gotten had he peddled Burba at a trading deadline instead of at the end of spring training. Casey struggled after the Opening Day beaning, but was fine once he returned. Looks like he should eventually be an adequate first baseman, but he'll have to continue to improve his hitting to be a good overall solution.

Brook Fordyce   C   Bats R   Age 29

YEAR	TEAM	LGE	AB	H	DB	TP	HR	BB	R	RBI	SB	CS	OUT	BA	OBA	SA	EQA	EQR	DEFENSE
1995	Buffalo	AA	177	41	10	0	0	13	13	11	1	0	136	.232	.284	.288	.197	12	
1996	Indianap	AA	375	94	13	1	12	24	33	41	2	1	282	.251	.296	.387	.234	37	
1997	Cincnnti	NL	95	19	4	0	1	9	7	5	2	0	76	.200	.269	.274	.191	6	
1998	Cincnnti	NL	145	37	6	0	4	12	13	16	0	1	109	.255	.312	.379	.237	15	41-C 102
1999	*Cincnnti*	*NL*	*184*	*47*	*6*	*0*	*7*	*15*	*17*	*23*	*1*	*1*	*138*	*.255*	*.312*	*.402*	*.248*	*21*	

Spare part, will keep a job until he gets all Carlos Hernandez-like and demands big money.

Mike Frank   CF   Bats L   Age 24

YEAR	TEAM	LGE	AB	H	DB	TP	HR	BB	R	RBI	SB	CS	OUT	BA	OBA	SA	EQA	EQR	DEFENSE
1997	Billings	Pio	253	48	3	1	3	18	12	10	5	3	208	.190	.244	.245	.158	10	65-OF 93
1998	Chattang	Sou	226	65	7	2	10	13	26	33	3	1	162	.288	.326	.469	.271	31	51-OF 105
1998	Indianap	Int	87	27	3	0	0	6	10	8	1	0	60	.310	.355	.345	.251	9	19-OF 110
1998	Cincnnti	NL	89	20	7	0	0	7	8	5	0	0	69	.225	.281	.303	.200	6	23-OF 110
1999	*Cincnnti*	*NL*	*323*	*91*	*13*	*1*	*8*	*19*	*33*	*38*	*4*	*2*	*234*	*.282*	*.322*	*.402*	*.253*	*38*	

Didn't belong in Triple-A this year, much less the majors, but McKeon's mid-summer freak-out meant Frank came up too soon and went on the 40-man roster a year earlier than he had to. The Reds deserve credit for jumping him to Double-A, and he performed very well there. Needs a year of Triple-A to get his bat up to the point where it doesn't negate his glove; the Cameron acquisition makes this likely.

Jeffrey Hammonds   OF/DL   Bats R   Age 28

YEAR	TEAM	LGE	AB	H	DB	TP	HR	BB	R	RBI	SB	CS	OUT	BA	OBA	SA	EQA	EQR	DEFENSE
1996	Rochestr	Int	125	30	3	0	3	16	14	12	2	1	96	.240	.326	.336	.236	13	28-OF 112
1996	Baltimor	AL	245	54	10	1	9	22	22	25	3	4	195	.220	.285	.380	.225	23	59-OF 105
1997	Baltimor	AL	392	103	19	2	22	33	53	58	15	1	290	.263	.320	.490	.278	59	102-OF 104
1998	Baltimor	AL	169	46	13	1	6	27	29	24	6	2	125	.272	.372	.467	.292	29	45-OF 101
1998	Cincnnti	NL	86	26	5	1	0	13	13	10	1	1	61	.302	.394	.384	.278	12	23-OF 114
1999	*Cincnnti*	*NL*	*294*	*75*	*15*	*1*	*11*	*35*	*40*	*37*	*11*	*3*	*222*	*.255*	*.334*	*.425*	*.269*	*41*	

So the Reds get him, and 100-odd plate appearances later, his season is over due to injury. Are we surprised? For all the praise Bowden gets for shrewd deal-making, this was a really ridiculous move. Hammonds is a worse player than Willie Greene, plays about half the time, is a year older, and doesn't hit well enough to separate himself from the Reds' other dozen out-fielders. He'll be extremely overpriced in roto leagues this year.

Damian Jackson   SS/2B   Bats R   Age 25

YEAR	TEAM	LGE	AB	H	DB	TP	HR	BB	R	RBI	SB	CS	OUT	BA	OBA	SA	EQA	EQR	DEFENSE
1996	Buffalo	AA	455	114	11	1	11	49	56	43	23	7	348	.251	.323	.352	.244	51	130-SS 103
1997	Buffalo	AA	270	79	7	0	5	35	44	28	19	7	198	.293	.374	.374	.272	38	66-SS 104
1997	Indianap	AA	71	18	5	1	0	10	11	6	4	1	54	.254	.346	.352	.256	9	
1998	Indianap	Int	513	122	29	6	6	54	60	44	17	8	399	.238	.310	.353	.234	53	129-SS 96
1998	Cincnnti	NL	38	12	6	0	0	6	9	4	2	0	26	.316	.409	.474	.316	7	
1999	*Cincnnti*	*NL*	*472*	*122*	*24*	*3*	*7*	*50*	*62*	*45*	*22*	*8*	*358*	*.258*	*.330*	*.367*	*.251*	*57*	

Heavily hyped Indians prospect who simply collapsed in his third year of Triple-A. Maybe he was just depressed about returning to Indianapolis. If either Larkin or Boone are still around, Pokey Reese is ahead of him, which would probably depress me too.

Austin Kearns   RF   Bats R   Age 19

YEAR	TEAM	LGE	AB	H	DB	TP	HR	BB	R	RBI	SB	CS	OUT	BA	OBA	SA	EQA	EQR	DEFENSE
1998	Billings	Pio	104	20	2	0	1	15	7	6	0	1	84	.192	.294	.240	.186	6	28-OF 80
1999	*Cincnnti*	*NL*	*79*	*20*	*0*	*0*	*2*	*10*	*7*	*9*	*0*	*1*	*60*	*.253*	*.337*	*.329*	*.237*	*8*	

The Reds' #1 pick this year, he signed late but had a good stint when he finally showed up in Billings. Kearns is extremely athletic and has a very high ceiling if he can harness his tools. Handled himself very well considering his age.

Paul Konerko   **1B**   **Bats R   Age 23**

YEAR	TEAM	LGE	AB	H	DB	TP	HR	BB	R	RBI	SB	CS	OUT	BA	OBA	SA	EQA	EQR	DEFENSE	
1996	SanAnton	Tex	474	137	14	1	25	64	65	81	1	2	339	.289	.374	.481	.292	78	120-1B 102	
1997	Albuquer	PCL	453	118	15	1	26	53	55	71	2	2	337	.260	.338	.470	.275	67	102-3B 88	23-1B 93
1998	LosAngls	NL	145	33	2	0	4	11	10	12	0	1	113	.228	.282	.324	.206	11		
1998	Albuquer	PCL	83	28	6	0	5	9	14	17	0	0	55	.337	.402	.590	.329	17	17-OF 92	
1998	Cincnnti	NL	73	16	4	0	3	6	6	8	0	0	57	.219	.278	.397	.230	7		
1998	Indianap	Int	148	46	6	0	7	17	22	25	1	0	102	.311	.382	.493	.301	25	35-3B 97	
1999	*ChiSox*	*AL*	*442*	*125*	*15*	*0*	*24*	*48*	*58*	*75*	*1*	*1*	*318*	*.283*	*.353*	*.480*	*.287*	*70*		

Not the next David McCarty, no matter what you've read, heard, or thought. Remember that the last David McCarty was Todd Walker, who is now, what, the next Craig Biggio? Konerko needs to have two things happen to succeed in 1999: he needs to get 500 plate appearances with one team, and he needs to play one position, preferably first. Neither condition would have been satisfied with in Cincinnati, so the Reds traded him to the White Sox for Mike Cameron, where it looks like he'll get both the time and the position.

Barry Larkin   **SS**   **Bats R   Age 35**

YEAR	TEAM	LGE	AB	H	DB	TP	HR	BB	R	RBI	SB	CS	OUT	BA	OBA	SA	EQA	EQR	DEFENSE
1996	Cincnnti	NL	517	153	31	4	33	97	108	97	30	11	375	.296	.407	.563	.325	113	142-SS 98
1997	Cincnnti	NL	223	69	17	3	4	47	51	31	12	3	157	.309	.430	.466	.319	45	54-SS 110
1998	Cincnnti	NL	537	165	34	9	19	82	107	86	28	3	375	.307	.399	.510	.317	106	140-SS 93
1999	*Cincnnti*	*NL*	*427*	*125*	*26*	*6*	*17*	*78*	*85*	*69*	*22*	*5*	*307*	*.293*	*.402*	*.501*	*.316*	*86*	

Hall of Famer working on being elected on the first ballot; a few more seasons like '98 won't hurt. Traded walks for power, which isn't a bad deal. The Reds say they won't trade him, but Bowden would be foolish not to check the market price, especially with LaRussa on the other side of the table.

Brandon Larson   **SS**   **Bats R   Age 23**

YEAR	TEAM	LGE	AB	H	DB	TP	HR	BB	R	RBI	SB	CS	OUT	BA	OBA	SA	EQA	EQR	DEFENSE
1997	Chattang	Sou	40	9	3	1	0	1	2	3	0	0	31	.225	.244	.350	.196	3	
1998	Burlingt	Mid	68	12	2	0	1	3	2	2	1	1	57	.176	.211	.250	.133	2	
1999	*Cincnnti*	*NL*	*51*	*10*	*1*	*0*	*1*	*2*	*2*	*2*	*0*	*1*	*42*	*.196*	*.226*	*.275*	*.151*	*2*	

Former #1 pick stalled out at Burlington before his season ended in June due to injury. Like so many other Red prospects, his major-league ETA is totally up in the air until we see if he's healthy.

Jason LaRue   **C**   **Bats R   Age 25**

YEAR	TEAM	LGE	AB	H	DB	TP	HR	BB	R	RBI	SB	CS	OUT	BA	OBA	SA	EQA	EQR	DEFENSE
1996	Charl-WV	SAL	126	23	2	0	2	8	5	5	1	0	103	.183	.231	.246	.149	4	
1997	Charl-WV	SAL	482	123	23	1	6	36	47	42	6	3	362	.255	.307	.344	.227	45	
1998	Chattang	Sou	375	118	24	3	11	26	50	57	3	2	259	.315	.359	.483	.287	57	92-C 94
1998	Indianap	Int	51	11	3	0	0	3	3	2	0	1	41	.216	.259	.275	.169	2	
1999	*Cincnnti*	*NL*	*394*	*112*	*23*	*1*	*9*	*27*	*45*	*48*	*5*	*2*	*284*	*.284*	*.330*	*.416*	*.261*	*49*	

We said last year that he needed a two-level jump this year to get noticed; he did it, and excelled at Double-A. Of course, we said the jump was doubtful, which shows what we know. The power increase was dramatic, and enough to make him a star behind the plate. Now the #1 catcher in the Reds' system, and a threat to Taubensee this summer.

Blane Layton   **CF**   **Bats L   Age 22**

YEAR	TEAM	LGE	AB	H	DB	TP	HR	BB	R	RBI	SB	CS	OUT	BA	OBA	SA	EQA	EQR	DEFENSE
1998	Billings	Pio	215	31	5	1	2	16	6	6	1	1	185	.144	.203	.205	.095	3	55-OF 83
1999	*Cincnnti*	*NL*	*174*	*40*	*8*	*1*	*3*	*13*	*14*	*15*	*1*	*1*	*135*	*.230*	*.283*	*.339*	*.216*	*15*	

Leadoff hitter and fan favorite in Billings. Covers a lot of ground in center, but his arm may not be major-league. Has a lot to prove, but this isn't exactly a system stacked with talent, so he'll move up as long as he performs.

James Matan   DH   Bats R   Age 23

YEAR	TEAM	LGE	AB	H	DB	TP	HR	BB	R	RBI	SB	CS	OUT	BA	OBA	SA	EQA	EQR	DEFENSE
1998	Billings	Pio	287	34	2	0	4	17	6	6	0	1	254	.118	.168	.167	—	-4	
1999	Cincnnti	NL	226	45	4	0	5	12	10	13	0	1	182	.199	.239	.283	.170	11	

Huge power prospect who spent most of the season at DH. Coaches focused on getting him to make contact this year, with some success, but they need to teach him to play left or first, because the Reds aren't headed for the American League any time soon.

Melvin Nieves   OF   Bats B   Age 27

YEAR	TEAM	LGE	AB	H	DB	TP	HR	BB	R	RBI	SB	CS	OUT	BA	OBA	SA	EQA	EQR	DEFENSE
1996	Detroit	AL	423	100	21	4	23	42	47	60	1	2	325	.236	.305	.468	.260	56	94-OF 95
1997	Detroit	AL	354	80	18	1	20	39	37	48	1	7	281	.226	.303	.452	.250	44	92-OF 96
1998	Indianap	Int	53	13	1	0	2	7	6	6	0	0	40	.245	.333	.377	.250	6	
1998	Cincnnti	NL	119	30	2	0	3	27	18	14	0	0	89	.252	.390	.345	.271	17	
1999	Cincnnti	NL	250	61	11	1	11	31	28	34	0	2	191	.244	.327	.428	.260	33	

Drew a lot of walks, but between injuries and the spring death of his infant son, he really struggled this year. Can help someone, but Cincinnati is not the place for him. Released.

Jon Nunnally   CF   Bats L   Age 27

YEAR	TEAM	LGE	AB	H	DB	TP	HR	BB	R	RBI	SB	CS	OUT	BA	OBA	SA	EQA	EQR	DEFENSE
1996	Omaha	AA	345	91	15	2	21	46	50	56	10	8	262	.264	.350	.501	.285	57	96-OF 94
1996	KansasCy	AL	88	18	5	0	5	13	10	12	0	0	70	.205	.307	.432	.253	11	22-OF 107
1997	Cincnnti	NL	199	62	10	3	13	27	35	40	6	3	140	.312	.394	.588	.323	42	49-OF 110
1998	Cincnnti	NL	174	36	7	0	8	35	23	21	3	5	143	.207	.340	.385	.251	23	51-OF 105
1998	Indianap	Int	289	62	10	1	8	38	29	27	4	3	230	.215	.306	.339	.227	28	73-OF 99
1999	Cincnnti	NL	444	109	21	3	21	67	64	63	14	7	342	.245	.344	.448	.276	68	

Can still hit, but McKeon dropped him like a bad habit when he started slowly. Like Nieves, Nunnally will help any team smart enough to give him a chance, but unlike him, Nunnally can also offer solid defense in center.

Eduardo Perez   1B   Bats R   Age 29

YEAR	TEAM	LGE	AB	H	DB	TP	HR	BB	R	RBI	SB	CS	OUT	BA	OBA	SA	EQA	EQR	DEFENSE
1996	Indianap	AA	456	122	20	3	15	47	59	58	10	1	335	.268	.336	.423	.266	61	113-3B 88
1997	Cincnnti	NL	295	72	14	0	17	30	35	42	4	1	224	.244	.314	.464	.265	40	65-1B 91
1998	Cincnnti	NL	172	41	2	0	5	22	16	18	0	1	132	.238	.325	.337	.233	17	
1999	Cincnnti	NL	232	61	9	0	10	24	27	32	2	1	172	.263	.332	.431	.266	31	

We hope the facination is finally over. On a team of six or seven first basemen, he's the worst, and even Dad can't save him this time.

Roberto Petagine   1B/OF   Bats L   Age 28

YEAR	TEAM	LGE	AB	H	DB	TP	HR	BB	R	RBI	SB	CS	OUT	BA	OBA	SA	EQA	EQR	DEFENSE	
1996	Norfolk	Int	314	91	16	2	9	45	47	45	3	1	224	.290	.379	.439	.287	49	93-1B 91	
1996	NY Mets	NL	100	24	4	0	4	9	9	12	0	2	78	.240	.303	.400	.235	10	28-1B 98	
1997	Norfolk	Int	439	125	15	1	23	69	64	76	0	1	315	.285	.382	.481	.296	75	114-1B 89	
1998	Indianap	Int	359	105	15	1	17	57	56	61	2	1	255	.292	.389	.482	.301	63	67-1B 100	16-OF 99
1998	Cincnnti	NL	62	16	3	1	3	16	12	11	1	0	46	.258	.410	.484	.313	13		
1999	Cincnnti	NL	404	119	19	1	21	66	63	74	1	1	286	.295	.394	.502	.309	76		

It seemed to good to be true: McKeon was talking about having Petagine come north with the Reds to be the fourth out-fielder, backup at first, and main pinch-hitter. The two-time defending IL MVP has deserved his shot for almost half a decade, but he's going to get it in Japan. Is on a track to be one of those "what could have been" types, like Orestes Destrade.

Pokey Reese   2B/IF   Bats R   Age 26

YEAR	TEAM	LGE	AB	H	DB	TP	HR	BB	R	RBI	SB	CS	OUT	BA	OBA	SA	EQA	EQR	DEFENSE
1996	Indianap	AA	281	63	7	0	3	22	21	17	5	2	220	.224	.281	.281	.195	18	73-SS 101
1997	Indianap	AA	72	16	2	0	3	9	8	8	3	0	56	.222	.309	.375	.247	8	
1997	Cincnnti	NL	394	84	9	0	6	33	35	23	22	7	317	.213	.274	.282	.200	28	103-SS 97
1998	Cincnnti	NL	133	35	2	2	1	14	15	12	3	2	100	.263	.333	.331	.236	14	24-3B 106
1999	Cincnnti	NL	226	52	5	1	5	19	22	19	10	3	177	.230	.290	.327	.223	21	

Spared Red fans the last 300 at bats of a dismal season by going down with an injury. Has no redeeming qualities as a starter, and I'd be hard-pressed to use him as a defensive replacement for Larkin or Boone. Despite all of this, he's the leading candidate to start at second with Boone gone.

Reggie Sanders   OF   Bats R   Age 31

YEAR	TEAM	LGE	AB	H	DB	TP	HR	BB	R	RBI	SB	CS	OUT	BA	OBA	SA	EQA	EQR	DEFENSE
1996	Cincnnti	NL	286	72	17	1	14	45	49	39	20	9	223	.252	.353	.465	.282	47	69-OF 108
1997	Cincnnti	NL	310	77	17	2	19	43	47	48	11	7	240	.248	.340	.500	.281	50	75-OF 108
1998	Cincnnti	NL	480	129	18	6	15	54	67	60	21	10	361	.269	.343	.425	.267	67	118-OF 99
1999	Cincnnti	NL	400	104	21	2	16	52	57	54	17	10	306	.260	.345	.442	.273	60	

An abysmal year, one when he couldn't stay healthy long enough for Bowden to kick him to the curb. Still a threat to be a rotisserie bargain in any season, but his value to real teams is pretty dubious because of the constant injuries.

Chris Stynes   UT   Bats R   Age 26

YEAR	TEAM	LGE	AB	H	DB	TP	HR	BB	R	RBI	SB	CS	OUT	BA	OBA	SA	EQA	EQR	DEFENSE	
1996	Omaha	AA	282	95	18	1	9	20	43	45	7	3	190	.337	.381	.504	.302	47	33-OF 97	25-3B 106
1996	KansasCy	AL	91	26	6	0	0	1	9	7	5	2	67	.286	.293	.352	.226	8		
1997	Omaha	AA	325	74	12	1	6	18	22	25	2	1	252	.228	.268	.326	.201	23	22-OF 108	20-2B 88
1997	Indianap	AA	86	30	3	0	2	2	11	12	4	1	57	.349	.364	.453	.286	12	19-2B 116	
1997	Cincnnti	NL	196	67	6	1	6	12	30	29	9	2	131	.342	.380	.474	.298	32	30-OF 114	
1998	Cincnnti	NL	346	88	8	1	7	34	42	32	16	1	259	.254	.321	.344	.243	38	61-OF 97	
1999	Cincnnti	NL	411	115	15	1	11	28	50	47	18	3	299	.280	.326	.401	.260	52		

Could be arrested for fraud. Tortured rotogeeks by stealing fourteen bases before June 1st, and stealing the grand total of one thereafter, to go with a tumbling average and just one more home run. Briefly a starting outfielder, he's now in a utility role, which is what he was suited for in the first place. The new Rex Hudler.

Tony Tarasco   OF   Bats L   Age 28

YEAR	TEAM	LGE	AB	H	DB	TP	HR	BB	R	RBI	SB	CS	OUT	BA	OBA	SA	EQA	EQR	DEFENSE
1996	Baltimor	AL	83	20	2	0	1	6	8	5	5	4	67	.241	.292	.301	.206	6	18-OF 115
1997	Baltimor	AL	164	33	9	1	7	25	19	19	2	2	133	.201	.307	.396	.243	19	67-OF 87
1998	Indianap	Int	315	85	11	1	11	35	37	42	2	2	232	.270	.343	.416	.263	41	66-OF 88
1998	Cincnnti	NL	24	5	2	0	1	3	2	3	0	0	19	.208	.296	.417	.244	3	
1999	Cincnnti	NL	285	72	10	0	12	34	32	38	4	3	216	.253	.332	.414	.261	37	

Deserves a chance; he can't be any worse than Reggie Sanders, and he would give the Reds a real defensive outfielder. I don't expect him to get the opportunity, and he was released in November.

Eddie Taubensee   C   Bats L   Age 30

YEAR	TEAM	LGE	AB	H	DB	TP	HR	BB	R	RBI	SB	CS	OUT	BA	OBA	SA	EQA	EQR	DEFENSE
1996	Cincnnti	NL	326	93	14	0	14	27	37	48	2	4	237	.285	.340	.457	.270	45	
1997	Cincnnti	NL	252	65	15	0	11	23	29	34	0	1	188	.258	.320	.448	.261	33	
1998	Cincnnti	NL	430	120	20	0	14	55	57	59	1	0	310	.279	.361	.423	.275	61	114-C 94
1999	Cincnnti	NL	351	100	15	0	15	44	46	55	1	1	252	.285	.365	.456	.285	55	

The hot start may have made it look like a breakout season, but it wasn't that much better as much as it was a case that he finally got to play every day for the first time. With his offense slipping and LaRue creeping up, Taubensee's trade bait, and could end up being the new Ron Hassey.

Justin Towle   C/DH   Bats R   Age 25

YEAR	TEAM	LGE	AB	H	DB	TP	HR	BB	R	RBI	SB	CS	OUT	BA	OBA	SA	EQA	EQR	DEFENSE
1996	WnstnSlm	Car	356	76	7	1	11	76	50	37	8	2	282	.213	.352	.331	.252	45	
1997	Chattang	Sou	407	103	24	2	8	44	47	43	4	3	307	.253	.326	.381	.247	46	
1998	Chattang	Sou	146	34	5	0	4	18	15	15	2	0	112	.233	.317	.349	.238	15	
1999	Cincnnti	NL	258	67	10	1	8	35	33	33	4	1	192	.260	.348	.399	.267	35	

Didn't play after mid-June due to a knee injury, which means his catching days may be over. He can hit and controls the strike zone extremely well, but his future is up in the air until we see what position he can play.

Pat Watkins   OF   Bats R   Age 26

YEAR	TEAM	LGE	AB	H	DB	TP	HR	BB	R	RBI	SB	CS	OUT	BA	OBA	SA	EQA	EQR	DEFENSE
1996	Chattang	Sou	492	124	21	1	8	21	40	41	10	7	375	.252	.283	.348	.215	40	121-OF 96
1997	Chattang	Sou	171	48	8	1	4	11	21	19	6	2	125	.281	.324	.409	.256	21	41-OF 93
1997	Indianap	AA	325	86	12	5	8	23	37	36	12	7	247	.265	.313	.406	.247	38	80-OF 100
1998	Indianap	Int	184	61	8	1	2	12	25	23	5	2	125	.332	.372	.418	.278	26	43-OF 109
1998	Cincnnti	NL	146	39	8	1	2	9	13	15	1	3	110	.267	.310	.377	.232	14	41-OF 102
1999	Cincnnti	NL	409	116	18	2	8	22	45	45	13	6	299	.284	.320	.396	.251	47	

A nice fourth outfielder on a team that needs fourth outfielders like it needs more first basemen.

Jason Williams   2B   Bats R   Age 25

YEAR	TEAM	LGE	AB	H	DB	TP	HR	BB	R	RBI	SB	CS	OUT	BA	OBA	SA	EQA	EQR	DEFENSE	
1997	Burlingt	Mid	252	59	7	0	4	14	17	18	4	3	196	.234	.274	.310	.198	17	43-SS 94	21-2B 100
1997	Chattang	Sou	264	67	11	1	4	13	22	23	4	3	200	.254	.289	.348	.218	22	65-2B 103	
1998	Indianap	Int	403	96	18	1	2	61	47	32	3	2	309	.238	.338	.303	.232	40	114-2B 93	
1999	Cincnnti	NL	396	106	17	1	4	39	43	39	5	3	293	.268	.333	.346	.243	43		

A sleeper who cooled off dramatically in the second half at Indianapolis. Still doesn't hit for much power; will probably get more Triple-A time this year, which isn't unwise given his limited pro exposure and inconsistency in '98.

Dewayne Wise   CF   Bats L   Age 21

YEAR	TEAM	LGE	AB	H	DB	TP	HR	BB	R	RBI	SB	CS	OUT	BA	OBA	SA	EQA	EQR	DEFENSE
1997	Billings	Pio	257	52	5	2	4	6	11	12	7	4	209	.202	.221	.284	.160	11	59-OF 99
1998	Burlingt	Mid	498	96	13	5	2	34	26	20	12	9	411	.193	.244	.251	.161	21	123-OF 101
1999	Cincnnti	NL	385	89	9	3	4	17	27	25	14	8	304	.231	.264	.301	.195	26	

Three-sport star in high school who chose the wrong one to pursue. Wise is athletic, has great speed, covers a ton of ground, but he doesn't really hit much and didn't adjust at all in a full season at Burlington. He's only 21 this year and will get more time, but is more likely to wind up someone's Rule 5 pick in the double-A round someday.

Dmitri Young   LF   Bats B   Age 25

YEAR	TEAM	LGE	AB	H	DB	TP	HR	BB	R	RBI	SB	CS	OUT	BA	OBA	SA	EQA	EQR	DEFENSE	
1996	Louisvil	AA	460	149	28	5	14	37	73	70	16	5	316	.324	.374	.498	.299	77	121-1B 105	
1997	Louisvil	AA	84	22	4	0	4	12	12	12	1	1	63	.262	.354	.452	.276	13		
1997	St Louis	NL	333	86	14	2	6	40	39	35	5	5	252	.258	.338	.366	.247	38	70-1B 88	
1998	Cincnnti	NL	535	166	41	2	17	50	76	83	2	5	374	.310	.369	.490	.291	85	93-OF 85	37-1B 96
1999	Cincnnti	NL	484	150	35	2	18	47	71	79	7	4	338	.310	.371	.502	.299	82		

I know it's not his fault, but Young is one horrible defensive outfielder. Fortunately for him, he smacked the hell out of the ball, having a season on par with his breakthrough '96. I think this was worth Jeff Brantley.

PITCHERS (Averages: 4.00 ERA, 9.00 H/9 1.00 HR/9, 3.00 BB/9,, 6.00 K/9, 1.00 KWH)

Stan Belinda — Throws R — Age 32

YEAR	TEAM	LGE	IP	H	ER	HR	BB	K	ERA	W	L	H/9	HR/9	BB/9	K/9	KWH	PERA
1996	Boston	AL	30.3	29	16	2	17	18	4.75	1	2	8.60	0.59	5.04	5.34	0.49	3.56
1997	Cincnnti	NL	102.3	84	35	11	30	102	3.08	7	4	7.39	0.97	2.64	8.97	3.10	2.81
1998	Cincnnti	NL	63.3	47	20	8	25	52	2.84	5	2	6.68	1.14	3.55	7.39	1.73	2.56

Diagnosed with multiple sclerosis. He's expected to pitch again in '99, and we're pulling for him.

Jason Bere — Throws R — Age 28

YEAR	TEAM	LGE	IP	H	ER	HR	BB	K	ERA	W	L	H/9	HR/9	BB/9	K/9	KWH	PERA
1996	ChiSox	AL	17.0	26	16	3	15	18	8.47	0	2	13.76	1.59	7.94	9.53	0.62	7.41
1997	Nashvill	AmA	19.3	27	14	2	7	10	6.52	1	1	12.57	0.93	3.26	4.66	0.40	5.59
1997	ChiSox	AL	29.7	20	12	4	14	20	3.64	2	1	6.07	1.21	4.25	6.07	1.07	2.43
1998	ChiSox	AL	86.7	99	59	13	53	52	6.13	3	7	10.28	1.35	5.50	5.40	0.39	5.19
1998	Cincnnti	NL	45.0	40	17	3	19	29	3.40	3	2	8.00	0.60	3.80	5.80	0.83	3.20

Yes, he looked good in a small sample. Yes, Don Gullett has gotten good at returning one-time star pitchers to form. The problem is that Bere's arm is still held together by twine and thread, none of his pitches are where they were pre-surgery, and his control is still weak. He'll stay in the Reds' rotation until June.

Jim Crowell — Throws L — Age 25

Year	Team	Lge	IP	H	ER	HR	BB	K	ERA	W	L	H/9	HR/9	BB/9	K/9	KWH	PERA
1996	Columbus	SAL	146.7	264	132	22	87	60	8.10	3	13	16.20	1.35	5.34	3.68	0.12	7.79
1997	Kinston	Car	104.0	135	55	5	27	61	4.76	5	7	11.68	0.43	2.34	5.28	0.77	4.67
1997	Chattang	Sou	18.3	21	5	2	5	11	2.45	1	1	10.31	0.98	2.45	5.40	0.86	4.42
1997	Indianap	AmA	19.7	21	7	1	7	5	3.20	1	1	9.61	0.46	3.20	2.29	0.13	3.66
1998	Charl-WV	SAL	12.3	41	31	1	13	5	22.62	0	1	29.92	0.73	9.49	3.65	0.04	10.95
1998	Chattang	Sou	22.7	46	27	2	15	7	10.72	0	3	18.26	0.79	5.96	2.78	0.05	7.94

Started 0-4, 8.51, then had surgery to repair tears on the inside of his rotator cuff. Needs at least a year to get back to where he was in '97, which puts him on a 2001 timetable—assuming he didn't leave his slider on the operating table.

Keith Glauber — Throws R — Age 27

YEAR	TEAM	LGE	IP	H	ER	HR	BB	K	ERA	W	L	H/9	HR/9	BB/9	K/9	KWH	PERA
1996	Peoria	Mid	55.7	87	48	3	32	46	7.76	1	5	14.07	0.49	5.17	7.44	0.57	6.14
1997	Arkansas	Tex	53.7	62	27	3	28	39	4.53	3	3	10.40	0.50	4.70	6.54	0.66	4.53
1997	Louisvil	AmA	15.3	21	15	2	4	11	8.80	0	2	12.33	1.17	2.35	6.46	1.08	5.87
1998	Indianap	Int	15.7	23	17	1	14	12	9.77	0	2	13.21	0.57	8.04	6.89	0.34	6.32
1998	Cincnnti	NL	7.7	6	2	0	1	4	2.35	1	0	7.04	0.00	1.17	4.70	2.00	1.17

A Rule 5 selection who was recovering from rotator cuff surgery—an interesting strategy, if you think about it. Bowden liked the pre-injury Glauber enough to reportedly offer the Cardinals Brantley for him. When healthy, he had a 93-mph heater and a plus slider. He'll get a trial in the Reds' pen this year.

Danny Graves — Throws R — Age 25

YEAR	TEAM	LGE	IP	H	ER	HR	BB	K	ERA	W	L	H/9	HR/9	BB/9	K/9	KWH	PERA
1996	Buffalo	AmA	77.7	68	16	1	25	40	1.85	7	2	7.88	0.12	2.90	4.64	0.71	2.67
1996	Clevelnd	AL	30.7	27	13	2	8	22	3.82	2	1	7.92	0.59	2.35	6.46	1.68	2.93
1997	Clevelnd	AL	11.7	16	7	2	7	4	5.40	0	1	12.34	1.54	5.40	3.09	0.11	6.17
1997	Buffalo	AmA	41.0	53	23	3	11	18	5.05	2	3	11.63	0.66	2.41	3.95	0.42	4.83
1997	Cincnnti	NL	15.7	27	13	0	11	7	7.47	0	2	15.51	0.00	6.32	4.02	0.12	6.32
1998	Cincnnti	NL	83.0	78	27	6	25	40	2.93	6	3	8.46	0.65	2.71	4.34	0.62	3.25

In the closer mix, with the crown of "closer of the future" resting on his head. Given that the Reds won't be contending in '99, there's no reason not to continue with the three-headed monster in the closer role, as long as Graves gets enough work to continue his development.

Pete Harnisch — Throws R — Age 32

YEAR	TEAM	LGE	IP	H	ER	HR	BB	K	ERA	W	L	H/9	HR/9	BB/9	K/9	KWH	PERA
1996	NY Mets	NL	192.3	211	98	31	57	102	4.59	9	12	9.87	1.45	2.67	4.77	0.65	4.59
1997	NY Mets	NL	25.7	39	24	6	10	11	8.42	1	2	13.68	2.10	3.51	3.86	0.23	7.36
1997	Milwauke	AL	14.7	13	7	1	11	10	4.30	1	1	7.98	0.61	6.75	6.14	0.52	3.68
1998	Cincnnti	NL	214.0	177	67	25	58	143	2.82	16	8	7.44	1.05	2.44	6.01	1.49	2.86

Perhaps his best season since 1991, and maybe his best ever. Harnisch regained his confidence and arm strength, pitching 200 innings for the first time since 1993 with no signs of late-season fatigue. Signed a two-year extension for a relatively low salary, giving the Reds a good front three behind Neagle and Tomko.

Josh Harris — Throws R — Age 21

YEAR	TEAM	LGE	IP	H	ER	HR	BB	K	ERA	W	L	H/9	HR/9	BB/9	K/9	KWH	PERA
1996	Billings	Pio	37.3	69	29	5	20	18	6.99	1	3	16.63	1.21	4.82	4.34	0.18	7.71
1997	Billings	Pio	75.7	136	58	3	32	32	6.90	2	6	16.18	0.36	3.81	3.81	0.18	6.66
1998	Burlingt	Mid	171.7	213	92	9	51	113	4.82	8	11	11.17	0.47	2.67	5.92	0.88	4.51

A big (6'3", 230) thrower who went through some dominating stretches this. The season translates less impressively than you might think because of the 22 unearned runs that don't show up in his ERA. The one concern is his workload, which was high for 20-year-old.

John Hudek — Throws R — Age 32

YEAR	TEAM	LGE	IP	H	ER	HR	BB	K	ERA	W	L	H/9	HR/9	BB/9	K/9	KWH	PERA
1996	Tucson	PCL	19.7	19	8	3	8	20	3.66	1	1	8.69	1.37	3.66	9.15	1.97	4.12
1996	Houston	NL	16.0	13	4	2	4	12	2.25	2	0	7.31	1.12	2.25	6.75	2.08	2.81
1997	New Orln	AmA	20.0	5	2	1	3	20	0.90	2	0	2.25	0.45	1.35	9.00	20.00	-1.35
1997	Houston	NL	41.0	43	25	9	30	32	5.49	2	3	9.44	1.98	6.59	7.02	0.60	5.27
1998	NY Mets	NL	27.7	25	11	2	17	26	3.58	2	1	8.13	0.65	5.53	8.46	1.19	3.58
1998	Cincnnti	NL	38.7	28	12	7	26	37	2.79	3	1	6.52	1.63	6.05	8.61	1.41	3.26

Before we all get excited about Hudek's "comeback," check out those walk totals: 47 in 64 IP, coupled with 50 hits and 4 HB. That's over 14 base runners every 9 innings. His ERA masks five unearned runs, behind just Harnisch (7) and Tomko (6). Factor those back in, Hudek's ERA shoots to 3.80, and people start getting less excited.

Rick Krivda — Throws L — Age 29

YEAR	TEAM	LGE	IP	H	ER	HR	BB	K	ERA	W	L	H/9	HR/9	BB/9	K/9	KWH	PERA
1996	Baltimor	AL	82.3	88	39	12	32	53	4.26	4	5	9.62	1.31	3.50	5.79	0.75	4.48
1997	Rochestr	Int	141.7	143	63	13	34	95	4.00	8	8	9.08	0.83	2.16	6.04	1.39	3.62
1997	Baltimor	AL	51.0	68	31	6	16	28	5.47	2	4	12.00	1.06	2.82	4.94	0.54	5.47
1998	Clevelnd	AL	26.7	23	8	2	15	10	2.70	2	1	7.76	0.68	5.06	3.38	0.22	3.37
1998	Cincnnti	NL	28.0	43	31	8	18	18	9.96	0	3	13.82	2.57	5.79	5.79	0.31	8.04

Much ado about nothing; the Reds gave up a moderate pitching prospect (Eddie Priest) for Krivda, who had already been designated for assignment, then realized Krivda wasn't all that after all. Released in November.

Marc Kroon — Throws R — Age 26

YEAR	TEAM	LGE	IP	H	ER	HR	BB	K	ERA	W	L	H/9	HR/9	BB/9	K/9	KWH	PERA
1996	Memphis	Sou	45.0	43	20	5	26	42	4.00	3	2	8.60	1.00	5.20	8.40	1.18	4.00
1997	LasVegas	PCL	42.0	33	17	5	20	43	3.64	3	2	7.07	1.07	4.29	9.21	2.10	3.00
1998	Indianap	Int	45.0	48	30	6	46	28	6.00	2	3	9.60	1.20	9.20	5.60	0.27	5.20

The wild man of San Diego found a new home, and all the Reds had to give up was their top pitching prospect, Buddy Carlyle. Kroon was sent back to the minors a few weeks after the Reds got him, although I expect they'll give him more chances once Carlyle reaches the majors.

Steve Parris — Throws R — Age 31

YEAR	TEAM	LGE	IP	H	ER	HR	BB	K	ERA	W	L	H/9	HR/9	BB/9	K/9	KWH	PERA
1996	Carolina	Sou	25.0	30	13	2	6	15	4.68	1	2	10.80	0.72	2.16	5.40	0.94	4.32
1996	Pittsbrg	NL	27.3	37	19	4	10	25	6.26	1	2	12.18	1.32	3.29	8.23	1.27	5.93
1997	Chattang	Sou	76.3	95	47	9	31	47	5.54	3	5	11.20	1.06	3.66	5.54	0.56	5.19
1997	Indianap	AmA	33.7	32	17	4	12	21	4.54	2	2	8.55	1.07	3.21	5.61	0.86	3.74
1998	Indianap	Int	81.0	88	40	8	26	78	4.44	4	5	9.78	0.89	2.89	8.67	1.99	4.11
1998	Cincnnti	NL	101.7	90	38	9	29	70	3.36	6	5	7.97	0.80	2.57	6.20	1.41	3.01

Similar to Hudek, in that his final stats belie how well he actually pitched. Parris beat up on a lot of bad teams down the stretch, drastically lowering his ERA against Florida, Montreal (twice), and Arizona, with one good start against Houston thrown in. Parris can certainly be an adequate pitcher at the back of a rotation, and the Reds could sorely use a #4 or #5 guy who can eat innings. That's a role Parris could excel at.

Eddie Priest — Throws L — Age 25

YEAR	TEAM	LGE	IP	H	ER	HR	BB	K	ERA	W	L	H/9	HR/9	BB/9	K/9	KWH	PERA
1997	Charl-WV	SAL	68.7	118	55	8	14	39	7.21	2	6	15.47	1.05	1.83	5.11	0.69	6.82
1997	Chattang	Sou	89.7	111	35	7	16	49	3.51	6	4	11.14	0.70	1.61	4.92	1.01	4.52
1998	Chattang	Sou	25.0	19	6	1	9	21	2.16	2	1	6.84	0.36	3.24	7.56	1.93	2.16
1998	Buffalo	Int	86.7	110	51	9	26	36	5.30	4	6	11.42	0.93	2.70	3.74	0.34	4.98
1998	Indianap	Int	33.3	40	18	6	6	17	4.86	2	2	10.80	1.62	1.62	4.59	0.90	5.13

In the spring, Bowden talked about how Priest would be a key member of the Reds' rotation of the future. Then he traded Priest to Cleveland for a throwaway waiver-wire pitcher (see Krivda). Then he reclaimed Priest off waivers down the stretch. Then he outrighted him off the 40-man roster to make room for Rob Bell, acquired in the Boone deal. Priest will probably start the '99 season on the DL with whiplash.

Mike Remlinger — Throws L — Age 33

YEAR	TEAM	LGE	IP	H	ER	HR	BB	K	ERA	W	L	H/9	HR/9	BB/9	K/9	KWH	PERA
1996	Indianap	AmA	86.7	78	33	4	52	76	3.43	6	4	8.10	0.42	5.40	7.89	1.07	3.43
1996	Cincnnti	NL	28.0	26	15	4	19	17	4.82	1	2	8.36	1.29	6.11	5.46	0.44	4.18
1997	Cincnnti	NL	128.7	102	52	12	54	130	3.64	8	6	7.13	0.84	3.78	9.09	2.30	2.80
1998	Cincnnti	NL	170.7	169	84	24	81	133	4.43	9	10	8.91	1.27	4.27	7.01	0.97	4.17

Another retread (remember Roger Craig's predictions of greatness for him?) whom Bowden probably wishes he had traded sooner; he went to Atlanta in the Neagle/Boone deal. His outlook as a reliever under Mazzone is bright, but he needs to cut his walk rate.

Dennis Reyes — Throws L — Age 22

YEAR	TEAM	LGE	IP	H	ER	HR	BB	K	ERA	W	L	H/9	HR/9	BB/9	K/9	KWH	PERA
1996	San Bern	Cal	160.3	190	96	12	71	119	5.39	6	12	10.67	0.67	3.99	6.68	0.79	4.60
1997	SanAnton	Tex	75.0	92	34	7	27	54	4.08	4	4	11.04	0.84	3.24	6.48	0.88	4.80
1997	Albuquer	PCL	59.7	63	28	3	30	38	4.22	3	4	9.50	0.45	4.53	5.73	0.57	3.92
1997	LosAngls	NL	46.0	57	21	5	16	32	4.11	2	3	11.15	0.98	3.13	6.26	0.84	4.89
1998	Albuquer	PCL	45.0	30	10	5	17	48	2.00	4	1	6.00	1.00	3.40	9.60	3.39	2.00
1998	LosAngls	NL	29.0	29	16	1	19	30	4.97	1	2	9.00	0.31	5.90	9.31	1.22	3.72
1998	Indianap	Int	24.0	22	9	1	13	23	3.38	2	1	8.25	0.38	4.88	8.62	1.39	3.37
1998	Cincnnti	NL	40.3	37	16	2	25	41	3.57	2	2	8.26	0.45	5.58	9.15	1.36	3.57

Top prospect pilfered with Konerko from the one-man blue wrecking crew (Tommy Lasorda). Reyes throws three pitches for strikes, including a devastating fastball/change-up combo. Worked significantly fewer innings this year, although whether it's enough to save his arm isn't clear.

Ted Rose   Throws R   Age 25

YEAR	TEAM	LGE	IP	H	ER	HR	BB	K	ERA	W	L	H/9	HR/9	BB/9	K/9	KWH	PERA
1996	Princetn	App	46.7	120	67	10	30	23	12.92	0	5	23.14	1.93	5.79	4.44	0.11	10.99
1997	Charl-WV	SAL	116.7	162	64	9	38	74	4.94	5	8	12.50	0.69	2.93	5.71	0.67	5.32
1998	Chattang	Sou	159.3	228	98	13	60	80	5.54	6	12	12.88	0.73	3.39	4.52	0.35	5.59

This passes for a top pitching prospect in this organization, especially with Buddy Carlyle thrown away. Rose is a filler who's been added to the 40-man roster for no apparent reason. While I'm hardly an advocate of the Rule 5 draft, I believe you can find better options there than Rose.

Scott Sullivan   Throws R   Age 28

YEAR	TEAM	LGE	IP	H	ER	HR	BB	K	ERA	W	L	H/9	HR/9	BB/9	K/9	KWH	PERA
1996	Indianap	AmA	105.7	114	41	10	43	62	3.49	7	5	9.71	0.85	3.66	5.28	0.59	4.26
1997	Indianap	AmA	26.7	19	4	0	4	17	1.35	3	0	6.41	0.00	1.35	5.74	2.85	1.35
1997	Cincnnti	NL	100.0	79	30	12	27	86	2.70	8	3	7.11	1.08	2.43	7.74	2.60	2.61
1998	Cincnnti	NL	105.0	100	54	14	33	79	4.63	5	7	8.57	1.20	2.83	6.77	1.42	3.69

Even sidearmers can be overworked, and Sullivan clearly showed the signs of overuse this season. I wouldn't count on his continued health if I were the Reds. Almost as troubling is that he gave up 12 home runs to right-handers; that's more Frohwirth than Quisenberry as far as sidearmers go.

Brett Tomko   Throws R   Age 26

YEAR	TEAM	LGE	IP	H	ER	HR	BB	K	ERA	W	L	H/9	HR/9	BB/9	K/9	KWH	PERA
1996	Chattang	Sou	150.0	163	78	22	50	123	4.68	7	10	9.78	1.32	3.00	7.38	1.39	4.50
1997	Indianap	AmA	60.0	59	21	7	9	50	3.15	4	3	8.85	1.05	1.35	7.50	3.53	3.45
1997	Cincnnti	NL	129.7	107	42	14	43	85	2.92	9	5	7.43	0.97	2.98	5.90	1.18	2.92
1998	Cincnnti	NL	216.3	200	96	22	58	148	3.99	12	12	8.32	0.92	2.41	6.16	1.42	3.29

Went through a horrendous midsummer blowup before mostly righting himself in August and September. Still has the great repertoire, fronted by a 92-mph fastball. I see no reason he can't get back on track to becoming a staff ace.

Gabe White   Throws L   Age 27

YEAR	TEAM	LGE	IP	H	ER	HR	BB	K	ERA	W	L	H/9	HR/9	BB/9	K/9	KWH	PERA
1996	Indianap	AmA	67.7	78	25	6	10	43	3.33	5	3	10.37	0.80	1.33	5.72	1.78	4.12
1997	Indianap	AmA	113.3	140	50	9	18	49	3.97	7	6	11.12	0.71	1.43	3.89	0.71	4.53
1997	Cincnnti	NL	41.7	40	17	6	7	22	3.67	3	2	8.64	1.30	1.51	4.75	1.30	3.46
1998	Cincnnti	NL	101.0	86	39	17	25	76	3.48	6	5	7.66	1.51	2.23	6.77	2.01	3.21

Successful in middle relief, but still better-suited for a starting role. The home run ratio will send McKeon for the Zantac if White continues to close. White is a rare example of a talented player whom the Expos gave away before he turned good, instead of after.

Todd Williams   Throws R   Age 28

YEAR	TEAM	LGE	IP	H	ER	HR	BB	K	ERA	W	L	H/9	HR/9	BB/9	K/9	KWH	PERA
1996	Edmonton	PCL	85.0	145	76	5	39	26	8.05	2	7	15.35	0.53	4.13	2.75	0.09	6.56
1997	Chattang	Sou	53.3	46	17	1	27	31	2.87	4	2	7.76	0.17	4.56	5.23	0.58	2.87
1997	Indianap	AmA	12.3	13	5	0	7	9	3.65	1	0	9.49	0.00	5.11	6.57	0.67	3.65
1998	Indianap	Int	56.0	64	21	0	24	27	3.38	4	2	10.29	0.00	3.86	4.34	0.36	3.86

Indianapolis's closer; the season wasn't as impressive as his '97 reign of terror in Double-A, but he's still worth having around. Will pop up on various rosters for the next few years, eventually having one breakout year to establish himself and start work on the pension.

Scott Williamson   **Throws R**   **Age 23**

YEAR	TEAM	LGE	IP	H	ER	HR	BB	K	ERA	W	L	H/9	HR/9	BB/9	K/9	KWH	PERA
1997	Billings	Pio	75.0	101	36	6	32	50	4.32	4	4	12.12	0.72	3.84	6.00	0.58	5.28
1998	Chattang	Sou	98.7	97	45	5	38	83	4.10	5	6	8.85	0.46	3.47	7.57	1.40	3.47
1998	Indianap	Int	20.7	22	8	2	8	14	3.48	1	1	9.58	0.87	3.48	6.10	0.84	3.92

Scouts thought he'd go much higher than the 9th round, where the Reds got him in '97, and he has done nothing to prove them wrong, racing through the system nearly untouched. The Reds were actually going to call him up in September before he suffered a minor finger injury. Throws a nasty split-fingered fastball, has two other plus offerings with great control. Almost ready.

Scott Winchester   **Throws R**   **Age 26**

YEAR	TEAM	LGE	IP	H	ER	HR	BB	K	ERA	W	L	H/9	HR/9	BB/9	K/9	KWH	PERA
1996	Columbus	SAL	53.0	87	45	10	22	32	7.64	1	5	14.77	1.70	3.74	5.43	0.40	7.47
1997	Kinston	Car	33.0	34	10	2	12	27	2.73	3	1	9.27	0.55	3.27	7.36	1.34	3.82
1998	Indianap	Int	28.0	46	24	7	7	9	7.71	1	2	14.79	2.25	2.25	2.89	0.19	7.71
1998	Cincnnti	NL	81.7	103	49	12	25	37	5.40	3	6	11.35	1.32	2.76	4.08	0.40	5.29

Had his season ruined by a slight tear under his right rotator cuff, which inhibited his ability to throw his slider for strikes and made him even more vulnerable to lefties. If healthy, he projects to be a #4-#5 starter.

SNWLP				CINCINNATI REDS							Park Effect: +2.0%	
PITCHER	GS	IP	R	SNW	SNL	SNPCT	W	L	RA	APW	SNVA	SNWAR
Bere, J.	7	39.7	17	3.2	2.0	.615	3	2	3.86	0.39	0.53	0.99
Cooke, S.	1	6.0	1	0.5	0.1	.893	1	0	1.50	0.21	0.23	0.28
Harnisch, P.	32	209.0	79	14.3	7.6	.653	13	7	3.40	3.08	3.11	4.99
Hutton, M.	2	2.3	7	0.1	0.9	.079	0	1	27.00	-0.56	-0.41	-0.35
Klingenbeck, S.	4	22.7	17	0.7	2.0	.260	1	3	6.75	-0.48	-0.54	-0.44
Krivda, R.	1	4.0	7	0.0	0.8	.024	0	1	15.75	-0.47	-0.36	-0.32
Parris, S.	16	95.0	44	5.5	5.2	.514	6	5	4.17	0.62	0.14	0.96
Priest, E.	2	6.0	8	0.1	1.2	.069	0	1	12.00	-0.47	-0.50	-0.46
Remlinger, M.	28	155.7	91	8.2	10.2	.447	7	15	5.26	-0.83	-0.75	0.41
Reyes, D.	7	37.0	19	2.1	2.3	.479	3	1	4.62	0.06	-0.08	0.24
Tomko, B.	34	210.7	111	12.4	12.3	.501	13	12	4.74	0.06	-0.03	1.89
Weathers, D.	9	49.7	35	2.3	3.9	.367	2	4	6.34	-0.84	-0.78	-0.36
White, G.	3	15.3	12	0.8	1.2	.390	0	2	7.04	-0.38	-0.22	-0.07
Winchester, S.	16	79.0	56	4.0	6.8	.369	3	6	6.38	-1.37	-1.45	-0.60
TOTALS	162	932.0	504	54.2	56.5	.490	52	60	4.87	-0.99	-1.11	7.16

This is not a huge improvement over the 1997 rotation, but things are looking up. While 1997's staff was heavily loaded with aging or fragile guys like Mike Morgan, Pete Schourek, and Kent Mercker, the 1998 rotation had a much younger cast. Bret Tomko followed up on his impressive 1997 half-season with a league-average full season. He showed signs of continued development during the year, as his SN record went from 6.1-7.0 (.465) before the All-Star break to 6.3-5.4 (.542) after. While Scott Winchester and Dennis Reyes weren't impressive, at least they weren't old. Not that youth is everything. The best story coming out of the Reds rotation in 1998 was 31-year-old Pete Harnisch, who bounced back from physical and mental problems to have his best season since 1991. Harnisch was probably the most underappreciated elite starter in 1998, as he earned the 6th best SNWAR in the NL, and 11th best in the majors. Of course, having a highly inconsistent pitcher like Harnisch account for such a high percentage of the staff's value is a source of concern. Substituting a replacement pitcher's numbers for Harnisch's would drop the Reds from 13th to 27th in the majors.

Pitcher Abuse Points

PITCHER	AGE	GS	PAP	PAP/S	AAW	MAX	115+	130+
Bere, Jason	27	7	32	4.57	8.38	119	1	0
Harnisch, Pete	31	32	218	6.81	7.95	125	5	0
Parris, Steve	30	16	95	5.94	7.92	120	2	0
Remlinger, Mike	32	28	356	12.71	12.71	133	7	1
Reyes, Dennis	21	7	21	3.00	8.50	109	0	0
Tomko, Brett	25	34	225	6.62	14.34	132	2	1
Weathers, David	28	9	0	0.00	0.00	121	2	0
Winchester, Scott	25	16	0	0.00	0.00	93	0	0
TOTALS		162	959	5.92	8.42	133	19	2
RANKING (NL)			13	13	14		13	7-T

Jack McKeon seems a rather strange choice to manage this young and motley bunch, but he did a fine job to keep the talent he had from evaporating. The highest AAW went to their best young pitcher, Brett Tomko, and he only reached 115 pitches twice all year. Mike Remlinger was worked hard, but he's 32 and it's the Braves' problem now. Pete Harnisch was well handled in his return to glory, and prize pickup Dennis Reyes was pampered after he was heisted from the Dodgers. Steve Parris wasn't worked all that hard, but his arm is so fragile I'd consider limiting him to five innings per start.

Houston Astros

Almost from the moment Gerry Hunsicker pulled the trigger and brought Randy Johnson to town, the Astros became the trendy pick to walk away with the NL pennant, if not a World Championship. After all, the team with the league's best offense, a deep rotation and Billy Wagner in the pen had just added the game's most unhittable pitcher. When Johnson went 10-1 with a 1.28 ERA, proving the best mid-season acquisition since Doyle Alexander or Rick Sutcliffe, the specter of the Big Unit taking the mound every third game in the playoffs seemed to chase away the curse over the franchise and guarantee the Astros' first-ever World Series appearance.

Oops. The Astros ran into the Padres and their ace pitcher, Kevin Brown. While Johnson got the Chinese water torture treatment from the Padres en route to a pair of losses, Brown forced his name on to the short list of big-game pitchers, and the Astros' postseason came crashing down after four games. What went wrong? And more importantly: what can they do to prevent it from happening again?

Trying to predict who's going to win a playoff series is a fool's game—it can't be done, not consistently. Ordinarily, trying to analyze a team's strengths and weakness for a short series is an exercise in futility—that's what the Astros tried to do when they acquired Johnson in the first place. But in the Astros' case, there was one undeniable flaw to an otherwise formidable squad. They just didn't have any left-handed hitters.

This didn't happen by design or indifference, but rather around the opportunities available to the Astros. The team was built around a foundation of Jeff Bagwell and Craig Biggio, both right-handers. Ken Caminiti and Steve Finley were traded away four years ago, which netted another right-handed hitter in Derek Bell—and after trying to cover a hole at third base, the Astros grabbed Sean Berry from the Expos. Richard Hidalgo developed into a fine prospect and played a good center field, so the Astros protected him while exposing lefty Bobby Abreu in the Expansion Draft. Then Moises Alou became available in the Marlins' fire sale, and was acquired

without sacrificing any of the Astros' most coveted prospects. And with left-handed hitters at a premium at catcher and shortstop, the Astros stood pat with Brad Ausmus and Ricky Gutierrez.

Individually the moves were not critical, but collectively they left the Astros with only two left-handed hitters in the starting lineup on even a semi-regular basis: platoon third baseman Billy Spiers and platoon center fielder Carl Everett. The result is that, while the Astros' lineup against left-handers had the platoon advantage nearly 100% of the time, against right-handers they had the platoon advantage just 22% of the time, by far the worst in baseball (only one other team was under 40%). Having six right-handed hitters in the lineup every-day didn't have much impact during the regular season—Bagwell and Biggio and Alou hit just fine either way, thank you—but certain right-handers can take advantage of that kind of lineup.

Remember how Kerry Wood made the Astros look like a 30-and-over sandlot team that fine May afternoon? Wood destroyed right-handed hitters to the tune of .169/.244/.295 all season, while left-handers fared okay with a .228/.371/.349 performance. You can guess which way the Astros' lineup was leaning that day. When Kevin Brown started dropping down and tearing a page out of David Cone's book, firing laredo-style from the hip, the Astros were meat: a two-hitter with 16 K's in just 8 innings in his first outing, and 6.2 excellent innings in his second. It was enough to dig the Astros a hole—and the Padres scratched out enough base runners in Game 4 to push them into it.

So what do the Astros do now? Good organizations seem to come up with the solutions to their problems internally, so seamlessly that it would appear to be a carefully choreographed transition. And sure enough, the Astros' prized catcher, Mitch Meluskey, is a switch-hitter, and should force Ausmus aside this season. Lance Berkman, a switch-hitter, is ready to pulverize major league pitching, although the restructuring of Alou's contract closes the only obvious vacancy he could fill. Ken Caminiti re-signed with his old

---

Astros Prospectus

1998 record: 102-60; First place, NL Central; Lost to San Diego Padres in Division Series, 3-1

Pythagorean W/L: 108-54

Runs scored: 874 (1st in NL)

Runs allowed: 620 (2nd in NL)

Team EQA: .279 (1st in NL)

Park: Astrodome (good pitchers')

1998: An excellent season, built around the league's best offense.

1999: The division favorite; only injuries can keep them out of October.

---

ballclub, substituting another replaceable right-handed bat with a switch-hitter. In short, with the Astros remodeling their kitchen this off-season, it doesn't matter if they didn't notice the cracks in the plumbing last year. They're getting them fixed anyway.

———◇———

Arguably the most incredible unnoticed accomplishment of the 1998 season is this: the Houston Astros led the National League in runs scored, by a comfortable margin. That's rather like saying the Colorado Rockies led baseball in ERA; it's an unbelievable testament to the Astros' offense that they paced the league while playing in the Astrodome. The explosiveness of their lineup—and the Astros' entrance on to the national stage as a perennial playoff contender—has finally attracted a spotlight for two of the greatest players in the game, Jeff Bagwell and Craig Biggio. Bagwell burst on the scene with a Rookie of the Year award and has picked up an MVP award, and has the image of the hulking power hitter that gets Hall of Fame attention. Biggio, on the other hand, hit around .270 with 6 homers a year for the first half of his career, and the perception is that while he has bloomed into a perennial All-Star, he did so too late in his career to attract much Hall of Fame attention. But is that the case?

Making a Hall of Fame argument for anyone is an exhaustive process, and I can't do it justice here. But a very direct method would simply be to compare his production with Hall of Fame second basemen at the same age. There are 14 Hall of Fame second baseman (counting Rod Carew) who weren't inducted for their success as managers. Biggio was 32 last year, and if we compare his stats to those of the Hall of Famers through age 32, he isn't embarassed. He ranks 11th (out of 15) in games played, a reflection of the late start to his career (most Hall of Famers reach the major leagues by the time they're 21, while Biggio was 23). He ranks 11th in hits, but 7th in doubles and 5th in homers. He's only 10th in runs and 11th in RBIs, but sixth in walks and 4th in stolen bases. In the rate categories, he places in the third quartile: 10th in average, 9th in OBP, 10th in slugging.

He hasn't reached the standards of a typical Hall of Famer—at least not yet. Keep in mind that we're comparing raw totals without adjusting for context, and the Astrodome in the 90s—or any decade—is a much harsher climate than what Rogers Hornsby or Tony Lazzeri or Charlie Gehringer faced. Biggio has hit just 54 of his 136 career homers—fewer than 40%—at home. Most importantly, Biggio is playing better at 32 than at any time in his career. He has scored over 110 runs each of the last four seasons, a feat accomplished by no other active player—not even Rickey Henderson. Bobby Doerr played his last season at 33, and Lazzeri lost his starting job at the same age. Even Hornsby played in more than a hundred games for the last time at 33. The second baseman whose career best mirrors the elevation of Biggio's game in

his late 20s also started his career as an Astro, only Joe Morgan needed to leave the stifling atmosphere under the dome before he became one of the game's best players. Morgan was the MVP of the National League in 1975–76, when he was 31 and 32 years old. Biggio was the same age in 1997 and 1998, and it really isn't ridiculous to suggest that, over the last two seasons, he might have been the best player in the league.

I'm not trying to suggest that Biggio is as good, was as good, or ever will be as good as Joe Morgan. But he might be almost as good at Joe Morgan—and that next level down from Joe Morgan might still be a Hall of Famer.

———◇———

In the two years under Larry Dierker's command, it has become flatly obvious that the much-ridiculed decision to pull him out of the announcer's booth and put him in uniform has been nothing short of brilliant. Under Terry Collins, the Astros made a habit of finishing in second (a trend Collins continues with the Angels). It's a general trend in baseball that teams that play for a high-tension manager for a few years frequently improve significantly when that manager is fired and replaced with a "player's manager" who stops barking orders and using intimidation tactics to get things done, and credits his players with knowing how to prepare for each game.

When you think about it, was there any team more poorly suited than the Astros for an intense manager like Collins? The attitudes of Bagwell and Biggio, and even second-line stars like Derek Bell, are echoed by the rest of the team. They don't break their bats or dump the water cooler after making out with the bases loaded; what they do is take batting practice until their hands bleed and field ground balls until they can barely walk. They are self-motivated, if a little stoic, and what they need is a manager who outlines what their job is and trusts them to do it right. Having a manager call team meetings after every two-game losing streak and single out players for key mistakes had to be grating after a while, and you certainly have to say the Astros have responded to having the leash taken off.

However, Dierker's success—smashing the team record with 102 wins—can't solely be attributed to a breath of fresh air. The consistency of their improvement on both sides of the ball is remarkable. As impressive as their offensive improvement has been—they set a franchise record with 777 runs in 1997, then broke that record by nearly 100 more runs in 1998—it is the pitching staff that is the interesting story here.

When Dierker took over two seasons ago, the Astros had finished 10th out of 14 teams in ERA—a terrible performance given that the Astrodome is one of the best pitcher's parks in the game. But in his first year, Dierker improved the team's ranking to third—and last year, only the Braves had a better pitching staff than Houston. Since Dierker himself was a pitcher—and a very effective one—his experience and wisdom on the mound have been credited for the staff's about-face.

But what really happened? The news that blew in from Houston in Dierker's first year was that he was sticking with his starters longer than anyone in baseball—Dierker, after all, was a workhorse himself—and that by allowing his starters to work out of their own jams, he was somehow imparting confidence that was cashed in for better performances. There was no denying the results: Ramon Garcia, who was 27 and had a career ERA over 6, went 9-8 with an ERA of 3.69. Rookie Chris Holt, who scouts derided as a finesse pitcher, posted an impressive 3.52 ERA in over 200 innings. After frustrating the Astros for years with his wildness and inconsistency, Darryl Kile broke through with a 19-7 record and a 2.57 ERA.

The down side to this strategy, of course, would be that he was forcing his starters to work too hard and wear down or injure their arms. It is fascinating to look at the parallels in Dierker's own career: Dierker made his major league debut on his 18th birthday, and at the tender age of 22 worked 305 innings. Guess what? His career was over by the time he was 30. And the aftermath of his first season as manager was grisly, as both Garcia and Holt basically missed 1998 with arm injuries.

Was it Dierker's fault? His pitching patterns were almost the first item we looked at when the PAP system was unveiled—and the results were surprising. Feel free to skip to the end of this chapter for the Astros numbers, but the short of it is that there is little, if any, evidence that Dierker worked his starters more strenuously than the league as a whole works starters. With the exception of Randy Johnson, Dierker kept his pitches on a fairly tight leash, at least for 1998. So now the question is posed: did Dierker learn to protect his pitchers better after losing Holt and Garcia to injury, or had he been protective all along?

So we dug up the 1997 PAP data, and if anything, Dierker sheltered his starters even more in his first year. The table below shows the Astros' six main starters that year, and a comparison with last season.

Obviously, Darryl Kile was worked much harder than anyone else—but he was the ace of the staff, was a pending free-agent, and moved on to Colorado—where he was worked nearly as hard. Kile is not really a concern; his falloff is at least partly explained by the enormous park differences involved. But look at Garcia and Holt. Garcia was not certainly not worked very hard by Dierker, and when you look at his record, you realize he's always had trouble staying healthy—that's why he had never been successful in the major leagues before. Holt was babied as much as possible by Dierker, never throwing more than 117 pitches in a game, so it's time to start looking elsewhere for answers for his injury.

So how has Dierker gotten the most out of his pitchers? While his starters aren't worked any harder, he gets more innings out of them—by preaching control, control, control, and getting it: the Astros, eighth in the NL with 539 walks allowed in 1996, gave up the fewest in in baseball in 1998, just 465. Better control means fewer pitches per batter, meaning Sean Bergman or Shane Reynolds can pitch seven innings while keeping their pitch counts in double digits, which means the Astros' starters get the luxury of regular work without straining their arms.

The way Dierker handles his bullpen is just as interesting. The Astros brought in a new reliever just 340 times last year, the lowest total in the league (an average number would be about 400), and did so mid-inning just 113 times, second-lowest in baseball behind the Braves. That means that the Astros' relievers, like their starters, consistently worked longer outings and had the opportunity to work on developing their slider or getting their curveball over for strikes without getting pulled after two hitters. Meanwhile, fewer pitching changes meant fewer instances of warming up a reliever several times before bringing him in a game, a heavy contributor to fatigue and burnout among relievers.

When an Astro reliever was brought in, he had the platoon advantage against his first hitter just 48% of the time—by far the lowest in baseball (only the Dodgers were below 56%). In other words, Dierker wasn't concerned about playing the percentages and bringing in his left-handed specialist to pitch against just Barry Bonds or Larry Walker. Besides, with

Pitcher	Age	GS	PAP	Max	115+	130+	PAP/S	AAW ('97)	AAW ('98)
Garcia, Ramon	27	20	150	122	6	0	7.50	13.75	—
Hampton, Mike	24	34	274	126	7	0	8.06	18.80	22.75
Holt, Chris	25	32	138	117	3	0	4.31	9.34	—
Kile, Darryl	28	34	664	133	15	1	19.53	32.55	26.53
Reynolds, Shane	29	29*	160	124	5	0	5.52	8.28	9.60
Wall, Donne	29	8	24	114	0	0	3.00	4.50	—

*One start missing

as many as four lefties in the bullpen and two in the rotation, if Dierker had waited for the platoon advantage some of his relievers would face five batters in a month. Dierker decided that the benefit of getting his relievers consistent work is greater than that of getting the platoon advantage 30 extra times a season. And you know what? It worked.

Dierker's philosophy is probably matched most closely by Felipe Alou, who does a wonderful job of protecting his young rotation, although he uses his relievers more often than Dierker. Between them, they have done a remarkable job of turning veteran Triple-A pitchers into quality middle relievers. Alou annually gets great seasons out of waiver-wire pickups like Anthony Telford or Marc Valdes or Steve Kline, and now Dierker has some successes to add to his own resume. In his first season, he stuck Mike Magnante—who had stowed away on major league rosters for six years—in his bullpen, and was rewarded with a 2.27 ERA. Last year, he took C.J. Nitkowski, whose career was going nowhere after

getting jerked around between Detroit and Cincinnati and the bullpen and the rotation—and found a role for him as one of the league's best long men.

The vote for Manager of the Year almost always comes down to who won the most games, with the result that the award frequently ends up in the hands of a one-year wonder, and everyone scratches their head when the same team finishes under .500 the following year. But Dierker is no flash in the pan. He's won 186 games in his first two seasons at the helm, and presides over a franchise with impressive depth and a farm system that hasn't run out of talent. Having lost Randy Johnson, Scott Elarton is ready to step in to the rotation, and no one on the staff is older than 31. The offense features a pair of superstars at the top of their game, and a bunch of youngsters ready if the supporting cast drops off. The Astros are giving every indication they're going to defend their NL Central crown pretty easily.

HITTERS (Averages: BA .260/ OBA .330/ SA .420, EQA .260)

Moises Alou   LF   Bats R   Age 32

YEAR	TEAM	LGE	AB	H	DB	TP	HR	BB	R	RBI	SB	CS	OUT	BA	OBA	SA	EQA	EQR	DEFENSE
1996	Montreal	NL	535	144	25	2	21	52	65	73	7	4	395	.269	.334	.441	.266	72	124-OF 104
1997	Florida	NL	539	158	29	5	24	73	83	90	7	5	386	.293	.377	.499	.298	93	136-OF 97
1998	Houston	NL	585	184	33	4	41	87	107	123	12	3	404	.315	.403	.595	.331	127	152-OF 90
1999	*Houston*	*NL*	*573*	*168*	*32*	*2*	*32*	*80*	*90*	*102*	*11*	*4*	*409*	*.293*	*.380*	*.524*	*.315*	*114*	

Must be a soccer fan, because he comes up with a career year for every World Cup. Alou has been driving analysts crazy for years, because as soon as he establishes himself at one level as a hitter, he goes on and reaches a new one. He's a wonderful player, not hurt at all by the Astrodome. He's right at the age where quality players just fall back from the ridge, but the improvement means he probably has two or three good years left. Much was made of the fact he didn't hit a homer after August, but he hit 8 doubles and had a .408 OBP in September, so I'm not worried.

Brad Ausmus   C   Bats R   Age 30

YEAR	TEAM	LGE	AB	H	DB	TP	HR	BB	R	RBI	SB	CS	OUT	BA	OBA	SA	EQA	EQR	DEFENSE
1996	Detroit	AL	222	52	8	0	5	24	21	20	3	5	175	.234	.309	.338	.223	21	
1996	SanDieg	NL	149	27	4	0	1	14	6	5	0	4	126	.181	.252	.228	.144	5	
1997	Houston	NL	426	115	24	1	5	40	52	41	12	6	317	.270	.333	.366	.247	48	
1998	Houston	NL	412	112	9	4	7	55	56	45	11	3	303	.272	.358	.364	.261	53	118-C 104
1999	*Houston*	*NL*	*400*	*101*	*12*	*1*	*6*	*47*	*46*	*37*	*10*	*5*	*304*	*.252*	*.331*	*.333*	*.247*	*46*	

His days as a starter may be running out. Meluskey is ready for the job, even though Ausmus is a fine defensive catcher and not an enormous liability batting 8th. He could definitely help teams lacking major league catchers (the Cubs or Devil Rays) in a starting role, but as an Astro, he better be preparing to hire a flak for the inevitable smear campaign. "Can we trust that our children will be safe with Tony Eusebio behind the plate? This April, vote Brad Ausmus!"

Jeff Bagwell   1B   Bats R   Age 31

YEAR	TEAM	LGE	AB	H	DB	TP	HR	BB	R	RBI	SB	CS	OUT	BA	OBA	SA	EQA	EQR	DEFENSE
1996	Houston	NL	577	187	46	2	34	138	135	121	18	8	398	.324	.455	.588	.349	144	158-1B 112
1997	Houston	NL	571	167	37	2	46	130	127	122	27	11	415	.292	.424	.606	.339	138	155-1B 104
1998	Houston	NL	541	166	27	1	38	113	112	111	21	8	383	.307	.427	.571	.335	124	149-1B 111
1999	*Houston*	*NL*	*524*	*154*	*29*	*1*	*35*	*119*	*108*	*102*	*23*	*10*	*380*	*.294*	*.425*	*.553*	*.339*	*127*	

(Jeff Bagwell *continued*)

There's almost nothing to say about Bagwell that you don't already know. He's as well-rounded as players get: he's about to crack the top 10 in steals among first basemen since 1920, and despite the perception that he breaks his hand every August, he's missed an average of nine games a season on his career. About the only bad thing you can say is that he's streaky, but so was Mike Schmidt. He should continue to be a MVP candidate for several more seasons.

Derek Bell RF Bats R Age 30

YEAR	TEAM	LGE	AB	H	DB	TP	HR	BB	R	RBI	SB	CS	OUT	BA	OBA	SA	EQA	EQR	DEFENSE
1996	Houston	NL	629	168	41	3	18	44	82	72	26	3	464	.267	.315	.428	.261	80	141-OF 100
1997	Houston	NL	494	138	29	3	16	43	65	65	13	7	363	.279	.337	.447	.269	68	80-OF 101
1998	Houston	NL	630	199	37	2	25	55	94	101	14	3	434	.316	.371	.500	.298	105	149-OF 98
1999	*Houston*	*NL*	*577*	*164*	*33*	*2*	*21*	*46*	*73*	*80*	*13*	*3*	*416*	*.284*	*.337*	*.458*	*.283*	*88*	

It's not a coincidence that Bell had his best season while drawing a career-high 51 walks. It's amazing how many undisciplined hitters spend years fighting their coaches while trying to hit homers on sliders in the dirt—and after giving in, find themselves teeing off on 2-0 and 3-1 counts and hitting for more power than ever. Bell set career highs with 41 doubles and 22 homers, and while he still makes too many outs to be a real star, as the third-best outfielder on a team he's an asset. His average may drop, but we may not have seen his best power years yet. A quality regular getting a star's salary, he figures to be the odd man out in Houston's outfield.

Lance Berkman LF Bats B Age 23

YEAR	TEAM	LGE	AB	H	DB	TP	HR	BB	R	RBI	SB	CS	OUT	BA	OBA	SA	EQA	EQR	DEFENSE
1997	Kissimme	Fla	188	53	4	0	11	32	28	33	1	1	136	.282	.386	.479	.298	33	43-OF 90
1998	Jackson	Tex	419	113	17	0	19	71	62	64	4	3	309	.270	.376	.446	.286	68	114-OF 93
1998	NewOrln	PCL	59	16	2	0	6	11	9	14	0	0	43	.271	.386	.610	.325	13	
1999	*Houston*	*NL*	*346*	*100*	*14*	*0*	*20*	*55*	*51*	*63*	*2*	*1*	*247*	*.289*	*.387*	*.503*	*.313*	*68*	

The umpteenth example why, even in amateur ranks, ignoring the numbers in favor of the scouts is a dumb idea. Berkman had a great college career at Rice, but slipped to the middle of the first round because he wasn't particularly agile on the base paths or in the field. It's ten times easier to teach a player to field well enough to get his bat in the lineup than to teach him to hit well enough to get his glove on the field. He's new to left field and it shows, but he has the kind of bat a good organization sees every five years or so. He was much more effective from the left side of the plate, so a platoon role may be the best way to break him in. How the Astros handle the Alou-Bell-Berkman-Everett-Hidalgo logjam will be one of the most interesting questions of the spring.

Sean Berry 3B Bats R Age 33

YEAR	TEAM	LGE	AB	H	DB	TP	HR	BB	R	RBI	SB	CS	OUT	BA	OBA	SA	EQA	EQR	DEFENSE
1996	Houston	NL	432	123	34	1	19	27	57	63	11	7	316	.285	.327	.500	.276	63	93-3B 100
1997	Houston	NL	301	78	22	1	9	27	33	37	0	5	228	.259	.320	.429	.251	36	66-3B 98
1998	Houston	NL	299	94	17	1	14	33	45	53	3	1	206	.314	.383	.518	.306	53	73-3B 93
1999	*Milwauke*	*NL*	*302*	*88*	*19*	*1*	*12*	*29*	*40*	*47*	*4*	*3*	*217*	*.291*	*.353*	*.480*	*.284*	*47*	

Proved he wasn't done after all, scorching the ball for a .368 average after the break. But he's fragile and not that nimble around the bag, and as a free agent in an era of increasingly stratified salaries, he's probably going to get the shaft. His age and health record suggest his bat could go at any time, and I suspect any team that signs him to a multi-year deal will be disappointed.

Craig Biggio 2B Bats R Age 33

YEAR	TEAM	LGE	AB	H	DB	TP	HR	BB	R	RBI	SB	CS	OUT	BA	OBA	SA	EQA	EQR	DEFENSE
1996	Houston	NL	610	179	25	4	16	79	95	80	22	8	439	.293	.374	.426	.283	93	156-2B 100
1997	Houston	NL	622	194	38	7	24	88	123	98	41	11	439	.312	.397	.511	.313	121	153-2B 104
1998	Houston	NL	646	211	48	2	23	68	130	96	54	9	444	.327	.391	.514	.315	124	154-2B 95
1999	*Houston*	*NL*	*579*	*174*	*35*	*3*	*20*	*72*	*101*	*83*	*34*	*7*	*412*	*.301*	*.378*	*.475*	*.308*	*108*	

One of the truly great players of our time. He started out as the fastest catcher in baseball, and his career has been on the less-travelled road ever since. You look over his career and what pops out at you is a man obsessed with helping his team win any way possible. He accepted the move to second base—one virtually unprecedented in baseball history—with grace, and slaved at his defense until he became a Gold Glover. He went from walking 50 times a year to 80, and learned to skirt the rules by piling on the arm guards and getting plunked 25 times a year. His power keeps going up—he drove in 88 runs last year out of the leadoff spot—and I don't think we've seen his slugging peak. He could hit 30 homers this season, and be an even more viable MVP candidate.

Tim Bogar   INF   Bats R   Age 32

YEAR	TEAM	LGE	AB	H	DB	TP	HR	BB	R	RBI	SB	CS	OUT	BA	OBA	SA	EQA	EQR	DEFENSE	
1996	NYMets	NL	90	20	5	0	0	8	6	5	0	3	73	.222	.286	.278	.183	5	17-1B 79	15-3B 87
1997	Houston	NL	241	60	14	3	5	26	29	26	3	1	182	.249	.322	.394	.250	28	70-SS 95	
1998	Houston	NL	155	24	5	1	1	10	4	4	2	1	132	.155	.206	.219	.114	3	33-SS 114	
1999	Houston	NL	159	33	7	1	2	15	12	11	1	1	127	.208	.276	.302	.208	13		

When you bat only 150 times, this is what can happen. He's not really a .150 hitter. He's an adequate utility player with tenure and a two-year contract; expect little more than that.

Dave Clark   PH/OF   Bats L   Age 36

YEAR	TEAM	LGE	AB	H	DB	TP	HR	BB	R	RBI	SB	CS	OUT	BA	OBA	SA	EQA	EQR	DEFENSE
1996	Pittsbrg	NL	210	56	11	2	8	32	31	31	2	1	155	.267	.364	.452	.283	33	48-OF 92
1997	ChiCubs	NL	141	40	5	0	6	20	20	22	1	0	101	.284	.373	.447	.287	22	17-OF 101
1998	Houston	NL	131	27	8	0	0	15	11	7	1	1	105	.206	.288	.267	.193	9	
1999	Houston	NL	141	32	5	0	4	22	16	15	1	0	109	.227	.331	.348	.253	18	

His unfortunate season really put a crimp in the Astros' bench, because other than Carl Everett and Billy Spiers, he was frequently the only hitter on the team that didn't bat right-handed. Looks done to me; he's come back from bad seasons before, but he's never been this bad or this old.

Tony Eusebio   C   Bats R   Age 32

YEAR	TEAM	LGE	AB	H	DB	TP	HR	BB	R	RBI	SB	CS	OUT	BA	OBA	SA	EQA	EQR	DEFENSE
1996	Houston	NL	153	42	8	2	1	19	19	17	0	1	112	.275	.355	.373	.256	19	
1997	Houston	NL	165	46	2	0	1	20	17	16	0	1	120	.279	.357	.309	.240	17	
1998	Houston	NL	182	47	6	1	1	19	18	16	1	0	135	.258	.328	.319	.231	17	44-C 102
1999	Houston	NL	169	43	5	1	1	19	17	15	0	0	126	.254	.330	.314	.239	18	

As good a backup catcher as you'll find. Eusebio threw out 37% of base runners and is okay at handling pitchers, and while he's not much more than a singles hitter, he has never hit below .250 in his career. He's almost indistinguishable from Ausmus as a player, but he's older and shakier behind the plate. With Meluskey arriving, he should land on his feet somewhere.

Carl Everett   CF   Bats B   Age 29

YEAR	TEAM	LGE	AB	H	DB	TP	HR	BB	R	RBI	SB	CS	OUT	BA	OBA	SA	EQA	EQR	DEFENSE
1996	NYMets	NL	194	48	9	1	1	22	23	15	5	0	146	.247	.324	.320	.235	19	40-OF 101
1997	NYMets	NL	442	109	27	3	15	34	50	50	14	9	342	.247	.300	.423	.246	52	111-OF 98
1998	Houston	NL	467	140	35	4	16	47	71	69	15	14	341	.300	.364	.495	.287	75	118-OF 115
1999	Houston	NL	405	109	27	2	13	37	52	51	12	9	304	.269	.330	.442	.272	59	

He has shown brief flashes of ability before, but never proved he could sustain it for an entire season. Getting out of New York was probably the best thing for him. He's a switch-hitter in name only—he has a .225 average from the right side over the last 5 years. As a role player in a deep outfield, he's got a lot of value.

Ricky Gutierrez   SS   Bats R   Age 29

YEAR	TEAM	LGE	AB	H	DB	TP	HR	BB	R	RBI	SB	CS	OUT	BA	OBA	SA	EQA	EQR	DEFENSE	
1996	Houston	NL	220	64	9	1	1	24	29	22	5	1	157	.291	.361	.355	.259	27	55-SS 85	
1997	Houston	NL	303	80	14	3	4	23	32	30	4	2	225	.264	.316	.370	.239	31	49-SS 94	15-3B 111
1998	Houston	NL	491	130	26	3	2	57	63	43	14	8	369	.265	.341	.342	.244	54	129-SS 101	
1999	Houston	NL	381	99	16	2	3	37	42	34	10	5	287	.260	.325	.336	.245	42		

Provides at short what Ausmus and Eusebio provided at catcher: a marginal hitter who made up what he lacks in offensive ability with consistency and reliability, preventing a revolving door from forming at the position. He might be just keeping the position warm for Julio Lugo, but he's an adequate short-term solution and miles better than alternatives like Tim Bogar.

Carlos Hernandez   2B   Bats R   Age 23

YEAR	TEAM	LGE	AB	H	DB	TP	HR	BB	R	RBI	SB	CS	OUT	BA	OBA	SA	EQA	EQR	DEFENSE	
1995	QuadCit	Mid	478	116	14	3	5	29	45	33	25	13	375	.243	.286	.316	.211	38	95-2B 103	23-SS 92
1996	QuadCit	Mid	459	111	10	3	6	17	37	31	22	9	357	.242	.269	.316	.204	33	109-2B 102	
1997	Jackson	Tex	357	90	6	1	4	28	34	27	12	5	272	.252	.306	.308	.219	30	91-2B 100	
1998	NewOrln	PCL	490	139	18	2	1	21	54	37	26	10	361	.284	.313	.335	.231	46	122-2B 96	
1999	*Houston*	*NL*	*450*	*122*	*14*	*2*	*3*	*20*	*49*	*34*	*27*	*8*	*336*	*.271*	*.302*	*.331*	*.237*	*46*		

Not to be confused with the Padres' catcher, this Hernandez plays great defense and on another team might be in line for a starting job. In Houston, they hope he lights up Triple-A his second time around so they can package him for whatever holes they've got in July.

Richard Hidalgo   CF   Bats R   Age 23

YEAR	TEAM	LGE	AB	H	DB	TP	HR	BB	R	RBI	SB	CS	OUT	BA	OBA	SA	EQA	EQR	DEFENSE
1996	Jackson	Tex	506	134	20	1	13	27	48	53	9	5	377	.265	.302	.385	.237	51	125-OF 110
1997	NewOrln	AA	530	148	33	5	10	34	59	61	6	8	390	.279	.323	.417	.252	62	122-OF 103
1997	Houston	NL	62	19	2	0	3	5	8	10	1	0	43	.306	.358	.484	.290	10	
1998	Houston	NL	211	65	11	0	9	18	28	33	3	4	150	.308	.362	.488	.286	33	53-OF 112
1999	*Houston*	*NL*	*384*	*109*	*19*	*1*	*12*	*24*	*41*	*50*	*5*	*4*	*279*	*.284*	*.326*	*.432*	*.268*	*52*	

Another reason why the Astros were one of the most enjoyable teams to watch in recent memory. A great center fielder, with excellent range and one of the best arms in the business. His all-out style cost him a few months; some players (Lenny Dykstra, Freddy Lynn) are unable to curb their aggression near the outfield walls and get constantly banged up. If he can avoid that, I think he's going to be great. He hit much better after he returned, and began to draw walks for the first time. If he keeps it up, he's going to make a half-dozen All-Star teams before he's through.

Pete Incaviglia   DH   Bats R   Age 35

YEAR	TEAM	LGE	AB	H	DB	TP	HR	BB	R	RBI	SB	CS	OUT	BA	OBA	SA	EQA	EQR	DEFENSE
1996	Philadel	NL	269	63	7	2	16	32	31	39	2	0	206	.234	.316	.454	.263	37	63-OF 82
1997	Baltimor	AL	136	33	4	0	5	12	13	15	0	0	103	.243	.304	.382	.237	14	
1998	NewOrln	PCL	280	84	6	1	16	29	41	47	9	3	199	.300	.366	.500	.295	47	41-OF 82
1999	*Houston*	*NL*	*244*	*61*	*8*	*1*	*11*	*24*	*25*	*33*	*2*	*1*	*184*	*.250*	*.317*	*.426*	*.264*	*33*	

Inky had never played in the minor leagues (save for rehab assignments) before last year—he went straight from the Oklahoma State campus to the majors. He's old and the only thing he's ever had is his bat, but he has some value as a lefty-mashing pinch-hitter.

Russ Johnson   INF   Bats R   Age 26

YEAR	TEAM	LGE	AB	H	DB	TP	HR	BB	R	RBI	SB	CS	OUT	BA	OBA	SA	EQA	EQR	DEFENSE
1996	Jackson	Tex	491	134	15	3	12	49	57	58	7	3	360	.273	.339	.389	.256	60	132-SS 97
1997	NewOrln	AA	452	123	13	5	4	61	58	47	6	3	332	.272	.359	.350	.255	54	104-3B 101
1998	NewOrln	PCL	455	127	19	1	6	78	69	51	9	9	337	.279	.385	.365	.269	63	109-3B 102
1999	*Houston*	*NL*	*470*	*127*	*19*	*3*	*7*	*65*	*63*	*52*	*9*	*5*	*348*	*.270*	*.359*	*.368*	*.269*	*65*	

A personal favorite. He's a good third baseman and is just a step slow to be a major-league shortstop. He hits for average and has learned to draw a ton of walks. He has shown steady improvement throughout his career, and deserves at least a bench job. He's capable of holding his own as a starter for a championship ballclub.

Julio Lugo   SS   Bats R   Age 23

YEAR	TEAM	LGE	AB	H	DB	TP	HR	BB	R	RBI	SB	CS	OUT	BA	OBA	SA	EQA	EQR	DEFENSE
1996	QuadCit	Mid	396	104	11	1	9	22	38	38	13	7	299	.263	.301	.364	.231	38	85-SS 95
1997	Kissimme	Fla	509	128	16	8	9	41	56	49	18	5	386	.251	.307	.367	.239	54	115-SS 107
1998	Kissimme	Fla	508	134	13	8	7	41	59	48	23	11	385	.264	.319	.362	.240	55	100-SS 90
1999	*Houston*	*NL*	*473*	*121*	*16*	*4*	*7*	*30*	*49*	*42*	*20*	*7*	*359*	*.256*	*.300*	*.351*	*.239*	*50*	

The Astros had three fine shortstop prospects—Lugo, Jhonny Perez and Carlos Guillen—which forced Lugo to repeat a level. He had another fine year, and after Guillen was traded Lugo was promoted to help the Zephyrs win the Triple-A World Series. Speed is his game, with 14 triples and 51 stolen bases, but he's not a weakling and draws a fair number of walks, so he can contribute in several ways. He needs to come on fast this season if he wants to win the coming battle with Perez for the starting job, but he has the edge defensively.

Mitch Meluskey — C — Bats B — Age 25

YEAR	TEAM	LGE	AB	H	DB	TP	HR	BB	R	RBI	SB	CS	OUT	BA	OBA	SA	EQA	EQR	DEFENSE
1996	Kissimme	Fla	236	74	10	0	3	24	30	30	1	1	163	.314	.377	.394	.273	32	
1996	Jackson	Tex	133	37	9	0	0	16	16	13	0	0	96	.278	.356	.346	.252	15	
1997	Jackson	Tex	236	72	9	0	11	26	32	39	1	2	166	.305	.374	.483	.292	38	
1997	NewOrln	AA	174	44	3	0	4	24	18	19	0	0	130	.253	.343	.339	.245	19	
1998	NewOrln	PCL	397	137	23	0	18	77	79	80	2	0	260	.345	.451	.539	.342	89	118-C 96
1999	*Houston*	*NL*	*398*	*122*	*15*	*1*	*16*	*58*	*58*	*67*	*1*	*1*	*277*	*.307*	*.395*	*.470*	*.309*	*74*	

The Astros may have finally gotten back at the Indians for stealing Kenny Lofton from them when they dealt Lofton for Eddie Taubensee. In 1995, the Astros acquired Meluskey for a nondescript outfielder named Buck McNabb—and now Meluskey may be the best catching prospect in baseball. His offense has always been good, but the overwhelming consensus it that his defense made huge strides last year. For the Astros, with their All-World offense, to be able to replace one of their lightest bats with this stud is almost unfair. I expect him to finish 3rd or 4th in Rookie of the Year voting, and have better years after that.

Ray Montgomery — OF — Bats R — Age 29

YEAR	TEAM	LGE	AB	H	DB	TP	HR	BB	R	RBI	SB	CS	OUT	BA	OBA	SA	EQA	EQR	DEFENSE
1996	Tucson	PCL	350	89	9	0	15	48	43	47	5	1	262	.254	.344	.409	.265	47	88-OF 100
1998	NewOrln	PCL	271	70	10	1	7	22	27	29	3	2	203	.258	.314	.380	.241	29	69-OF 101
1999	*Houston*	*NL*	*234*	*60*	*8*	*0*	*9*	*25*	*25*	*30*	*2*	*1*	*175*	*.256*	*.328*	*.406*	*.264*	*31*	

A Quadruple-A hitter who puts up big numbers during his rare healthy streaks, but he's a flyball hitter who has yet to have a good year in a park at a low elevation. If his agent is shrewd, he'll get a minor league contract with Colorado Springs or Albuquerque.

Jhonny Perez — SS/2B — Bats R — Age 22

YEAR	TEAM	LGE	AB	H	DB	TP	HR	BB	R	RBI	SB	CS	OUT	BA	OBA	SA	EQA	EQR	DEFENSE	
1996	Kissimme	Fla	326	85	10	1	13	23	33	39	10	11	252	.261	.309	.417	.244	37	44-SS 91	
1997	Kissimme	Fla	273	66	13	3	3	12	22	21	4	3	210	.242	.274	.344	.210	21		
1997	Jackson	Tex	152	33	3	0	3	10	10	10	3	2	121	.217	.265	.296	.190	10	19-OF 89	
1998	Jackson	Tex	433	104	8	1	8	37	40	35	14	7	336	.240	.300	.319	.218	37	64-2B 90	53-SS 85
1999	*Houston*	*NL*	*417*	*104*	*12*	*1*	*11*	*28*	*39*	*41*	*13*	*8*	*320*	*.249*	*.297*	*.362*	*.237*	*44*		

He's a year younger than Lugo and played at the higher level last year, but the Astros are dissatisfied with his defense at shortstop, and he split time at second. He's an accomplished hitter for his age and his glove is the only barrier to a starting job by 2000. But erratic arms are usually a chronic condition, and if his persists, he's trade bait.

J.R. Phillips — 1B/OF — Bats L — Age 29

YEAR	TEAM	LGE	AB	H	DB	TP	HR	BB	R	RBI	SB	CS	OUT	BA	OBA	SA	EQA	EQR	DEFENSE	
1996	Scran-WB	Int	197	49	8	0	9	17	20	25	1	2	150	.249	.308	.426	.249	23	47-OF 97	
1997	NewOrln	AA	415	113	15	0	17	34	43	57	0	1	303	.272	.327	.431	.260	52	56-OF 83	37-1B 105
1998	NewOrln	PCL	224	64	11	0	15	18	28	40	1	1	161	.286	.339	.536	.290	36	37-1B 98	
1998	Houston	NL	58	11	1	0	2	7	4	5	0	0	47	.190	.277	.310	.203	4		
1999	*Houston*	*NL*	*309*	*78*	*11*	*0*	*18*	*29*	*32*	*46*	*0*	*1*	*232*	*.252*	*.317*	*.463*	*.272*	*45*		

Its pretty clear he can pummel minor league pitching, but he keeps failing major league trials. Without anything else to offer besides his bat, he might want to start looking across the Pacific. If he's willing to hold on in Triple-A, he'll probably get another chance, but he'll have to hit like gangbusters when it's offered to him.

Jamie Saylor — 2B/SS — Bats L — Age 24

YEAR	TEAM	LGE	AB	H	DB	TP	HR	BB	R	RBI	SB	CS	OUT	BA	OBA	SA	EQA	EQR	DEFENSE	
1996	Kissimme	Fla	182	36	3	1	2	9	8	8	5	4	150	.198	.236	.258	.157	7	39-3B 101	
1997	Jackson	Tex	202	45	8	2	4	17	17	17	2	1	158	.223	.283	.342	.216	17	23-2B 90	15-3B 121
1998	Jackson	Tex	454	111	12	3	12	32	40	44	9	7	350	.244	.294	.363	.226	42	48-2B 101	46-SS 95
1999	*Houston*	*NL*	*370*	*88*	*12*	*3*	*10*	*22*	*31*	*36*	*8*	*5*	*287*	*.238*	*.281*	*.368*	*.231*	*37*		

(Jamie Saylor *continued*)

He's been in the organization for years without ever getting serious consideration, but he added power last year, and might yet have a career. A natural second baseman, but flip-flopped with Jhonny Perez mid-season.

Bill Spiers — INF — Bats L — Age 33

YEAR	TEAM	LGE	AB	H	DB	TP	HR	BB	R	RBI	SB	CS	OUT	BA	OBA	SA	EQA	EQR	DEFENSE	
1996	Houston	NL	219	56	9	1	7	21	27	25	6	0	163	.256	.321	.402	.256	27	46-3B 102	
1997	Houston	NL	294	96	27	4	5	62	66	46	8	5	203	.327	.444	.497	.326	62	63-3B 99	19-SS 93
1998	Houston	NL	384	106	26	4	5	47	58	43	12	2	280	.276	.355	.404	.271	53	83-3B 94	
1999	*Houston*	*NL*	*314*	*87*	*19*	*3*	*5*	*49*	*50*	*38*	*10*	*3*	*230*	*.277*	*.375*	*.404*	*.288*	*51*		

The only left-handed hitting infielder on the team, which can be tough for the lineup against hard-throwing right-handers, from Kerry Wood to Todd Van Poppel. Should go back to his pinch-hitting and sub role now that Caminiti's been signed; he could start at shortstop without giving up too much in the field.

Chris Truby — 3B — Bats R — Age 25

YEAR	TEAM	LGE	AB	H	DB	TP	HR	BB	R	RBI	SB	CS	OUT	BA	OBA	SA	EQA	EQR	DEFENSE	
1996	QuadCit	Mid	365	74	7	0	7	18	16	19	3	5	296	.203	.240	.279	.165	16	62-1B 83	46-3B 92
1997	QuadCit	Mid	268	56	7	0	4	15	15	15	5	2	214	.209	.251	.280	.177	14	68-3B 103	
1997	Kissimme	Fla	199	42	5	0	2	7	9	9	4	2	159	.211	.238	.266	.162	8	54-3B 89	
1998	Kissimme	Fla	211	54	6	0	8	14	20	24	3	1	158	.256	.302	.398	.242	23	51-3B 106	
1998	Jackson	Tex	302	72	10	2	10	16	26	30	5	2	232	.238	.277	.384	.226	28	70-3B 97	
1999	*Houston*	*NL*	*459*	*111*	*14*	*1*	*13*	*23*	*37*	*44*	*9*	*3*	*351*	*.242*	*.278*	*.362*	*.229*	*44*		

Truby went from organizational soldier to prospect in one year; after never reaching double figures in homers, he hit 14 in 52 games with Kissimmee, and continued from there. It didn't come a moment too soon. He's a consistently good fielder, and at 25 he may have a career. Caminiti's return is a big blow to his chances as an Astro.

Daryle Ward — LF/1B — Bats L — Age 24

YEAR	TEAM	LGE	AB	H	DB	TP	HR	BB	R	RBI	SB	CS	OUT	BA	OBA	SA	EQA	EQR	DEFENSE	
1996	Lakeland	Fla	466	124	19	1	12	48	51	55	1	1	343	.266	.335	.388	.253	55	119-1B 116	
1997	Jackson	Tex	414	123	12	0	17	39	51	62	3	1	292	.297	.358	.449	.279	60	109-1B 96	
1998	NewOrln	PCL	461	138	22	1	22	39	59	76	2	0	323	.299	.354	.495	.289	72	56-OF 95	48-1B 110
1999	*Houston*	*NL*	*469*	*139*	*17*	*0*	*25*	*43*	*58*	*79*	*2*	*0*	*330*	*.296*	*.355*	*.493*	*.298*	*80*		

I don't know what the Astros plan for Ward. They're still trying to find playing time for both Everett and Hidalgo, and if they open up an outfield spot, Berkman gets first dibs. Ward's a hitting machine, but he's on the hefty side and as a converted first baseman, I doubt he'll ever be a serviceable outfielder. The Astros are wasting his time if they return him to the minor leagues. A trade is the only realistic option here.

PITCHERS (Averages: 4.00 ERA, 9.00 H/9, 1.00 HR/9, 3.00 BB/9, 6.00 K/9, 1.00 KWH)

Sean Bergman — Throws R — Age 29

YEAR	TEAM	LGE	IP	H	ER	HR	BB	K	ERA	W	L	H/9	HR/9	BB/9	K/9	KWH	PERA
1996	SanDieg	NL	111.7	133	62	14	31	76	5.00	5	7	10.72	1.13	2.50	6.13	1.05	4.76
1997	SanDieg	NL	99.3	133	67	12	34	66	6.07	3	8	12.05	1.09	3.08	5.98	0.72	5.53
1998	Houston	NL	174.7	189	73	20	38	92	3.76	10	9	9.74	1.03	1.96	4.74	0.88	4.07

Surprise #1 in the Astros' rotation: he was picked for nothing from San Diego, and was 8-4 with a 3.01 ERA at the break. He tailed off after that and lost his rotation spot in September, and to be honest I'm not optimistic about his future. Even at his best he puts on a lot of base runners, and if he can't give up less than a hit an inning in the Astrodome, he better not rock the boat with any outrageous contract demands. Dierker should be able to get another servicable year out of him.

Sean Duncan   Throws L   Age 26

YEAR	TEAM	LGE	IP	H	ER	HR	BB	K	ERA	W	L	H/9	HR/9	BB/9	K/9	KWH	PERA
1996	SthBend	Mid	49.0	68	44	5	27	32	8.08	1	4	12.49	0.92	4.96	5.88	0.42	5.88
1997	QuadCit	Mid	41.3	58	26	5	19	26	5.66	2	3	12.63	1.09	4.14	5.66	0.46	5.88
1998	Kissimme	Fla	28.7	42	18	2	21	13	5.65	1	2	13.19	0.63	6.59	4.08	0.14	5.97
1998	Jackson	Tex	36.3	35	16	6	23	26	3.96	2	2	8.67	1.49	5.70	6.44	0.63	4.46

Pitched very impressively at two levels, and as a lefty there's always going to be interest. I do not expect him to have a successful career; he just had his first taste of Double-A at 25, he doesn't have impressive K/BB ratios, and his arm breaks down with alarming regularity. He could hang out on the fringes for a few years, but the Astros could re-sign Mike Magnante if they want that.

Scott Elarton   Throws R   Age 23

YEAR	TEAM	LGE	IP	H	ER	HR	BB	K	ERA	W	L	H/9	HR/9	BB/9	K/9	KWH	PERA
1996	Kissimme	Fla	163.0	195	76	21	58	101	4.20	9	9	10.77	1.16	3.20	5.58	0.68	4.91
1997	Jackson	Tex	127.3	117	55	7	46	116	3.89	7	7	8.27	0.49	3.25	8.20	1.87	3.11
1997	NewOrln	AmA	51.7	61	39	5	16	42	6.79	2	4	10.63	0.87	2.79	7.32	1.36	4.53
1998	NewOrln	PCL	87.7	80	41	6	38	81	4.21	5	5	8.21	0.62	3.90	8.32	1.62	3.29
1998	Houston	NL	57.7	43	19	5	18	51	2.97	4	2	6.71	0.78	2.81	7.96	2.52	2.34

GET SCOTT ELARTON. That's my #1 piece of advice this year for fantasy leaguers. Let's get the caveat on its way: pitchers are unpredictable. Even so, Elarton has everything you look for in a young pitcher. He's a power pitcher all the way—throws in the low 90s, excellent change up, baffling curveball. He's very tall—6'7"—but his control is very good and improving. He was outstanding in the minor leagues, with a 53-27 career record. He's working in a great pitcher's park. He has an outstanding manager who has a knack for getting the most out of his pitchers without overworking them. He has already has a half-season in the major leagues as a middle reliever, the ideal spot for a rookie pitcher. He has an unblemished health record. The only concern is that he works up in the zone, but with the Astrodome's dimensions and tough hitting background, a lot of those potential long drives turn into strikeouts or flyball outs. I don't want to raise expectations unrealistically—he is, after all, 23 and not yet guaranteed a spot in the rotation. But if he stays healthy all season, I think he'll win 15 games easy.

Ramon Garcia   Throws R   Age 29

YEAR	TEAM	LGE	IP	H	ER	HR	BB	K	ERA	W	L	H/9	HR/9	BB/9	K/9	KWH	PERA
1996	NewOrln	AmA	37.7	37	11	2	15	25	2.63	3	1	8.84	0.48	3.58	5.97	0.84	3.58
1996	Milwauke	AL	78.0	78	43	15	17	40	4.96	4	5	9.00	1.73	1.96	4.62	0.90	4.15
1997	Houston	NL	158.0	166	67	21	47	107	3.82	9	9	9.46	1.20	2.68	6.09	1.10	4.16

The reason he's never been able to sustain success is simple: his mechanics are awful. Anytime you see a pitcher's arm hurled across his body on follow-through until his arm hits his chest, you can go ahead and book the appointment with Dr. Jobe. The shock isn't that he broke down, but that the Astros were able to get 159 good innings out of him. He may resurface, but unless someone re-teaches him how to pitch, I doubt he'll ever stay healthy long enough to succeed.

Mike Grzanich   Throws R   Age 26

YEAR	TEAM	LGE	IP	H	ER	HR	BB	K	ERA	W	L	H/9	HR/9	BB/9	K/9	KWH	PERA
1996	Jackson	Tex	68.0	74	51	11	46	68	6.75	2	6	9.79	1.46	6.09	9.00	1.02	5.03
1997	Jackson	Tex	92.7	136	71	11	49	56	6.90	3	7	13.21	1.07	4.76	5.44	0.35	6.22
1998	NewOrln	PCL	36.7	33	14	2	21	29	3.44	2	2	8.10	0.49	5.15	7.12	0.91	3.44
1998	Houston	NL	1.0	1	2	0	2	1	18.00	0	0	9.00	0.00	18.00	9.00	0.37	9.00

Came back from an injury to pitch well for the Zephyrs down the stretch, and the Astros are in the unusual position of having more left-handed than right-handed options in the bullpen. I'm not saying Grzanich is going to have a career, but he's in the right place for it to happen.

John Halama — Throws L — Age 27

YEAR	TEAM	LGE	IP	H	ER	HR	BB	K	ERA	W	L	H/9	HR/9	BB/9	K/9	KWH	PERA
1995	QuadCit	Mid	53.0	80	25	9	27	34	4.25	3	3	13.58	1.53	4.58	5.77	0.40	6.79
1996	Jackson	Tex	150.0	190	91	11	67	89	5.46	6	11	11.40	0.66	4.02	5.34	0.47	4.98
1997	NewOrln	AmA	160.0	188	71	9	33	99	3.99	9	9	10.58	0.51	1.86	5.57	1.18	4.11
1998	NewOrln	PCL	110.0	143	56	11	17	63	4.58	5	7	11.70	0.90	1.39	5.15	1.22	4.91
1998	Houston	NL	33.0	39	19	0	12	19	5.18	1	3	10.64	0.00	3.27	5.18	0.58	4.09

Halama was sent to the Mariners after the season as the PTNBL in the Johnson deal. He's an excellent control pitcher who has nothing left to prove in the minors after going 25-6 the last two years. He's old for a prospect (four months older than Andy Pettite) and has little star potential, but he may be a perfect fit in Seattle, being cut from the same mold as Jamie Moyer. If any young pitcher is going to get past Lou Piniella, it's going to be one who doesn't beat himself with walks.

Mike Hampton — Throws L — Age 26

YEAR	TEAM	LGE	IP	H	ER	HR	BB	K	ERA	W	L	H/9	HR/9	BB/9	K/9	KWH	PERA
1996	Houston	NL	161.0	183	71	12	47	91	3.97	9	9	10.23	0.67	2.63	5.09	0.72	4.19
1997	Houston	NL	221.7	234	100	16	69	124	4.06	12	13	9.50	0.65	2.80	5.03	0.71	3.82
1998	Houston	NL	216.3	237	83	18	74	126	3.45	14	10	9.86	0.75	3.08	5.24	0.68	4.12

He continues to be successful despite giving up a boatload of base runners every season. Last year, batters had a 742 OPS against him—the NL average was 741—yet he nearly cracked the top 10 in ERA. How? Partly because he is a tremendous ground ball pitcher, and led the league with 31 double play balls. But mostly because he did much better from the stretch—hitters had a puny 639 OPS with runners on, and with runners in scoring position their OPS was 589.

It's a team-wide phenomenon—with runners in scoring position, the Astros held opposing batters to .217/.294/.342, by far the best numbers in either league. It may be coincidence, but with a sample size of over 1500 plate appearances, maybe not. Between Dierker and pitching coach Vern Ruhle, the Astros get more out of mediocre talent than anyone this side of Montreal, and Hampton isn't mediocre. My gut tells me he could be one of the top lefties in baseball as soon as this year.

Reggie Harris — Throws R — Age 30

YEAR	TEAM	LGE	IP	H	ER	HR	BB	K	ERA	W	L	H/9	HR/9	BB/9	K/9	KWH	PERA
1996	Trenton	Eas	34.7	25	8	3	21	30	2.08	3	1	6.49	0.78	5.45	7.79	1.29	2.60
1997	Philadel	NL	55.3	61	31	1	39	41	5.04	2	4	9.92	0.16	6.34	6.67	0.53	4.23
1998	NewOrln	PCL	48.0	48	31	7	30	39	5.81	2	3	9.00	1.31	5.63	7.31	0.79	4.50

He seems to have been on the verge of a break out since he was a rookie nine years ago, and it still hasn't happened. He's got nasty stuff, but his control is just bad enough that major league hitters can sit on his high fastball and wax him. Has maybe a 15% chance of ever having a good year, and that's only if he gets an opportunity in a big ballpark that will forgive a 400-foot mistake.

Doug Henry — Throws R — Age 35

YEAR	TEAM	LGE	IP	H	ER	HR	BB	K	ERA	W	L	H/9	HR/9	BB/9	K/9	KWH	PERA
1996	NYMets	NL	74.7	89	46	8	34	52	5.54	3	5	10.73	0.96	4.10	6.27	0.67	4.94
1997	SanFran	NL	71.7	75	41	6	37	62	5.15	3	5	9.42	0.75	4.65	7.79	1.04	4.14
1998	Houston	NL	72.3	58	23	10	32	54	2.86	5	3	7.22	1.24	3.98	6.72	1.18	3.11

(Doug Henry *continued*)

Henry has never strung together two good seasons in a row, and I think part of the problem is that he throws that high fastball and has little margin of error if his command is off. If he doesn't place the pitch just right, it's off the wall for a double. Dierker used him wisely, and all those flyballs he gave up in the Astrodome were chased down—he had a 2.27 ERA at home. He's also never learned to stop the running game, but I expect another good year from him.

Chris Holt — Throws R — Age 27

YEAR	TEAM	LGE	IP	H	ER	HR	BB	K	ERA	W	L	H/9	HR/9	BB/9	K/9	KWH	PERA
1995	Jackson	Tex	30.0	33	10	3	5	21	3.00	2	1	9.90	0.90	1.50	6.30	2.00	3.90
1995	Tucson	PCL	122.0	150	50	6	32	67	3.69	8	6	11.07	0.44	2.36	4.94	0.70	4.35
1996	Tucson	PCL	186.0	210	72	13	37	115	3.48	12	9	10.16	0.63	1.79	5.56	1.28	3.97
1997	Houston	NL	207.7	225	93	18	55	85	4.03	11	12	9.75	0.78	2.38	3.68	0.44	3.99

Holt averaged 173 innings a year from 1993 to 1996—high for a young pitcher whose season only ran until Labor Day. In the off-season before his rookie year, he pitched winter ball, which is where he attracted Dierker's attention in the first place. Between April 1996 and the September 1997, Holt threw over 400 innings without ever giving his arm a few months to recuperate. The majors now have a policy restricting hitters from playing in the winter leagues—but they should be more concerned about pitchers wearing down their arms. Holt may come back, but he was never a power pitcher to begin with, and it would be a surprise if he had another quality season.

Eric Ireland   Throws R   Age 22

YEAR	TEAM	LGE	IP	H	ER	HR	BB	K	ERA	W	L	H/9	HR/9	BB/9	K/9	KWH	PERA
1997	Auburn	NYP	100.3	152	68	7	29	46	6.10	3	8	13.63	0.63	2.60	4.13	0.36	5.74
1998	QuadCit	Mid	187.7	253	109	22	81	124	5.23	8	13	12.13	1.06	3.88	5.95	0.56	5.61

Ireland led all of minor league baseball with 206 innings last season, all of them in the Midwest League. Why do organizations do stuff like this? If you want to challenge your pitcher, promote him out of a league he's wasting his time in. Don't do dumb stuff like training him to throw nine innings. The track record of minor league pitchers who throw 200 innings, from Bill Pulsipher on down, is grisly. Ireland's a good pitcher, but as a power pitcher who hasn't polished his control, he throws a lot of pitches in an inning, making him an even more serious injury risk.

Randy Johnson   Throws L   Age 35

YEAR	TEAM	LGE	IP	H	ER	HR	BB	K	ERA	W	L	H/9	HR/9	BB/9	K/9	KWH	PERA
1996	Seattle	AL	63.0	45	20	8	20	84	2.86	5	2	6.43	1.14	2.86	12.00	5.88	2.29
1997	Seattle	AL	220.3	140	45	19	66	282	1.84	20	4	5.72	0.78	2.70	11.52	6.45	1.63
1998	Seattle	AL	166.3	139	70	18	54	207	3.79	9	9	7.52	0.97	2.92	11.20	4.28	2.92
1998	Houston	NL	85.3	60	11	4	24	106	1.16	8	1	6.33	0.42	2.53	11.18	5.85	1.79

If Johnson had re-signed with the Astros, with the bad hitting background and no DH, and stayed healthy, he could have made a serious run at Nolan Ryan's single-season K record (383). Now that he's with Arizona, he might still become only the third man (after Ryan and Koufax) to reach 350 K's in a season. He proved that his arm wasn't the problem once he left Seattle. He's 35, but unless his back gives out, I see no evidence that he won't last into his 40s.

Jose Lima   Throws R   Age 26

YEAR	TEAM	LGE	IP	H	ER	HR	BB	K	ERA	W	L	H/9	HR/9	BB/9	K/9	KWH	PERA
1996	Toledo	Int	69.3	99	47	11	12	49	6.10	2	6	12.85	1.43	1.56	6.36	1.52	5.97
1996	Detroit	AL	75.0	80	35	11	18	58	4.20	4	4	9.60	1.32	2.16	6.96	1.75	4.20
1997	Houston	NL	74.7	83	42	10	15	56	5.06	3	5	10.00	1.21	1.81	6.75	1.89	4.34
1998	Houston	NL	235.3	235	90	34	29	154	3.44	15	11	8.99	1.30	1.11	5.89	2.61	3.71

Surprise #2, and I think Lima's for real. He has always had good stuff and excellent control, but it took him a few years to figure out that control doesn't always mean throwing the ball down the middle. His ERA and K/BB ratio have both improved three straight seasons, and last year he had the best K/BB ratio (5.28) in the NL. As the Astros' most pronounced flyball pitcher, he did much better at home (3.16 ERA vs. 4.33 on the road). I don't think his stuff is good enough to ever give up less than a hit an inning, but in the situation he's in right now, he's a good bet for 13-16 wins.

Mike Magnante   Throws L   Age 34

YEAR	TEAM	LGE	IP	H	ER	HR	BB	K	ERA	W	L	H/9	HR/9	BB/9	K/9	KWH	PERA
1996	KansasCy	AL	54.7	57	29	4	19	32	4.77	2	4	9.38	0.66	3.13	5.27	0.71	3.79
1997	NewOrln	AmA	22.0	39	18	0	6	18	7.36	0	2	15.95	0.00	2.45	7.36	1.04	6.14
1997	Houston	NL	47.3	42	15	2	10	38	2.85	3	2	7.99	0.38	1.90	7.23	2.58	2.66
1998	Houston	NL	53.3	59	25	2	24	36	4.22	3	3	9.96	0.34	4.05	6.08	0.69	4.05

A slop pitcher who gets by with a strange uncoiling motion as he heads to the plate. 1997 looks like a huge fluke, and I don't see the Astros re-signing him. He could land somewhere as the 11th man, because he is good at keeping the ball down and his motion works to confuse left-handers. Not a good bet for any sustained success.

Trever Miller   **Throws L**   **Age 26**

YEAR	TEAM	LGE	IP	H	ER	HR	BB	K	ERA	W	L	H/9	HR/9	BB/9	K/9	KWH	PERA
1996	Toledo	Int	166.0	178	86	19	65	100	4.66	8	10	9.65	1.03	3.52	5.42	0.65	4.28
1997	NewOrln	AmA	154.7	214	82	15	53	82	4.77	7	10	12.45	0.87	3.08	4.77	0.44	5.53
1998	Houston	NL	54.3	59	19	4	19	28	3.15	4	2	9.77	0.66	3.15	4.64	0.52	3.98

He's not supremely talented, but he brings certain talents that can be exploited in middle relief. He throws a good sinker and gets double play balls, and allowed just 4 of 22 inherited runners to score. He cuts off the running game, and he was exceptional against left-handers (.217 with no power). With Magnante on his way out, Miller should have some security.

Wade Miller   **Throws R**   **Age 22**

YEAR	TEAM	LGE	IP	H	ER	HR	BB	K	ERA	W	L	H/9	HR/9	BB/9	K/9	KWH	PERA
1997	QuadCit	Mid	56.3	56	29	8	11	33	4.63	3	3	8.95	1.28	1.76	5.27	1.33	3.83
1997	Kissimme	Fla	94.3	103	35	5	16	57	3.34	6	4	9.83	0.48	1.53	5.44	1.48	3.63
1998	Jackson	Tex	59.7	56	22	7	27	38	3.32	4	3	8.45	1.06	4.07	5.73	0.72	3.77

This is your arm. This is your arm on too many pitches. Wade was one of the jewels of the Astros' farm system in 1997, but threw 159 innings in just 22 starts, and you can't expect a 20-year-old who isn't particularly big (6'2", 185) to shoulder that kind of load. Pitching well before his arm came up lame, and he strikes me as the kind of pitcher who could return from the injury and still make the big leagues.

Tony Mounce   **Throws L**   **Age 24**

YEAR	TEAM	LGE	IP	H	ER	HR	BB	K	ERA	W	L	H/9	HR/9	BB/9	K/9	KWH	PERA
1996	Kissimme	Fla	147.3	177	75	13	74	80	4.58	7	9	10.81	0.79	4.52	4.89	0.37	4.89
1997	Jackson	Tex	136.3	185	86	20	65	96	5.68	5	10	12.21	1.32	4.29	6.34	0.57	5.94
1998	Kissimme	Fla	22.7	48	27	3	15	10	10.72	0	3	19.06	1.19	5.96	3.97	0.10	8.74
1998	Jackson	Tex	103.7	147	72	14	49	63	6.25	3	9	12.76	1.22	4.25	5.47	0.41	6.08

Mounce had a fabulous season in the Midwest League in 1995, but the whispers were that he didn't throw hard enough to make the adjustments on the way up the ladder. With pitchers, you have to take the scouts seriously, and Mounce has regressed badly. He's a longshot for any major league success at this point, and the Astros have plenty of better options.

C.J. Nitkowski   **Throws L**   **Age 26**

YEAR	TEAM	LGE	IP	H	ER	HR	BB	K	ERA	W	L	H/9	HR/9	BB/9	K/9	KWH	PERA
1996	Toledo	Int	111.7	111	53	13	53	89	4.27	6	6	8.95	1.05	4.27	7.17	1.01	4.03
1996	Detroit	AL	47.7	61	34	6	31	36	6.42	1	4	11.52	1.13	5.85	6.80	0.51	5.66
1997	NewOrln	AmA	165.3	221	93	10	55	117	5.06	7	11	12.03	0.54	2.99	6.37	0.84	5.01
1998	Houston	NL	60.3	52	24	4	21	40	3.58	4	3	7.76	0.60	3.13	5.97	1.10	2.83

Nitkowski is the most talented of the Astros' middle relievers. He was always a power lefty, and his struggles in the major leagues were a result of organizational impatience. The Reds couldn't wait to bring him up, and when he struggled they couldn't wait to send him away. The Astros' bullpen was full of converted ex-starters—Nitkowski and Trever Miller were starters the year before, Elarton was a starter getting his feet wet in middle relief, and even Billy Wagner was as a starting pitcher. This is the way relievers used to be molded, it works, and it means Dierker can use his relievers for extended outings without worrying about their fragility.

Jay Powell   **Throws R**   **Age 27**

YEAR	TEAM	LGE	IP	H	ER	HR	BB	K	ERA	W	L	H/9	HR/9	BB/9	K/9	KWH	PERA
1996	Florida	NL	72.0	75	37	5	35	47	4.62	3	5	9.38	0.62	4.38	5.88	0.63	4.00
1997	Florida	NL	80.7	73	30	3	27	58	3.35	5	4	8.14	0.33	3.01	6.47	1.28	2.90
1998	Florida	NL	37.0	39	17	5	20	22	4.14	2	2	9.49	1.22	4.86	5.35	0.47	4.62
1998	Houston	NL	34.3	24	8	1	14	35	2.10	3	1	6.29	0.26	3.67	9.17	2.73	1.83

Powell has been a closer since college and has the two-pitch repertoire you'd expect, but the Orioles did force him into the rotation for a year. Throws hard, stays healthy, gets righties and lefties out well, and as the right-handed set-up man for a lefty closer, is bound to pick up a few saves this year.

Shane Reynolds　　Throws R　　Age 31

YEAR	TEAM	LGE	IP	H	ER	HR	BB	K	ERA	W	L	H/9	HR/9	BB/9	K/9	KWH	PERA
1996	Houston	NL	240.0	234	91	20	41	182	3.41	16	11	8.78	0.75	1.54	6.82	2.59	3.26
1997	Houston	NL	179.7	203	88	20	42	135	4.41	9	11	10.17	1.00	2.10	6.76	1.60	4.31
1998	Houston	NL	237.3	266	89	25	48	192	3.38	15	11	10.09	0.95	1.82	7.28	2.17	4.21

Terry Collins tested his limits, and Reynolds is only now fully recovered. Consistently has pretty K/BB ratios and, along with Hampton, was the main reason the Astros were one of the most groundball-oriented staffs in baseball, behind only Atlanta and San Diego. There's a lesson in the knowledge that the three best pitching staffs in the NL also got the most grounders. He's not going to sneak up on anyone after a 19-8 record last year, but I think he's due for a big year.

Roberto Rivera　　Throws L　　Age 30

YEAR	TEAM	LGE	IP	H	ER	HR	BB	K	ERA	W	L	H/9	HR/9	BB/9	K/9	KWH	PERA
1995	Orlando	Sou	62.3	71	26	5	12	24	3.75	4	3	10.25	0.72	1.73	3.47	0.51	4.04
1996	Iowa	AmA	31.7	33	11	3	9	14	3.13	2	2	9.38	0.85	2.56	3.98	0.49	3.98
1998	NewOrln	PCL	56.7	71	25	5	16	28	3.97	3	3	11.28	0.79	2.54	4.45	0.52	4.76

A career minor league reliever with just five major league innings despite having an ERA over 3 just once in the last five years. A soft-tosser with good control, he could be effective in a limited role. Signed by San Diego, where he'll get a better shot at a job.

Wilfredo Rodriguez　　Throws L　　Age 20

YEAR	TEAM	LGE	IP	H	ER	HR	BB	K	ERA	W	L	H/9	HR/9	BB/9	K/9	KWH	PERA
1998	QuadCit	Mid	153.0	177	91	11	69	113	5.35	6	11	10.41	0.65	4.06	6.65	0.78	4.47

Still a few years away, which is actually a good thing, because the Astros aren't going to get to his application soon. He led the Gulf Coast League in wins in his pro debut, then had a spectacular year for a teenager in the Midwest League. Has a chance to be an impact pitcher in three years.

Derek Root　　Throws L　　Age 24

YEAR	TEAM	LGE	IP	H	ER	HR	BB	K	ERA	W	L	H/9	HR/9	BB/9	K/9	KWH	PERA
1996	QuadCit	Mid	58.7	76	31	2	27	32	4.76	3	4	11.66	0.31	4.14	4.91	0.37	4.76
1997	Kissimme	Fla	118.7	177	96	14	48	50	7.28	3	10	13.42	1.06	3.64	3.79	0.22	6.22
1998	Kissimme	Fla	74.7	90	34	4	24	54	4.10	4	4	10.85	0.48	2.89	6.51	1.01	4.34
1998	Jackson	Tex	42.0	52	23	4	18	24	4.93	2	3	11.14	0.86	3.86	5.14	0.46	4.93

Root's actually a converted first baseman, and really came on last year when he added zip to his fastball. The Astros are high on him and moved him back into the rotation after a promotion to Double-A, which left him unfazed. It's going to be a year or two before the Astros clear some space for him, but he should have a career.

Roger Salkeld　　Throws R　　Age 28

YEAR	TEAM	LGE	IP	H	ER	HR	BB	K	ERA	W	L	H/9	HR/9	BB/9	K/9	KWH	PERA
1996	Cincnnti	NL	119.3	120	61	18	51	74	4.60	6	7	9.05	1.36	3.85	5.58	0.67	4.22
1997	Indianap	AmA	83.7	114	85	16	65	69	9.14	1	8	12.26	1.72	6.99	7.42	0.48	6.56
1998	NewOrln	PCL	73.7	101	64	8	67	58	7.82	2	6	12.34	0.98	8.19	7.09	0.37	6.11

The former All-World prospect never recovered from reconstructive surgery, and his stamina seems to drop every year. If he took a year off entirely and just let his arm rest, he could probably work his way back into a bullpen role. They should add him to the Spring Training lecture circuit, addressing minor league pitchers on what can happen if they give in to peer pressure and "pitch through the pain."

Brian Sikorski　　Throws R　　Age 24

YEAR	TEAM	LGE	IP	H	ER	HR	BB	K	ERA	W	L	H/9	HR/9	BB/9	K/9	KWH	PERA
1996	QuadCit	Mid	154.3	198	97	18	72	101	5.66	6	11	11.55	1.05	4.20	5.89	0.54	5.37
1997	Kissimme	Fla	62.7	86	37	3	18	34	5.31	3	4	12.35	0.43	2.59	4.88	0.56	5.03
1997	Jackson	Tex	88.3	102	53	9	30	61	5.40	4	6	10.39	0.92	3.06	6.22	0.91	4.48
1998	Jackson	Tex	92.3	97	49	13	45	61	4.78	4	6	9.45	1.27	4.39	5.95	0.64	4.48
1998	NewOrln	PCL	78.7	96	56	9	30	52	6.41	3	6	10.98	1.03	3.43	5.95	0.70	4.92

(Brian Sikorski *continued*)

The Astros' entry in the "gee, if he could only cut down those walks a little" pool of pitchers. Sikorski is well thought of by the organization. I think his future is in the pen, but regardless of his role, he's going to have to step it up to get a shot with this team.

Billy Wagner   Throws L   Age 27

YEAR	TEAM	LGE	IP	H	ER	HR	BB	K	ERA	W	L	H/9	HR/9	BB/9	K/9	KWH	PERA
1996	Tucson	PCL	74.0	63	27	2	33	72	3.28	5	3	7.66	0.24	4.01	8.76	1.87	2.80
1996	Houston	NL	52.0	31	14	7	28	60	2.42	4	2	5.37	1.21	4.85	10.38	3.11	2.08
1997	Houston	NL	66.7	54	22	6	27	94	2.97	5	2	7.29	0.81	3.65	12.69	4.54	2.83
1998	Houston	NL	61.3	49	17	7	22	88	2.49	5	2	7.19	1.03	3.23	12.91	5.39	2.79

I couldn't understand why everyone was worried that after taking the line drive off his noggin, that he would somehow be too "scared" to pitch. I'd worry about a long-term injury, but worry about Wagner's psyche? The man comes from a turbulent childhood, getting passed around from relative to relative, he's had to battle the knock of being too short (5'11") to pitch in the majors, and his wife's father and stepmom were killed by another relative a few years ago. I don't think he wastes time worrying about a liner through the box. A wonderful pitcher who has averaged over two strikeouts a hit every season of his career, and trained as a starter, Wagner could handle an 85-90 inning load as a closer without much difficulty.

Kent Wallace   Throws R   Age 28

YEAR	TEAM	LGE	IP	H	ER	HR	BB	K	ERA	W	L	H/9	HR/9	BB/9	K/9	KWH	PERA
1995	Norwich	Eas	86.7	120	49	12	24	54	5.09	4	6	12.46	1.25	2.49	5.61	0.76	5.71
1995	Columbus	Int	50.7	50	19	9	12	27	3.38	4	2	8.88	1.60	2.13	4.80	0.91	4.09
1996	Columbus	Int	65.0	82	37	14	16	27	5.12	3	4	11.35	1.94	2.22	3.74	0.42	5.68
1998	Jackson	Tex	46.3	47	20	4	12	35	3.88	3	2	9.13	0.78	2.33	6.80	1.63	3.69

A former Yankees' farmhand let go after arm troubles, Wallace was rescued from the independent leagues last year and pitched extremely well. Normally a guy like this is strictly minor league filler, but Wallace was a decent starter with the Yankees before his injury, and as a reliever was able to keep his arm strength for most of the year. He's not in the Astros' plans, but Kerry Ligtenberg wasn't exactly the Braves' closer of the future either.

SNWLP — HOUSTON ASTROS — Park Effect: -10.4%

PITCHER	GS	IP	R	SNW	SNL	SNPCT	W	L	RA	APW	SNVA	SNWAR
Bergman, S.	27	168.0	80	9.5	9.3	.505	12	8	4.29	0.37	0.14	1.50
Elarton, S.	2	12.3	9	0.6	0.7	.468	0	0	6.57	-0.29	-0.05	0.05
Halama, J.	6	32.3	21	1.5	2.5	.364	1	1	5.85	-0.49	-0.53	-0.24
Hampton, M.	32	211.7	92	12.8	10.5	.548	11	7	3.91	1.34	0.92	2.87
Johnson, R.	11	84.3	12	7.6	1.1	.875	10	1	1.28	3.01	3.10	3.93
Lima, J.	33	233.3	100	13.3	11.0	.546	16	8	3.86	1.62	1.03	2.94
Miller, Trev.	1	4.0	2	0.2	0.3	.384	0	0	4.50	-0.00	-0.03	-0.02
Reynolds, S.	35	233.3	99	14.0	11.3	.554	19	8	3.82	1.72	1.24	3.25
Schourek, P.	15	80.0	43	4.7	5.2	.477	7	6	4.84	-0.32	-0.26	0.51
TOTALS	162	1059.3	458	64.0	51.8	.553	76	39	3.89	6.96	5.57	14.78

Flash back to opening day 1998. The Astros had had a pretty good rotation the year before, but they had lost their best starter to free agency, two other solid starters from 1997 were out indefinitely with injuries, and they had made no significant acquisitions to fill the holes. You predicted the rotation was going to (a) improve from the previous year, (b) stay the same, (c) fall off so badly they'd long for the "good old days" of Doug Drabek. Of course, the answer was (a), because the Astros had secret weapons: Sean Bergman, Jose Lima, and Pete Schourek. In the five years prior to 1998, Bergman's SNPcts were .218, .406, .427, .369, and .307. Lima's only two years with more than one start gave him SNPcts of .447 and .228. Schourek was coming off injury-riddled years of .342 and .353. So naturally, they put up solid seasons. I swear Larry Dierker is doing it with mirrors. One 1998 Astro starter who actually had a history of success prior to 1998 was Randy Johnson. Even with that history, it was hard to imagine that he'd be as good as he was. If you take Johnson's time with the Astros as a season by itself (i.e., ignore what he did in 1998 with the Mariners), his .875 SNPct represents the best SNPct recorded among pitchers with five or more starts. In case you're wondering who gets the record if the threshold is lowered, Jeff Brantley of all people had a .939 SNPct in four starts in 1992.

Pitcher Abuse Points

PITCHER	AGE	GS	PAP	PAP/S	AAW	MAX	115+	130+
Bergman, Sean	28	27	72	2.67	4.44	119	1	0
Halama, John	26	6	0	0.00	0.00	99	0	0
Hampton, Mike	25	32	336	10.50	22.75	136	6	3
Johnson, Randy	34	11	472	42.91	42.91	136	8	4
Lima, Jose	25	33	310	9.39	20.35	127	6	0
Reynolds, Shane	30	35	252	7.20	9.60	128	5	0
Schourek, Pete	29	15	25	1.67	2.50	115	1	0
TOTAL		162	1581	9.76	14.83	136	27	7
RANKING (NL)			6	6	4		7	2-T

The Astros actually rank higher in PAP than I expected them to all season—they ranked in the bottom half midway through the year, but it's amazing what even a little Randy Johnson can do for your team. Ignore his 11 starts, and the Astros would rank 8th in PAP/S and 7th in AAW, a reasonable spot for a deep rotation. The key, though, was that the abuse was dispersed among everyone in the rotation. Bergman and Reynolds came out almost unscathed, but even Jose Lima did very well given he averaged over seven innings per start. The only guy I'm concerned about is Hampton, who put on a lot of base runners last year. I am not that concerned about Johnson, even though he led baseball in PAP. His back is always a concern, but I think his arm will last at least another five years.

Milwaukee Brewers

What do you have to do to be relevant? There's a timeless sense of fun that going to a ballgame in County Stadium can give you. I got hooked on County Stadium when I drove to Milwaukee with a friend to catch a doubleheader against the Orioles. Maybe it's the relatively low-tech scoreboard, or the sausage races. Maybe it's Bernie Brewer in what another friend calls "Bernie's love shack." Maybe it's singing "Roll Out the Barrel" after "Take Me Out to the Ballgame." Maybe it's the bratwursts. Maybe it's the happy cheeseheads tailgating in the parking lot, or the native Midwestern courtesy people seem to treat each other with that's so very different from the reception you get at other ballparks. My wife loves going to County Stadium, and she doesn't even like baseball all that much. She's jealous when I go without her on days she's stuck at work. What does that say about the place? It isn't like we ever go to Milwaukee for any other reason.

But what does any of that mean for the team on the field? It isn't easy being one of the two dozen teams Ken Burns forgot. What does any of this mean as far as winning or trying to win? What about baseball for those Brewers fans still muttering about Pete Ladd or the roller coaster ride of '87 or the almost-something '92 Brew Crew? At what point do the Brewers matter?

It would easy or cynical to say that the Brewers are only the logical extension of Bud Selig and the larger economic issues that he says need to be resolved in his lifetime. We could pretend that they're just the physical representation of the argument that teams with old stadiums and small budgets can't compete with the Braves and the Yankees. We could claim that the Brewers are merely designed to illustrate the need for revenue-sharing and new stadiums.

That's a pretty cold-hearted way of looking of things, and I don't believe it for a minute. As much as Bud Selig is publicly flogged around the country for his role in the game's labor wars, I'm willing to guess that he is not so Machiavellian that he'd let his franchise serve as little more than a major league ghetto to illustrate the dangers of radical financial disparities between franchises. The man has consis-

tently come across as deeply interested in seeing his Brewers win. It has been his misfortune that the franchise hasn't really gone anywhere or done anything since they finally fired Harry Dalton and Tom Trebelhorn in 1991. Shaking things up (and they did need to be shaken up) helped to produce 92 wins in '92, but since then the Brewers have played along from year to year, without actually doing much to make themselves significantly better. Although I've commended them in the past for having the good sense to go year-to-year with John Jaha instead of ever giving him a multi-year deal, I'd be concerned that how they've handled Jaha reflects the absence of any plan from the Bando/Garner regime. It seems as if they just stumble along from year to year, sort of hoping things work out. It may also reflect the organization's sense of priorities that the front office is increasingly populated with Brewers of bygone days, representatives of the proud tradition created by the strong teams of the late 70s and early 80s. On one level, I think that's kind of cool.

Brewers Prospectus

1998 record: 74-88; Fifth place, NL Central

Pythagorean W/L: 70-92

Runs scored: 707 (10th in NL)

Runs allowed: 812 (t-13th in NL)

Team EQA: .251 (t-11th in NL)

Park: County Stadium (moderate hitters')

1998: Faceless team meandered aimlessly through a meaningless season.

1999: No reason to expect significant improvement; franchise is looking towards 2000.

Who doesn't think its fun to still have Cecil Cooper or Mike Caldwell or Jim Gantner or Don Money or even Dwight Bernard around in some capacity? The danger is that the selection of old favorites doesn't necessarily mean that the Brewers have the best people running the organization, just some well regarded and popular ones.

On that level, the Brewers have always observed a certain loyalty to their own, and although I respect that (and envy it—who wouldn't want to work for an organization that values and has a sense of its past?), it hasn't helped them so far. Perhaps it is critical to remember the historical legacy of bringing in Dalton and George Bamberger from the outside, because it was the two ex-Orioles who built the Brewers' first great teams, and their legacy still towers over anything Bando and Garner have ever accomplished. Perhaps they know that, because scarcely a week goes by during a baseball season where Bando or Garner won't blame their troubles on small-market woes.

The small-market excuse is a thin reed to lean on year after year, but it can also handicap how the Brewers address a future with Miller Park on the horizon. It is easy to say the Brewers should be smarter with their money and use better judgment in selecting the players they can afford as well as use. That's because it is equally easy to see that if you're blowing money on Marquis Grissom and Darrin Jackson, the point isn't what you're spending, it's whether the Brewers know which players are any good in the first place. Player acquisition has been scattershot: while getting Jeromy Burnitz seems to compare with old pickups like Ben Oglivie and Cecil Cooper, you see far too much of the Brewers bringing in guys like Marc Newfield or Bill Pulsipher or Paul Wagner, bad gambles that turn out even worse than expected.

The future riches that Miller Park should infuse into the franchise aren't going to make the Brewers smarter. They have to focus on how to improve the team, instead of lazily claiming that money solves everybody's problems. Until they do, the Brewers won't be anything more than an afternoon of fun.

———o———

Because the most common response to Bud Selig anywhere in the country is booing, jeering, and catcalls, it will probably surprise some of you that Selig seems to be a popular guy in Milwaukee. There shouldn't be any cognitive dissonance on this score. Selig's place in baseball history is going to end up being an uncomfortable balance between his public image as the man who canceled the World Series, and the incremental but real progress that is slowly taking place in major league operations. In that sense, being hated nationally and valuable to the industry isn't too strange a combination for a career that will reflect other strange combinations.

Because Czar Bud isn't exactly a dynamic leader but is nevertheless the game's commissioner, let's ask the question. What has Bud Selig done for us lately?

Did he save baseball in Milwaukee? Maybe he did, and maybe he didn't. North Carolina is nowhere near the viable threat for franchise relocation that the Tampa/St. Petersburg area was in the 80s. Indeed, the absence of a viable, ready-to-go destination for major league teams trying to bully their way into getting a new stadium meant that nobody had to take Carl Pohlad too seriously last year. But nobody doubts that Selig wanted to stay in Milwaukee, and as questionable as his methods may have been, the Brewers will remain in Milwaukee. In a country already saddled with corporate welfare as a way of life, I can't really begrudge Selig for using the tools of his time to procure what is, on a governmental scale, petty cash. That isn't to dismiss the expenses taxpayers are going to have to pick up, but if America's citizenry spent as much time getting involved in public works and infrastructure projects as they do arguing about high-profile stadiums, everyone would be better off.

Are labor relations going to ever get ironed out under Selig? If there is any workable solution to baseball's continu-ing cold war between labor or management, it is probably going to come during Selig's watch. The commissioner's office is little more than a connection between an unwieldy and loosely federated group of associations, franchises, and unions whose interests obviously don't coincide in all areas. Selig is on top because he's been an owner, in a position that owes its existence to the owners. Keeping the commissioner's office from becoming a wild card in populist plays for short-term non-solutions to the game's labor wars, as it was under the dopey, ineffective tyranny of Fay Vincent, is in the game's best business interests. If the owners and the player's union are ever going to create a long-term business plan for the industry that profits players, owners, and by extension the game and its fans, it is going to be in a situation where neither side can abuse the commissioner's office as the source for a cop-out from persistent and intractable labor problems. As the ugliness of 1994 laid bare, knights on white horses, whether they're federal negotiators or the President or a congressional committee, cannot provide easy answers for what is, at root, an uneasy and untrusting business relationship between players and owners. By ascending the throne, Bud Selig may have exposed that relationship for everyone to see, but the solutions to the game's problems are only going to come from direct negotiation between the players and owners.

How is the commissioner's office going to work now? The early indications are that it will work better than it ever has. Bud Selig may be many things, but stupid doesn't seem to one of them. From experience, he knows two things. First, he knows to try to rule through consensus. There aren't any easy solutions, so he'll get to plug away at creating working coalitions that produce acceptable solutions. Second, he's smart enough to know that there are people smarter than he is, which is why Paul Beeston and Sandy Alderson are working for him instead of in their individual fiefdoms. All three men have made sacrifices to take a crack at solving the game's issues, whether those issues are the quality of umpiring, player development, the draft, the relationships with the unions, or the relationship with the minor leagues through the National Association. They may screw up. They may not pull it off. But it is at least an improvement over a commissioner's office run by a dilettante and his embezzling agent sidekick.

Hate him, dislike him, or ignore him, but get used to the idea that Bud Selig is here to stay. There won't be any campaigns worth mentioning for George Mitchell or Bob Costas or Joe Morgan or Boog Powell for commissioner. Not until after the important stuff gets taken care of. That is what Selig was hired to do, and in five or six years, we'll have a better idea about whether or not he's doing it.

HITTERS (Averages: BA .260/ OBA .330/ SA .420, EQA .260)

Alex Andreopoulos   C   Bats L   Age 26

YEAR	TEAM	LGE	AB	H	DB	TP	HR	BB	R	RBI	SB	CS	OUT	BA	OBA	SA	EQA	EQR	DEFENSE
1995	Beloit	Mid	167	39	2	0	2	25	17	13	2	2	130	.234	.333	.281	.222	15	
1996	Stockton	Cal	288	68	9	0	4	27	26	22	5	2	222	.236	.302	.309	.216	24	
1998	El Paso	Tex	360	74	11	1	5	38	25	24	1	2	288	.206	.281	.283	.194	24	86-C 90
1999	*Milwauke*	*NL*	*246*	*60*	*6*	*0*	*5*	*21*	*20*	*23*	*1*	*1*	*187*	*.244*	*.303*	*.329*	*.222*	*22*	

Sort of lost in the shuffle, because the Brewers are already more excited by Jeff Alfano's tools, but considering the weak major league catching situation and Alfano's struggles, Andreopolous may enter the picture. He hit as well as everybody who plays at El Paso hits, but if the Brewers finally get tired of Matheny, he has a chance to claim a platoon role.

Brian Banks   UT   Bats B   Age 28

YEAR	TEAM	LGE	AB	H	DB	TP	HR	BB	R	RBI	SB	CS	OUT	BA	OBA	SA	EQA	EQR	DEFENSE
1996	New Orln	AA	490	119	21	4	12	60	61	51	15	7	378	.243	.325	.376	.247	58	125-OF 97
1997	Tucson	PCL	364	82	14	0	7	27	28	28	5	3	285	.225	.279	.321	.206	28	72-OF 97
1998	Louisvil	Int	297	77	10	1	14	43	43	42	10	3	223	.259	.353	.441	.278	45	26-OF 91
1999	*Milwauke*	*NL*	*379*	*100*	*17*	*2*	*16*	*44*	*51*	*53*	*11*	*4*	*283*	*.264*	*.340*	*.446*	*.273*	*55*	

Handy, in that he has some sock, can play some outfield, and was smart enough to pick up the tools of ignorance so that he can be a team's emergency catcher.

Kevin Barker   1B   Bats L   Age 23

YEAR	TEAM	LGE	AB	H	DB	TP	HR	BB	R	RBI	SB	CS	OUT	BA	OBA	SA	EQA	EQR	DEFENSE
1996	Ogden	Pio	269	43	5	1	3	25	8	8	0	1	227	.160	.231	.219	.132	7	66-1B 95
1997	Stockton	Cal	267	76	15	2	11	20	32	40	3	2	193	.285	.334	.479	.275	38	59-1B 84
1997	El Paso	Tex	230	52	9	2	8	23	22	25	2	2	180	.226	.296	.387	.234	24	46-1B 94
1998	El Paso	Tex	81	19	4	0	3	3	6	8	1	1	63	.235	.262	.395	.219	7	17-1B 112
1998	Louisvil	Int	459	120	20	3	20	31	46	62	1	4	343	.261	.308	.449	.254	56	110-1B 100
1999	*Milwauke*	*NL*	*477*	*128*	*21*	*2*	*21*	*34*	*50*	*67*	*3*	*3*	*352*	*.268*	*.317*	*.453*	*.262*	*62*	

Barker may be one good camp away from becoming the Brewers' starting first baseman. They're fed up with Nilsson's injuries and his tendency to go stone cold for months at a time, Jaha's gone, and it isn't like there are any other great internal candidates. Since being converted from the outfield, Barker has slowly improved with his glovework at first.

Ronnie Belliard   2B   Bats R   Age 24

YEAR	TEAM	LGE	AB	H	DB	TP	HR	BB	R	RBI	SB	CS	OUT	BA	OBA	SA	EQA	EQR	DEFENSE
1996	El Paso	Tex	406	92	14	4	3	52	48	29	18	6	320	.227	.314	.303	.226	39	107-2B 103
1997	Tucson	PCL	427	100	23	2	4	52	47	35	8	6	333	.234	.317	.326	.228	41	113-2B 94
1998	Louisvil	Int	501	153	29	5	13	61	85	69	23	10	358	.305	.381	.461	.292	83	128-2B 104
1999	*Milwauke*	*NL*	*471*	*133*	*30*	*3*	*9*	*52*	*69*	*56*	*18*	*7*	*345*	*.282*	*.354*	*.416*	*.272*	*67*	

A potential superstar at second, Belliard is as good right now as Fernando Vina was in his career year. Don't think that the Brewers haven't noticed. He was named the #4 prospect in the International League, and he's growing into a great fielder after early concerns that he was careless at times. At the plate, he sprays the ball around to all fields out of an open stance, hits for power and average, draws a walk or two, and he's fast.

Jeromy Burnitz   RF   Bats L   Age 30

YEAR	TEAM	LGE	AB	H	DB	TP	HR	BB	R	RBI	SB	CS	OUT	BA	OBA	SA	EQA	EQR	DEFENSE
1996	Clevelnd	AL	124	33	8	0	7	23	21	21	2	1	92	.266	.381	.500	.300	23	21-OF 98
1996	Milwauke	AL	70	15	3	0	2	8	8	6	2	0	55	.214	.295	.343	.229	7	16-OF 100
1997	Milwauke	AL	486	136	35	8	28	75	88	86	20	14	363	.280	.376	.558	.307	95	142-OF 94
1998	Milwauke	NL	606	158	22	1	41	73	79	102	7	5	453	.261	.340	.503	.283	97	159-OF 96
1999	*Milwauke*	*NL*	*479*	*128*	*26*	*2*	*28*	*64*	*70*	*80*	*13*	*8*	*359*	*.267*	*.354*	*.505*	*.290*	*81*	

Okay, I'm easily amused, but there was a stretch of games where every time I showed up in Milwaukee, Burnitz would jack a pitch into the cheap seats. That streak was finally broken, but in the meantime Bob Hamelin had started a similar streak. Some think he was pressing after the All-Star break, and his OBP dropped like a rock. The perfect example of the kind of player "small market" teams need to find, trade for, and develop.

Jeff Cirillo   3B   Bats R   Age 29

YEAR	TEAM	LGE	AB	H	DB	TP	HR	BB	R	RBI	SB	CS	OUT	BA	OBA	SA	EQA	EQR	DEFENSE
1996	Milwauke	AL	549	173	44	5	14	54	80	84	3	11	387	.315	.376	.490	.290	88	139-3B 92
1997	Milwauke	AL	571	164	44	2	11	61	78	73	4	3	410	.287	.356	.429	.273	80	147-3B 113
1998	Milwauke	NL	601	192	27	1	16	82	96	90	11	5	414	.319	.401	.448	.298	101	148-3B 109
1999	*Milwauke*	*NL*	*577*	*182*	*38*	*2*	*16*	*67*	*89*	*89*	*8*	*4*	*399*	*.315*	*.387*	*.471*	*.298*	*97*	

How do you turn 45 double plays from third and not win the Gold Glove? Probably because you aren't smarmy enough to get on Fox's "In the Zone." Cirillo is the George Kell of the '90s: a line-drive hitter who whistles the ball all over the infield, a brilliant defensive player, and frankly somebody I hope gets into the limelight.

Todd Dunn   OF   Bats R   Age 28

YEAR	TEAM	LGE	AB	H	DB	TP	HR	BB	R	RBI	SB	CS	OUT	BA	OBA	SA	EQA	EQR	DEFENSE
1996	El Paso	Tex	348	91	12	1	11	34	40	41	8	3	260	.261	.327	.397	.253	42	69-OF 83
1997	Tucson	PCL	319	78	15	2	11	30	34	37	4	4	245	.245	.309	.408	.245	36	82-OF 91
1997	Milwauke	AL	117	27	2	0	4	2	8	9	3	0	90	.231	.244	.350	.203	8	20-OF 92
1998	El Paso	Tex	281	60	10	1	6	19	21	20	4	1	222	.214	.263	.320	.200	20	66-OF 83
1999	*Milwauke*	*NL*	*357*	*91*	*18*	*1*	*11*	*25*	*36*	*41*	*6*	*2*	*268*	*.255*	*.304*	*.403*	*.245*	*40*	

A great minor league slugger in every sense of the word. He can't hit any pitch with a wiggle in it, and he can't really play the field. The downward spiral of his career is just another anecdote about what's turned out to be a really lousy decade for Brewers player development. Off the 40-man roster and optioned back to Louisville.

Chad Green   CF   Bats B   Age 24

YEAR	TEAM	LGE	AB	H	DB	TP	HR	BB	R	RBI	SB	CS	OUT	BA	OBA	SA	EQA	EQR	DEFENSE
1997	Stockton	Cal	513	112	22	7	2	29	40	29	20	9	410	.218	.260	.300	.193	34	126-OF 105
1998	Stockton	Cal	150	43	9	1	0	9	21	12	11	4	111	.287	.327	.360	.247	17	33-OF 99
1999	*Milwauke*	*NL*	*240*	*59*	*11*	*3*	*1*	*13*	*25*	*17*	*13*	*4*	*185*	*.246*	*.285*	*.329*	*.220*	*21*	

A broken tibia and a sore hamstring nearly wiped out the whole year for Green, and subsequently derailed plans to have him play in the Arizona Fall League. For now, he's ticketed to open the year at Huntsville. As things stand now, the Brewers are trotting out the usual "he's fast so he needs to hit the ball on the ground more often" line about what he needs to do to improve, and they're disappointed that he can't bunt. On the plus side, he's very good in center.

Marquis Grissom   CF   Bats R   Age 32

YEAR	TEAM	LGE	AB	H	DB	TP	HR	BB	R	RBI	SB	CS	OUT	BA	OBA	SA	EQA	EQR	DEFENSE
1996	Atlanta	NL	666	200	31	8	24	45	90	96	23	12	478	.300	.345	.479	.280	99	149-OF 109
1997	Clevelnd	AL	553	147	28	6	13	44	69	60	23	14	420	.266	.320	.409	.251	66	142-OF 110
1998	Milwauke	NL	539	145	24	1	12	27	54	54	14	9	403	.269	.304	.384	.237	55	133-OF 108
1999	*Milwauke*	*NL*	*553*	*151*	*23*	*3*	*14*	*34*	*61*	*62*	*18*	*9*	*411*	*.273*	*.315*	*.401*	*.249*	*64*	

The Anti-Burnitz, in that getting Grissom was exactly the sort of thing a team that claims it has financial strictures should not pick up if making itself better is part of the program. Struggled with an injured buttock through May. The great speed isn't going to reappear, and unless you have a large number of great rookies, you can't afford to carry a player who hits like this when he's as expensive as Grissom is. I think he can bounce back as well as this projection says; that still isn't very good.

Bob Hamelin   1B/PH   Bats L   Age 31

YEAR	TEAM	LGE	AB	H	DB	TP	HR	BB	R	RBI	SB	CS	OUT	BA	OBA	SA	EQA	EQR	DEFENSE
1996	KansasCy	AL	233	58	14	1	8	52	41	32	5	2	177	.249	.386	.421	.287	39	23-1B 105
1997	Detroit	AL	312	83	13	0	19	48	45	53	2	1	230	.266	.364	.490	.291	53	
1998	Milwauke	NL	145	31	4	0	8	17	13	18	0	1	115	.214	.296	.407	.239	16	27-1B 73
1999	*Milwauke*	*NL*	*214*	*54*	*8*	*0*	*13*	*35*	*29*	*36*	*1*	*1*	*161*	*.252*	*.357*	*.472*	*.285*	*35*	

(Bob Hamelin *continued*)

The right player in the right place. It wasn't that he had a great season, but the Brewers desperately needed a pinch-hitter more menacing than Jeff Huson. The Hammer was definitely that, setting the team record (and leading the National League) with four pinch-hit homers. A credit to Garner for using him, and to Hamelin for adapting to the role.

Bobby Hughes   C   Bats R   Age 28

YEAR	TEAM	LGE	AB	H	DB	TP	HR	BB	R	RBI	SB	CS	OUT	BA	OBA	SA	EQA	EQR	DEFENSE
1996	El Paso	Tex	231	54	8	0	8	23	22	24	2	2	179	.234	.303	.372	.233	24	
1996	New Orln	AA	124	22	2	0	3	5	4	5	1	1	103	.177	.209	.266	.140	4	
1997	Tucson	PCL	279	67	14	1	5	18	22	25	0	0	212	.240	.286	.351	.218	24	
1998	Milwauke	NL	217	49	7	1	10	17	18	25	1	2	170	.226	.282	.406	.232	22	59-C 93
1999	*Milwauke*	*NL*	*246*	*61*	*12*	*1*	*8*	*17*	*23*	*28*	*1*	*1*	*186*	*.248*	*.297*	*.402*	*.240*	*26*	

Hughes initially made the team to avoid having to be sent down through waivers, but he promptly engaged in a bitter battle with Mike Matheny for the starting catcher's job. Yes, it wasn't exactly a clash of titans in Beertown. Hughes impressed people by finally starting to take conditioning seriously. Had the misfortune of being Jeff Juden's personal catcher, which helped frag his throwing stats (24 steals and 4 CS with Juden on the mound).

Anthony Iapoce   CF   B   Age 25

YEAR	TEAM	LGE	AB	H	DB	TP	HR	BB	R	RBI	SB	CS	OUT	BA	OBA	SA	EQA	EQR	DEFENSE
1996	Beloit	Mid	274	64	3	2	1	31	27	17	11	7	217	.234	.311	.270	.209	22	69-OF 94
1997	Stockton	Cal	387	83	8	2	1	22	22	17	11	6	310	.214	.257	.253	.170	18	91-OF 92
1998	El Paso	Tex	549	113	11	1	2	25	25	22	15	10	446	.206	.240	.240	.152	20	132-OF 93
1999	*Milwauke*	*NL*	*454*	*105*	*11*	*1*	*1*	*22*	*31*	*23*	*17*	*9*	*358*	*.231*	*.267*	*.267*	*.184*	*26*	

The next Greg Martinez? He's fast, a good glove with a strong arm in center, and Phil Garner's kind of dirty-uniformed scrapper. Moved to left when Chad Green came up. Not really a good bet to ever beat out Darrell Nicholas, let alone the great Greg Martinez.

Darrin Jackson   OF   Bats R   Age 35

YEAR	TEAM	LGE	AB	H	DB	TP	HR	BB	R	RBI	SB	CS	OUT	BA	OBA	SA	EQA	EQR	DEFENSE
1997	Minnesot	AL	128	32	1	1	3	5	10	11	2	0	96	.250	.278	.344	.215	10	35-OF 108
1997	Milwauke	AL	80	22	4	0	3	2	7	10	2	1	59	.275	.293	.438	.247	9	21-OF 113
1998	Milwauke	NL	203	48	14	1	4	10	17	18	1	1	156	.236	.272	.374	.218	17	51-OF 100
1999	*Milwauke*	*NL*	*215*	*52*	*11*	*1*	*5*	*9*	*17*	*20*	*2*	*1*	*164*	*.242*	*.272*	*.372*	*.220*	*19*	

As of this writing, he's considering retirement, so hopefully you can toss that projection into the dumpster.

Bucky Jacobsen   RF   Bats R   Age 23

YEAR	TEAM	LGE	AB	H	DB	TP	HR	BB	R	RBI	SB	CS	OUT	BA	OBA	SA	EQA	EQR	DEFENSE
1997	Ogden	Pio	232	36	2	0	3	23	7	7	2	2	198	.155	.231	.203	.126	6	56-OF 84
1998	Beloit	Mid	510	130	10	1	20	64	57	66	2	1	381	.255	.338	.396	.257	64	130-OF 90
1999	*Milwauke*	*NL*	*363*	*95*	*9*	*0*	*13*	*40*	*38*	*47*	*1*	*1*	*269*	*.262*	*.335*	*.394*	*.256*	*44*	

Beloit's most popular Snapper. He's got a fan club with their own website (the "Bucky Backers"), and he was the best power hitter in the Midwest League. He's a shade on the old side, so he'll have to progress quickly to have a good future, but power is as good a ticket as any.

John Jaha   1B   Bats R   Age 33

YEAR	TEAM	LGE	AB	H	DB	TP	HR	BB	R	RBI	SB	CS	OUT	BA	OBA	SA	EQA	EQR	DEFENSE
1996	Milwauke	AL	526	151	23	1	33	80	81	98	3	1	376	.287	.381	.523	.306	97	81-1B 103
1997	Milwauke	AL	160	39	5	0	12	25	22	28	1	0	121	.244	.346	.500	.287	27	22-1B 90
1998	Milwauke	NL	215	44	6	0	8	50	29	24	1	3	174	.205	.355	.344	.251	27	50-1B 82
1999	*Milwauke*	*NL*	*252*	*63*	*6*	*0*	*16*	*49*	*37*	*43*	*1*	*1*	*190*	*.250*	*.372*	*.464*	*.290*	*43*	

As we've mentioned in the past, the Brewers have been right to never give Jaha a long-term contract. He was never a good bet to age well, even before you consider he's missed significant portions of three of the last four seasons. He'd be the perfect Angel signing if Gene Autry were still in the saddle.

Geoff Jenkins   OF   Bats L   Age 24

YEAR	TEAM	LGE	AB	H	DB	TP	HR	BB	R	RBI	SB	CS	OUT	BA	OBA	SA	EQA	EQR	DEFENSE
1996	Stockton	Cal	135	40	5	2	3	15	19	18	2	2	97	.296	.367	.430	.276	19	
1997	Tucson	PCL	338	66	15	2	8	28	23	24	0	2	274	.195	.257	.322	.193	23	66-OF 95
1998	Louisvil	Int	212	66	9	3	6	12	25	31	1	1	147	.311	.348	.467	.278	30	46-OF 99
1998	Milwauke	NL	261	59	10	1	10	21	22	28	1	3	205	.226	.284	.387	.226	25	66-OF 92
1999	*Milwauke*	*NL*	*371*	*98*	*15*	*3*	*12*	*28*	*37*	*47*	*2*	*3*	*276*	*.264*	*.316*	*.418*	*.252*	*44*	

Nagging injuries have had a way of holding Jenkins back in the past, but the Brett Favre look-alike ended up getting a shot at the LF job. Although he's considered the best power prospect in the organization, his awful plate discipline has kept him from being very helpful. He acknowledged his tendency to hack early in the count, and has promised to work on it. Ordinarily I'd scoff at that, but '98 was a good reminder of what a player can do if he really works on improving his game (Sosa, Galarraga, or Vina, to note three guys we were dead wrong about last year).

Josh Klimek   3B   Bats L   Age 25

YEAR	TEAM	LGE	AB	H	DB	TP	HR	BB	R	RBI	SB	CS	OUT	BA	OBA	SA	EQA	EQR	DEFENSE	
1997	Beloit	Mid	444	88	12	1	7	25	20	23	2	4	360	.198	.241	.277	.165	20	111-3B 89	
1998	Stockton	Cal	440	94	11	2	6	25	24	26	2	1	347	.214	.256	.289	.180	24	80-3B 76	17-SS 83
1999	*Milwauke*	*NL*	*380*	*88*	*12*	*1*	*7*	*17*	*23*	*29*	*1*	*2*	*294*	*.232*	*.264*	*.324*	*.198*	*26*		

Non-prospect, but Klimek was named the best defensive third baseman in the California League, and I guess I have to write about a certain number of Brewers. Starred in the Big 10 at Illinois, so he might a good example of why Big 10 athletic programs seem to be falling behind in all sorts of sports.

Toby Kominek   OF/1B   Bats R   Age 26

YEAR	TEAM	LGE	AB	H	DB	TP	HR	BB	R	RBI	SB	CS	OUT	BA	OBA	SA	EQA	EQR	DEFENSE	
1996	Stockton	Cal	354	81	8	3	5	34	30	28	5	4	277	.229	.296	.311	.212	29	92-OF 98	
1997	Stockton	Cal	476	112	13	2	9	34	40	38	11	7	371	.235	.286	.328	.212	39	125-OF 90	
1998	El Paso	Tex	476	90	13	0	8	52	34	26	10	8	394	.189	.269	.267	.184	28	64-OF 84	64-1B 82
1999	*Milwauke*	*NL*	*434*	*101*	*15*	*1*	*9*	*37*	*39*	*37*	*10*	*7*	*340*	*.233*	*.293*	*.334*	*.219*	*38*		

Kominek is a great platoon mate in the making, because he absolutely kills left-handed junk, getting almost everything into the air. A good athlete, he wasn't a great outfielder, which encouraged the Brewers to move him to first. Potentially a nifty platoon mate with Kevin Barker, and coming off a good '98 AFL.

Scott Krause   OF   Bats R   Age 25

YEAR	TEAM	LGE	AB	H	DB	TP	HR	BB	R	RBI	SB	CS	OUT	BA	OBA	SA	EQA	EQR	DEFENSE
1996	Stockton	Cal	421	108	13	1	14	20	40	44	13	4	317	.257	.290	.392	.236	43	96-OF 89
1997	El Paso	Tex	449	131	19	4	13	17	48	57	8	3	321	.292	.318	.439	.259	55	115-OF 97
1998	Louisvil	Int	386	106	19	1	21	40	52	61	8	3	283	.275	.343	.492	.283	60	89-OF 91
1999	*Milwauke*	*NL*	*425*	*123*	*23*	*2*	*17*	*25*	*52*	*61*	*10*	*3*	*305*	*.289*	*.329*	*.473*	*.275*	*60*	

An International League All-Star in '98, Krause made significant improvements in his game, particularly in working a pitcher for a base on balls. He's a good glove in either OF corner, has good power, and he should be given the opportunity to either beat out, job-share, or platoon with Jenkins.

Mark Loretta   INF   Bats R   Age 27

YEAR	TEAM	LGE	AB	H	DB	TP	HR	BB	R	RBI	SB	CS	OUT	BA	OBA	SA	EQA	EQR	DEFENSE	
1996	Milwaukee	AL	150	39	0	0	2	13	12	13	2	1	112	.260	.319	.300	.220	13	18-2B 109	12-3B 101
1997	Milwaukee	AL	411	117	17	5	5	48	53	48	5	5	299	.285	.359	.387	.262	53	57-2B 102	32-SS 91
1998	Milwaukee	NL	432	136	18	0	10	44	61	58	10	7	303	.315	.378	.426	.281	63	43-SS 105	40-1B 84
1999	*Milwaukee*	*NL*	*380*	*116*	*17*	*1*	*9*	*40*	*52*	*52*	*8*	*5*	*269*	*.305*	*.371*	*.426*	*.280*	*56*		

Northwestern's best major leaguer, Loretta should be the Brewers' everyday shortstop right now. That puts the Brewers in a difficult situation with Jose Valentin, but neither player is that young. The Brewers problem is similar to what it was in the mid-80s: a group of infielders who can outhit their outfield. It isn't because their infielders are the Joe Morgan and Honus

(Mark Loretta *continued*)

Wagner and Mike Schmidt, so we'll call this the Curse of Charlie Moore. It isn't a hard problem to fix, but the Brewers run the risk of blowing the best years of their core players because they need to make some choices, instead of farting around with everybody all at once.

Greg Martinez   CF   Bats B   Age 27

Year	Team	Lge	AB	H	DB	TP	HR	BB	R	RBI	SB	CS	Out	BA	OBA	SA	EQA	EQR	Defense
1996	Stockton	Cal	283	54	3	0	0	17	12	10	11	5	234	.191	.237	.201	.135	8	68-OF 100
1996	El Paso	Tex	161	38	0	1	1	11	13	9	8	3	126	.236	.285	.267	.197	11	40-OF 107
1997	El Paso	Tex	367	71	5	4	1	23	22	14	19	5	301	.193	.241	.237	.164	16	94-OF 106
1998	Louisvil	Int	374	82	4	6	3	42	43	23	26	6	298	.219	.298	.286	.218	33	102-OF 101
1999	*Milwauke*	*NL*	*395*	*94*	*6*	*5*	*2*	*33*	*47*	*24*	*34*	*7*	*308*	*.238*	*.297*	*.294*	*.223*	*36*	

Regarded as the best center fielder in the organization, Martinez has that and his speed to get him a shot at being a fifth outfielder now that Darrin Jackson is probably retiring. He's fast, bunts well, and Garner likes him already.

Mike Matheny   C   Bats Far Too Often   Age 28

YEAR	TEAM	LGE	AB	H	DB	TP	HR	BB	R	RBI	SB	CS	OUT	BA	OBA	SA	EQA	EQR	DEFENSE
1996	Milwauke	AL	309	59	15	2	7	12	16	18	3	2	252	.191	.221	.320	.174	16	
1997	Milwauke	AL	316	76	16	1	4	18	24	25	0	1	241	.241	.281	.335	.209	24	
1998	Milwauke	NL	318	75	10	0	7	13	21	25	1	0	243	.236	.266	.333	.202	22	91-C 95
1999	*Milwauke*	*NL*	*294*	*69*	*10*	*0*	*7*	*12*	*18*	*25*	*1*	*1*	*226*	*.235*	*.265*	*.340*	*.205*	*21*	

The new "Tomato Face?" He played the night after getting hit in the face with a Rich Loiselle fastball; his mask barely fit over the swelling. Guttiness aside, he doesn't hit like Gabby Hartnett, or even Gabby Hayes. That its taken the Brewers three years to prove in their own minds that Matheny can't play is not to their credit.

Marc Newfield   OF   Bats R   Age 26

YEAR	TEAM	LGE	AB	H	DB	TP	HR	BB	R	RBI	SB	CS	OUT	BA	OBA	SA	EQA	EQR	DEFENSE
1996	San Dieg	NL	191	48	8	0	6	18	19	22	1	1	144	.251	.316	.387	.243	21	38-OF 89
1996	Milwauke	AL	175	52	10	0	8	10	20	27	0	1	124	.297	.335	.491	.277	25	36-OF 107
1997	Milwauke	AL	155	35	6	0	2	14	12	11	0	0	120	.226	.290	.303	.205	11	21-OF 99
1998	Milwauke	NL	185	43	5	0	4	20	15	17	0	1	143	.232	.307	.324	.220	16	41-OF 92
1999	*Milwauke*	*NL*	*193*	*48*	*5*	*0*	*6*	*17*	*17*	*21*	*0*	*1*	*146*	*.249*	*.310*	*.368*	*.235*	*20*	

Flashback to '94, when a debate raged as to who had the better future between two PCL hackers: Garret Anderson or Newfield. Now its five years later, and neither of them is that valuable, so as the Reverend Jackson might, the question is moot. If Newfield gets kept ahead of Krause, the Brewers aren't interested in results.

Darrell Nicholas   OF   Bats R   Age 27

YEAR	TEAM	LGE	AB	H	DB	TP	HR	BB	R	RBI	SB	CS	OUT	BA	OBA	SA	EQA	EQR	DEFENSE
1996	El Paso	Tex	232	45	6	1	2	22	15	11	5	5	192	.194	.264	.254	.173	12	66-OF 101
1997	El Paso	Tex	495	110	20	2	8	20	33	33	10	4	389	.222	.252	.319	.193	32	114-OF 99
1998	Louisvil	Int	491	123	18	4	9	32	50	43	20	10	378	.251	.296	.358	.228	47	109-OF 95
1999	*Milwauke*	*NL*	*433*	*113*	*22*	*2*	*9*	*24*	*45*	*43*	*16*	*7*	*327*	*.261*	*.300*	*.383*	*.239*	*45*	

Not really a prospect, but the Brewers are probably going to end up taking one of Nicholas, Greg Martinez, or Iapoce north. My pick would be Nicholas, if only because he's probably better suited to pinch-hit as well as pinch-run and be a defensive replacement.

Dave Nilsson   1B/LF/C   Bats L   Age 29

YEAR	TEAM	LGE	AB	H	DB	TP	HR	BB	R	RBI	SB	CS	OUT	BA	OBA	SA	EQA	EQR	DEFENSE	
1996	Milwauke	AL	438	139	31	2	16	53	69	74	2	3	303	.317	.391	.507	.305	78	45-OF 100	16-1B 102
1997	Milwauke	AL	545	151	25	0	23	66	70	81	2	3	397	.277	.355	.450	.277	80	67-1B 86	16-OF 97
1998	Milwauke	NL	307	81	12	1	13	35	37	43	2	2	228	.264	.339	.436	.267	42	38-1B 82	29-OF 91
1999	*Milwauke*	*NL*	*392*	*111*	*14*	*0*	*18*	*48*	*50*	*62*	*1*	*2*	*283*	*.283*	*.361*	*.457*	*.282*	*60*		

If he hadn't finished the season hot (six homers in September), we might not even be talking about his future with the team. On the other hand, his slow start came as he recovered from knee surgery. Excuses abound when talking about Nilsson, and it doesn't help that much in management's eyes if they're valid. The Brewers expect to have him at first in '99, but he'll need a platoon mate.

Santiago Perez   SS   Bats B   Age 23

YEAR	TEAM	LGE	AB	H	DB	TP	HR	BB	R	RBI	SB	CS	OUT	BA	OBA	SA	EQA	EQR	DEFENSE
1996	Lakeland	Fla	416	93	15	0	2	14	20	20	3	3	326	.224	.249	.274	.167	19	120-SS 80
1997	Lakeland	Fla	442	108	15	7	5	19	36	35	10	5	339	.244	.275	.344	.212	35	108-SS 91
1998	El Paso	Tex	435	101	13	5	8	22	35	34	12	6	341	.232	.269	.340	.209	34	106-SS 84
1998	Louisvil	Int	132	33	4	2	3	5	12	12	4	2	101	.250	.277	.379	.225	12	31-SS 97
1999	*Milwauke*	*NL*	*522*	*134*	*21*	*6*	*9*	*19*	*47*	*48*	*15*	*7*	*395*	*.257*	*.283*	*.372*	*.226*	*48*	

A throw-in from the Tigers, Perez impressed people with his defense, but keep in mind they were used to watching Danny Klassen airmail things all over the place. Named the best glove at short in the Texas League, and like most bipeds, he hit well in El Paso. Not really a great prospect at this point, just an alternative should the Brewers trade Jose Valentin and suffer an injury or two.

Jose Valentin   SS   Bats B   Age 29

YEAR	TEAM	LGE	AB	H	DB	TP	HR	BB	R	RBI	SB	CS	OUT	BA	OBA	SA	EQA	EQR	DEFENSE
1996	Milwauke	AL	539	133	31	7	22	62	75	71	18	5	411	.247	.324	.453	.268	77	147-SS 98
1997	Milwauke	AL	487	122	21	1	18	40	56	55	19	8	373	.251	.307	.409	.248	57	130-SS 97
1998	Milwauke	NL	426	95	20	0	18	65	54	50	11	8	339	.223	.326	.397	.251	54	119-SS 99
1999	*Milwauke*	*NL*	*445*	*110*	*22*	*1*	*20*	*56*	*59*	*59*	*15*	*7*	*342*	*.247*	*.331*	*.436*	*.266*	*63*	

Platoon shortstops are relatively rare birds, but Valentin can be a good player for a team that needs power from the left side of the plate . . . hey, isn't that the Brewers? Garner gets down on him because he's always going to be streaky, but when he didn't play regularly in the second half, his power evaporated. The Brewers need to come to a decision about what to do with Valentin pronto; he'll make them look bad and bust out if he heads for a good homerun ballpark, but Loretta's the better player. Moving him to center, à la Jose Hernandez, would probably help the lineup, but that would mean admitting they were wrong to get Grissom.

Fernando Vina   2B   Bats L   Age 30

YEAR	TEAM	LGE	AB	H	DB	TP	HR	BB	R	RBI	SB	CS	OUT	BA	OBA	SA	EQA	EQR	DEFENSE
1996	Milwauke	AL	541	146	18	10	6	35	58	53	16	8	403	.270	.314	.373	.240	57	135-2B 102
1997	Milwauke	AL	320	87	12	2	4	13	29	29	8	7	240	.272	.300	.359	.225	29	74-2B 103
1998	Milwauke	NL	634	197	38	7	8	57	92	78	23	18	455	.311	.368	.431	.275	90	157-2B 99
1999	*Milwauke*	*NL*	*529*	*157*	*32*	*5*	*6*	*37*	*67*	*60*	*17*	*13*	*385*	*.297*	*.343*	*.410*	*.261*	*67*	

The ultimate scrapper, and a good example of why analysts shouldn't take players for granted. Vina acknowledged his past problems at reaching base, and wound up being one of the NL's best leadoff men. Wisely enough, the Brewers are trying to cash him in after the best year of his career (and with Ronnie Belliard waiting in the wings). Is he a great defensive player? He's probably the best man in baseball on turning the pivot, and that's very valuable, but he doesn't have tremendous range. He's got a better case for the Gold Glove than Bret Boone.

Antone Williamson   1B   Bats L   Age 25

YEAR	TEAM	LGE	AB	H	DB	TP	HR	BB	R	RBI	SB	CS	OUT	BA	OBA	SA	EQA	EQR	DEFENSE
1996	New Orln	AA	199	49	9	1	4	19	20	20	1	0	150	.246	.312	.362	.236	20	23-1B 100
1997	Tucson	PCL	292	70	14	3	4	43	36	29	2	1	223	.240	.337	.349	.245	33	62-1B 95
1998	Louisvil	Int	103	19	5	1	2	11	8	7	0	0	84	.184	.263	.311	.196	7	
1999	*Milwauke*	*NL*	*182*	*44*	*9*	*1*	*4*	*22*	*20*	*20*	*1*	*0*	*138*	*.242*	*.324*	*.368*	*.245*	*21*	

What was it this year, in the now-annual Antone derailment? A broken wrist. Okay, maybe life isn't fair when the undertall or the overly-adipose-gifted don't find that life is one big happy cakewalk, but the Brewers are rightfully angry about Williamson's poor conditioning. That still doesn't explain their unrealistic expectations of him. Taken off of the 40-man roster and optioned back to Louisville in October, at this point he's looking done.

PITCHERS (Averages: 4.00 ERA, 9.00 H/9, 1.00 HR/9, 3.00 BB/9, 6.00 K/9, 1.00 KWH)

Valerio Delossantos   **Throws L**   **Age 23**

YEAR	TEAM	LGE	IP	H	ER	HR	BB	K	ERA	W	L	H/9	HR/9	BB/9	K/9	KWH	PERA
1996	Beloit	Mid	153.7	219	97	17	60	94	5.68	6	11	12.83	1.00	3.51	5.51	0.50	5.86
1997	El Paso	Tex	116.7	146	67	7	39	52	5.17	5	8	11.26	0.54	3.01	4.01	0.36	4.63
1998	El Paso	Tex	70.0	81	26	2	26	50	3.34	5	3	10.41	0.26	3.34	6.43	0.89	4.11
1998	Milwauke	NL	11.7	8	6	2	18	3	4.63	0	1	6.17	1.54	13.89	2.31	0.05	4.63

Coming off of a '97 where he struggled with a staph infection, the Brewers pushed their luck and tried to keep developing him as a starter. He flopped, mostly because his slider is meat. Still, lefties with 90+ fastballs don't grow on trees, and he's a major asset as a reliever. He'll almost certainly be the second lefty in the pen for '99, and should be dominating. He's a very good example of a lefty who should just be used as a long or middle reliever, instead of getting shoe-horned into a situation Fossas/Honeycutt role.

Cal Eldred   **Throws R**   **Age 31**

YEAR	TEAM	LGE	IP	H	ER	HR	BB	K	ERA	W	L	H/9	HR/9	BB/9	K/9	KWH	PERA
1996	Milwauke	AL	87.3	78	33	7	31	50	3.40	6	4	8.04	0.72	3.19	5.15	0.78	3.09
1997	Milwauke	AL	208.7	203	96	29	77	118	4.14	11	12	8.76	1.25	3.32	5.09	0.67	3.92
1998	Milwauke	NL	139.0	161	71	14	56	80	4.60	6	9	10.42	0.91	3.63	5.18	0.53	4.60

He's expected to be as healthy as he's ever going to be in time for camp, which is more than you can say for Jeff D'Amico. Hittable, wilder than you'd like from somebody now relying on junk. At this point, the most you can really hope for is for him to be a living reminder to Garner about what not to do to your starting pitchers.

Horacio Estrada   **Throws L**   **Age 23**

YEAR	TEAM	LGE	IP	H	ER	HR	BB	K	ERA	W	L	H/9	HR/9	BB/9	K/9	KWH	PERA
1996	Beloit	Mid	27.7	29	9	3	11	23	2.93	2	1	9.43	0.98	3.58	7.48	1.24	4.23
1996	Stockton	Cal	46.7	55	30	7	19	42	5.79	2	3	10.61	1.35	3.66	8.10	1.27	5.01
1997	El Paso	Tex	158.0	173	73	12	71	107	4.16	9	9	9.85	0.68	4.04	6.09	0.70	4.22
1998	El Paso	Tex	51.7	50	21	3	21	30	3.66	3	3	8.71	0.52	3.66	5.23	0.64	3.48
1998	Louisvil	Int	11.7	12	4	1	4	3	3.09	1	0	9.26	0.77	3.09	2.31	0.14	3.86

Hampered by a broken hand he suffered in camp, Estrada missed most of the year. When healthy, he has good control of his curve, fastball, and slider. Added to the 40-man roster. Probably won't get a clean shot at a rotation spot until they move to Miller Park in '00.

Chad Fox   **Throws R**   **Age 28**

YEAR	TEAM	LGE	IP	H	ER	HR	BB	K	ERA	W	L	H/9	HR/9	BB/9	K/9	KWH	PERA
1996	Richmond	Int	89.0	108	59	9	52	69	5.97	3	7	10.92	0.91	5.26	6.98	0.64	5.06
1997	Richmond	Int	23.3	30	11	1	14	19	4.24	1	2	11.57	0.39	5.40	7.33	0.64	5.01
1997	Atlanta	NL	27.3	27	11	4	15	25	3.62	2	1	8.89	1.32	4.94	8.23	1.16	4.28
1998	Milwauke	NL	59.0	57	23	4	18	59	3.51	4	3	8.69	0.61	2.75	9.00	2.54	3.36

A good example of an okay minor league starter turning into a very good major league reliever. Nearly unhittable at the start, but an inflamed shoulder shelved him in June, and he struggled through August. Fox has a plus fastball and a sharp-breaking curve, and should be a great setup man in '99.

Jose Garcia   **Throws R**   **Age 21**

YEAR	TEAM	LGE	IP	H	ER	HR	BB	K	ERA	W	L	H/9	HR/9	BB/9	K/9	KWH	PERA
1997	Beloit	Mid	147.7	189	99	12	73	85	6.03	5	11	11.52	0.73	4.45	5.18	0.39	5.12
1998	Stockton	Cal	160.0	184	95	16	96	108	5.34	6	12	10.35	0.90	5.40	6.07	0.50	4.84

Very popular very quickly, Garcia is one of those "battlers" on the mound that some people can't get enough of. He mixes a good fastball with the best curve in the organization. He's agressive on the mound, and he isn't afraid to throw inside. Right now, he's a big, wild kid, but if he survives Huntsville in '99, he'll be in major league boxscores pretty quickly.

Rick Greene   Throws R   Age 28

YEAR	TEAM	LGE	IP	H	ER	HR	BB	K	ERA	W	L	H/9	HR/9	BB/9	K/9	KWH	PERA
1996	Jacksnvl	Sou	51.0	90	52	9	40	29	9.18	1	5	15.88	1.59	7.06	5.12	0.18	8.12
1997	Toledo	Int	66.0	63	33	4	31	37	4.50	3	4	8.59	0.55	4.23	5.05	0.53	3.55
1998	Louisvil	Int	63.7	87	33	6	33	34	4.66	3	4	12.30	0.85	4.66	4.81	0.30	5.65

Hasn't really made progress since his days as LSU's closer on their '91 championship team. He gets lots of grounders when he gets his forkball working, so he could have a career on a team with a good infield (like the Brewers). About even with Curtis King in terms of prospectdom.

Rod Henderson   Throws R   Age 28

YEAR	TEAM	LGE	IP	H	ER	HR	BB	K	ERA	W	L	H/9	HR/9	BB/9	K/9	KWH	PERA
1996	Ottawa	Int	115.3	138	78	12	56	66	6.09	4	9	10.77	0.94	4.37	5.15	0.42	4.92
1997	Ottawa	Int	118.7	162	75	18	49	77	5.69	4	9	12.29	1.37	3.72	5.84	0.56	5.92
1998	Louisvil	Int	116.0	118	48	4	39	52	3.72	7	6	9.16	0.31	3.03	4.03	0.44	3.41

Taken off the 40-man roster after enjoying a good season for the final edition of the Louisville Redbirds (they'll be the River Bats from here on out). He's getting to the age that pitching well isn't going to be good enough for most teams to give him a shot, and it isn't like he's got Rick Reed's control.

Doug Johnston   Throws R   Age 21

YEAR	TEAM	LGE	IP	H	ER	HR	BB	K	ERA	W	L	H/9	HR/9	BB/9	K/9	KWH	PERA
1997	Helena	Pio	67.0	87	45	6	42	37	6.04	2	5	11.69	0.81	5.64	4.97	0.28	5.37
1998	Beloit	Mid	87.3	99	33	9	31	47	3.40	6	4	10.20	0.93	3.19	4.84	0.54	4.43
1998	Stockton	Cal	57.7	58	21	4	27	35	3.28	4	2	9.05	0.62	4.21	5.46	0.59	3.75

The Brewers' best pitching prospect, Johnston's season ended early with a strained elbow. He's got a good mix, with a decent curve, fastball, and change, but mostly he's been successful because he knows how to use his assortment. He's been spared a future bump in the road with the Double-A affiliation switch from El Paso to Huntsville in '99, which should do wonders in terms of pitcher development for the organization.

Scott Karl   Throws L   Age 27

YEAR	TEAM	LGE	IP	H	ER	HR	BB	K	ERA	W	L	H/9	HR/9	BB/9	K/9	KWH	PERA
1996	Milwauke	AL	212.7	208	94	25	58	120	3.98	12	12	8.80	1.06	2.45	5.08	0.90	3.68
1997	Milwauke	AL	199.7	205	83	21	58	116	3.74	12	10	9.24	0.95	2.61	5.23	0.85	3.88
1998	Milwauke	NL	199.7	222	90	21	61	94	4.06	11	11	10.01	0.95	2.75	4.24	0.49	4.28

The only survivor from the rotation on Opening Day, but he's beginning to look like he's breaking down. He's fooling fewer hitters with the palmball, his strikeout rates are down, and he's having a harder time getting into the sixth and seventh innings. He had fewer quality starts in '98 than in '97, without having to face the DH. I don't think there's much Garner can do either way, or should be held responsible if he flames out; it may be too late to do anything about it.

Allen Levrault   Throws R   Age 21

YEAR	TEAM	LGE	IP	H	ER	HR	BB	K	ERA	W	L	H/9	HR/9	BB/9	K/9	KWH	PERA
1996	Helena	Pio	65.7	86	40	9	21	41	5.48	2	5	11.79	1.23	2.88	5.62	0.70	5.48
1997	Beloit	Mid	123.3	183	98	22	42	75	7.15	3	11	13.35	1.61	3.06	5.47	0.55	6.57
1998	Stockton	Cal	93.0	92	34	10	28	55	3.29	6	4	8.90	0.97	2.71	5.32	0.88	3.68
1998	El Paso	Tex	65.0	78	42	7	18	37	5.82	2	5	10.80	0.97	2.49	5.12	0.73	4.71

A big guy who throws hard, Levrault began making the adjustment from thrower to pitcher this year. Shoulder tightness and a really bad two months in El Paso combined to end his year early. A mechanic in the off-season, so a potential blue collar hero in a town that loves blue collar heroes.

Jose Mercedes — Throws R — Age 28

YEAR	TEAM	LGE	IP	H	ER	HR	BB	K	ERA	W	L	H/9	HR/9	BB/9	K/9	KWH	PERA
1996	New Orln	AmA	99.3	130	62	13	33	38	5.62	4	7	11.78	1.18	2.99	3.44	0.25	5.44
1996	Milwauke	AL	17.0	19	13	6	4	6	6.88	1	1	10.06	3.18	2.12	3.18	0.36	5.82
1997	Milwauke	AL	163.3	141	61	22	46	78	3.36	11	7	7.77	1.21	2.53	4.30	0.70	3.14
1998	Milwauke	NL	33.3	42	22	6	9	10	5.94	1	3	11.34	1.62	2.43	2.70	0.20	5.40

Some folks are claiming he'll be 100% by spring training, and some are claiming he may never pitch again. For those of us in the public sphere, that means you shouldn't count on him, but you already knew that after his fluky '97. Even if healthy, his forgetting to show up to the ballpark on time on the day he was starting wins him both the Pascual Perez Award (for cluelessness in the line of duty), and a spot in Garner's doghouse.

Greg Mullins — Throws L — Age 27

YEAR	TEAM	LGE	IP	H	ER	HR	BB	K	ERA	W	L	H/9	HR/9	BB/9	K/9	KWH	PERA
1996	El Paso	Tex	27.3	35	25	7	20	23	8.23	1	2	11.52	2.30	6.59	7.57	0.57	6.59
1997	Stockton	Cal	29.3	33	13	2	14	30	3.99	2	1	10.13	0.61	4.30	9.20	1.46	4.30
1997	El Paso	Tex	22.7	21	7	3	13	16	2.78	2	1	8.34	1.19	5.16	6.35	0.70	3.97
1998	Louisvil	Int	63.7	68	28	5	23	66	3.96	4	3	9.61	0.71	3.25	9.33	2.09	3.96

Owns a nasty curveball, which helped him strike out almost half of the left-handed batters he faced all year. He'll give the Brewers a very interesting decision in camp, in that they could come north with three good lefties in their pen, keeping Mullins as well as Delossantos and Myers. If Mullins looks good enough, he could give Bando the freedom of action to trade Myers for a (choose one: catcher, center fielder, first baseman).

Mike Myers — Throws L — Age 30

YEAR	TEAM	LGE	IP	H	ER	HR	BB	K	ERA	W	L	H/9	HR/9	BB/9	K/9	KWH	PERA
1996	Detroit	AL	67.0	66	30	5	28	68	4.03	3	4	8.87	0.67	3.76	9.13	1.88	3.63
1997	Detroit	AL	54.7	60	30	11	22	49	4.94	2	4	9.88	1.81	3.62	8.07	1.36	4.94
1998	Milwauke	NL	51.3	46	16	5	20	37	2.81	4	2	8.06	0.88	3.51	6.49	1.12	3.33

Although the Brewers' miserable total of complete games (a NL-record low of two) was interpreted as a weakness, it wasn't like Garner had to leave his starter out there. He had good middle relievers for the bulk of the season, his closer was only a problem as long as it was Doug Jones, and why leave the starters on the mound when he had an excellent lefty like Myers? Trading Florie to get Myers worked, because Florie's looking like waiver bait, while Myers is the front man for an organization awash in quality lefty relievers at a time when everyone wants one. On the down side, Garner has to learn when to pick his spots; he used Myers in 28 of the Brewers' first 53 games, and that wore him down.

Brian Passini — Throws L — Age 24

YEAR	TEAM	LGE	IP	H	ER	HR	BB	K	ERA	W	L	H/9	HR/9	BB/9	K/9	KWH	PERA
1996	Helena	Pio	66.3	123	42	5	30	37	5.70	2	5	16.69	0.68	4.07	5.02	0.28	7.19
1997	Beloit	Mid	113.0	158	59	17	40	72	4.70	5	8	12.58	1.35	3.19	5.73	0.62	5.97
1997	Stockton	Cal	41.7	52	31	8	21	23	6.70	1	4	11.23	1.73	4.54	4.97	0.36	5.83
1998	Stockton	Cal	82.7	109	45	9	35	55	4.90	4	5	11.87	0.98	3.81	5.99	0.59	5.44
1998	El Paso	Tex	82.7	68	28	5	29	40	3.05	6	3	7.40	0.54	3.16	4.35	0.61	2.61

Passini doesn't throw hard, but when he and Levrault were promoted from Stockton, it was the lefty control artist who adapted quickly. There's a reasonable chance that he'll crack the major league rotation in '99.

Bronswell Patrick — Throws R — Age 28

YEAR	TEAM	LGE	IP	H	ER	HR	BB	K	ERA	W	L	H/9	HR/9	BB/9	K/9	KWH	PERA
1996	Tucson	PCL	115.7	144	53	8	35	65	4.12	6	7	11.20	0.62	2.72	5.06	0.63	4.67
1997	New Orln	AmA	92.3	139	57	10	32	68	5.56	3	7	13.55	0.97	3.12	6.63	0.78	6.14
1998	Louisvil	Int	35.7	51	22	6	9	21	5.55	1	3	12.87	1.51	2.27	5.30	0.72	6.06
1998	Milwauke	NL	81.7	84	37	9	27	45	4.08	4	5	9.26	0.99	2.98	4.96	0.67	3.97

Throws four kinds of slow, some of which wiggles. Came in as a non-roster invitee, and wound up being the Brewers' twelfth man, coming up for injuries to Chad Fox and later Al Reyes. Removed from the major league roster after the season, he's a minor league free agent.

Kyle Peterson   **Throws R**   **Age 23**

YEAR	TEAM	LGE	IP	H	ER	HR	BB	K	ERA	W	L	H/9	HR/9	BB/9	K/9	KWH	PERA
1998	Stockton	Cal	90.0	124	60	6	36	69	6.00	3	7	12.40	0.60	3.60	6.90	0.80	5.30
1998	El Paso	Tex	44.7	40	19	2	17	27	3.83	3	2	8.06	0.40	3.43	5.44	0.80	3.02

Coming out of Stanford, Peterson was named the '97 pick closest to the majors before the season. Although he didn't make it, he did show the poise and the solid curve he was expected to have. There are concerns that he throws across his body, but with Jeff D'Amico's second surgery taking him out of the picture for the '99 rotation, Peterson will have an excellent opportunity to claim a spot with a good camp.

Eric Plunk   **Throws R**   **Age 35**

YEAR	TEAM	LGE	IP	H	ER	HR	BB	K	ERA	W	L	H/9	HR/9	BB/9	K/9	KWH	PERA
1996	Clevelnd	AL	80.0	54	15	5	27	84	1.69	8	1	6.08	0.56	3.04	9.45	3.63	1.80
1997	Clevelnd	AL	67.7	62	31	12	31	64	4.12	4	4	8.25	1.60	4.12	8.51	1.60	3.99
1998	Clevelnd	AL	43.7	41	17	6	14	37	3.50	3	2	8.45	1.24	2.89	7.63	1.79	3.71
1998	Milwauke	NL	33.3	34	12	4	13	33	3.24	2	2	9.18	1.08	3.51	8.91	1.85	4.05

One of my personal favorites, and currently the oldest veteran on the Brewers. He can still pump gas from time to time, but he's always going to have those bouts of wildness which can leave his managers weeping. A solid middle reliever.

Bill Pulsipher   **Throws L**   **Age 25**

YEAR	TEAM	LGE	IP	H	ER	HR	BB	K	ERA	W	L	H/9	HR/9	BB/9	K/9	KWH	PERA
1997	St Lucie	Fla	35.0	39	32	2	42	25	8.23	1	3	10.03	0.51	10.80	6.43	0.29	5.14
1997	Norfolk	Int	28.3	28	27	1	35	15	8.58	1	2	8.89	0.32	11.12	4.76	0.17	4.45
1998	Norfolk	Int	87.0	98	45	12	38	48	4.66	4	6	10.14	1.24	3.93	4.97	0.46	4.76
1998	NY Mets	NL	15.0	23	9	2	5	12	5.40	1	1	13.80	1.20	3.00	7.20	0.94	6.60
1998	Milwauke	NL	60.3	65	26	6	24	35	3.88	4	3	9.70	0.90	3.58	5.22	0.59	4.18

Maybe he led a sheltered life as a star prospect, because few players "play dumb" as much as Pulsipher does. Routinely costs himself by forgetting to cover first or back up throws to third or home. After giving up a run or two, he starts getting angry and goes head-hunting. Before you have your elbow reconstructed, maybe you can get away with that. He should have a three-month window of opportunity, after which the Brewers will know if they have Doug Johns or somebody they can use. Physically, he's trying to compensate for the elbow by contorting his back like a wishbone to get his pitches over the top; it doesn't look healthy.

Al Reyes   **Throws R**   **Age 28**

YEAR	TEAM	LGE	IP	H	ER	HR	BB	K	ERA	W	L	H/9	HR/9	BB/9	K/9	KWH	PERA
1995	Milwauke	AL	34.7	19	7	3	15	30	1.82	3	1	4.93	0.78	3.89	7.79	2.37	1.30
1997	Tucson	PCL	53.7	58	36	11	34	52	6.04	2	4	9.73	1.84	5.70	8.72	1.03	5.20
1997	Milwauke	AL	30.7	31	15	4	8	27	4.40	1	2	9.10	1.17	2.35	7.92	2.20	3.82
1998	Milwauke	NL	59.3	57	22	9	29	54	3.34	4	3	8.65	1.37	4.40	8.19	1.32	4.10

Proved he was healthy by racking up 11 saves in winter ball in the Domincan Republic, then enjoyed his finest major league season. A good bit player in what was top to bottom one of the league's best bullpens. Runner-up for most ridiculous facial hair in the majors (a sculpted trace beard), but his wife probably loves him anyway.

Frankie Rodriguez   **Throws R**   **Age 26**

YEAR	TEAM	LGE	IP	H	ER	HR	BB	K	ERA	W	L	H/9	HR/9	BB/9	K/9	KWH	PERA
1996	El Paso	Tex	36.3	48	29	1	27	35	7.18	1	3	11.89	0.25	6.69	8.67	0.71	5.20
1997	El Paso	Tex	50.3	48	20	2	14	31	3.58	3	3	8.58	0.36	2.50	5.54	1.07	3.04
1997	Tucson	PCL	45.7	53	21	1	17	33	4.14	2	3	10.45	0.20	3.35	6.50	0.91	4.14
1998	Louisvil	Int	87.3	104	40	10	37	69	4.12	5	5	10.72	1.03	3.81	7.11	0.93	4.84

Small righties are a generally unfortunate lot. Scouting biases on this score seem to work out: short righties don't seem to make it to the majors as rotation regulars. Frankie's ticket is currently punched as a reliever, and he could be a good middle man if given the chance.

Rafael Roque   Throws L   Age 27

YEAR	TEAM	LGE	IP	H	ER	HR	BB	K	ERA	W	L	H/9	HR/9	BB/9	K/9	KWH	PERA
1996	St Lucie	Fla	70.7	80	28	3	49	40	3.57	4	4	10.19	0.38	6.24	5.09	0.31	4.46
1996	Binghmtn	Eas	58.0	93	65	9	43	35	10.09	1	5	14.43	1.40	6.67	5.43	0.23	7.29
1997	St Lucie	Fla	71.3	112	54	10	33	35	6.81	2	6	14.13	1.26	4.16	4.42	0.25	6.69
1997	Binghmtn	Eas	24.7	44	27	7	19	16	9.85	0	3	16.05	2.55	6.93	5.84	0.23	9.12
1998	El Paso	Tex	94.3	125	51	8	40	50	4.87	4	6	11.93	0.76	3.82	4.77	0.37	5.25
1998	Louisvil	Int	47.7	50	23	2	19	33	4.34	2	3	9.44	0.38	3.59	6.23	0.86	3.78
1998	Milwauke	NL	49.7	43	24	10	22	31	4.35	3	3	7.79	1.81	3.99	5.62	0.76	3.81

Could be a very intersting example of how much of a difference instruction can mean between organizations. With the Mets, Roque was wild when he wasn't just hittable. After being signed as a minor league free agent by the Brewers, he suddenly had improved command of a good fastball, curve, and changeup. He isn't a great prospect, but he can obviously pitch, but why he could in higher levels, and in El Paso of all places, is basically a mystery. In the running for a rotation spot, and helped by the injuries.

Dave Weathers   Throws R   Age 29

YEAR	TEAM	LGE	IP	H	ER	HR	BB	K	ERA	W	L	H/9	HR/9	BB/9	K/9	KWH	PERA
1996	Florida	NL	72.3	89	37	8	26	36	4.60	3	5	11.07	1.00	3.24	4.48	0.42	4.98
1996	NY Yanks	AL	18.0	22	14	1	12	13	7.00	0	2	11.00	0.50	6.00	6.50	0.48	5.00
1997	Columbus	Int	34.7	43	19	3	7	26	4.93	2	2	11.16	0.78	1.82	6.75	1.68	4.67
1997	Buffalo	AmA	63.0	92	47	7	18	39	6.71	2	5	13.14	1.00	2.57	5.57	0.69	5.86
1998	Cincnnti	NL	65.0	89	41	3	25	47	5.68	2	5	12.32	0.42	3.46	6.51	0.74	5.12
1998	Milwauke	NL	49.0	45	19	3	13	40	3.49	3	2	8.27	0.55	2.39	7.35	2.05	2.94

Pitched better mopping up as a Brewer than I thought we'd ever see him pitch. He still has a good sinker, but he never has added a breaking pitch to freeze lefties. That isn't as much of a problem in long relief as it is as a starter or short reliever, so he may have finally found his niche.

Bob Wickman   Throws R   Age 30

YEAR	TEAM	LGE	IP	H	ER	HR	BB	K	ERA	W	L	H/9	HR/9	BB/9	K/9	KWH	PERA
1995	NY Yanks	AL	81.0	79	32	6	27	52	3.56	5	4	8.78	0.67	3.00	5.78	0.95	3.44
1996	NY Yanks	AL	82.3	87	30	6	27	60	3.28	5	4	9.51	0.66	2.95	6.56	1.15	3.83
1996	Milwauke	AL	17.0	12	7	3	8	14	3.71	1	1	6.35	1.59	4.24	7.41	1.53	2.65
1997	Milwauke	AL	98.7	87	26	7	36	76	2.37	8	3	7.94	0.64	3.28	6.93	1.38	3.01
1998	Milwauke	NL	85.3	81	33	5	36	65	3.48	5	4	8.54	0.53	3.80	6.86	1.09	3.37

A quick run of converting seven of seven save opportunities, and bingo! You're rich! He isn't exactly your classic closer: he's a power/groundball pitcher, but he's wild and more hittable than you'd like. Now that the Brewers got outmaneuvered and had to pay him top dollar, he's a great candidate to trade should they get frustrated with him or if a contender comes shopping.

Brad Woodall   Throws L   Age 30

YEAR	TEAM	LGE	IP	H	ER	HR	BB	K	ERA	W	L	H/9	HR/9	BB/9	K/9	KWH	PERA
1996	Richmond	Int	125.3	149	64	10	40	57	4.60	6	8	10.70	0.72	2.87	4.09	0.41	4.52
1997	Richmond	Int	140.0	219	110	19	52	87	7.07	4	12	14.08	1.22	3.34	5.59	0.50	6.62
1998	Louisvil	Int	28.7	38	20	3	16	21	6.28	1	2	11.93	0.94	5.02	6.59	0.54	5.65
1998	Milwauke	NL	143.0	146	70	25	43	78	4.41	7	9	9.19	1.57	2.71	4.91	0.73	4.28

Take a long look, because this is that rarest of pitchers (as in, he's just about the only one): a guy who had his best year on the mound after the Braves' organization had him. Signed as a minor league free agent on a tip from his old UNC teammate, Jesse Levis, he ended up becoming an excellent jack-of-all-trades for the Brewers. Pitching coach Don Rowe noticed that in his best year, back in '94, Woodall used to have a hitch in his delivery that set up driving off his back leg, and getting back to that has been used as a reason for his success.

Steve Woodard   **Throws R**   **Age 24**

YEAR	TEAM	LGE	IP	H	ER	HR	BB	K	ERA	W	L	H/9	HR/9	BB/9	K/9	KWH	PERA
1996	Stockton	Cal	164.3	244	94	15	29	95	5.15	7	11	13.36	0.82	1.59	5.20	0.96	5.70
1997	El Paso	Tex	138.7	133	42	8	25	81	2.73	10	5	8.63	0.52	1.62	5.26	1.48	3.05
1997	Milwauke	AL	37.3	38	20	5	5	31	4.82	2	2	9.16	1.21	1.21	7.47	3.79	3.86
1998	Milwauke	NL	170.7	170	71	19	30	124	3.74	10	9	8.96	1.00	1.58	6.54	2.26	3.59

Woodard's a finesse pitcher, but one who nevertheless racks up plenty of strikeouts by setting up a killer changeup that can embarass the best of them. There was no sign of the back woes that slowed him down in '97, but the Brewers are concerned about his conditioning. We've been plugging him for awhile, and we aren't stopping now.

Kelly Wunsch   **Throws L**   **Age 26**

YEAR	TEAM	LGE	IP	H	ER	HR	BB	K	ERA	W	L	H/9	HR/9	BB/9	K/9	KWH	PERA
1997	Stockton	Cal	122.0	204	90	12	70	58	6.64	4	10	15.05	0.89	5.16	4.28	0.18	6.86
1998	El Paso	Tex	100.3	144	77	10	36	50	6.91	3	8	12.92	0.90	3.23	4.49	0.36	5.74
1998	Louisvil	Int	49.3	62	24	5	15	28	4.38	2	3	11.31	0.91	2.74	5.11	0.63	4.93

Frustrated by his injuries and a lack of development, the Brewers are considering switching him to relief. Could end up surprising some people, in that he's good at keeping the ball low and in the infield. At worst he'll be the new Blaise Illsley, but lefties are lefties, so he can look forward to years of spring training invites.

SNWLP					MILWAUKEE BREWERS						Park Effect: +2.2%		
PITCHER	GS	IP	R	SNW	SNL	SNPCT	W	L	RA	APW	SNVA	SNWAR
Eldred, C.	23	133.0	82	6.4	9.2	.410	4	8	5.55	-1.11	-1.38	-0.24
Juden, J.	24	138.3	91	7.2	10.1	.417	7	11	5.92	-1.71	-1.38	-0.14
Karl, S.	33	192.3	104	10.9	11.2	.492	10	11	4.87	-0.19	-0.30	1.47
Mercedes, J.	5	27.7	21	1.6	2.0	.433	2	2	6.83	-0.61	-0.27	0.03
Patrick, B.	3	20.0	11	0.9	1.1	.453	1	1	4.95	-0.04	-0.06	0.06
Pulsipher, B.	10	56.0	30	3.4	3.5	.493	3	4	4.82	-0.03	-0.07	0.47
Roque, R.	9	48.0	28	2.4	3.2	.427	4	2	5.25	-0.25	-0.35	0.01
Wagner, P.	9	50.0	44	1.8	4.5	.292	1	5	7.92	-1.70	-1.29	-0.84
Woodall, B.	20	118.3	74	5.9	7.6	.440	5	8	5.63	-1.09	-0.87	0.21
Woodard, S.	26	151.0	82	8.9	8.5	.511	8	12	4.89	-0.19	0.23	1.50
TOTALS	162	934.7	567	49.4	60.9	.448	45	64	5.46	-6.93	-5.74	2.52

Last year I wrote a fairly glowing review of the Brewers starting pitchers, calling them "a good staff that had a collective off year" in 1997. If that was true, they must have really had an off year in 1998. The one defense I can use to save face is that I put the important disclaimer "if they can stay healthy" before my rosy predictions. As usual, the Brewers were anything but healthy in 1998. Jeff D'Amico missed the entire year. Ben McDonald was traded to Cleveland, and missed the entire year. Cal Eldred fought with and ultimately lost to his usual set of ailments. Jose Mercedes followed his surprising 1997 with a rotator cuff injury. Scott Karl, who was at least healthy enough to make 33 starts, continued his career-long downward trend. His SNPcts since his rookie season in 1995: .598, .541, .517, .492. The end result was that the Brewers' SNVA dropped by over six wins, from 0.80 in 1997 to -5.74 in 1998, and their major league rank dropped from 11th in 1997 to 27th in 1998. One good bit of news was the pitching of Steve Woodard. He was good enough to rank third among NL rookies, behind Kerry Wood and Masato Yoshii.

Pitcher Abuse Points

PITCHER	AGE	GS	PAP	PAP/S	AAW	MAX	115+	130+
Eldred, Cal	30	23	115	5.00	6.67	120	2	0
Juden, Jeff	27	24	274	11.42	20.93	126	6	0
Karl, Scott	26	33	157	4.76	9.52	121	4	0
Mercedes, Jose	27	5	0	0.00	0.00	94	0	0
Pulsipher, Bill	24	10	4	0.40	0.93	104	0	0
Roque, Rafael	26	9	2	0.22	0.44	102	0	0
Wagner, Paul	30	9	97	10.78	14.37	123	2	0
Woodall, Brad	29	20	46	2.30	3.45	113	0	0
Woodard, Steve	23	26	51	1.96	4.90	118	1	0
TOTAL		162	746	4.60	8.08	126	15	0
RANKING (NL)			15	15	15		15	14-T

Maybe Phil Garner did learn from Cal Eldred after all. Eldred, you may recall, was an amazing 11-2 with a 1.79 ERA as a rookie—and the next year, Garner made him lead the league in starts, innings, and batters faced. He went under the knife two years later. Garner has publicly stated that he learned from the experience to be more careful, and he sure has—only Felipe Alou took better care of his starters. His two hardest-worked starters, Jeff Juden and Paul Wagner, have already been sent packing. Bill Pulsipher needs that kind of TLC if he's going to return to form. Steve Woodard conserves his pitches like nuclear winter was coming—only 51 PAPs despite averaging nearly 6.5 innings a start—and is a good bet to improve on his rookie season.

Pittsburgh Pirates

One good season changes everything. Expectations of new players run as high as the bar set by previous newcomers. Overachievers are expected to meet or exceed their prior levels of performance. And luck, or the lack thereof, is no excuse when these expectations are inevitably left unmet. All of these phenomena surrounded the Pirates as they came off a season that, if nothing else, thoroughly beat their fans' expectations and saw the team stay in the playoff race until the season's final two weeks.

But as easily as one good season can create a house of unrealistic expectations, one bad month can bring the whole structure down to a pile of smoldering embers. The Pirates had one really, truly bad month to close out an already disappointing 1998 season, which has stepped up the pressure on a team that previously had received tremendous leeway to undergo a rebuilding process.

On the whole, the Pirates did have a disappointing season. Several key players failed to build on their 1997 gains. Jose Guillen completely stagnated, slugging under .400 after June 1 and continuing his struggles with controlling the strike zone. Rich Loiselle struggled with his control all season. Al Martin, reliably mediocre for the past five seasons, was awful when he wasn't hurt. And Kevin Polcovich, one of the team's biggest overachievers in '97, couldn't hit his weight and was absolutely dismal in the field.

Of course, there were positives as well—Jason Kendall, Jason Christiansen, Francisco Cordova—which leaves the Bucs with the difficult task of deciding where to fish and where to cut bait:

- How much longer can the team suffer with the worst-hitting right fielder in baseball? Guillen is still only 23, but showed no cause for optimism in his second season, and will be arbitration-eligible after 1999.
- Should the team stick Aramis Ramirez back at the hot corner, or use a stopgap solution from within (Freddy Garcia) or without (Joe Randa rumors never seem to die)?

- Is Tony Womack the team's second baseman? Center fielder? Or just an alumnus?
- Can the team survive with an offensive nonfactor (Abraham Nunez) at shortstop?

The team's decision—tacit or explicit—not to address some of these questions last winter or even in July led directly to the Pirates' overall struggles at the plate and on the field.

The Pirates may not have had the worst offense in the NL last year, but they certainly had the most inexcusably bad offense. They were second to last in the NL in runs scored, just six ahead of Montreal. Their team slugging percentage was just .001 ahead of the league-worst Marlins, whose problems were somewhat more severe than Pittsburgh's. Even so, the Marlins still out-homered the Pirates in 1998. But their most damaging attribute was their lack of plate discipline: the Pirates finished dead last in the NL in walks with 393, a full 46 behind the Expos, and were third from the bottom in OBP.

The same players who contributed to the poor offensive showing weren't exactly making up for it on the field. The Pirates' groundball-oriented pitching staff generated more double-play opportunities than any other staff but the Rockies, but the infield had one of the worst DP conversion ratios in the NL, ranking ahead of just four teams. While Womack's inability to turn the deuce consistently was clearly a driver, part of the blame has to fall on the shortstop shuffle and the fielding woes of the players shuffling in and out. Collier, Polcovich, and Nunez combined for 45 errors this year, with Polcovich's 20 coming in just 55 games. The outfield defensive unit was subpar as a whole, with Al Martin's struggles worsening due to vision problems (now corrected). In fact, only Jason Kendall and Kevin Young provided above-average defense, further handicapping a pitching staff already suffering from a criminal lack of run support.

Viewed in the abstract and from the outside, these decisions seem easy. Womack's perceived value far exceeds his actual value. Ramirez is the long-term solution at third and will not benefit from more time in AAA. But what do you do

Pirates Prospectus

1998 record: 69-93; Sixth place, NL Central

Pythagorean W/L: 73-89

Runs scored: 650 (15th in NL)

Runs allowed: 718 (6th in NL)

Team EQA: .240 (16th in NL)

Park: Three Rivers Stadium (good hitters')

1998: A disappointment, as a number of young players did not develop.

1999: A rebound to .500 or so is likely with expected offensive improvements.

when the public's appetite for success and excitement has been whetted ahead of schedule? The fans love Guillen's strong and increasingly accurate arm. They consider Womack to be the sparkplug for an offense nearly devoid of power threats. They look to Kevin Young—he of the .481 slugging percentage—as the team's power threat. They saw Freddy Garcia's August rampage and decided he was a future star. None of these sentiments are particularly accurate or helpful, but the fans are becoming more vocal, and the team needs their support to bring attendance up and negotiate a new cable-television deal to replace the worst-in-the-majors deal in place now.

At the same time, the team is fighting to preserve the contentious Plan B to provide public funding and land-clearing for a new stadium, the abysmally named and universally booed PNC Park. Continued strip-mining at the major-league level would not help the team's cause politically, nor is it likely to satisfy increasingly hungry fans. For the first time in years, sports-talk radio in Pittsburgh comprises some baseball talk in addition to football and hockey, but much of it expresses fear and loathing of the day when Womack and Young will be discarded for cheaper and potentially better alternatives.

The result of this conflict is a change in the team's rebuilding timetable—or, more accurately, a reversion to the old "win in '99 timetable." The team backed off that mantra after the 1997 season showed them that some prospects weren't going to be productive major-leaguers as quickly as they had hoped, if at all. So, while the team's 1999 payroll budget of about $23 million won't exactly vault the club into the world of high salaries and free-agent follies, it portends a philosophical shift away from the school of thought that salaries should stay low until the new park opens. We can see similar escalations of cost in the expectations of plenty in Milwaukee, Seattle, and even Montreal. In practice, this is a dangerous trend on the field and on the books. With eleven players under contract for 1999 and few, if any, headed for arbitration-induced raises, the extra funds could be used to import expensive alternatives to adequate or superior home-grown solutions. If the team decided to import a truly superior player—say, a Bernie Williams to plug the center field hole—they would have a different problem, one of a single player whose salary nearly exceeds that of his 24 teammates.

In parallel, the Pirates are moving towards a tenuous financial situation. Although the team was profitable and cashflow-positive the last two seasons, the practice of increasing payrolls to meet expected revenues the year that a new stadium opens is risky for two reasons. First, the team is planning on a revenue stream similar to that of Baltimore's or Cleveland's, where a new stadium led to a flood of new fans at the ballpark and over the airwaves that, for Cleveland, has yet to ebb. Second, that experience may not be perfectly reproducible in other cities, particularly if the hometown team isn't a contender when the new park opens as the O's and Indians were. If the Pirates or Brewers or any other team that importuned its way into public funding for a private-enterprise ballpark spend $50 million on a .450 team, they'll find themselves saddled with an empty park, substantial wage liabilities, and the threat of bankruptcy.

The Pirates are staring at both edges of the sword: the benefits of fiscal prudence and a focus on building from within on one side; the PR advantages, quick-fix appeal, and momentum-generating possibilities of bringing in expensive outside talent on the other. To us, it's clear that the former path is desirable, but we don't have to walk in Cam Bonifay's shoes, nor do we have to stare a huge commitment like a new stadium in the face every day the team loses another game in amateurish fashion.

The flashpoints on the diamond are clear: all the main position players besides Kendall are on watch, and prospects of note and promise are advancing at every position but shortstop (unless you count Nunez for his defense). The team has begun to address the problem by importing Brian Giles, an outfielder with some power and excellent control of the strike zone. However, rumors that the team is looking at importing other veterans offer scant hope of continued patience with the farm-centric approach that is close to fruition. Striking the right balance between competitiveness today and contention in the future, between building a fan base and maintaining a focus on the future, is a difficult task fraught with potential failure. The Pirates have little room for error, and throwing away the rebuilding effort now could have a devastating impact on the team tomorrow.

HITTERS (Averages: BA .260/ OBA .330/ SA .420, EQA .260)

Adrian Brown   OF   Bats B   Age 25

YEAR	TEAM	LGE	AB	H	DB	TP	HR	BB	R	RBI	SB	CS	OUT	BA	OBA	SA	EQA	EQR	DEFENSE
1996	Lynchbrg	Car	214	59	4	2	3	11	21	20	8	5	160	.276	.311	.355	.232	21	47-OF 103
1996	Carolina	Sou	340	93	9	2	3	19	37	28	18	7	254	.274	.312	.338	.232	33	80-OF 109
1997	Carolina	Sou	142	35	2	2	2	14	16	12	6	3	110	.246	.314	.331	.230	14	34-OF 98
1997	Calgary	PCL	233	55	7	0	1	23	27	13	14	3	181	.236	.305	.279	.217	20	60-OF 112
1997	Pittsbrg	NL	146	27	3	0	2	14	10	6	7	4	123	.185	.256	.247	.173	8	34-OF 113
1998	Nashvill	PCL	306	79	8	3	3	26	39	24	21	6	233	.258	.316	.333	.237	32	79-OF 111
1998	Pittsbrg	NL	151	43	4	1	0	10	17	12	4	0	108	.285	.329	.325	.237	15	35-OF 109
1999	*Pittsbrg*	*NL*	*443*	*115*	*10*	*3*	*4*	*31*	*47*	*35*	*24*	*8*	*336*	*.260*	*.308*	*.323*	*.229*	*42*	

Would be the perfect center field solution for the Bucs if he could just hit. He can field like a dream, which puts him worlds ahead of Tony Womack in center. In the mix for a slot in the '99 outfield, and a great fourth outfielder if that's his role.

Emil Brown   OF   Bats R   Age 24

YEAR	TEAM	LGE	AB	H	DB	TP	HR	BB	R	RBI	SB	CS	OUT	BA	OBA	SA	EQA	EQR	DEFENSE
1996	Modesto	Cal	207	53	4	1	7	24	25	24	7	3	157	.256	.333	.386	.254	26	54-OF 104
1997	Pittsbrg	NL	94	16	2	1	2	11	8	5	4	1	79	.170	.257	.277	.190	6	31-OF 97
1998	Carolina	Sou	454	129	18	1	12	35	57	53	15	5	330	.284	.335	.407	.261	57	105-OF 93
1998	Pittsbrg	NL	39	10	1	0	0	1	2	2	0	0	29	.256	.275	.282	.184	2	
1999	*Pittsbrg*	*NL*	*344*	*96*	*14*	*1*	*9*	*26*	*42*	*40*	*12*	*4*	*252*	*.279*	*.330*	*.404*	*.259*	*43*	

The Pirates are aggressive Rule 5 participants, and so far, Emil looks like the best one they've gotten. It looks like the year off didn't hurt him much. He had a monstrous campaign in AA, heating up as the season went along. He has star potential, but is more likely to be a very good all-around player.

Lou Collier   SS   Bats R   Age 25

YEAR	TEAM	LGE	AB	H	DB	TP	HR	BB	R	RBI	SB	CS	OUT	BA	OBA	SA	EQA	EQR	DEFENSE	
1996	Carolina	Sou	443	115	16	2	3	38	51	34	19	6	334	.260	.318	.325	.232	43	116-SS 87	
1997	Calgary	PCL	373	94	20	3	1	30	38	29	9	5	284	.252	.308	.330	.224	34	85-SS 95	26-2B 83
1998	Pittsbrg	NL	333	81	15	6	2	33	34	29	2	2	254	.243	.311	.342	.228	32	97-SS 101	
1999	*Pittsbrg*	*NL*	*358*	*92*	*17*	*3*	*2*	*30*	*39*	*30*	*9*	*4*	*270*	*.257*	*.314*	*.338*	*.232*	*35*		

I think he needs glasses. He doesn't read balls off the bat correctly, and his offensive statistics certainly don't disprove the theory. He had one chance to grab the spotlight and earn himself a starting role somewhere, and he did nothing with it.

J.J. Davis   1B   Bats R   Age 20

YEAR	TEAM	LGE	AB	H	DB	TP	HR	BB	R	RBI	SB	CS	OUT	BA	OBA	SA	EQA	EQR	DEFENSE
1998	Erie	NYP	197	45	5	1	6	16	16	19	2	1	153	.228	.286	.355	.221	18	49-OF 87
1998	Augusta	SAL	106	18	3	0	3	3	3	4	1	1	89	.170	.193	.283	.137	3	19-OF 95
1999	*Pittsbrg*	*NL*	*210*	*51*	*4*	*0*	*7*	*9*	*15*	*20*	*2*	*1*	*160*	*.243*	*.274*	*.362*	*.218*	*18*	

A questionable pick to begin with, Davis has tools that haven't translated into professional success. One and a half years into his career, he can't get out of short-season ball, and he's stuck playing first. Maybe he'll go back to pitching. The Bucs have a bad history with first-rounders, and Davis appears to be no exception.

Kory Dehaan   OF   Bats L   Age 22

YEAR	TEAM	LGE	AB	H	DB	TP	HR	BB	R	RBI	SB	CS	OUT	BA	OBA	SA	EQA	EQR	DEFENSE
1997	Erie	NYP	210	37	6	2	1	28	15	9	5	5	178	.176	.273	.238	.176	11	51-OF 98
1998	Augusta	SAL	484	133	25	5	6	56	67	51	15	8	359	.275	.350	.384	.260	62	125-OF 100
1999	*Pittsbrg*	*NL*	*359*	*94*	*17*	*2*	*4*	*39*	*45*	*34*	*14*	*8*	*273*	*.262*	*.334*	*.354*	*.246*	*41*	

A '97 seventh-rounder who obviously took a little time to adjust to the wooden bat. Probably a year old for the Sally League, but his performance was still impressive, and the outfield mess upstairs will only help him. The skills are there for him to jump to Carolina, and this organization is the type to do it.

Luis Figueroa			SS				Bats B		Age 25								
YEAR	TEAM	LGE	AB	H	DB	TP	HR	BB	R	RBI	SB	CS	OUT	BA	OBA	SA	EQA	EQR	DEFENSE
1997	Augusta	SAL	257	46	4	0	0	26	13	9	8	3	214	.179	.254	.195	.148	9	66-SS 87
1997	Lynchbrg	Car	89	20	3	0	0	5	5	4	0	1	70	.225	.266	.258	.168	4	20-2B 95
1998	Carolina	Sou	346	63	6	1	0	53	25	13	3	3	286	.182	.291	.205	.174	18	86-SS 93 28-2B 100
1999	Pittsbrg	NL	314	68	2	0	2	36	23	18	5	3	249	.217	.297	.242	.192	20	

Fielding whiz who obviously believes if you can do one thing at the plate, do it well. Figueroa drew 71 walks at AA this year while slugging .291. Worked hard on developing patience and bunting skills, but he'll be limited to a glorified Raffy Belliard role if he even makes the majors.

Eddy Furniss			1B				Bats L		Age 23								
YEAR	TEAM	LGE	AB	H	DB	TP	HR	BB	R	RBI	SB	CS	OUT	BA	OBA	SA	EQA	EQR	DEFENSE
1998	Augusta	SAL	89	38	3	0	6	18	20	24	0	1	52	.427	.523	.663	.395	25	
1998	Lynchbrg	Car	112	21	4	0	2	15	9	7	1	0	91	.188	.283	.277	.198	8	
1998	Carolina	Sou	44	5	0	0	0	3	1	1	0	0	39	.114	.170	.114	—	-1	
1999	Pittsbrg	NL	200	55	7	0	8	29	26	30	0	1	146	.275	.367	.430	.278	30	

A long year combined with some poor pitch recognition led to a disappointing ending to Furniss's season. He struggled after his promotion, but that should be remedied with experience. Looked extremely slow at Double-A, which may have been a function of combining a full college season with his pro debut. A big guy with gap power to all fields well; his defense at first will be good enough if he can continue to develop as a hitter.

Freddy Garcia			3B				Bats R		Age 26								
YEAR	TEAM	LGE	AB	H	DB	TP	HR	BB	R	RBI	SB	CS	OUT	BA	OBA	SA	EQA	EQR	DEFENSE
1996	Lynchbrg	Car	474	121	14	1	15	34	43	53	2	1	354	.255	.305	.384	.238	49	109-3B 98
1997	Carolina	Sou	276	68	8	2	12	13	22	33	0	1	209	.246	.280	.420	.235	28	68-3B 99
1997	Calgary	PCL	116	20	3	0	3	8	4	6	0	0	96	.172	.226	.276	.158	5	29-3B 75
1998	Nashvill	PCL	321	78	15	2	16	22	30	43	0	2	245	.243	.292	.452	.248	38	66-3B 91 18-1B 104
1998	Pittsbrg	NL	171	43	9	1	10	19	20	27	0	2	130	.251	.326	.491	.271	25	45-3B 105
1999	Pittsbrg	NL	469	117	19	1	25	34	45	66	0	2	354	.249	.300	.454	.255	58	

At times this year, the Pirates played the worst infield defense I have ever seen on a major-league diamond: Garcia at third, Womack at second, and Collier at short. It was easier to go through those three than security at Lagos International Airport. Garcia's entire production came in a .383/.449/.833 August, and one would hope that's not enough to fool the Pirates into demoting Ramirez.

Jose Guillen			OF				Bats R		Age 23								
YEAR	TEAM	LGE	AB	H	DB	TP	HR	BB	R	RBI	SB	CS	OUT	BA	OBA	SA	EQA	EQR	DEFENSE
1996	Lynchbrg	Car	524	149	9	1	17	17	47	61	12	8	383	.284	.307	.403	.242	55	121-OF 96
1997	Pittsbrg	NL	494	128	18	4	15	21	41	55	1	2	368	.259	.289	.403	.234	49	125-OF 101
1998	Pittsbrg	NL	570	152	37	2	15	25	54	64	3	6	424	.267	.297	.418	.241	60	143-OF 99
1999	Pittsbrg	NL	532	150	24	1	18	21	51	68	5	4	386	.282	.309	.432	.253	62	

Rob Neyer has said what few else have: Jose Guillen was a really bad ballplayer this year. Yes, the arm is awesome, and we all love to see Kirt Manwaring get gunned down at first by the right fielder, but he completely atrophied at the plate, slugging under .400 after about mid-May. There's no one pushing him at the moment, but the Pirates will need to look elsewhere for solutions if he doesn't step forward.

Yamid Haad			C				Bats R		Age 21								
YEAR	TEAM	LGE	AB	H	DB	TP	HR	BB	R	RBI	SB	CS	OUT	BA	OBA	SA	EQA	EQR	DEFENSE
1997	Erie	NYP	153	34	4	1	1	6	7	8	1	2	121	.222	.252	.281	.170	7	
1998	Lynchbrg	Car	300	70	5	1	5	15	18	21	1	3	233	.233	.270	.307	.192	19	83-C 98
1999	Pittsbrg	NL	223	57	7	1	4	8	16	20	1	2	168	.256	.281	.350	.214	18	

Defensive specialist who has yet to turn the corner offensively; some in the organization are afraid he never will. Haad is a dead fastball hitter who was easily fooled by offspeed stuff, a bad harbinger for the future. On the plus side, his defense is nearly major-league. Worth watching.

Kevin Haverbusch   **SS**   **Bats L**   **Age 23**

YEAR	TEAM	LGE	AB	H	DB	TP	HR	BB	R	RBI	SB	CS	OUT	BA	OBA	SA	EQA	EQR	DEFENSE	
1997	Erie	NYP	238	55	5	0	6	10	15	18	2	2	185	.231	.262	.328	.197	16	50-SS 72	
1998	Lynchbrg	Car	183	57	7	1	7	9	21	28	2	1	127	.311	.344	.475	.279	26	31-SS 87	
1998	Carolina	Sou	162	53	5	0	3	9	18	21	1	2	111	.327	.363	.414	.268	21	39-3B 93	
1999	*Pittsbrg*	*NL*	*271*	*82*	*6*	*0*	*10*	*11*	*26*	*38*	*3*	*2*	*191*	*.303*	*.330*	*.435*	*.263*	*34*		

A '97 20th-rounder who has hit everywhere he's played and may not be finished filling out yet. His weaknesses: the strike zone and defense. He walked more in his brief time at Double-A than he has anywhere else. As for defense, his range at short isn't great, prompting a move to third; his arm is strong but not that accurate yet. The Bucs are covered at third and possibly second, so moving him seems questionable. Where he plays obviously determines how long he remains a Pirate prospect.

Chad Hermansen   **OF**   **Bats R**   **Age 21**

YEAR	TEAM	LGE	AB	H	DB	TP	HR	BB	R	RBI	SB	CS	OUT	BA	OBA	SA	EQA	EQR	DEFENSE	
1996	Augusta	SAL	238	60	5	1	12	29	29	33	5	2	180	.252	.333	.433	.265	33	57-SS 79	
1996	Lynchbrg	Car	252	62	4	2	8	24	24	28	2	1	191	.246	.312	.373	.238	27	63-SS 79	
1997	Carolina	Sou	479	114	20	1	16	57	58	52	13	4	369	.238	.319	.384	.248	57	57-OF 99	32-SS 69
1998	Nashvill	PCL	452	110	18	4	24	47	60	62	19	4	346	.243	.315	.460	.267	64	109-OF 91	
1999	*Pittsbrg*	*NL*	*462*	*124*	*21*	*2*	*22*	*48*	*64*	*67*	*17*	*4*	*342*	*.268*	*.337*	*.465*	*.278*	*70*		

His strikeouts drew the ire of many a writer and fan, but Hermansen actually had a pretty good season. His main problem is consistency—he was ice cold until late May, got hot, got cold again, etc.—but having one position should make that easier. Will return to Triple-A to start '99 now that Giles has been brought in.

Alex Hernandez   **OF**   **Bats L**   **Age 22**

YEAR	TEAM	LGE	AB	H	DB	TP	HR	BB	R	RBI	SB	CS	OUT	BA	OBA	SA	EQA	EQR	DEFENSE	
1996	Erie	NYP	227	55	9	1	4	15	19	19	3	4	176	.242	.289	.344	.215	19	30-OF 89	28-1B 94
1997	Lynchbrg	Car	521	138	27	2	5	20	45	44	8	5	388	.265	.292	.353	.221	45	126-OF 95	
1998	Carolina	Sou	446	99	16	3	8	29	34	33	7	3	350	.222	.269	.325	.204	33	109-OF 96	
1999	*Pittsbrg*	*NL*	*423*	*110*	*18*	*2*	*8*	*22*	*38*	*41*	*7*	*4*	*317*	*.260*	*.297*	*.369*	*.231*	*40*		

Excellent defense will bring him to the majors someday, but the hole in his swing is so big you could drive LeAnn Rimes through it.

Jason Kendall   **C**   **Bats R**   **Age 25**

YEAR	TEAM	LGE	AB	H	DB	TP	HR	BB	R	RBI	SB	CS	OUT	BA	OBA	SA	EQA	EQR	DEFENSE
1996	Pittsbrg	NL	411	120	22	5	3	38	52	46	4	2	293	.292	.352	.392	.262	51	
1997	Pittsbrg	NL	483	139	35	3	9	52	72	59	15	6	350	.288	.357	.429	.275	69	
1998	Pittsbrg	NL	533	174	36	3	13	54	96	75	28	6	365	.326	.388	.478	.303	93	143-C 99
1999	*Pittsbrg*	*NL*	*480*	*150*	*39*	*3*	*11*	*47*	*79*	*68*	*19*	*5*	*335*	*.312*	*.374*	*.475*	*.296*	*80*	

The best story on the Pirates. Kendall took huge steps forward at the plate, on the bases, in the field, and in the clubhouse, becoming the team's unquestioned leader and occasional mouthpiece. He's a player you lock up long-term and build around, and the Pirates are trying to do just that.

Garrett Long   **OF/1B**   **Bats R**   **Age 22**

YEAR	TEAM	LGE	AB	H	DB	TP	HR	BB	R	RBI	SB	CS	OUT	BA	OBA	SA	EQA	EQR	DEFENSE	
1997	Augusta	SAL	294	83	6	1	7	54	44	39	2	1	212	.282	.394	.381	.280	44	29-1B 89	21-OF 85
1998	Lynchbrg	Car	317	86	18	0	9	46	46	41	4	1	232	.271	.364	.413	.275	46	62-1B 92	
1998	Carolina	Sou	96	24	2	0	0	8	8	6	1	0	72	.250	.308	.271	.205	7	23-OF 88	
1999	*Pittsbrg*	*NL*	*362*	*104*	*17*	*1*	*10*	*47*	*50*	*50*	*4*	*1*	*259*	*.287*	*.369*	*.423*	*.280*	*54*		

Aside from his questionable academic credentials, this Eli looks like a pretty good ballplayer. He's in a pattern of moving up, struggling, adjusting, and moving up again, which is generally a positive thing. However, his defense limits him to first or left, so he needs to build on the power he showed at Lynchburg this year to stay in the team's plans.

Al Martin   LF   Bats L   Age 31

YEAR	TEAM	LGE	AB	H	DB	TP	HR	BB	R	RBI	SB	CS	OUT	BA	OBA	SA	EQA	EQR	DEFENSE
1996	Pittsbrg	NL	626	184	31	2	20	58	93	81	32	13	455	.294	.354	.446	.278	92	139-OF 87
1997	Pittsbrg	NL	421	120	23	6	14	47	66	59	19	7	308	.285	.357	.468	.285	67	99-OF 86
1998	Pittsbrg	NL	438	103	14	2	13	35	48	41	21	3	338	.235	.292	.365	.235	45	104-OF 96
1999	*Pittsbrg*	*NL*	*451*	*124*	*19*	*2*	*14*	*38*	*58*	*55*	*18*	*6*	*333*	*.275*	*.331*	*.419*	*.264*	*59*	

The power of hindsight says the Bucs should have traded him last winter, but the team probably hoped to trade him in July to a contender, and that's actually a pretty good strategy. Unfortunately, Martin imploded, hitting righties as poorly as he hits lefties with continued execrable defense. He's in Hermansen's spot, and at this point, the Pirates may have to swallow some salary to move him.

Manny Martinez   OF   Bats R   Age 28

YEAR	TEAM	LGE	AB	H	DB	TP	HR	BB	R	RBI	SB	CS	OUT	BA	OBA	SA	EQA	EQR	DEFENSE
1996	Tacoma	PCL	274	75	9	0	4	20	30	25	12	7	206	.274	.323	.350	.237	28	64-OF 116
1997	Calgary	PCL	394	93	13	0	10	25	34	33	12	7	308	.236	.282	.345	.216	33	103-OF 102
1998	Nashvill	PCL	74	14	2	0	1	6	5	3	4	2	62	.189	.250	.257	.175	4	15-OF 95
1998	Pittsbrg	NL	179	45	11	2	6	10	17	21	0	3	137	.251	.291	.436	.240	19	44-OF 100
1999	*Pittsbrg*	*NL*	*311*	*80*	*16*	*1*	*9*	*20*	*33*	*34*	*10*	*6*	*237*	*.257*	*.302*	*.402*	*.243*	*34*	

Filler, essentially Adrian Brown but two years older with less offense. May return if Martin is dealt, but otherwise, the Pirates have better internal options.

Warren Morris   2B   Bats L   Age 25

YEAR	TEAM	LGE	AB	H	DB	TP	HR	BB	R	RBI	SB	CS	OUT	BA	OBA	SA	EQA	EQR	DEFENSE
1997	Charlott	Fla	502	136	16	4	11	51	59	57	8	3	369	.271	.338	.384	.255	60	97-2B 84
1998	Carolina	Sou	147	40	5	1	4	17	19	18	3	1	108	.272	.348	.401	.264	19	40-2B 86
1998	Tulsa	Tex	383	103	12	2	9	33	42	42	7	5	285	.269	.327	.381	.247	43	88-2B 95
1999	*Pittsbrg*	*NL*	*440*	*123*	*17*	*2*	*9*	*38*	*50*	*51*	*8*	*4*	*321*	*.280*	*.337*	*.389*	*.255*	*53*	

His fielding earns mixed reviews, but unless he becomes worse than Womack (is it possible?), Morris should be the Pirates' Opening Day second baseman. Morris is small and thus unloved by many scouts, but the man hits, and should have a good career as an above-average second baseman. Led the AFL in slugging, and impressed his AFL manager (Ken Griffey) with his defense, especially on the deuce.

Abraham Nunez   SS   Bats B   Age 23

YEAR	TEAM	LGE	AB	H	DB	TP	HR	BB	R	RBI	SB	CS	OUT	BA	OBA	SA	EQA	EQR	DEFENSE	
1996	St Cath	NYP	303	74	3	1	4	23	29	21	16	9	238	.244	.298	.300	.212	25	52-SS 90	23-2B 117
1997	Lynchbrg	Car	306	73	7	2	3	18	27	20	16	9	242	.239	.281	.304	.204	23	74-SS 102	
1997	Carolina	Sou	193	53	3	1	1	16	21	16	7	3	143	.275	.330	.316	.232	19	48-SS 81	
1997	Pittsbrg	NL	40	9	2	2	0	3	5	3	1	0	31	.225	.279	.375	.229	4		
1998	Nashvill	PCL	361	80	9	2	3	37	34	22	14	7	288	.222	.294	.283	.205	28	94-SS 91	
1998	Pittsbrg	NL	52	10	3	0	1	12	9	4	4	2	44	.192	.344	.308	.243	6		
1999	*Pittsbrg*	*NL*	*404*	*97*	*10*	*2*	*3*	*34*	*41*	*27*	*20*	*8*	*315*	*.240*	*.299*	*.297*	*.216*	*34*		

As nervous as I've ever seen a rookie, and it was all the more surprising because he had already had a cup of joe in '97. Even if his glove comes back, he's pretty much an absolute zero with the bat, and that's pretty cold. Probable Opening Day shortstop and SportsCenter highlight fave.

Keith Osik   C   Bats R   Age 30

YEAR	TEAM	LGE	AB	H	DB	TP	HR	BB	R	RBI	SB	CS	OUT	BA	OBA	SA	EQA	EQR	DEFENSE
1996	Pittsbrg	NL	139	39	13	1	1	15	19	16	1	0	100	.281	.351	.410	.267	18	
1997	Pittsbrg	NL	104	26	8	1	0	10	11	9	0	1	79	.250	.316	.346	.229	10	
1998	Pittsbrg	NL	98	21	5	0	0	13	8	6	1	2	79	.214	.306	.265	.200	7	19-C 102
1999	*Pittsbrg*	*NL*	*102*	*25*	*8*	*0*	*0*	*11*	*11*	*8*	*0*	*1*	*78*	*.245*	*.319*	*.324*	*.225*	*9*	

Signed to a long-term deal, after which he promptly had his worst season. A little embarrassing, don't you think? Has one more year to show he's worth keeping around, and he's certainly more worthwhile than '98 demonstrated.

Jeff Patzke   2B   Bats R   Age 25

YEAR	TEAM	LGE	AB	H	DB	TP	HR	BB	R	RBI	SB	CS	OUT	BA	OBA	SA	EQA	EQR	DEFENSE	
1996	Knoxvill	Sou	417	104	23	1	4	65	55	39	4	3	316	.249	.351	.338	.248	48	117-2B 100	
1997	Syracuse	Int	315	86	21	2	2	46	43	34	0	2	231	.273	.366	.371	.262	40	77-2B 98	
1998	Dunedin	Fla	62	12	0	0	0	6	2	2	0	0	50	.194	.265	.194	.143	2		
1998	Nashvill	PCL	356	95	8	0	7	43	39	38	4	5	266	.267	.346	.348	.245	40	101-2B 101	
1999	*Pittsbrg*	*NL*	*374*	*103*	*19*	*1*	*6*	*49*	*48*	*44*	*3*	*3*	*274*	*.275*	*.359*	*.380*	*.263*	*49*		

After some shoddy treatment by the Jays, Patzke found refuge in the Pirates' system and did what he always does: drew some walks, hit for average, fielded well. Better than Womack in all dimensions but baserunning. Should at least be Womack's backup/defensive caddy unless Morris claims the job this year.

Corey Pointer   OF   Bats R   Age 23

YEAR	TEAM	LGE	AB	H	DB	TP	HR	BB	R	RBI	SB	CS	OUT	BA	OBA	SA	EQA	EQR	DEFENSE
1996	Eugene	Nwn	237	49	4	1	9	25	21	22	6	2	190	.207	.282	.346	.220	22	64-OF 83
1997	Augusta	SAL	253	46	5	0	6	23	18	14	11	2	209	.182	.250	.273	.184	15	65-OF 88
1998	Lynchbrg	Car	383	83	15	1	16	49	41	43	7	6	306	.217	.306	.386	.239	43	109-OF 99
1999	*Pittsbrg*	*NL*	*333*	*68*	*7*	*0*	*14*	*34*	*29*	*32*	*9*	*4*	*269*	*.204*	*.278*	*.351*	*.220*	*31*	

The poor man's Rob Deer? Hits homers but nothing else, draws walks, strikes out a lot—I mean, a lot: 177 times in 375 AB. If he's drawing walks, a decent coach should be able to work on his selectiveness, but the Pirates have not had success teaching kids the strike zone, and this is something of an advanced case.

Kevin Polcovich SS   Bats R   Age 29

YEAR	TEAM	LGE	AB	H	DB	TP	HR	BB	R	RBI	SB	CS	OUT	BA	OBA	SA	EQA	EQR	DEFENSE	
1996	Calgary	PCL	327	69	13	1	1	15	17	14	5	4	262	.211	.246	.266	.164	14	64-SS 94	28-2B 100
1997	Pittsbrg	NL	243	64	16	1	4	23	27	26	1	2	181	.263	.327	.387	.247	27	77-SS 99	
1998	Pittsbrg	NL	211	40	12	0	0	16	12	8	4	3	174	.190	.247	.246	.160	9	47-SS 104	
1999	*Pittsbrg*	*NL*	*250*	*58*	*11*	*0*	*3*	*16*	*19*	*18*	*5*	*3*	*195*	*.232*	*.278*	*.312*	*.204*	*18*		

Another overachiever who went back to his bad old self in '98. Off the 40-man roster, and out of the team's plans.

Aramis Ramirez   3B   Bats R   Age 21

YEAR	TEAM	LGE	AB	H	DB	TP	HR	BB	R	RBI	SB	CS	OUT	BA	OBA	SA	EQA	EQR	DEFENSE	
1996	Erie	NYP	226	60	7	1	8	24	25	30	0	0	166	.265	.336	.412	.260	29	59-3B 86	
1997	Lynchbrg	Car	488	128	15	1	24	66	62	73	3	2	362	.262	.350	.445	.274	71	129-3B 96	
1998	Nashvill	PCL	166	42	6	0	5	22	18	20	0	2	126	.253	.340	.380	.250	20	45-3B 85	
1998	Pittsbrg	NL	250	59	9	1	6	19	20	23	0	1	192	.236	.290	.352	.220	22	68-3B 89	
1999	*Pittsbrg*	*NL*	*415*	*113*	*15*	*1*	*16*	*47*	*49*	*59*	*1*	*2*	*304*	*.272*	*.346*	*.429*	*.269*	*57*		

So now people are calling in to local sports-gab stations, complaining about how Ramirez "didn't do nothing" this year. Never mind the fact that he still can't walk into a bar and get himself a drink (except on the Strip), or that he was two months removed from A-ball when he was called up in May. Between adjusting to defending 3B on turf and adjusting to major-league pitchers, he held his own, and he still looks like a star in the making if he can handle the inevitable struggles of an early call-up.

Mark Smith   OF/1B   Bats R   Age 29

YEAR	TEAM	LGE	AB	H	DB	TP	HR	BB	R	RBI	SB	CS	OUT	BA	OBA	SA	EQA	EQR	DEFENSE
1996	Rochestr	Int	130	41	8	0	6	12	22	21	7	1	90	.315	.373	.515	.306	23	31-OF 89
1996	Baltimor	AL	77	18	2	0	4	3	5	9	0	2	61	.234	.262	.416	.219	7	16-OF 117
1997	Calgary	PCL	127	37	7	0	8	15	19	23	2	1	91	.291	.366	.535	.302	23	30-OF 99
1997	Pittsbrg	NL	192	53	12	1	9	29	30	31	2	1	140	.276	.371	.490	.294	33	31-OF 102
1998	Nashvill	PCL	91	29	7	1	5	9	16	17	3	1	63	.319	.380	.582	.319	18	
1998	Pittsbrg	NL	127	24	4	0	3	11	12	7	8	0	103	.189	.254	.291	.201	9	20-OF 101
1999	*Pittsbrg*	*NL*	*256*	*71*	*15*	*1*	*13*	*26*	*37*	*40*	*8*	*2*	*187*	*.277*	*.344*	*.496*	*.287*	*41*	

Couldn't hit a beach ball with a tennis racket before June, after which he returned to his normal self. Like Ward, he's replaceable; unlike Ward, he's already off the 40-man roster. Not in the team's plans, but he and his reverse platoon split can help someone off the bench.

T.J. Staton — OF — Bats L — Age 24

YEAR	TEAM	LGE	AB	H	DB	TP	HR	BB	R	RBI	SB	CS	OUT	BA	OBA	SA	EQA	EQR	DEFENSE
1996	Carolina	Sou	385	112	16	2	14	48	58	55	12	5	278	.291	.370	.452	.286	61	103-OF 94
1997	Carolina	Sou	203	51	6	1	5	9	17	19	6	3	155	.251	.283	.365	.223	18	46-OF 95
1997	Calgary	PCL	191	30	6	0	2	19	7	6	2	2	163	.157	.233	.220	.138	6	59-OF 89
1998	Carolina	Sou	218	56	10	0	6	18	23	23	4	3	165	.257	.314	.385	.241	24	52-OF 84
1998	Nashvill	PCL	184	40	6	0	5	14	14	15	4	3	147	.217	.273	.332	.207	14	51-OF 95
1999	*Montreal*	*NL*	*379*	*93*	*14*	*1*	*11*	*29*	*37*	*39*	*10*	*5*	*291*	*.245*	*.299*	*.375*	*.241*	*41*	

Can't hit Triple-A pitching. When he reached Calgary in '97, he lost all his plate discipline, and he's never gotten it back. Fooled a lot of smart people, but now he's just getting fooled. Claimed by Montreal on waivers in November.

Doug Strange — 3B — Bats B — Age 35

YEAR	TEAM	LGE	AB	H	DB	TP	HR	BB	R	RBI	SB	CS	OUT	BA	OBA	SA	EQA	EQR	DEFENSE
1996	Seattle	AL	180	41	6	1	3	13	14	14	1	0	139	.228	.280	.322	.207	14	28-3B 90
1997	Montreal	NL	325	81	15	2	12	38	37	42	0	2	246	.249	.328	.418	.256	41	98-3B 97
1998	Pittsbrg	NL	184	32	8	0	0	11	6	6	1	0	152	.174	.221	.217	.121	4	33-3B 88
1999	*Pittsbrg*	*NL*	*215*	*44*	*4*	*0*	*5*	*21*	*14*	*16*	*0*	*0*	*171*	*.205*	*.275*	*.293*	*.197*	*15*	

Signed to provide a stopgap in case Garcia and Ramirez weren't ready, but Strange turned out to be the least ready of all. He can't play short and plays a lousy second, so his role on the '99 Pirates is unclear. I'd just release him.

Turner Ward — OF — Bats B — Age 34

YEAR	TEAM	LGE	AB	H	DB	TP	HR	BB	R	RBI	SB	CS	OUT	BA	OBA	SA	EQA	EQR	DEFENSE
1996	Milwauke	AL	66	11	1	1	2	12	8	5	3	0	55	.167	.295	.303	.224	6	23-OF 100
1997	Calgary	PCL	195	48	9	1	5	18	22	20	5	1	148	.246	.310	.379	.243	22	50-OF 95
1997	Pittsbrg	NL	166	57	16	1	7	19	31	32	3	1	110	.343	.411	.578	.331	35	43-OF 98
1998	Pittsbrg	NL	281	74	11	3	10	29	33	37	5	5	212	.263	.332	.431	.260	37	66-OF 111
1999	*Pittsbrg*	*NL*	*261*	*70*	*13*	*2*	*9*	*29*	*34*	*35*	*5*	*2*	*193*	*.268*	*.341*	*.437*	*.271*	*37*	

Came back to earth, of course, of course. The two-year contract was silly, but at least it wasn't three. Should get squeezed out by the Browns this summer.

Rico Washington — 3B — Bats L — Age 21

YEAR	TEAM	LGE	AB	H	DB	TP	HR	BB	R	RBI	SB	CS	OUT	BA	OBA	SA	EQA	EQR	DEFENSE
1998	Erie	NYP	197	53	5	1	5	12	17	22	0	1	145	.269	.311	.381	.237	20	43-3B 107
1998	Augusta	SAL	51	14	2	1	1	6	7	6	1	0	37	.275	.351	.412	.270	7	
1999	*Pittsbrg*	*NL*	*198*	*61*	*8*	*0*	*6*	*12*	*22*	*28*	*1*	*1*	*138*	*.308*	*.348*	*.439*	*.272*	*27*	

Tenth-rounder from 1997 who is being converted from shortstop to . . . well, to something. Could be third, which he played at Erie; could be catching, which he did in instructional league. The team was pleased with his defense behind the plate, and they really like his bat; his power is just developing. An emerging top prospect who just needs a permanent position.

Craig Wilson — C — Bats R — Age 22

YEAR	TEAM	LGE	AB	H	DB	TP	HR	BB	R	RBI	SB	CS	OUT	BA	OBA	SA	EQA	EQR	DEFENSE
1996	Hagerstn	SAL	502	115	14	2	10	24	34	37	7	5	392	.229	.264	.325	.199	34	45-OF 93
1997	Lynchbrg	Car	404	100	15	1	16	31	39	48	4	3	307	.248	.301	.408	.243	44	
1998	Lynchbrg	Car	223	59	8	1	11	21	25	33	1	1	165	.265	.328	.457	.267	30	40-C 96
1998	Carolina	Sou	144	42	5	0	5	10	17	19	3	1	103	.292	.338	.431	.266	19	29-C 91
1999	*Pittsbrg*	*NL*	*396*	*108*	*16*	*1*	*16*	*26*	*42*	*53*	*5*	*2*	*290*	*.273*	*.318*	*.439*	*.260*	*50*	

He was moving himself towards the upper echelon of hitting prospects and presenting the Pirates with a pleasant dilemma behind the plate, smashing the ball consistently at AA, before he went down with an elbow injury that required Tommy John surgery. They're bravely saying he'll be hitting again this season, but that seems ridiculously optimistic, and there's no guarantee he'll hit or catch at the same level again.

Tony Womack   2B   Bats L   Age 29

YEAR	TEAM	LGE	AB	H	DB	TP	HR	BB	R	RBI	SB	CS	OUT	BA	OBA	SA	EQA	EQR	DEFENSE	
1996	Calgary	PCL	490	114	15	5	1	26	42	27	25	8	384	.233	.271	.290	.198	34	75-SS 95	34-2B 91
1996	Pittsbrg	NL	30	10	2	1	0	6	7	4	2	0	20	.333	.444	.467	.332	6		
1997	Pittsbrg	NL	637	174	27	7	7	47	92	56	51	7	470	.273	.323	.370	.255	77	145-2B 90	
1998	Pittsbrg	NL	652	183	28	7	3	42	99	51	62	9	478	.281	.324	.359	.254	78	149-2B 105	
1999	*Pittsbrg*	*NL*	*613*	*169*	*24*	*8*	*3*	*38*	*86*	*50*	*53*	*7*	*451*	*.276*	*.318*	*.356*	*.251*	*71*		

Still awful. Easily the worst defensive second baseman in the game today, and probably the worst leadoff hitter as well. "It's a soft roller to Womack's left and it's THROUGH!" Cordova has a special right to have Rincon and Lieber hold Womack down once a week so Cordova can smack him upside the head. Arbitration-eligible, so he's about to become ridiculously overpaid.

Ron Wright   1B   Bats R   Age 23

YEAR	TEAM	LGE	AB	H	DB	TP	HR	BB	R	RBI	SB	CS	OUT	BA	OBA	SA	EQA	EQR	DEFENSE
1996	Durham	Car	240	59	6	1	14	30	28	36	1	0	181	.246	.330	.454	.269	34	64-1B 104
1996	Greenvil	Sou	231	55	6	1	13	31	27	34	1	0	176	.238	.328	.442	.265	32	53-1B 105
1997	Calgary	PCL	318	77	13	0	13	20	27	36	0	2	243	.242	.287	.406	.233	32	78-1B 104
1998	Nashvill	PCL	56	11	2	0	0	8	4	3	0	0	45	.196	.297	.232	.187	3	
1999	*Pittsbrg*	*NL*	*185*	*48*	*7*	*0*	*9*	*18*	*19*	*27*	*0*	*1*	*138*	*.259*	*.325*	*.443*	*.262*	*24*	

Lost almost the entire season to a back injury that required surgery. It's obviously a serious problem, probably related to the fact that he's just plain fat. Coupled with his stalled progress from '97, it puts him on a late summer timetable at the earliest— and that's only if his power returns.

Kevin Young   1B   Bats R   Age 30

YEAR	TEAM	LGE	AB	H	DB	TP	HR	BB	R	RBI	SB	CS	OUT	BA	OBA	SA	EQA	EQR	DEFENSE
1996	Omaha	AA	185	51	7	0	9	11	21	26	3	0	134	.276	.316	.459	.266	24	31-1B 100
1996	KansasCy	AL	130	31	5	0	8	10	14	17	3	4	103	.238	.293	.462	.248	16	18-1B 112
1997	Pittsbrg	NL	331	98	17	3	18	18	45	54	9	2	235	.296	.332	.529	.289	53	70-1B 97
1998	Pittsbrg	NL	589	158	35	2	30	48	76	86	16	8	439	.268	.323	.487	.273	86	153-1B 85
1999	*Pittsbrg*	*NL*	*483*	*135*	*24*	*1*	*24*	*34*	*60*	*72*	*12*	*5*	*353*	*.280*	*.327*	*.482*	*.275*	*70*	

It looked nice on the surface, but you can see it wasn't up to his '97 season, and he's bordering on replacement-level at this point. He should be moved out by July. The defensive number is deceiving: Young has to deal with some serious crap from Womack, Garcia, and the shortstops, and it's to his credit that he fields as well as he does.

PITCHERS (Averages: 4.00 ERA, 9.00 H/9 1.00 HR/9, 3.00 BB/9,, 6.00 K/9, 1.00 KWH)

Paul Ah Yat   Throws L   Age 25

YEAR	TEAM	LGE	IP	H	ER	HR	BB	K	ERA	W	L	H/9	HR/9	BB/9	K/9	KWH	PERA
1996	Erie	NYP	25.7	36	21	2	8	18	7.36	1	2	12.62	0.70	2.81	6.31	0.84	5.26
1997	Augusta	SAL	79.3	127	52	9	23	66	5.90	3	6	14.41	1.02	2.61	7.49	1.12	6.47
1997	Lynchbrg	Car	45.3	48	10	3	4	25	1.99	4	1	9.53	0.60	0.79	4.96	2.44	3.37
1998	Lynchbrg	Car	92.3	138	57	12	18	46	5.56	3	7	13.45	1.17	1.75	4.48	0.64	6.04
1998	Carolina	Sou	82.0	94	39	10	19	44	4.28	4	5	10.32	1.10	2.09	4.83	0.81	4.50

Forced to return to Lynchburg because of a bad spring, one of the worst decisions this organization has made in the past few years. Ah Yat did eventually make it to AA and pitched reasonably well, although the higher H/IP rate is of concern. His stuff isn't overpowering, but his control and intelligence are. Gets little respect within the organization, obviously, but he will be a major-league pitcher.

Jimmy Anderson   Throws L   Age 23

YEAR	TEAM	LGE	IP	H	ER	HR	BB	K	ERA	W	L	H/9	HR/9	BB/9	K/9	KWH	PERA
1996	Lynchbrg	Car	64.0	59	25	3	22	41	3.52	4	3	8.30	0.42	3.09	5.77	0.97	3.09
1996	Carolina	Sou	94.7	108	39	3	39	61	3.71	6	5	10.27	0.29	3.71	5.80	0.66	4.09
1997	Carolina	Sou	24.7	17	5	1	8	18	1.82	2	1	6.20	0.36	2.92	6.57	1.79	1.82
1997	Calgary	PCL	110.0	104	51	8	58	60	4.17	6	6	8.51	0.65	4.75	4.91	0.45	3.60
1998	Nashvill	PCL	121.0	150	77	7	69	51	5.73	4	9	11.16	0.52	5.13	3.79	0.19	4.91

Converted to the bullpen with the same ugly results. There really is no such thing as a pitching prospect, as he looked like a lock after a strong '96 in Double-A.

Bronson Arroyo   Throws R   Age 22

YEAR	TEAM	LGE	IP	H	ER	HR	BB	K	ERA	W	L	H/9	HR/9	BB/9	K/9	KWH	PERA
1996	Augusta	SAL	123.7	182	87	16	41	65	6.33	4	10	13.25	1.16	2.98	4.73	0.42	6.11
1997	Lynchbrg	Car	153.3	192	75	19	32	86	4.40	8	9	11.27	1.12	1.88	5.05	0.90	4.99
1998	Carolina	Sou	127.3	168	76	19	43	72	5.37	5	9	11.87	1.34	3.04	5.09	0.54	5.65

Gave back his '97 gains and then some. His arm was hurting for part of the season, so we can't throw him out entirely, but the Double-A barrier smacked him around pretty good.

Kris Benson   Throws R   Age 24

YEAR	TEAM	LGE	IP	H	ER	HR	BB	K	ERA	W	L	H/9	HR/9	BB/9	K/9	KWH	PERA
1997	Lynchbrg	Car	57.3	62	23	1	13	50	3.61	3	3	9.73	0.16	2.04	7.85	2.33	3.45
1997	Carolina	Sou	68.0	87	42	11	30	52	5.56	3	5	11.51	1.46	3.97	6.88	0.78	5.69
1998	Nashvill	PCL	152.3	169	90	25	48	105	5.32	6	11	9.98	1.48	2.84	6.20	1.02	4.73

The Pirates are happy with Benson's season, pointing out that he stayed healthy, held his own in Triple-A in just his second season, etc. However, his mechanics aren't completely ironed out, and Triple-A has been a cemetery for Pirate pitchers lately. He has three major-league pitches, but didn't have command of them in at least a half-dozen starts this year. Will return to Triple-A for at least another half-season.

Jason Christiansen   Throws L   Age 29

YEAR	TEAM	LGE	IP	H	ER	HR	BB	K	ERA	W	L	H/9	HR/9	BB/9	K/9	KWH	PERA
1996	Pittsbrg	NL	46.3	58	30	7	19	35	5.83	2	3	11.27	1.36	3.69	6.80	0.83	5.44
1997	Carolina	Sou	14.3	20	7	1	5	17	4.40	1	1	12.56	0.63	3.14	10.67	2.17	5.65
1997	Pittsbrg	NL	35.7	36	8	2	16	33	2.02	3	1	9.08	0.50	4.04	8.33	1.42	3.79
1998	Pittsbrg	NL	66.3	53	19	2	25	65	2.58	5	2	7.19	0.27	3.39	8.82	2.39	2.44

As good as he ever was pre-injury. Christiansen remains effective against lefties and righties, and can easily throw two innings per stint. He struggled after a 4-inning, 54-pitch outing in July, although he was still above-average. Has campaigned openly for a shot at the closer role, which he deserves more than Loiselle.

Francisco Cordova — Throws R — Age 27

YEAR	TEAM	LGE	IP	H	ER	HR	BB	K	ERA	W	L	H/9	HR/9	BB/9	K/9	KWH	PERA
1996	Pittsbrg	NL	101.3	106	42	10	19	86	3.73	6	5	9.41	0.89	1.69	7.64	2.75	3.73
1997	Pittsbrg	NL	186.3	165	61	14	44	108	2.95	14	7	7.97	0.68	2.13	5.22	1.20	2.85
1998	Pittsbrg	NL	225.3	210	80	22	63	144	3.20	15	10	8.39	0.88	2.52	5.75	1.18	3.32

One of the best right-handed starters in baseball. His lack of run support is criminal: under four runs per game this year, well under five for his career. He didn't tire down the stretch this year as he did last year, although he still starts to bog down around the 95-105 pitch mark. An extreme groundballer, he'll be a star if the Pirates upgrade their infield defense.

Elmer Dessens — Throws R — Age 27

YEAR	TEAM	LGE	IP	H	ER	HR	BB	K	ERA	W	L	H/9	HR/9	BB/9	K/9	KWH	PERA
1996	Calgary	PCL	34.0	42	12	5	15	13	3.18	2	2	11.12	1.32	3.97	3.44	0.20	5.29
1996	Pittsbrg	NL	26.0	42	21	2	4	12	7.27	1	2	14.54	0.69	1.38	4.15	0.64	6.23
1998	Nashvill	PCL	28.3	36	12	2	6	10	3.81	2	1	11.44	0.64	1.91	3.18	0.35	4.76
1998	Pittsbrg	NL	77.0	93	44	10	23	40	5.14	3	6	10.87	1.17	2.69	4.68	0.56	4.91

Alternated stretches of dominating relief with stretches of total hittability. Won't put the fastball past anyone; he needs pin-point control, wild swingers, and Tom Glavine's umpires for any kind of protracted success. In the pen for '99; will post hot streaks now and then for the rest of his career.

Jason Haynie — Throws L — Age 25

YEAR	TEAM	LGE	IP	H	ER	HR	BB	K	ERA	W	L	H/9	HR/9	BB/9	K/9	KWH	PERA
1996	Erie	NYP	73.7	129	49	4	30	40	5.99	2	6	15.76	0.49	3.67	4.89	0.31	6.60
1997	Augusta	SAL	76.0	119	60	7	34	45	7.11	2	6	14.09	0.83	4.03	5.33	0.38	6.28
1997	Lynchbrg	Car	78.3	90	50	9	24	45	5.74	3	6	10.34	1.03	2.76	5.17	0.70	4.60
1998	Carolina	Sou	78.0	92	33	8	25	33	3.81	5	4	10.62	0.92	2.88	3.81	0.36	4.62

When healthy, Haynie has intriguing stuff, including a sinking fastball and a plus breaking ball. He had a strong first half but developed elbow soreness, and never got back to his original level. He rehabbed in the fall, and the team is optimistic he'll be fine for spring training. If so, he's a prospect.

Sean Lawrence — Throws L — Age 28

YEAR	TEAM	LGE	IP	H	ER	HR	BB	K	ERA	W	L	H/9	HR/9	BB/9	K/9	KWH	PERA
1996	Carolina	Sou	75.7	105	46	12	37	55	5.47	3	5	12.49	1.43	4.40	6.54	0.58	6.19
1997	Calgary	PCL	146.3	142	60	15	57	88	3.69	9	7	8.73	0.92	3.51	5.41	0.72	3.69
1998	Nashvill	PCL	138.3	175	88	19	61	93	5.73	5	10	11.39	1.24	3.97	6.05	0.61	5.40
1998	Pittsbrg	NL	20.3	27	14	4	9	11	6.20	1	1	11.95	1.77	3.98	4.87	0.37	6.20

Spent a year and a half getting Triple-A hitters out, so the Bucs gave him a chance, with which he did nothing. Throws a lot of junk and is prone to the longball, but you could have said the same of Mike Williams before '98, and he had a fantastic year under the Pete Vuckovich.

Jon Lieber — Throws R — Age 29

YEAR	TEAM	LGE	IP	H	ER	HR	BB	K	ERA	W	L	H/9	HR/9	BB/9	K/9	KWH	PERA
1996	Pittsbrg	NL	145.7	160	61	19	26	85	3.77	8	8	9.89	1.17	1.61	5.25	1.30	4.20
1997	Pittsbrg	NL	196.7	183	80	23	46	143	3.66	12	10	8.37	1.05	2.11	6.54	1.82	3.34
1998	Pittsbrg	NL	175.3	186	82	23	37	127	4.21	9	10	9.55	1.18	1.90	6.52	1.76	4.11

Came back from a groin injury for two ill-advised September starts that blew his ERA over 4. The great sign with Lieber is that he cured his home run problem after April, after giving up 8 of his 23 homers allowed in that month. If he can pitch the way he did after April and before the injury, he'll be an extremely valuable starter.

Rich Loiselle   Throws R   Age 27

YEAR	TEAM	LGE	IP	H	ER	HR	BB	K	ERA	W	L	H/9	HR/9	BB/9	K/9	KWH	PERA
1996	Jackson	Tex	90.3	134	55	7	31	53	5.48	3	7	13.35	0.70	3.09	5.28	0.51	5.78
1996	Calgary	PCL	50.0	67	25	3	16	34	4.50	3	3	12.06	0.54	2.88	6.12	0.81	5.04
1996	Tucson	PCL	33.3	28	17	1	11	26	4.59	2	2	7.56	0.27	2.97	7.02	1.65	2.43
1996	Pittsbrg	NL	21.0	24	7	3	7	8	3.00	1	1	10.29	1.29	3.00	3.43	0.29	4.71
1997	Pittsbrg	NL	76.0	73	22	7	22	59	2.61	6	2	8.64	0.83	2.61	6.99	1.63	3.43
1998	Pittsbrg	NL	57.3	59	23	2	34	45	3.61	3	3	9.26	0.31	5.34	7.06	0.76	3.92

One-trick pony who fell behind hitters a little too often. He can't throw anything but the heater for strikes, which is fine if the heater was about 98 with movement (see below), but it's not. Loiselle could be an adequate short-relief righty out of the pen, but he's not likely to have another protracted stretch of success like he did in '97.

Javier Martinez   Throws R   Age 22

YEAR	TEAM	LGE	IP	H	ER	HR	BB	K	ERA	W	L	H/9	HR/9	BB/9	K/9	KWH	PERA
1996	Rockford	Mid	56.7	64	27	7	30	36	4.29	3	3	10.16	1.11	4.76	5.72	0.51	4.76
1997	Rockford	Mid	76.0	108	65	9	53	48	7.70	2	6	12.79	1.07	6.28	5.68	0.30	6.16
1997	Daytona	Fla	52.0	76	39	10	31	27	6.75	2	4	13.15	1.73	5.37	4.67	0.23	6.92
1998	Pittsbrg	NL	43.3	41	28	6	32	39	5.82	2	3	8.52	1.25	6.65	8.10	0.87	4.36

The man cooks with gas. Throws up to 98 with movement, plus a slider he's learning to control. As a Rule 5er, he was up before he was ready, but Lamont tried to use him more and more down the stretch so he'd be ready for winter ball. Could be back as soon as this fall, and if he can handle his newfound power, he will be very, very good.

Brian O'Connor   Throws L   Age 22

YEAR	TEAM	LGE	IP	H	ER	HR	BB	K	ERA	W	L	H/9	HR/9	BB/9	K/9	KWH	PERA
1996	Erie	NYP	66.3	105	70	7	56	39	9.50	1	6	14.25	0.95	7.60	5.29	0.19	6.78
1997	Augusta	SAL	79.7	124	66	8	48	60	7.46	2	7	14.01	0.90	5.42	6.78	0.45	6.44
1997	Lynchbrg	Car	12.7	14	5	0	6	10	3.55	1	0	9.95	0.00	4.26	7.11	0.89	3.55
1998	Lynchbrg	Car	83.7	109	39	4	26	58	4.20	4	5	11.73	0.43	2.80	6.24	0.89	4.73
1998	Carolina	Sou	65.3	95	56	12	45	33	7.71	1	6	13.09	1.65	6.20	4.55	0.19	6.89

Pirate player development folk think O'Connor has some of the best stuff of any lefty in the system. Showed signs that he was learning how to pitch in Lynchburg, but was not ready for Double-A. The Pirates are grooming him for the LH middle-relief role that Tabaka filled last year.

Chris Peters   Throws L   Age 27

YEAR	TEAM	LGE	IP	H	ER	HR	BB	K	ERA	W	L	H/9	HR/9	BB/9	K/9	KWH	PERA
1996	Carolina	Sou	88.0	90	40	5	33	49	4.09	5	5	9.20	0.51	3.38	5.01	0.61	3.68
1996	Calgary	PCL	27.3	19	2	0	8	13	0.66	3	0	6.26	0.00	2.63	4.28	0.83	1.65
1996	Pittsbrg	NL	65.7	75	38	9	24	25	5.21	3	4	10.28	1.23	3.29	3.43	0.26	4.80
1997	Calgary	PCL	52.7	48	23	4	29	43	3.93	3	3	8.20	0.68	4.96	7.35	1.00	3.59
1997	Pittsbrg	NL	39.3	37	19	7	19	15	4.35	2	2	8.47	1.60	4.35	3.43	0.24	4.12
1998	Pittsbrg	NL	152.0	147	56	13	50	95	3.32	10	7	8.70	0.77	2.96	5.62	0.92	3.49

The Pirates' second-best starter this year, and an absolute savior after Silva went down. Peters repeatedly said he wanted his chance to start, and unlike many such complainants, he did something with it. Doesn't throw hard, but has three pitches with movement, and throws them all for strikes at will. He rattles less easily than any other Pirate pitcher, which is key on a young staff like this.

Jason Phillips Throws R Age 25

YEAR	TEAM	LGE	IP	H	ER	HR	BB	K	ERA	W	L	H/9	HR/9	BB/9	K/9	KWH	PERA
1996	Augusta	SAL	79.3	125	53	5	36	42	6.01	3	6	14.18	0.57	4.08	4.76	0.29	6.13
1996	Lynchbrg	Car	71.3	98	51	4	39	46	6.43	2	6	12.36	0.50	4.92	5.80	0.42	5.43
1997	Lynchbrg	Car	130.0	172	80	12	37	92	5.54	5	9	11.91	0.83	2.56	6.37	1.00	5.12
1997	Carolina	Sou	30.7	22	7	1	9	17	2.05	2	1	6.46	0.29	2.64	4.99	1.09	1.76
1998	Carolina	Sou	147.3	182	82	15	47	84	5.01	6	10	11.12	0.92	2.87	5.13	0.62	4.89
1998	Nashvill	PCL	30.3	40	9	3	12	17	2.67	2	1	11.87	0.89	3.56	5.04	0.45	5.34

Not a terrible year, but not one marked by great progress. Throws a plus fastball and a hard curve, but he lost ground gained in '97 with his control. Still needs to learn how to pitch, instead of just throw. He's got the stuff, but his learning curve so far has been steep.

Kevin Pickford Throws L Age 24

YEAR	TEAM	LGE	IP	H	ER	HR	BB	K	ERA	W	L	H/9	HR/9	BB/9	K/9	KWH	PERA
1996	Lynchbrg	Car	167.3	225	102	19	26	74	5.49	7	12	12.10	1.02	1.40	3.98	0.70	5.22
1997	Lynchbrg	Car	70.0	90	35	3	11	34	4.50	4	4	11.57	0.39	1.41	4.37	0.88	4.37
1997	Carolina	Sou	29.0	52	25	3	14	19	7.76	1	2	16.14	0.93	4.34	5.90	0.37	7.14
1998	Carolina	Sou	57.3	52	22	7	12	33	3.45	3	3	8.16	1.10	1.88	5.18	1.31	3.14
1998	Nashvill	PCL	78.3	86	29	7	20	48	3.33	5	4	9.88	0.80	2.30	5.51	1.00	4.02

A real breakthrough year, moving up to Triple-A a year after he started his third season in A-ball. Pickford's fastball is only in the mid-80s, but it has good tailing movement, and he works inside very effectively, especially to right-handers. His breaking pitch would be bleacher-food in the majors, so they have to keep working with him. Considered the best-hitting pitcher in the chain.

Ricardo Rincon Throws L Age 29

YEAR	TEAM	LGE	IP	H	ER	HR	BB	K	ERA	W	L	H/9	HR/9	BB/9	K/9	KWH	PERA
1997	Pittsbrg	NL	62.7	49	20	5	22	64	2.87	5	2	7.04	0.72	3.16	9.19	2.85	2.59
1998	Pittsbrg	NL	66.7	52	27	6	27	59	3.65	4	3	7.02	0.81	3.65	7.97	1.86	2.70

When he came off the DL, he was unhittable. When August rolled around, he was erratic. Irregular use in July was a contributing factor, but not the only one; even when his usage patterns returned to normal, he still couldn't find the handle. That said, he is still one of the best LH relievers in baseball, and I see no reason to expect that to change now that he's in Cleveland.

Jason Schmidt Throws R Age 26

YEAR	TEAM	LGE	IP	H	ER	HR	BB	K	ERA	W	L	H/9	HR/9	BB/9	K/9	KWH	PERA
1996	Richmond	Int	44.7	40	16	2	19	35	3.22	3	2	8.06	0.40	3.83	7.05	1.21	3.02
1996	Atlanta	NL	61.0	74	43	8	31	44	6.34	2	5	10.92	1.18	4.57	6.49	0.63	5.16
1996	Pittsbrg	NL	39.0	41	16	2	20	24	3.69	2	2	9.46	0.46	4.62	5.54	0.53	3.92
1997	Pittsbrg	NL	197.0	185	84	16	69	122	3.84	11	11	8.45	0.73	3.15	5.57	0.87	3.38
1998	Pittsbrg	NL	220.3	235	94	24	65	146	3.84	12	12	9.60	0.98	2.66	5.96	1.05	4.08

Took a step forward, then one back, then a half-step forward at the end of the season. Unlike Peters, Schmidt seemed to rattle easily, running off five or six scoreless innings, then completely losing his cool after a tough-luck play.

Jose Silva Throws R Age 25

YEAR	TEAM	LGE	IP	H	ER	HR	BB	K	ERA	W	L	H/9	HR/9	BB/9	K/9	KWH	PERA
1996	Knoxvill	Sou	45.3	50	24	3	21	21	4.76	2	3	9.93	0.60	4.17	4.17	0.31	4.17
1997	Calgary	PCL	70.3	60	15	3	20	45	1.92	7	1	7.68	0.38	2.56	5.76	1.27	2.56
1997	Pittsbrg	NL	38.7	51	21	4	15	27	4.89	2	2	11.87	0.93	3.49	6.28	0.71	5.35
1998	Pittsbrg	NL	103.0	107	48	7	27	59	4.19	5	6	9.35	0.61	2.36	5.16	0.90	3.67

Don't believe the numbers: Silva posted an 8.38 ERA in four September starts after returning from the injury. Before that, he performed above expectations, with a 3.44 ERA in 14 starts. He was on track for over 170 innings, so the injury may have helped him in that roundabout manner. When his arm isn't broken, he throws into the mid-90s with a nasty slider and a developing changeup.

Jeff Tabaka   Throws L   Age 35

YEAR	TEAM	LGE	IP	H	ER	HR	BB	K	ERA	W	L	H/9	HR/9	BB/9	K/9	KWH	PERA
1996	Tucson	PCL	42.0	44	14	2	22	40	3.00	3	2	9.43	0.43	4.71	8.57	1.24	3.86
1996	Houston	NL	20.3	31	17	6	13	16	7.52	0	2	13.72	2.66	5.75	7.08	0.48	7.97
1997	Indianap	AmA	55.3	54	21	5	21	52	3.42	3	3	8.78	0.81	3.42	8.46	1.79	3.58
1998	Pittsbrg	NL	52.3	38	17	7	20	37	2.92	4	2	6.54	1.20	3.44	6.36	1.35	2.58

Another unheralded but effective reliever in the Pirates' pen. In one of the more unusual splits you'll see, Tabaka posted a 1.44 ERA and a .155 opponent's BA when he appeared in the first six innings of a game, but a 4.56 ERA and a .247 OpBA in innings seven and later. Come to think of it, that's not the ideal profile for an effective reliever.

Todd Van Poppel   Throws R   Age 27

YEAR	TEAM	LGE	IP	H	ER	HR	BB	K	ERA	W	L	H/9	HR/9	BB/9	K/9	KWH	PERA
1996	Oakland	AL	65.0	84	44	11	27	37	6.09	2	5	11.63	1.52	3.74	5.12	0.45	5.68
1996	Detroit	AL	37.7	51	39	10	24	16	9.32	1	3	12.19	2.39	5.73	3.82	0.16	6.93
1997	Charlott	Fla	31.0	54	28	4	13	21	8.13	1	2	15.68	1.16	3.77	6.10	0.47	7.26
1997	Tulsa	Tex	39.0	63	28	2	17	19	6.46	1	3	14.54	0.46	3.92	4.38	0.25	6.23
1997	Omaha	AmA	38.7	58	36	10	26	23	8.38	1	3	13.50	2.33	6.05	5.35	0.26	7.68
1998	Oklahoma	PCL	81.3	103	46	10	27	51	5.09	3	6	11.40	1.11	2.99	5.64	0.70	5.20
1998	Pittsbrg	NL	48.3	55	28	4	17	30	5.21	2	3	10.24	0.74	3.17	5.59	0.72	4.28
1998	Texas	AL	20.7	25	15	5	9	10	6.53	1	1	10.89	2.18	3.92	4.35	0.33	6.10

Needs help. The stuff is there, but the command and control aren't, and sometimes the stuff isn't there after all. Pushed off the 40-man roster in October; could be a Rule 5 pick, could spend '99 at the Bucs' Triple-A club trying to find new life in relief.

Marc Wilkins   Throws R   Age 28

YEAR	TEAM	LGE	IP	H	ER	HR	BB	K	ERA	W	L	H/9	HR/9	BB/9	K/9	KWH	PERA
1996	Pittsbrg	NL	77.7	78	32	6	35	56	3.71	5	4	9.04	0.70	4.06	6.49	0.86	3.82
1997	Pittsbrg	NL	79.0	62	25	7	30	42	2.85	6	3	7.06	0.80	3.42	4.78	0.71	2.62
1998	Pittsbrg	NL	16.0	14	5	1	8	16	2.81	1	1	7.88	0.56	4.50	9.00	1.71	3.37

Out with a shoulder injury, unrelated to his May prize fight with Tabaka. Given the success of Williams, Tabaka, and other castoffs living in the pen, Wilkins will have to fight for a job when he returns. Jeff Wallace is also expected back next spring after missing the year with reconstructive surgery, but as a lefty, he'll get a few more lives.

Mike Williams   Throws R   Age 30

YEAR	TEAM	LGE	IP	H	ER	HR	BB	K	ERA	W	L	H/9	HR/9	BB/9	K/9	KWH	PERA
1996	Philadel	NL	169.0	200	98	26	64	93	5.22	7	12	10.65	1.38	3.41	4.95	0.51	5.06
1997	Omaha	AmA	81.7	78	38	9	41	54	4.19	4	5	8.60	0.99	4.52	5.95	0.68	3.86
1997	KansasCy	AL	15.0	20	9	1	7	10	5.40	1	1	12.00	0.60	4.20	6.00	0.54	5.40
1998	Nashvill	PCL	34.3	43	25	11	14	25	6.55	1	3	11.27	2.88	3.67	6.55	0.78	6.55
1998	Pittsbrg	NL	52.0	41	11	1	14	54	1.90	5	1	7.10	0.17	2.42	9.35	3.81	2.08

Changeups and a pretty nasty slurve added up to the best statistical relief season of any Pirate. He kept heating up down the stretch, allowing just four earned runs while striking out 34 in 25.2 August and September innings. He's the #1 righty reliever behind Loiselle going into '99.

SNWLP					PITTSBURGH PIRATES							Park Effect: +0.4%	
PITCHER	GS	IP	R	SNW	SNL	SNPCT	W	L	RA	APW	SNVA	SNWAR
Cordova, F.	33	220.0	91	14.4	9.8	.596	13	14	3.72	2.40	2.29	4.13
Dessens, E.	5	26.7	20	1.3	2.2	.361	0	4	6.75	-0.58	-0.42	-0.23
Lawrence, S.	3	13.3	11	0.5	1.4	.256	1	1	7.43	-0.39	-0.47	-0.32
Lieber, J.	28	170.7	93	10.0	10.2	.494	8	14	4.90	-0.32	-0.20	1.39
Loaiza, E.	14	78.3	45	4.2	5.5	.429	4	5	5.17	-0.37	-0.63	0.04
Peters, C.	21	124.7	57	7.4	6.1	.548	8	8	4.11	0.83	0.66	1.65
Schmidt, J.	33	214.3	106	12.0	11.4	.514	11	14	4.45	0.65	0.25	2.08
Silva, J.	18	100.3	55	6.4	6.2	.507	6	7	4.93	-0.22	-0.07	1.03
VanPoppel, T.	7	37.0	26	1.7	3.1	.359	1	1	6.32	-0.64	-0.64	-0.32
Williams, M.	1	5.0	1	0.4	0.1	.766	1	0	1.80	0.16	0.11	0.18
TOTALS	163	990.3	505	58.2	56.1	.509	53	68	4.59	1.52	0.88	9.66

In 1997 the Pirates had the most consistent and dependable rotation in the majors. Their rotation at the beginning of the season took all but five of the team's starts, and each member of the rotation finished within 60 points of a .500 SNPct. Because of injuries and the Loaiza trade, the Pirates lost some of that consistency last year, and it hurt them. The four guys who made spot starts—Dessens, Lawrence, Williams, and the legendary Todd Van Poppel—had a combined SN record of 3.9-6.8 (.364). The continued development of the young core members of the Pirates rotation compensated for the lousy spot starters. From 1997 to 1998, Francisco Cordova improved his SNVA by a full game, and Jason Schmidt was up .35. Only Esteban Loaiza saw a meaningful decline in his numbers, and he was shipped off to the desperate Rangers in July. Chris Peters and Jose Silva each saw extended duty in the rotation for the first time, and each responded with a solid season. The overall result was that the Pirates' numbers improved from 1997, up 0.7 games in SNVA and up from 15th to 12th in their major league rank.

Pitcher Abuse Points

PITCHER	AGE	GS	PAP	PAP/S	AAW	MAX	115+	130+
Cordova, Francisco	26	33	257	7.79	15.58	138	5	1
Dessens, Elmer	26	5	0	0.00	0.00	94	0	0
Lieber, Jon	28	28	139	4.96	8.27	116	2	0
Loaiza, Esteban	26	14	30	2.14	4.29	116	1	0
Peters, Chris	26	21	47	2.24	4.48	116	1	0
Schmidt, Jason	25	33	648	19.64	42.55	139	14	1
Silva, Jose	24	18	21	1.17	2.72	110	0	0
Van Poppel, Todd	26	7	6	0.86	1.71	105	0	0
TOTAL		163	1148	7.04	14.51	139	23	2
RANKING-NL			9	9	6		9	7

Gene Lamont, friend and disciple of Jim Leyland, is fortunately nothing like him in terms of how he treats his starters. With one major exception, Lamont had the kid gloves on. Francisco Cordova blossomed into the staff ace in 1997, and Jose Silva was pitching extremely well before going out with a non-arm-related injury. But Jason Schmidt must have irked Lamont somewhere along the way, or else he thinks the ex-Brave keeps a packet of Mazzone's Magical Medicine in his back pocket. Schmidt still has the best stuff on the team and could yet become a 20-game winner, but only if he avoids injury.

St. Louis Cardinals

Mark McGwire's tremendous season has already killed more than its share of trees, so let's talk about what's really interesting about the Cardinals. Are they creating a future where major league organizations no longer need their own farm systems?

It would be ironic for the organization that created the modern minors under Branch Rickey to be the first to come to the conclusion that you don't need the status quo with the minor leagues to build a successful organization. In effect, that's a potential repercussion of what's happening with the Cardinals right now, because the way they're playing the player development game is redefining the relationship between professional baseball and amateur talent as well as the relationship between the major and minor leagues.

The many gripes about "small market" versus "big market" have generally skipped over a growing trend in player development. The June amateur draft has become a two-tiered setup where the division between the haves and have-nots is becoming even more dramatic than it is anywhere else in organized baseball. Every summer, we get to hear various euphemisms for poverty from general managers with early picks who kick around their choices about who they're going to select. The usual claim is that teams are concerned with a player's "signability," especially and none-too-coincidentally if he happens to have a heavy hitter like Scott Boras representing or "advising" him. As a result, the amateur draft has become meaningless in terms of what it is supposed to do. Whereas it's supposed to give losing teams the chance to rebuild themselves with amateur talent, it's turned into a sham where teams who want to spend big money on player development will, and where teams that aren't spending that kind of money get to build farm systems like the Phillies'. The draft has become a question not of teams selecting the best available amateur talent to help themselves, but of some teams doing it while others select the best available and affordable amateur talent.

The issue of how much cash teams are willing to spend for talent has played out on a lesser scale (but with more publicity) with expensive foreign amateur signings, whether they're Japanese veterans or Cuban émigrés or Australian or Korean teen-agers. Some organizations have elected to stay out of this field, while others had the foresight to build baseball academies and player development programs in talent pipelines like Venezuela or the Dominican Republic years ago.

That doesn't necessarily mean that teams spending money in the draft or on foreign talent will reap all the benefits, sign all the real prospects, or re-create the miseries of baseball in the '50s, when only the few competed and contended. One of the nice things about player development is how often organizations, scouts, and people like you and I end up being surprised by who the sleepers and the washouts turn out to be. As smart as some organizations may be, they're still going to crank out their share of turkeys. "Signability" issues seems to be making some pretty disappointing players high draft picks, which has more to do with their willingness to ink a contract than it may with actual talent. For that reason, it would be cavalier to merely dismiss bad drafts these days as the products of bad front office decisions, because money and its discontents have more to do with sudden fame and equally sudden disappointment for players like Phil Nevin than just talent. But the flip side of the coin is that big financial investments do not consistently or automatically yield big payoffs when it comes to amateur and foreign talent, if you wanted to talk about Glenn Williams or Robinson Checo or Ariel Prieto or Katsuhiro Maeda, among others.

Even with those concerns, there is big-ticket domestic talent about which some sort of consensus about their major league potential greatness exists, which is where economic disparities between major league teams entering the amateur draft becomes an issue. Perhaps J.D. Drew brought this to the fore by telling the Phillies he could afford to wait for a year, but his case wasn't really as unique as it was invested with media drama. Pete Incaviglia told the Expos he wasn't interested in them, which got him on the Rangers without spending a day in the minors. As a result, we got a few years' worth of poisonous articles about Inky's "bad attitude" from gray-bearded eminences from Jerome Holtzman on down.

Cardinals Prospectus

1998 record: 83-79; Third place, NL Central

Pythagorean W/L: 84-78

Runs scored: 810 (5th in NL)

Runs allowed: 782 (9th in NL)

Team EQA: .271 (4th in NL)

Park: Busch Stadium (neutral)

1998: The team was a forgotten sideshow to the Greatest Show on Earth.

1999: Quietly getting younger, the Cardinals should be part of the wild-card chase.

College players who decide to stick with their amateur careers instead of accepting whatever they're offered by major league teams (A.J. Hinch or Jason Varitek, for example) end up having their "commitment to baseball" questioned. These are the same sour grapes that the owners have been stomping to crank out some fine media whines since Curt Flood. What the J.D. Drew case really means for baseball is that the secret is out: there is a significant division within baseball between the teams that want to throw money at player development and those who don't. And everyone—players, prospects, agents, scouts, and front office personnel—knows it.

No team illustrates that as boldly as the Cardinals in the last two years. The meaning of the selections and signings of players who other teams thought they couldn't sign, like Rick Ankiel and J.D. Drew and Chad Hutchinson in the last two drafts, boils down to this: the Cardinals can pay top dollar for outstanding amateur talent where other teams are hesitant to do so. They're also clearly unafraid of haggling with Scott Boras. Both points are to their significant advantage in terms of procuring talent. As other teams fall into the trap of feeling they have to perpetuate their weakness in the standings by scrimping on player development costs, the Cardinals skip gut checks and get straight to the bottom line. Signing Ankiel and Drew probably gives them the best tandem of prospects in baseball today, and that's without mentioning their Dominican find, Pablo Ozuna.

This aggressive policy stands in contrast to the spotty record of Cardinals' player development when pursued through "normal" means. We could keep kicking Carl Dale or Bret Wagner or Corey Avrard or Mike Busby or Sean Lowe. That isn't fair, because the Cardinals aren't that much different from other teams on this score, if you want to judge them in terms of what they've done when they aren't taking advantage of other teams' tight purse strings. In the last five years, probably their best pick that wasn't one of the "unsignables" like Drew or Ankiel or Hutchinson was 1994 22nd-rounder: Jose Leon out of Puerto Rico.

What's intriguing about the Cardinals' organization is the big gap between the prospects who they're clearly invested in, and the draft picks who serve little better purpose than to give the prospects teammates. The message here is that the Cardinals, like every team, have a few dozen "organizational soldiers," whose professional existence is defined and limited to their contributions on fields in Peoria or Prince William or Arkansas.

The question is why teams have to bother with employing them at all. Because it's traditional? Or because someone like a Jose Leon might fall through the cracks? Whether or not the divisions over the amateur draft lead to its abolition, there's no requirement that major league organizations field teams or sign everybody. The player's association is almost completely unengaged on the subject of minor league employment and compensation, which gives owners room to maneuver and change their relationship with the National Association in terms of how the minor leagues are operated.

Say the amateur draft gets abolished, what could happen? Major league teams could disengage from the ownership and operation of minor league teams, focusing only on signing high-risk, high-yield talent, and negotiating for jobs for their prospects with minor league operators. That would leave generation after generation of organizational soldiers to find work for themselves in the minor leagues. That may sound uncertain or rotten for those guys, but what that could create would be good, and not dissimilar from how the Caribbean winter leagues work out each season. Amateurs would have to earn their jobs and prove themselves in the minors, at which point they would have the freedom to sign contracts with major league teams at any stage of their minor league careers. That's potentially much more lucrative for these guys in terms of signing bonuses. Major league teams would no longer have to operate minor league teams, but could create working agreements with minor league operators to provide some (but not all) of the players for their rosters. Minor league operators would have greater freedom to put together their own teams, and by having a greater say in who they're going to have, could re-invest the pennant races of their leagues with some significance.

Things won't end up this way, but the potential to create a system that creates greater freedom for both players and management is there. One way or another, major changes to the way player development works are going happen within the next ten years.

What about the Cardinals and their major league team? As feared, Tony LaRussa continued fragging and slagging his starters, proving yet again that if we want to talk about what he's going to do, we have to remember his entire career as a manager: his overuse of a good young rotation in Chicago, as well as his subsequent overreliance on veterans in Oakland. For Cardinals fans, that means they get the best of both worlds: not only will they get to see a widely hailed genius blow out an Alan Benes or abuse a Matt Morris, they also get to appreciate Bobby Witt's golden years.

LaRussa goofed off with batting the pitcher eighth after the All-Star break, but it worked after a fashion: their runs scored per game dropped infinitesimally (from 4.98 to 4.96 per game), but their record in games they used the pitcher in the eighth slot was 43-30. That could also be meaningless: I think it's more significant that Matt Morris was in the rotation or that the staff ERA was a run lower after the break in terms of wins or losses than this sort of tactical chicanery.

If LaRussa continues to plow through his rotation and his roster as if every game was the seventh game of the World Series, the Cardinals will continue to undermine their ability to push the Astros or compete for the wild card. But by making room for J.D. Drew in the major leagues right now, the Cardinals are building up a potentially great team for the next six to ten years. They've made room for young players like Eli Marrero, and they're in a position to make more room for players like Pablo Ozuna or Jose Leon. As long as they don't waste Rick Ankiel like they wasted Alan Benes, they have the foundation for an unmatched mix of top-notch major league talent (McGwire, Lankford) and the best young talent in baseball today. If LaRussa has the patience to let it happen, the Astros' budding dynasty is going to have some competition.

HITTERS (Averages: BA .260/ OBA .330/ SA .420, EQA .260)

Brent Butler — SS — Bats R — Age 21

YEAR	TEAM	LGE	AB	H	DB	TP	HR	BB	R	RBI	SB	CS	OUT	BA	OBA	SA	EQA	EQR	DEFENSE
1996	JohnsnCy	App	249	69	9	0	6	15	24	28	3	1	181	.277	.318	.386	.245	27	55-SS 84
1997	Peoria	Mid	481	129	19	0	14	50	55	58	3	2	354	.268	.337	.395	.256	59	123-SS 99
1998	Pr Willm	Car	483	132	17	1	12	39	49	56	2	2	353	.273	.328	.387	.248	54	112-SS 103
1999	St Louis	NL	450	129	19	1	12	37	51	58	4	2	323	.287	.341	.413	.266	59	

Butler has no real holes in his game to iron out. He was supposed to work on hitting to all fields, and he can. There are concerns about his arm, which is why the Cardinals have reservations about leaving him at short. That's going to happen when you also have Pablo Ozuna and Adam Kennedy and Jason Woolf. In that crowd, Butler's the second-best prospect, but still good enough to be one of the five best prospects at short in the minors today.

Stubby Clapp — 2B — Bats L — Age 26

YEAR	TEAM	LGE	AB	H	DB	TP	HR	BB	R	RBI	SB	CS	OUT	BA	OBA	SA	EQA	EQR	DEFENSE	
1997	Pr Willm	Car	273	71	11	3	3	37	35	28	4	2	204	.260	.348	.355	.252	32	40-2B 85	27-OF 89
1998	Arkansas	Tex	509	101	13	3	7	63	42	32	9	6	414	.198	.287	.277	.198	36	136-2B 100	
1999	St Louis	NL	403	91	15	2	7	50	43	35	10	5	317	.226	.311	.325	.230	40		

A patient hitter, Stubby does things to entertain folks: pregame backflips, hustling, getting his uniform dirty. You can't help but hope he gets the cup of coffee someday, so that he can take an honored place in baseball history alongside Shooty Babbitt and Slammin' Sammy Khalifa.

Delino Deshields — 2B — Bats L — Age 30

YEAR	TEAM	LGE	AB	H	DB	TP	HR	BB	R	RBI	SB	CS	OUT	BA	OBA	SA	EQA	EQR	DEFENSE
1996	LosAngls	NL	585	137	13	8	6	57	71	41	43	12	460	.234	.302	.315	.227	56	145-2B 100
1997	St Louis	NL	573	172	28	12	13	58	101	72	47	15	416	.300	.365	.459	.288	93	136-2B 95
1998	St Louis	NL	418	121	20	8	8	58	75	51	28	11	308	.289	.376	.433	.285	67	101-2B 92
1999	Baltimor	AL	478	130	19	7	9	55	75	53	29	12	360	.272	.347	.397	.266	66	

Even now, folks are still calling him an underachiever. If this isn't a race thing, I don't know what is. He's one of the league's best and fastest base runners, an adequate fielder, and a good hitter. Since only one team gets to have Craig Biggio, I don't understand what the problem is. I hope he gets his due in Baltimore.

Nate Dishington — 1B — Bats L — Age 24

YEAR	TEAM	LGE	AB	H	DB	TP	HR	BB	R	RBI	SB	CS	OUT	BA	OBA	SA	EQA	EQR	DEFENSE
1996	Peoria	Mid	211	41	7	1	3	18	13	12	1	1	171	.194	.258	.280	.179	12	16-1B 72
1997	Pr Willm	Car	457	117	11	3	23	66	60	68	5	3	343	.256	.350	.444	.274	68	98-1B 88
1998	Arkansas	Tex	235	51	4	0	11	32	25	27	4	1	185	.217	.311	.374	.242	27	63-1B 92
1998	Memphis	PCL	197	49	9	1	9	23	24	27	1	1	149	.249	.327	.442	.263	26	27-1B 95
1999	St Louis	NL	390	99	15	1	19	46	47	56	5	2	293	.254	.333	.444	.271	56	

Probably the best power-hitting prospect in the organization, in the organization with the best power hitter on the planet coincidentally playing his position. Rats. He's not really a candidate to move to another position, so he's trade bait.

J.D. Drew   **OF**   **Bats L   Age 23**

YEAR	TEAM	LGE	AB	H	DB	TP	HR	BB	R	RBI	SB	CS	OUT	BA	OBA	SA	EQA	EQR	DEFENSE
1997	St Paul	Nrt	165	47	3	1	10	23	23	29	2	2	120	.285	.372	.497	.294	28	
1998	St Paul	Nrt	109	35	6	1	5	16	21	19	4	1	75	.321	.408	.532	.321	22	
1998	Arkansas	Tex	66	20	0	1	4	10	10	13	1	1	47	.303	.395	.515	.307	12	
1998	Memphis	PCL	78	23	6	1	2	20	16	13	1	2	58	.295	.439	.474	.313	16	23-OF 116
1998	St Louis	NL	36	15	3	1	5	4	9	13	0	0	21	.417	.475	.972	.430	13	
1999	*St Louis*	*NL*	*226*	*73*	*11*	*1*	*15*	*38*	*41*	*48*	*5*	*3*	*156*	*.323*	*.420*	*.580*	*.336*	*51*	

Is that all? Call me greedy, but I wanted more from his projection. His few weeks in the Texas League were enough to get him named its #3 prospect. I'm sure that's got a hundred kids wondering how they can get Scott Boras on their side, rather than cave in and take $10,000 to skip college or something. Drew is the complete package: strong arm, good range, and a compact, vicious swing that generates tremendous power. He's good enough in the field to push Lankford out of center right now, but it looks like he'll be in right.

Ron Gant   **LF**   **Bats R   Age 34**

YEAR	TEAM	LGE	AB	H	DB	TP	HR	BB	R	RBI	SB	CS	OUT	BA	OBA	SA	EQA	EQR	DEFENSE
1996	St Louis	NL	420	103	14	2	30	75	67	72	11	4	321	.245	.360	.502	.293	74	101-OF 98
1997	St Louis	NL	502	115	19	4	18	61	58	56	12	6	393	.229	.313	.390	.245	58	113-OF 102
1998	St Louis	NL	381	90	16	1	27	53	53	62	9	0	291	.236	.329	.496	.282	61	91-OF 89
1999	*Philadel*	*NL*	*396*	*90*	*15*	*1*	*22*	*60*	*51*	*56*	*10*	*3*	*309*	*.227*	*.329*	*.437*	*.268*	*58*	

Considered a big disappointment, but it isn't that much of a stretch to just recalibrate the ol' disappointometer to find that he was a useful player in '96 and '98. His hamstring cost him about a month, and he's always going to lose that kind of time to injuries. Traded to the Phillies in the Bottalico deal, he'll definitely help give them the power they thought they'd get from Danny Tartabull, if he's healthy enough to play in 120 games.

Chris Haas   **3B**   **Bats L   Age 22**

YEAR	TEAM	LGE	AB	H	DB	TP	HR	BB	R	RBI	SB	CS	OUT	BA	OBA	SA	EQA	EQR	DEFENSE
1996	Peoria	Mid	428	91	7	1	10	48	34	34	2	1	338	.213	.292	.304	.208	34	114-3B 99
1997	Peoria	Mid	116	33	4	0	5	17	17	18	2	0	83	.284	.376	.448	.290	19	20-3B 114
1997	Pr Willm	Car	366	82	6	1	12	34	29	35	1	1	285	.224	.290	.344	.219	32	97-3B 104
1998	Arkansas	Tex	439	103	15	2	15	60	49	51	1	1	337	.235	.327	.380	.248	52	104-3B 97
1999	*St Louis*	*NL*	*443*	*108*	*14*	*1*	*15*	*54*	*47*	*53*	*2*	*1*	*336*	*.244*	*.326*	*.381*	*.251*	*53*	

If the Cards are creative, they'll give Haas every opportunity to work his way into a platoon with Tatis at third. He isn't a terrible third baseman; he has a very strong arm, but he is relatively heavy and immobile. He's got very good power, good strike-zone judgment, and he hits lefty. His name isn't up in lights like the Cards' top prospects, but Haas is a very good prospect in his own right.

Tyrone Horne   **OF**   **Bats L   Age 28**

YEAR	TEAM	LGE	AB	H	DB	TP	HR	BB	R	RBI	SB	CS	OUT	BA	OBA	SA	EQA	EQR	DEFENSE
1996	Edmonton	PCL	202	37	5	1	3	26	16	11	4	2	167	.183	.276	.262	.189	13	43-OF 94
1996	Binghmtn	Eas	125	27	3	0	3	11	9	10	2	0	98	.216	.279	.312	.207	10	16-OF 83
1997	KaneCnty	Mid	477	107	7	1	11	70	50	43	7	4	374	.224	.324	.312	.229	47	31-OF 88
1998	Arkansas	Tex	436	106	5	1	19	51	48	53	10	5	335	.243	.322	.390	.249	52	88-OF 88
1999	*Philadel*	*NL*	*422*	*100*	*9*	*1*	*14*	*50*	*44*	*46*	*8*	*3*	*325*	*.237*	*.318*	*.363*	*.243*	*47*	

After years of being ignored in the Expos' chain, where they don't care much for people who draw walks, Horne has bounced through six organizations in four years, and hitting wherever he goes. He's a minor league free agent, which means he'll probably get snookered to sign with Boston, where he'll get ten at-bats with the Red Sox before being stranded in Pawtucket for the year. He isn't quite good enough to be the next Matt Stairs, but he can hit well enough to help a team as a spare part and pinch-hitter.

David Howard   **SS**   **Bats B** **Age 32**

YEAR	TEAM	LGE	AB	H	DB	TP	HR	BB	R	RBI	SB	CS	OUT	BA	OBA	SA	EQA	EQR	DEFENSE	
1996	KansasCy	AL	414	86	13	5	4	38	30	26	5	7	335	.208	.274	.292	.192	27	129-SS 102	
1997	KansasCy	AL	159	37	7	1	1	11	12	11	2	2	124	.233	.282	.308	.202	11	28-2B 94	17-OF 81
1998	St Louis	NL	101	24	2	1	2	13	10	10	0	0	77	.238	.325	.337	.235	10		
1999	St Louis	NL	167	38	6	1	2	16	14	13	1	2	131	.228	.295	.311	.213	14		

From the "Things Could Have Been Worse" file: what if Howard doesn't reinjure his shoulder in July and miss the rest of the year ? After trading Clayton, they could have wasted their time playing Howard every day, instead of taking a gander at Ordaz and Polanco. Not that it's important, but Ordaz and Polanco are young enough to have value in trades.

Brian Jordan   **OF**   **Bats R** **Age 32**

YEAR	TEAM	LGE	AB	H	DB	TP	HR	BB	R	RBI	SB	CS	OUT	BA	OBA	SA	EQA	EQR	DEFENSE
1996	St Louis	NL	512	158	32	1	19	33	74	74	19	6	360	.309	.350	.486	.286	79	125-OF 107
1997	St Louis	NL	145	34	5	0	0	11	12	8	5	1	112	.234	.288	.269	.199	10	33-OF 111
1998	St Louis	NL	561	175	34	7	26	44	86	95	18	6	392	.312	.362	.537	.302	98	130-OF 98
1999	Atlanta	NL	422	128	27	2	18	32	59	67	12	4	298	.303	.352	.505	.294	70	

With a season this good under his belt, he's finally lived up to the considerable hype, providing good defense and solid power. Potentially the big ticket turkey in this year's free agent shopping season, in terms of what it cost to get him, and how that doesn't match up with a season like the one forecast here.

Pat Kelly   **2B**   **Bats R** **Age 31**

YEAR	TEAM	LGE	AB	H	DB	TP	HR	BB	R	RBI	SB	CS	OUT	BA	OBA	SA	EQA	EQR	DEFENSE
1995	NY Yanks	AL	267	63	12	1	4	21	26	21	8	3	207	.236	.292	.333	.220	23	83-2B 106
1997	NY Yanks	AL	119	29	7	1	2	14	18	11	8	1	91	.244	.323	.370	.254	15	33-2B 99
1998	Syracuse	Int	288	71	13	2	11	31	38	34	12	5	222	.247	.320	.420	.257	37	79-2B 88
1998	St Louis	NL	152	32	3	0	5	14	13	13	5	1	121	.211	.277	.329	.214	13	34-2B 98
1999	St Louis	NL	320	79	15	1	13	33	41	39	13	4	245	.247	.317	.422	.261	43	

One of the bizarre signings by the Blue Jays before the year, when they were intent on bringing in as many second basemen as possible at once: Kelly, Tony Fernandez, Craig Grebeck, even Juan Bell. After muddling through that overstock, Kelly was sent off to the Cards when Delino DeShields got hurt at the start of August. A nice platoon partner for either DeShields or Adam Kennedy.

Adam Kennedy   **2B/SS**   **Bats L** **Age 23**

YEAR	TEAM	LGE	AB	H	DB	TP	HR	BB	R	RBI	SB	CS	OUT	BA	OBA	SA	EQA	EQR	DEFENSE
1997	New Jrsy	NYP	115	30	3	2	0	9	12	9	3	1	86	.261	.315	.322	.227	11	26-SS 104
1997	Pr Willm	Car	155	45	7	2	1	4	14	15	2	2	112	.290	.308	.381	.235	15	35-SS 93
1998	Arkansas	Tex	201	47	5	1	5	6	14	16	4	1	155	.234	.256	.343	.204	14	50-SS 98
1998	Memphis	PCL	299	85	17	5	4	12	37	31	13	4	218	.284	.312	.415	.253	35	60-SS 95
1999	St Louis	NL	425	120	23	5	5	16	48	43	17	5	310	.282	.308	.395	.249	48	

Named one of the top hitters to come out of the '97, Kennedy is considered a great athlete but not a great shortstop. The Cardinals were thinking about moving him to second at the start of the year, but then Jason Woolf got hurt, so he moved up to Arkansas to play short, and then he wasn't so bad there, and suddenly he's still a shortstop. A separated shoulder suffered in the Arizona Fall League isn't going to require surgery, so he'll get a look in camp at both second and short for the major league squad.

Tom Lampkin   **C**   **Bats L** **Age 35**

YEAR	TEAM	LGE	AB	H	DB	TP	HR	BB	R	RBI	SB	CS	OUT	BA	OBA	SA	EQA	EQR	DEFENSE
1996	San Fran	NL	177	41	5	0	7	20	16	20	0	5	141	.232	.310	.379	.230	18	
1997	St Louis	NL	229	56	8	0	8	29	26	27	2	1	174	.245	.329	.384	.251	27	
1998	St Louis	NL	215	49	10	1	7	25	23	23	3	2	168	.228	.308	.381	.240	24	53-C 99
1999	St Louis	NL	213	49	8	0	7	27	21	24	1	2	166	.230	.317	.366	.241	24	

A handy backup, Lampkin will make a very good caddy for Eli Marrero should the Cards re-sign him. Since much has been made of his friendship with Mark McGwire, he's already on the ins with LaRussa's mercenary crew.

Ray Lankford · CF · Bats L · Age 32

YEAR	TEAM	LGE	AB	H	DB	TP	HR	BB	R	RBI	SB	CS	OUT	BA	OBA	SA	EQA	EQR	DEFENSE
1996	St Louis	NL	546	151	36	7	22	82	99	81	30	8	403	.277	.371	.489	.297	97	136-OF 111
1997	St Louis	NL	468	139	34	3	33	97	98	96	17	11	340	.297	.418	.594	.331	107	123-OF 106
1998	St Louis	NL	531	154	31	1	34	89	103	96	28	6	383	.290	.392	.544	.318	109	137-OF 105
1999	*St Louis*	*NL*	*502*	*142*	*33*	*2*	*30*	*91*	*96*	*90*	*24*	*8*	*368*	*.283*	*.393*	*.536*	*.318*	*105*	

We've trumpeted him as an underacknowledged great for years, and we aren't about to stop. Already re-signed to a five-year extension, another way of saying the Cardinals have their act together. Signing Jordan might have been popular, but Lankford's the significantly better and more consistent player. His huge second half got lost in the shuffle as far as the Maris chase was concerned, but it was critical to the Cardinals' strong finish.

Jose Leon · 3B · Bats R · Age 22

YEAR	TEAM	LGE	AB	H	DB	TP	HR	BB	R	RBI	SB	CS	OUT	BA	OBA	SA	EQA	EQR	DEFENSE
1996	JohnsnCy	App	224	43	4	0	6	10	9	12	2	2	183	.192	.226	.290	.163	10	42-3B 96
1997	Peoria	Mid	400	82	11	1	15	25	26	34	3	3	321	.205	.252	.350	.201	29	101-3B 87
1998	Pr Willm	Car	447	128	20	1	21	50	60	71	3	2	321	.286	.358	.477	.285	70	117-3B 116
1999	*St Louis*	*NL*	*404*	*106*	*14*	*1*	*19*	*33*	*43*	*56*	*4*	*2*	*300*	*.262*	*.318*	*.443*	*.263*	*53*	

A definite sleeper right now, and the man who could eventually push aside Tatis and/or Chris Haas. He's got great power, and he's shown decisive improvement with his command of the strike zone. Keep in mind the translation process tends to be merciless to A-ball players, and that Prince William is one of the toughest places to hit in, so don't be surprised if he muscles his way into the Beltre/Aramis stratosphere as far as potential.

Mark Little · CF · Bats R · Age 26

YEAR	TEAM	LGE	AB	H	DB	TP	HR	BB	R	RBI	SB	CS	OUT	BA	OBA	SA	EQA	EQR	DEFENSE
1996	Tulsa	Tex	404	101	14	0	11	42	48	40	16	7	310	.250	.321	.366	.243	45	94-OF 106
1997	Oklahoma	AA	411	98	17	3	12	36	46	41	18	7	320	.238	.300	.382	.239	45	115-OF 102
1998	Oklahoma	PCL	269	69	13	2	6	14	27	26	8	5	205	.257	.293	.387	.233	27	63-OF 114
1998	Memphis	PCL	62	14	2	2	0	5	4	5	0	2	50	.226	.284	.323	.198	4	
1999	*St Louis*	*NL*	*363*	*89*	*15*	*2*	*9*	*27*	*38*	*35*	*15*	*7*	*281*	*.245*	*.297*	*.372*	*.237*	*38*	

A throw-in on the back end of the deal with the Rangers. In the Rangers' organization, this is a prospect. In the Cardinals' organization, this is someone who hopes Willie McGee is tired of playing baseball, or that John Mabry gets squashed by loose air conditioner.

John Mabry · OF/1B/3B · Bats L · Age 28

YEAR	TEAM	LGE	AB	H	DB	TP	HR	BB	R	RBI	SB	CS	OUT	BA	OBA	SA	EQA	EQR	DEFENSE	
1996	St Louis	NL	543	160	28	2	14	40	63	72	2	2	385	.295	.343	.431	.267	71	132-1B 86	
1997	St Louis	NL	388	110	13	0	7	42	44	45	0	1	279	.284	.353	.371	.256	46	61-OF 96	35-1B 91
1998	St Louis	NL	375	93	17	0	11	32	35	41	0	2	284	.248	.307	.381	.236	39	47-OF 97	29-3B 84
1999	*St Louis*	*NL*	*365*	*101*	*13*	*0*	*11*	*32*	*38*	*47*	*0*	*1*	*265*	*.277*	*.335*	*.403*	*.259*	*45*		

Like Joel Youngblood or Kenny Williams before him, he's an outfielder who can't really play third. You have to respect him for trying, but he isn't good at it. A very good spare part, pinch-hitter and part-time regular.

Eli Marrero · C · Bats R · Age 25

YEAR	TEAM	LGE	AB	H	DB	TP	HR	BB	R	RBI	SB	CS	OUT	BA	OBA	SA	EQA	EQR	DEFENSE
1996	Arkansas	Tex	369	89	9	2	15	29	35	42	7	4	284	.241	.296	.398	.239	39	
1997	Louisvil	AA	393	103	17	5	18	24	41	55	4	3	293	.262	.305	.468	.260	50	
1998	Memphis	PCL	128	27	4	0	5	12	11	12	4	3	104	.211	.279	.359	.219	12	29-C 105
1998	St Louis	NL	253	61	19	1	4	29	32	24	6	2	194	.241	.319	.372	.244	29	69-C 105
1999	*St Louis*	*NL*	*362*	*90*	*19*	*2*	*13*	*28*	*40*	*43*	*10*	*4*	*276*	*.249*	*.303*	*.420*	*.252*	*44*	

Beating a malignant tumor found in his neck in spring training was one of the biggest challenges any player had to confront in '98. A nimble backstop, termed "catlike," and possessing a strong arm, Marrero is an excellent catcher. If he's healthy he should be more valuable over his career than Sandy Alomar.

Joe McEwing   OF   Bats R Age 26

YEAR	TEAM	LGE	AB	H	DB	TP	HR	BB	R	RBI	SB	CS	OUT	BA	OBA	SA	EQA	EQR	DEFENSE
1996	Arkansas	Tex	214	36	5	1	2	11	7	7	2	2	180	.168	.209	.229	.117	4	85-OF 87
1997	Arkansas	Tex	258	50	3	1	3	15	10	10	1	2	210	.194	.238	.248	.149	9	57-OF 94
1998	Arkansas	Tex	216	60	10	1	5	15	23	25	2	1	157	.278	.325	.403	.252	25	47-OF 110
1998	Memphis	PCL	322	94	19	4	5	18	38	37	9	8	236	.292	.329	.422	.256	39	70-OF 106
1999	*St Louis*	*NL*	*397*	*99*	*18*	*3*	*8*	*22*	*35*	*38*	*8*	*6*	*304*	*.249*	*.289*	*.370*	*.229*	*38*	

An unheralded pick out of a New Jersey community college, '98 was shaping like the year that he was going to be run out of baseball if he didn't improve. He improved, and he's in that same pool of barracudas waiting for Willie McGee to fall apart like a dried-out old rubber band.

Willie McGee   OF   Bats B Age 40

YEAR	TEAM	LGE	AB	H	DB	TP	HR	BB	R	RBI	SB	CS	OUT	BA	OBA	SA	EQA	EQR	DEFENSE
1996	St Louis	NL	309	94	15	2	5	20	37	38	4	2	217	.304	.347	.414	.265	39	68-OF 90
1997	St Louis	NL	300	90	20	4	3	24	41	36	7	2	212	.300	.352	.423	.271	41	64-OF 88
1998	St Louis	NL	267	67	10	1	3	16	25	21	8	2	202	.251	.293	.330	.220	23	52-OF 92
1999	*St Louis*	*NL*	*246*	*59*	*10*	*1*	*3*	*19*	*22*	*20*	*5*	*2*	*189*	*.240*	*.294*	*.325*	*.221*	*22*	

Still wrestling with whether or not he'll retire. Before getting goofy about batting the pitcher in the eighth slot, LaRussa would routinely use McGee as half of the double-switch. It isn't for me to say "enough already," but here's hoping McGee steps aside and lets somebody else get some major league time. Just imagine if he's around for twenty years as a first base coach; he'll be the Un-Zimmer.

Mark McGwire   1B   Bats R Age 35

YEAR	TEAM	LGE	AB	H	DB	TP	HR	BB	R	RBI	SB	CS	OUT	BA	OBA	SA	EQA	EQR	DEFENSE
1996	Oakland	AL	405	122	18	0	49	110	90	116	0	0	283	.301	.450	.709	.369	117	98-1B 88
1997	Oakland	AL	358	100	19	0	35	58	60	82	1	0	258	.279	.380	.626	.326	78	97-1B 98
1997	St Louis	NL	175	45	6	0	23	44	35	47	2	0	130	.257	.406	.686	.347	46	42-1B 93
1998	St Louis	NL	508	151	24	0	70	164	126	159	1	0	357	.297	.469	.758	.384	164	149-1B 91
1999	*St Louis*	*NL*	*490*	*136*	*22*	*0*	*56*	*140*	*104*	*132*	*1*	*0*	*354*	*.278*	*.438*	*.665*	*.360*	*137*	

Anyone want to sit down and count how many times people said he couldn't do it because he's "too patient?" I wonder how everyone will put 70 into context if McGwire actually lives up to that projection. All in all, another great example of what history tells us about expansion years: offensive levels don't go up, but uniquely talented hitters are well-positioned to take unique advantage of the circumstances.

    I hope we all realize that the guy who was complaining about media attention in June and basking in it by August was the same man. That's not a knock on Big Red. The media needs to realize that insinuating itself into the story is wrong. When reporters make themselves a nuisance to generate news, they've crossed the line that separates Ed Murrow from Vince McMahon. A great player did a great thing, and whether or not he'd had enough of being asked "when" or "how" should not be made part of the story. The media owes McGwire an apology for turning his excellence into another excuse for a summer-long content-free junket.

Juan Munoz   OF   Bats L Age 25

YEAR	TEAM	LGE	AB	H	DB	TP	HR	BB	R	RBI	SB	CS	OUT	BA	OBA	SA	EQA	EQR	DEFENSE
1996	St Pete	Fla	340	81	11	1	2	32	29	24	3	3	262	.238	.304	.294	.209	26	85-OF 87
1997	Pr Willm	Car	257	71	11	4	3	14	25	27	2	1	187	.276	.314	.385	.242	27	58-OF 97
1997	Arkansas	Tex	211	48	4	1	5	13	15	16	4	6	169	.227	.272	.327	.200	15	51-OF 106
1998	Arkansas	Tex	116	22	5	0	0	3	4	4	0	0	94	.190	.210	.233	.114	2	21-OF 102
1998	Memphis	PCL	393	93	12	4	3	27	32	28	7	3	303	.237	.286	.310	.207	30	102-OF 101
1999	*St Louis*	*NL*	*469*	*118*	*19*	*3*	*4*	*28*	*40*	*38*	*8*	*5*	*356*	*.252*	*.294*	*.330*	*.220*	*40*	

One of those whippets they used to always crank out in the Cardinals' system. Not really a great prospect, but one of the better potential heirs to Willie McGee's spot should E.T. retire.

Luis Ordaz   SS   Bats R   Age 23

YEAR	TEAM	LGE	AB	H	DB	TP	HR	BB	R	RBI	SB	CS	OUT	BA	OBA	SA	EQA	EQR	DEFENSE
1996	St Pete	Fla	432	116	11	2	4	27	38	38	6	3	319	.269	.312	.331	.225	38	118-SS 88
1997	Arkansas	Tex	381	92	14	3	4	19	29	28	8	6	295	.241	.278	.325	.205	28	105-SS 91
1998	Memphis	PCL	210	56	8	1	5	16	21	23	3	3	157	.267	.319	.386	.243	23	57-SS 93
1998	St Louis	NL	152	30	6	0	0	13	9	6	2	0	122	.197	.261	.237	.167	7	44-SS 110
1999	*St Louis*	*NL*	*378*	*98*	*12*	*1*	*6*	*22*	*35*	*34*	*10*	*4*	*284*	*.259*	*.300*	*.344*	*.229*	*36*	

The Cardinals' answer to Rey Ordonez. Cardinals fans, bless'em, don't go bonkers when they see a shortstop better than Raffy Santana take the field. Probably has something to do with seeing lots of the good Ozzie for awhile. Luis can take notes from Manny Alexander if things break his way, and that can be taken as proof that life is more fair for some than others.

Pablo Ozuna   SS   Bats R   Age 20

YEAR	TEAM	LGE	AB	H	DB	TP	HR	BB	R	RBI	SB	CS	OUT	BA	OBA	SA	EQA	EQR	DEFENSE
1997	JohnsnCy	App	226	50	5	0	3	7	13	12	8	3	179	.221	.245	.283	.177	12	55-SS 86
1998	Peoria	Mid	538	172	18	5	10	24	72	64	29	15	381	.320	.349	.428	.269	71	123-SS 94
1999	*St Louis*	*NL*	*402*	*132*	*14*	*2*	*8*	*13*	*54*	*49*	*26*	*11*	*281*	*.328*	*.349*	*.433*	*.276*	*56*	

If this organization that didn't already have J.D. Drew or Rick Ankiel, you'd hear more about Ozuna. Named the best prospect in the Midwest League, he's the best glove at short in the organization, has great speed, and potentially a great offensive player. He won't make people forget the AL trio of ARod, Nomar, and Jeter, but within the next two years, the Cardinals are going to have someone who deserves to get mentioned with them.

Tom Pagnozzi   C   Bats R   Age 36

YEAR	TEAM	LGE	AB	H	DB	TP	HR	BB	R	RBI	SB	CS	OUT	BA	OBA	SA	EQA	EQR	DEFENSE
1996	St Louis	NL	406	108	17	0	15	27	42	50	4	1	299	.266	.312	.419	.251	47	
1997	Arkansas	Tex	61	15	0	0	3	3	4	7	0	0	46	.246	.281	.393	.229	6	
1998	St Louis	NL	159	34	7	0	2	15	12	11	0	0	125	.214	.282	.296	.199	11	41-C 98
1999	*St Louis*	*NL*	*181*	*39*	*6*	*0*	*5*	*15*	*13*	*16*	*1*	*0*	*142*	*.215*	*.276*	*.331*	*.213*	*15*	

The big mistake, in that Walt Jocketty had no business giving injury-prone Pags a multi-year contract after his first healthy season ('96) since '92. Released on August 16, his career is probably over.

Placido Polanco   2B/SS   Bats R   Age 23

YEAR	TEAM	LGE	AB	H	DB	TP	HR	BB	R	RBI	SB	CS	OUT	BA	OBA	SA	EQA	EQR	DEFENSE
1996	St Pete	Fla	549	157	25	3	2	22	48	51	2	3	395	.286	.313	.353	.230	50	124-2B 108
1997	Arkansas	Tex	496	122	12	1	2	25	37	30	12	4	378	.246	.282	.286	.197	33	126-2B 109
1998	Memphis	PCL	242	62	14	1	1	15	23	19	5	3	183	.256	.300	.335	.220	21	55-2B 101
1998	St Louis	NL	113	28	4	2	1	6	10	9	2	0	85	.248	.286	.345	.220	10	22-SS 114
1999	*St Louis*	*NL*	*397*	*107*	*18*	*2*	*2*	*19*	*36*	*34*	*8*	*3*	*293*	*.270*	*.303*	*.340*	*.228*	*36*	

Polanco was only really moved to second to make room for Ordaz, but neither of them are looking like they're more than utility infielders or fill-ins before one of the kids claims the shortstop job for the next six or ten years. At the plate, he's more likely to hack or make contact than Ordaz, but not much more of a hitter.

Luis Saturria   CF   Bats R   Age 22

YEAR	TEAM	LGE	AB	H	DB	TP	HR	BB	R	RBI	SB	CS	OUT	BA	OBA	SA	EQA	EQR	DEFENSE
1996	JohnsnCy	App	230	44	3	0	3	15	11	9	4	1	187	.191	.241	.243	.156	9	46-OF 83
1997	Peoria	Mid	446	106	11	2	10	34	40	38	12	6	346	.238	.292	.339	.220	39	107-OF 94
1998	Pr Willm	Car	468	132	18	5	13	29	54	57	15	8	344	.282	.324	.425	.258	58	125-OF 99
1999	*St Louis*	*NL*	*398*	*104*	*13*	*2*	*11*	*25*	*40*	*43*	*13*	*6*	*300*	*.261*	*.305*	*.387*	*.244*	*44*	

Acquitted himself well in the Maryland Fall League after finishing up his regular season with a hot second half. He was good enough in Peoria in to draw a Rule 5 excursion courtesy of the Blue Jays, who couldn't coax the Cardinals into accepting some compensation so that they could keep him in their own minors. Probably the Cardinals' best outfield prospect, other than that Drew character.

Mike Stefanski   C   Bats R   Age 29

YEAR	TEAM	LGE	AB	H	DB	TP	HR	BB	R	RBI	SB	CS	OUT	BA	OBA	SA	EQA	EQR	DEFENSE
1996	Louisvil	AA	127	23	5	1	1	10	6	5	1	2	106	.181	.241	.260	.158	5	
1997	Louisvil	AA	195	52	4	0	5	11	15	21	0	1	144	.267	.306	.364	.230	18	
1998	Memphis	PCL	294	64	11	1	4	19	19	19	1	2	232	.218	.265	.303	.190	18	97-C 100
1999	*St Louis*	*NL*	*244*	*59*	*6*	*0*	*7*	*16*	*18*	*24*	*1*	*2*	*187*	*.242*	*.288*	*.352*	*.222*	*22*	

A good glove and now a minor league free agent, Stefanski would be a very solid backup catcher for somebody if they ever got tired of handing service time to Pat Borders or Mark Parent.

Fernando Tatis   3B   Bats R   Age 24

YEAR	TEAM	LGE	AB	H	DB	TP	HR	BB	R	RBI	SB	CS	OUT	BA	OBA	SA	EQA	EQR	DEFENSE
1996	Charlott	Fla	330	92	11	1	13	26	38	45	6	2	240	.279	.331	.436	.265	43	78-3B 86
1997	Tulsa	Tex	373	104	14	1	19	39	51	56	12	6	275	.279	.347	.475	.280	57	99-3B 97
1997	Texas	AL	220	55	6	0	9	14	21	25	3	0	165	.250	.295	.400	.240	23	58-3B 83
1998	Texas	AL	323	82	16	2	3	13	26	26	5	2	243	.254	.283	.344	.215	26	93-3B 111
1998	St Louis	NL	201	57	14	2	9	25	32	32	7	3	147	.284	.363	.507	.295	35	53-3B 100
1999	*St Louis*	*NL*	*511*	*148*	*29*	*2*	*20*	*39*	*66*	*74*	*13*	*5*	*368*	*.290*	*.340*	*.472*	*.281*	*77*	

Is he a prospect? To be honest, at this point I'm not really certain. What do you choose, the two months with the Cardinals, when he was new to the league, or his pathetic four months with the Rangers? With a gun to my head, I'd say he could live up to that projection, but that the Rangers won't miss him that badly.

Jason Woolf   SS   Bats B   Age 22

YEAR	TEAM	LGE	AB	H	DB	TP	HR	BB	R	RBI	SB	CS	OUT	BA	OBA	SA	EQA	EQR	DEFENSE
1996	Peoria	Mid	368	83	10	4	2	43	39	24	14	7	292	.226	.307	.291	.215	31	104-SS 88
1997	Pr Willm	Car	257	61	7	2	6	46	41	25	15	4	200	.237	.353	.350	.260	34	70-SS 99
1998	Arkansas	Tex	290	65	15	3	3	28	35	20	17	4	229	.224	.292	.328	.225	28	74-SS 104
1999	*St Louis*	*NL*	*284*	*68*	*10*	*2*	*4*	*32*	*36*	*23*	*17*	*5*	*221*	*.239*	*.316*	*.331*	*.240*	*31*	

How unfair is life? Woolf is merely a good shortstop in an organization filled with great ones. In a few years, we can start talking about ex-Cardinals' shortstops in the same way we talk about "Third basemen Wade Boggs chased off" or "Catchers Geno Petralli outlasted in Texas" or "Orioles minor league shortstops of the '80s."

PITCHERS (Averages: 4.00 ERA, 9.00 H/9, 1.00 HR/9, 3.00 BB/9, 6.00 K/9, 1.00 KWH)

Juan Acevedo   Throws R   Age 29

YEAR	TEAM	LGE	IP	H	ER	HR	BB	K	ERA	W	L	H/9	HR/9	BB/9	K/9	KWH	PERA
1996	Norfolk	Int	94.7	146	79	15	59	65	7.51	2	9	13.88	1.43	5.61	6.18	0.37	6.94
1997	Norfolk	Int	113.7	129	56	7	34	73	4.43	6	7	10.21	0.55	2.69	5.78	0.91	4.12
1997	NY Mets	NL	47.7	57	23	7	20	30	4.34	2	3	10.76	1.32	3.78	5.66	0.59	5.10
1998	St Louis	NL	100.7	84	25	7	26	51	2.24	8	3	7.51	0.63	2.32	4.56	0.89	2.59

After doing good work as a starter, Acevedo got hurt again, so he's going to be left in the bullpen as the team's closer, which is sort of an in-your-face gesture to all of the Cardinals' minor league closers. But this is where closers come from, besides the waiver wire: decent starters with endurance problems or who can't come up with a third pitch. Among today's closers, 21 of 30 were starters for most of their careers or minor league careers before going to the pen. Some of the names would surprise you: even guys like Rod Beck or Jerry DiPoto were starters once upon a time. The point is that Acevedo should end up being a very wealthy and successful guy.

Armando Almanza   **Throws L**   **Age 26**

YEAR	TEAM	LGE	IP	H	ER	HR	BB	K	ERA	W	L	H/9	HR/9	BB/9	K/9	KWH	PERA
1996	Peoria	Mid	54.3	81	41	3	38	40	6.79	2	4	13.42	0.50	6.29	6.63	0.39	5.96
1997	Pr Willm	Car	60.0	57	25	4	36	50	3.75	4	3	8.55	0.60	5.40	7.50	0.91	3.75
1998	Arkansas	Tex	30.0	35	15	3	20	32	4.50	1	2	10.50	0.90	6.00	9.60	1.10	5.10
1998	Memphis	PCL	34.0	40	18	1	20	34	4.76	2	2	10.59	0.26	5.29	9.00	1.08	4.50

Throws hard for a lefty, in that his fastball tops out in the high 80s with wicked movement, leaving most batters flailing. The Cardinals will be much better off if they let him run Lance Painter out of town to take the spot as the second lefty in the pen behind Scott Radinsky.

Rich Ankiel   **Throws L**   **Age 19**

YEAR	TEAM	LGE	IP	H	ER	HR	BB	K	ERA	W	L	H/9	HR/9	BB/9	K/9	KWH	PERA
1998	Peoria	Mid	33.7	21	10	0	14	27	2.67	3	1	5.61	0.00	3.74	7.22	1.86	1.34
1998	Pr Willm	Car	119.3	126	60	11	44	124	4.53	6	7	9.50	0.83	3.32	9.35	2.08	4.07

Probably the best pitching prospect in the minor leagues right now. He's got a great fastball, one of the best curves you'll see, and a nice changeup that he occasionally tips off. He's supposed to be an apt pupil when it comes to learning his craft. The Cards have been careful with him, keeping him on a pitch count. On the other hand, the danger should he make the majors to face LaRussa's tender mercies is one of those moments pregnant with possibility. Some people argue that LaRussa and Duncan should be fired the minute Ankiel's ready, which might sound drastic until you think about Alan Benes and Matt Morris.

Manny Aybar   **Throws R**   **Age 24**

YEAR	TEAM	LGE	IP	H	ER	HR	BB	K	ERA	W	L	H/9	HR/9	BB/9	K/9	KWH	PERA
1996	Arkansas	Tex	117.3	135	52	11	36	73	3.99	7	6	10.36	0.84	2.76	5.60	0.82	4.37
1996	Louisvil	AmA	31.0	28	12	1	8	22	3.48	2	1	8.13	0.29	2.32	6.39	1.62	2.61
1997	Louisvil	AmA	138.0	143	56	9	43	98	3.65	8	7	9.33	0.59	2.80	6.39	1.17	3.65
1997	St Louis	NL	68.7	69	30	9	26	37	3.93	4	4	9.04	1.18	3.41	4.85	0.57	4.06
1998	Memphis	PCL	80.3	67	22	6	16	51	2.46	7	2	7.51	0.67	1.79	5.71	1.82	2.46
1998	St Louis	NL	85.0	92	50	6	39	53	5.29	3	6	9.74	0.64	4.13	5.61	0.59	4.13

Like most position players who've been converted into pitchers, Aybar's best pitch is his fastball. He mixes in a slider well against lefties, but his changeup isn't fooling anyone, and his fastball doesn't have that much movement. I don't expect a great career, but he could end up being a good fourth or fifth starter.

Brian Barnes   **Throws L**   **Age 32**

YEAR	TEAM	LGE	IP	H	ER	HR	BB	K	ERA	W	L	H/9	HR/9	BB/9	K/9	KWH	PERA
1996	Jacksnvl	Sou	69.3	96	43	9	26	50	5.58	3	5	12.46	1.17	3.38	6.49	0.75	5.84
1996	Toledo	Int	85.3	99	50	8	32	55	5.27	3	6	10.44	0.84	3.38	5.80	0.72	4.54
1997	Toledo	Int	106.0	178	112	17	57	64	9.51	2	10	15.11	1.44	4.84	5.43	0.30	7.39
1998	Memphis	PCL	131.7	162	70	14	42	114	4.78	6	9	11.07	0.96	2.87	7.79	1.43	4.85

That Brian Barnes? Yes indeed, the same guy who looked like a prospect at the beginning of the decade with the Expos. He's still very effective at keeping the ball down, and if Brad Woodall can come back, Barnes might too.

Alan Benes   **Throws R**   **Age 27**

YEAR	TEAM	LGE	IP	H	ER	HR	BB	K	ERA	W	L	H/9	HR/9	BB/9	K/9	KWH	PERA
1995	Louisvil	AmA	56.0	40	15	5	15	50	2.41	4	2	6.43	0.80	2.41	8.04	3.12	2.09
1996	St Louis	NL	191.3	213	115	28	83	118	5.41	7	14	10.02	1.32	3.90	5.55	0.59	4.75
1997	St Louis	NL	163.0	136	54	14	61	142	2.98	12	6	7.51	0.77	3.37	7.84	1.82	2.87

He's had surgery (again), and as of early December his status is still very uncertain. The worst crime to charge LaRussa with as the Cardinal's manager is that he fragged Benes for a '97 team going nowhere.

Kent Bottenfield   Throws R   Age 30

YEAR	TEAM	LGE	IP	H	ER	HR	BB	K	ERA	W	L	H/9	HR/9	BB/9	K/9	KWH	PERA
1996	Iowa	AmA	23.7	24	11	0	9	11	4.18	1	2	9.13	0.00	3.42	4.18	0.42	3.42
1996	ChiCubs	NL	62.0	65	24	3	18	30	3.48	4	3	9.44	0.44	2.61	4.35	0.58	3.63
1997	ChiCubs	NL	88.3	81	32	13	32	67	3.26	6	4	8.25	1.32	3.26	6.83	1.30	3.67
1998	St Louis	NL	138.7	130	62	13	53	90	4.02	7	8	8.44	0.84	3.44	5.84	0.88	3.50

Although we're generally critical of LaRussa's work with his pitching staff, Bottenfield was the right sort of guy to get out of the bullpen and use as a starter. He came up as a starter with the Expos, and has never had his career derailed by injuries. As a swingman he's much more valuable than just as a middle reliever, and the Cardinals can now use him as an answer to any problem that comes up.

Jeff Brantley   Throws R   Age 35

YEAR	TEAM	LGE	IP	H	ER	HR	BB	K	ERA	W	L	H/9	HR/9	BB/9	K/9	KWH	PERA
1995	Cincnnti	NL	71.3	54	20	12	19	57	2.52	6	2	6.81	1.51	2.40	7.19	2.37	2.65
1996	Cincnnti	NL	72.3	57	18	8	26	68	2.24	6	2	7.09	1.00	3.24	8.46	2.34	2.74
1998	St Louis	NL	52.3	40	22	13	16	44	3.78	3	3	6.88	2.24	2.75	7.57	2.27	3.27

Traded to the Phillies after being picked up for Dmitri Young. He still knows how to pitch, but the flesh isn't quite so willing these days, as you can see from the exciting big fly fun he brought to the ballpark. This is a downward trade spiral for the Cards; if Bottalico flops, they got nothing for Dmitri Young but a salary dump.

Mike Busby   Throws R   Age 26

YEAR	TEAM	LGE	IP	H	ER	HR	BB	K	ERA	W	L	H/9	HR/9	BB/9	K/9	KWH	PERA
1995	Arkansas	Tex	133.0	130	56	10	35	87	3.79	8	7	8.80	0.68	2.37	5.89	1.25	3.38
1996	Louisvil	AmA	73.0	101	57	11	48	47	7.03	2	6	12.45	1.36	5.92	5.79	0.34	6.29
1997	Louisvil	AmA	93.0	107	48	11	30	55	4.65	4	6	10.35	1.06	2.90	5.32	0.71	4.65
1998	St Louis	NL	47.3	46	20	3	14	30	3.80	3	2	8.75	0.57	2.66	5.70	1.05	3.42

Busby finally had his day in the sun, being healthy enough in consecutive months to make the team and pitch well as a middle reliever. Naturally, in the chaotic situation LaRussa had created on the pitching staff, he was asked to start, and he almost instantly blew out his elbow.

Rick Croushore   Throws R   Age 28

YEAR	TEAM	LGE	IP	H	ER	HR	BB	K	ERA	W	L	H/9	HR/9	BB/9	K/9	KWH	PERA
1996	Arkansas	Tex	98.7	145	88	19	61	66	8.03	2	9	13.23	1.73	5.56	6.02	0.37	6.93
1997	Arkansas	Tex	81.0	144	63	8	42	49	7.00	2	7	16.00	0.89	4.67	5.44	0.30	7.22
1997	Louisvil	AmA	42.7	44	15	3	14	32	3.16	3	2	9.28	0.63	2.95	6.75	1.25	3.80
1998	Memphis	PCL	27.3	25	17	3	9	29	5.60	1	2	8.23	0.99	2.96	9.55	2.80	3.29
1998	St Louis	NL	56.3	45	27	7	27	43	4.31	3	3	7.19	1.12	4.31	6.87	1.14	3.04

Righties who throw screwballs are rare and usually kept at a distance, usually a few stops away from the majors. His brief shot at greatness as a closer went up in flames after a few titanic home runs in July. Still potentially a good reliever, but he won't get entrusted with a major role again any time soon.

John Frascatore   Throws R   Age 29

YEAR	TEAM	LGE	IP	H	ER	HR	BB	K	ERA	W	L	H/9	HR/9	BB/9	K/9	KWH	PERA
1996	Louisvil	AmA	150.7	221	120	22	50	75	7.17	4	13	13.20	1.31	2.99	4.48	0.38	6.21
1997	St Louis	NL	80.3	79	23	5	29	52	2.58	6	3	8.85	0.56	3.25	5.83	0.89	3.47
1998	St Louis	NL	99.0	96	41	11	33	45	3.73	6	5	8.73	1.00	3.00	4.09	0.48	3.64

His season wasn't really all that bad, which probably has Cardinals' fans cringing as I say it, but other than an especially grisly contribution in April, he was what he is, an adequate middle reliever. Being a paisan' probably helped keep him out of LaRussa's doghouse.

Tristan Jerue   Throws R   Age 23

YEAR	TEAM	LGE	IP	H	ER	HR	BB	K	ERA	W	L	H/9	HR/9	BB/9	K/9	KWH	PERA
1997	New Jrsy	NYP	63.7	110	49	5	30	31	6.93	2	5	15.55	0.71	4.24	4.38	0.22	6.79
1998	Peoria	Mid	119.7	159	67	10	58	62	5.04	5	8	11.96	0.75	4.36	4.66	0.31	5.34
1998	Pr Willm	Car	39.3	44	19	0	14	23	4.35	2	2	10.07	0.00	3.20	5.26	0.64	3.66

A converted outfielder, Jerue is a sinker/slider pitcher. In other words, he probably already has a better idea of what he's doing than Felix Rodriguez, since he knows that there are second pitches. Keeps the ball down and in the yard, and although superficially similar to Manny Aybar, I expect him to turn out better.

Jose Jimenez   Throws R   Age 25

YEAR	TEAM	LGE	IP	H	ER	HR	BB	K	ERA	W	L	H/9	HR/9	BB/9	K/9	KWH	PERA
1996	Peoria	Mid	155.0	232	103	9	58	83	5.98	5	12	13.47	0.52	3.37	4.82	0.38	5.69
1997	Pr Willm	Car	135.0	172	89	14	44	53	5.93	5	10	11.47	0.93	2.93	3.53	0.28	5.07
1998	Arkansas	Tex	166.0	195	81	9	73	65	4.39	8	10	10.57	0.49	3.96	3.52	0.22	4.45
1998	St Louis	NL	22.0	22	7	0	8	11	2.86	1	1	9.00	0.00	3.27	4.50	0.52	3.27

There's a considerable amount of argument about whether Jimenez is really a prospect. He has a great late-breaking sinker—and that's it, except that he uses it to keep his infielders busy and his outfielders snoozing. He's got a funky delivery and he throws strikes, but his stuff will never get much respect. With so many other problems on the major league staff, he's exactly the right kind of dark horse to ride in and claim a rotation spot, winning big if he has a tight infield and some run support. I've always liked one-trick ponies as long as the one trick is a showstopper.

Curtis King   Throws R   Age 28

YEAR	TEAM	LGE	IP	H	ER	HR	BB	K	ERA	W	L	H/9	HR/9	BB/9	K/9	KWH	PERA
1996	St Pete	Fla	47.0	67	35	1	29	18	6.70	1	4	12.83	0.19	5.55	3.45	0.13	5.36
1997	Arkansas	Tex	31.7	51	23	7	11	21	6.54	1	3	14.49	1.99	3.13	5.97	0.59	7.39
1997	Louisvil	AmA	21.3	22	5	1	7	7	2.11	2	0	9.28	0.42	2.95	2.95	0.24	3.37
1997	St Louis	NL	29.3	40	13	0	10	12	3.99	2	1	12.27	0.00	3.07	3.68	0.27	4.60
1998	Memphis	PCL	24.0	36	6	1	6	17	2.25	2	1	13.50	0.38	2.25	6.38	1.00	5.25
1998	St Louis	NL	52.7	51	17	5	18	26	2.91	4	2	8.72	0.85	3.08	4.44	0.55	3.59

Hittable reliever with no dominating pitch, throws hard and straight. Any story about Curtis King talks about his "confidence." Custer was confident. Todd Marinovich is probably still confident, if lucid. A team can use somebody like Curtis King to pitch complete innings when they don't have the lead or the lead is comfortable.

Braden Looper   Throws R   Age 24

YEAR	TEAM	LGE	IP	H	ER	HR	BB	K	ERA	W	L	H/9	HR/9	BB/9	K/9	KWH	PERA
1997	Pr Willm	Car	61.0	91	43	7	25	40	6.34	2	5	13.43	1.03	3.69	5.90	0.53	6.20
1997	Arkansas	Tex	19.7	28	14	3	7	17	6.41	1	1	12.81	1.37	3.20	7.78	1.11	5.95
1998	Memphis	PCL	39.7	46	15	3	12	35	3.40	2	2	10.44	0.68	2.72	7.94	1.66	4.31

Still a very good prospect; guys who can dial up a 95 mph fastball with great movement usually are. His delivery creates concerns about his ability to stay healthy, which he's failed to do each of the last two years. Still trying to add a slider or change so that he can mix things up. Among prospects, pre-packaged closers are among the ones least likely to work out.

Kevin Lovingier   Throws L   Age 27

YEAR	TEAM	LGE	IP	H	ER	HR	BB	K	ERA	W	L	H/9	HR/9	BB/9	K/9	KWH	PERA
1996	Arkansas	Tex	60.0	74	33	4	55	60	4.95	3	4	11.10	0.60	8.25	9.00	0.66	5.40
1997	Arkansas	Tex	67.3	87	33	5	30	60	4.41	3	4	11.63	0.67	4.01	8.02	1.03	5.08
1998	Arkansas	Tex	22.0	26	11	3	15	18	4.50	1	1	10.64	1.23	6.14	7.36	0.62	5.32
1998	Memphis	PCL	55.7	46	23	7	35	46	3.72	3	3	7.44	1.13	5.66	7.44	0.99	3.56

There aren't many left-handed forkballers, but Lovingier's one of the few. Because he can use it well against righties, he could be successful as a normal middle reliever. Which means he'll never get used by LaRussa.

Sean Lowe   Throws R   Age 28

YEAR	TEAM	LGE	IP	H	ER	HR	BB	K	ERA	W	L	H/9	HR/9	BB/9	K/9	KWH	PERA
1996	Arkansas	Tex	30.7	40	29	3	18	20	8.51	1	2	11.74	0.88	5.28	5.87	0.42	5.58
1996	Louisvil	AmA	112.7	151	79	7	60	62	6.31	4	9	12.06	0.56	4.79	4.95	0.32	5.27
1997	Louisvil	AmA	129.0	168	79	12	57	92	5.51	5	9	11.72	0.84	3.98	6.42	0.66	5.23
1998	Memphis	PCL	142.7	173	61	16	65	84	3.85	8	8	10.91	1.01	4.10	5.30	0.47	5.05

One of the organization's big disappointments. Lowe doesn't throw that hard or have good stuff, and he's prone to concentration lapses. That wasn't what the Cardinals expected when they made him their top pick in '92. If you remember ex-Cardinals' farmhand Jeff Matranga, keep in mind that Matranga was the #1 starter on Arizona State that year, not Lowe. Very tough on righthanders, so he may do well in the pen.

Kent Mercker   Throws L   Age 31

YEAR	TEAM	LGE	IP	H	ER	HR	BB	K	ERA	W	L	H/9	HR/9	BB/9	K/9	KWH	PERA
1995	Atlanta	NL	147.7	145	64	16	58	95	3.90	8	8	8.84	0.98	3.53	5.79	0.80	3.84
1996	Baltimor	AL	58.3	73	45	11	28	22	6.94	1	5	11.26	1.70	4.32	3.39	0.18	5.71
1997	Cincnnti	NL	149.3	137	56	17	56	68	3.38	10	7	8.26	1.02	3.38	4.10	0.45	3.50
1998	St Louis	NL	167.3	204	87	11	49	67	4.68	8	11	10.97	0.59	2.64	3.60	0.34	4.52

What's life like when you grow up and you're the left-handed answer to Mike Morgan? "Heheh, low and outside, that'll get him. Damn, that got out to right pretty quick. Okay, I can get this guy with something up and in. Damn, Gant isn't going to get to that, is he? Next guy's gonna line out for sure. Yessir. Oh man . . ." Works fast and dirty, emphasis on the dirt, and on hitting the showers fast.

Matt Morris   Throws R   Age 24

YEAR	TEAM	LGE	IP	H	ER	HR	BB	K	ERA	W	L	H/9	HR/9	BB/9	K/9	KWH	PERA
1996	Arkansas	Tex	161.7	201	78	15	51	106	4.34	8	10	11.19	0.84	2.84	5.90	0.82	4.84
1997	St Louis	NL	217.7	218	80	12	62	133	3.31	14	10	9.01	0.50	2.56	5.50	0.98	3.39
1998	St Louis	NL	117.0	103	32	8	38	73	2.46	9	4	7.92	0.62	2.92	5.62	1.02	2.92

The Cardinals' priorities came to the fore pretty quickly—they rushed Morris back in April only to have to wait until mid-July to really get him back. He was as good as new once he was actually healed up, and he generates lots of grounders with a good four-pitch assortment. You just have to hope that the Cardinals learned from what happened, because they probably cost themselves an extra month of Morris, and that meant something in terms of the wild card.

Darren Oliver   Throws L   Age 28

YEAR	TEAM	LGE	IP	H	ER	HR	BB	K	ERA	W	L	H/9	HR/9	BB/9	K/9	KWH	PERA
1996	Texas	AL	182.7	176	70	17	62	112	3.45	11	9	8.67	0.84	3.05	5.52	0.86	3.55
1997	Texas	AL	210.7	202	86	27	71	101	3.67	12	11	8.63	1.15	3.03	4.31	0.53	3.72
1998	Texas	AL	111.3	132	64	10	40	57	5.17	4	8	10.67	0.81	3.23	4.61	0.46	4.61
1998	St Louis	NL	59.3	65	27	7	21	27	4.10	3	4	9.86	1.06	3.19	4.10	0.40	4.40

Overall, things seem to be getting worse and worse: although offensive levels have been relatively constant, he's more hittable, wilder, giving up more runs, becoming more fragile. Hand him over to Tony LaRussa, and you've got a formula for major surgery.

Donovan Osborne   Throws L   Age 30

YEAR	TEAM	LGE	IP	H	ER	HR	BB	K	ERA	W	L	H/9	HR/9	BB/9	K/9	KWH	PERA
1996	St Louis	NL	198.0	210	85	22	54	121	3.86	11	11	9.55	1.00	2.45	5.50	0.97	4.05
1997	St Louis	NL	81.0	87	42	11	21	46	4.67	4	5	9.67	1.22	2.33	5.11	0.87	4.22
1998	St Louis	NL	86.0	85	36	11	20	55	3.77	5	5	8.90	1.15	2.09	5.76	1.33	3.77

His signing almost makes the Pagnozzi multi-year deal look good. He may never be healthy for any length of time, and it isn't like I'd say he's as good as John Tudor when he is healthy. He's entering the last year of his contract, so don't be surprised if he tries to pitch through the inevitable injuries.

Lance Painter   Throws L   Age 31

YEAR	TEAM	LGE	IP	H	ER	HR	BB	K	ERA	W	L	H/9	HR/9	BB/9	K/9	KWH	PERA
1996	Colorado	NL	58.3	51	26	11	25	46	4.01	3	3	7.87	1.70	3.86	7.10	1.24	3.70
1997	Louisvil	AmA	20.0	22	15	2	4	17	6.75	1	1	9.90	0.90	1.80	7.65	2.46	4.05
1997	St Louis	NL	17.0	14	8	1	7	10	4.24	1	1	7.41	0.53	3.71	5.29	0.77	2.65
1998	St Louis	NL	49.3	43	21	6	26	36	3.83	3	2	7.84	1.09	4.74	6.57	0.87	3.47

Handed the Honeycutt/Fossas role, he was the ultimately inoffensive lefty specialist. He wasn't too good, or too bad. Bad enough that teams wouldn't automatically yank left-handed hitters, but how much do you gain doing that? A tactical advantage inside of an inning, and a strategic loss in that you didn't get the other guy to pull his left-handed hitters. Probably headed out of town now that Scott Radinsky's signed.

Mark Petkovsek   Throws R   Age 33

YEAR	TEAM	LGE	IP	H	ER	HR	BB	K	ERA	W	L	H/9	HR/9	BB/9	K/9	KWH	PERA
1996	St Louis	NL	88.3	92	36	10	33	41	3.67	5	5	9.37	1.02	3.36	4.18	0.42	4.08
1997	St Louis	NL	96.3	114	56	14	28	46	5.23	4	7	10.65	1.31	2.62	4.30	0.50	4.86
1998	St Louis	NL	110.0	133	54	9	33	51	4.42	5	7	10.88	0.74	2.70	4.17	0.44	4.58

Having spent as many years in the minors as he has, he's accepted every role he's been given. He's been overused in the past, jerked into and out of the rotation, and he never says boo about it. Probably cultivating a future as a coach. One of the most extreme groundball pitchers in the majors. It's enough to have a career with.

Cliff Politte   Throws R   Age 25

YEAR	TEAM	LGE	IP	H	ER	HR	BB	K	ERA	W	L	H/9	HR/9	BB/9	K/9	KWH	PERA
1996	Peoria	Mid	136.3	163	70	12	51	96	4.62	6	9	10.76	0.79	3.37	6.34	0.83	4.69
1997	Pr Willm	Car	112.7	121	45	12	32	77	3.59	7	6	9.67	0.96	2.56	6.15	1.15	4.07
1997	Arkansas	Tex	35.0	42	16	3	9	21	4.11	2	2	10.80	0.77	2.31	5.40	0.87	4.63
1998	St Louis	NL	38.7	46	28	7	17	20	6.52	1	3	10.71	1.63	3.96	4.66	0.38	5.35
1998	Memphis	PCL	49.0	76	43	10	23	33	7.90	1	4	13.96	1.84	4.22	6.06	0.47	7.16
1998	Arkansas	Tex	62.3	70	28	5	17	45	4.04	3	4	10.11	0.72	2.45	6.50	1.28	4.19

Clearly wasn't ready, but you can see why people make the comparisons to Scott Bankhead: a short righty who can throw 90 and who only drops to 85 on his slider. Still, it was impressive that he got to beat out Steve Ontiveros; LaRussa doesn't give up on an ex-A unless compelled. Traded to the Phillies in the Bottalico deal.

Brady Raggio   Throws R   Age 26

YEAR	TEAM	LGE	IP	H	ER	HR	BB	K	ERA	W	L	H/9	HR/9	BB/9	K/9	KWH	PERA
1996	Arkansas	Tex	156.0	185	70	19	43	105	4.04	8	9	10.67	1.10	2.48	6.06	1.04	4.73
1997	Louisvil	AmA	137.3	161	67	17	32	76	4.39	7	8	10.55	1.11	2.10	4.98	0.84	4.59
1997	St Louis	NL	31.7	47	23	1	15	19	6.54	1	3	13.36	0.28	4.26	5.40	0.38	5.40
1998	Memphis	PCL	143.3	178	59	10	32	76	3.70	9	7	11.18	0.63	2.01	4.77	0.76	4.52

A finesse pitcher, throwing several types of junk to set up his change-up. It says quite a bit about how much the organization values him that despite their season-long pitching troubles, they never plugged him into the rotation.

Bobby Witt   Throws R   Age 34

YEAR	TEAM	LGE	IP	H	ER	HR	BB	K	ERA	W	L	H/9	HR/9	BB/9	K/9	KWH	PERA
1996	Texas	AL	211.0	219	94	24	78	157	4.01	11	12	9.34	1.02	3.33	6.70	1.08	4.09
1997	Texas	AL	219.7	231	92	30	65	118	3.77	13	11	9.46	1.23	2.66	4.83	0.70	4.18
1998	Texas	AL	75.0	90	48	13	30	30	5.76	3	5	10.80	1.56	3.60	3.60	0.25	5.28
1998	St Louis	NL	49.3	56	28	7	19	26	5.11	2	3	10.22	1.28	3.47	4.74	0.48	4.74

Star of the soon-to-be-released horror series Batting Practice Bloodbath. "C'mon kids, just let me toss another half hour." "No! How many times to we have to take you yard anyways?" "Don't say that. Don't ever say that." "Eeeeeek! He's got a machete! Just let him pitch, okay?" "Too much premarital sex makes Jack and Jill struggle with breaking stuff." "Run! Run! He can't be reasoned with!"

SNWLP				ST. LOUIS CARDINALS								Park Effect: -7.9%
PITCHER	GS	IP	R	SNW	SNL	SNPCT	W	L	RA	APW	SNVA	SNWAR
Acevedo, J.	9	50.0	14	3.9	1.6	.702	4	1	2.52	1.12	0.96	1.52
Aybar, M.	14	69.3	53	3.6	5.4	.402	5	6	6.88	-1.80	-0.89	-0.21
Bottenfield, K.	17	99.3	51	5.2	6.1	.458	3	4	4.62	-0.09	-0.46	0.37
Busby, M.	2	10.7	6	0.5	0.7	.422	1	1	5.06	-0.06	-0.10	-0.00
Jimenez, J.	3	18.3	8	1.0	0.9	.546	3	0	3.93	0.12	0.10	0.23
Lowe, S.	1	1.7	5	0.0	0.8	.007	0	1	27.00	-0.41	-0.38	-0.34
Mercker, K.	29	160.7	96	8.4	11.0	.432	11	10	5.38	-1.49	-1.35	0.13
Morris, M.	17	113.7	37	8.2	3.8	.683	7	5	2.93	2.02	2.08	3.08
Oliver, D.	10	57.0	31	3.1	3.7	.461	4	4	4.89	-0.22	-0.28	0.24
Osborne, D.	14	83.7	42	4.9	5.2	.487	5	4	4.52	0.02	-0.10	0.62
Petkovsek, M.	10	48.3	34	3.6	4.1	.464	3	4	6.33	-0.96	-0.35	0.30
Politte, C.	8	37.0	32	1.7	3.5	.329	2	3	7.78	-1.33	-0.90	-0.51
Raggio, B.	1	0.7	7	0.0	0.9	.000	0	1	94.50	-0.66	-0.45	-0.39
Stottlemyre, T.	23	161.3	74	9.1	8.2	.528	9	9	4.13	0.73	0.34	1.78
Witt, B.	5	24.3	21	0.9	2.5	.272	1	4	7.77	-0.87	-0.79	-0.52
TOTALS	163	936.0	511	54.1	58.4	.481	58	57	4.91	-3.87	-2.56	6.31

Once again, the Cardinals couldn't keep their starters healthy. They had 15 different pitchers make at least one start, tops in the majors. Occasionally one of the experiments would work (Juan Acevedo), but usually it was back to the drawing board. The Cardinals' bottom six starters in terms of number of starts made had a combined SN record of 4.1-9.3 (.305). The result overall was a big drop in SNVA from 1.23 in 1997 to -2.56 in 1998, declining from 10th in the majors to 15th. Matt Morris did manage to put together two consecutive months of good health, and he made the most of it. Morris's SNPct of .683 represented the fifth-best rate of production in the majors (minimum of 15 starts), behind only Glavine, Leiter, Maddux, and Clemens—not exactly bad company. Morris was 1997's top rookie pitcher, and last year he showed that wasn't a fluke.

Pitcher Abuse Points

PITCHER	AGE	GS	PAP	PAP/S	AAW	MAX	115+	130+
Acevedo, Juan	28	9	5	0.56	0.93	102	0	0
Aybar, Manny	23	14	49	3.50	8.75	122	1	0
Bottenfield, Kent	29	17	77	4.53	6.79	121	1	0
Mercker, Kent	30	29	60	2.07	2.76	119	1	0
Morris, Matt	23	17	187	11.00	27.50	135	3	1
Oliver, Darren	27	10	34	3.40	6.23	115	1	0
Osborne, Donovan	29	14	65	4.64	6.96	121	2	0
Petkovsek, Mark	32	10	25	2.50	2.50	113	0	0
Politte, Cliff*	24	9	0	0.00	0.00	93	0	0
Stottlemyre, Todd	33	23	476	20.70	20.70	129	12	0
Witt, Bobby	34	5	0	0.00	0.00	100	0	0
TOTAL		164	992	6.05	9.07	135	20	1
RANKING (NL)			12	12	12		11-T	11-T

*includes rainout start

They did not adequately replace Matt Morris (who threw 217 innings as a 22-year-old rookie) for half the season and Alan Benes (who averaged over 7 innings per start in 1997). The departed Todd Stottlemyre had just over 20 PAPs per start, standard fare for the over-30 staff ace, but Matt Morris came back in the second half and got worked as if he had never been gone. If Tony LaRussa is such a genius, why can't he learn from his mistakes? Donovan Osborne is the epitome of brittle, and was used with a little more restraint, but in his case I wonder if it even matters.

Arizona Diamondbacks

The Diamondbacks's 97-loss inaugural season had to be a bitter pill for the organization to swallow. After parading through much of 1997 and early 1998 as if they were going to reinvent baseball, they discovered to their horror that the team they'd assembled—gasp!—wasn't all that good.

What went wrong has been pretty well dissected by minds great and small, so we'll leave the kicking of Jay Bell and Matt Williams to others. Mistakes were made, and while the repercussions are going to be felt for a while, there's already been some recovery, and it's apparent that Arizona is going to eventually be a good baseball team in spite of itself.

Let's focus on where the team is headed. While 1998 was a disappointment, it did serve a couple of purposes. One, it appeared to humble the architects of the disaster: Buck Showalter, Joe Garagiola Jr., and Jerry Colangelo. Sure, Buck, it would be nice to have an entire team full of scrappy white guys who are Gil Thorp's wet dream and who tithe a third of every paycheck to the United Way. The reality is that good baseball players are not all choirboys, and the choirboys who can play baseball don't necessarily help you win.

Joe, you're no saint, either. That Expansion Draft was so bad, there's plenty of blame to go around. Next time somebody gives you free shots at the 16th-most desirable player in half of the organizations in baseball, make sure you actually take people who can lay claim to the title. Edwin Diaz? Yamil Benitez? Sorry, but "organ donor" isn't a position you needed to fill 18 months ago. And to trade actual baseball talent, plus Tom Martin, for Matt Williams?

And Jerry, what the hell were you thinking? Five years, $35 million for Jay Bell, whose good 1997 screamed "fluke?" Five years, $45 million for Matt Williams, who was so happy to be close to his kids again he would have played for half that? Tossing out Jorge Fabregas's arbitration loss and giving him what he'd asked for? For two years? Jerry, there's times to be generous to a fault—the first month of dating, when people are watching, when the write-off is too good to pass up—but these deals just used up working capital and roster spots

on people who should have been with the Twins or Royals. Especially the Royals.

So 1998 cut down some of the organizational arrogance, and for a little while, it established a more realistic timetable for success. The team showed a knack for turning people with checkered pasts into usable pitchers. Omar Daal and Amaury Telemaco couldn't have gotten arrested a year ago; Daal emerged as one of the better left-handers in the league, while Telemaco was effective after the Cubs waived him, showing he could handle a rotation slot. Both of these guys have all kinds of talent, but couldn't get consistent opportunities. Pitching coach Mark Connor deserves a chunk of the credit here, as does Garagiola, who brought both players in.

It wasn't just starting pitchers. The bullpen looked like a waiver wire had tossed its cookies into it. How much did Gregg Olson, Willie Banks, Bobby Chouinard, and Aaron Small go for in your rotisserie league? All of these guys joined the Diamond-backs after the first of the year, and all posted below-average ERAs pitching out of the pen. Olson might have been Comeback Player of the Year had the national media paid any attention to Phoenix after about April 15.

So the D'backs did a heck of a job building a pitching staff, or at least parts of one. So why were they 13th in the league in ERA, despite the BOB actually showing up as only a slight hitters' park, and not the anticipated Coors Light? Mostly because two big-ticket pitchers, free agent signee Willie Blair and #2 Expansion Draft pick Jeff Suppan, combined for 36 starts of...um...five plus four is...carry the one...some really, really bad baseball. Suppan, in particular, was a disappointment, both to the Diamondbacks and to analysts who thought he was a breakout candidate. You may have read something like that in this book, actually. It was probably Gary.

The flops of the Opening Day #2 and #4 starters contributed heavily to the D'backs 17-38 start. By the time they started playing well, everybody was paying attention to some guys having good power years, and the effectiveness of their rotation in the second half remained a secret. So much

---

Diamondbacks Prospectus

1998 record: 65-97; Fifth place, NL West

Pythagorean W/L: 65-97

Runs scored: 665 (14th in NL)

Runs allowed: 812 (t-13th in NL)

Team EQA: .245 (15th in NL)

Park: Bank One Ballpark (slight hitters')

1998: An expensive disappointment with enough bright spots to keep hope alive.

1999: High expectations after writing some big checks, but the offense is still a problem.

---

so that the Diamondbacks didn't even recognize how good they were.

Displaying a terrifying ignorance of the team's strengths and weaknesses, the Diamondbacks went on an unholy spending spree in November, signing Todd Stottlemyre and Randy Johnson to four-year, big-money deals, and Armando Reynoso to a two-year deal. This leaves the team with a legit-imate seven-man rotation, which is actually about twice as deep as their lineup. Signing one of these pitchers wasn't necessarily a bad idea; it would enable Telemaco to be used as the fifth starter, and let the team use Vladimir Nunez in a long-relief role.

But now, the Diamondbacks have committed more than $90 million to high-risk properties without addressing their primary problem: scoring runs. Even if Johnson can continue to pitch at his 1997-98 level for a few more years, is he $13 million better than Brian Anderson? Even if Reynoso stays healthy and effective, the marginal gain over Telemaco is almost nil. These moves solved a problem that didn't exist at a tremendous cost, especially with the gaping lineup holes the D'backs have in the lineup.

The Diamondbacks desperately need hitters. They scored an abysmal 665 runs, 14th in the league. Nobody posted a .360 OBP, and just two players broke a .450 slugging percentage. One of those two, Tony Batista, had to have a meteor destroy half the infield before he was allowed to play. They've signed Steve Finley, two years into the decline phase of his career, to a four-year deal. While it will help defensively, add another millstone to the dead weight on offense.

So it looks like the Diamondbacks will have an above-average pitching staff. They have talent in the rotation and have shown the ability to get production out of nondescript relievers. But to score the 800 runs or so that are necessary to compete, even in a division like the NL West, they're going to have to rebuild the offense. Their best offensive prospects, like outfielder Jason Conti, second baseman Jackie Rexrode and first baseman Jack Cust, are at least a year away, so they'll have to scramble for a year.

An infield of Travis Lee, Batista, Bell, and Williams isn't optimal, but at least the two young players have consider-able upside. In the outfield, the Diamondbacks still have the disappointing Karim Garcia, entering a critical year for him. He's worth playing, because the team needs to learn about him, and there's still a chance he could slug .540. David Dellucci showed a nice mix of offensive skills in 1998. A ter-rible second half wiped out his numbers, but at 25 there's still some expected growth, and he could become Andy Van Slyke Lite. He's certainly a better risk than Steve Finley.

In left field, the D'backs are committed to the remnants of Bernard Gilkey, who has suffered a sharp decline from his great 1996. Vision correction surgery at the end of 1998 provides some hope for the future, but at best he'll be a platoon player.

By midseason, the team could have another young player, Conti, ready to step into at least a platoon with Gilkey. Behind the plate, Kelly Stinnett is an underrated contributor, good defensively and capable of an above-average season at the plate. In this division, he's one of the best solutions.

Looking at the expected lineup, you can see why the D'backs should be optimistic, and why there should also be head-shaking. They have good players with considerable growth left at four positions. But the two expensive veterans block cheaper solutions like Danny Klassen, Rexrode and Junior Spivey. The Diamondbacks have a lot of talent below the Triple-A level, so much so that it's easy to see this team winning three or four division titles at the start of the next decade. But they're going to have to resist the urge to waste resources chasing past-prime talent, especially in pursuit of nebulous "character" goals.

In addition to the aforementioned minor leaguers who can expect to be wearing the purple, aqua, black, gold soon (when did Stevie Wonder start designing uniforms, anyway?), the D'backs have two of the top ten young arms in baseball in John Patterson and Brad Penny. Both pitched exceptionally at High Desert this year, and both should move up to the new Double-A team at El Paso. Penny is the better prospect, but was mildly overworked this year.. The handling of these two will give us a good idea of the quality of Arizona's player development system. One of the two will probably get hurt no matter what the D'Backs do; they're pitchers.

What may be underestimated is just how tough a divi-sion this is going to be. Right now, it's not much. The Rockies and Dodgers are a bit lost at sea, the Padres and Giants are old teams on the brink of collapse. If the Diamondbacks can get serious, they can steal a few division crowns in the next three years.

But come 2002 or so, you are going to have:

- the Dodgers, with the Fox bankroll and a new or redesigned ballpark;
- the Giants, two years into the PacBell Park era;
- the Padres, either on the brink of opening or having opened their new downtown park;
- the Rockies, with their moneymaker called Coors.

Two new parks, one redesigned with a new owner, and a park that is already a significant source of revenue. The D'backs can hang in this crowd, with the BOB and potentially some success to grow the revenue base on. What the American League East is perceived as now is what the NL West is going to be in a few years: five teams with unholy rev-enue streams, packed houses and ownership that, at least in Los Angeles, Colorado and Arizona, has already shown a will-ingness to write big checks.

In a situation like that, what will probably

success is who chooses to do what the Braves and Yankees have done: developing your best players from within, so that you can have a relatively inexpensive core to build around. Both of those teams have high payrolls and have brought in talent from the outside, but as you look at the rosters, you see the core players are home-grown. For the Braves, you have Jones x 2, Lopez, Klesko, Glavine, and Smoltz. For the Yankees, it's Jeter, Williams, Posada, Pettitte, and Rivera. Having players like this for the first six years of their careers makes it easier to spend for a Maddux or trade for a Knoblauch.

The Diamondbacks obviously have the money to put into player development, particularly internationally, which is where the real battleground is. If they put their focus and

their resources on establishing a talent pipeline instead of signing past-prime free agents, they'll have the under priced core that will free them to sign a 26-year-old Andruw Jones or a 27-year-old Vladimir Guerrero. For the cost of a superfluous Armando Reynoso (two years, $5.5 million), they can establish an academy and scouting network in the Dominican, or Antigua, or Korea, that will provide dividends long after Reynoso is a pitching coach somewhere.

That's how good teams become great. I'm convinced that Arizona has everything they need to be that kind of organization, but after November, I'm less convinced that they will make the right decisions.

HITTERS (Averages: BA .260/ OBA .330/ SA .420, EQA .260)

Rod Barajas — C — Bats R — Age 23

YEAR	TEAM	LGE	AB	H	DB	TP	HR	BB	R	RBI	SB	CS	OUT	BA	OBA	SA	EQA	EQR	DEFENSE
1996	Lethbrid	Pio	166	34	3	0	4	5	7	9	1	0	132	.205	.228	.295	.167	8	
1997	High Des	Cal	194	41	5	0	5	6	9	12	0	1	154	.211	.235	.314	.176	10	
1998	High Des	Cal	430	104	10	0	15	19	30	42	1	1	327	.242	.274	.370	.218	36	96-C 98
1999	Arizona	NL	347	93	7	0	13	13	27	41	1	1	255	.268	.294	.401	.238	35	

Catching suspect who took a step forward as a high-A repeater. His defense gets good marks, and there are some serious opportunities for a quality catcher in this organization. Especially if Damian Miller loses the pictures he has of Joe Garagiola Jr., Wendy Selig-Prieb, and all that Jell-o. Mmm . . . lime.

Tony Batista — IF — Bats R — Age 25

YEAR	TEAM	LGE	AB	H	DB	TP	HR	BB	R	RBI	SB	CS	OUT	BA	OBA	SA	EQA	EQR	DEFENSE	
1996	Edmonton	PCL	199	59	12	2	8	14	26	31	2	1	141	.296	.343	.497	.284	30	57-SS 109	
1996	Oakland	AL	232	66	8	2	6	18	28	28	7	4	170	.284	.336	.414	.260	29	44-2B 108	
1997	Oakland	AL	185	36	9	1	4	15	12	13	2	2	151	.195	.255	.319	.193	12	49-SS 103	
1997	Edmonton	PCL	117	29	6	0	3	15	14	13	2	2	90	.248	.333	.376	.248	14	30-SS 95	
1998	Arizona	NL	292	79	15	1	19	19	33	49	1	1	214	.271	.315	.524	.278	44	32-2B 94	28-SS 111
1999	Arizona	NL	323	89	18	1	15	24	38	48	5	2	236	.276	.326	.477	.273	46		

Boy, good thing they signed Jay Bell to a nine-year, $145 million contract, or whatever it was. Batista got a shot when Matt Williams and Travis Lee went down with injuries, and ended the year as the starting shortstop. He has significant power, and will walk more than that projection indicates. Only Barry Larkin is clearly better among National League shortstops.

Juan Bautista — IF — Bats R — Age 20

YEAR	TEAM	LGE	AB	H	DB	TP	HR	BB	R	RBI	SB	CS	OUT	BA	OBA	SA	EQA	EQR	DEFENSE	
1997	Lethbrid	Pio	134	13	0	0	1	8	2	2	1	0	121	.097	.148	.119	—	-4	40-SS 88	
1997	Sth Bend	Mid	93	10	0	1	0	4	2	2	0	0	83	.108	.144	.129	—	-3	22-SS 107	
1998	Sth Bend	Mid	238	46	6	0	2	16	11	9	3	3	195	.193	.244	.244	.154	9	28-SS 91	24-2B 84
1999	Arizona	NL	240	45	5	0	3	13	9	9	1	2	197	.188	.229	.246	.144	8		

Not shown above are cups of coffee at high-A and Triple-A, where he was even more overmatched. Bautista's prospect status is entirely a function of his youth. The Diamondbacks are set in the infield at the major league level and Triple-A, so they can take their time with him. I'd leave him in the Midwest League and let him get some success to build on. I'd also make him run laps or do pushups or cook dinner for all of South Bend every time he saw fewer than 10 pitches in a game, but that's just me.

Jay Bell   SS/2B   Bats R   Age 33

YEAR	TEAM	LGE	AB	H	DB	TP	HR	BB	R	RBI	SB	CS	OUT	BA	OBA	SA	EQA	EQR	DEFENSE
1996	Pittsbrg	NL	524	127	28	3	13	57	58	56	5	4	401	.242	.317	.382	.243	58	147-SS 99
1997	KansasCy	AL	560	159	27	3	21	71	81	82	10	6	407	.284	.365	.455	.283	87	146-SS 105
1998	Arizona	NL	547	137	27	5	22	84	74	77	3	6	416	.250	.350	.439	.271	79	134-SS 105
1999	*Arizona*	*NL*	*516*	*135*	*30*	*3*	*19*	*75*	*72*	*73*	*6*	*5*	*386*	*.262*	*.355*	*.442*	*.276*	*78*	

Saved his season with a strong second half, which still doesn't make his contract make any sense. Bell is already being asked to move to second base, with Tony Batista moving over to short. He'll be even less valuable as a second baseman. The walk rate spike sometimes signals a sharp decline, and he's at an age when non-superstars fall off a cliff, so I see him as an enormous risk.

Yamil Benitez   OF   Bats R   Age 26

YEAR	TEAM	LGE	AB	H	DB	TP	HR	BB	R	RBI	SB	CS	OUT	BA	OBA	SA	EQA	EQR	DEFENSE
1996	Ottawa	Int	436	117	14	1	21	29	47	60	8	3	322	.268	.314	.450	.261	56	106-OF 94
1997	Omaha	AA	321	83	11	1	15	22	37	41	10	2	240	.259	.306	.439	.257	40	86-OF 90
1997	KansasCy	AL	188	49	7	1	8	10	18	24	2	2	141	.261	.298	.436	.247	21	41-OF 105
1998	Arizona	NL	205	41	7	1	9	15	15	19	2	2	166	.200	.255	.376	.211	17	45-OF 100
1999	*Arizona*	*NL*	*320*	*79*	*12*	*1*	*15*	*20*	*31*	*40*	*6*	*2*	*243*	*.247*	*.291*	*.431*	*.248*	*37*	

Low-OBP slugger, and not a particularly special one. Benitez didn't even reach the modest expectations his half-season in Kansas City raised. He has real power, but unless they start awarding extra runs for distance-hitting, Benitez shouldn't be in the lineup. Would make a good Royal. Again.

Brent Brede   OF   Bats L   Age 27

YEAR	TEAM	LGE	AB	H	DB	TP	HR	BB	R	RBI	SB	CS	OUT	BA	OBA	SA	EQA	EQR	DEFENSE	
1996	SaltLake	PCL	464	139	27	4	10	74	80	65	11	4	329	.300	.396	.440	.295	78	92-OF 88	25-1B 102
1997	SaltLake	PCL	309	85	14	2	6	36	38	37	3	2	226	.275	.351	.392	.261	39	40-OF 92	38-1B 87
1997	Minnesot	AL	187	51	11	1	3	21	27	20	7	2	138	.273	.346	.390	.263	24	32-OF 92	
1998	Arizona	NL	211	48	9	3	2	25	21	18	1	0	163	.227	.309	.327	.225	20	42-OF 90	
1998	Tucson	PCL	92	22	4	1	1	17	13	9	1	1	71	.239	.358	.337	.251	11	21-OF 102	
1999	*Arizona*	*NL*	*379*	*104*	*19*	*2*	*8*	*49*	*52*	*46*	*7*	*2*	*277*	*.274*	*.357*	*.398*	*.269*	*52*		

Buck Showalter gushed over Brede, with his generic mix of Texas League singles, two-pitch at-bats and indifferent defense. Up close, all of those things didn't look nearly as enticing. Brede didn't hit and was shipped off to Japan in November.

Jason Conti   OF   Bats L   Age 24

YEAR	TEAM	LGE	AB	H	DB	TP	HR	BB	R	RBI	SB	CS	OUT	BA	OBA	SA	EQA	EQR	DEFENSE
1996	Lethbrid	Pio	212	38	4	0	1	14	9	7	7	3	177	.179	.230	.212	.136	6	48-OF 87
1997	Sth Bend	Mid	460	116	14	4	3	32	42	35	14	10	354	.252	.301	.320	.216	38	116-OF 104
1997	High Des	Cal	57	16	2	0	2	7	7	8	1	1	42	.281	.359	.421	.270	8	
1998	Tulsa	Tex	522	140	19	5	12	51	62	59	12	9	391	.268	.333	.393	.252	63	114-OF 97
1999	*Arizona*	*NL*	*454*	*123*	*16*	*3*	*11*	*37*	*52*	*51*	*14*	*8*	*339*	*.271*	*.326*	*.392*	*.251*	*54*	

The D'backs didn't field a Double-A team in 1998, so Conti spent the year with the Texas Rangers' affiliate. While there, he became the organization's best prospect, showing a broad base of skills and significantly increasing his power. Devon White's departure briefly opened center field. The D'backs could have done worse than handing the job to Conti for a year, but Finley won't be worse for the first year or two he's around.

Jack Cust   LF/1B   Bats L   Age 20

YEAR	TEAM	LGE	AB	H	DB	TP	HR	BB	R	RBI	SB	CS	OUT	BA	OBA	SA	EQA	EQR	DEFENSE
1998	Sth Bend	Mid	63	13	3	0	0	4	3	3	0	0	50	.206	.254	.254	.163	3	
1998	Lethbrid	Pio	213	47	6	1	5	55	35	22	5	4	170	.221	.381	.329	.262	30	58-OF 85
1999	*Arizona*	*NL*	*213*	*58*	*10*	*1*	*4*	*44*	*37*	*26*	*5*	*3*	*158*	*.272*	*.397*	*.385*	*.284*	*34*	

Arizona's #1 draft pick in 1997. Cust is learning left field on the fly and will probably never be better than adequate. When you hit like this, it doesn't really matter. Tremendous plate discipline and above-average power, even as a teenager. After last year's problems at South Bend, the Diamondbacks will move him up slowly, starting him this year back in middle A-ball. ETA: 2001.

David Dellucci   OF   Bats L   Age 25

YEAR	TEAM	LGE	AB	H	DB	TP	HR	BB	R	RBI	SB	CS	OUT	BA	OBA	SA	EQA	EQR	DEFENSE
1996	Frederck	Car	186	49	4	1	3	31	25	20	2	3	140	.263	.369	.344	.256	23	53-OF 96
1996	Bowie	Eas	252	68	10	1	2	24	26	24	2	4	188	.270	.333	.341	.235	25	59-OF 101
1997	Bowie	Eas	385	118	21	2	15	47	60	62	8	3	270	.306	.382	.488	.299	66	86-OF 97
1998	Arizona	NL	414	107	18	12	6	36	44	47	3	6	313	.258	.318	.403	.246	47	105-OF 99
1999	*Arizona*	*NL*	*434*	*120*	*22*	*7*	*8*	*42*	*54*	*53*	*8*	*6*	*320*	*.276*	*.340*	*.415*	*.262*	*56*	

One of the few good players the Diamondbacks took in the Expansion Draft, Dellucci hits OK for a center fielder, but probably not well enough to carry a corner spot. In limited action during a Devon White owie, he wasn't anything special with the glove. I thought he'd be more patient; in fact, Dellucci, Batista, and Travis Lee all walked less than I thought they would. Given the history of Buck Showalter, it's hard to imagine this would be the result of instruction, and all three players should draw more walks this year. Dellucci should out perform the projection above.

Edwin Diaz   2B   Bats R   Age 24

YEAR	TEAM	LGE	AB	H	DB	TP	HR	BB	R	RBI	SB	CS	OUT	BA	OBA	SA	EQA	EQR	DEFENSE
1996	Tulsa	Tex	492	115	21	2	14	24	38	45	7	6	383	.234	.269	.370	.216	41	121-2B 91
1997	Tulsa	Tex	431	102	15	1	13	28	35	41	5	6	335	.237	.283	.367	.220	38	105-2B 105
1998	Tucson	PCL	494	106	23	7	2	26	32	28	7	5	393	.215	.254	.302	.185	29	107-2B 95
1999	*Arizona*	*NL*	*489*	*117*	*25*	*3*	*9*	*22*	*39*	*42*	*9*	*5*	*377*	*.239*	*.272*	*.358*	*.216*	*41*	

Another head-scratcher from the Expansion Draft, Diaz is a good defensive second baseman who just isn't going to hit enough to contribute. The projection above is a good reflection of how well he'll play, but overestimates his playing time by about 400%. Young enough to eventually catch on somewhere and start for a bad team, like the 2002 Indians.

Andy Fox   UT   Bats L   Age 28

YEAR	TEAM	LGE	AB	H	DB	TP	HR	BB	R	RBI	SB	CS	OUT	BA	OBA	SA	EQA	EQR	DEFENSE	
1996	NY Yanks	AL	186	33	3	0	3	19	14	8	11	3	157	.177	.254	.242	.177	10	43-2B 90	18-3B 113
1997	Columbus	Int	319	76	7	2	5	44	42	26	20	9	252	.238	.331	.320	.238	35	48-3B 90	22-2B 99
1998	Arizona	NL	500	138	20	6	10	46	63	57	15	8	370	.276	.337	.400	.257	62	50-2B 89	35-OF 99
1999	*Arizona*	*NL*	*385*	*101*	*14*	*2*	*9*	*39*	*48*	*41*	*17*	*8*	*292*	*.262*	*.330*	*.379*	*.252*	*46*		

Fox may have been the Diamondbacks' MVP, contributing offensively while starting at six positions. He wore down in September, possibly due to playing more than he had in years. With the D'backs set at second base, look for him to reprise his super-sub role, picking up 500 plate appearances all over the field and lineup. Extremely valuable.

Hanley Frias   SS   Bats B   Age 25

YEAR	TEAM	LGE	AB	H	DB	TP	HR	BB	R	RBI	SB	CS	OUT	BA	OBA	SA	EQA	EQR	DEFENSE
1996	Tulsa	Tex	497	124	19	7	2	28	41	38	7	6	379	.249	.290	.328	.212	39	133-SS 103
1997	Oklahoma	AA	479	115	15	3	4	53	58	34	29	12	376	.240	.316	.309	.228	46	128-SS 95
1998	Tucson	PCL	244	55	5	3	1	21	23	14	12	5	194	.225	.287	.283	.204	18	55-SS 90
1999	*Arizona*	*NL*	*343*	*83*	*11*	*3*	*2*	*27*	*35*	*24*	*17*	*6*	*266*	*.242*	*.297*	*.309*	*.219*	*30*	

Part of the Diamondbacks' plot to ruin the Texas Rangers included drafting all their overrated middle infield prospects. Frias is better than Edwin Diaz - he plays shortstop, he walks more—and while I wouldn't want him starting for me, he would make a serviceable utility infielder. With Andy Fox on the roster, he'll probably have to go elsewhere to get that chance.

Karim Garcia   RF   Bats L   Age 23

YEAR	TEAM	LGE	AB	H	DB	TP	HR	BB	R	RBI	SB	CS	OUT	BA	OBA	SA	EQA	EQR	DEFENSE
1996	Albuquer	PCL	312	76	12	4	11	26	32	37	5	3	239	.244	.302	.413	.245	35	75-OF 96
1996	SanAnton	Tex	129	30	4	0	5	8	10	13	1	1	100	.233	.277	.380	.223	12	30-OF 100
1997	Albuquer	PCL	248	62	10	2	15	19	30	36	9	4	190	.250	.303	.488	.266	35	59-OF 92
1998	Arizona	NL	331	73	10	7	10	20	26	32	5	5	263	.221	.265	.384	.218	29	87-OF 100
1998	Tucson	PCL	102	28	2	1	8	13	16	19	4	1	75	.275	.357	.549	.303	19	24-OF 107
1999	*Arizona*	*NL*	*388*	*100*	*13*	*7*	*17*	*28*	*45*	*53*	*13*	*5*	*293*	*.258*	*.308*	*.459*	*.262*	*52*	

(Karim Garcia *continued*)

The good news is that he's still just 23, and the Diamondbacks appear willing to give him a chance. The bad news is that he didn't hit much. Garcia is one of the few Diamondbacks with a high upside, so they'd be better off giving him another 500 at-bats this year to develop. If they do, I like his chances of taking a big step forward.

Bernard Gilkey — LF — Bats R — Age 32

YEAR	TEAM	LGE	AB	H	DB	TP	HR	BB	R	RBI	SB	CS	OUT	BA	OBA	SA	EQA	EQR	DEFENSE
1996	NY Mets	NL	580	191	43	3	33	76	105	115	14	10	399	.329	.407	.584	.327	122	138-OF 103
1997	NY Mets	NL	518	128	26	1	20	72	63	67	5	11	402	.247	.339	.417	.258	68	119-OF 102
1998	NY Mets	NL	265	62	11	0	6	33	30	25	6	1	204	.234	.319	.343	.238	28	68-OF 93
1998	Arizona	NL	101	25	1	0	1	11	11	7	4	2	78	.248	.321	.287	.220	9	26-OF 94
1999	*Arizona*	*NL*	*444*	*120*	*21*	*1*	*16*	*58*	*60*	*61*	*10*	*6*	*330*	*.270*	*.355*	*.430*	*.274*	*65*	

His decline may have been exacerbated by vision problems. He underwent laser surgery in September in the hope of correcting the problem and sat out the remainder of the season. Obviously 1996 was his peak, but if his eyes are working again he can probably be a league-average left fielder. His value to the Diamondbacks lies in how much they get for him at the next trade deadline.

Danny Klassen — 2B/SS — Bats R — Age 23

YEAR	TEAM	LGE	AB	H	DB	TP	HR	BB	R	RBI	SB	CS	OUT	BA	OBA	SA	EQA	EQR	DEFENSE	
1995	Beloit	Mid	219	53	10	1	2	12	18	16	5	2	168	.242	.281	.324	.210	17	54-SS 79	
1996	Stockton	Cal	428	94	16	1	2	23	26	22	7	4	338	.220	.259	.276	.178	23	119-SS 94	
1997	El Paso	Tex	495	131	19	2	11	40	53	52	10	6	370	.265	.320	.378	.243	54	130-SS 83	
1998	Tucson	PCL	271	67	17	1	8	18	28	29	5	2	206	.247	.294	.406	.240	29	51-SS 89	18-2B 114
1998	Arizona	NL	107	20	3	1	3	10	7	8	1	1	88	.187	.256	.318	.194	7	27-2B 93	
1999	*Arizona*	*NL*	*404*	*109*	*19*	*2*	*10*	*27*	*43*	*46*	*9*	*4*	*299*	*.270*	*.316*	*.401*	*.250*	*47*		

Klassen was handled in a haphazard manner, being moved from short to second in June, and being called up to the majors a month later. On-the-job training is hard. On-the-job training while trying to prove yourself in the major leagues...I don't envy Danny. He didn't hit, and was sent back to Tucson, which opened the door for Tony Batista. Right now, he's blocked, and needs a Bell trade or a Batista flop to get another chance. His upside is Jay Bell, without the big 1993.

Travis Lee — 1B — Bats L — Age 24

YEAR	TEAM	LGE	AB	H	DB	TP	HR	BB	R	RBI	SB	CS	OUT	BA	OBA	SA	EQA	EQR	DEFENSE
1997	HighDes	Cal	217	66	7	1	12	36	37	40	3	1	152	.304	.403	.512	.314	42	54-1B 128
1997	Tucson	PCL	218	57	11	1	11	27	30	33	2	0	161	.261	.343	.472	.280	33	38-1B 106
1998	Arizona	NL	560	150	19	2	23	70	74	78	9	1	411	.268	.349	.432	.273	80	144-1B 101
1999	*Arizona*	*NL*	*484*	*145*	*22*	*1*	*27*	*63*	*74*	*88*	*7*	*1*	*340*	*.300*	*.380*	*.517*	*.307*	*89*	

A strained groin, and the decision to come back too soon from it, derailed what was becoming a fine season. Lee was getting on base and slugging .366/.484 before the injury, .303/.324 after. A healthy Lee will be a great player, starting right now. My impression is that the average will develop faster than the power.

Garry Maddox — OF — Bats L — Age 24

YEAR	TEAM	LGE	AB	H	DB	TP	HR	BB	R	RBI	SB	CS	OUT	BA	OBA	SA	EQA	EQR	DEFENSE
1997	High Des	Cal	397	95	14	4	6	41	43	35	12	4	306	.239	.311	.340	.232	40	95-OF 104
1998	Jackson	Tex	92	27	2	0	3	4	10	11	2	1	66	.293	.323	.413	.254	11	21-OF 101
1998	Tucson	PCL	260	56	8	3	3	15	16	17	3	2	206	.215	.258	.304	.188	16	67-OF 94
1999	*Arizona*	*NL*	*337*	*87*	*13*	*3*	*6*	*23*	*34*	*33*	*8*	*3*	*253*	*.258*	*.306*	*.368*	*.237*	*34*	

The name garners him some extra attention. Non-prospect, since he won't hit and he doesn't field like his dad. He'll show up in the major leagues this year, so don't say you weren't warned.

Damian Miller   C   Bats R   Age 29

YEAR	TEAM	LGE	AB	H	DB	TP	HR	BB	R	RBI	SB	CS	OUT	BA	OBA	SA	EQA	EQR	DEFENSE
1996	SaltLake	PCL	373	82	14	1	5	21	22	24	1	3	294	.220	.261	.303	.187	22	
1997	SaltLake	PCL	297	75	9	1	7	22	28	29	4	1	223	.253	.304	.360	.232	29	
1997	Minnesot	AL	65	17	2	0	2	2	5	7	0	0	48	.262	.284	.385	.227	6	
1998	Tucson	PCL	60	16	3	1	0	7	7	6	0	0	44	.267	.343	.350	.247	7	
1998	Arizona	NL	167	47	15	2	3	12	21	21	1	0	120	.281	.330	.449	.267	22	44-C100
1999	*Arizona*	*NL*	*289*	*78*	*16*	*1*	*7*	*21*	*30*	*34*	*2*	*1*	*212*	*.270*	*.319*	*.405*	*.251*	*34*	

Cemented a nice little six-year career as a backup catcher with his 1998. Getting established is the hard thing; once you do that, you acquire the label "major leaguer" and get jobs based on that, irrespective of performance. Miller's a serviceable backup catcher who shouldn't be extended beyond that role.

Abraham Nunez   OF   Bats B   Age 19

YEAR	TEAM	LGE	AB	H	DB	TP	HR	BB	R	RBI	SB	CS	OUT	BA	OBA	SA	EQA	EQR	DEFENSE
1998	Sth Bend	Mid	374	86	7	1	9	56	39	36	5	8	296	.230	.330	.326	.231	38	108-OF 100
1999	*Arizona*	*NL*	*230*	*59*	*4*	*0*	*6*	*34*	*27*	*26*	*3*	*4*	*175*	*.257*	*.352*	*.352*	*.251*	*28*	

Young'un who displayed good plate discipline and power for his age and level. Normally, young players excel in one area or another-high average, great speed, etc.; Nunez doesn't do any one thing spectacularly, but also has no significant weakness. Steady development could have him knocking on BOB's door in late 2000. Watch him.

Mark Osborne   C/DH   Bats L   Age 21

YEAR	TEAM	LGE	AB	H	DB	TP	HR	BB	R	RBI	SB	CS	OUT	BA	OBA	SA	EQA	EQR	DEFENSE
1997	Sth Bend	Mid	337	79	15	0	8	34	32	32	1	1	259	.234	.305	.350	.228	32	
1997	High Des	Cal	42	6	1	0	1	8	3	2	0	0	36	.143	.280	.238	.184	3	
1998	Sth Bend	Mid	276	60	3	0	4	36	23	20	2	2	218	.217	.308	.272	.206	21	
1999	*Arizona*	*NL*	*276*	*67*	*7*	*0*	*7*	*31*	*26*	*29*	*1*	*1*	*210*	*.243*	*.319*	*.344*	*.235*	*28*	

His inability to pass Barajas on the depth chart is a bad sign, despite a significant organizational halo. They sent him to the AFL in 1997, making him one of the league's youngest players, but he didn't hit there, or anywhere in 1998. Prospect status and career are hanging by a thread.

Jackie Rexrode   2B   Bats L   Age 20

YEAR	TEAM	LGE	AB	H	DB	TP	HR	BB	R	RBI	SB	CS	OUT	BA	OBA	SA	EQA	EQR	DEFENSE
1997	Lethbrid	Pio	87	17	1	0	1	20	12	5	3	1	71	.195	.346	.241	.227	9	
1997	Sth Bend	Mid	335	83	7	3	2	44	39	27	8	3	255	.248	.335	.304	.233	33	92-2B 90
1998	Sth Bend	Mid	182	51	4	1	1	37	34	17	10	2	133	.280	.402	.330	.278	27	49-2B 85
1998	High Des	Cal	203	56	3	2	1	36	34	19	9	1	148	.276	.385	.325	.269	28	42-2B 90
1999	*Arizona*	*NL*	*353*	*104*	*10*	*2*	*2*	*60*	*62*	*36*	*17*	*3*	*252*	*.295*	*.397*	*.351*	*.281*	*53*	

Tremendous leadoff hitter prospect. Comparable to Quilvio Veras at a similar age, although Veras was a much better fielder. With the D'backs relative lack of outfield prospects, and Rexrode's less-than-stellar glove, he could end up in the outfield at the upper levels.

Rob Ryan   OF   Bats L   Age 26

YEAR	TEAM	LGE	AB	H	DB	TP	HR	BB	R	RBI	SB	CS	OUT	BA	OBA	SA	EQA	EQR	DEFENSE
1996	Lethbrid	Pio	204	18	0	0	1	21	3	3	4	2	188	.088	.173	.103	****	-5	52-OF 93
1997	Sth Bend	Mid	430	101	16	1	5	60	48	36	5	1	330	.235	.329	.312	.232	43	109-OF 91
1998	Tucson	PCL	378	93	9	1	11	53	45	42	6	2	287	.246	.339	.362	.250	45	107-OF 92
1999	*Arizona*	*NL*	*363*	*92*	*9*	*0*	*12*	*50*	*46*	*43*	*10*	*2*	*273*	*.253*	*.344*	*.377*	*.260*	*47*	

Needed to make a big jump and did. Ryan is too old to be a significant prospect, but his combination of plate discipline and left-handed pop would make him a good fourth outfielder, or platoon partner for Gilkey. The Dante Powell acquisition clouds his future.

Jhensy Sandoval   OF   Bats R   Age 20

YEAR	TEAM	LGE	AB	H	DB	TP	HR	BB	R	RBI	SB	CS	OUT	BA	OBA	SA	EQA	EQR	DEFENSE
1997	Lethbrid	Pio	152	41	6	0	4	5	13	16	3	2	113	.270	.293	.388	.232	15	38-OF 98
1997	Sth Bend	Mid	72	17	1	0	1	1	4	4	2	2	57	.236	.247	.292	.173	4	
1998	High Des	Cal	389	83	10	1	4	11	16	18	5	5	311	.213	.235	.275	.160	16	104-OF 95
1999	Arizona	NL	307	85	7	0	6	5	23	29	7	5	227	.277	.288	.358	.221	26	

Toolsy outfielder with no plate discipline, still learning the game. The Diamondbacks would love to believe he's a young Raul Mondesi; not indefensible, but Mondesi's development wasn't typical. Players who don't control the strike zone and succeed are the exception, not the rule. Sandoval will be overrated for a while.

Junior Spivey   2B   Bats R   Age 24

YEAR	TEAM	LGE	AB	H	DB	TP	HR	BB	R	RBI	SB	CS	OUT	BA	OBA	SA	EQA	EQR	DEFENSE
1996	Lethbrid	Pio	102	15	1	0	1	12	4	3	2	1	88	.147	.237	.186	.128	3	27-2B 71
1997	High Des	Cal	480	97	13	2	5	54	37	28	7	4	387	.202	.283	.269	.192	31	134-2B 89
1998	High Des	Cal	282	55	6	1	4	48	33	17	15	7	234	.195	.312	.266	.215	25	75-2B 89
1998	Tulsa	Tex	118	31	6	1	2	23	21	13	5	3	90	.263	.383	.381	.274	18	33-2B 89
1999	Arizona	NL	390	92	13	2	7	55	50	35	17	7	305	.236	.330	.333	.242	44	

Another good Diamondback second base prospect. Spivey gets more attention for his speed than his walks, which is OK; at least he's getting noticed. Rexrode has a higher upside and is much younger, so I doubt Spivey has a future in this organization. Had a terrible AFL season.

Andy Stankiewicz   2B   Bats R   Age 34

YEAR	TEAM	LGE	AB	H	DB	TP	HR	BB	R	RBI	SB	CS	OUT	BA	OBA	SA	EQA	EQR	DEFENSE
1996	Montreal	NL	76	20	5	1	0	7	9	7	1	0	56	.263	.325	.355	.242	8	
1997	Montreal	NL	106	23	6	0	2	5	7	7	1	1	84	.217	.252	.330	.193	7	13-2B 110
1998	Arizona	NL	144	30	5	0	0	8	7	6	1	0	114	.208	.250	.243	.158	6	34-2B 97
1999	Arizona	NL	121	26	2	0	2	6	6	7	1	0	95	.215	.252	.281	.178	6	

Has no business in the majors at this point, especially given the young infielders in this system. Hanley Frias would be an infinitely better choice as a utility infielder; if Stankiewicz is on the roster this year, it's a sign the D'backs aren't serious about winning.

Kelly Stinnett   C   Bats R   Age 29

YEAR	TEAM	LGE	AB	H	DB	TP	HR	BB	R	RBI	SB	CS	OUT	BA	OBA	SA	EQA	EQR	DEFENSE
1996	NewOrln	AA	334	88	11	1	19	28	37	50	3	3	249	.263	.320	.473	.267	46	
1997	Tucson	PCL	200	50	9	1	6	33	27	25	1	1	151	.250	.356	.395	.265	27	
1998	Arizona	NL	273	70	12	1	12	37	34	39	0	1	204	.256	.345	.440	.270	39	81-C 104
1999	Arizona	NL	266	69	12	1	12	34	33	39	1	1	198	.259	.343	.447	.273	39	

Nice to see him get a chance after taking apart the American Association for two years. Stinnett is the best catcher the D'backs have at the upper levels, and should settle in as an above-average catcher for the next few years. He'll have one big year in the next few, bouncing up around a .900 OPS.

Mike Stoner   OF   Bats R   Age 26

YEAR	TEAM	LGE	AB	H	DB	TP	HR	BB	R	RBI	SB	CS	OUT	BA	OBA	SA	EQA	EQR	DEFENSE
1996	Bakrsfld	Cal	144	32	3	0	4	4	7	10	0	1	113	.222	.243	.326	.184	8	35-1B 93
1997	High Des	Cal	542	143	18	1	16	23	45	59	3	2	401	.264	.294	.389	.233	53	120-OF 89
1998	Tucson	PCL	378	90	13	2	3	23	27	27	2	0	288	.238	.282	.307	.202	26	93-OF 82
1999	Arizona	NL	374	98	14	1	8	17	30	38	1	1	277	.262	.294	.369	.228	34	

Don't believe the hype. Stoner gets some positive reviews as a prospect, but as you can see, he's taken advantage of good hitting environments and being older than the competition.

Devon White   CF   Bats B   Age 36

Year	Team	Lge	AB	H	DB	TP	HR	BB	R	RBI	SB	CS	Out	BA	OBA	SA	EQA	EQR	Defense
1996	Florida	NL	554	154	38	6	18	42	76	73	19	7	407	.278	.329	.466	.272	78	132-OF 110
1997	Florida	NL	265	65	14	1	6	34	35	27	11	5	205	.245	.331	.374	.250	32	65-OF 111
1998	Arizona	NL	561	156	26	1	25	45	75	77	24	9	414	.278	.332	.462	.272	80	139-OF 109
1999	*LosAngls*	*NL*	*475*	*118*	*24*	*1*	*16*	*41*	*54*	*53*	*17*	*7*	*364*	*.248*	*.308*	*.404*	*.260*	*63*	

Much of the hope for the Malone Era in La-La Land died with this signing. White has held much of his value into his mid-30s, and his glove makes him a bit above average in center. But he adds to the Dodger OBP problem, and expecting him to be worth $4 million at age 38 (his deal is for three years plus an option) is optimistic. He'll hit the above projection, and everyone will wonder why the team can't score.

Matt Williams   3B   Bats R   Age 33

YEAR	TEAM	LGE	AB	H	DB	TP	HR	BB	R	RBI	SB	CS	OUT	BA	OBA	SA	EQA	EQR	DEFENSE
1996	San Fran	NL	403	120	15	1	22	41	53	70	1	2	285	.298	.363	.504	.292	66	91-3B 101
1997	Clevelnd	AL	591	158	33	2	34	35	70	89	12	4	437	.267	.308	.503	.272	84	148-3B 105
1998	Arizona	NL	508	135	22	1	22	46	59	70	5	1	374	.266	.327	.443	.265	67	128-3B 115
1999	*Arizona*	*NL*	*453*	*122*	*20*	*1*	*21*	*36*	*52*	*65*	*6*	*1*	*332*	*.269*	*.323*	*.457*	*.268*	*62*	

Clearly a second-tier third baseman at this point, and a real problem for the Diamondbacks. In a year's time, they're going to have a bunch of good, cheap infielders who need to play knocking on the door. Williams will be blocking them and sucking up 15% of the payroll. Time to test the bigger fool theory, I guess. "Herk? Hi, it's Joe. Listen I want to talk to you about a player…"

PITCHERS (Averages: 4.00 ERA, 9.00 H/9, 1.00 HR/9, 3.00 BB/9, 6.00 K/9, 1.00 KWH)

Joel Adamson   Throws L   Age 27

YEAR	TEAM	LGE	IP	H	ER	HR	BB	K	ERA	W	L	H/9	HR/9	BB/9	K/9	KWH	PERA
1996	Charlott	Int	101.3	110	39	14	29	72	3.46	6	5	9.77	1.24	2.58	6.39	1.22	4.35
1997	Tucson	PCL	31.0	40	15	4	8	18	4.35	1	2	11.61	1.16	2.32	5.23	0.76	5.23
1997	Milwauke	AL	78.7	75	29	12	16	54	3.32	5	4	8.58	1.37	1.83	6.18	1.82	3.66
1998	Arizona	NL	23.3	27	19	5	10	13	7.33	1	2	10.41	1.93	3.86	5.01	0.47	5.40

Turned a corner in 1997 when he got a fair shot in Milwaukee. Unfortunately, he's a pitcher: after five bad starts for the D'backs, he underwent rotator cuff surgery and missed the rest of the year. Even if Adamson's healthy, his opportunity here may be gone.

Brian Anderson   Throws L   Age 27

YEAR	TEAM	LGE	IP	H	ER	HR	BB	K	ERA	W	L	H/9	HR/9	BB/9	K/9	KWH	PERA
1996	Buffalo	AmA	124.0	151	64	14	31	72	4.65	6	8	10.96	1.02	2.25	5.23	0.83	4.79
1996	Clevelnd	AL	53.0	54	22	8	11	21	3.74	3	3	9.17	1.36	1.87	3.57	0.56	3.91
1997	Buffalo	AmA	79.3	100	41	13	15	47	4.65	4	5	11.34	1.47	1.70	5.33	1.10	5.33
1997	Clevelnd	AL	49.0	53	23	7	10	21	4.22	2	3	9.73	1.29	1.84	3.86	0.62	4.22
1998	Arizona	NL	210.0	229	100	39	21	87	4.29	11	12	9.81	1.67	0.90	3.73	1.18	4.46

About as good a year as you can have when you give up 39 bombs. Anderson throws strikes and flyballs, kind of an extreme version of Denny Neagle. As someone who works on the edge, he could be very volatile. Until they contend, the D'backs can handle the risk. Impossible to run on. Rumored to be on the move after the signings of Johnson, Stottlemyre, and Reynoso.

Willie Banks   Throws R   Age 30

YEAR	TEAM	LGE	IP	H	ER	HR	BB	K	ERA	W	L	H/9	HR/9	BB/9	K/9	KWH	PERA
1995	Florida	NL	51.3	45	24	8	28	28	4.21	3	3	7.89	1.40	4.91	4.91	0.47	3.86
1995	LosAngls	NL	29.0	40	20	2	15	21	6.21	1	2	12.41	0.62	4.66	6.52	0.55	5.59
1997	Columbus	Int	145.7	201	96	18	45	97	5.93	5	11	12.42	1.11	2.78	5.99	0.78	5.68
1998	NYYanks	AL	14.7	21	14	4	11	8	8.59	0	2	12.89	2.45	6.75	4.91	0.21	7.36
1998	Arizona	NL	44.7	37	19	2	23	29	3.83	3	2	7.46	0.40	4.63	5.84	0.74	2.82

(Willie Banks *continued*)

One of several reclamation projects who pitched well out in the bullpen. The Diamondbacks were a perfect example of the interchangeability of relievers, assembling an effective bullpen from retreads and washouts. Hopefully, they've learned from the experience and will be the rare team that rejects the closer myth. Don't get excited about Banks; he gave up a handful of unearned runs and had lousy peripherals.

Andy Benes   Throws R   Age 31

YEAR	TEAM	LGE	IP	H	ER	HR	BB	K	ERA	W	L	H/9	HR/9	BB/9	K/9	KWH	PERA
1996	StLouis	NL	229.7	237	103	28	73	144	4.04	13	13	9.29	1.10	2.86	5.64	0.90	4.04
1997	StLouis	NL	177.7	159	59	9	54	156	2.99	13	7	8.05	0.46	2.74	7.90	2.13	2.89
1998	Arizona	NL	235.3	232	101	25	68	151	3.86	13	13	8.87	0.96	2.60	5.77	1.08	3.67

Benes has been one of the most reliable starters in baseball for nine years, and has carried a pretty heavy workload in that time. I don't know that I would predict an arm injury, but I would be very wary. His career had paralleled Kevin Appier's up until last year.

Nick Bierbrodt   Throws R   Age 21

YEAR	TEAM	LGE	IP	H	ER	HR	BB	K	ERA	W	L	H/9	HR/9	BB/9	K/9	KWH	PERA
1997	SthBend	Mid	71.0	101	48	6	38	43	6.08	2	6	12.80	0.76	4.82	5.45	0.36	5.83
1998	HighDes	Cal	129.7	144	64	9	70	59	4.44	6	8	9.99	0.62	4.86	4.10	0.26	4.37

One of several good pitching prospects in the D'backs' low minors, I'm less impressed with Bierbrodt than a lot of other analysts. He's had some pretty unimpressive ratios, even before adjustments, and he's tall and thin, which makes me think he's an injury risk.

Chris Cervantes   Throws L   Age 20

YEAR	TEAM	LGE	IP	H	ER	HR	BB	K	ERA	W	L	H/9	HR/9	BB/9	K/9	KWH	PERA
1998	SthBend	Mid	32.3	37	8	0	6	24	2.23	3	1	10.30	0.00	1.67	6.68	1.95	3.62

Fifth-round draft pick who danced all over the Midwest League. Yes, it was only 32 innings, but his performance and age are tough to ignore. High Desert is a tough park, so we'll know a lot more about him in six months.

Bobby Chouinard   Throws R   Age 27

YEAR	TEAM	LGE	IP	H	ER	HR	BB	K	ERA	W	L	H/9	HR/9	BB/9	K/9	KWH	PERA
1996	Edmonton	PCL	80.7	78	32	8	24	38	3.57	5	4	8.70	0.89	2.68	4.24	0.58	3.57
1996	Oakland	AL	60.7	73	32	9	26	32	4.75	3	4	10.83	1.34	3.86	4.75	0.40	5.19
1997	Edmonton	PCL	96.0	134	69	17	25	45	6.47	3	8	12.56	1.59	2.34	4.22	0.45	6.09
1998	Louisvil	Int	39.7	62	33	5	15	25	7.49	1	3	14.07	1.13	3.40	5.67	0.50	6.58
1998	Arizona	NL	39.0	43	21	6	10	24	4.85	2	2	9.92	1.38	2.31	5.54	1.00	4.62

Like Willie Banks, Chouinard started the year somewhere else, found his way to Arizona, and pitched serviceable low-leverage relief. Mark Connor earned his salary and more by getting usable innings out of guys like this. I don't think Chouinard is a good bet to repeat.

Chris Clemons   Throws R   Age 26

YEAR	TEAM	LGE	IP	H	ER	HR	BB	K	ERA	W	L	H/9	HR/9	BB/9	K/9	KWH	PERA
1996	PrWillm	Car	32.7	49	20	7	9	18	5.51	1	3	13.50	1.93	2.48	4.96	0.55	6.89
1996	Birmnghm	Sou	89.0	113	43	8	37	52	4.35	5	5	11.43	0.81	3.74	5.26	0.49	5.06
1997	Nashvill	AmA	127.0	127	69	14	65	59	4.89	6	8	9.00	0.99	4.61	4.18	0.32	4.11
1998	Tucson	PCL	87.7	108	60	12	46	61	6.16	3	7	11.09	1.23	4.72	6.26	0.56	5.34

Non-prospect, one of many the Diamondbacks bored us with during the Expansion Draft. Given their success at developing pitchers and the significant revenue streams they can access to acquire stars, the mind boggles at how successful they could have been had they had even a mediocre draft. Clemons is a big guy with a good fastball and nothing else of note.

Bryan Corey   **Throws R**   **Age 25**

YEAR	TEAM	LGE	IP	H	ER	HR	BB	K	ERA	W	L	H/9	HR/9	BB/9	K/9	KWH	PERA
1996	Fayettvl	SAL	75.0	79	28	3	20	55	3.36	5	3	9.48	0.36	2.40	6.60	1.44	3.48
1997	Jacksnvl	Sou	62.3	91	45	8	21	28	6.50	2	5	13.14	1.16	3.03	4.04	0.31	6.06
1998	Tucson	PCL	91.3	113	47	12	24	41	4.63	4	6	11.14	1.18	2.36	4.04	0.46	5.03

Converted shortstop who got a cameo at the BOB. Unlike most converted infielders, he's not a hard thrower, relying more on a good sinker and command. I'd rather bet on him than on the Chouinard/Banks class, which is exactly what Detroit did by claiming him on waivers.

Omar Daal   **Throws L**   **Age 27**

Year	Team	Lge	IP	H	ER	HR	BB	K	ERA	W	L	H/9	HR/9	BB/9	K/9	KWH	PERA
1996	Montreal	NL	90.0	78	35	10	35	74	3.50	6	4	7.80	1.00	3.50	7.40	1.50	3.20
1997	Montreal	NL	31.3	51	32	4	14	15	9.19	0	3	14.65	1.15	4.02	4.31	0.24	6.89
1997	Syracuse	Int	32.7	22	2	0	9	22	0.55	4	0	6.06	0.00	2.48	6.06	1.83	1.38
1997	Toronto	AL	27.3	34	11	3	5	27	3.62	2	1	11.20	0.99	1.65	8.89	3.22	4.94
1998	Arizona	NL	165.7	153	55	12	47	121	2.99	12	6	8.31	0.65	2.55	6.57	1.53	3.15

Daal finally got the rotation slot he deserved and ran with it. In addition to putting him in the rotation, Showalter and Connor did a good job of slowly stretching him out in his first month. Daal can pitch at this level for a while, and may even get better.

Alan Embree   **Throws L**   **Age 29**

YEAR	TEAM	LGE	IP	H	ER	HR	BB	K	ERA	W	L	H/9	HR/9	BB/9	K/9	KWH	PERA
1996	Buffalo	AmA	32.7	34	20	1	16	36	5.51	1	3	9.37	0.28	4.41	9.92	1.79	3.86
1996	Cleveind	AL	33.0	28	19	10	17	33	5.18	1	3	7.64	2.73	4.64	9.00	1.72	4.36
1997	Atlanta	NL	45.7	40	13	1	18	40	2.56	4	1	7.88	0.20	3.55	7.88	1.67	2.76
1998	Atlanta	NL	19.0	25	13	2	10	18	6.16	1	1	11.84	0.95	4.74	8.53	0.97	5.68
1998	Arizona	NL	36.0	34	16	6	12	22	4.00	2	2	8.50	1.50	3.00	5.50	0.89	4.00

Traded to San Francisco for non-prospect Dante Powell. I think 1997 is his real level of ability, but I can be stubborn. Embree throws very hard and has reasonable command. I stand by this: he needs more work and should not be restricted to the one-out lefty role. He'd be a much better pitcher at 90 innings than he is at 50. Maybe Dusty will surprise us.

Nelson Figueroa   **Throws R**   **Age 25**

YEAR	TEAM	LGE	IP	H	ER	HR	BB	K	ERA	W	L	H/9	HR/9	BB/9	K/9	KWH	PERA
1996	Columbia	SAL	168.7	200	88	14	71	112	4.70	8	11	10.67	0.75	3.79	5.98	0.66	4.64
1997	Binghmtn	Eas	141.0	157	71	13	65	88	4.53	7	9	10.02	0.83	4.15	5.62	0.57	4.47
1998	Binghmtn	Eas	118.3	165	81	20	46	84	6.16	4	9	12.55	1.52	3.50	6.39	0.70	6.16
1998	Tucson	PCL	42.7	45	17	7	16	24	3.59	3	2	9.49	1.48	3.38	5.06	0.60	4.43

His stock dropped after an amazing 1996, far enough that the Mets added him to the execrable Blair/Fabregas deal. He's still young enough to have a good career. Lacks a dominant fastball, but he throws four pitches, including a very good curveball. Saying he'll be the Omar Daal of 1999 is pushing it, but I think he's eventually going to be a credible major league starting pitcher.

Ben Ford   **Throws R**   **Age 23**

YEAR	TEAM	LGE	IP	H	ER	HR	BB	K	ERA	W	L	H/9	HR/9	BB/9	K/9	KWH	PERA
1995	Oneonta	NYP	50.0	50	26	2	19	33	4.68	3	3	9.00	0.36	3.42	5.94	0.86	3.42
1996	Greensbr	SAL	75.0	115	67	5	38	52	8.04	2	6	13.80	0.60	4.56	6.24	0.46	6.00
1997	Tampa	Fla	35.7	35	9	2	16	28	2.27	3	1	8.83	0.50	4.04	7.07	1.05	3.53
1997	Norwich	Eas	41.3	40	27	1	18	29	5.88	2	3	8.71	0.22	3.92	6.31	0.88	3.27
1998	Tucson	PCL	71.7	64	31	5	32	52	3.89	4	4	8.04	0.63	4.02	6.53	0.99	3.27

Closer prospect, and like most of the breed, vastly overrated. Ford's a big guy who throws hard and has a good slider. He's perfectly capable of stepping into the bullpen and throwing 80 good innings, and he might even end up as the closer if Olson falls apart. An interesting player in March.

Russell Jacob   Throws R   Age 24

YEAR	TEAM	LGE	IP	H	ER	HR	BB	K	ERA	W	L	H/9	HR/9	BB/9	K/9	KWH	PERA
1996	Wisconsn	Mid	63.7	95	57	4	56	43	8.06	1	6	13.43	0.57	7.92	6.08	0.26	6.22
1997	Wisconsn	Mid	69.7	95	53	9	66	48	6.85	2	6	12.27	1.16	8.53	6.20	0.28	6.33
1998	HighDes	Cal	66.0	96	44	2	31	40	6.00	2	5	13.09	0.27	4.23	5.45	0.40	5.45

Relief suspect, listed here because the D'backs saw fit to use an AFL slot on him, where he got blistered. His good year at High Desert is partially attributable to his age. Non-prospect, no matter what you might read. The only good thing about sending him to the AFL is it kept Brad Penny, already a bit overworked, from tacking on more innings.

Cory Lidle   Throws R   Age 27

YEAR	TEAM	LGE	IP	H	ER	HR	BB	K	ERA	W	L	H/9	HR/9	BB/9	K/9	KWH	PERA
1996	Binghmtn	Eas	181.0	239	93	13	52	104	4.62	9	11	11.88	0.65	2.59	5.17	0.65	4.97
1997	Norfolk	Int	41.0	52	20	1	10	26	4.39	2	3	11.41	0.22	2.20	5.71	0.97	4.39
1997	NYMets	NL	81.3	93	37	7	18	48	4.09	4	5	10.29	0.77	1.99	5.31	1.03	4.20

Power groundball pitcher who looked like one of the better Expansion Draft picks, but missed most of the season with shoulder and elbow problems. If healthy, he joins the cast of thousands fighting for jobs bailing out Brian Anderson.

Vladimir Nunez   Throws R   Age 24

YEAR	TEAM	LGE	IP	H	ER	HR	BB	K	ERA	W	L	H/9	HR/9	BB/9	K/9	KWH	PERA
1996	Lethbrid	Pio	74.3	110	32	4	12	48	3.87	4	4	13.32	0.48	1.45	5.81	1.31	5.33
1996	Visalia	Cal	50.7	73	41	10	16	25	7.28	1	5	12.97	1.78	2.84	4.44	0.40	6.57
1997	HighDes	Cal	155.7	198	94	35	41	97	5.43	6	11	11.45	2.02	2.37	5.61	0.87	5.90
1998	Tucson	PCL	100.0	97	43	11	36	65	3.87	6	5	8.73	0.99	3.24	5.85	0.91	3.69

Nunez started the year being babied because of a mild elbow strain but pitched well upon his return. Fastball/curveball mix, working on adding a change up. High upside, although his opportunities for 1998 took a turn for the worse after the pitcher signings. Would be a prime candidate for Connorization (trademark pending) in a long relief role.

Gregg Olson   Throws R   Age 32

YEAR	TEAM	LGE	IP	H	ER	HR	BB	K	ERA	W	L	H/9	HR/9	BB/9	K/9	KWH	PERA
1996	Detroit	AL	44.7	41	19	6	23	29	3.83	3	2	8.26	1.21	4.63	5.84	0.67	3.83
1997	Omaha	AmA	36.3	32	11	4	11	16	2.72	3	1	7.93	0.99	2.72	3.96	0.55	3.22
1997	KansasCy	AL	43.0	40	15	3	14	27	3.14	3	2	8.37	0.63	2.93	5.65	0.98	3.14
1998	Arizona	NL	69.7	60	23	4	23	50	2.97	5	3	7.75	0.52	2.97	6.46	1.36	2.84

Forget McGwire, Sammy and El Duque—this was the feel-good hit of the summer. Olson has been bouncing around since ruining his elbow in 1993, pitching in seven major league and countless minor league cities. After some success with KC in 1997, he hooked on with the D'backs, won the closer role in May and never looked back. He pitched better in the second half, so I'm not going to say he can't keep it up.

John Patterson   Throws R   Age 21

YEAR	TEAM	LGE	IP	H	ER	HR	BB	K	ERA	W	L	H/9	HR/9	BB/9	K/9	KWH	PERA
1997	SthBend	Mid	74.7	82	35	4	35	63	4.22	4	4	9.88	0.48	4.22	7.59	1.04	4.10
1998	HighDes	Cal	126.7	120	52	14	45	98	3.69	8	6	8.53	0.99	3.20	6.96	1.33	3.62

One of the CBA-violation free agents of 1996, Patterson used a great curve to abuse the California League. With Brad Penny, he was part of a killer one-two punch. The guy above should serve as a cautionary tale for any young curveball pitcher, so don't get too excited about him. Yet.

Brad Penny   Throws R   Age 21

YEAR	TEAM	LGE	IP	H	ER	HR	BB	K	ERA	W	L	H/9	HR/9	BB/9	K/9	KWH	PERA
1997	SthBend	Mid	113.0	118	49	6	45	77	3.90	7	6	9.40	0.48	3.58	6.13	0.84	3.74
1998	HighDes	Cal	164.3	160	61	18	38	136	3.34	11	7	8.76	0.99	2.08	7.45	2.28	3.51

Owned the Cal League with excellent command and a 90-plus fastball, and did so in the league's best hitters' park. I'm concerned about the workload, although he didn't walk many batters and threw only one complete game. One of the three or four best pitching prospects in the game.

Stephen Randolph   Throws L   Age 25

YEAR	TEAM	LGE	IP	H	ER	HR	BB	K	ERA	W	L	H/9	HR/9	BB/9	K/9	KWH	PERA
1996	Greensbr	SAL	88.7	117	70	13	120	64	7.11	2	8	11.88	1.32	12.18	6.50	0.22	6.60
1997	Tampa	Fla	88.0	105	69	10	77	76	7.06	2	8	10.74	1.02	7.88	7.77	0.54	5.42
1998	HighDes	Cal	80.3	97	53	7	53	60	5.94	3	6	10.87	0.78	5.94	6.72	0.53	5.04
1998	Tucson	PCL	23.7	15	9	1	19	19	3.42	2	1	5.70	0.38	7.23	7.23	0.95	2.28

A perfectly good starting pitcher being converted to relief. Randolph was effective in the rotation at High Desert, but was sent to the bullpen when called up to Tucson. He throws hard and is working on a slider to use against left-handers, since getting lefties will be his job from now on. Trading Embree removes one obstacle from his path, and signing Swindell adds one.

Felix Rodriguez   Throws R   Age 26

YEAR	TEAM	LGE	IP	H	ER	HR	BB	K	ERA	W	L	H/9	HR/9	BB/9	K/9	KWH	PERA
1996	Albuquer	PCL	111.7	111	57	17	60	57	4.59	5	7	8.95	1.37	4.84	4.59	0.37	4.35
1997	Indianap	AmA	26.3	26	10	0	16	22	3.42	2	1	8.89	0.00	5.47	7.52	0.87	3.42
1997	Cincnnti	NL	48.0	49	20	2	26	31	3.75	3	2	9.19	0.38	4.88	5.81	0.57	3.75
1998	Arizona	NL	45.7	47	28	6	27	33	5.52	2	3	9.26	1.18	5.32	6.50	0.64	4.53

More overrated than anything by Robert James Waller. Rodriguez has been on prospect lists for years, basically because he was a Dodger. He hasn't shown the ability to be effective, displaying only a live arm with no real pitching skills. He'll get more chances to burn teams.

Aaron Small   Throws R   Age 27

YEAR	TEAM	LGE	IP	H	ER	HR	BB	K	ERA	W	L	H/9	HR/9	BB/9	K/9	KWH	PERA
1996	Edmonton	PCL	114.7	124	64	10	27	69	5.02	5	8	9.73	0.78	2.12	5.42	1.07	3.92
1996	Oakland	AL	30.0	36	21	3	18	17	6.30	1	2	10.80	0.90	5.40	5.10	0.33	5.10
1997	Oakland	AL	102.3	102	38	6	35	56	3.34	6	5	8.97	0.53	3.08	4.93	0.66	3.52
1998	Oakland	AL	36.7	51	28	3	12	18	6.87	1	3	12.52	0.74	2.95	4.42	0.40	5.40
1998	Arizona	NL	32.0	34	13	5	8	13	3.66	2	2	9.56	1.41	2.25	3.66	0.47	4.22

Another mediocrity who was surprisingly effective in Arizona. I wouldn't bet on Small being a reliable contributor. He'll bounce around for a while, and if he ends up somewhere with a good defense behind him he'll have a year like 1997 again. Be still my heart.

Clint Sodowsky   Throws R   Age 26

YEAR	TEAM	LGE	IP	H	ER	HR	BB	K	ERA	W	L	H/9	HR/9	BB/9	K/9	KWH	PERA
1996	Toledo	Int	119.7	135	59	8	52	51	4.44	6	7	10.15	0.60	3.91	3.84	0.28	4.29
1996	Detroit	AL	25.7	38	26	5	17	9	9.12	0	3	13.32	1.75	5.96	3.16	0.09	7.01
1997	Pittsbrg	NL	54.7	49	17	7	31	46	2.80	4	2	8.07	1.15	5.10	7.57	1.04	3.79
1998	Arizona	NL	79.7	92	51	5	36	39	5.76	3	6	10.39	0.56	4.07	4.41	0.34	4.41

Turned the corner in 1997, and kept turning corners until he was back at 1996. There's no reason to expect effectiveness, just an arm with a decent sinker that somebody will look at and say, "I can make him a pitcher."

Amaury Telemaco   Throws R   Age 25

YEAR	TEAM	LGE	IP	H	ER	HR	BB	K	ERA	W	L	H/9	HR/9	BB/9	K/9	KWH	PERA
1996	Iowa	AmA	49.3	45	20	6	19	36	3.65	3	2	8.21	1.09	3.47	6.57	1.14	3.47
1996	ChiCubs	NL	98.3	118	62	20	29	58	5.67	4	7	10.80	1.83	2.65	5.31	0.74	5.40
1997	Iowa	AmA	110.7	141	73	20	37	64	5.94	4	8	11.47	1.63	3.01	5.20	0.59	5.61
1997	ChiCubs	NL	40.0	46	21	4	10	26	4.72	2	2	10.35	0.90	2.25	5.85	1.10	4.27
1998	ChiCubs	NL	28.0	25	11	5	12	16	3.54	2	1	8.04	1.61	3.86	5.14	0.64	3.86
1998	Arizona	NL	123.0	133	57	13	30	55	4.17	7	7	9.73	0.95	2.20	4.02	0.57	4.10

The Cubs releasing him might have been the dumbest personnel move of the year. Why would you dump a product of your system who's finally pitching well for you? Telemaco joined Arizona's rotation in June and pitched okay. He was much more effective as a reliever, despite having the broad repertoire of a starter. He'll be effective in whatever role the Diamondbacks use him in.

Neil Weber   Throws L   Age 26

YEAR	TEAM	LGE	IP	H	ER	HR	BB	K	ERA	W	L	H/9	HR/9	BB/9	K/9	KWH	PERA
1996	Harrisbg	Eas	103.7	112	40	8	44	57	3.47	7	5	9.72	0.69	3.82	4.95	0.49	4.17
1997	Harrisbg	Eas	108.7	114	56	16	51	87	4.64	5	7	9.44	1.33	4.22	7.21	0.98	4.47
1997	Ottawa	Int	39.7	54	44	8	37	22	9.98	1	3	12.25	1.82	8.39	4.99	0.18	6.81
1998	Tucson	PCL	115.0	118	69	15	58	61	5.40	5	8	9.23	1.17	4.54	4.77	0.41	4.30

Left-handed, throws hard, would benefit from the cloning of Eric Gregg. We've been writing about Weber for four years, and his outlook hasn't changed one bit. Converted to relief at Tucson; since he only has two pitches (fastball, curve), maybe he'll have success as a specialist and make some money. Don't lose sleep waiting, because he's been released.

Bob Wolcott   Throws R   Age 25

YEAR	TEAM	LGE	IP	H	ER	HR	BB	K	ERA	W	L	H/9	HR/9	BB/9	K/9	KWH	PERA
1996	Seattle	AL	153.0	168	76	22	43	77	4.47	8	9	9.88	1.29	2.53	4.53	0.62	4.47
1997	Tacoma	PCL	35.0	40	20	4	6	24	5.14	2	2	10.29	1.03	1.54	6.17	1.80	4.37
1997	Seattle	AL	104.3	123	56	20	25	56	4.83	5	7	10.61	1.73	2.16	4.83	0.76	5.18
1998	Tucson	PCL	133.3	151	61	11	26	81	4.12	7	8	10.19	0.74	1.76	5.47	1.25	4.05
1998	Arizona	NL	34.0	33	24	8	12	19	6.35	1	3	8.74	2.12	3.18	5.03	0.68	4.50

Six starts spread across three separate stints with the team; it's got to be nice to know they believe in you. Wolcott has the potential to be a #3 starter, along the lines of Brian Anderson. He's not going to impress radar guns. He does have pretty good control, three major league pitches and a good health record. I'd like to see him left alone for 30 starts with a good outfield defense behind him. Traded to Boston, which has the good outfield defense.

SNWLP				ARIZONA DIAMONDBACKS						Park Effect: +0.9%		
PITCHER	**GS**	**IP**	**R**	**SNW**	**SNL**	**SNPCT**	**W**	**L**	**RA**	**APW**	**SNVA**	**SNWAR**
Adamson, J.	5	23.0	21	0.6	2.6	.191	0	3	8.22	-0.86	-0.95	-0.77
Anderson, B.	32	208.0	109	11.8	11.5	.507	12	13	4.72	0.06	0.14	1.91
Benes, A.	34	231.3	111	14.0	11.8	.543	14	13	4.32	1.06	1.04	3.05
Blair, W.	23	146.7	91	6.5	9.9	.397	4	15	5.58	-1.34	-1.58	-0.46
Chouinard, B.	2	6.0	4	0.4	0.4	.464	0	0	6.00	-0.08	-0.04	0.03
Daal, O.	23	152.0	57	10.9	5.2	.677	8	10	3.38	2.25	2.66	4.07
Sodowsky, C.	6	28.7	24	1.1	2.7	.286	1	2	7.53	-0.87	-0.78	-0.53
Suppan, J.	13	66.0	55	2.8	6.6	.295	1	7	7.50	-1.97	-1.89	-1.22
Telemaco, A.	18	104.3	58	5.4	6.7	.446	5	9	5.00	-0.29	-0.55	0.26
Wolcott, B.	6	33.0	27	1.4	3.2	.305	1	3	7.36	-0.94	-0.84	-0.56
TOTALS	162	999.0	557	54.9	60.7	.475	46	75	5.02	-2.98	-2.79	5.79

The D-Backs put together a respectable pitching staff for their inaugural year, ranking 18th in the majors. It isn't surprising that an expansion team can do that. Expansion owners willing to chase top-dollar free agents from the outset allow their first-year teams to find at least two or three pitchers who will be better than average, and two or three pitchers is more than some major league teams have. In fact, the average expansion team in the 90's has had their starting rotation rank in the 42nd percentile of the league—i.e., about 42% of major league rotations are worse than an average expansion team rotation in the 90's. This year, both expansion teams had rotations that were much better than one of the division winners' (Texas). I get the feeling that Andy Benes is perceived as having a disappointing career so far. That may be true, but that's related more to sky-high expectations—he was touted as the next Tom Seaver—than poor performance. Benes has actually been a model of consistency during his career, with a SNPct well over .500 in all but one of the past seven years, and at least 25 starts in each of them. That doesn't include 1991, which was probably his best year. Benes's SN record since 1992 is 87-75 (.528), which ranks him 18th in SNWAR among starters over that period. Not Tom Seaver, but hardly what you'd expect from a big disappointment.

Pitcher Abuse Points

PITCHER	**AGE**	**GS**	**PAP**	**PAP/S**	**AAW**	**MAX**	**115+**	**130+**
Adamson, Joel	26	5	0	0.00	0.00	93	0	0
Anderson, Brian	26	32	10	0.31	0.63	104	0	0
Benes, Andy	30	34	537	15.79	21.06	138	10	1
Blair, Willie	32	23	168	7.30	7.30	125	3	0
Daal, Omar	26	23	220	9.57	19.13	127	6	0
Sodowsky, Clint	25	6	10	1.67	3.61	110	0	0
Suppan, Jeff	23	13	28	2.15	5.38	115	1	0
Telemaco, Amaury	24	18	31	1.72	4.02	113	0	0
Wolcott, Bob	24	6	2	0.33	0.78	101	0	0
TOTAL		162	1006	6.21	9.34	138	20	1
RANKING (NL)			11	11	10		7	11-T

The Diamondbacks got served a much-needed slice of humble pie in their first season, but Buck Showalter did an outstanding job of protecting a staff largely made up of youngsters. Andy Benes was the only starter worked particularly hard, but at 30 and the undisputed ace of the staff didn't take on an unreasonable burden. The only other starter anywhere near the danger zone was Omar Daal, who despite a breakout season was kept within reasonable limits. The three shining young talents, Brian Anderson, Amaury Telemaco, and Jeff Suppan, were handled brilliantly, and I expect at least one of them will break out this year. The Diamondbacks better hope it's not Suppan, who was given away to Kansas City late in the year.

Colorado Rockies

The Rockies have never afraid to go out and buy the biggest name on the market. So it came as no surprise when they made the first managerial change in the history of the franchise this October, hiring noted Barney Fife clone Jim Leyland. Is he the right manager for this team, given its composition, its organization, and its goals?

At first, it seems like a match made in heaven. The Rockies' immediate goal is contention, at least for a division title, and ostensibly for a shot at a World Series. In today's NL West, teams are throwing a lot of money around, but no team is really head and shoulders above the rest. Colorado is probably one or two key acquisitions and some tactical improvements away from moving themselves to the head of the NL West class. Leyland is, in general, one of the better managers of talent in the game today, particularly veteran talent, and the Rockies are nothing else if not veteran.

On the other hand, there are dangerous signs in Leyland's history that the Rockies may not have fully considered in making their decision. The gravest issue is his epic mishandling of his young starters last season, particularly Livan Hernandez and Jesus Sanchez. Both pitchers threw over 140 pitches in a start last season, something only one other NL pitcher can claim—Curt Schilling, about ten years their senior. Either Leyland was asleep at the wheel, or he simply ceased to care. Neither of those is sufficient explanation for abusing his employer's top two young pitchers. Additionally, Leyland's fuse in working with young relievers appears to have gotten shorter. His Opening Day roster featured Oscar Henriquez and Gabe Gonzalez. Both struggled early, and both found themselves demoted to Triple-A (Gonzalez after facing five major league batters). He used Felix Heredia as a starter for two games, then gave up on the idea and put him back in short relief, then reduced him to mopping up.

Although many thought that Don Baylor would take the Rockies' managing job with him into his next life, owner Jerry McMorris finally pulled Baylor out of the job, effectively removing him from the organization he had served since its inception. That he wasn't a great tactical manager or a great handler of a pitching staff is beside the point; he had one

---

Rockies Prospectus

1998 record: 77-85; Fourth place, NL West

Pythagorean W/L: 78-84

Runs scored: 826 (5th in NL)

Runs allowed: 855 (15th in NL)

Team EQA: .261 (t-12th in NL)

Park: Coors Field (excellent hitters')

1998: Altitude chewed up a few more starting pitchers and the hitters were overrated. Again.

1999: Still no sign that the Rockies get it: it's the offense, stupid.

---

playoff appearance in his tenure in Denver, and with the kind of money McMorris is pouring into payroll, better results were expected. So Baylor fell victim not only to his own flaws as a field boss, but to Bob Gebhard's annual parade of questionable free-agent signings and the ongoing problems the team has had developing players—especially hitters—through its farm system.

Despite some very public protestations to the contrary, the Rockies are a team primarily built around relief pitching and defense. The team led the NL in double plays and were above-average in DP-turned ratio, thanks to Neifi Perez's work at short. Vinny Castilla's glove work has slipped from his peak, but the team still considers him a top defender. Darryl Hamilton and Larry Walker are both pluses in the outfield. Mean-while, the team's bullpen—often the source of ire among the team's fans—had an incredible season, posting a 3.61 ERA before park-adjustments. Four relievers had DT-ERAs under 3, and Curt Leskanic was nearly there at 3.23.

The Rockies certainly have two very good hitters in Larry Walker and Todd Helton, both of whom project to be well above league average for their positions in '99. They'll also have the best leadoff on-base threat in their history with Darryl Hamilton. But the team has offensive holes at short and catcher, and they have to hope that Lansing gets his health back so they don't have to write him off as a total loss.

The team does have some starting pitching talent, but not at the level that McMorris wants or is paying for. John Thomson carried his 1997 success over to have an excellent but unheralded first full season in the majors, and the team should look forward to having him as their ace for the next three or four years. However, Darryl Kile saw his ERA more than double, which is as much a function of him returning to his actual (Dierkerless) level of performance as it is a park effect; the Rockies simply bought high and carried the wrong expectations into the season as a result. Down the rotation, Pedro Astacio was mediocre, leading the NL in runs allowed, earned runs allowed, homers allowed, and batters hit. Talented but enigmatic Jamey Wright gave him a run for his money in all of these categories, racking up a workload to make Dallas Green proud. Now the team has struck again, buying journeyman Brian Bohanon as he comes off a career year spent in two pitchers' parks.

How does the current state of the Rockies correspond to Leyland's strengths and weaknesses? The picture isn't all that positive. Leyland's pattern of abusing starting pitchers is of great concern, given the Rockies' drafting and developmental tendency toward high-ceiling hurlers. John Thomson is the best of all worlds for Colorado: a good young pitcher whose arm isn't too abused and who can handle pitching in Coors. If Leyland abuses him like he did Hernandez or Sanchez, it would be criminal and irreparably damaging to the franchise, as he's the best pitching prospect the Rockies' system has produced to date. On the other side of the spectrum, Jamey Wright is already in danger because of heavy workloads in the past two seasons; while he may never produce much value for Colorado, he should be attractive in trade to other teams. Letting Leyland blow him out and destroy Wright's remaining value would be irresponsible.

Leyland's decreasing patience with relievers does not gel with his tenure in Pittsburgh, where he could take Sir Pour-a-Lot out of the stands and make him a righty setup man. Because he's inheriting a veteran bullpen, he probably won't be nearly as impatient, but there's still going to be an adjustment period for him in Coors. The altitude can make a decent reliever seem maddening at times, and it's unclear how well Leyland understands the park's impact on relief decisions. Leyland's typical pattern of using multiple relievers to close out games may be an asset, as he probably won't hang himself with a struggling closer.

Finally, Leyland's general preference for veterans over rookies, which he could scarcely indulge in Florida last year, probably won't pose any problems in Colorado, at least in 1999. Helton is well established at first base, and there's no immediate backup available as there was in '98 with Greg Colbrunn. Neifi Perez shouldn't get too much slack at the plate, but he doesn't deserve much; his defense is good, but not enough to carry an empty bat. Ben Petrick, the only

major hitting prospect in the system's upper levels, is at least a year away.

The lack of major hitting prospects in the system has a major impact on what the team's goals for 1999 should be. The upper levels of the Rockies' organization are quite barren, with their one solid Triple-A prospect (Steve Shoemaker) failing his first altitude test badly, and the two mediocre hitting prospects at Triple-A (Derrick Gibson and Edgard Velazquez-Clemente) both hitting well below expectations. There were a few interesting pitchers at Double-A—Lariel Gonzalez and Heath Bost in the pen, Shoemaker and Mike Kusiewicz in the rotation—but all have the huge hurdle of Colorado Springs between them and the Show. While there is more talent in A-ball, there's no revolution building, and the trade of three top young arms in the Lansing deal limits the depth or strength of any wave of pitching help.

The conclusion is that the Rockies should swing for the fences this year. This is made all the more urgent if Larry Walker doesn't sign an extension and intends to walk after the season. The team is as good now as it's going to get for the next few years, and an ideal strategy would be to follow one or two competitive seasons with a dump-and-rebuild effort to stack the farm system. As much as purists and journalists decried the strategy, and as much as the Leyland complained the whole way through, the Marlins dumped their way into an impressive array of minor-league talent. They will contend again, and could embarrass the Rockies with a second World Series appearance before the Rockies get their first if Colorado doesn't go for the brass ring right now.

The answer to the question posed at the start—whether Leyland is the right man for this job—isn't clear. He's a good choice for a veteran team that's going for it all, and for any team that needs order in its bullpen management. He's a poor choice for a team with significant pitching issues like a 9% distance subsidy on fly balls, or a team with good young arms in its rotation. Leyland will probably figure out how to deal with the latter, and the Rockies will put up better records as a result of the change.

HITTERS (Averages: BA .260/ OBA .330/ SA .420, EQA .260)

Kurt Abbott UT Bats R Age 30

YEAR	TEAM	LGE	AB	H	DB	TP	HR	BB	R	RBI	SB	CS	OUT	BA	OBA	SA	EQA	EQR	DEFENSE	
1996	Florida	NL	321	82	17	7	9	24	34	40	2	3	242	.255	.307	.436	.251	38	40-SS 96	23-3B 86
1997	Florida	NL	252	69	18	1	7	15	28	31	3	1	184	.274	.315	.437	.257	31	45-2B 98	
1998	Oakland	AL	122	33	7	1	2	11	15	13	2	1	90	.270	.331	.393	.253	14	25-SS 91	
1998	Colorado	NL	69	15	4	0	3	3	5	7	0	0	54	.217	.250	.406	.219	6		
1999	*Colorado*	*NL*	*244*	*71*	*18*	*1*	*8*	*17*	*30*	*35*	*3*	*2*	*175*	*.291*	*.337*	*.471*	*.251*	*28*		

(Kurt Abbott *continued*)

Apparently suffered from an undiagnosed case of astigmatism until late in the season, after which he started hitting again. If that's all the problem was, then Abbott could easily be a huge Rockie-esque "surprise," maybe outhitting Lansing in the process. I'd like to see the "screw-defense" middle infield of Lansing and Abbott, with Neifi Perez on the bench, but it won't happen. As much as Leyland liked Abbott in Florida, he didn't play him regularly.

Dante Bichette   LF   Bats R   Age 35

YEAR	TEAM	LGE	AB	H	DB	TP	HR	BB	R	RBI	SB	CS	OUT	BA	OBA	SA	EQA	EQR	DEFENSE
1996	Colorado	NL	607	161	32	2	26	47	76	79	22	11	457	.265	.318	.453	.263	81	141-OF 96
1997	Colorado	NL	549	156	26	2	25	33	61	81	4	5	398	.284	.325	.475	.269	75	114-OF 101
1998	Colorado	NL	639	188	36	2	22	32	77	87	14	4	455	.294	.328	.460	.270	86	150-OF 95
1999	*Colorado*	*NL*	*593*	*184*	*29*	*2*	*28*	*34*	*76*	*99*	*11*	*4*	*413*	*.310*	*.348*	*.508*	*.265*	*75*	

The guy you trade. Bichette's season had some good points: he came back to play a full year, and he hasn't shown his age yet, with many of his unadjusted stats up over his '97 totals. That, of course, is why you trade him now, to one of the many GMs who don't understand Coors Field. Signed to three-year extension in August '98.

Vinny Castilla   3B   Bats R   Age 31

YEAR	TEAM	LGE	AB	H	DB	TP	HR	BB	R	RBI	SB	CS	OUT	BA	OBA	SA	EQA	EQR	DEFENSE
1996	Colorado	NL	605	156	22	0	35	37	62	86	5	2	451	.258	.301	.468	.259	77	157-3B 115
1997	Colorado	NL	599	168	21	2	37	47	69	101	1	4	435	.280	.333	.508	.280	90	156-3B 93
1998	Colorado	NL	623	178	23	3	42	43	74	109	4	9	454	.286	.332	.535	.284	97	162-3B 96
1999	*Colorado*	*NL*	*608*	*188*	*24*	*3*	*41*	*43*	*79*	*121*	*3*	*4*	*424*	*.309*	*.355*	*.561*	*.278*	*87*	

A better year than many expected. While Castilla isn't the best third baseman around, his contract isn't so gaudy anymore, he plays solid defense, and he's more productive than guys like Bichette. If the Rockies get it together at other positions, Castilla won't hold them back.

Edgard Clemente OF   Bats R   Age 23

YEAR	TEAM	LGE	AB	H	DB	TP	HR	BB	R	RBI	SB	CS	OUT	BA	OBA	SA	EQA	EQR	DEFENSE	
1996	New Havn	Eas	489	136	22	3	17	45	60	67	5	1	354	.278	.339	.440	.269	67	121-OF	100
1997	ColSprin	PCL	418	93	14	4	14	28	34	41	5	2	327	.222	.271	.376	.221	37	112-OF	101
1998	ColSprin	PCL	475	96	13	4	16	38	34	41	4	4	383	.202	.261	.347	.206	37	126-OF	98
1999	*Colorado*	*NL*	*441*	*124*	*21*	*4*	*19*	*31*	*52*	*66*	*6*	*3*	*320*	*.281*	*.328*	*.476*	*.249*	*50*		

You can call yourself Babe Aaron Cobb, for all I care, Ed—you still can't hit Triple-A pitching. He's very young, so it's early to give up on him completely, but the last two years of non-production speak pretty strongly about the impact of his failure to control the strike zone.

Angel Echevarria   OF   Bats R   Age 28

YEAR	TEAM	LGE	AB	H	DB	TP	HR	BB	R	RBI	SB	CS	OUT	BA	OBA	SA	EQA	EQR	DEFENSE	
1996	ColSprin	PCL	397	107	8	1	12	32	39	47	3	2	292	.270	.324	.385	.247	44	101-OF 87	
1997	ColSprin	PCL	278	65	8	0	8	21	23	26	4	2	215	.234	.288	.349	.220	24	60-OF 96	
1998	ColSprin	PCL	286	71	10	1	9	12	22	29	0	1	216	.248	.279	.385	.224	26	45-1B 87	28-OF 85
1999	*Colorado*	*NL*	*323*	*100*	*12*	*1*	*13*	*21*	*39*	*51*	*3*	*1*	*224*	*.310*	*.352*	*.474*	*.259*	*38*		

Could easily poke 20 homers and hit .280 in Coors, which would earn him about $2.5 million a year in today's climate. To be so close to that opportunity and never attain it must be painful. Can help someone in need of a cheap right-handed bat off the bench.

Derrick Gibson   OF   Bats R   Age 24

YEAR	TEAM	LGE	AB	H	DB	TP	HR	BB	R	RBI	SB	CS	OUT	BA	OBA	SA	EQA	EQR	DEFENSE
1996	New Havn	Eas	451	108	16	3	13	26	36	44	4	7	350	.239	.281	.375	.220	40	115-OF 89
1997	New Havn	Eas	449	121	17	1	16	28	50	53	15	8	336	.269	.312	.419	.251	53	113-OF 89
1997	ColSprin	PCL	72	26	2	0	3	4	9	13	0	2	48	.361	.395	.514	.299	12	
1998	ColSprin	PCL	476	111	13	2	10	33	39	39	11	5	370	.233	.283	.332	.213	39	116-OF 91
1999	*Colorado*	*NL*	*492*	*151*	*19*	*1*	*18*	*29*	*61*	*71*	*15*	*7*	*348*	*.307*	*.345*	*.459*	*.252*	*56*	

Colorado Springs isn't exactly a tough park for hitters, but it sure laid Gibson and Velazquez—er, Clemente—pretty low this year. Gibson has more fans in the front office, so he'll get a shot in left if Bichette is dealt. Despite his struggles this year, Coors Field is all-forgiving: one hot streak and he'll be getting Rookie of the Year votes.

Curtis Goodwin OF Bats L Age 26

YEAR	TEAM	LGE	AB	H	DB	TP	HR	BB	R	RBI	SB	CS	OUT	BA	OBA	SA	EQA	EQR	DEFENSE
1996	Indianap	AA	341	86	17	3	2	54	63	25	38	11	266	.252	.354	.337	.261	46	80-OF 100
1996	Cincnnti	NL	136	31	3	0	0	19	18	6	12	6	111	.228	.323	.250	.216	12	31-OF 99
1997	Cincnnti	NL	263	66	5	0	3	25	29	18	18	14	211	.251	.316	.304	.219	24	62-OF 113
1997	Indianap	AA	117	30	2	1	1	14	16	9	10	6	93	.256	.336	.316	.236	13	26-OF 102
1998	Colorado	NL	154	32	5	0	1	17	14	8	5	1	123	.208	.287	.260	.197	11	44-OF 112
1999	*Colorado*	*NL*	*249*	*69*	*11*	*1*	*2*	*28*	*40*	*20*	*24*	*10*	*190*	*.277*	*.350*	*.353*	*.233*	*25*	

Found his niche: fifth outfielder. I can't see the Leyland putting up with Goodwin's crap for very long, although the Mouth would be useful to a few teams in a defensive replacement/pinch-runner/occasional lefty pinch-hitter role.

Darryl Hamilton CF Bats L Age 34

YEAR	TEAM	LGE	AB	H	DB	TP	HR	BB	R	RBI	SB	CS	OUT	BA	OBA	SA	EQA	EQR	DEFENSE
1996	Texas	AL	607	164	26	4	5	50	69	55	15	6	449	.270	.326	.351	.240	63	139-OF 109
1997	San Fran	NL	461	125	22	3	6	64	64	49	12	10	346	.271	.360	.371	.259	59	106-OF 103
1998	San Fran	NL	369	112	21	2	1	62	63	41	10	9	266	.304	.404	.379	.280	55	91-OF 104
1998	Colorado	NL	186	55	6	1	5	24	27	25	4	1	132	.296	.376	.419	.282	28	46-OF 102
1999	*Colorado*	*NL*	*508*	*158*	*23*	*4*	*6*	*71*	*82*	*64*	*16*	*10*	*360*	*.311*	*.396*	*.407*	*.261*	*62*	

If his knees don't give out and he doesn't slow appreciably during his tenure in Coors, this might be a pretty good signing. They need someone who'll cover a lot of ground, which he does. They need a guy who'll draw walks, which he has really done since coming over to the NL. And they need someone old who Leyland won't try to demote to A-ball, which he is. Not a bad fit.

Todd Helton 1B Bats L Age 25

YEAR	TEAM	LGE	AB	H	DB	TP	HR	BB	R	RBI	SB	CS	OUT	BA	OBA	SA	EQA	EQR	DEFENSE	
1996	New Havn	Eas	322	101	19	1	7	44	50	47	2	3	224	.314	.396	.444	.293	52	93-1B 100	
1996	ColSprin	PCL	68	21	2	1	2	9	10	11	0	0	47	.309	.390	.456	.295	11	16-1B 115	
1997	ColSprin	PCL	365	105	18	1	12	50	52	53	2	1	261	.288	.373	.441	.284	56	79-1B 100	20-OF 103
1997	Colorado	NL	91	23	3	1	4	8	9	12	0	1	69	.253	.313	.440	.253	11		
1998	Colorado	NL	511	143	27	1	24	54	67	79	3	3	371	.280	.349	.477	.281	77	137-1B 117	
1999	*Colorado*	*NL*	*464*	*155*	*25*	*2*	*24*	*53*	*75*	*94*	*3*	*2*	*311*	*.334*	*.402*	*.552*	*.297*	*75*		

Helton's very, very good, but there was no justification for him nearly toppling Kerry Wood in the Rookie of the Year voting. He tore it up after the All-Star Break: .359/.420/.579 before adjustments. There isn't anything you shouldn't like about Helton; he'll improve dramatically this year, and win a few batting titles before he's through.

Chris Kirgan 1B Bats L Age 26

YEAR	TEAM	LGE	AB	H	DB	TP	HR	BB	R	RBI	SB	CS	OUT	BA	OBA	SA	EQA	EQR	DEFENSE
1996	High Des	Cal	509	107	8	0	18	35	32	42	1	1	403	.210	.261	.332	.200	36	130-1B 93
1997	Bowie	Eas	507	100	14	0	13	46	32	36	0	0	407	.197	.264	.302	.192	33	134-1B 93
1998	New Havn	Eas	429	104	16	0	16	35	39	49	1	1	326	.242	.300	.392	.237	45	111-1B 87
1998	ColSprin	PCL	83	20	3	0	2	3	6	7	0	0	63	.241	.267	.349	.208	6	19-1B 92
1999	*Colorado*	*NL*	*454*	*119*	*15*	*0*	*19*	*32*	*41*	*58*	*0*	*1*	*336*	*.262*	*.311*	*.421*	*.226*	*41*	

Signed as a minor-league free agent before the season, Kirgan is a former fringe prospect from the Orioles chain who bought himself a second chance when he came into his own in New Haven, working hard and taking a leadership role—the kind of thing that earns points with decision-makers. Could hit 30 homers in Coors given a starting job, but so could all sorts of people.

Mike Lansing   2B   Bats R   Age 31

YEAR	TEAM	LGE	AB	H	DB	TP	HR	BB	R	RBI	SB	CS	OUT	BA	OBA	SA	EQA	EQR	DEFENSE
1996	Montreal	NL	635	174	37	1	12	47	75	67	19	8	469	.274	.324	.392	.250	74	150-2B 91
1997	Montreal	NL	568	156	41	2	21	49	74	78	9	5	417	.275	.332	.465	.271	80	137-2B 101
1998	Colorado	NL	567	138	30	2	12	41	55	53	10	3	432	.243	.294	.367	.230	55	145-2B 94
1999	*Colorado*	*NL*	*555*	*165*	*34*	*2*	*17*	*43*	*73*	*78*	*12*	*4*	*394*	*.297*	*.348*	*.458*	*.254*	*64*	

A back injury robbed him of everything: power, average, defense. Of course, he's also 30 years old, and was coming off a career year that clearly set expectations too high. If the problem is cleared up, he should put up strong superficial numbers this year, but all indications were that the back problem isn't going to go away soon.

Kirt Manwaring   C   Bats R   Age 33

YEAR	TEAM	LGE	AB	H	DB	TP	HR	BB	R	RBI	SB	CS	OUT	BA	OBA	SA	EQA	EQR	DEFENSE
1996	San Fran	NL	145	33	4	0	2	16	12	11	0	1	113	.228	.304	.297	.209	11	
1996	Houston	NL	82	18	3	0	0	4	4	4	0	0	64	.220	.256	.256	.164	3	
1997	Colorado	NL	331	67	7	3	1	32	18	17	0	5	269	.202	.273	.251	.172	16	
1998	Colorado	NL	282	60	11	2	2	39	25	20	1	5	227	.213	.308	.287	.208	22	90-C 100
1999	*Colorado*	*NL*	*277*	*69*	*9*	*1*	*1*	*33*	*24*	*21*	*1*	*4*	*212*	*.249*	*.329*	*.300*	*.196*	*18*	

The Colorado Out Machine™, or living proof that some people can't hit anywhere, even Coors. He's been cut, although the Rockies are reportedly trying to bring him back for a lower salary, which, if more than food and lodging, will be too much.

Elvis Pena   2B   Bats B   Age 22

YEAR	TEAM	LGE	AB	H	DB	TP	HR	BB	R	RBI	SB	CS	OUT	BA	OBA	SA	EQA	EQR	DEFENSE	
1996	Salem VA	Car	347	67	5	2	1	51	31	16	13	8	288	.193	.296	.228	.190	23	97-2B 94	
1997	Salem VA	Car	283	57	8	1	1	30	22	13	9	4	230	.201	.278	.247	.185	17	36-2B 99	27-SS 90
1998	Ashevlle	SAL	428	97	14	2	4	56	49	30	17	7	338	.227	.316	.297	.223	40	110-2B 87	
1999	*Colorado*	*NL*	*385*	*104*	*15*	*1*	*3*	*45*	*51*	*33*	*19*	*8*	*289*	*.270*	*.347*	*.338*	*.224*	*34*		

Had a great start but struggled with groin and hamstring injuries. They claim he's phenomenal in the field, earning big points for his range. His coaches all say he's probably at least 24 years old; if true, his performance is a lot less impressive.

Neifi Perez   SS   Bats B   Age 24

Year	Team	Lge	AB	H	DB	TP	HR	BB	R	RBI	SB	CS	Out	BA	OBA	SA	EQA	EQR	Defense	
1996	ColSprin	PCL	548	147	22	6	7	21	50	50	13	9	410	.268	.295	.369	.227	51	132-SS 103	
1997	ColSprin	PCL	284	85	15	2	6	13	33	35	6	2	201	.299	.330	.430	.262	35	68-SS 95	
1997	Colorado	NL	306	82	14	8	5	23	34	36	3	3	227	.268	.319	.415	.251	36	39-SS 108	35-2B 104
1998	Colorado	NL	628	152	22	7	9	41	50	54	5	6	482	.242	.288	.342	.216	52	158-SS 105	
1999	*Colorado*	*NL*	*616*	*188*	*31*	*9*	*12*	*34*	*74*	*81*	*13*	*8*	*436*	*.305*	*.342*	*.443*	*.245*	*65*		

Couldn't even put up respectable offensive numbers, although his glove has lived up to the hype. The question here is whether his range will be enough to appease Leyland when or if he realizes that Perez isn't far removed from Luis Castillo as a hitter.

Ben Petrick   C   Bats R   Age 22

YEAR	TEAM	LGE	AB	H	DB	TP	HR	BB	R	RBI	SB	CS	OUT	BA	OBA	SA	EQA	EQR	DEFENSE
1996	Ashevlle	SAL	457	92	11	1	11	57	40	35	8	4	369	.201	.290	.302	.209	37	
1997	Salem VA	Car	417	97	15	2	13	51	52	42	18	7	327	.233	.316	.372	.244	48	
1998	New Havn	Eas	352	83	16	2	17	51	46	48	6	5	274	.236	.333	.438	.264	49	81-C 89
1999	*Colorado*	*NL*	*401*	*109*	*19*	*2*	*19*	*51*	*58*	*61*	*12*	*7*	*299*	*.272*	*.354*	*.471*	*.258*	*51*	

An interesting package of tools and skills. Petrick controls the strike zone well and has power, but hasn't hit much for average, although part of that was probably due to a pitch that nailed his wrist in the spring. His defense is still developing, but his arm is already quite good. He's got good speed, but doesn't steal bases well. The Rockies are very high on him, but they've had prospects blow out in Triple-A before, so they would do well to move slowly with Petrick.

Jeff Reed   **C**   **Bats L**   **Age 36**

YEAR	TEAM	LGE	AB	H	DB	TP	HR	BB	R	RBI	SB	CS	OUT	BA	OBA	SA	EQA	EQR	DEFENSE
1996	Colorado	NL	327	77	15	1	7	43	35	33	1	2	252	.235	.324	.352	.238	35	
1997	Colorado	NL	250	68	7	0	16	36	35	43	2	1	183	.272	.364	.492	.291	42	
1998	Colorado	NL	250	64	12	1	9	37	33	34	0	0	186	.256	.352	.420	.270	35	71-C 102
1999	*Colorado*	*NL*	*254*	*73*	*10*	*1*	*12*	*38*	*37*	*44*	*0*	*0*	*181*	*.287*	*.380*	*.476*	*.271*	*35*	

No repeat was in the works, and at 35, he's not likely to do it this year either. A perfectly adequate solution while they wait for Petrick. Anybody else remember when he came up as a glove man with the Twins, during the Reagan administration? First term? Or that he was Joe Oliver's caddy on the 1990 champion Reds?

Todd Sears   **1B**   **Bats L**   **Age 23**

YEAR	TEAM	LGE	AB	H	DB	TP	HR	BB	R	RBI	SB	CS	OUT	BA	OBA	SA	EQA	EQR	DEFENSE
1997	Portland	Nwn	202	33	5	0	1	25	10	6	1	0	169	.163	.256	.203	.148	7	55-1B 78
1998	Ashevlle	SAL	459	97	11	1	7	55	38	32	4	2	364	.211	.296	.285	.205	35	105-3B 81
1999	*Colorado*	*NL*	*319*	*81*	*9*	*0*	*6*	*35*	*31*	*30*	*3*	*1*	*239*	*.254*	*.328*	*.339*	*.212*	*25*	

Big kid who sprays the ball well to all fields. It looks like he'll continue to develop power as he adjusts. The Rockies are very high on him but are trying to make him a third baseman; he made 31 errors there this year, so the team has its work cut out for it. Could show up on top-prospects lists at this time next year.

Terry Shumpert   **UT**   **Bats R**   **Age 32**

YEAR	TEAM	LGE	AB	H	DB	TP	HR	BB	R	RBI	SB	CS	OUT	BA	OBA	SA	EQA	EQR	DEFENSE	
1996	Iowa	AA	248	61	9	2	4	22	29	21	11	3	190	.246	.307	.347	.234	25	46-2B 104	21-3B 87
1996	ChiCubs	NL	31	7	1	0	2	2	2	4	0	1	25	.226	.273	.452	.232	3		
1997	LasVegas	PCL	104	19	3	0	1	7	5	4	2	0	85	.183	.234	.240	.153	4		
1997	SanDieg	NL	33	9	4	0	1	3	4	5	0	0	24	.273	.333	.485	.277	5		
1998	ColSprin	PCL	359	81	15	4	7	29	32	30	8	8	286	.226	.284	.348	.215	31	41-2B 92	29-OF 78
1999	*Colorado*	*NL*	*300*	*80*	*13*	*3*	*8*	*24*	*33*	*35*	*7*	*4*	*224*	*.267*	*.321*	*.410*	*.229*	*28*		

The organization is full of guys like this—Nelson Liriano, Steve Pegues, Jeff Barry—and meanwhile, they already keep people like Kurt Abbott and Jason Bates on the major-league roster. Is there really such a shortage that a team has to stockpile utility players? Who's next, Bob Bailor? Bill Almon? Probably John Wehner, if you think about it . . .

Juan Sosa   **SS**   **Bats R**   **Age 23**

YEAR	TEAM	LGE	AB	H	DB	TP	HR	BB	R	RBI	SB	CS	OUT	BA	OBA	SA	EQA	EQR	DEFENSE	
1996	Savannah	SAL	380	87	13	0	7	23	27	28	6	6	299	.229	.273	.318	.200	27	42-2B 102	29-SS 90
1997	VeroBch	Fla	249	49	2	1	5	13	14	12	10	4	204	.197	.237	.273	.171	12	43-SS 87	28-2B 97
1998	SalemVA	Car	533	138	14	7	9	42	66	48	32	9	404	.259	.313	.362	.242	58	121-SS 89	
1999	*Colorado*	*NL*	*450*	*129*	*15*	*5*	*10*	*27*	*60*	*49*	*31*	*9*	*330*	*.287*	*.327*	*.409*	*.237*	*45*		

Has two things going for him: speed (he stole 67 bags last year) and a great last name. Does not have the arm or range to play short; will probably return to second in the next year or so.

Larry Walker   **OF**   **Bats L**   **Age 32**

YEAR	TEAM	LGE	AB	H	DB	TP	HR	BB	R	RBI	SB	CS	OUT	BA	OBA	SA	EQA	EQR	DEFENSE
1996	Colorado	NL	262	61	14	3	15	21	35	35	14	2	203	.233	.290	.481	.264	36	73-OF 105
1997	Colorado	NL	552	188	39	3	46	79	117	128	27	8	372	.341	.423	.672	.354	138	126-OF 99
1998	Colorado	NL	434	141	39	2	21	64	85	82	13	4	297	.325	.412	.569	.329	92	115-OF 98
1999	*Colorado*	*NL*	*447*	*158*	*37*	*3*	*30*	*62*	*98*	*106*	*18*	*4*	*293*	*.353*	*.432*	*.651*	*.331*	*92*	

The one guy you keep. He had a great season, so his bum elbow didn't slow him down that much. Trade talks are out of line here: the Rockies only have two great hitters, and Walker's one of them. Trading him instead of Bichette surrenders the opportunity to hose some GM who doesn't quite grasp Planet Coors. Moving into his option year and toward a very substantial payday.

Derrick White — OF — Bats R — Age 29

YEAR	TEAM	LGE	AB	H	DB	TP	HR	BB	R	RBI	SB	CS	OUT	BA	OBA	SA	EQA	EQR	DEFENSE	
1996	WMichgn	Mid	270	55	5	0	6	28	20	19	5	2	217	.204	.279	.289	.198	19	20-OF 93	
1996	Modesto	Cal	194	40	6	0	4	18	15	13	3	2	156	.206	.274	.299	.197	13	28-1B 121	
1997	Vancouvr	PCL	401	106	18	1	8	34	44	41	9	6	301	.264	.322	.374	.243	44	81-OF 96	
1998	Iowa	PCL	244	76	9	1	12	31	36	43	3	4	172	.311	.389	.504	.301	43	53-OF 101	
1998	ColSprin	PCL	78	16	2	0	1	8	5	5	1	1	63	.205	.279	.269	.188	5		
1999	Colorado	NL	390	114	13	0	17	40	50	60	7	4	280	.292	.358	.456	.256	47		

0-for-9 with the Rockies, so take that, rotogeeks. Missed his chance to become Dante Bichette, and at White's age, his shot at anything more than a pinch-hitting role is probably gone.

PITCHERS (Averages: 4.00 ERA, 9.00 H/9, 1.00 HR/9, 3.00 BB/9, 6.00 K/9, 1.00 KWH)

Pedro Astacio — Throws R — Age 29

YEAR	TEAM	LGE	IP	H	ER	HR	BB	K	ERA	W	L	H/9	HR/9	BB/9	K/9	KWH	PERA
1996	LosAngls	NL	209.0	225	83	19	63	116	3.57	13	10	9.69	0.82	2.71	5.00	0.71	4.05
1997	LosAngls	NL	150.7	166	73	15	42	102	4.36	8	9	9.92	0.90	2.51	6.09	1.12	4.18
1997	Colorado	NL	52.3	46	17	9	12	46	2.92	4	2	7.91	1.55	2.06	7.91	2.87	3.44
1998	Colorado	NL	233.0	237	123	37	70	163	4.75	11	15	9.15	1.43	2.70	6.30	1.20	4.17

Even though his performance was roughly on par with that of the previous few years, he has been judged a total failure because 1) he pitched very well with Colorado in '97, mostly outside of Coors, and 2) people still don't understand park effects. Of course, he wasn't really all that special in the first place, because LA had made him look better than he is, but the Rockies need someone to blame again, and they usually start with the pitchers.

Roger Bailey — Throws R — Age 28

YEAR	TEAM	LGE	IP	H	ER	HR	BB	K	ERA	W	L	H/9	HR/9	BB/9	K/9	KWH	PERA
1996	ColSprin	PCL	47.7	66	33	5	21	22	6.23	1	4	12.46	0.94	3.97	4.15	0.26	5.66
1996	Colorado	NL	97.7	85	46	7	53	43	4.24	5	6	7.83	0.65	4.88	3.96	0.31	3.32
1997	Colorado	NL	207.0	195	76	26	64	77	3.30	14	9	8.48	1.13	2.78	3.35	0.36	3.57

Injured badly in a spring car wreck, and not recovering quickly. Not likely to repeat '97 under any circumstances.

Heath Bost — Throws R — Age 24

YEAR	TEAM	LGE	IP	H	ER	HR	BB	K	ERA	W	L	H/9	HR/9	BB/9	K/9	KWH	PERA
1996	Ashevlle	SAL	73.3	68	18	4	22	60	2.21	6	2	8.35	0.49	2.70	7.36	1.80	3.07
1997	Salem VA	Car	14.3	12	5	1	2	6	3.14	1	1	7.53	0.63	1.26	3.77	1.12	2.51
1997	New Havn	Eas	43.0	49	17	3	9	35	3.56	3	2	10.26	0.63	1.88	7.33	2.08	3.98
1998	New Havn	Eas	44.7	50	21	2	11	36	4.23	2	3	10.07	0.40	2.22	7.25	1.77	3.83

A tailing fastball in the high-80s and a groundball-inducing slider make Bost a good prospect for the Rockies' pen, but he lost two months to a broken ankle and as a result didn't reach Triple-A this year. Given the usual adjustments at Colorado Springs, he's probably two years away.

Mark Brownson — Throws L — Age 24

YEAR	TEAM	LGE	IP	H	ER	HR	BB	K	ERA	W	L	H/9	HR/9	BB/9	K/9	KWH	PERA
1996	New Havn	Eas	141.7	162	72	11	41	122	4.57	7	9	10.29	0.70	2.60	7.75	1.68	4.26
1997	New Havn	Eas	183.3	195	93	22	52	133	4.57	9	11	9.57	1.08	2.55	6.53	1.31	4.12
1998	ColSprin	PCL	130.7	125	63	19	36	69	4.34	7	8	8.61	1.31	2.48	4.75	0.79	3.72
1998	Colorado	NL	14.3	16	5	2	2	8	3.14	1	1	10.05	1.26	1.26	5.02	1.50	4.40

Great control, pretty good stuff, but a hard adjustment to the thin air in Colorado Springs. The Rockies aren't likely to stick him in their Opening Day rotation, which should give Brownson what he needs—another year in Triple-A. In any other organization, a grade B prospect.

Mike DeJean — Throws R — Age 28

YEAR	TEAM	LGE	IP	H	ER	HR	BB	K	ERA	W	L	H/9	HR/9	BB/9	K/9	KWH	PERA
1996	New Havn	Eas	20.3	27	11	2	9	8	4.87	1	1	11.95	0.89	3.98	3.54	0.20	5.31
1996	ColSprin	PCL	40.0	56	22	3	22	25	4.95	2	2	12.60	0.68	4.95	5.62	0.38	5.62
1997	Colorado	NL	73.3	68	25	4	23	35	3.07	5	3	8.35	0.49	2.82	4.30	0.59	3.07
1998	Colorado	NL	81.3	75	22	4	23	26	2.43	7	2	8.30	0.44	2.55	2.88	0.29	2.99

It sounds heretical, but DeJean may be more valuable in Colorado than in many other locales. He boasts a deadly forkball and a heavy fastball, both of which work pretty well in thin air. DeJean isn't going to overpower anyone, so I'd be surprised if Leyland gave him much closing duty, but he's likely to continue on this path of success in middle relief.

Jerry Dipoto — Throws R — Age 31

YEAR	TEAM	LGE	IP	H	ER	HR	BB	K	ERA	W	L	H/9	HR/9	BB/9	K/9	KWH	PERA
1996	NY Mets	NL	76.7	101	43	6	42	47	5.05	3	6	11.86	0.70	4.93	5.52	0.39	5.28
1997	Colorado	NL	104.0	100	42	6	31	68	3.63	7	5	8.65	0.52	2.68	5.88	1.12	3.29
1998	Colorado	NL	77.3	58	23	8	23	46	2.68	6	3	6.75	0.93	2.68	5.35	1.19	2.33

A.k.a. "Sliderman." Overcame some May-June struggles to reclaim the closer job in July and wind up with his best season in Colorado. Will have his ups and downs, like any Rockie pitcher, but as long as the slider keeps sliding, he'll be fine.

Lariel Gonzalez — Throws R — Age 23

YEAR	TEAM	LGE	IP	H	ER	HR	BB	K	ERA	W	L	H/9	HR/9	BB/9	K/9	KWH	PERA
1996	Asheville	SAL	44.0	58	27	3	44	34	5.52	2	3	11.86	0.61	9.00	6.95	0.34	5.73
1997	Salem VA	Car	56.0	53	20	4	22	56	3.21	4	2	8.52	0.64	3.54	9.00	2.02	3.37
1998	New Havn	Eas	57.3	55	30	6	39	49	4.71	3	3	8.63	0.94	6.12	7.69	0.84	4.08

Considered the Rox closer-of-the-future, Gonzalez gave up the gains he had made in his control in '97. Throws a devastating split-fingered fastball, sometimes for strikes. Pitched poorly in the spring, which was attributed to the cold weather of New Haven.

Bobby Jones — Throws L — Age 27

YEAR	TEAM	LGE	IP	H	ER	HR	BB	K	ERA	W	L	H/9	HR/9	BB/9	K/9	KWH	PERA
1996	ColSprin	PCL	89.7	91	47	9	64	66	4.72	4	6	9.13	0.90	6.42	6.62	0.56	4.42
1997	ColSprin	PCL	131.3	136	74	14	69	81	5.07	6	9	9.32	0.96	4.73	5.55	0.52	4.25
1997	Colorado	NL	21.3	30	14	2	11	5	5.91	1	1	12.66	0.84	4.64	2.11	0.06	5.91
1998	Colorado	NL	157.3	149	67	11	63	105	3.83	9	8	8.52	0.63	3.60	6.01	0.88	3.43

Lefty pitcher who isn't particularly effective against lefty hitters. Doesn't throw hard, doesn't induce groundballs, doesn't throw strikes. Not a great pitcher in any ballpark, much less in Denver.

Josh Kalinowski — Throws L — Age 22

YEAR	TEAM	LGE	IP	H	ER	HR	BB	K	ERA	W	L	H/9	HR/9	BB/9	K/9	KWH	PERA
1997	Portland	Nwn	16.7	23	8	0	10	14	4.32	1	1	12.42	0.00	5.40	7.56	0.64	4.86
1998	Asheville	SAL	166.7	207	103	17	80	132	5.56	6	13	11.18	0.92	4.32	7.13	0.79	5.13

Left-hander with a knee-knocking curve and an above-average fastball. Kalinowski changes speeds well and works inside effectively, so the Rox are very high on him . . . so high that they worked him to death with 172 innings. Showed signs of fatigue down the stretch, so they've already started to damage him.

Darryl Kile — Throws R — Age 30

YEAR	TEAM	LGE	IP	H	ER	HR	BB	K	ERA	W	L	H/9	HR/9	BB/9	K/9	KWH	PERA
1995	Houston	NL	125.0	128	79	6	68	103	5.69	5	9	9.22	0.43	4.90	7.42	0.91	3.89
1996	Houston	NL	221.7	247	102	17	92	197	4.14	12	13	10.03	0.69	3.74	8.00	1.28	4.26
1997	Houston	NL	254.7	225	83	20	84	182	2.93	18	10	7.95	0.71	2.97	6.43	1.31	3.04
1998	Colorado	NL	256.7	248	108	26	92	151	3.79	15	14	8.70	0.91	3.23	5.29	0.75	3.65

The Rockies should be pleased with Kile's 1998: he threw a ton of innings, keeping the bullpen's workload down, and he was better than league-average for the season. The problem is what they paid for his 1997.

Mike Kusiewicz   **Throws L**   **Age 22**

YEAR	TEAM	LGE	IP	H	ER	HR	BB	K	ERA	W	L	H/9	HR/9	BB/9	K/9	KWH	PERA
1996	New Havn	Eas	74.3	96	38	4	27	51	4.60	3	5	11.62	0.48	3.27	6.17	0.75	4.84
1997	Salem VA	Car	114.7	122	47	6	30	75	3.69	7	6	9.58	0.47	2.35	5.89	1.15	3.69
1997	New Havn	Eas	28.0	47	26	2	9	9	8.36	1	2	15.11	0.64	2.89	2.89	0.14	6.43
1998	New Havn	Eas	174.0	183	60	4	34	117	3.10	12	7	9.47	0.21	1.76	6.05	1.65	3.31

A third time around New Haven was the charm. Kusiewicz has always had the arm—his fastball runs into the upper 80s, and he throws a nasty curve—but he drew criticism for his work ethic. He started listening to his pitching coach and broke through Double-A for good. Serious groundball pitcher, which bodes well. Threw 178+ innings this year, which doesn't.

Curt Leskanic   **Throws R**   **Age 31**

YEAR	TEAM	LGE	IP	H	ER	HR	BB	K	ERA	W	L	H/9	HR/9	BB/9	K/9	KWH	PERA
1995	Colorado	NL	108.0	73	25	6	32	101	2.08	9	3	6.08	0.50	2.67	8.42	3.27	1.75
1996	Colorado	NL	85.0	75	36	11	38	72	3.81	5	4	7.94	1.16	4.02	7.62	1.36	3.49
1997	Colorado	NL	63.3	55	27	8	22	48	3.84	4	3	7.82	1.14	3.13	6.82	1.43	3.27
1998	Colorado	NL	84.0	73	28	8	39	53	3.00	6	3	7.82	0.86	4.18	5.68	0.74	3.32

His peripherals were all off, and he was significantly less consistent in '98 than he was in '97. Tapered off badly in September, which may indicate that his arm wasn't all the way back from the injury. If he's healthy, a great bet to flourish under Leyland.

Chuck McElroy   **Throws L**   **Age 31**

YEAR	TEAM	LGE	IP	H	ER	HR	BB	K	ERA	W	L	H/9	HR/9	BB/9	K/9	KWH	PERA
1996	Cincnnti	NL	12.7	14	9	2	10	12	6.39	0	1	9.95	1.42	7.11	8.53	0.77	4.97
1996	Calfrnia	AL	37.3	30	9	2	11	32	2.17	3	1	7.23	0.48	2.65	7.71	2.33	2.41
1997	Anaheim	AL	16.3	16	6	2	3	18	3.31	1	1	8.82	1.10	1.65	9.92	5.06	3.31
1997	ChiSox	AL	61.0	54	23	3	16	42	3.39	4	3	7.97	0.44	2.36	6.20	1.53	2.80
1998	Colorado	NL	75.0	65	17	3	23	58	2.04	6	2	7.80	0.36	2.76	6.96	1.69	2.64

Like Leskanic, he broke down in September, prompting all sorts of angst over whether it was related to his signing of a three-year contract. No, it wasn't, but it was related to Baylor's bizarre usage patterns. It was an outstanding season, bad month or no. Like Leskanic, McElroy could benefit from more adept bullpen management practices.

Mike Munoz   **Throws L**   **Age 33**

YEAR	TEAM	LGE	IP	H	ER	HR	BB	K	ERA	W	L	H/9	HR/9	BB/9	K/9	KWH	PERA
1996	Colorado	NL	51.7	50	23	4	16	43	4.01	3	3	8.71	0.70	2.79	7.49	1.73	3.48
1997	Colorado	NL	49.7	48	18	4	12	24	3.26	4	2	8.70	0.72	2.17	4.35	0.75	3.26
1998	Colorado	NL	46.3	52	25	2	15	23	4.86	2	3	10.10	0.39	2.91	4.47	0.51	3.88

Lefty-killer who got killed by lefties for the second year in a row. I don't fault the Rockies for liking groundball pitchers, but a bad groundball pitcher is nothing to covet.

Mike Porzio   **Throws L**   **Age 26**

YEAR	TEAM	LGE	IP	H	ER	HR	BB	K	ERA	W	L	H/9	HR/9	BB/9	K/9	KWH	PERA
1998	DanvillC	Car	89.0	106	47	9	41	56	4.75	4	6	10.72	0.91	4.15	5.66	0.54	4.85
1998	Salem VA	Car	39.3	56	26	7	16	28	5.95	1	3	12.81	1.60	3.66	6.41	0.66	6.41

Came over from Atlanta in the waiver-deadline deal for Colbrunn; obviously, he missed a good bit of time in '97 with injuries. He was old for fast-A, but pitched adequately; the Rockies should bump him up quickly to see if he's got a future.

Scott Randall   **Throws R**   **Age 23**

YEAR	TEAM	LGE	IP	H	ER	HR	BB	K	ERA	W	L	H/9	HR/9	BB/9	K/9	KWH	PERA
1995	Portland	Nwn	85.7	121	51	3	29	48	5.36	4	6	12.71	0.32	3.05	5.04	0.49	5.15
1996	Ashevlle	SAL	148.3	179	68	15	58	84	4.13	8	8	10.86	0.91	3.52	5.10	0.51	4.85
1997	Salem VA	Car	170.0	210	100	9	64	91	5.29	7	12	11.12	0.48	3.39	4.82	0.46	4.61
1998	NewHavn	Eas	196.7	240	104	16	60	105	4.76	9	13	10.98	0.73	2.75	4.81	0.57	4.62

Randall wasn't a great prospect to begin with, but what pray tell are the Rockies thinking? At 22, he faced nearly 30 batters per start and threw over 200 innings. This was the second year in a row that Randall faced over 29 batters per start. Not only is that inhumane, but if you treat all your non-star pitching prospects like this, you eliminate any chance of any of them lasting long enough to surprise you.

Fred Rath   Throws R   Age 26

YEAR	TEAM	LGE	IP	H	ER	HR	BB	K	ERA	W	L	H/9	HR/9	BB/9	K/9	KWH	PERA
1996	Ft Wayne	Mid	37.7	41	18	2	12	37	4.30	2	2	9.80	0.48	2.87	8.84	2.09	3.82
1996	Ft Myers	Fla	26.3	36	14	2	12	21	4.78	1	2	12.30	0.68	4.10	7.18	0.77	5.47
1997	Ft Myers	Fla	19.0	29	7	3	3	14	3.32	1	1	13.74	1.42	1.42	6.63	1.69	6.63
1997	New Brit	Eas	46.0	55	20	1	13	23	3.91	3	2	10.76	0.20	2.54	4.50	0.55	4.11
1998	ColSprin	PCL	29.3	38	15	2	17	16	4.60	1	2	11.66	0.61	5.22	4.91	0.30	5.22
1998	SaltLake	PCL	32.0	37	14	4	8	12	3.94	2	2	10.41	1.12	2.25	3.38	0.36	4.50

The Twins gave up on Rath in a hurry, never even trying him in the major-league pen, so the Rockies saw the talent and grabbed him. He throws a fastball with good tailing movement that produces groundballs, exactly the type of guy the Rockies crave. Rath struggled some with his control at Colorado Springs, so he's probably not ready to step into the lion's den.

Kevin Ritz   Throws R   Age 34

YEAR	TEAM	LGE	IP	H	ER	HR	BB	K	ERA	W	L	H/9	HR/9	BB/9	K/9	KWH	PERA
1996	Colorado	NL	245.3	212	93	22	105	100	3.41	16	11	7.78	0.81	3.85	3.67	0.34	3.15
1997	Colorado	NL	118.7	134	55	16	43	52	4.17	6	7	10.16	1.21	3.26	3.94	0.35	4.63
1998	New Havn	Eas	15.3	23	8	3	3	10	4.70	1	1	13.50	1.76	1.76	5.87	1.09	6.46
1998	ColSprin	PCL	18.0	26	21	2	10	5	10.50	0	2	13.00	1.00	5.00	2.50	0.07	6.00
1998	Colorado	NL	10.7	17	9	1	2	3	7.59	0	1	14.34	0.84	1.69	2.53	0.20	5.91

One year left on the contract he signed after his '96 season, which was immediately followed by a complete arm blowout. Showed no indication at any level that he was close to returning, which means he probably won't be ready until after he's a free agent again.

Mike Saipe   Throws R   Age 25

YEAR	TEAM	LGE	IP	H	ER	HR	BB	K	ERA	W	L	H/9	HR/9	BB/9	K/9	KWH	PERA
1996	New Havn	Eas	135.3	132	53	13	40	99	3.52	8	7	8.78	0.86	2.66	6.58	1.39	3.52
1997	New Havn	Eas	134.0	147	55	16	28	94	3.69	8	7	9.87	1.07	1.88	6.31	1.61	4.16
1997	ColSprin	PCL	61.0	70	31	9	21	34	4.57	3	4	10.33	1.33	3.10	5.02	0.59	4.87
1998	ColSprin	PCL	147.0	164	75	17	51	102	4.59	7	9	10.04	1.04	3.12	6.24	0.93	4.47
1998	Colorado	NL	11.7	22	10	5	0	2	7.71	0	1	16.97	3.86	0.00	1.54	—	10.80

He doesn't throw gas or a real sinking pitch of any sort, making him a terrible pitcher for Coors Field. However, his stuff is far from pedestrian, particularly his curveball, and the Rockies would be wise to unlock Saipe's value by dealing him for something they need. Booted off the 40-man roster; a great pickup for a team that needs pitching, which is pretty much everyone.

Ryan Seifert   Throws R   Age 23

YEAR	TEAM	LGE	IP	H	ER	HR	BB	K	ERA	W	L	H/9	HR/9	BB/9	K/9	KWH	PERA
1997	Portland	Nwn	61.7	134	65	10	35	26	9.49	1	6	19.56	1.46	5.11	3.79	0.11	9.19
1998	Ashevlle	SAL	83.3	89	51	9	47	52	5.51	3	6	9.61	0.97	5.08	5.62	0.48	4.43

Had an incredible second-half, lowering his ERA by over a run in the process. Doesn't have great stuff, but changes speeds well and keeps hitters off balance. Not a Coors Field prospect, but he could surprise somewhere else.

Steve Shoemaker   Throws R   Age 26

YEAR	TEAM	LGE	IP	H	ER	HR	BB	K	ERA	W	L	H/9	HR/9	BB/9	K/9	KWH	PERA
1996	Salem VA	Car	80.0	88	63	8	72	72	7.09	2	7	9.90	0.90	8.10	8.10	0.61	4.95
1997	Salem VA	Car	48.3	47	28	4	28	46	5.21	2	3	8.75	0.74	5.21	8.57	1.21	3.91
1997	New Havn	Eas	93.3	81	37	5	53	81	3.57	6	4	7.81	0.48	5.11	7.81	1.15	3.18
1998	New Havn	Eas	79.0	92	74	8	70	59	8.43	2	7	10.48	0.91	7.97	6.72	0.41	5.24
1998	ColSprin	PCL	66.0	83	59	6	69	45	8.05	1	6	11.32	0.82	9.41	6.14	0.27	5.73

Was probably his own worst enemy at Colorado Springs, trying to finesse hitters when he was ahead in the count. His fastball runs up to 97, and his slurve is just about major-league, so he should be able blow hitters away at Double-A or Triple-A. Needs to re-establish himself and get back on track.

Jim Stoops — Throws R — Age 27

YEAR	TEAM	LGE	IP	H	ER	HR	BB	K	ERA	W	L	H/9	HR/9	BB/9	K/9	KWH	PERA
1996	Burlingt	Mid	52.7	76	39	3	49	41	6.66	2	4	12.99	0.51	8.37	7.01	0.34	5.98
1997	SanJose	Cal	83.0	121	67	4	51	67	7.27	2	7	13.12	0.43	5.53	7.27	0.55	5.75
1998	SanJose	Cal	50.7	43	11	0	30	53	1.95	5	1	7.64	0.00	5.33	9.41	1.63	2.84
1998	ColSprin	PCL	15.0	6	5	0	8	13	3.00	1	1	3.60	0.00	4.80	7.80	2.64	0.60
1998	Colorado	NL	4.7	5	1	1	3	0	1.93	1	0	9.64	1.93	5.79	0.00	0.00	5.79

Came over in the Burks/Hamilton swap in the midst of a phenomenal run he was having in the California League at age 26. The Rockies moved him up quickly, and he continued to pitch well until he hit the majors. Throws an extremely heavy ball with great control, but the dirt on him is that he's a one-inning pitcher. That isn't really a problem, since Leyland can work with that.

Mark Thompson — Throws R — Age 28

YEAR	TEAM	LGE	IP	H	ER	HR	BB	K	ERA	W	L	H/9	HR/9	BB/9	K/9	KWH	PERA
1996	Colorado	NL	194.7	170	75	23	74	94	3.47	13	9	7.86	1.06	3.42	4.35	0.53	3.28
1997	Colorado	NL	32.7	38	21	8	12	8	5.79	1	3	10.47	2.20	3.31	2.20	0.11	5.51
1998	SalemVA	Car	12.3	25	10	3	4	6	7.30	0	1	18.24	2.19	2.92	4.38	0.27	9.49
1998	Colorado	NL	27.0	36	17	8	12	14	5.67	1	2	12.00	2.67	4.00	4.67	0.34	7.00

He had a partially torn labrum in '93, so with that in mind, the Rox worked him really hard in '96 to finish the job. Looked awful everywhere he pitched this year, and is probably too damaged to contribute in the near future.

John Thomson — Throws R — Age 25

YEAR	TEAM	LGE	IP	H	ER	HR	BB	K	ERA	W	L	H/9	HR/9	BB/9	K/9	KWH	PERA
1996	NewHavn	Eas	95.3	95	35	9	26	67	3.30	7	4	8.97	0.85	2.45	6.33	1.36	3.59
1996	ColSprin	PCL	71.0	76	37	6	26	54	4.69	3	5	9.63	0.76	3.30	6.85	1.11	4.06
1997	ColSprin	PCL	42.7	34	13	4	12	41	2.74	3	2	7.17	0.84	2.53	8.65	3.09	2.53
1997	Colorado	NL	180.3	179	69	15	47	97	3.44	11	9	8.93	0.75	2.35	4.84	0.84	3.49
1998	Colorado	NL	177.3	167	66	20	46	101	3.35	12	8	8.48	1.02	2.33	5.13	1.00	3.40

The Rockies' best pitcher, even though he didn't come with several years and millions of dollars attached to him (yet). The one concern coming into '98 was his workload, but he was healthy most of the year, and pitched almost 40 fewer innings in '98 than he had the year before. Will be the Rockies' ace as long as his arm holds up.

Dave Veres — Throws R — Age 32

YEAR	TEAM	LGE	IP	H	ER	HR	BB	K	ERA	W	L	H/9	HR/9	BB/9	K/9	KWH	PERA
1996	Montreal	NL	80.7	90	34	10	30	74	3.79	5	4	10.04	1.12	3.35	8.26	1.52	4.57
1997	Montreal	NL	63.7	71	25	5	25	43	3.53	4	3	10.04	0.71	3.53	6.08	0.78	4.24
1998	Colorado	NL	83.3	63	20	6	26	70	2.16	7	2	6.80	0.65	2.81	7.56	2.24	2.27

It took two years, but he finally recovered from the case of terrycollinsitis he contracted in '95. Should be an anchor for the Rockies in middle relief this season and a favorite of the Leyland, although he may see fewer lefties.

Doug Walls — Throws R — Age 25

YEAR	TEAM	LGE	IP	H	ER	HR	BB	K	ERA	W	L	H/9	HR/9	BB/9	K/9	KWH	PERA
1996	Salem VA	Car	12.7	23	14	4	11	12	9.95	0	1	16.34	2.84	7.82	8.53	0.43	9.24
1997	Portland	Nwn	17.7	32	5	0	13	10	2.55	1	1	16.30	0.00	6.62	5.09	0.18	6.62
1997	Asheville	SAL	47.7	74	31	5	32	36	5.85	2	3	13.97	0.94	6.04	6.80	0.41	6.61
1998	Salem VA	Car	146.3	206	125	13	87	102	7.69	3	13	12.67	0.80	5.35	6.27	0.44	5.84

Missed a huge chunk of time with arm woes in '97, retarding his development so that he still hasn't escaped fast-A. The Rockies should just push him to Double-A and let him sink or swim.

Jamey Wright			**Throws R**			**Age 24**											
YEAR	TEAM	LGE	IP	H	ER	HR	BB	K	ERA	W	L	H/9	HR/9	BB/9	K/9	KWH	PERA
1996	NewHavn	Eas	44.0	31	6	0	12	42	1.23	5	0	6.34	0.00	2.45	8.59	3.56	1.64
1996	ColSprin	PCL	61.0	51	16	4	21	35	2.36	5	2	7.52	0.59	3.10	5.16	0.86	2.80
1996	Colorado	NL	104.7	96	41	7	41	43	3.53	7	5	8.25	0.60	3.53	3.70	0.35	3.27
1997	Colorado	NL	165.3	187	87	19	67	55	4.74	7	11	10.18	1.03	3.65	2.99	0.18	4.57
1998	Colorado	NL	230.0	229	111	22	92	83	4.34	12	14	8.96	0.86	3.60	3.25	0.25	3.80

Didn't belong in the majors in '96, and the Rockies screwed him up by rushing him. Wright threw so many pitches in so many innings—he faced over 900 batters, and it only seemed like he walked half of them—that this year he's probably headed for a breakdown, physical or emotional. Still has the plus fastball and slider, he could find himself in another organization.

SNWLP				COLORADO ROCKIES								Park Effect: +38.2%
PITCHER	GS	IP	R	SNW	SNL	SNPCT	W	L	RA	APW	SNVA	SNWAR
Astacio, P.	34	208.0	159	9.8	14.8	.398	13	14	6.88	-2.64	-2.28	-0.66
Brownson, M.	2	13.3	7	1.0	0.7	.567	1	0	4.73	0.12	0.14	0.24
Dejean, M.	1	3.0	1	0.3	0.1	.779	0	0	3.00	0.08	0.10	0.12
Jones, B. M.	20	121.0	76	6.7	6.7	.500	7	8	5.65	-0.06	0.04	1.00
Kile, D.	35	228.3	140	13.8	12.5	.525	13	17	5.52	0.20	0.57	2.61
Ritz, K.	2	9.0	11	0.1	1.3	.092	0	2	11.00	-0.48	-0.57	-0.48
Saipe, M.	2	10.0	12	0.4	1.1	.264	0	1	10.80	-0.52	-0.33	-0.24
Thompson, M.	6	23.3	22	0.9	2.3	.280	1	2	8.49	-0.67	-0.65	-0.46
Thomson, J.	26	161.0	86	10.9	7.9	.580	7	11	4.81	1.28	1.38	2.90
Wright, Jamey	34	206.3	143	10.5	13.6	.436	9	14	6.24	-1.30	-1.48	0.27
TOTALS	162	983.3	657	54.3	61.0	.471	51	69	6.01	-3.99	-3.08	5.31

Many thought Darryl Kile would be a catastrophe in Colorado, reverting to mediocrity but with the additional problem of being unable to snap off his curve in the thin air of Coors. I certainly had doubts. Now the results are in, and while he may not be worth the gazillion dollars he got, he wasn't bad either. His line from last year represents the fourth best season by a starter in the Rockies' short history. Pundits seem to have been right when predicting he'd be ill-suited for Coors, though. Kile's SN record on the road was 8.1-5.8, for a .585 SNPct—not out of line with what he did in 1997. In Coors, however, he was 5.6-6.7, for a .457 SNPct. John Thomson's year represents the second-best season by a Rockies starter ever, ranking only behind Marvin Freeman's 18 starts in strike-shortened 1994. Thomson had similar Coors problems to Kile, going 7.2-3.7 (.661) on the road but 3.6-4.2 (.466) at home. So did any Rocky starter pitch effectively in Coors? No, but at least Jamey Wright was an equal opportunity offender, going .433 on the road and .440 at home. There was a lot of pre-season and in-season buzz that this would be the best-ever Rockies rotation, but they ended up falling short of the 1995 wild-card winners. The 1995 rotation was ranked fifth in the NL by Support-Neutral numbers, while the 1998 group finished fifth from the bottom.

Pitcher Abuse Points

PITCHER	AGE	GS	PAP	PAP/S	AAW	MAX	115+	130+
Astacio, Pedro	28	34	311	9.15	15.25	128	6	0
Jones, Bobby M.	26	20	111	5.55	11.10	124	2	0
Kile, Darryl	29	35	619	17.69	26.53	140	12	3
Thompson, Mark	27	6	0	0.00	0.00	81	0	0
Thomson, John*	24	27	96	3.56	8.30	117	2	0
Wright, Jamey	23	34	174	5.12	12.79	129	4	0
TOTAL		163	1311	8.04	14.28	140	26	3
RANKING (NL)			8	8	7		8	6

*includes rainout start

In the thin air of Colorado, you have to wonder if a starter is bound to throw more pitches because he has to face more hitters—or if he's bound to throw fewer because he's more likely to be pulled early. It looks like a wash. Don Baylor had his boys right in the middle of the NL, although Baylor used his bullpen as much as any manager in history, and look who's coming to town but Jim Leyland. Be afraid, Rockies fans. Kile was worked hard, but that's why they signed him, and they need to be more attentive to his arm this year. John Thomson, one of the great pitching secrets in baseball, was handled very nicely by Baylor—more so than Jamey Wright, who was so bad last year you have to wonder about his health.

Los Angeles Dodgers

Had this Dodger essay been written November 1, it would have looked much different. There was a considerable amount of optimism with the hiring of Kevin Malone as general manager and long-suffering Davey Johnson as manager. Surely Johnson, with his respect for OBP and ability to find roles for young players, would be able to solve the recent Dodger problems with scoring and develop players like Roger Cedeno or Adrian Beltre. Malone was a welcome respite from the Fox/Lasorda combination that ripped a hole in the farm system and inflated the payroll without significantly improving the team.

A month later, the Dodgers have budgeted over $40 million to secure the services of some vastly overrated 30-somethings. Devon White (three years, $12 million) and Jeff Shaw (contract restructured to avoid trade demand, now three years, $15 million) are expensive, almost sure to decline and aren't much better then what the in-house solutions, Cedeno and Antonio Osuna, were. They threw $6 million and a three-year contract at Alan Mills, who's no better than any number of pitchers trapped in Triple-A. They dumped Charles Johnson (along with Cedeno) in exchange for Todd Hundley, who hit .151 last year and may or may not be able to throw. But he is signed for two more years at $5 million per.

This is not progress. Malone, in particular, seems very enamored of being considered the savior, after the unfunny circus that was Dodger baseball in 1998. He's determined to do things that make the press and fans happy, it doesn't appear he's entirely focused on the baseball ramifications of his actions, and he certainly doesn't appear to be looking any further ahead than about mid-May. His moves have added payroll, age and uncertainty to the Dodger roster, without improving the team in any significant way. While it's apparent he has been given a lot of leeway by a chastened Fox management, it's less apparent that he's going to use that free rein, and the resources at his disposal, wisely.

There is the positive of the Bobby Bonilla trade. Bonilla was sent back to Queens in exchange for Mel Rojas, who like Bonilla is expensive and had been a disappointment. Even if Rojas doesn't find his 1996 form, the trade takes away an excuse for the Dodgers to keep Adrian Beltre out of the major league lineup. Beltre wasn't spectacular after his midseason callup, but he's going to be an excellent third baseman, and he'll be a big part of any success the Dodgers are going to have in the next five years.

In spite of most of the moves, the Dodgers are going to be an improved team, quite possibly enough to win the NL West going away. That's how strong the Davey Johnson effect is. There is no doubt that Johnson can convert random collections of mismatched talent into a winning team, and what is certain in L.A. is that there is talent. Johnson maximizes baseball players, getting good performances out of marginal guys (Danny Heep, 1986; Mark Lewis, 1995; Lenny Webster, 1997), building an offense that gets on base—and not over-managing—and assembling bullpens that let him control the late stages of a game.

That last point could be key in Los Angeles, because the Dodger rotation isn't what it once was. Ismael Valdes, Chan Ho Park, and Carlos Perez will be the top three guys, but after that there are some question marks. They have talent, including hard-throwing but fragile Darren Dreifort, innings-muncher Dave Mlicki and a handful of B prospects like Mike Judd and Ricky Stone. In the bullpen, Johnson has any number of live arms to get the game to Shaw, including Osuna, Jeff Kubenka, and Sean Maloney. The staff doesn't have the top one or two starters like Atlanta, and it doesn't have a veteran bullpen like the Yankees, but it has the tools Johnson will need to win games.

And he's going to win. He's going to sift through the flotsam of the Dodger offense until he finds the guys who can put runs on the board. He'll play those players, even if there's a defensive cost. It's how he wins. In ten full seasons as manager, his teams have led the league in runs scored four times. They've finished in the top three eight times. The comparable numbers for runs allowed? Three times and six times. Only three times have his teams ranked better in runs allowed than runs scored; two of those came while he managed in Shea Stadium, a very good pitchers' park. His 1986-88 Mets teams led the league in runs scored three straight times, a remarkable achievement in that park.

Dodgers Prospectus

1998 record: 83-79; Third place, NL West

Pythagorean W/L: 80-82

Runs scored: 669 (12th in NL)

Runs allowed: 678 (5th in NL)

Team EQA: .255 (10th in NL)

Park: Dodger Stadium (excellent pitchers')

1998: Tumultuous year left the team older, more expensive, and not much improved.

1999: Outlook could change a dozen times before you turn the page.

If he can do it there, he can do it in Los Angeles, which presents similar challenges to his stint as Mets manager. Both teams are transitioning out of difficult eras: the 1984 Mets from the post-Seaver malaise, and the 1999 Dodgers from the bloodbath that occurred last season. Both teams' best player is a right fielder who doesn't receive proper credit for his contributions. Both teams have pitching staffs with a lot of upside, with young breakout starter candidates.

To be sure, there are some significant differences, not the least of which is the changes that have occurred in baseball since 1984. Johnson has placed himself in a situation where there are great expectations, in part due to his track record. With the Mets in 1984, he was an unknown quantity taking over a team that had been downright brutal for years. The Dodgers have not been nearly as bad, and there's an unspoken pressure, a feeling that this team can get right back to the top of its division. That's unrealistic—you don't trade one of the best players in the game's history and not feel that—but unavoidable. Dodger fans, Fox, the Los Angeles media all expect this team to win 90-95 games in 1999, and aren't going to want to hear about the problems in building an offense with at least three OBP sink-holes in the lineup, or how Davey's hands were tied by the White and Shaw contracts, or how Glenn Hoffman burnt out Chan Ho Park, leaving him without one of his rotation anchors.

You know what? It doesn't matter. In Davey We Trust. Why?

- Walks. In 1984, four of the six regulars who Davey carried over from 1983 increased their walk rate. Of the two who didn't, Keith Hernandez's dropped slightly, but he still walked a lot; George Foster's decreased a bit more, but he was 35 and unlikely to change much. At second base, Wally Backman replaced Brian Giles, a net increase in walk rate, while Mike Fitzgerald replaced Ron Hodges, a net decrease in walk rate, but an overall gain.

It's reasonable to expect the 1999 Dodgers to walk more, either by playing players who will do so, or getting the current players to walk more. I expect Karros, Young, Beltre, Mondesi, White and Johnson to increase their walk rates, in some cases significantly. I also expect Johnson to have players on his bench with good plate discipline.

- Young pitchers. Johnson arrived at a fortunate time, in that the Mets' system was about to burp up about 5000 high-quality innings to replace an aging staff. Johnson swapped Tom Seaver and Mike Torrez for Dwight Gooden and Ron Darling, increased the role of Walt Terrell at the expense of Ed Lynch, and swapped Craig Swan for Sid Fernandez. For a better upgrade, you need frequent flier miles.

The Dodgers don't have that kind of talent coming up, but they do have options for Johnson to choose from. Mike Judd is ready to step into a rotation spot, preferably the one occupied by Dave Mlicki. Osuna, Kubenka, Maloney, Eric Weaver, and Onan Masaoka all have the stuff to be part of a deep and talented bullpen. Johnson has had good pens, especially in his last few stops. That should continue here.

- No over-managing. Johnson played under Earl Weaver, and it shows. He underplays one-run strategies, never squeezes and uses the intentional walk less than his peers. He understands how an offense works, and isn't going to give away outs by having Devon White bunt Eric Young over to second base in the bottom of the first with nobody out.

This will take on additional importance because of the makeup of the Dodger roster. Even with expected bumps in walk rate, this is a team that will struggle to have a league-average OBP. Not wasting outs on one-run strategies is a good way to make the extra base runners go further.

- Arrogance. Without putting too much weight on it, Johnson has won as a player and as a manager. In the locker room, that counts for something, and probably gives Johnson a level of respect that Glenn Hoffman would never have. It also gives him the benefit of the doubt from the press and public. At least for a little while.

Success isn't guaranteed. The Dodgers have plenty of flaws, and could find themselves scuffling through another lost season. But Johnson is not that type of manager. When obstacles arise, he's more likely to find solutions than excuses, and he'll expect his team to be the same way. I think the Dodgers are going to win 90 games, which might win the division, but if they sign Gary Gaetti and Tim Belcher before you read this, all bets are off.

HITTERS (Averages: BA .260/ OBA .330/ SA .420, EQA .260)

Luke Allen — OF — Bats R — Age 20

YEAR	TEAM	LGE	AB	H	DB	TP	HR	BB	R	RBI	SB	CS	OUT	BA	OBA	SA	EQA	EQR	DEFENSE
1997	GreatFls	Pio	247	56	5	1	4	13	16	16	5	5	196	.227	.265	.304	.190	15	61-3B 80
1998	San Bern	Cal	395	99	17	2	4	24	36	31	10	6	302	.251	.294	.334	.218	33	101-OF 97
1998	SanAnton	Tex	77	23	1	1	2	5	8	10	1	1	55	.299	.341	.416	.260	10	
1999	LosAngls	NL	379	96	15	2	6	20	33	34	9	6	289	.253	.291	.351	.233	38	

Moved out from behind the Beltre roadblock, he picked up his hitting a bit. Dodger prospects are either fast-tracked or doomed; we should know by midseason which way Allen is going to go. I'm less than optimistic, especially with the all-long-term-deal outfield.

Ricky Bell   3B   Bats R   Age 20

YEAR	TEAM	LGE	AB	H	DB	TP	HR	BB	R	RBI	SB	CS	OUT	BA	OBA	SA	EQA	EQR	DEFENSE
1997	Yakima	Nwn	262	47	8	0	1	7	9	9	3	0	215	.179	.201	.221	.104	4	66-SS 80
1998	San Bern	Cal	478	89	10	0	5	13	17	17	3	5	394	.186	.208	.238	.116	9	133-3B 101
1999	LosAngls	NL	424	90	12	1	4	10	19	21	5	3	337	.212	.230	.274	.173	21	

I'm thrilled to see him here, since I was a big fan of his growing up in New York. My friends and I would listen to New Edition, and then Bell Biv De . . . what? . . . oh. . . . Bell's best chance to make a lot of money is to go into music; being younger than the league is a good thing, but you have to perform adequately. Bell was overmatched in the Cal League, and needs to stay there, maybe even take a step backwards, until he's walking at least once a week.

Adrian Beltre   3B   Bats R   Age 21

YEAR	TEAM	LGE	AB	H	DB	TP	HR	BB	R	RBI	SB	CS	OUT	BA	OBA	SA	EQA	EQR	DEFENSE
1996	Savannah	SAL	255	75	6	1	13	27	33	42	2	2	182	.294	.362	.478	.286	40	66-3B 98
1996	San Bern	Cal	234	49	7	0	7	13	15	17	2	2	187	.209	.251	.329	.193	15	58-3B 97
1997	Vero Bch	Fla	436	126	13	1	22	58	66	69	13	5	315	.289	.372	.475	.292	73	119-3B 95
1998	SanAnton	Tex	244	72	14	0	11	33	43	37	13	3	175	.295	.379	.488	.301	44	59-3B 94
1998	LosAngls	NL	196	44	9	0	8	15	18	21	3	1	153	.224	.280	.393	.231	20	59-3B 96
1999	LosAngls	NL	448	124	17	1	23	47	61	67	15	4	328	.277	.345	.473	.294	77	

Beltre vs. Rolen is going to be the National League's A-Rod vs. Nomar for years to come. The Bonilla trade removes a convenient excuse for the Dodgers to mess with him, although I expect him to hit enough next year to make it a non-issue. Better defensive player than the numbers above indicate, with a strong arm. Might already be the best player on the team.

Hiram Bocachica   OF   Bats R   Age 23

YEAR	TEAM	LGE	AB	H	DB	TP	HR	BB	R	RBI	SB	CS	OUT	BA	OBA	SA	EQA	EQR	DEFENSE	
1996	W Palm B	Fla	272	88	16	3	3	30	47	35	12	2	186	.324	.391	.438	.296	44	26-SS 92	
1997	Harrisbg	Eas	438	106	15	2	8	32	44	36	20	8	340	.242	.294	.340	.224	40	54-SS 76	27-2B 102
1998	Harrisbg	Eas	296	75	16	3	4	20	34	26	15	6	227	.253	.301	.368	.235	31	71-OF 110	
1998	Albuquer	PCL	98	19	4	1	3	12	11	8	4	2	81	.194	.282	.347	.221	9	24-OF 136	
1999	LosAngls	NL	409	105	21	2	7	32	49	38	21	7	311	.257	.311	.369	.254	51		

No shot to start in Los Angeles, not that he was a good bet to contribute. Bocachica would be a good player to develop as a utility guy, someone who can legitimately play five or six positions, come off the bench and pinch-run or slap singles. It's a hard thing to groom a 23-year-old for, but a player like that would be valuable. Didn't hit at all after elbow surgery, so watch him carefully this spring.

Bobby Bonilla   3B/OF   Bats B   Age 36

YEAR	TEAM	LGE	AB	H	DB	TP	HR	BB	R	RBI	SB	CS	OUT	BA	OBA	SA	EQA	EQR	DEFENSE
1996	Baltimor	AL	584	167	27	5	27	71	80	96	1	4	421	.286	.363	.488	.288	94	95-OF 94
1997	Florida	NL	564	168	39	3	18	76	88	86	5	6	402	.298	.381	.473	.293	93	137-3B 83
1998	Florida	NL	97	27	4	0	5	13	13	16	0	1	71	.278	.364	.474	.284	15	24-3B 90
1998	LosAngls	NL	238	59	6	1	8	31	26	29	1	1	180	.248	.335	.382	.252	29	53-3B 78
1999	NYMets	NL	411	105	19	1	14	55	49	54	1	2	308	.255	.343	.409	.269	58	

Because injuries took such a toll on his season, it's hard to say whether we should expect him to rebound. He's going to have trouble finding a position, now that he's inadequate at third. He's been traded to the Mets for Mel Rojas, where he will play an outfield corner. He was a pretty brutal outfielder three years ago; it's unlikely that's changed. Anybody know what Bob Klapisch is doing these days?

Juan Castro   SS/2B   Bats R   Age 27

YEAR	TEAM	LGE	AB	H	DB	TP	HR	BB	R	RBI	SB	CS	OUT	BA	OBA	SA	EQA	EQR	DEFENSE	
1996	LosAngls	NL	133	27	6	3	0	10	10	7	1	0	106	.203	.259	.293	.187	8	24-SS 108	
1997	Albuquer	PCL	96	21	3	1	1	3	5	6	1	0	75	.219	.242	.302	.180	5	18-SS 104	
1997	LosAngls	NL	75	11	3	1	0	8	2	2	0	0	64	.147	.229	.213	.130	2	14-SS 102	
1998	LosAngls	NL	221	46	5	0	3	16	11	13	0	0	175	.208	.262	.271	.177	12	34-SS 100	24-2B 98
1999	*LosAngls*	*NL*	*184*	*38*	*5*	*1*	*2*	*12*	*11*	*11*	*1*	*0*	*146*	*.207*	*.255*	*.277*	*.191*	*12*		

Superior defensive shortstop, possibly the best in the NL. His lateral range is fantastic, and he turns a great pivot. He could be the Rafael Belliard of the '00s, because he hits like Rany Jazayerli on a NyQuil bender. Has value on a team with Mark Grudzielanek, who fields like Rany Jaza....

Roger Cedeno   CF   Bats B   Age 24

YEAR	TEAM	LGE	AB	H	DB	TP	HR	BB	R	RBI	SB	CS	OUT	BA	OBA	SA	EQA	EQR	DEFENSE
1996	Albuquer	PCL	121	20	2	1	1	13	7	4	5	3	104	.165	.246	.223	.157	5	30-OF 110
1996	LosAngls	NL	213	55	12	1	2	25	27	20	4	1	159	.258	.336	.352	.247	24	55-OF 101
1997	Albuquer	PCL	104	28	3	1	2	19	16	12	4	4	80	.269	.382	.375	.267	15	25-OF 103
1997	LosAngls	NL	196	55	9	2	4	26	32	23	8	1	142	.281	.365	.408	.278	29	58-OF 106
1998	LosAngls	NL	242	61	13	1	2	29	32	20	9	2	183	.252	.332	.339	.244	27	54-OF 91
1999	*NYMets*	*NL*	*274*	*70*	*16*	*2*	*3*	*33*	*37*	*26*	*9*	*3*	*207*	*.255*	*.336*	*.361*	*.257*	*35*	

For a few weeks it looked like his chance had arrived. In the past, Davey Johnson had crafted roles for people like Wally Backman and Lenny Dykstra, and didn't fear young players, so maybe he would rescue Cedeno. Then Devon White was signed. Traded to the Mets, where he's expected to be the fourth outfielder. With Bobby Bonilla and Butch Huskey on the corners, he should play a lot. Cedeno's skills are still there, he just needs a real opportunity.

Alex Cora   SS   Bats L   Age 23

YEAR	TEAM	LGE	AB	H	DB	TP	HR	BB	R	RBI	SB	CS	OUT	BA	OBA	SA	EQA	EQR	DEFENSE
1996	Vero Bch	Fla	214	50	4	2	1	11	13	13	3	3	167	.234	.271	.285	.186	12	59-SS 97
1997	SanAnton	Tex	442	87	15	1	3	21	19	17	8	6	361	.197	.233	.256	.153	17	127-SS 106
1998	Albuquer	PCL	290	63	12	4	4	14	22	19	8	5	232	.217	.253	.328	.196	20	80-SS 101
1999	*LosAngls*	*NL*	*346*	*76*	*14*	*3*	*4*	*16*	*24*	*23*	*8*	*5*	*275*	*.220*	*.254*	*.312*	*.204*	*26*	

A left-handed-hitting Juan Castro. Cora's no prospect, but he advanced through the system thanks to a good glove. It's hard to say he has a role as a bench player in Los Angeles, but if he improves his hitting or his base-stealing, he should be able to be a fifth infielder someday. Hey, it pays well.

Bubba Crosby   OF   Bats L   Age 22

YEAR	TEAM	LGE	AB	H	DB	TP	HR	BB	R	RBI	SB	CS	OUT	BA	OBA	SA	EQA	EQR	DEFENSE
1998	San Bern	Cal	199	34	7	1	0	13	6	6	2	3	168	.171	.222	.216	.119	4	50-OF 101
1999	*LosAngls*	*NL*	*154*	*28*	*5*	*1*	*0*	*9*	*5*	*5*	*1*	*2*	*128*	*.182*	*.227*	*.227*	*.147*	*5*	

The Dodgers' 1998 #1 draft pick from Rice University. I wouldn't put too much weight on his initial performance, which was awful. Like a lot of college draftees, he needs to progress quickly, at least a level per year, or risk falling off the prospect track. A center fielder in college, he projects as a corner outfielder in the pros.

Glenn Davis   1B/LF   Bats B   Age 23

YEAR	TEAM	LGE	AB	H	DB	TP	HR	BB	R	RBI	SB	CS	OUT	BA	OBA	SA	EQA	EQR	DEFENSE	
1997	San Bern	Cal	227	48	6	0	8	38	27	23	4	2	181	.211	.325	.344	.239	25	57-1B 100	
1998	Vero Bch	Fla	377	76	6	1	14	57	37	37	6	3	304	.202	.306	.334	.228	38	49-OF 94	30-1B 101
1998	SanAnton	Tex	69	19	3	0	4	8	10	11	1	0	50	.275	.351	.493	.288	11		
1999	*LosAngls*	*NL*	*320*	*71*	*9*	*0*	*12*	*44*	*35*	*35*	*6*	*2*	*251*	*.222*	*.316*	*.363*	*.253*	*40*		

The reason the Dodgers considered Jon Tucker expendable. Davis was their 1997 #1, and is a first baseman in the David Segui mold; now he's a left fielder in the Todd Hundley mold. OK, he's not that bad, but learning the new position may have negative impact on his development. As with Allen, his chance at playing time in Los Angeles is slim, given the Dodger outfield. He really isn't a great prospect, anyway. Lousy in the AFL.

Jim Eisenreich   OF/PH   Bats L   Age 40

YEAR	TEAM	LGE	AB	H	DB	TP	HR	BB	R	RBI	SB	CS	OUT	BA	OBA	SA	EQA	EQR	DEFENSE
1996	Philadel	NL	340	123	26	3	3	33	63	50	10	1	218	.362	.418	.482	.317	62	83-OF 93
1997	Florida	NL	293	82	20	1	2	32	37	31	0	0	211	.280	.351	.375	.257	35	41-OF 96 15-1B 107
1998	Florida	NL	64	17	1	0	1	4	7	5	2	0	47	.266	.309	.328	.229	6	
1998	LosAngls	NL	128	27	2	2	0	12	11	6	5	0	101	.211	.279	.258	.195	8	
1999	*LosAngls*	*NL*	*232*	*57*	*9*	*1*	*2*	*23*	*23*	*20*	*3*	*0*	*175*	*.246*	*.314*	*.319*	*.239*	*24*	

Looking back, he really had a heck of a career, one that makes you think about what could have happened if he'd been able to control the Tourette's Syndrome sooner.

My wife is a counselor at a school for troubled kids, one of whom has a mild form of Tourette's, and we happened to be watching a Dodger game when the subject came up. A week later, I clipped an L.A. Times article on Eisenreich, gave it to her, and she took it to school for the student. As she put it, "It made him feel like he wasn't so weird, that there was somebody famous and popular with the same thing he had. It was probably the first time he realized what he had could be controlled, and he could be 'normal.'" Jim, your time in Los Angeles was successful, no matter what the numbers say.

Kevin Gibbs   OF   Bats B   Age 25

YEAR	TEAM	LGE	AB	H	DB	TP	HR	BB	R	RBI	SB	CS	OUT	BA	OBA	SA	EQA	EQR	DEFENSE
1996	Vero Bch	Fla	429	106	10	5	2	54	60	30	32	12	335	.247	.331	.308	.237	46	119-OF 107
1997	SanAnton	Tex	351	99	16	3	2	60	68	31	31	13	265	.282	.387	.362	.275	53	98-OF 103
1999	*LosAngls*	*NL*	*174*	*45*	*6*	*2*	*1*	*25*	*28*	*14*	*14*	*5*	*134*	*.259*	*.352*	*.333*	*.266*	*25*	

Missed almost all of 1998 after blowing out his knee. A good chunk of his value was in his legs, so it's possible his career is essentially over. We're not as optimistic about him as we were a year ago. Even if he's healthy, he'll have to go elsewhere to play.

Mark Grudzielanek   SS   Bats R   Age 29

YEAR	TEAM	LGE	AB	H	DB	TP	HR	BB	R	RBI	SB	CS	OUT	BA	OBA	SA	EQA	EQR	DEFENSE
1996	Montreal	NL	650	192	32	4	6	30	79	64	28	7	465	.295	.326	.385	.252	74	150-SS 97
1997	Montreal	NL	644	172	51	3	5	28	70	56	21	9	481	.267	.298	.379	.234	64	152-SS 96
1998	Montreal	NL	399	116	16	1	9	24	46	46	12	6	289	.291	.331	.404	.255	48	101-SS 97
1998	LosAngls	NL	194	53	5	0	3	6	19	16	8	0	141	.273	.295	.345	.229	18	50-SS 107
1999	*LosAngls*	*NL*	*594*	*157*	*30*	*2*	*7*	*26*	*59*	*52*	*21*	*6*	*443*	*.264*	*.295*	*.357*	*.241*	*63*	

Wildly overrated, as most high-average hitters are. Of course, Grudzielanek doesn't hit for that high an average, so your guess is as good as mine why people still think he's good. The Dodgers may be looking to trade him, as he's arbitration-eligible and a good bet to be overpaid. Wherever he is, he'll be the starting shortstop, sucking up about 450 outs.

Kip Harkrider   SS/2B   Bats L   Age 23

YEAR	TEAM	LGE	AB	H	DB	TP	HR	BB	R	RBI	SB	CS	OUT	BA	OBA	SA	EQA	EQR	DEFENSE
1997	Savannah	SAL	71	11	0	0	0	2	2	2	0	0	60	.155	.178	.155	—	-1	
1997	Vero Bch	Fla	102	24	4	0	0	5	7	5	1	0	79	.235	.271	.275	.184	6	27-SS 81
1998	SanAnton	Tex	341	69	12	2	3	26	22	18	5	3	275	.202	.259	.276	.180	19	62-SS 92 38-2B 99
1999	*LosAngls*	*NL*	*254*	*54*	*9*	*1*	*2*	*16*	*16*	*15*	*3*	*2*	*202*	*.213*	*.259*	*.280*	*.194*	*17*	

Probably a non-prospect, but I include him here because left-handed hitting shortstops are rare, and make valuable fifth infielders. Harkrider is a marginally better offensive player than Joey Cora, and could still develop enough offensively to make some noise in spring training. Of course, he'd still be named Kip....

Todd Hollandsworth   OF   Bats L   Age 26

YEAR	TEAM	LGE	AB	H	DB	TP	HR	BB	R	RBI	SB	CS	OUT	BA	OBA	SA	EQA	EQR	DEFENSE
1996	LosAngls	NL	483	146	28	4	13	44	73	65	18	7	344	.302	.361	.458	.283	73	126-OF 91
1997	LosAngls	NL	297	75	19	2	5	19	28	29	4	5	227	.253	.297	.380	.230	29	84-OF 99
1998	LosAngls	NL	176	50	5	4	4	10	20	21	5	4	130	.284	.323	.426	.255	21	43-OF 99
1999	*LosAngls*	*NL*	*257*	*72*	*16*	*2*	*5*	*18*	*30*	*30*	*7*	*5*	*190*	*.280*	*.327*	*.416*	*.268*	*35*	

(Todd Hollandsworth *continued*)

Another vested participant in the "lose a year to injury" club, Hollandsworth's left shoulder gained him entry. In his absence, the Dodgers acquired about $100 million worth of outfielders, so what he comes back to could be his perfect role: fourth outfielder. Might not be a bad gamble for the next few years; his peak could look something like a bad Rusty Greer season.

Damon Hollins — OF — Bats R — Age 25

YEAR	TEAM	LGE	AB	H	DB	TP	HR	BB	R	RBI	SB	CS	OUT	BA	OBA	SA	EQA	EQR	DEFENSE
1996	Richmond	Int	146	27	7	0	0	15	8	5	1	2	121	.185	.261	.233	.160	6	38-OF 115
1997	Richmond	Int	496	127	25	1	19	39	54	61	6	2	371	.256	.310	.425	.253	60	130-OF 108
1998	Richmond	Int	428	98	18	2	10	39	40	39	7	2	332	.229	.293	.350	.225	40	109-OF 99
1999	LosAngls	NL	418	96	20	1	13	31	37	42	5	2	324	.230	.283	.376	.239	45	

Acquired to cover the organization during a late-season rash of injuries, Hollins adds to the collection of fourth-outfielder, fifth-infielder candidates the Dodgers have. Unlikely to see daylight in this organization, although I think he'll be around for a while in others. Zero star potential.

Trent Hubbard — CF/LF — Bats R — Age 33

YEAR	TEAM	LGE	AB	H	DB	TP	HR	BB	R	RBI	SB	CS	OUT	BA	OBA	SA	EQA	EQR	DEFENSE
1996	ColSprin	PCL	181	43	8	1	5	23	21	19	5	5	143	.238	.324	.376	.242	21	24-OF 108
1996	Colorado	NL	58	10	3	1	1	9	7	4	2	0	48	.172	.284	.310	.217	5	
1997	Buffalo	AA	382	111	15	1	12	48	61	49	22	9	280	.291	.370	.429	.281	59	88-OF 106
1998	LosAngls	NL	210	65	9	1	8	20	32	31	10	6	151	.310	.370	.476	.288	34	
1999	LosAngls	NL	263	70	11	1	8	31	36	31	12	6	199	.266	.344	.407	.275	40	

Hubbard is pretty much what Damon Hollins aspires to be, and did a good job last year, playing a bit more than expected but doing well. The Dodgers would be better served with a left-handed hitting fourth outfielder, like Hollandsworth, so Hubbard may move on again. Deserves to be on a roster, just not playing everyday.

Charles Johnson — C — Bats R — Age 27

YEAR	TEAM	LGE	AB	H	DB	TP	HR	BB	R	RBI	SB	CS	OUT	BA	OBA	SA	EQA	EQR	DEFENSE
1996	Florida	NL	387	85	14	1	13	43	36	39	1	0	302	.220	.298	.362	.229	38	
1997	Florida	NL	417	105	21	1	21	62	55	63	0	2	314	.252	.349	.458	.276	63	
1998	Florida	NL	113	25	4	0	8	17	13	18	0	1	89	.221	.323	.469	.266	16	30-C 100
1998	LosAngls	NL	348	79	12	0	14	31	30	38	0	1	270	.227	.290	.382	.230	34	100-C 107
1999	Baltimor	AL	419	99	16	0	21	49	46	58	0	1	321	.236	.316	.425	.256	53	

His offense has really been a disappointment to those of us who keep thinking he's turned the corner. He's not bad the way most catchers are bad, hitting an empty .260. Johnson can drive the ball and take pitches. He strikes out 25-30% of the time, keeping him from hitting the .250 that would make him good. I'm think it's just an odd learning curve, and say he still has a .360 on-base and .480 slugging peak in him. Traded to Baltimore, an excellent park for him.

Eric Karros — 1B — Bats R — Age 31

YEAR	TEAM	LGE	AB	H	DB	TP	HR	BB	R	RBI	SB	CS	OUT	BA	OBA	SA	EQA	EQR	DEFENSE
1996	LosAngls	NL	613	164	26	1	37	57	77	98	8	0	449	.268	.330	.494	.280	93	154-1B 105
1997	LosAngls	NL	632	173	23	0	35	65	82	97	13	8	467	.274	.341	.476	.277	95	160-1B 105
1998	LosAngls	NL	512	157	20	1	26	51	73	87	8	2	357	.307	.369	.502	.297	86	133-1B 104
1999	LosAngls	NL	512	135	17	0	26	53	60	74	9	3	380	.264	.333	.449	.281	80	

Like Tino Martinez's deal, his contract doesn't look nearly as bad now, and Karros's performance last year was his best since 1995. Trading him isn't such a bad idea; his perceived value is fairly high and he is replaceable. Unbelievably slow.

Paul LoDuca — C — Bats R — Age 27

YEAR	TEAM	LGE	AB	H	DB	TP	HR	BB	R	RBI	SB	CS	OUT	BA	OBA	SA	EQA	EQR	DEFENSE	
1996	Vero Bch	Fla	446	107	7	0	4	51	41	33	4	1	340	.240	.318	.283	.215	37		
1997	SanAnton	Tex	377	95	12	1	5	34	38	32	9	5	287	.252	.314	.329	.227	35		
1998	Albuquer	PCL	434	104	15	2	5	48	47	35	13	5	335	.240	.315	.318	.227	41	103-C 98	17-1B 105
1999	LosAngls	NL	396	98	16	1	6	46	46	36	12	5	303	.247	.326	.338	.251	48		

Organizational soldier who will battle Angel Pena for the backup job this spring. Pena's a much better prospect, so LoDuca could end up backing up Hundley because he's the one the Dodgers would rather see rotting away on the bench. He's not a bad player, and should hang around for a few years, maybe even start for a bad team for a couple of years.

Matt Luke   LF   Bats L   Age 28

YEAR	TEAM	LGE	AB	H	DB	TP	HR	BB	R	RBI	SB	CS	OUT	BA	OBA	SA	EQA	EQR	DEFENSE
1996	Columbus	Int	259	63	9	1	13	16	23	33	1	1	197	.243	.287	.436	.244	29	46-OF 87
1997	Columbus	Int	337	67	11	2	6	23	18	21	0	2	272	.199	.250	.297	.179	18	61-OF 91
1998	LosAngls	NL	238	59	13	1	13	19	26	34	2	1	180	.248	.304	.475	.262	32	50-OF 102
1999	*LosAngls*	*NL*	*277*	*64*	*14*	*1*	*13*	*21*	*26*	*34*	*1*	*1*	*214*	*.231*	*.285*	*.430*	*.254*	*35*	

It was nice to see Luke get a shot after some good years in the Yankees chain. Of course, his good start masked the fact that he was an abysmal player for much of the year. Might have crossed the line from "borderline" to "major leaguer" this year. Remember: that's more about perception than ability or performance. In reality, Luke's a one-trick pony whose trick isn't very good.

Mike Metcalfe   2B   Bats R   Age 26

YEAR	TEAM	LGE	AB	H	DB	TP	HR	BB	R	RBI	SB	CS	OUT	BA	OBA	SA	EQA	EQR	DEFENSE
1995	Vero Bch	Fla	439	117	8	1	4	49	61	33	35	16	338	.267	.340	.317	.241	48	118-SS 82
1995	SanAnton	Tex	41	9	1	0	0	7	5	2	1	1	33	.220	.333	.244	.211	3	
1997	San Bern	Cal	513	100	14	2	2	38	34	20	28	15	428	.195	.250	.242	.168	25	126-2B 91
1998	SanAnton	Tex	213	43	2	2	2	22	17	11	10	8	178	.202	.277	.258	.185	13	56-2B 83
1999	*LosAngls*	*NL*	*315*	*65*	*8*	*3*	*2*	*26*	*30*	*16*	*23*	*10*	*260*	*.206*	*.267*	*.270*	*.206*	*25*	

Non-prospect the Dodgers wasted an AFL spot on. Metcalfe isn't even as good a utility infield prospect as Cora or Harkrider, so it's hard to see what the Dodgers expect to happen here. With Eric Young apparently staying, Metcalfe's future involves waiting to be a six-year minor league free agent and hoping for expansion in 2002. More coaching jobs, dontcha know....

Raul Mondesi   RF   Bats R   Age 28

YEAR	TEAM	LGE	AB	H	DB	TP	HR	BB	R	RBI	SB	CS	OUT	BA	OBA	SA	EQA	EQR	DEFENSE
1995	LosAngls	NL	538	157	23	5	29	37	78	85	24	4	385	.292	.337	.515	.290	87	125-OF 109
1996	LosAngls	NL	639	195	40	7	26	37	85	100	12	8	452	.305	.343	.512	.286	99	147-OF 105
1997	LosAngls	NL	620	197	43	5	32	49	101	107	27	16	439	.318	.368	.558	.305	113	147-OF 102
1998	LosAngls	NL	584	170	28	5	33	34	76	94	18	12	426	.291	.330	.526	.283	91	143-OF 100
1999	*LosAngls*	*NL*	*593*	*169*	*33*	*4*	*31*	*34*	*73*	*91*	*18*	*11*	*435*	*.285*	*.324*	*.511*	*.290*	*98*	

I've left in the 1995 line to further illustrate the outlier. In 1997, Mondesi was a heck of player, improving across the board, most notably a distinct bump in the walk rate. It appears that the improved discipline helped the rest of his game. He gave back most of those gains in 1998. The difference between Mondesi 1997 and 1998 is the difference between a great player worth his price and an overrated one. I think the projection is accurate: he'll split the difference in 1999.

Juan Moreta   OF   Bats R   Age 23

YEAR	TEAM	LGE	AB	H	DB	TP	HR	BB	R	RBI	SB	CS	OUT	BA	OBA	SA	EQA	EQR	DEFENSE
1997	GreatFls	Pio	253	39	1	1	0	10	7	7	7	5	219	.154	.186	.166	—	-1	61-OF 88
1998	San Bern	Cal	533	109	12	4	1	34	33	21	23	13	437	.205	.252	.248	.168	25	131-OF 109
1999	*LosAngls*	*NL*	*426*	*90*	*9*	*2*	*1*	*19*	*26*	*18*	*21*	*11*	*347*	*.211*	*.245*	*.249*	*.179*	*24*	

Base stealing prospect, looks enough like Brian Hunter to give any self-respecting stathead the shakes. Like the rest of the Dodger outfield prospects, he's blocked at the major league level. If he keeps running, you'll hear his name as a prospect. Don't be fooled.

Tony Mota   OF   Bats B   Age 21

YEAR	TEAM	LGE	AB	H	DB	TP	HR	BB	R	RBI	SB	CS	OUT	BA	OBA	SA	EQA	EQR	DEFENSE
1996	Yakima	Nwn	228	53	6	1	3	9	15	15	7	5	180	.232	.262	.307	.191	14	36-OF 94
1997	San Bern	Cal	416	83	10	7	4	24	23	22	6	4	337	.200	.243	.286	.174	21	107-OF 107
1998	Vero Bch	Fla	250	69	12	2	6	15	28	28	6	5	186	.276	.317	.412	.249	29	53-OF 102
1998	SanAnton	Tex	220	46	8	3	2	10	15	12	10	5	179	.209	.243	.300	.184	13	55-OF 92
1999	*LosAngls*	*NL*	*424*	*105*	*17*	*5*	*7*	*19*	*39*	*37*	*14*	*7*	*326*	*.248*	*.280*	*.361*	*.233*	*43*	

(Tony Mota *continued*)

Took a step backward and had some success; you'd like to see teams do this a little more with their young prospects. Mota's better than Moreta, but not as good as Crosby, who he'll have to hold off. He'll be playing in excellent hitting environments, so there's a good chance he'll pick up a "prospect" tag.

Angel Pena   C   Bats R   Age 24

YEAR	TEAM	LGE	AB	H	DB	TP	HR	BB	R	RBI	SB	CS	OUT	BA	OBA	SA	EQA	EQR	DEFENSE
1996	Savannah	SAL	130	25	3	0	4	4	5	7	0	0	105	.192	.216	.308	.164	6	
1997	San Bern	Cal	318	75	13	1	12	25	29	35	2	3	246	.236	.292	.396	.234	32	
1998	SanAnton	Tex	477	142	17	1	17	39	58	68	6	4	339	.298	.351	.444	.274	66	112-C 97
1999	*LosAngls*	*NL*	*363*	*97*	*11*	*1*	*14*	*25*	*34*	*47*	*2*	*2*	*268*	*.267*	*.314*	*.419*	*.263*	*48*	

It was a heck of a year for Pena: not only did he take a big step forward with the bat, he no longer has to beat out the game's best catcher. That sure beats Newt Gingrich's 1998. Pena should start the year at Albuquerque, and his chances depend on the condition of Todd Hundley's elbow.

Tom Prince   C   Bats R   Age 34

YEAR	TEAM	LGE	AB	H	DB	TP	HR	BB	R	RBI	SB	CS	OUT	BA	OBA	SA	EQA	EQR	DEFENSE
1996	LosAngls	NL	65	20	4	0	2	6	8	10	0	0	45	.308	.366	.462	.285	10	
1997	LosAngls	NL	100	22	3	0	4	6	7	10	0	0	78	.220	.264	.370	.214	8	
1998	LosAngls	NL	81	16	5	1	0	8	6	4	0	0	65	.198	.270	.284	.188	5	23-C 114
1999	*LosAngls*	*NL*	*101*	*22*	*3*	*0*	*3*	*11*	*8*	*10*	*0*	*0*	*79*	*.218*	*.295*	*.337*	*.233*	*10*	

Why would you want a good-field, no-hit, slow right-handed catcher backing up Charles Johnson? Nothing against Prince, but generally should have a backup who gives you things your starter doesn't.

Adam Riggs   2B   Bats R   Age 26

YEAR	TEAM	LGE	AB	H	DB	TP	HR	BB	R	RBI	SB	CS	OUT	BA	OBA	SA	EQA	EQR	DEFENSE
1996	SanAnton	Tex	506	132	21	2	13	33	53	53	13	5	379	.261	.306	.387	.241	54	126-2B 100
1997	Albuquer	PCL	214	50	3	1	9	24	25	24	9	2	166	.234	.311	.383	.247	25	56-2B 96
1998	Albuquer	PCL	162	48	8	1	3	17	24	19	9	5	119	.296	.363	.414	.272	23	43-2B 88
1999	*LosAngls*	*NL*	*228*	*58*	*11*	*1*	*5*	*20*	*27*	*23*	*10*	*4*	*174*	*.254*	*.315*	*.377*	*.256*	*29*	

Riggs was having another fine season when he injured his shoulder in June, knocking him out for the year. Despite out best efforts, the Dodgers steadfastly refuse to give him a chance to play, so we're considering more forceful means. That's all I can tell you without incriminating you. If healthy, he's an Eric Young injury away from being a big surprise.

Damian Rolls   3B   Bats R   Age 21

YEAR	TEAM	LGE	AB	H	DB	TP	HR	BB	R	RBI	SB	CS	OUT	BA	OBA	SA	EQA	EQR	DEFENSE
1996	Yakima	Nwn	259	58	4	1	3	4	11	13	4	2	203	.224	.236	.282	.165	11	64-3B 103
1997	Savannah	SAL	483	95	12	2	6	35	26	24	5	2	390	.197	.251	.267	.171	24	130-3B 104
1998	Vero Bch	Fla	264	53	4	0	1	19	13	10	6	2	213	.201	.254	.227	.158	11	74-3B 121
1998	SanAnton	Tex	159	28	3	0	1	5	5	5	1	0	131	.176	.201	.214	.094	2	49-3B 104
1999	*LosAngls*	*NL*	*405*	*83*	*6*	*1*	*4*	*21*	*20*	*20*	*7*	*2*	*324*	*.205*	*.244*	*.254*	*.177*	*21*	

Draft picks like this are killing the Dodgers, and led to the firing of Charlie Blaney as farm director. Rolls was their 1996 #1, and as you can see he hasn't been much. Being a good defensive third baseman isn't going to get you far in this organization. He might benefit by going back to the Florida State League, or even back to rookie ball, to start over. Check back in 2001. Or don't.

Rich Saitta   IF   Bats R   Age 23

YEAR	TEAM	LGE	AB	H	DB	TP	HR	BB	R	RBI	SB	CS	OUT	BA	OBA	SA	EQA	EQR	DEFENSE	
1996	Yakima	Nwn	167	33	1	0	1	8	6	6	3	3	137	.198	.234	.222	.133	4	41-2B 96	
1997	Yakima	Nwn	180	36	5	0	1	7	7	7	2	1	145	.200	.230	.244	.143	6	23-2B 95	
1998	San Bern	Cal	443	106	10	2	5	41	40	33	12	9	346	.239	.304	.305	.213	36	54-2B 94	45-SS 94
1999	*LosAngls*	*NL*	*358*	*78*	*10*	*1*	*2*	*23*	*24*	*20*	*9*	*6*	*286*	*.218*	*.265*	*.268*	*.194*	*24*		

In another organization Saitta might be a halfway decent prospect, moving up steadily and eventually positioning himself for a job as a fifth infielder. Unfortunately, the Dodgers have a long line for that job. Saitta's a year off radar, but remember the name, because if he can handle shortstop, I think he'll hit enough to make himself a prospect.

Gary Sheffield RF Bats R Age 30

YEAR	TEAM	LGE	AB	H	DB	TP	HR	BB	R	RBI	SB	CS	OUT	BA	OBA	SA	EQA	EQR	DEFENSE
1996	Florida	NL	528	171	29	1	46	144	125	131	13	10	367	.324	.469	.644	.363	145	143-OF 94
1997	Florida	NL	447	113	19	1	23	123	88	73	9	7	341	.253	.414	.454	.304	87	118-OF 102
1998	Florida	NL	137	38	10	1	7	27	26	24	4	2	101	.277	.396	.518	.310	27	36-OF 93
1998	LosAngls	NL	307	102	17	1	18	72	75	61	20	6	211	.332	.459	.570	.350	77	88-OF 94
1999	LosAngls	NL	429	123	20	1	25	110	88	79	16	7	313	.287	.432	.513	.338	104	

A wonderful hitter who needs to fire his PR firm and get one that will actually do something about his image. The whole flap about Sheffield wanting extra money to go to Los Angeles was reported as just another "greedy ballplayer" story. But the fact is that Sheffield had a no-trade clause in his contract, and the trade to Los Angeles was going to cost him around a million dollars a year in state income tax. If your company wanted you to make a move that was going to effectively cut your pay 10%, would you take it lying down? Sheffield's raw numbers will be down, but that's all park effect; he's still a great hitter.

Eric Stuckenschneider OF Bats R Age 27

YEAR	TEAM	LGE	AB	H	DB	TP	HR	BB	R	RBI	SB	CS	OUT	BA	OBA	SA	EQA	EQR	DEFENSE
1996	Savannah	SAL	503	111	11	2	9	73	56	40	17	9	401	.221	.319	.304	.226	48	99-OF 82
1997	Vero Bch	Fla	461	97	13	1	4	75	53	29	15	6	370	.210	.321	.269	.218	41	111-OF 94
1998	SanAnton	Tex	282	60	9	3	2	33	28	18	8	2	224	.213	.295	.287	.210	23	
1998	Albuquer	PCL	260	62	7	4	5	35	34	25	13	6	204	.238	.329	.354	.245	30	
1999	LosAngls	NL	486	108	16	4	7	70	61	39	22	7	385	.222	.320	.315	.245	57	

Late bloomer who needs to get to another organization before he becomes Webster Garrison with an even cooler name. Stuckenschneider is good enough to help most teams as an extra outfielder, and could even be an effective platoon partner. None of this will happen in Los Angeles.

Bernie Torres SS/2B Bats R Age 19

YEAR	TEAM	LGE	AB	H	DB	TP	HR	BB	R	RBI	SB	CS	OUT	BA	OBA	SA	EQA	EQR	DEFENSE	
1997	GreatFls	Pio	171	24	1	0	1	8	4	4	2	2	149	.140	.179	.164	—	-2	48-SS 103	
1998	Vero Bch	Fla	410	84	5	1	1	23	16	16	4	4	330	.205	.247	.229	.146	14	70-SS 93	45-2B 83
1999	LosAngls	NL	290	63	4	1	1	11	13	13	4	3	230	.217	.246	.248	.171	14		

Super-young shortstop who didn't embarrass himself in the Florida State League. The Dodgers are easy to read: if he hits San Antonio this year, he's a serious prospect in their eyes. I think I'd start him back at Vero Beach and see if he can start the year with a bang. Intangibles at the major league level have a high silliness quotient, but when you're messing with kids—and at 19, you're a kid—there's nothing wrong with building their confidence.

Jose Vizcaino SS Bats B Age 31

YEAR	TEAM	LGE	AB	H	DB	TP	HR	BB	R	RBI	SB	CS	OUT	BA	OBA	SA	EQA	EQR	DEFENSE
1996	NY Mets	NL	367	115	14	6	1	30	48	42	7	5	257	.313	.365	.392	.266	47	88-2B 100
1996	Clevelnd	AL	175	47	4	2	0	6	15	12	6	2	130	.269	.293	.314	.213	14	40-2B 100
1997	San Fran	NL	568	151	19	6	6	52	59	55	6	8	425	.266	.327	.352	.237	58	138-SS 106
1998	LosAngls	NL	239	66	8	0	4	18	27	23	8	4	177	.276	.327	.360	.242	26	63-SS 97
1999	LosAngls	NL	362	95	11	2	3	28	35	31	8	6	273	.262	.315	.329	.238	38	

A double whammy. His signing was a bad decision, since he can't hit much and is well past the point of expected improvement. But when he went down with the sprained ankle from hell, the Dodgers panicked and traded for Mark Grudzielanek, giving up two excellent prospects, a decent one, and a good ballplayer's little brother. Vizcaino couldn't have done much more damage without an Uzi. The Dodgers have a set infield without him, so it's hard to see where Vizcaino fits in. He's a bit expensive for the supersub role, which is where I'd put him. He'll have no trade value until he shows he's healthy, and even then he's not exactly Barry Larkin. An interesting dilemma for Malone and Johnson.

Eric Young			2B			Bats R		Age 32									
YEAR	TEAM	LGE	AB	H	DB	TP	HR	BB	R	RBI	SB	CS	OUT	BA	OBA	SA	EQA	EQR	DEFENSE
1996	Colorado	NL	543	148	18	3	7	49	73	48	38	17	412	.273	.333	.355	.247	62	135-2B 100
1997	Colorado	NL	458	119	26	5	6	58	69	44	25	12	351	.260	.343	.378	.257	58	115-2B 101
1997	LosAngls	NL	155	44	5	2	2	15	25	15	12	2	113	.284	.347	.381	.267	21	32-2B 98
1998	LosAngls	NL	456	136	24	1	10	49	84	49	47	15	335	.298	.366	.421	.282	71	110-2B 94
1999	LosAngls	NL	509	132	24	2	9	56	73	47	38	14	391	.259	.333	.367	.265	71	

A better year than we had any reason to expect from him. It doesn't justify the signing, but it does mean he isn't hurting the team yet. He's at an age where second basemen stumble, so the decline in the projection is not surprising. In fact, it looks dead on.

PITCHERS (Averages: 4.00 ERA, 9.00 H/9, 1.00 HR/9, 3.00 BB/9, 6.00 K/9, 1.00 KWH)

Brian Bohanon			Throws L			Age 30									
YEAR	TEAM	LGE	IP	H	ER	HR	BB	K	ERA	W	L	H/9	HR/9	BB/9	K/9	KWH	PERA
1996	Syracuse	Int	56.0	65	30	4	19	30	4.82	2	4	10.45	0.64	3.05	4.82	0.55	4.34
1997	Norfolk	Int	93.0	104	38	9	32	62	3.68	5	5	10.06	0.87	3.10	6.00	0.87	4.35
1997	NY Mets	NL	94.0	104	47	9	30	59	4.50	4	6	9.96	0.86	2.87	5.65	0.84	4.21
1998	NY Mets	NL	55.7	47	18	5	19	36	2.91	4	2	7.60	0.81	3.07	5.82	1.09	2.91
1998	LosAngls	NL	98.0	77	31	10	32	65	2.85	7	4	7.07	0.92	2.94	5.97	1.29	2.66

Another late-developing left-hander who improved a bit just in time to pitch in two exceptional pitchers' parks. Would that we all could have such karma. And that we wouldn't be so stupid about messing with it as Bohanon, who signed a three-year deal to ruin his career on Planet Coors. "I'm a groundball pitcher." Yeah, and so was Bill Swift. It was nice knowing you.

Allen Davis			Throws L			Age 23									
YEAR	TEAM	LGE	IP	H	ER	HR	BB	K	ERA	W	L	H/9	HR/9	BB/9	K/9	KWH	PERA
1998	Yakima	Nwn	14.3	16	6	0	3	8	3.77	1	1	10.05	0.00	1.88	5.02	1.00	3.77
1998	SanBern	Cal	29.3	39	15	2	7	22	4.60	1	2	11.97	0.61	2.15	6.75	1.33	4.91
1998	SanAnton	Tex	29.3	36	13	2	9	26	3.99	2	1	11.05	0.61	2.76	7.98	1.56	4.60

Davis was a 24th-round draft pick last year, and apparently should have gone a bit higher. Davis's year is an excellent example of how the Dodgers treat their top prospects. He's going to get a lot of attention, probably just in time for his adjustment period, so don't get trampled when the bandwagon empties.

Toby Dollar			Throws R			Age 24									
YEAR	TEAM	LGE	IP	H	ER	HR	BB	K	ERA	W	L	H/9	HR/9	BB/9	K/9	KWH	PERA
1996	GreatFls	Pio	40.3	96	60	2	27	22	13.39	0	4	21.42	0.45	6.02	4.91	0.14	8.70
1997	Savannah	SAL	81.7	113	45	9	16	40	4.96	4	5	12.45	0.99	1.76	4.41	0.66	5.40
1998	SanAnton	Tex	130.3	202	102	18	39	50	7.04	3	11	13.95	1.24	2.69	3.45	0.24	6.49

Dollar jumped to the Texas League because of the lack of credible Dodger pitching prospects. He is not a prospect, despite which he'll probably show up in Albuquerque's rotation this year.

Darren Dreifort			Throws R			Age 27									
YEAR	TEAM	LGE	IP	H	ER	HR	BB	K	ERA	W	L	H/9	HR/9	BB/9	K/9	KWH	PERA
1996	Albuquer	PCL	89.7	89	41	6	54	65	4.12	5	5	8.93	0.60	5.42	6.52	0.66	3.91
1996	LosAngls	NL	23.3	26	13	2	12	22	5.01	1	2	10.03	0.77	4.63	8.49	1.16	4.63
1997	LosAngls	NL	62.3	51	21	3	31	56	3.03	4	3	7.36	0.43	4.48	8.09	1.49	2.89
1998	LosAngls	NL	181.0	177	74	12	52	152	3.68	11	9	8.80	0.60	2.59	7.56	1.88	3.38

Really not a good year for someone whose stuff is described the way Dreifort's is. He's very inconsistent (his Support-Neutral data looks better than his conventional numbers), and despite being babied for a few years, still had to be shut down in September with arm stiffness. There's two ways to go with him: plug him in the rotation in April, let him go 6-1, 2.15, and trade him before he gets hurt, or make him a high-leverage reliever like Mariano Rivera 1996 or Arthur Rhodes 1997 and see if you can't shorten games to six innings. He'd be awesome in that role.

Eric Gagne   Throws R   Age 23

YEAR	TEAM	LGE	IP	H	ER	HR	BB	K	ERA	W	L	H/9	HR/9	BB/9	K/9	KWH	PERA
1996	Savannah	SAL	104.3	150	70	16	49	80	6.04	4	8	12.94	1.38	4.23	6.90	0.65	6.30
1998	VeroBch	Fla	134.0	148	75	19	55	104	5.04	6	9	9.94	1.28	3.69	6.99	1.00	4.63

Returned from arm surgery and picked up right where he left off, more or less. No star potential, but he could take advantage of the organization's lack of talent to make himself into a prospect. Won't see another pitchers' environment for a while, though.

Mark Guthrie   Throws L   Age 33

YEAR	TEAM	LGE	IP	H	ER	HR	BB	K	ERA	W	L	H/9	HR/9	BB/9	K/9	KWH	PERA
1996	LosAngls	NL	72.0	71	20	3	21	50	2.50	6	2	8.88	0.38	2.63	6.25	1.26	3.25
1997	LosAngls	NL	68.0	79	44	13	27	37	5.82	3	5	10.46	1.72	3.57	4.90	0.48	5.29
1998	LosAngls	NL	54.7	59	23	3	21	41	3.79	3	3	9.71	0.49	3.46	6.75	1.02	3.95

He won't be back for the Dodgers, and neither party is losing any sleep over it. Guthrie would prefer to have an opportunity to start, although he's had all of his success as a reliever. He's not much different than Greg Swindell, who got a nice three-year deal from the Diamondbacks, so there are definitely jobs out there for him.

Mike Judd   Throws R   Age 24

YEAR	TEAM	LGE	IP	H	ER	HR	BB	K	ERA	W	L	H/9	HR/9	BB/9	K/9	KWH	PERA
1996	Greensbr	SAL	25.7	35	21	3	9	21	7.36	1	2	12.27	1.05	3.16	7.36	1.05	5.61
1996	Savannah	SAL	50.3	63	31	3	18	36	5.54	2	4	11.26	0.54	3.22	6.44	0.86	4.65
1997	VeroBch	Fla	84.7	84	41	5	45	77	4.36	4	5	8.93	0.53	4.78	8.19	1.18	3.72
1997	SanAnton	Tex	74.0	81	28	1	32	54	3.41	5	3	9.85	0.12	3.89	6.57	0.84	3.77
1998	Albuquer	PCL	98.0	96	49	16	43	64	4.50	5	6	8.82	1.47	3.95	5.88	0.74	4.22

For an organization with a reputation for developing pitchers, the Dodgers do some funny things. Judd is probably their best pitching prospect. Fighting injuries and trying desperately to hold on to playoff hopes, the Dodgers called him up to pitch mop-up relief in June, not to break him in, but because they were panicked over their bullpen problems. That was Tommy Lasorda, I guess: extremely short-sighted and stupid. Judd's still a good prospect, and will fight for a rotation slot.

Jeff Kubenka   Throws L   Age 24

Year	Team	Lge	IP	H	ER	HR	BB	K	ERA	W	L	H/9	HR/9	BB/9	K/9	KWH	PERA
1996	Yakima	Nwn	29.3	33	16	3	11	32	4.91	1	2	10.13	0.92	3.38	9.82	2.12	4.30
1997	SanBern	Cal	38.0	30	5	1	10	41	1.18	4	0	7.11	0.24	2.37	9.71	4.20	2.13
1997	SanAnton	Tex	24.7	12	2	1	6	31	0.73	3	0	4.38	0.36	2.19	11.31	10.01	0.36
1998	Albuquer	PCL	41.3	31	8	1	11	33	1.74	4	1	6.75	0.22	2.40	7.19	2.39	1.96

Being shopped around, as the Dodgers make "major improvements" to their team. Kubenka has been six kinds of hell on hitters everywhere he's pitched, up to and including a cup of coffee with the Dodgers last year. He's going to be in somebody's bullpen this year and he's going to be effective; on the right team he could end up as a closer. I love his chances if he stays here, because Johnson is very good with relievers.

Sean Maloney   Throws R   Age 28

YEAR	TEAM	LGE	IP	H	ER	HR	BB	K	ERA	W	L	H/9	HR/9	BB/9	K/9	KWH	PERA
1996	ElPaso	Tex	55.7	56	10	1	14	44	1.62	5	1	9.05	0.16	2.26	7.11	1.85	3.07
1997	Tucson	PCL	17.3	26	9	3	3	16	4.67	1	1	13.50	1.56	1.56	8.31	2.46	6.23
1997	Milwauke	AL	7.0	7	3	1	2	5	3.86	1	0	9.00	1.29	2.57	6.43	1.34	3.86
1998	Albuquer	PCL	34.7	41	18	5	9	29	4.67	2	2	10.64	1.30	2.34	7.53	1.71	4.93
1998	LosAngls	NL	13.0	13	6	2	5	10	4.15	0	1	9.00	1.38	3.46	6.92	1.15	4.15

Finding his way back after appendicitis ruined his 1997. Maloney could have a short, effective career if he dropped everything but his splitter and fastball. The splitter is his out pitch, and looks like a good one. It isn't the recipe for a long career, but he could get 280 innings and a couple of high-six-figure contracts before his elbow explodes. See above about Johnson and relievers.

Ramon Martinez   Throws R   Age 31

YEAR	TEAM	LGE	IP	H	ER	HR	BB	K	ERA	W	L	H/9	HR/9	BB/9	K/9	KWH	PERA
1996	LosAngls	NL	167.3	169	72	12	81	119	3.87	10	9	9.09	0.65	4.36	6.40	0.78	3.87
1997	LosAngls	NL	132.3	137	63	15	61	107	4.28	7	8	9.32	1.02	4.15	7.28	1.03	4.22
1998	LosAngls	NL	102.3	79	37	9	37	82	3.25	7	4	6.95	0.79	3.25	7.21	1.73	2.55

Has made more rehab visits the past three years than Robert Downey, Jr. This year, no rehab: just a torn rotator cuff and really bad surgery. In an interesting twist, the Dodgers declined Martinez's option, no surprise, but Martinez declined to file for free agency. At this writing, it's hard to tell how it will play out, but if Martinez thinks the Dodgers are going to offer him arbitration just for being a loyal soldier, he clearly missed a memo. Unlikely to be effective in 1999.

Onan Masaoka   Throws L   Age 21

YEAR	TEAM	LGE	IP	H	ER	HR	BB	K	ERA	W	L	H/9	HR/9	BB/9	K/9	KWH	PERA
1996	Savannah	SAL	58.7	89	49	10	40	49	7.52	2	5	13.65	1.53	6.14	7.52	0.51	6.90
1997	VeroBch	Fla	146.3	138	75	20	61	99	4.61	7	9	8.49	1.23	3.75	6.09	0.87	3.81
1998	SanAnton	Tex	102.0	135	81	11	63	74	7.15	3	8	11.91	0.97	5.56	6.53	0.48	5.65

Half the battle is staying healthy, which Masaoka has accomplished, in part by being ineffective and removed from the rotation. His best pitch is his fastball, so he may find himself moved to the pen full-time. He's still young enough to repeat Double-A and keep his prospect status, and left-handers who throw 90 don't grow on trees, so pay attention.

Dean Mitchell   Throws R   Age 24

YEAR	TEAM	LGE	IP	H	ER	HR	BB	K	ERA	W	L	H/9	HR/9	BB/9	K/9	KWH	PERA
1996	Yakima	Nwn	43.3	88	36	5	32	31	7.48	1	4	18.28	1.04	6.65	6.44	0.26	8.31
1997	Savannah	SAL	107.0	170	72	8	35	67	6.06	4	8	14.30	0.67	2.94	5.64	0.57	6.14
1998	SanAnton	Tex	71.7	94	34	8	23	54	4.27	4	4	11.80	1.00	2.89	6.78	1.01	5.27

Closer suspect who the organization liked enough to send to Arizona, where he didn't really hurt or help himself. Mitchell fights the size bias, but his performance has been good so far. He'll move up to Albuquerque this year, and has a clear path to the majors if he continues to keep the ball down.

Dave Mlicki   Throws R   Age 31

YEAR	TEAM	LGE	IP	H	ER	HR	BB	K	ERA	W	L	H/9	HR/9	BB/9	K/9	KWH	PERA
1996	NY Mets	NL	89.7	103	44	10	31	74	4.42	5	5	10.34	1.00	3.11	7.43	1.29	4.62
1997	NY Mets	NL	194.0	211	86	22	69	141	3.99	11	11	9.79	1.02	3.20	6.54	1.02	4.31
1998	NY Mets	NL	59.3	68	33	8	23	36	5.01	3	4	10.31	1.21	3.49	5.46	0.62	4.85
1998	LosAngls	NL	124.7	125	59	16	34	71	4.26	7	7	9.02	1.16	2.45	5.13	0.89	3.83

I'm off the bandwagon. Mlicki's been a personal favorite for years, but I really don't know how he's even been this effective. He has a good, hard fastball that's straighter than Mr. Rogers, a major league curveball, and nothing else you haven't seen at a good American Legion game. If he ever has to pitch in a park that doesn't save him, he'll look like Frank Castillo. Might make a good reliever, but the lack of movement is a real problem.

Matt Montgomery   Throws R   Age 23

YEAR	TEAM	LGE	IP	H	ER	HR	BB	K	ERA	W	L	H/9	HR/9	BB/9	K/9	KWH	PERA
1997	GreatFls	Pio	19.0	37	16	1	5	3	7.58	0	2	17.53	0.47	2.37	1.42	0.04	7.11
1997	Yakima	Nwn	49.0	71	30	4	19	19	5.51	2	3	13.04	0.73	3.49	3.49	0.20	5.69
1998	San Bern	Cal	74.7	89	36	8	30	52	4.34	4	4	10.73	0.96	3.62	6.27	0.76	4.82

Closer suspect #2, Montgomery may have leapfrogged Mitchell this year. He looks more like a closer, a big guy who throws hard, and he got a cameo with Albuquerque towards the end of the year. Montgomery's a better prospect, but neither guy is going to be saving games in Los Angeles anytime soon. Both pitchers are good examples of how easy it is to find relief pitchers.

Antonio Osuna — Throws R — Age 26

YEAR	TEAM	LGE	IP	H	ER	HR	BB	K	ERA	W	L	H/9	HR/9	BB/9	K/9	KWH	PERA
1996	LosAngls	NL	83.0	72	31	6	30	76	3.36	5	4	7.81	0.65	3.25	8.24	2.01	2.93
1997	LosAngls	NL	61.0	51	15	7	16	60	2.21	5	2	7.52	1.03	2.36	8.85	3.31	2.80
1998	LosAngls	NL	65.7	52	23	9	29	65	3.15	4	3	7.13	1.23	3.97	8.91	2.10	3.02

One of the better relievers in the league, and gets less respect than Chris Kahrl at a Mensa meeting. Osuna throws hard, mixes in a nice breaking ball and tries really hard not to do bad things, like kill everyone in the Dodger front office, no matter how justified he would be. He's going to save 120 games over three years for somebody, and it would be nice if 15 of those could come against the Dodgers. Needs a change of scenery.

Chan Ho Park — Throws R — Age 26

YEAR	TEAM	LGE	IP	H	ER	HR	BB	K	ERA	W	L	H/9	HR/9	BB/9	K/9	KWH	PERA
1996	LosAngls	NL	108.3	93	46	8	67	106	3.82	6	6	7.73	0.66	5.57	8.81	1.35	3.32
1997	LosAngls	NL	188.7	166	79	25	63	147	3.77	11	10	7.92	1.19	3.01	7.01	1.55	3.34
1998	LosAngls	NL	222.7	207	90	17	88	173	3.64	14	11	8.37	0.69	3.56	6.99	1.23	3.35

Quality pitcher who didn't improve as much as expected in 1998. Despite this, it was a good year: he stayed healthy, kept the ball in the park more—mostly by dumping the AckerCurve ™ he'd occasionally throw—and finished strong. That finish is actually the only concern: he averaged almost eight innings per start in August and September, including three straight 136-pitch starts. If healthy, I think there's a step forward coming. I just don't know if he'll stay healthy, and I think he's a bad risk.

Carlos Perez — Throws L — Age 28

YEAR	TEAM	LGE	IP	H	ER	HR	BB	K	ERA	W	L	H/9	HR/9	BB/9	K/9	KWH	PERA
1995	Montreal	NL	143.0	145	54	18	27	98	3.40	9	7	9.13	1.13	1.70	6.17	1.84	3.78
1997	Montreal	NL	209.0	213	97	21	43	99	4.18	11	12	9.17	0.90	1.85	4.26	0.80	3.66
1998	Montreal	NL	161.3	186	75	12	30	74	4.18	9	9	10.38	0.67	1.67	4.13	0.74	4.13
1998	LosAngls	NL	78.3	69	26	9	27	42	2.99	6	3	7.93	1.03	3.10	4.83	0.71	3.22

Also did yeoman's work during September, averaging almost nine innings per start, albeit with much lower pitch counts. I've never understood the hype surrounding Perez: he'd put in two season with ERAs in the high threes, and was generally discussed as if he was a premier starter. He's above average, a quality #3 guy, but with Tim Belcher's strikeout rates it's hard to see how long it can last. He's in the right park, and having Devo and Mondesi around won't hurt.

Luke Prokopec — Throws R — Age 21

YEAR	TEAM	LGE	IP	H	ER	HR	BB	K	ERA	W	L	H/9	HR/9	BB/9	K/9	KWH	PERA
1997	Savannah	SAL	39.0	51	25	10	15	29	5.77	1	3	11.77	2.31	3.46	6.69	0.82	6.46
1998	San Bern	Cal	105.7	124	46	13	35	97	3.92	6	6	10.56	1.11	2.98	8.26	1.63	4.77
1998	SanAnton	Tex	24.7	19	5	0	13	20	1.82	2	1	6.93	0.00	4.74	7.30	1.21	2.55

Converted catcher who took apart the Cal League with a tremendous fastball/curveball mix. Still developing, so it would be nice if the Dodgers showed some restraint and let him get a full year in at San Antonio. It could happen. The Dodgers' second-best prospect, after Judd.

Scott Radinsky — Throws L — Age 31

YEAR	TEAM	LGE	IP	H	ER	HR	BB	K	ERA	W	L	H/9	HR/9	BB/9	K/9	KWH	PERA
1996	LosAngls	NL	51.7	57	18	2	16	43	3.14	4	2	9.93	0.35	2.79	7.49	1.52	3.83
1997	LosAngls	NL	61.0	60	22	4	19	39	3.25	4	3	8.85	0.59	2.80	5.75	1.00	3.39
1998	LosAngls	NL	62.3	65	18	5	18	41	2.60	5	2	9.39	0.72	2.60	5.92	1.08	3.75

Like Guthrie, Radinsky has been effective over the past three years. And yet, you get the feeling the Dodgers are disappointed with him for not being Billy Wagner. Signed a two-year deal with the Cardinals. It's unclear how LaRussa will use him, but if it's as a one-batter specialist, it's a waste. Radinsky is a top-tier left-handed reliever.

Gary Rath   Throws L   Age 26

YEAR	TEAM	LGE	IP	H	ER	HR	BB	K	ERA	W	L	H/9	HR/9	BB/9	K/9	KWH	PERA
1996	Albuquer	PCL	187.3	176	78	14	89	110	3.75	11	10	8.46	0.67	4.28	5.28	0.58	3.51
1997	Albuquer	PCL	136.0	164	79	15	45	82	5.23	6	9	10.85	0.99	2.98	5.43	0.68	4.83
1998	Albuquer	PCL	158.7	191	78	15	55	92	4.42	8	10	10.83	0.85	3.12	5.22	0.60	4.71

Longtime prospect who's been ready for a job since I was single. Still only 26, he's got to be getting tired of New Mexico by now. His name has popped up in a couple of trade rumors, and it would be nice if something was worked out. Rath is a back-of-the-rotation guy who could help 20 teams. Needs to go someplace like Kansas City where he's much better than the competition, and doesn't have to look over his shoulder every time he goes 2-0 on someone.

Jeff Shaw   Throws R   Age 32

YEAR	TEAM	LGE	IP	H	ER	HR	BB	K	ERA	W	L	H/9	HR/9	BB/9	K/9	KWH	PERA
1995	Montreal	NL	63.3	60	31	4	25	42	4.41	3	4	8.53	0.57	3.55	5.97	0.88	3.41
1996	Cincnnti	NL	106.7	102	30	8	28	62	2.53	9	3	8.61	0.68	2.36	5.23	1.01	3.29
1997	Cincnnti	NL	96.3	78	21	7	10	66	1.96	9	2	7.29	0.65	0.93	6.17	4.19	2.15
1998	Cincnnti	NL	50.3	41	9	2	11	26	1.61	5	1	7.33	0.36	1.97	4.65	1.12	2.32
1998	LosAngls	NL	35.0	36	9	6	7	24	2.31	3	1	9.26	1.54	1.80	6.17	1.71	4.11

Baseball people are a funny breed. They'll preach on about how you need a "proven" closer to win, and how only certain people have what it takes to pitch the ninth inning. They'll give lots of money to those pitchers who have the magical "closer" label, irrespective of performance or the presence of other capable pitchers. And every year, a handful of guys without that label will be forced into the role and be outstanding. What happens? Those pitchers are dubbed "closers" and the cycle repeats itself. No one ever looks back and notices, "Hey, he didn't have the scarlet 'C' on his chest. Maybe it doesn't mean that much." Shaw was the shining example from 1997, pressed into the role when Jeff Brantley's shoulder blew. Now, he'll make $6 million per year while his performance slowly deteriorates and Antonio Osuna blows people away in the eighth inning. And he will deteriorate—his peripherals are already in a slow retreat. The park and the save totals will mask his decline for awhile.

Ricky Stone   Throws R   Age 24

YEAR	TEAM	LGE	IP	H	ER	HR	BB	K	ERA	W	L	H/9	HR/9	BB/9	K/9	KWH	PERA
1996	Savannah	SAL	28.0	53	22	3	11	19	7.07	1	2	17.04	0.96	3.54	6.11	0.46	7.71
1996	VeroBch	Fla	109.7	141	63	15	50	59	5.17	4	8	11.57	1.23	4.10	4.84	0.37	5.50
1997	SanAnton	Tex	49.0	73	33	4	30	38	6.06	2	3	13.41	0.73	5.51	6.98	0.49	6.06
1997	SanBern	Cal	51.3	49	23	4	10	27	4.03	3	3	8.59	0.70	1.75	4.73	1.12	3.16
1998	SanAnton	Tex	76.0	92	43	7	26	53	5.09	3	5	10.89	0.83	3.08	6.28	0.88	4.74
1998	Albuquer	PCL	109.3	116	54	12	40	71	4.45	5	7	9.55	0.99	3.29	5.84	0.81	4.20

Hasn't spent a full year in one place as a professional, and not always for the good reasons. Stone did two things right this year: he survived the San Antonio/Albuquerque route, which has derailed better pitchers, and he pitched very well in the Arizona Fall League, which has become a starmaker. The Dodgers rotation is going to be in flux for a while, so he may get an opportunity. He's good, but has generally needed adjustment periods at every level.

Ismael Valdes   Throws R   Age 25

YEAR	TEAM	LGE	IP	H	ER	HR	BB	K	ERA	W	L	H/9	HR/9	BB/9	K/9	KWH	PERA
1996	LosAngls	NL	222.0	237	90	21	50	154	3.65	14	11	9.61	0.85	2.03	6.24	1.50	3.89
1997	LosAngls	NL	191.7	189	69	17	42	124	3.24	13	8	8.87	0.80	1.97	5.82	1.45	3.43
1998	LosAngls	NL	175.7	177	73	18	59	111	3.74	11	9	9.07	0.92	3.02	5.69	0.88	3.84

Made the long-awaited trip to the disabled list, but it was for a pulled stomach muscle, not the arm injury that's been "inevitable" for so long. Despite the off year, I'd still take him over just about any non-Brave in the league, and fully expect him to run off a few Cy Young seasons, starting now.

Eric Weaver · Throws R · Age 25

YEAR	TEAM	LGE	IP	H	ER	HR	BB	K	ERA	W	L	H/9	HR/9	BB/9	K/9	KWH	PERA
1996	SanAnton	Tex	112.7	131	59	7	46	60	4.71	5	8	10.46	0.56	3.67	4.79	0.45	4.39
1996	Albuquer	PCL	49.3	63	32	5	22	34	5.84	2	3	11.49	0.91	4.01	6.20	0.63	5.29
1997	SanAnton	Tex	78.3	95	45	5	39	48	5.17	3	6	10.91	0.57	4.48	5.51	0.47	4.71
1997	Albuquer	PCL	72.0	91	38	6	34	45	4.75	3	5	11.38	0.75	4.25	5.62	0.49	5.00
1998	Albuquer	PCL	63.7	65	33	6	32	51	4.66	3	4	9.19	0.85	4.52	7.21	0.94	4.10

Middle-relief fodder. The catch is, guys like this are more valuable in a place like Chavez Ravine than almost anywhere else. All kinds of scrubs have stepped up and had decent years for the Dodgers throwing low-leverage relief lately: Darren Hall, Jim Bruske, John Cummings, so why not Eric Weaver? Needs to cut one walk per nine innings to be taken more seriously. Traded to Seattle; if given a chance, he'll be effective, and I guarantee you he'll be the closer for at least a week.

Pete Zamora · Throws L · Age 23

YEAR	TEAM	LGE	IP	H	ER	HR	BB	K	ERA	W	L	H/9	HR/9	BB/9	K/9	KWH	PERA
1997	GreatFls	Pio	58.3	92	41	4	42	36	6.33	2	4	14.19	0.62	6.48	5.55	0.25	6.48
1998	San Bern	Cal	78.3	57	25	2	36	49	2.87	6	3	6.55	0.23	4.14	5.63	0.88	2.18
1998	SanAnton	Tex	62.0	83	53	6	26	37	7.69	1	6	12.05	0.87	3.77	5.37	0.48	5.37

Not a bad selection, and since he went to UCLA, if he makes it there's a good story. Zamora got slapped around at San Antonio, but as a left-hander with better command than stuff, that'll probably happen at every level. I like Zamora's chances to eventually be a rotation starter (there go my USC alumni benefits), but the Dodgers will have to be patient. Not a factor until 2001.

SNWLP   LOS ANGELES DODGERS   Park Effect: -20.3%

PITCHER	GS	IP	R	SNW	SNL	SNPCT	W	L	RA	APW	SNVA	SNWAR
Bohanon, B.	14	97.3	35	6.3	4.0	.611	4	7	3.24	1.13	1.08	1.92
Dreifort, D.	26	165.0	83	8.6	10.2	.459	8	12	4.53	-0.52	-0.70	0.64
Martinez, R.	15	101.7	42	5.8	4.8	.549	7	3	3.72	0.62	0.47	1.32
Mlicki, D.	20	124.3	64	6.7	7.7	.464	7	3	4.63	-0.54	-0.52	0.57
Nomo, H.	12	67.3	39	3.8	4.6	.455	2	7	5.21	-0.74	-0.44	0.26
Park, C.	34	220.7	101	12.8	11.7	.523	15	9	4.12	0.34	0.54	2.38
Perez, C.	11	77.7	30	5.7	3.1	.649	4	4	3.48	0.69	1.31	1.95
Reyes, D.	3	15.3	10	0.9	0.7	.579	0	2	5.87	-0.28	0.10	0.24
Valdes, I.	27	174.0	82	10.1	9.2	.523	11	9	4.24	0.02	0.27	1.89
TOTALS	162	1043.3	486	60.7	55.9	.521	58	56	4.19	0.72	2.11	11.17

1998 was a good year for Dodgers starters, a big improvement over the previous year despite the fact that by the season's end they lost all but one member of their touted (and overrated) rotation from 1997. Nomo, Astacio, and Candiotti all ended up on other teams and struggled, and Ramon Martinez sat out the last half of 1998 with an injury. The mostly unheralded pitchers they brought in to replace those four were more than adequate. The combined SN record for the three new Dodgers brought in through trades—Bohanon, Mlicki, and Perez—was 18.7-14.8 (.558). The only two Dodger pitchers who were full-time starters both before and after the Piazza trade were Ismael Valdes and Chan Ho Park. How did the trade suit them? Valdes had a .466 SNPct before the trade, .544 after. Park was .434 before the trade, .550 after. I don't claim that proves anything; it's just interesting to know.

Pitcher Abuse Points

PITCHER	AGE	GS	PAP	PAP/S	AAW	MAX	115+	130+
Bohanon, Brian	29	14	196	14.00	21.00	133	3	1
Dreifort, Darren	26	26	217	8.35	16.69	131	4	1
Martinez, Ramon	30	15	294	19.60	26.13	126	6	0
Mlicki, Dave	30	20	96	4.80	6.40	126	2	0
Nomo, Hideo	29	12	156	13.00	19.50	136	3	1
Park, Chan Ho	25	34	500	14.71	31.86	137	9	3
Perez, Carlos	27	11	150	13.64	25.00	130	3	1
Valdes, Ismael	24	27	305	11.30	26.36	129	6	0
Manager								
Russell, Bill		74	772	10.43	17.95	136	16	1
Hoffman, Glenn		88	1142	12.98	25.27	137	20	6
TOTAL		162	1914	11.81	21.93	137	36	7
RANKING (NL)			2	2	2		2	2-T

The Dodgers never learn. Tommy Lasorda worked his pitchers like galley slaves, and learned nothing from Fernando Valenzuela's slow demise or Orel Hershiser's sudden breakdown. He abused Ramon Martinez for years. Last year, Bill Russell finished him off: Martinez led the team in PAP per start with an already-diagnosed partial tear in his rotator cuff. For that alone Russell should have been canned—but Glenn Hoffman, his successor, was even more brutal than Russell had been. Ismael Valdes continued to be pushed, and while Russell actually handled Chan Ho Park fairly well—57 PAPs in 16 starts—Hoffman turned up the treadmill, getting an average of 25.2 Abuse Points per start. His AAW under Hoffman was 54.53, which over a full season would have ranked fifth in all of baseball. Darren Dreifort had to be shut down after one start in September with arm soreness. I don't know if Davey Johnson will counteract the damage already done to a young rotation that was forced to grow up too fast. But I know this: he can't be any worse.

San Diego Padres

From the ashes of a disappointing 1997 came a season full of positives for Padres fans. The team went to the World Series for only the second time in its history, and the voters of San Diego approved a new stadium for the Padres just in time to keep talk of moving to Virginia from getting serious. The hometown team gave its best effort in over a decade, and they're going to remain the hometown team for the time being. So today's baseball fan can't ask for much more than what the Pads gave their fans in 1998, but questions about the team's immediate future—and how much they might have sacrificed to get their 1998 showing and subsequent electoral victory—abound.

When viewing the 1998 Padre season, we can't forget about 1997, or 1996 (when the Padres won the National League West but were swept out of the playoffs by the Cardinals). Truth be told, the Padres recent history resembles nothing so much as Anna Nicole Smith's silhouette ("They're up! Now they're down! Now they're up!"). While there have been more highs than lows, the team has hardly given its fans reason to consider them a stable contender. For all success the Padres experienced on the field, the biggest win was at the polls, where the voters of San Diego passed Proposition C by a large margin. Ignoring, for a moment, the general axiom that public funding for private-enterprise stadia is a questionable use of tax money, Proposition C isn't the hatchet job that some teams that shall remain nameless (but who play in a city with a twin) tried to pull over on their home towns. By comparison, the new ballpark in the East Village will be relatively cheap for the community. As part of the proposition, the Padres are now obligated to stay in San Diego until 2024, which makes John Moores a very happy and popular man.

To reach this point, the Padres clearly made a decision before the season to try to replicate the on- and off-field success of the Seattle Mariners' franchise in 1995. That club squeaked out a divisional title for the team's first-ever playoff appearance just in time for an Election Day vote on funding for a new stadium. The sudden success of the previously woebegone M's packed the stadium nightly and turned certain defeat at the polls into the most narrow of victories.

> ## Padres Prospectus
>
> **1998 record:** 98-64; First place, NL West; Lost to New York Yankees in World Series, 4-0
>
> **Pythagorean W/L:** 94-68
>
> **Runs scored:** 749 (8th in NL)
>
> **Runs allowed:** 635 (3rd in NL)
>
> **Team EQA:** .274 (4th in NL)
>
> **Park:** Qualcomm Stadium (excellent pitchers')
>
> **1998:** The offense aged gracefully, and improved pitching sent them to the Series.
>
> **1999:** Can reasonably expect to improve at only one position. A big falloff is likely.

The Padres came into the season with a team designed to win the division and fare better in the playoffs. They traded two of their top four prospects, Derrek Lee and Rafael Medina, to Florida for one year of Kevin Brown's time. They hung onto several older players entering their contract years, such as Finley, Caminiti, Joyner. And they chose to stick it out with Greg Vaughn in left rather than break in rookie Ruben Rivera, instead electing to use Rivera as a valuable bat and glove off the bench.

As a result, the Padres enjoyed their finest season in history overall. They crushed all comers in the NL West, winning the title by almost ten games, improving by 22 games on their record, and setting a franchise record for wins in the process. The team's fortunes only got better in the playoffs, as San Diego beat two arguably superior teams in the Astros and the Braves before falling to the Yankee juggernaut in the World Series.

Most of the difference was the return to competence on the part of the pitching staff. Led by Head Intimidator Dave Stewart (who has since taken a job as assistant general manager with Toronto) and Rent-An-Ace employee Kevin Brown, the entire staff was superb in 1998. Andy Ashby's development into a money pitcher, highlighted by a 75-pitch complete game effort against Colorado on July 5, was particularly gratifying. Ashby later pulled a muscle and was ineffective for the last two months of the season, but he rebounded in the playoffs and may be San Diego's new ace in 1999—by rights and by default. In the bullpen, solid work by previous enigmas like Donne Wall and Dan Miceli bridged the gap between the starters and the ninth inning. Then terminator Trevor Hoffman would take over, while posting a season good enough to merit Cy Young consideration.

The offense vindicated the front office's go-for-it strategy by producing despite several key contributors getting long in the tooth. Greg Vaughn's career year managed to gloss over some other players' hitting woes. Most observers (BP included) thought Vaughn was through after his putrid 1997 season, but he had the last laugh, setting a club record with 50 home runs and leading the Padres' offense through Ken Caminiti's annual injury woes. Tony Gwynn was again large, both in stature and talent, hitting .321 for the season and ensuring that he'll reach 3000 hits in 1999. Quilvio Veras came through with a season more befitting his role as leadoff hitter, although nagging injuries remained a problem for him.

The front office gets good marks for most of their moves last season. The Kevin Brown trade was essential to the team's success, and picking up Jim "The King" Leyritz on the cheap was an inspired move. If the team's player-acquisition strategy has a flaw, it's an inability to find an effective left-hander for the pen. After Ed Vosberg hit the disabled list for the season, the team looked at Roberto Ramirez, and then Ben Van Ryn for about a week to prove he belonged before unceremoniously dumping him. The lefty out of the pen ended up being Randy Myers, a horrendously expensive and ineffective late season pickup. The team had done fine without a portsider in the pen, but that didn't stop Kevin Towers and company from trying.

Everybody in San Diego seems to love Padres owner John Moores. Virtually deified by the local media, he seems to be a hands-off owner who lets the people he has hired to run the team run it—refreshing in an era where a kinder, gentler George Steinbrenner is hailed as the exemplary sports team owner. It is locally expected that the passing of the new stadium deal will open up Moores's pockets, which seems tautological. Of course, the new stadium didn't get Ken Caminiti or Steve Finley the contracts they wanted, but in the end, that's probably to Moores's credit—while he's known as a huge fan of both Caminiti and Finley, he left the decision up to the people paid to make such decisions. Letting both walk away was the right call, moreso in Finley's case than in Caminiti's.

Having spent significant talent capital to make their 1998 push, the Padres find themselves in a difficult spot for 1999. Turning to the minor leagues for help won't be the answer; if the cupboard was bare last year, there isn't even a cupboard this year, as the farm system is barren. The Padres affiliates at Mobile and Rancho Cucamonga both won their respective leagues, but they were led in large part by filler

veterans who were a good half-decade older than their competition. Ruben Rivera is ready to take over an outfield spot, and coveted pitching prospect Matt Clement will be with the major-league team in 1999, but after that, there's little on its way for 1999. On the mound, Ashby, playoff hero Sterling Hitchcock, and Joey Hamilton will all be returning, and they form a competent top three to a starting rotation. Clement is expected to take a spot, leaving the other slot open to question, as the Pads are unlikely to be able to retain Brown.

As it always is with this team, offense is the big question. Age is still a huge factor, as Joyner, Gwynn, and Steve Finley are all approaching AARP membership (with great prescription discounts). Finley has been healthy but increasingly ineffective, and the Pads aren't likely to re-sign him. Joyner and Gwynn have had their troubles over the last few seasons. Vaughn was obviously worth the money last year, but do you bet a long shot like that twice? I'd expect Quilvio Veras to have a fine season leading off and playing second, and Chris Gomez to be steady at short and inoffensive at the plate. Third base remains another question, with Caminiti gone to Houston and the team's commitment to George Arias tentative at best.

In the abstract, the Padres' best course of action is clear: let the free agents go, trade Vaughn and Joyner, and start a rebuilding process to put a winning team on the field when the new park opens. However, on the heels of a pennant and an electoral victory, the Padres might find that full retreat alienates many of the fans they just won over. In all likelihood, the Pads will straddle the line. Caminiti, Finley, and Brown won't be back, and the team will probably try to move Randy Myers to get out from under his contract. At the same time, the team will probably try to fill some holes via free agency, hoping to trade those players in a year to restock the farm system's upper levels. In the weak NL West, the middling strategy might work for '99 if they're lucky again, but the aging Padres face some sort of slump between now and the new stadium's opening, and denying it isn't going to help the team one bit.

HITTERS (Averages: BA .260/ OBA .330/ SA .420, EQA .260)

Dusty Allen   OF-1B   Bats R   Age 26

YEAR	TEAM	LGE	AB	H	DB	TP	HR	BB	R	RBI	SB	CS	OUT	BA	OBA	SA	EQA	EQR	DEFENSE	
1996	Clinton	Mid	253	51	3	1	6	45	26	21	2	3	205	.202	.322	.292	.221	24	77-1B 93	
1996	R Cucmng	Cal	204	46	7	1	5	26	20	20	1	1	159	.225	.313	.343	.231	20	42-1B 85	
1997	Mobile	Sou	471	93	16	1	11	62	39	37	1	2	380	.197	.291	.306	.208	38	76-1B 96	54-OF 76
1998	Mobile	Sou	154	32	6	1	4	23	16	15	1	0	122	.208	.311	.338	.231	16	35-OF 85	
1998	LasVegas	PCL	285	63	10	1	11	26	24	30	0	2	224	.221	.286	.379	.226	27	42-OF 76	33-1B 90
1999	SanDieg	NL	409	88	17	1	13	48	37	42	1	2	323	.215	.298	.357	.240	45		

Not likely to make the cut in FOX's new reality special, "When Prospects Attack!" By all accounts he's an easy-going fellow, but he's not really a prospect at this point. Originally a 30th-round pick out of Stanford, is a similar player to Rob Deer—minus a little bit of everything.

George Arias 3B Bats R Age 27

YEAR	TEAM	LGE	AB	H	DB	TP	HR	BB	R	RBI	SB	CS	OUT	BA	OBA	SA	EQA	EQR	DEFENSE
1996	Vancouvr	PCL	242	80	14	0	10	19	35	41	2	1	163	.331	.379	.512	.303	41	61-3B 115
1996	Calfrnia	AL	248	56	7	1	6	15	18	20	2	0	192	.226	.270	.335	.207	19	79-3B 127
1997	Vancouvr	PCL	391	90	15	2	8	31	31	34	2	3	304	.230	.287	.340	.215	32	99-3B 116
1998	LasVegas	PCL	421	110	18	1	23	31	45	62	0	1	312	.261	.312	.473	.264	56	107-3B 100
1998	San Dieg	NL	36	7	2	1	1	4	3	4	0	0	29	.194	.275	.389	.227	4	
1999	*SanDieg*	*NL*	*473*	*123*	*21*	*1*	*22*	*34*	*48*	*65*	*2*	*1*	*351*	*.260*	*.310*	*.448*	*.270*	*66*	

Arias had what looks like another breakout season in the PCL, hitting for power at Las Vegas. With Caminiti's departure from San Diego, he'll get a crack at the job at third with the Padres. Not a good long-term answer because he won't take a walk, but his chances of being a quality short-time player because of the power he should put up for the next year or two. Very solid defensively.

Ken Caminiti 3B Bats B Age 36

YEAR	TEAM	LGE	AB	H	DB	TP	HR	BB	R	RBI	SB	CS	OUT	BA	OBA	SA	EQA	EQR	DEFENSE
1996	San Dieg	NL	550	182	34	2	42	81	102	125	9	6	374	.331	.417	.629	.341	127	144-3B 109
1997	San Dieg	NL	491	146	24	0	29	83	86	91	10	2	347	.297	.399	.523	.315	97	127-3B 113
1998	San Dieg	NL	460	124	26	0	35	75	76	89	7	2	338	.270	.372	.554	.309	90	119-3B 87
1999	*Houston*	*NL*	*471*	*125*	*20*	*0*	*33*	*81*	*73*	*86*	*8*	*2*	*348*	*.265*	*.373*	*.518*	*.311*	*94*	

It was another frustrating, injury-riddled season for Ken Caminiti. He missed 31 games due to various scrapes and pulls, and was obviously not himself much of the time he played. His range took a huge hit while he was active, and watching him leg out grounders was painful. Caminiti still hit for power and took walks, but serious questions need to be asked about his health after the last two seasons. He spurned the Tigers and went back to the Astros after the season, where he'll help them with their overly right-handed lineup.

Mike Darr OF Bats L Age 23

YEAR	TEAM	LGE	AB	H	DB	TP	HR	BB	R	RBI	SB	CS	OUT	BA	OBA	SA	EQA	EQR	DEFENSE
1996	Lakeland	Fla	312	70	13	4	1	24	25	20	4	2	244	.224	.280	.301	.200	22	79-OF 90
1997	R Cucmng	Cal	512	156	22	5	13	45	71	70	13	4	360	.305	.361	.443	.280	75	130-OF 91
1998	Mobile	Sou	516	145	30	3	6	46	69	53	18	6	377	.281	.340	.386	.257	63	126-OF 102
1999	*SanDieg*	*NL*	*487*	*134*	*26*	*4*	*7*	*39*	*59*	*51*	*15*	*5*	*358*	*.275*	*.329*	*.388*	*.265*	*65*	

Cemented his status as one of the team's few real hitting prospects with a nice 1998. He's hit a load of doubles over the last two years, which is a great sign for his future power development. An All-Star with Mobile this season, he's on track for a nice career in an outfield corner.

Ben Davis C Bats B Age 22

YEAR	TEAM	LGE	AB	H	DB	TP	HR	BB	R	RBI	SB	CS	OUT	BA	OBA	SA	EQA	EQR	DEFENSE
1996	R Cucmng	Cal	350	50	6	0	4	22	10	10	0	0	300	.143	.194	.194	.059	1	
1997	R Cucmng	Cal	468	114	14	1	14	22	35	45	2	1	355	.244	.278	.368	.219	40	
1998	Mobile	Sou	429	112	19	1	13	30	43	49	3	1	318	.261	.309	.401	.245	47	116-C 107
1999	*SanDieg*	*NL*	*415*	*105*	*13*	*1*	*13*	*21*	*33*	*45*	*1*	*1*	*311*	*.253*	*.289*	*.383*	*.242*	*45*	

Davis looked like a blown pick at the start of his career, but had another year where he made progress. He still doesn't hit much and won't take a walk, but has good doubles power that should turn into home runs at peak age. Defensively awesome; everything from his arm to his footwork is top-notch.

Kevin Eberwein 3B Bats R Age 22

YEAR	TEAM	LGE	AB	H	DB	TP	HR	BB	R	RBI	SB	CS	OUT	BA	OBA	SA	EQA	EQR	DEFENSE
1998	Clinton	Mid	250	67	11	1	9	21	28	32	2	1	184	.268	.325	.428	.259	31	52-3B 93
1999	*SanDieg*	*NL*	*194*	*58*	*11*	*1*	*8*	*12*	*23*	*30*	*1*	*1*	*137*	*.299*	*.340*	*.490*	*.292*	*32*	

(Kevin Eberwein *continued*)

A fifth-round pick out of UNLV who started higher in the system than any other draft choice, Eberwein had an excellent first pro season. He hit for power in limited playing time at Clinton. He had some elbow troubles in high school, which may become a factor as he moves up the chain.

Steve Finley　　CF　　Bats L　Age 34

YEAR	TEAM	LGE	AB	H	DB	TP	HR	BB	R	RBI	SB	CS	OUT	BA	OBA	SA	EQA	EQR	DEFENSE
1996	San Dieg	NL	657	198	44	8	32	60	102	111	19	9	468	.301	.360	.539	.300	115	157-OF 109
1997	San Dieg	NL	562	150	24	5	30	47	71	85	13	3	415	.267	.323	.488	.275	83	134-OF 111
1998	San Dieg	NL	626	166	43	6	17	50	78	76	14	4	464	.265	.320	.435	.260	80	152-OF 111
1999	*Arizona*	*NL*	*553*	*148*	*30*	*5*	*21*	*46*	*67*	*76*	*11*	*4*	*409*	*.268*	*.324*	*.454*	*.267*	*76*	

Finley's drop-off accelerated last season. He's gone from one of the better players in the league in 1996 to a drag on the team's offense in 1998, and it didn't help that he got lots of playing time batting high in the order (something he's never really been suited for). He's still awesome defensively, but so is Ruben Rivera. Signed with Arizona for four years, where he'll be part of their problem as far as getting on base and scoring runs.

Ed Giovanola　　IF　　Bats L　Age 30

YEAR	TEAM	LGE	AB	H	DB	TP	HR	BB	R	RBI	SB	CS	OUT	BA	OBA	SA	EQA	EQR	DEFENSE	
1996	Richmond	Int	211	53	10	1	2	32	26	20	1	4	162	.251	.350	.336	.242	23	26-SS 108	
1997	Richmond	Int	395	98	17	2	2	51	43	34	1	1	298	.248	.334	.316	.233	39	79-3B 92	22-SS 112
1998	San Dieg	NL	141	36	5	3	1	23	19	15	1	2	107	.255	.360	.355	.254	17	20-2B 122	
1999	*SanDieg*	*NL*	*221*	*53*	*6*	*2*	*1*	*34*	*25*	*19*	*1*	*2*	*170*	*.240*	*.341*	*.299*	*.244*	*25*		

The Padres picked up Giovanola from the Braves to sub for their regular middle infielders, and he was adequate for that in 1998. He's not much of a hitter, but as a defensive substitute he brings more to the party than Rafael Belliard (or Ozzie Guillen) at this point.

Chris Gomez　　SS　　Bats R　Age 28

YEAR	TEAM	LGE	AB	H	DB	TP	HR	BB	R	RBI	SB	CS	OUT	BA	OBA	SA	EQA	EQR	DEFENSE
1996	Detroit	AL	125	28	4	0	1	18	12	9	1	1	98	.224	.322	.280	.216	11	44-SS 89
1996	San Dieg	NL	329	87	17	1	3	41	39	33	1	2	244	.264	.346	.350	.247	37	88-SS 95
1997	San Dieg	NL	525	136	19	2	6	56	53	50	3	8	397	.259	.330	.337	.233	52	145-SS 93
1998	San Dieg	NL	456	131	36	3	5	55	64	55	1	4	329	.287	.364	.412	.270	62	134-SS 101
1999	*SanDieg*	*NL*	*451*	*122*	*24*	*1*	*6*	*53*	*53*	*49*	*2*	*4*	*333*	*.271*	*.347*	*.368*	*.264*	*60*	

Gomez hit well after the All-Star break, and turned in the finest season of his career overall. He was very steady on defense, though his range remains pedestrian. It's probably all downhill from here, but if nothing else, Gomez peaked at the right time for the organization.

Creighton Gubanich　　C　　Bats R　Age 27

YEAR	TEAM	LGE	AB	H	DB	TP	HR	BB	R	RBI	SB	CS	OUT	BA	OBA	SA	EQA	EQR	DEFENSE
1996	Huntsvil	Sou	216	52	9	0	7	23	22	24	1	0	164	.241	.314	.380	.242	24	
1996	Edmonton	PCL	115	25	6	1	3	5	9	9	2	0	90	.217	.250	.365	.210	9	
1997	Edmonton	PCL	137	35	4	0	5	11	12	16	0	2	104	.255	.311	.394	.238	14	
1998	LasVegas	PCL	284	68	11	0	12	25	27	34	1	1	217	.239	.301	.405	.242	31	76-C 90
1999	*SanDieg*	*NL*	*280*	*68*	*9*	*0*	*13*	*22*	*25*	*35*	*1*	*1*	*213*	*.243*	*.298*	*.414*	*.255*	*35*	

Gubanich added to his qualifications by playing some first base and third base with the Stars last season, and he certainly wouldn't be the worst utility player/backup catcher in the majors. He's got good power, which helps make up for his low batting average, and it wouldn't be surprising to see him finally end up on a major league roster somewhere next season.

Aaron Guiel　　OF　　Bats L　Age 26

YEAR	TEAM	LGE	AB	H	DB	TP	HR	BB	R	RBI	SB	CS	OUT	BA	OBA	SA	EQA	EQR	DEFENSE	
1996	Midland	Tex	428	90	17	2	8	47	38	33	8	4	342	.210	.288	.315	.212	35	79-3B 85	33-2B 91
1997	Midland	Tex	400	100	17	2	14	45	47	48	9	7	307	.250	.326	.407	.253	49	61-OF 90	
1998	LasVegas	PCL	178	46	9	3	3	23	24	20	4	1	133	.258	.343	.393	.261	23	45-OF 87	
1999	*SanDieg*	*NL*	*278*	*67*	*15*	*2*	*7*	*33*	*34*	*30*	*7*	*3*	*214*	*.241*	*.322*	*.385*	*.261*	*37*		

Guiel missed most of the season in Las Vegas due to injury. Although his defense is really poor no matter where he plays, his power has spiked since the move to the outfield, which has him looking like a major-league quality pinch-hitter.

Tony Gwynn RF Bats L Age 39

YEAR	TEAM	LGE	AB	H	DB	TP	HR	BB	R	RBI	SB	CS	OUT	BA	OBA	SA	EQA	EQR	DEFENSE
1996	San Dieg	NL	453	161	28	2	3	42	73	63	9	4	296	.355	.410	.446	.301	74	98-OF 94
1997	San Dieg	NL	597	225	46	2	20	48	103	113	10	5	377	.377	.423	.561	.332	120	127-OF 91
1998	San Dieg	NL	469	159	27	0	22	39	71	86	4	1	311	.339	.390	.537	.314	86	101-OF 88
1999	SanDieg	NL	484	149	27	1	14	46	65	70	6	2	337	.308	.368	.455	.298	81	

Gwynn's injury woes continued in 1998, when he played in only 127 games. It's par for the course for him, since he's played in 130 or more games only twice in the past seven seasons. There was talk that he was through after his midseason slump, when he hit under .280 in June and July, and he wasn't a factor in the batting race, but then he rebounded in September and during the playoffs. A leadfoot on the base paths, he isn't even getting a good jump in RF anymore.

Matt Halloran SS Bats R Age 21

YEAR	TEAM	LGE	AB	H	DB	TP	HR	BB	R	RBI	SB	CS	OUT	BA	OBA	SA	EQA	EQR	DEFENSE
1997	Clinton	Mid	154	27	1	0	2	6	5	5	5	2	129	.175	.206	.221	.120	3	46-SS 78
1998	Clinton	Mid	462	92	15	1	2	28	23	18	9	7	377	.199	.245	.249	.158	19	123-SS 83
1999	SanDieg	NL	340	71	7	0	4	15	18	17	8	5	274	.209	.242	.265	.179	19	

Halloran had a rough season in 1998. The Padres' first pick in 1997, he lost most of that season because of shoulder surgery. He's 6'1" and not great defensively, so a change of positions may be coming. He's a spray hitter with a very slow bat. Some straight-out-of-high-school players catch up after a couple of seasons with wooden bats, and hopefully Halloran will be one of them.

Carlos Hernandez C Bats R Age 32

YEAR	TEAM	LGE	AB	H	DB	TP	HR	BB	R	RBI	SB	CS	OUT	BA	OBA	SA	EQA	EQR	DEFENSE
1996	Albuquer	PCL	225	37	5	0	3	9	7	7	3	2	190	.164	.197	.227	.105	3	
1997	San Dieg	NL	134	43	7	1	3	4	14	19	0	2	93	.321	.341	.455	.267	17	
1998	San Dieg	NL	394	110	11	0	12	19	35	46	2	3	287	.279	.312	.398	.243	42	105-C 98
1999	SanDieg	NL	269	65	6	0	7	11	17	24	1	2	206	.242	.271	.342	.219	23	

Mike Piazza's former caddy turned in an lame season as the number one catcher for San Diego. He got the most playing time of his career, and Hernandez's build indicates he might not be able to handle it without tiring—he's short and stocky, and he may have the largest arms this side of Mark McGwire. He swings at the first pitch a dishearteningly high percentage of the time.

Wally Joyner 1B Bats L Age 37

YEAR	TEAM	LGE	AB	H	DB	TP	HR	BB	R	RBI	SB	CS	OUT	BA	OBA	SA	EQA	EQR	DEFENSE
1996	San Dieg	NL	436	122	27	0	10	71	67	57	4	3	317	.280	.381	.411	.280	66	117-1B 101
1997	San Dieg	NL	459	153	30	2	14	54	73	77	2	5	311	.333	.404	.499	.307	81	116-1B 100
1998	San Dieg	NL	447	142	30	1	15	55	69	74	1	2	307	.318	.392	.490	.302	77	115-1B 93
1999	SanDieg	NL	430	121	23	1	11	57	56	58	1	2	311	.281	.366	.416	.286	68	

Joyner reupped with a two-year deal just days after the World Series ended. Much was made in the local press that he "didn't get a raise," like perhaps there is an untapped demand for slap-hitting 37-year-old first basemen out there. He had a fine season overall, though he had some mobility problems around first base and more nagging injuries. He may finally sit against portsiders now that the Padres have Jim Leyritz locked up for 1999.

Jim Leyritz 1B-C Bats R Age 35

YEAR	TEAM	LGE	AB	H	DB	TP	HR	BB	R	RBI	SB	CS	OUT	BA	OBA	SA	EQA	EQR	DEFENSE
1996	NY Yanks	AL	259	65	8	0	7	28	27	28	2	0	194	.251	.324	.363	.243	28	
1997	Anaheim	AL	288	77	6	0	11	38	34	39	1	1	212	.267	.353	.403	.265	38	
1998	Boston	AL	127	36	6	0	8	21	20	24	0	0	91	.283	.385	.520	.307	24	
1998	San Dieg	NL	146	42	7	0	6	22	22	23	0	0	104	.288	.381	.459	.292	24	
1999	SanDieg	NL	273	65	7	0	11	43	32	35	1	0	208	.238	.342	.385	.270	39	

(Jim Leyritz *continued*)

Kevin Towers acquired Leyritz from Boston for the stretch run, and "The King" was his usual reliable self. You probably didn't miss the inspiring four-home-run playoff series against the Astros; graybeards might sniff it had nothing on Gene Tenace's four-home-run gig in the '72 World Series. His option was picked up for 1999, and he'll be starting against left-handers at first, and at catcher whenever possible.

Gary Matthews Jr.   OF   Bats B   Age 24

YEAR	TEAM	LGE	AB	H	DB	TP	HR	BB	R	RBI	SB	CS	OUT	BA	OBA	SA	EQA	EQR	DEFENSE
1996	R Cucmng	Cal	427	90	12	5	6	44	34	31	3	4	341	.211	.285	.304	.203	32	120-OF 89
1997	R Cucmng	Cal	266	68	9	2	6	39	35	30	5	2	200	.256	.351	.372	.258	34	66-OF 100
1998	Mobile	Sou	250	69	10	1	7	43	41	33	7	1	182	.276	.382	.408	.284	39	67-OF 119
1999	*SanDieg*	*NL*	*290*	*72*	*11*	*1*	*7*	*39*	*36*	*31*	*7*	*2*	*220*	*.248*	*.337*	*.366*	*.264*	*39*	

Matthews injured his wrist April 25, and missed 60 games. In the time he played, he was awesome at the plate and in the field, with his power and his walk rate spiking. He'll probably start the season in Las Vegas, where he'll get a chance to show that his improvement is for real. He's an organizational favorite, so he'll be given every chance to succeed.

Juan Melo   SS   Bats B   Age 22

YEAR	TEAM	LGE	AB	H	DB	TP	HR	BB	R	RBI	SB	CS	OUT	BA	OBA	SA	EQA	EQR	DEFENSE
1996	R Cucmng	Cal	490	118	16	3	6	12	29	34	3	4	376	.241	.259	.322	.192	30	128-SS 106
1997	Mobile	Sou	448	108	13	1	6	22	30	33	5	6	346	.241	.277	.315	.199	31	113-SS 98
1998	LasVegas	PCL	454	104	17	0	6	24	31	30	8	6	356	.229	.268	.306	.194	29	125-SS 87
1999	*SanDieg*	*NL*	*459*	*113*	*16*	*1*	*8*	*18*	*33*	*38*	*6*	*5*	*351*	*.246*	*.275*	*.338*	*.220*	*40*	

Just another Juan Melo season. A little bit of pop, and a whole load of hype. Melo is a reasonable prospect. He's very young for Triple-A, but he hasn't really hit, and he's not a great defensive player. This is the kind of Neifi Perez-ish prospect who gets press clippings but doesn't really contribute. The Padres would be wise to deal Melo while he's still the flavor of the week.

James Mouton   OF   Bats R   Age 30

YEAR	TEAM	LGE	AB	H	DB	TP	HR	BB	R	RBI	SB	CS	OUT	BA	OBA	SA	EQA	EQR	DEFENSE
1996	Houston	NL	302	82	14	1	4	40	46	29	18	10	230	.272	.357	.364	.258	39	92-OF 92
1997	Houston	NL	180	39	10	1	3	19	18	14	7	7	148	.217	.291	.333	.215	16	52-OF 93
1998	LasVegas	PCL	184	52	10	1	3	15	27	19	11	1	133	.283	.337	.397	.265	24	40-OF 86
1998	San Dieg	NL	64	14	3	1	0	7	6	4	4	4	54	.219	.296	.297	.204	5	
1999	*SanDieg*	*NL*	*224*	*57*	*13*	*1*	*2*	*23*	*29*	*19*	*12*	*6*	*173*	*.254*	*.324*	*.348*	*.252*	*28*	

Mouton was acquired from the Astros for Sean Bergman before the season began, and was slated to be the fourth outfielder and defensive sub with the Padres. He tore up the Cactus League, but couldn't carry it over to the regular season, and was soon replaced by Ruben Rivera. At best, he's a useful spare part; he's very tough on left handed pitching, and a plus base-stealer.

Greg Myers   C   Bats L   Age 33

YEAR	TEAM	LGE	AB	H	DB	TP	HR	BB	R	RBI	SB	CS	OUT	BA	OBA	SA	EQA	EQR	DEFENSE
1996	Minnesot	AL	321	86	22	3	5	17	32	34	0	0	235	.268	.305	.402	.242	34	
1997	Minnesot	AL	162	42	11	1	5	17	19	21	0	0	120	.259	.330	.432	.262	21	
1998	San Dieg	NL	173	45	7	0	6	19	19	22	0	1	129	.260	.333	.405	.255	21	38-C 103
1999	*SanDieg*	*NL*	*186*	*44*	*5*	*0*	*6*	*17*	*16*	*20*	*0*	*0*	*142*	*.237*	*.300*	*.360*	*.242*	*20*	

Myers spent time on the DL in June and July, and played like Greg Myers when he wasn't hurt. He's solid defensively, and his batting lefty is a neat oddity, but it doesn't really translate to a platoon advantage anymore. He's a better bet than Carlos Hernandez in 1999, but Leyritz should have the inside track at playing time.

Kevin Nicholson   SS   Bats B   Age 23

YEAR	TEAM	LGE	AB	H	DB	TP	HR	BB	R	RBI	SB	CS	OUT	BA	OBA	SA	EQA	EQR	DEFENSE
1997	R Cucmng	Cal	64	18	3	0	1	3	6	6	1	1	47	.281	.313	.375	.236	6	
1998	Mobile	Sou	488	93	18	2	5	33	26	22	6	3	398	.191	.242	.266	.165	22	129-SS 97
1999	*SanDieg*	*NL*	*313*	*66*	*17*	*1*	*3*	*18*	*22*	*19*	*4*	*2*	*249*	*.211*	*.254*	*.300*	*.199*	*22*	

Nicholson was the Padres' 1996 #1 pick, and the team had him rated near the top of college hitters. Like Halloran, he had his problems offensively in 1998; unlike Halloran, he was solid defensively and will probably remain a shortstop. Expect him to start next season in Mobile again.

Ruben Rivera OF Bats R Age 25

YEAR	TEAM	LGE	AB	H	DB	TP	HR	BB	R	RBI	SB	CS	OUT	BA	OBA	SA	EQA	EQR	DEFENSE
1996	Columbus	Int	357	74	14	2	9	38	33	29	11	7	290	.207	.284	.333	.215	31	100-OF 110
1998	LasVegas	PCL	103	11	2	0	2	10	2	2	3	0	92	.107	.186	.184	.084	1	28-OF 101
1998	San Dieg	NL	174	39	8	2	7	30	26	22	6	1	136	.224	.338	.414	.267	25	52-OF 101
1999	*SanDieg*	*NL*	*241*	*47*	*10*	*2*	*7*	*27*	*24*	*20*	*9*	*3*	*197*	*.195*	*.276*	*.340*	*.230*	*25*	

He didn't make the Padres out of spring training, went to Las Vegas, and was terrible there, swinging at anything. The Padres called him up anyway, and he responded by being very selective and hitting well, while playing excellent defense. Whatever works, I guess. He'll be the everyday center fielder now that Finley has skipped town, and he should significantly outperform that projection.

Andy Sheets IF Bats R Age 27

YEAR	TEAM	LGE	AB	H	DB	TP	HR	BB	R	RBI	SB	CS	OUT	BA	OBA	SA	EQA	EQR	DEFENSE
1996	Tacoma	PCL	229	77	14	3	5	23	37	36	5	3	155	.336	.397	.489	.304	39	55-SS 93
1996	Seattle	AL	109	20	7	0	0	9	7	4	2	0	89	.183	.246	.248	.165	5	21-3B 103
1997	Tacoma	PCL	393	83	11	0	10	36	31	30	5	2	312	.211	.277	.316	.205	30	107-SS 96
1997	Seattle	AL	88	21	4	0	4	7	10	10	2	0	67	.239	.295	.420	.248	10	15-3B 101
1998	San Dieg	NL	197	51	6	3	8	22	27	26	8	2	148	.259	.333	.442	.270	28	28-SS 106
1999	*SanDieg*	*NL*	*279*	*67*	*13*	*2*	*8*	*27*	*31*	*30*	*8*	*2*	*214*	*.240*	*.307*	*.387*	*.256*	*36*	

The Padres picked Sheets up in the John Flaherty trade, and he enjoyed his new surroundings, hitting seven home runs in just 194 at-bats while adding solid defense. He allowed Chris Gomez to take some time off, which was probably partially responsible for Gomez's good season.

Mark Sweeney OF-1B Bats L Age 29

YEAR	TEAM	LGE	AB	H	DB	TP	HR	BB	R	RBI	SB	CS	OUT	BA	OBA	SA	EQA	EQR	DEFENSE
1996	St Louis	NL	171	45	7	0	4	33	28	20	3	0	126	.263	.382	.374	.277	25	28-OF 98
1997	San Dieg	NL	104	34	1	0	3	12	15	15	2	2	72	.327	.397	.423	.286	16	
1998	San Dieg	NL	195	50	10	3	2	27	24	21	1	2	147	.256	.347	.369	.252	23	19-OF 101
1999	*SanDieg*	*NL*	*166*	*43*	*7*	*1*	*3*	*24*	*22*	*18*	*3*	*2*	*125*	*.259*	*.353*	*.367*	*.269*	*23*	

Mark Sweeney began the year as the team's top pinch hitter, but he had a rough season and ended it behind John Vanderwal as far as left-handers off the bench are concerned. Expect a rebound in for him, but remember that keeping your hitting edge as a fifth outfielder is never easy.

John VanderWal OF Bats L Age 33

YEAR	TEAM	LGE	AB	H	DB	TP	HR	BB	R	RBI	SB	CS	OUT	BA	OBA	SA	EQA	EQR	DEFENSE
1996	Colorado	NL	146	30	7	1	4	19	14	14	1	2	118	.205	.297	.349	.223	14	18-OF 100
1997	Colorado	NL	91	14	2	0	1	10	3	3	1	1	78	.154	.238	.209	.136	3	
1998	Colorado	NL	100	25	7	1	5	16	15	16	0	0	75	.250	.353	.490	.287	17	
1998	San Dieg	NL	26	7	4	0	0	6	5	3	0	0	19	.269	.406	.423	.296	5	
1999	*SanDieg*	*NL*	*141*	*32*	*9*	*1*	*3*	*20*	*16*	*15*	*1*	*1*	*110*	*.227*	*.323*	*.369*	*.255*	*18*	

Cemented his reputation as one of the top pinch hitters in the league with his stint in San Diego after being acquired late in the season. He's tough on right-handed pitching, doesn't mind his limited role, can actually play the field decently enough, and won't clog up the base paths. It was nice to see him get some recognition for his postseason heroics.

Greg Vaughn — LF — Bats R — Age 33

YEAR	TEAM	LGE	AB	H	DB	TP	HR	BB	R	RBI	SB	CS	OUT	BA	OBA	SA	EQA	EQR	DEFENSE
1996	Milwauke	AL	364	98	15	0	29	55	56	70	5	2	268	.269	.365	.549	.304	69	83-OF 99
1996	San Dieg	NL	142	30	4	1	10	24	19	22	3	1	113	.211	.325	.465	.270	21	28-OF 112
1997	San Dieg	NL	363	81	10	0	19	58	45	47	6	4	286	.223	.330	.408	.257	48	78-OF 98
1998	San Dieg	NL	583	170	29	4	57	84	102	134	12	5	418	.292	.381	.648	.330	131	147-OF 98
1999	*SanDieg*	*NL*	*471*	*115*	*18*	*1*	*35*	*70*	*64*	*81*	*7*	*3*	*359*	*.244*	*.342*	*.510*	*.298*	*87*	

Last year, we said that the Padres should release Vaughn in this space. Oops. That probably isn't being considered now after his excellent season in 1998. I'd try to move him anyway, because of his age and spotty recent history, but I've been called stubborn before.

Quilvio Veras — 2B — Bats B — Age 28

YEAR	TEAM	LGE	AB	H	DB	TP	HR	BB	R	RBI	SB	CS	OUT	BA	OBA	SA	EQA	EQR	DEFENSE
1996	Florida	NL	256	67	7	1	5	52	39	29	6	9	198	.262	.386	.355	.264	35	66-2B 94
1997	San Dieg	NL	543	150	22	1	4	75	84	48	29	13	406	.276	.364	.343	.258	68	136-2B 95
1998	San Dieg	NL	527	153	27	2	7	89	96	58	27	11	385	.290	.393	.389	.283	82	128-2B 108
1999	*SanDieg*	*NL*	*509*	*139*	*23*	*1*	*8*	*79*	*83*	*52*	*29*	*11*	*381*	*.273*	*.371*	*.369*	*.282*	*80*	

A fine leadoff hitter, Veras had a nice year in 1998. For some reason, he has a rap with the local media of not being patient enough at the plate, though he's always drawn lots of walks. This year was no exception, and he hit for some pop besides. He's got an ugly, ugly swing, and looks like he's dislocating his shoulders while he's swinging through, so maybe it isn't a coincidence that he's having offseason surgery on both his shoulders.

PITCHERS (Averages: 4.00 ERA, 9.00 H/9, 1.00 HR/9, 3.00 BB/9, 6.00 K/9, 1.00 KWH)

Andy Ashby — Throws R — Age 31

YEAR	TEAM	LGE	IP	H	ER	HR	BB	K	ERA	W	L	H/9	HR/9	BB/9	K/9	KWH	PERA
1996	San Dieg	NL	148.0	164	61	17	32	76	3.71	9	7	9.97	1.03	1.95	4.62	0.83	4.20
1997	San Dieg	NL	199.0	219	102	18	43	128	4.61	9	13	9.90	0.81	1.94	5.79	1.30	4.03
1998	San Dieg	NL	222.0	241	88	24	51	136	3.57	14	11	9.77	0.97	2.07	5.51	1.13	4.09

Maybe it was Kevin Brown's arrival, or maybe it was Dave Stewart. Whatever the reason, Ashby responded with the best four months of his career to open 1998. Unfortunately, he pulled a muscle while pitching in late July, and was a different pitcher through the end of the regular season. He was tough in the playoffs, and with Brown's departure, figures to be the ace of the staff in 1999.

Brian Boehringer — Throws R — Age 30

YEAR	TEAM	LGE	IP	H	ER	HR	BB	K	ERA	W	L	H/9	HR/9	BB/9	K/9	KWH	PERA
1996	Columbus	Int	148.7	184	82	13	63	104	4.96	7	10	11.14	0.79	3.81	6.30	0.70	4.90
1996	NY Yanks	AL	48.3	42	20	6	17	37	3.72	3	2	7.82	1.12	3.17	6.89	1.44	3.17
1997	NY Yanks	AL	49.0	40	13	4	28	51	2.39	4	1	7.35	0.73	5.14	9.37	1.74	3.12
1998	San Dieg	NL	75.3	83	37	11	41	61	4.42	4	4	9.92	1.31	4.90	7.29	0.82	4.90

Picked up the nickname "Ballfouringer" in 1998 due to his problems with the unintentional walk. He didn't really do too much worse in that department than previously, but he gave up a lot more hits and home runs than he had before. He was a big disappointment, and the Padres will be looking for improvement in 1999.

Kevin Brown — Throws R — Age 34

YEAR	TEAM	LGE	IP	H	ER	HR	BB	K	ERA	W	L	H/9	HR/9	BB/9	K/9	KWH	PERA
1996	Florida	NL	233.7	191	51	8	30	141	1.96	21	5	7.36	0.31	1.16	5.43	2.60	2.08
1997	Florida	NL	240.7	216	65	11	59	182	2.43	20	7	8.08	0.41	2.21	6.81	1.95	2.77
1998	San Dieg	NL	251.3	245	77	8	44	231	2.76	19	9	8.77	0.29	1.58	8.27	3.71	2.94

It was business as usual for Brown last year, who was among the league leaders in every important pitching statistic. He's as steady as they come, but a long-term deal for Brown (through his 40th birthday, if Boras gets what he's asking) might not be in this team's best interests. Wherever he pitches in 1999, expect more of the same, except on Planet Coors.

Buddy Carlyle   Throws R   Age 21

YEAR	TEAM	LGE	IP	H	ER	HR	BB	K	ERA	W	L	H/9	HR/9	BB/9	K/9	KWH	PERA
1996	Princetn	App	42.7	68	40	5	17	23	8.44	1	4	14.34	1.05	3.59	4.85	0.34	6.54
1997	Charl-WV	SAL	136.0	170	59	12	33	72	3.90	8	7	11.25	0.79	2.18	4.76	0.69	4.76
1998	Mobile	Sou	174.3	206	75	14	38	77	3.87	10	9	10.63	0.72	1.96	3.98	0.57	4.34

The Padres stole Carlyle from the Reds for Marc Kroon a week into the season. He pitched well as part of the strong Mobile staff last season, and will be promoted in 1999. He doesn't strike anyone out, but his control of the strike zone is impressive. It will be interesting to see what he does at higher levels, when control pitchers tend to struggle through some pretty harsh adjustment periods.

Matt Clement   Throws R   Age 24

YEAR	TEAM	LGE	IP	H	ER	HR	BB	K	ERA	W	L	H/9	HR/9	BB/9	K/9	KWH	PERA
1996	Clinton	Mid	90.3	95	37	5	54	73	3.69	5	5	9.46	0.50	5.38	7.27	0.78	4.08
1996	R Cucmng	Cal	54.0	71	36	8	24	51	6.00	2	4	11.83	1.33	4.00	8.50	1.14	5.67
1997	R Cucmng	Cal	98.3	87	29	3	31	73	2.65	8	3	7.96	0.27	2.84	6.68	1.48	2.75
1997	Mobile	Sou	86.3	91	33	4	30	72	3.44	6	4	9.49	0.42	3.13	7.51	1.42	3.75
1998	LasVegas	PCL	176.0	153	74	11	82	132	3.78	11	9	7.82	0.56	4.19	6.75	1.04	3.12
1998	San Dieg	NL	13.7	16	8	0	7	12	5.27	1	1	10.54	0.00	4.61	7.90	0.96	3.95

Call him "The Future." Clement is far and away the Padres' top prospect. He has good velocity and his slider is a thing of beauty, but his control needs work. He's never been seriously injured, and hasn't been overworked. Led all of Triple-A with 160 strikeouts, it's expected he'll get 30 starts for the Padres in 1999.

Will Cunnane   Throws R   Age 25

YEAR	TEAM	LGE	IP	H	ER	HR	BB	K	ERA	W	L	H/9	HR/9	BB/9	K/9	KWH	PERA
1996	Portland	Eas	150.3	181	72	15	29	81	4.31	8	9	10.84	0.90	1.74	4.85	0.94	4.55
1997	San Dieg	NL	92.0	121	64	12	45	71	6.26	3	7	11.84	1.17	4.40	6.95	0.69	5.67
1998	LasVegas	PCL	37.0	45	22	1	19	24	5.35	1	3	10.95	0.24	4.62	5.84	0.51	4.62

A Rule V pick from the Marlins, Cunnane lost most of 1998 to injury. He's been a prospect forever, but he's still deserving of the tag. He's suffered from a bit of wildness since he arrived in San Diego, but he could be a factor in the rotation or the pen if he keeps his walks under control.

Bubba Dixon   Throws L   Age 27

YEAR	TEAM	LGE	IP	H	ER	HR	BB	K	ERA	W	L	H/9	HR/9	BB/9	K/9	KWH	PERA
1996	Memphis	Sou	60.0	69	37	7	27	55	5.55	2	5	10.35	1.05	4.05	8.25	1.22	4.80
1997	Mobile	Sou	71.0	83	33	4	40	61	4.18	4	4	10.52	0.51	5.07	7.73	0.84	4.56
1998	LasVegas	PCL	51.3	64	35	3	35	32	6.14	2	4	11.22	0.53	6.14	5.61	0.34	5.08

He finally made it to Triple-A, and pitched about as well as could have been expected. He doesn't have a fastball to speak of, and it cost him dearly in the PCL. His change-up is strong, and he's supposedly very coachable, but how many more lefties can you say that about?

Rickey Guttormson   Throws R   Age 22

YEAR	TEAM	LGE	IP	H	ER	HR	BB	K	ERA	W	L	H/9	HR/9	BB/9	K/9	KWH	PERA
1997	IdahoFls	Pio	23.0	50	32	2	14	10	12.52	0	3	19.57	0.78	5.48	3.91	0.11	8.22
1998	Clinton	Mid	151.3	200	74	13	47	91	4.40	8	9	11.89	0.77	2.80	5.41	0.66	5.11

Guttormson started the season in the bullpen, moved into the Clinton rotation when Kevin Walker was promoted, and turned in an excellent season. He really improved on his location, but doesn't have the stuff to blow hitters away, so he has to be careful.

Joey Hamilton   Throws R   Age 28

YEAR	TEAM	LGE	IP	H	ER	HR	BB	K	ERA	W	L	H/9	HR/9	BB/9	K/9	KWH	PERA
1996	San Dieg	NL	209.7	232	99	19	78	166	4.25	11	12	9.96	0.82	3.35	7.13	1.14	4.29
1997	San Dieg	NL	192.7	209	92	23	62	110	4.30	10	11	9.76	1.07	2.90	5.14	0.70	4.30
1998	San Dieg	NL	213.3	243	111	16	96	133	4.68	10	14	10.25	0.68	4.05	5.61	0.57	4.43

It was a tale of two seasons for Hamilton. His pre- and post-All Star break ERA: 5.15 vs. 3.13. What happened? Apparently, Dave Stewart worked with Hamilton to slow down his delivery and improve his concentration. Whatever the case, he kept baserunners to a minimum in the second half. I've been predicting a monster breakout for years, and I'll do it again this year.

Harry Herndon Jr.   Throws R   Age 20

YEAR	TEAM	LGE	IP	H	ER	HR	BB	K	ERA	W	L	H/9	HR/9	BB/9	K/9	KWH	PERA
1998	Clinton	Mid	127.3	149	64	5	38	67	4.52	6	8	10.53	0.35	2.69	4.74	0.59	4.10
1998	R Cucmng	Cal	37.7	47	20	6	14	19	4.78	2	2	11.23	1.43	3.35	4.54	0.41	5.50

Moved on to Rancho Cucamonga after a solid season in Clinton's rotation. Herndon occasionally lets a defensive miscue rattle him, which he needs to work on. He also gave up the long ball after his call-up, so we'll see if he makes the adjustment this year.

Sterling Hitchcock   Throws L   Age 28

YEAR	TEAM	LGE	IP	H	ER	HR	BB	K	ERA	W	L	H/9	HR/9	BB/9	K/9	KWH	PERA
1996	Seattle	AL	202.3	229	98	23	59	130	4.36	10	12	10.19	1.02	2.62	5.78	0.94	4.45
1997	San Dieg	NL	160.7	181	95	26	49	94	5.32	6	12	10.14	1.46	2.74	5.27	0.75	4.76
1998	San Dieg	NL	173.3	183	81	31	42	142	4.21	9	10	9.50	1.61	2.18	7.37	1.97	4.41

Hitchcock started the season in the bullpen, and pitched poorly. After Pete Smith was dealt to Baltimore, he moved into the rotation and improved markedly, but nobody was prepared for his inspiring run through the playoffs. He shut down the Braves, won the National League Series MVP, and allowed two runs to a talented Yankee lineup in his World Series start. If he pitches like that next year, the Padres won't need Kevin Brown.

Trevor Hoffman   Throws R   Age 31

YEAR	TEAM	LGE	IP	H	ER	HR	BB	K	ERA	W	L	H/9	HR/9	BB/9	K/9	KWH	PERA
1996	San Dieg	NL	87.0	58	24	7	29	99	2.48	7	3	6.00	0.72	3.00	10.24	4.37	1.86
1997	San Dieg	NL	81.7	62	23	10	21	98	2.53	6	3	6.83	1.10	2.31	10.80	5.53	2.42
1998	San Dieg	NL	72.0	46	12	2	18	77	1.50	7	1	5.75	0.25	2.25	9.62	5.37	1.25

The best closer in the league had another excellent season. His new introductory music at Qualcomm Stadium (AC/DC's "Hell's Bells") smacks of pro wrestling, but the crowd loves it, so what the heck? He blew his lone save right after they started playing his new intro. A four-pitch repertoire makes him the most dangerous closer in the league.

Mark Langston   Throws L   Age 38

YEAR	TEAM	LGE	IP	H	ER	HR	BB	K	ERA	W	L	H/9	HR/9	BB/9	K/9	KWH	PERA
1996	Calfrnia	AL	125.7	110	51	16	36	82	3.65	8	6	7.88	1.15	2.58	5.87	1.27	3.22
1997	Anaheim	AL	50.3	61	28	8	25	29	5.01	2	4	10.91	1.43	4.47	5.19	0.41	5.36
1998	San Dieg	NL	79.3	118	54	11	37	51	6.13	3	6	13.39	1.25	4.20	5.79	0.45	6.35

Langston completely lost it this season, and it was a joke that he was included on the postseason roster over Matt Clement or Stan Spencer. He's still a good athlete, which I suppose means he's more useful as a pinch-runner than a pitcher.

Dan Miceli   Throws R   Age 28

YEAR	TEAM	LGE	IP	H	ER	HR	BB	K	ERA	W	L	H/9	HR/9	BB/9	K/9	KWH	PERA
1996	Pittsbrg	NL	88.3	106	59	15	43	60	6.01	3	7	10.80	1.53	4.38	6.11	0.59	5.40
1997	Detroit	AL	84.7	79	42	12	33	77	4.46	4	5	8.40	1.28	3.51	8.19	1.71	3.72
1998	San Dieg	NL	71.7	69	27	6	25	63	3.39	5	3	8.67	0.75	3.14	7.91	1.73	3.52

Miceli did not disappoint in 1998, ending the season as Trevor Hoffman's setup man. He kept the strikeouts up and the hits down, and the key to his success was setting up opposing batters with his fastball, and then finishing them off with his off-speed stuff. If he's as effective this year, the Padres will be in good shape to kill rallies after the sixth inning.

Jason Middlebrook **Throws R** **Age 24**

YEAR	TEAM	LGE	IP	H	ER	HR	BB	K	ERA	W	L	H/9	HR/9	BB/9	K/9	KWH	PERA
1997	Clinton	Mid	76.3	101	54	6	45	54	6.37	2	6	11.91	0.71	5.31	6.37	0.48	5.42
1998	R Cucmng	Cal	137.3	218	119	13	73	81	7.80	3	12	14.29	0.85	4.78	5.31	0.31	6.49

The bonus baby out of Stanford, Middlebrook was a certain first round pick until he hurt his elbow. The Padres grabbed him in the ninth round and made him a rich young man. The investment hasn't worked out so far: his control is very suspect, but he's got an excellent fastball and his breaking stuff is solid.

Heath Murray **Throws L** **Age 26**

YEAR	TEAM	LGE	IP	H	ER	HR	BB	K	ERA	W	L	H/9	HR/9	BB/9	K/9	KWH	PERA
1996	Memphis	Sou	166.3	190	89	15	55	117	4.82	7	11	10.28	0.81	2.98	6.33	0.98	4.38
1997	LasVegas	PCL	108.7	137	56	9	37	81	4.64	5	7	11.35	0.75	3.06	6.71	0.97	4.89
1997	San Dieg	NL	33.7	54	24	3	19	14	6.42	1	3	14.44	0.80	5.08	3.74	0.14	6.42
1998	LasVegas	PCL	161.7	200	91	12	65	93	5.07	7	11	11.13	0.67	3.62	5.18	0.50	4.79

A reliable Triple-A starter, and shouldn't be counted on for anything else. He's got some good breaking stuff, and keeps his defense busy, but his fastball is Bob Tewksbury slow—and he doesn't have Tewksbury's control to make up for it.

Randy Myers **Throws L** **Age 36**

YEAR	TEAM	LGE	IP	H	ER	HR	BB	K	ERA	W	L	H/9	HR/9	BB/9	K/9	KWH	PERA
1996	Baltimor	AL	59.3	60	19	6	23	73	2.88	5	2	9.10	0.91	3.49	11.07	2.90	3.94
1997	Baltimor	AL	60.3	49	11	2	19	54	1.64	6	1	7.31	0.30	2.83	8.06	2.35	2.39
1998	Toronto	AL	43.7	43	17	4	17	31	3.50	3	2	8.86	0.82	3.50	6.39	0.99	3.71
1998	San Dieg	NL	14.0	17	10	2	6	8	6.43	1	1	10.93	1.29	3.86	5.14	0.47	5.14

Toronto signed Myers to an ill-advised three-year $18 million contract to be their closer. Myers didn't pitch well there. He was picked up by the Padres, reportedly to block the Braves from getting him, and pitched poorly down the stretch. He's obviously lost a few feet on his fastball; sometimes pitchers can recover from that, but Myers doesn't seem like a likely candidate to do so. The Padres are looking to move him during the offseason.

Alan Newman **Throws L** **Age 29**

YEAR	TEAM	LGE	IP	H	ER	HR	BB	K	ERA	W	L	H/9	HR/9	BB/9	K/9	KWH	PERA
1997	Birmnghm	Sou	67.0	70	39	0	43	44	5.24	3	4	9.40	0.00	5.78	5.91	0.48	3.76
1998	LasVegas	PCL	75.7	61	26	2	54	57	3.09	5	3	7.26	0.24	6.42	6.78	0.74	2.97

Newman put three years sitting around in the Texas-Louisiana League under his belt before he was signed by the White Sox. He came to the Padres in 1998 and turned in an excellent season for Las Vegas. He's got size (6'6", 240 pounds) and he's a lefty, so he could make a career for himself.

Roberto Ramirez **Throws L** **Age 26**

YEAR	TEAM	LGE	IP	H	ER	HR	BB	K	ERA	W	L	H/9	HR/9	BB/9	K/9	KWH	PERA
1998	LasVegas	PCL	29.3	24	13	2	11	25	3.99	2	1	7.36	0.61	3.38	7.67	1.78	2.76
1998	San Dieg	NL	14.7	14	13	5	11	15	7.98	0	2	8.59	3.07	6.75	9.20	1.10	5.52

A star pitcher in the Mexican League, Ramirez was the subject of a nasty little tiff between the Padres and the Rockies early in 1998. The Rockies thought they had a deal with him, and accused the Padres of underhandedness, but in the end, with a guy like this, who really cares? Don't these two teams have more important things to worry about? Ramirez signed with the Rockies after the season, so they get some pretty feeble bragging rights.

Jim Sak **Throws R** **Age 25**

YEAR	TEAM	LGE	IP	H	ER	HR	BB	K	ERA	W	L	H/9	HR/9	BB/9	K/9	KWH	PERA
1996	Clinton	Mid	60.0	71	40	3	49	46	6.00	2	5	10.65	0.45	7.35	6.90	0.46	4.95
1997	R Cucmng	Cal	67.7	55	31	6	31	72	4.12	4	4	7.32	0.80	4.12	9.58	2.28	2.93
1998	Mobile	Sou	46.3	45	31	4	32	41	6.02	2	3	8.74	0.78	6.22	7.96	0.88	4.08

Sak moved on to Mobile after his excellent season in Rancho Cucamonga. He still allowed few hits, but the hitters in the Southern League drew more walks off him than the California League did in 1997. A tenth-round pick from Illinois Benedictine in 1995, Sak will probably start the season in Mobile and end it in Las Vegas.

Scott Sanders — Throws R — Age 30

YEAR	TEAM	LGE	IP	H	ER	HR	BB	K	ERA	W	L	H/9	HR/9	BB/9	K/9	KWH	PERA
1996	San Dieg	NL	142.7	132	57	10	45	141	3.60	9	7	8.33	0.63	2.84	8.89	2.51	3.15
1997	Seattle	AL	68.7	71	38	15	33	60	4.98	3	5	9.31	1.97	4.33	7.86	1.15	4.85
1997	Detroit	AL	75.7	80	38	13	21	56	4.52	4	4	9.52	1.55	2.50	6.66	1.40	4.40
1998	Detroit	AL	10.0	25	16	1	6	6	14.40	0	1	22.50	0.90	5.40	5.40	0.18	9.00
1998	San Dieg	NL	30.3	35	19	6	4	23	5.64	1	2	10.38	1.78	1.19	6.82	2.83	5.04

Sanders came back from Detroit on waivers not even two years since he was traded to Seattle for Sterling Hitchcock. Coming off his strong 1996, the trade looked like a mistake for the Padres, but like most pitchers, Sanders hasn't been the same since meeting Lou Piniella. He did some good work with the Padres in 1998 in long relief. Signed by the Cubs, where he'll get a look as a fifth starter and long reliever.

Wascar Serrano — Throws R — Age 21

YEAR	TEAM	LGE	IP	H	ER	HR	BB	K	ERA	W	L	H/9	HR/9	BB/9	K/9	KWH	PERA
1998	Clinton	Mid	151.0	190	81	9	61	95	4.83	7	10	11.32	0.54	3.64	5.66	0.58	4.77

A lanky Dominican, Serrano has a good fastball with jaw-dropping movement. He came into the season as Clinton's second or third starter, but pitched well all season and may get fast-tracked this year. He needs to work on his control, but his ceiling is very high.

Stan Spencer — Throws R — Age 30

YEAR	TEAM	LGE	IP	H	ER	HR	BB	K	ERA	W	L	H/9	HR/9	BB/9	K/9	KWH	PERA
1997	R Cucmng	Cal	37.0	50	21	6	5	27	5.11	2	2	12.16	1.46	1.22	6.57	2.19	5.59
1997	LasVegas	PCL	46.7	50	20	4	18	36	3.86	3	2	9.64	0.77	3.47	6.94	1.08	4.05
1998	LasVegas	PCL	135.3	129	61	15	45	101	4.06	7	8	8.58	1.00	2.99	6.72	1.32	3.59
1998	San Dieg	NL	30.0	31	16	6	3	28	4.80	1	2	9.30	1.80	0.90	8.40	6.32	4.20

Spencer's career has been one injury after another, but he experienced a revival in Las Vegas last year, outpitching Matt Clement. He wasn't overmatched in his brief major league appearance, so expect him to get another crack at the majors. Watching him throw warm-up pitches without the ball is one of the more surreal things you'll see in baseball.

Brendan Sullivan — Throws R — Age 24

YEAR	TEAM	LGE	IP	H	ER	HR	BB	K	ERA	W	L	H/9	HR/9	BB/9	K/9	KWH	PERA
1996	IdahoFls	Pio	35.3	62	30	6	30	21	7.64	1	3	15.79	1.53	7.64	5.35	0.18	7.90
1997	Clinton	Mid	58.3	74	39	1	39	34	6.02	2	4	11.42	0.15	6.02	5.25	0.30	4.78
1998	R Cucmng	Cal	39.0	32	9	0	22	22	2.08	3	1	7.38	0.00	5.08	5.08	0.52	2.77
1998	Mobile	Sou	37.0	35	8	1	13	18	1.95	3	1	8.51	0.24	3.16	4.38	0.53	3.16

Sullivan had a fine year as a reliever at both Rancho Cucamonga and Mobile. Yet another Padres minor leaguer out of Stanford, Sullivan has a marginal fastball, but his submarine delivery is very deceptive, and he doesn't give up the long ball. He's a no-nonsense, goal-oriented young pitcher who should make it to Las Vegas this year.

Ed Vosberg — Throws L — Age 37

YEAR	TEAM	LGE	IP	H	ER	HR	BB	K	ERA	W	L	H/9	HR/9	BB/9	K/9	KWH	PERA
1996	Texas	AL	46.7	47	12	4	17	32	2.31	4	1	9.06	0.77	3.28	6.17	0.96	3.66
1997	Texas	AL	42.7	42	18	3	13	28	3.80	3	2	8.86	0.63	2.74	5.91	1.08	3.37
1997	Florida	NL	12.3	16	6	0	5	7	4.38	0	1	11.68	0.00	3.65	5.11	0.46	4.38

Vosberg missed all of 1998 with shoulder problems. The Padres, who had thought he would be the end to their perennial searches for a left-hander, will be counting on him in 1999. He's supposed to be healthy, and is a reliable if not overpowering pitcher.

Kevin Walker   **Throws L**   **Age 22**

YEAR	TEAM	LGE	IP	H	ER	HR	BB	K	ERA	W	L	H/9	HR/9	BB/9	K/9	KWH	PERA
1996	Clinton	Mid	70.7	107	53	13	34	30	6.75	2		13.63	1.66	4.33	3.82	0.19	6.88
1997	Clinton	Mid	106.0	163	84	12	40	54	7.13	3	9	13.84	1.02	3.40	4.58	0.34	6.28
1998	R Cucmng	Cal	114.7	155	68	13	51	62	5.34	5	8	12.17	1.02	4.00	4.87	0.36	5.65

Walker can thank Cubs rookie pitching phenom Kerry Wood for his being drafted in the sixth round in 1996; scouts who came to Grand Prairie High in Texas to see Wood took note of Walker, his teammate, as well. He suffered from some shoulder soreness in 1997, but didn't seem to be any worse for wear in 1998. He'll probably be converted to a reliever due to questions about his ability to handle a heavy workload.

Donne Wall   **Throws R**   **Age 31**

YEAR	TEAM	LGE	IP	H	ER	HR	BB	K	ERA	W	L	H/9	HR/9	BB/9	K/9	KWH	PERA
1996	Houston	NL	150.7	177	76	17	32	89	4.54	7	1	10.57	1.02	1.91	5.32	1.05	4.54
1997	Houston	NL	41.7	57	30	9	15	22	6.48	1	4	12.31	1.94	3.24	4.75	0.42	6.48
1997	New Orln	AmA	101.0	141	63	13	25	64	5.61	4	7	12.56	1.16	2.23	5.70	0.87	5.70
1998	San Dieg	NL	69.3	56	20	7	29	51	2.60	6	2	7.27	0.91	3.76	6.62	1.20	2.86

After being traded around like a wooden nickel following the 1997 season, Wall had an excellent season in the bullpen. He benefited from a stingy defense while posting the best strikeout rate of his career. He's still vulnerable to the long ball, as seen in the playoffs; hopefully the organization hasn't soured on him because of it.

Bryan Wolff   **Throws R**   **Age 27**

YEAR	TEAM	LGE	IP	H	ER	HR	BB	K	ERA	W	L	H/9	HR/9	BB/9	K/9	KWH	PERA
1996	Wilmngtn	Car	55.7	72	50	2	47	36	8.08	1	5	11.64	0.32	7.60	5.82	0.29	5.34
1997	R Cucmng	Cal	31.3	26	7	2	6	23	2.01	2	1	7.47	0.57	1.72	6.61	2.54	2.30
1997	Mobile	Sou	27.7	42	19	6	21	26	6.18	1	2	13.66	1.95	6.83	8.46	0.57	7.48
1998	Mobile	Sou	124.3	120	47	8	40	93	3.40	8	6	8.69	0.58	2.90	6.73	1.35	3.33

Wolff was Southern League Pitcher of the Week three times this year for the Baybears, and it's not hard to see why: he dominated the league. Unfortunately, he was still in Double-A ball at 27, so that's kind of like beating up little kids to take their Halloween candy. He'll get an extended look at Las Vegas, and there's still time for a career if he's really as good as he looked in Mobile.

SNWLP	SAN DIEGO PADRES											Park Effect: -23.9%
PITCHER	GS	IP	R	SNW	SNL	SNPCT	W	L	RA	APW	SNVA	SNWAR
Ashby, A.	33	226.7	90	13.8	10.5	.567	17	9	3.57	1.56	1.51	3.47
Boehringer, B.	1	4.0	5	0.0	0.7	.059	0	1	11.25	-0.33	-0.34	-0.28
Brown, K.	35	256.0	77	17.5	9.1	.657	18	7	2.71	4.32	3.88	6.18
Clement, M.	2	11.7	5	0.5	0.8	.357	1	0	3.86	0.04	-0.13	-0.09
Hamilton, J.	34	217.3	113	10.8	13.6	.443	13	13	4.68	-1.28	-1.43	0.44
Hitchcock, S.	27	166.3	78	9.2	9.3	.497	9	7	4.22	-0.10	-0.11	1.33
Langston, M.	16	78.3	53	3.4	6.9	.331	4	6	6.09	-1.74	-1.70	-0.97
Smith, P.	8	39.7	22	2.1	2.9	.415	3	2	4.99	-0.38	-0.46	-0.05
Spencer, S.	5	28.7	16	1.3	2.1	.392	1	0	5.02	-0.28	-0.33	-0.11
Wall, D.	1	5.0	1	0.3	0.1	.695	1	0	1.80	0.14	0.11	0.13
TOTALS	162	1033.7	460	59.0	56.1	.512	67	45	4.01	1.96	1.00	10.04

No surprise to find out that the Padres were 1998's most improved starting pitching staff, boosting their major league ranking from 27th in 1997 to 10th in 1998. How did they do it? First, all of the returning members of their rotation bounced back from disappointing years. Andy Ashby's SNVA improved by 2.4 games, Joey Hamilton's by 0.5 games, and Sterling Hitchcock's by 1.7 games. That's an expected improvement of over 4 1/2 games in the standings just from those three, but an even larger source of improvement came from adding Kevin Brown. In 1997, the Padres had one slot in their pitching rotation that was filled by 13 starts from Fernando Valenzuela, 9 starts from Danny Jackson, and 8 starts from Will Cunnane. I can't find a word or phrase that does justice to their performance, but let's just say they weren't good. They had a combined SNVA of -4.7. It's reasonable to think of Brown as taking over that slot in the rotation. Since Brown had an SNVA of 3.9, he represented an improvement of 8.6 games in the standings. Who says one player can't make a difference? The sum total of these changes was that the Padres' starters improved by almost 12 games according to SNVA, which accounts for more than half of the 22 games they actually gained in the standings. The Padres' improvement could have been even greater, but Ashby had one of the biggest second-half collapses you're likely to see. Before the All-Star break, he was among the elite starters in the game, with an SN record of 9.5-4.9 (.662). Afterwards, he was barely above replacement level, going 4.3-5.7 (.430). Hamilton picked up some of the slack by going 5.9-4.6 (.561) post-break after recording a 4.9-9.0 (.354) before.

Pitcher Abuse Points

PITCHER	AGE	GS	PAP	PAP/S	AAW	MAX	115+	130+
Ashby, Andy	30	33	136	4.12	5.49	120	4	0
Brown, Kevin	33	35	511	14.60	14.60	128	11	0
Hamilton, Joey	27	34	239	7.03	12.89	122	4	0
Hitchcock, Sterling	27	27	148	5.48	10.05	129	3	0
Langston, Mark	37	16	6	0.38	0.38	104	0	0
Smith, Pete	32	8	10	1.25	1.25	110	0	0
Spencer, Stan	28	5	4	0.80	1.33	104	0	0
TOTAL		162	1054	6.51	8.79	129	22	0
RANKING (NL)			10	10		13	10	14-T

Give Bruce Bochy—and pitching coach Dave Stewart—a lot of credit here: the Padres engineered a remarkable turn-around in their rotation in one season without overworking any one pitcher. Kevin Brown was given the workload of a typical staff ace. Andy Ashby had a bearable burden and bounced back nicely. Sterling Hitchcock was last October's Mariano Rivera, coming out of anonymity to beat three different Cy Young winners. Joey Hamilton didn't respond, but then Hamilton has been frustrating a lot of people for several years now. Matt Clement, the Padres' hot prospect who brings nasty stuff but less intimidating control, needs a manager to guard his pitch counts carefully, and it looks like he has one.

San Francisco Giants

Quick, name the most important San Francisco Giant. Barry Bonds hopefully comes quickly to mind, although Barry has many detractors in the local media, who seem to prefer Jeff Kent. You hear folks claim that Dusty Baker is the heart and soul of the team. General Manager Brian Sabean is always doing something; perhaps he's your choice. Hell, judging by how often he is trotted out for good publicity, Willie Mays might still be the most important San Francisco Giant.

Bonds, Kent, Baker, Sabean, Mays... in fact, none of them are the most important San Francisco Giant. The most important San Francisco Giant isn't a player. It isn't even a person. It's Pacific Bell Park, home of the Giants beginning in the year 2000. Don't believe me? Stop by the Giants "Virtual Dugout" and check out the "incredible Pacific Bell Park Seat View Generator [which] enables you to see our new ballpark—18 months before the first pitch will be thrown!" Instead of Spahn and Sain and pray for rain, it's Bonds and Baker and pray for 2000, when Pac Bell Park will make everything right in the Giants' world. While ownership says all the right things about fielding a contender, there is a stop-gap feeling to many of the moves the front office makes, a fact that is somewhat hidden by the team's "pennant drives" in the last two seasons.

The Giants have put a lot of money into Barry Bonds, and they are putting a lot of money into the new ballpark. They don't have a lot of money for anything else, so they muddle along with a crew of average journeymen, Grade B prospects, and mid-season trades for the pennant push. In '97, the blockbuster trade for Roberto Hernandez and Wilson Alvarez might have suggested a spending spree, but when 1998 arrived, only the inexpensive Danny Darwin was left on the club. Similarly, all of the major players picked up in mid-season last year (Jose Mesa, Joe Carter, Ellis Burks) were in the last season of their contracts, leaving the club with plenty of room to maneuver in the off-season. Indeed, with the departure of Mesa and Shawon Dunston, it appears the Giants traded Steve Reed and Jacob Cruz for 31 innings of Joe Table, the putrid remains of Dunston and Alvin Morman,

and a supplemental draft pick that is the only possible salvation for the deal.

You can compete in the majors with a mid-range budget, if you are smart about player acquisition (more about that later). But are the Giants being intelligent when they place so much of their future on the new ballpark? They clearly think so. They've sold virtually all of the personal seat licenses that will guarantee an acceptable bottom line for attendance, and surely in the first couple of years, the novelty of Pac Bell Park (and the long-awaited absence of Candlestick Park) will lead to many full houses. Nonetheless, once the novelty wears off, will Pac Bell Park be enough on its own to make the team a success? Or will Bay Area fans demand a winner before they will plunk down their money? The evidence suggests the team better concentrate on building that winner: the only team in the area with consistently excellent attendance is the 49ers, who have been in the NFL elite for almost two decades, and who are trying to move into a new stadium themselves.

Is the current brain trust capable of bringing about that success on the field? Can the combination of Brian Sabean in the front office and Dusty Baker in the dugout move the Giants to the top of the National League?

We spoke at length about Baker in last year's book, calling him the "King of Intangibles." His strengths remain the same as they've been for years: players seem to love to play for him, and he seems to have a knack for extracting the best performance out of his players. He defeats these positives to a certain extent by his apparent preference for mediocre veterans with "character" and his ongoing abuse of his pitching staff, but ultimately Dusty is idiosyncratic, not dumb. He isn't as dogmatic about this stuff as folks might think: two years ago, he reduced the playing time of Glenallen Hill, and last season he resisted the temptation to put the names Dunston and Carter in the lineup every day.

Which leaves us with Brian Sabean, who made such an eventful first impression on Giants' fans when he traded their beloved Matt Williams and then uttered the immortal statement, "I am not an idiot." Sabean has been fighting off

---

Giants Prospectus

1998 record: 89-74; Second place, NL West; Lost one-game wild-card playoff to Chicago, 5-2.

Pythagorean W/L: 92-70

Runs scored: 845 (2nd in NL)

Runs allowed: 739 (7th in NL)

Team EQA: .278 (2nd in NL)

Park: 3Com Park (moderate pitchers')

1998: Fairly anonymous offense got the Giants within three runs of the playoffs.

1999: Expect them to regress, but that was the case twelve months ago too.

the implications of that statement for the last two years, and while in last year's book we called the battle a draw, after going through another year of the Sabean Era, the idiot seems to have the upper hand.

What are Sabean's positive qualities as a General Manager? He is an active GM; it was no accident that when the White Sox decided to make their salary dump in '97, Sabean was there to make his move. He is less concerned with public opinion than you might think after hearing his defensive "idiot" statement. Trading Matt Williams was a good idea, no matter what fans thought, and to give credit where it is due, Jeff Kent has worked out well. Not only is Sabean willing to make things happen, he understands the simple fact that something does indeed need to happen. He is not overly impressed by the team's good record over the last two years, each time making mid-season trades because he knew the team as it was constituted wasn't good enough to go all the way. Of course, you could even say his record speaks for itself: one NL West title and one wild-card playoff game in two seasons.

Yes, his record does speak for itself, but ultimately, that record isn't very good. For all his activity, and for all the team's limited success in the standings, the tendencies Sabean has shown in his tenure with the Giants, while not entirely negative, are disappointing.

No GM is perfect. The most logical plans will sometimes fail. But there are ways to maximize the possibility that good will result from your actions. This is particularly important for those teams who operate with less money than the richest elite of MLB. If the Yankees decide to blow millions on Joe Girardi, they have a mediocre catcher on the roster, but they'll survive the hit to their pocketbook. If a team like the Giants misspends those millions, they won't have the extra cash to fix the problem.

So there are players (call them "proven veterans" if you like) who are known mediocrities. They have been mostly average to below-average major-leaguers. They have played long enough to establish within reasonable certainty their level of play. Often, they are old enough that they're past their

prime. A smart general manager begins with a simple position: that he will not sign any player who fits the above description (downsliding veteran with little upside potential). Almost everything is preferable to known mediocrity, even the uncertainty that comes from giving a job to a younger player.

Brian Sabean loves these kinds of "proven veterans," though. Joe Carter, J.T. Snow, Shawon Dunston, Brian Johnson, Jose Vizcaino, Rey Sanchez...when their names come up, Brian Sabean should say "no thanks" and move on, but he not only continues the conversation, he signs them. Even when he gets a good player like Steve Reed, his judgment seems off: Reed was traded away for guys Cleveland didn't want. Sometimes some of these guys work out. Snow had one good year out of two so far, and Carter did well for a few weeks in September, and Johnson once hit a memorable home run against the Dodgers. But those things don't last. You cannot waste roster spot after roster spot on Proven Mediocrity. Yet that is precisely what Brian Sabean does.

What is the outlook for the Giants in the near, pre-Pac Bell future? They still have Barry Bonds (for Pac Bell reasons, it appears; each time Bonds's name comes up in trade talks, ownership states that they need one superstar to help open the new stadium). They have the usual batch of veterans like Snow and Charlie Hayes. The pitching is unpredictable, a mishmash of third starters, middle relievers, young and mostly unknown quantities like Russ Ortiz and Shawn Estes, and Robb Nen. There isn't much in the farm system. The most highly-touted players (Calvin Murray and the recently departed Dante Powell) have more tools than skills, while others like Mike Caruso were traded away. Giuseppe Chiaramonte could be a sleeper behind the plate, while pitchers Jason Grilli and Robbie Crabtree might become the next Shawn Estes and Rod Beck. But what the team really needs is a general manager who understands the true value of the J.T. Snows of baseball, especially before they enter PacBell Park. And the Giants don't have that general manager. Instead, they have a man who protests too loudly when he blurts out, "I am not an idiot."

HITTERS (Averages: BA .260/ OBA .330/ SA .420, EQA .260)

Rich Aurilia   SS   Bats R Age 27

YEAR	TEAM	LGE	AB	H	DB	TP	HR	BB	R	RBI	SB	CS	OUT	BA	OBA	SA	EQA	EQR	DEFENSE
1996	San Fran	NL	317	74	7	1	3	27	25	22	3	1	244	.233	.294	.290	.204	23	80-SS 100
1997	San Fran	NL	102	28	5	0	6	9	13	16	1	1	75	.275	.333	.500	.279	15	24-SS 116
1998	San Fran	NL	411	113	29	2	10	34	49	51	3	3	302	.275	.330	.428	.260	52	102-SS 99
1999	SanFran	NL	310	80	15	1	8	26	32	35	4	2	232	.258	.315	.390	.252	37	

The type of player who is simultaneously underrated (by the Giants, who keep signing other more expensive shortstops to take his place) and overrated (by those of us who find those signings pointless). Aurilia is a mid-level shortshop who will be at his peak during the next few years. If the Giants are smart, the days of Shawon Dunston, Jose Vizcaino, and Rey Sanchez are over.

Marvin Benard   OF   Bats L   Age 28

Year	Team	Lge	AB	H	DB	TP	HR	BB	R	RBI	SB	CS	Out	BA	OBA	SA	EQA	EQR	Defense
1996	San Fran	NL	487	120	17	3	6	61	60	41	20	12	379	.246	.330	.331	.237	52	126-OF 106
1997	Phoenix	PCL	57	13	3	0	0	8	7	3	3	2	46	.228	.323	.281	.219	5	
1997	San Fran	NL	114	26	4	0	1	14	12	8	3	1	89	.228	.312	.289	.218	10	22-OF 79
1998	San Fran	NL	288	95	21	1	4	36	53	38	12	5	198	.330	.404	.451	.301	49	59-OF 95
1999	*SanFran*	*NL*	*265*	*74*	*14*	*1*	*3*	*31*	*38*	*27*	*11*	*5*	*196*	*.279*	*.355*	*.374*	*.267*	*36*	

Benard failed in full-time duty in '96, but performed extremely well as a part-timer last year. He has hit well as a pinch-hitter, and when used properly can be an effective spot starter and pinch-hitter. Dusty Baker often plays these guys more than he should, but he found the right balance with Benard.

Barry Bonds   LF   Bats L   Age 34

YEAR	TEAM	LGE	AB	H	DB	TP	HR	BB	R	RBI	SB	CS	OUT	BA	OBA	SA	EQA	EQR	DEFENSE
1996	San Fran	NL	519	159	26	2	43	152	137	116	34	8	368	.306	.463	.613	.360	143	141-OF 96
1997	San Fran	NL	537	159	26	3	43	147	133	116	32	8	386	.296	.447	.596	.350	140	142-OF 98
1998	San Fran	NL	553	174	44	7	41	135	138	123	31	14	393	.315	.449	.642	.355	147	149-OF 99
1999	*SanFran*	*NL*	*513*	*147*	*33*	*3*	*36*	*145*	*123*	*105*	*28*	*9*	*375*	*.287*	*.444*	*.573*	*.350*	*136*	

Among the people the local media promoted as the team's MVP last year: Jeff Kent, Robb Nen, Charlie Hayes, J.T Snow, and P.A. announcer Sherry Davis. Bonds had his usual terrific September (OPS 1.269); the media credited Joe Carter for the Giants' late-season pennant run. The greatest San Francisco Giant since his godfather, Willie Mays, another player who never managed to win the World Series as a Giant. If the same people were writing about the Giants back then, Mays probably wasn't called the MVP of those SF teams; that honor probably went to Jose Pagan. Or was it Hobie Landrith? They say Jim Duffalo was good in the clubhouse...

Ellis Burks   RF   Bats R   Age 34

YEAR	TEAM	LGE	AB	H	DB	TP	HR	BB	R	RBI	SB	CS	OUT	BA	OBA	SA	EQA	EQR	DEFENSE
1996	Colorado	NL	584	172	37	6	33	61	97	101	24	6	418	.295	.361	.548	.305	108	138-OF 102
1997	Colorado	NL	415	111	17	2	29	48	58	73	6	2	306	.267	.343	.528	.291	70	98-OF 105
1998	Colorado	NL	345	87	17	4	15	40	42	48	3	7	265	.252	.330	.455	.263	47	91-OF 98
1998	San Fran	NL	148	46	5	1	6	19	26	23	9	1	103	.311	.389	.480	.307	27	39-OF 106
1999	*SanFran*	*NL*	*459*	*122*	*22*	*2*	*24*	*55*	*62*	*71*	*11*	*5*	*342*	*.266*	*.344*	*.479*	*.287*	*76*	

Burks is a good player; it wasn't just the thin Colorado air that gave him those big numbers. Unfortunately he's not a great player, he's getting old, and his late-season injury leaves him a question mark yet again after a career already filled with injuries, mostly to his back. Worth a one-year deal, the Giants gave him two to play right.

Jay Canizaro   2B   Bats R   Age 25

YEAR	TEAM	LGE	AB	H	DB	TP	HR	BB	R	RBI	SB	CS	OUT	BA	OBA	SA	EQA	EQR	DEFENSE	
1996	Phoenix	PCL	354	80	14	1	7	42	39	30	11	3	277	.226	.308	.331	.229	35	50-2B 106	40-SS 97
1996	San Fran	NL	119	23	4	1	2	10	7	7	0	2	98	.193	.256	.294	.179	7	26-2B 103	
1997	Shrevprt	Tex	174	39	5	0	8	22	18	21	2	1	136	.224	.311	.391	.244	20	31-2B 84	
1997	Phoenix	PCL	79	12	2	0	2	8	4	3	2	2	69	.152	.230	.253	.155	3		
1998	Shrevprt	Tex	283	50	5	0	7	41	22	18	3	1	234	.177	.281	.269	.194	19	79-2B 99	
1998	Fresno	PCL	104	21	5	0	5	15	11	12	0	1	84	.202	.303	.394	.238	12	21-2B 102	
1999	*SanFran*	*NL*	*357*	*77*	*12*	*1*	*12*	*41*	*35*	*36*	*7*	*2*	*282*	*.216*	*.296*	*.356*	*.236*	*38*		

Once upon a time, he was going to be the next Robby Thompson. Now he only deserves mention because some people remember once upon a time. He's going backwards, and wouldn't get 384 at-bats in the majors next season even if they had another expansion draft and added eight teams.

Joe Carter   OF/1B   Bats R   Age 39

YEAR	TEAM	LGE	AB	H	DB	TP	HR	BB	R	RBI	SB	CS	OUT	BA	OBA	SA	EQA	EQR	DEFENSE	
1996	Toronto	AL	613	148	33	7	28	41	62	79	7	7	472	.241	.289	.455	.249	73	99-OF 88	29-1B 89
1997	Toronto	AL	606	142	30	4	22	42	58	66	8	2	466	.234	.284	.406	.236	63	46-OF 99	41-1B 92
1998	Baltimor	AL	280	69	16	1	11	20	29	34	3	1	212	.246	.297	.429	.247	32	43-OF 105	
1998	San Fran	NL	101	31	6	0	8	6	14	20	1	0	70	.307	.346	.604	.310	19		
1999	*SanFran*	*NL*	*459*	*103*	*25*	*2*	*18*	*33*	*42*	*50*	*5*	*2*	*358*	*.224*	*.276*	*.405*	*.239*	*50*		

The most overrated player of his day, Carter will be missed by everyone: the folks who believed in the inherent value of his RBI, and those who used him as a punching bag for his many flaws. His home run against Mitch Williams will be trotted out as evidence of the existence of "clutch" ability until we're all dead and gone. His useful and lovable contributions to the Giants' stretch run put the perfect cap to a career that was maddeningly less substantial than his admirers think. Retires with a lifetime OBA of .306.

Giuseppe Chiaramonte C   Bats R   Age 23

YEAR	TEAM	LGE	AB	H	DB	TP	HR	BB	R	RBI	SB	CS	OUT	BA	OBA	SA	EQA	EQR	DEFENSE
1997	San Jose	Cal	224	47	7	1	9	20	18	22	0	0	177	.210	.275	.371	.220	20	
1998	San Jose	Cal	503	121	16	1	17	37	44	53	3	1	383	.241	.293	.378	.231	49	105-C 96
1999	*SanFran*	*NL*	*356*	*85*	*14*	*1*	*11*	*23*	*29*	*37*	*1*	*0*	*271*	*.239*	*.285*	*.376*	*.234*	*36*	

An All-American out of Fresno State, Chiaramonte's numbers after translation aren't overwhelming in a year-and-a-half of A-ball, but he impressed observers with his defense and power potential, leading San Jose in several offensive categories. One of many catching prospects in the Arizona Fall League in '98, where he struggled early. Could make the big club within two years.

Wilson Delgado   SS   Bats B   Age 23

YEAR	TEAM	LGE	AB	H	DB	TP	HR	BB	R	RBI	SB	CS	OUT	BA	OBA	SA	EQA	EQR	DEFENSE
1996	San Jose	Cal	462	106	15	3	2	34	34	29	4	1	357	.229	.282	.288	.197	31	120-SS 97
1997	Phoenix	PCL	400	94	15	2	7	20	30	31	7	3	309	.235	.271	.335	.207	30	110-SS 103
1998	Fresno	PCL	499	120	15	1	10	49	48	45	8	4	383	.240	.308	.335	.226	47	127-SS 99
1999	*SanFran*	*NL*	*486*	*121*	*18*	*1*	*8*	*35*	*45*	*43*	*10*	*4*	*369*	*.249*	*.299*	*.340*	*.231*	*47*	

He isn't going to hit. Shortstops who can't hit are kinda like catchers who can't hit: their defensive reputation grows as their offensive production plummets. Last year we said he was still young enough to improve, and he did improve, but now there are rumors that he's really 27, not 23, at which point he's a stiff, not a prospect.

Alex Diaz   OF   Bats B   Age 30

YEAR	TEAM	LGE	AB	H	DB	TP	HR	BB	R	RBI	SB	CS	OUT	BA	OBA	SA	EQA	EQR	DEFENSE	
1996	Tacoma	PCL	174	34	3	0	0	6	6	6	4	4	144	.195	.222	.213	.116	3	38-OF 95	
1996	Seattle	AL	78	18	1	0	1	2	6	4	7	4	64	.231	.250	.282	.184	5	20-OF 109	
1997	Oklahoma	AA	421	103	17	1	8	28	44	35	20	6	324	.245	.292	.347	.227	40	77-OF 89	15-2B 89
1998	San Fran	NL	62	8	3	0	0	0	1	1	1	1	55	.129	.129	.177	—	-2		
1999	*SanFran*	*NL*	*243*	*55*	*4*	*0*	*5*	*12*	*18*	*17*	*11*	*5*	*193*	*.226*	*.263*	*.305*	*.204*	*18*		

You don't care about Alex Diaz, but he belongs here as Exhibit 42B in the People vs. Idiot Sabean. In 1997, at the age of 28, Alex Diaz spent most of the year at Triple-A and posted his fourth-consecutive sub-.300 OBA in his major-league stints. His career major-league OPS at that point was .621 over 302 games. Brian Sabean signed him to play baseball.

Shawon Dunston   SS   Bats R   Age 36

YEAR	TEAM	LGE	AB	H	DB	TP	HR	BB	R	RBI	SB	CS	OUT	BA	OBA	SA	EQA	EQR	DEFENSE
1996	San Fran	NL	286	84	13	2	5	15	33	33	7	0	202	.294	.329	.406	.259	34	68-SS 105
1997	ChiCubs	NL	414	114	17	4	9	11	46	41	24	7	307	.275	.294	.401	.243	45	88-SS 92
1997	Pittsbrg	NL	70	26	4	1	5	1	11	16	2	1	45	.371	.380	.671	.336	15	
1998	Clevelnd	AL	153	34	10	3	3	7	15	13	8	2	121	.222	.256	.386	.223	14	
1998	San Fran	NL	50	8	3	0	3	0	3	3	0	2	44	.160	.160	.400	.160	2	
1999	*SanFran*	*NL*	*271*	*68*	*12*	*2*	*7*	*8*	*24*	*26*	*9*	*3*	*206*	*.251*	*.272*	*.387*	*.234*	*27*	

He almost made sense in 1996; in 1998 he was a joke. He hit a double and a home run in his first start after re-joining the club, but Dusty Baker showed remarkable restraint and never gave Dunston a shot at a regular job. Young son Shawon Jr. looked cute in the clubhouse, and would have been just as useful as his father in taking up a roster spot.

Mike Glendenning   OF   Bats R   Age 22

YEAR	TEAM	LGE	AB	H	DB	TP	HR	BB	R	RBI	SB	CS	OUT	BA	OBA	SA	EQA	EQR	DEFENSE
1996	Bellnghm	Nwn	274	64	11	1	9	29	26	30	2	4	215	.234	.307	.380	.235	29	60-OF 81
1997	Bakrsfld	Cal	500	115	13	0	25	51	47	62	1	2	387	.230	.301	.406	.242	56	130-OF 91
1998	San Jose	Cal	178	40	3	0	8	19	16	20	1	1	139	.225	.299	.376	.233	18	47-OF 94
1998	Shrevprt	Tex	253	53	6	1	6	30	21	21	0	0	200	.209	.293	.312	.212	21	66-OF 85
1999	*SanFran*	*NL*	*422*	*97*	*12*	*0*	*17*	*44*	*39*	*48*	*1*	*2*	*327*	*.230*	*.303*	*.379*	*.242*	*47*	

He's hit lots of homers in parks that make it easy, but hasn't done much otherwise, and he didn't hit very well in his first try at Double A. Was moved from third to the outfield a few seasons ago, but it hasn't helped his defense. Will remind some of Rob Deer, but he's not going to be that good.

Charlie Hayes   3B/1B   Bats R   Age 34

YEAR	TEAM	LGE	AB	H	DB	TP	HR	BB	R	RBI	SB	CS	OUT	BA	OBA	SA	EQA	EQR	DEFENSE	
1996	Pittsbrg	NL	456	110	20	2	10	39	44	44	5	0	346	.241	.301	.360	.231	45	116-3B 110	
1996	NY Yanks	AL	66	18	2	0	2	1	5	7	0	0	48	.273	.284	.394	.229	6		
1997	NY Yanks	AL	350	92	13	0	13	41	41	46	3	2	260	.263	.340	.411	.262	45	89-3B 96	
1998	San Fran	NL	327	96	8	0	13	36	41	49	2	1	232	.294	.364	.437	.279	48	37-1B 109	35-3B 98
1999	*SanFran*	*NL*	*343*	*88*	*10*	*0*	*12*	*36*	*36*	*42*	*2*	*1*	*256*	*.257*	*.327*	*.391*	*.257*	*43*		

Still a useful platoon player (.338/.407/.492 vs. lefties last year), especially on a team with J.T. Snow. Hayes is the kind of player who Dusty Baker would have played too frequently in the past. If Hayes plays too much against righties in '99, it will be a bad sign.

Stan Javier   OF   Bats B   Age 35

YEAR	TEAM	LGE	AB	H	DB	TP	HR	BB	R	RBI	SB	CS	OUT	BA	OBA	SA	EQA	EQR	DEFENSE
1996	San Fran	NL	273	72	15	0	5	27	38	26	13	2	203	.264	.330	.374	.254	33	65-OF 112
1997	San Fran	NL	441	127	15	4	9	59	72	52	22	3	317	.288	.372	.401	.280	66	116-OF 101
1998	San Fran	NL	417	125	13	5	5	66	75	48	23	6	298	.300	.395	.391	.287	66	105-OF 100
1999	*SanFran*	*NL*	*376*	*103*	*11*	*2*	*6*	*55*	*59*	*39*	*20*	*4*	*277*	*.274*	*.367*	*.362*	*.275*	*55*	

I don't know about clubhouse influence, but this is the kind of player I want filling my roster: good glove, makes the most of his abilities, gets on base, intelligent basestealer (84% career success rate). He ain't Joe Carter, for better and for worse, but he has been cost-effective for the Giants.

Brian Johnson   C   Bats R   Age 31

YEAR	TEAM	LGE	AB	H	DB	TP	HR	BB	R	RBI	SB	CS	OUT	BA	OBA	SA	EQA	EQR	DEFENSE
1996	San Dieg	NL	243	66	13	1	8	6	21	29	0	0	177	.272	.289	.432	.243	26	
1997	Detroit	AL	137	32	5	1	2	6	10	10	1	0	105	.234	.266	.328	.202	10	
1997	San Fran	NL	179	50	8	2	11	15	22	31	0	1	130	.279	.335	.531	.286	28	
1998	San Fran	NL	307	75	9	1	14	30	30	40	0	2	234	.244	.312	.417	.248	36	85-C 101
1999	*SanFran*	*NL*	*301*	*76*	*12*	*1*	*12*	*22*	*28*	*38*	*0*	*1*	*226*	*.252*	*.303*	*.419*	*.252*	*36*	

Regressed to his former crappy level as a hitter, and in the end, Giants' fans didn't care. He hit The Home Run against the Dodgers in '97, and for that he'll always be popular in San Francisco. Not the worst catcher in the league, but needs to lose some of his playing time to Mayne.

Chris Jones   PH/OF   Bats R   Age 33

YEAR	TEAM	LGE	AB	H	DB	TP	HR	BB	R	RBI	SB	CS	OUT	BA	OBA	SA	EQA	EQR	DEFENSE
1996	NY Mets	NL	150	37	6	0	5	13	14	17	1	0	113	.247	.307	.387	.241	16	51-OF 78
1997	San Dieg	NL	153	38	8	0	8	17	21	21	6	2	117	.248	.324	.458	.269	22	45-OF 88
1998	Arizona	NL	31	6	1	0	0	3	2	1	0	0	25	.194	.265	.226	.160	1	
1998	Fresno	PCL	59	13	0	2	2	5	6	6	2	1	47	.220	.281	.390	.231	6	
1998	San Fran	NL	90	17	3	1	2	9	7	6	2	1	74	.189	.263	.311	.198	6	
1999	SanFran	NL	161	35	5	1	5	17	15	16	3	1	127	.217	.292	.354	.233	17	

Acquired for a flame-throwing relief prospect who couldn't find the plate. Jones, unlike many of Sabean's Proven Veterans, seemed to have some usefulness when they got him; he'd had a few years of success as a pinch-hitter. Alas, he was only 3-for-25 in that role last season.

Jeff Kent   2B   Bats R   Age 31

YEAR	TEAM	LGE	AB	H	DB	TP	HR	BB	R	RBI	SB	CS	OUT	BA	OBA	SA	EQA	EQR	DEFENSE
1996	NY Mets	NL	338	101	19	1	10	23	40	47	3	3	240	.299	.343	.450	.271	46	86-3B 100
1996	Clevelnd	AL	100	25	3	0	4	9	10	12	2	1	76	.250	.312	.400	.246	11	13-1B 100
1997	San Fran	NL	580	146	33	2	31	51	70	83	10	3	437	.252	.312	.476	.267	80	142-2B 98
1998	San Fran	NL	524	160	36	3	34	52	83	101	10	5	369	.305	.368	.580	.312	100	131-2B 101
1999	SanFran	NL	520	143	27	1	28	48	66	82	10	4	381	.275	.336	.492	.287	84	

I sat next to Kent's parents at a game a few years ago when he was a Met having a great start. Fans brought signs to the park reading "Jeff Kent Is God." I asked his parents what it was like having a son that people referred to as God. Mr. Kent just beamed proudly, but Mrs. Kent replied, "Well, when he comes home, he's just Jeff." Just Jeff was plenty good enough last year; Brian Sabean gets to gloat about this one. Even so, Just Jeff wasn't the team MVP.

Chris Magruder   OF   Bats B   Age 22

YEAR	TEAM	LGE	AB	H	DB	TP	HR	BB	R	RBI	SB	CS	OUT	BA	OBA	SA	EQA	EQR	DEFENSE
1998	Salem OR	Nwn	176	42	4	2	2	23	19	15	4	4	138	.239	.327	.318	.228	17	42-OF 99
1998	Bakrsfld	Cal	92	24	4	0	1	10	11	8	2	0	68	.261	.333	.337	.243	10	20-OF 108
1999	SanFran	NL	210	59	9	1	2	24	27	22	6	3	154	.281	.355	.362	.263	27	

Chosen out of Washington in the June draft, Magruder could be the leadoff man of the future for the Giants. They haven't had a good one since Brett Butler left. Switch-hitter with speed and a good batting eye, compared to Chad Curtis, but not Butler.

Ramon Martinez   2B   Bats R   Age 26

YEAR	TEAM	LGE	AB	H	DB	TP	HR	BB	R	RBI	SB	CS	OUT	BA	OBA	SA	EQA	EQR	DEFENSE
1996	Wichita	Tex	91	27	1	1	1	6	11	9	3	1	65	.297	.340	.363	.250	10	24-2B 109
1996	Omaha	AA	318	75	11	2	5	23	26	26	3	2	245	.236	.287	.330	.213	26	84-2B 90
1997	Shrevprt	Tex	396	103	19	2	4	32	39	36	3	3	296	.260	.315	.348	.231	38	104-SS 113
1998	Fresno	PCL	354	92	12	1	10	32	34	41	0	2	264	.260	.321	.384	.244	39	
1998	San Fran	NL	19	6	2	0	0	4	4	2	0	0	13	.316	.435	.421	.309	3	
1999	SanFran	NL	379	98	14	1	10	33	38	43	4	2	283	.259	.318	.380	.250	44	

Went 3-for-3 in his major-league debut, 3-for-16 after that. Has never hit in the minors, but people like his glove and his attitude, so he might find a home at the bottom of a major-league roster.

Brent Mayne   C   Bats L   Age 31

YEAR	TEAM	LGE	AB	H	DB	TP	HR	BB	R	RBI	SB	CS	OUT	BA	OBA	SA	EQA	EQR	DEFENSE
1996	NY Mets	NL	100	27	4	0	2	13	11	12	0	1	74	.270	.354	.370	.254	12	
1997	Oakland	AL	251	71	9	0	7	19	27	31	1	0	180	.283	.333	.402	.256	30	
1998	San Fran	NL	274	76	11	0	5	39	37	32	2	1	199	.277	.367	.372	.265	36	73-C 94
1999	SanFran	NL	234	60	4	0	6	27	23	26	1	1	175	.256	.333	.350	.249	27	

Not every team gets to have Mike Piazza. The idea is to get a couple of decent guys to platoon at catcher, rather than a handful of non-hitters with good defensive reputations. Brent Mayne has held up his end of such platoons for a few years now.

Arturo McDowell   **OF**   **Bats L**   **Age 19**

YEAR	TEAM	LGE	AB	H	DB	TP	HR	BB	R	RBI	SB	CS	OUT	BA	OBA	SA	EQA	EQR	DEFENSE
1998	Salem OR	Nwn	173	27	1	1	0	20	7	5	5	1	147	.156	.244	.173	.131	5	42-OF 100
1999	*SanFran*	*NL*	*137*	*26*	*2*	*1*	*0*	*14*	*10*	*5*	*5*	*1*	*112*	*.190*	*.265*	*.219*	*.178*	*7*	

High-schooler was a first-round pick in the June draft, thanks to amazing speed and a reputation as a ballhawk on defense. *Baseball America* called him "late-blooming," hard to imagine for a teenager. McDowell is likely to prove the adage that you can't steal first base. Could be another in the line of Calvin Murray and Dante Powell.

Damon Minor   **1B**   **Bats L**   **Age 25**

YEAR	TEAM	LGE	AB	H	DB	TP	HR	BB	R	RBI	SB	CS	OUT	BA	OBA	SA	EQA	EQR	DEFENSE
1996	Bellnghm	Nwn	281	50	4	0	6	30	14	15	0	1	232	.178	.257	.256	.170	14	74-1B 81
1997	Bakrsfld	Cal	529	128	13	1	20	66	56	64	1	1	402	.242	.326	.384	.248	62	129-1B 81
1998	San Jose	Cal	178	38	4	0	4	20	14	14	0	0	140	.213	.293	.303	.208	14	44-1B 91
1998	Shrevprt	Tex	288	56	5	0	9	23	17	20	1	0	232	.194	.254	.306	.188	18	71-1B 85
1999	*SanFran*	*NL*	*408*	*89*	*8*	*0*	*13*	*41*	*32*	*39*	*1*	*0*	*319*	*.218*	*.290*	*.333*	*.224*	*38*	

Minor had terrific raw numbers for Bakersfield in '97, including 31 homers and a .923 OPS. But the DTs didn't buy it, and with good reason judging by the 1998 numbers. Even if Minor was hitting well, he's old for Double-A. Non-prospect.

Doug Mirabelli   **C**   **Bats R**   **Age 28**

YEAR	TEAM	LGE	AB	H	DB	TP	HR	BB	R	RBI	SB	CS	OUT	BA	OBA	SA	EQA	EQR	DEFENSE
1996	Shrevprt	Tex	384	95	8	0	14	58	44	48	0	1	290	.247	.346	.378	.256	48	
1996	Phoenix	PCL	46	11	5	0	0	3	5	3	0	0	35	.239	.286	.348	.217	4	
1997	Phoenix	PCL	320	59	11	0	5	45	24	20	1	1	262	.184	.285	.266	.193	21	
1998	Fresno	PCL	261	54	7	1	8	43	28	26	1	0	207	.207	.319	.333	.234	27	96-C 104
1999	*SanFran*	*NL*	*314*	*73*	*12*	*0*	*12*	*47*	*36*	*39*	*1*	*1*	*242*	*.232*	*.332*	*.385*	*.259*	*41*	

Mirabelli has shown occasional signs that he would make a good, inexpensive part-time option at catcher. As the projection above shows, the Giants could do worse than give him the opportunity.

Bill Mueller   **3B**   **Bats B**   **Age 28**

YEAR	TEAM	LGE	AB	H	DB	TP	HR	BB	R	RBI	SB	CS	OUT	BA	OBA	SA	EQA	EQR	DEFENSE
1996	Phoenix	PCL	428	103	10	3	3	36	33	32	2	3	328	.241	.300	.299	.207	32	82-3B 102
1996	San Fran	NL	200	65	13	2	0	25	32	25	0	0	135	.325	.400	.410	.289	30	40-3B 103
1997	San Fran	NL	391	115	27	3	7	50	58	52	3	3	279	.294	.374	.432	.281	58	112-3B 96
1998	San Fran	NL	536	162	19	0	13	83	80	75	3	4	378	.302	.396	.410	.286	83	128-3B 100
1999	*SanFran*	*NL*	*495*	*145*	*23*	*1*	*10*	*65*	*67*	*65*	*3*	*2*	*352*	*.293*	*.375*	*.404*	*.283*	*75*	

Still my favorite Giant. A subject of trade rumors, which seems odd, since third basemen like Mueller, who make the plays on defense and get on base regularly but don't have much power, would seem to be underrated rather than overrated, and thus poor candidates for trade bait. Will be a fan favorite wherever he ends up.

Calvin Murray   **OF**   **Bats R**   **Age 27**

YEAR	TEAM	LGE	AB	H	DB	TP	HR	BB	R	RBI	SB	CS	OUT	BA	OBA	SA	EQA	EQR	DEFENSE
1996	Shrevprt	Tex	170	37	4	0	5	20	16	15	4	3	136	.218	.300	.329	.221	16	39-OF 94
1996	Phoenix	PCL	305	62	12	3	3	38	30	20	10	4	247	.203	.292	.292	.209	25	77-OF 109
1997	Shrevprt	Tex	416	88	11	1	7	50	49	27	30	6	334	.212	.296	.293	.220	38	104-OF 94
1998	Shrevprt	Tex	336	79	12	1	5	43	42	26	18	10	267	.235	.322	.321	.232	34	88-OF 105
1998	Fresno	PCL	89	15	2	0	2	10	5	5	2	1	75	.169	.253	.258	.174	5	
1999	*SanFran*	*NL*	*439*	*101*	*18*	*2*	*8*	*51*	*56*	*36*	*27*	*8*	*346*	*.230*	*.310*	*.335*	*.242*	*50*	

Calvin Murray has been touted as the next big thing ever since he was the team's first-round draft choice in 1992. He's got tools, you know. Here's an even more useful bit of knowledge: he's not a good baseball player. About as deserving of the above-projected 490 AB as Marge Schott's dog.

Dante Powell   CF   Bats R   Age 25

YEAR	TEAM	LGE	AB	H	DB	TP	HR	BB	R	RBI	SB	CS	OUT	BA	OBA	SA	EQA	EQR	DEFENSE
1996	Shrevprt	Tex	508	129	17	1	18	64	74	56	34	16	395	.254	.337	.398	.259	68	127-OF 102
1997	Phoenix	PCL	437	83	15	1	9	45	41	26	27	9	363	.190	.266	.291	.200	33	105-OF 107
1997	San Fran	NL	39	12	1	0	1	4	5	5	1	1	28	.308	.372	.410	.271	5	13-OF 95
1998	Fresno	PCL	440	84	12	2	10	64	54	29	32	8	364	.191	.294	.295	.220	41	131-OF 100
1999	*Arizona*	*NL*	*429*	*97*	*14*	*1*	*12*	*51*	*56*	*38*	*33*	*11*	*343*	*.226*	*.308*	*.347*	*.240*	*48*	

Unlike former teammate Calvin Murray, Powell would probably be better than Marge Schott's dog. A former #1 draft choice with the ever-popular "tools." If tools were all that mattered, my gardener would be in the Hall of Fame. Traded to Arizona for Alan Embree, which looks like a steal for the Giants.

Armando Rios   OF   Bats L   Age 27

YEAR	TEAM	LGE	AB	H	DB	TP	HR	BB	R	RBI	SB	CS	OUT	BA	OBA	SA	EQA	EQR	DEFENSE
1996	Shrevprt	Tex	329	79	11	1	9	36	35	33	7	6	256	.240	.315	.362	.236	34	83-OF 89
1997	Shrevprt	Tex	456	103	15	2	9	47	43	38	10	5	358	.226	.298	.327	.220	41	112-OF 87
1998	Fresno	PCL	434	107	12	1	16	45	50	49	13	4	331	.247	.317	.389	.249	51	111-OF 87
1999	*SanFran*	*NL*	*420*	*106*	*16*	*1*	*16*	*44*	*50*	*52*	*12*	*4*	*318*	*.252*	*.323*	*.410*	*.263*	*56*	

A lesson in sample size. In his first-ever at-bat against the Dodgers, Rios hit a pinch-hit homer. In his second-ever at-bat against the Dodgers, Rios hit a pinch-hit homer. In his third-ever at-bat against the Dodgers, he got a single. His career numbers against LA: 1.000/1.000/3.000. Naturally, there's talk of his taking over in center for the Giants.

Rey Sanchez   SS/2B   Bats R   Age 31

YEAR	TEAM	LGE	AB	H	DB	TP	HR	BB	R	RBI	SB	CS	OUT	BA	OBA	SA	EQA	EQR	DEFENSE	
1996	ChiCubs	NL	287	59	5	0	2	24	18	13	6	1	229	.206	.267	.244	.175	15	84-SS 110	
1997	ChiCubs	NL	203	48	6	0	2	12	15	13	3	2	157	.236	.279	.296	.196	13	36-SS 88	25-2B 99
1997	NY Yanks	AL	137	44	7	0	3	5	13	18	0	5	98	.321	.345	.438	.257	16	29-2B 111	
1998	San Fran	NL	317	93	16	2	2	18	33	33	0	0	224	.293	.331	.375	.246	34	56-SS 103	21-2B 114
1999	*KansasCy*	*AL*	*296*	*79*	*13*	*1*	*3*	*18*	*27*	*28*	*2*	*2*	*219*	*.267*	*.309*	*.348*	*.223*	*26*		

Sanchez was hitting .382 in late May, resulting in more playing time. His glove and ability to play two positions make him useful if his manager understands that 317 AB is about 217 too many. Seeing the light, the Giants declined to exercise a $1.4 million option on Sanchez.

J.T. Snow   1B   Bats B/L   Age 31

YEAR	TEAM	LGE	AB	H	DB	TP	HR	BB	R	RBI	SB	CS	OUT	BA	OBA	SA	EQA	EQR	DEFENSE
1996	Calfrnia	AL	564	140	17	1	17	53	51	62	0	7	431	.248	.313	.372	.234	57	152-1B 103
1997	San Fran	NL	533	150	30	1	31	99	91	97	5	4	387	.281	.394	.516	.309	102	151-1B 96
1998	San Fran	NL	434	110	22	0	19	60	55	61	1	2	326	.253	.344	.435	.269	61	116-1B 106
1999	*SanFran*	*NL*	*460*	*121*	*18*	*1*	*24*	*69*	*62*	*73*	*3*	*3*	*342*	*.263*	*.359*	*.463*	*.289*	*77*	

You can read: look at the above line and ask yourself how good this player is. What's missing are the Gold Gloves, the death of his mother, his grit, his famous father. He didn't get his average over .200 until June, and put a stop to his resurgence by going 4-for-43 in a long August slump. The Giants looked at this evidence and decided J.T. is worth $3 million in 1999. You can read: you decide if they are right. Snow's thinking of giving up switch-hitting.

Tony Torcato   3B   Bats L   Age 19

YEAR	TEAM	LGE	AB	H	DB	TP	HR	BB	R	RBI	SB	CS	OUT	BA	OBA	SA	EQA	EQR	DEFENSE
1998	Salem OR	Nwn	217	48	8	1	2	8	12	12	1	1	170	.221	.249	.295	.177	11	52-3B 100
1999	*SanFran*	*NL*	*170*	*46*	*10*	*1*	*2*	*3*	*14*	*16*	*1*	*1*	*125*	*.271*	*.283*	*.376*	*.230*	*16*	

Torcato was the Giants' first pick in the June draft. He is often referred to as a "pure hitter," which in his case apparently means he hit a lot of homers in high school. But he only hit three homers in 220 AB for the Salem-Keizer Volcanoes, and he has shoulder problems which may result in a move to first base. At this point he looks to be an odd choice for a top draft pick.

Yorvit Torrealba   C   Bats R   Age 20

YEAR	TEAM	LGE	AB	H	DB	TP	HR	BB	R	RBI	SB	CS	OUT	BA	OBA	SA	EQA	EQR	DEFENSE
1997	Bakrsfld	Cal	441	101	11	0	4	25	25	27	2	1	341	.229	.270	.281	.185	25	
1998	San Jose	Cal	69	16	1	0	0	1	3	3	1	1	54	.232	.243	.246	.148	2	
1998	Shrevprt	Tex	195	36	5	0	0	15	7	7	0	3	162	.185	.243	.210	.128	5	58-C 101
1999	SanFran	NL	333	83	9	1	2	18	24	24	3	3	253	.249	.288	.300	.208	25	

Came up quickly through the ranks last season, but he sure didn't do it with his bat. He gets lots of attention for his glove, which may just be Nichols's Law at work: If a catcher isn't hitting, he'll get a rep as a great defensive player. Regardless, his hitting makes Kirt Manwaring look like Yogi Berra, which means Yorvit's glove must be a lot better than Manwaring's.

PITCHERS (Averages: 4.00 ERA, 9.00 H/9, 1.00 HR/9, 3.00 BB/9, 6.00 K/9, 1.00 KWH)

Cory Bailey   Throws R   Age 28

YEAR	TEAM	LGE	IP	H	ER	HR	BB	K	ERA	W	L	H/9	HR/9	BB/9	K/9	KWH	PERA
1996	Louisvil	AmA	33.3	35	24	1	23	22	6.48	1	3	9.45	0.27	6.21	5.94	0.45	4.05
1996	St Louis	NL	57.3	64	21	1	28	34	3.30	4	2	10.05	0.16	4.40	5.34	0.48	3.92
1997	Oklahoma	AmA	50.0	58	22	1	25	30	3.96	3	3	10.44	0.18	4.50	5.40	0.47	4.14
1997	Phoenix	PCL	16.3	18	4	0	5	10	2.20	2	0	9.92	0.00	2.76	5.51	0.83	3.31
1998	Fresno	PCL	92.0	87	30	3	19	56	2.93	7	3	8.51	0.29	1.86	5.48	1.42	2.84

Cory Bailey has a lot of minor-league saves. Cory Bailey has pitched in parts of six different major-league seasons. Cory Bailey has no major-league saves. This should tell you all you need to know about pitchers who get a lot of minor-league saves.

Chris Brock   Throws R   Age 29

YEAR	TEAM	LGE	IP	H	ER	HR	BB	K	ERA	W	L	H/9	HR/9	BB/9	K/9	KWH	PERA
1996	Richmond	Int	140.7	168	104	20	67	87	6.65	4	12	10.75	1.28	4.29	5.57	0.50	5.18
1997	Richmond	Int	112.3	124	56	9	50	62	4.49	5	7	9.93	0.72	4.01	4.97	0.46	4.33
1997	Atlanta	NL	30.3	39	22	2	17	14	6.53	1	2	11.57	0.59	5.04	4.15	0.22	5.04
1998	Fresno	PCL	111.7	123	45	10	36	83	3.63	7	5	9.91	0.81	2.90	6.69	1.17	4.19
1998	San Fran	NL	28.0	33	12	3	6	17	3.86	2	1	10.61	0.96	1.93	5.46	1.09	4.50

Brock has gotten some attention as a young starter out of the Atlanta system. He seems to have recovered from earlier injury problems, and his control was as good last season as it has ever been. Brock isn't young, so his future would appear to be in long relief.

Troy Brohawn   Throws L   Age 26

YEAR	TEAM	LGE	IP	H	ER	HR	BB	K	ERA	W	L	H/9	HR/9	BB/9	K/9	KWH	PERA
1996	Shrevprt	Tex	143.7	201	110	32	53	70	6.89	4	12	12.59	2.00	3.32	4.39	0.34	6.58
1997	Shrevprt	Tex	152.0	188	68	11	69	75	4.03	8	9	11.13	0.65	4.09	4.44	0.33	4.86
1998	Fresno	PCL	118.7	157	69	16	37	67	5.23	5	8	11.91	1.21	2.81	5.08	0.58	5.54

A difficult pitcher to judge, Brohawn led the Texas League in ERA in '97, finally earning his shot at Triple-A. His control, always decent, got even better, and he posted a 10-8 record, but he didn't pitch that well. Since he doesn't have a great fastball, he needs to impress. A longshot.

Nate Bump   Throws R   Age 22

YEAR	TEAM	LGE	IP	H	ER	HR	BB	K	ERA	W	L	H/9	HR/9	BB/9	K/9	KWH	PERA
1998	San Jose	Cal	57.7	51	17	3	25	39	2.65	4	2	7.96	0.47	3.90	6.09	0.89	3.12

Look out for this guy. Pitched great in college, was drafted by the Giants in the first round, and pitched great for San Jose. He doesn't have much experience, but what he has looks very good. Virtually every time his name comes up, people talk about how quickly they expect to see him shoot up through the system. Given the Giants' rotation problems, Bump might get promoted to the big club even sooner than folks think.

Robby Crabtree   Throws R   Age 26

YEAR	TEAM	LGE	IP	H	ER	HR	BB	K	ERA	W	L	H/9	HR/9	BB/9	K/9	KWH	PERA
1996	Bellnghm	Nwn	42.3	72	33	9	19	34	7.02	1	4	15.31	1.91	4.04	7.23	0.63	7.87
1997	Bakrsfld	Cal	101.7	165	91	11	67	69	8.06	2	9	14.61	0.97	5.93	6.11	0.32	6.82
1998	San Jose	Cal	48.7	59	10	1	9	37	1.85	4	1	10.91	0.18	1.66	6.84	1.93	4.07
1998	Shrevprt	Tex	49.7	41	14	4	18	39	2.54	4	2	7.43	0.72	3.26	7.07	1.55	2.72

Before 1998, who had even heard of Crabtree? He was terrific with San Jose, then terrific in Shreveport, then terrific in the Arizona Fall League. He's entertaining in a cagey veteran sort of way. The Giants keep their bullpen well-stocked; look for Crabtree to get at least a cup of coffee in '99.

Danny Darwin   Throws R   Age 43

YEAR	TEAM	LGE	IP	H	ER	HR	BB	K	ERA	W	L	H/9	HR/9	BB/9	K/9	KWH	PERA
1996	Pittsbrg	NL	124.0	120	41	8	15	62	2.98	9	5	8.71	0.58	1.09	4.50	1.60	3.05
1996	Houston	NL	42.7	45	29	8	10	24	6.12	1	4	9.49	1.69	2.11	5.06	0.96	4.43
1997	ChiSox	AL	116.7	125	48	20	26	60	3.70	7	6	9.64	1.54	2.01	4.63	0.83	4.40
1997	San Fran	NL	44.3	54	24	5	12	27	4.87	2	3	10.96	1.02	2.44	5.48	0.84	4.87
1998	San Fran	NL	149.3	187	91	23	45	74	5.48	6	11	11.27	1.39	2.71	4.46	0.49	5.30

His career had to end somewhere with somebody, and as old as he was, it was no surprise he pitched poorly in '98. He continued to have no adequate wiggling pitch to mix lefties up, and his good stuff had gotten stale. When you last this long, it happens. Sayonara, Mr. Darwin. It was a treat to watch you when you were on.

Shawn Estes   Throws L   Age 26

YEAR	TEAM	LGE	IP	H	ER	HR	BB	K	ERA	W	L	H/9	HR/9	BB/9	K/9	KWH	PERA
1996	Phoenix	PCL	106.3	104	43	8	37	82	3.64	7	5	8.80	0.68	3.13	6.94	1.31	3.55
1996	San Fran	NL	72.3	65	26	3	38	54	3.24	5	3	8.09	0.37	4.73	6.72	0.89	3.24
1997	San Fran	NL	203.0	172	72	13	91	162	3.19	14	9	7.63	0.58	4.03	7.18	1.26	2.97
1998	San Fran	NL	151.3	162	83	15	73	125	4.94	7	10	9.63	0.89	4.34	7.43	0.99	4.34

Now he's had his first serious arm problems. Will he come back? He was mostly awful in a September return (four bad outings and one beautiful 1-0 loss to the Dodgers), but he struck out 21 men in 23 innings. More important, though, he still has trouble with his control; he could use a few lessons from Mark Gardner.

Aaron Fultz   Throws L   Age 25

YEAR	TEAM	LGE	IP	H	ER	HR	BB	K	ERA	W	L	H/9	HR/9	BB/9	K/9	KWH	PERA
1996	San Jose	Cal	92.0	133	59	8	50	67	5.77	3	7	13.01	0.78	4.89	6.55	0.51	5.87
1997	Shrevprt	Tex	64.3	79	32	6	19	48	4.48	3	4	11.05	0.84	2.66	6.72	1.15	4.76
1998	Shrevprt	Tex	56.3	73	45	4	31	44	7.19	1	5	11.66	0.64	4.95	7.03	0.64	5.11
1998	Fresno	PCL	15.7	23	9	2	2	10	5.17	1	1	13.21	1.15	1.15	5.74	1.63	5.74

Former starter, converted to the bullpen a couple of years ago. Fultz has decent control, but hasn't shown enough of anything else to suggest he'll ever be more than a mop-up man in the majors.

Mark Gardner   Throws R   Age 37

YEAR	TEAM	LGE	IP	H	ER	HR	BB	K	ERA	W	L	H/9	HR/9	BB/9	K/9	KWH	PERA
1996	San Fran	NL	185.0	204	90	28	54	131	4.38	10	11	9.92	1.36	2.63	6.37	1.17	4.52
1997	San Fran	NL	181.7	196	84	29	51	121	4.16	10	10	9.71	1.44	2.53	5.99	1.10	4.46
1998	San Fran	NL	212.7	215	99	30	59	138	4.19	11	13	9.10	1.27	2.50	5.84	1.13	3.98

You could exaggerate and call Gardner underrated, but he's a decent third or fourth starter with excellent control despite his heavy reliance on breaking stuff. Keep an eye on the K/9 numbers; they've dropped slightly but consistently for a few years now, and his margin of error isn't that great to begin with.

Jason Grilli   Throws R   Age 22

YEAR	TEAM	LGE	IP	H	ER	HR	BB	K	ERA	W	L	H/9	HR/9	BB/9	K/9	KWH	PERA
1998	Shrevprt	Tex	115.3	134	62	11	36	78	4.84	5	8	10.46	0.86	2.81	6.09	0.95	4.45
1998	Fresno	PCL	42.3	50	25	7	17	31	5.31	2	3	10.63	1.49	3.61	6.59	0.85	5.10

Grilli was the first starting pitcher taken in the 1997 draft. He pitched okay at Double-A and didn't embarrass himself in the PCL. Some feel he is already good enough to pitch for the Giants, but that says more about San Francisco's problems than it does about Grilli's performance thus far. Still on track for a solid career.

Jason Grote   Throws R   Age 24

YEAR	TEAM	LGE	IP	H	ER	HR	BB	K	ERA	W	L	H/9	HR/9	BB/9	K/9	KWH	PERA
1996	Burlingt	Mid	127.0	215	103	24	59	71	7.30	3	11	15.24	1.70	4.18	5.03	0.30	7.65
1997	Bakrsfld	Cal	150.3	183	76	12	59	78	4.55	7	10	10.96	0.72	3.53	4.67	0.42	4.73
1998	San Jose	Cal	78.7	119	41	3	25	53	4.69	4	5	13.61	0.34	2.86	6.06	0.71	5.49
1998	Shrevprt	Tex	47.7	99	46	5	15	21	8.69	1	4	18.69	0.94	2.83	3.97	0.22	8.12

Grote's raw numbers were eye-popping in San Jose: 7-2 2.45, a strikeout per inning with a 4:1 K/BB ratio. Then he went to Double-A and it all fell apart. He'll get more chances, but he needs to show that Shreveport was a fluke, but chances are it was the California League that was an anomaly.

Orel Hershiser   Throws R   Age 40

YEAR	TEAM	LGE	IP	H	ER	HR	BB	K	ERA	W	L	H/9	HR/9	BB/9	K/9	KWH	PERA
1996	Clevelnd	AL	212.3	222	85	17	47	124	3.60	13	11	9.41	0.72	1.99	5.26	1.11	3.69
1997	Clevelnd	AL	199.0	196	88	25	59	103	3.98	11	11	8.86	1.13	2.67	4.66	0.69	3.80
1998	San Fran	NL	203.3	214	98	23	78	115	4.34	11	12	9.47	1.02	3.45	5.09	0.59	4.16

Beginning in early May, he won six straight starts with an ERA of 1.29. Outside of that run, he was 5-10 with a 5.23 ERA on the season. May-December romances are nice, but as a pitcher, Orel is a lot closer to winter than he is to springtime.

John Johnstone   Throws R   Age 30

YEAR	TEAM	LGE	IP	H	ER	HR	BB	K	ERA	W	L	H/9	HR/9	BB/9	K/9	KWH	PERA
1996	Tucson	PCL	54.0	64	26	2	24	55	4.33	3	3	10.67	0.33	4.00	9.17	1.48	4.33
1996	Houston	NL	13.0	18	7	2	5	4	4.85	0	1	12.46	1.38	3.46	2.77	0.13	6.23
1997	Phoenix	PCL	35.7	38	17	3	15	23	4.29	2	2	9.59	0.76	3.79	5.80	0.70	4.04
1997	San Fran	NL	18.7	16	6	1	6	13	2.89	1	1	7.71	0.48	2.89	6.27	1.32	2.89
1998	San Fran	NL	88.3	78	30	11	35	78	3.06	6	4	7.95	1.12	3.57	7.95	1.67	3.36

The kind of pitcher who makes a bullpen better without costing his team a fortune. It took forever for Johnstone to get a full season in the majors; now that he's done it, he'll be around for at least five more years, giving his teams 80 innings of solid relief.

Scott Linebrink   Throws R   Age 22

YEAR	TEAM	LGE	IP	H	ER	HR	BB	K	ERA	W	L	H/9	HR/9	BB/9	K/9	KWH	PERA
1997	San Jose	Cal	27.3	34	11	3	9	27	3.62	2	1	11.20	0.99	2.96	8.89	1.79	4.94
1998	Shrevprt	Tex	106.3	120	66	12	57	100	5.59	4	8	10.16	1.02	4.82	8.46	1.10	4.74

Jason Grilli got most of the attention after the '97 draft. Linebrink was drafted in the second round of the same year, and is maturing faster than his more-noted colleague. His upside might not be as high as Grilli's; on the other hand, he did strike out 128 in 113 innings for Shreveport.

Mike McMullen   Throws R   Age 25

YEAR	TEAM	LGE	IP	H	ER	HR	BB	K	ERA	W	L	H/9	HR/9	BB/9	K/9	KWH	PERA
1996	Burlingt	Mid	50.3	75	33	5	31	22	5.90	2	4	13.41	0.89	5.54	3.93	0.16	6.26
1997	San Jose	Cal	85.3	104	40	1	34	45	4.22	4	5	10.97	0.11	3.59	4.75	0.43	4.22
1998	Shrevprt	Tex	62.3	60	27	1	44	55	3.90	4	3	8.66	0.14	6.35	7.94	0.86	3.61

The Giants sent him to the Arizona Fall League, which must mean something. His control fluctuates, and before last season he wasn't a big strikeout pitcher. Has shown consistent improvement, in any event, and the Giants need bodies who can pitch.

Jose Mesa   Throws R   Age 33

YEAR	TEAM	LGE	IP	H	ER	HR	BB	K	ERA	W	L	H/9	HR/9	BB/9	K/9	KWH	PERA
1996	Clevelnd	AL	74.7	65	24	5	23	64	2.89	5	3	7.83	0.60	2.77	7.71	2.05	2.89
1997	Clevelnd	AL	84.0	81	23	7	24	67	2.46	7	2	8.68	0.75	2.57	7.18	1.73	3.43
1998	Clevelnd	AL	57.0	58	28	6	19	35	4.42	3	3	9.16	0.95	3.00	5.53	0.83	3.95
1998	San Fran	NL	31.0	33	13	1	17	26	3.77	2	1	9.58	0.29	4.94	7.55	0.90	4.06

He's no Steve Reed, but then few pitchers are. Although a handful of terrible outings made it seem bad, Mesa allowed only one home run and had only one blown save with the Giants. Still a good pitcher to have in the bullpen, as long as you aren't paying him closer wages, which Seattle will do for a few years. Has a great chance to go Ayala on the Mariners; tonight's forecast is hail storms in the power alleys.

Alvin Morman   Throws L   Age 30

YEAR	TEAM	LGE	IP	H	ER	HR	BB	K	ERA	W	L	H/9	HR/9	BB/9	K/9	KWH	PERA
1996	Houston	NL	42.3	46	22	9	23	28	4.68	2	3	9.78	1.91	4.89	5.95	0.56	5.10
1997	Clevelnd	AL	18.7	19	11	2	13	13	5.30	1	1	9.16	0.96	6.27	6.27	0.51	4.34
1998	Clevelnd	AL	23.3	24	10	1	11	16	3.86	2	1	9.26	0.39	4.24	6.17	0.73	3.86
1998	San Fran	NL	7.0	9	4	4	3	6	5.14	0	1	11.57	5.14	3.86	7.71	1.00	9.00

Hey, wait a minute, this guy stinks. But then, everyone but Sabean knew that. Morman has had some success in the past against lefties, which is why he'll be in the majors until his arm falls off. Morman and Mesa do not equal Steve Reed.

Robb Nen   Throws R   Age 29

YEAR	TEAM	LGE	IP	H	ER	HR	BB	K	ERA	W	L	H/9	HR/9	BB/9	K/9	KWH	PERA
1996	Florida	NL	83.3	70	18	2	20	82	1.94	7	2	7.56	0.22	2.16	8.86	3.60	2.38
1997	Florida	NL	75.3	76	30	7	36	72	3.58	4	4	9.08	0.84	4.30	8.60	1.42	3.94
1998	San Fran	NL	89.0	63	20	4	22	100	2.02	8	2	6.37	0.40	2.22	10.11	5.41	1.72

It'll never happen, but Robb Nen would make great trade bait. He is a magnificent, awesome pitcher, a genuine premier closer. But the actual value of a closer is nowhere near his market value, and the better the closer, the better deal you ought to be able to pull off, and the Giants' needs are many.

Eddie Oropesa   Throws L   Age 27

YEAR	TEAM	LGE	IP	H	ER	HR	BB	K	ERA	W	L	H/9	HR/9	BB/9	K/9	KWH	PERA
1996	San Bern	Cal	142.3	175	84	8	82	78	5.31	6	10	11.07	0.51	5.19	4.93	0.32	4.87
1997	Shrevprt	Tex	108.0	160	72	8	72	47	6.00	4	8	13.33	0.67	6.00	3.92	0.14	6.08
1998	Shrevprt	Tex	126.3	186	88	6	76	72	6.27	4	10	13.25	0.43	5.41	5.13	0.28	5.77

Oropesa might remind you of Luis Tiant, if Luis Tiant wasn't any good. Should be ready for the majors about the year 2001, at which time he will get a half-page story in *Baseball America*. You read it here first.

Russ Ortiz   Throws R   Age 25

YEAR	TEAM	LGE	IP	H	ER	HR	BB	K	ERA	W	L	H/9	HR/9	BB/9	K/9	KWH	PERA
1996	San Jose	Cal	34.3	23	3	0	19	41	0.79	4	0	6.03	0.00	4.98	10.75	2.88	1.83
1996	Shrevprt	Tex	25.3	27	15	0	22	25	5.33	1	2	9.59	0.00	7.82	8.88	0.79	4.26
1997	Shrevprt	Tex	52.0	63	30	3	38	40	5.19	2	4	10.90	0.52	6.58	6.92	0.50	5.02
1997	Phoenix	PCL	82.3	97	47	10	30	58	5.14	3	6	10.60	1.09	3.28	6.34	0.87	4.81
1998	Fresno	PCL	50.7	37	9	3	21	47	1.60	5	1	6.57	0.53	3.73	8.35	2.13	2.31
1998	San Fran	NL	89.3	97	48	12	43	69	4.84	4	6	9.77	1.21	4.33	6.95	0.86	4.63

Have the Giants actually developed a pitcher in their farm system? Ortiz started as a reliever, so he hasn't had to carry a heavy workload yet. His control is improving gradually, he's a year younger than Shawn Estes, and his arm is a lot healthier. He's not there yet, but by Giants' standards, he's already a stud.

Joe Roa — Throws R — Age 27

YEAR	TEAM	LGE	IP	H	ER	HR	BB	K	ERA	W	L	H/9	HR/9	BB/9	K/9	KWH	PERA
1996	Buffalo	AmA	159.7	195	75	19	40	70	4.23	9	9	10.99	1.07	2.25	3.95	0.47	4.85
1997	Phoenix	PCL	33.7	47	20	4	10	12	5.35	1	3	12.56	1.07	2.67	3.21	0.23	5.61
1997	San Fran	NL	66.3	89	36	9	18	30	4.88	3	4	12.08	1.22	2.44	4.07	0.42	5.56
1998	Fresno	PCL	155.3	216	99	23	34	72	5.74	6	11	12.52	1.33	1.97	4.17	0.53	5.79

Roa has excellent control, but nothing else about his game stands out. He's had chances with two major-league teams already. If he was a lefty, he'd get chances with at least two more. He's a righty, and probably the envy of Kennie Steenstra and Brady Raggio for getting even two chances.

Rich Rodriguez — Throws L — Age 36

YEAR	TEAM	LGE	IP	H	ER	HR	BB	K	ERA	W	L	H/9	HR/9	BB/9	K/9	KWH	PERA
1996	Omaha	AmA	68.3	92	45	11	25	54	5.93	3	5	12.12	1.45	3.29	7.11	0.95	5.93
1997	San Fran	NL	65.3	68	22	7	19	29	3.03	4	3	9.37	0.96	2.62	3.99	0.49	3.99
1998	San Fran	NL	66.0	73	26	7	19	40	3.55	4	3	9.95	0.95	2.59	5.45	0.87	4.23

He's been decent in the lefty reliever role since his comeback from rotator cuff surgery a few years ago. The next time he has two bad months in a row, he's gone. Anyone else looking forward to the next matchup between Rodriguez and Matt Mieske?

Kirk Rueter — Throws L — Age 28

YEAR	TEAM	LGE	IP	H	ER	HR	BB	K	ERA	W	L	H/9	HR/9	BB/9	K/9	KWH	PERA
1996	Montreal	NL	81.0	96	40	12	21	27	4.44	4	5	10.67	1.33	2.33	3.00	0.27	4.89
1996	Phoenix	PCL	23.7	31	14	3	13	12	5.32	1	2	11.79	1.14	4.94	4.56	0.27	5.70
1996	San Fran	NL	23.7	18	5	0	5	14	1.90	2	1	6.85	0.00	1.90	5.32	1.63	1.90
1997	San Fran	NL	191.3	202	75	17	46	103	3.53	12	9	9.50	0.80	2.16	4.84	0.86	3.81
1998	San Fran	NL	188.3	204	93	28	52	93	4.44	9	12	9.75	1.34	2.48	4.44	0.61	4.40

He's been lucky in the W-L department for two straight years; it's unlikely to continue. His numbers were a little worse across the board last season, despite the 16-9 record. He had the highest run support per 9 innings in the NL by more than a run over the next guy. Top candidate for a disappointing 1999.

Steve Soderstrom — Throws R — Age 27

YEAR	TEAM	LGE	IP	H	ER	HR	BB	K	ERA	W	L	H/9	HR/9	BB/9	K/9	KWH	PERA
1996	Phoenix	PCL	162.7	204	96	15	58	67	5.31	7	11	11.29	0.83	3.21	3.71	0.28	4.92
1996	San Fran	NL	14.3	16	10	1	6	8	6.28	1	1	10.05	0.63	3.77	5.02	0.50	4.40
1997	Phoenix	PCL	99.0	152	75	11	50	60	6.82	3	8	13.82	1.00	4.55	5.45	0.36	6.36
1998	Fresno	PCL	133.0	148	68	18	42	71	4.60	6	9	10.02	1.22	2.84	4.80	0.61	4.53

You would like to see Soderstrom have some success, as he's coming back from several injuries. He pitched better for Fresno than he has in many years, but the fastball is a memory, he didn't really pitch that well in Fresno, and his career will likely be no more than a footnote.

Julian Tavarez — Throws R — Age 26

YEAR	TEAM	LGE	IP	H	ER	HR	BB	K	ERA	W	L	H/9	HR/9	BB/9	K/9	KWH	PERA
1996	Buffalo	AmA	13.7	12	2	0	3	9	1.32	2	0	7.90	0.00	1.98	5.93	1.69	2.63
1996	Clevelnd	AL	83.0	95	37	7	18	46	4.01	4	5	10.30	0.76	1.95	4.99	0.93	4.23
1997	San Fran	NL	89.0	95	39	7	31	34	3.94	5	5	9.61	0.71	3.13	3.44	0.29	3.94
1998	San Fran	NL	85.7	103	39	5	33	48	4.10	5	5	10.82	0.53	3.47	5.04	0.51	4.52

What's to like? Tavarez throws in the 90s and gets into "hot streaks," two items which make him a fan favorite. But at the end of the season, his numbers are no different than the Jose Bautistas of the world that Tavarez is supposed to be an improvement upon. It's hard to think that there are overrated middle relievers, but Tavarez is the poster boy for the concept.

Jeff Urban   Throws L   Age 22

YEAR	TEAM	LGE	IP	H	ER	HR	BB	K	ERA	W	L	H/9	HR/9	BB/9	K/9	KWH	PERA
1998	Salem OR	Nwn	19.3	30	17	1	9	13	7.91	0	2	13.97	0.47	4.19	6.05	0.47	6.05
1998	San Jose	Cal	21.0	35	16	3	6	15	6.86	1	1	15.00	1.29	2.57	6.43	0.80	6.86

He's a big ol' guy, a second-round draft pick who draws differing opinions from various observers. Everyone agrees that if his size translates into an extra foot on his fastball, he could be an excellent pitcher. That foot hasn't arrived yet.

Ryan Vogelsong   Throws R   Age 21

YEAR	TEAM	LGE	IP	H	ER	HR	BB	K	ERA	W	L	H/9	HR/9	BB/9	K/9	KWH	PERA
1998	Salem OR	Nwn	52.3	53	18	6	16	41	3.10	4	2	9.11	1.03	2.75	7.05	1.49	3.96
1998	San Jose	Cal	17.3	30	18	4	4	17	9.35	0	2	15.58	2.08	2.08	8.83	1.81	7.79

Unhittable for Salem-Keizer, but for San Jose, while he had excellent peripheral numbers (26 K and 4 BB in 19 IP), he got banged around pretty hard. A pitcher who can throw but not pitch, but he has time to learn.

SNWLP				SAN FRANCISCO GIANTS							Park Effect: -9.3%	
PITCHER	GS	IP	R	SNW	SNL	SNPCT	W	L	RA	APW	SNVA	SNWAR
Darwin, D.	25	138.0	89	6.6	10.9	.378	8	10	5.80	-1.99	-1.97	-0.82
Estes, S.	25	149.3	89	8.0	10.0	.444	7	12	5.36	-1.42	-0.93	0.35
Gardner, M.	33	212.0	106	12.9	11.5	.529	13	6	4.50	0.02	0.49	2.54
Hershiser, O.	34	202.0	105	11.2	11.8	.486	11	10	4.68	-0.38	-0.29	1.41
Ortiz, R.	13	75.7	50	3.0	5.4	.360	4	4	5.95	-1.21	-1.06	-0.55
Rueter, K.	33	187.7	100	10.8	11.4	.487	16	9	4.80	-0.60	-0.45	1.37
TOTALS	163	964.7	539	52.5	61.0	.463	59	51	5.03	-5.59	-4.21	4.29

This was not a great year for Giants starters, but considering that their rotation consisted of old veterans (Darwin, Hershiser, Gardner) coupled with two decent peak-age players (Estes, Rueter), it could have been worse. Their rotation ranked just 22nd in the league, and it dropped by about 2 1/2 games' worth of SNVA from the year before. But the durability of the starters and Dusty Baker's patience with them allowed the Giants to avoid the dreaded spot starts from minor leaguers or middle relievers that hurt other teams. Only six pitchers made starts all year, the lowest number in the league. The Giants were not able to avoid using replacement pitchers in their rotation entirely: Russ Ortiz was called up to take Sean Estes's spot in the rotation when Estes was hurt, and he did not pitch well. Estes's situation demonstrates the double whammy effect of some injuries—Estes pitched hurt with reduced effectiveness, and Ortiz represented another step down. If you'd replace the 1998 numbers of Estes and Ortiz with the 1997 version of Estes, the Giants rotation would have ranked 13th in the majors instead of 22nd. Orel Hershiser has done an admirable job of returning from his 1990 rotator cuff injury and putting together a fine tail end to his career. He has never rediscovered the Cy Young level he had in the 80's, but he has been valuable as a league average (or better) workhorse in every year since 1992. He is declining—his SNPcts for the last four years are .590, .538, .503, .486—but it's a very slow decline, so that you could imagine him being a contributor for another two or three years. Mark Gardner, on the other hand, is doing anything but declining. He's getting better as he ages. He's improved his SNPct every year since 1995—.380, .392, .481, .522—and 1998 was probably his best season ever. He even improved within the season: he was a crummy 5.9-7.5 (.442) before the break, but came back for a stellar 7.0-4.1 (.632) afterwards.

Pitcher Abuse Points

PITCHER	AGE	GS	PAP	PAP/S	AAW	MAX	115+	130+
Darwin, Danny	42	25	38	1.52	1.52	116	1	0
Estes, Shawn	25	25	317	12.68	27.47	130	7	1
Gardner, Mark	36	33	355	10.76	10.76	135	6	1
Hershiser, Orel	39	34	90	2.65	2.65	123	1	0
Ortiz, Russ	24	13	94	7.23	16.87	120	2	0
Rueter, Kirk	27	33	62	1.88	3.44	110	0	0
TOTAL		163	956	5.87	9.22	135	17	2
RANKING (NL)			14	14	11		14	7-T

The stability of the rotation is a tribute to Dusty Baker's heavy reliance on his bullpen. Better to make Julian Tavarez or Rich Rodriguez suffer than Russ Ortiz or Kirk Rueter. I would say "or Shawn Estes," but Baker's one mistake was in letting Estes work harder per start than anyone else. Another case of the young starter with major league experience fooling his manager into thinking he can take on the workload of a veteran. The Giants can only hope Estes comes back with his best stuff, and Giant fans can only hope Baker has learned to think twice when deciding whether to leave him in or pinch-hit for him in the seventh.

Baltimore Orioles

I blame Sidney Ponson. I could instead blame the devastating injuries to Jimmy Key and Scott Kamieniecki, which limited them to a combined 134 innings. I could blame the extreme ineffectiveness of Doug Drabek—it's tough to toss more than 108 innings when you're always leaving the game by the fourth inning. But it was Ponson, due to his ability, his performance (not all that great, but the Orioles were desperate), and above all, his extreme youthfulness (a mere 21 years old), that cost the 1998 Orioles their chance at a title: the Oldest Team of All Time.

I calculated the age of a team's offense by looking at each individual and multiplying their age by their plate appearances. For pitchers, I multiplied by innings pitched. Sum up all the players, divide by total team PA or innings, as appropriate, and voilà—you get the average age of the team, weighted by playing time. Combine the hitting age and pitching age equally, and you have the age of the entire team. (See Table 1).

The Oriole offense did its part, averaging 33.35 years of age, the highest ever. Three teams had contended for the title, with ages between 32.36 and 32.45: two California Angels teams (1982 and 1985) and the 1945 Detroit Tigers. (See Table 2). The Orioles blew that away by having a regular lineup that featured no players under 30. And on the bench, Jeffrey Hammonds, a sprightly 27, was the only under-30 player to get as many as 140 plate appearances, before he was sent packing to Cincinnati.

One thing that distinguished the Orioles from the rest of these teams was their lack of success. The Tigers won the World Series, the '82 Angels won their division, the '85 Angels lost to the Royals by one game. Going further down the list, the '83 Phillies were winners, the '88 Tigers fell short by a game, the '84 Angels finished three games out, the '97 O's were division winners, the '08 White Sox were third, a game and a half out of first. Only the '45 White Sox, who lagged the Tigers by 15 games, were a bad team, and the teams from 1944 and 1945 were the result of World War II.

The pitching staff dragged the O's down, averaging a paltry 30.16 years of age. That leaves the overall Oriole total of 31.75 years in third place, behind the amazing 1983 Angels (31.43 batting, 32.79 pitching, 32.11 total) and 1982 Angels (32.36 batting, 31.80 pitching, 32.08 overall). Those Angel teams had aged arms as well—their top three winning pitchers in 1982—Geoff Zahn, Ken Forsch and Steve Renko—were all over 35, and they added a 40-year-old Tommy John the following year.

Like I said, it was Ponson's fault. Hold him to 50 innings, give the remainder of his time to Key, Drabek, or even Doug Johns, and they take those Angel teams. So in a year of many disappointments at the Yards, the O's were unable to achieve even this modest bit of infamy.

Of course, this wasn't the close race Peter Angelos had in mind when he ratcheted up the payroll prior to the 1998 season. He wrote the checks to add a number of players who could not reasonably have been expecte to contribute to a championship team, most notably Drabek and analyst bête noir Joe Carter. While these players were instrumental in the chase of the 1983 Angels for a bit of history, they did little to help the team catch the 1998 Yankees or Red Sox. They merely added to the core of expensive, overrated, past-prime "talent" that Angelos and outgoing GM Pat Gillick had assembled. This Oriole team had failed, and with a number of 30-somethings reaching free agency, a complete rebuilding seemed in order.

The rebuilding of the Orioles will be the first test for their new general manager, Frank Wren. Wren is a product of the Expos organization; he was a run-of-the-mill outfielder in their minor league system before a brain tumor brought his career to a halt. He intended to go into coaching, and the Expos had a job for him, but then they decided to cut one team from their minor league system: goodbye, job. They made it up to him by offering him the GM job at Jamestown in the New York-Penn League. From that humble beginning, he eventually reached the Expos's front office, primarily on the scouting side (executive assistant for scouting in 1986-87, assistant director of scouting in 1988-90, assistant director of scouting and director of Latin American operations in 1991). This was while the

Table 1. Players with 150+ Plate Appearances

	1998 BALTIMORE	1945 TIGERS	1985 ANGELS	1982 ANGELS
1B	Palmeiro, 33	York, 31	Carew, 39	Carew, 36
2B	Alomar, 31	Mayo, 35	Grich, 36	Grich, 33
3B	Ripken, 37	Maier, 29	DeCinces, 34	DeCinces, 31
SS	Bordick, 32	Webb, 35	Schofield, 22	Foli, 31
LF	Surhoff, 33	Outlaw, 32	Downing, 34	Downing, 31
CF	Anderson, 34	Cramer, 39	Pettis, 27	Lynn, 30
RF	Davis, 36	Cullenbine, 31	Jackson, 39	Re. Jackson, 36
C	Webster, 33	Swift, 30	Boone, 37	Boone, 34
	Hoiles, 33	Richards, 36	Jones, 30	Baylor, 33
	Baines, 39	Greenberg, 34	Beniquez, 35	Beniquez, 32
	Carter, 38	Hoover, 30	Wilfong, 31	Ro. Jackson, 29
	Hammonds, 27		Brown, 25	
Weighted Average	33.35	32.45	32.40	32.36

Expos had both Dave Dombrowski and Dan Duquette in their front office. Wren was a Dombrowski man, and followed him to Florida to spend six years as an assistant GM.

Now he's a GM in an organization where independence is not part of the title. It is quite clear that Peter Angelos has the final word on all things Oriole. I don't necessarily think that's a bad thing—after all, you can be certain that I'd have the last word on something in which I had invested $170 million. Of more concern is where the decisions actually get made (as opposed to where they end). The previous GM, Pat Gillick, seemed mortally offended that Angelos not only didn't accept as gospel whatever pearls of baseball wisdom Gillick deigned to offer, but had the audacity to question and even reject some of Gillick's ideas. The record on that decision is mixed: Angelos was right to reject Gillick at least once, vetoing the trade of Bobby Bonilla prior to the Orioles' 1996 wild-card run). There was at least one decision that seems all Gillick that Angelos should have rejected (signing Joe Carter), and several more Gillick deals that worked out well, in particular, signing Roberto Alomar.

Furthermore, remember that Angelos was not a close follower of baseball prior to buying the team, and so there is legitimate concern about who he gets his information from. It obviously was not only Gillick. Much of the talk in Baltimore concerns his son, John Angelos, an enthusiastic rotisserie player, who certainly has his father's ear. It is not at all clear just how knowledgeable John is about baseball, although the local media ridicules him for being a fantasy player, and papa Pete for involving him in team decisions in any way. However, when you consider that Angelos is pushing 70 and has expressed the desire to leave the team to his son to run, involving him in decisions seems an obvious necessity.

Another suspect is Director of Player Development Syd Thrift. Thrift has been around baseball for years, and was formerly a GM himself. He was also somewhat unorthodox and had fallen out of favor with mainstream baseball ownership, making him a natural pal of a maverick owner like Angelos. He definitely has more sway over the ownership than does the typical director of player development; in many ways, he ran the Oriole minor league system almost as his personal fiefdom, a separate entity from the parent organization. He was here before Gillick, brought in by Angelos, and apparently didn't have to answer to Gillick. This is a definite chain-of-command problem for which the blame must ultimately lie with Angelos. And Thrift's performance as DPP hasn't been anything special. The Oriole system has still not produced a regular position player in the 1990s; Calvin Pickering is the only one who has shown any sign of development prior to 1998, though several players made significant progress in the last year. It does appear that Thrift's status was a subject of Wren's job interview, though, and as of November, Thrift seems unlikely to keep his job.

The early returns on the Wren Era have been disappointing. After Eric Davis and Roberto Alomar left Baltimore, it looked like the O's might follow through with a complete house-cleaning, giving players like Pickering, Jerry Hairston, and Willie Greene chances to contribute. But in a flurry of action, the team signed Albert Belle and Delino DeShields,

Table 2. Top 10 Oldest Teams

	BATTING		PITCHING		OVERALL	
1.	1998 Orioles	33.35	1935 Braves	33.00	1983 Angels	32.11
2.	1945 Tigers	32.45	1945 Cubs	32.85	1982 Angels	32.08
3.	1985 Angels	32.40	1988 Astros	32.82	1998 Orioles	31.75
4.	1982 Angels	32.36	1983 Angels	32.79	1988 Tigers	31.52
5.	1983 Phillies	32.07	1947 Pirates	32.76	1982 Phillies	31.44
6.	1988 Tigers	32.02	1945 Reds	32.72	1988 Yankees	31.42
7.	1945 White Sox	31.80	1989 Astros	32.52	1960 White Sox	31.42
8.	1984 Angels	31.77	1947 Phillies	32.50	1983 Phillies	31.36
9.	1997 Orioles	31.73	1944 Pirates	32.49	1945 Cubs	31.36
10.	1908 White Sox	31.73	1931 Dodgers	32.37	1984 Angels	31.30

each 30 or over, then gave B.J. Surhoff a four-year contract to be a below-average corner outfielder, and Will Clark a two-year deal to be alternately declining and injured. These signings ratcheted the team's average age back up, and probably doomed the Orioles to a few more years of disappointment.

You can't build an entire lineup around past-prime players, and the Orioles will start eight of these on Opening Day. It's going to be a long year by Chesapeake Bay. Juan Beniquez, if you're out there, you better watch your dentures: there's another challenge coming to the late, great, early 80s Angels.

HITTERS (Averages: BA .260/ OBA .330/ SA .420, EQA .260)

Chip Alley   C   Bats B   Age 22

YEAR	TEAM	LGE	AB	H	DB	TP	HR	BB	R	RBI	SB	CS	OUT	BA	OBA	SA	EQA	EQR	DEFENSE
1996	Bluefld	App	70	9	1	0	0	10	1	1	0	1	62	.129	.237	.143	.084	1	
1997	Delmarva	SAL	256	55	11	1	3	30	24	18	3	1	202	.215	.297	.301	.212	21	
1998	Frederck	Car	349	87	13	1	10	56	44	42	0	1	263	.249	.353	.378	.259	45	92-C 95
1999	Baltimor	AL	330	81	13	1	9	46	40	39	1	1	250	.245	.338	.373	.253	40	

"Alley CAT," as he humorously appeared in one on-line boxscore source, pounced into prospectdom with a breakout offensive season. The secret to his success is an excellent eye: he was fifth in the Carolina League in both walks and OBP. His defense needs work, since he led the league in passed balls, and the Frederick team led the league in wild pitches.

Roberto Alomar   2B   Bats B   Age 31

YEAR	TEAM	LGE	AB	H	DB	TP	HR	BB	R	RBI	SB	CS	OUT	BA	OBA	SA	EQA	EQR	DEFENSE
1996	Baltimor	AL	574	188	44	4	21	85	110	99	18	7	393	.328	.414	.528	.321	115	135-2B 107
1997	Baltimor	AL	405	135	21	2	15	41	65	68	9	3	273	.333	.395	.506	.309	72	102-2B 103
1998	Baltimor	AL	582	166	30	2	16	62	82	74	17	5	421	.285	.354	.426	.274	83	142-2B 102
1999	Clevelnd	AL	512	153	31	2	15	61	85	75	16	4	363	.299	.373	.455	.290	82	

See below.

Brady Anderson   CF   Bats L   Age 35

YEAR	TEAM	LGE	AB	H	DB	TP	HR	BB	R	RBI	SB	CS	OUT	BA	OBA	SA	EQA	EQR	DEFENSE
1996	Baltimor	AL	567	169	37	5	49	72	103	122	22	10	408	.298	.377	.640	.326	124	135-OF 108
1997	Baltimor	AL	580	167	38	7	19	85	96	86	18	13	425	.288	.379	.476	.292	98	114-OF 105
1998	Baltimor	AL	475	114	27	3	19	77	75	60	20	7	368	.240	.346	.429	.272	71	123-OF 103
1999	Baltimor	AL	488	119	27	2	22	80	76	70	14	8	377	.244	.350	.443	.276	76	

After the 1997 season, Cal Ripken went to the front office and asked that the core of the team be kept together for 1998, a plea that meant keeping both of these players. Anderson could have left as a free agent; Alomar was highly sought by other teams in trade. This stands as a testament to the idiocy of making personnel decisions based on clubhouse influence, especially after the Oriole clubhouse fractured into cliques along racial and linguistic lines, factions of which these two were leaders.

The end of Alomar's Oriole tenure was cemented in August when he engaged in a clubhouse row with Ray Miller, sparked by allegations of lackadaisical play against Robby. Anderson, meanwhile, was held out by management as a shining example for his attempts to play through the pain of a shoulder injury. Never mind that he went 4-for-60 and crippled the team by doing so. In the end they had similar numbers to each other, but while Anderson will be an Oriole again next year, Alomar will not, having signed a four-year deal to play with the Indians. His reputation far outstrips his contributions at this point.

Harold Baines   DH   Bats L   Age 40

YEAR	TEAM	LGE	AB	H	DB	TP	HR	BB	R	RBI	SB	CS	OUT	BA	OBA	SA	EQA	EQR	DEFENSE
1996	ChiSox	AL	486	152	24	0	24	70	78	88	3	1	335	.313	.399	.510	.311	91	
1997	ChiSox	AL	313	96	13	0	14	42	45	54	0	1	218	.307	.389	.482	.299	53	
1997	Baltimor	AL	132	39	5	0	4	14	16	19	0	0	93	.295	.363	.424	.275	18	
1998	Baltimor	AL	290	88	13	0	11	33	39	46	0	0	202	.303	.375	.462	.289	46	
1999	Baltimor	AL	356	93	9	0	14	48	44	50	0	0	263	.261	.349	.404	.267	48	

Contrary to rumor in the fall of '97, he did not retire, and had yet another productive season. He's expected to be back in Baltimore again in 1999, possibly splitting DH duties with Chris Hoiles. His basic skill, hitting right-handed pitching, is still intact.

Rich Becker OF Bats L Age 27

YEAR	TEAM	LGE	AB	H	DB	TP	HR	BB	R	RBI	SB	CS	OUT	BA	OBA	SA	EQA	EQR	DEFENSE
1996	Minnesot	AL	508	139	28	4	11	64	77	59	20	6	375	.274	.355	.409	.271	72	142-OF 107
1997	Minnesot	AL	435	113	22	3	10	63	66	49	17	5	327	.260	.353	.393	.267	60	123-OF 105
1998	NYMets	NL	100	19	4	3	3	22	15	11	3	1	82	.190	.336	.380	.257	14	26-OF 103
1998	Baltimor	AL	112	23	2	0	3	22	14	10	2	0	89	.205	.336	.304	.237	12	31-OF 96
1999	*Baltimor*	*AL*	*302*	*75*	*15*	*2*	*8*	*45*	*44*	*36*	*8*	*2*	*229*	*.248*	*.346*	*.391*	*.265*	*41*	

People like me have been touting Becker for several years as an example of a player with clear limitations—hitting left-handers—but definite skills—fielding, plate discipline. But when he hits below the Mendoza line, it's hard for him to be taken seriously, even when his secondary average is an excellent .352. A problem with his skill set is that pitchers can attack it, and he found himself taking more pitches and getting behind in the count more often than in previous years.

Mike Bordick SS Bats R Age 33

YEAR	TEAM	LGE	AB	H	DB	TP	HR	BB	R	RBI	SB	CS	OUT	BA	OBA	SA	EQA	EQR	DEFENSE
1996	Oakland	AL	514	115	15	4	5	49	41	36	5	7	406	.224	.291	.298	.203	38	149-SS 100
1997	Baltimor	AL	503	118	19	1	7	34	36	39	0	2	387	.235	.283	.318	.204	37	147-SS 98
1998	Baltimor	AL	461	121	28	1	14	41	51	56	5	7	347	.262	.323	.419	.253	56	143-SS 101
1999	*Baltimor*	*AL*	*475*	*113*	*18*	*1*	*12*	*41*	*43*	*47*	*2*	*4*	*366*	*.238*	*.298*	*.356*	*.226*	*45*	

Fortunately for the Orioles, '98 was not the final year of his contract, as this was exactly the type of season that leads to heightened expectations and silly renewals. The improvement was real, in that there was no identifiable cause: he didn't get platooned vs. left-handers, who he cannot hit; he didn't work himself into any more hitters' counts. He just got on a roll after the All-Star break. I don't expect it to continue.

Danny Clyburn OF Bats R Age 25

YEAR	TEAM	LGE	AB	H	DB	TP	HR	BB	R	RBI	SB	CS	OUT	BA	OBA	SA	EQA	EQR	DEFENSE
1996	Bowie	Eas	365	88	12	3	15	14	29	41	3	2	279	.241	.269	.414	.229	35	57-OF 86
1997	Rochestr	Int	515	147	26	4	18	47	69	72	11	3	371	.285	.345	.456	.277	75	133-OF 91
1998	Rochestr	Int	320	86	14	1	12	29	39	41	8	4	238	.269	.330	.431	.262	42	70-OF 94
1999	*Baltimor*	*AL*	*403*	*111*	*19*	*2*	*16*	*30*	*52*	*56*	*10*	*3*	*295*	*.275*	*.326*	*.452*	*.269*	*56*	

He had hoped that his breakthrough '97 would land him in Baltimore; instead, it was the young Clyburn, not one of his aged opponents for the right field and DH jobs, who broke his foot in spring training. He didn't do as well as in '97, but that was to be expected: when a player's EQA jumps 50 points in one year like Clyburn's did, the chance that it will drop the next year is about 80%. Having maintained most of his gain, he's a good bet to hit at least as well again. I think the projection is low, overly weighting his poor 1996.

Evanon Coffie IF Bats L Age 22

YEAR	TEAM	LGE	AB	H	DB	TP	HR	BB	R	RBI	SB	CS	OUT	BA	OBA	SA	EQA	EQR	DEFENSE	
1997	Delmarva	SAL	308	77	10	3	3	22	28	25	8	6	237	.250	.300	.331	.219	27	74-SS 96	
1998	Frederck	Car	480	116	12	1	15	46	47	50	9	6	370	.242	.308	.365	.234	49	52-3B 72	50-SS 96
1999	*Baltimor*	*AL*	*375*	*94*	*12*	*1*	*10*	*32*	*40*	*39*	*8*	*5*	*286*	*.251*	*.310*	*.368*	*.237*	*39*		

A native of Curacao, Coffie reminds me of Jose Valentin: a slugging middle infielder with middling patience and a poor batting average. The attempt to use him at third was a disaster, largely due to the errors he made there. I expect them to try again; his glove does not look good enough for him to make it in the majors.

Eric Davis OF Bats R Age 37

YEAR	TEAM	LGE	AB	H	DB	TP	HR	BB	R	RBI	SB	CS	OUT	BA	OBA	SA	EQA	EQR	DEFENSE
1996	Cincnnti	NL	414	117	17	0	27	72	74	73	19	10	307	.283	.389	.519	.306	80	118-OF 107
1997	Baltimor	AL	156	47	9	0	9	14	24	27	6	0	109	.301	.359	.532	.304	28	20-OF 94
1998	Baltimor	AL	447	149	25	1	30	46	72	93	6	6	304	.333	.396	.595	.324	91	65-OF 96
1999	*StLouis*	*NL*	*354*	*102*	*15*	*0*	*22*	*46*	*53*	*63*	*8*	*4*	*256*	*.288*	*.370*	*.517*	*.302*	*64*	

Nobody could have expected he'd return from cancer and have a season like this, one in which he finished fifth in the league in EQA, topped off by a team-record 30-game hitting streak. Stayed healthy all year, splitting time between right field and DH.

(Eric Davis *continued*)

Miller had him in a strict "don't play the field three games in a row" role all season. Signed by the Cardinals to play left field, so he won't have the DH option; this may cut into his playing time. A bargain at the price (two years, $8 million).

Tim DeCinces   **C**   **Bats R**   **Age 22**

YEAR	TEAM	LGE	AB	H	DB	TP	HR	BB	R	RBI	SB	CS	OUT	BA	OBA	SA	EQA	EQR	DEFENSE
1996	Bluefld	App	131	31	3	0	4	16	13	14	1	1	101	.237	.320	.351	.236	14	
1997	Delmarva	SAL	433	102	10	0	12	84	55	49	1	2	333	.236	.360	.342	.254	54	
1998	Frederck	Car	383	98	13	0	16	55	48	52	2	2	287	.256	.349	.415	.267	53	30-C 101
1999	Baltimor	AL	404	105	9	0	16	60	52	57	2	2	301	.260	.356	.401	.268	56	

The knock on DeCinces, son of the former third baseman, is his defense, though it's unclear what he needs to do. He doesn't give up passed balls, with just four in the past two years combined. He stops the running game; his .395 caught-stealing rate was second-best in the Carolina League. However, he once again spent more time as a DH than he did behind the plate, as well as playing three infield positions.

P.J. Forbes   **IF**   **Bats R**   **Age 31**

YEAR	TEAM	LGE	AB	H	DB	TP	HR	BB	R	RBI	SB	CS	OUT	BA	OBA	SA	EQA	EQR	DEFENSE	
1996	Vancouvr	PCL	410	98	15	1	1	35	33	27	3	2	314	.239	.299	.288	.205	30	109-2B 87	
1997	Rochestr	Int	431	100	14	1	6	27	34	30	10	3	334	.232	.277	.311	.204	32	56-3B 98	56-2B 93
1998	Rochestr	Int	456	116	25	1	5	28	42	39	6	2	342	.254	.298	.346	.224	41	83-2B 101	17-SS 90
1999	Baltimor	AL	453	112	20	1	5	31	40	38	5	2	343	.247	.295	.329	.218	38		

The best year of his career, and one of the shinier examples of the dross that inhabited Rochester last season. He's been released, and at this point has as much chance of showing up as a coach as he does as a player.

Eddy Garabito   **2B**   **Bats B**   **Age 20**

YEAR	TEAM	LGE	AB	H	DB	TP	HR	BB	R	RBI	SB	CS	OUT	BA	OBA	SA	EQA	EQR	DEFENSE
1997	Bluefld	App	228	47	4	1	3	14	14	12	9	5	186	.206	.252	.272	.177	12	59-2B 87
1998	Delmarva	SAL	483	101	13	3	8	37	34	31	11	8	390	.209	.265	.298	.192	31	130-2B 97

This is the same guy who is listed in many publications as Garavito, thanks to an error a year ago by the Oriole public relations department. Defensively, he's got a good arm for a second baseman, with decent range. At the plate, he's really a right-handed hitter but is trying to switch-hit. My unprofessional opinion is that he should go back to batting right-handed full time.

Willie Greene   **3B/OF**   **Bats L**   **Age 27**

YEAR	TEAM	LGE	AB	H	DB	TP	HR	BB	R	RBI	SB	CS	OUT	BA	OBA	SA	EQA	EQR	DEFENSE	
1996	Cincnnti	NL	286	68	6	5	18	37	34	46	0	1	219	.238	.325	.483	.272	42	60-3B 112	
1997	Cincnnti	NL	492	120	20	1	26	79	68	73	5	0	372	.244	.349	.447	.277	75	102-3B 93	30-OF 109
1998	Cincnnti	NL	355	96	17	1	15	58	55	53	6	3	262	.270	.373	.451	.286	57	70-3B 101	22-OF 95
1998	Baltimor	AL	40	6	2	0	1	13	7	3	1	0	34	.150	.358	.275	.247	5		
1999	Baltimor	AL	391	96	16	1	18	62	56	57	5	1	296	.246	.349	.430	.275	58		

Greene was traded from the Reds in exchange for Jeffrey Hammonds, in a swap of two highly-touted players who never lived up to expectations and had been scapegoated for that failing. He was one of three players the Orioles acquired during the year who were primarily third basemen, but who had to play elsewhere to accommodate His Ironness. Greene was the middle one in terms of luck; he only ran into the outfield fence and suffered a mild concussion.

Jerry Hairston   **2B**   **Bats R**   **Age 23**

YEAR	TEAM	LGE	AB	H	DB	TP	HR	BB	R	RBI	SB	CS	OUT	BA	OBA	SA	EQA	EQR	DEFENSE
1997	Bluefld	App	216	36	3	1	1	12	7	7	3	3	183	.167	.211	.204	.100	3	55-SS 109
1998	Frederck	Car	297	78	15	2	5	27	35	30	7	4	223	.263	.324	.377	.245	33	65-SS 110
1998	Bowie	Eas	218	66	9	2	5	18	28	29	4	3	155	.303	.356	.431	.272	30	52-2B 102
1999	Baltimor	AL	388	106	16	2	6	29	44	40	9	6	288	.273	.324	.371	.244	42	

Hairston, whose dad and granddad both played in the majors, was a 1997 11th-round pick. I have a great fondness for players who explode in their second professional seasons, even though I haven't done the study to show that they always succeed.

Many seem to. His hitting improved all season long, continuing into a strong Arizona Fall League campaign. He's a classic #2 hitter, putting the ball in play, neither walking or striking out too much. Moved from short to second just before being called up to Bowie, due to a weak arm. The DeShields signing slows his train down; with Bordick's contract up after 1999, a move back to shortstop isn't out of the question.

Chris Hoiles — C/DH — Bats R — Age 34

YEAR	TEAM	LGE	AB	H	DB	TP	HR	BB	R	RBI	SB	CS	OUT	BA	OBA	SA	EQA	EQR	DEFENSE
1996	Baltimor	AL	400	102	11	0	25	54	49	65	0	1	299	.255	.344	.470	.277	60	
1997	Baltimor	AL	315	82	13	0	13	51	44	45	1	0	233	.260	.363	.425	.277	47	
1998	Baltimor	AL	264	70	9	0	16	40	36	45	0	1	195	.265	.362	.481	.287	43	74-C 91
1999	Baltimor	AL	279	68	8	0	16	46	37	45	0	0	211	.244	.351	.444	.278	43	

He can still hit, and at many of the tasks involved he's a great catcher. What he cannot do is throw. There were times in 1998 when he literally could not throw the ball to second base, and with the Charles Johnson acquisition it appears that he will not be called on to catch at all in 1999. He may play first, he may DH; in limited time over the last two years, he's hit better when playing a position other than catcher.

Eugene Kingsale — CF — Bats B — Age 22

YEAR	TEAM	LGE	AB	H	DB	TP	HR	BB	R	RBI	SB	CS	OUT	BA	OBA	SA	EQA	EQR	DEFENSE
1996	Frederck	Car	166	39	4	3	0	16	19	10	10	3	130	.235	.302	.295	.219	15	48-OF 99
1998	Bowie	Eas	424	102	9	4	1	43	45	27	20	9	331	.241	.310	.288	.216	36	110-OF 112
1998	Rochestr	Int	55	11	1	1	0	3	3	2	2	2	46	.200	.241	.255	.158	2	
1999	Baltimor	AL	306	80	8	4	0	29	39	23	17	7	233	.261	.325	.314	.234	31	

My fear that he is really Curtis Goodwin in disguise is looking more and more like reality. Look for him on the waiver wire in the spring of 2000: the O's have already burned two of his three options for a grand total of two plate appearances.

David Lamb — SS — Bats B — Age 23

YEAR	TEAM	LGE	AB	H	DB	TP	HR	BB	R	RBI	SB	CS	OUT	BA	OBA	SA	EQA	EQR	DEFENSE	
1996	High	Des	Cal	447	78	13	1	2	35	15	15	2	3	372	.174	.234	.221	.135	12	116-SS 101
1997	Frederck	Car	250	58	14	1	2	20	22	18	2	1	193	.232	.289	.320	.211	20	59-2B 97	
1997	Bowie	Eas	268	83	16	2	3	28	37	35	0	0	185	.310	.375	.418	.279	38	45-SS 98	19-3B 80
1998	Bowie	Eas	239	65	7	1	2	24	24	23	1	2	176	.272	.338	.335	.238	24	64-SS 101	
1998	Rochestr	Int	177	49	5	1	1	15	17	16	1	4	132	.277	.333	.333	.230	17	38-SS 95	
1999	Baltimor	AL	446	119	19	2	4	40	48	43	3	3	330	.267	.327	.345	.238	46		

The heir apparent to Jeff Reboulet, Lamb has always been a disappointment. He was a second-round pick, big enough that you'd have expected some power, but no trace of it has shown up yet. With Reboulet signed for two more years, Lamb's ETA looks like late 2000, if ever.

Eddy Martinez — SS — Bats R — Age 21

YEAR	TEAM	LGE	AB	H	DB	TP	HR	BB	R	RBI	SB	CS	OUT	BA	OBA	SA	EQA	EQR	DEFENSE
1996	Bluefld	App	124	21	0	0	1	8	4	4	5	3	106	.169	.220	.194	.116	2	35-SS 87
1996	Frederck	Car	244	44	1	0	2	17	8	8	5	4	204	.180	.234	.209	.130	6	73-SS 95
1997	Frederck	Car	175	36	1	0	2	16	10	9	3	4	143	.206	.272	.246	.172	9	52-SS 75
1998	Delmarva	SAL	362	80	11	1	1	28	26	19	9	4	286	.221	.277	.265	.188	22	110-SS 97
1999	Baltimor	AL	354	82	4	0	4	26	26	23	9	5	277	.232	.284	.277	.196	23	

When the Orioles signed him at 17, the thinking was that he'd fill out as he matured, get stronger and be able to hit with more authority. He was a skinny, 6'2", 150-lb kid then; four years later he's 6'2", 150, and while he hits a little better than he used to, it's not authoritative. He continues to win raves for his defense, but it won't be enough.

Luis Matos — CF — Bats R — Age 20

YEAR	TEAM	LGE	AB	H	DB	TP	HR	BB	R	RBI	SB	CS	OUT	BA	OBA	SA	EQA	EQR	DEFENSE
1997	Bluefld	App	237	42	3	1	1	14	8	8	8	2	197	.177	.223	.211	.132	6	60-OF 106
1997	Delmarva	SAL	120	21	2	1	0	9	4	4	3	3	102	.175	.233	.208	.129	3	30-OF 108
1998	Delmarva	SAL	503	118	16	3	6	33	44	35	19	9	394	.235	.282	.314	.208	39	130-OF 103
1999	Baltimor	AL	428	102	13	2	5	25	36	31	14	8	334	.238	.280	.313	.206	32	

(Luis Matos *continued*)

That's not exactly what I mean when I talk about a "second-year improvement," but at least it is improvement. He's a lot like Kingsale—a speedster with great range in center, slaps the ball around. Maybe it was a bad day, but he looked slow and confused, playing very deep in center, when I saw him in August.

Darnell McDonald   OF   Bats R   Age 20

YEAR	TEAM	LGE	AB	H	DB	TP	HR	BB	R	RBI	SB	CS	OUT	BA	OBA	SA	EQA	EQR	DEFENSE
1998	Delmarva	SAL	527	118	17	2	5	29	38	31	16	7	416	.224	.264	.292	.191	33	115-OF 86
1999	Baltimor	AL	462	111	16	2	6	23	38	34	13	7	358	.240	.276	.323	.207	35	

The hype was immense, and the Orioles took a chance in luring him away from a University of Texas football scholarship. His debut was not what they wanted to see; especially troubling were the 117-33 K/BB ratio and the 11 outfield errors. Looking at it from the positive side, very few players make their professional debut in a full-season league. There's a lot to adjust to in pro ball: wooden bats, bus trips, curveballs. I wouldn't panic yet.

Ryan Minor   3B   Bats R   Age 25

YEAR	TEAM	LGE	AB	H	DB	TP	HR	BB	R	RBI	SB	CS	OUT	BA	OBA	SA	EQA	EQR	DEFENSE
1996	Bluefld	App	87	13	2	0	1	4	2	2	0	0	74	.149	.187	.207	.060	0	20-3B 104
1997	Delmarva	SAL	496	125	13	1	15	40	45	54	3	2	373	.252	.308	.373	.236	50	111-3B 91
1998	Bowie	Eas	517	111	11	2	13	28	29	38	1	2	408	.215	.255	.319	.191	32	133-3B 98
1999	Baltimor	AL	444	106	12	2	13	27	35	45	1	1	339	.239	.282	.363	.221	39	

Coming off an overhyped '97, Minor turned into the Human Whiff Machine this year, racking up a league-leading 152 during the regular season before fanning in nearly half of his Arizona Fall League at-bats. His defense gets good reviews—*Baseball America* called him the best third baseman in the Eastern League—but the evidence doesn't back it up. "They" say he'll take over for Cal at third base, and in a sense he already has, since he was the starter when Cal sat, but They are full of it. He would probably not be a disaster of Booty-an proportions—more Pittaroesque.

Lyle Mouton   OF   Bats R   Age 30

YEAR	TEAM	LGE	AB	H	DB	TP	HR	BB	R	RBI	SB	CS	OUT	BA	OBA	SA	EQA	EQR	DEFENSE
1996	ChiSox	AL	211	62	8	1	7	21	28	30	3	0	149	.294	.358	.441	.279	31	28-OF 96
1997	ChiSox	AL	239	64	7	0	6	15	22	25	4	4	179	.268	.311	.372	.235	24	54-OF 94
1998	Rochestr	Int	136	39	6	1	5	10	16	19	1	1	98	.287	.336	.456	.269	18	27-OF 100
1998	Baltimor	AL	39	12	3	0	2	4	6	7	0	0	27	.308	.372	.538	.306	7	
1999	Baltimor	AL	211	62	8	0	9	17	26	33	2	1	150	.294	.346	.460	.279	31	

Mouton found himself with no job in the States after a poor 1997, so he gave Japan a try. After 30 games with the Yakult Swallows, he decided to give the States a second chance. His skill set is unchanged; he could help a team needing a platoon partner in left field.

Ntema Ndungidi   LF   Bats B   Age 20

YEAR	TEAM	LGE	AB	H	DB	TP	HR	BB	R	RBI	SB	CS	OUT	BA	OBA	SA	EQA	EQR	DEFENSE
1998	Bluefld	App	209	45	5	1	4	24	18	16	2	3	167	.215	.296	.306	.209	17	46-OF 77
1999	Baltimor	AL	169	40	5	1	3	20	17	16	1	2	131	.237	.317	.331	.228	16	

The best name in baseball, assuming you can pronounce it. "Pappy" is an extremely raw player with enormous physical talent. Born in northern Zaire (when it was still called that), his family moved to Montreal when he was four. He became one of that city's best-ever high school athletes, and was essentially the Orioles' third first-round draft pick in 1997.

Augie Ojeda   SS   Bats B   Age 24

YEAR	TEAM	LGE	AB	H	DB	TP	HR	BB	R	RBI	SB	CS	OUT	BA	OBA	SA	EQA	EQR	DEFENSE
1997	Frederck	Car	128	38	6	1	1	15	16	15	1	3	93	.297	.371	.383	.262	16	33-SS 99
1997	Bowie	Eas	204	55	6	1	2	26	26	20	5	0	149	.270	.352	.338	.253	24	57-SS 104
1998	Bowie	Eas	253	57	8	1	1	32	22	17	0	2	198	.225	.312	.277	.207	19	69-SS 104
1999	Baltimor	AL	269	69	10	1	2	33	31	25	2	2	202	.257	.338	.323	.238	28	

A 1996 Olympian, he was supposed to be an all-glove, no-hit infielder, but he surprised everyone in '97 with his ability to work pitchers. Unfortunately, he broke a bone in his wrist and missed the first half of the year. While he still worked pitchers well after his return, he was unable to drive anything. My usual rule of thumb is that any season with a wrist injury can be ignored; they have horrible effects on hitting until they're fully healed, which usually takes an off-season. Reserve judgment until spring.

Willis Otanez   3B   Bats R   Age 26

YEAR	TEAM	LGE	AB	H	DB	TP	HR	BB	R	RBI	SB	CS	OUT	BA	OBA	SA	EQA	EQR	DEFENSE
1996	Bowie	Eas	508	126	18	0	20	37	46	59	3	4	386	.248	.299	.402	.239	54	132-3B 96
1997	Bowie	Eas	78	23	4	0	3	6	8	12	0	1	56	.295	.345	.462	.272	11	
1997	Rochestr	Int	168	32	5	0	5	12	9	11	0	0	136	.190	.244	.310	.183	10	40-3B 93
1998	Rochestr	Int	478	124	16	1	20	33	46	61	1	0	354	.259	.307	.423	.250	55	116-3B 110
1999	*Baltimor*	*AL*	*375*	*93*	*11*	*0*	*16*	*26*	*35*	*46*	*1*	*1*	*283*	*.248*	*.297*	*.405*	*.241*	*41*	

Otanez's career has involved an oscillation between prospect (when healthy) and suspect (when injured, which is often). Had seemingly returned to prospect status by getting off to a blazing start, but suffered a prolonged drought through the summer. Called up anyway, but tried in right field. In his second game he attempted a diving catch and broke his wrist. On-the-job training at the major league level is stupid.

Rafael Palmeiro   1B   Bats L   Age 34

YEAR	TEAM	LGE	AB	H	DB	TP	HR	BB	R	RBI	SB	CS	OUT	BA	OBA	SA	EQA	EQR	DEFENSE
1996	Baltimor	AL	613	176	38	3	38	91	102	115	9	0	437	.287	.379	.545	.312	119	157-1B 103
1997	Baltimor	AL	606	154	23	2	39	68	75	98	5	2	454	.254	.329	.492	.277	92	152-1B 105
1998	Baltimor	AL	613	184	31	1	46	81	99	124	10	7	436	.300	.382	.579	.316	122	158-1B 104
1999	*Texas*	*AL*	*605*	*163*	*23*	*1*	*41*	*84*	*90*	*113*	*6*	*3*	*445*	*.269*	*.358*	*.514*	*.289*	*100*	

Palmeiro was without question the O's most effective hitter all season, a nice rebound from an awful '97. So it was surprising that he was consistently blamed for the team's problems during '98. He was—you know the routine—a selfish performer, interested only in his statistics. He was practically run out of town for all the wrong reasons; with Pickering's emergence, he needed to be moved anyway, but that wasn't why he was under attack. Signed to a five-year, $45 million by the Rangers.

Richard Paz   3B   Bats R   Age 21

YEAR	TEAM	LGE	AB	H	DB	TP	HR	BB	R	RBI	SB	CS	OUT	BA	OBA	SA	EQA	EQR	DEFENSE	
1996	Bluefld	App	175	38	3	0	1	29	18	11	3	2	139	.217	.328	.251	.213	15	26-SS 104	
1997	Delmarva	SAL	395	87	12	2	2	34	30	23	6	3	311	.220	.282	.276	.193	26	44-SS 95	20-3B 101
1998	Delmarva	SAL	332	91	7	2	4	62	53	35	9	4	245	.274	.388	.343	.270	46	88-3B 98	
1998	Frederck	Car	146	34	5	0	4	20	16	15	3	2	114	.233	.325	.349	.239	16	28-3B 80	
1999	*Baltimor*	*AL*	*438*	*113*	*11*	*1*	*6*	*59*	*54*	*43*	*8*	*5*	*330*	*.258*	*.346*	*.329*	*.245*	*49*		

Not really a prospect. His only solid season came while repeating a league, and at 5'8" he's considered too small, although not as small as some publications think; a Howe Sportsdata misprint put him at 130 pounds instead of his true 180. This Venezuelan is a sort of anti-Guillen: he uses his stature to force walks from the opposition.

Calvin Pickering   1B   Bats L   Age 22

YEAR	TEAM	LGE	AB	H	DB	TP	HR	BB	R	RBI	SB	CS	OUT	BA	OBA	SA	EQA	EQR	DEFENSE
1996	Bluefld	App	202	55	5	0	10	18	23	29	3	1	148	.272	.332	.446	.267	27	49-1B 80
1997	Delmarva	SAL	453	132	15	0	22	48	58	72	3	2	323	.291	.359	.470	.284	69	114-1B 82
1998	Bowie	Eas	485	141	20	1	27	87	80	88	3	4	348	.291	.399	.503	.307	91	126-1B 79
1998	Baltimor	AL	21	5	1	0	2	3	3	4	1	0	16	.238	.333	.571	.302	4	
1999	*Baltimor*	*AL*	*440*	*129*	*14*	*0*	*27*	*65*	*69*	*84*	*3*	*2*	*313*	*.293*	*.384*	*.509*	*.306*	*81*	

I can remember a picture from the 1930s of a player who looked just like Pickering. I think it was Mule Suttles, even though he was seven inches and 70 pounds smaller. Everything looks small on him; his hat sort of perches on top of his head, he looks like he's wearing a child's glove; he wears his uniform really loose, perhaps out of sensitivity over his weight; he completes the picture by wearing his pants tucked in at the knees. A young Mo Vaughn, complete with the horrible defense. The Will Clark signing means that if he plays, it'll be as the DH; he should be up by midseason.

Jeff Reboulet   IF   Bats R   Age 35

YEAR	TEAM	LGE	AB	H	DB	TP	HR	BB	R	RBI	SB	CS	OUT	BA	OBA	SA	EQA	EQR	DEFENSE	
1996	Minnesot	AL	229	46	8	0	0	23	16	9	4	2	185	.201	.274	.236	.174	12	24-3B 107	21-SS 77
1997	Baltimor	AL	225	53	6	0	5	24	22	20	3	0	172	.236	.309	.329	.227	21	45-2B 102	12-SS 89
1998	Baltimor	AL	125	31	4	0	2	19	15	12	0	1	95	.248	.347	.328	.241	14		
1999	Baltimor	AL	154	35	4	0	2	19	15	12	1	1	120	.227	.312	.292	.216	13		

Signed for the next two years to cover the all-important utility infield position. Reboulet is actually one of the best utility infielders in the game, but as a class there's really no reason to give any of them that kind of job security. Unless they have a cute sister or something.

Cal Ripken   3B   Bats R   Age 38

YEAR	TEAM	LGE	AB	H	DB	TP	HR	BB	R	RBI	SB	CS	OUT	BA	OBA	SA	EQA	EQR	DEFENSE
1996	Baltimor	AL	630	173	33	2	27	55	73	92	1	2	459	.275	.333	.462	.270	87	152-SS 99
1997	Baltimor	AL	607	163	22	0	20	57	65	76	1	0	444	.269	.331	.404	.256	73	150-3B 107
1998	Baltimor	AL	595	163	25	1	15	54	63	72	0	2	434	.274	.334	.395	.253	70	157-3B 92
1999	Baltimor	AL	552	130	17	0	18	55	52	60	0	1	423	.236	.305	.364	.234	56	

One excuse for his decline went by the boards on September 20, when number 2,633 didn't happen. Now, perhaps, we can analyze Cal the way we do everyone else, an aging player whose offense has been declining for years and whose defense collapsed this year.

B.J. Surhoff   OF   Bats L   Age 34

YEAR	TEAM	LGE	AB	H	DB	TP	HR	BB	R	RBI	SB	CS	OUT	BA	OBA	SA	EQA	EQR	DEFENSE	
1996	Baltimor	AL	528	153	28	6	20	44	65	81	0	1	376	.290	.344	.479	.279	78	104-3B 89	19-OF 104
1997	Baltimor	AL	520	147	28	4	19	50	66	76	1	1	374	.283	.346	.462	.276	75	119-OF 100	
1998	Baltimor	AL	567	160	30	1	24	52	71	83	8	7	414	.282	.342	.466	.274	82	150-OF 93	
1999	Baltimor	AL	528	138	25	2	21	54	64	74	3	2	392	.261	.330	.436	.265	71		

Re-signed by the Orioles after a bidding war with the Pirates for his services. They pulled it out by offering a fourth year. Running the projection for 2000 based on the projection for 1999, and so on, produces a .230 EQA for that fourth year.

Lenny Webster   C   Bats R   Age 34

YEAR	TEAM	LGE	AB	H	DB	TP	HR	BB	R	RBI	SB	CS	OUT	BA	OBA	SA	EQA	EQR	DEFENSE
1996	Montreal	NL	173	38	6	0	3	25	17	15	0	0	135	.220	.318	.306	.223	16	
1997	Baltimor	AL	256	65	9	1	7	22	24	28	0	1	192	.254	.313	.379	.239	27	
1998	Baltimor	AL	306	88	11	1	11	17	31	42	0	0	218	.288	.325	.438	.261	38	82-C 94
1999	Baltimor	AL	245	60	8	0	9	20	23	29	0	0	185	.245	.302	.388	.239	26	

He became the Orioles' regular catcher last season, getting into 20 more games than Hoiles. His reputation as a strong defender is tough to support; his caught stealing rate is hardly any better than Hoiles's and he gives up a lot more passed balls. He does have a better CERA, although that has a lot to do with not catching Doug Drabek as often as Hoiles did.

Jayson Werth   C   Bats R   Age 20

YEAR	TEAM	LGE	AB	H	DB	TP	HR	BB	R	RBI	SB	CS	OUT	BA	OBA	SA	EQA	EQR	DEFENSE
1998	Delmarva	SAL	411	93	12	1	7	42	38	32	9	4	322	.226	.298	.311	.215	35	107-C 101
1999	Baltimor	AL	344	89	15	1	6	34	41	35	9	4	259	.259	.325	.360	.244	38	

The Oriole scouting department really has a bias towards bloodlines. There's Luzinski and Hairston and DeCinces, and Ripken of course. Darnell McDonald's older brother is a Yankee. As for Werth, the other first-round pick from '97, his mother is Dick Schofield's sister, his grandfather is Ducky Schofield, and his stepfather is Dennis Werth, who had a 139 AB career over four years in the early 1980s. He's a good catcher; he nailed 64 would-be base thieves, second most in pro ball last year. Since he's big, athletic, and has a lot of potential as a hitter, he may not remain behind the plate.

PITCHERS (Averages: 4.00 ERA, 9.00 H/9, 1.00 HR/9, 3.00 BB/9, 6.00 K/9, 1.00 KWH)

Armando Benitez — Throws R — Age 26

YEAR	TEAM	LGE	IP	H	ER	HR	BB	K	ERA	W	L	H/9	HR/9	BB/9	K/9	KWH	PERA
1997	Baltimor	AL	75.3	51	19	8	37	103	2.27	6	2	6.09	0.96	4.42	12.31	4.22	2.39
1998	Baltimor	AL	69.7	49	24	10	35	84	3.10	5	3	6.33	1.29	4.52	10.85	3.09	2.71

Another Oriole who got an undeserved share of the blame for 1998, despite doing his job better than most of his teammates did theirs. That was all overshadowed by how spectacular his few failures were, especially the notorious night in New York when he lashed out at Tino Martinez. It was inexcusable, and in the eyes of many in Baltimore, unforgivable. Unfortunately, following emotions in lieu of impassive evaluation leads to suboptimal decisions like sending Benitez to the Mets for an arbitration-eligible Charles Johnson. Power pitchers have had a lot of success in Shea; I think Benitez will have a monster year.

Darin Blood — Throws R — Age 24

YEAR	TEAM	LGE	IP	H	ER	HR	BB	K	ERA	W	L	H/9	HR/9	BB/9	K/9	KWH	PERA
1996	San Jose	Cal	153.7	182	67	5	64	128	3.92	9	8	10.66	0.29	3.75	7.50	1.05	4.28
1997	Shrevprt	Tex	144.0	181	92	14	82	74	5.75	5	11	11.31	0.88	5.13	4.62	0.28	5.25
1998	Fresno	PCL	114.3	140	53	8	36	52	4.17	6	7	11.02	0.63	2.83	4.09	0.40	4.57
1998	Rochestr	Int	31.7	28	11	2	12	12	3.13	2	2	7.96	0.57	3.41	3.41	0.32	3.13

He's got one big shining success in his career, which means he has ability; it's a matter of finding the right pitching coach to show him how to do it again. Whether he can or not, simply getting any humanoid for Joe Carter was a neat trick.

Derek Brown — Throws R — Age 22

YEAR	TEAM	LGE	IP	H	ER	HR	BB	K	ERA	W	L	H/9	HR/9	BB/9	K/9	KWH	PERA
1997	Bluefld	App	37.0	63	31	3	17	23	7.54	1	3	15.32	0.73	4.14	5.59	0.37	6.81
1998	Delmarva	SAL	63.3	75	24	4	16	38	3.41	4	3	10.66	0.57	2.27	5.40	0.90	4.26

Brown was a 40th-round pick in 1994, a second baseman from a Maryland high school. He spent two years playing the infield, never getting out of the Gulf Coast League, never hitting a lick. He had a good arm, so they gave him a shot as a pitcher. 33 saves later, with an impressive 4.8 K/W ratio, it looks like a good idea. He's all fastball at the moment, so don't get too excited.

Rocky Coppinger — Throws R — Age 25

YEAR	TEAM	LGE	IP	H	ER	HR	BB	K	ERA	W	L	H/9	HR/9	BB/9	K/9	KWH	PERA
1996	Rochestr	Int	73.7	69	31	6	39	70	3.79	4	4	8.43	0.73	4.76	8.55	1.37	3.67
1996	Baltimor	AL	125.7	126	61	22	48	102	4.37	6	8	9.02	1.58	3.44	7.31	1.29	4.30
1997	Baltimor	AL	20.7	22	12	2	14	21	5.23	1	1	9.58	0.87	6.10	9.15	1.07	4.35
1998	Bowie	Eas	30.0	33	19	4	11	22	5.70	1	2	9.90	1.20	3.30	6.60	1.00	4.50
1998	Rochestr	Int	84.3	93	38	11	40	53	4.06	4	5	9.92	1.17	4.27	5.66	0.57	4.70
1998	Baltimor	AL	16.0	16	7	3	6	13	3.94	1	1	9.00	1.69	3.38	7.31	1.32	4.50

Rocky's road through 1997 was destroyed by shoulder surgery first, and fights with management second. Not all was forgiven in 1998; his rehab dragged on through an extended stay in Rochester, despite the need for a starter in Baltimore, primarily because Ray Miller didn't want to see him. Assuming he keeps his weight down, thus depriving management of their best excuse to hold him back, he should return to the rotation in 1999.

Doug Drabek — Lobs R — Age 36

YEAR	TEAM	LGE	IP	H	ER	HR	BB	K	ERA	W	L	H/9	HR/9	BB/9	K/9	KWH	PERA
1996	Houston	NL	177.0	218	92	22	57	123	4.68	8	12	11.08	1.12	2.90	6.25	0.91	5.03
1997	ChiSox	AL	174.3	164	88	28	60	82	4.54	8	11	8.47	1.45	3.10	4.23	0.51	3.82
1998	Baltimor	AL	110.3	137	75	19	25	53	6.12	4	8	11.18	1.55	2.04	4.32	0.62	5.30

I was optimistic about Drabek, in that I thought he was the most likely to succeed of the four Hell's Agents the Orioles acquired in December of '97 (Ozzie Guillen, Joe Carter, Norm Charlton). Since he's the only one who was still an Oriole at the end of the season, you could say that he was the most successful.

Radhames Dykhoff — Throws L — Age 24

YEAR	TEAM	LGE	IP	H	ER	HR	BB	K	ERA	W	L	H/9	HR/9	BB/9	K/9	KWH	PERA
1996	Frederck	Car	60.3	94	49	9	24	56	7.31	2	5	14.02	1.34	3.58	8.35	1.04	6.71
1997	Frederck	Car	66.0	62	20	5	38	68	2.73	5	2	8.45	0.68	5.18	9.27	1.47	3.68
1998	Bowie	Eas	93.0	99	53	11	53	75	5.13	4	6	9.58	1.06	5.13	7.26	0.80	4.55

Deceptive season. Dykhoff is another Aruban find for the Orioles, and had an exceptional year in relief through July. He got called up, spent one miserable inning being punched around by the Braves, and then went back to Bowie. He was used as a starter to get more work, and watched his ERA climb three runs before the season mercifully ended.

Scott Erickson — Throws R — Age 31

YEAR	TEAM	LGE	IP	H	ER	HR	BB	K	ERA	W	L	H/9	HR/9	BB/9	K/9	KWH	PERA
1996	Baltimor	AL	222.0	257	111	18	52	98	4.50	11	14	10.42	0.73	2.11	3.97	0.54	4.26
1997	Baltimor	AL	223.7	222	88	15	52	127	3.54	14	11	8.93	0.60	2.09	5.11	1.05	3.34
1998	Baltimor	AL	255.3	281	104	21	61	180	3.67	15	13	9.90	0.74	2.15	6.34	1.42	3.98

Ironic that the guy who "takes no-hit stuff to the mound every night," to quote one famous Boston columnist, should lead the league in hits allowed. He did lead the league in innings pitched by a fair margin, but that's not the main reason for his dubious achievement. The league hit .288 off of him.

Chris Fussell — Throws R — Age 23

YEAR	TEAM	LGE	IP	H	ER	HR	BB	K	ERA	W	L	H/9	HR/9	BB/9	K/9	KWH	PERA
1996	Frederck	Car	84.7	87	38	10	47	70	4.04	4	5	9.25	1.06	5.00	7.44	0.90	4.36
1997	Frederck	Car	49.3	53	23	6	31	39	4.20	2	3	9.67	1.09	5.66	7.11	0.69	4.74
1997	Bowie	Eas	77.3	124	72	12	54	55	8.38	2	7	14.43	1.40	6.28	6.40	0.34	7.22
1998	Bowie	Eas	93.3	101	53	14	52	66	5.11	4	6	9.74	1.35	5.01	6.36	0.62	4.82
1998	Rochestr	Int	57.3	57	29	4	25	43	4.55	3	3	8.95	0.63	3.92	6.75	0.97	3.77
1998	Baltimor	AL	9.7	12	8	1	8	8	7.45	0	1	11.17	0.93	7.45	7.45	0.50	5.59

A well-regarded prospect who has a lot of pitches, but no one pitch dominant enough to carry him to the majors yet. The biggest problem, as always, is control. If it comes around, he'll be a fine pitcher. Otherwise he'll stay at this level.

Juan Guzman — Throws R — Age 32

YEAR	TEAM	LGE	IP	H	ER	HR	BB	K	ERA	W	L	H/9	HR/9	BB/9	K/9	KWH	PERA
1996	Toronto	AL	192.0	148	50	17	43	164	2.34	16	5	6.94	0.80	2.02	7.69	3.17	2.30
1997	Toronto	AL	61.3	48	35	14	27	50	5.14	3	4	7.04	2.05	3.96	7.34	1.45	3.52
1998	Toronto	AL	150.7	128	66	18	59	110	3.94	9	8	7.65	1.08	3.52	6.57	1.20	3.17
1998	Baltimor	AL	67.3	60	28	4	29	53	3.74	4	3	8.02	0.53	3.88	7.08	1.21	3.07

After showing up healthy in '98, exchanged for Nerio Rodriguez in July for the stretch run that never happened. He'll be in the Oriole rotation for the next two years, and I expect he'll be as good as he was in 1998.

Doug Johns — Throws L — Age 31

YEAR	TEAM	LGE	IP	H	ER	HR	BB	K	ERA	W	L	H/9	HR/9	BB/9	K/9	KWH	PERA
1996	Oakland	AL	162.0	181	87	18	56	71	4.83	7	11	10.06	1.00	3.11	3.94	0.37	4.44
1997	Omaha	AmA	44.0	63	33	6	12	19	6.75	1	4	12.89	1.23	2.45	3.89	0.36	5.93
1997	Rochestr	Int	53.7	66	25	5	13	31	4.19	3	3	11.07	0.84	2.18	5.20	0.84	4.70
1998	Baltimor	AL	88.3	107	39	8	29	33	3.97	5	5	10.90	0.82	2.95	3.36	0.26	4.69

A soft-tosser who arrived in Rochester after a visa problem delayed his joining an Italian baseball league. Johns showed up when the Orioles needed a starter and he, unlike Nerio Rodriguez, did well in his first two starts. He had less success in relief after a disabled list stint for insomnia.

Scott Kamieniecki   Throws R   Age 35

YEAR	TEAM	LGE	IP	H	ER	HR	BB	K	ERA	W	L	H/9	HR/9	BB/9	K/9	KWH	PERA
1996	Tampa	Fla	20.3	30	10	2	5	11	4.43	1	1	13.28	0.89	2.21	4.87	0.60	5.75
1996	Columbus	Int	29.7	39	21	4	9	21	6.37	1	2	11.83	1.21	2.73	6.37	0.94	5.46
1996	NYYanks	AL	23.7	35	22	5	16	15	8.37	1	2	13.31	1.90	6.08	5.70	0.30	7.23
1997	Baltimor	AL	181.7	183	73	19	58	106	3.62	11	9	9.07	0.94	2.87	5.25	0.79	3.81
1998	Baltimor	AL	56.0	67	35	7	23	24	5.62	2	4	10.77	1.12	3.70	3.86	0.28	4.98

He was fine through spring training and his first few starts, when he came down with a strained groin and an inflamed elbow, netting him a three-week stint on the disabled list. He was back for two ineffective weeks before a bulging disk in his neck put him back on the DL for two months; another ineffective month and the same injury put him on the DL for the third and final time.

Jimmy Key   Threw L   Age 38

YEAR	TEAM	LGE	IP	H	ER	HR	BB	K	ERA	W	L	H/9	HR/9	BB/9	K/9	KWH	PERA
1996	NYYanks	AL	175.0	157	68	18	47	115	3.50	11	8	8.07	0.93	2.42	5.91	1.34	3.14
1997	Baltimor	AL	215.0	216	80	22	71	137	3.35	14	10	9.04	0.92	2.97	5.73	0.92	3.81
1998	Baltimor	AL	80.3	76	32	5	20	51	3.59	5	4	8.51	0.56	2.24	5.71	1.28	3.14

His signing prior to 1997 was a calculated risk: that his surgically repaired shoulder (from '95) could last through a two-year deal. They got one good year out of him before the pain came back, and Key was vehemently opposed to putting himself through another surgery and rehab. He came back to do what he could for the team in relief, before it overwhelmed him.

Alan Mills   Throws R   Age 32

YEAR	TEAM	LGE	IP	H	ER	HR	BB	K	ERA	W	L	H/9	HR/9	BB/9	K/9	KWH	PERA
1996	Baltimor	AL	55.3	40	21	10	29	49	3.42	3	3	6.51	1.63	4.72	7.97	1.55	2.93
1997	Baltimor	AL	39.7	44	20	5	29	31	4.54	2	2	9.98	1.13	6.58	7.03	0.56	4.99
1998	Baltimor	AL	78.3	56	27	8	45	55	3.10	6	3	6.43	0.92	5.17	6.32	0.90	2.64

When his slider is working, it's as good a pitch as anyone throws. He'll now be throwing it for the Dodgers, which should help the long flyballs he allows turn into noisy outs. A silly signing: three years, $6.7 million.

Gabe Molina   Throws R   Age 24

YEAR	TEAM	LGE	IP	H	ER	HR	BB	K	ERA	W	L	H/9	HR/9	BB/9	K/9	KWH	PERA
1996	Bluefld	App	25.0	49	18	1	17	16	6.48	1	2	17.64	0.36	6.12	5.76	0.23	7.20
1997	Delmarva	SAL	84.3	89	34	4	41	72	3.63	5	4	9.50	0.43	4.38	7.68	1.07	3.95
1998	Bowie	Eas	61.3	57	24	5	27	57	3.52	4	3	8.36	0.73	3.96	8.36	1.58	3.52

Started the season as Bowie's co-closer, but since he was doing the job and Kohlmeier wasn't, took the job for himself at mid-season. Not big enough to be considered a real prospect, doesn't throw hard enough to be a real prospect (he relies on a changeup), and he got his head handed to him in the AFL in '98.

Steve Montgomery   Throws R   Age 28

YEAR	TEAM	LGE	IP	H	ER	HR	BB	K	ERA	W	L	H/9	HR/9	BB/9	K/9	KWH	PERA
1996	Edmonton	PCL	52.0	62	22	8	12	32	3.81	3	3	10.73	1.38	2.08	5.54	1.03	4.85
1997	Edmonton	PCL	44.7	65	27	5	17	29	5.44	2	3	13.10	1.01	3.43	5.84	0.57	6.04
1998	Rochestr	Int	82.7	97	55	13	24	50	5.99	3	6	10.56	1.42	2.61	5.44	0.81	4.90

Last year I wrote about a surprising Oriole prospect named Steve Montgomery. This isn't him; that Steve Montgomery hurt his shoulder, and was put on waivers to give Ozzie Guillen a spot on the 40-man roster. He was claimed by the Dodgers and spent the entire year on the DL. This Steve Montgomery is the guy who wasn't a prospect when he was with Oakland, and he isn't one now.

Bobby Munoz   **Throws R**   **Age 31**

YEAR	TEAM	LGE	IP	H	ER	HR	BB	K	ERA	W	L	H/9	HR/9	BB/9	K/9	KWH	PERA
1996	Scran-WB	Int	48.3	60	25	6	8	27	4.66	2	3	11.17	1.12	1.49	5.03	1.14	4.84
1996	Philadel	NL	25.3	46	27	6	6	7	9.59	0	3	16.34	2.13	2.13	2.49	0.13	8.53
1997	Philadel	NL	34.0	50	33	4	14	18	8.74	1	3	13.24	1.06	3.71	4.76	0.35	6.09
1997	Albuquer	PCL	31.0	42	13	2	15	15	3.77	2	1	12.19	0.58	4.35	4.35	0.27	5.23
1998	Rochestr	Int	56.0	50	11	5	12	35	1.77	5	1	8.04	0.80	1.93	5.62	1.53	2.89
1998	Baltimor	AL	12.3	18	11	4	6	6	8.03	0	1	13.14	2.92	4.38	4.38	0.25	8.03

An overpowering closer in Rochester, where he was apparently able to bring the ball with mid-90s velocity once again. It didn't work in Baltimore. He'll show up somewhere this spring; there are worse pitchers to take a flyer on.

Mike Mussina   **Throws R**   **Age 30**

YEAR	TEAM	LGE	IP	H	ER	HR	BB	K	ERA	W	L	H/9	HR/9	BB/9	K/9	KWH	PERA
1996	Baltimor	AL	244.0	258	110	27	55	201	4.06	13	14	9.52	1.00	2.03	7.41	2.14	3.95
1997	Baltimor	AL	227.0	199	76	25	47	211	3.01	16	9	7.89	0.99	1.86	8.37	3.57	2.97
1998	Baltimor	AL	208.7	185	70	21	37	169	3.02	15	8	7.98	0.91	1.60	7.29	3.13	2.93

Mussina made two trips to the DL last season, neither one of which had anything to do with his arm. One trip was for a wart on his finger, the other was courtesy of his nemesis, Sandy Alomar, whose line drive gave him a broken nose and a cut requiring over 30 stitches. The rest of the time he was the same old Mussina.

Jesse Orosco   **Throws L**   **Age 42**

YEAR	TEAM	LGE	IP	H	ER	HR	BB	K	ERA	W	L	H/9	HR/9	BB/9	K/9	KWH	PERA
1996	Baltimor	AL	56.0	42	18	5	23	51	2.89	4	2	6.75	0.80	3.70	8.20	2.02	2.57
1997	Baltimor	AL	51.0	31	12	6	26	44	2.12	5	1	5.47	1.06	4.59	7.76	1.80	1.94
1998	Baltimor	AL	57.3	47	16	6	25	48	2.51	4	2	7.38	0.94	3.92	7.53	1.47	2.98

Promoted by one of us as the best left-handed reliever of all time, and a plausible argument it is. He's gone to the mound for 19 seasons, of which only three can be called poor. Barring an injury, he should set the record for career games pitched right around August . . . hmm . . . 8th.

Sidney Ponson   **Throws R**   **Age 22**

YEAR	TEAM	LGE	IP	H	ER	HR	BB	K	ERA	W	L	H/9	HR/9	BB/9	K/9	KWH	PERA
1996	Frederck	Car	105.0	116	60	8	30	82	5.14	5	7	9.94	0.69	2.57	7.03	1.45	4.03
1997	Bowie	Eas	70.3	92	52	11	30	43	6.65	2	6	11.77	1.41	3.84	5.50	0.50	5.76
1998	Baltimor	AL	137.3	155	68	18	38	82	4.46	7	8	10.16	1.18	2.49	5.37	0.86	4.52

Another Aruban find for the Orioles, Ponson was one of three Birds who spent part of his 1997–98 offseason at Duke University's Sports Nutrition Center—a roundabout way of saying the Orioles were concerned about his weight. He was a surprise call-up to the Orioles in April. He has what all the scouts call a "live arm," and when he wasn't immediately overwhelmed he managed to stay up for the rest of the year. He needs to work on his control, but not to cut his walks; he gets into trouble grooving pitches.

Arthur Rhodes   **Throws L**   **Age 29**

YEAR	TEAM	LGE	IP	H	ER	HR	BB	K	ERA	W	L	H/9	HR/9	BB/9	K/9	KWH	PERA
1996	Baltimor	AL	53.3	48	22	6	18	61	3.71	3	3	8.10	1.01	3.04	10.29	3.23	3.37
1997	Baltimor	AL	96.3	76	28	8	22	99	2.62	8	3	7.10	0.75	2.06	9.25	4.40	2.34
1998	Baltimor	AL	78.7	65	25	8	30	80	2.86	6	3	7.44	0.92	3.43	9.15	2.46	2.97

I want to write in this comment that Rhodes is one of the premier left-handed relievers in the game today, a statement which is pretty much true. This is the third season, though, in which he has injured his elbow and missed time, and I have to believe that he's on the brink of a major injury.

Matthew Riley   Throws L   Age 19

YEAR	TEAM	LGE	IP	H	ER	HR	BB	K	ERA	W	L	H/9	HR/9	BB/9	K/9	KWH	PERA
1998	Delmarva	SAL	78.7	61	24	0	51	84	2.75	6	3	6.98	0.00	5.83	9.61	1.70	2.63

A third-round pick in '97, but didn't sign until just before he would have re-entered the draft for '98. Once aboard, his performance was staggering. He flashed a mid-90s fastball, sharp curve, and reasonable changeup that was too much for the Sally League to handle. His raw numbers were outrageous: 136 strikeouts and 42 hits in 83 innings, the highest strikeout rate and the second-best opponent batting average (.151) in professional baseball.

Pete Smith   Throws R   Age 33

YEAR	TEAM	LGE	IP	H	ER	HR	BB	K	ERA	W	L	H/9	HR/9	BB/9	K/9	KWH	PERA
1996	LasVegas	PCL	162.3	216	107	18	46	74	5.93	6	12	11.98	1.00	2.55	4.10	0.41	5.32
1997	LasVegas	PCL	32.7	39	13	4	6	18	3.58	2	2	10.74	1.10	1.65	4.96	1.04	4.68
1997	San Dieg	NL	118.0	127	61	17	47	61	4.65	6	7	9.69	1.30	3.58	4.65	0.47	4.50
1998	San Dieg	NL	42.7	49	22	6	16	33	4.64	2	3	10.34	1.27	3.38	6.96	1.04	4.85
1998	Baltimor	AL	46.0	56	26	7	15	28	5.09	2	3	10.96	1.37	2.93	5.48	0.70	5.09

Slopballer was acquired by the Orioles in a desperation; they had seen 60% of their rotation go down with injuries, and Smith had lost his job in San Diego. He gave them replacement-level starts until the acquisition of Guzman forced him into the pen.

Matt Snyder   Throws R   Age 24

YEAR	TEAM	LGE	IP	H	ER	HR	BB	K	ERA	W	L	H/9	HR/9	BB/9	K/9	KWH	PERA
1996	High Des	Cal	71.3	70	31	6	36	64	3.91	4	4	8.83	0.76	4.54	8.07	1.22	3.79
1997	Bowie	Eas	75.3	107	49	11	39	53	5.85	3	5	12.78	1.31	4.66	6.33	0.50	6.21
1998	Bowie	Eas	118.7	147	67	15	30	89	5.08	5	8	11.15	1.14	2.28	6.75	1.35	5.01
1998	Rochestr	Int	19.3	19	9	3	5	11	4.19	1	1	8.84	1.40	2.33	5.12	0.96	3.72

There are lots of pitchers who have good arms, wash out as starters and try to convert to closer. Snyder is trying the opposite: a closer for two years who turned to starting this year. That has about as much chance of working as winning ten grand in a ballpark giveaway. Of course, some guy in Bowie did win $10,000 this year when Snyder struck out the side in a promotional inning, soyouneverknow.

Josh Towers   Throws R   Age 22

YEAR	TEAM	LGE	IP	H	ER	HR	BB	K	ERA	W	L	H/9	HR/9	BB/9	K/9	KWH	PERA
1996	Bluefld	App	48.0	96	45	11	5	32	8.44	1	4	18.00	2.06	0.94	6.00	1.60	9.00
1997	Frederck	Car	52.7	89	37	5	18	46	6.32	2	4	15.21	0.85	3.08	7.86	0.99	6.66
1998	Frederck	Car	140.0	170	66	15	11	84	4.24	8	8	10.93	0.96	0.71	5.40	2.83	4.50

Towers is, at the moment, a freak show; descriptions of him start and end with the incredible control he displayed, walking just nine batters in 145 innings while striking out 122. Those who worship at the K/BB altar go into ecstatic convulsions at such numbers, but I call it "freaky" because such control has not been an indicator of future success. Granted, it's a limited sample: only three other pitchers this decade have managed to have a translated walk rate under 1.25 and a translated strikeout rate above 5.00 in the minors. Neither Elvin Hernandez, Jose Martinez (not the one now in the Texas system), nor Jose Parra really improved after their extraordinary seasons. None of them were as effective at preventing runs as Towers was this year, but I don't expect big things.

SNWL		BALTIMORE ORIOLES									Park Effect: -2.4%
PITCHER	**GS**	**IP**	**R**	**SNW**	**SNL**	**SNPCT**	**W**	**L**	**RA**	**APW**	**SNVA**	**SNWAR**
Coppinger, R.	1	5.0	4	0.1	0.5	.184	0	0	7.20	-0.12	-0.17	-0.15
Drabek, D.	21	101.3	83	4.7	9.6	.328	6	11	7.37	-2.70	-2.25	-1.39
Erickson, S.	36	251.3	125	15.1	13.1	.536	16	13	4.48	1.08	0.93	3.13
Fussell, C.	2	6.7	7	0.3	0.9	.269	0	1	9.45	-0.33	-0.25	-0.19
Guzman, J.	11	66.0	34	4.1	3.6	.534	4	4	4.64	0.17	0.22	0.84
Johns, D.	10	50.0	25	3.1	3.1	.497	2	2	4.50	0.20	-0.00	0.45
Kamieniecki, S.	11	50.7	40	2.8	4.4	.389	2	6	7.11	-1.20	-0.82	-0.26
Key, J.	11	65.0	33	4.5	2.9	.608	4	3	4.57	0.21	0.69	1.37
Lewis, R.	1	4.3	7	0.0	0.8	.025	0	0	14.54	-0.45	-0.36	-0.32
Munoz, B.	1	3.0	5	0.0	0.7	.026	0	0	15.00	-0.32	-0.31	-0.29
Mussina, M.	29	206.3	85	13.1	8.6	.603	13	10	3.71	2.58	2.17	3.86
Ponson, S.	20	113.0	68	6.0	7.0	.463	8	8	5.42	-0.65	-0.44	0.50
Rodriguez, N.	4	15.3	13	0.9	1.6	.352	1	3	7.63	-0.45	-0.32	-0.18
Smith, P.	4	18.0	19	0.4	2.2	.143	0	3	9.50	-0.89	-0.86	-0.73
TOTALS	162	956.0	548	55.2	59.0	.483	56	64	5.16	-2.87	-1.77	6.65

The Orioles' rotation went into a mini-freefall in 1998, sliding from baseball's fifth-best in 1997 to 14th best in 1998. The team SNVA dropped from +4.5 to -1.8, meaning that the rotation accounted for a loss of 6.3 games in the standings. What accounted for that loss? Drop-offs by Mike Mussina and Scott Erickson, and Jimmy Key's injury. Neither Mussina nor Erickson were bad in 1998, but they didn't pitch at their 1997 levels. Key was excellent in his few starts, but when he went down he was replaced by Sidney Ponson's below-average performance. According to SNVA, the difference between Key's '97 and Key+Ponson in '98 is 2.1 games. One other key to the decline was Doug Drabek, who doesn't belong in the majors. His SNPcts from 1995 to 1997 were .442, .413 and .414. That's in 30+ starts each season, so it's not like those numbers are skewed by a bad couple of games. It should have been pretty clear from his consistently bad numbers, or equally bad and equally consistent ERAs, that his glory days are now well past him, and that he has almost zero up-side.

Pitcher Abuse Points

PITCHER	AGE	GS	PAP	PAP/S	AAW	MAX	115+	130+
Drabek, Doug	35	21	2	0.10	0.10	102	0	0
Erickson, Scott	30	36	733	20.36	27.15	149	11	3
Guzman, Juan	31	11	104	9.45	11.03	127	2	0
Johns, Doug	30	10	0	0.00	0.00	89	0	0
Kamieniecki, Scott	34	11	0	0.00	0.00	97	0	0
Key, Jimmy	37	11	5	0.45	0.45	105	0	0
Mussina, Mike	29	29	520	17.93	26.90	136	10	2
Ponson, Sidney	21	20	123	6.15	17.43	125	3	0
TOTAL		162	1487	9.18	13.79	149	26	5
RANKING (AL)			8	8	9		9	6-T

Scott Erickson led all of baseball in games started and the AL in innings and complete games, so it's not a surprise that his workload is as high as it was. If you were going to lay a load on somebody's shoulder, Erickson is who I'd pick to carry it. He was 30, he'd been in the majors for nine years and he's a sinkerball pitcher who puts less strain on his shoulder than guys who rely on high heat. Erickson seems to thrive on lots of work, and his strikeout rate last season was by far the best of his career. Mussina was not worked as hard. The only other guys worth mentioning on this injury-riddled and largely ineffective staff are Juan Guzman, who was treated far more sensibly by Miller than he was by Blue Jays's skipper Tim Johnson, and Sidney Ponson, who got an aggressive but sensible workload in his rookie season.

Boston Red Sox

The Red Sox made the playoffs in 1998 and had the second best record in the league. Not that you'd know it if you were in Boston last year. You see, what should have been a great story was sullied by the strange soap opera between first baseman Mo Vaughn and Red Sox management.

General Manager Dan Duquette and Vaughn could never be accused of being chummy even in good times, but the epic battle between the strong-willed superstar and the measured GM took a variety of turns for the worse, and occasionally even into the bizarre. After '97, the off-season began with an oft-replayed comment from Vaughn claiming he would play for $5.5 million if the team showed a commitment to winning. Of course, such a statement should never be taken at face value. Does landing a reigning Cy Young winner qualify as showing a commitment towards winning? Apparently not, as the $75 million deal Pedro signed after the trade prompted an increase in Vaughn's asking price. Now it was about "respect."

With the battle lines drawn, the public soon took sides and debated their positions on talk radio, in the papers, and on the Internet. Over the course of the season, Vaughn vs. Duquette became the dominant issue, dwarfing the ongoing heroics by Nomar Garciaparra, Pedro Martinez, and the rest of an exciting Sox club. Each day, the Fenway faithful tried to answer the key questions in the brouhaha:

- Is Mo the heart and soul of the club? Will the premier power hitter dominate for the next five to seven years the way he's done for the past four? Or is he a loud-mouthed, overweight slugger heading into decline? A bully who tried to run the front office from the papers and TV?
- What of the enigmatic Dan Duquette? Is he an intelligent general manager and skillful roster strategist who recognizes the value of performance or a control freak who runs players out of town when they don't kowtow to him? Is he a cold, heartless computer geek running the Sox like his personal Rotisserie team? Or is he the fall guy for Sox management, handcuffed by budgetary restraints handed down from above and taking the blame that rightfully belongs to John Harrington?

The war of words stretched into the off-season, finally ending in a bitter divorce when Vaughn spurned the Sox, citing what amounted to hurt feelings. Two weeks after breaking off talks, he became the highest-paid player in baseball, signing a six-year, $80 million contract to play for Anaheim in the shadow of The Happiest Place on Earth. In light of the past 18 months, that has to have a lot of appeal.

Being spurned by Vaughn was the biggest blow in what has been a difficult winter for the Sox. While they have signed Jose Offerman to fill their leadoff hole, the loss of Vaughn and inability to sign a power-hitting free agent outfielder left them woefully short on sock.

The strength of the team is its few genuine superstars: Garciaparra and Martinez, plus the emergence of Tom Gordon as a top closer. Then there's the tier of average-plus players who can and will help a team—Tim Wakefield, Mike Stanley, John Valentin, and Scott Hatteberg. Continued performance at their established levels can reasonably be expected, and shouldn't hurt the team's chances.

Duquette has a fondness for picking up the infirm and hoping they can be nursed back to health. So as usual, there's a whole slew of players on the Hospital Squad—Reggie Jefferson, Jeff Frye, Lou Merloni, Butch Henry, Brian Rose, Pete Schourek, Robinson Checo, and Rich Garces. Henry and Frye missed almost the entire season after being pencilled in as key players.

Duquette's strategy can work. Bret Saberhagen was this year's shining success, throwing 175 innings of sub-4.00 ERA ball after missing all of 1996 and most of 1997. So far this off-season, Scavenger Dan's been looking at Kevin Appier (intriguing, expensive) and Mark Gubicza (ambulatory). The success of the team depends in large part of how many of these players can get healthy, stay healthy, and perform at close to their pre-injury level. Unfortunately, a significant portion of the starting rotation lies in this group. I call these

---

Red Sox Prospectus

1998 record: 92-70; Second place, AL East; Lost to Cleveland Indians in Division Series, 3-1

Pythagorean W/L: 96-66

Runs scored: 876 (3rd in AL)

Runs allowed: 729 (2nd in AL)

Team EQA: .274 (4th in AL)

Park: Fenway Park (moderate hitters')

1998: Pleasantly surprising season built around three stars and some overacheivers.

1999: Loss of Mo Vaughn and expected decline of outfielders will show up in the standings.

pitchers "lottery arms" because they're cheap and have great upsides, but rarely pay off. Which means the starting pitching could be anywhere from barely adequate to a real strength, depending on how many winning tickets Duquette can pick.

Then there's the Sox who had career years in '98 and who shouldn't be expected to contribute at a comparable level—Darren Lewis, Damon Buford, Midre Cummings, and Mike Benjamin. To be fair, Lewis and Buford, along with Darren Bragg, gave Sox fans outfield defense like they haven't seen this decade, but hit so far over their heads that a repeat is unlikely.

When you add Troy O'Leary's disappointing year to the mix, the outfield becomes a major concern for 1999. If Troy can't break a .340 OBP as a corner outfielder, he's a drag on the team. Maybe Duquette can pawn him off on a team that sees the 20+ home run season and a couple of .300 batting averages in the past and thinks he's useful. Hoping lightning will strike the Lewis/Buford/Cummings trio again is wishful thinking; none of them should be full-time players at this point, and all are expendable.

My wild card player for 1999 is John Valentin. He signed a four-year, $28 million contract before the 1998 season, but never really got out of the gate, posting a disappointing .247/.340/.442 instead of his usual .300/.370/.480. After posting an MVP-caliber performance in 1995, and above-average ones in the years since, he should have earned a reputation as one of the best middle infielders in the game. Instead he seems best-known as the whiner who was blocking Nomar's arrival in Boston.

In reality, Valentin is an excellent player when healthy, and he needs to rebound if the Sox want to get back to the post-season in 1999. He is fully capable of being one of the top third basemen in the league next year. That assumes that his perennial use as trade bait doesn't finally put him on some other team. A good John Valentin year gives the team four credible offensive threats (to support Nomar, Offerman, and Stanley), two of them playing tough defensive positions.

A handful of '98 role players might improve and balance the expected declines of last year's overachievers. They include Donnie Sadler, Darren Bragg, Jason Varitek, Jim Corsi, and Derek Lowe. Trot Nixon has a shot at improving the dismal outfield situation. Prospects like Cole Liniak and Dernell Stenson might get a taste of the majors. Korean import Jin Ho Cho turned a lot of heads in Trenton and could be ready by mid-season. James Chamblee and David Eckstein are moving up through the minors as well.

The Sox needed to do three things in the off-season: replace Vaughn, overhaul the outfield, and stabilize the pitching staff. As of mid-December, none of these things have been done. They probably have enough lottery arms to stitch together a makeshift rotation behind Pedro. With Mo gone, replacing his bat and overhauling the outfield could be combined into a single step with the right move. The Sox are a team on the cusp. Without making major moves, they could still threaten for the wild-card, but would probably fall short. A couple of key upgrades could make them into the favorites for the wild card, and even get them into contention for the division if the Yankees return to mortality.

Particularly important in evaluating the Red Sox is understanding their uncertain ownership and ballpark situations. John Harrington doesn't own the team—he's running it on behalf of the Yawkey trust, and he's bound in ways other teams aren't by certain fiscal responsibilities in administering the trust. He's presumably looking for new ownership, though there are doubts about how quickly the search is progressing. Meanwhile, Fenway Park is ancient and decaying, and won't provide the luxury box revenues a team needs to support an upper-tier payroll. The flip side of this is that Fenway is still beloved by legions of fans. They'll resist any effort to replace the little bandbox. Expect a concerted effort to create a definitive plan for a new ballpark during 1999 despite increasing opposition from the rank-and-file fans.

A triple whammy of losing Clemens, Vaughn, and Fenway within five years could be enough to do long-term damage to the team's regional popularity. Retaining Vaughn would have been a public relations boost to help push through a new ballpark, much as the Giants locked up Barry Bonds until Pacific Bell Park is ready. Breaking the bank to get a team to the World Series once or twice in the next couple of years might be prudent as well, just as the Padres's World Series appearance boosted the stadium ballot measure in San Diego this year. Securing a new ballpark on favorable terms is worth a lot more long-term than a couple of years' expense for a top-heavy payroll.

Losing Vaughn in a nasty Clemens-like divorce could hamper efforts to win support for a new home for the Red Sox. In Duquette's worst-case scenario, Vaughn could add insult to injury by triumphantly returning to Fenway in an Angel uniform for the 1999 All-Star game, and letting loose with some long-ball heroics. That kind of return will be a lot easier to take if the Sox are playing well. Unless they can add power, it's unlikely they will be.

HITTERS (Averages: BA .260/ OBA .330/ SA .420, EQA .260)

Billy Ashley   DH/1B   Bats R   Age 28

YEAR	TEAM	LGE	AB	H	DB	TP	HR	BB	R	RBI	SB	CS	OUT	BA	OBA	SA	EQA	EQR	DEFENSE
1996	LosAngls	NL	111	23	4	1	9	22	15	20	0	0	88	.207	.338	.505	.283	19	26-OF 84
1997	LosAngls	NL	131	33	7	0	6	9	13	17	0	0	98	.252	.300	.443	.252	16	25-OF 84
1998	Pawtuckt	Int	216	50	7	0	9	28	23	26	1	0	166	.231	.320	.389	.248	25	20-1B 91
1998	Boston	AL	24	7	3	0	3	2	5	6	0	0	17	.292	.346	.792	.345	6	
1999	*Boston*	*AL*	*197*	*48*	*8*	*0*	*12*	*26*	*25*	*32*	*1*	*0*	*149*	*.244*	*.332*	*.467*	*.271*	*28*	

Starred in a spring training mini-drama in which it was unclear if the Sox were going to trade for him or if the Dodgers were going to simply release him. Duquette waited and scooped him up after he was cut. A prototypical all-or-nothing slugger, Ashley's a free agent and not likely to return.

Mike Benjamin   IF   Bats R   Age 33

YEAR	TEAM	LGE	AB	H	DB	TP	HR	BB	R	RBI	SB	CS	OUT	BA	OBA	SA	EQA	EQR	DEFENSE
1996	Philadel	NL	103	23	5	1	4	13	13	12	3	1	81	.223	.310	.408	.250	13	24-SS 118
1997	Pawtuckt	Int	104	22	1	1	3	6	7	8	3	1	83	.212	.255	.327	.200	7	27-SS 99
1997	Boston	AL	115	26	10	1	0	4	8	7	2	3	92	.226	.252	.330	.190	7	
1998	Boston	AL	344	92	13	0	7	17	30	34	3	0	252	.267	.302	.366	.232	33	73-2B 94
1999	*Pittsbrg*	*NL*	*268*	*68*	*13*	*1*	*6*	*15*	*24*	*27*	*4*	*2*	*202*	*.254*	*.293*	*.377*	*.232*	*26*	

Benjamin picked a good time to have a career year. With Frye lost for the season in spring training, he got a chance to get 300 at bats. He proved that, on his good days, he's replacement-level. For his trouble he received a two-year contract with the Pirates.

Darren Bragg   RF   Bats L   Age 29

YEAR	TEAM	LGE	AB	H	DB	TP	HR	BB	R	RBI	SB	CS	OUT	BA	OBA	SA	EQA	EQR	DEFENSE
1996	Tacoma	PCL	71	18	3	0	3	12	10	10	1	0	53	.254	.361	.423	.277	11	16-OF 98
1996	Seattle	AL	190	51	11	1	7	32	32	26	8	6	145	.268	.374	.447	.282	31	53-OF 98
1996	Boston	AL	215	50	11	1	3	34	28	19	6	5	170	.233	.337	.335	.240	24	49-OF 117
1997	Boston	AL	505	129	35	2	9	62	67	53	10	6	382	.255	.337	.386	.254	62	145-OF 108
1998	Boston	AL	402	110	29	3	8	44	53	49	4	3	295	.274	.345	.420	.266	54	111-OF 96
1999	*Boston*	*AL*	*450*	*118*	*27*	*2*	*11*	*58*	*64*	*55*	*9*	*5*	*337*	*.262*	*.346*	*.404*	*.261*	*58*	

Long ago, I had hopes that Bragg would turn out to be a better hitter when given a chance to play full-time. He got that chance, and it didn't happen. He's not the biggest problem on the team, but as a league-average hitter and corner outfielder, he's very replaceable.

Damon Buford   CF   Bats R   Age 29

YEAR	TEAM	LGE	AB	H	DB	TP	HR	BB	R	RBI	SB	CS	OUT	BA	OBA	SA	EQA	EQR	DEFENSE
1996	Texas	AL	140	37	6	0	6	14	19	17	8	6	109	.264	.331	.436	.260	19	66-OF 81
1997	Texas	AL	361	79	12	0	10	30	36	28	19	7	289	.219	.279	.335	.218	32	112-OF 104
1998	Boston	AL	212	59	14	4	10	23	30	35	4	5	158	.278	.349	.524	.287	35	55-OF 107
1999	*Boston*	*AL*	*240*	*60*	*12*	*1*	*9*	*25*	*30*	*30*	*7*	*5*	*185*	*.250*	*.321*	*.421*	*.252*	*29*	

I wasn't all that enthralled with the Buford acquisition, but he went out and made a fool out of me. Solid defense in center field and a nice blast of unexpected power, entirely against left-handers. I expect some regression to the mean next year. The projection looks about right if he doesn't stick to a platoon role.

James Chamblee   2B   Bats R   Age 24

YEAR	TEAM	LGE	AB	H	DB	TP	HR	BB	R	RBI	SB	CS	OUT	BA	OBA	SA	EQA	EQR	DEFENSE	
1996	Michigan	Mid	308	60	11	1	1	10	12	12	1	1	249	.195	.220	.247	.134	8	85-SS 85	
1997	Michigan	Mid	491	127	14	1	16	38	50	55	9	3	367	.259	.312	.389	.244	54	103-2B 94	22-SS 101
1998	Trenton	Eas	491	112	25	2	15	54	52	51	7	4	383	.228	.305	.379	.237	53	131-2B 92	
1999	*Boston*	*AL*	*476*	*118*	*19*	*1*	*13*	*40*	*49*	*51*	*6*	*2*	*360*	*.248*	*.306*	*.374*	*.234*	*48*		

(James Chamblee *continued*)

Chamblee's a walking optical illusion. He looks tall and lanky out on the field, but up close you can see that his 6'4" frame is filled out. A free swinger, he doesn't hit for average and strikes out a lot, but he has some pop. He's squeezed at second base by the Offerman signing above him and by Eckstein below, so they may try him in center field next year.

Michael Coleman   CF   Bats R   Age 23

YEAR	TEAM	LGE	AB	H	DB	TP	HR	BB	R	RBI	SB	CS	OUT	BA	OBA	SA	EQA	EQR	DEFENSE
1996	Sarasota	Fla	409	94	17	3	2	32	37	26	13	4	319	.230	.286	.301	.207	31	108-OF 102
1997	Trenton	Eas	384	108	14	6	11	34	52	49	15	5	281	.281	.340	.435	.270	53	100-OF 107
1997	Pawtuckt	Int	112	34	7	1	7	10	17	21	3	2	80	.304	.361	.571	.305	21	27-OF 96
1998	Pawtuckt	Int	335	77	8	0	12	24	27	32	8	7	265	.230	.281	.361	.219	30	86-OF 99
1999	*Boston*	*AL*	*354*	*92*	*14*	*2*	*11*	*27*	*41*	*41*	*10*	*5*	*267*	*.260*	*.312*	*.404*	*.245*	*40*	

After a breakthrough 1997 season, Coleman ended 1998 branded with the scarlet letter "A" for "Attitude Problem." He regressed substantially in his first full season at Triple-A. He can be outstanding when he plays hard. If he can revert to 1997 form, all will be forgiven; another disappointing campaign will probably cement his reputation.

Midre Cummings   PH/RF   Bats L   Age 27

YEAR	TEAM	LGE	AB	H	DB	TP	HR	BB	R	RBI	SB	CS	OUT	BA	OBA	SA	EQA	EQR	DEFENSE
1996	Calgary	PCL	357	94	16	2	7	19	33	36	5	3	266	.263	.301	.378	.234	35	77-OF 102
1997	Pittsbrg	NL	105	19	5	2	3	9	8	8	0	0	86	.181	.246	.352	.201	8	20-OF 105
1996	Pittsbrg	NL	84	18	2	1	3	1	4	7	0	0	66	.214	.224	.369	.192		517-OF 119
1997	Philadel	NL	208	63	17	4	1	24	31	27	1	3	148	.303	.375	.438	.280	31	43-OF 109
1998	Boston	AL	118	33	5	0	6	17	17	19	3	3	88	.280	.370	.475	.286	19	
1999	*Boston*	*AL*	*209*	*54*	*11*	*1*	*6*	*19*	*24*	*25*	*2*	*2*	*157*	*.258*	*.320*	*.407*	*.247*	*24*	

Cummings hit .350/.458/.700 as a pinch hitter, and made Jimy Williams look like a genius several times early in the season. He was another Duquette pickup that had me scratching my head at the time, but which paid dividends. Melding Cummings with Buford would yield a pretty decent outfielder, so it's a shame they have to consume two roster spots.

Joe DePastino   C   Bats R   Age 25

YEAR	TEAM	LGE	AB	H	DB	TP	HR	BB	R	RBI	SB	CS	OUT	BA	OBA	SA	EQA	EQR	DEFENSE
1996	Sarasota	Fla	345	80	9	1	7	24	25	28	1	2	267	.232	.282	.325	.207	26	
1997	Trenton	Eas	277	65	8	1	13	25	26	34	1	1	213	.235	.298	.412	.242	31	
1998	Trenton	Eas	275	73	7	0	9	23	27	33	2	0	202	.265	.322	.389	.249	31	56-C 102
1999	*Boston*	*AL*	*298*	*76*	*9*	*0*	*9*	*22*	*28*	*33*	*1*	*1*	*223*	*.255*	*.306*	*.376*	*.232*	*29*	

A favorite with Trenton pitchers, who apparently love throwing to him. That kind of reputation may get him to the majors faster than his bat, and he isn't all that terrible as a hitter. An injury may have prevented him from having a breakout season; that projection looks low to me.

David Eckstein   2B   Bats R   Age 24

YEAR	TEAM	LGE	AB	H	DB	TP	HR	BB	R	RBI	SB	CS	OUT	BA	OBA	SA	EQA	EQR	DEFENSE
1997	Lowell	NYP	252	52	5	1	2	22	17	13	7	3	203	.206	.270	.258	.183	14	64-2B 99
1998	Sarasota	Fla	501	119	17	1	3	67	59	35	18	9	391	.238	.327	.293	.226	48	115-2B 101
1999	*Boston*	*AL*	*379*	*96*	*12*	*1*	*3*	*44*	*46*	*31*	*14*	*6*	*289*	*.253*	*.331*	*.314*	*.231*	*37*	

He may be inheriting the organization's mantle of "second baseman of the future" from Donnie Sadler, despite Sadler's playing in the majors while Eckstein's in A-ball at the same age. Finished in the top 10 in the league in hitting, and is considered solid defensively. Set a Sarasota team record for steals. Eckstein made a nice jump in production from 1997, but he needs to follow it up with a similar jump this year at Double-A.

Jeff Frye   2B   Bats R   Age 32

YEAR	TEAM	LGE	AB	H	DB	TP	HR	BB	R	RBI	SB	CS	OUT	BA	OBA	SA	EQA	EQR	DEFENSE
1995	Texas	AL	307	83	14	2	4	22	31	31	3	3	227	.270	.319	.368	.238	31	79-2B 100
1996	Boston	AL	405	107	23	2	4	51	60	37	19	5	303	.264	.346	.360	.257	51	100-2B 106
1997	Boston	AL	397	123	37	2	3	28	62	44	19	8	282	.310	.355	.436	.275	56	79-2B 102
1999	*Boston*	*AL*	*191*	*52*	*14*	*1*	*2*	*20*	*27*	*20*	*6*	*3*	*142*	*.272*	*.341*	*.387*	*.254*	*23*	

The official "big blow" that threatened the Red Sox season came during spring training, when Frye went down with a knee injury. Fresh off signing a three-year contract, Jeff was supposed to be the starting second baseman. Instead, the Sox paraded Lemke, Benjamin, Merloni, and Sadler through the position, and still made it to the playoffs. Frye owes his career to Duquette, who plucked him out of Texas's minors in 1996. Even if he's healthy, he'll be hard-pressed to do much more than win a utility role now that Jose Offerman is under contract.

Nomar Garciaparra　　SS　　　Bats R　Age 25

YEAR	TEAM	LGE	AB	H	DB	TP	HR	BB	R	RBI	SB	CS	OUT	BA	OBA	SA	EQA	EQR	DEFENSE
1996	Pawtuckt	Int	168	55	10	1	14	14	27	38	2	1	114	.327	.379	.649	.331	36	42-SS 104
1996	Boston	AL	85	19	2	2	4	4	10	9	5	0	66	.224	.258	.435	.244	10	18-SS 99
1997	Boston	AL	673	205	42	11	31	37	96	110	23	9	477	.305	.341	.538	.293	111	151-SS 99
1998	Boston	AL	593	190	36	8	35	36	87	113	11	6	409	.320	.359	.585	.309	109	143-SS 99
1999	*Boston*	*AL*	*584*	*180*	*37*	*9*	*33*	*34*	*92*	*114*	*15*	*0*	*404*	*.318*	*.350*	*.582*	*.307*	*105*	

As a fan, the most bittersweet moment of the entire season came at the end of the Division Series Game 4, watching Nomar waving and rallying the crowd until the very end, then coming out of the dugout after the game to thank the fans. As much as it hurt to lose, you had to feel like the future is in good hands with this kid. Sure you'd like him to take a few more walks, but a shortstop who hits like Jim Rice in his prime and shows as much class as this one is someone more than special.

David Gibralter　　1B　　　Bats R　Age 24

YEAR	TEAM	LGE	AB	H	DB	TP	HR	BB	R	RBI	SB	CS	OUT	BA	OBA	SA	EQA	EQR	DEFENSE
1996	Sarasota	Fla	451	118	18	1	14	27	42	51	5	5	338	.262	.303	.399	.240	47	93-1B 96
1997	Trenton	Eas	478	120	17	1	12	35	43	48	3	3	361	.251	.302	.366	.230	46	114-1B 104
1998	Trenton	Eas	384	93	8	0	14	22	29	40	2	2	293	.242	.283	.372	.223	34	90-1B 83
1999	*Boston*	*AL*	*423*	*114*	*14*	*1*	*14*	*25*	*42*	*52*	*3*	*2*	*311*	*.270*	*.310*	*.407*	*.243*	*45*	

Gibralter was frustrated about not being at Triple-A in '98, but was very professional about it. He has a good defensive reputation, which runs counter to his rating above, but is still overmatched on offense. He must reverse the decline of the past three years in order to salvage any chance at a career.

Scott Hatteberg　　C　　　Bats L　Age 29

YEAR	TEAM	LGE	AB	H	DB	TP	HR	BB	R	RBI	SB	CS	OUT	BA	OBA	SA	EQA	EQR	DEFENSE
1996	Pawtuckt	Int	285	62	8	0	8	49	32	29	1	1	224	.218	.332	.330	.238	31	
1997	Boston	AL	344	94	21	1	11	41	45	47	0	1	251	.273	.351	.436	.272	48	
1998	Boston	AL	353	96	19	1	13	44	46	50	0	0	257	.272	.353	.442	.275	51	103-C 100
1999	*Boston*	*AL*	*335*	*88*	*15*	*0*	*14*	*46*	*45*	*50*	*0*	*0*	*247*	*.263*	*.352*	*.433*	*.270*	*47*	

Talk about consistency...Bill James developed a measure called Similarity Scores to compare career or season totals. Hatteberg's 1997–98 was the fourth-most-similar season pair in history, and the closest since Red Kress's 1930–31 seasons (thanks to Tom Ruane for the details). Hatteberg is a good bet to make it three in a row.

Reggie Jefferson　　DH　　　Bats L　Age 30

YEAR	TEAM	LGE	AB	H	DB	TP	HR	BB	R	RBI	SB	CS	OUT	BA	OBA	SA	EQA	EQR	DEFENSE
1996	Boston	AL	372	122	28	4	17	23	53	69	0	0	250	.328	.367	.562	.309	66	32-OF 94
1997	Boston	AL	481	153	30	1	14	25	58	71	1	2	330	.318	.352	.472	.280	69	
1998	Boston	AL	192	58	15	1	8	22	29	33	0	0	134	.302	.374	.516	.301	33	
1999	*Boston*	*AL*	*307*	*96*	*21*	*1*	*12*	*21*	*42*	*52*	*0*	*0*	*211*	*.313*	*.357*	*.505*	*.289*	*48*	

Reggie Jefferson has exactly one skill—hitting right-handed pitching. He can't run, he can't field, he can't throw, and he can't hit left-handers. But he does his one trick so well that he's still valuable to have around. He may have to put on a first baseman's glove on a Vaughn-less Red Sox team, sharing duties with Mike Stanley.

Mark Lemke   2B   Bats B   Age 33

YEAR	TEAM	LGE	AB	H	DB	TP	HR	BB	R	RBI	SB	CS	OUT	BA	OBA	SA	EQA	EQR	DEFENSE
1996	Atlanta	NL	495	122	10	0	7	55	46	43	4	2	375	.246	.322	.309	.225	45	128-2B 116
1997	Atlanta	NL	351	86	17	1	2	35	34	28	2	0	265	.245	.313	.316	.223	31	95-2B 122
1998	Boston	AL	90	16	4	0	0	6	3	3	0	1	75	.178	.229	.222	.125	2	27-2B 95
1999	*Boston*	*AL*	*205*	*46*	*5*	*0*	*3*	*21*	*17*	*15*	*1*	*1*	*160*	*.224*	*.296*	*.293*	*.202*	*15*	

Possibly the most execrable decision of last season was signing Lemke and actually letting him onto the field for 100 at-bats. It was a concession from the front office to manager Jimy Williams, who worked with Lemke in Atlanta, and represented cronyism at its worst. Mercifully, Lemke got injured and didn't play after May. While I wish him a full recovery, I hope he enjoys his health in retirement.

Darren Lewis   CF   Bats R   Age 31

YEAR	TEAM	LGE	AB	H	DB	TP	HR	BB	R	RBI	SB	CS	OUT	BA	OBA	SA	EQA	EQR	DEFENSE
1996	ChiSox	AL	333	75	12	2	4	43	44	23	23	6	264	.225	.314	.309	.232	34	117-OF 98
1997	ChiSox	AL	76	18	1	0	0	11	13	3	11	4	62	.237	.333	.250	.230	8	51-OF 84
1997	LosAngls	NL	78	24	4	1	1	6	10	10	2	2	56	.308	.357	.423	.267	10	18-OF 111
1998	Boston	AL	575	152	25	3	8	73	81	55	26	12	435	.264	.347	.360	.254	71	150-OF 108
1999	*Boston*	*AL*	*409*	*108*	*17*	*2*	*7*	*52*	*60*	*42*	*19*	*9*	*310*	*.264*	*.347*	*.367*	*.253*	*50*	

Deserves every bit of his considerable defensive reputation. The Sox picked up a bonus with a smidgen of offense out of him in '98, but don't expect that to hold up. Re-signed for three years, at the end of which he'll be no better than fourth outfielder material. Mistakenly classified as a leadoff hitter.

Cole Liniak   3B   Bats R   Age 22

YEAR	TEAM	LGE	AB	H	DB	TP	HR	BB	R	RBI	SB	CS	OUT	BA	OBA	SA	EQA	EQR	DEFENSE	
1996	Michigan	Mid	449	109	17	1	4	45	42	36	4	3	343	.243	.312	.312	.220	39	111-3B	103
1997	Sarasota	Fla	216	65	6	0	7	19	26	30	1	1	152	.301	.357	.426	.272	29	58-3B	95
1997	Trenton	Eas	200	51	5	0	3	13	15	17	0	1	150	.255	.300	.325	.215	16	45-3B	91
1998	Pawtuckt	Int	423	101	21	1	15	34	40	47	3	3	325	.239	.295	.400	.237	45	107-3B	88
1999	*Boston*	*AL*	*420*	*114*	*14*	*0*	*15*	*33*	*45*	*55*	*2*	*2*	*308*	*.271*	*.325*	*.412*	*.251*	*49*		

Along with Stenson, the top position player prospect in the system. He had an excellent season for a 21-year-old at Triple-A. His defense improved during the season, so I'm not too worried about that rating. Since he's blocked by Valentin, Liniak may see some time in the outfield in '99.

Steve Lomasney   C   Bats R   Age 21

YEAR	TEAM	LGE	AB	H	DB	TP	HR	BB	R	RBI	SB	CS	OUT	BA	OBA	SA	EQA	EQR	DEFENSE
1996	Lowell	NYP	180	22	3	0	4	33	10	7	1	0	158	.122	.258	.206	.159	8	
1997	Michigan	Mid	327	82	15	2	10	24	31	37	2	2	247	.251	.302	.401	.240	35	
1998	Sarasota	Fla	441	92	9	1	17	49	38	43	6	3	352	.209	.288	.349	.222	41	83-C 98
1999	*Boston*	*AL*	*416*	*98*	*11*	*0*	*20*	*45*	*44*	*54*	*4*	*2*	*320*	*.236*	*.310*	*.406*	*.245*	*47*	

The Sox system has several good catching prospects: Lomasney, Sapp, Chevalier, McKeel, and Depastino. Lomasney is one of the better ones. He set a single season home run record at Sarasota last year, and is willing to take a walk.

Walt McKeel   C/1B   Bats R   Age 27

YEAR	TEAM	LGE	AB	H	DB	TP	HR	BB	R	RBI	SB	CS	OUT	BA	OBA	SA	EQA	EQR	DEFENSE	
1996	Trenton	Eas	468	125	11	1	12	48	49	54	2	2	345	.267	.335	.372	.248	53	36-1B	86
1997	Pawtuckt	Int	236	52	8	0	5	28	21	20	0	1	185	.220	.303	.318	.217	20	16-1B	73
1998	Pawtuckt	Int	167	39	7	1	2	17	15	14	1	1	129	.234	.304	.323	.219	15	33-C	88
1999	*Boston*	*AL*	*235*	*57*	*6*	*0*	*7*	*24*	*23*	*25*	*1*	*1*	*179*	*.243*	*.313*	*.357*	*.231*	*23*		

McKeel lost a couple of months to back surgery in '98. The big expectations the Sox had for him heading into 1997 have diminished. Offensively, he looked out of whack at the plate after the surgery, and looked rusty behind the plate. The good news is that he can still catch, which might buy him a little more time to put it all together.

Lou Merloni   IF   Bats R   Age 28

YEAR	TEAM	LGE	AB	H	DB	TP	HR	BB	R	RBI	SB	CS	OUT	BA	OBA	SA	EQA	EQR	DEFENSE
1996	Trenton	Eas	96	19	2	1	2	7	5	6	0	1	78	.198	.252	.302	.181	5	19-3B 105
1996	Pawtuckt	Int	113	22	3	0	1	9	5	5	0	1	92	.195	.254	.248	.160	5	
1997	Trenton	Eas	255	65	10	2	3	21	25	23	2	1	191	.255	.312	.345	.230	24	53-3B 92
1997	Pawtuckt	Int	163	41	4	0	4	12	13	16	0	1	123	.252	.303	.350	.224	15	33-2B 97
1998	Pawtuckt	Int	86	29	2	1	5	12	14	18	1	1	58	.337	.418	.558	.327	18	
1998	Boston	AL	94	26	5	0	1	8	11	9	1	0	68	.277	.333	.362	.247	10	24-2B 95
1999	*Boston*	*AL*	*243*	*65*	*7*	*1*	*7*	*24*	*27*	*30*	*1*	*2*	*180*	*.267*	*.333*	*.391*	*.248*	*28*	

Local kid makes good. Merloni got off to a red-hot start at Pawtucket, got called up, and played well in Boston. Then he injured his knee. He has a good defensive rep at second base, and can also play third. He'll be in the backup infielder mix, battling Frye and Sadler.

Keith Mitchell   OF   Bats R   Age 29

YEAR	TEAM	LGE	AB	H	DB	TP	HR	BB	R	RBI	SB	CS	OUT	BA	OBA	SA	EQA	EQR	DEFENSE	
1996	Indianap	AA	365	100	15	1	12	57	56	49	8	1	266	.274	.372	.419	.282	56	43-OF 89	21-1B 90
1997	Indianap	AA	413	99	15	1	11	61	52	44	8	3	317	.240	.338	.361	.250	49	79-OF 97	
1998	Pawtuckt	Int	208	55	8	0	8	35	30	29	2	2	155	.264	.370	.418	.276	31	39-OF 99	
1998	Boston	AL	32	9	1	0	0	7	6	3	1	0	23	.281	.410	.312	.278	5		
1999	*Boston*	*AL*	*328*	*85*	*9*	*0*	*14*	*55*	*48*	*48*	*4*	*1*	*244*	*.259*	*.366*	*.415*	*.274*	*48*		

Good minor league hitter who's hasn't gotten a real shot yet: fewer than 250 at-bats in the majors spread over seven years. Nothing special defensively. Too old to be a prospect, but impressed enough people in Boston during his call-up that he's likely to be a useful bench player next year.

Tim Naehring   3B   Bats R   Age 32

YEAR	TEAM	LGE	AB	H	DB	TP	HR	BB	R	RBI	SB	CS	OUT	BA	OBA	SA	EQA	EQR	DEFENSE
1995	Boston	AL	424	130	25	2	11	74	71	66	0	2	296	.307	.410	.453	.302	74	121-3B 102
1996	Boston	AL	416	111	13	0	16	46	48	55	2	1	306	.267	.340	.413	.262	54	113-3B 100
1997	Boston	AL	254	72	18	1	9	39	40	39	1	1	183	.283	.379	.469	.292	42	65-3B 94
1999	*Boston*	*AL*	*129*	*35*	*6*	*0*	*5*	*18*	*18*	*19*	*0*	*0*	*94*	*.271*	*.361*	*.434*	*.275*	*19*	

What kind of career could Tim Naehring have had if he'd stayed healthy? A back-of-the-envelope estimate puts him in Bob Watson and Bill Madlock territory. Not Cooperstown material, but if his career is over, as it appears now, he deserved better. Well-liked in Boston for taking less money to stay in Boston instead of jumping to Cleveland.

Trot Nixon   OF   Bats L   Age 25

YEAR	TEAM	LGE	AB	H	DB	TP	HR	BB	R	RBI	SB	CS	OUT	BA	OBA	SA	EQA	EQR	DEFENSE
1996	Trenton	Eas	442	105	9	2	10	43	39	41	6	5	342	.238	.305	.335	.223	40	116-OF 100
1997	Pawtuckt	Int	472	108	13	2	18	56	51	52	9	3	367	.229	.311	.379	.242	53	129-OF 102
1998	Pawtuckt	Int	499	139	18	3	18	66	73	68	18	10	370	.279	.363	.435	.277	75	124-OF 93
1998	Boston	AL	27	7	1	0	0	1	2	2	0	0	20	.259	.286	.296	.197	2	
1999	*Boston*	*AL*	*479*	*124*	*14*	*2*	*18*	*57*	*61*	*63*	*10*	*6*	*361*	*.259*	*.338*	*.409*	*.258*	*61*	

Maybe the nagging back injuries are gone, because he finally had the breakthrough year that's been expected of him. He and Andy Abad were both 20-20 players at Pawtucket, but Nixon got there first. He is well-rounded—hits well, runs well, throws well. He was on the post-season roster, demonstrating the club's confidence in his maturity, and he may be handed a starting job in spring training.

Troy O'Leary   LF   Bats L   Age 29

YEAR	TEAM	LGE	AB	H	DB	TP	HR	BB	R	RBI	SB	CS	OUT	BA	OBA	SA	EQA	EQR	DEFENSE
1996	Boston	AL	484	116	27	5	13	43	49	53	3	2	370	.240	.302	.397	.240	52	129-OF 92
1997	Boston	AL	491	151	30	4	16	40	63	76	0	5	345	.308	.360	.483	.284	74	129-OF 97
1998	Boston	AL	602	160	34	8	23	39	66	82	2	2	444	.266	.310	.463	.261	77	153-OF 96
1999	*Boston*	*AL*	*558*	*148*	*32*	*4*	*19*	*43*	*63*	*75*	*1*	*3*	*413*	*.265*	*.318*	*.439*	*.255*	*68*	

(Troy O'Leary *continued*)

The prototypical Duquette success story: a waiver-wire pickup that turned into a solid major leaguer. He's got an annoying habit of alternating good years with bad ones. He's "due" for a good year, but if I were Duquette, I'd try to parlay his 23-homer season and two previous .300 batting averages into something cheaper. One of Duquette's worst decisions was long-terming him after his 27-year-old career year in 1997.

Arquimedez Pozo   2B   Bats R   Age 25

YEAR	TEAM	LGE	AB	H	DB	TP	HR	BB	R	RBI	SB	CS	OUT	BA	OBA	SA	EQA	EQR	DEFENSE
1996	Tacoma	PCL	363	98	10	2	15	36	42	50	3	2	267	.270	.336	.433	.265	48	74-3B 80
1997	Pawtuckt	Int	373	100	11	1	20	33	42	56	3	3	276	.268	.328	.464	.268	51	85-3B 99
1998	Pawtuckt	Int	341	93	15	3	10	19	34	42	3	2	250	.273	.311	.422	.250	39	53-2B 92
1999	*Boston*	*AL*	*351*	*97*	*15*	*2*	*13*	*24*	*40*	*49*	*3*	*2*	*256*	*.276*	*.323*	*.442*	*.258*	*43*	

One of the biggest mysteries in Boston last year was why Pozo never even got a shot at second base after Frye went down. A good hitter who's been ready to bat against major league pitching for three years. Presumably, his defense was holding him back, though I don't see it in the ratings above. Sold to Japan.

Donnie Sadler   2B   Bats R   Age 24

YEAR	TEAM	LGE	AB	H	DB	TP	HR	BB	R	RBI	SB	CS	OUT	BA	OBA	SA	EQA	EQR	DEFENSE	
1996	Trenton	Eas	456	116	17	5	6	33	55	38	26	6	346	.254	.305	.353	.237	47	78-SS 100	27-OF 117
1997	Pawtuckt	Int	479	93	15	1	10	50	39	30	16	11	397	.194	.270	.292	.195	33	79-2B 101	46-SS 97
1998	Pawtuckt	Int	130	26	3	1	2	23	18	9	8	1	105	.200	.320	.285	.231	13	32-2B 99	
1998	Boston	AL	122	27	3	4	3	7	11	12	4	0	95	.221	.264	.385	.226	12	37-2B 92	
1999	*Boston*	*AL*	*350*	*82*	*13*	*3*	*7*	*34*	*41*	*31*	*15*	*5*	*273*	*.234*	*.302*	*.349*	*.229*	*34*		

Still considered a good prospect by some, but has gotten jerked around so much both in level and position that you wonder if it's affecting his development. The Offerman signing probably closes his window in this organization. Sadler is fast and excellent defensively, but must start hitting.

Damian Sapp   C   Bats R   Age 23

YEAR	TEAM	LGE	AB	H	DB	TP	HR	BB	R	RBI	SB	CS	OUT	BA	OBA	SA	EQA	EQR	DEFENSE
1996	Michigan	Mid	343	106	11	2	16	28	44	57	2	1	238	.309	.361	.493	.290	54	
1998	Sarasota	Fla	126	26	5	0	5	13	10	13	0	0	100	.206	.281	.365	.222	12	
1998	Trenton	Eas	91	21	3	0	5	8	8	12	0	0	70	.231	.293	.429	.245	10	19-C 79
1999	*Boston*	*AL*	*174*	*45*	*7*	*0*	*7*	*16*	*20*	*23*	*1*	*0*	*129*	*.259*	*.321*	*.420*	*.254*	*21*	

A huge rock of a man whose season was cut short by injury. He was involved in a brawl during the Eastern League all-star game and was hit by a retaliatory pitch the next day that knocked him out for the rest of the season. He looked overmatched at Trenton, both offensively and defensively. Still very raw behind the plate.

Mike Stanley   DH/1B   Bats R   Age 36

YEAR	TEAM	LGE	AB	H	DB	TP	HR	BB	R	RBI	SB	CS	OUT	BA	OBA	SA	EQA	EQR	DEFENSE
1996	Boston	AL	383	96	19	1	21	65	56	61	2	0	287	.251	.359	.470	.286	63	
1997	Boston	AL	255	76	13	1	14	39	40	47	0	1	180	.298	.391	.522	.309	48	23-1B 97
1997	NY Yanks	AL	86	25	6	0	4	15	14	15	0	0	61	.291	.396	.500	.308	16	
1998	Boston	AL	153	43	8	0	8	27	25	26	1	0	110	.281	.389	.490	.303	28	
1998	Toronto	AL	335	79	11	0	22	57	45	54	2	1	257	.236	.347	.466	.279	53	20-1B 94
1999	*Boston*	*AL*	*392*	*97*	*14*	*0*	*24*	*73*	*59*	*68*	*1*	*1*	*296*	*.247*	*.366*	*.467*	*.285*	*64*	

Since Stanley doesn't catch anymore, he can now legally use the phrase "professional hitter" on his business card. A stathead favorite for some time, Boston will look to him to share the first base duties now that Vaughn has left.

Dernell Stenson   OF   Bats L   Age 21

YEAR	TEAM	LGE	AB	H	DB	TP	HR	BB	R	RBI	SB	CS	OUT	BA	OBA	SA	EQA	EQR	DEFENSE
1997	Michigan	Mid	477	125	18	1	14	58	57	58	3	2	354	.262	.342	.392	.258	60	105-OF 83
1998	Trenton	Eas	507	125	14	1	22	76	63	68	4	2	384	.247	.345	.408	.264	69	129-OF 92
1999	*Boston*	*AL*	*461*	*129*	*15*	*0*	*21*	*60*	*63*	*74*	*2*	*1*	*333*	*.280*	*.363*	*.449*	*.279*	*69*	

The most coveted prospect in the Boston system. Has power and patience rarely found in such a young player. Stenson adds another rare dimension—maturity. Not fast afoot, and has had some problems tracking fly balls. He's more comfortable in right field, and has a good arm. Moving him to first base, as has been rumored, would be a waste. Trivia: Stenson's the only player in Trenton history to hit a ball over the ballpark's scoreboard.

John Valentin 3B Bats R Age 32

YEAR	TEAM	LGE	AB	H	DB	TP	HR	BB	R	RBI	SB	CS	OUT	BA	OBA	SA	EQA	EQR	DEFENSE	
1996	Boston	AL	509	141	26	3	12	59	65	63	8	12	379	.277	.352	.411	.262	67	117-SS 102	
1997	Boston	AL	565	172	45	5	19	59	87	89	7	4	397	.304	.370	.503	.296	95	78-2B 108	63-3B 98
1998	Boston	AL	579	140	35	2	25	79	73	79	3	5	444	.242	.333	.439	.264	79	152-3B 117	
1999	Boston	AL	564	146	36	2	22	71	77	81	4	5	423	.259	.342	.447	.267	78		

Overlooked as an MVP candidate back in 1995, Valentin still hasn't earned the respect he deserves. He's finally found a home at third base, where his defensive play was exceptional. My favorite player since Jim Rice, but I recognize that his big new contract makes him trade bait, but I still hold out hope that Valentin will finish his career in a Boston uniform.

Jason Varitek C Bats B Age 27

YEAR	TEAM	LGE	AB	H	DB	TP	HR	BB	R	RBI	SB	CS	OUT	BA	OBA	SA	EQA	EQR	DEFENSE
1996	PortCity	Sou	507	117	18	0	11	50	45	44	5	4	394	.231	.300	.331	.220	45	
1997	Tacoma	PCL	301	63	6	0	10	27	21	26	0	1	239	.209	.274	.329	.206	23	
1998	Boston	AL	220	55	9	0	8	18	22	25	2	2	167	.250	.307	.400	.242	24	57-C 93
1999	Boston	AL	284	69	7	0	11	28	28	34	1	1	216	.243	.311	.384	.238	30	

Now that he's spent a year in the majors, he's no longer known as the former Scott Boras holdout. After all the hype surrounding him, he's turned out to be nothing special as a player. Some of that is due to the lost year, but he didn't look like Mike Piazza on draft day, either.

Mo Vaughn 1B Bats L Age 31

YEAR	TEAM	LGE	AB	H	DB	TP	HR	BB	R	RBI	SB	CS	OUT	BA	OBA	SA	EQA	EQR	DEFENSE
1996	Boston	AL	609	187	23	1	41	89	97	123	2	0	422	.307	.395	.550	.318	121	145-1B 84
1997	Boston	AL	516	162	19	0	37	87	88	110	2	2	356	.314	.413	.566	.328	109	127-1B 89
1998	Boston	AL	597	199	29	2	40	64	93	128	0	0	398	.333	.398	.590	.327	122	142-1B 95
1999	Anaheim	AL	583	180	24	1	37	79	94	120	1	0	403	.309	.391	.544	.316	113	

The short list of the best hitters the Red Sox have had since Ted Williams retired: Carl Yastrzemski, Jim Rice, Wade Boggs, Mo Vaughn. There's no sign of a decline here—his 1995 EQA was actually his lowest of the past four years. He's leaving Boston while he's clearly still at the top of his game. Contrast this with Clemens, who at least appeared to be in the early stages of decline before roaring back. I don't envy Dan Duquette right now.

Wilton Veras 3B Bats R Age 21

YEAR	TEAM	LGE	AB	H	DB	TP	HR	BB	R	RBI	SB	CS	OUT	BA	OBA	SA	EQA	EQR	DEFENSE
1996	Lowell	NYP	251	50	8	0	1	10	10	10	1	1	202	.199	.230	.243	.140	7	66-3B 92
1997	Michigan	Mid	490	124	12	1	8	24	36	41	2	1	367	.253	.288	.331	.212	38	128-3B 91
1998	Trenton	Eas	467	130	21	3	15	14	44	57	4	3	340	.278	.299	.433	.248	52	126-3B 105
1999	Boston	AL	449	124	17	1	13	17	42	53	3	2	327	.276	.303	.405	.239	46	

Veras had one of those years that should make you eligible for the comeback award within a single season. He started out hot in April, winning Trenton's Player of the Month award, then fell into a horrific slump in May, June, and July. He rebounded by putting up what one observer called an "all-time hot stretch" for the rest of the year. He has a good arm, but is erratic defensively. He's started to fill out physically, gaining size and strength as the year went on. A free swinger blocked by Valentin and Liniak at third base, so he'll need to be moved to another position unless a trade opens up a spot.

PITCHERS (Averages: 4.00 ERA, 9.00 H/9, 1.00 HR/9, 3.00 BB/9, 6.00 K/9, 1.00 KWH)

Steve Avery   Throws L   Age 29

YEAR	TEAM	LGE	IP	H	ER	HR	BB	K	ERA	W	L	H/9	HR/9	BB/9	K/9	KWH	PERA
1996	Atlanta	NL	133.7	156	65	10	39	78	4.38	7	8	10.50	0.67	2.63	5.25	0.75	4.31
1997	Boston	AL	101.7	123	62	14	43	50	5.49	4	7	10.89	1.24	3.81	4.43	0.35	5.13
1998	Boston	AL	127.7	128	62	13	58	56	4.37	6	8	9.02	0.92	4.09	3.95	0.32	3.95

Won a second chance thanks to Jimy Williams, who ran him out there for his 18th start of 1997, triggering his 1998 contract. Avery improved all the way from awful to below-average. He was the best left-handed pinch-runner in the bullpen, though.

Brian Barkley   Throws L Age 23

YEAR	TEAM	LGE	IP	H	ER	HR	BB	K	ERA	W	L	H/9	HR/9	BB/9	K/9	KWH	PERA
1996	Trenton	Eas	114.0	157	86	19	54	70	6.79	3	10	12.39	1.50	4.26	5.53	0.43	6.16
1997	Trenton	Eas	169.3	244	113	17	73	93	6.01	6	13	12.97	0.90	3.88	4.94	0.36	5.85
1998	Pawtuckt	Int	140.3	170	70	20	46	75	4.49	7	9	10.90	1.28	2.95	4.81	0.54	5.07
1998	Boston	AL	11.3	17	11	2	8	2	8.74	0	1	13.50	1.59	6.35	1.59	0.02	7.15

Got off to an excellent start at Pawtucket, then was called up to Boston for infrequent use. He suffered from the lack of regular work, yet still put together a good season. He throws hard, has good control, and should have a future as a starter in the majors before too long.

Robinson Checo   Throws R Age 27

YEAR	TEAM	LGE	IP	H	ER	HR	BB	K	ERA	W	L	H/9	HR/9	BB/9	K/9	KWH	PERA
1997	Sarasota	Fla	50.0	80	49	10	36	42	8.82	1	5	14.40	1.80	6.48	7.56	0.46	7.56
1997	Pawtuckt	Int	53.7	49	22	8	16	43	3.69	3	3	8.22	1.34	2.68	7.21	1.77	3.52
1997	Boston	AL	14.0	11	4	0	3	14	2.57	1	1	7.07	0.00	1.93	9.00	4.45	1.93
1998	Pawtuckt	Int	51.0	58	32	9	27	36	5.65	2	4	10.24	1.59	4.76	6.35	0.62	5.12
1998	Boston	AL	8.0	11	6	3	5	5	6.75	0	1	12.38	3.38	5.63	5.62	0.34	7.87

The organization has sunk a lot of money into him without much to show for it. He shows flashes of brilliance, but wasn't healthy long enough in '98 to shake the "inconsistent" label. Occasionally rumored to be a closer candidate.

Jin Ho Cho   Throws R   Age 23

YEAR	TEAM	LGE	IP	H	ER	HR	BB	K	ERA	W	L	H/9	HR/9	BB/9	K/9	KWH	PERA
1998	Sarasota	Fla	31.0	40	15	2	6	22	4.35	1	2	11.61	0.58	1.74	6.39	1.51	4.65
1998	Trenton	Eas	72.3	68	21	4	18	48	2.61	6	2	8.46	0.50	2.24	5.97	1.41	3.11
1998	Boston	AL	19.0	28	14	4	3	15	6.63	1	1	13.26	1.89	1.42	7.11	2.01	6.63

One of the real jewels of the Bosox system. Cho throws four pitches (fastball/curve/slider/change), all well, all for strikes. He hits 91-93 on the radar gun. He dominated the Eastern League, and probably shouldn't have been there last year. He has a good work ethic and demeanor. If he's got a fault, it's that he's too relaxed on the mound, and was often seen laughing and smiling while pitching. I think he could be a crowd favorite in Boston real soon.

Jim Corsi   Throws R   Age 37

YEAR	TEAM	LGE	IP	H	ER	HR	BB	K	ERA	W	L	H/9	HR/9	BB/9	K/9	KWH	PERA
1996	Oakland	AL	75.3	69	26	5	28	43	3.11	5	3	8.24	0.60	3.35	5.14	0.72	3.23
1997	Boston	AL	59.7	54	20	1	18	39	3.02	4	3	8.15	0.15	2.72	5.88	1.17	2.72
1998	Boston	AL	67.0	58	19	5	21	48	2.55	5	2	7.79	0.67	2.82	6.45	1.42	2.96

Found life after 30 as a quality right arm in the bullpen, and has made a nice career out of it. The team picked up his option for 1999, so he'll be back in the pen working middle relief/set-up.

Paxton Crawford   Throws R   Age 21

YEAR	TEAM	LGE	IP	H	ER	HR	BB	K	ERA	W	L	H/9	HR/9	BB/9	K/9	KWH	PERA
1996	Michigan	Mid	115.3	169	80	8	42	71	6.24	4	9	13.19	0.62	3.28	5.54	0.53	5.62
1997	Sarasota	Fla	63.3	87	47	8	31	43	6.68	2	5	12.36	1.14	4.41	6.11	0.51	5.83
1998	Trenton	Eas	106.3	119	54	9	38	64	4.57	5	7	10.07	0.76	3.22	5.42	0.68	4.23

The organization is pretty high on this guy, and they've pushed him pretty hard. Maybe too hard. He pitched in the instructional league and in winter ball, and his arm just died during the summer. He has the best changeup in the organization, and hits the low 90s with his fastball. 1999 will be important, to see whether he can rebound from the overwork or not.

Dennis Eckersley		Throws R			Age 44											
YEAR	TEAM	LGE	IP	H	ER	HR	BB	K	ERA	W	L	H/9	HR/9	BB/9	K/9	KWH	PERA
1996	St Louis	NL	59.7	70	25	8	5	44	3.77	4	3	10.56	1.21	0.75	6.64	4.15	4.53
1997	St Louis	NL	52.7	51	21	9	7	40	3.59	3	3	8.72	1.54	1.20	6.84	3.36	3.76
1998	Boston	AL	40.3	46	17	6	7	21	3.79	2	2	10.26	1.34	1.56	4.69	1.03	4.46

Retired. When Dennis Eckersley was a rookie in 1975, a couple of grizzled vets were winding down their Hall of Fame careers: Hank Aaron and Harmon Killebrew, both of whom broke in way back in 1954. In fact, you can trace the entire history of organized baseball through six players: Cap Anson to Honus Wagner to Babe Ruth to Phil Cavaretta to Hank Aaron to Dennis Eckersley is one such list. All but Cavaretta and Eckersley are in Cooperstown, and the Eck will get there. Which active player will extend the chain longest? Send your guess to: info@baseballprospectus.com

Rich Garces		Throws R			Age 28											
YEAR	TEAM	LGE	IP	H	ER	HR	BB	K	ERA	W	L	H/9	HR/9	BB/9	K/9	KWH	PERA
1996	Boston	AL	47.3	38	18	5	28	55	3.42	3	2	7.23	0.95	5.32	10.46	2.13	3.23
1997	Pawtuckt	Int	30.3	29	6	0	13	31	1.78	3	0	8.60	0.00	3.86	9.20	1.91	2.97
1997	Boston	AL	14.3	14	7	2	8	12	4.40	1	1	8.79	1.26	5.02	7.53	0.96	4.40
1998	Boston	AL	47.3	36	16	6	25	33	3.04	3	2	6.85	1.14	4.75	6.27	0.91	3.04

The save he recorded on May 8th was his first major league save since 1990. He visited the disabled list three times in '98, finally succumbing for the season in August with bone chips in his elbow. He'll be up and down again in 1999.

Tom Gordon		Throws R			Age 31											
YEAR	TEAM	LGE	IP	H	ER	HR	BB	K	ERA	W	L	H/9	HR/9	BB/9	K/9	KWH	PERA
1996	Boston	AL	229.3	226	101	24	86	171	3.96	13	12	8.87	0.94	3.38	6.71	1.13	3.77
1997	Boston	AL	189.3	149	67	9	68	154	3.18	13	8	7.08	0.43	3.23	7.32	1.76	2.42
1998	Boston	AL	80.7	55	20	2	22	76	2.23	7	2	6.14	0.22	2.45	8.48	3.58	1.56

The latest exhibit in the case for closers being made, not born. Gordon was a quality starting pitcher, to be sure, but he turned into one of the top closers in the American League. I'm still not enamored of exchanging 200+ general innings for 75 high-leverage innings, but in a case like Gordon's, where there have been concerns about his durability for years, the conversion can work well for everyone involved.

Butch Henry		Throws L			Age 30											
YEAR	TEAM	LGE	IP	H	ER	HR	BB	K	ERA	W	L	H/9	HR/9	BB/9	K/9	KWH	PERA
1995	Montreal	NL	128.3	136	41	11	26	55	2.88	9	5	9.54	0.77	1.82	3.86	0.64	3.79
1997	Boston	AL	87.3	84	28	6	16	49	2.89	7	3	8.66	0.62	1.65	5.05	1.34	3.09
1998	Boston	AL	9.0	8	3	2	3	6	3.00	1	0	8.00	2.00	3.00	6.00	1.12	4.00

He has thrown just 1⅓ more innings over the past four years than Pedro Martinez threw in 1998 alone. Still generally considered to have a quality arm, although questions exist about whether he'll ever put together a full season again. Still, he's left handed, and thus will get lots of opportunities to restart his career. Boston will try to bring him back in '99.

Derek Lowe		Throws R			Age 26											
YEAR	TEAM	LGE	IP	H	ER	HR	BB	K	ERA	W	L	H/9	HR/9	BB/9	K/9	KWH	PERA
1996	PortCity	Sou	59.7	73	32	8	15	25	4.83	3	4	11.01	1.21	2.26	3.77	0.43	4.98
1996	Tacoma	PCL	97.3	132	64	8	35	46	5.92	3	8	12.21	0.74	3.24	4.25	0.34	5.27
1997	Tacoma	PCL	54.0	56	24	3	18	39	4.00	3	3	9.33	0.50	3.00	6.50	1.13	3.67
1997	Seattle	AL	55.3	56	34	10	18	38	5.53	2	4	9.11	1.63	2.93	6.18	1.07	4.39
1997	Pawtuckt	Int	29.7	27	8	3	10	17	2.43	2	1	8.19	0.91	3.03	5.16	0.80	3.34
1998	Boston	AL	126.3	125	54	5	37	75	3.85	7	7	8.91	0.36	2.64	5.34	0.91	3.28

Stolen from Seattle along with Jason Varitek in return for Heathcliff Slocumb. The improvement first seen in 1997 seems to be for real. Lowe had a Jekyll and Hyde season—Jekyll in relief (2.88 ERA in 53 games), and Hyde starting (5.81 ERA in 10

(Derek Lowe *continued*)

starts). A return to the starting role may be in his future. Generated an insane number of groundballs last year; if he can keep that up, he could be dominant. Lowe is drawing trade interest from other teams, and may not be in Boston in 1999.

Ron Mahay   Throws L   Age 28

YEAR	TEAM	LGE	IP	H	ER	HR	BB	K	ERA	W	L	H/9	HR/9	BB/9	K/9	KWH	PERA
1996	Sarasota	Fla	64.0	90	47	8	45	47	6.61	2	5	12.66	1.12	6.33	6.61	0.41	6.19
1997	Trenton	Eas	37.7	38	20	0	14	32	4.78	2	2	9.08	0.00	3.35	7.65	1.44	3.35
1997	Boston	AL	25.7	19	5	3	9	21	1.75	3	0	6.66	1.05	3.16	7.36	1.93	2.45
1998	Pawtuckt	Int	40.0	43	20	8	20	32	4.50	2	2	9.68	1.80	4.50	7.20	0.89	4.95
1998	Boston	AL	27.0	26	13	2	14	14	4.33	1	2	8.67	0.67	4.67	4.67	0.40	3.67

The former outfielder is a strong candidate to join the Boston bullpen for good next year. In limited exposure at the major league level over the past two years, he's been effective in the specialist role. He's going to have a long career.

Pedro Martinez   Throws R   Age 27

YEAR	TEAM	LGE	IP	H	ER	HR	BB	K	ERA	W	L	H/9	HR/9	BB/9	K/9	KWH	PERA
1996	Montreal	NL	223.0	197	88	19	67	201	3.55	14	11	7.95	0.77	2.70	8.11	2.30	3.03
1997	Montreal	NL	244.3	164	57	16	60	272	2.10	21	6	6.04	0.59	2.21	10.02	5.64	1.66
1998	Boston	AL	239.0	184	66	24	60	243	2.49	19	8	6.93	0.90	2.26	9.15	4.01	2.41

The early returns on that massive contract he signed before the season are in, and yes, he was worth it. The '97 NL Cy Young winner adjusted to the AL without missing a beat, designated hitter and all. He's a joy to watch on the mound, and even given a chance to do it over again, I'd rather have Pedro Martinez over the next five years than Roger Clemens.

Juan Pena   Throws R   Age 22

YEAR	TEAM	LGE	IP	H	ER	HR	BB	K	ERA	W	L	H/9	HR/9	BB/9	K/9	KWH	PERA
1996	Michigan	Mid	170.3	209	91	23	34	105	4.81	8	11	11.04	1.22	1.80	5.55	1.16	4.91
1997	Sarasota	Fla	89.0	84	43	10	26	66	4.35	5	5	8.49	1.01	2.63	6.67	1.50	3.44
1997	Trenton	Eas	92.0	115	56	12	29	61	5.48	3	7	11.25	1.17	2.84	5.97	0.84	5.18
1998	Pawtuckt	Int	141.3	148	63	16	46	124	4.01	8	8	9.42	1.02	2.93	7.90	1.69	4.08

The youngest player in the International League last year. He pitched a no-hitter and led the league in strikeouts. Pena doesn't throw hard, but has good movement and control. Not yet a prospect of Pavano/Rose caliber, but with a little more improvement he could be a major contributor in the starting rotation for years to come.

Robert Ramsay   Throws L   Age 25

YEAR	TEAM	LGE	IP	H	ER	HR	BB	K	ERA	W	L	H/9	HR/9	BB/9	K/9	KWH	PERA
1996	Sarasota	Fla	32.3	57	27	2	31	26	7.52	1	3	15.87	0.56	8.63	7.24	0.29	7.24
1997	Sarasota	Fla	126.7	183	110	20	77	82	7.82	3	11	13.00	1.42	5.47	5.83	0.36	6.54
1998	Trenton	Eas	156.7	167	74	11	52	119	4.25	8	9	9.59	0.63	2.99	6.84	1.22	3.91

The #1 starter in Trenton before Cho arrived, Ramsay set a club record for strikeouts last year. A 6'5" left-hander who hits 92 mph with his fastball. He exudes a quiet confidence and is very composed on the mound. Will start for the PawSox at Triple-A next year.

Carlos Reyes   Throws R   Age 30

YEAR	TEAM	LGE	IP	H	ER	HR	BB	K	ERA	W	L	H/9	HR/9	BB/9	K/9	KWH	PERA
1996	Oakland	AL	125.3	131	55	16	49	77	3.95	7	7	9.41	1.15	3.52	5.53	0.69	4.24
1997	Edmonton	PCL	29.7	32	13	2	3	17	3.94	2	1	9.71	0.61	0.91	5.16	2.26	3.64
1997	Oakland	AL	82.0	94	39	12	22	42	4.28	4	5	10.32	1.32	2.41	4.61	0.64	4.72
1998	San Dieg	NL	26.7	26	11	4	5	22	3.71	2	1	8.78	1.35	1.69	7.43	2.79	3.71
1998	Boston	AL	39.0	35	12	2	13	22	2.77	3	1	8.08	0.46	3.00	5.08	0.80	3.00

The sadist in me would love to see post-season interviews with players like Reyes who were traded away from teams that went on to make it to the World Series. Maybe Fox could plant them in the crowd in attendance to showcase the same way they shamelessly plug their fall lineup. "Oh look, there's Gillian Anderson of 'The X-Files,' which can be seen Sundays on Fox. And with her is Don Wengert, who was traded from the Padres to the Cubs back on May 5th. Boy, doesn't he look bitter."

Brian L. Rose   Throws R   Age 23

YEAR	TEAM	LGE	IP	H	ER	HR	BB	K	ERA	W	L	H/9	HR/9	BB/9	K/9	KWH	PERA
1996	Trenton	Eas	155.7	193	90	23	44	90	5.20	6	11	11.16	1.33	2.54	5.20	0.72	5.20
1997	Pawtuckt	Int	189.3	207	70	21	41	96	3.33	12	9	9.84	1.00	1.95	4.56	0.81	4.14
1998	Pawtuckt	Int	17.7	26	17	5	3	14	8.66	0	2	13.25	2.55	1.53	7.13	1.88	7.13
1998	Boston	AL	38.7	43	26	9	12	18	6.05	1	3	10.01	2.09	2.79	4.19	0.47	5.12

Rose started the season touted as the top pitching prospect in the system, but now he may be damaged goods. He has been seeing a number of doctors, but hasn't gone under the knife as of this writing. He's still far from coming back from his season-ending injury.

Bret Saberhagen   Throws R   Age 35

YEAR	TEAM	LGE	IP	H	ER	HR	BB	K	ERA	W	L	H/9	HR/9	BB/9	K/9	KWH	PERA
1995	NY Mets	NL	107.7	115	45	13	19	65	3.76	6	6	9.61	1.09	1.59	5.43	1.45	4.01
1995	Colorado	NL	49.7	55	24	8	13	28	4.35	3	3	9.97	1.45	2.36	5.07	0.82	4.53
1997	Boston	AL	27.0	29	16	5	9	14	5.33	1	2	9.67	1.67	3.00	4.67	0.56	4.67
1998	Boston	AL	178.3	177	67	20	26	97	3.38	12	8	8.93	1.01	1.31	4.90	1.53	3.48

After missing all of 1996, Saberhagen became one of Duquette's most successful reclamation projects. He was kept on a strict pitch count, only topping 100 pitches five times all year. The side effect of this was an average of just about 5.5 innings per start. Signed to a risky three-year extension, which means it's prudent to keep babying his arm.

Pete Schourek   Throws L   Age 30

YEAR	TEAM	LGE	IP	H	ER	HR	BB	K	ERA	W	L	H/9	HR/9	BB/9	K/9	KWH	PERA
1996	Cincnnti	NL	69.3	83	43	7	23	49	5.58	3	5	10.77	0.91	2.99	6.36	0.94	4.67
1997	Cincnnti	NL	87.3	79	50	18	35	53	5.15	4	6	8.14	1.85	3.61	5.46	0.76	4.02
1998	Houston	NL	81.7	86	39	10	33	54	4.30	4	5	9.48	1.10	3.64	5.95	0.77	4.30
1998	Boston	AL	45.0	44	17	7	13	35	3.40	3	2	8.80	1.40	2.60	7.00	1.61	4.00

He avoided becoming another chapter in Boston's post-season misery parade when he acquitted himself admirably in Game Four of the Division Series. Schourek is a good pitcher with a dubious health record. Naturally, this makes him irresistible to Duquette.

Greg Swindell   Throws L   Age 34

YEAR	TEAM	LGE	IP	H	ER	HR	BB	K	ERA	W	L	H/9	HR/9	BB/9	K/9	KWH	PERA
1996	Houston	NL	23.0	38	24	6	11	14	9.39	0	3	14.87	2.35	4.30	5.48	0.35	8.22
1996	Clevelnd	AL	29.3	30	15	7	6	21	4.60	1	2	9.20	2.15	1.84	6.44	1.84	4.60
1997	Minnesot	AL	118.0	99	37	11	21	73	2.82	9	4	7.55	0.84	1.60	5.57	1.92	2.59
1998	Minnesot	AL	68.3	65	22	9	16	44	2.90	5	3	8.56	1.19	2.11	5.80	1.40	3.56
1998	Boston	AL	24.7	25	11	3	12	18	4.01	1	2	9.12	1.09	4.38	6.57	0.81	4.01

Obtained along with Orlando Merced for three minor leaguers in a trade that inspired a few quizzical looks and one of the biggest collective yawns of the year. At least it wasn't another Bagwell-for-Andersen deal. Swindell has discovered baseball's Elixir of Eternal Life—become a left-handed middle reliever. Consequently, he'll have a job until he dies, and maybe longer if it's an expansion year. Gone to Arizona as a free agent.

Carlos Valdez   Throws R   Age 27

YEAR	TEAM	LGE	IP	H	ER	HR	BB	K	ERA	W	L	H/9	HR/9	BB/9	K/9	KWH	PERA
1996	Phoenix	PCL	57.3	72	38	4	34	32	5.97	2	4	11.30	0.63	5.34	5.02	0.31	5.02
1997	Pawtuckt	Int	77.0	89	51	7	45	49	5.96	3	6	10.40	0.82	5.26	5.73	0.45	4.79
1998	Pawtuckt	Int	72.7	86	38	11	22	58	4.71	3	5	10.65	1.36	2.72	7.18	1.33	4.95

Valdez caught fire the last two months of the season. He racks up lots of strikeouts, particularly with a nasty slider to right-handed batters. Designated for assignment, he's someone you'll want to look for this spring.

Dario Veras — Throws R — Age 26

YEAR	TEAM	LGE	IP	H	ER	HR	BB	K	ERA	W	L	H/9	HR/9	BB/9	K/9	KWH	PERA
1996	Memphis	Sou	41.0	46	15	4	8	35	3.29	3	2	10.10	0.88	1.76	7.68	2.50	4.17
1996	LasVegas	PCL	40.0	42	15	1	6	26	3.38	2	2	9.45	0.22	1.35	5.85	2.01	3.15
1996	San Dieg	NL	28.7	27	10	3	10	21	3.14	2	1	8.48	0.94	3.14	6.59	1.22	3.45
1997	San Dieg	NL	24.7	30	17	6	11	19	6.20	1	2	10.95	2.19	4.01	6.93	0.82	5.84
1998	LasVegas	PCL	35.3	38	13	5	12	22	3.31	2	2	9.68	1.27	3.06	5.60	0.80	4.33
1998	Pawtuckt	Int	28.7	34	12	4	11	21	3.77	2	1	10.67	1.26	3.45	6.59	0.88	5.02

Acquired in the Jim Leyritz trade, Veras is a thin pitcher with a good slider and curve. Will be given a shot to make the pen in spring training. If he can just get a job, he's an excellent bet for 80 good innings.

Tim Wakefield — Throws R — Age 32

YEAR	TEAM	LGE	IP	H	ER	HR	BB	K	ERA	W	L	H/9	HR/9	BB/9	K/9	KWH	PERA
1996	Boston	AL	224.3	214	106	33	74	140	4.25	12	13	8.59	1.32	2.97	5.62	0.93	3.81
1997	Boston	AL	209.0	186	86	22	75	147	3.70	12	11	8.01	0.95	3.23	6.33	1.16	3.27
1998	Boston	AL	222.0	208	101	28	71	142	4.09	12	13	8.43	1.14	2.88	5.76	1.02	3.57

League-average, inning-chewing pitchers have a lot of value, and Wakefield should be able to continue doing just what he's done the past couple of years for another decade. My prediction: Wakefield will put up at least one more season like his Cy Young runner-up performance in 1995 before he's through.

John Wasdin — Throws R — Age 26

YEAR	TEAM	LGE	IP	H	ER	HR	BB	K	ERA	W	L	H/9	HR/9	BB/9	K/9	KWH	PERA
1996	Edmonton	PCL	48.0	57	22	7	16	26	4.12	2	3	10.69	1.31	3.00	4.88	0.56	5.06
1996	Oakland	AL	135.0	138	73	21	40	74	4.87	6	9	9.20	1.40	2.67	4.93	0.74	4.20
1997	Boston	AL	129.0	115	54	17	33	81	3.77	7	7	8.02	1.19	2.30	5.65	1.30	3.28
1998	Boston	AL	98.7	109	47	13	24	57	4.29	5	6	9.94	1.19	2.19	5.20	0.93	4.38

I expected good things for Wasdin after a strong second-half performance in 1997, but instead he fell apart. I'm actually surprised his season translated so well, considering the painful general impression it left on most observers. Wasdin has bounced around between starting and relieving, but hasn't found his niche in either yet.

SNWL				BOSTON RED SOX								Park Effect: +3.3%
PITCHER	GS	IP	R	SNW	SNL	SNPCT	W	L	RA	APW	SNVA	SNWAR
Avery, S.	23	117.0	67	7.4	7.3	.503	10	7	5.15	-0.16	0.09	1.15
Checo, R.	2	7.7	8	0.2	1.0	.169	0	2	9.39	-0.35	-0.32	-0.31
Cho, J.	4	18.7	17	0.7	2.0	.258	0	3	8.20	-0.62	-0.61	-0.45
Henry, B.	2	9.0	4	0.5	0.5	.486	0	0	4.00	0.10	0.03	0.06
Lowe, D.	10	48.0	35	2.4	4.1	.368	0	7	6.56	-0.78	-0.85	-0.37
Martinez, P.	33	233.7	82	16.9	8.3	.670	19	7	3.16	4.58	3.99	6.18
Rose, B.	8	37.7	32	1.6	3.6	.310	1	4	7.65	-1.04	-0.94	-0.60
Saberhagen, B.	31	175.0	82	11.7	8.5	.580	15	8	4.22	1.48	1.43	3.13
Schourek, P.	8	41.3	20	2.7	2.2	.553	1	2	4.35	0.29	0.25	0.62
Wakefield, T.	33	210.0	118	11.5	11.9	.491	17	8	5.06	-0.08	-0.16	1.55
Wasdin, J.	8	39.7	26	2.3	2.6	.467	1	2	5.90	-0.37	-0.25	0.21
TOTALS	162	937.7	491	57.9	52.0	.527	64	50	4.71	3.05	2.66	11.18

The 1998 Red Sox starting staff had a completely new look. The only regulars who were held over from the 1997 rotation were Wakefield and Avery. It was the newcomers, $70-million-man Pedro Martinez and 70-million-injuries man Bret Saberhagen, who made the difference. Martinez did everything that was expected of him, and Saberhagen exceeded expectations. The result was that the Red Sox rotation improved by about 3½ games in SNVA, and rose 10 places in the major league rankings to #7. It is a good staff, but still not terribly deep in quality. Without Martinez (or, if you prefer, with an average starter in his place), the staff is well below average. They'd also be significantly worse than the 1997 rotation if Martinez were replaced by an average starter. I don't want to take away from Martinez's outstanding season, but he did have a little help from his friends, particularly his bullpen. In 1998, Martinez left 14 runners for his relievers to handle. Based on what base those runners occupied and how many outs there were, the number of them that would be expected to score is 5.4. Only one actually scored, and that was the third-best bullpen support in the league last year for any starter.

Pitcher Abuse Points

PITCHER	AGE	GS	PAP	PAP/S	AAW	MAX	115+	130+
Avery, Steve	28	23	0	0.00	0.00	99	0	0
Lowe, Derek	25	10	4	0.40	0.87	104	0	0
Martinez, Pedro	26	33	957	29.00	58.00	146	19	3
Rose, Brian	22	8	1	0.13	0.33	101	0	0
Saberhagen, Bret	34	31	23	0.74	0.74	110	0	0
Schourek, Pete	29	8	0	0.00	0.00	91	0	0
Wakefield, Tim	31	33	155	4.70	5.48	123	4	0
Wasdin, John	25	8	0	0.00	0.00	98	0	0
TOTAL		162	1140	7.04	13.14	146	23	3
RANKING (AL)			11	11	11		10	8-T

Jimy Williams may never entirely live down his collapse with the Blue Jays twelve years ago, but he deserves credit for pampering a staff full of youngsters and rehab cases. Pedro Martinez recorded 84% of his team's total PAPs, easily the highest total of any starter, so I'm a little worried about him. He doesn't have a huge body frame, and he wore down a bit in September (4.15 ERA). In fairness, he was brought up to his current workload over a period of years by Felipe Alou, and in fact he faced more batters per start in 1997 than he did last season. But everyone else on the staff was treated with the utmost care. Williams's caution is a big reason why Bret Saberhagen pitched better during the second half (4.78 ERA before the break, 3.19 ERA after), as well as Pete Schourek.

New York Yankees

Given the two World Championships in three years, and the American League-record 114 wins in 1998, I feel the Yankees's place in history is an area that has not been explored nearly enough by the media. I'd like to take the next 2000 words to analyze the 1998 champs, and compare them to some of the...wait...what are you doing?...Put those matches down!...Hey, that hurts!

Let's just say that the 1998 Yankees were one of the best teams in baseball history, thanks to a deep lineup, exceptional team plate discipline, and tremendous starting pitching. For many readers—and many authors, for that matter—this was the first team in their personal baseball histories that they could make this claim for. We were all fortunate to experience this team, and whether you're a Yankee fan or Yankee hater, it was a team and a season you might tell your kids and grandkids about.

But now comes the hard part. As we pointed out a year ago, the Yankees are a relatively old team, despite a core of young, home-grown players. With the addition of a past-prime Chuck Knoblauch and the continued inability to work Ricky Ledee into the lineup, the team has grown older and more expensive. Despite the continued good play of 30-somethings Paul O'Neill, David Wells, Scott Brosius, and Darryl Strawberry, expecting this level of performance to continue is a pipe dream. The Yankees have already decided to dream, giving Brosius a three-year, $16 million deal, and renegotiating David Cone's option.

The one essential player the Yankees retained is center fielder Bernie Williams. Williams, who appeared certain to go elsewhere in the days after the World Series, returned to New York after receiving a seven-year deal worth just under $90 million. Williams is the best player on the team, a switch-hitter with a complete offensive package and an excellent glove. He is also the only player the Yankees did not have a ready in-house replacement for. The organization is flush with infielders and corner outfielders, but the only legitimate center field prospect, Donzell McDonald, is at least a year away.

Williams's departure would have set in motion events that would have left the Yankees inferior both offensively and defensively, while making them older, and quite possibly more expensive. Williams fills some key roles for the team: he is the cleanup hitter, combining a high average with good plate discipline and power. His range in center field helps make up for the aging Yankee corner outfielders. Scott Brosius's year notwithstanding, he's the only bat from the right side of the plate that can scare left-handing pitching within the lineup.

His durability is a concern, with an average of 30 missed games a year since 1996. However, Williams will probably be enough of an offensive force that he can be moved to an outfield corner in a few years, saving wear and tear on him and still providing well-above-average production. The signing was expensive, and projecting any player to be a star at 36 and 37 is risky, but Williams was the one irreplaceable Yankee, and keeping him lets them head into 1999 as the favorite in the AL East.

Even with Williams, the team is going to decline significantly in 1999, although it will still be a postseason contender. Any team that plays nearly .700 ball is going to decline. The Yankees's preponderance of players in their thirties just makes it likely that the decline will be steeper. Even a 20-game slide would make them the favorite in the wild-card race, assuming one of the lost souls in the AL East can even get to 95 wins to beat them out for the division.

Even with their age issues, the Yankees are in excellent shape. The core of good starting pitching, Williams, Derek Jeter, Jorge Posada, and Chuck Knoblauch is easy to build around, especially with the resources the New York market provides. Even as Knoblauch and Williams decline, the farm system will be burping up good, young, cheap players such as Nick Johnson who can step in and ease the burden of their large contracts. In two years, Ken Griffey and Chipper Jones will be free agents; in three years, Alex Rodriguez steps out, and Andruw Jones and Vladimir Guerrero not long after that.

The Yankees (and any successful team, really) would go a long way towards sustaining success by taking a careful look at what parts of that success are integral, and what parts are secondary. The aura of success that builds around mediocre players who happen to play for good teams can lead

---

Yankees Prospectus

1998 record: 114-48; First place, AL East; Beat San Diego Padres in the World Series, 4-0

Pythagorean W/L: 111-51

Runs scored: 965 (1st in AL)

Runs allowed: 656 (1st in AL)

Team EQA: .287 (1st in AL)

Park: Yankee Stadium (moderate pitchers')

1998: Not a bad little year.

1999: Some decline from aging is certain, but not enough to keep them out of October.

to some terrible player personnel decisions. The Braves have carried Rafael Belliard around like a mascot for eight years, and attached an unnatural value to Mark Lemke for almost as long.

In a similar fashion, the Yankees, and especially Joe Torre, have been blinded to how bad a player Joe Girardi is. They gave him a two-year contract after the first World Championship and picked up a $3.4 million option after this one. Rather than view Scott Brosius as a fluke, to be appreciated, feted, and allowed to go play for the Royals or Giants, he was given an absurd three-year deal. Davids Cone and Wells are both likely to get contract extensions beyond 1999, and it's possible Tino Martinez will be extended past 2000 as well.

These players fall into one of three categories: non-critical elements (Girardi); readily replaceable talent (Brosius, Martinez); or bad risks to maintain their performance level (Cone, Wells). Most successful teams have five to seven players than are truly mission-critical. The rest usually belong to one of the above categories, and should be traded, allowed to walk away as free agents, or merely released. Or shot.

Try this exercise with any of the playoff teams . . . let's take the Braves, since they've been guilty. Who is mission-critical? Both Joneses, Lopez, Maddux, Smoltz, Glavine. That's six. Weiss, Galarraga and probably Neagle (now traded) are risks; the entire bullpen and bench, with the possible exception of Gerald Williams, are readily replaceable. The second basemen and Michael Tucker are non-critical.

How about the other great team of the 1990s, the Cleveland Indians? Jim Thome and Manny Ramirez are their only essential elements. Maybe Bartolo Colon and Jaret Wright. Both Alomars, Kenny Lofton, Dave Justice, Travis Fryman, and Charles Nagy are risks. Their bench, the back end of the rotation and most of the bullpen are readily replaceable. Omar Vizquel is non-critical.

And yet, these players' value is inflated by their association with success, while management teams that fear public relations problems, "unproven" young players, or the perception of "messing with success" fall over themselves to keep an aging team intact. A few years later, that team is meandering towards .500, and no one can figure out why these "winners" aren't performing as well. The concept that players decline as they age, a given among analysts and a seemingly obvious point, gets overlooked as a team decides they need to guarantee themselves the services of a 38-year-old Paul O'Neill or a 36-year-old Chuck Knoblauch or a 37-year-old David Cone.

Are all late-career signings a bad idea? Of course not, but it's only truly great players who continue to be worth the money deep into their thirties. Roger Clemens, a free agent at 34, was a great signing, and many analysts would have told you so at the time. Extending Barry Bonds through 2000, as the Giants did, gives them the services of the best player of his generation through 36. There are also some players who take atypical career paths, making them credible bets even as they approach 40. Tony Phillips and Chili Davis are recent examples of this.

But for the most part, trying to keep the second-tier of a successful team together is a bad idea, because those players are the ones most likely to decline beyond usefulness. The costs involved, in money and roster spots, limit the other things you can do to improve the team. Avoiding this pitfall can go a long way towards long-term success.

Since it doesn't look like the Yankees are going to avoid this mistake, they'll just have to rely on spending whatever it takes to get the best available talent, both in the conventional free agent market, and the international market they've exploited so deftly. They'll also have to continue to pump funds into scouting an development, so their farm system can continue to crank out players like Jeter, Posada, and Andy Pettitte. The Yankees's revenue streams are going to impact their success in more ways than one.

HITTERS (Averages: BA .260/ OBA .330/ SA .420, EQA .260)

Scott Brosius   3B   Bats R   Age 32

YEAR	TEAM	LGE	AB	H	DB	TP	HR	BB	R	RBI	SB	CS	OUT	BA	OBA	SA	EQA	EQR	DEFENSE	
1996	Oakland	AL	415	121	19	0	22	56	64	70	8	2	296	.292	.376	.496	.299	72	107-3B 110	
1997	Oakland	AL	473	93	19	1	11	35	32	31	9	4	384	.197	.252	.311	.191	31	96-3B 107	17-SS 84
1998	NY Yanks	AL	523	157	24	0	23	55	73	82	10	8	374	.300	.367	.478	.287	83	150-3B 107	
1999	NYYanks	AL	494	125	19	1	20	53	58	65	6	5	374	.253	.325	.417	.258	63		

Well, it could be worse: it could be Devon White signing. Brosius is a nice little player with a top-notch glove and reasonable secondary skills who had a good year at the right time. Smart teams say "Thanks" and bring up the comparable player from Triple-A at 3% of the cost. Dumb teams attach all sorts of value to the individual, pay no attention to his career pattern or age or available talent or opportunity cost, and sign him to a three-year $16 million contract. That projection looks dead on.

Homer Bush — IF — Bats B — Age 26

YEAR	TEAM	LGE	AB	H	DB	TP	HR	BB	R	RBI	SB	CS	OUT	BA	OBA	SA	EQA	EQR	DEFENSE
1996	LasVegas	PCL	111	34	6	1	2	3	12	13	3	4	80	.306	.325	.432	.253	13	28-2B 96
1997	LasVegas	PCL	149	32	6	1	2	5	9	9	4	1	118	.215	.240	.309	.185	9	34-2B 98
1997	Columbus	Int	275	63	8	2	2	21	24	17	9	5	217	.229	.284	.295	.202	20	74-2B 108
1998	NY Yanks	AL	70	27	3	0	1	5	12	10	5	3	46	.386	.427	.471	.309	12	
1999	NYYanks	AL	178	47	7	1	3	11	19	17	7	4	135	.264	.307	.365	.236	18	

A career .378 hitter. OK, it's 82 at-bats, but when he tells his grandkids, do you think they'll care? Credit Torre for seeing what Bush could do—run, field, slap singles—and giving him a role he could succeed in. As long as he's kept in his role he can contribute.

Chad Curtis — LF/CF — Bats R — Age 30

YEAR	TEAM	LGE	AB	H	DB	TP	HR	BB	R	RBI	SB	CS	OUT	BA	OBA	SA	EQA	EQR	DEFENSE
1996	Detroit	AL	391	99	17	1	10	51	52	41	17	12	304	.253	.339	.379	.252	48	97-OF 102
1996	LosAngls	NL	105	23	3	0	3	18	13	10	2	1	83	.219	.333	.333	.241	12	28-OF 104
1997	NY Yanks	AL	317	94	21	1	13	37	51	48	12	6	229	.297	.370	.492	.294	53	82-OF 101
1998	NY Yanks	AL	451	110	18	1	11	76	69	46	20	5	346	.244	.353	.361	.261	60	132-OF 105
1999	NYYanks	AL	436	106	19	1	12	64	60	49	13	7	337	.243	.340	.374	.255	56	

Like a lot of good fourth outfielders, if he plays too much he wears down and loses a lot of his value. Curtis was setting the world on fire when Bernie Williams went down, hitting .280/.406/.434 on June 11, the day Williams went on the DL. From that day forward, he hit .221/.313/.313. He is one of the two or three best fourth outfielders in baseball, and the return of Williams keeps him in that role. May be traded.

Chili Davis — DH — Bats B — Age 39

YEAR	TEAM	LGE	AB	H	DB	TP	HR	BB	R	RBI	SB	CS	OUT	BA	OBA	SA	EQA	EQR	DEFENSE
1996	Calfrnia	AL	516	147	19	0	28	82	79	88	5	2	371	.285	.383	.484	.299	90	
1997	KansasCy	AL	465	126	15	0	31	85	75	84	6	3	342	.271	.384	.503	.302	86	
1998	NY Yanks	AL	102	30	4	0	4	14	14	16	0	1	73	.294	.379	.451	.286	16	
1999	NYYanks	AL	295	73	10	0	15	54	44	46	2	1	223	.247	.364	.434	.281	47	

A right ankle injury destroyed his season. When he played, he was pretty much the same old Chili Davis. With a year left on his contract, he'll probably exceed that projection. The term "professional hitter" gets wasted on people like Paul Molitor nowadays; Chili Davis is a professional hitter.

Mike Figga — C — Bats R — Age 28

YEAR	TEAM	LGE	AB	H	DB	TP	HR	BB	R	RBI	SB	CS	OUT	BA	OBA	SA	EQA	EQR	DEFENSE
1995	Norwich	Eas	411	110	14	2	13	34	42	51	1	0	301	.268	.324	.406	.253	48	
1997	Columbus	Int	388	81	8	2	9	14	19	24	2	2	309	.209	.236	.309	.176	20	
1998	Columbus	Int	453	108	17	2	17	27	38	49	1	2	347	.238	.281	.397	.229	44	100-C 88
1999	NYYanks	AL	411	96	15	2	16	21	33	45	1	2	317	.234	.271	.397	.226	38	

His 1998 is not his real level of ability, but given the success the Yankees had with Jorge Posada, would it have been so difficult to make Figga the backup catcher, at a savings of $3.2 million? Like Chris Turner and others, Figga is in limbo between career minor leaguer and major league backup catcher. Guys like this deserve your good wishes, because they tend to lose out to...

Joe Girardi — C — Bats R — Age 34

YEAR	TEAM	LGE	AB	H	DB	TP	HR	BB	R	RBI	SB	CS	OUT	BA	OBA	SA	EQA	EQR	DEFENSE
1996	NY Yanks	AL	412	116	19	3	2	28	48	37	14	5	301	.282	.327	.357	.243	44	
1997	NY Yanks	AL	395	107	24	1	1	27	39	34	2	3	291	.271	.318	.344	.230	37	
1998	NY Yanks	AL	251	69	11	4	3	15	25	26	2	4	186	.275	.316	.386	.239	26	74-C 98
1999	NYYanks	AL	304	79	15	2	2	22	30	27	4	3	228	.260	.310	.342	.228	28	

To those of you who heard the bi-coastal primal scream on November 1, courtesy Keith Law and me, we apologize. Bringing back this wildly overrated out machine at $3.4 million is a bad joke. You want him on the roster, fine, but decline the option and get him back at a reasonable price. The Rockies cut loose Kirt Manwaring, so it can be done. Girardi's a passable backup catcher who gets too much playing time.

Rudy Gomez — 2B — Bats B — Age 24

YEAR	TEAM	LGE	AB	H	DB	TP	HR	BB	R	RBI	SB	CS	OUT	BA	OBA	SA	EQA	EQR	DEFENSE
1996	Tampa	Fla	134	38	8	0	2	22	21	16	2	1	97	.284	.385	.388	.277	20	38-2B 89
1997	Norwich	Eas	393	108	15	5	4	51	53	42	8	5	290	.275	.358	.369	.259	49	91-2B 99
1998	Columbus	Int	232	42	5	1	5	23	14	13	3	4	194	.181	.255	.276	.176	13	63-2B 91
1998	Norwich	Eas	189	54	8	1	3	15	23	20	6	4	139	.286	.338	.386	.253	22	
1999	*NYYanks*	*AL*	*370*	*96*	*13*	*2*	*8*	*38*	*43*	*40*	*7*	*6*	*280*	*.259*	*.328*	*.370*	*.246*	*42*	

A personal favorite, he ran into his first difficulty as a pro at Columbus, resulting in a July demotion. Bounced back at Norwich, but he's blocked at the major league level and has to deal with the possible move of D'Angelo Jimenez to his position. Basically, he's screwed, and we may never know if he could have been the player I thought he would be. Played well in the AFL...maybe the A's will notice.

Derek Jeter — SS — Bats R — Age 25

YEAR	TEAM	LGE	AB	H	DB	TP	HR	BB	R	RBI	SB	CS	OUT	BA	OBA	SA	EQA	EQR	DEFENSE
1996	NY Yanks	AL	567	172	24	6	9	44	73	69	14	8	403	.303	.354	.414	.268	75	155-SS 101
1997	NY Yanks	AL	648	193	32	7	11	75	99	80	24	13	468	.298	.371	.420	.277	95	155-SS 96
1998	NY Yanks	AL	617	201	25	7	20	60	102	95	28	6	422	.326	.386	.486	.303	107	147-SS 92
1999	*NYYanks*	*AL*	*600*	*192*	*30*	*7*	*14*	*61*	*101*	*88*	*24*	*9*	*417*	*.320*	*.383*	*.463*	*.297*	*100*	

He took a big step forward this year; the Brosius signing means he won't be moving to third base anytime soon, but his defense at shortstop warrants the discussion at least. He has excellent hands and a strong arm, but isn't anything special on the pivot and seems to struggle going to his left. The arm hides some of this. Jeter could improve the same way Ken Griffey, whose defense was overrated for many years, did. Even with a below-average glove, Jeter is a special player. That projection is low.

D'Angelo Jimenez — SS — Bats B — Age 21

YEAR	TEAM	LGE	AB	H	DB	TP	HR	BB	R	RBI	SB	CS	OUT	BA	OBA	SA	EQA	EQR	DEFENSE
1996	Greensbr	SAL	555	121	17	2	6	42	36	35	6	8	442	.218	.273	.288	.189	34	135-SS 91
1997	Tampa	Fla	355	88	11	3	6	44	38	35	4	7	274	.248	.331	.346	.236	37	93-SS 100
1998	Norwich	Eas	153	39	4	2	2	22	19	15	4	4	117	.255	.349	.346	.247	18	40-SS 98
1998	Columbus	Int	339	77	14	3	7	40	34	32	4	5	267	.227	.309	.348	.228	33	87-SS 100

A fantastic example of a player making a slow, steady climb through the system, improving at every level, and now ready to...to...spend a lot of time at Columbus. Jimenez, like Gomez, is blocked, with the infielders in Yankee Stadium under contract through at least 2001. For his sake and ours I hope he's traded, because he could be a special player. There are thirty major league infields; based solely on expected 1999 production, I'd probably take Johnson-Gomez-Jimenez-Lowell over a half-dozen of them.

Nick Johnson — 1B — Bats L — Age 20

YEAR	TEAM	LGE	AB	H	DB	TP	HR	BB	R	RBI	SB	CS	OUT	BA	OBA	SA	EQA	EQR	DEFENSE
1997	Greensbr	SAL	448	115	13	0	15	67	59	55	7	2	335	.257	.353	.386	.264	60	124-1B 80
1998	Tampa	Fla	304	85	7	1	13	57	45	49	0	2	221	.280	.393	.438	.291	50	91-1B 90
1999	*NYYanks*	*AL*	*323*	*98*	*8*	*0*	*16*	*51*	*51*	*59*	*2*	*2*	*227*	*.303*	*.398*	*.477*	*.305*	*58*	

That .291 EQA might have been higher if not for a separated shoulder that cost Johnson six weeks, and probably some power once he returned. Johnson has drawn comparisons to Will Clark, but I see him more as Jim Thome, without the fashion statement. Johnson is going to be great; the only question is opportunity.

Chuck Knoblauch   2B   Bats R Age 30

YEAR	TEAM	LGE	AB	H	DB	TP	HR	BB	R	RBI	SB	CS	OUT	BA	OBA	SA	EQA	EQR	DEFENSE
1996	Minnesot	AL	554	180	31	13	12	91	123	80	46	16	390	.325	.420	.493	.318	111	141-2B 100
1997	Minnesot	AL	599	172	26	10	9	85	121	63	63	10	437	.287	.376	.409	.289	98	149-2B 95
1998	NY Yanks	AL	596	159	24	4	18	78	88	72	28	12	449	.267	.352	.411	.269	84	147-2B 101
1999	NYYanks	AL	572	156	28	7	14	81	99	71	32	10	426	.273	.363	.420	.280	89	

There's no nice way to say this: Like Roberto Alomar, he appears to be into his decline phase and is unlikely to see the heights of 1994-96 again. I don't think he'll continue to lose 20 points of EQA a year, either, but at $6 million per through 2001, and $9 million for 2002-03, he's unlikely to be worth the money. I would have let him demand a trade and test the market. He might have come back anyway and saved the team a contract extension.

Ricky Ledee   LF   Bats L Age 25

YEAR	TEAM	LGE	AB	H	DB	TP	HR	BB	R	RBI	SB	CS	OUT	BA	OBA	SA	EQA	EQR	DEFENSE
1996	Norwich	Eas	138	49	8	1	7	14	24	28	2	1	90	.355	.414	.580	.332	29	30-OF 95
1996	Columbus	Int	352	91	16	2	19	42	46	54	4	2	263	.259	.338	.477	.277	53	64-OF 86
1997	Columbus	Int	169	51	9	1	9	19	26	30	3	0	118	.302	.372	.527	.306	30	32-OF 90
1998	Columbus	Int	354	90	13	1	15	46	44	48	5	2	266	.254	.340	.424	.266	48	75-OF 92
1998	NY Yanks	AL	78	19	4	2	1	8	10	8	3	1	60	.244	.314	.385	.246	9	23-OF 102
1999	NYYanks	AL	366	98	19	2	16	45	54	55	7	2	270	.268	.348	.462	.281	57	

I don't have problems with Bob Costas like some people do, but did anyone else do a double take when he suggested that Ledee could take over in center field for the Yankees if they lost Bernie Williams? Uh, sure, Bob. Ledee can hit, and was a nice story in the World Series. He and Spencer are a painfully obvious, unbelievably cheap left field solution that would be better than league-average for the position. Ledee will outperform that projection, given a reasonably regular job.

Mike Lowell   3B   Bats R Age 25

YEAR	TEAM	LGE	AB	H	DB	TP	HR	BB	R	RBI	SB	CS	OUT	BA	OBA	SA	EQA	EQR	DEFENSE
1996	Greensbr	SAL	448	108	11	0	8	32	34	37	4	2	342	.241	.292	.319	.212	35	111-3B 118
1997	Norwich	Eas	284	90	10	0	12	39	43	49	2	1	195	.317	.399	.479	.304	50	64-3B 94
1997	Columbus	Int	209	56	11	1	13	21	27	35	2	3	156	.268	.335	.517	.281	33	42-3B 85
1998	Columbus	Int	499	136	24	1	21	32	54	68	3	0	363	.273	.316	.451	.262	64	117-3B 109
1999	NYYanks	AL	476	128	19	1	19	36	53	65	3	1	349	.269	.320	.433	.260	60	

Screwed, and now must go to bed every night rooting for Scott Brosius's evil twin to return. Actually, he's likely to be elsewhere by the time you read this, as his trade value is peaking and he has almost no value to the Yankees. Some enterprising team can get themselves a cheap six-year solution at third base if they're quick. Lowell will hit about like Tim Wallach and play average defense; that will push a lot of teams towards a championship.

Tino Martinez   1B   Bats L Age 31

YEAR	TEAM	LGE	AB	H	DB	TP	HR	BB	R	RBI	SB	CS	OUT	BA	OBA	SA	EQA	EQR	DEFENSE
1996	NY Yanks	AL	580	163	22	0	25	64	73	86	2	1	418	.281	.352	.448	.276	84	148-1B 99
1997	NY Yanks	AL	588	178	32	2	46	77	95	126	3	1	411	.303	.383	.599	.323	121	146-1B 110
1998	NY Yanks	AL	524	147	28	1	30	64	74	90	2	1	378	.281	.359	.510	.293	88	139-1B 103
1999	NYYanks	AL	544	149	23	1	34	67	77	98	2	1	396	.274	.354	.507	.293	92	

Average, maybe a little above, so at $4 million per year he's an absolute bargain in this market. Any efforts to give Martinez an extension past 2000 should be met with short-range nuclear weapons. Nick Johnson is going to be knocking on the door by September; maybe one of the Yankees's prospects can be allowed to break through?

Donzell McDonald   OF   Bats R Age 24

YEAR	TEAM	LGE	AB	H	DB	TP	HR	BB	R	RBI	SB	CS	OUT	BA	OBA	SA	EQA	EQR	DEFENSE
1996	Oneonta	NYP	294	74	6	5	3	31	42	23	24	5	225	.252	.323	.337	.245	33	73-OF 101
1997	Tampa	Fla	300	79	19	4	3	41	48	29	19	10	231	.263	.352	.383	.261	40	77-OF 104
1998	Norwich	Eas	496	116	16	4	6	49	53	36	25	16	396	.234	.303	.319	.220	45	127-OF 102
1999	NYYanks	AL	405	98	16	5	5	42	52	34	22	10	317	.242	.313	.343	.236	43	

Double-A is the wall for prospects; some make it over easily, some run into it and others need a little extra time to climb. McDonald looks like he'll one of the strugglers. He didn't get beaten by the Eastern League, but he did scuffle and will be back at Norwich in 1999. I expect him to conquer the league this year, and advance to Columbus by August. ETA: mid-2000.

Jackson Melian   OF   Bats R   Age 19

YEAR	TEAM	LGE	AB	H	DB	TP	HR	BB	R	RBI	SB	CS	OUT	BA	OBA	SA	EQA	EQR	DEFENSE
1998	Greensbr	SAL	470	101	11	1	6	35	30	28	6	6	375	.215	.269	.281	.185	28	127-OF 92
1999	NYYanks	AL	365	88	7	0	7	24	28	30	4	4	281	.241	.288	.318	.209	28	

While on a visit from Venezuela to see him play, Melian's parents were killed in a car accident on August 28 in North Carolina. The best wishes of the *Baseball Prospectus* family go out to him.

Paul O'Neill   RF   Bats L   Age 36

YEAR	TEAM	LGE	AB	H	DB	TP	HR	BB	R	RBI	SB	CS	OUT	BA	OBA	SA	EQA	EQR	DEFENSE
1996	NY Yanks	AL	528	153	30	1	19	97	87	84	0	1	376	.290	.400	.458	.300	93	135-OF 102
1997	NY Yanks	AL	547	182	33	0	26	76	96	101	11	8	373	.333	.414	.536	.321	108	136-OF 103
1998	NY Yanks	AL	594	189	39	2	25	60	96	100	14	1	406	.318	.381	.517	.308	106	147-OF 98
1999	NYYanks	AL	544	154	28	1	23	75	83	87	5	2	392	.283	.370	.465	.291	90	

Some players take atypical career paths. O'Neill's walk rate regressed some more last year, but he also did things like steal 15 bases in 16 attempts, and hit his most home runs since 1991. Predicting what some players are going to do is nearly impossible, and O'Neill falls into that category. That pesky problem with left-handers is re-emerging, so getting him out of the three hole against southpaws would be a good idea.

Jorge Posada   C   Bats B   Age 27

YEAR	TEAM	LGE	AB	H	DB	TP	HR	BB	R	RBI	SB	CS	OUT	BA	OBA	SA	EQA	EQR	DEFENSE
1996	Columbus	Int	350	83	16	2	10	71	51	43	2	2	269	.237	.366	.380	.267	49	
1997	NY Yanks	AL	186	47	8	0	8	31	26	26	1	2	141	.253	.359	.425	.272	27	
1998	NY Yanks	AL	354	95	18	0	19	48	48	57	0	1	260	.268	.356	.480	.284	56	88-C 106
1999	NYYanks	AL	318	81	15	1	15	49	46	49	1	1	238	.255	.354	.450	.280	49	

The second-best catcher in the league behind Ivan Rodriguez. Posada has great secondary skills, is a legitimate switch-hitter, throws well, and is getting better at the other aspects of catching. I think he'll peak around a .900 OPS in the next few years. He's thin, and wore down late this year, so I think having a quality backup around is a good idea. Maybe Girardi knows someone.

Tim Raines   DH/LF   Bats B   Age 39

YEAR	TEAM	LGE	AB	H	DB	TP	HR	BB	R	RBI	SB	CS	OUT	BA	OBA	SA	EQA	EQR	DEFENSE
1996	NY Yanks	AL	195	53	8	0	9	32	35	28	11	1	143	.272	.374	.451	.294	34	39-OF 98
1997	NY Yanks	AL	268	88	22	2	4	42	51	39	8	5	185	.328	.419	.470	.309	49	47-OF 90
1998	NY Yanks	AL	317	92	13	1	5	56	52	39	7	3	228	.290	.397	.385	.283	49	38-OF 88
1999	NYYanks	AL	271	68	11	1	5	51	42	30	4	2	205	.251	.370	.354	.265	37	

Now a valuable spare part. I engaged in a brief debate with another analyst last summer over Raines's Hall of Fame chances, a subject that subsequently came up during postseason television coverage. To my mind there is no debate: Raines is one of the top ten left fielders ever, the second-best base stealer in history, and an easy selection. He was probably the best player in the game in 1986-87. I'd be interested in hearing a cogent case against him; send yours to info@baseballprospectus.com

While I'm at it, the whole idea that the 1998 Yankees had no Hall of Famers is patently absurd. Raines is a Hall of Famer, David Cone is on track, and Derek Jeter is off to a Hall of Fame start. And that doesn't count guys like Bernie Williams or Andy Pettitte, who you can't make good cases for yet, but who have the skeleton of an argument in place.

Juan Rivera   OF   Bats R   Age 20

YEAR	TEAM	LGE	AB	H	DB	TP	HR	BB	R	RBI	SB	CS	OUT	BA	OBA	SA	EQA	EQR	DEFENSE
1998	Oneonta	NYP	18	4	0	0	1	1	1	2	0	1	15	.222	.263	.389	.202	1	
1999	NYYanks	AL	14	4	0	0	1	1	1	3	0	0	10	.286	.333	.500	.283	2	

Rivera was named the top prospect in the Gulf Coast League by *Baseball America*, and is another product of the Yankees international scouting and development efforts. He was a little old for the GCL; before we get too excited, I'd like to see him play in a full-season league. Then we can all genuflect.

Luis Sojo   IF   Bats R   Age 33

YEAR	TEAM	LGE	AB	H	DB	TP	HR	BB	R	RBI	SB	CS	OUT	BA	OBA	SA	EQA	EQR		DEFENSE	
1996	Seattle	AL	245	49	7	1	1	8	9	9	2	2	198	.200	.225	.249	.140	7		29-3B 104	19-2B 105
1997	NY Yanks	AL	213	67	6	1	2	17	26	25	3	1	147	.315	.365	.380	.265	27		58-2B 95	
1998	NY Yanks	AL	145	33	3	1	0	5	7	7	1	0	112	.228	.253	.262	.167	6			
1999	*NYYanks*	*AL*	*186*	*44*	*6*	*1*	*1*	*9*	*13*	*12*	*2*	*1*	*143*	*.237*	*.272*	*.296*	*.193*	*12*			

Having him and Homer Bush around on a team with middle infielders as good as the Yankees have is a bit redundant. Sojo's value is his ability to play all the infield slots and hit singles. He only did one of those things last year, so I hope he was doing people's taxes or arbitrating marital disputes or something else to make up for being useless on the field. D'Angelo Jimenez would be a better use of both roster spots.

Alfonso Soriano   SS   Bats R   Age 21

Shortstop who apparently plays defense like Ozzie Smith's big brother. As with any well-publicized foreign free agent, don't believe the hype. These guys have been a lot more Glenn Williams than Orlando Hernandez. He wasn't overmatched in the Arizona Fall League; even if he's good, he's in the wrong organization. He's already being mentioned in trade talks.

Shane Spencer   LF   Bats R   Age 27

YEAR	TEAM	LGE	AB	H	DB	TP	HR	BB	R	RBI	SB	CS	OUT	BA	OBA	SA	EQA	EQR	DEFENSE
1996	Norwich	Eas	457	107	11	0	21	55	47	57	3	1	351	.234	.316	.396	.248	54	90-OF 90
1997	Columbus	Int	454	103	23	2	23	59	51	62	0	2	353	.227	.316	.438	.257	59	107-OF 91
1998	Columbus	Int	334	90	15	1	12	33	38	45	1	2	246	.269	.335	.428	.262	43	63-OF 94
1998	NY Yanks	AL	66	25	6	0	10	5	13	22	0	1	42	.379	.423	.924	.393	20	
1999	*NYYanks*	*AL*	*417*	*109*	*20*	*1*	*24*	*49*	*55*	*69*	*1*	*2*	*310*	*.261*	*.339*	*.487*	*.281*	*65*	

He can play Ron Roenicke to Ricky Ledee's John Lowenstein, and become a cult hero by doing it. Spencer is not going to have a long career—his skills are walks and power, and he's pretty slow. Players like that are valuable, but tend to fade in their early thirties. For the next few years, he's a cheap power source.

Darryl Strawberry   DH/LF   Bats L   Age 37

YEAR	TEAM	LGE	AB	H	DB	TP	HR	BB	R	RBI	SB	CS	OUT	BA	OBA	SA	EQA	EQR	DEFENSE
1996	NY Yanks	AL	197	50	11	0	11	29	28	30	6	6	153	.254	.350	.477	.277	31	23-OF 95
1998	NY Yanks	AL	291	72	11	2	24	48	45	54	7	7	226	.247	.354	.546	.294	53	
1999	*NYYanks*	*AL*	*202*	*46*	*6*	*0*	*13*	*34*	*27*	*32*	*3*	*3*	*159*	*.228*	*.339*	*.450*	*.272*	*31*	

It's hard to believe 1998 was his first 20-homerun or .500-slugging season since 1991. In the six intervening seasons, he'd racked up just 669 at-bats. I've been saying for years that Strawberry's skills were still intact, and he just needed regular playing time to produce. Bringing in Straw is one of the best things George Steinbrenner has ever done. Here's hoping he makes a full recovery from colon cancer.

Bernie Williams   CF   Bats B   Age 30

YEAR	TEAM	LGE	AB	H	DB	TP	HR	BB	R	RBI	SB	CS	OUT	BA	OBA	SA	EQA	EQR	DEFENSE
1996	NY Yanks	AL	534	157	25	7	27	78	93	92	18	5	382	.294	.384	.519	.308	100	136-OF 107
1997	NY Yanks	AL	504	170	35	6	23	74	99	96	16	9	343	.337	.422	.567	.331	108	123-OF 104
1998	NY Yanks	AL	492	168	29	5	27	75	95	101	13	9	333	.341	.429	.585	.336	109	125-OF 106
1999	*NYYanks*	*AL*	*499*	*160*	*31*	*4*	*25*	*76*	*95*	*97*	*12*	*9*	*348*	*.321*	*.410*	*.549*	*.324*	*104*	

A truly great player; you'd be hard-pressed to find one more complete. He's going to make an unholy amount of money over the next few years, so I feel obligated to point out one problem: he's only played an average of 133 games over the past three seasons. That's a full month of each year he's missed. Durability is the only question; I think that you'll be able to move him from center field to an outfield corner in about four years, and he'll be one of those players, like Chili Davis or Paul Molitor, who hits even better once he gets away from the tough defensive role. I think there are a few 35-homer seasons in him.

PITCHERS (Averages: 4.00 ERA, 9.00 H/9, 1.00 HR/9, 3.00 BB/9, 6.00 K/9, 1.00 KWH)

Jose Alberro Throws R Age 30

YEAR	TEAM	LGE	IP	H	ER	HR	BB	K	ERA	W	L	H/9	HR/9	BB/9	K/9	KWH	PERA
1996	Oklahoma	AmA	166.7	188	83	12	69	111	4.48	8	11	10.15	0.65	3.73	5.99	0.71	4.32
1997	Oklahoma	AmA	90.3	106	52	6	32	46	5.18	4	6	10.56	0.60	3.19	4.58	0.47	4.38
1997	Texas	AL	30.0	36	26	4	14	11	7.80	1	2	10.80	1.20	4.20	3.30	0.18	5.10
1998	Columbus	Int	125.0	143	76	13	70	71	5.47	5	9	10.30	0.94	5.04	5.11	0.38	4.75

Quadruple-A pitcher who's just about out of chances. Alberro was never allowed to settle into a role with Texas, and the constant shifting has damaged his career. Not everyone is Kerry Wood; some pitchers need an opportunity to fail, to learn from that failure and improve, all without looking over their shoulder. Alberro never got that.

Ricardo Aramboles Throws R Age 19

YEAR	TEAM	LGE	IP	H	ER	HR	BB	K	ERA	W	L	H/9	HR/9	BB/9	K/9	KWH	PERA
1998	Oneonta	NYP	5.3	7	3	1	1	5	5.06	0	1	11.81	1.69	1.69	8.44	2.68	5.06

The latest high-priced international signing, Aramboles was Marlins's property until his agent notified MLB that he had signed early to make money for his family. It's hard to fault the kid for this, but the rules that make him a free agent are silly, especially when it seems he knew he was breaking the rules, and the signing was approved by the Dominican government. Fine both parties, dock the Marlins a draft pick and move on. Armaboles is a 19-year-old pitching prospect with no pro experience. Anybody who tells you they know anything definitive about him is lying.

Ryan Bradley Throws R Age 23

YEAR	TEAM	LGE	IP	H	ER	HR	BB	K	ERA	W	L	H/9	HR/9	BB/9	K/9	KWH	PERA
1997	Oneonta	NYP	23.3	35	8	2	7	12	3.09	2	1	13.50	0.77	2.70	4.63	0.44	5.79
1998	Tampa	Fla	92.3	71	30	6	34	80	2.92	7	3	6.92	0.58	3.31	7.80	1.99	2.44
1998	Norwich	Eas	24.7	10	4	1	7	19	1.46	3	0	3.65	0.36	2.55	6.93	3.87	0.00
1998	Columbus	Int	16.0	17	12	4	12	10	6.75	1	1	9.56	2.25	6.75	5.62	0.37	5.62
1998	NY Yanks	AL	13.0	12	7	2	8	13	4.85	0	1	8.31	1.38	5.54	9.00	1.32	4.15

The Yankees had an 18½ game lead over the Red Sox on August 21st, and the bullpen was in tatters thanks to twin back injuries to Jeff Nelson and Darren Holmes. Rather than call up one of the many staff fillers on the Columbus Clippers, they brought their 1997 first-round pick to his fourth city in six weeks. Why would you do this? You don't need him, it's obviously a panic move, and it starts the clock ticking on his arbitration and free agent eligibility, plus uses an option. An extremely rash decision.

When not packing and unpacking, Bradley moved from the bullpen into Tampa's rotation, and chewed up the Florida State and Eastern leagues. He's as good a pitching prospect as you'll find—insert the usual health caveats associated with "pitching prospect" here—with a 95-mph fastball that moves, a split-finger fastball, and a slider. It's not clear if his future is as a starter or reliever; he's got the arm and the repertoire to be excellent in either role.

Jim Bruske Throws R Age 34

YEAR	TEAM	LGE	IP	H	ER	HR	BB	K	ERA	W	L	H/9	HR/9	BB/9	K/9	KWH	PERA
1996	Albuquer	PCL	62.3	68	32	3	23	41	4.62	3	4	9.82	0.43	3.32	5.92	0.81	3.90
1997	LasVegas	PCL	66.0	76	36	7	21	51	4.91	3	4	10.36	0.95	2.86	6.95	1.22	4.50
1997	San Dieg	NL	44.7	40	21	5	23	28	4.23	2	3	8.06	1.01	4.63	5.64	0.64	3.63
1998	LosAngls	NL	44.7	49	16	2	17	28	3.22	3	2	9.87	0.40	3.43	5.64	0.71	4.03

Just another faceless automaton who can step into a bullpen and give you 70 innings with a 4.00 ERA. Bruske had been a bit of a ping-pong ball between the Dodgers and Padres the past two years before being sent to the Yankees at the trade deadline. Deserves a job, so watch where he ends up this spring.

Mike Buddie Throws R Age 28

YEAR	TEAM	LGE	IP	H	ER	HR	BB	K	ERA	W	L	H/9	HR/9	BB/9	K/9	KWH	PERA
1996	Norwich	Eas	148.0	224	119	11	78	72	7.24	4	12	13.62	0.67	4.74	4.38	0.22	6.02
1997	Columbus	Int	71.3	103	27	4	25	50	3.41	5	3	13.00	0.50	3.15	6.31	0.73	5.43
1998	Columbus	Int	42.0	40	15	0	15	23	3.21	3	2	8.57	0.00	3.21	4.93	0.66	3.00
1998	NY Yanks	AL	42.3	46	24	5	12	19	5.10	2	3	9.78	1.06	2.55	4.04	0.49	4.25

(Mike Buddie *continued*)

Jim Bruske, without the frequent flyer miles on Southwest. Buddie throws harder than Bruske, but has the same outlook: he can be an effective middle reliever and contribute to a winning team. Buddie has the added advantage of recent starting experience, so he could be a valuable swingman. He's close to establishing himself.

David Cone   Throws R   Age 36

YEAR	TEAM	LGE	IP	H	ER	HR	BB	K	ERA	W	L	H/9	HR/9	BB/9	K/9	KWH	PERA
1996	NY Yanks	AL	74.0	47	18	3	28	70	2.19	6	2	5.72	0.36	3.41	8.51	2.79	1.58
1997	NY Yanks	AL	198.7	155	55	16	74	214	2.49	16	6	7.02	0.72	3.35	9.69	2.99	2.58
1998	NY Yanks	AL	211.3	184	74	19	53	202	3.15	14	9	7.84	0.81	2.26	8.60	3.14	2.90

There's evidence of decline, although a good chunk of the difference between 1997 and 1998 was a terrible April, and he may have been coming back too quickly from off-season surgery on his right shoulder. The rest of the year, he was David Cone. I still think the four months he missed in 1996 will help him in the long-term. Good bet to continue at this level in 1999.

Rick Cremer   Throws R   Age 22

YEAR	TEAM	LGE	IP	H	ER	HR	BB	K	ERA	W	L	H/9	HR/9	BB/9	K/9	KWH	PERA
1998	Greensbr	SAL	75.0	74	32	6	30	47	3.84	4	4	8.88	0.72	3.60	5.64	0.75	3.72

Was impressing Sally League hitters and the organization with a nasty deuce when an injury cut two months out of his season. If you're looking for a guy who could advance quickly, this is a good candidate, health pending; the Yankees don't have a lot of pitching prospects at the upper levels.

Luis De los Santos   Throws R   Age 21

YEAR	TEAM	LGE	IP	H	ER	HR	BB	K	ERA	W	L	H/9	HR/9	BB/9	K/9	KWH	PERA
1996	Oneonta	NYP	53.7	66	37	5	24	38	6.20	2	4	11.07	0.84	4.02	6.37	0.68	4.86
1996	Greensbr	SAL	28.0	60	24	6	12	13	7.71	1	2	19.29	1.93	3.86	4.18	0.18	9.64
1997	Greensbr	SAL	85.0	116	52	4	16	40	5.51	3	6	12.28	0.42	1.69	4.24	0.65	4.87
1997	Tampa	Fla	59.0	62	22	5	9	29	3.36	4	3	9.46	0.76	1.37	4.42	1.13	3.66
1997	Norwich	Eas	23.7	27	8	4	6	12	3.04	2	1	10.27	1.52	2.28	4.56	0.67	4.94
1998	Norwich	Eas	78.3	107	48	4	23	40	5.51	3	6	12.29	0.46	2.64	4.60	0.49	5.06
1998	Tampa	Fla	64.7	80	40	2	12	24	5.57	2	5	11.13	0.28	1.67	3.34	0.45	4.18

A bad back contributed to his tough year, one that saw him get demoted back to A-ball. He was young for Double-A, and he did fight injuries, so I wouldn't worry too much about 1998. Despite good stuff, he's never struck out a lot of hitters. Now that I would worry about.

Todd Erdos   Throws R   Age 25

YEAR	TEAM	LGE	IP	H	ER	HR	BB	K	ERA	W	L	H/9	HR/9	BB/9	K/9	KWH	PERA
1996	R Cucmng	Cal	65.0	74	31	2	35	54	4.29	3	4	10.25	0.28	4.85	7.48	0.84	4.29
1997	Mobile	Sou	57.3	51	20	4	21	37	3.14	4	2	8.01	0.63	3.30	5.81	0.96	3.14
1998	Columbus	Int	49.3	56	25	4	19	42	4.56	2	3	10.22	0.73	3.47	7.66	1.24	4.38

Erdos had a golden opportunity snatched away from him on March 8th, when he was traded by the D'backs to the Yankees. Sometimes, you're just not in the right place at the right time. He throws hard, and is young enough that he has time to find an organization a bit less deep than the Yankees.

Orlando Hernandez   Throws R   Age 29

YEAR	TEAM	LGE	IP	H	ER	HR	BB	K	ERA	W	L	H/9	HR/9	BB/9	K/9	KWH	PERA
1998	Columbus	Int	41.7	47	19	2	17	46	4.10	2	3	10.15	0.43	3.67	9.94	1.99	4.10
1998	NY Yanks	AL	143.7	112	44	10	47	127	2.76	11	5	7.02	0.63	2.94	7.96	2.30	2.44

He and Rolando Arrojo re-established the credibility of Cuban pitchers. I was convinced there would be a learning curve, that the league would catch up to him, but so far I'm wrong: he was 3-1, 3.20 in second starts against teams. Even if he's older than 29, I think his short-term outlook is very good, a top 15 AL starter for the next two or three years. Very fun to watch.

Darren Holmes   Throws R   Age 33

YEAR	TEAM	LGE	IP	H	ER	HR	BB	K	ERA	W	L	H/9	HR/9	BB/9	K/9	KWH	PERA
1996	Colorado	NL	87.0	70	28	7	28	68	2.90	7	3	7.24	0.72	2.90	7.03	1.77	2.59
1997	Colorado	NL	98.3	107	44	12	33	64	4.03	5	6	9.79	1.10	3.02	5.86	0.87	4.30
1998	NY Yanks	AL	52.0	53	16	4	12	30	2.77	4	2	9.17	0.69	2.08	5.19	1.06	3.63

Underrated because of the years spent in Colorado, and because he doesn't have much of a physical presence. He gets groundballs and strikeouts, keeps the ball in the park, and is usually healthy. A bulging disk wiped out his August, but he was fine in September. A reliable reliever.

Hideki Irabu   Throws R   Age 30

YEAR	TEAM	LGE	IP	H	ER	HR	BB	K	ERA	W	L	H/9	HR/9	BB/9	K/9	KWH	PERA
1997	NY Yanks	AL	54.7	68	39	14	17	54	6.42	2	4	11.20	2.30	2.80	8.89	1.89	6.09
1998	NY Yanks	AL	176.3	147	66	26	69	122	3.37	12	8	7.50	1.33	3.52	6.23	1.10	3.27

This is about the top of his range, in my opinion. He seemed to be throwing harder at the start of the year, but there's still nothing about him that screams "superstar." The Yankees would be well-served to trade him for talent with more up-side; they have the rotation depth. His second half fade scares me.

Marty Janzen   Throws R   Age 26

YEAR	TEAM	LGE	IP	H	ER	HR	BB	K	ERA	W	L	H/9	HR/9	BB/9	K/9	KWH	PERA
1996	Syracuse	Int	55.0	80	49	12	24	29	8.02	1	5	13.09	1.96	3.93	4.75	0.33	6.87
1996	Toronto	AL	77.0	89	48	14	31	47	5.61	3	6	10.40	1.64	3.62	5.49	0.60	5.14
1997	Syracuse	Int	64.0	87	55	12	33	45	7.73	1	6	12.23	1.69	4.64	6.33	0.53	6.33
1997	Toronto	AL	25.3	23	9	4	12	16	3.20	2	1	8.17	1.42	4.26	5.68	0.70	3.91
1998	Norwich	Eas	32.7	53	33	4	21	26	9.09	1	3	14.60	1.10	5.79	7.16	0.46	6.89
1998	Columbus	Int	68.0	89	47	8	38	43	6.22	2	6	11.78	1.06	5.03	5.69	0.41	5.56

Like Todd Erdos, Janzen went from a golden opportunity to the bowels of hell (or Ohio) when he was traded from Arizona to New York. Unlike Erdos, he's unlikely to contribute in the majors. He's a pretty good example for trading pitching prospects for current value; the Yankees got David Cone for him and change back in 1995, and none of what they gave up turned into anything.

Mike Jerzembeck   Throws R   Age 27

YEAR	TEAM	LGE	IP	H	ER	HR	BB	K	ERA	W	L	H/9	HR/9	BB/9	K/9	KWH	PERA
1996	Tampa	Fla	64.3	100	40	7	16	40	5.60	2	5	13.99	0.98	2.24	5.60	0.75	6.16
1996	Norwich	Eas	66.0	91	42	10	27	47	5.73	2	5	12.41	1.36	3.68	6.41	0.67	6.00
1997	Norwich	Eas	39.7	28	12	1	16	28	2.72	3	1	6.35	0.23	3.63	6.35	1.31	2.04
1997	Columbus	Int	125.7	148	57	14	35	89	4.08	7	7	10.60	1.00	2.51	6.37	1.15	4.58
1998	Columbus	Int	136.7	184	83	19	55	83	5.47	5	10	12.12	1.25	3.62	5.47	0.51	5.73

The only thing vaguely resembling a pitching prospect at Columbus; the rest of the rotation there included Jose Alberro, Ricardo Jordan, Wilson Heredia, and Frank Lankford. Jerzembeck is another Yankee arm who is going to have to go elsewhere to get an opportunity. If he ends up somewhere with a job, he'll be a league-average starter. That's valuable.

Graeme Lloyd   Throws L   Age 32

YEAR	TEAM	LGE	IP	H	ER	HR	BB	K	ERA	W	L	H/9	HR/9	BB/9	K/9	KWH	PERA
1996	Milwauke	AL	52.0	47	14	3	13	24	2.42	4	2	8.13	0.52	2.25	4.15	0.71	2.94
1997	NY Yanks	AL	50.0	54	20	6	18	25	3.60	3	3	9.72	1.08	3.24	4.50	0.48	4.32
1998	NY Yanks	AL	37.7	26	8	3	5	19	1.91	3	1	6.21	0.72	1.19	4.54	2.08	1.67

There's not much you can say about Lloyd: he gets left-handed hitters out, controls the running game, and resists the urge to preach Scientology in the clubhouse. His stats will vary, because in 40 innings a year anything can happen, but he'll contribute to many more winning teams.

Katsuhiro Maeda   Throws R   Age 28

YEAR	TEAM	LGE	IP	H	ER	HR	BB	K	ERA	W	L	H/9	HR/9	BB/9	K/9	KWH	PERA
1996	Norwich	Eas	49.3	63	29	4	24	21	5.29	2	3	11.49	0.73	4.38	3.83	0.22	5.11
1997	Norwich	Eas	113.0	153	87	13	65	52	6.93	3	10	12.19	1.04	5.18	4.14	0.20	5.81
1998	Norwich	Eas	34.7	57	43	4	35	19	11.16	0	4	14.80	1.04	9.09	4.93	0.14	7.27
1998	Columbus	Int	14.3	15	5	1	8	12	3.14	1	1	9.42	0.63	5.02	7.53	0.90	4.40

If his name was Bob Smith, would he be in the book? Probably not. Maeda hasn't been notably impressive at any level or in any role. Until and unless he has a heart-to-heart with home plate, he's not going to be a good pitcher. You would think the opportunity to leave Norwich, Connecticut, would be a bigger motivator.

Ramiro Mendoza   Throws R   Age 27

YEAR	TEAM	LGE	IP	H	ER	HR	BB	K	ERA	W	L	H/9	HR/9	BB/9	K/9	KWH	PERA
1996	Columbus	Int	96.7	105	29	2	20	52	2.70	8	3	9.78	0.19	1.86	4.84	0.97	3.44
1996	NY Yanks	AL	55.0	73	32	4	8	34	5.24	2	4	11.95	0.65	1.31	5.56	1.48	4.91
1997	NY Yanks	AL	135.7	153	56	14	24	79	3.71	8	7	10.15	0.93	1.59	5.24	1.27	4.18
1998	NY Yanks	AL	132.0	130	42	8	26	54	2.86	10	5	8.86	0.55	1.77	3.68	0.65	3.20

A big part of the championship staff, moving between the rotation and bullpen as needed and pitching in a variety of relief roles. Regular readers know how high we've been on him, and that hasn't changed, even with the dip in strikeout rate. Gets lots of groundballs and skewers the running game. It would be nice to see him get a more glamorous role.

Jeff Nelson   Throws R   Age 32

YEAR	TEAM	LGE	IP	H	ER	HR	BB	K	ERA	W	L	H/9	HR/9	BB/9	K/9	KWH	PERA
1996	NY Yanks	AL	77.7	70	27	5	29	90	3.13	6	3	8.11	0.58	3.36	10.43	2.99	3.13
1997	NY Yanks	AL	79.7	54	27	7	32	78	3.05	6	3	6.10	0.79	3.62	8.81	2.64	2.15
1998	NY Yanks	AL	41.3	45	15	1	19	34	3.27	3	2	9.80	0.22	4.14	7.40	1.01	3.92

Like the rest of the Yankee bullpen, when healthy he's among the best at his job. Nelson is the primary setup man for Mariano Rivera, and uses a plus fastball and wicked slider out of a sidearm delivery. The control issues that he's had in the past bothered him last year, but not as much as the bad back and broken toe that cost him two months. The slight decline isn't worrisome; he was his old self in September and the postseason.

Andy Pettitte   Throws L   Age 27

YEAR	TEAM	LGE	IP	H	ER	HR	BB	K	ERA	W	L	H/9	HR/9	BB/9	K/9	KWH	PERA
1996	NY Yanks	AL	228.3	211	76	19	58	161	3.00	16	9	8.32	0.75	2.29	6.35	1.59	3.15
1997	NY Yanks	AL	243.0	230	71	6	55	160	2.63	19	8	8.52	0.22	2.04	5.93	1.52	2.85
1998	NY Yanks	AL	220.7	225	92	19	78	142	3.75	13	12	9.18	0.77	3.18	5.79	0.86	3.79

Pettitte was extremely streaky this year; three months with ERAs of 2.31 or under, three at 5.71 or higher. Since there was no report of an injury, and he didn't look hurt in the postseason, I'm inclined to believe he just got himself out of whack at times. My observation is that he didn't seem to be as aggressive in the strike zone as in the past, and that he was carrying extra weight. Both problems are easily solved, and I expect Pettitte to bounce back towards his 1997 level in 1999.

Brian Reith   Throws R   Age 21

YEAR	TEAM	LGE	IP	H	ER	HR	BB	K	ERA	W	L	H/9	HR/9	BB/9	K/9	KWH	PERA
1998	Greensbr	SAL	113.0	111	47	8	37	71	3.74	7	6	8.84	0.64	2.95	5.65	0.92	3.50

Do you know how hard it is to have a DT-ERA of 3.74 while pitching in the Sally League? About as hard as getting Rany Jazayerli to attend a meeting of the Herk Robinson Fan Club. Unarmed. Reith didn't get a whole lot of ink for his performance, and standard caveats apply, so the Yankees's system has been thinned out, and he could be on everyone's list by June.

Mariano Rivera   Throws R   Age 29

YEAR	TEAM	LGE	IP	H	ER	HR	BB	K	ERA	W	L	H/9	HR/9	BB/9	K/9	KWH	PERA
1996	NY Yanks	AL	110.3	68	17	1	27	129	1.39	11	1	5.55	0.08	2.20	10.52	6.80	1.06
1997	NY Yanks	AL	72.7	64	14	5	17	66	1.73	7	1	7.93	0.62	2.11	8.17	3.00	2.85
1998	NY Yanks	AL	61.7	48	11	3	15	35	1.61	6	1	7.01	0.44	2.19	5.11	1.28	2.19

Something very bad is happening here. A declining strikeout rate is red flag #1 in predicting a pitcher's future success. Rivera's rate isn't declining: it's dropping like consumer confidence in Jakarta. He had a big drop in effectiveness in the second half, and all of this is with a diminishing workload. Subjectively, he seemed to have a very hard time getting strike three, or for that matter any swing-and-miss strike. His fastball is straight, and he doesn't have a great second pitch. This could just be small sample size, or a dramatic change in approach, but I don't think so. I think Rivera is experiencing a loss in effectiveness, one that is going to start showing up on the scoreboard this season.

Anthony Shelby   Throws L   Age 25

YEAR	TEAM	LGE	IP	H	ER	HR	BB	K	ERA	W	L	H/9	HR/9	BB/9	K/9	KWH	PERA
1996	Greensbr	SAL	23.3	27	8	0	12	14	3.09	2	1	10.41	0.00	4.63	5.40	0.45	4.24
1996	Tampa	Fla	27.7	35	16	2	8	14	5.20	1	2	11.39	0.65	2.60	4.55	0.52	4.88
1997	Tampa	Fla	64.0	93	30	6	19	40	4.22	3	4	13.08	0.84	2.67	5.62	0.68	5.77
1998	Columbus	Int	48.0	50	17	1	12	32	3.19	3	2	9.38	0.19	2.25	6.00	1.28	3.37

Another pitcher who became much more effective once moved to the bullpen. Shelby isn't a hot prospect by any means, but an excellent example of the kinds of free talent available at Triple-A. He is an injury away from stepping up to a role in major league bullpen, and could be 1999's Brian Edmondson. Anybody who keeps the ball in the park like this can work for me.

Cam Spence   Throws R   Age 24

YEAR	TEAM	LGE	IP	H	ER	HR	BB	K	ERA	W	L	H/9	HR/9	BB/9	K/9	KWH	PERA
1997	Greensbr	SAL	44.7	59	29	5	13	21	5.84	2	3	11.89	1.01	2.62	4.23	0.43	5.24
1997	Tampa	Fla	46.7	54	19	3	12	23	3.66	3	2	10.41	0.58	2.31	4.44	0.61	4.24
1998	Greensbr	SAL	35.7	49	14	2	7	22	3.53	2	2	12.36	0.50	1.77	5.55	1.06	5.05
1998	Tampa	Fla	119.3	160	76	8	45	72	5.73	4	9	12.07	0.60	3.39	5.43	0.54	5.13

Spence, like Brian Reith and Rick Cremer, has a chance to advance quickly because of the dearth of Yankee pitching prospects above A-ball. His stuff isn't impressive, but his command is; this helps when you're 23 in A-ball, but is not as significant at Double-A. Of the three pitchers, I think Spence is the one most likely to flop.

Mike Stanton   Throws L   Age 32

YEAR	TEAM	LGE	IP	H	ER	HR	BB	K	ERA	W	L	H/9	HR/9	BB/9	K/9	KWH	PERA
1996	Boston	AL	59.3	52	16	8	19	46	2.43	5	2	7.89	1.21	2.88	6.98	1.61	3.34
1996	Texas	AL	23.0	18	6	2	3	14	2.35	2	1	7.04	0.78	1.17	5.48	2.72	2.35
1997	NY Yanks	AL	67.7	51	15	3	29	67	2.00	6	2	6.78	0.40	3.86	8.91	2.28	2.39
1998	NY Yanks	AL	80.0	71	42	12	23	67	4.72	4	5	7.99	1.35	2.59	7.54	2.06	3.37

Saw more big flies than a garbage dump in August, and developed a nasty habit of letting left-handed hitters share in the fun, giving up six homers to them in 99 at-bats. A left-handed setup man who does this is about as useful as Joe Girardi. Pitched better in September and October. Stanton's got nasty stuff and should bounce back in 1999. If I'm right about Rivera, he could see "S" next to his name a dozen times.

Brien Taylor   Throws L   Age 27

YEAR	TEAM	LGE	IP	H	ER	HR	BB	K	ERA	W	L	H/9	HR/9	BB/9	K/9	KWH	PERA
1996	Greensbr	SAL	25.3	8	22	1	67	7	7.82	1	2	2.84	0.36	23.80	2.49	0.07	3.91
1997	Greensbr	SAL	22.0	52	68	8	78	12	27.82	0	2	21.27	3.27	31.91	4.91	0.03	12.27
1998	Greensbr	SAL	20.3	42	43	5	37	9	19.03	0	2	18.59	2.21	16.38	3.98	0.04	10.18

May have turned the corner, cutting his translated walk rate in half and his translated ERA by almost a third. He is without a doubt a better prospect than Eric Cartman.

Jay Tessmer   Throws R   Age 26

YEAR	TEAM	LGE	IP	H	ER	HR	BB	K	ERA	W	L	H/9	HR/9	BB/9	K/9	KWH	PERA
1996	Tampa	Fla	90.0	96	26	4	22	74	2.60	7	3	9.60	0.40	2.20	7.40	1.94	3.60
1997	Norwich	Eas	58.3	94	44	7	24	37	6.79	2	4	14.50	1.08	3.70	5.71	0.46	6.63
1998	Norwich	Eas	47.3	62	9	0	14	39	1.71	4	1	11.79	0.00	2.66	7.42	1.31	4.37
1998	Columbus	Int	17.7	9	2	1	1	11	1.02	2	0	4.58	0.51	0.51	5.60	10.08	0.00

(Jay Tessmer *continued*)

Tessmer added a changeup and was good again. He's the type of pitcher I like, keeping the ball in the park and throwing strikes for groundballs. That he was able to adjust and be successful after getting hit hard speaks well for him. I'm still not convinced, but ignoring performance like this is what gets teams in trouble. I expect a significant adjustment period, followed by a few years of serviceable relief. He's not going to be Steve Reed.

David Wells   Throws L   Age 36

YEAR	TEAM	LGE	IP	H	ER	HR	BB	K	ERA	W	L	H/9	HR/9	BB/9	K/9	KWH	PERA
1996	Baltimor	AL	224.0	240	106	27	41	128	4.26	12	13	9.64	1.08	1.65	5.14	1.25	4.02
1997	NY Yanks	AL	221.3	232	90	22	39	150	3.66	14	11	9.43	0.89	1.59	6.10	1.86	3.74
1998	NY Yanks	AL	216.7	191	71	27	25	157	2.95	16	8	7.93	1.12	1.04	6.52	3.87	2.91

The most popular baseball player in New York since the Dwight Gooden/Don Mattingly peak in the mid-1980s. On the mound, Wells has become a power/control pitcher, a deadly combination. Not as much of a flyball pitcher as you'd think, given his penchant for working up in the zone. When he goes bad, he's going to go quickly. There's a good chance he'll be a terrible free agent signing for someone after 1999.

SNWL				NEW YORK YANKEES							Park Effect: -1.9%	
PITCHER	GS	IP	R	SNW	SNL	SNPCT	W	L	RA	APW	SNVA	SNWAR
Bradley, R.	1	5.0	6	0.1	0.7	.085	0	1	10.80	-0.31	-0.28	-0.25
Bruske, J.	1	5.0	1	0.4	0.1	.822	1	0	1.80	0.16	0.16	0.20
Buddie, M.	2	10.3	11	0.3	1.1	.192	0	1	9.58	-0.52	-0.44	-0.32
Cone, D.	31	207.7	89	13.9	8.5	.620	20	7	3.86	2.29	2.55	4.36
Hernandez, O.	21	141.0	53	10.8	5.1	.680	12	4	3.38	2.27	2.72	4.04
Irabu, H.	28	171.0	77	11.9	8.8	.577	13	9	4.05	1.53	1.43	3.13
Mendoza, R.	14	88.3	41	5.6	4.2	.572	6	1	4.18	0.67	0.70	1.45
Pettitte, A.	32	213.3	110	12.6	11.4	.525	16	11	4.64	0.57	0.52	2.39
Wells, D.	30	214.3	86	14.1	8.6	.622	18	4	3.61	2.92	2.77	4.47
TOTALS	162	1061.3	483	69.6	49.6	.584	86	39	4.10	8.99	9.59	18.94

No, the "Greatest Team of All Time" did not feature the greatest starting rotation of all time. But the Yankees's rotation was awfully good, gaining five games in SNVA from their already-fine 1997 total. The 1998 staff had the second-best season of the past seven years by a non-Atlanta rotation, according to SNVA. The best was the McDowell/Fernandez/Alvarez/Bere White Sox of 1993, which had a 10.3 SNVA. The Braves have beaten the Yankee total of 9.6 in all but one of the past seven years, and they've beaten the White Sox 1993 SNVA of 10.3 in four of those seven years. The '98 Yankees were also probably the deepest starting staff since the advent of the five-man rotation. They were the only team since the beginning of the SN stats to have five 10-game SN Winners. As impossible as it may sound, the Yankees could have won even more ballgames in 1998 if Hideki Irabu and Andy Pettitte had just maintained their first-half levels. Irabu was 6.5-3.3 (.664) before the break, and 5.3-5.4 (.498) after. Pettitte was 7.8-5.4 (.592) before the break, and 4.7-6.0 (.442) after.

Pitcher Abuse Points

PITCHER	AGE	GS	PAP	PAP/S	AAW	MAX	115+	130+
Cone, David	35	31	455	14.68	14.68	133	8	1
Hernandez, Orlando	"28"	21	537	25.57	42.62	142	10	2
Irabu, Hideki*	29	29	78	2.69	4.03	122	3	0
Mendoza, Ramiro	26	14	21	1.50	3.00	115	1	0
Pettite, Andy	26	32	641	20.03	40.06	143	10	2
Wells, David	35	30	419	13.97	13.97	134	9	2
TOTAL		163	2158	13.24	19.79	143	41	7
RANKING (AL)			4	4	3		3-T	4

*includes rainout start

Joe Torre is a deserving Manager of the Year after the Yankees's record-breaking season, but you have to wonder: was it really necessary to work his starters as hard as he did? I realize it was a largely veteran staff, but the irony is that the older starters—35-year-olds David Cone and David Wells—were worked the least (although extra care needs to be taken with Cone, who has already battled an aneurysm in his shoulder). I think major league baseball has a vendetta against the Hernandez brothers for proving that some Cuban pitchers actually deserve the hype—although again, Orlando's age is a fiction pulled from the mind of Joe Cubas. The guy to really worry about here is Pettitte, who pitched like he was hurt down the stretch, although he did have a couple of fine postseason outings. He's got good mechanics and may recover, but not if Torre continues to flog him.

Tampa Bay Devil Rays

Be careful what you wish for. Tampa Bay general manager Chuck Lamar went into the expansion draft claiming that he wanted to build the new team around pitching and defense. The foundation for that was well-laid before the draft: the Rays had committed $20 million for Cuban defector Rolando Arrojo and high school pitchers-turned-free-agents Bobby Seay and Matt White.

So on into the Expansion Draft, and pitchers are the order of the day. First pick: Tony Saunders, thank you and what were you thinking, Florida Marlins? If you're going to have a strong defense, you have to be strong up the middle, so catcher Mike Difelice, second baseman Miguel Cairo, and center fielder Quinton McCracken were brought in. Gotta have a second strong catcher—trade for John Flaherty. Must have a shortstop—trade for Kevin Stocker. To the extent that they got what they wanted, it was a perfectly executed draft.

They didn't stop there, locking up free agents Wilson Alvarez and Roberto Hernandez, who seem to travel as a two-fer package deal. Nothing was allowed to interfere with building a good defense up the middle, and offense wasn't a consideration; save that for the infield and outfield corners.

There's nothing wrong with that approach in principle, although I would always be looking to maximize the hitting plus defense combination, rather than either in isolation. The problem is that they were not willing to make the same commitment to offense at the hitting positions that they had made to defense up the middle. A pitcher had to be good to be chosen for the team, but apparently a hitter only had to be from central Florida. Sentiment has always been a useful promotion for a team with no hope of contending, and for expansion teams in particular. For a new team in a region like Tampa, where baseball is a year-round sport, the use of locals to build interest would attract some viewers. So the Devil Ray offense was founded upon the past prime (McGriff at first, Boggs at third) and the second-rate (Sorrento at DH).

The end result was that Tampa Bay cruised to the second worst adjusted EQA of any expansion team in history, behind

only the the '69 Padres, and one of the worst performances since World War II (See Table 1).

It gets worse. Of the 20 teams listed above, 16 of them scored more runs than was predicted for them; there appears to be something in any run prediction procedure that exaggerates their failure. Not just, or even primarily, in EqR alone: the 20 teams above scored an aggregate of 10,921 runs. Their equivalent runs total 10,841, a shortage of about 4 runs per team. Use linear weights to calculate runs scored, and you get just 10,637, a shortage of 14 per team; they have a total of 10,699 runs created, for a minus 11 run bias.

The exceptions were the '67 Mets and '52 Pirates, who were short by small amounts (two and 13 runs of EQR, respectively), and the two expansion teams: the Padres fell 34 runs short of their EqR total, while the Devil Rays were a whopping 52 runs behind their projection. That is an unusually large error, the 25th-worst since World War II. It means that while their predicted rate of run scoring was the 13th-worst in the last half-century, their true rate of run scoring (relative to their league) was third-worst, behind only those Padres and the truly dreadful '81 Blue Jays, holders of the all-time low team EQA.

The blame for that shortfall in runs can mostly be blamed on their hitting with runners in scoring position. The average team gains about 20 points of raw EQA with runners in scoring position; the 1998 Devil Rays lost 51 points, the worst of any team in the last six years. To see how those teams did in terms of expected run scoring refer to Table 2.

It is obvious that there is a strong (r=.64) relationship between poor situational hitting and not scoring as many runs as expected. That relationship is not as strong overall as it is here at the extreme end of the spectrum, dropping to about .44 for all 1993-98 teams.

How important is that? We can use the RISP information to make a further correction to equivalent runs (or to any other run prediction scheme you care to use; the principles are the same). Calculate a raw EQA from the RISP data; you can simply ignore the stolen base terms. The league RISP data should be used for the league raw score; plate appear-

Devil Rays Prospectus

1998 record: 63-99; Fifth place, AL East

Pythagorean W/L: 66-96

Runs scored: 620 (14th in AL)

Runs allowed: 751 (3rd in AL)

Team EQA: .238 (14rd in AL)

Park: Tropicana Field (good hitters')

1998: A great job of putting together a pitching staff and an unspeakably bad offense.

1999: Likely to get worse if the pitching regresses, with nothing done to help the lineup.

Table 1. Bottom Ten Teams, Adjusted EqA, 1946-98

	American League		National League	
1.	1981 Toronto	.221	1965 New York	.228
2.	1992 California	.231	1963 New York	.232
3.	1948 Washington	.231	1964 Houston	.233
4.	1979 Toronto	.232	1953 Pittsburgh	.233
5.	1981 Minnesota	.232	1960 Philadelphia	.233
6.	1950 St Louis	.234	1969 San Diego	.234
7.	1951 St Louis	.235	1952 Pittsburgh	.235
8.	1998 TAMPA BAY	.235	1977 Atlanta	.236
9.	1980 Seattle	.235	1951 Cincinnati	.238
10.	1954 Philadelphia	.236	1967 New York	.238

Table 2. Team Comparison of Expected Run Scoring

Team	REQAw/RISP-REQA	R-EQR
'98 Tampa Bay	-52	-51
'94 San Diego	-45	-45
'96 Texas	-33	-27
'97 Oakland	-27	-29
'97 Atlanta	-21	-2
'96 California	-21	-50
'94 Colorado	-20	-18
'95 Pittsburgh	-15	+3
'97 Cincinnati	-13	-15
'95 Toronto	-12	-28

REQAw/RISP-REQA = Raw EQA with Runners in Scoring Position minus Raw EQA
R-EQR = Runs minus Equivalent Runs

ances with RISP should be used in place of regular plate appearances. Keep the total league runs per plate appearance, though. Now you can set up an equation that looks like

$$delR = \left[\left(\frac{REQAsp}{LgREQAsp} \right)^2 - \left(\frac{REQA}{LgREQA} \right)^2 \right] \times PAsp \times LgRPA \times .5$$

where

REQAsp = raw EQA with RISP
LgREQAsp = league raw EQA with RISP
PAsp = PA with RISP

For Tampa Bay, we have a raw overall EqA of .719, and .660 with RISP. League values are .782 and .787, respectively; the league RPA was .1319, and the Rays had 1580 plate appearances with RISP. So, [$(.660/.787)^2 - (.719/.782)^2$] times 1580 times .1319 times .5 gives us –15 runs: a healthy chunk of that original 52 run error.

On the whole, doing this extra work will only shave a run and a half off of the average error, not 15 runs (the root-mean-square error for the regular EqR for all 1993-98 teams is 22.52; adding the delR value given above cuts that to 20.96). To give you an idea of how important that is, it is a little larger than the difference between calculating EqR with and without any stolen base or caught stealing information.

The good fortune for the Devil Rays is that poor situa-

tional hitting is more a matter of chance than lack of special skill; teams which do poorly in a year are as likely to be above average the next year as they are to be below average again (Table 3).

What does this mean for the Devil Rays? Well, most of the team that was so good at preventing runs and so horrid at producing them is returning in 1999. The pitching will be virtually unchanged, which should be a net wash, as Wilson Alvarez and Roberto Hernandez improve and cover for the probable slippage from Rolando Arrojo and the anonymous relievers who fared so well in '98.

Unfortunately, the same offense is returning as well. As of mid-December, the Devil Rays are one of just a few teams in baseball that hasn't made a major transaction, or lost a player of significance to free agency. So the terrible offense of '98 will come back, a year older in what should be a worse hitters' park—the fences in the power alleys will be moved back a dozen feet or so to compensate for an architects' error. Six hundred runs will have to be considered a real upset.

Until the D-Rays get serious about putting runs on the board, they aren't going to come close to being competitive. Assembling a credible defense and a good, unsung pitching staff is just half of building a baseball team. The other half is finding guys who can hit. Whether Chuck Lamar can will determine the fate of Tampa Bay. We're not optimistic.

Table 3.

Team	Actual R	EQR	Diff	EQR+delR	New Diff
Anaheim	787	766	+21	762	+25
Arizona	665	658	+7	662	+3
Atlanta	826	837	-11	836	-10
Baltimore	817	848	-31	845	-28
Boston	876	886	-10	884	-8
Cubs	831	817	+14	820	+11
Cincinnati	750	750	0	763	-13
Cleveland	850	881	-31	874	-24
Colorado	826	868	-42	883	-57
White Sox	861	836	+25	837	+24
Detroit	722	738	-16	735	-13
Florida	667	654	+13	662	+5
Houston	874	877	-3	885	-11
Kansas City	714	710	+4	705	+9
Los Angeles	669	654	+15	649	+20
Milwaukee	707	705	+2	719	-12
Minnesota	734	710	+24	708	+26
Montreal	644	644	0	640	+4
Mets	706	709	-3	712	-6
Yankees	965	948	+17	958	+7
Oakland	804	748	+56	759	+45
Philadelphia	713	716	+3	722	+9
Pittsburgh	650	626	+24	624	+26
San Diego	749	742	+7	744	+5
Seattle	859	898	-39	895	-36
San Francisco	845	844	+1	860	+15
St Louis	810	859	-49	851	-41
Tampa Bay	620	672	-52	658	-38
Texas	940	919	+21	935	+5
Toronto	816	842	-26	848	-32

HITTERS (Averages: BA .260/ OBA .330/ SA .420, EQA .260)

Wade Boggs   3B   Bats L   Age 41

YEAR	TEAM	LGE	AB	H	DB	TP	HR	BB	R	RBI	SB	CS	OUT	BA	OBA	SA	EQA	EQR	DEFENSE
1996	NYYanks	AL	486	145	26	2	2	63	67	55	1	2	343	.298	.379	.372	.269	64	114-3B 103
1997	NYYanks	AL	350	105	25	1	4	48	52	45	0	1	246	.300	.384	.411	.281	52	64-3B 106
1998	TampaBay	AL	425	114	21	4	7	48	52	48	3	2	313	.268	.342	.386	.256	52	72-3B 101
1999	*TampaBay*	*AL*	*378*	*97*	*21*	*2*	*3*	*51*	*47*	*38*	*1*	*2*	*283*	*.257*	*.345*	*.347*	*.242*	*41*	

He's strictly playing for 3,000 hits now, which is no big deal; an expansion club like this is the ideal place to indulge in a meaningless milestone chase. He'll enter 1999 with a contract for the year, a club option for 2000, the need for 78 more hits to get the mark, and talk of being a batting coach in the years to follow.

Rich Butler   OF   Bats L   Age 26

YEAR	TEAM	LGE	AB	H	DB	TP	HR	BB	R	RBI	SB	CS	OUT	BA	OBA	SA	EQA	EQR	DEFENSE
1995	Knoxvill	Sou	215	51	9	2	4	22	25	19	7	2	166	.237	.308	.353	.235	22	47-OF 101
1995	Syracuse	Int	198	30	2	1	3	10	6	6	2	2	170	.152	.192	.217	.091	2	54-OF 98
1997	Syracuse	Int	535	153	22	6	22	52	75	79	16	6	388	.286	.349	.473	.282	82	130-OF 97
1998	TampaBay	AL	213	46	2	3	7	16	17	19	4	2	169	.216	.271	.352	.214	18	56-OF 103
1998	Durham	Int	144	38	5	0	6	18	19	19	4	2	108	.264	.346	.424	.268	20	34-OF 87
1999	*TampaBay*	*AL*	*424*	*116*	*16*	*3*	*18*	*39*	*57*	*61*	*13*	*6*	*314*	*.274*	*.335*	*.453*	*.267*	*58*	

Part of the left-field trio Tampa Bay carried into April, he got off to a better start than Trammell and won a platoon role. He was doing reasonably well before a Greg Swindell pitch broke his hand, and wasn't the same when he came back. I don't expect to see him have a year as good as 1997 again.

Miguel Cairo   2B   Bats R   Age 25

YEAR	TEAM	LGE	AB	H	DB	TP	HR	BB	R	RBI	SB	CS	OUT	BA	OBA	SA	EQA	EQR	DEFENSE	
1996	Syracuse	Int	461	120	11	3	3	27	45	34	19	7	348	.260	.301	.317	.219	39	83-2B 98	31-3B 93
1997	Iowa	AA	568	154	31	4	4	24	67	45	36	13	427	.271	.301	.361	.234	57	106-2B 106	28-SS 98
1998	TampaBay	AL	505	130	24	5	5	27	50	42	17	8	383	.257	.295	.354	.226	47	141-2B 104	
1999	*TampaBay*	*AL*	*493*	*136*	*23*	*3*	*6*	*25*	*55*	*47*	*18*	*8*	*365*	*.276*	*.311*	*.371*	*.234*	*49*		

The Tampa Bay prototype: Small, fast, good glove, hacker at the plate. He did exactly as well as should have been expected. It wasn't worth all that much, and he won't get much better.

Humberto Cota   C   Bats R   Age 20

YEAR	TEAM	LGE	AB	H	DB	TP	HR	BB	R	RBI	SB	CS	OUT	BA	OBA	SA	EQA	EQR	DEFENSE
1998	Princetn	App	242	57	6	1	8	22	21	25	1	2	187	.236	.299	.368	.229	23	50-C 95
1999	*TampaBay*	*AL*	*170*	*46*	*4*	*0*	*5*	*14*	*17*	*21*	*1*	*1*	*125*	*.271*	*.326*	*.382*	*.242*	*18*	

Cota is a long way from the majors, but any catcher who ranks among the league leaders in offense deserves mention as a prospect. The young Mexican was second in the league in homers and RBI, third in extra-base hits and slugging average, and fifth in total bases. Not a bad catcher, either.

Steve Cox   1B   Bats L   Age 24

YEAR	TEAM	LGE	AB	H	DB	TP	HR	BB	R	RBI	SB	CS	OUT	BA	OBA	SA	EQA	EQR	DEFENSE
1996	Huntsvil	Sou	378	96	12	1	11	42	40	44	1	1	283	.254	.329	.378	.247	43	100-1B 99
1997	Edmonton	PCL	444	95	18	1	11	75	50	43	1	2	351	.214	.328	.333	.236	47	126-1B 87
1998	Durham	Int	427	101	19	0	12	50	44	45	2	3	329	.237	.317	.365	.238	45	114-1B 97
1999	*TampaBay*	*AL*	*428*	*106*	*20*	*1*	*14*	*55*	*52*	*54*	*1*	*2*	*324*	*.248*	*.333*	*.397*	*.251*	*51*	

Cox looked like a player in 1995, but he hasn't done a thing since. Back injuries have been a problem, and he is woefully short of power for his position. He'd give McGriff a run in a fair fight, not that he'd be a great improvement over the Crime Dog.

Mike Difelice   C   Bats R   Age 30

YEAR	TEAM	LGE	AB	H	DB	TP	HR	BB	R	RBI	SB	CS	OUT	BA	OBA	SA	EQA	EQR	DEFENSE
1996	Louisvil	AA	247	62	7	0	7	19	20	26	0	2	187	.251	.305	.364	.229	23	
1997	StLouis	NL	260	62	11	1	4	20	22	22	1	1	199	.238	.293	.335	.216	22	
1998	TampaBay	AL	244	53	10	3	3	16	17	17	0	0	191	.217	.265	.320	.197	17	76-C 104
1999	*TampaBay*	*AL*	*230*	*58*	*9*	*1*	*5*	*17*	*21*	*24*	*0*	*1*	*173*	*.252*	*.304*	*.365*	*.226*	*21*	

A strong defensive catcher who has never hit at any level. Except for the small and fast part, fits the team prototype. He appears to have established himself, so look for him in BP 2007.

John Flaherty   C   Bats R   Age 31

YEAR	TEAM	LGE	AB	H	DB	TP	HR	BB	R	RBI	SB	CS	OUT	BA	OBA	SA	EQA	EQR	DEFENSE
1996	Detroit	AL	150	36	8	0	5	7	13	15	1	0	114	.240	.274	.393	.227	14	
1996	SanDieg	NL	264	80	10	0	10	11	26	38	1	3	187	.303	.331	.455	.264	34	
1997	SanDieg	NL	441	123	21	1	10	36	48	52	3	4	322	.279	.333	.399	.253	52	
1998	TampaBay	AL	299	58	7	0	4	23	13	14	0	5	246	.194	.252	.258	.160	13	86-C 105
1999	*TampaBay*	*AL*	*327*	*80*	*8*	*0*	*9*	*23*	*27*	*32*	*1*	*2*	*249*	*.245*	*.294*	*.352*	*.217*	*27*	

Like Difelice, he's always had a strong defensive reputation. He had never shown any ability to hit prior to his arrival in San Diego in 1996, and he hasn't since. He did suffer a gruesome dislocated thumb injury after being hit by a foul tip, but he wasn't hitting before it happened, and he isn't likely to start hitting now.

Aubrey Huff   3B   Bats L   Age 22

YEAR	TEAM	LGE	AB	H	DB	TP	HR	BB	R	RBI	SB	CS	OUT	BA	OBA	SA	EQA	EQR	DEFENSE
1998	Charl-SC	SAL	265	74	9	1	9	20	28	35	1	1	192	.279	.330	.423	.259	33	69-3B 96
1999	*TampaBay*	*AL*	*215*	*70*	*9*	*1*	*10*	*15*	*30*	*39*	*1*	*1*	*146*	*.326*	*.370*	*.516*	*.296*	*35*	

A first team All-American from Miami, Huff was chosen in the fifth round in '98. He didn't waste any time adjusting to the wood bat, hitting .321 and slugging .547. It was an outstanding debut, but too short to know if it was real. Check back in August.

Kenny Kelly   OF   Bats R   Age 20

YEAR	TEAM	LGE	AB	H	DB	TP	HR	BB	R	RBI	SB	CS	OUT	BA	OBA	SA	EQA	EQR	DEFENSE
1998	Charl-SC	SAL	218	52	4	3	3	17	21	17	9	3	169	.239	.294	.326	.220	19	54-OF 110
1999	*TampaBay*	*AL*	*177*	*50*	*5*	*1*	*3*	*12*	*21*	*19*	*7*	*2*	*129*	*.282*	*.328*	*.373*	*.245*	*19*	

Very fast and strong-armed, hasn't shown an ability to hit yet. None of which should be a surprising description for a college quarterback, which Kelly was for the University of Miami. On the baseball field, he's an outstanding center fielder, but he'll have to commit to baseball full-time to go forward.

Mike Kelly   OF   Bats R   Age 29

YEAR	TEAM	LGE	AB	H	DB	TP	HR	BB	R	RBI	SB	CS	OUT	BA	OBA	SA	EQA	EQR	DEFENSE
1996	Indianap	AA	295	55	8	1	5	27	22	15	11	2	242	.186	.255	.271	.185	18	69-OF 91
1997	Indianap	AA	94	31	6	0	5	19	23	17	6	1	64	.330	.442	.553	.343	22	22-OF 100
1997	Cincnnti	NL	139	40	12	2	6	11	21	22	5	1	100	.288	.340	.532	.294	23	46-OF 96
1998	TampaBay	AL	274	63	9	2	10	23	29	28	12	6	217	.230	.290	.387	.234	29	70-OF 100
1999	*TampaBay*	*AL*	*305*	*74*	*15*	*2*	*11*	*32*	*40*	*36*	*11*	*4*	*235*	*.243*	*.315*	*.413*	*.250*	*37*	

After a strong spring, he was the right-handed half of the left-field platoon. As the season went on he moved down the depth chart, eventually becoming a pinch-hitter and defensive replacement. He was probably the Rays's worst mistake on Draft Day—they should have tried to get Dmitri Young for themselves.

Aaron Ledesma   INF   Bats R   Age 28

YEAR	TEAM	LGE	AB	H	DB	TP	HR	BB	R	RBI	SB	CS	OUT	BA	OBA	SA	EQA	EQR	DEFENSE
1996	Vancouvr	PCL	438	121	22	2	1	28	42	39	2	2	319	.276	.320	.342	.231	41	95-SS 82
1997	Rochestr	Int	322	90	16	0	3	28	39	31	8	2	234	.280	.337	.357	.248	36	81-SS 94
1997	Baltimor	AL	86	30	5	1	2	13	16	15	1	0	56	.349	.434	.500	.327	17	14-2B 98
1998	TampaBay	AL	292	92	12	3	1	11	33	30	8	7	207	.315	.340	.387	.250	32	51-SS 104
1999	*TampaBay*	*AL*	*342*	*104*	*16*	*2*	*2*	*23*	*43*	*37*	*7*	*4*	*242*	*.304*	*.348*	*.380*	*.252*	*39*	

(Aaron Ledesma *continued*)

The Rays's utility infielder, he finally got a chance to be a big leaguer. He can play all four infield spots, though he's never before played defense as well as he did this year. He should probably start against left-handed pitching: his batting average is 75 points higher against them over the last two seasons.

Dave Martinez   RF   Bats L   Age 34

YEAR	TEAM	LGE	AB	H	DB	TP	HR	BB	R	RBI	SB	CS	OUT	BA	OBA	SA	EQA	EQR	DEFENSE	
1996	ChiSox	AL	433	140	20	8	10	49	72	64	16	9	302	.323	.392	.476	.299	74	100-OF 97	15-1B 101
1997	ChiSox	AL	497	143	15	6	13	56	68	65	12	6	360	.288	.360	.421	.273	70	92-OF 99	38-1B 94
1998	TampaBay	AL	303	74	7	0	4	36	30	25	7	7	236	.244	.324	.307	.223	28	80-OF 103	
1999	*TampaBay*	*AL*	*361*	*96*	*11*	*2*	*7*	*45*	*45*	*40*	*7*	*8*	*273*	*.266*	*.347*	*.366*	*.246*	*41*		

Martinez had been a reliable hitter, but fell into the same morass as the rest of the Devil Rays. Bad karma. Seriously, he suffered from back spasms all season, including one notorious incident in which he was injured by an airline seat; then he tore his quadriceps in July, and it didn't heal before season's end.

Scott McClain   3B   Bats R   Age 27

YEAR	TEAM	LGE	AB	H	DB	TP	HR	BB	R	RBI	SB	CS	OUT	BA	OBA	SA	EQA	EQR	DEFENSE	
1996	Rochestr	Int	460	118	15	2	15	57	55	56	6	4	346	.257	.338	.396	.257	58	132-3B 107	
1997	Norfolk	Int	428	108	19	1	16	53	51	55	1	2	322	.252	.335	.414	.259	55	92-3B 93	20-SS 98
1998	Durham	Int	468	124	18	0	24	53	58	70	4	2	346	.265	.340	.457	.273	67	123-3B 93	
1999	*TampaBay*	*AL*	*456*	*120*	*16*	*0*	*23*	*53*	*58*	*70*	*3*	*2*	*338*	*.263*	*.340*	*.450*	*.268*	*63*		

McClain has to be one of the unluckiest guys around. He's a quality third baseman, an OK hitter who probably deserved a major league job about three years ago. His original team, the Orioles, moved Cal Ripken to third. They traded him to the Mets, just in time for Edgardo Alfonzo to have a great year, at third. He gets picked up by the Devil Rays, and they sign Wade Boggs. He got a trivial callup in July, to back up Boggs when Bobby Smith pulled a hamstring, and that cost him the International League home run title.

Quinton McCracken   OF   Bats B   Age 29

YEAR	TEAM	LGE	AB	H	DB	TP	HR	BB	R	RBI	SB	CS	OUT	BA	OBA	SA	EQA	EQR	DEFENSE
1996	Colorado	NL	272	66	9	5	3	32	34	24	12	6	212	.243	.322	.346	.238	29	78-OF 92
1997	Colorado	NL	318	86	9	1	3	43	48	27	22	11	243	.270	.357	.333	.252	39	108-OF 96
1998	TampaBay	AL	601	170	35	7	7	44	74	64	17	10	441	.283	.332	.399	.254	72	150-OF 109
1999	*TampaBay*	*AL*	*472*	*130*	*25*	*4*	*6*	*43*	*62*	*50*	*16*	*10*	*352*	*.275*	*.336*	*.383*	*.248*	*54*	

That Devil Ray prototype rears its head again. He got off to a blistering start, which generated delusions about him deserving to be on the All-Star team. As the season went on he returned to form. The center fielder for the first half of the season, he spent much of the second half in left, which gave the team outstanding defense and even less offense than it started off with.

Fred McGriff   1B   Bats L   Age 35

YEAR	TEAM	LGE	AB	H	DB	TP	HR	BB	R	RBI	SB	CS	OUT	BA	OBA	SA	EQA	EQR	DEFENSE
1996	Atlanta	NL	613	175	31	1	29	71	85	97	6	3	441	.285	.360	.481	.287	97	152-1B 106
1997	Atlanta	NL	564	155	21	1	24	71	74	83	4	0	409	.275	.356	.443	.278	83	137-1B 95
1998	TampaBay	AL	551	151	23	0	21	80	78	78	6	2	402	.274	.366	.430	.279	83	135-1B 95
1999	*TampaBay*	*AL*	*537*	*139*	*19*	*0*	*23*	*74*	*70*	*78*	*3*	*1*	*399*	*.259*	*.349*	*.423*	*.266*	*73*	

Traded to Tampa Bay from Atlanta for a player to be named later, who turned out to be Twenty K. Cash. Like Boggs, he's a Bay area native receiving a sinecure with the Rays.

Carlos Mendoza   OF   Bats L   Age 24

YEAR	TEAM	LGE	AB	H	DB	TP	HR	BB	R	RBI	SB	CS	OUT	BA	OBA	SA	EQA	EQR	DEFENSE
1996	Columbia	SAL	312	89	5	1	1	43	44	27	12	6	229	.285	.372	.317	.253	37	46-OF 80
1997	Binghmtn	Eas	221	72	8	1	1	11	28	23	10	8	156	.326	.358	.385	.258	26	43-OF 104
1998	Durham	Int	199	48	7	0	0	14	16	11	6	7	158	.241	.291	.276	.192	13	47-OF 98
1998	Orlando	Sou	135	40	1	2	1	14	21	13	10	2	97	.296	.362	.356	.266	18	23-OF 99
1999	*TampaBay*	*AL*	*328*	*95*	*10*	*1*	*1*	*30*	*44*	*29*	*16*	*8*	*241*	*.290*	*.349*	*.335*	*.243*	*35*	

Another classic Devil Ray. He started the season at Durham and was horrible, but returned to his normal form after being loaned out to Orlando. He's fast enough and has just enough patience to be a useful hitter, even without power.

Alex Sanchez   CF   Bats L   Age 22

YEAR	TEAM	LGE	AB	H	DB	TP	HR	BB	R	RBI	SB	CS	OUT	BA	OBA	SA	EQA	EQR	DEFENSE
1997	Charl-SC	SAL	543	144	12	3	1	35	60	35	40	23	422	.265	.310	.304	.219	47	129-OF 102
1998	StPete	Fla	539	155	13	5	2	27	60	44	30	19	403	.288	.322	.341	.232	53	127-OF 102
1999	TampaBay	AL	480	141	12	3	1	24	58	39	30	17	355	.294	.327	.338	.232	46	

His escape from Cuba was decidedly less glamorous than those of some other players. Sanchez was only 16 when he tried to raft his way off the island, only to be picked up by the U.S. Coast Guard and spend 16 months in a Guantanamo refugee camp. A pure speed player at this time, without the baseball skill to use it well. He stole 92 bases in 1997, more than anyone this decade, but got caught 40 times; in '98 he was 66-33. He can outrun most of his many defensive mistakes.

Jared Sandberg   3B   Bats R   Age 21

YEAR	TEAM	LGE	AB	H	DB	TP	HR	BB	R	RBI	SB	CS	OUT	BA	OBA	SA	EQA	EQR	DEFENSE
1997	Princetn	App	267	58	5	1	8	28	24	24	5	2	211	.217	.292	.333	.219	24	40-2B 104
1998	Charl-SC	SAL	194	30	4	0	3	22	9	7	2	0	164	.155	.241	.222	.149	7	56-3B 81
1998	HudsnVal	NYP	279	71	7	1	9	32	33	32	6	2	210	.254	.331	.384	.252	34	69-3B 110
1999	TampaBay	AL	371	88	6	0	12	39	36	39	5	2	285	.237	.310	.350	.228	35	

Sandberg—yes, Ryne's his uncle—was the Appalachian League's MVP a year ago as a second baseman. This year, the Rays tried to take advantage of his arm by moving him to third, while advancing him to the Sally League. It didn't work out, as he was lost at the plate (76 Ks in 56 games) and the field (22 errors in those same 56 games). Sent back to the New York-Penn League, he was again a dominant offensive force, and improved afield.

Dave Silvestri   UT   Bats R   Age 31

YEAR	TEAM	LGE	AB	H	DB	TP	HR	BB	R	RBI	SB	CS	OUT	BA	OBA	SA	EQA	EQR	DEFENSE
1996	Montreal	NL	161	31	1	0	2	34	18	10	2	1	131	.193	.333	.236	.214	14	31-3B 124
1997	Oklahoma	AA	465	94	16	2	11	46	35	35	3	4	375	.202	.274	.316	.202	34	87-3B 104
1998	Durham	Int	476	110	18	1	6	49	43	37	7	7	373	.231	.303	.311	.214	40	95-2B 98
1999	TampaBay	AL	457	102	15	1	9	52	42	39	4	4	359	.223	.303	.319	.213	38	

There was a time when he was a regarded as a good-hitting middle infielder with stone hands. Now, the Tampa papers call him someone whose glove was "never in doubt" but whose hitting was, and near as I can tell they're not wrong. Silvestri isn't a serious part of anybody's future.

Bobby Smith   3B/SS   Bats R   Age 25

YEAR	TEAM	LGE	AB	H	DB	TP	HR	BB	R	RBI	SB	CS	OUT	BA	OBA	SA	EQA	EQR	DEFENSE	
1996	Richmond	Int	443	108	16	0	9	32	40	38	11	7	342	.244	.295	.341	.220	39	76-3B 99	39-SS 96
1997	Richmond	Int	356	83	8	1	11	39	34	36	5	4	277	.233	.309	.354	.231	36	98-SS 107	
1998	TampaBay	AL	362	96	13	3	11	36	41	45	4	3	269	.265	.332	.409	.256	45	85-3B 105	
1999	TampaBay	AL	370	98	15	1	12	33	43	46	6	4	276	.265	.325	.408	.250	43		

One of the team's most pleasant surprises, Smith was their leading hitter prior to a September collapse (.179/.247/.274). He has always been hyped more than his performance justified, but had never before made good use of his tools. Good enough in the field to play a respectable shortstop. His glove is the main reason he probably should start ahead of Boggs, although not ahead of McClain.

Paul Sorrento   DH/1B   Bats L   Age 33

YEAR	TEAM	LGE	AB	H	DB	TP	HR	BB	R	RBI	SB	CS	OUT	BA	OBA	SA	EQA	EQR	DEFENSE
1996	Seattle	AL	461	130	29	1	23	54	63	76	0	2	333	.282	.357	.499	.289	75	125-1B 98
1997	Seattle	AL	449	119	17	0	32	52	57	79	0	2	332	.265	.341	.517	.286	73	118-1B 120
1998	TampaBay	AL	427	92	20	0	18	55	45	48	2	3	338	.215	.305	.389	.239	47	25-1B 111
1999	TampaBay	AL	455	110	18	0	25	60	56	69	1	2	347	.242	.330	.446	.262	61	

Primarily a DH last year, a position he said he detests, and his hitting collapsed . . . or so it appears. For one thing, as noted last year, Sorrento has a very large platoon split; the Rays allowed him to try and hit left-handed pitchers in 88 of his 489 plate

(Paul Sorrento *continued*)

appearances, a higher ratio than in any of the previous three years, and he was no better or worse than usual in the attempt (1993-97 vs. LHP: .683 OPS; 1998: .660). For another, his home/road splits over the last two years were huge (EQAs of .317 and .310 in 1996 and 1997 at home, .260 and .245 on the road), even though the Kingdome was essentially a neutral park. His '98 road performance was just like '97, with a few extra plate appearances against left-handers to drag him down even further.

Kevin Stocker   SS   Bats B   Age 29

YEAR	TEAM	LGE	AB	H	DB	TP	HR	BB	R	RBI	SB	CS	OUT	BA	OBA	SA	EQA	EQR	DEFENSE
1996	Philadel	NL	395	101	22	5	6	45	48	42	5	4	298	.256	.332	.382	.250	46	117-SS 109
1997	Philadel	NL	504	134	23	4	5	54	60	49	9	6	376	.266	.337	.357	.245	56	145-SS 95
1998	TampaBay	AL	330	65	9	3	6	29	22	21	4	3	268	.197	.262	.297	.189	21	107-SS 103
1999	*TampaBay*	*AL*	*373*	*93*	*17*	*3*	*6*	*39*	*41*	*38*	*5*	*4*	*284*	*.249*	*.320*	*.359*	*.234*	*38*	

Another in the prototype, and another in which their choice was clear: they traded away Bobby Abreu to get him. He provided them his usual excellent defense, but his on-again/off-again hitting took the year off. His problems came entirely from the left side of the plate—he was actually better than usual from his natural right-handed side—and he was considering (not for the first time) abandoning switch-hitting. His season ended in August when a Justin Thompson fastball broke his hand.

Bubba Trammell   OF/DH   Bats R   Age 27

YEAR	TEAM	LGE	AB	H	DB	TP	HR	BB	R	RBI	SB	CS	OUT	BA	OBA	SA	EQA	EQR	DEFENSE
1996	Jacksnvl	Sou	309	93	13	1	19	23	40	55	2	1	217	.301	.349	.534	.295	51	66-OF 88
1996	Toledo	Int	178	48	10	1	5	21	25	22	4	1	131	.270	.347	.421	.269	25	45-OF 97
1997	Toledo	Int	322	79	9	1	22	31	36	50	2	2	245	.245	.312	.484	.266	45	74-OF 82
1997	Detroit	AL	121	27	5	0	4	15	14	12	3	1	95	.223	.309	.364	.238	13	19-OF 108
1998	TampaBay	AL	195	54	16	1	12	17	26	34	0	2	143	.277	.335	.554	.290	32	31-OF 93
1998	Durham	Int	216	56	7	0	11	30	29	32	4	1	161	.259	.350	.444	.276	32	55-OF 94
1999	*TampaBay*	*AL*	*434*	*118*	*18*	*1*	*28*	*48*	*60*	*78*	*4*	*2*	*318*	*.272*	*.344*	*.512*	*.284*	*69*	

The Devil Rays came out of spring training planning on using Mike Kelly in left field against left-handers, with Trammell and Butler still competing for the rest of the playing time. Trammell got off to a slow start, batting .176 and striking out half the time. A two-month refresher course in Durham got his patience back, and with it his stroke, and when he was recalled at the All-Star break he proceeded to set the league on its ear. The only instance where the Rays chose a player for offense instead of defense, speed, or sentiment.

Randy Winn   CF   Bats B   Age 25

YEAR	TEAM	LGE	AB	H	DB	TP	HR	BB	R	RBI	SB	CS	OUT	BA	OBA	SA	EQA	EQR	DEFENSE
1995	Elmira	NYP	215	54	4	1	1	10	16	14	7	4	165	.251	.284	.293	.199	15	50-OF 98
1996	KaneCnty	Mid	517	109	8	1	1	31	26	21	13	9	417	.211	.255	.236	.160	21	130-OF 95
1997	Brevard	Fla	144	38	6	1	0	14	17	11	7	4	110	.264	.329	.319	.232	14	35-OF 110
1997	Portland	Eas	376	88	9	3	6	32	41	27	24	12	300	.234	.294	.322	.219	34	89-OF 101
1998	Durham	Int	122	30	4	1	1	13	15	9	7	3	95	.246	.319	.320	.231	12	27-OF 95
1998	TampaBay	AL	331	89	8	9	1	30	45	28	23	12	254	.269	.330	.356	.244	37	82-OF 109
1999	*TampaBay*	*AL*	*452*	*116*	*16*	*5*	*2*	*37*	*55*	*34*	*27*	*13*	*349*	*.257*	*.313*	*.327*	*.225*	*42*	

Another prototype, Winn was the team's most surprising player in 1998, as he leapt out to a .363 average through his first 25 games. That set off all manner of wild speculation about what a steal he was, which didn't die down when he returned to normal, hitting .219 over the last two months. Winn is a pure speedster who keeps the ball on the ground and outruns it to first, then tries to steal second. Other players in that mold—Curtis Goodwin and Alex Cole come to mind—have had similar initial success before teams realized that they were really pretty easy to defend. The Rays are relying on him for 1999, a serious mistake.

PITCHERS (Averages: 4.00 ERA, 9.00 H/9, 1.00 HR/9, 3.00 BB/9, 6.00 K/9, 1.00 KWH)

Scott Aldred   Throws L   Age 31

YEAR	TEAM	LGE	IP	H	ER	HR	BB	K	ERA	W	L	H/9	HR/9	BB/9	K/9	KWH	PERA
1996	Detroit	AL	45.0	57	39	8	21	36	7.80	1	4	11.40	1.60	4.20	7.20	0.81	5.80
1996	Minnesot	AL	126.0	127	55	17	34	75	3.93	7	7	9.07	1.21	2.43	5.36	0.98	3.93
1997	SaltLake	PCL	37.7	59	36	4	15	17	8.60	1	3	14.10	0.96	3.58	4.06	0.24	6.45
1997	Minnesot	AL	80.0	101	55	19	24	32	6.19	3	6	11.36	2.14	2.70	3.60	0.32	5.96
1998	Durham	Int	34.0	51	27	3	14	15	7.15	1	3	13.50	0.79	3.71	3.97	0.24	6.09
1998	TampaBay	AL	32.3	33	11	1	11	21	3.06	3	1	9.19	0.28	3.06	5.85	0.91	3.34

He didn't survive the Rays's final spring training cut, but was called up in April to take Ramon Tatis's place as the bullpen's designated lefty-killer. Even though he had no history of a platoon split, it worked: he held left-handers to a .182 EQA, while right-handers had a .306.

Wilson Alvarez   Throws L   Age 29

YEAR	TEAM	LGE	IP	H	ER	HR	BB	K	ERA	W	L	H/9	HR/9	BB/9	K/9	KWH	PERA
1996	ChiSox	AL	217.3	215	86	18	78	178	3.56	13	11	8.90	0.75	3.23	7.37	1.42	3.64
1997	ChiSox	AL	149.7	122	48	8	47	106	2.89	11	6	7.34	0.48	2.83	6.37	1.47	2.53
1997	SanFran	NL	67.3	58	33	10	32	62	4.41	3	4	7.75	1.34	4.28	8.29	1.55	3.61
1998	TampaBay	AL	147.3	131	65	17	62	105	3.97	8	8	8.00	1.04	3.79	6.41	1.02	3.42

With a $35 million contract, he was supposed to be the ace of the staff. He started out well enough, but started getting hit hard in May. He eventually admitted he'd been pitching in pain, so he missed six weeks with what was called either shoulder tendinitis or an inflamed rotator cuff, depending on who you listen to. He probably should have stayed out longer, as it took another two months before he began to pitch well again. Alvarez was awfully hard-headed about it; he never wanted to go on the disabled list at all, and was indignant that he was on a pitch count when he returned. Rothschild saved him from himself.

Rolando Arrojo   Throws R   Age 30

YEAR	TEAM	LGE	IP	H	ER	HR	BB	K	ERA	W	L	H/9	HR/9	BB/9	K/9	KWH	PERA
1997	StPete	Fla	80.0	109	60	8	17	47	6.75	2	7	12.26	0.90	1.91	5.29	0.89	5.29
1998	TampaBay	AL	207.7	195	71	19	59	149	3.08	14	9	8.45	0.82	2.56	6.46	1.45	3.34

Arrojo deserved to be Rookie of the Year. His secret is his arsenal; none of the weapons are overpowering alone, but the variety is overwhelming. Five pitches—a two-seam fastball that goes to the right, a four-seamer that goes left, a slider, sinker, and curve are only the start of the problem. You also have to contend with a delivery that comes from anywhere between full over-hand to submarine. The sidearm and underhand stuff was especially deadly on right-handed hitters, who managed just a .190 EQA off him (left-handers hit .280). You would think that a pitcher like this would be more vulnerable the second time a team sees him, but you'd be wrong: he allowed more runs, more hits, and more walks per nine innings the first time he faced a team than the second. He did fade a bit before being shut down in September, so watch him carefully this spring.

Cedrick Bowers   Throws L   Age 21

YEAR	TEAM	LGE	IP	H	ER	HR	BB	K	ERA	W	L	H/9	HR/9	BB/9	K/9	KWH	PERA
1997	Charl-SC	SAL	147.7	170	93	15	95	108	5.67	5	11	10.36	0.91	5.79	6.58	0.54	4.94
1998	StPete	Fla	143.0	179	95	18	88	116	5.98	5	11	11.27	1.13	5.54	7.30	0.64	5.48

Bowers is a big, strong pitcher who has been sheltered from attention by the much richer Matt White and Bobby Seay, even though he's accomplished more to date than either of them. His fastball is good; his curve is big but out of control. Not a great prospect, but you never know with pitchers.

John Daniels   Throws R   Age 25

YEAR	TEAM	LGE	IP	H	ER	HR	BB	K	ERA	W	L	H/9	HR/9	BB/9	K/9	KWH	PERA
1996	Lancastr	Cal	94.7	100	43	9	28	67	4.09	5	6	9.51	0.86	2.66	6.37	1.20	3.99
1997	StPete	Fla	56.7	74	33	5	17	50	5.24	2	4	11.75	0.79	2.70	7.94	1.49	5.08
1998	StPete	Fla	37.3	43	16	4	14	29	3.86	2	2	10.37	0.96	3.38	6.99	1.05	4.58
1998	Orlando	Sou	17.7	18	12	4	8	14	6.11	1	1	9.17	2.04	4.08	7.13	1.02	4.58

(John Daniels *continued*)

Daniels led the Florida State League in 1997 with 29 saves, and he racked up another 20 this year. His hit ratio is a little high, but the rest of his numbers are very respectable. Nobody regards him as a prospect. Part of that is that he's a minor league closer; part is that he was closing against younger kids; part is that he's a sinker/changeup guy with a lousy fastball.

Michael Duvall   Throws L Age 24

YEAR	TEAM	LGE	IP	H	ER	HR	BB	K	ERA	W	L	H/9	HR/9	BB/9	K/9	KWH	PERA
1996	KaneCnty	Mid	45.3	59	24	1	22	31	4.76	2	3	11.71	0.20	4.37	6.15	0.56	4.76
1997	Portland	Eas	67.7	71	19	3	19	38	2.53	6	2	9.44	0.40	2.53	5.05	0.80	3.59
1998	Durham	Int	72.7	79	28	3	29	47	3.47	5	3	9.78	0.37	3.59	5.82	0.72	3.84

Duvall was expected to contend for a bullpen role following an impressive 1997, but was bothered by tendinitis in the spring and was an early cut. He recovered to have a fine season for Durham, working as a left-handed set-up man, and would have been next in line if Aldred failed. Aldred didn't fail, so Duvall stayed in Durham until September.

Mark Eichhorn   Throws R   Age 38

YEAR	TEAM	LGE	IP	H	ER	HR	BB	K	ERA	W	L	H/9	HR/9	BB/9	K/9	KWH	PERA
1996	LkElsin	Cal	14.0	20	11	1	2	12	7.07	0	2	12.86	0.64	1.29	7.71	2.70	5.14
1996	Calfrnia	AL	31.0	34	13	3	9	24	3.77	2	1	9.87	0.87	2.61	6.97	1.41	4.06
1998	Durham	Int	55.7	68	28	7	11	34	4.53	3	3	10.99	1.13	1.78	5.50	1.16	4.85

One of those guys who just doesn't want to give up, even after the rotator cuff surgery which wiped out 1995 or a visit to the Taiwanese professional leagues last year that ended when he tried to catch a line drive with his eye. He still sidearms, notching 18 saves, but the long ride is just about over.

Dave Eiland   Throws R   Age 32

YEAR	TEAM	LGE	IP	H	ER	HR	BB	K	ERA	W	L	H/9	HR/9	BB/9	K/9	KWH	PERA
1996	Columbus	Int	89.3	91	39	9	15	59	3.93	5	5	9.17	0.91	1.51	5.94	1.91	3.63
1996	Louisvil	AmA	23.3	33	20	2	10	14	7.71	1	2	12.73	0.77	3.86	5.40	0.45	5.79
1997	Columbus	Int	58.3	97	51	8	14	32	7.87	1	5	14.97	1.23	2.16	4.94	0.57	6.94
1998	Durham	Int	164.7	203	72	12	27	86	3.94	9	9	11.10	0.66	1.48	4.70	1.01	4.43

Another veteran slop-baller—I can't believe he's only 32—Eiland had his best season in years, going 13-5 and keeping his ERA under 3.00. From the good news/bad news department, he got his 100th career win this season—his 100th career minor league win.

Trevor Enders   Throws L   Age 24

YEAR	TEAM	LGE	IP	H	ER	HR	BB	K	ERA	W	L	H/9	HR/9	BB/9	K/9	KWH	PERA
1996	Butte	Pio	24.3	43	23	1	14	12	8.51	1	2	15.90	0.37	5.18	4.44	0.18	6.66
1997	Charl-SC	SAL	61.7	81	26	3	23	44	3.79	4	3	11.82	0.44	3.36	6.42	0.78	4.82
1998	StPete	Fla	64.7	62	23	5	18	41	3.20	4	3	8.63	0.70	2.51	5.71	1.13	3.34

If minor league closers get no respect, how much less is accorded to minor league set-up men? Especially older ones? Even if they do their job well and accumulate a 10-1 record? There is a good reason for it, though. When I went looking through the database for 23-year-old Florida State League pitchers with 40-90 innings and a DT-ERA between 2.70 and 3.70, I got 18 names besides Enders. Five made it to the majors; only one, Larry Thomas, had any success at all, and that was brief. It helps that like Thomas, Enders is left-handed.

Eddie Gaillard   Throws R   Age 28

YEAR	TEAM	LGE	IP	H	ER	HR	BB	K	ERA	W	L	H/9	HR/9	BB/9	K/9	KWH	PERA
1996	Jacksnvl	Sou	82.0	108	46	9	52	52	5.05	3	6	11.85	0.99	5.71	5.71	0.36	5.71
1997	Toledo	Int	49.3	66	30	7	23	40	5.47	2	3	12.04	1.28	4.20	7.30	0.79	5.84
1997	Detroit	AL	20.7	17	10	2	9	12	4.35	1	1	7.40	0.87	3.92	5.23	0.71	3.05
1998	Durham	Int	19.0	32	18	5	11	16	8.53	0	2	15.16	2.37	5.21	7.58	0.55	8.53

Waived by Detroit at the end of spring training, claimed by the Rays and sent to Durham, he played "twelfth pitcher" for the Rays, as in, "we need a twelfth pitcher, bring up Gaillard." "Now we don't, send him back." Even when he was in Tampa he didn't get much work. His season ended in June with a strained forearm, probably from lifting luggage.

Rick Gorecki   Throws R   Age 25

YEAR	TEAM	LGE	IP	H	ER	HR	BB	K	ERA	W	L	H/9	HR/9	BB/9	K/9	KWH	PERA
1995	VeroBch	Fla	26.0	26	7	0	9	19	2.42	2	1	9.00	0.00	3.12	6.58	1.16	3.12
1997	SanBern	Cal	48.3	50	25	5	34	37	4.66	2	3	9.31	0.93	6.33	6.89	0.60	4.47
1997	SanAnton	Tex	42.7	32	9	4	15	26	1.90	4	1	6.75	0.84	3.16	5.48	1.06	2.53
1998	TampaBay	AL	17.0	16	8	1	9	7	4.24	1	1	8.47	0.53	4.76	3.71	0.26	3.71

In 1995, it was a hernia, followed by shoulder surgery that wiped out 1996. This year, he made three starts before "biceps tendinitis" forced him to the sidelines, and it wouldn't heal. He'd throw, there'd be pain. Wait ten days, try again, same result. After three months of this he had arthroscopic surgery which removed a bone spur and, in the words of his doctor, "tightened up some loose things." No reason to be optimistic.

Roberto Hernandez   Throws R   Age 34

YEAR	TEAM	LGE	IP	H	ER	HR	BB	K	ERA	W	L	H/9	HR/9	BB/9	K/9	KWH	PERA
1996	ChiSox	AL	84.7	65	17	2	31	84	1.81	7	2	6.91	0.21	3.30	8.93	2.63	2.23
1997	ChiSox	AL	49.3	38	12	5	21	46	2.19	4	1	6.93	0.91	3.83	8.39	1.99	2.74
1997	SanFran	NL	33.0	31	8	2	13	31	2.18	3	1	8.45	0.55	3.55	8.45	1.79	3.27
1998	TampaBay	AL	73.7	56	27	5	37	54	3.30	5	3	6.84	0.61	4.52	6.60	1.06	2.69

Hernandez's season was one of extremes. From the start of the season through May 8, he was dreadful: 15 innings with an ERA of 7.80 and a ratio of 2.33, saving two while blowing three opportunities. Then he found his split-finger, and went the next 24+ innings without allowing an earned run, with as many saves (15) as baserunners. Then he lost it again; the next 23 innings yielded a 7.33 ERA, with four of ten saves blown; then September came and he finished the year with 8 2/3 scoreless innings and a 10-2 K/BB ratio. He was twice publicly demoted from the closer's role; his resurgences coincided with those demotions almost to the day.

Jason Johnson   Throws R   Age 25

YEAR	TEAM	LGE	IP	H	ER	HR	BB	K	ERA	W	L	H/9	HR/9	BB/9	K/9	KWH	PERA
1996	Augusta	SAL	74.3	128	59	3	31	47	7.14	2	6	15.50	0.36	3.75	5.69	0.42	6.42
1996	Lynchbrg	Car	42.7	67	40	7	13	20	8.44	1	4	14.13	1.48	2.74	4.22	0.34	6.75
1997	Lynchbrg	Car	93.0	131	52	5	31	61	5.03	4	6	12.68	0.48	3.00	5.90	0.69	5.23
1997	Carolina	Sou	56.7	60	27	6	16	48	4.29	3	3	9.53	0.95	2.54	7.62	1.80	3.97
1998	TampaBay	AL	62.3	75	32	8	24	35	4.62	3	4	10.83	1.16	3.47	5.05	0.51	5.05

A lightly regarded high school prospect who spent four years as a lightly regarded pro prospect before finally getting it together in 1997, when he went from A-ball to a cup of major-league coffee. It might be that it took until then for him to get his diabetes under control; it might be that an auto accident in December of 1996, which left him in the hospital with a fractured skull, was the literal knock upside the head he needed to start taking his profession more seriously. Gorecki's injury gave him a chance, which was largely wasted by nervousness early and increasing back pain late. The injury turned out to be a broken bone. It ended his season, but then he pitched well in the '98 Arizona Fall League.

Albie Lopez   Throws R   Age 27

YEAR	TEAM	LGE	IP	H	ER	HR	BB	K	ERA	W	L	H/9	HR/9	BB/9	K/9	KWH	PERA
1996	Buffalo	AmA	102.0	110	60	13	44	76	5.29	4	7	9.71	1.15	3.88	6.71	0.89	4.50
1996	Clevelnd	AL	64.3	75	36	12	18	45	5.04	3	4	10.49	1.68	2.52	6.30	1.12	5.04
1997	Clevelnd	AL	79.0	101	52	11	35	61	5.92	3	6	11.51	1.25	3.99	6.95	0.79	5.47
1998	TampaBay	AL	82.0	74	26	6	28	61	2.85	6	3	8.12	0.66	3.07	6.70	1.35	3.07

1998 was the first year of his career in which he played the entire season with one team, and the first time since 1994 that he wasn't shuffled between the rotation and the bullpen. He said he liked it that way; the numbers say he was telling the truth. His two-pitch arsenal, one of which is a very good fastball, is better suited to relief anyway.

Jim Mecir　　　　　Throws R　　　Age 29

YEAR	TEAM	LGE	IP	H	ER	HR	BB	K	ERA	W	L	H/9	HR/9	BB/9	K/9	KWH	PERA
1996	Columbus	Int	46.3	44	15	2	17	41	2.91	3	2	8.55	0.39	3.30	7.96	1.69	3.30
1996	NYYanks	AL	42.0	40	17	5	19	38	3.64	3	2	8.57	1.07	4.07	8.14	1.42	3.86
1997	Columbus	Int	26.3	17	5	0	6	25	1.71	3	0	5.81	0.00	2.05	8.54	4.60	1.03
1997	NYYanks	AL	34.0	36	19	5	8	24	5.03	2	2	9.53	1.32	2.12	6.35	1.50	4.24
1998	TampaBay	AL	86.3	68	25	6	30	75	2.61	7	3	7.09	0.63	3.13	7.82	2.07	2.50

As with Lopez, 1998 was the first time Mecir has been able to spend an entire year in the major leagues. The right-handed screwballer was Hernandez's primary setup man, and probably should have been left in to close a few. But they're not paying him $22 million.

Brad Pennington　　　Throws L　　　Age 30

YEAR	TEAM	LGE	IP	H	ER	HR	BB	K	ERA	W	L	H/9	HR/9	BB/9	K/9	KWH	PERA
1996	Vancouvr	PCL	24.7	26	23	3	23	33	8.39	1	2	9.49	1.09	8.39	12.04	1.37	5.11
1997	Omaha	AmA	52.3	45	26	6	46	39	4.47	3	3	7.74	1.03	7.91	6.71	0.55	3.96
1998	Durham	Int	97.0	93	57	12	66	96	5.29	4	7	8.63	1.11	6.12	8.91	1.13	4.18

Still around, still the same old "throw it as hard as I can and hope the umpire misses it and calls it a strike" philosophy. His late season callup resulted in a classic line: 20 pitches, three walks, 1 hit, no batters retired, and amazingly, only one run.

Bryan Rekar　　　　Throws R　　　Age 27

YEAR	TEAM	LGE	IP	H	ER	HR	BB	K	ERA	W	L	H/9	HR/9	BB/9	K/9	KWH	PERA
1996	ColSprin	PCL	124.0	140	57	14	36	63	4.14	7	7	10.16	1.02	2.61	4.57	0.59	4.43
1996	Colorado	NL	68.7	83	44	10	26	24	5.77	3	5	10.88	1.31	3.41	3.15	0.20	5.11
1997	ColSprin	PCL	142.3	171	79	18	38	90	5.00	6	10	10.81	1.14	2.40	5.69	0.93	4.81
1998	TampaBay	AL	89.3	94	46	15	19	54	4.63	4	6	9.47	1.51	1.91	5.44	1.22	4.33

Good news, Bryan, you don't have to pitch in Coors Field anymore. Even if Tropicana Field is a "joke," to use Tampa Bay pitchers' favorite description, it has to beat trying to throwing a curve in thin air. It's tough to judge this season; he strained his back in the spring, then his shoulder while on rehab, and didn't make it to the big club until the All-Star break. A good bet to improve next season, if healthy. Experienced shoulder stiffness in winter ball.

Ryan Rupe　　　　　Throws R　　　Age 24

YEAR	TEAM	LGE	IP	H	ER	HR	BB	K	ERA	W	L	H/9	HR/9	BB/9	K/9	KWH	PERA
1998	HudsnVal	NYP	11.7	14	2	0	3	9	1.54	1	0	10.80	0.00	2.31	6.94	1.45	3.86
1998	Charl-SC	SAL	51.3	51	27	4	13	32	4.73	2	4	8.94	0.70	2.28	5.61	1.16	3.51

There was a time, after his sophomore year in college, when the 6'5", 230-pound Rupe was seen as a first-round pick. Then there was the elbow surgery that wiped out his junior year. Then there was a blood clot under his collarbone that cost him a rib and his senior season. He pitched well in his redshirt senior year last spring, but a lot of teams were reluctant to take a chance on him. Watch out for guys who have something to prove.

Julio Santana　　　　Throws R　　　Age 26

YEAR	TEAM	LGE	IP	H	ER	HR	BB	K	ERA	W	L	H/9	HR/9	BB/9	K/9	KWH	PERA
1996	Oklahoma	AmA	187.7	190	100	12	71	99	4.80	9	12	9.11	0.58	3.40	4.75	0.54	3.64
1997	Texas	AL	110.3	135	68	15	43	63	5.55	4	8	11.01	1.22	3.51	5.14	0.51	5.14
1998	TampaBay	AL	144.3	145	61	17	53	59	3.80	8	8	9.04	1.06	3.30	3.68	0.34	3.93

Texas's celebrated shortstop-turned-pitcher found himself on waivers in April, when the pennant-hungry Rangers decided they didn't have time to wait for his development, he was out of options, and they couldn't arrange a trade. The Rays got a steal. Still unrefined but with a great arm, he worked from the pen for the first month, then moved into the rotation when Alvarez got hurt and Durham callups couldn't cut it. A sure thing for this year's rotation.

Tony Saunders Throws L Age 25

YEAR	TEAM	LGE	IP	H	ER	HR	BB	K	ERA	W	L	H/9	HR/9	BB/9	K/9	KWH	PERA
1996	Portland	Eas	167.3	143	51	10	61	124	2.74	13	6	7.69	0.54	3.28	6.67	1.32	2.85
1997	Florida	NL	114.0	103	55	13	58	91	4.34	6	7	8.13	1.03	4.58	7.18	1.04	3.63
1998	TampaBay	AL	200.7	192	79	14	102	169	3.54	12	10	8.61	0.63	4.57	7.58	1.09	3.63

Lucky enough to be the first pick in the Expansion Draft, after which his luck ran out. Saunders pitched much better than his 6-15 record indicates. He was supported by a paltry 3.5 runs per game. He was, by SNWL, easily the unluckiest pitcher in the majors. Looking only at quality starts, he was 5-8 with six no-decisions: that's five more quality starts, in two fewer opportunities, than 20-game winner Rick Helling. It got so bad he started messing with his head: turning his brown hair blond didn't end an eight-game losing streak, but turning it red did. He had surgery to clean out elbow chips at the end of the season, but expects to be fully recovered by spring training.

Bobby Seay Throws L Age 21

YEAR	TEAM	LGE	IP	H	ER	HR	BB	K	ERA	W	L	H/9	HR/9	BB/9	K/9	KWH	PERA
1997	Charl-SC	SAL	58.3	77	42	3	46	43	6.48	2	4	11.88	0.46	7.10	6.63	0.39	5.40
1998	Charl-SC	SAL	64.0	82	47	11	34	46	6.61	2	5	11.53	1.55	4.78	6.47	0.57	5.91

The guy who started the sweepstakes that Travis Lee and Matt White cashed in on, but so far he's a primer on all the things that can go wrong with a high school pitcher. He's suffered repeated injuries, most having nothing to do with his arm. He broke his foot in '97. In the off-season he needed an appendectomy; infection set in, and the surgeons had to go in again to repair a perforated colon. Those are nuisances, hurting his development without doing permanent damage. More worrisome is the ulnar nerve problem he had in '98.

Dennis Springer Throws R Age 34

YEAR	TEAM	LGE	IP	H	ER	HR	BB	K	ERA	W	L	H/9	HR/9	BB/9	K/9	KWH	PERA
1996	Vancouvr	PCL	97.7	113	44	11	38	59	4.05	5	6	10.41	1.01	3.50	5.44	0.61	4.70
1996	Calfrnia	AL	97.3	86	50	22	35	63	4.62	5	6	7.95	2.03	3.24	5.83	0.99	3.88
1997	Anaheim	AL	201.7	193	95	29	64	73	4.24	10	12	8.61	1.29	2.86	3.26	0.32	3.79
1998	TampaBay	AL	119.7	122	64	19	54	45	4.81	5	8	9.18	1.43	4.06	3.38	0.23	4.36
1998	Durham	Int	36.3	40	13	1	15	18	3.22	2	2	9.91	0.25	3.72	4.46	0.40	3.96

He never really got the knuckleball working, and was repeatedly pounded to fully earn his 3-11 record. He lost his spot in the rotation and the roster to Rekar at the break. When he was recalled, he worked from the pen and was much more successful.

Ramon Tatis Throws L Age 26

YEAR	TEAM	LGE	IP	H	ER	HR	BB	K	ERA	W	L	H/9	HR/9	BB/9	K/9	KWH	PERA
1996	StLucie	Fla	70.0	95	43	7	45	34	5.53	3	5	12.21	0.90	5.79	4.37	0.20	5.79
1997	ChiCubs	NL	59.0	66	30	13	27	30	4.58	3	4	10.07	1.98	4.12	4.58	0.38	5.34
1998	TampaBay	AL	12.7	25	17	2	15	5	12.08	0	1	17.76	1.42	10.66	3.55	0.05	8.53
1998	Durham	Int	59.7	75	29	4	23	35	4.37	3	4	11.31	0.60	3.47	5.28	0.53	4.83

Tatis started the year as the only left-hander in the pen, but when you are left-handed and opposing left-handers smack you around for a .308 EQA, you don't keep your roster spot. He pitched better at Durham, and was actually called back before elbow tendinitis ended his season.

Terrell Wade Throws L Age 26

YEAR	TEAM	LGE	IP	H	ER	HR	BB	K	ERA	W	L	H/9	HR/9	BB/9	K/9	KWH	PERA
1996	Atlanta	NL	72.0	62	26	10	46	72	3.25	5	3	7.75	1.25	5.75	9.00	1.36	3.75
1997	Atlanta	NL	42.3	65	29	6	14	32	6.17	1	4	13.82	1.28	2.98	6.80	0.84	6.59
1998	StPete	Fla	13.0	19	12	3	9	10	8.31	0	1	13.15	2.08	6.23	6.92	0.44	6.92
1998	Durham	Int	19.3	24	12	1	12	11	5.59	1	1	11.17	0.47	5.59	5.12	0.32	5.12
1998	TampaBay	AL	11.0	14	5	3	2	8	4.09	0	1	11.45	2.45	1.64	6.55	1.71	6.55

Wade almost missed the entire season trying to recover from rotator cuff surgery. It was August before he was well enough to pitch in rehab, and mid-September before he got back into the bigs. He appeared to be all right. He started all nine games he pitched in 1998, but that was just to ensure regular work; he figures to pitch in relief in '99.

Matt White   Throws R   Age 20

Year	Team	Lge	IP	H	ER	HR	BB	K	ERA	W	L	H/9	HR/9	BB/9	K/9	KWH	PERA
1997	HudsnVal	NYP	76.0	114	59	5	38	49	6.99	2	6	13.50	0.59	4.50	5.80	0.42	5.92
1998	Charl-SC	SAL	69.7	98	50	1	25	37	6.46	2	6	12.66	0.13	3.23	4.78	0.42	4.91
1998	StPete	Fla	91.0	130	74	12	46	48	7.32	2	8	12.86	1.19	4.55	4.75	0.29	6.13

Scouts continue to rave about him, but the performance, in terms of ERA and strikeouts, doesn't match up. Nobody in the '90s who has put up a 7.00 ERA at age 19 has gone on to a successful career. There are several who have had good seasons, notably Jeremi Gonzalez, Gabe White, and Scott Elarton. Most have not made the majors at all. If that weren't enough, 170 innings of mediocre pitching means an awful lot of pitches for a 19-year-old, regardless of size; none of the 18 pitchers this decade who faced this many batters in a season at age 19 have had a successful career as a starter, and only Ugueth Urbina made it at all.

Rick White   Throws R   Age 30

YEAR	TEAM	LGE	IP	H	ER	HR	BB	K	ERA	W	L	H/9	HR/9	BB/9	K/9	KWH	PERA
1997	Orlando	Sou	77.3	118	63	7	23	45	7.33	2	7	13.73	0.81	2.68	5.24	0.56	5.94
1998	Durham	Int	51.3	71	30	3	11	24	5.26	2	4	12.45	0.53	1.93	4.21	0.55	5.08
1998	TampaBay	AL	70.3	66	27	7	21	38	3.45	5	3	8.45	0.90	2.69	4.86	0.78	3.33

The old junkballer was called up for what was supposed to be one start in May, when the Rays had a pitching crunch due to Alvarez's injury. Three terrible starts somehow didn't get him sent back to Durham; instead he became an outstanding addition to the bullpen.

Esteban Yan   Throws R   Age 25

YEAR	TEAM	LGE	IP	H	ER	HR	BB	K	ERA	W	L	H/9	HR/9	BB/9	K/9	KWH	PERA
1996	Rochestr	Int	72.0	79	32	6	17	52	4.00	4	4	9.88	0.75	2.13	6.50	1.51	4.00
1997	Rochestr	Int	120.0	115	48	13	33	107	3.60	7	6	8.63	0.98	2.48	8.02	2.26	3.52
1998	TampaBay	AL	91.7	78	34	10	38	75	3.34	6	4	7.66	0.98	3.73	7.36	1.42	3.14

Yan got off to a great start, allowing just one run and two hits in his first 15 innings. He then gave up a run in six of the next eight appearances, and a month later had another stretch in which he allowed runs in seven of eight appearances. The big problem was getting into a set pattern of pitches, especially first-pitch fastballs. Correcting the error could be worth millions of dollars to him; a bad Roberto Hernandez start could make him the closer.

SNWL				TAMPA BAY DEVIL RAYS							Park Effect: +10.8%	
PITCHER	GS	IP	R	SNW	SNL	SNPCT	W	L	RA	APW	SNVA	SNWAR
Alvarez, W.	25	142.7	78	8.9	9.0	.499	6	14	4.92	0.43	-0.02	1.32
Arrojo, R.	32	202.0	84	14.5	8.2	.638	14	12	3.74	3.06	3.06	4.83
Eiland, D.	1	2.7	6	0.0	0.6	.053	0	1	20.25	-0.41	-0.28	-0.24
Gorecki, R.	3	16.7	9	1.1	0.9	.535	1	2	4.86	0.06	0.03	0.22
Johnson, J.	13	60.0	38	3.7	4.2	.471	2	5	5.70	-0.30	-0.18	0.36
Rekar, B.	15	85.7	56	4.2	5.6	.432	2	8	5.88	-0.59	-0.65	0.07
Ruebel, M.	1	4.3	4	0.1	0.6	.138	0	1	8.31	-0.14	-0.24	-0.19
Santana, J.	19	116.7	64	6.9	6.1	.531	4	6	4.94	0.33	0.51	1.38
Saunders, T.	31	192.3	95	12.0	8.9	.573	6	15	4.45	1.52	1.33	3.11
Springer, D.	17	93.0	68	3.8	7.6	.333	3	11	6.58	-1.31	-1.83	-1.05
Wade, T.	2	10.7	6	0.5	0.6	.446	1	1	5.06	0.02	-0.09	0.02
White, R.	3	14.3	11	0.5	1.3	.301	0	3	6.91	-0.25	-0.33	-0.22
TOTALS	162	941.0	519	56.3	53.5	.513	39	79	4.96	2.41	1.32	9.62

I don't have SNWL numbers going back further than 1992, but I'll go out on a limb and say that this is the best starting pitching performance by an expansion team in a long time. That's not to say they're without competition. The Florida Marlins also got better than average starting pitching in their inaugural season. I think the Devil Rays were a bit better: the '98 D-Rays had an SNVA of 1.32 to rank 10th in a 30-team league; the '93 Marlins had an SNVA of 0.16 to rank 12th in a 28-team league. If you adjust for park and league, as the SN stats do, Rolando Arrojo's rookie season looks an awful lot like Hideo Nomo's. Nomo's SNPct was .660, Arrojo's was .638. Nomo had 4.9 SN Wins above Replacement, Arrojo had 4.8. The only stat in which they were not close was televised appearances. The comparison would have been even more favorable for Arrojo if he hadn't faded down the stretch. Before the All-Star break, he was 9.3-3.9 (.703), and after the break, he was 5.2-4.3 (.548).

Pitcher Abuse Points

PITCHER	AGE	GS	PAP	PAP/S	AAW	MAX	115+	130+
Alvarez, Wilson	28	25	214	8.56	14.27	127	5	0
Arrojo, Rolando	"29"	32	350	10.94	16.41	129	7	0
Johnson, Jason	24	13	17	1.31	3.05	112	0	0
Rekar, Bryan	26	15	82	5.47	10.93	118	1	0
Santana, Julio	25	19	228	12.00	26.00	128	4	0
Saunders, Tony	24	31	496	16.00	37.33	130	13	1
Springer, Dennis	33	17	38	2.24	2.24	110	0	0
TOTAL		162	1444	8.91	17.35	130	30	1
RANKING (AL)			9	9	5		7	11-T

Larry Rothschild is a former pitching coach, and he's supposed to have a good rapport with his pitchers, but he needs to extend that relationship to their rotator cuffs and elbow ligaments. Tony Saunders got too much work in his sophomore season, and I wonder if Rothschild didn't simply look at his innings and ignore his 111 walks when deciding when to remove him from a game. Julio Santana was claimed off waivers from the Rangers early in the year and was ridden hard, though to be fair he wasn't much of a prospect before and Rothschild deserves some credit for getting the year he did out of him. Wilson Alvarez was the veteran the Devil Rays hoped would lead the staff, had a manageable burden, but still struggled with injuries and effectiveness all year. Rolando Arrojo went through Joe Cubas's time machine on his way out of Cuba, "losing" three years of age, but he was not overworked.

Toronto Blue Jays

For better or for worse, Canadian soap operas don't get much circulation south of the border. Like many things in life, that isn't entirely fair, because the '98 Blue Jays holds all sorts of lessons for baseball fans. They can tell us a thing or two about how teams win ballgames, how organizations can build winning teams, and how misunderstandings about how you got to be good in the first place can derail your progress before you really get started.

Last year, we wrote that the Blue Jays were well positioned to make a run for at least the wild card. Our expectation was that they'd take advantage of a solid rotation, a good bullpen, and a core of good young hitters to push themselves into contention. Our hope was that they would tire of their unfortunate commitments to veterans like Ed Sprague, and choose to put their best team on the field, instead of their most expensive one. Our disappointment was that for the first four months of the season, they did not try to put that team on the field.

The Jays, for many of the same reasons, also believed they were capable of contending. But they misidentified some of their weaknesses. Rather than try to contend with the team's strengths—good young players at positions where they needed them, including Tom Evans, Jose Cruz, Jr., and to a lesser extent Jeff Patzke—the Jays took advantage of the sudden generosity of their corporate parent, Interbrew SA, to buy a few veteran players. At great expense, they brought in closer Randy Myers, infielder Tony Fernandez, designated hitter Mike Stanley, infielders Pat Kelly and Craig Grebeck, and to cover for the previous season's free agent mistake (Benito Santiago), catcher Darrin Fletcher. Finally, expecting that slugger Carlos Delgado would be out for the first two months of the season, and at the request of Roger Clemens and their new manager, Tim Johnson, they signed their friend from the '95 Boston Red Sox, designated hitter Jose Canseco.

Independently, almost all of the moves were good ideas. On paper, each decision has a reasonable explanation. Signing Fletcher to compensate for Santiago might be expensive, but the Jays did not have a viable internal alternative to Santiago. Santiago's subsequent injury in a car accident made the decision look even better. The Jays also needed to help their offense, and creating potential competition for jobs between rookies and with veterans isn't a bad idea. But things didn't work out that way. Rather than let Evans or Patzke compete for jobs, none of the veterans were ever really challenged. Tony Fernandez, Ed Sprague, and Alex Gonzalez would all start; past mediocrity would be forgiven and forgotten. The differences between Tim Johnson and Cito Gaston suddenly didn't seem to be much more than cosmetic.

Two things happened in April that made the Jays' season different than what they'd initially expected. First, they stumbled out of the gate while watching the Yankees race out to a huge lead; they were already 8 1/2 games back by the end of April. Second, Carlos Delgado healed far faster than anybody expected, returning to the lineup before month's end. The twin signings of Canseco and Stanley were suddenly redundant; they didn't need both of them. A good manager can take advantage of this kind of depth. It may not be the happiest thing in the world for the players involved, but it can be put to good advantage, keeping everyone fresh and taking advantage of matchups. Tim Johnson didn't choose to do that. The Blue Jays stuck with what they had already done during the winter, and what they'd decided to do in spring training. They decided the best way for them to compete was to make sure that they shoehorn the players they felt were their best offensive players into the lineup. And the players they felt were their best offensive players included three designated hitters and Ed Sprague.

One of the most frequent insults tossed in the dirction of any of us smart-alecky second guessers is that we're guided by "rotisserie" sensibilities. This misunderstanding is either unfortunate or deliberate, and is in part the product of a sports media unhappy with the idea that outsiders may know more about their area of expertise. What's important is that it's wrong. It doesn't take much more than a cursory knowledge of the two to know that rotisserie baseball may be

---

Blue Jays Prospectus

1998 record: 88-74; Third place, AL East

Pythagorean W/L: 86-76

Runs scored: 816 (8th in AL)

Runs allowed: 768 (4th in AL)

Team EQA: .267 (7rd in AL)

Park: Skydome (slight pitchers')

1998: Took too long to dispense with the dead wood and play their best players.

1999: Likely departure of Roger Clemens might cost them the division, but they'll be contenders.

baseball-flavored, but it isn't baseball. What makes a winning rotisserie team is not related to what makes a winning baseball team. In real baseball, teams are more than the sum of offensive categories like stolen bases or runs batted in. Real baseball teams win because of their ability to score and prevent runs. Most importantly, that means defense and the relationship between pitching and defense matters. Rotisserie skips over that, and so did Tim Johnson.

With Delgado back in the fold by May 1st, somebody was going to lose playing time. That somebody ended up being the team's best defensive outfielders, Jose Cruz, Jr. and Shannon Stewart. The Jays were already a bad defensive ballclub; there are few praises to sing about the glovework of Shawn Green or Mike Stanley or Ed Sprague or Carlos Delgado or Tony Fernandez. Although Cruz contributed very little offensively in the first two months of the season, and it's far from clear whether he's going to be a good center fielder, the alternatives Johnson turned to were bad news for his pitching staff. He alternated Shawn Green and Shannon Stewart in center, and put Jose Canseco in an outfield corner, Stanley at DH and Delgado at first. On June 14th, Cruz was banished to Syracuse and Tim Johnson reached a point of no return: the Jays were going to try to play softball.

A team can probably survive having a player playing out of position. But the Blue Jays weren't playing just one player out of position, they were playing four bad defensive players (Sprague, Fernandez, Canseco, and Green). Bringing in Tony Phillips on July 17 only made a bad situation worse, since that meant the Jays' remaining adequate glove in the outfield, Shannon Stewart, lost more playing time. To a limited extent, the decision worked: the Jays went from scoring 4.3 runs per game in the first two months to averaging 5.0 runs per game in June and July. But the defensive cost was too high: they went from allowing 4.6 runs per game to 5.2 runs per game. This despite the fact that Roger Clemens didn't really heat up until July, which means the defensive problems were even worse than these figures indicate. The pressure on the defense, combined with Johnson's inclination to ride his rotation as hard as Cito Gaston ever had, led to the Jays' pitching staff giving up more hits in June and July than during any other two months. By July's end, not only were they almost ten games behind the Red Sox for the wildcard, they'd dropped to fourth in the AL East behind the wheezing geezers, the Orioles. The best-offensive-lineup gambit, so productive in rotisserie or in a Strat-O-Matic league, had flopped.

The Jays needed to make some changes, and to his credit, Gord Ash made them. He traded off Phillips, Stanley, and Sprague—and Juan Guzman, for good measure—and suddenly they had a baseball team again. Jose Canseco returned to DH, Jose Cruz, Jr. was recalled and put back in center, Shawn Green went to right, Shannon Stewart went to left,

Tony Fernandez went to third base, and Craig Grebeck started playing second base regularly. The changes produced dramatic results. They were a younger team, improving defensively (allowing only 4.3 runs per game over the last two months) and offensively (scoring 5.7 runs per game). Roger Clemens's red-hot finish helps make the contrast even more stark, but so did letting Stewart and Cruz play every day, on both sides of the ledger.

The moves were correct, and ultimately successful, but at the time were not greeted happily. The Jays were immediately accused by fans and the media of giving up on the season. Tim Johnson pointed the finger at Gord Ash, the media decried this apparent betrayal of Roger Clemens and his oft-stated desire to play for a winner, and one writer described the Jays as "rudderless." Comparisons to the White Sox and their infamous July '97 "white flag" trade with the Giants were made. It's important to note that the pundits were wrong, and that Gord Ash deserves credit for scrapping what didn't work.

This isn't the first time a team has made itself more competitive at the end of July and gotten less credit than they deserved for it. The '95 Royals got noticeably better down the stretch when they replaced useless veterans with Johnny Damon, Jon Nunnally, Michael Tucker, and Keith Lockhart. What's significant now is whether the Jays will take the lesson to heart, because the Royals did not. The Royals didn't learn anything from the experience, having dumped Lockhart, Tucker, and Nunnally for Scooby Snacks. Clemens couldn't figure it out, and forced a trade out of Toronto because he felt the absence of veterans was a sign the team would not be competitive.

Sorry, Roger. If there's one thing the Jays need to take from the '98 season, it is that veteran players are not the answer. This team has a young outfield that should recall the great trio of Lloyd Moseby, Jesse Barfield, and George Bell. It has a great power hitter in Carlos Delgado and an oustanding group of young pitchers in Chris Carpenter, Kelvim Escobar, and Roy Halladay. Pile all that up behind Clemens, and you've got a team that should be the favorite for the wild card, and is poised to make the Yankees sweat a little if the World Champs begin to feel their age.

Unfortunately, Clemens won't be there, and his absence may well be the difference between 94 wins and the postseason, and 88 wins and frustration. Yes, Interbrew SA put the team up for sale again, and the Jays stayed out of the bidding for Bernie Williams, Mo Vaughn, and Roberto Alomar. But only Alomar would have filled a need, and it's an open question what he has left. The Blue Jay team that finished the season on a 34-18 kick would have returned essentially intact had the Rocket evaluated his teammates based on their talent and not their service time.

Clemens may turn out to be correct; if the Belgians dictate

that Ash dump salary, it's going to make it difficult for the Jays to get the best value for the veterans he'd have to trade. But that isn't nearly as unfortunate as losing a shot at winning the AL East or the wild card in '99. This team isn't going to have to play against the Yankees of '98—as good as that team was, you only win the World Series once a year. The Jays could still contend, but the loss of the best pitcher of his generation is a crushing blow, made more painful for the fact that it didn't have to happen.

For the Jays to stay in the hunt now, they have to avoid letting loyalty to faltering veterans or rotisserie sensibilities dictate who they play. They need to put their best baseball team on the field, and that's something that more money isn't going to buy.

HITTERS (Averages: BA .260/ OBP .330/ SLG .420, EqA .260)

Brent Abernathy — 2B — Bats R — Age 21

YEAR	TEAM	LGE	AB	H	DB	TP	HR	BB	R	RBI	SB	CS	OUT	BA	OBA	SA	EQA	EQR	DEFENSE
1997	Hagerstn	SAL	381	103	20	1	1	28	40	31	9	7	285	.270	.320	.336	.230	36	
1998	Dunedin	Fla	477	132	23	1	3	37	55	42	16	8	353	.277	.329	.348	.240	50	121-2B 93
1999	Toronto	AL	457	136	24	1	4	35	60	49	14	8	329	.298	.348	.381	.256	54	

The Jays are already in love with him, because he's got every "classic" attribute teams say they want from their second basemen. He's called heady and scrappy and couple of other flinty, tough-sounding names that you'd slap on a team of angry bad-ass diamond dwarves. He'd be a lot better off drawing more walks, but the Jays have encouraged him to be more aggressive at the plate and in the field, so he may end up being the Anglo version of Damaso Garcia. It may not be Roberto Alomar in his prime, but it's a good player to have around.

Casey Blake — 3B — Bats R — Age 25

YEAR	TEAM	LGE	AB	H	DB	TP	HR	BB	R	RBI	SB	CS	OUT	BA	OBA	SA	EQA	EQR	DEFENSE
1996	Hagerstn	SAL	174	35	6	0	2	8	8	8	2	1	140	.201	.236	.270	.162	7	45-3B 87
1997	Dunedin	Fla	450	86	7	0	7	39	25	22	8	5	369	.191	.256	.253	.170	22	119-3B 84
1998	Dunedin	Fla	332	86	12	0	7	22	30	32	3	3	249	.259	.305	.358	.229	31	86-3B 93
1998	Knoxvill	Sou	165	52	8	2	5	15	26	25	6	0	113	.315	.372	.479	.298	27	44-3B 90
1999	Toronto	AL	426	113	17	1	10	32	47	46	9	4	317	.265	.317	.380	.243	46	

He had an excellent season after he gave up on trying to pull everything, as he had been doing in his first two years. He's come along much better than most scouts expected, and he's become a much more consistent defensive player. Nevertheless, keep in mind that he's neither the hitter nor the defensive player that Tom Evans is, and he's both older and behind Evans in the chain.

Kevin Brown — C — Bats R — Age 26

YEAR	TEAM	LGE	AB	H	DB	TP	HR	BB	R	RBI	SB	CS	OUT	BA	OBA	SA	EQA	EQR	DEFENSE
1996	Tulsa	Tex	457	106	12	1	20	63	49	57	0	2	353	.232	.325	.394	.250	55	
1997	Oklahoma	AA	400	88	14	1	15	35	33	41	2	2	314	.220	.283	.373	.224	37	
1998	Toronto	AL	108	28	6	1	2	10	12	12	0	0	80	.259	.322	.389	.247	12	35-C 98
1999	Toronto	AL	241	56	9	0	9	25	23	28	0	1	186	.232	.305	.382	.236	25	

After getting rescued from the Rangers in exchange for Tim Crabtree, Brown finally got a shot at the role he's best suited for: backup catcher. He's good at it, and he'll be handy to have around for several seasons.

Jose Canseco — DH/OF — Bats R — Age 34

YEAR	TEAM	LGE	AB	H	DB	TP	HR	BB	R	RBI	SB	CS	OUT	BA	OBA	SA	EQA	EQR	DEFENSE
1996	Boston	AL	346	93	18	1	26	60	57	68	3	1	254	.269	.377	.552	.310	68	
1997	Oakland	AL	381	87	15	0	24	52	49	55	8	2	296	.228	.321	.457	.267	55	33-OF 98
1998	Toronto	AL	574	134	23	0	46	67	77	91	26	17	457	.233	.314	.514	.273	89	60-OF 92
1999	TampaBay	AL	475	109	16	0	35	66	64	78	11	7	373	.229	.323	.484	.268	70	

I've always liked Canseco, but he's about one big contract demand away from professional extinction. Sort of like Strawberry before Steinbrenner felt charitable, he's basically going to be offered a job not on the basis of whether not he can help a team, but whether or not a team thinks it can put up with him. With 397 career homeruns, has a good chance of being the first man to hit 500 home runs and not be in the Hall of Fame. I don't agree with that idea, but I think it's likely. Signed by the Devil Rays, a team whose offense is so bad he can actually help them.

Felipe Crespo   UT   Bats B   Age 26

YEAR	TEAM	LGE	AB	H	DB	TP	HR	BB	R	RBI	SB	CS	OUT	BA	OBA	SA	EQA	EQR	DEFENSE	
1996	Syracuse	Int	354	93	14	0	9	54	48	41	7	8	269	.263	.360	.379	.260	46	38-2B 93	28-OF 96
1997	Syracuse	Int	290	70	7	0	11	41	34	34	6	6	226	.241	.335	.379	.249	35	26-OF 98	24-2B 100
1998	Toronto	AL	128	33	7	1	1	15	16	12	4	3	98	.258	.336	.352	.243	14	26-OF 99	
1999	*Toronto*	*AL*	*228*	*58*	*9*	*1*	*6*	*30*	*29*	*27*	*5*	*4*	*174*	*.254*	*.341*	*.382*	*.253*	*28*		

He had to masquerade as a defensive replacement in the outfield, which cost the Jays a game or two early on. On a team pretending Canseco could play one corner and Shawn Green another, and with Juan Samuel doing some limp Yoda schtick on the bench, the Jays did need a defensive replacement, and Crespo really deserved to be in the majors. But talk about hammering a square peg through a round hole. If the Jays don't bring in a veteran, they should have Crespo share second with Grebeck.

Bobby Cripps   C   Bats L   Age 22

YEAR	TEAM	LGE	AB	H	DB	TP	HR	BB	R	RBI	SB	CS	OUT	BA	OBA	SA	EQA	EQR	DEFENSE
1996	GreatFls	Pio	133	21	0	1	1	4	4	4	1	2	114	.158	.182	.195	—	0	
1997	GreatFls	Pio	139	26	1	1	2	4	5	5	2	2	115	.187	.210	.252	.131	4	
1998	Hagerstn	SAL	422	95	9	1	18	34	34	45	1	2	329	.225	.283	.379	.225	40	51-C 101
1999	*Toronto*	*AL*	*312*	*72*	*5*	*1*	*12*	*20*	*24*	*32*	*2*	*2*	*242*	*.231*	*.277*	*.369*	*.218*	*27*	

Cue up Ralph Edwards for "This is Your Life," because what we have here is a kid who hits with power, swings left-handed, and who isn't the best catcher in the world. In fact, he may have to move to DH or first eventually, and . . . wait a minute, you're not Carlos Delgado, are you? No?

Jose Cruz, Jr.   CF/LF   Bats B   Age 25

YEAR	TEAM	LGE	AB	H	DB	TP	HR	BB	R	RBI	SB	CS	OUT	BA	OBA	SA	EQA	EQR	DEFENSE
1996	Lancastr	Cal	194	47	7	1	4	28	24	20	3	1	148	.242	.338	.351	.247	22	40-OF 92
1996	PortCity	Sou	182	49	9	1	3	22	24	20	3	0	133	.269	.348	.379	.260	23	42-OF 103
1997	Tacoma	PCL	185	44	12	1	5	30	27	21	3	0	141	.238	.344	.395	.263	25	46-OF 90
1997	Seattle	AL	180	47	12	1	12	14	23	30	1	0	133	.261	.314	.539	.282	28	37-OF 103
1997	Toronto	AL	210	49	6	0	15	28	28	32	6	2	163	.233	.324	.476	.272	32	50-OF 95
1998	Toronto	AL	346	86	13	3	11	58	51	43	10	4	264	.249	.356	.399	.268	49	101-OF 105
1998	Syracuse	Int	139	38	10	0	6	28	27	21	6	3	104	.273	.395	.475	.301	26	40-OF 119
1999	*Toronto*	*AL*	*483*	*119*	*26*	*2*	*19*	*74*	*72*	*66*	*9*	*3*	*367*	*.246*	*.346*	*.427*	*.270*	*70*	

Criminy. Difficult-to-please media types are already bleating that he's a disappointment, but the expectations of what he could do were overstated. He's an adequate center fielder, which is better than expected. He has a good eye and solid power, but sort of like getting the wrong impression about Wally Joyner from the start of his career, power isn't going to be his central skill.

Mark Dalesandro   C/UT   Bats R   Age 31

YEAR	TEAM	LGE	AB	H	DB	TP	HR	BB	R	RBI	SB	CS	OUT	BA	OBA	SA	EQA	EQR	DEFENSE
1995	Vancouvr	PCL	123	39	9	1	1	5	15	15	2	0	84	.317	.344	.431	.270	16	
1996	Columbus	Int	250	58	19	1	2	15	20	19	1	0	192	.232	.275	.340	.210	19	14-3B 102
1997	Iowa	AA	406	93	6	0	7	28	25	29	0	0	313	.229	.279	.296	.195	26	28-3B 98
1998	Syracuse	Int	162	38	6	1	6	9	14	17	1	0	124	.235	.275	.395	.228	15	
1998	Toronto	AL	66	20	4	0	2	1	6	9	0	0	46	.303	.313	.455	.260	8	
1999	*Toronto*	*AL*	*267*	*66*	*7*	*0*	*9*	*18*	*23*	*29*	*0*	*0*	*201*	*.247*	*.295*	*.375*	*.229*	*25*	

A regular for Tim Johnson at Iowa in '97, and like any manager, Johnson wanted as many familiar faces around as possible so that he'd have a good number of guys to work on the players he didn't know, to convince them that the new fearless leader was a good guy.

Carlos Delgado   1B   Bats L   Age 27

YEAR	TEAM	LGE	AB	H	DB	TP	HR	BB	R	RBI	SB	CS	OUT	BA	OBA	SA	EQA	EQR	DEFENSE
1996	Toronto	AL	476	123	27	2	23	55	60	71	0	0	353	.258	.335	.468	.274	69	23-1B 86
1997	Toronto	AL	513	136	43	3	31	65	75	90	0	3	380	.265	.348	.542	.294	89	117-1B 89
1998	Toronto	AL	520	150	35	2	39	75	86	107	3	0	370	.288	.378	.588	.319	106	141-1B 94
1999	*Toronto*	*AL*	*571*	*156*	*35*	*1*	*40*	*76*	*88*	*112*	*1*	*1*	*416*	*.273*	*.359*	*.548*	*.302*	*104*	

Delgado's fast comeback was a huge surprise, and he went on to enjoy his best season yet. For sluggers, doing this at this age isn't extraordinary. He's consistently improved parts of his game; in '98 he started hitting left-handers well, and worked his way to being adequate in the field. Statistically, the expectation should be that he won't be much better than he's been, but I can't shake the feeling that he's going to have a better career than your typical slow slugger.

Tom Evans   3B   Bats R   Age 24

YEAR	TEAM	LGE	AB	H	DB	TP	HR	BB	R	RBI	SB	CS	OUT	BA	OBA	SA	EQA	EQR	DEFENSE
1996	Knoxvill	Sou	383	90	14	0	14	95	63	51	2	0	293	.235	.387	.381	.279	60	71-3B 104
1997	Syracuse	Int	376	96	13	1	14	47	43	49	1	2	282	.255	.338	.407	.259	48	104-3B 109
1998	Syracuse	Int	394	110	21	1	14	44	53	54	8	6	290	.279	.352	.444	.273	57	110-3B 96
1999	*Toronto*	*AL*	*416*	*112*	*18*	*0*	*18*	*57*	*58*	*63*	*3*	*3*	*307*	*.269*	*.357*	*.442*	*.276*	*62*	

If it isn't one thing, its another. Once again, injuries cut into Evans's opportunity to lay claim to the Jays' third base job. This time it was recovering from rotator cuff surgery and a knee injury. Although Tim Johnson has said he likes what he's seen of Evans, he doesn't exactly have a great profile for a long career: he's godawful slow, and he has yet to be healthy for an entire season. But Evans is, right now, a great defensive player and capable of contributing much more to an offense than Ed Sprague ever dreamed of. Whether and how the Jays make room for him is one of the team's major issues entering the '99 season.

Tony Fernandez   IF   Bats B   Age 37

YEAR	TEAM	LGE	AB	H	DB	TP	HR	BB	R	RBI	SB	CS	OUT	BA	OBA	SA	EQA	EQR	DEFENSE	
1995	NY Yanks	AL	379	92	21	2	5	40	40	34	6	7	294	.243	.315	.348	.230	37	101-SS 97	
1997	Clevelnd	AL	405	118	20	1	12	23	45	52	6	6	293	.291	.329	.435	.260	50	106-2B 97	
1998	Toronto	AL	477	151	35	2	9	47	73	65	11	8	334	.317	.378	.455	.287	74	77-2B 104	49-3B 92
1999	*Toronto*	*AL*	*390*	*110*	*22*	*1*	*9*	*36*	*49*	*49*	*6*	*8*	*288*	*.282*	*.343*	*.413*	*.259*	*49*		

His defense at second was abysmal. Routinely out of position to pivot on the deuce, he lacks the arm strength to compensate for it. That doesn't have to kill you if he's only playing second twice a week, but day-in, day-out, it can be a back-breaker. Fernandez has considerable value as somebody who could start five or six times a week, alternating among second, short, and third, depending on whoever else is hot or cold and who's pitching.

Darrin Fletcher   C   Bats L   Age 32

YEAR	TEAM	LGE	AB	H	DB	TP	HR	BB	R	RBI	SB	CS	OUT	BA	OBA	SA	EQA	EQR	DEFENSE
1996	Montreal	NL	390	99	14	0	14	29	36	46	0	0	291	.254	.305	.397	.242	42	
1997	Montreal	NL	308	83	18	0	18	19	34	48	1	1	226	.269	.312	.503	.272	43	
1998	Toronto	AL	400	110	23	1	9	27	41	47	0	0	290	.275	.321	.405	.250	46	112-C 96
1999	*Toronto*	*AL*	*366*	*98*	*13*	*0*	*15*	*25*	*37*	*50*	*0*	*0*	*268*	*.268*	*.315*	*.426*	*.253*	*43*	

Although he'll never get good marks for his glovework, Fletcher's a handy source of left-handed pop from behind the plate. You could gripe that signing him when Santiago was already under contract was a case of throwing good money after bad. Ash may understand the idea of sunk costs, though, and decided to get at least a good platoon or some real offense out of the position. Then Santiago got hurt, and he snagged Kevin Brown. Given the choice between spending money or keeping Sandy Martinez around, I'd say Ash made the right choice.

Ryan Freel   UT   Bats R   Age 23

YEAR	TEAM	LGE	AB	H	DB	TP	HR	BB	R	RBI	SB	CS	OUT	BA	OBA	SA	EQA	EQR	DEFENSE
1996	Dunedin	Fla	382	88	16	2	5	29	33	28	11	9	303	.230	.285	.322	.209	30	92-2B 86
1997	Dunedin	Fla	183	46	6	1	3	40	34	18	11	3	140	.251	.386	.344	.274	27	23-SS 98
1998	Knoxvill	Sou	247	61	13	2	3	24	30	21	11	6	192	.247	.314	.352	.235	26	52-OF 97
1998	Syracuse	Int	117	23	2	0	2	23	15	8	6	3	97	.197	.329	.265	.223	11	27-OF 93
1999	*Toronto*	*AL*	*358*	*92*	*14*	*1*	*7*	*46*	*50*	*36*	*16*	*9*	*275*	*.257*	*.342*	*.360*	*.250*	*43*	

Working towards becoming a super-sub, Freel is already known for his diving, athletic play in the field. Between his ability to get on base and his roving from position to position, he's looking like the new Lance Blankenship. Like Blankenship, he's best suited to play second base or the outfield. Like Blankenship, he can be a very handy guy to have around.

Tim Giles   1B   Bats L   Age 23

YEAR	TEAM	LGE	AB	H	DB	TP	HR	BB	R	RBI	SB	CS	OUT	BA	OBA	SA	EQA	EQR	DEFENSE
1996	Med Hat	Pio	250	34	3	0	4	8	6	6	1	0	216	.136	.163	.196	—	-2	55-1B 87
1997	Hagerstn	SAL	385	112	13	0	12	40	46	53	1	1	274	.291	.358	.418	.271	52	50-1B 93
1998	Dunedin	Fla	358	92	10	1	13	25	33	42	1	1	267	.257	.305	.399	.242	38	70-1B 115
1999	*Toronto*	*AL*	*363*	*97*	*11*	*0*	*13*	*26*	*36*	*46*	*1*	*1*	*267*	*.267*	*.316*	*.405*	*.248*	*41*	

The Jays don't get nearly as much attention for their first base flops as they do for their outfield flops—there are only so many hours in the day—but they have had their fair share of first base non-prospects. Let's call them the Domingo Martinez product line. Giles is probably going to turn out better than Martinez or Chris Weinke or Ryan Jones, but he has problems with his strike zone judgment and power that make it doubtful whether he's going to make it in the majors. He gets the ball up in the air whenever he makes contact, though, so if he can handle the pitching at Double-A, he could surprise.

Alex Gonzalez   SS   Bats R   Age 26

YEAR	TEAM	LGE	AB	H	DB	TP	HR	BB	R	RBI	SB	CS	OUT	BA	OBA	SA	EQA	EQR	DEFENSE
1996	Toronto	AL	517	115	28	5	13	42	52	47	16	7	409	.222	.281	.371	.226	50	147-SS 111
1997	Toronto	AL	422	102	22	2	13	35	48	44	16	6	326	.242	.300	.396	.242	47	124-SS 106
1998	Toronto	AL	560	131	24	1	14	31	51	47	19	6	435	.234	.274	.355	.219	49	157-SS 99
1999	*Toronto*	*AL*	*477*	*112*	*24*	*2*	*13*	*32*	*50*	*45*	*18*	*7*	*372*	*.235*	*.283*	*.375*	*.228*	*46*	

His career is stalled, and at this point I don't think he'll come out of it. Although his defense is good, it isn't so good that he's off the hook for being this inadequate with the bat. I'd compare him to Dick Schofield, except Schofield had had a better year than Gonzalez has ever had before his 26th birthday.

Craig Grebeck   IF   Bats R   Age 34

YEAR	TEAM	LGE	AB	H	DB	TP	HR	BB	R	RBI	SB	CS	OUT	BA	OBA	SA	EQA	EQR	DEFENSE	
1996	Florida	NL	95	20	1	0	1	5	4	4	0	0	75	.211	.250	.253	.159	4	24-2B 91	
1997	Anaheim	AL	124	33	6	0	2	18	15	14	0	1	92	.266	.359	.363	.256	15	21-2B 102	11-SS 103
1998	Toronto	AL	296	74	16	2	2	30	31	26	2	2	224	.250	.319	.338	.231	29	82-2B 107	
1999	*Toronto*	*AL*	*206*	*49*	*8*	*0*	*3*	*22*	*20*	*18*	*1*	*1*	*158*	*.238*	*.311*	*.320*	*.221*	*18*		

His window of opportunity to be a good regular has long since come and gone. In 1993, he had a great chance to become the everyday second baseman for the White Sox; he got hurt, and Joey Cora got rich. It was nice to finally see him get a break, and it was nice to see the Jays reward him a two-year contract to be their utility infielder.

Shawn Green   RF/CF   Bats L   Age 26

YEAR	TEAM	LGE	AB	H	DB	TP	HR	BB	R	RBI	SB	CS	OUT	BA	OBA	SA	EQA	EQR	DEFENSE
1996	Toronto	AL	413	110	32	3	10	30	49	49	5	1	304	.266	.316	.431	.257	51	111-OF 103
1997	Toronto	AL	424	123	21	4	17	37	61	62	15	3	304	.290	.347	.479	.285	66	86-OF 96
1998	Toronto	AL	619	169	31	4	35	53	90	94	32	12	462	.273	.330	.506	.282	98	151-OF 96
1999	*Toronto*	*AL*	*527*	*143*	*31*	*3*	*26*	*43*	*74*	*80*	*19*	*8*	*392*	*.271*	*.326*	*.490*	*.276*	*78*	

Freed from Cito's tyranny, he had the big year prospect hounds have been waiting for. We've bashed Tim Johnson a lot in these pages, but if there was one thing I thought was really cool, it was Johnson's decision to slap Green into the #2 slot in the line-up and essentially leave him there for the year. Why bunt Stewart over when you can move around with an extra-base hit?

Jose Herrera   OF   Bats L   Age 26

YEAR	TEAM	LGE	AB	H	DB	TP	HR	BB	R	RBI	SB	CS	OUT	BA	OBA	SA	EQA	EQR	DEFENSE
1996	Oakland	AL	314	80	13	1	6	18	30	29	8	2	236	.255	.295	.360	.229	30	82-OF 99
1997	Edmonton	PCL	401	89	11	1	3	35	30	24	5	4	316	.222	.284	.277	.193	26	111-OF 90
1998	Syracuse	Int	467	109	15	3	9	25	39	36	17	9	367	.233	.272	.336	.210	37	115-OF 105
1999	*Toronto*	*AL*	*428*	*104*	*16*	*1*	*9*	*30*	*41*	*38*	*11*	*6*	*330*	*.243*	*.293*	*.348*	*.222*	*38*	

(Jose Herrera *continued*)

Prospect washout emeritus, so that's Dr. Herrera to you, bub. Spectacularly non-prospect-like in a quintessentially Syracuse kind of way.

Joe Lawrence — SS — Bats R — Age 22

YEAR	TEAM	LGE	AB	H	DB	TP	HR	BB	R	RBI	SB	CS	OUT	BA	OBA	SA	EQA	EQR	DEFENSE
1996	St Cath	NYP	101	20	6	1	0	11	7	6	0	1	82	.198	.277	.277	.187	6	23-SS 84
1997	Hagerstn	SAL	451	89	14	1	7	44	29	27	4	6	368	.197	.269	.279	.185	27	116-SS 85
1998	Dunedin	Fla	452	117	18	3	10	87	69	54	7	7	342	.259	.378	.378	.270	65	119-SS 88
1999	*Toronto*	*AL*	*416*	*110*	*21*	*1*	*9*	*56*	*56*	*50*	*5*	*5*	*311*	*.264*	*.352*	*.385*	*.259*	*53*	

The Jays '96 first-rounder, Lawrence had a huge breakout in Dunedin, pasting 31 doubles and drawing 103 walks from a new Henderson Crouch ™. He's still extremely raw at shortstop (48 errors), showing little more than a great throwing arm. The arm has been good enough to tease the Jays into having him catch in instructional league, but his eventual destination is probably third base.

Patrick Lennon — OF — Bats R — Age 31

YEAR	TEAM	LGE	AB	H	DB	TP	HR	BB	R	RBI	SB	CS	OUT	BA	OBA	SA	EQA	EQR	DEFENSE	
1996	Edmonton	PCL	244	67	8	0	9	23	28	32	3	2	179	.275	.337	.418	.261	31	34-OF	86
1997	Edmonton	PCL	126	33	4	0	5	17	16	17	0	0	93	.262	.350	.413	.267	17		
1997	Oakland	AL	114	33	5	1	1	15	15	13	0	1	82	.289	.372	.377	.265	15	27-OF	91
1998	Syracuse	Int	434	108	13	2	18	71	61	58	8	3	329	.249	.354	.412	.270	63	79-OF	93
1999	*Toronto*	*AL*	*373*	*98*	*15*	*1*	*15*	*59*	*55*	*55*	*4*	*2*	*277*	*.263*	*.363*	*.429*	*.277*	*56*		

Another career-long Kenny Phelps All-Star kind of guy, Lennon has continued to hit, hit, and hit some more. He's basically everything Jose Herrera isn't: he's slower, not as good in the field, doesn't throw well, and can play baseball. Even Geronimo Berroa got his first break at 29, so Lennon doesn't look like he'll ever get his. Sort of like Shane Spencer, but more deserving.

Luis Lopez — 1B — Bats R — Age 25

YEAR	TEAM	LGE	AB	H	DB	TP	HR	BB	R	RBI	SB	CS	OUT	BA	OBA	SA	EQA	EQR	DEFENSE	
1996	St Cath	NYP	265	58	6	0	5	18	16	18	1	2	209	.219	.269	.298	.190	16	67-1B 101	
1997	Hagerstn	SAL	508	141	21	1	8	46	54	55	2	4	371	.278	.338	.370	.247	56	88-1B 102	
1998	Knoxvill	Sou	439	110	12	1	11	39	39	46	0	1	330	.251	.312	.358	.233	43	60-1B 97	28-3B 90
1999	*Toronto*	*AL*	*444*	*119*	*14*	*1*	*10*	*42*	*47*	*51*	*1*	*2*	*327*	*.268*	*.331*	*.372*	*.245*	*49*		

One of the organization's better hitters for average, Lopez gets credit for a good work ethic. Not much of a prospect as a first baseman, but the Jays are keeping their options open by having him work at third base. Hoping to avoid the Russ Morman Trail of Tears.

Adam Melhuse — C — Bats B — Age 27

YEAR	TEAM	LGE	AB	H	DB	TP	HR	BB	R	RBI	SB	CS	OUT	BA	OBA	SA	EQA	EQR	DEFENSE
1996	Dunedin	Fla	324	67	8	1	9	51	32	30	1	1	258	.207	.315	.321	.226	31	
1997	Syracuse	Int	118	25	3	0	2	10	8	8	1	1	94	.212	.273	.288	.191	7	
1998	Knoxvill	Sou	235	54	8	0	9	50	34	30	2	2	183	.230	.365	.379	.266	33	51-C 94
1998	Syracuse	Int	38	9	1	0	1	5	4	4	0	0	29	.237	.326	.342	.237	4	
1999	*Toronto*	*AL*	*268*	*59*	*8*	*0*	*9*	*43*	*31*	*30*	*2*	*1*	*210*	*.220*	*.328*	*.351*	*.241*	*30*	

Between injuries and waiting for the Jays to get over Sandy Martinez, Melhuse has needed a break. He got one this year, earning a berth in the Double-A All-Star game. There aren't many teams that couldn't use a switch-hitting catcher who can play the position, and if the Jays deal Fletcher, he and Brown would make a very good platoon to hold down the catching duties for a few years until the arrival of Venezuelan wonderboy Guillermo Quiroz.

Michael Peeples — 2B — Bats R — Age 22

YEAR	TEAM	LGE	AB	H	DB	TP	HR	BB	R	RBI	SB	CS	OUT	BA	OBA	SA	EQA	EQR	DEFENSE
1996	Hagerstn	SAL	276	58	8	1	3	28	22	17	6	3	221	.210	.283	.279	.197	19	
1997	Dunedin	Fla	477	107	21	0	3	47	44	29	13	8	378	.224	.294	.287	.205	36	121-2B 89
1998	Knoxvill	Sou	390	83	10	2	6	25	27	24	12	6	313	.213	.260	.295	.190	25	108-2B 95
1999	*Toronto*	*AL*	*401*	*93*	*15*	*1*	*7*	*32*	*37*	*32*	*11*	*6*	*314*	*.232*	*.289*	*.327*	*.214*	*33*	

He's been moving up through the organization relatively quickly at a young age, so getting squashed in his first year at Double-A isn't career-ending. He does a few things well: he can pick it at second, he's pretty quick, he's a good bunter, and he's drawn a walk or two before. He could still grow up to be a solid player.

Tomas Perez		SS				Bats B		Age 25										
YEAR	TEAM	LGE	AB	H	DB	TP	HR	BB	R	RBI	SB	CS	OUT	BA	OBA	SA	EQA	EQR	DEFENSE
1996	Syracuse	Int	122	31	8	1	1	7	14	10	6	1	92	.254	.295	.361	.234	12	31-SS 86
1996	Toronto	AL	289	68	12	4	1	23	24	21	1	2	223	.235	.292	.315	.208	22	73-2B 103
1997	Syracuse	Int	303	64	5	0	3	33	21	18	3	3	242	.211	.289	.257	.189	19	89-SS 100
1997	Toronto	AL	122	24	3	2	0	11	7	6	1	1	99	.197	.263	.254	.172	6	30-SS 113
1998	Syracuse	Int	399	88	12	2	3	15	19	21	2	5	316	.221	.249	.283	.169	19	100-SS 124
1999	*Toronto*	*AL*	*372*	*86*	*14*	*2*	*2*	*25*	*27*	*24*	*3*	*4*	*290*	*.231*	*.280*	*.296*	*.193*	*24*	

Defensively, he's even better than Gonzalez, so it says volumes about his hitting skills that he doesn't get even momentary consideration for the job when Gonzalez is scuffling as badly as he has been. At this stage, the Jays may make them both a little better by throwing the shortstop job up for grabs between the two of them.

Benito Santiago		C				Bats R		Age 34										
YEAR	TEAM	LGE	AB	H	DB	TP	HR	BB	R	RBI	SB	CS	OUT	BA	OBA	SA	EQA	EQR	DEFENSE
1996	Philadel	NL	482	128	21	2	30	52	61	81	2	0	354	.266	.337	.504	.284	76	
1997	Toronto	AL	338	83	8	0	14	18	26	38	1	0	255	.246	.284	.393	.231	33	
1998	Toronto	AL	28	8	5	0	0	2	4	3	0	0	20	.286	.333	.464	.272	4	
1999	*ChiCubs*	*NL*	*203*	*50*	*6*	*0*	*10*	*16*	*19*	*27*	*1*	*0*	*153*	*.246*	*.301*	*.424*	*.247*	*23*	

Think the Jays wouldn't mind giving Santiago an appropriate sendoff? How about a Viking funeral on the shores of Lake Erie, with xeroxed copies of his contract for kindling? All in all, he didn't exactly turn out the way Gord Ash had in mind, and even when healthy, a major turkey. Signed by the Cubs, where he'll keep the seat warm for Pat Cline.

Shannon Stewart		OF				Bats R		Age 25										
YEAR	TEAM	LGE	AB	H	DB	TP	HR	BB	R	RBI	SB	CS	OUT	BA	OBA	SA	EQA	EQR	DEFENSE
1996	Syracuse	Int	418	119	23	4	7	52	70	47	25	6	305	.285	.364	.409	.278	62	110-OF 111
1997	Syracuse	Int	207	69	10	1	5	32	38	31	7	5	143	.333	.423	.464	.308	38	54-OF 106
1997	Toronto	AL	166	48	14	7	0	19	31	19	10	3	121	.289	.362	.458	.287	27	40-OF 104
1998	Toronto	AL	507	140	29	3	12	68	91	55	46	18	385	.276	.362	.416	.276	77	130-OF 100
1999	*Toronto*	*AL*	*453*	*132*	*28*	*4*	*10*	*57*	*83*	*57*	*29*	*11*	*332*	*.291*	*.371*	*.437*	*.284*	*72*	

He finally got his opportunity, after having to put in extra time at Syracuse to satisfy He Who Could Not Be Pleased, Sleepy Cito. His defense in left was good enough to encourage some in the front office to push for putting him in center, but his throwing arm makes Lance Johnson's look like a cannon. The Jays will have to settle for having a great leadoff hitter in left for several years, which is fine.

Andy Thompson		3B/OF/1B				Bats R		Age 23										
YEAR	TEAM	LGE	AB	H	DB	TP	HR	BB	R	RBI	SB	CS	OUT	BA	OBA	SA	EQA	EQR	DEFENSE
1996	Dunedin	Fla	429	113	16	2	13	51	55	52	9	3	319	.263	.342	.401	.262	56	114-3B 98
1997	Knoxvill	Sou	434	98	15	2	10	51	40	41	0	3	339	.226	.307	.339	.225	40	104-3B 84
1998	Knoxvill	Sou	472	116	19	1	13	39	45	49	5	2	358	.246	.303	.373	.235	48	
1999	*Toronto*	*AL*	*443*	*113*	*17*	*1*	*13*	*42*	*48*	*52*	*3*	*2*	*332*	*.255*	*.320*	*.386*	*.245*	*49*	

Thompson is a bit of a problem. He's flashed some power, and this is without counting the eight taters he smashed in the '97 Arizona Fall League. An erratic arm has made him a public nuisance at the hot corner, and he hasn't hit well enough yet to really make him worth considering as a regular outfielder or first baseman. So what do you do with him?

Pete Tucci   OF   Bats R   Age 23

YEAR	TEAM	LGE	AB	H	DB	TP	HR	BB	R	RBI	SB	CS	OUT	BA	OBA	SA	EQA	EQR	DEFENSE
1996	St Cath	NYP	210	47	3	2	7	17	17	20	2	2	165	.224	.282	.357	.218	18	51-OF 94
1997	Hagerstn	SAL	468	107	16	2	9	32	35	37	4	3	364	.229	.278	.329	.207	36	107-OF 87
1998	Dunedin	Fla	349	99	15	1	17	24	40	53	4	3	253	.284	.330	.479	.273	49	89-OF 91
1998	Knoxvill	Sou	138	35	5	2	6	9	14	18	2	1	104	.254	.299	.449	.253	17	34-OF 91
1999	Toronto	AL	466	126	17	3	17	28	50	61	5	3	343	.270	.312	.429	.253	55	

With a huge uppercut that finally started getting results in '98, Tucci has been named the best power prospect in the organization. A weak arm probably limits him to left. There are concerns about the holes in his swing, but he's looking like a good power threat, and he may be up by the end of the year.

Vernon Wells   CF   Bats R   Age 20

YEAR	TEAM	LGE	AB	H	DB	TP	HR	BB	R	RBI	SB	CS	OUT	BA	OBA	SA	EQA	EQR	DEFENSE
1997	St Cath	NYP	269	71	7	1	8	24	28	31	4	4	202	.264	.324	.387	.246	30	60-OF 99
1998	Hagerstn	SAL	508	119	19	1	9	41	43	42	6	4	393	.234	.291	.329	.215	42	127-OF 107
1999	Toronto	AL	388	105	12	0	11	29	40	46	4	4	287	.271	.321	.387	.244	42	

In his first full season, the Jays' 1997 first-round pick ended up looking pretty good. He showed decent power and patience, and was named the Sally League's eighth-best prospect. He's still learning the mechanics of basestealing, but the Jays are hoping he'll be able to put his speed to work. He can easily handle center and has a great throwing arm.

Kevin Witt   1B   Bats L   Age 23

YEAR	TEAM	LGE	AB	H	DB	TP	HR	BB	R	RBI	SB	CS	OUT	BA	OBA	SA	EQA	EQR	DEFENSE	
1996	Dunedin	Fla	447	112	10	3	14	34	41	49	5	3	338	.251	.304	.380	.236	46	118-SS 90	
1997	Knoxvill	Sou	485	117	16	2	21	35	44	58	1	0	368	.241	.292	.412	.240	52	65-1B 110	32-3B 81
1998	Syracuse	Int	449	113	14	2	20	47	49	60	2	2	338	.252	.323	.425	.257	56	102-1B 100	
1999	Toronto	AL	444	112	14	1	20	37	46	60	2	1	333	.252	.310	.423	.251	52		

For a while, it looked like the Jays had a left-handed power threat for the left side of their infield. But just like Andy Thompson, Witt played his way over to first, and may be best suited to DH. The Jays are looking at moving him to the outfield in instructional league. He's basically a platoon hitter so far, so although he's shown considerable offensive potential at a young age, he isn't really a very good prospect.

PITCHERS (Averages: 4.00 ERA, 9.00 H/9, 3.00 BB/9, 1.00 HR/9, 6.00 K/9, 1.00 KWH)

Carlos Almanzar   Throws R   Age 25

YEAR	TEAM	LGE	IP	H	ER	HR	BB	K	ERA	W	L	H/9	HR/9	BB/9	K/9	KWH	PERA
1996	Knoxvill	Sou	98.3	116	51	14	30	83	4.67	5	6	10.62	1.28	2.75	7.60	1.48	4.85
1997	Knoxvill	Sou	26.0	31	12	2	5	19	4.15	1	2	10.73	0.69	1.73	6.58	1.75	4.15
1997	Syracuse	Int	50.3	32	8	2	7	38	1.43	5	1	5.72	0.36	1.25	6.79	4.83	1.07
1998	Syracuse	Int	49.3	51	21	7	12	44	3.83	3	2	9.30	1.28	2.19	8.03	2.37	4.01
1998	Toronto	AL	30.0	32	14	4	8	20	4.20	1	2	9.60	1.20	2.40	6.00	1.17	4.20

Almanzar is one of the products of the Jays' Dominican academy. He has exceptional control, but has always been hittable. He should be somebody who can make the Jays' middle relief in '99 a major strength—if Johnson is willing to use him.

Clayton Andrews   Throws L   Age 21

YEAR	TEAM	LGE	IP	H	ER	HR	BB	K	ERA	W	L	H/9	HR/9	BB/9	K/9	KWH	PERA
1996	Med Hat	Pio	23.7	42	19	4	9	8	7.23	1	2	15.97	1.52	3.42	3.04	0.13	7.61
1997	Hagerstn	SAL	108.7	168	87	11	59	75	7.21	3	9	13.91	0.91	4.89	6.21	0.43	6.38
1998	Hagerstn	SAL	154.0	154	72	8	55	119	4.21	8	9	9.00	0.47	3.21	6.95	1.25	3.51

A short left-hander with good control. There's concern that Andrews will need a fourth pitch to complement his curve, fastball, and change-up. He was named the #5 prospect in the Sally League this year after striking out 193 men in 162 innings, and is ticketed for Knoxville in '99.

Chris Carpenter   **Throws R**   **Age 24**

YEAR	TEAM	LGE	IP	H	ER	HR	BB	K	ERA	W	L	H/9	HR/9	BB/9	K/9	KWH	PERA
1996	Knoxvill	Sou	178.0	178	82	15	85	119	4.15	10	10	9.00	0.76	4.30	6.02	0.70	3.89
1997	Syracuse	Int	119.3	125	59	16	47	79	4.45	6	7	9.43	1.21	3.54	5.96	0.80	4.30
1997	Toronto	AL	83.3	109	47	6	32	53	5.08	3	6	11.77	0.65	3.46	5.72	0.60	5.08
1998	Toronto	AL	181.3	171	77	17	55	132	3.82	10	10	8.49	0.84	2.73	6.55	1.39	3.37

Bounced from the rotation after two starts to make way for Erik Hanson, the Jays had wanted to leave Carpenter in the pen for as long as possible. By the end of May, they decided Carpenter was already effectively starting since Hanson usually needed relief in the fourth inning. Note to Johnson: keep him away from Texas. They've hammered him to the tune of 24 runs allowed in 17⅔ innings over four starts.

Roger Clemens   **Throws R**   **Age 36**

YEAR	TEAM	LGE	IP	H	ER	HR	BB	K	ERA	W	L	H/9	HR/9	BB/9	K/9	KWH	PERA
1995	Boston	AL	145.0	137	54	14	48	135	3.35	9	7	8.50	0.87	2.98	8.38	2.08	3.48
1996	Boston	AL	255.7	195	72	16	86	256	2.53	20	8	6.86	0.56	3.03	9.01	2.93	2.32
1997	Toronto	AL	268.0	201	53	8	58	282	1.78	25	5	6.75	0.27	1.95	9.47	5.12	1.85
1998	Toronto	AL	241.7	163	61	10	79	263	2.27	20	7	6.07	0.37	2.94	9.79	4.03	1.71

Another year, another Cy Young, another war of words with a mute multinational conglomerate busy ruining Labatt's. Belgian beer is sweet to the point of being a bad cola, so I'm not surprised the Rocket isn't a happy employee. I'm guessing it'll take five years for him to get to 300 wins, at which point we can start arguing if anyone can ever get there again. It's amazing to think that in this great season, he still had nine starts that were not quality; he ran off thirteen quality starts in a row from June 30 to September 11.

Tom Davey   **Throws R**   **Age 25**

YEAR	TEAM	LGE	IP	H	ER	HR	BB	K	ERA	W	L	H/9	HR/9	BB/9	K/9	KWH	PERA
1996	Hagerstn	SAL	141.0	215	112	11	115	57	7.15	4	12	13.72	0.70	7.34	3.64	0.10	6.38
1997	Dunedin	Fla	37.7	58	25	5	19	26	5.97	1	3	13.86	1.19	4.54	6.21	0.46	6.69
1997	Knoxvill	Sou	94.0	116	56	5	49	56	5.36	4	6	11.11	0.48	4.69	5.36	0.41	4.79
1998	Knoxvill	Sou	75.3	84	33	2	48	58	3.94	4	4	10.04	0.24	5.73	6.93	0.63	4.30

After moving into the bullpen, Davey had a good year, making the Double-A All-Star squad. The huge right-hander finally started to harness command of his four pitches—a plus fastball, a forkball, a curve, and a change-up—to generate one of those tasty power/groundball combos that I like. He was red-hot in the Arizona Fall League, so he figures to get a long look in camp.

Kelvim Escobar   **Throws R**   **Age 23**

YEAR	TEAM	LGE	IP	H	ER	HR	BB	K	ERA	W	L	H/9	HR/9	BB/9	K/9	KWH	PERA
1996	Dunedin	Fla	107.7	124	48	9	36	89	4.01	6	6	10.37	0.75	3.01	7.44	1.33	4.35
1996	Knoxvill	Sou	56.0	67	32	7	23	35	5.14	2	4	10.77	1.12	3.70	5.62	0.60	4.98
1997	Knoxvill	Sou	25.0	21	11	1	16	25	3.96	2	1	7.56	0.36	5.76	9.00	1.39	3.24
1997	Toronto	AL	31.7	29	10	1	16	35	2.84	3	1	8.24	0.28	4.55	9.95	1.98	3.13
1998	Toronto	AL	82.7	70	29	5	31	70	3.16	6	3	7.62	0.54	3.38	7.62	1.69	2.83
1998	Syracuse	Int	59.0	58	25	7	22	54	3.81	4	3	8.85	1.07	3.36	8.24	1.71	3.81

Struggled mightily as Randy Myers's setup man, so back to Syracuse, back to starting and—presto!—he's back to being a good-looking prospect. He came up in August to replace Juan Guzman in the rotation, and became a major component of the Jays' late push for the wild card. As Rany has pointed out, he was probably overused, but I'm not as frightened...yet. If Johnson continues to push him to eight innings and 120 pitches every night out, I agree that we'll never get to know Escobar very well.

Isabel Giron   **Throws R**   **Age 21**

YEAR	TEAM	LGE	IP	H	ER	HR	BB	K	ERA	W	L	H/9	HR/9	BB/9	K/9	KWH	PERA
1998	Hagerstn	SAL	118.7	151	69	13	32	80	5.23	5	8	11.45	0.99	2.43	6.07	0.99	5.01
1998	Knoxvill	Sou	35.0	32	13	6	11	28	3.34	2	2	8.23	1.54	2.83	7.20	1.67	3.60

This wa the skinny right-hander's first season here in the States after starring for the Blue Jays' Dominican academy team. He opened people's eyes by tossing three shutouts in the Sally League. He's a better prospect than Hartshorn.

Gary Glover		Throws R				Age 22										
YEAR	TEAM	LGE	IP	H	ER	HR	BB	K	ERA	W	L	H/9	HR/9	BB/9	K/9	KWH	PERA
1996	Med Hat	Pio	76.3	139	84	14	28	31	9.90	1	7	16.39	1.65	3.30	3.66	0.19	8.02
1997	Hagerstn	SAL	164.3	231	117	12	72	103	6.41	5	13	12.65	0.66	3.94	5.64	0.48	5.53
1998	Dunedin	Fla	105.0	146	72	10	40	66	6.17	4	8	12.51	0.86	3.43	5.66	0.56	5.57
1998	Knoxvill	Sou	38.0	45	31	3	24	11	7.34	1	3	10.66	0.71	5.68	2.61	0.08	4.97

A big kid, Glover's wrestled with back troubles. He's occasionally tantalized the JUGS gun with a 97, but usually he's in the low 90s, and also flashes a power slider. He's still working on a useful changeup. The Jays' tendency to push kids up young isn't helpful for a pitcher like Glover; he's still filling out and he's barely getting enough time to figure out what works.

Beiker Graterol		Throws R				Age 24										
YEAR	TEAM	LGE	IP	H	ER	HR	BB	K	ERA	W	L	H/9	HR/9	BB/9	K/9	KWH	PERA
1997	Dunedin	Fla	78.7	107	51	12	31	40	5.83	3	6	12.24	1.37	3.55	4.58	0.36	5.95
1997	Knoxvill	Sou	17.0	26	10	1	8	9	5.29	1	1	13.76	0.53	4.24	4.76	0.29	5.82
1998	Knoxvill	Sou	66.3	84	41	8	19	41	5.56	2	5	11.40	1.09	2.58	5.56	0.79	5.16
1998	Syracuse	Int	94.0	116	53	9	29	53	5.07	4	6	11.11	0.86	2.78	5.07	0.63	4.79

With 17 hit batsmen in 28 starts, I guess you could say he knows what a purpose pitch is. Another product of the Dominican program, but obviously not a great prospect.

Roy Halladay		Throws R				Age 22										
YEAR	TEAM	LGE	IP	H	ER	HR	BB	K	ERA	W	L	H/9	HR/9	BB/9	K/9	KWH	PERA
1996	Dunedin	Fla	160.3	193	82	12	50	86	4.60	8	10	10.83	0.67	2.81	4.83	0.57	4.55
1997	Knoxvill	Sou	37.3	48	22	4	11	24	5.30	1	3	11.57	0.96	2.65	5.79	0.82	5.06
1997	Syracuse	Int	125.0	145	68	13	47	52	4.90	6	8	10.44	0.94	3.38	3.74	0.30	4.61
1998	Syracuse	Int	114.0	122	51	10	48	60	4.03	6	7	9.63	0.79	3.79	4.74	0.46	4.18
1998	Toronto	AL	14.3	9	3	2	1	12	1.88	2	0	5.65	1.26	0.63	7.53	12.00	1.26

A near-perfect game on the last day of the season is a good way to make everyone remember you. Named the International League's top pitching prospect. Halladay flashes one of the best sinking fastballs in the minors. He gets it up to 97, throws the cutter to get movement, has a great slider and mixes in a knuckle-curve. He's still figuring out how to change speeds. Halladay is a lock for the Jays rotation in '99, and an early candidate for Rookie of the Year if Tim Johnson doesn't burn him out. To put it another way, Dave Stewart will be just as smart for coming over to join Toronto's front office this year as he was for being Kevin Brown's pitching coach last year.

Ty Hartshorn		Throws R				Age 24										
YEAR	TEAM	LGE	IP	H	ER	HR	BB	K	ERA	W	L	H/9	HR/9	BB/9	K/9	KWH	PERA
1996	Hagerstn	SAL	134.7	235	116	21	78	67	7.75	3	12	15.71	1.40	5.21	4.48	0.18	7.62
1997	Dunedin	Fla	154.0	248	113	24	47	76	6.60	5	12	14.49	1.40	2.75	4.44	0.37	6.90
1998	Dunedin	Fla	59.3	69	20	1	20	37	3.03	4	3	10.47	0.15	3.03	5.61	0.74	3.94
1998	Knoxvill	Sou	106.0	148	66	16	37	43	5.60	4	8	12.57	1.36	3.14	3.65	0.25	6.03

Hartshorn succeeds by mixing a good four-seam fastball with a sinker, and when he's on he's generating a huge number of groundball outs. His shutout at Dunedin had 17 groundouts to shortstop. Standard operating procedure for the Jays is to promote at the first sign of success, so Hartshorn got pasted in the Southern League, but was named the top pitching prospect in the Florida State League.

Pat Hentgen		Throws R				Age 30										
YEAR	TEAM	LGE	IP	H	ER	HR	BB	K	ERA	W	L	H/9	HR/9	BB/9	K/9	KWH	PERA
1995	Toronto	AL	209.7	226	99	23	73	139	4.25	11	12	9.70	0.99	3.13	5.97	0.88	4.21
1996	Toronto	AL	272.3	224	78	17	76	176	2.58	21	9	7.40	0.56	2.51	5.82	1.36	2.54
1997	Toronto	AL	268.3	248	96	29	61	155	3.22	18	12	8.32	0.97	2.05	5.20	1.19	3.25
1998	Toronto	AL	185.0	201	87	26	62	92	4.23	10	11	9.78	1.26	3.02	4.48	0.51	4.48

We can go after Johnson, but most of the damage was undoubtedly done by Cito in the course of the epic 183 consecutive starts streak. He had only two quality starts in his last twelve before finally agreeing that he needed rest. So far, the Jays don't think surgery will be necessary, but I'm not optimistic.

Billy Koch — Throws R — Age 24

YEAR	TEAM	LGE	IP	H	ER	HR	BB	K	ERA	W	L	H/9	HR/9	BB/9	K/9	KWH	PERA
1997	Dunedin	Fla	21.3	33	11	2	4	15	4.64	1	1	13.92	0.84	1.69	6.33	1.28	5.91
1998	Dunedin	Fla	116.3	160	79	10	49	75	6.11	4	9	12.38	0.77	3.79	5.80	0.54	5.49

Tentatively pencilled in as the closer of the future. After having "Tommy John surgery" to reconstruct his elbow in '97, it was pretty remarkable that Koch came back as well as he did this year. The surgeon's knife has claimed the 100+ heat he was supposed to have when drafted, but he's still throwing in the 90s.

Yan Lachapelle — Throws L — Age 23

YEAR	TEAM	LGE	IP	H	ER	HR	BB	K	ERA	W	L	H/9	HR/9	BB/9	K/9	KWH	PERA
1997	Hagerstn	SAL	111.7	110	70	9	93	75	5.64	4	8	8.87	0.73	7.50	6.04	0.41	4.27
1998	Dunedin	Fla	120.0	148	76	19	67	92	5.70	4	9	11.10	1.42	5.03	6.90	0.64	5.55

A left-hander with good breaking stuff?!? Gee, we never hear about enough guys like that. The Expos are definitely jealous, since Lachapelle's a French Canadian. He is wild enough that he isn't quite the next Jamie Moyer or Doug Johns, but he could end up being a decent prospect if he survives the make-or-break contact with Double-A in '99.

Peter Munro — Throws R — Age 24

YEAR	TEAM	LGE	IP	H	ER	HR	BB	K	ERA	W	L	H/9	HR/9	BB/9	K/9	KWH	PERA
1996	Sarasota	Fla	149.0	197	89	8	68	92	5.38	6	11	11.90	0.48	4.11	5.56	0.47	5.07
1997	Trenton	Eas	111.0	134	76	11	43	84	6.16	4	8	10.86	0.89	3.49	6.81	0.92	4.78
1998	Pawtuckt	Int	107.7	116	42	9	32	64	3.51	7	5	9.70	0.75	2.67	5.35	0.83	4.01
1998	Syracuse	Int	44.0	65	39	6	21	36	7.98	1	4	13.30	1.23	4.30	7.36	0.71	6.34

Sheesh, one good AFL campaign and every goes bonkers in a mad scramble to anoint Boston pitching prospects as the new mother lode. He throws hard but hasn't exactly been consistent enough to live up to the media hype. There's been some talk of moving him to the pen.

Robert Person — Throws R — Age 30

YEAR	TEAM	LGE	IP	H	ER	HR	BB	K	ERA	W	L	H/9	HR/9	BB/9	K/9	KWH	PERA
1996	Norfolk	Int	40.0	43	19	7	23	25	4.28	2	2	9.68	1.58	5.18	5.62	0.47	4.95
1996	NY Mets	NL	89.0	94	48	18	33	68	4.85	4	6	9.51	1.82	3.34	6.88	1.12	4.75
1997	Toronto	AL	131.0	125	72	18	52	96	4.95	6	9	8.59	1.24	3.57	6.60	1.06	3.85
1998	Syracuse	Int	55.7	51	21	9	29	42	3.40	3	3	8.25	1.46	4.69	6.79	0.89	4.04
1998	Toronto	AL	40.3	44	25	9	20	30	5.58	1	3	9.82	2.01	4.46	6.69	0.77	5.13

It was a rotten year for Person almost any way you slice it. Dumped from the rotation, shipped off to Syracuse, surviving a concussion and a car accident... The move to relief seems to have done him good, although he leaves his fastball over the plate far too often for him to really turn into a reliable closer. He could easily be the new Alan Mills, which isn't exactly greatness, but can be useful and lucrative.

Dan Plesac — Throws L — Age 37

YEAR	TEAM	LGE	IP	H	ER	HR	BB	K	ERA	W	L	H/9	HR/9	BB/9	K/9	KWH	PERA
1996	Pittsbrg	NL	72.3	69	30	4	23	69	3.73	4	4	8.59	0.50	2.86	8.59	2.25	3.24
1997	Toronto	AL	51.3	47	18	8	16	59	3.16	4	2	8.24	1.40	2.81	10.34	3.47	3.68
1998	Toronto	AL	51.7	40	18	4	14	53	3.14	4	2	6.97	0.70	2.44	9.23	3.76	2.26

Life as a lefty specialist: 41 of his 70 appearances were for less than 10 pitches. He only had to toss more than 20 pitches four times, and even then, he never pitched two innings in a single game. Another 250 innings over five years at this rate would get him to over 1,100 games, but Orosco is so far ahead (and still effective) that Plesac won't catch him.

Paul Quantrill — Throws R — Age 30

YEAR	TEAM	LGE	IP	H	ER	HR	BB	K	ERA	W	L	H/9	HR/9	BB/9	K/9	KWH	PERA
1996	Toronto	AL	139.0	162	68	23	41	85	4.40	7	8	10.49	1.49	2.65	5.50	0.82	4.99
1997	Toronto	AL	89.7	100	21	5	15	54	2.11	8	2	10.04	0.50	1.51	5.42	1.46	3.81
1998	Toronto	AL	83.0	84	20	5	20	58	2.17	7	2	9.11	0.54	2.17	6.29	1.50	3.47

(Paul Quantrill *continued*)

Maybe he's better throwing from the stretch, maybe not. This year, he was worse than league average as far as allowing inherited runners to score, which is what you'd expect from someone as hittable as Bloody Paul. Nevertheless, he's gone from being a bad starter to a useful middle reliever. That isn't an unusual transmogrification.

Bill Risley　　Throws R　　Age 32

YEAR	TEAM	LGE	IP	H	ER	HR	BB	K	ERA	W	L	H/9	HR/9	BB/9	K/9	KWH	PERA
1996	Toronto	AL	43.0	31	15	7	21	29	3.14	3	2	6.49	1.47	4.40	6.07	0.97	2.93
1998	Toronto	AL	57.0	51	29	7	31	41	4.58	3	3	8.05	1.11	4.89	6.47	0.80	3.63

If Quantrill's the pitcher who gets brought into tight spots, Risley is the mop-up guy. Johnson was careful with his tender arm, so that Risley only pitched twice on back-to-back days all season while enjoying only his second season without a trip to the disabled list. He also gave up runs in 20 of 44 appearances, and was almost never asked to protect a lead. Combine those results with his limitations, and he might be too much of a pain in the ass to keep around.

Nerio Rodriguez　　Throws R　　Age 26

YEAR	TEAM	LGE	IP	H	ER	HR	BB	K	ERA	W	L	H/9	HR/9	BB/9	K/9	KWH	PERA
1996	Frederck	Car	106.7	106	48	12	46	78	4.05	6	6	8.94	1.01	3.88	6.58	0.94	3.97
1996	Baltimor	AL	16.7	18	9	2	6	12	4.86	1	1	9.72	1.08	3.24	6.48	1.00	4.32
1997	Rochestr	Int	167.3	139	76	23	57	128	4.09	9	10	7.48	1.24	3.07	6.88	1.55	3.07
1997	Baltimor	AL	22.0	22	13	2	7	11	5.32	1	1	9.00	0.82	2.86	4.50	0.59	3.68
1998	Rochestr	Int	23.3	29	17	6	10	15	6.56	1	2	11.19	2.31	3.86	5.79	0.58	6.17
1998	Baltimor	AL	19.3	25	14	0	9	8	6.52	1	1	11.64	0.00	4.19	3.72	0.21	4.66
1998	Toronto	AL	8.7	10	7	1	7	3	7.27	0	1	10.38	1.04	7.27	3.12	0.10	5.19

Another converted position player, Rodriguez is still figuring some things out. He's got a good, hard sinker and a nicely developing change, but he has a tendency to let his slider flatten out. It then gets hammered. For now, he'll be in the bullpen, where he may or may not ever have to get his slider working.

Mark Sievert　　Throws R　　Age 26

YEAR	TEAM	LGE	IP	H	ER	HR	BB	K	ERA	W	L	H/9	HR/9	BB/9	K/9	KWH	PERA
1995	Hagerstn	SAL	143.7	198	88	20	57	82	5.51	6	10	12.40	1.25	3.57	5.14	0.45	5.89
1996	Knoxvill	Sou	102.7	92	30	7	49	58	2.63	8	3	8.06	0.61	4.30	5.08	0.56	3.24
1996	Syracuse	Int	54.7	67	36	6	33	40	5.93	2	4	11.03	0.99	5.43	6.59	0.54	5.27
1998	Syracuse	Int	90.7	115	53	7	58	29	5.26	4	6	11.42	0.69	5.76	2.88	0.09	5.26

It's been rough going for Sievert. A second major surgery, to remove bone chips, cost him the '97 season, and doctors don't think they got all of them. Signed with the Devil Rays as a minor league free agent.

Steve Sinclair　　Throws L　　Age 27

YEAR	TEAM	LGE	IP	H	ER	HR	BB	K	ERA	W	L	H/9	HR/9	BB/9	K/9	KWH	PERA
1995	Dunedin	Fla	67.0	98	36	7	20	37	4.84	3	4	13.16	0.94	2.69	4.97	0.52	5.91
1997	Dunedin	Fla	64.0	85	45	5	35	43	6.33	2	5	11.95	0.70	4.92	6.05	0.47	5.34
1998	Syracuse	Int	47.7	46	17	2	23	35	3.21	3	2	8.69	0.38	4.34	6.61	0.87	3.40
1998	Toronto	AL	15.3	13	6	0	4	8	3.52	1	1	7.63	0.00	2.35	4.70	0.92	2.35

Those wacky left-handers. Sinclair retired in '96, and came back throwing harder (93 mph) after a year playing amateur ball for the fun of it. He's now good enough to be used in a larger role than the "get Griffey" spot reserved for most left-handers. The Jays are planning on letting him take much of the pressure off of Plesac, who they felt was overworked by season's end.

John Sneed　　Throws R　　Age 23

YEAR	TEAM	LGE	IP	H	ER	HR	BB	K	ERA	W	L	H/9	HR/9	BB/9	K/9	KWH	PERA
1997	Med Hat	Pio	62.7	62	25	5	28	39	3.59	4	3	8.90	0.72	4.02	5.60	0.66	3.73
1998	Hagerstn	SAL	149.0	181	80	10	74	121	4.83	7	10	10.93	0.60	4.47	7.31	0.82	4.77

It's hard to say Sneed was the Jays' big sleeper of the '97 draft, because everyone has been touting him from day one since he was picked out of Texas A&M. He was named the Sally League's #6 prospect, and the term "bulldog" gets tossed around. He's got a solid fastball, and command of a slider and changeup. He was far too advanced for the Sally League, so it'll be interesting to see if the Jays are as aggressive in promoting him as they have been with other pitching prospects in the past.

Dave Stieb   Throws R   Age 41

YEAR	TEAM	LGE	IP	H	ER	HR	BB	K	ERA	W	L	H/9	HR/9	BB/9	K/9	KWH	PERA
1998	Syracuse	Int	62.7	55	26	5	17	36	3.73	4	3	7.90	0.72	2.44	5.17	1.04	2.87
1998	Toronto	AL	52.3	56	25	6	15	26	4.30	3	3	9.63	1.03	2.58	4.47	0.60	4.13

Not bad for a guy brought into camp to be an instructor. Stieb was called up in mid-June to avoid losing him to the Rangers. He showed up as his old ornery self as a long reliever, plunking five batters in half a season. He knew what he was doing; he has to back people off the plate so he can hit the outside corner. Knows his craft, and though I love rooting for him, not somebody the Jays should count on.

Ben VanRyn   Throws L   Age 27

YEAR	TEAM	LGE	IP	H	ER	HR	BB	K	ERA	W	L	H/9	HR/9	BB/9	K/9	KWH	PERA
1996	Vancouvr	PCL	32.0	40	19	3	12	23	5.34	1	3	11.25	0.84	3.38	6.47	0.83	5.06
1996	Louisvil	AmA	66.0	79	44	9	30	36	6.00	2	5	10.77	1.23	4.09	4.91	0.41	5.05
1997	Iowa	AmA	76.0	109	50	9	27	51	5.92	3	5	12.91	1.07	3.20	6.04	0.66	5.92
1998	Syracuse	Int	39.0	42	18	3	13	23	4.15	2	2	9.69	0.69	3.00	5.31	0.73	3.92

Useful, not a bad guy to have around as your second left-hander. The Cubs shouldn't have traded him, and the Padres shouldn't have cut him. Another of Johnson's Iowa vets, so a good bet to stick around the organization.

Woody Williams   Throws R   Age 32

YEAR	TEAM	LGE	IP	H	ER	HR	BB	K	ERA	W	L	H/9	HR/9	BB/9	K/9	KWH	PERA
1996	Syracuse	Int	31.0	26	5	4	8	26	1.45	3	0	7.55	1.16	2.32	7.55	2.44	2.90
1996	Toronto	AL	61.0	60	24	7	17	43	3.54	4	3	8.85	1.03	2.51	6.34	1.36	3.69
1997	Toronto	AL	198.7	198	82	29	57	120	3.71	12	10	8.97	1.31	2.58	5.44	0.96	3.94
1998	Toronto	AL	217.3	189	89	34	72	147	3.69	13	11	7.83	1.41	2.98	6.09	1.19	3.40

Best-suited to be a fifth starter, because as the season wore on he had to take his regular turn every fifth day; that combined with the highest pitch count of his injury-riddled career left him almost useless during the summer. He finished up strong, but Williams was probably the starter least-suited to Johnson's usage patterns, and I'm worried about him going into '99.

Jay Yennaco   Throws R   Age 23

Year	Team	Lge	IP	H	ER	HR	BB	K	ERA	W	L	H/9	HR/9	BB/9	K/9	KWH	PERA
1996	Michigan	Mid	149.7	273	141	20	68	80	8.48	3	14	16.42	1.20	4.09	4.81	0.26	7.64
1997	Sarasota	Fla	43.0	38	13	4	22	31	2.72	3	2	7.95	0.84	4.60	6.49	0.86	3.35
1997	Trenton	Eas	115.7	171	89	8	50	56	6.93	3	10	13.31	0.62	3.89	4.36	0.28	5.76
1998	Trenton	Eas	52.3	58	31	9	19	18	5.33	2	4	9.97	1.55	3.27	3.10	0.22	4.82
1998	Pawtuckt	Int	60.7	80	38	6	15	29	5.64	2	5	11.87	0.89	2.23	4.30	0.53	5.19
1998	Syracuse	Int	37.7	61	26	4	9	23	6.21	1	3	14.58	0.96	2.15	5.50	0.72	6.45

He didn't embarrass himself in the AFL, but is essentially an overrated, hard-throwing Red Sox pitcher that we get to hear about because you-know-who will tout anybody from the Red Sox organization, especially after Dan Duquette trades them. The Jays think a move to the pen will do him good.

SNWL							TORONTO BLUE JAYS					Park Effect: +1.5%
PITCHER	GS	IP	R	SNW	SNL	SNPCT	W	L	RA	APW	SNVA	SNWAR
Carpenter, C.	24	152.3	91	8.4	9.2	.478	11	7	5.38	-0.64	-0.32	0.93
Clemens, R.	33	234.7	78	17.5	7.6	.697	20	6	2.99	4.92	4.86	6.85
Escobar, K.	10	69.0	22	5.1	2.0	.712	6	2	2.87	1.54	1.38	2.04
Guzman, J.	22	145.0	83	8.0	8.2	.493	6	12	5.15	-0.27	-0.15	1.10
Halladay, R.	2	14.0	4	1.1	0.3	.788	1	0	2.57	0.36	0.39	0.53
Hanson, E.	8	45.0	30	2.0	3.5	.357	0	2	6.00	-0.49	-0.75	-0.37
Hentgen, P.	29	177.7	109	9.4	11.7	.445	12	11	5.52	-1.02	-1.25	0.42
Stieb, D.	3	15.7	14	0.4	1.6	.208	1	2	8.04	-0.51	-0.57	-0.43
Williams, W.	32	209.7	112	12.0	11.0	.521	10	9	4.81	0.37	0.38	2.22
TOTALS	163	1063.0	543	63.9	55.2	.536	67	51	4.60	4.25	3.98	13.28

The Blue Jays had a very nice starting staff in 1998, but not quite on par with the excellent 1997 group. They were second in the majors with a 7.4 SNVA in 1997, and dropped to sixth with a 4.0 SNVA last year. A big part of the drop was Pat Hentgen, who lost over four games in SNVA, from 2.9 to -1.3. The other big decline came from that huge disappointment Roger Clemens, who lost around three games of SNVA. As a result of his mammoth collapse, Clemens was merely the Cy Young Award winner, as opposed to the Cy-Young-Can't-Carry-My-Jock Award winner.... Compensating for some of the decline of Hentgen and Clemens was Kelvim Escobar, who had an outstanding 10 starts. Escobar's season was the second best among AL rookies, and he was one of only four pitchers (with Maddux, Glavine, and Al Leiter) who had more than 10 starts and a .700+ SNPct.... From the Modern Greats Making Comebacks Trivia Department: Dave Stieb and Kevin Appier had almost identical Support Neutral lines in their brief 1998 campaigns.

Pitcher Abuse Points

PITCHER	AGE	GS	PAP	PAP/S	AAW	MAX	115+	130+
Carpenter, Chris	23	24	357	14.88	37.19	133	7	1
Clemens, Roger	35	33	1206	36.55	36.55	147	21	10
Escobar, Kelvim	22	10	274	27.40	73.07	137	6	1
Guzman, Juan	31	22	431	19.59	22.86	134	9	2
Hanson, Erik	33	8	108	13.50	13.50	125	3	0
Hentgen, Pat	29	29	318	10.97	16.45	131	7	1
Williams, Woody	31	32	584	18.25	21.29	134	13	2
TOTAL		163	3283	20.14	28.24	147	66	17
RANKING (AL)			1	1	1		1	1

The jury is in, and it's unanimous: Tim Johnson, however better he was than Cito Gaston at letting the young'uns (Shawn Green, Shannon Stewart) play, gives it all back with the reckless way he handles his rotation. Even if we set aside his treatment of veterans Clemens, Hentgen, Guzman, and Williams, he has a lot to explain. Chris Carpenter: nearly 15 PAPs a start for a 24-year-old in his first full major league season is dangerously high, and unforgivable. Kelvim Escobar? In just 10 starts, Escobar recorded nearly as many PAPs as Hentgen did—as a 22-year-old who had never started a major league game before this year. His AAW was the second-highest in baseball. Absolutely unforgivable. PAP really sheds light on how the Blue Jays' pennant hopes in 1998, and possibly future pennant hopes as well, were damaged by their manager's inability to go out to the mound and say, "Give me the ball."

Chicago White Sox

When the Sox finally cast Terry Bevington aside, there were all sorts of hopes that they would finally get their collective act together. It was expected that they'd bring in a manager who would be an active participant in shepherding the franchise towards contention as the Indians come back to the pack in their post-greatness phase. The Sox surprised almost everyone with their choice: Jerry Manuel.

For a baseball lifer, Manuel came across as well-read, thoughtful, and deft with the press. Even the Sox exulted that he got the job on the basis of a great interview. In short, he's everything Terry Bevington wasn't. And his credentials were impeccable: he'd worked with Felipe Alou and Jim Leyland, and although the contrasts between these two potential mentors are dramatic, they're the right names to have as references nowadays.

But the education of Jerry Manuel was no easy task. Although the ability to communicate with other humanoids was almost a necessity for anyone following in Bevington's footsteps, Manuel was far too accommodating with the press in his first few months. He went into spring training trashing or challenging his players in print. Maybe it's just me, but if a manager has a problem with a player, or wants that player to do something new, dragging them into the manager's office for a serious discussion seems to work for the better managers around today. As much fun as it may be to have a good laugh about Sparky Anderson's quotes about the greatness of a Marty Castillo or a Chris Pittaro, the point of those comments was never that Sparky believed them. The point was that Sparky wouldn't use the press to belittle his players. If the press wanted to say Chris Pittaro was lousy, they'd have to do it themselves, and not armed with a quote from the old man.

It's a rare day when Davey Johnson or Bobby Cox rip into their men for the record, and then only when it seems an absolute necessity (like Cox with Andruw Jones). A manager's job description does not include a clause demanding that he provide good copy, and Manuel's stunts were both ill-considered in terms of how to motivate players to do better, and unprofessional in the sense that their only goal seemed to be to help make him popular with a local media happy to be talking to anyone not named Terry Bevington.

More unsettling, Manuel didn't seem to understand the job he was taking on, the league he was entering, the strengths and weaknesses of the players he had, or any aspect of his job as it related to managing a roster. None of these were crippling problems in themselves. With experience, he could sort these things out. What was disappointing was the way in which he virtually blackmailed the team into acquiring one of his personal favorites, Wil Cordero. This was as clear a sign as any that he had absolutely no idea what the team's needs were (good offensive players to compensate for a weak pitching staff), and a troubling sign that he might not understand what makes players valuable (the ability to put runs on the board or play a position; preferably both).

How bad was the early going? Manuel goofed off with Ruben Sierra, he jerked people out of the rotation, kept and then demoted scrubs like Todd Rizzo, and eventually, grudgingly recognized he needed to have Bill Simas around after all. He put Magglio Ordonez in center field, as if to prove to himself that Ordonez couldn't do it. He got frustrated with players quickly and easily, saying he was "miffed" that other people in the organization were so patient. "When I was coming up . . . they'd give a player 15 at bats and at that point they'd know. Now it's 'give'm a few weeks or give'm a few months or give'm a year.' I wrestle with this continually." One has to wonder whether he thought he was taking the job with Dan Duquette's use'm and lose'm Red Sox. His new friends in the media helped him out, popping off rounds at the easy targets: Albert Belle for "not running out grounders," Frank Thomas for being human, and Jaime Navarro for being himself. By July 1st, the team was tied with the Tigers at 31-48, worst in the American League.

Perhaps the big moves had already happened by the end of May, because things only got better from that point forward. Von Joshua and Nardi Contreras were brought in to coach the hitting and pitching. Both men are well-respected

White Sox Prospectus

1998 record: 80-82; Second place, AL Central

Pythagorean W/L: 75-87

Runs scored: 861 (4th in AL)

Runs allowed: 931 (14th in AL)

Team EQA: .269 (6th in AL)

Park: Comiskey Park (good pitchers')

1998: A difficult season ended positively as some young players showed promise.

1999: A reverse: below-average offense and improved pitching, and the same results.

instructors, and Joshua is well-known for his work in the Sox minor leagues and with the Dodgers before that. For whatever reason, after they came in, Manuel seemed to be less glib with the press. Stiffs like Ruben Sierra were cut loose, the reclamation project of Jason Bere was mercifully ended, and Navarro was removed from the rotation. And like almost any team that removes some of the league's worst players from the group it uses regularly, the team got dramatically better. Albert Belle became the hottest hitter in baseball for the last three months, the Sox finally settled on a rotation and bullpen, and suddenly they weren't playing like it was spring training. They roared down the stretch at 24-9. But as soon as the season ended, Manuel got back to yapping about players he didn't like, or sharing his disappointment that poor old Wil Cordero wasn't going to be re-signed to continue his two-way millstone act.

I'm willing to give managers the same benefit of the doubt as I give players. As a manager, Manuel may figure things out, but we'll have to see. He's going to have to learn that playing Cordero or Greg Norton at first base costs his team too many runs. A decision like that means more to a team's runs scored than the total Manuel can snag with tactical decisions on an entire season. He's going to have to learn to shrug off Mike Caruso's errors like Jim Leyland learned to live with Jay Bell's ten years ago. As much as his mistakes may frustrate Sox fans, at least none of them rivaled Phil Garner's slagging of Cal Eldred early in his managerial career.

The bigger issue for the organization is how they're going to get people into the stands. As expected, the "payoff" of the previous season's misnamed "white flag" trades was the loss of almost 500,000 fannies in the seats. This was the short-term repercussion, and the Sox can still hope to reap the long-term benefits of having significantly improved both their farm system and their chances of being the team to beat in the AL Central as the Indians get old. Certainly what they chose to do stands in stark contrast to the Cubs' cynically orchestrated banzai charge of '98.

Unfortunately, they've gotten too concerned with public appearances, because they've let Albert Belle walk away for big Bal'mer bucks. Because of the persistent media campaign of going after Belle for past transgressions, and his unwillingness to participate in pre- and post-game nonsense, Belle is going to consistently draw negative publicity to his team. While this will almost certainly help the Sox in terms of getting the local media to be more enthusiastic about them (with the hoped-for effect that good publicity will lead to more ticket sales), for Sox fans who want to see their team push Cleveland sooner rather than later, it's a big loss. The Indians aren't invincible, and a Sox team with Belle and without Cordero or Cameron's struggles or locked into starting Jaime Navarro and Jason Bere could give them trouble. Move beyond addition by subtraction, and think about a team with Belle as well as Mario Valdez or Mark Johnson or Carlos Lee, with Jeff Abbott in a more regular role, and it's not hard to envision a team with the potential to upset the Tribe. That team will now never take the field, and the Sox have to be considered better bets to start their push in 2000, or about the same time the Royals and possibly the Twins will be in better shape as well.

I'm not really sold on the idea that the Sox need to apologize for the trades of '97, or have to go out of their way to placate their fans' hurt feelings. Memory is a tricky thing; most fans have probably forgotten what a bad idea it was to fire Gene Lamont, while they remember Ozzie Guillen as some sort of useful player. What's important to realize about the Sox is that their attendance problems offer a potentially chilling lesson for teams stumping for new stadiums. Their average attendance dropped in 1996, the year after the year after the strike; the Sox were almost alone in that. Although they can blame the trade or keep blaming the strike or the neighborhood or the stadium, it's time for them to blame themselves, or at least marketing yutz Ron Gallas.

A trip to Comiskey isn't pleasant. It's an endless cacophony of canned music and scoreboard cartoons. Sox promotions border on the idiotic, even for advertising. Maybe it's just me, but I don't know anyone who thinks Tim Kazurinsky is funny, yet one of Saturday Night Live's most feeble graduates routinely pops up in Sox commercials. Why? Maybe he's a good golf partner.

With attendance plummeting while Snugglies fans pile into Wrigley to drink bad beer at worse prices while coincidentally watching baseball, you would think the Sox would understand that they have to start cutting ticket prices and marketing themselves aggressively on the basis of their product, major league baseball. Instead they spend more money on a high-tech ad campaign featuring . . . Tim Kazurinsky. It's just this sort of genius that can put the Sox in third place in professional baseball attendance in the Chicago area, behind the Kane County Cougars. With the expansion of the Northern League to Chicago, it seems the issue isn't fan interest in baseball in Chicago, it's getting the fans to come to this ballpark. The Sox are a tough sale determined to make themselves a tougher sale, and for what is shaping up as a good, young, competitive team, that's a bigger betrayal than anything people think Ron Schueler has done to them.

HITTERS (Averages: BA .260/ OBP .330/ SLG .420, EqA .260)

Jeff Abbott   OF   Bats R   Age 26

YEAR	TEAM	LGE	AB	H	DB	TP	HR	BB	R	RBI	SB	CS	OUT	BA	OBA	SA	EQA	EQR	DEFENSE
1996	Nashvill	AA	442	140	21	1	13	35	62	63	12	4	306	.317	.367	.457	.286	67	101-OF 91
1997	Nashvill	AA	459	137	28	2	9	38	61	57	10	6	328	.298	.352	.427	.270	62	110-OF 100
1998	ChiSox	AL	240	66	13	1	12	11	26	35	3	3	177	.275	.307	.488	.264	32	57-OF 99
1999	*ChiSox*	*AL*	*347*	*98*	*20*	*1*	*12*	*23*	*42*	*48*	*6*	*3*	*252*	*.282*	*.327*	*.450*	*.269*	*47*	

Not a bad debut, and he did it while fighting off a sporadic pinch-hitting role and a shoulder injury in June that almost landed him on the disabled list. Initially, he was very cautious in the field, and he figured out pretty early that the way to stay on the roster was going to hit the ball hard during his weekly start. I expect him to improve in both areas now that Belle's gone, and he's expected to play every day in left or center.

Albert Belle   LF   Bats R   Age 32

YEAR	TEAM	LGE	AB	H	DB	TP	HR	BB	R	RBI	SB	CS	OUT	BA	OBA	SA	EQA	EQR	DEFENSE
1996	Clevelnd	AL	581	173	37	3	44	93	108	122	12	0	408	.298	.395	.599	.330	127	144-OF 99
1997	ChiSox	AL	626	172	37	2	33	55	78	99	4	4	458	.275	.333	.498	.279	94	142-OF 96
1998	ChiSox	AL	598	196	43	2	50	83	110	141	5	4	406	.328	.410	.657	.343	140	155-OF 95
1999	*Baltimor*	*AL*	*595*	*168*	*31*	*1*	*42*	*78*	*93*	*118*	*5*	*2*	*429*	*.282*	*.366*	*.550*	*.308*	*113*	

He caught plenty of flak for not running out grounders, but that's mostly media sniping over not getting to interview him. It would be hard to envision a player more focused on the outcome of each individual ballgame than Belle. The man's consuming passion is to play baseball, and I can't really blame him for putting his focus ahead of putting in the time to say "we just have to play one game at a time, take things day by day and do what we have to do." If you're the schlub whose life depends on getting that fodder, I don't have much sympathy for you. The game on the field comes first, and that's where Belle wants to be. What's wrong with that?

Mike Cameron   CF   Bats R   Age 26

YEAR	TEAM	LGE	AB	H	DB	TP	HR	BB	R	RBI	SB	CS	OUT	BA	OBA	SA	EQA	EQR	DEFENSE
1996	Birmnghm	Sou	475	136	22	6	25	57	80	76	28	11	350	.286	.363	.516	.297	84	119-OF 99
1997	Nashvill	AA	119	30	5	2	5	17	17	17	4	2	91	.252	.346	.454	.275	18	26-OF 108
1997	ChiSox	AL	374	97	17	3	15	56	65	49	24	2	279	.259	.356	.441	.285	61	105-OF 111
1998	ChiSox	AL	391	80	16	5	8	39	42	28	24	11	322	.205	.277	.332	.216	35	112-OF 111
1999	*Cincnnti*	*NL*	*422*	*103*	*22*	*6*	*14*	*50*	*63*	*49*	*29*	*9*	*328*	*.244*	*.324*	*.424*	*.266*	*60*	

By June, Manuel was itching to send him down. Cameron got overly pull-conscious, and not even Von Joshua could get him to take the bit out from between his teeth on that score. Manuel's constant in-print needling probably wasn't helpful, but trashing your players for the beat writers' benefit never is. A hand injury on a diving catch on the Fourth of July created more problems. Mercifully, he's been traded for Paul Konerko, and he should be the Reds' everyday center fielder. I still expect him to thrive. Even as Cameron was headed out, Manuel couldn't help but take a parting shot or two. If this is how the manager handles development, Sox fans, be very afraid.

Mike Caruso   SS   Bats L   Age 22

YEAR	TEAM	LGE	AB	H	DB	TP	HR	BB	R	RBI	SB	CS	OUT	BA	OBA	SA	EQA	EQR	DEFENSE
1996	Bellnghm	Nwn	316	79	9	1	1	11	23	19	12	7	244	.250	.275	.294	.195	21	72-SS 108
1997	San Jose	Cal	438	128	20	6	2	30	49	45	7	8	318	.292	.338	.379	.248	49	106-SS 92
1997	WnstnSlm	Car	119	24	3	1	0	3	4	4	2	0	95	.202	.221	.244	.140	3	26-SS 91
1998	ChiSox	AL	515	156	17	6	5	17	58	53	20	6	365	.303	.325	.388	.251	58	128-SS 93
1999	*ChiSox*	*AL*	*503*	*148*	*17*	*5*	*3*	*21*	*55*	*50*	*15*	*7*	*362*	*.294*	*.323*	*.366*	*.244*	*53*	

Caruso has extraordinary hand-eye coordination, which causes all sorts of problems right now because he can react to almost any pitch and can snap up almost any ball hit at him. The problem is that he doesn't always seem to know what to do after he's reacted. At season's start, his throws had a weird, wobbling spin on them, which probably didn't make Wil Cordero's life any easier. Jerry Manuel was all smiles in camp when he cracked that Caruso might make 30 errors, and the manager got

(Mike Caruso *continued*)

more and more sullen about being right as the season progressed. Caruso is still learning how to play the field, how to hit and how to run the bases, so he could end up making significant improvements as he matures and gains experience. Not bad, when you consider he's already one of the best shortstops in the American League not named Rodriguez, Garciaparra, or Jeter.

McKay Christensen   CF   Bats L   Age 23

YEAR	TEAM	LGE	AB	H	DB	TP	HR	BB	R	RBI	SB	CS	OUT	BA	OBA	SA	EQA	EQR	DEFENSE
1997	Hickory	SAL	512	126	8	7	5	46	46	42	11	11	397	.246	.308	.318	.218	44	123-OF 103
1998	WnstnSlm	Car	368	96	12	3	5	48	48	36	10	5	277	.261	.346	.351	.250	43	95-OF 105
1999	*ChiSox*	*AL*	*432*	*117*	*13*	*3*	*7*	*46*	*53*	*47*	*10*	*7*	*322*	*.271*	*.341*	*.363*	*.252*	*51*	

He missed all of camp with a broken thumb, but still managed to put together an OK season. He's a good center fielder, and he's shown a good line-drive stroke and patience at the plate. Health and surviving Double-A will give the Sox a good read on whether he'll be able to push his way into the center field picture by 2000.

Wil Cordero   1B/OF   Bats R   Age 27

YEAR	TEAM	LGE	AB	H	DB	TP	HR	BB	R	RBI	SB	CS	OUT	BA	OBA	SA	EQA	EQR	DEFENSE
1996	Boston	AL	193	52	8	0	4	10	17	20	2	1	142	.269	.305	.373	.234	19	35-2B 101
1997	Boston	AL	562	156	25	3	19	32	56	73	1	3	409	.278	.316	.434	.255	67	124-OF 96
1998	ChiSox	AL	336	88	18	2	13	24	36	44	2	1	249	.262	.311	.443	.257	42	78-1B 107
1999	*ChiSox*	*AL*	*369*	*97*	*19*	*1*	*13*	*26*	*39*	*48*	*2*	*1*	*273*	*.263*	*.311*	*.425*	*.255*	*45*	

Heading downhill and picking up steam, he was only on the roster at the new manager's behest in the first place. He was brutal in the field, doing a lousy job of scooping low throws, and contributing plenty to Caruso's error count. Offensively, he has never been good enough to put up with if he isn't playing shortstop or second. Naturally, Manuel's singing his praises as he leaves.

Joe Crede   3B   Bats R   Age 21

YEAR	TEAM	LGE	AB	H	DB	TP	HR	BB	R	RBI	SB	CS	OUT	BA	OBA	SA	EQA	EQR	DEFENSE
1997	Hickory	SAL	405	98	10	0	7	23	28	32	1	1	308	.242	.283	.319	.205	29	112-3B 101
1998	WnstnSlm	Car	499	148	19	2	19	51	65	75	5	4	355	.297	.362	.457	.281	75	128-3B 113
1999	*ChiSox*	*AL*	*448*	*137*	*20*	*1*	*16*	*36*	*58*	*70*	*2*	*2*	*313*	*.306*	*.357*	*.462*	*.284*	*67*	

Named the best hitting prospect and the best defensive third baseman in the Carolina League, he wound up the Sox' minor league player of the year. His development has him being considered the eventual replacement for Robin Ventura, but a word of warning: he's faded badly in the second half in each of the last two seasons.

Jason Dellaero   SS   Bats B   Age 22

YEAR	TEAM	LGE	AB	H	DB	TP	HR	BB	R	RBI	SB	CS	OUT	BA	OBA	SA	EQA	EQR	DEFENSE
1997	Hickory	SAL	194	50	6	1	6	15	19	22	1	1	145	.258	.311	.392	.242	21	53-SS 93
1998	WnstnSlm	Car	429	83	13	2	10	26	25	26	7	2	348	.193	.240	.303	.181	24	120-SS 82
1999	*ChiSox*	*AL*	*317*	*71*	*11*	*1*	*9*	*20*	*24*	*29*	*3*	*1*	*247*	*.224*	*.270*	*.350*	*.214*	*26*	

When they first picked him, the Sox expected he'd have to move to third as he grew up and filled out. But between not hitting a lick, and being named the best defensive shortstop in his league, the Sox can kick around leaving him at short for the time being. His best tool is a strong throwing arm. This is the year we find out if he's adapted to hitting with wood.

Ray Durham   2B   Bats B   Age 27

YEAR	TEAM	LGE	AB	H	DB	TP	HR	BB	R	RBI	SB	CS	OUT	BA	OBA	SA	EQA	EQR	DEFENSE
1996	ChiSox	AL	550	151	33	5	10	55	85	59	33	5	404	.275	.340	.407	.269	76	147-2B 106
1997	ChiSox	AL	626	171	26	5	12	63	87	65	34	17	472	.273	.340	.388	.257	79	153-2B 104
1998	ChiSox	AL	625	177	32	8	20	75	102	84	33	9	457	.283	.360	.456	.285	99	155-2B 101
1999	*ChiSox*	*AL*	*606*	*166*	*33*	*5*	*15*	*68*	*93*	*74*	*26*	*10*	*450*	*.274*	*.347*	*.419*	*.272*	*87*	

The Little Bull finally had the year we've said he had in him for the last two years, and with Alomar and Knoblauch both getting gray, the best player at second base in the American League. Although the defensive numbers are down, he improved noticeably at turning the double play, or more accurately, he finally had a shortstop with quick hands.

Benji Gil — SS — Bats R — Age 26

YEAR	TEAM	LGE	AB	H	DB	TP	HR	BB	R	RBI	SB	CS	OUT	BA	OBA	SA	EQA	EQR	DEFENSE
1996	Oklahoma	AA	291	60	13	1	5	23	21	19	4	5	236	.206	.264	.309	.193	19	82-SS 102
1997	Texas	AL	313	68	13	2	5	18	20	22	1	2	247	.217	.260	.319	.193	20	104-SS 105
1998	Calgary	PCL	447	84	14	2	9	36	28	26	8	3	366	.188	.248	.289	.181	26	114-SS 89
1999	*ChiSox*	*AL*	*365*	*75*	*14*	*1*	*8*	*26*	*25*	*26*	*4*	*3*	*293*	*.205*	*.258*	*.315*	*.195*	*25*	

A nice insurance policy; the Sox deserve credit for having him in place. By acquiring Gil for two scrapheap pitchers, they got an adequate veteran fill-in just in case Caruso didn't look ready in camp, and kept him for the year as an alternative in case Caruso faltered. Caruso never did, so the Sox never had to use Gil. Having redundancy isn't gripping drama, but it is sound organizational policy. Now they have a solid veteran replacement to barter with, and a great young shortstop. That's better than anything that's happened at shortstop for the Sox since they blew the opportunity to replace Guillen with Craig Grebeck.

Jeff Inglin — OF — Bats R — Age 23

YEAR	TEAM	LGE	AB	H	DB	TP	HR	BB	R	RBI	SB	CS	OUT	BA	OBA	SA	EQA	EQR	DEFENSE
1996	Bristol	App	193	41	3	0	4	5	8	10	3	3	155	.212	.232	.290	.165	9	
1997	Hickory	SAL	544	164	21	3	14	44	71	71	14	5	385	.301	.354	.428	.273	75	84-OF 87
1998	Birmnghm	Sou	491	109	13	3	21	61	50	58	2	1	383	.222	.308	.389	.242	55	113-OF 93
1999	*ChiSox*	*AL*	*481*	*130*	*17*	*1*	*17*	*44*	*57*	*64*	*6*	*2*	*353*	*.270*	*.331*	*.416*	*.263*	*63*	

He's not getting much attention as a prospect, but he hit better at Birmingham than Ordonez did at the same age. He's short and has a vicious swing, so he doesn't get "tool time" attention. Looks like he has the makings of a good major league hitter.

Mark Johnson — C — Bats L — Age 23

YEAR	TEAM	LGE	AB	H	DB	TP	HR	BB	R	RBI	SB	CS	OUT	BA	OBA	SA	EQA	EQR	DEFENSE
1996	Sth Bend	Mid	219	50	11	2	2	30	25	18	2	2	171	.228	.321	.324	.229	21	
1997	WnstnSlm	Car	381	86	20	2	4	89	59	36	2	1	296	.226	.372	.320	.257	50	
1998	Birmnghm	Sou	376	95	11	2	8	86	59	46	0	1	282	.253	.392	.356	.274	55	103-C 91
1999	*ChiSox*	*AL*	*388*	*95*	*14*	*2*	*6*	*77*	*57*	*42*	*1*	*1*	*294*	*.245*	*.370*	*.338*	*.262*	*51*	

Johnson is what's referred to as a "quiet" catcher: he sets up and frames pitches well, and doesn't move much as he receives the ball. He's also the perfect "silent" contributor on offense, because very few hitters ever learn to be as selective as Johnson is. There are already the usual complaints that he's "too passive" as a hitter, but that's the "Mike Matheny has value" lunatic fringe of baseball evaluation talking.

Carlos Lee — 3B — Bats R — Age 23

YEAR	TEAM	LGE	AB	H	DB	TP	HR	BB	R	RBI	SB	CS	OUT	BA	OBA	SA	EQA	EQR	DEFENSE
1996	Hickory	SAL	489	136	13	3	8	16	41	48	8	6	359	.278	.301	.366	.229	45	113-3B 97
1997	WnstnSlm	Car	544	157	33	2	15	28	61	69	7	3	390	.289	.323	.439	.261	68	133-3B 93
1998	Birmnghm	Sou	542	149	20	1	19	25	53	66	7	3	396	.275	.307	.421	.249	61	126-3B 85
1999	*ChiSox*	*AL*	*526*	*149*	*22*	*1*	*16*	*25*	*54*	*67*	*6*	*4*	*381*	*.283*	*.316*	*.420*	*.255*	*62*	

Lee struggled mightily in his first few months at Double-A, then rebounded to have a very good second half. There are some doubts about his glovework, and whether he remains at third is up in the air. He worked out at first base and in left field in the Arizona Fall League, which combined with his error-prone ways at third have helped to reinforce some trendy comparisons to Bobby Bonilla.

Jeff Liefer — OF — Bats L — Age 24

YEAR	TEAM	LGE	AB	H	DB	TP	HR	BB	R	RBI	SB	CS	OUT	BA	OBA	SA	EQA	EQR	DEFENSE
1996	Sth Bend	Mid	280	82	5	0	12	21	31	40	3	3	201	.293	.342	.439	.267	37	35-3B 68
1997	Birmnghm	Sou	471	101	17	5	12	30	34	39	1	0	370	.214	.261	.348	.206	36	104-OF 84
1998	Birmnghm	Sou	465	121	21	2	18	44	51	62	1	1	345	.260	.324	.430	.259	59	99-1B 92
1999	*ChiSox*	*AL*	*489*	*122*	*20*	*2*	*17*	*36*	*47*	*59*	*1*	*1*	*368*	*.249*	*.301*	*.403*	*.244*	*54*	

The comparisons to Robin Ventura that were made when he was drafted out of Long Beach State are deader than Elvis. He's looking like a DH after having been a brutal fielder at third base, the outfield, and now first base. He was a Southern League All-Star in '98, but it was his second time through the league. May still have a career.

Robert Machado   C   Bats R   Age 26

YEAR	TEAM	LGE	AB	H	DB	TP	HR	BB	R	RBI	SB	CS	OUT	BA	OBA	SA	EQA	EQR	DEFENSE
1996	Birmnghm	Sou	310	67	9	0	6	14	16	20	1	2	245	.216	.250	.303	.181	17	
1997	Nashvill	AA	304	75	9	0	8	12	23	27	4	0	229	.247	.275	.355	.217	25	
1998	Calgary	PCL	232	46	6	0	4	17	12	13	2	2	188	.198	.253	.276	.174	12	70-C 106
1998	ChiSox	AL	110	23	5	0	3	7	7	9	0	0	87	.209	.256	.336	.199	8	32-C 99
1999	*ChiSox*	*AL*	*320*	*73*	*7*	*0*	*10*	*18*	*22*	*29*	*2*	*1*	*248*	*.228*	*.269*	*.344*	*.211*	*25*	

The White Sox have what they may perceive as a very difficult set of choices ahead of them at catcher. They can choose some combination of signing a veteran journeyman, playing Mark Johnson or playing Machado. The worst solution is signing someone like Terry Steinbach. The next worst is not letting either Johnson or Machado play. The next worst after that is picking Machado over Johnson, because even if everything breaks Machado's way you've got a Pat Borders clone on your hands, and that isn't something that makes you a better team. Machado was named a Pacific Coast League All-Star and the best defensive catcher in that circuit.

J.R. Mounts   OF   Bats R   Age 20

YEAR	TEAM	LGE	AB	H	DB	TP	HR	BB	R	RBI	SB	CS	OUT	BA	OBA	SA	EQA	EQR	DEFENSE
1998	Hickory	SAL	430	88	12	0	9	23	25	25	9	4	346	.205	.245	.295	.180	24	105-OF 95
1999	*ChiSox*	*AL*	*338*	*80*	*8*	*0*	*10*	*16*	*27*	*30*	*7*	*3*	*261*	*.237*	*.271*	*.349*	*.215*	*28*	

The Sox' third-round pick in '97, he's a tools player who was initially compared to Mike Cameron when that wasn't an insult in this organization. So far, he's known for his great throwing arm and little else.

Greg Norton   1B/3B   Bats B   Age 26

YEAR	TEAM	LGE	AB	H	DB	TP	HR	BB	R	RBI	SB	CS	OUT	BA	OBA	SA	EQA	EQR	DEFENSE
1996	Birmnghm	Sou	288	75	9	2	7	26	30	32	4	3	216	.260	.322	.378	.244	32	76-SS 94
1996	Nashvill	AA	165	47	12	2	6	18	23	25	2	3	121	.285	.355	.491	.283	26	35-SS 86
1997	Nashvill	AA	411	105	19	1	21	52	52	61	3	4	310	.255	.339	.460	.271	60	93-3B 91
1998	ChiSox	AL	295	69	17	2	9	27	30	32	3	3	229	.234	.298	.397	.238	31	71-1B 90
1999	*ChiSox*	*AL*	*355*	*86*	*18*	*2*	*13*	*35*	*40*	*44*	*3*	*3*	*272*	*.242*	*.310*	*.414*	*.251*	*43*	

One of the Sox' two creatine users. Highlight of the year: a two-homer game against Randy Johnson, so now he can say "I own the Big Unit." Acquiring Paul Konerko for Cameron has happily killed off talk about having him play every day at first base next year. He can be an adequate fill-in at third until either Carlos Lee or Joe Crede look ready.

Magglio Ordonez   RF   Bats R   Age 25

YEAR	TEAM	LGE	AB	H	DB	TP	HR	BB	R	RBI	SB	CS	OUT	BA	OBA	SA	EQA	EQR	DEFENSE
1996	Birmnghm	Sou	480	120	22	1	18	30	45	55	7	7	367	.250	.294	.412	.239	51	127-OF 94
1997	Nashvill	AA	516	158	22	3	12	31	63	66	13	8	366	.306	.346	.430	.267	68	120-OF 104
1998	ChiSox	AL	527	147	24	2	14	31	55	62	8	7	387	.279	.319	.412	.250	60	139-OF 102
1999	*ChiSox*	*AL*	*516*	*147*	*21*	*1*	*17*	*29*	*57*	*68*	*9*	*7*	*376*	*.285*	*.323*	*.428*	*.260*	*64*	

Like Jose Canseco before him, Ordonez was once "The Man of a Thousand Stances." Von Joshua got him away from that, at which point (1996) he started to become a prospect. Unfortunately, that's all he's ever going to have in common with Canseco. Ordonez can play a good right field, flashes a strong arm, and has a little power. His problem is that he needs to be considerably better than he is to really help his team if it doesn't have several better offensive players in the lineup, and the '99 Sox don't look like they'll be that team.

Josh Paul   C   Bats R   Age 24

YEAR	TEAM	LGE	AB	H	DB	TP	HR	BB	R	RBI	SB	CS	OUT	BA	OBA	SA	EQA	EQR	DEFENSE
1996	Hickory	SAL	232	68	6	0	7	16	27	29	6	2	166	.293	.339	.409	.262	29	19-OF 101
1997	Birmnghm	Sou	114	29	4	0	1	9	11	9	4	1	86	.254	.309	.316	.224	10	
1998	WnstnSlm	Car	448	101	10	3	10	34	37	36	10	4	351	.225	.280	.328	.211	36	108-C 98
1999	*ChiSox*	*AL*	*321*	*77*	*8*	*1*	*7*	*23*	*29*	*29*	*7*	*2*	*246*	*.240*	*.291*	*.336*	*.222*	*29*	

Drafted before A.J. Hinch, Paul hasn't worked out very well so far because of persistent wrist injuries. Behind the plate, he's still considered a work in progress, and if things work out offensively you're looking at a John Stearns type. Not a bad player, but he's already been less than expected. You can guarantee he'll get a cup of coffee, or even some time as a backup, at some point.

Liu Rodriguez   2B   Bats B   Age 22

YEAR	TEAM	LGE	AB	H	DB	TP	HR	BB	R	RBI	SB	CS	OUT	BA	OBA	SA	EQA	EQR	DEFENSE	
1996	Hickory	SAL	446	98	10	0	1	46	33	23	6	6	354	.220	.293	.249	.187	27	90-2B 101	29-SS 82
1997	Hickory	SAL	461	118	17	4	1	58	52	39	5	7	350	.256	.339	.317	.233	46	124-2B 96	
1998	WnstnSlm	Car	425	110	21	1	3	43	48	36	8	5	320	.259	.327	.334	.234	43	93-2B 95	
1999	*ChiSox*	*AL*	*454*	*121*	*18*	*2*	*2*	*48*	*53*	*41*	*8*	*6*	*339*	*.267*	*.337*	*.328*	*.239*	*48*		

The Sox are intrigued by his ability to get on base and his speed, but he's got a Durham ahead of him and a Durham (Ray's kid brother Chad) behind him, and there are nagging rumors that some folks want to move Caruso to second base, so there are lots of things out of Liu's control that keep us from talking seriously about his future. Liu is a prospect at a position with lots of good players and adequate prospects.

Aaron Rowand   OF   Bats R   Age 21

YEAR	TEAM	LGE	AB	H	DB	TP	HR	BB	R	RBI	SB	CS	OUT	BA	OBA	SA	EQA	EQR	DEFENSE
1998	Hickory	SAL	218	65	8	2	4	18	26	27	3	2	155	.298	.352	.408	.265	28	45-OF 98
1999	*ChiSox*	*AL*	*171*	*57*	*7*	*1*	*4*	*13*	*24*	*26*	*3*	*2*	*116*	*.333*	*.380*	*.456*	*.293*	*27*	

A supplemental first-rounder in the '98 draft, Rowand has already garnered early comparisons to Tim Salmon and Raul Mondesi, mostly because they expect him to hit for more power once he figures out how to drive pitches with wood. He's a name to remember for now. Should probably skip past Hickory in '99, because he didn't have much to learn from the Sally League.

Olmedo Saenz   3B   Bats R   Age 28

YEAR	TEAM	LGE	AB	H	DB	TP	HR	BB	R	RBI	SB	CS	OUT	BA	OBA	SA	EQA	EQR	DEFENSE
1995	Nashvill	AA	415	120	18	1	13	45	52	58	0	2	297	.289	.359	.431	.273	58	111-3B 111
1996	Nashvill	AA	480	115	18	0	15	50	48	51	4	2	367	.240	.311	.371	.238	51	120-3B 105
1998	Calgary	PCL	448	112	13	0	18	38	42	54	2	2	338	.250	.309	.400	.243	49	114-3B 96
1999	*Oakland*	*AL*	*320*	*82*	*11*	*0*	*14*	*30*	*34*	*44*	*1*	*1*	*239*	*.256*	*.320*	*.422*	*.256*	*39*	

After missing all of '97 with a torn Achilles tendon, '98 was a bittersweet success story for Saenz. He had a good season in Calgary, but he had to know that he could have been in Chris Snopek's or Greg Norton's shoes when Robin Ventura went down in '97. Signed by Oakland as a minor league free agent, where they're expecting him to make the roster and add some needed right-handed power platooning with Stairs and/or Chavez.

Ruben Sierra   DH   Bats Too Often   Age 33

YEAR	TEAM	LGE	AB	H	DB	TP	HR	BB	R	RBI	SB	CS	OUT	BA	OBA	SA	EQA	EQR	DEFENSE
1996	NY Yanks	AL	352	87	16	1	10	38	37	39	1	4	269	.247	.321	.384	.242	39	24-OF 107
1996	Detroit	AL	155	32	8	1	1	19	15	10	3	1	124	.206	.293	.290	.208	12	18-OF 106
1997	Cincnnti	NL	89	21	4	1	2	7	8	9	0	0	68	.236	.292	.371	.228	8	18-OF 101
1998	ChiSox	AL	73	15	4	1	4	4	8	8	2	0	58	.205	.247	.452	.237	8	
1998	Norfolk	Int	107	23	2	0	2	10	9	7	2	0	84	.215	.282	.290	.202	8	24-OF 101
1999	*ChiSox*	*AL*	*215*	*46*	*6*	*1*	*7*	*23*	*20*	*21*	*2*	*1*	*170*	*.214*	*.290*	*.349*	*.225*	*20*	

Classic Manuel doublethink from late May, during the stretch where the Sox decided they'd be better off with Sierra playing regularly: "I think I know what the kids can do. I want to see what the veterans will do so I can justify playing the kids." The Bad Bald One wouldn't help most Northern League teams, but in the post-Bevington era, the Sox went out of their way to be accommodating to Manuel.

Brian Simmons   CF   Bats B   Age 25

YEAR	TEAM	LGE	AB	H	DB	TP	HR	BB	R	RBI	SB	CS	OUT	BA	OBA	SA	EQA	EQR	DEFENSE	
1996	Sth Bend	Mid	362	94	12	2	13	33	40	44	8	6	274	.260	.322	.412	.252	44	90-OF	99
1996	Pr Willm	Car	131	22	1	2	3	8	5	6	1	0	109	.168	.216	.275	.154	5	31-OF	100
1997	Birmnghm	Sou	543	123	19	6	12	71	60	52	11	8	428	.227	.316	.350	.234	57	135-OF	104
1998	Calgary	PCL	343	82	14	3	9	36	38	35	8	5	266	.239	.311	.376	.239	37	91-OF	98
1999	*ChiSox*	*AL*	*394*	*94*	*15*	*2*	*13*	*41*	*44*	*45*	*8*	*5*	*305*	*.239*	*.310*	*.386*	*.245*	*45*		

He's come along slowly, but could claim the center field job after a '98 that started off with his impressing folks in the 1997 Arizona Fall League, and finished with his hitting homers from both sides of the plate in a game during his September

(Brian Simmons *continued*)

callup. He gets high marks for hustle and intelligence. Simmons is a better hitter from the left side of the plate, so a platoon with Abbott isn't out of the question, especially if the Sox add a token veteran to their outfield.

Demond Smith					CF			**Bats B**	**Age 26**								
YEAR	TEAM	LGE	AB	H	DB	TP	HR	BB	R	RBI	SB	CS	OUT	BA	OBA	SA	EQA	EQR	DEFENSE
1996	Huntsvil	Sou	445	102	13	8	8	43	48	38	19	9	352	.229	.297	.348	.228	43	108-OF 93
1997	Huntsvil	Sou	320	71	11	2	6	50	45	26	20	7	256	.222	.327	.325	.240	36	82-OF 95
1997	Edmonton	PCL	146	23	2	1	4	19	12	8	7	2	125	.158	.255	.267	.187	9	28-OF 101
1998	Birmnghm	Sou	317	77	11	3	4	32	35	26	14	9	249	.243	.312	.334	.228	31	82-OF 98
1999	*ChiSox*	*AL*	*378*	*86*	*13*	*4*	*7*	*41*	*43*	*33*	*17*	*9*	*301*	*.228*	*.303*	*.339*	*.230*	*38*	

Smith has the makings of a good fourth outfielder. He can handle center, has good speed, no platoon problems and patience at the plate. Currently a minor league free agent.

Jim Terrell					3B			**Bats L**	**Age 21**								
YEAR	TEAM	LGE	AB	H	DB	TP	HR	BB	R	RBI	SB	CS	OUT	BA	OBA	SA	EQA	EQR	DEFENSE	
1997	Bristol	App	176	19	0	0	1	11	3	3	1	0	157	.108	.160	.125	—	-5	47-2B 80	
1998	Hickory	SAL	501	146	14	2	10	45	61	58	11	5	360	.291	.350	.387	.260	62	84-3B 91	19-2B 93
1999	*ChiSox*	*AL*	*380*	*109*	*8*	*1*	*7*	*32*	*44*	*43*	*7*	*3*	*274*	*.287*	*.342*	*.368*	*.255*	*45*		

A third-round pick in '96, Terrell played short in high school. Because the Sox already have Crede and Lee ahead of him, they've been kicking around where to play Terrell, including a potential move to the outfield. The Sox have time to sort out their options, but Terrell's moving along fast enough that he may push his way into Birmingham in '99.

Frank Thomas					DH			**Bats R**	**Age 31**								
YEAR	TEAM	LGE	AB	H	DB	TP	HR	BB	R	RBI	SB	CS	OUT	BA	OBA	SA	EQA	EQR	DEFENSE
1996	ChiSox	AL	514	182	22	0	41	105	105	130	1	1	333	.354	.464	.636	.364	133	136-1B 99
1997	ChiSox	AL	520	182	30	0	38	109	109	127	1	1	339	.350	.463	.627	.362	134	92-1B 91
1998	ChiSox	AL	575	151	33	2	29	112	98	94	7	0	424	.263	.383	.478	.299	104	
1999	*ChiSox*	*AL*	*547*	*161*	*25*	*1*	*36*	*111*	*103*	*115*	*2*	*0*	*386*	*.294*	*.413*	*.541*	*.328*	*119*	

It was a rough year for Frank in all sorts of ways. His divorce was a distraction, he crabbed about the attitudes of the younger players on the team, bemoaned the release of Ruben Sierra, whined about the wider strike zone he thought umps were giving him, and denied any need to even speak to hitting coach Von Joshua. All season long, observers kvetched that he'd screwed up his stance: he was squatting too much, standing too straight, or he'd moved back off the plate. Most of that is just well-intentioned nonsense. Thomas had a bad year by his own lofty standards. Although I doubt he'll get back to where he was, he lost most of the ground in his at-bats against left-handers, which won't last. That projection is probably the low end of what you should expect.

Mario Valdez					1B			**Bats L**	**Age 24**								
YEAR	TEAM	LGE	AB	H	DB	TP	HR	BB	R	RBI	SB	CS	OUT	BA	OBA	SA	EQA	EQR	DEFENSE
1996	Sth Bend	Mid	205	69	7	0	9	27	31	38	1	2	138	.337	.414	.502	.313	38	51-1B 114
1996	Birmnghm	Sou	169	44	8	1	3	27	22	20	0	0	125	.260	.362	.373	.263	22	33-1B 101
1997	Nashvill	AA	280	74	15	1	13	40	39	43	1	1	207	.264	.356	.464	.281	44	74-1B 98
1997	ChiSox	AL	114	28	4	0	2	17	14	11	1	0	86	.246	.344	.333	.245	13	30-1B 91
1998	Calgary	PCL	429	122	17	0	17	54	56	64	1	2	309	.284	.364	.443	.279	64	117-1B 96
1999	*ChiSox*	*AL*	*381*	*105*	*12*	*0*	*17*	*49*	*50*	*59*	*1*	*1*	*277*	*.276*	*.358*	*.441*	*.280*	*58*	

The guy who lost the most in the one-year fling with Wil Cordero. Valdez could have a career very similar to Tino Martinez, and his glovework gets high marks. The acquisition of Konerko doesn't make things easy for him; he isn't really a platoon player, and the Sox would probably be best off trying to get both Valdez and Konerko in the lineup, with Konerko in left field, rather than play Abbott, Simmons, and Ordonez all at once in the outfield.

Robin Ventura 3B Bats L Age 31

YEAR	TEAM	LGE	AB	H	DB	TP	HR	BB	R	RBI	SB	CS	OUT	BA	OBA	SA	EQA	EQR	DEFENSE
1996	ChiSox	AL	577	167	31	2	34	75	84	105	1	4	414	.289	.371	.527	.300	102	143-3B 102
1997	ChiSox	AL	180	47	11	1	6	35	29	26	0	0	133	.261	.381	.433	.287	29	53-3B 105
1998	ChiSox	AL	581	151	30	4	21	81	77	81	1	1	431	.260	.350	.434	.272	83	157-3B 113
1999	*NYMets*	*NL*	*412*	*105*	*21*	*1*	*18*	*63*	*54*	*61*	*0*	*1*	*308*	*.255*	*.354*	*.442*	*.282*	*65*	

It's depressing to accept the implacable logic that dictates Robin's departure from the Sox. The organization is loaded with third base prospects, Ventura expected a huge chunk of change over several years, and his reactions at the plate are not the same as they were three years ago. He is no longer one of the best offensive second bananas in baseball. I can't help but get depressed about this, because Ventura has been the greatest third baseman and one of the greatest players in franchise history. The ankle injury has not had any lasting effects on his fielding.

Craig Wilson IF Bats R Age 28

YEAR	TEAM	LGE	AB	H	DB	TP	HR	BB	R	RBI	SB	CS	OUT	BA	OBA	SA	EQA	EQR	DEFENSE	
1996	Birmnghm	Sou	205	48	2	0	3	29	20	17	1	1	158	.234	.329	.288	.222	18	40-SS 91	
1996	Nashvill	AA	123	19	2	1	1	10	3	3	0	0	104	.154	.218	.211	.116	2	37-SS 87	
1997	Nashvill	AA	450	101	14	1	4	41	34	30	3	3	352	.224	.289	.287	.199	31	113-SS 95	
1998	Calgary	PCL	416	97	11	1	8	31	31	34	3	2	321	.233	.286	.322	.210	32	49-2B 89	27-SS 101
1998	ChiSox	AL	46	22	2	0	4	3	10	14	1	0	24	.478	.510	.783	.421	14		
1999	*ChiSox*	*AL*	*423*	*108*	*16*	*1*	*10*	*37*	*43*	*46*	*3*	*2*	*317*	*.255*	*.315*	*.369*	*.241*	*45*		

Shared shortstop on the '92 edition of Team USA with some guy named Garciaparra. Benji Gil's demotion pushed Wilson into a utility job at Calgary, which was probably the best thing that could have happened to him. The next best thing was playing in the Pacific Coast League, in PCL ballparks, because that made his hitting numbers interesting enough to the organization to finally get him called up. He isn't a great player, but he's a much better utility infielder than Chris Snopek could hope to be.

PITCHERS (Averages: 4.00 ERA, 9.00 H/9, 3.00 BB/9, 1.00 HR/9, 6.00 K/9, 1.00 KWH)

Jim Abbott Throws L Age 31

YEAR	TEAM	LGE	IP	H	ER	HR	BB	K	ERA	W	L	H/9	HR/9	BB/9	K/9	KWH	PERA
1996	Calfrnia	AL	146.0	164	99	20	63	57	6.10	5	11	10.11	1.23	3.88	3.51	0.24	4.75
1998	Birmnghm	Sou	38.7	65	35	2	20	25	8.15	1	3	15.13	0.47	4.66	5.82	0.36	6.52
1998	Calgary	PCL	30.7	33	8	1	10	15	2.35	2	1	9.68	0.29	2.93	4.40	0.51	3.82
1998	ChiSox	AL	32.7	35	13	2	11	14	3.58	2	2	9.64	0.55	3.03	3.86	0.38	3.86

Okay, folks, time to stop twanging the old heartstrings. He hasn't gotten his velocity back, so we're still talking about a junk-tossing left-hander. His 5-0 record was nifty, but three of those five starts were against the Twins and Royals, so keep in mind what happened to Jason Bere in '98 after he got a few token starts against the AL's worst offensive teams at the tail end of '97.

Luis Andujar Throws R Age 26

YEAR	TEAM	LGE	IP	H	ER	HR	BB	K	ERA	W	L	H/9	HR/9	BB/9	K/9	KWH	PERA
1996	ChiSox	AL	22.7	32	18	4	12	6	7.15	1	2	12.71	1.59	4.76	2.38	0.07	6.35
1996	Toronto	AL	14.7	12	6	4	1	5	3.68	1	1	7.36	2.45	0.61	3.07	1.56	3.07
1997	Syracuse	Int	38.0	43	25	7	12	23	5.92	1	3	10.18	1.66	2.84	5.45	0.77	4.97
1997	Toronto	AL	51.3	76	38	8	18	27	6.66	2	4	13.32	1.40	3.16	4.73	0.40	6.31
1998	Syracuse	Int	32.3	28	10	5	6	19	2.78	3	1	7.79	1.39	1.67	5.29	1.61	3.06
1998	Calgary	PCL	50.3	66	34	7	16	36	6.08	2	4	11.80	1.25	2.86	6.44	0.92	5.54

Andujar was coming off having his ever-troublesome elbow 'scoped in '97. The Jays put him into the bullpen to Syracuse and he had his first good run in years. After rejoining the Sox, they tossed him into the rotation at Calgary, with predictable results. In a bullpen, he's a major asset.

James Baldwin — Throws R — Age 27

YEAR	TEAM	LGE	IP	H	ER	HR	BB	K	ERA	W	L	H/9	HR/9	BB/9	K/9	KWH	PERA
1996	ChiSox	AL	168.3	166	72	21	46	125	3.85	10	9	8.88	1.12	2.46	6.68	1.53	3.74
1997	ChiSox	AL	206.0	199	103	17	72	136	4.50	10	13	8.69	0.74	3.15	5.94	0.97	3.50
1998	ChiSox	AL	163.7	174	85	17	54	105	4.67	8	10	9.57	0.93	2.97	5.77	0.88	4.07

The demotion to the pen was very rewarding, because it gave Baldwin the chance to learn a good two-seam fastball from Nardi Contreras. Baldwin's breaking stuff has never been in doubt, but his need to set it up to make it effective has been a consistent problem that may finally be resolved. It would have been nice if Jerry Manuel could have managed to keep his mouth shut early in the year; Baldwin, like Cameron, was one of the players Manuel enjoyed dogging with press quotes.

Kevin Beirne — Throws R — Age 25

YEAR	TEAM	LGE	IP	H	ER	HR	BB	K	ERA	W	L	H/9	HR/9	BB/9	K/9	KWH	PERA
1996	Sth Bend	Mid	129.7	219	111	8	66	71	7.70	3	11	15.20	0.56	4.58	4.93	0.26	6.52
1997	WnstnSlm	Car	78.7	89	45	8	29	49	5.15	3	6	10.18	0.92	3.32	5.61	0.70	4.46
1997	Birmnghm	Sou	71.0	89	51	4	40	37	6.46	2	6	11.28	0.51	5.07	4.69	0.29	4.94
1998	Birmnghm	Sou	160.3	172	76	14	79	113	4.27	8	10	9.65	0.79	4.43	6.34	0.70	4.27

The fight for rotation spots in '99 should be tough. Baldwin, Sirotka, Parque, and Snyder are tentatively penciled in, but Beirne should be able to push his way in. His overhand curve was considered the best breaking pitch in the Southern League in '98, and he complements it with a 92 mph fastball and an improving changeup. He's never had serious arm problems as a pro after essentially not pitching at Texas A&M (he played football). I like his chances.

Chad Bradford — Throws R — Age 24

YEAR	TEAM	LGE	IP	H	ER	HR	BB	K	ERA	W	L	H/9	HR/9	BB/9	K/9	KWH	PERA
1996	Hickory	SAL	28.0	32	10	2	8	16	3.21	2	1	10.29	0.64	2.57	5.14	0.75	4.18
1997	WnstnSlm	Car	53.3	65	32	2	25	30	5.40	2	4	10.97	0.34	4.22	5.06	0.42	4.56
1998	Calgary	PCL	52.0	48	9	3	11	22	1.56	5	1	8.31	0.52	1.90	3.81	0.69	2.94
1998	ChiSox	AL	31.3	26	13	0	7	11	3.73	2	1	7.47	0.00	2.01	3.16	0.50	2.01

He was promoted to Calgary early to cover for a rash of injuries, and created an opportunity for himself from there that led to a major league job. Not just a sidearmer, but a genuine submariner. He's a lot of fun to watch, in that he can throw four pitches for strikes from the submarine delivery, particularly a wicked circle change. He's also fun because he almost brags about his lack of velocity; now that we've lost the great Dan Quisenberry to history, he's sort of a cocky 90s edition of the old master. I'm pretty heavily biased in wanting him to have a career, so take what I'm saying with a grain of salt.

Carlos Castillo — Throws R — Age 24

YEAR	TEAM	LGE	IP	H	ER	HR	BB	K	ERA	W	L	H/9	HR/9	BB/9	K/9	KWH	PERA
1996	Sth Bend	Mid	122.3	178	91	17	30	85	6.69	4	10	13.10	1.25	2.21	6.25	1.01	6.03
1996	Pr Willm	Car	41.3	55	25	0	4	22	5.44	2	3	11.98	0.00	0.87	4.79	1.65	4.14
1997	ChiSox	AL	68.3	67	28	8	29	42	3.69	4	4	8.82	1.05	3.82	5.53	0.68	3.95
1998	ChiSox	AL	102.3	93	50	16	32	62	4.40	5	6	8.18	1.41	2.81	5.45	0.97	3.61

Optioned to Calgary towards the end of August. Was his potential to get to salary arbitration after '99 a consideration? Schueler angrily denied it. This isn't the first time the Sox have been down this road before: there are lingering suspicions that well-timed demotions were aimed at keeping Jack McDowell, Alex Fernandez, and Wilson Alvarez away from arbitration for an extra year. It may or may not actually be the case; I happen to think it is, but I could be wrong. The point is that the Sox are so generally distrusted that nobody will believe anything they have to say. "Baby Huey" is one of baseball's biggest pitchers; one of baseball's most entertaining bits of physical comedy is seeing him standing next to diminutive Jim Parque.

Pat Daneker — Throws R — Age 23

YEAR	TEAM	LGE	IP	H	ER	HR	BB	K	ERA	W	L	H/9	HR/9	BB/9	K/9	KWH	PERA
1997	Bristol	App	54.7	120	70	5	29	24	11.52	1	5	19.76	0.82	4.77	3.95	0.12	8.40
1998	Hickory	SAL	105.7	163	65	16	21	54	5.54	4	8	13.88	1.36	1.79	4.60	0.64	6.47
1998	WnstnSlm	Car	51.3	64	15	4	6	29	2.63	4	2	11.22	0.70	1.05	5.08	1.64	4.56

The number two starter behind Seth Greisinger on a pretty good '96 University of Virginia team, Daneker is beginning to look like the better pro prospect than his old teammate. Of course, he was also blowing away kids in the Sally League. A sinker/slider pitcher, he was called for an incredible ten balks last year.

Scott Eyre — Throws L — Age 27

YEAR	TEAM	LGE	IP	H	ER	HR	BB	K	ERA	W	L	H/9	HR/9	BB/9	K/9	KWH	PERA
1996	Birmnghm	Sou	145.0	223	105	14	77	98	6.52	4	12	13.84	0.87	4.78	6.08	0.42	6.33
1997	Birmnghm	Sou	115.7	142	69	14	59	88	5.37	5	8	11.05	1.09	4.59	6.85	0.69	5.21
1997	ChiSox	AL	62.3	61	29	10	27	35	4.19	3	4	8.81	1.44	3.90	5.05	0.56	4.19
1998	ChiSox	AL	110.7	114	65	23	58	71	5.29	4	8	9.27	1.87	4.72	5.77	0.57	4.88

His big-breaking curve can be especially sharp, and perhaps typically, Nardi Contreras wants to get him to learn how to set it up with a two-seam fastball. He gets good movement on his fastball and he also flashes a nice changeup. And to think they got all of this from Texas for Esteban Beltre. One of the players that management and Contreras had to convince Jerry Manuel to keep around, Eyre looks like he's always going to be wild, but he can be a very effective spot starter and long reliever.

Tom Fordham — Throws L — Age 25

YEAR	TEAM	LGE	IP	H	ER	HR	BB	K	ERA	W	L	H/9	HR/9	BB/9	K/9	KWH	PERA
1996	Birmnghm	Sou	35.7	33	14	5	12	28	3.53	2	2	8.33	1.26	3.03	7.07	1.48	3.53
1996	Nashvill	AmA	138.7	139	64	15	75	103	4.15	7	8	9.02	0.97	4.87	6.69	0.76	4.15
1997	Nashvill	AmA	117.3	121	58	13	52	78	4.45	6	7	9.28	1.00	3.99	5.98	0.73	4.14
1998	Calgary	PCL	57.3	38	17	6	26	31	2.67	4	2	5.97	0.94	4.08	4.87	0.73	2.20
1998	ChiSox	AL	49.7	53	31	7	38	22	5.62	2	4	9.60	1.27	6.89	3.99	0.18	4.89

He's frustrating, in that he can toss a nice overhand curve, but his mechanics are a mess that nobody before Nardi Contreras seemed to have noticed and/or tried to do anything about. He misses high with his change-up way too often, and his fastball is really only in the 80s.

Keith Foulke — Throws R — Age 26

YEAR	TEAM	LGE	IP	H	ER	HR	BB	K	ERA	W	L	H/9	HR/9	BB/9	K/9	KWH	PERA
1996	Shrevprt	Tex	170.7	182	70	18	38	109	3.69	10	9	9.60	0.95	2.00	5.75	1.29	3.96
1997	Phoenix	PCL	73.0	82	33	10	13	44	4.07	4	4	10.11	1.23	1.60	5.42	1.36	4.44
1997	San Fran	NL	45.3	63	38	9	17	30	7.54	1	4	12.51	1.79	3.38	5.96	0.63	6.35
1997	ChiSox	AL	29.3	27	9	4	4	20	2.76	2	1	8.28	1.23	1.23	6.14	2.78	3.37
1998	ChiSox	AL	66.7	50	25	9	18	55	3.38	4	3	6.75	1.22	2.43	7.43	2.52	2.43

Foulke was pitching in pain all season, working through a bone spur in his shoulder that first cropped up in '97. Despite surgery, the Sox expect he'll be healthy in camp for '99. Foulke simply knows how to pitch well, mixing a great curve and an adequate fastball. If there's a big question for the Sox going into camp, it's whether or not to put Foulke into the rotation. They had him relieve in '98 because of the injury, and initially they may be inclined to leave him in the pen until they're confident he's healthy. Foulke in the rotation could have a large impact on the Sox in 1998.

Jon Garland — Throws R — Age 19

YEAR	TEAM	LGE	IP	H	ER	HR	BB	K	ERA	W	L	H/9	HR/9	BB/9	K/9	KWH	PERA
1998	Rockford	Mid	98.3	174	86	16	51	47	7.87	2	9	15.93	1.46	4.67	4.30	0.19	7.78
1998	Hickory	SAL	24.7	47	23	3	16	12	8.39	1	2	17.15	1.09	5.84	4.38	0.14	8.03

The Cubs' #1 pick in the '97 draft, and the bounty for letting journeyman Matt Karchner close for five months over two seasons. For his age, Garland has impressed some folks. He's got good command of a 95 mph fastball and curve, and he has good mechanics. After seeing how much flak they were catching over the trade, Cubs scouts started trashing him anonymously, saying he was never going to develop. Garland may never make it, because of injuries as likely as not, but organizations who try to stomp out second-guessing by roasting their own ex-prospects are being cowardly.

Mike Heathcott   Throws R   Age 30

YEAR	TEAM	LGE	IP	H	ER	HR	BB	K	ERA	W	L	H/9	HR/9	BB/9	K/9	KWH	PERA
1996	Birmnghm	Sou	133.3	188	92	11	57	73	6.21	4	11	12.69	0.74	3.85	4.93	0.37	5.60
1997	Birmnghm	Sou	54.3	63	22	2	27	32	3.64	3	3	10.44	0.33	4.47	5.30	0.45	4.31
1997	Nashvill	AmA	26.7	46	24	5	14	18	8.10	1	2	15.53	1.69	4.73	6.08	0.38	7.76
1998	Calgary	PCL	108.3	122	60	11	55	58	4.98	5	7	10.14	0.91	4.57	4.82	0.38	4.65

Mike Heathcott made his major league debut, and that doesn't mean much to some people. He's a control artist who was the ace pitcher for Jim Hendry's great Creighton team from '91 (along with Scott Stahoviak at third, young Alan Benes in the rotation, and Dax Jones and Chad McConnell). That Creighton squad was probably my favorite college baseball team ever. They finished third, losing to Wichita State ace Tyler Green before Green went on to lose to LSU. Now Hendry's with the Cubs, Benes is hurt, and everyone else has basically washed out, but I'm still enough of a sentimental schmuck that I hope Heathcott can make it.

Russ Herbert   Throws R   Age 27

YEAR	TEAM	LGE	IP	H	ER	HR	BB	K	ERA	W	L	H/9	HR/9	BB/9	K/9	KWH	PERA
1996	Pr Willm	Car	128.7	187	102	15	77	95	7.13	3	11	13.08	1.05	5.39	6.65	0.47	6.23
1997	Birmnghm	Sou	144.7	176	82	14	85	87	5.10	6	10	10.95	0.87	5.29	5.41	0.38	5.10
1998	Calgary	PCL	162.3	199	92	22	81	111	5.10	7	11	11.03	1.22	4.49	6.15	0.57	5.27

Herbert almost seems lost in the shuffle after his first genuinely poor season in his career. He throws hard, mixing in a slider and change, but he works high and gives up a bunch of fly balls. In the PCL, that's trouble. He could still sneak in, but he's going to have to open some eyes in camp.

Bobby Howry   Throws R   Age 25

YEAR	TEAM	LGE	IP	H	ER	HR	BB	K	ERA	W	L	H/9	HR/9	BB/9	K/9	KWH	PERA
1996	Shrevprt	Tex	145.7	195	98	19	58	50	6.05	5	11	12.05	1.17	3.58	3.09	0.17	5.62
1997	Shrevprt	Tex	49.7	71	37	6	21	35	6.70	2	4	12.87	1.09	3.81	6.34	0.62	5.98
1998	Calgary	PCL	32.0	25	10	2	10	18	2.81	3	1	7.03	0.56	2.81	5.06	0.97	2.25
1998	ChiSox	AL	55.0	37	16	7	17	49	2.62	4	2	6.05	1.15	2.78	8.02	2.86	2.13

Sometimes winter ball tells you nothing at all: Howry got crushed in the '97 Arizona Fall League. Six months later, he was in the majors, being looked at as a closer. Not bad for a guy who'd flopped as a starter. He's got an OK fastball and an OK slider. Leave him in to see batters several times in the same game and he's going to get punished, but make him a short man and he only has to get a few hitters to guess wrong.

Jason Lakman   Throws R   Age 22

YEAR	TEAM	LGE	IP	H	ER	HR	BB	K	ERA	W	L	H/9	HR/9	BB/9	K/9	KWH	PERA
1996	Bristol	App	60.0	106	59	6	43	35	8.85	1	6	15.90	0.90	6.45	5.25	0.20	7.35
1996	Hickory	SAL	57.7	103	74	10	51	27	11.55	1	5	16.08	1.56	7.96	4.21	0.10	8.12
1997	Hickory	SAL	147.0	190	99	15	85	111	6.06	5	11	11.63	0.92	5.20	6.80	0.57	5.45
1998	WnstnSlm	Car	84.3	77	42	1	35	68	4.48	4	5	8.22	0.11	3.74	7.26	1.29	2.99
1998	Birmnghm	Sou	70.3	101	63	16	34	63	8.06	2	6	12.92	2.05	4.35	8.06	0.87	6.91

A big guy who throws a wild 96 mph fastball, and changes pace with a bunch of balls when he tries to get his breaking stuff over. Drafted out of high school in '95, the Sox have brought him along slowly, but he clearly couldn't handle Double-A the first time through. He's somebody who could move up quickly.

David Lundquist   Throws R   Age 26

YEAR	TEAM	LGE	IP	H	ER	HR	BB	K	ERA	W	L	H/9	HR/9	BB/9	K/9	KWH	PERA
1995	Sth Bend	Mid	105.7	158	73	4	43	40	6.22	4	8	13.46	0.34	3.66	3.41	0.18	5.54
1996	Pr Willm	Car	24.7	42	21	3	16	16	7.66	1	2	15.32	1.09	5.84	5.84	0.29	7.30
1997	WnstnSlm	Car	43.3	92	52	8	27	25	10.80	1	4	19.11	1.66	5.61	5.19	0.19	9.14
1998	Birmnghm	Sou	39.0	35	16	1	14	29	3.69	2	2	8.08	0.23	3.23	6.69	1.29	2.77
1998	Calgary	PCL	15.0	13	5	0	7	9	3.00	1	1	7.80	0.00	4.20	5.40	0.67	3.00

An elbow injury cost him his chance as a starter, but surgery didn't rob him of his mid-90s heat, so he was been converted to closer. Lundquist should make people forget Matt Karchner pretty quickly, except that Sox fans will be ribbing Cubs fans about Karchner for years.

Aaron Myette — Throws R — Age 21

YEAR	TEAM	LGE	IP	H	ER	HR	BB	K	ERA	W	L	H/9	HR/9	BB/9	K/9	KWH	PERA
1997	Bristol	App	43.7	54	30	9	25	25	6.18	1	4	11.13	1.85	5.15	5.15	0.35	5.98
1997	Hickory	SAL	30.3	26	7	2	13	17	2.08	2	1	7.71	0.59	3.86	5.04	0.64	2.97
1998	Hickory	SAL	96.3	111	50	5	36	64	4.67	5	6	10.37	0.47	3.36	5.98	0.77	4.20
1998	WnstnSlm	Car	43.7	40	15	5	17	37	3.09	3	2	8.24	1.03	3.50	7.63	1.51	3.50

The Sox' best pitching prospect, Myette is a tall, gangly right-hander who throws hard. His slider is called the best breaking pitch in the organization. He was nabbed with one of the compensation picks for Alex Fernandez. Don't think that Ron Schueler doesn't take a bit of satisfaction in that. He has a chance to sneak into the rotation this year.

Jaime Navarro — Throws R — Age 32

YEAR	TEAM	LGE	IP	H	ER	HR	BB	K	ERA	W	L	H/9	HR/9	BB/9	K/9	KWH	PERA
1996	ChiCubs	NL	238.7	266	110	25	68	143	4.15	13	14	10.03	0.94	2.56	5.39	0.85	4.30
1997	ChiSox	AL	217.0	259	126	20	63	138	5.23	9	15	10.74	0.83	2.61	5.72	0.88	4.56
1998	ChiSox	AL	178.7	222	112	28	69	69	5.64	7	13	11.18	1.41	3.48	3.48	0.23	5.39

He tried Sutcliffe-style wrist snaps in his delivery. It didn't work. He tried a big lead-arm windmill action. It didn't work. He tried to be less bouncy in his delivery. It didn't work. Now he's claiming he just needs to get back to bringing his hands over his head in his windup, "just like he did with the Cubs." At this point, he may as well be counting on the power of prayer, Scientology, or faith in the giant badger gods of the Yu-kuki tribe for all the good any of it has done. He's been consistently awful despite having a great ballpark, an improved defense, and an offense that can hand him a lead. If you can't say Navarro is bad, the word "bad" has no meaning.

Jason Olsen — Throws R — Age 24

YEAR	TEAM	LGE	IP	H	ER	HR	BB	K	ERA	W	L	H/9	HR/9	BB/9	K/9	KWH	PERA
1996	Sth Bend	Mid	52.3	56	21	5	14	36	3.61	3	3	9.63	0.86	2.41	6.19	1.24	3.96
1996	Pr Willm	Car	75.3	93	45	7	33	41	5.38	3	5	11.11	0.84	3.94	4.90	0.41	4.90
1997	Birmnghm	Sou	152.7	207	96	14	54	95	5.66	6	11	12.20	0.83	3.18	5.60	0.61	5.36
1998	Birmnghm	Sou	153.0	213	89	21	45	104	5.24	6	11	12.53	1.24	2.65	6.12	0.85	5.82

Another of several converted position players who are bouncing around these days. Like many of them, he has good velocity. He's extremely wild with the breaking stuff he tries to run past left-handers. Olsen may break through as a reliever, but the Sox are willing to see if he can come around as a starter.

Jim Parque — Throws L — Age 23

YEAR	TEAM	LGE	IP	H	ER	HR	BB	K	ERA	W	L	H/9	HR/9	BB/9	K/9	KWH	PERA
1997	WnstnSlm	Car	60.7	38	20	4	22	53	2.97	5	2	5.64	0.59	3.26	7.86	2.52	1.63
1998	Calgary	PCL	49.7	48	21	7	24	26	3.81	3	3	8.70	1.27	4.35	4.71	0.44	3.99
1998	ChiSox	AL	116.7	134	60	13	44	75	4.63	6	7	10.34	1.00	3.39	5.79	0.72	4.63

They claim he's 5'11", and I suppose if he stood on a phone book or two he would be. Parque spent '98 figuring out which of his four pitches (good fastball, plus change, curve, slider) work in which order and situation. He's also messing around with a cut fastball, and he's pretty good at changing speeds. I'm betting he's going to improve significantly in '99.

Jesus Pena — Throws L — Age 24

YEAR	TEAM	LGE	IP	H	ER	HR	BB	K	ERA	W	L	H/9	HR/9	BB/9	K/9	KWH	PERA
1996	Erie	NYP	33.3	49	31	5	30	20	8.37	1	3	13.23	1.35	8.10	5.40	0.20	6.75
1997	Hickory	SAL	59.7	80	32	4	25	35	4.83	3	4	12.07	0.60	3.77	5.28	0.46	5.13
1998	WnstnSlm	Car	30.3	27	14	3	15	24	4.15	1	2	8.01	0.89	4.45	7.12	1.07	3.56
1998	Birmnghm	Sou	22.3	24	12	4	8	22	4.84	1	1	9.67	1.61	3.22	8.87	1.89	4.84

An escapee from the Pirates, and now a dark horse candidate to become a left-handed reliever in the major league pen. There's some competition for the job.

Todd Rizzo		Throws L				Age 28										
YEAR	TEAM	LGE	IP	H	ER	HR	BB	K	ERA	W	L	H/9	HR/9	BB/9	K/9	KWH	PERA
1996	Birmnghm	Sou	62.3	84	35	1	41	33	5.05	3	4	12.13	0.14	5.92	4.76	0.24	5.05
1997	Nashvill	AmA	69.7	75	41	5	36	47	5.30	3	5	9.69	0.65	4.65	6.07	0.61	4.26
1998	Calgary	PCL	72.0	110	57	5	43	44	7.12	2	6	13.75	0.62	5.38	5.50	0.31	6.12

Surprised some by making the team, but Rizzo throws pretty hard and he's left-handed. An ugly debut against the Rangers earned a demotion, and he never really got on track after that. A minor league free agent after the season, so he could end up anywhere.

Mark Roberts		Throws R				Age 23										
YEAR	TEAM	LGE	IP	H	ER	HR	BB	K	ERA	W	L	H/9	HR/9	BB/9	K/9	KWH	PERA
1996	Hickory	SAL	65.7	105	56	16	22	38	7.68	1	6	14.39	2.19	3.02	5.21	0.47	7.68
1997	Hickory	SAL	20.7	31	14	4	12	9	6.10	1	1	13.50	1.74	5.23	3.92	0.16	6.97
1997	WnstnSlm	Car	88.7	101	51	11	44	46	5.18	4	6	10.25	1.12	4.47	4.67	0.36	4.77
1998	WnstnSlm	Car	159.3	212	103	20	61	97	5.82	6	12	11.97	1.13	3.45	5.48	0.55	5.54

The pitching ace of the University of South Florida team that finished up 16th in the country in '96, Roberts was a teammate of Jason Dellaero and the Marlins' Ross Gload. Making the jump up to Birmingham doesn't look like it will be easy for him, so I'll hold off on calling him a prospect.

Bill Simas		Throws R				Age 27										
YEAR	TEAM	LGE	IP	H	ER	HR	BB	K	ERA	W	L	H/9	HR/9	BB/9	K/9	KWH	PERA
1996	ChiSox	AL	72.7	75	32	4	32	64	3.96	4	4	9.29	0.50	3.96	7.93	1.28	3.84
1997	ChiSox	AL	43.0	45	18	6	21	37	3.77	3	2	9.42	1.26	4.40	7.74	1.09	4.40
1998	ChiSox	AL	72.0	53	23	11	20	54	2.88	5	3	6.63	1.38	2.50	6.75	2.06	2.50

Simas belonged on the Opening Day roster, but he was sent down so that people like Rizzo, Fordham and both Castillos could stick around. Simas wasn't afraid to say Manuel had made a mistake, and Manuel, to his credit, didn't hold it against him. What's not to like? He's unhittable when he's on, but he occasionally gets too focused on racking up strikeouts.

Mike Sirotka		Throws L				Age 28										
YEAR	TEAM	LGE	IP	H	ER	HR	BB	K	ERA	W	L	H/9	HR/9	BB/9	K/9	KWH	PERA
1996	Nashvill	AmA	86.0	113	52	10	28	47	5.44	4	6	11.83	1.05	2.93	4.92	0.52	5.34
1996	ChiSox	AL	26.3	34	22	3	9	11	7.52	1	2	11.62	1.03	3.08	3.76	0.30	5.13
1997	Nashvill	AmA	110.7	134	51	12	23	72	4.15	6	6	10.90	0.98	1.87	5.86	1.26	4.64
1997	ChiSox	AL	32.7	35	7	4	4	23	1.93	3	1	9.64	1.10	1.10	6.34	2.83	3.86
1998	ChiSox	AL	217.0	251	113	28	42	125	4.69	10	14	10.41	1.16	1.74	5.18	1.11	4.52

My idea of a replacement-level pitcher, but like Jerry Manuel, I like him for his bulldog approach on the mound. He changes speeds, uses everything he's got, and he's straightforward in talking about how everyone on the Sox needs to be pitching for their jobs. One of the Sox' acknowledged creatine users. I made the comparison to Jamie Moyer last year, and it still applies in that he could be better in his thirties than he is now.

John Snyder		Throws R				Age 24										
YEAR	TEAM	LGE	IP	H	ER	HR	BB	K	ERA	W	L	H/9	HR/9	BB/9	K/9	KWH	PERA
1996	Birmnghm	Sou	51.0	72	37	11	14	45	6.53	2	4	12.71	1.94	2.47	7.94	1.51	6.53
1997	Birmnghm	Sou	109.0	147	72	9	40	70	5.94	4	8	12.14	0.74	3.30	5.78	0.62	5.28
1998	Calgary	PCL	99.7	110	39	10	34	53	3.52	6	5	9.93	0.90	3.07	4.79	0.56	4.24
1998	ChiSox	AL	88.7	94	40	13	21	51	4.06	5	5	9.54	1.32	2.13	5.18	0.99	4.26

Snyder's entire repertoire revolves around his heavy sinker, which he can work inside and out at will. He complements it with a curve, change-up, and fastball, but they're basically trotted out for show. The sinker's a good pitch, good enough to have some front office types making comparisons to Jack McDowell, except that despite his past injuries he's still throwing across his body. Manuel credited him with "knowing how to set hitters up." After a disastrous debut in relief, he put up a 4.25 ERA as a starter.

Ken Vining   Throws L   Age 24

YEAR	TEAM	LGE	IP	H	ER	HR	BB	K	ERA	W	L	H/9	HR/9	BB/9	K/9	KWH	PERA
1996	Bellnghm	Nwn	52.7	75	26	5	27	37	4.44	3	3	12.82	0.85	4.61	6.32	0.51	5.81
1997	San Jose	Cal	129.7	167	78	10	60	95	5.41	5	9	11.59	0.69	4.16	6.59	0.68	5.07
1997	WnstnSlm	Car	33.7	45	19	3	11	26	5.08	2	2	12.03	0.80	2.94	6.95	1.02	5.35
1998	Birmnghm	Sou	166.7	217	97	9	78	103	5.24	7	12	11.72	0.49	4.21	5.56	0.47	4.97

The third starter at Clemson behind Kris Benson and Billy Koch in '96. He can reach 90 with the fastball, so he's not just another soft-tossing left-hander. He's another part of the bounty for the "white flag" trade that has given the Sox such a good-looking farm system and a chance to beat Cleveland in the future.

Bryan Ward   Throws L   Age 27

YEAR	TEAM	LGE	IP	H	ER	HR	BB	K	ERA	W	L	H/9	HR/9	BB/9	K/9	KWH	PERA
1996	Portland	Eas	141.3	213	106	23	34	92	6.75	4	12	13.56	1.46	2.17	5.86	0.88	6.43
1997	Portland	Eas	71.3	92	42	15	20	48	5.30	3	5	11.61	1.89	2.52	6.06	0.94	5.93
1997	Charlott	Int	74.7	117	60	17	29	37	7.23	2	6	14.10	2.05	3.50	4.46	0.30	7.35
1998	Birmnghm	Sou	39.7	42	21	0	24	28	4.76	2	2	9.53	0.00	5.45	6.35	0.58	3.86
1998	ChiSox	AL	27.7	30	11	4	6	17	3.58	2	1	9.76	1.30	1.95	5.53	1.20	4.23

Claimed on waivers, Ward was not only an outstanding "free talent" pickup in terms of what he can do, but deserves special mention as winner of the major league's coveted "Most Ridiculous Facial Hair" award. When you get the Elvis sideburns going, and then grow a goatee without letting the two groups grow together by neatly trimming the space between them (avoiding the Abe Lincoln look), you end up with a getup no self-respecting extra on Xena: Warrior Princess would sport. Best suited for long relief, he'll be battling Scott Eyre and Tom Fordham for a spot.

SNWL						CHICAGO WHITE SOX					Park Effect: +1.2%	
PITCHER	GS	IP	R	SNW	SNL	SNPCT	W	L	RA	APW	SNVA	SNWAR
Abbott, J.	5	31.7	16	1.8	1.5	.555	5	0	4.55	0.14	0.15	0.43
Baldwin, J.	24	137.3	77	8.0	8.2	.495	13	6	5.05	-0.11	-0.07	1.13
Bere, J.	15	76.7	60	3.2	6.6	.327	3	7	7.04	-1.68	-1.63	-0.96
Castillo, C.	2	9.7	7	0.4	0.9	.318	1	1	6.52	-0.16	-0.19	-0.14
Eyre, S.	17	87.0	65	3.7	7.7	.326	2	7	6.72	-1.62	-1.86	-1.12
Fordham, T.	5	17.3	12	0.8	1.7	.319	0	2	6.23	-0.23	-0.35	-0.27
Navarro, J.	27	153.7	118	7.0	13.0	.349	8	15	6.91	-3.16	-2.85	-1.51
Parque, J.	21	113.0	72	5.6	8.2	.405	7	5	5.73	-0.92	-1.25	-0.27
Sirotka, M.	33	211.7	137	10.8	14.4	.429	14	15	5.83	-1.92	-1.82	0.09
Snyder, J.	14	84.7	43	5.6	4.4	.562	7	2	4.57	0.36	0.47	1.36
TOTALS	163	922.7	607	47.0	66.5	.414	60	60	5.92	-9.29	-9.40	-1.25

You'd think that a team that loses Doug Drabek would improve, but not the White Sox, who actually lost ground compared to their awful Drabek-led 1997 band. One bright note is that James Baldwin bounced back from his disappointing sophomore season to have an inning-eating league-average season. Another encouraging sign is that he got much better as the season went on. In his first 12 starts he was 3.2-4.8 (.404); in his last 12 he was 4.8-3.4 (.584). Jim Parque also improved, going 2.6-4.7 (.360) in his first 11 starts, and 3.0-3.5 (.457) in his last 10. I don't think these splits constitute strong evidence of anything, but improvement over the course of a season is somewhat more encouraging than the alternative. Jaime Navarro sticks out like a sore thumb: his two-year stay with the White Sox has resulted in an SN record of 16.5-29.7 (.357). As far as I can tell, that's the worst two-year stretch of the last seven years (by SNWAR). Lots of guys have really awful single years, but their teams usually have the common sense to not give them 27 starts the following year.

Pitcher Abuse Points

PITCHER	AGE	GS	PAP	PAP/S	AAW	MAX	115+	130+
Abbott, Jim	30	5	0	0.00	0.00	96	0	0
Baldwin, James	26	24	162	6.75	13.50	119	4	0
Bere, Jason	27	15	91	6.07	11.12	125	2	0
Eyre, Scott	26	17	60	3.53	7.06	120	1	0
Fordham, Tom	24	5	0	0.00	0.00	90	0	0
Navarro, Jaime	30	27	148	5.48	7.31	118	2	0
Parque, Jim	23	21	37	1.76	4.40	112	0	0
Sirotka, Mike	27	33	382	11.58	21.22	128	10	0
Snyder, John	23	14	55	3.93	9.82	117	1	0
TOTAL		163	935	5.77	10.67	128	20	0
RANKING (AL)			14	14	14		12-T	14

Jerry Manuel didn't do any better in the standings than his predecessor, Terry Bevington, but he did a much better job of running a pitching staff. Bevington would either run a pitcher into a ground or let him waste away from lack of work. Manuel protected his starters better than anyone in the league. The White Sox rotation was a melange of old rookies and young veterans; none of them pitched particularly well, though Mike Sirotka showed sparks of talent and Jim Parque is a good prospect. The White Sox need somebody like Fordham or Eyre to step it up by cutting their walks in half, and they need Baldwin to pitch like he did as a rookie. That's a tall order, but if they don't accomplish it, at least it won't be from exhaustion.

Cleveland Indians

What do you do with a pygmy dynasty? Once the strike killed off any chance of a great confrontation between the Tribe and the White Sox down the stretch in '94, the Indians have enjoyed a four-year run relatively free of challenges, and essentially free to keep an eye on what they can do to beat the Braves. Comfortably armed with sharpened hindsight, we could lay into John Hart about how the Indians have not actually capitalized on their opportunities. We could complain about some of his decisions: long-term contracts for David Justice, Omar Vizquel, Travis Fryman, and Marquis Grissom that seem like very bad risks. We could note that the Indians only managed to win 89 games, scant improvement over the previous season's 86 wins. Considering that the Indians had a much more stable rotation in '98, this was disappointing.

That's an awful lot of knee-biting for a team that's enjoyed a pretty good run. Are we closet Tribe fans, aching for that first big win? My old man's bitter disappointments aside (an Ohioan, he seems to have given up on baseball after the heartbreak of '54), the Indians deserve credit for slowly building a great organization and taking it for a ride. In part because of their weak divisional rivals, the Indians can brag about their successes while teams like the Angels, Mariners, or Red Sox, also armed with a few great core offensive players, have little of their own to show for the careers of Tim Salmon, Ken Griffey, or Mo Vaughn.

More importantly, Hart's Indians deserve credit for not being afraid to make changes. Bringing a team through the tail end of a successful run and bridging a potential gap to your next successful run is one of the most difficult transitions in professional sports. Some of the big American League winners from earlier in this decade, particularly the A's and the Blue Jays, did a bad job of it, and the White Sox went out with a whimper. The Yankees appear determined to keep their roster intact deep into the 2000s.

Baseball history isn't well-stocked with great teams that outlasted their core players. Perhaps the only genuine exception was the Yankee dynasty that stretched from Ruth and Gehrig to DiMaggio to Mantle. In the era of divisional play, all of the teams with any sustained success (Weaver's Orioles, Finley's A's, the Big Red Machine, the 70s Pirates, the Martin/Lemon Yankees) finally got old and fell apart. By contrast, the successful peers that Hart's Indians will be compared to, the Braves, have already retooled around the Joneses. With those comparisons to draw on, the Indians have reason to worry. Unlike Weaver's Orioles or Cox's Braves, and like the other teams on the list, the Indians are greatly dependent on their offensive core of Manny Ramirez and Jim Thome. Once they go, so goes the Tribe.

I suppose it depends on whether you call it positive or negative reinforcement, but the experience of consistently falling short of victory hasn't left Hart afraid to change around his rosters every year (see table 1).

Not many teams have shared Hart's willingness to make dramatic changes to a winning roster, but now more than ever, Hart is leaving well enough alone. Whereas previous Indians squads would see a routine shakeup of the teams' veteran cadre, the Indians will go into '99 with only two changes to their lineup, and with the same rotation that started '98.

In some respects, that's good. On the pitching side of the ledger, the rotation isn't as dependent on a distinguished gentleman like Black Jack or El Presidente, at least until Dave Burba earns some sort of intimidating nickname. There are reasons to be concerned: Bartolo Colon and Jaret Wright have never had to bounce back from pitching as much as they did last season, and Burba's workload was the heaviest of his career as well. Dwight Gooden probably won't pitch as well as he did last year, and although Charles Nagy seemed to stop giving up three home runs per start in the second half, he still pitched badly. The Indians could easily see their solid rotation of '98 become a season-long problem in '99. While the Chad Ogea trade cost the Indians their favorite rotation temp, it looks like Jason Rakers will handle that job well if asked. Behind him, Willie Martinez may not be too far off.

Perhaps in anticipation of some problems in the rotation, Hart has made some very cagey moves to reinforce his

---

Indians Prospectus

1998 record: 89-73; First place, AL Cental; Lost to New York Yankees in ALCS, 4-2

Pythagorean W/L: 88-74

Runs scored: 850 (6th in AL)

Runs allowed: 779 (5th in AL)

Team EQA: .264 (8th in AL)

Park: Jacobs Field (moderate hitters')

1998: Another division title thanks to the lack of competition; the team is passing its peak.

1999: Might hold off the Twins for another title. Might.

bullpen. By bringing in Jerry Spradlin and Ricardo Rincon to support Mike Jackson, Steve Reed, Paul Assenmacher, and Paul Shuey, the Indians probably have built the best bullpen in the majors. The potential to ease the burden on the rotation early and often is there. This is a better group of relievers than previous successful Tribe pens, which relied on castoffs like Mesa, Eric Plunk, and Jim Poole. Jackson and Reed are two of the best—and most unsung—right-handed relievers in baseball, and Rincon belongs on the short list of best left-handed relievers in the game. Your '99 Indians don't have Alvin Morman to kick around anymore.

What about the changes that have been made in the lineup? Bringing in Roberto Alomar may be a nice public relations story. Certainly it isn't the same as bringing in Bip Roberts or Jose Vizcaino. But it's also ill-timed. Alomar is not the same offensive player at 31 that he was when he was the core of the '92-93 champion Blue Jays. He's drawn 60 walks in a season only once in the past five years. He hasn't stolen 20 bases since '95, when even Newt Gingrich thought all sorts of things were attainable. Is a renaissance possible? Sure, anything's possible. But with the information at hand, Alomar's looking like a player the Indians didn't need. It's disappointing that he's blocking Enrique Wilson. As for trading Brian Giles away, I'm not as disappointed as some of my colleagues. Giles is a good offensive player, but not significantly better than Richie Sexson.

What's particularly interesting about the '99 Indians is that Hart seems to be consciously trying to put together a lineup of middle-aged veterans. The lineup's average age will be 30, with Richie Sexson being the only young player, and with core offensive performers Ramirez and Thome at 27 and 28. This isn't an old team, but if Hart stops tinkering and that's the lineup of your 2001 Indians, don't be surprised when they finish third. If the White Sox had kept Albert Belle, they would have put up a good fight, and the Royals and Twins seem to have finally figured out that rebuilding is something you don't do with Hal Morris or Otis Nixon. The American League Central is going to be tougher to win in the years to come that it has been for the last four.

Going into '99, the Indians have an improved bullpen and what passes for a reliable rotation in the non-Braves portion of the universe. Their lineup that should be able to put runs on the board. But it isn't a young team, and the farm system holds little in the way of quality players who could break through. The Indians' good prospects, like Russ Branyan or Willie Martinez, have major questions about their health. They have other players they can use as trade bait, like Enrique Wilson or Marcus Scutaro, because they're permanently blocked by Roberto Alomar and Omar Vizquel. But overall, the Indians will have to make their stand with the group they have. Like other teams that have had their runs, the Indians are only going to last as long as their stars, Ramirez and Thome, do. Their window of opportunity, when they can take their division title almost for granted, is fading fast. For the Indians, 1999 is the make-or-break year. If they don't do it this year, Manny Ramirez and Jim Thome will take their places alongside Al Rosen and Larry Doby in Indians history as great players on great teams that never won anything.

Table 1. Cleveland Indian Roster 1995–99

Lineup	1995	1996	1997	1998	1999
C	S. Alomar	S. Alomar	S. Alomar	S. Alomar	S. Alomar
1B	Sorrento/Perry	J. Franco	Thome	Thome	Thome
2B	Baerga	Baerga/Vizcaino	Fernandez	Da. Bell/Cora	R. Alomar
3B	Thome	Thome	Ma. Williams	Fryman	Fryman
SS	Vizquel	Vizquel	Vizquel	Vizquel	Vizquel
CF	Lofton	Lofton	Grissom	Lofton	Lofton
RF	M. Ramirez	M. Ramirez	M. Ramirez	M. Ramirez	M. Ramirez
LF	Belle	Belle	Giles	Giles	Sexson/A. Ramirez
DH	E. Murray	Murray/Seitzer	Justice	Justice	Justice
Pitching					
SP	Nagy	Nagy	Nagy	Nagy	Nagy
SP	Hershiser	Hershiser	Hershiser	Gooden	Gooden
SP	D. Martinez	McDowell	Ogea	Burba	Burba
SP	M. Clark	Ogea	J. Wright	Colon	Colon
SP	Ogea/K. Hill	D. Martinez	Colon	J. Wright	J. Wright
Closer	Mesa	Mesa	Mesa	Jackson	Jackson

HITTERS (Averages: BA .260/ OBP .330/ SLG .420, EqA .260)

Sandy Alomar   C   Bats R   Age 33

YEAR	TEAM	LGE	AB	H	DB	TP	HR	BB	R	RBI	SB	CS	OUT	BA	OBA	SA	EQA	EQR	DEFENSE
1996	Clevelnd	AL	410	102	16	0	12	17	31	41	1	0	308	.249	.279	.376	.222	36	
1997	Clevelnd	AL	446	146	29	0	25	21	58	83	0	2	302	.327	.358	.561	.303	76	
1998	Clevelnd	AL	401	88	22	2	6	20	26	28	0	3	316	.219	.257	.329	.193	26	106-C 101
1999	*Clevelnd*	*AL*	*414*	*102*	*23*	*1*	*15*	*21*	*38*	*48*	*0*	*1*	*313*	*.246*	*.283*	*.415*	*.235*	*42*	

Call me unsympathetic, but I wasn't overly impressed with Alomar's midseason blast against the fans who have voted him into the All-Star game in the past. He rates an honorable mention as one of the most overrated players of the decade. Played hurt most of the season, so the Indians would be better off carrying a better caddy than either Borders or Einar Diaz if he looks like this in '99.

Bruce Aven   OF   Bats R   Age 27

YEAR	TEAM	LGE	AB	H	DB	TP	HR	BB	R	RBI	SB	CS	OUT	BA	OBA	SA	EQA	EQR	DEFENSE
1996	Canton	Eas	479	126	19	2	16	34	55	55	16	4	357	.263	.312	.411	.252	57	128-OF 102
1997	Buffalo	AA	437	119	22	2	13	45	56	55	9	3	321	.272	.340	.421	.266	58	104-OF 95
1998	Buffalo	Int	15	3	0	0	1	5	4	2	2	0	12	.200	.400	.400	.308	3	
1999	*Florida*	*NL*	*206*	*55*	*12*	*1*	*7*	*19*	*27*	*26*	*6*	*2*	*153*	*.267*	*.329*	*.437*	*.272*	*29*	

Missed most of '98 with a fractured elbow. A right-handed hitter armed with moderate power, Aven also has good range in left field. After the season, Aven was waived and picked up by the Marlins, whose three starting outfielders all bat left-handed. For that reason, he's a good bet to be on their roster as a spare part.

Todd Betts   3B   Bats L   Age 26

YEAR	TEAM	LGE	AB	H	DB	TP	HR	BB	R	RBI	SB	CS	OUT	BA	OBA	SA	EQA	EQR	DEFENSE
1996	Canton	Eas	239	53	7	0	2	32	21	17	0	1	187	.222	.314	.276	.209	19	63-3B 77
1997	Akron	Eas	440	91	13	1	13	57	39	40	1	2	351	.207	.298	.330	.219	39	94-3B 94
1998	Akron	Eas	319	73	9	2	11	51	37	38	1	0	246	.229	.335	.373	.251	39	57-3B 88
1999	*Clevelnd*	*AL*	*354*	*79*	*11*	*1*	*13*	*48*	*38*	*41*	*1*	*1*	*276*	*.223*	*.316*	*.370*	*.240*	*39*	

Barely adequate afield and old for his league, Betts could catch on as a spare part because he bats left-handed. Branyan's injury was the only thing that allowed him to get serious playing time in '98, and the Indians don't see him as much more than an organizational soldier.

Pat Borders   C   Bats R   Age 36

YEAR	TEAM	LGE	AB	H	DB	TP	HR	BB	R	RBI	SB	CS	OUT	BA	OBA	SA	EQA	EQR	DEFENSE
1996	Calfrnia	AL	56	12	2	0	2	3	3	5	0	1	45	.214	.254	.357	.199	4	
1996	ChiSox	AL	93	26	0	0	3	5	7	11	0	0	67	.280	.316	.376	.240	9	
1996	St Louis	NL	69	22	3	0	0	1	6	7	0	1	48	.319	.329	.362	.234	6	
1997	Clevelnd	AL	157	47	7	1	4	10	17	21	0	2	112	.299	.341	.433	.263	20	
1998	Clevelnd	AL	157	35	5	0	0	10	9	7	0	2	124	.223	.269	.255	.169	7	43-C 96
1999	*Clevelnd*	*AL*	*150*	*35*	*3*	*0*	*3*	*9*	*9*	*12*	*0*	*1*	*116*	*.233*	*.277*	*.313*	*.197*	*10*	

Probably finished, but... some things are hard to kill. Once upon a time, I'm fishing with a buddy, and I reel in this catfish. I haul him onto the muddy bank, and it's clearly an old, stubborn, good-sized, angry fish. My buddy grabs him to unhook him and toss him into the bucket, and the fish or the hook draws blood. My friend, with a wisdom only country folk appreciate, whips out a pistol and shoots the fish. That just made it really mad, and they both freak out. At the end of the fracas, there wasn't much left of the fish, and I knew who not to fish with in the future. But I'm reminded that catfish have whiskers, sort of like Pat Borders, and although I might want to pronounce him finished, sometimes these things need helping along.

Russ Branyan — 3B — Bats L — Age 23

YEAR	TEAM	LGE	AB	H	DB	TP	HR	BB	R	RBI	SB	CS	OUT	BA	OBA	SA	EQA	EQR	DEFENSE
1996	Columbus	SAL	496	125	11	1	28	47	53	71	3	2	373	.252	.317	.448	.260	64	116-3B 91
1997	Kinston	Car	304	89	16	1	23	43	48	63	2	1	216	.293	.380	.579	.317	61	69-3B 81
1997	Akron	Eas	137	30	3	0	9	24	17	21	0	0	107	.219	.335	.438	.267	20	39-3B 114
1998	Akron	Eas	162	46	7	2	14	31	29	37	1	1	117	.284	.399	.611	.329	36	
1999	Clevelnd	AL	300	84	11	1	22	43	46	61	2	1	217	.280	.370	.543	.306	56	

A slow-healing but "not serious" bout of tendinitis in his wrist kept Branyan shelved most of the year, and prematurely ended his '98 Arizona Fall League stint as well. Even when he's healthy, some folks pile on the negatives: he'll swing through fastballs, and he's absent-minded or flaky to the point that he drives some minor league martinets ape. But he's also one of the game's top power prospects and an improving defensive player, the kind of guy who can blossom into a tremendous player. That's if he's healthy, which at this point is becoming a bigger and bigger "if."

Jolbert Cabrera — SS — Bats R — Age 26

YEAR	TEAM	LGE	AB	H	DB	TP	HR	BB	R	RBI	SB	CS	OUT	BA	OBA	SA	EQA	EQR	DEFENSE
1996	Harrisbg	Eas	353	75	14	0	3	19	21	18	7	3	281	.212	.253	.278	.177	19	102-SS 94
1997	Harrisbg	Eas	170	33	2	0	2	22	12	9	3	3	140	.194	.286	.241	.183	10	25-2B 90
1997	Ottawa	Int	190	50	9	3	0	9	21	14	12	4	144	.263	.296	.342	.228	18	42-3B 113
1998	Buffalo	Int	489	134	15	0	8	56	61	49	16	11	366	.274	.349	.354	.250	57	121-SS 89
1999	Clevelnd	AL	433	110	15	1	6	39	48	38	14	8	331	.254	.316	.335	.229	42	

Cabrera was an International League All-Star in '98, and is Montreal infielder Orlando Cabrera's older brother. A patient hitter who can handle any infield position, Cabrera could be an excellent utility infielder in the majors. He'll fight Enrique Wilson for the job.

Joey Cora — 2B — Bats B — Age 34

YEAR	TEAM	LGE	AB	H	DB	TP	HR	BB	R	RBI	SB	CS	OUT	BA	OBA	SA	EQA	EQR	DEFENSE
1995	Seattle	AL	420	125	20	2	3	35	57	42	18	8	303	.298	.352	.376	.259	52	107-2B 90
1996	Seattle	AL	520	147	35	6	6	33	58	58	5	6	379	.283	.325	.408	.251	60	124-2B 93
1997	Seattle	AL	564	168	41	4	11	54	77	75	6	7	403	.298	.359	.443	.275	80	130-2B 88
1998	Seattle	AL	511	143	23	6	6	63	71	57	12	5	373	.280	.359	.384	.264	67	125-2B 83
1998	Cleveland	AL	81	17	4	0	0	11	8	4	2	1	65	.210	.304	.259	.203	6	18-2B 87
1999	Clevelnd	AL	576	153	28	4	8	64	72	62	7	5	428	.266	.339	.370	.249	66	

How to threaten and cajole your way onto a postseason-bound roster: Joey blathered about retiring, jerking a tear or two somewhere. I don't understand how anyone takes him seriously, what with his ten-minute long orations on how he's a leader because leaders don't talk about leadership. Joey Cora is baseball's Adam Sandler: expensive for what he does, and not very good at it in the first place.

Edgar Cruz — C — Bats R — Age 20

YEAR	TEAM	LGE	AB	H	DB	TP	HR	BB	R	RBI	SB	CS	OUT	BA	OBA	SA	EQA	EQR	DEFENSE
1997	BlngtnNC	App	171	21	2	0	2	9	4	4	0	0	150	.123	.167	.170	—	-2	
1998	Columbus	SAL	395	82	11	0	12	29	25	31	0	0	313	.208	.262	.327	.199	28	97-C 89
1999	Clevelnd	AL	330	72	9	0	10	19	21	28	0	0	258	.218	.261	.336	.199	23	

An extremely young and extremely raw catcher, he's considered the best choice within the organization to be Sandy Alomar's heir. He has some folks in the front office raving about his offensive and defensive improvements.

Jacob Cruz — RF — Bats L — Age 26

YEAR	TEAM	LGE	AB	H	DB	TP	HR	BB	R	RBI	SB	CS	OUT	BA	OBA	SA	EQA	EQR	DEFENSE
1996	Phoenix	PCL	423	104	18	2	7	56	49	41	5	6	325	.246	.334	.348	.240	46	113-OF 100
1996	San Fran	NL	77	18	2	0	3	12	9	9	0	1	60	.234	.337	.377	.248	9	16-OF 110
1997	Phoenix	PCL	464	138	26	1	10	52	70	59	14	3	329	.297	.368	.422	.280	68	111-OF 99
1998	Fresno	PCL	333	83	9	2	12	39	40	40	9	4	254	.249	.328	.396	.254	41	81-OF 92
1998	Buffalo	Int	167	50	6	0	10	10	20	28	1	2	119	.299	.339	.515	.283	25	41-OF 86
1999	Clevelnd	AL	490	131	23	2	16	51	64	64	10	4	363	.267	.336	.420	.263	65	

Just waiting his turn until somebody notices he's as good as Luis Gonzalez. Like Gonzo, he can play the field, has a nice left-handed stroke, isn't afraid to draw a walk and doesn't have as much power as you'd like from a corner outfielder. Better than Gonzalez because he can hit left-handers. Must have given Dusty a hot foot on the bench; there's no good reason why he isn't playing for the Giants.

Einar Diaz — C — Bats R — Age 26

YEAR	TEAM	LGE	AB	H	DB	TP	HR	BB	R	RBI	SB	CS	OUT	BA	OBA	SA	EQA	EQR	DEFENSE
1996	Canton	Eas	392	99	20	0	3	9	26	28	2	1	294	.253	.269	.327	.200	26	
1997	Buffalo	AA	338	84	15	1	3	17	24	26	2	5	259	.249	.285	.325	.205	25	
1998	Buffalo	Int	409	111	14	2	6	17	34	39	2	2	300	.271	.300	.359	.226	37	111-C 100
1998	Clevelnd	AL	47	10	1	0	2	3	4	4	0	0	37	.213	.260	.362	.210	4	
1999	*Clevelnd*	*AL*	*401*	*103*	*17*	*1*	*6*	*16*	*31*	*36*	*2*	*2*	*300*	*.257*	*.285*	*.349*	*.215*	*32*	

A good throwing arm is his major defensive asset, but Diaz is hardly going to be the player who can replace Sandy if the Indians want either to: A) contend, or B) prevent dangerous Andy Allanson flashbacks. He's good enough to hold down the Tony Pena roster spot for a couple of years.

Cecil Fielder — DH/1B — Bats R — Age 35

YEAR	TEAM	LGE	AB	H	DB	TP	HR	BB	R	RBI	SB	CS	OUT	BA	OBA	SA	EQA	EQR	DEFENSE
1996	Detroit	AL	382	92	11	0	25	60	50	61	2	0	290	.241	.344	.466	.278	59	70-1B 104
1996	NY Yanks	AL	195	48	6	0	13	23	23	31	0	0	147	.246	.326	.477	.272	28	
1997	NY Yanks	AL	358	95	12	0	15	52	46	52	0	0	263	.265	.359	.425	.274	52	
1998	Anaheim	AL	377	92	16	1	17	53	46	52	0	1	286	.244	.337	.427	.264	51	70-1B 100
1999	*Clevelnd*	*AL*	*401*	*92*	*11*	*0*	*21*	*61*	*48*	*57*	*0*	*0*	*309*	*.229*	*.331*	*.414*	*.259*	*53*	

Time for a trip back to Japan for Cecil-san, don't you think? His production with the Angels was predictably disappointing, and his joining the Indians in mid-August a waste of time. Should be done, barring something silly involving a team that doesn't know what its doing, like the Devil Rays. Since they were busy signing Jose Canseco, Fielder is trying to get the Tigers interested.

Travis Fryman — 3B — Bats R — Age 30

YEAR	TEAM	LGE	AB	H	DB	TP	HR	BB	R	RBI	SB	CS	OUT	BA	OBA	SA	EQA	EQR	DEFENSE	
1996	Detroit	AL	604	157	31	3	21	53	67	76	4	4	451	.260	.320	.425	.255	74	128-3B 121	26-SS 100
1997	Detroit	AL	585	158	27	3	22	48	73	76	16	3	430	.270	.325	.439	.265	78	152-3B 108	
1998	Clevelnd	AL	543	148	28	2	27	46	66	81	9	8	403	.273	.329	.481	.272	78	145-3B 95	
1999	*Clevelnd*	*AL*	*577*	*156*	*33*	*2*	*26*	*52*	*75*	*87*	*8*	*4*	*425*	*.270*	*.331*	*.470*	*.272*	*82*		

Fryman had a great season because of an almost unnoticed second half. He expressed a willingness to play second base if the Indians had acquired a good third baseman, but the signing of Robby Alomar takes him off the hook for that promise. Fryman is an interesting test case for two different theories about player development: do young players who have old players' skills fade out sooner than you'd expect, and/or do young players with old players' skills end up lasting longer when they come up as young as Fryman did (at 21)? I won't be surprised if Fryman pulls a Gaetti on us and has a few more useful seasons left in him.

Brian Giles — OF — Bats L — Age 28

YEAR	TEAM	LGE	AB	H	DB	TP	HR	BB	R	RBI	SB	CS	OUT	BA	OBA	SA	EQA	EQR	DEFENSE
1996	Buffalo	AA	322	96	13	4	15	39	46	56	1	0	226	.298	.374	.503	.299	55	78-OF 87
1996	Clevelnd	AL	116	40	11	1	5	18	25	23	3	0	76	.345	.433	.586	.345	27	
1997	Clevelnd	AL	373	102	15	3	18	63	63	59	13	3	274	.273	.378	.475	.297	66	106-OF 95
1998	Clevelnd	AL	340	86	15	0	16	72	58	50	9	5	259	.253	.383	.438	.288	58	
1999	*Pittsbrg*	*NL*	*344*	*92*	*15*	*1*	*17*	*61*	*55*	*55*	*7*	*2*	*254*	*.267*	*.378*	*.465*	*.294*	*60*	

Traded to Pittsburgh for Ricardo Rincon, which was a great deal for the Indians. Giles is a good player, but he's not irreplaceable, especially now that Sexson has arrived. Finding corner outfielders who are solid offensive players (as opposed to great ones) is relatively easy, but getting a pitcher as good as Rincon is a rare opportunity. With Pittsburgh, he'd probably help them most hitting leadoff, but that isn't going to happen.

Mike Glavine — 1B — Bats L — Age 26

YEAR	TEAM	LGE	AB	H	DB	TP	HR	BB	R	RBI	SB	CS	OUT	BA	OBA	SA	EQA	EQR	DEFENSE
1996	Columbus	SAL	126	27	3	0	3	18	12	11	0	0	99	.214	.312	.310	.221	11	
1997	Columbus	SAL	411	77	6	0	13	58	32	33	0	0	334	.187	.288	.297	.205	32	
1998	Kinston	Car	416	82	8	1	15	59	37	39	1	2	336	.197	.297	.329	.219	38	104-1B 88
1999	Clevelnd	AL	371	74	7	0	14	47	31	36	0	1	298	.199	.289	.332	.215	32	

Named the best power prospect in the Carolina League, which at his age is sort of like naming a chain-smoking Filipino father of three the best power hitter in the Little League World Series. Short form: non-prospect, laugh track not included.

Phil Hiatt — 1B — Bats R — Age 30

YEAR	TEAM	LGE	AB	H	DB	TP	HR	BB	R	RBI	SB	CS	OUT	BA	OBA	SA	EQA	EQR	DEFENSE
1996	Toledo	Int	549	126	15	1	28	44	53	65	12	5	428	.230	.287	.413	.240	60	140-3B 104
1998	Buffalo	Int	450	98	10	0	21	33	35	47	3	1	353	.218	.271	.380	.222	41	73-1B 109
1999	Clevelnd	AL	325	74	8	0	16	27	30	39	3	1	252	.228	.287	.400	.235	34	

After a '97 Japanese adventure in which he couldn't adapt to breaking stuff, breaking stuff, and more breaking stuff, he's almost ready to grow up to be Jeff Manto. He's a minor league free agent, and will probably end up slugging for any team looking for a shot at the Triple-A World Series.

Dave Justice — DH — Bats L — Age 33

YEAR	TEAM	LGE	AB	H	DB	TP	HR	BB	R	RBI	SB	CS	OUT	BA	OBA	SA	EQA	EQR	DEFENSE
1996	Atlanta	NL	139	43	6	0	7	22	23	25	1	1	97	.309	.404	.504	.310	26	31-OF 125
1997	Clevelnd	AL	489	164	27	1	36	80	90	112	3	5	330	.335	.429	.616	.342	113	69-OF 92
1998	Clevelnd	AL	525	138	33	2	21	77	78	75	8	3	390	.263	.357	.453	.281	81	
1999	Clevelnd	AL	459	127	24	2	25	75	75	83	3	2	334	.277	.378	.501	.300	82	

Okay, so he's a fragile DH who could probably use some platooning. On the other hand, we could have said the same sort of thing about Harold Baines at 33. At 32, Baines was in his last year in Oakland. He was looking slow, weak-kneed, and underpowered. Only one thing got better, of course, but power's a handy thing. As much as we'd like to think Baines is remarkable, with the advances in sports medicine we've seen over the past fifteen years I wouldn't write anyone off, and especially not if they hit well enough to DH. Physically, it seems like Justice is better off now than Baines was then.

Kenny Lofton — CF — Bats L — Age 32

YEAR	TEAM	LGE	AB	H	DB	TP	HR	BB	R	RBI	SB	CS	OUT	BA	OBA	SA	EQA	EQR	DEFENSE
1996	Clevelnd	AL	642	194	32	4	13	57	120	67	78	20	468	.302	.359	.425	.283	100	150-OF 107
1997	Atlanta	NL	494	164	20	5	6	67	84	65	21	21	351	.332	.412	.429	.290	80	106-OF 113
1998	Clevelnd	AL	583	155	26	6	12	88	105	61	48	10	438	.266	.362	.393	.276	88	150-OF 101
1999	Clevelnd	AL	570	165	29	4	11	76	102	68	36	13	417	.289	.373	.412	.280	87	

Not really a deserving All-Star last season, but with Hargrove picking the team we can't be too surprised. Hart isn't getting too much credit for sending Lofton away rather than giving in to his huge contract demands in '96. Now he's back, seems reasonably happy, and for the beancounters he's cheaper than what he was asking for back then.

Jeff Manto — IF — Bats R — Age 34

YEAR	TEAM	LGE	AB	H	DB	TP	HR	BB	R	RBI	SB	CS	OUT	BA	OBA	SA	EQA	EQR	DEFENSE
1995	Baltimor	AL	250	63	9	0	17	23	26	40	0	3	190	.252	.315	.492	.267	35	63-3B 97
1997	Syracuse	Int	133	23	3	1	2	18	9	7	1	1	111	.173	.272	.256	.181	8	
1997	Buffalo	AA	191	60	6	0	15	26	29	41	0	2	133	.314	.396	.581	.321	39	26-3B 92
1998	Buffalo	Int	209	59	8	0	15	47	39	42	3	2	152	.282	.414	.536	.321	44	33-1B 106
1998	Clevelnd	AL	36	7	1	0	2	2	2	3	0	1	30	.194	.237	.389	.199	3	
1999	Clevelnd	AL	279	71	9	0	18	50	42	50	2	2	210	.254	.368	.480	.290	47	

Already released by the Indians, he may resurface anywhere a team wants some corner infield sock to keep in reserve. Crafting a reputation as the wise old man of the minor leagues; maybe he'll turn that into advocacy for benefits for career minor leaguers, but more likely he'll cash it in for a minor league coaching job.

John McDonald   SS   Bats R   Age 24

YEAR	TEAM	LGE	AB	H	DB	TP	HR	BB	R	RBI	SB	CS	OUT	BA	OBA	SA	EQA	EQR	DEFENSE	
1996	Watertwn	NYP	287	65	3	0	3	23	21	17	5	1	223	.226	.284	.268	.193	18	75-SS 106	
1997	Kinston	Car	549	130	19	1	5	40	41	39	3	3	422	.237	.289	.302	.203	39	129-SS 103	
1998	Akron	Eas	511	104	13	2	2	38	31	22	12	4	411	.204	.259	.249	.171	25	133-SS 106	
1999	*Clevelnd*	*AL*	*492*	*113*	*15*	*1*	*4*	*33*	*35*	*32*	*7*	*3*	*382*	*.230*	*.278*	*.289*	*.193*	*31*		

A very flashy defensive player, McDonald is such a weak hitter that he shouldn't become much more than the new Doug Baker. Vizquel's under contract until 2002, so it isn't like McDonald is going to get an opportunity.

David Miller   OF   Bats L   Age 25

YEAR	TEAM	LGE	AB	H	DB	TP	HR	BB	R	RBI	SB	CS	OUT	BA	OBA	SA	EQA	EQR	DEFENSE	
1996	Kinston	Car	493	110	10	1	6	30	30	30	6	4	387	.223	.268	.284	.186	29	83-OF 88	33-1B 86
1997	Akron	Eas	505	132	20	6	3	37	54	42	16	7	380	.261	.312	.343	.231	49	130-OF 93	
1998	Buffalo	Int	412	99	13	1	8	54	44	39	4	6	319	.240	.328	.335	.234	42	115-OF 98	
1999	*Clevelnd*	*AL*	*443*	*107*	*15*	*2*	*7*	*39*	*42*	*39*	*7*	*6*	*342*	*.242*	*.303*	*.332*	*.220*	*39*		

He lost time to shoulder surgery before the season. He's starting to do some things well and is a much better fielder now than when he was first moved from first base. His hitting still hasn't come around, and he's getting old enough that you have stop making excuses for him and start believing he's a first-round bust.

Scott Morgan   OF   Bats R   Age 25

YEAR	TEAM	LGE	AB	H	DB	TP	HR	BB	R	RBI	SB	CS	OUT	BA	OBA	SA	EQA	EQR	DEFENSE
1996	Columbus	SAL	315	86	8	1	14	33	37	45	4	3	232	.273	.342	.438	.268	43	68-OF 85
1997	Kinston	Car	375	110	18	1	17	35	48	60	2	1	266	.293	.354	.483	.285	58	82-OF 93
1998	Akron	Eas	453	118	19	3	18	46	52	61	3	4	339	.260	.329	.435	.261	59	107-OF 92
1999	*Clevelnd*	*AL*	*436*	*117*	*17*	*2*	*18*	*43*	*52*	*63*	*2*	*3*	*322*	*.268*	*.334*	*.440*	*.265*	*58*	

A huge player (one inch shorter than Sexson), Morgan's been hampered by thoracic outlet syndrome, also known as the affliction that finally ended Lenny Dykstra's career. A good reason to not be excited about his future.

Danny Peoples   OF   Bats R   Age 24

YEAR	TEAM	LGE	AB	H	DB	TP	HR	BB	R	RBI	SB	CS	OUT	BA	OBA	SA	EQA	EQR	DEFENSE
1996	Watertwn	NYP	124	26	2	0	3	21	13	11	1	1	99	.210	.324	.298	.224	12	
1997	Kinston	Car	420	103	10	1	27	70	59	68	5	1	318	.245	.353	.467	.283	67	72-OF 77
1998	Akron	Eas	221	56	10	0	8	25	25	28	1	1	166	.253	.329	.407	.255	27	42-OF 90
1999	*Clevelnd*	*AL*	*278*	*70*	*9*	*0*	*15*	*38*	*36*	*43*	*2*	*1*	*209*	*.252*	*.342*	*.446*	*.271*	*40*	

Although he flashes excellent bat speed, the complaint has been that he gets overly pull-conscious, and he got into the bad habit of pulling off on pitches as he made contact. He also struggled with back and knee injuries, so his introduction to Double-A wasn't conclusive one way or another.

Alex Ramirez   OF   Bats R   Age 24

YEAR	TEAM	LGE	AB	H	DB	TP	HR	BB	R	RBI	SB	CS	OUT	BA	OBA	SA	EQA	EQR	DEFENSE
1996	Canton	Eas	508	155	21	8	13	13	58	66	14	6	359	.305	.322	.455	.265	65	125-OF 92
1997	Buffalo	AA	419	121	17	6	11	23	49	53	10	4	302	.289	.326	.437	.262	53	95-OF 89
1998	Buffalo	Int	515	148	17	5	30	13	53	82	4	3	370	.287	.305	.515	.271	71	108-OF 95
1999	*Clevelnd*	*AL*	*477*	*141*	*21*	*5*	*21*	*15*	*56*	*74*	*8*	*3*	*339*	*.296*	*.317*	*.493*	*.273*	*66*	

Despite playing on a bad knee for much of '98, he was clearly (and was named) the Indians' best minor league player. Repeating Buffalo at 23, he showed dramatic improvement in driving the ball, but he still hasn't figured out the strike zone. He's gone from being a borderline prospect to a guy worth giving 250 plate appearances, if you pick your spots with him. The Giles trade creates the opening for a guy who ought to be the new Glenallen Hill.

Manny Ramirez — RF — Bats R — Age 27

YEAR	TEAM	LGE	AB	H	DB	TP	HR	BB	R	RBI	SB	CS	OUT	BA	OBA	SA	EQA	EQR	DEFENSE
1996	Clevelnd	AL	531	157	44	3	30	81	93	100	8	6	380	.296	.389	.559	.315	106	141-OF 96
1997	Clevelnd	AL	554	185	31	1	30	80	95	112	2	3	372	.334	.418	.556	.328	114	137-OF 95
1998	Clevelnd	AL	555	155	30	2	43	77	86	111	4	3	403	.279	.367	.573	.309	107	149-OF 93
1999	*Clevelnd*	*AL*	*576*	*171*	*30*	*1*	*40*	*84*	*97*	*120*	*4*	*3*	*408*	*.297*	*.386*	*.561*	*.316*	*114*	

Okay, so his glovework is a laughing matter. Like Jose Canseco and Darryl Strawberry in their primes, his defensive short-comings are overstated. As with those two, postseason exposure is going to make people who only get their sports from Sportscenter remember plays like Jeter's triple more than everything else he's done. A great player in the prime of his career not getting nearly enough credit.

David Roberts — OF — Bats L — Age 27

YEAR	TEAM	LGE	AB	H	DB	TP	HR	BB	R	RBI	SB	CS	OUT	BA	OBA	SA	EQA	EQR	DEFENSE
1996	Visalia	Cal	474	77	9	1	3	64	34	15	24	11	408	.162	.262	.205	.165	23	98-OF 92
1997	Jacksnvl	Sou	409	91	12	0	3	32	32	23	13	4	322	.222	.279	.274	.194	27	33-OF 99
1998	Jacksnvl	Sou	278	74	8	2	4	37	39	27	12	6	210	.266	.352	.353	.254	34	48-OF 100
1998	Akron	Eas	224	68	7	2	5	28	40	27	17	5	161	.304	.381	.420	.287	36	55-OF 101
1999	*Clevelnd*	*AL*	*457*	*114*	*15*	*2*	*6*	*53*	*58*	*40*	*21*	*9*	*352*	*.249*	*.327*	*.330*	*.237*	*48*	

Swiped from the Tigers for Geronimo Berroa, the Tribe was more than surprised with what they got. A short sparkplug of a hitter, Roberts had an All-Star season, and showed good enough range afield that they're considering letting him play center full-time. Caution: he's been old for his leagues and was a Southern League repeater.

Marcos Scutaro — 2B — Bats R — Age 23

YEAR	TEAM	LGE	AB	H	DB	TP	HR	BB	R	RBI	SB	CS	OUT	BA	OBA	SA	EQA	EQR	DEFENSE
1996	Columbus	SAL	324	73	7	1	8	28	25	28	3	1	252	.225	.287	.327	.213	26	77-2B 89
1997	Kinston	Car	384	101	12	3	10	28	43	41	14	5	288	.263	.313	.388	.246	43	73-2B 97
1998	Akron	Eas	457	133	22	3	11	42	67	54	24	12	336	.291	.351	.425	.270	64	118-2B 97
1999	*Clevelnd*	*AL*	*455*	*124*	*16*	*2*	*13*	*37*	*56*	*54*	*16*	*9*	*340*	*.273*	*.327*	*.402*	*.253*	*55*	

In his first exposure to Double-A, he improved in almost every phase of the game. His opportunity to have a career with the Tribe is stillborn now that Roberto Alomar's under contract for the next four years. Right now, he looks like a guy GMs should demand as a throw-in in any stretch-drive deal with John Hart.

Richie Sexson — 1B/LF — Bats R — Age 24

YEAR	TEAM	LGE	AB	H	DB	TP	HR	BB	R	RBI	SB	CS	OUT	BA	OBA	SA	EQA	EQR	DEFENSE	
1996	Canton	Eas	517	133	24	2	14	32	48	56	2	1	385	.257	.301	.393	.238	53	104-1B 100	
1997	Buffalo	AA	437	116	18	2	28	26	49	69	5	1	322	.265	.307	.508	.272	62	111-1B 98	
1998	Buffalo	Int	341	97	13	1	19	44	46	59	1	2	246	.284	.366	.496	.292	57	67-OF 93	20-1B 134
1998	Clevelnd	AL	170	51	11	1	11	6	20	31	1	1	120	.300	.324	.571	.292	28	39-1B 106	
1999	*Clevelnd*	*AL*	*512*	*144*	*21*	*1*	*30*	*42*	*65*	*88*	*3*	*1*	*369*	*.281*	*.336*	*.502*	*.282*	*78*		

We can dispense with the Dann Howitt jokes. He learned how to turn on pitches and fist inside stuff to the opposite field, all while becoming more patient. He even learned to play a creditable left field, flashing a good arm. Named the most exciting player of the International League in '98, as well as its #2 prospect. Upon his promotion he was less patient, but if he adjusts as well as he did in Buffalo in '98 he'll be a good regular. The trade of Giles means he'll be getting a lot of playing time.

Jim Thome — 1B — Bats L — Age 28

YEAR	TEAM	LGE	AB	H	DB	TP	HR	BB	R	RBI	SB	CS	OUT	BA	OBA	SA	EQA	EQR	DEFENSE
1996	Clevelnd	AL	484	144	26	5	35	116	99	108	2	2	342	.298	.433	.589	.340	116	141-3B 97
1997	Clevelnd	AL	490	143	22	0	43	120	98	115	1	1	348	.292	.431	.600	.342	119	143-1B 98
1998	Clevelnd	AL	426	118	30	1	29	88	78	86	1	0	308	.277	.401	.556	.321	90	116-1B 100
1999	*Clevelnd*	*AL*	*449*	*129*	*25*	*1*	*34*	*100*	*90*	*101*	*1*	*1*	*321*	*.287*	*.417*	*.575*	*.332*	*102*	

Clearly the Indians' most important player, although losing him with a broken hand to a Wilson Alvarez fastball did give them the opportunity to run Sexson out there and see that he could play. His at-bats in Game Six of the ALCS were probably the most exciting of the entire season by anybody, but then maybe I'm just not learning to love the Yankees.

Omar Vizquel — SS — Bats B — Age 32

YEAR	TEAM	LGE	AB	H	DB	TP	HR	BB	R	RBI	SB	CS	OUT	BA	OBA	SA	EQA	EQR	DEFENSE
1996	Clevelnd	AL	527	148	32	1	9	52	83	53	36	10	389	.281	.345	.397	.266	71	148-SS 100
1997	Clevelnd	AL	559	159	25	6	5	59	91	52	45	13	413	.284	.353	.377	.266	75	149-SS 95
1998	Clevelnd	AL	560	152	27	6	2	64	83	48	32	11	419	.271	.346	.352	.254	68	150-SS 102
1999	Clevelnd	AL	535	147	24	3	6	59	80	52	28	10	398	.275	.347	.364	.256	66	

Probably the best bat-control artist in the American League, but in a league populated by Jeter, Rodriguez, and Garciaparra, the Davey Concepcion of his day tends to get overlooked. In case you were worrying, the Indians have already picked up his option . . . for 2002.

Mark Whiten — OF — Bats B — Age 32

YEAR	TEAM	LGE	AB	H	DB	TP	HR	BB	R	RBI	SB	CS	OUT	BA	OBA	SA	EQA	EQR	DEFENSE
1996	PHILADEL	NL	183	44	5	0	8	34	31	22	12	3	142	.240	.359	.399	.275	28	43-OF 99
1996	Atlanta	NL	90	22	5	1	3	16	12	12	1	5	73	.244	.358	.422	.258	12	20-OF 100
1996	Seattle	AL	137	40	5	0	12	20	23	29	2	1	98	.292	.382	.591	.320	28	30-OF 113
1997	NY Yanks	AL	213	58	9	0	6	31	30	27	4	2	157	.272	.365	.399	.271	30	50-OF 98
1998	Clevelnd	AL	220	59	9	0	7	29	29	28	2	1	162	.268	.353	.405	.266	30	55-OF 101
1999	Clevelnd	AL	236	60	9	0	9	35	32	32	3	2	178	.254	.351	.407	.265	32	

He still has that great throwing arm, as seen when he struck out the side in a mop-up appearance. He's actually done a great job of sustaining his career as a fourth outfielder. Whiten has hit the most home runs of any outfielder developed by the Blue Jays in this decade, which is sort of like being the tallest midget in the circus.

Enrique Wilson — 2B/SS — Bats B — Age 23

YEAR	TEAM	LGE	AB	H	DB	TP	HR	BB	R	RBI	SB	CS	OUT	BA	OBA	SA	EQA	EQR	DEFENSE	
1996	Canton	Eas	481	132	13	3	5	26	48	42	18	10	359	.274	.312	.345	.230	46	113-SS 106	
1997	Buffalo	AA	455	138	18	2	11	41	59	60	9	7	324	.303	.361	.424	.272	63	64-SS 96	50-2B 104
1998	Buffalo	Int	219	58	6	0	5	17	23	22	6	3	164	.265	.318	.361	.238	23	47-2B 95	
1998	Clevelnd	AL	88	27	3	0	3	4	9	12	2	4	65	.307	.337	.443	.256	11		
1999	Clevelnd	AL	388	115	13	1	10	28	48	49	11	8	281	.296	.344	.412	.261	49		

A great defensive player at short; the move to second wastes his great arm. A thumb injury cost him his chance to simply win the Indians' second base job outright. The nonsense about fitting an "offensive profile" had to be galling. He's a better hitter than Joey Cora or David Bell. He's a better defensive player. He's a better player, period. Now has to fight for a utility role now that Roberto Alomar's signed, unless he's traded.

PITCHERS (Averages: 4.00 ERA, 9.00 H/9, 3.00 BB/9, 1.00 HR/9, 6.00 K/9, 1.00 KWH)

Paul Assenmacher — Throws L — Age 38

YEAR	TEAM	LGE	IP	H	ER	HR	BB	K	ERA	W	L	H/9	HR/9	BB/9	K/9	KWH	PERA
1996	Clevelnd	AL	48.0	43	13	1	11	44	2.44	4	1	8.06	0.19	2.06	8.25	3.07	2.62
1997	Clevelnd	AL	49.7	43	14	5	12	51	2.54	4	2	7.79	0.91	2.17	9.24	3.78	2.90
1998	Clevelnd	AL	50.0	52	17	5	17	42	3.06	4	2	9.36	0.90	3.06	7.56	1.50	3.96

There isn't an awful lot to say about Assenmacher. We know what he does, and he's generally good at it. I wonder if we could have all the veteran left-handed relievers playing gunslingers in a western, sitting around the "Portside Saloon." Assenmacher would be the killer with the kind eyes, which 30 years ago would have meant Hollywood would cast Robert Vaughn, and now probably means Brad Pitt, which either way sort of ruins the whole thing for me.

Mike Bacsik — Throws L — Age 21

YEAR	TEAM	LGE	IP	H	ER	HR	BB	K	ERA	W	L	H/9	HR/9	BB/9	K/9	KWH	PERA
1996	BlngtnNC	App	65.7	71	28	4	15	33	3.84	4	3	9.73	0.55	2.06	4.52	0.77	3.70
1997	Columbus	SAL	134.3	214	106	20	59	67	7.10	4	11	14.34	1.34	3.95	4.49	0.27	6.90
1998	Kinston	Car	155.3	193	79	23	43	88	4.58	7	10	11.18	1.33	2.49	5.10	0.70	5.21

(Mike Bacsik *continued*)

A soft-tossing left-hander who lives on location and a great changeup, so this is one Texan high school pick who won't get mentioned with Kerry Wood and Nolan Ryan. Named the Indians' minor league pitcher of the year.

Jim Brower Throws R Age 26

YEAR	TEAM	LGE	IP	H	ER	HR	BB	K	ERA	W	L	H/9	HR/9	BB/9	K/9	KWH	PERA
1996	Charlott	Fla	125.3	223	103	18	47	63	7.40	3	11	16.01	1.29	3.38	4.52	0.28	7.47
1997	Tulsa	Tex	130.0	183	102	14	45	79	7.06	3	11	12.67	0.97	3.12	5.47	0.57	5.68
1998	Akron	Eas	146.3	185	76	10	42	63	4.67	7	9	11.38	0.62	2.58	3.87	0.38	4.74

Brower isn't really a prospect, but he gets the most out of a poor repertoire, generating a good number of groundballs with a sinker/slider combo. He's looking like he could end up on Terry Clark's wild ride through almost every organization on the planet. Naturally, he's a minor league free agent, so buckle up.

Jamie Brown Throws R Age 22

YEAR	TEAM	LGE	IP	H	ER	HR	BB	K	ERA	W	L	H/9	HR/9	BB/9	K/9	KWH	PERA
1997	Watertwn	NYP	65.0	100	49	9	20	33	6.78	2	5	13.85	1.25	2.77	4.57	0.41	6.51
1998	Kinston	Car	162.0	212	111	17	51	102	6.17	5	13	11.78	0.94	2.83	5.67	0.72	5.22

A community college draft-and-follow from the '96 draft. He's survived so far by mixing a good fastball with a changeup, but he still lacks a quality breaking pitch. That's the profile of a good reliever, but the Indians think Brown is savvy enough to wing it or perfect something with movement.

Dave Burba Throws R Age 32

YEAR	TEAM	LGE	IP	H	ER	HR	BB	K	ERA	W	L	H/9	HR/9	BB/9	K/9	KWH	PERA
1996	Cincnnti	NL	200.3	189	85	18	92	134	3.82	12	10	8.49	0.81	4.13	6.02	0.77	3.59
1997	Cincnnti	NL	166.0	160	75	22	67	118	4.07	9	9	8.67	1.19	3.63	6.40	0.97	3.90
1998	Clevelnd	AL	214.7	199	76	27	63	130	3.19	15	9	8.34	1.13	2.64	5.45	1.01	3.48

A Don Gullett renovation project, in that Gullett cleaned up his delivery, and suddenly he seems more durable. He rapped out 10 quality starts in his first 13, but what's really interesting is his sustained control improvements. The Indians rewarded him with a two-year contract. I think the improvement's real, but I said that after '96; there's just more reason to believe it now.

Bartolo Colon Throws R Age 24

YEAR	TEAM	LGE	IP	H	ER	HR	BB	K	ERA	W	L	H/9	HR/9	BB/9	K/9	KWH	PERA
1996	Canton	Eas	61.0	53	17	2	25	44	2.51	5	2	7.82	0.30	3.69	6.49	1.10	2.80
1997	Buffalo	AmA	54.3	55	17	4	22	46	2.82	4	2	9.11	0.66	3.64	7.62	1.31	3.81
1997	Clevelnd	AL	96.3	106	55	11	39	64	5.14	4	7	9.90	1.03	3.64	5.98	0.74	4.48
1998	Clevelnd	AL	215.3	196	69	13	71	155	2.88	16	8	8.19	0.54	2.97	6.48	1.29	3.05

Credited with the best fastball in the AL in 1998 *Baseball America* polling, what really makes it special is its hard, sinking action and that he learned to set it up with an improved changeup. Jeff Bower and I have been working on new ways to track pitching in terms of results, and Colon's pattern was particularly interesting. Hargrove tried to leave him in games longer early in the season, with longer rest between starts, and Colon was very effective. As the season progressed, Hargrove tried using Colon every four days and he wore out. Was it the early high pitch counts, the regular work, or his perpetually tender elbow? I don't have a good answer for you. If I was Bob Feller, I'd probably blame it on Bill Clinton or fluoridated water or Hale-Bopp.

Tim Drew Throws R Age 20

YEAR	TEAM	LGE	IP	H	ER	HR	BB	K	ERA	W	L	H/9	HR/9	BB/9	K/9	KWH	PERA
1998	Columbus	SAL	68.0	89	48	6	32	40	6.35	2	6	11.78	0.79	4.24	5.29	0.42	5.29
1998	Kinston	Car	83.7	138	70	12	37	47	7.53	2	7	14.84	1.29	3.98	5.06	0.32	7.10

The kid brother of you-know-who-Drew, and considered the closest to the majors of the high school pitchers taken in the '97 draft. His 95 mph fastball doesn't have much movement, so he uses it to set up a slider and changeup. It's very early to guess whether or not he's going to make it, and high school pitchers as a group are bad bets to pan out.

Alberto Garza — Throws R — Age 22

YEAR	TEAM	LGE	IP	H	ER	HR	BB	K	ERA	W	L	H/9	HR/9	BB/9	K/9	KWH	PERA
1996	BlngtnNC	App	36.0	52	30	6	17	18	7.50	1	3	13.00	1.50	4.25	4.50	0.27	6.50
1997	Columbus	SAL	92.7	94	38	9	39	70	3.69	5	5	9.13	0.87	3.79	6.80	1.00	3.98
1998	Kinston	Car	106.0	106	54	10	70	76	4.58	5	7	9.00	0.85	5.94	6.45	0.58	4.25
1998	Akron	Eas	21.0	28	12	1	9	15	5.14	1	1	12.00	0.43	3.86	6.43	0.67	5.14

Garza hasn't gotten the same kind of attention as Willie Martinez, but may be the better prospect at this point. He has sound mechanics, a good curve, and an improving change-up. Garza was almost unhittable at Kinston.

Dwight Gooden — Throws R — Age 34

YEAR	TEAM	LGE	IP	H	ER	HR	BB	K	ERA	W	L	H/9	HR/9	BB/9	K/9	KWH	PERA
1996	NY Yanks	AL	177.7	157	73	16	71	125	3.70	11	9	7.95	0.81	3.60	6.33	1.05	3.19
1997	NY Yanks	AL	108.7	115	51	13	46	64	4.22	8	8	9.52	1.08	3.81	5.30	0.58	4.31
1998	Clevelnd	AL	141.7	128	45	12	46	82	2.86	11	5	8.13	0.76	2.92	5.21	0.86	3.18

Gooden probably pitched better than he has since hurting his shoulder in '89, despite playing the last two months with a hernia he was having taped up before games. I can't imagine pitching through that kind of pain, and at this point his career has been much too wild to make any useful guesses about what's going to happen next.

Jimmy Hamilton — Throws L — Age 23

YEAR	TEAM	LGE	IP	H	ER	HR	BB	K	ERA	W	L	H/9	HR/9	BB/9	K/9	KWH	PERA
1996	BlngtnNC	App	39.3	71	28	8	19	25	6.41	1	3	16.25	1.83	4.35	5.72	0.35	8.24
1997	Columbus	SAL	119.0	166	80	13	84	90	6.05	4	9	12.55	0.98	6.35	6.81	0.44	6.05
1998	Kinston	Car	70.7	82	32	7	25	55	4.08	4	4	10.44	0.89	3.18	7.00	1.11	4.58

A reliever with outstanding control, Hamilton allowed a mere 16 unintentional walks in '98. Drafted in '96 after starring at Ferrum College. With Assenmacher and Rincon in hand, he won't enter the picture for another year or two, assuming he survives the jump to Double-A.

Mike Jackson — Throws R — Age 34

YEAR	TEAM	LGE	IP	H	ER	HR	BB	K	ERA	W	L	H/9	HR/9	BB/9	K/9	KWH	PERA
1996	Seattle	AL	73.7	56	23	10	20	69	2.81	5	3	6.84	1.22	2.44	8.43	3.19	2.57
1997	Clevelnd	AL	76.3	59	27	3	25	71	3.18	5	3	6.96	0.35	2.95	8.37	2.56	2.24
1998	Clevelnd	AL	66.0	40	8	4	12	54	1.09	7	0	5.45	0.55	1.64	7.36	4.56	1.09

Throws hard—OK, not as hard as he used to—comes from Texas, and doesn't get mentioned as one of the hard-throwing Texans. Now why is that? He's probably had more career value than Rod Beck, but that isn't going to help him get remembered. Does he have a place in history as a great reliever in a time with a lot of great relievers? Or as a reflection that it's easier to find or make a great reliever than is commonly accepted? We'll have to see.

Doug Jones — Throws R — Age 42

YEAR	TEAM	LGE	IP	H	ER	HR	BB	K	ERA	W	L	H/9	HR/9	BB/9	K/9	KWH	PERA
1996	ChiCubs	NL	32.3	45	19	4	7	24	5.29	1	3	12.53	1.11	1.95	6.68	1.37	5.57
1996	Milwauke	AL	32.3	30	10	2	11	34	2.78	3	1	8.35	0.56	3.06	9.46	2.63	3.06
1997	Milwauke	AL	81.7	59	16	4	7	79	1.76	8	1	6.50	0.44	0.77	8.71	11.33	1.54
1998	Milwauke	NL	56.0	65	28	15	10	40	4.50	3	3	10.45	2.41	1.61	6.43	1.85	5.46
1998	Clevelnd	AL	33.0	32	9	2	5	27	2.45	3	1	8.73	0.55	1.36	7.36	3.42	3.00

The classic "fools some of the people some of the time" pitcher. Being the world's greatest palmball artist is a tough cross to bear. Once again, Jones jumped leagues midseason and pitched more effectively. It seems like more, but it was "only" the third time that he's switched leagues and shaved a run or more off of his ERA. He'll probably keep this up for another two years or until everyone starts getting nervous about whether their clubhouses need AARP seals of approval. "Where's the Metamucil?"

Steve Karsay   Throws R   Age 27

YEAR	TEAM	LGE	IP	H	ER	HR	BB	K	ERA	W	L	H/9	HR/9	BB/9	K/9	KWH	PERA
1996	Modesto	Cal	31.0	44	18	2	1	18	5.23	1	2	12.77	0.58	0.29	5.23	5.52	4.94
1997	Oakland	AL	141.0	154	70	18	41	90	4.47	7	9	9.83	1.15	2.62	5.74	0.96	4.34
1998	Buffalo	Int	76.3	100	39	5	15	48	4.60	3	5	11.79	0.59	1.77	5.66	1.15	4.72
1998	Clevelnd	AL	26.0	29	12	3	6	13	4.15	1	2	10.04	1.04	2.08	4.50	0.73	4.15

By July, he'd already been on the DL twice. There's little reason to expect that he's ever going to have a healthy season. Probably coveted by the Brewers for Hart's next sucker deal. "Sal, my man, how's it hangin'? Have I got a pitcher for you. Tasty curveball, great instincts on the mound. He'll make you forget Moose Haas."

Tom Martin   Throws L   Age 29

YEAR	TEAM	LGE	IP	H	ER	HR	BB	K	ERA	W	L	H/9	HR/9	BB/9	K/9	KWH	PERA
1996	Jackson	Tex	67.3	94	44	9	50	45	5.88	2	5	12.56	1.20	6.68	6.01	0.32	6.28
1997	Houston	NL	55.7	56	13	2	21	32	2.10	5	1	9.05	0.32	3.40	5.17	0.65	3.40
1998	Buffalo	Int	34.7	52	25	4	13	27	6.49	1	3	13.50	1.04	3.38	7.01	0.81	6.23
1998	Clevelnd	AL	16.3	29	17	3	11	9	9.37	0	2	15.98	1.65	6.06	4.96	0.19	8.27

Acquired in Hart's multiple redundancy campaign for left-handed relief help. It was sort of silly to get Martin and Villone, and then not let either one of them beat out the great Alvin Morman. He's got a wild curve and an adequate fastball, so he isn't just a postsurgical junkball left-hander.

Willie Martinez   Throws R   Age 21

YEAR	TEAM	LGE	IP	H	ER	HR	BB	K	ERA	W	L	H/9	HR/9	BB/9	K/9	KWH	PERA
1996	Watertwn	NYP	81.0	121	37	9	24	56	4.11	4	5	13.44	1.00	2.67	6.22	0.81	6.00
1997	Kinston	Car	127.7	166	72	15	40	84	5.08	5	9	11.70	1.06	2.82	5.92	0.80	5.29
1998	Akron	Eas	152.7	194	92	16	44	92	5.42	6	11	11.44	0.94	2.59	5.42	0.74	5.01

Since elbow surgery at the start of '97, the Tribe tried to avoid more damage last winter by putting him through a strength and conditioning program. He still came down with tendinitis in '98, as well as suffering a hip flexor. His low-90s fastball has wicked movement, but depending on who you talk to, either he's still learning to set it up or he just needs to be healthy to use it consistently.

Mike Matthews   Throws L   Age 25

YEAR	TEAM	LGE	IP	H	ER	HR	BB	K	ERA	W	L	H/9	HR/9	BB/9	K/9	KWH	PERA
1996	Canton	Eas	159.0	213	99	14	73	89	5.60	6	12	12.06	0.79	4.13	5.04	0.38	5.38
1997	Akron	Eas	112.3	125	53	12	55	52	4.25	6	6	10.01	0.96	4.41	4.17	0.29	4.57
1998	Buffalo	Int	129.3	148	71	18	63	71	4.94	6	8	10.30	1.25	4.38	4.94	0.41	4.94

A soft-tossing left-hander who has trouble keeping right-handed batters from getting the ball into the air. That's major league trouble with a tateriffic flavor.

Ben McDonald   Throws R   Age 31

YEAR	TEAM	LGE	IP	H	ER	HR	BB	K	ERA	W	L	H/9	HR/9	BB/9	K/9	KWH	PERA
1995	Baltimor	AL	82.3	67	32	10	31	64	3.50	5	4	7.32	1.09	3.39	7.00	1.48	2.95
1996	Milwauke	AL	226.7	215	78	21	54	145	3.10	16	9	8.54	0.83	2.14	5.76	1.36	3.30
1997	Milwauke	AL	136.3	116	55	12	31	106	3.63	8	7	7.66	0.79	2.05	7.00	2.34	2.71

Well, we had to mention him somewhere. Might get an invite from a team that likes having a good business relationship with Scott Boras. Resort to tea leaves if you want to know what he's going to do in '99.

Charles Nagy   Throws R   Age 32

YEAR	TEAM	LGE	IP	H	ER	HR	BB	K	ERA	W	L	H/9	HR/9	BB/9	K/9	KWH	PERA
1996	Clevelnd	AL	228.0	202	66	18	49	166	2.61	18	7	7.97	0.71	1.93	6.55	2.09	2.84
1997	Clevelnd	AL	231.7	249	96	25	66	144	3.73	14	12	9.67	0.97	2.56	5.59	0.95	4.12
1998	Clevelnd	AL	223.0	238	107	31	59	118	4.32	12	13	9.61	1.25	2.38	4.76	0.74	4.24

It was an awful season for Nagy, except for the paycheck part. Started off regularly hanging his splitter, and then he started nibbling. Although he got a four-year contract extension during the season, by July Hargrove was threatening to send him to the pen, at which point he settled down somewhat. We're talking about his post-operative career, so I'm not betting against him improving.

Chad Ogea — Throws R — Age 28

YEAR	TEAM	LGE	IP	H	ER	HR	BB	K	ERA	W	L	H/9	HR/9	BB/9	K/9	KWH	PERA
1996	Clevelnd	AL	151.0	140	61	19	34	100	3.64	9	8	8.34	1.13	2.03	5.96	1.58	3.34
1997	Clevelnd	AL	128.7	138	66	12	40	77	4.62	6	8	9.65	0.84	2.80	5.39	0.81	4.06
1998	Buffalo	Int	40.7	47	19	2	5	26	4.20	2	3	10.40	0.44	1.11	5.75	2.16	3.76
1998	Clevelnd	AL	73.0	71	34	8	22	42	4.19	4	4	8.75	0.99	2.71	5.18	0.85	3.58

After being kicked around as the contingency fifth starter for the last few years (as in: after the Jack McDowells and John Smileys and Jeff Judens don't work out, it's back to Ogea), he's been traded to the Phillies to get a shot at regular starts. He seems to attract injuries: they haven't all been arm injuries, and since we aren't talking about a guy built like Chris Bosio, the knee injuries may not kill him either.

Jim Poole — Throws L — Age 33

YEAR	TEAM	LGE	IP	H	ER	HR	BB	K	ERA	W	L	H/9	HR/9	BB/9	K/9	KWH	PERA
1996	Cleveland	AL	28.0	27	11	3	12	19	3.54	2	1	8.68	0.96	3.86	6.11	0.84	3.86
1996	San Fran	NL	24.3	15	6	2	13	17	2.22	2	1	5.55	0.74	4.81	6.29	1.11	1.85
1997	San Fran	NL	50.3	77	40	6	23	23	7.15	1	5	13.77	1.07	4.11	4.11	0.22	6.44
1998	San Fran	NL	32.0	41	19	5	8	15	5.34	1	3	11.53	1.41	2.25	4.22	0.51	5.34
1998	Clevelnd	AL	7.7	9	3	0	2	11	3.52	1	0	10.57	0.00	2.35	12.91	5.04	3.52

Made the cut for the Indians chapter solely on the expectation that he'd probably make the team, right up until they traded Brian Giles for Ricardo Rincon. A free agent who'll be coming soon to a ballpark near you.

Jason Rakers — Throws R — Age 26

YEAR	TEAM	LGE	IP	H	ER	HR	BB	K	ERA	W	L	H/9	HR/9	BB/9	K/9	KWH	PERA
1996	Columbus	SAL	66.3	140	61	7	23	34	8.28	1	6	18.99	0.95	3.12	4.61	0.27	8.28
1997	Kinston	Car	90.0	140	61	12	20	63	6.10	3	7	14.00	1.20	2.00	6.30	1.06	6.40
1997	Akron	Eas	40.0	40	20	3	11	22	4.50	2	2	9.00	0.68	2.48	4.95	0.82	3.60
1998	Akron	Eas	30.0	44	12	3	8	19	3.60	2	1	13.20	0.90	2.40	5.70	0.77	5.70
1998	Buffalo	Int	122.3	150	68	12	37	70	5.00	5	9	11.04	0.88	2.72	5.15	0.66	4.78

Rakers isn't known for any single "out" pitch, just his skill at mixing a solid fastball with an inconsistent slider. He hasn't been touted by scouts (being a 25th round pick out of New Mexico State does that to some guys), but the Ogea trade has made him the first alternate for the rotation.

Steve Reed — Throws R — Age 33

YEAR	TEAM	LGE	IP	H	ER	HR	BB	K	ERA	W	L	H/9	HR/9	BB/9	K/9	KWH	PERA
1996	Colorado	NL	83.0	57	25	10	19	47	2.71	6	3	6.18	1.08	2.06	5.10	1.53	1.95
1997	Colorado	NL	67.0	44	20	10	25	39	2.69	5	2	5.91	1.34	3.36	5.24	1.04	2.15
1998	San Fran	NL	54.3	33	9	4	17	45	1.49	5	1	5.47	0.66	2.82	7.45	2.71	1.49
1998	Clevelnd	AL	27.0	25	14	4	7	23	4.67	1	2	8.33	1.33	2.33	7.67	2.27	3.67

Despite a circulatory problem that left the tips of his fingers numb and required surgery at the end of the season—he couldn't feel his slider leaving his fingertips—the Giants got rooked. Reed is one of the best relievers in baseball today, and he should do a great job handling the Mike Jackson setup role for Mike Jackson.

David Riske — Throws R — Age 22

Year	Team	Lge	IP	H	ER	HR	BB	K	ERA	W	L	H/9	HR/9	BB/9	K/9	KWH	PERA
1997	Kinston	Car	68.3	78	27	4	32	63	3.56	4	4	10.27	0.53	4.21	8.30	1.19	4.35
1998	Kinston	Car	51.0	63	19	6	18	46	3.35	4	2	11.12	1.06	3.18	8.12	1.40	4.94

A big surprise since being picked in the 56th round, and was named the Carolina League's best reliever in '98 after racking up 33 saves. Using a three-quarters delivery, he mixes a splitter fastball, and slider. Moving him to the closer's role limited his innings, and he's going to need more work than this to develop into a useful major league pitcher.

Frankie Sanders   Throws R   Age 23

YEAR	TEAM	LGE	IP	H	ER	HR	BB	K	ERA	W	L	H/9	HR/9	BB/9	K/9	KWH	PERA
1996	Columbus	SAL	113.3	154	70	11	43	67	5.56	4	9	12.23	0.87	3.41	5.32	0.51	5.48
1997	Kinston	Car	137.0	175	85	13	64	90	5.58	5	10	11.50	0.85	4.20	5.91	0.54	5.19
1998	Akron	Eas	184.0	205	85	16	70	85	4.16	10	10	10.03	0.78	3.42	4.16	0.38	4.30

Although it sort of looks like progress, he's got to get better control of his fastball/curve mix. Sanders is under six feet tall, so he's always going to run into the bias against short right-handed pitchers. Does all of the extra things well: holds runners, fields his position, and stays cool on the mound to get a "bulldog" reputation.

Jeff Sexton   Throws R   Age 27

YEAR	TEAM	LGE	IP	H	ER	HR	BB	K	ERA	W	L	H/9	HR/9	BB/9	K/9	KWH	PERA
1996	Canton	Eas	46.3	59	33	6	25	25	6.41	1	4	11.46	1.17	4.86	4.86	0.32	5.44
1997	Akron	Eas	45.0	65	27	4	15	26	5.40	2	3	13.00	0.80	3.00	5.20	0.52	5.60
1997	Buffalo	AmA	22.3	22	16	3	12	12	6.45	1	1	8.87	1.21	4.84	4.84	0.41	4.03
1998	Akron	Eas	54.3	54	16	2	21	34	2.65	4	2	8.94	0.33	3.48	5.63	0.76	3.48
1998	Buffalo	Int	23.3	29	16	1	15	12	6.17	1	2	11.19	0.39	5.79	4.63	0.25	5.01

An Eastern League All-Star in '98, Sexton was also named the league's best relief pitcher in his third year there. Not likely to turn up on the major league roster now that the Indians have acquired Jerry Spradlin from the Phillies.

Paul Shuey   Throws R   Age 28

YEAR	TEAM	LGE	IP	H	ER	HR	BB	K	ERA	W	L	H/9	HR/9	BB/9	K/9	KWH	PERA
1996	Buffalo	AmA	32.7	18	5	1	10	45	1.38	4	0	4.96	0.28	2.76	12.40	8.44	0.83
1996	Clevelnd	AL	55.7	42	14	6	22	44	2.26	5	1	6.79	0.97	3.56	7.11	1.57	2.59
1997	Clevelnd	AL	46.0	53	26	5	25	45	5.09	2	3	10.37	0.98	4.89	8.80	1.15	4.89
1998	Clevelnd	AL	54.0	42	15	6	23	57	2.50	4	2	7.00	1.00	3.83	9.50	2.52	2.83

Widely credited for nasty stuff, although he doesn't get enough notice for his wildness or his ability to hang a pitch. Shuey is good, but the praise he's garnered is more than he deserves (à la "unhittable" Scott Erickson), and he's not half the pitcher Mike Jackson or Steve Reed have been over the last several years.

John Smiley   Throws L   Age 34

YEAR	TEAM	LGE	IP	H	ER	HR	BB	K	ERA	W	L	H/9	HR/9	BB/9	K/9	KWH	PERA
1995	Cincnnti	NL	178.3	179	65	11	37	114	3.28	12	8	9.03	0.56	1.87	5.75	1.47	3.33
1996	Cincnnti	NL	221.7	213	87	20	52	154	3.53	14	11	8.65	0.81	2.11	6.25	1.61	3.33
1997	Cincnnti	NL	121.0	140	65	18	28	85	4.83	5	8	10.41	1.34	2.08	6.32	1.38	4.69
1997	Clevelnd	AL	37.7	45	19	8	9	25	4.54	2	2	10.75	1.91	2.15	5.97	1.16	5.26

After missing all of '98 with a broken arm, he was optioned by the Tribe to Buffalo in November. He's still under contract for a few years, so the Indians will simply have to wait and see if he ever heals. A good ping-pong partner for Karsay.

Ron Villone   Throws L   Age 29

YEAR	TEAM	LGE	IP	H	ER	HR	BB	K	ERA	W	L	H/9	HR/9	BB/9	K/9	KWH	PERA
1996	San Dieg	NL	18.0	20	6	2	6	17	3.00	1	1	10.00	1.00	3.00	8.50	1.81	4.50
1996	Milwauke	AL	25.3	14	7	4	15	19	2.49	2	1	4.97	1.42	5.33	6.75	1.29	2.13
1997	Milwauke	AL	55.0	54	19	4	31	39	3.11	4	2	8.84	0.65	5.07	6.38	0.68	3.93
1998	Buffalo	Int	21.7	23	11	2	11	21	4.57	1	1	9.55	0.83	4.57	8.72	1.31	4.15
1998	Clevelnd	AL	29.0	30	14	3	20	15	4.34	1	2	9.31	0.93	6.21	4.66	0.28	4.34

I've been stubbornly singing his praises for several years, so don't expect me to stop now. In fairness, some guys make a comparison to Jeff Juden, in that there may be something nobody wants to put up with, but left-handers who throw this hard can be legitimate full-time setup men. That passes for unconventional nowadays, but Villone's stuff is nasty.

Jaret Wright			Throws R			Age 23											
YEAR	TEAM	LGE	IP	H	ER	HR	BB	K	ERA	W	L	H/9	HR/9	BB/9	K/9	KWH	PERA
1996	Kinston	Car	94.3	90	41	2	58	80	3.91	5	5	8.59	0.19	5.53	7.63	0.92	3.53
1997	Akron	Eas	54.0	46	22	4	21	46	3.67	3	3	7.67	0.67	3.50	7.67	1.64	3.00
1997	Buffalo	AmA	43.3	37	18	4	19	40	3.74	3	2	7.68	0.83	3.95	8.31	1.71	3.12
1997	Clevelnd	AL	92.0	80	37	9	30	61	3.62	5	5	7.83	0.88	2.93	5.97	1.16	3.03
1998	Clevelnd	AL	204.7	198	84	20	79	138	3.69	12	11	8.71	0.88	3.47	6.07	0.91	3.65

Although he teases us with a fastball that can get up around 98, he isn't finishing his delivery consistently. He troubles some because he's gutty in the Alex Fernandez/Rick Reuschel sense of the word. However, other than Bob Feller's cranky "when I was pitching, we sat in tubs filled with fire ants on our off-days, not like these sissies" shtick, everyone likes Wright's work habits. He was wildly inconsistent in the second half, alternating quality starts with blowouts. His workload has been high for a pitcher his age, but he wasn't asked to do the same sort of things Bartolo Colon was, and he doesn't have Colon's injury history.

SNWL | CLEVELAND INDIANS | Park Effect: +10.5%

PITCHER	GS	IP	R	SNW	SNL	SNPCT	W	L	RA	APW	SNVA	SNWAR
Burba, D.	31	200.0	99	12.1	9.5	.560	14	10	4.46	1.55	1.23	2.90
Colon, B.	31	204.0	91	13.7	8.6	.614	14	9	4.01	2.51	2.62	4.23
Gooden, D.	23	134.0	59	9.1	5.6	.618	8	6	3.96	1.72	1.71	2.84
Jacome, J.	1	5.0	8	0.0	0.9	.026	0	1	14.40	-0.48	-0.42	-0.35
Karsay, S.	1	6.7	2	0.5	0.1	.757	0	1	2.70	0.17	0.18	0.20
Krivda, R.	1	5.0	2	0.3	0.2	.536	0	0	3.60	0.08	0.04	0.06
Nagy, C.	33	210.3	139	11.1	13.0	.461	15	10	5.95	-1.62	-1.05	0.86
Ogea, C.	9	47.7	32	2.4	3.5	.405	3	4	6.04	-0.41	-0.55	-0.12
Wright, Jaret	32	192.7	109	11.5	10.5	.522	12	10	5.09	0.22	0.47	2.14
TOTALS	162	1005.3	541	60.7	52.0	.538	66	51	4.84	3.75	4.24	12.76

In 1997, the Indians proved you don't need pitching to win, riding a powerhouse offense and poor starting pitching to the seventh game of the World Series. In 1998, they were almost as successful, but with a different formula—they got plenty of starting pitching. The turnaround of the Indians rotation from 1997 to 1998 was the most dramatic in baseball. They went from being 23rd in the majors with an SNVA of -3.9, to being 5th (out of 30) with an SNVA of 4.2. The Indians were one of only four teams who had three starters with an SNVA of 1.0 or greater. The others were the Braves, Yankees, and Astros. Bartolo Colon's high workload and second-half collapse were well-documented. Colon was 9.9-3.3 (.747) before the All-Star break, and 3.9-5.3 (.421) after. Jaret Wright also declined in the second half, although not so dramatically: 7.0-5.2 (.573) before the break, 4.5-5.3 (.459) after.

Pitcher Abuse Points

PITCHER	AGE	GS	PAP	PAP/S	AAW	MAX	115+	130+
Burba, Dave	31	31	369	11.90	13.89	132	8	1
Colon, Bartolo	23	31	606	19.55	48.87	140	10	4
Gooden, Dwight	33	23	151	6.57	6.57	127	3	0
Nagy, Charles	31	33	284	8.61	10.04	130	6	1
Ogea, Chad	27	9	4	0.44	0.81	104	0	0
Wright, Jaret	22	32	444	13.88	37.00	128	9	0
TOTAL		162	1858	11.47	22.34	140	36	6
RANKING (AL)			5	5	2		5	5

Mike Hargrove does many things well, and the Indians have four division titles and two World Series berths in the last four years. But he is squarely to blame for the Indians' inability to develop a #1 starter. In 1992, Charles Nagy went 17-10 with a 2.96 ERA and a K/BB ratio of nearly 3.00; Hargrove made him throw 252 innings in just 33 starts, a heavy burden for a 25-year-old who was just coming into his own. Nagy made just nine starts the following year, and when he showed signs of recovery in 1996 (3.41 ERA), Hargrove wore him down again. Nagy, as fine a pitcher as he was, was never the prospect that Colon and Wright are. Colon, in particular, is a small guy and there was so much worry about his elbow that he missed half of 1996 and was briefly moved to the bullpen to protect his arm. Yet there he was in April and May, throwing six complete games. On any other team I'd be screaming about Jaret Wright's usage, but on the Indians he took a back seat to Colon. Colon and Wright, the future of this franchise on the mound, better hope the past doesn't repeat itself this year.

Detroit Tigers

Rebuilding is hard. If you don't believe me, just ask Buddy Bell.... If it feels like the Tigers have been rebuilding for years now, that's because they have. Their failure to realize the fruits of their labor on the field is not a reflection of wasted effort so much as an indication of just how dreadful this franchise had become in the mid-90s. The Tigers' last division title in 1987 represented the last gasp for an organization that had generated an enormous amount of talent—Alan Trammell, Lou Whitaker, Jack Morris, Lance Parrish, Kirk Gibson—in the late 70s, yet with the exception of one remarkable season had not quite achieved the greatness projected of them. Almost to a man, their great core of players were hailed as "gamers" and savvy, intelligent veterans who won by doing the little things correctly.

Because the Tigers were largely successful throughout the 80s, a mindset formed in Detroit that the road out of the moribund swamp they found themselves in lay with the veterans, with bringing in guys who excelled at the mental aspect of the game, who didn't hit for high averages but worked the strike zone and hit for power. For the offense, it worked: guys like Mickey Tettleton, Cecil Fielder, and Tony Phillips were brought in and established themselves as stars. But this led to neglect of the farm system. The only everyday player the team developed over a decade was Travis Fryman, who fit the same profile by being considered thinking man's player.

The Tigers had actually discovered something extraordinarily valuable, but the transmission was disrupted by the inability of the team to finish higher than third place, and was ultimately lost. The message, of course, was that secondary skills—power, the ability to draw walks, and speed—are the key to a successful offense. Unfortunately, the Tigers went wrong in two ways:

1. They used the same tack to build their pitching staff, using pitchers with good control but average velocity—the pitcher's answer to the low-average hitter. Those guys disappeared faster than a one-hit band in the '80s. Think of John Doherty as Kajagoogoo in spikes.

2. They were building their team around old players. Every year they had to scramble to replace someone who had finally lost his skills, coming closer and closer to group collapse, while the farm system was completely unproductive.

The result was unavoidable. The Tigers finally had to scrap the team and rebuild in the most brutal fashion. Yet in finally discarding their old philosophy of building around veterans, they also threw out the offensive principles that had worked so well for them. So while the rebuilt farm system has churned out power pitchers like Justin Thompson and Matt Anderson, the new organization focus on hitters with athleticism and "tools," but not necessarily plate discipline, is undermining the rebuilding process.

Nowhere is this more evident than at center field and shortstop, where the Tigers have installed Brian Hunter and Deivi Cruz to be the centerpieces of their new and improved defense. Cruz is an outstanding shortstop, but contributes little to the offense beyond his singles: he walked just 13 times all year. Cruz plays a position where offense is a bonus, and he's still young enough to improve with the bat. No such excuses exist for Brian Hunter, who was arguably the most burdensome everyday player in the AL. He hit .254 last season, and aside from an impressive-but-not-terribly-meaningful stolen base total, did nothing else for the offense. He had a .298 OBP, an unacceptable performance, yet led off the entire season, killing scoring opportunities before they even developed.

Faced with almost no production from shortstop, center field, and catcher, the Tigers had to rely on the bats of their corner players. What they got at third base was mostly bunk, negating the benefit of another strong year from Damion Easley at second base. They got reasonable output from Tony Clark and Bobby Higginson, but what they lacked was one hitter good enough to build a lineup around. What happened last year was that each player was forced into an offensive role that taxed his abilities just a bit, and the expectations on each player was reflected in a drop in walks as each hitter tried to make up for those around him. Higginson and Clark

---

Tigers Prospectus

1998 record: 65-97; Fifth place, AL Central

Pythagorean W/L: 67-95

Runs scored: 722 (12th in AL)

Runs allowed: 863 (10th in AL)

Team EQA: .250 (11th in AL)

Park: Tiger Stadium (neutral)

1998: Outsized expectations and some gaping holes led to Buddy Bell's downfall.

1999: They'll be better, just not enough to contend in 1999.

are probably both suited for the #5 spot—but they had to bat third and fourth. Easley, an excellent #6 hitter, was forced into the middle of the lineup. With Hunter and Joe Randa at the top of the lineup, the big guns frequently found themselves batting with no one on and little faith that the hitters behind them could score them. So they had to take it on themselves to produce the offense themselves, and their collective walk total dropped from 231 to 165. As a team the Tigers walked just 455 times, fewest in the AL.

As admirable as the Tigers are for attempting a philosophy that runs counter to the way things have been done at Michigan and Trumbull for decades, they need to find an equilibrium that brings out the best in their new generation of pitchers, while preserving a time-honored tradition of good offenses in Detroit. The signing of Dean Palmer is an indication that the Tigers understand their need to get offense at every position, but Palmer's main weakness is his poor OBP. That means the Tigers have spent $36 million without addressing their most fundamental issue: how to get more baserunners. Unless they suddenly get religion and dump ciphers like Hunter for less athletic but more effective hitters, the Tigers are playing a zero-sum game here: their improvement at preventing runs is being paralleled by their waning ability to score them.

What makes the Tigers' difficulties galling is that they had an opportunity to make an acquisition that might have meant five or even ten wins in the standings, and he could have been signed at a bargain price. Yet out of ego and a lack of appreciation for his talents, they let him go without a fight.

I speak, of course, of the decision to not hire Davey Johnson as manager. Johnson's managerial career remains one of the great riddles of our time. Here is a man who has had a record of consistent success unparalleled by any manager in the game with the exception of Bobby Cox, yet has to go hat-in-hand looking for a job every couple of years. It is true that Johnson's deftness with front office personnel does not match his skill with players; it is also true that his last two tenures have ended due to bizarre episodes with less-than-stable ownership. His term with the Reds ended in a lame-duck season because Marge Schott liked Ray Knight's moral character and, presumably, Schottzie 02 didn't yelp at Knight as much. His success in Baltimore came to an end because Peter Angelos was unwilling to share credit for that success, and Johnson was not thick-skinned enough to be the dutiful organization man.

But the man wins. He doesn't just win under favorable circumstances. He took over a Mets team that had finished at the bottom of the division for the previous seven seasons, and won 90 games his first year. The Reds went 73-89 in 1993; they would go 66-48 and 85-59 in his two years there. The Orioles, after five frustrating seasons with top-tier talent but

no playoff appearances, made the postseason both years under Johnson, losing in the ALCS twice.

That the Tigers decided not to hire Johnson despite his willingness to work can be traced to two factors: a possible personality conflict between Johnson and GM Randy Smith, a man also confident in his own talents, and an organizational decision that Parrish was better suited for the job because he was a superior teacher. The Tigers, building as they were with young talent, felt they needed a manager who would do things like "get to the ballpark before any of his players" to "nurture" that talent.

Yet that logic flies squarely in the face of Johnson's track record. When he took over the Mets in 1984, they were in the midst of a youth movement far more dramatic than the one the Tigers are undergoing. It was Johnson who broke in Dwight Gooden, not two years out of high school, and "nurtured" him into a Rookie of the Year. He was also instrumental in the development of Ron Darling, Sid Fernandez, Lenny Dykstra, Kevin Mitchell, and a half-dozen other players who contributed to the 1986 championship. But more fundamental than overlooking Johnson's résumé is a mistaken assumption about the manager's function in guiding his team.

Success as a manager is not steeped in taking raw talent and molding it into star players—that's what scouts and the farm system are for. If the horses haven't learned to run by the time they hit the track, the manager is scarcely in position to help. Johnson's success—indeed, the success of almost every great manager—comes from picking the right horses and placing them in roles that maximize their success and their contribution. Larry Parrish can spend the entire winter trying to teach Kimera Bartee to hit, and Davey Johnson can spend ten minutes on the phone optioning Bartee to Triple-A and finding out what Pat Lennon is up to, and Johnson's solution will, nine times out of 10, be more successful.

Look at what happened after Johnson took over the Reds, like the Tigers a team with financial constraints and with even less immediate help from the farm system. When Johnson made the postseason with the Reds in 1995, only four players—Hal Morris, Barry Larkin, Reggie Sanders, and John Smiley—had carried over from the previous administration. With almost no help from the minor leagues, Johnson put together the NL Central champions with players acquired on the cheap. Benito Santiago, who almost couldn't find work after the strike, platooned with Ed Taubensee behind the plate. At second base was Bret Boone, acquired along with Erik Hanson from Seattle, and in left field Ron Gant was signed after missing all of 1994 with a gruesome leg injury. The entire bullpen had been rebuilt, with Jeff Brantley, shrewdly acquired from the Giants, closing behind castoffs like Mike Jackson and Chuck McElroy. Hector Carrasco, who jumped all the way from A-ball to the major leagues the previous year, was a part of that pen. And the rotation, which lost Jose Rijo but gained mid-season acquisitions Dave Burba, David Wells, and Mark Portugal, was captained by Pete Schourek, who blossomed into an 18-game winner just a year after the Mets had let him go.

The closer you look at the Reds' surprising success under Johnson, the clearer it is that Johnson's work was made easier by having a GM in Dave Bowden who had the creativity and speculative bent to get players when their stock was low. Gant, Santiago, Brantley, and Schourek were all high-odds, low-cost gambles that Bowden has always delighted into making. It was Johnson who fit the jigsaw together; Bowden's wagers have crapped out more often than not since Johnson left. But the two worked in a symbiosis that carried a losing team with little depth and arguably the worst farm system in baseball to at least one great year.

And that chemistry may never have materialized between Johnson and Smith, not out of an inability to work together, but because Smith has yet to show the genius he was lauded for in San Diego. He deserves credit for bringing the Tigers' minor league system out of the pit it had dwelt in for 15 years. He has ruthlessly tried to acquire every available arm in the desperate hope that one or two would pan out. But he has yet to make trades with anyone but the Padres and Astros, and he has yet to show talent evaluation at the major league level, running off to sign stopgaps like Bip Roberts and Luis Gonzalez at every opportunity. The shaft that Buddy Bell got for 1998 was a clear sign that Smith expected better, meaning he thought the talent was there to do so. Larry Parrish is ostensibly on board to teach that talent to win; but you can't win if you don't have the horses, and their inability to see that dooms the Tigers to more years of running in place.

HITTERS (Averages: BA .260/ OBA .330/ SA .420, EQA .260)

Richard Almanzar   2B   Bats R   Age 23

YEAR	TEAM	LGE	AB	H	DB	TP	HR	BB	R	RBI	SB	CS	OUT	BA	OBA	SA	EQA	EQR	DEFENSE
1996	Lakeland	Fla	471	132	19	0	2	42	63	37	29	12	351	.280	.339	.333	.244	52	121-2B 111
1997	Jacksnvl	Sou	384	80	14	1	4	30	30	21	14	4	308	.208	.266	.281	.192	25	103-2B 96
1998	Toledo	Int	304	58	12	1	1	25	18	12	8	5	251	.191	.252	.247	.166	14	92-2B 102
1999	*Detroit*	*AL*	*347*	*80*	*8*	*0*	*5*	*27*	*30*	*24*	*13*	*6*	*273*	*.231*	*.286*	*.297*	*.202*	*25*	

A one-time hot prospect because of his speed and defense at second base, but epitomizes the precarious philosophy of developing athletes. The Tigers tried pushing him up the system quickly and he hasn't responded well. He's only 23, but his stolen bases have dropped from 53 to 20 to 11. Do that when speed is your calling card and you might as well turn off the cell phone.

Gabe Alvarez   3B   Bats R   Age 25

YEAR	TEAM	LGE	AB	H	DB	TP	HR	BB	R	RBI	SB	CS	OUT	BA	OBA	SA	EQA	EQR	DEFENSE
1996	Memphis	Sou	369	84	15	1	8	53	40	36	2	2	287	.228	.325	.339	.235	39	93-3B 80
1997	Mobile	Sou	419	107	16	1	11	40	43	46	1	1	313	.255	.320	.377	.243	45	108-3B 91
1998	Toledo	Int	247	64	10	1	16	26	30	41	2	1	184	.259	.330	.502	.279	38	68-3B 106
1998	Detroit	AL	196	44	7	0	6	19	16	19	1	3	155	.224	.293	.352	.220	18	51-3B 92
1999	*Detroit*	*AL*	*416*	*105*	*17*	*1*	*16*	*42*	*47*	*54*	*2*	*2*	*313*	*.252*	*.321*	*.413*	*.250*	*49*	

Alvarez has legitimate power and I expect he would adjust to major league pitching in time. But his defense at third base is beyond awful; he had an .873 fielding percentage last year, with a double-play-to-error ratio of 6 to 19. The typical ratio for third basemen is about 3 to 2. He also struck out 65 times in 58 games, and at his age it's doubtful he'll ever have the bat for first base or left field. I just don't see him hitting and fielding well enough to ever be an effective regular, and the Palmer signing seems to mean the Tigers agree.

Paul Bako   C   Bats L   Age 27

YEAR	TEAM	LGE	AB	H	DB	TP	HR	BB	R	RBI	SB	CS	OUT	BA	OBA	SA	EQA	EQR	DEFENSE
1996	Chattang	Sou	361	93	12	0	8	37	37	38	1	0	268	.258	.327	.357	.241	38	
1997	Indianap	AA	323	71	10	1	6	30	23	25	0	4	256	.220	.286	.313	.203	24	
1998	Detroit	AL	300	79	11	1	3	24	28	27	1	1	222	.263	.318	.337	.229	28	86-C 101
1999	*Detroit*	*AL*	*308*	*78*	*9*	*1*	*6*	*25*	*27*	*31*	*0*	*1*	*231*	*.253*	*.309*	*.347*	*.225*	*28*	

(Paul Bako *continued*)

He's been touted as one of the bright spots of the season, but he's no long-term answer. His dexterity behind the plate doesn't compensate for a weak bat, and he's already 27. If he draws the walks he did in 1994–95 he could stick in a platoon role. Left-handed hitters are valuable behind the plate; Rob Fick, also a left-handed hitter, has grabbed onto his collar and is ready to pull.

Kimera Bartee   OF   Bats B   Age 26

YEAR	TEAM	LGE	AB	H	DB	TP	HR	BB	R	RBI	SB	CS	OUT	BA	OBA	SA	EQA	EQR	DEFENSE
1996	Detroit	AL	213	52	5	1	1	16	24	12	21	12	173	.244	.297	.291	.212	18	90-OF 100
1997	Toledo	Int	505	107	11	6	3	45	46	27	26	8	406	.212	.276	.275	.198	36	135-OF 111
1998	Toledo	Int	213	44	5	0	2	13	11	10	4	2	171	.207	.252	.258	.168	10	46-OF 110
1998	Detroit	AL	97	18	5	1	3	6	9	6	8	5	84	.186	.233	.351	.199	7	
1999	*Detroit*	*AL*	*315*	*66*	*7*	*2*	*4*	*26*	*26*	*18*	*15*	*7*	*256*	*.210*	*.270*	*.283*	*.190*	*20*	

The epitome of Randy Smith's get-the-athletes philosophy, with predictable results. Bartee needed everything to break right for him to develop as a hitter, and getting jerked around by the Rule 5 draft kept him from the opportunity to play every day against a level of competition he might have learned to hit against. A useless major league player, but the Tigers haven't formally given up.

Trey Beamon   OF   Bats L   Age 25

YEAR	TEAM	LGE	AB	H	DB	TP	HR	BB	R	RBI	SB	CS	OUT	BA	OBA	SA	EQA	EQR	DEFENSE
1996	Calgary	PCL	368	92	10	2	5	49	47	33	12	2	278	.250	.338	.329	.244	41	94-OF 87
1997	LasVegas	PCL	310	81	13	2	4	41	42	30	11	5	234	.261	.348	.355	.253	37	73-OF 91
1997	San Dieg	NL	65	18	3	0	0	3	5	5	1	2	49	.277	.309	.323	.213	5	13-OF 84
1998	Toledo	Int	206	44	4	0	3	24	21	13	11	2	164	.214	.296	.277	.212	17	43-OF 95
1998	Detroit	AL	41	11	3	0	0	5	6	3	1	0	30	.268	.348	.341	.252	5	
1999	*Detroit*	*AL*	*312*	*80*	*8*	*0*	*6*	*38*	*41*	*30*	*13*	*4*	*236*	*.256*	*.337*	*.340*	*.243*	*34*	

A speedy, singles-hitting ex-Padre outfielder, so how could Randy Smith resist? He's always hit for good averages, but he has to hit .320 to help a team, and he's not even valuable as a defensive replacement.

Geronimo Berroa   OF/DH   Bats R   Age 34

YEAR	TEAM	LGE	AB	H	DB	TP	HR	BB	R	RBI	SB	CS	OUT	BA	OBA	SA	EQA	EQR	DEFENSE
1996	Oakland	AL	572	159	28	1	35	43	66	96	0	3	416	.278	.328	.514	.280	86	44-OF 97
1997	Oakland	AL	255	78	8	0	17	36	39	50	3	2	179	.306	.392	.537	.312	49	32-OF 99
1997	Baltimor	AL	296	77	11	0	11	40	36	39	1	2	221	.260	.348	.409	.264	39	29-OF 106
1998	Clevelnd	AL	64	12	2	1	0	7	4	3	1	0	52	.188	.268	.250	.180	4	
1998	Detroit	AL	124	29	3	1	1	17	12	10	0	1	96	.234	.326	.298	.222	11	
1999	*Toronto*	*AL*	*312*	*78*	*11*	*1*	*13*	*37*	*36*	*43*	*1*	*1*	*235*	*.250*	*.330*	*.417*	*.258*	*40*	

I know they didn't give up much to get him, but what exactly did he do to help the Tigers? Berroa has no defensive value, and old designated hitters don't usually make the priority list for rebuilding teams. He had old player's skills when he was 25; now that he's 34 and coming off a bad year, he may be finished. After not getting a major league job until he was 29, I imagine Berroa won't be convinced until 30 organizations tell him so. The Blue Jays are next in line; he'll be in Dunedin trying to get a job.

Javier Cardona   C   Bats R   Age 23

YEAR	TEAM	LGE	AB	H	DB	TP	HR	BB	R	RBI	SB	CS	OUT	BA	OBA	SA	EQA	EQR	DEFENSE
1996	Fayettvl	SAL	360	93	10	0	5	21	27	31	1	2	269	.258	.299	.328	.215	29	
1997	Lakeland	Fla	283	72	7	0	7	23	25	29	1	1	212	.254	.310	.353	.231	27	
1998	Jacksnvl	Sou	162	51	11	1	4	10	20	24	0	0	111	.315	.355	.469	.282	23	37-C 100
1998	Toledo	Int	161	28	4	0	4	8	5	7	0	0	133	.174	.213	.273	.146	5	47-C 100
1999	*Detroit*	*AL*	*322*	*81*	*10*	*0*	*8*	*19*	*26*	*32*	*0*	*1*	*242*	*.252*	*.293*	*.357*	*.219*	*27*	

A young catcher whose hot start was an early factor in Jacksonville's success. He had a devil of a time adjusting to Triple-A itching, hitting .191 with a terrible strikeout-to-walk ratio. He doesn't figure in the Tigers' short-term plans, which may be a blessing: he needs a year or two at Triple-A to figure things out. It wouldn't surprise me if he has a future.

Raul Casanova   C   Bats B   Age 26

YEAR	TEAM	LGE	AB	H	DB	TP	HR	BB	R	RBI	SB	CS	OUT	BA	OBA	SA	EQA	EQR	DEFENSE
1996	Toledo	Int	159	40	7	0	7	19	18	22	0	1	120	.252	.331	.428	.260	21	
1996	Detroit	AL	84	15	0	0	4	6	4	6	0	0	69	.179	.233	.321	.182	5	
1997	Detroit	AL	299	71	10	1	5	27	25	26	1	1	229	.237	.301	.328	.219	26	
1998	Detroit	AL	41	5	2	0	1	6	2	2	0	0	36	.122	.234	.244	.156	2	
1998	Toledo	Int	170	38	5	0	5	18	14	16	0	1	133	.224	.298	.341	.221	15	46-C 97
1999	*Detroit*	*AL*	*249*	*58*	*6*	*0*	*9*	*24*	*22*	*27*	*0*	*1*	*192*	*.233*	*.300*	*.365*	*.226*	*23*	

He's got one full season on his résumé that suggests he can hit, and that was in A-ball four years ago. Fair defense, and one of the few switch-hitting catchers around, but the Tigers have lost patience with him. He isn't out of chances yet, but they're punching "Hell's Bells" into the sound system as we speak.

Frank Catalanotto   IF   Bats L   Age 25

YEAR	TEAM	LGE	AB	H	DB	TP	HR	BB	R	RBI	SB	CS	OUT	BA	OBA	SA	EQA	EQR	DEFENSE	
1996	Jacksnvl	Sou	496	137	24	3	16	61	69	66	11	9	368	.276	.355	.433	.272	71	133-2B 96	
1997	Toledo	Int	503	150	27	2	16	41	65	70	11	9	362	.298	.351	.455	.275	72	96-2B 104	36-3B 92
1998	Toledo	Int	104	32	4	2	4	12	15	18	0	0	72	.308	.379	.500	.300	18		
1998	Detroit	AL	209	57	13	2	6	13	24	26	3	2	154	.273	.315	.440	.257	26		
1999	*Detroit*	*AL*	*394*	*116*	*24*	*2*	*12*	*36*	*56*	*57*	*7*	*5*	*283*	*.294*	*.353*	*.457*	*.275*	*56*		

The *Baseball Prospectus* poster boy showed a lot of promise last season, despite having no defined role. Re-signing of Damion Easley closed off his natural position, and the Tigers had made up their minds to go with Joe Randa at third base. So Catalanotto pinch-hit, then proved himself once again in Triple-A until August, when the Tigers' desperation forced him to first base. He's only a fair hitter for first base, and his defensive skills are wasted there. The Palmer acquisition screws him. It almost makes too much sense for the Tigers to trade him for more pitching, but we'll continue to hope that he gets a chance to shine somewhere.

Tony Clark   1B   Bats B   Age 27

YEAR	TEAM	LGE	AB	H	DB	TP	HR	BB	R	RBI	SB	CS	OUT	BA	OBA	SA	EQA	EQR	DEFENSE
1996	Toledo	Int	192	53	4	1	11	29	27	33	1	1	140	.276	.371	.479	.291	32	44-1B 94
1996	Detroit	AL	370	89	11	0	27	27	36	57	0	1	282	.241	.292	.489	.260	48	84-1B 97
1997	Detroit	AL	569	155	28	3	32	93	86	100	1	3	417	.272	.375	.501	.297	100	154-1B 91
1998	Detroit	AL	590	168	28	0	36	66	80	103	3	3	425	.285	.357	.515	.293	99	142-1B 94
1999	*Detroit*	*AL*	*600*	*164*	*25*	*1*	*39*	*75*	*85*	*111*	*2*	*2*	*438*	*.273*	*.354*	*.513*	*.290*	*99*	

He's got about three full seasons in the books and remains a bit of a mystery. Clark has great power from both sides of the plate, but he's prone to huge slumps and his terrible April (.232, no power) was a big factor in the Tigers' 6-18 start. He's an extremely agile, if error-prone, first baseman. Clark is slightly above-average for his position; if he can take his game one step further, he'll be a star. But he's not capable of being the sole anchor of a championship lineup.

Deivi Cruz   SS   Bats R   Age 24

YEAR	TEAM	LGE	AB	H	DB	TP	HR	BB	R	RBI	SB	CS	OUT	BA	OBA	SA	EQA	EQR	DEFENSE
1996	Burlingt	Mid	514	125	12	1	8	23	34	39	6	3	392	.243	.276	.317	.202	36	120-SS 114
1997	Detroit	AL	430	102	14	1	5	16	24	29	3	7	335	.237	.265	.309	.188	26	134-SS 102
1998	Detroit	AL	447	113	21	3	5	15	33	36	2	4	338	.253	.277	.347	.209	34	133-SS 106
1999	*Detroit*	*AL*	*465*	*119*	*21*	*1*	*7*	*17*	*35*	*41*	*3*	*4*	*350*	*.256*	*.282*	*.351*	*.210*	*36*	

The Tigers would love to get some much-needed offense from shortstop, and they could technically play Easley at shortstop and Catalanotto at second. But they can't afford to dispense with Cruz's glove as they break in a young pitching staff. He was a huge factor in Brian Moehler's success last year, and the Tigers feel his value to guys like Greisinger and Powell is immeasurable. There isn't another shortstop with any promise in the system, and his offense, bad as it is, is considerably better than that of Rey Ordonez, who couldn't slug .355 in batting practice.

Damion Easley   2B   Bats R   Age 29

YEAR	TEAM	LGE	AB	H	DB	TP	HR	BB	R	RBI	SB	CS	OUT	BA	OBA	SA	EQA	EQR	DEFENSE	
1996	Detroit	AL	65	22	0	0	2	4	9	9	3	1	44	.338	.377	.431	.285	10		
1997	Detroit	AL	518	135	37	3	22	68	84	70	28	13	396	.261	.346	.471	.280	82	130-2B 101	9-SS 80
1998	Detroit	AL	584	155	35	2	27	42	71	81	14	5	434	.265	.315	.471	.267	80	135-2B 104	
1999	*Detroit*	*AL*	*497*	*132*	*31*	*2*	*24*	*50*	*71*	*75*	*13*	*7*	*372*	*.266*	*.333*	*.481*	*.273*	*73*		

He's not part of the problem, but it's debatable whether he's going to be part of the solution. After two fine seasons, he cannot be written off as a fluke; nevertheless, it's clear that what we're seeing is the best he has to offer. His walks dropped a whole bunch last year, which just aggravates the team-wide problem with getting baserunners. If the Tigers can find some real table-setters to bat at the top of the order, they can drop Easley in the lineup to where he belongs. By the time that happens, Easley will be 32 or 33 and past the point of contributing.

Juan Encarnacion   RF/CF   Age 23

YEAR	TEAM	LGE	AB	H	DB	TP	HR	BB	R	RBI	SB	CS	OUT	BA	OBA	SA	EQA	EQR	DEFENSE
1996	Lakeland	Fla	497	110	14	1	16	22	33	41	7	4	391	.221	.254	.350	.203	36	122-OF 97
1997	Jacksnvl	Sou	484	142	20	2	21	34	63	71	13	3	345	.293	.340	.473	.279	71	110-OF 94
1998	Toledo	Int	352	95	15	2	7	26	45	35	17	3	261	.270	.320	.384	.251	41	88-OF 93
1998	Detroit	AL	161	52	9	4	7	8	23	28	6	4	113	.323	.355	.559	.300	28	38-OF 89
1999	*Detroit*	*AL*	*522*	*151*	*21*	*4*	*20*	*33*	*69*	*75*	*17*	*5*	*376*	*.289*	*.332*	*.460*	*.270*	*71*	

He could be a whopping good player. He dealt with an injury early, which hurt his production at Triple-A, then came up in August and was impressive. Raul Mondesi, the year before his rookie season, had a distinctly unimpressive minor league season; he played that year through a wrist injury, and with an off-season of rest won the Rookie of the Year award. Encarnacion could follow the same path, and like Mondesi he's an excellent right fielder, stretched a bit in center. If the Tigers replace Hunter with him, that's three wins easy, defense be damned.

Robert Fick   C/1B   Bats L   Age 25

YEAR	TEAM	LGE	AB	H	DB	TP	HR	BB	R	RBI	SB	CS	OUT	BA	OBA	SA	EQA	EQR	DEFENSE
1996	Jamestwn	NYP	135	25	1	0	1	8	5	5	1	1	111	.185	.231	.215	.126	3	
1997	W Michgn	Mid	470	130	19	1	11	51	57	56	6	3	343	.277	.347	.391	.260	59	100-1B 84
1998	Jacksnvl	Sou	512	145	28	2	15	50	65	68	5	3	370	.283	.347	.434	.270	70	79-C 88
1998	Detroit	AL	21	7	0	0	3	3	4	6	1	0	14	.333	.417	.762	.372	6	
1999	*Detroit*	*AL*	*458*	*132*	*24*	*1*	*16*	*45*	*62*	*68*	*4*	*2*	*328*	*.288*	*.352*	*.450*	*.274*	*65*	

An excellent prospect, with two caveats: he's too old to develop into a superstar, and his lack of a clearly-defined position gives the Tigers ample opportunity to stunt his career. He has alternated between catcher and first base throughout his minor league career, and last season he started at first base until Cardona was promoted to Triple-A. The 98 doubles he's pounded in the last two years lead organized baseball. I saw him catch in September, and didn't see a problem; he's got a strong arm and good mobility. He hit .312 with power against left-handers at Double-A, so that's not even an issue. His excellent cup of coffee opened some eyes in Detroit, and if he gets the catching job he's a sleeper pick for Rookie of the Year.

Luis Garcia   SS   Bats R   Age 24

YEAR	TEAM	LGE	AB	H	DB	TP	HR	BB	R	RBI	SB	CS	OUT	BA	OBA	SA	EQA	EQR	DEFENSE
1996	Jacksnvl	Sou	521	117	16	2	9	5	26	31	10	7	411	.225	.232	.315	.176	27	130-SS 98
1997	Jacksnvl	Sou	449	102	11	1	4	7	20	23	2	1	348	.227	.239	.283	.165	19	125-SS 89
1998	Toledo	Int	403	96	15	3	3	6	21	25	2	2	309	.238	.249	.313	.183	22	106-SS 94
1999	*Detroit*	*AL*	*426*	*105*	*15*	*1*	*5*	*6*	*25*	*29*	*3*	*2*	*323*	*.246*	*.257*	*.322*	*.187*	*24*	

The worst kind of prospect, because he has just enough ability to get touted as a future shortstop, but with plate discipline that makes Ozzie Guillen look finicky. He has 50 walks in a pro career that has spanned nearly 2100 at-bats. The American League had a shortstop like this about 10 years ago, Angel Salazar, who was just good enough to be the worst shortstop in the league for about three seasons.

Luis Gonzalez   LF   Bats L   Age 31

YEAR	TEAM	LGE	AB	H	DB	TP	HR	BB	R	RBI	SB	CS	OUT	BA	OBA	SA	EQA	EQR	DEFENSE
1996	ChiCubs	NL	481	127	29	4	15	63	66	64	7	6	360	.264	.349	.435	.270	68	122-OF 94
1997	Houston	NL	552	144	31	2	11	74	72	62	8	7	415	.261	.348	.384	.257	70	137-OF 101
1998	Detroit	AL	537	140	32	5	23	59	72	76	11	7	404	.261	.334	.467	.272	78	130-OF 93
1999	*Detroit*	*AL*	*536*	*142*	*30*	*3*	*19*	*71*	*76*	*76*	*7*	*7*	*401*	*.265*	*.351*	*.438*	*.269*	*75*	

He had one of his best seasons and set a career high in homers. At his best Gonzalez is a valuable player when you're getting a lot of offense from other positions. That's the rub: with the exception of second base, the Tigers got next to nothing up the middle, and their corner players, while not liabilities, were not able to compensate. If Higginson and Tony Clark aren't making up for having three zeroes in the lineup, what can you say about Gonzalez? His bat is replaceable, providing just enough offense to move from team to team and stay in a lineup. He's going to end up with a team that can't offer him 500 at-bats, and when that happens his career will deteriorate rapidly.

Bob Higginson   RF   Bats L   Age 28

YEAR	TEAM	LGE	AB	H	DB	TP	HR	BB	R	RBI	SB	CS	OUT	BA	OBA	SA	EQA	EQR	DEFENSE
1996	Detroit	AL	427	134	27	0	27	62	74	85	6	4	297	.314	.401	.567	.322	87	112-OF 92
1997	Detroit	AL	535	158	29	5	27	71	86	92	12	7	384	.295	.378	.520	.302	97	134-OF 99
1998	Detroit	AL	600	166	34	4	25	66	79	91	3	3	437	.277	.348	.472	.279	90	153-OF 98
1999	*Detroit*	*AL*	*556*	*162*	*34*	*2*	*28*	*72*	*89*	*99*	*6*	*5*	*399*	*.291*	*.373*	*.511*	*.296*	*95*	

If he could play center field, or if the Tigers could find hitters capable sustaining a nine-man offense, he would make a terrific second-line star. He's not any less a player than Paul O'Neill, but whereas O'Neill plays with Bernie Williams, Derek Jeter, Jorge Posada, Chuck Knoblauch, and Scott Brosius, Higginson gets to share clubhouse space with Brian Hunter and Joe Randa. He's a good right fielder whose 18 assists ranked second in the league. The Tigers have about a three-year window to surround him with a complete offense.

Brian Hunter   CF   Bats R   Age 28

YEAR	TEAM	LGE	AB	H	DB	TP	HR	BB	R	RBI	SB	CS	OUT	BA	OBA	SA	EQA	EQR	DEFENSE
1996	Houston	NL	527	149	28	1	6	21	64	46	31	10	388	.283	.310	.374	.242	56	118-OF 107
1997	Detroit	AL	647	172	29	7	4	67	110	48	75	19	494	.266	.335	.351	.256	82	160-OF 107
1998	Detroit	AL	585	145	27	3	4	39	66	40	38	12	452	.248	.295	.325	.223	53	
1999	*Detroit*	*AL*	*611*	*160*	*32*	*4*	*6*	*43*	*82*	*51*	*43*	*13*	*464*	*.262*	*.310*	*.357*	*.238*	*64*	

Despite decades of evidence that getting on base is the most valuable offensive skill—the essential skill for a leadoff man—here are still those who think that stolen bases, speed and "disrupting the pitcher's concentration" make a speedster like Hunter an effective leadoff hitter. But the whole point of leading off—hell, the point of the game—is to score runs to win, and Hunter scored 67 of them. Gary DiSarcina, batting at the bottom of the Angels' lineup, scored 73.

Gabe Kapler   OF   Bats R   Age 23

YEAR	TEAM	LGE	AB	H	DB	TP	HR	BB	R	RBI	SB	CS	OUT	BA	OBA	SA	EQA	EQR	DEFENSE
1996	Fayettvl	SAL	548	159	21	0	23	48	68	80	7	3	392	.290	.347	.454	.276	78	127-OF 90
1997	Lakeland	Fla	519	139	24	2	18	47	59	67	4	3	383	.268	.329	.426	.259	66	136-OF 94
1998	Jacksnvl	Sou	543	168	34	3	26	49	77	95	4	3	378	.309	.367	.527	.300	93	137-OF 102
1999	*Detroit*	*AL*	*547*	*160*	*27*	*2*	*22*	*44*	*71*	*85*	*5*	*2*	*389*	*.293*	*.345*	*.470*	*.276*	*78*	

Kapler combined with Fick to give Jacksonville the best duo in minor league baseball. No other minor league team had a pair of teammates score or drive in 100 runs each, and Kapler and Fick did both for the Suns. Kapler's story is well-known by now. A 58th-round draft pick, a fitness maniac, and now the *Baseball Weekly* Minor League Player of the Year. He's a fine prospect, but that's overstated, and proof that some people may still rate RBIs over everything else; his 146 led the minor leagues by a comfortable margin. He's ready, and should force Gonzalez off the team.

Jose Macias   2B   Bats B   Age 25

YEAR	TEAM	LGE	AB	H	DB	TP	HR	BB	R	RBI	SB	CS	OUT	BA	OBA	SA	EQA	EQR	DEFENSE	
1996	Delmarva	SAL	385	81	8	2	1	40	31	19	14	7	311	.210	.285	.249	.189	24	64-OF 93	24-2B 101
1997	Lakeland	Fla	426	90	10	1	2	42	28	22	4	6	342	.211	.282	.254	.182	24	118-2B 99	
1998	Jacksnvl	Sou	508	134	18	5	10	35	47	54	4	6	380	.264	.311	.378	.236	52	126-2B 97	
1999	Detroit	AL	487	122	17	2	8	38	46	45	7	6	371	.251	.305	.343	.221	43		

Macias developed some power last season, and he's pretty well-rounded offensively. If he were 22 I'd like his chances of developing, but he's 24 and still not major-league caliber. Easley is going to be forced off of second base someday, but methinks Macias is not the man destined to do so.

Joe Randa   3B   Bats R   Age 29

YEAR	TEAM	LGE	AB	H	DB	TP	HR	BB	R	RBI	SB	CS	OUT	BA	OBA	SA	EQA	EQR	DEFENSE
1996	KansasCy	AL	330	97	23	1	6	24	46	38	14	5	238	.294	.342	.424	.268	44	79-3B 86
1997	Pittsbrg	NL	440	130	26	8	8	44	60	60	3	2	312	.295	.360	.445	.278	64	115-3B 100
1998	Detroit	AL	452	112	19	2	9	43	46	44	7	7	347	.248	.313	.358	.233	45	108-3B 105
1999	KansasCy	AL	415	114	22	2	8	37	51	48	6	4	305	.275	.334	.395	.250	48	

The Tigers gambled that he would be an adequate replacement for Fryman, sacrificing power but hitting for a better average. They lost. Tweeners like Randa, who can hit for average but have little power and don't get on base enough, are constantly vulnerable to the variability of batting average. Randa is sure-handed, committing only seven errors last season, but moves like molasses in February. Traded twice in one December week, he's back in Kansas City and will be the starting third baseman.

Billy Ripken   IF   Bats R   Age 34

YEAR	TEAM	LGE	AB	H	DB	TP	HR	BB	R	RBI	SB	CS	OUT	BA	OBA	SA	EQA	EQR	DEFENSE	
1996	Baltimor	AL	133	29	5	0	3	9	9	10	0	0	104	.218	.268	.323	.200	9	17-3B 110	17-2B 108
1997	Texas	AL	200	54	9	1	3	9	16	20	0	1	147	.270	.301	.370	.229	18	22-SS 102	20-2B 121
1998	Detroi	AL	73	19	3	0	0	5	7	5	3	2	56	.260	.308	.301	.214	6		
1999	Detroit	AL	117	29	3	0	3	6	9	11	1	1	89	.248	.285	.350	.213	9		

He is what he's always been: a versatile glove man who needs to be kept as far away from the plate as possible. He's managed to keep his skill base even as his brother has melted away from superstar to borderline regular, a dubious distinction. His ability to stay in the majors has less to do with his talent than with some teams' desperation for a utilityman.

Joe Siddall   C   Bats R   Age 31

YEAR	TEAM	LGE	AB	H	DB	TP	HR	BB	R	RBI	SB	CS	OUT	BA	OBA	SA	EQA	EQR	DEFENSE
1996	Charlott	Int	184	40	6	1	2	10	11	11	1	1	145	.217	.258	.293	.183	10	
1997	Ottawa	Int	164	38	7	1	1	17	15	12	1	1	127	.232	.304	.305	.213	13	
1998	Toledo	Int	128	26	2	0	3	9	7	8	1	1	103	.203	.255	.289	.181	7	29-C 92
1998	Detroit	AL	64	11	3	0	1	7	4	3	0	0	53	.172	.254	.266	.173	3	20-C 109
1999	Detroit	AL	182	40	4	0	4	15	13	14	1	1	143	.220	.279	.308	.197	12	

Our obligatory third-string-catcher-who-needs-a-lucky-break-reference. There are dozens of guys like him along the major league fringe; if you want to know which ones will get a chance this year, feel free to call the Psychic Frauds' Network at 1-888-RIPUOFF.

Carlos Villalobos   3B   Bats R   Age 25

YEAR	TEAM	LGE	AB	H	DB	TP	HR	BB	R	RBI	SB	CS	OUT	BA	OBA	SA	EQA	EQR	DEFENSE
1996	Lancastr	Cal	401	82	12	2	3	35	25	22	4	2	321	.204	.268	.267	.182	23	100-3B 84
1997	Lakeland	Fla	147	29	2	0	1	9	5	5	0	0	118	.197	.244	.231	.145	5	27-3B 87
1997	Lancastr	Cal	289	77	9	1	7	45	38	35	2	3	215	.266	.365	.377	.263	38	71-3B 85
1998	Jacksnvl	Sou	493	140	19	1	14	37	55	62	5	0	353	.284	.334	.412	.260	61	125-3B 107
1999	Detroit	AL	436	114	13	1	12	38	45	51	3	1	323	.261	.321	.378	.241	46	

Villalobos showed an impressive skill set last year, but he's too old to be classified as a top prospect. He has a track record of success and he is a former Mariner prospect, which is probably evidence that he does have ability. The commitment to Palmer means he'll have to move to another position or city. Or profession.

Jason Wood   IF   Bats R   Age 29

YEAR	TEAM	LGE	AB	H	DB	TP	HR	BB	R	RBI	SB	CS	OUT	BA	OBA	SA	EQA	EQR	DEFENSE	
1996	Huntsvil	Sou	491	102	9	0	13	51	34	39	1	3	392	.208	.282	.305	.202	36	81-3B 103	25-SS 98
1997	Edmonton	PCL	479	114	16	2	12	33	37	45	1	3	368	.238	.287	.355	.219	41	115-3B 101	
1998	Edmonton	PCL	301	70	8	0	12	31	28	34	1	1	232	.233	.304	.379	.236	31	41-3B 99	20-2B 105
1998	Toledo	Int	167	40	4	0	5	13	13	17	0	0	127	.240	.294	.353	.224	15	27-3B 88	
1998	Detroit	AL	22	7	2	0	1	4	4	4	0	1	16	.318	.423	.545	.313	4		
1999	*Detroit*	*AL*	*481*	*118*	*17*	*1*	*18*	*47*	*50*	*59*	*1*	*2*	*365*	*.245*	*.312*	*.397*	*.242*	*52*		

Acquired from the Athletics for Bip Roberts. Given that he's an ambulatory biped and not under indictment, it was a good trade. Wood is 29, but he has marginal power and can play all over the infield in a pinch. Good in a brief callup, imperative at his age, and could be the 25th man with a hot spring training.

PITCHERS (Averages: 4.00 ERA, 9.00 H/9, 1.00 HR/9, 3.00 BB/9, 6.00 K/9, 1.00 KWH)

Matt Anderson   Throws R   Age 22

YEAR	TEAM	LGE	IP	H	ER	HR	BB	K	ERA	W	L	H/9	HR/9	BB/9	K/9	KWH	PERA
1998	Lakeland	Fla	25.3	22	4	0	9	25	1.42	3	0	7.82	0.00	3.20	8.88	2.37	2.49
1998	Jacksnvl	Sou	14.0	10	2	1	4	9	1.29	2	0	6.43	0.64	2.57	5.79	1.52	1.93
1998	Detroit	AL	45.7	39	13	3	28	43	2.56	4	1	7.69	0.59	5.52	8.47	1.27	3.35

He's only a year out of college, yet he has as much chance as anyone of being the premier closer of the next decade. Anderson has supposedly hit 103 on the radar gun, and I'm not sure even Troy Percival throws harder. His control is still 18 months away. The Tigers should stop delaying the inevitable and make him the closer in April. The last pitcher to step off campus and into a closer's role so quickly was Gregg Olson. Anderson doesn't throw the knee-bending, elbow-rending curveball, so unless he throws 110 innings this year his long-term prospects are bright.

Kym Ashworth   Throws L   Age 22

YEAR	TEAM	LGE	IP	H	ER	HR	BB	K	ERA	W	L	H/9	HR/9	BB/9	K/9	KWH	PERA
1995	Vero Bch	Fla	116.0	152	69	14	71	77	5.35	5	8	11.79	1.09	5.51	5.97	0.41	5.66
1997	San Bern	Cal	29.7	42	26	4	23	18	7.89	1	2	12.74	1.21	6.98	5.46	0.25	6.37
1998	Lakeland	Fla	154.3	207	102	17	67	84	5.95	5	12	12.07	0.99	3.91	4.90	0.38	5.54

A crafty Australian southpaw who was a Dodger stud until he hurt his arm. Still young, still getting a feel for the mound, still several years away if at all. Needs to make a big jump this year; staying healthy may be taxing enough for him.

Doug Bochtler   Throws R   Age 28

YEAR	TEAM	LGE	IP	H	ER	HR	BB	K	ERA	W	L	H/9	HR/9	BB/9	K/9	KWH	PERA
1996	San Dieg	NL	65.3	52	25	7	37	61	3.44	4	3	7.16	0.96	5.10	8.40	1.45	3.17
1997	San Dieg	NL	61.0	56	32	3	46	41	4.72	3	4	8.26	0.44	6.79	6.05	0.49	3.69
1998	Detroit	AL	70.0	74	40	16	38	44	5.14	3	5	9.51	2.06	4.89	5.66	0.52	5.14

This is the ugly side of Randy Smith's penchant for arms. Bochtler had no control, and gave up a home run every four innings and a triple every 11; both ratios were the worst in baseball (min: 40 IP). Never overestimate a no-movement fastball.

David Borkowski   Throws R   Age 22

Year	Team	Lge	IP	H	ER	HR	BB	K	ERA	W	L	H/9	HR/9	BB/9	K/9	KWH	PERA
1996	Fayettvl	SAL	162.7	231	115	11	62	71	6.36	5	13	12.78	0.61	3.43	3.93	0.26	5.48
1997	W Michgn	Mid	148.7	200	101	19	32	69	6.11	5	12	12.11	1.15	1.94	4.18	0.56	5.45
1998	Jacksnvl	Sou	162.7	248	105	27	45	76	5.81	6	12	13.72	1.49	2.49	4.20	0.39	6.58

He's advanced quickly at a young age. Borkowski is a finesse pitcher and still adjusting to Double-A. The Tigers have high hopes for him, but he's going to need another year or two before taking on any kind of major league role. He'll have at least one successful season; his ceiling is low.

Doug Brocail Throws R Age 32

YEAR	TEAM	LGE	IP	H	ER	HR	BB	K	ERA	W	L	H/9	HR/9	BB/9	K/9	KWH	PERA
1996	Houston	NL	53.7	61	28	8	21	30	4.70	3	3	10.23	1.34	3.52	5.03	0.53	4.86
1997	Detroit	AL	79.7	76	27	9	32	58	3.05	6	3	8.59	1.02	3.62	6.55	1.04	3.73
1998	Detroit	AL	64.0	47	19	2	16	53	2.67	5	2	6.61	0.28	2.25	7.45	2.80	1.83

This is the dazzling side of Randy Smith's penchant for arms. Unlike Bochtler, who's more of a flyball pitcher, Brocail has generally been able to keep the ball down. Last season, for the first time, he kept ball in the park. He's finding that early-thirties groove that a lot of groundball pitchers discover, with improved control, handling of the running game, and plenty of rally-killing double plays. In short, he's the perfect middle reliever, and may have more good years ahead.

Clay Bruner Throws R Age 22

YEAR	TEAM	LGE	IP	H	ER	HR	BB	K	ERA	W	L	H/9	HR/9	BB/9	K/9	KWH	PERA
1996	Fayettvl	SAL	143.7	189	86	10	87	92	5.39	6	10	11.84	0.63	5.45	5.76	0.39	5.32
1997	W Michgn	Mid	151.7	189	69	15	50	90	4.09	8	9	11.22	0.89	2.97	5.34	0.64	4.93
1998	Jacksnvl	Sou	156.7	215	96	17	54	71	5.51	6	11	12.35	0.98	3.10	4.08	0.33	5.57

See Borkowski, David. Their similarities are striking: same age, both went 15-3 with a dominant West Michigan team in 1996, both skipped a level to Double-A and struggled. Bruner had a slightly better year and is a better bet for the future, with nastier stuff and a slightly more advanced mental approach. He needs to start embarrassing hitters again or the gloss will be gone.

William Brunson Throws L Age 29

YEAR	TEAM	LGE	IP	H	ER	HR	BB	K	ERA	W	L	H/9	HR/9	BB/9	K/9	KWH	PERA
1996	SanAnton	Tex	36.7	45	18	2	18	29	4.42	2	2	11.05	0.49	4.42	7.12	0.78	4.66
1996	Albuquer	PCL	54.3	58	27	7	26	38	4.47	3	3	9.61	1.16	4.31	6.29	0.72	4.47
1997	SanAnton	Tex	65.0	89	37	8	15	52	5.12	3	4	12.32	1.11	2.08	7.20	1.52	5.54
1997	Albuquer	PCL	26.3	39	15	3	9	19	5.13	1	2	13.33	1.03	3.08	6.49	0.77	6.15
1998	Albuquer	PCL	120.3	143	62	10	43	75	4.64	6	7	10.70	0.75	3.22	5.61	0.69	4.56

Another arm claimed from the Dodgers, Brunson is almost too old to have a career. "Almost" because he's left-handed, and finally figured out how to pitch in Albuquerque, an impressive feat. He has a habit of putting together great runs for half-seasons at a time.

Frank Castillo Throws R Age 30

YEAR	TEAM	LGE	IP	H	ER	HR	BB	K	ERA	W	L	H/9	HR/9	BB/9	K/9	KWH	PERA
1996	ChiCubs	NL	184.3	226	105	28	44	126	5.13	8	12	11.03	1.37	2.15	6.15	1.20	5.08
1997	ChiCubs	NL	103.3	113	54	9	41	61	4.70	5	6	9.84	0.78	3.57	5.31	0.60	4.18
1997	Colorado	NL	94.3	100	43	16	23	54	4.10	5	5	9.54	1.53	2.19	5.15	0.95	4.39
1998	Detroit	AL	120.3	149	75	16	40	79	5.61	4	9	11.14	1.20	2.99	5.91	0.79	5.16

What is it about pitching in Colorado? The park effects seem to be so strong they actually stretch into the fourth dimension. Castillo is only the most recent pitcher to end up in Denver for a few months and lose so much confidence in his breaking stuff that even a return to thicker air can't revive his career. I've been a big fan of his for years, but there's nothing in his record last year worth defending. It's non-roster invite time, baby.

Francisco Cordero Throws R Age 21

YEAR	TEAM	LGE	IP	H	ER	HR	BB	K	ERA	W	L	H/9	HR/9	BB/9	K/9	KWH	PERA
1997	W Michgn	Mid	50.7	51	17	3	15	44	3.02	4	2	9.06	0.53	2.66	7.82	1.90	3.55
1998	Jacksnvl	Sou	15.3	24	12	1	7	14	7.04	0	2	14.09	0.59	4.11	8.22	0.87	5.87

He was major-league closer material a year ago, then kept hitting the disabled list with elbow problems and was shelved for the season with a stress fracture in his shoulder. Still very young and quite capable of a comeback this year, but minor league closersespecially in the low minorsare historically bad bets. And his arm has to heal in two places first.

Dean Crow   Throws R   Age 26

YEAR	TEAM	LGE	IP	H	ER	HR	BB	K	ERA	W	L	H/9	HR/9	BB/9	K/9	KWH	PERA
1996	PortCity	Sou	63.0	82	41	5	18	32	5.86	2	5	11.71	0.71	2.57	4.57	0.52	5.00
1997	Tacoma	PCL	40.3	58	22	3	17	29	4.91	2	2	12.94	0.67	3.79	6.47	0.64	5.58
1998	Toledo	Int	23.3	24	8	1	3	9	3.09	2	1	9.26	0.39	1.16	3.47	0.84	3.09
1998	Detroit	AL	47.0	55	18	5	15	18	3.45	3	2	10.53	0.96	2.87	3.45	0.29	4.60

Former minor league closer in the Mariner systemdamning words, thosewho made considerable strides last season after he was sent to Detroit. Crow relies on a good sinking fastball, and is going to need a second pitch if he's thinking of staying in the majors. Trying to be Doug Brocail; with a strikeout rate that low, I'm skeptical.

Matt Drews   Throws R   Age 24

YEAR	TEAM	LGE	IP	H	ER	HR	BB	K	ERA	W	L	H/9	HR/9	BB/9	K/9	KWH	PERA
1996	Norwich	Eas	45.3	47	26	5	33	29	5.16	2	3	9.33	0.99	6.55	5.76	0.41	4.57
1996	Columbus	Int	20.7	21	24	4	28	6	10.45	0	2	9.15	1.74	12.19	2.61	0.05	5.66
1996	Jacksnvl	Sou	30.7	31	17	4	17	31	4.99	1	2	9.10	1.17	4.99	9.10	1.37	4.40
1997	Jacksnvl	Sou	133.7	193	110	23	47	67	7.41	3	12	13.00	1.55	3.16	4.51	0.37	6.40
1998	Toledo	Int	148.0	191	110	25	71	73	6.69	4	12	11.61	1.52	4.32	4.44	0.29	5.78

Enormous (6'8") right-hander, once a Yankees phenom, whose mechanics and confidence are so messed up he could have Jack Llewellyn, Leo Mazzone, and Billy Graham on the mound next to him and it wouldn't help. Taken by the Diamondbacks in the Expansion Draft, but the Tigers wanted him back in the Fryman deal, so clearly they thought he could turn it around. Wrong answer.

Mike Drumright   Throws R   Age 25

YEAR	TEAM	LGE	IP	H	ER	HR	BB	K	ERA	W	L	H/9	HR/9	BB/9	K/9	KWH	PERA
1996	Jacksnvl	Sou	97.7	95	50	13	44	84	4.61	5	6	8.75	1.20	4.05	7.74	1.27	3.96
1997	Jacksnvl	Sou	26.7	22	8	0	12	18	2.70	2	1	7.43	0.00	4.05	6.08	0.92	2.36
1997	Toledo	Int	130.3	155	75	23	81	94	5.18	5	9	10.70	1.59	5.59	6.49	0.53	5.52
1998	Toledo	Int	151.7	210	124	21	88	76	7.36	4	13	12.46	1.25	5.22	4.51	0.23	6.11

The similarities to Drews are eerie, and to a Tigers fan, depressing. Another big guy, former first-rounder, great sinking fastball and overhand curve, but he's regressed badly each of the last two years. He had a nagging shoulder problem in 1997, and I think he's trying to throw through an injury. His velocity was supposedly fine last year, but his command disappeared. Injury or no, if you look at the careers of every star pitcher in the major leagues, you'll find probably none ever had a season at any level that was remotely as awful as Drews and Drumright were last year. They combined to go 9-36, and unless the Toledo lineup was made up only of guys named "Rey" and "Rafael," that's really, really bad.

Roberto Duran   Throws L   Age 26

YEAR	TEAM	LGE	IP	H	ER	HR	BB	K	ERA	W	L	H/9	HR/9	BB/9	K/9	KWH	PERA
1996	Dunedin	Fla	46.0	42	10	2	22	39	1.96	4	1	8.22	0.39	4.30	7.63	1.23	3.33
1996	Knoxvill	Sou	83.7	84	48	9	59	58	5.16	3	6	9.04	0.97	6.35	6.24	0.51	4.41
1997	Jacksnvl	Sou	56.3	56	22	2	39	69	3.51	3	3	8.95	0.32	6.23	11.02	1.63	3.83
1998	Detroit	AL	16.0	9	8	0	16	12	4.50	1	1	5.06	0.00	9.00	6.75	0.75	2.25

A left-hander with wicked stuff who was this close to establishing himself as a major league reliever before slamming into the injury wall. You'll find with wild pitchers that just as they seem to harness their control, all those innings of high pitch counts and inconsistent mechanics catch up to them. If he comes back healthy, he may yet establish himself. Then again, if Ron Villone hasn't done it after all these years, I'm skeptical that Duran will.

Bryce Florie   Throws R   Age 29

YEAR	TEAM	LGE	IP	H	ER	HR	BB	K	ERA	W	L	H/9	HR/9	BB/9	K/9	KWH	PERA
1996	San Dieg	NL	49.3	51	23	1	26	46	4.20	2	3	9.30	0.18	4.74	8.39	1.20	3.65
1996	Milwauke	AL	20.0	19	12	3	11	12	5.40	1	1	8.55	1.35	4.95	5.40	0.52	4.05
1997	Milwauke	AL	78.0	73	35	4	36	51	4.04	4	5	8.42	0.46	4.15	5.88	0.74	3.35
1998	Detroit	AL	137.3	141	66	15	53	95	4.33	7	8	9.24	0.98	3.47	6.23	0.91	4.00

(Bryce Florie *continued*)

Another ex-Padre arm; with so many of them in the bullpen, it only made sense to try one of them in the rotation. I think the Tigers made a good choice: Florie is a far more extreme groundball pitcher than even Brocail, and he showed the best control of his career last year. He turns 29 in May; if the Tigers leave him in the rotation all season, I think they could be very surprised.

Seth Greisinger   Throws R   Age 23

YEAR	TEAM	LGE	IP	H	ER	HR	BB	K	ERA	W	L	H/9	HR/9	BB/9	K/9	KWH	PERA
1997	Jacksnvl	Sou	147.3	232	105	29	50	82	6.41	4	12	14.17	1.77	3.05	5.01	0.43	7.15
1998	Toledo	Int	58.3	54	19	5	19	31	2.93	4	2	8.33	0.77	2.93	4.78	0.70	3.24
1998	Detroit	AL	133.7	142	66	16	43	65	4.44	7	8	9.56	1.08	2.90	4.38	0.52	4.17

Wasn't especially impressive in his rookie season, but it was just his second pro season and was rushed to the majors by the Tigers' desperation for another starter. He did have a 4.34 ERA after August 1, despite a strikeout rate too low to sustain success. A young pitcher who doesn't strike out at least six men per nine innings is living on the edge, and Greisinger was at 4.57 last year. Most rookie pitchers improve on that rate as sophomores; if he follows suit he could have a career.

Denny Harriger   Throws R   Age 29

YEAR	TEAM	LGE	IP	H	ER	HR	BB	K	ERA	W	L	H/9	HR/9	BB/9	K/9	KWH	PERA
1996	LasVegas	PCL	158.3	205	91	13	56	80	5.17	7	11	11.65	0.74	3.18	4.55	0.42	5.00
1997	Toledo	Int	155.3	198	97	19	62	80	5.62	6	11	11.47	1.10	3.59	4.64	0.39	5.27
1998	Toledo	Int	135.3	178	82	14	49	67	5.45	5	10	11.84	0.93	3.26	4.46	0.39	5.32

He's got a 41-47 career record at Triple-A, which is probably a fair assessment of his ability. He did make his major league debut last season, but the surge of pitching depth in the farm system means the next time they need an emergency starter, they're likely to give a prospect the shot.

Todd Jones   Throws R   Age 31

YEAR	TEAM	LGE	IP	H	ER	HR	BB	K	ERA	W	L	H/9	HR/9	BB/9	K/9	KWH	PERA
1996	Houston	NL	58.0	65	27	5	30	40	4.19	3	3	10.09	0.78	4.66	6.21	0.62	4.50
1997	Detroit	AL	71.7	62	25	3	30	68	3.14	5	3	7.79	0.38	3.77	8.54	1.86	2.89
1998	Detroit	AL	65.7	58	31	7	33	56	4.25	3	4	7.95	0.96	4.52	7.68	1.23	3.43

Here's another example of the fallacy in thinking that "closers" somehow have a special talent that other relievers don't. He sported an ERA near 5.00 and scared the Tiger faithful every time he came in. Despite that, or that other pitchers were pitching far more effectively, Jones was never in danger of losing his closer role. He did only blow 4 saves, and he's certainly better than his ERA last year. I imagine he'll rebound this year, but he doesn't merit his role, or the salary that it comes with. As a middle reliever on a middle reliever's salary, he's quite an asset.

Greg Keagle   Throws R   Age 28

YEAR	TEAM	LGE	IP	H	ER	HR	BB	K	ERA	W	L	H/9	HR/9	BB/9	K/9	KWH	PERA
1996	Toledo	Int	26.0	49	32	7	12	20	11.08	0	3	16.96	2.42	4.15	6.92	0.51	9.00
1996	Detroit	AL	91.3	100	58	12	56	69	5.72	3	7	9.85	1.18	5.52	6.80	0.64	4.83
1997	Toledo	Int	142.0	170	77	8	60	103	4.88	6	10	10.77	0.51	3.80	6.53	0.78	4.50
1997	Detroit	AL	46.3	60	28	8	15	32	5.44	2	3	11.65	1.55	2.91	6.22	0.85	5.63
1998	Detroit	AL	40.0	47	21	5	18	25	4.72	2	2	10.58	1.12	4.05	5.62	0.55	4.95
1998	Toledo	Int	77.7	111	50	11	32	47	5.79	3	6	12.86	1.27	3.71	5.45	0.47	6.14

The Tigers have been trying for years to find a role he's able to handle, but it has become clear that that role is in Triple-A. The left-handers on the bench draw lots for the right to pinch-hit against him; they hit .355/.434/.591 against Keagle last year, and that's a typical performance for them. Off the 40-man roster, having major knee surgery.

Matt Miller   Throws L   Age 24

YEAR	TEAM	LGE	IP	H	ER	HR	BB	K	ERA	W	L	H/9	HR/9	BB/9	K/9	KWH	PERA
1998	W Michgn	Mid	84.0	97	34	1	33	57	3.64	5	4	10.39	0.11	3.54	6.11	0.76	3.96
1998	Jacksnvl	Sou	55.7	91	51	7	42	38	8.25	1	5	14.71	1.13	6.79	6.14	0.28	7.11

After making the Midwest League look silly all spring, he skipped a level to Double-A and was put in his place a bit. It's still a hell of a debut, but he's getting a late start to his career and needs to keep the afterburners on. Like a lot of polished college pitchers that dominate early on, what he does in his second season, against good minor league competition, will tell us everything. I think he'll have a career.

Brian Moehler   Throws R   Age 27

YEAR	TEAM	LGE	IP	H	ER	HR	BB	K	ERA	W	L	H/9	HR/9	BB/9	K/9	KWH	PERA
1996	Jacksnvl	Sou	164.0	226	86	10	49	86	4.72	8	10	12.40	0.55	2.69	4.72	0.50	5.16
1997	Detroit	AL	178.7	201	84	20	53	94	4.23	9	11	10.13	1.01	2.67	4.74	0.62	4.38
1998	Detroit	AL	226.3	218	86	28	50	120	3.42	14	11	8.67	1.11	1.99	4.77	0.99	3.54

"Coming up next on 'Whatever Happened To?' on VH-1: Dexy's Midnight Runners, A Flock of Seagulls, and that wonderful duet between Jeff Ballard and Mike Dunne, 'That WAS My Fastball'." Baseball is littered with the carcasses of starting pitchers who had success without striking anyone out and petered out soon thereafter. Moehler isn't quite in the Ballard class of finesse, but he has yet to strike out more than five men per nine innings, and at 27 is unlikely to improve on that. He does have a fine sinker that could still fool people for another year or two. I certainly wouldn't want to sign him to any five-year deals.

Adam Pettyjohn   Throws L   Age 22

YEAR	TEAM	LGE	IP	H	ER	HR	BB	K	ERA	W	L	H/9	HR/9	BB/9	K/9	KWH	PERA
1998	Jamestwn	NYP	20.3	30	13	0	5	13	5.75	1	1	13.28	0.00	2.21	5.75	0.84	4.87
1998	W Michgn	Mid	45.7	66	20	4	10	41	3.94	3	2	13.01	0.79	1.97	8.08	1.91	5.52

What a great nameasking for Adam Tommyjohn would probably be greedy. The Tigers' first- and second-round picks in last year's draft (Pettyjohn and Jeff Weaver) both came out of Fresno State, and both pitched extremely well in their debuts. Weaver's got the better stuff, but Pettyjohn is younger, has a few more innings under his belt, and is left-handed. If the Tigers want to see if Pettyjohn has star potential, they need to push him to Double-A this year.

Brian Powell   Throws R   Age 25

YEAR	TEAM	LGE	IP	H	ER	HR	BB	K	ERA	W	L	H/9	HR/9	BB/9	K/9	KWH	PERA
1996	Lakeland	Fla	166.0	252	127	20	53	65	6.89	5	13	13.66	1.08	2.87	3.52	0.24	6.23
1997	Lakeland	Fla	170.7	212	93	12	42	85	4.90	8	11	11.18	0.63	2.21	4.48	0.61	4.59
1998	Jacksnvl	Sou	84.0	111	46	6	21	37	4.93	4	5	11.89	0.64	2.25	3.96	0.44	4.93
1998	Detroit	AL	86.7	101	55	16	33	45	5.71	3	7	10.49	1.66	3.43	4.67	0.46	5.19

Brian Moehler, three years ago. Powell's been successful in his minor league career, but his fastball is nothing special. He doesn't have a great sinker, relying instead on a full repertoire, but none of them are out pitches. He got rocked in his debut, and while I think he may adjust and be a league-average pitcher for a year or two, I am very skeptical about his long-term chances.

Brandon Reed   Throws R   Age 24

YEAR	TEAM	LGE	IP	H	ER	HR	BB	K	ERA	W	L	H/9	HR/9	BB/9	K/9	KWH	PERA
1996	Jacksnvl	Sou	25.3	20	6	1	2	14	2.13	2	1	7.11	0.36	0.71	4.97	3.67	1.78
1997	Jacksnvl	Sou	163.0	229	104	25	51	71	5.74	6	12	12.64	1.38	2.82	3.92	0.32	6.02
1998	Toledo	Int	116.7	170	76	16	41	59	5.86	4	9	13.11	1.23	3.16	4.55	0.37	6.17

This is why finesse pitchers don't succeed. Reed had a phenomenal year as a closer in 1995, but was pitching in the Midwest League, where teenage hitters wave at breaking stuff like it's a good friend driving by. He doesn't throw particularly hard, and the arm injury he suffered in 1996 probably ended what little chance he had of making it.

Sean Runyan   Throws L   Age 25

YEAR	TEAM	LGE	IP	H	ER	HR	BB	K	ERA	W	L	H/9	HR/9	BB/9	K/9	KWH	PERA
1996	Quad Cit	Mid	119.3	182	80	14	33	66	6.03	4	9	13.73	1.06	2.49	4.98	0.54	6.18
1997	Mobile	Sou	60.3	61	23	4	27	40	3.43	4	3	9.10	0.60	4.03	5.97	0.73	3.73
1998	Detroit	AL	52.0	47	19	7	25	38	3.29	4	2	8.13	1.21	4.33	6.58	0.92	3.63

(Sean Runyan *continued*)

He set the major league record for appearances by a rookie with 88, facing an average of 2.5 batters per appearance. It's got to be hard to be typecast as a one-out left-hander in your rookie season. He looks completely miscast in that role, too: lefties hit .271/.367/.430 against him, compared to .234/.323/.390 for the more conventional swingers. He fared worse against the first hitter he faced than he did overall, and pitched very well on those rare occasions he was allowed to pitch an inning or more. Throwing every other day is going to catch up to his arm at some point. It will be very interesting to see how Parrish handles him this year.

A.J. Sager — Throws R — Age 34

YEAR	TEAM	LGE	IP	H	ER	HR	BB	K	ERA	W	L	H/9	HR/9	BB/9	K/9	KWH	PERA
1996	Toledo	Int	36.3	44	14	5	4	19	3.47	2	2	10.90	1.24	0.99	4.71	1.54	4.71
1996	Detroit	AL	81.3	86	35	9	23	51	3.87	5	4	9.52	1.00	2.55	5.64	0.99	3.98
1997	Detroit	AL	85.0	83	37	9	20	51	3.92	5	4	8.79	0.95	2.12	5.40	1.18	3.49
1998	Detroit	AL	61.3	79	39	6	21	23	5.72	2	5	11.59	0.88	3.08	3.38	0.24	5.14
1998	Toledo	Int	23.0	32	8	1	13	12	3.13	2	1	12.52	0.39	5.09	4.70	0.26	5.48

He was in the perfect situation for two years, pitching in non-stressful situations in front of a good defense, which allowed him to milk two good seasons out of a Triple-A arm. That's all gone now. He's old to sign as a Triple-A veteran and hope to find another opportunity, but he has yet to make big money in this game and I imagine he'll try to latch on as a closer in Indianapolis or Buffalo.

Marino Santana — Throws R — Age 27

YEAR	TEAM	LGE	IP	H	ER	HR	BB	K	ERA	W	L	H/9	HR/9	BB/9	K/9	KWH	PERA
1996	Lancastr	Cal	147.0	207	107	24	62	99	6.55	4	12	12.67	1.47	3.80	6.06	0.57	6.24
1997	Jacksnvl	Sou	66.7	78	34	8	45	68	4.59	3	4	10.53	1.08	6.08	9.18	0.99	5.13
1998	Toledo	Int	66.0	54	31	10	34	72	4.23	3	4	7.36	1.36	4.64	9.82	2.12	3.41

He's a right-handed, healthy Roberto Duran: throws hard, without much movement on his fastball. He can't resist trying to get guys out up in the strike zone. If he learns to hit the corners a little better, or gets a little sink to his fastball, he could be a tremendous reliever. Even if he avoids injury, the track record of pitchers with his profile is ugly.

Victor Santos — Throws R — Age 22

YEAR	TEAM	LGE	IP	H	ER	HR	BB	K	ERA	W	L	H/9	HR/9	BB/9	K/9	KWH	PERA
1996	Lakeland	Fla	27.0	25	12	3	10	20	4.00	2	1	8.33	1.00	3.33	6.67	1.20	3.67
1997	Lakeland	Fla	138.7	177	86	14	67	82	5.58	5	10	11.49	0.91	4.35	5.32	0.43	5.26
1998	Lakeland	Fla	96.7	107	40	11	27	55	3.72	6	5	9.96	1.02	2.51	5.12	0.79	4.28
1998	Jacksnvl	Sou	33.7	50	21	2	12	29	5.61	1	3	13.37	0.53	3.21	7.75	1.05	5.61

Another good young arm who is still several years away. Credit the Tigers for making the commitment to find these talents, but with the notable exception of Justin Thompson they have yet to see much return on their investment. Long-term, Santos could be the real deal; for 1999, I would be impressed with a September callup.

Justin Thompson — Throws L — Age 26

YEAR	TEAM	LGE	IP	H	ER	HR	BB	K	ERA	W	L	H/9	HR/9	BB/9	K/9	KWH	PERA
1996	Toledo	Int	84.7	78	32	2	26	59	3.40	5	4	8.29	0.21	2.76	6.27	1.29	2.87
1996	Detroit	AL	61.0	59	26	6	25	44	3.84	4	3	8.70	0.89	3.69	6.49	0.98	3.69
1997	Detroit	AL	225.7	192	72	18	57	147	2.87	16	9	7.66	0.72	2.27	5.86	1.48	2.75
1998	Detroit	AL	228.3	226	94	18	71	145	3.71	13	12	8.91	0.71	2.80	5.72	0.98	3.55

A phenomenal pitcher when healthy. Two years ago, the only thing more imposing than his pitching had been his inability to stay off the disabled list. Now, he hasn't missed a start in two seasons. I still think that his arm is fragile: after going 9-8 with a 3.70 ERA through July, he went 2-7 with a 5.03 ERA the rest of the way, finishing with numbers way off his terrific 1997. He was not worked particularly hard by Buddy Bell. The Tigers need to accept that he has to be a six-inning pitcher to be successful. I think he's going to be fine, and come back with a big year.

Jeff Weaver   Throws R   Age 22

YEAR	TEAM	LGE	IP	H	ER	HR	BB	K	ERA	W	L	H/9	HR/9	BB/9	K/9	KWH	PERA
1998	Jamestwn	NYP	11.7	8	6	0	2	6	4.63	0	1	6.17	0.00	1.54	4.63	1.69	1.54
1998	W Michgn	Mid	12.3	11	5	2	0	13	3.65	1	0	8.03	1.46	0.00	9.49	—	2.92

The Tigers' first-round selection last June, he didn't break a sweat while ringing up hitters at two levels, and was even better in the Midwest League playoffs, going 16 innings without allowing an earned run. First-round college pitchers, especially a senior like Weaver was, should dominate the low minors right from the get-go. He was the only pitcher from the 1998 draft assigned to the Arizona Fall League, where he more than held his own. On the very fast track, could be in Detroit by September.

Alan Webb   Throws L   Age 19

YEAR	TEAM	LGE	IP	H	ER	HR	BB	K	ERA	W	L	H/9	HR/9	BB/9	K/9	KWH	PERA
1998	W Michgn	Mid	160.0	160	91	14	63	132	5.12	7	11	9.00	0.79	3.54	7.43	1.30	3.77

Moxie. He doesn't throw all that hard, and being 5'10" he's going to have that little chip on his shoulder, but he was one of only five minor league pitchers to record over 200 strikeouts, while allowing less than a baserunner an inning. A left-hander with his poise, an excellent changeup and curveball, and outstanding mound awareness can survive just fine in the majors. Webb needs a full year at Double-A before we can promote him as the next Jimmy Key or Tom Glavine.

SNWL DETROIT TIGERS   Park Effect: +4.7%

PITCHER	GS	IP	R	SNW	SNL	SNPCT	W	L	RA	APW	SNVA	SNWAR
Castillo, F.	19	92.0	88	3.5	9.4	.274	3	9	8.61	-3.42	-2.82	-1.95
Florie, B.	16	92.0	56	5.2	5.5	.486	5	8	5.48	-0.41	-0.17	0.66
Greisinger, S.	21	130.0	79	6.7	7.9	.459	6	9	5.47	-0.56	-0.59	0.50
Harriger, D.	2	10.0	10	0.3	1.1	.195	0	2	9.00	-0.41	-0.34	-0.30
Keagle, G.	7	35.3	23	1.5	2.6	.364	0	5	5.86	-0.30	-0.45	-0.25
Moehler, B.	33	221.3	103	14.0	10.1	.580	14	13	4.19	2.02	1.99	3.74
Powell, B.	16	82.7	67	3.8	6.9	.352	3	8	7.29	-1.94	-1.52	-0.78
Sager, A.	3	11.0	13	0.4	1.6	.193	1	1	10.64	-0.64	-0.62	-0.47
Sanders, S.	2	8.7	19	0.0	1.7	.025	0	2	19.73	-1.33	-0.82	-0.69
Thompson, J.	34	222.0	114	14.1	10.6	.570	11	15	4.62	1.01	1.64	3.58
Worrell, T.	9	47.7	36	2.4	3.8	.392	2	6	6.80	-0.87	-0.73	-0.21
TOTALS	162	952.7	608	52.0	61.3	.459	45	78	5.74	-6.86	-4.42	3.83

The most surprising rotation of 1997 was one of 1998's biggest disappointments, as the Tigers slipped back to their accustomed spot near the bottom of the league, losing a whopping 6.6 games of value according to SNVA. Much of the decline was by Justin Thompson, who followed his superstar-level 1997 with merely a star-level 1998. Another big part was the lack of a decent third starter. In 1997, Willie Blair filled that role effectively, but the Tigers found no adequate replacement when Blair signed with the Diamondbacks. The third reason? Frank Castillo. Even with Justin Thompson's decline, if the other owners in your fantasy league haven't figured out how good this guy is, grab him now. In his limited time in the majors, he ranks as the fifth unluckiest pitcher of the last seven years, deserving a record of about 32-22 but actually getting a record of 27-32. He's not going to pitch into that kind of bad luck forever. Even his RA last year is reflective of bad luck, as he received the fifth-worst bullpen support in the majors. Sooner or later his luck will change and the W's will come.

Pitcher Abuse Points

PITCHER	AGE	GS	PAP	PAP/S	AAW	MAX	115+	130+
Castillo, Frank	29	19	109	5.74	8.61	127	2	0
Florie, Bryce	28	16	110	6.88	11.46	123	2	0
Greisinger, Seth	22	21	115	5.48	14.60	120	2	0
Keagle, Greg	27	7	12	1.71	3.14	109	0	0
Moehler, Brian	26	33	319	9.67	19.33	123	8	0
Powell, Brian	24	16	27	1.69	3.94	112	0	0
Thompson, Justin	25	34	341	10.03	21.73	130	7	1
Worrell, Tim*	30	10	29	2.90	3.87	115	1	0
Manager								
Bell, Buddy		138	929	6.73	13.61	130	20	1
Parrish, Larry		25	143	5.72	11.55	118	2	0
TOTAL		163	1072	6.58	13.30	130	22	1
RANKING (AL)			12	12	10		11	11-T

*includes rainout start

Well, Buddy Bell may be gone, but you can't blame the Tigers' record on the way he managed his rotation. The team's AAW leader, Justin Thompson wasn't exactly mauled last year. Brian Moehler was handled with similar prudence, and had a season few thought he was capable of. Larry Parrish actually worked the staff even less vigorously than Bell did, but it was September and he had an expanded bullpen to work with. It's a good sign that with Parrish in the dugout, Tiger fans can sleep easy about the state of Thompson's arm, and be reasonably confident Seth Greisinger and the rest of the kids aren't going to be using the words "labrum," "ulna," or "rehab start," anytime soon.

Kansas City Royals

Humans are fascinated by disasters. Consider the three-hour bottleneck created by drivers gawking at an accident scene: we have a powerful desire to observe suffering and tragedy from a safe distance. But when the moment of high drama has passed and all that remains to watch is the clearing of debris and the methodical search for what went wrong, we find the denouement unfulfilling and drive on.

Such is the case with the Kansas City Royals of the late 1990s. The considerable enthusiasm for this franchise in the middle of the decade crashed into a wall of questionable talent judgments, mishandled young players and, perhaps most importantly, a lack of vision for the organization as a whole. The mangled, unsightly mess of 1997 deservedly cost Bob Boone his job, while damaging both the Royals' talent base and their play-off aspirations considerably.

The cleanup began last year, as far away from the public's consciousness as possible in a season of 70 home runs and 114 wins and a Cubs' postseason appearance. While no one was watching, the Royals were slowly piecing together the clues left behind in the litter. Though many questions still linger, they did find at least one answer that they've been after for years. Tony Muser has thus far proven to be the Royals' best manager in a decade, because he makes every decision with an eye towards building a foundation for the franchise's future.

When Muser was hired, Mike Sweeney had been banished to the minor leagues for perceived defensive shortcomings, despite a potentially explosive bat. Muser immediately put him back in the lineup. While his own evaluation of Sweeney's defense has kept Sweeney from being a first-stringer, Muser has understood that patience is required to develop Sweeney's offense. Muser was told that Scott Service was not a major leaguer. He saw a pitcher with an outstanding history of success in the minor leagues, and with little to lose gave him the opportunity to pitch himself out of a job. Service didn't; he was the set-up man all season, and in his first full year in the major leagues had a 3.48 ERA and struck out 95 men in 83 innings.

Perhaps most importantly, Muser rescued Johnny Damon from the crisis of confidence created by Bob Boone's mistreatment. Damon was the only Royal to play in every game, and despite continued trouble with left-handers, finally had a year reflective of his talents. He ranked second on the team with 58 extra-base-hits and scored 104 runs, the highest total in Kansas City in 11 years. How Muser handles budding stars like Damon will have a long-term impact on the franchise. For the first time in a while, the Royals appear to have a manager who understands that the Royals will only get off the treadmill when they consider long-term impact in every decision they make.

It's not easy to put a positive spin on a 72-89 record, but consider this: the Royals had a road record of 43-38. The only better road team in the AL was the Yankees. But at home, the Royals were so hospitable to visitors you expected Donna Reed to dust off home plate before each game. They went just 29-51 at Kauffman Stadium, the worst home record in baseball.

Their home field "advantage" (13.5 games) was a remarkable achievement, given that no other team in the major leagues played more than one game worse at home than on the road. Could it be a fluke? Possibly, though the Royals were also slightly better on the road in both 1996 and 1997. But I think there's more to the story, and it has to do with the ballpark itself.

Kauffman Stadium was remodeled in 1995, when the artificial turf was finally taken out and the power alleys moved in ten feet. The park was always thought of as a pitchers' park because it was one of the toughest places in baseball to hit a home run, but the fast turf helped grounders scoot through and encouraged leg triples, so overall it was a neutral ballpark for offense. For the first two years after the remodeling, it appeared nothing had changed: the fast grass kept batting averages a little higher, while homers were still hard to

Royals Prospectus

1998 record: 72-89; Third place, AL Central

Pythagorean W/L: 63-99

Runs scored: 714 (13th in AL)

Runs allowed: 899 (13th in AL)

Team EQA: .244 (13th in AL)

Park: Kauffman Stadium (moderate hitters')

1998: Lost franchise drifted aimlessly for the most part, playing high-upside youth with useless veterans.

1999: Sale of team has created hope; still, look forward to 75 wins.

come by. But over the last two years Kauffman has been the best hitter's park in the league. The difference is that the stadium is now a good power park. Over the last two seasons, the Royals and their AL opponents have hit 333 homers in Kansas City and just 278 on the road—an increase of 20%.

If the Royals are even aware of the change, they have yet to respond. The Royals have historically built their team to suit their surroundings by emphasizing speed and average over power. The Royals have always been outhomered by their opponents, a disadvantage that was diminished at home. The last two seasons, they've been outhomered 162-116 on the road—and been bludgeoned 192-141 in their own digs. Yet they have continued their brand of Turfball that has been out of date for ten years. They signed Hal Morris, one of the most prolific groundball hitters at any position, to be their designated hitter. Their #1 starter last year, Tim Belcher, is a pronounced flyball pitcher: over the last two years he is 16-9 with a 3.65 ERA on the road, just 11-17 with a 5.70 ERA at home. That's not a coincidence—that's a connection. It's time for the Royals to get with the 1990s. Whitey Herzog isn't the manager anymore, and Willie Wilson isn't cranking out inside-the-park home runs. It's time to build the offense around guys who get on base and hit for power, and it's time to build the pitching staff around guys who keep the ball down. In other words, it's time to start acting like every other American League team.

———◇———

I have nothing personal against Herk Robinson. He is, by all accounts, an extremely friendly, personable individual, deeply committed to the franchise, and he has nothing but good intentions in his work for the Royals. I am sure that the failure of the Royals to accomplish anything during his tenure as general manager is as painful for him as it has been for all of Royal fandom.

That said, there's no easy way to put it: he has no business being the GM of a major league baseball team. The primary role of a GM is to acquire as much talent as possible and assemble that talent into the framework of a baseball team. Robinson has shown a spectacular inability to fulfill either task on a consistent basis. An exhaustive look at his résumé would force the editors to execute me, and besides we write about it every year in the Royals' essay. But Herk certainly added to his dubious résumé last season when, after DH Chili Davis walked away, Robinson signed Hal Morris, with the result that the Royals had virtually no offense from their designated hitters.

It has become increasingly clear that Robinson's incompetence is just the first step into the abyss for the Royals' front office. Start at the top with the Royals' owner. The Royals don't have one. You can't be a successful professional sports team without direction, a sense of vision as to the organization's priorities and goals. And how can you have

that vision when the seat of the owner, the ultimate arbiter of every decision, stands empty? The death of Ewing Kauffman five years ago tore the roof off this franchise, and the elements have poured in and formed a rusty residue of inertia, indecisiveness, and incompetence.

Kauffman left a significant portion of his immense estate—easily $80 million—to keep the Royals afloat long enough to provide adequate time to find a suitable new owner. His board instead used this as an opportunity to drag their heels, waiting almost four years to even place the team up for sale, and only then after every interested party spoke out against the holdup. They were ostensibly waiting for a good season to raise the team's value—after all, the proceeds from the sale go to charity. But the very success they held out for could not exist without the guidance they were withholding. Their unrealistic expectations for that success in 1997 were met with disaster, which finally prompted the sale to begin. By then, the perceived value of the team had dropped such that the minimum required bid of $75 million would only be met by third party entry Miles Prentice, at first written off as "the New York lawyer," who appears to have emerged victorious.

Prentice's bid bid hit a snag that revealed volumes about the board's inability to effectively govern the sale process. After Prentice was hailed as the winning bidder, the board revealed that the rules of the sale required him to restructure his ownership group so that at least 50% of the capital came from local investors. This was a bombshell dropped on the competing buyers, none of whom were aware of the provision, and who, like George Brett's group, might not have wasted the effort of putting together a bid had they known their attempt would be futile.

Prentice hurdled the speed bump with plenty to spare. He dispelled the initial distrust towards an outsider with impressive ease, and charmed so many of the wealthier families in Kansas City that his final bid was nearly 75% local. He has come across as a likable man with a deep love for the game, and his public statements reveal a better understanding of the game's economics than that of many long-term owners. To quote him: "You can still afford one or two guys who make $6 million to $8 million as long as you're wise in other decisions. You know, maybe you don't spent $1 million on a Hal Morris . . . but we have to build our team around our own farm products . . . the way the Royals teams in the 70s were built." If he can crystallize these statements into action, he may yet succeed Kauffman as one of the most progressive-thinking owners in the game.

The 1999 Royals represent one of the most difficult predictions in recent memory. I do not recall a team which had so much dormant talent, and so many unsettled positions. Consider that the Royals may (and should) play the season with three rookies in the starting lineup: Jeremy Giambi,

Carlos Febles, and Carlos Beltran. Breaking in three rookies in one year isn't unique. The Marlins did it with Kotsay, Lee, and Dunwoody last year, and the 1982 Twins had six, but it certainly adds to the uncertainty. Consider also that:

- Kevin Appier, the Royals' best pitcher of the decade, may or may not be at full health, and may or may not be traded away.
- Three-fifths of the likely rotation—Jose Rosado, Glendon Rusch, and Jeff Suppan—are all just 24.
- Two potential stars—Damon and Sweeney—could regress as easily as they could flourish.
- The Royals have a scar at shortstop, and whether they find a steady, everyday player or get by with last year's debris again could mean several games in the standings.
- The third-base hole could be resolved by trade, a promotion of Kit Pellow, or just a nod from Jeff King.
- The Royals' #1 overall pick last year, Stanford right-hander Jeff Austin, has yet to sign. If he does, he has the ability to reach the major leagues in his first pro season.

Those are just the decisions that need to be made at the player level. At the management level, there is the matter of ownership. While Prentice has been given the green light by the organization, the history of this sport has proven that until a purchase is ratified by the two leagues, it's anything but a done deal. The decision at the top trickles down to the resolution of the GM's job, the distribution of payroll, and the team's determination to play for respectability in 1999 or success further down the road.

There's a lot of talent on this team; under ideal management conditions, there's no reason the Royals couldn't win 88 games this year. But that's just it: "ideal management" is a fairy tale in Kansas City, told to children who wonder why their team hasn't won anything in their lifetime. The Royals' spiraling descent into the Third World of baseball is not the fault of a barren farm system, or even a spiraling salary structure that the franchise couldn't afford to keep up with. It's squarely the fault of a front office that can't distinguish between their real prospects and Phil Hiatt, that can't discern between a player worth acquiring and Jermaine Dye, that can't differentiate between a free agent worth buying and Hal Morris. The talent is here, but so is the same management team that has run this franchise into the ground, and until someone gets rid of them, the Royals may be doomed to remain at the bottom of the American League. If Prentice's first order of business is to "re-assign" Herk Robinson and bring in a new GM, it will be a clear sign that a new movement is afoot. But if he values Robinson's loyalty more than his track record and leaves him in place, it will be evidence that, new owner or not, it remains business as usual in Kansas City.

HITTERS (Averages: BA .260/ OBA .330/ SA .420, EQA .260)

Carlos Beltran — CF — Bats B — Age 22

YEAR	TEAM	LGE	AB	H	DB	TP	HR	BB	R	RBI	SB	CS	OUT	BA	OBA	SA	EQA	EQR	DEFENSE
1996	Spokane	Nwn	219	50	4	1	5	22	20	19	5	2	171	.228	.299	.324	.220	19	50-OF 96
1997	Wilmngtn	Car	426	93	10	3	10	37	36	34	10	5	338	.218	.281	.326	.211	35	117-OF 101
1998	Wilmngtn	Car	198	53	8	0	6	24	26	24	6	4	149	.268	.347	.399	.261	26	49-OF 112
1998	Wichita	Tex	174	52	8	1	10	19	26	31	4	1	123	.299	.368	.529	.303	31	44-OF 94
1998	KansasCy	AL	57	15	5	3	0	3	8	6	3	0	42	.263	.300	.456	.265	8	
1999	KansasCy	AL	414	108	16	2	12	40	51	49	11	5	311	.261	.326	.396	.249	48	

Beltran is a five-tool player who, to borrow a term from John Sickels, has converted those tools into useful baseball skills. He's also the poster child for the importance of understanding ballpark effects when evaluating minor league players. Wilmington has one of the best pitchers' parks in the minor leagues, while Wichita has incredibly short power alleys and plays at almost the same elevation as Phoenix. So Beltran hit "just" .276 at Wilmington, yet after a mid-season promotion hit .352 with outstanding power at Wichita. He is an excellent defensive center fielder with great speed and a rapidly improving batting eye. He may be a little raw to start the year in the major leagues, but he has already shown the capacity for sudden, dramatic improvement.

Dermal Brown — OF — Bats L — Age 21

YEAR	TEAM	LGE	AB	H	DB	TP	HR	BB	R	RBI	SB	CS	OUT	BA	OBA	SA	EQA	EQR	DEFENSE
1997	Spokane	Nwn	291	70	9	1	8	24	28	28	6	3	224	.241	.298	.361	.229	28	65-OF 83
1998	Wilmngtn	Car	453	116	20	2	11	51	57	49	14	6	343	.256	.331	.382	.252	55	102-OF 79
1999	KansasCy	AL	375	100	19	1	9	34	47	43	10	5	280	.267	.328	.395	.248	43	

(Dermal Brown *continued*)

Keeping the ballpark effects of Wilmington in mind, Brown is a sleeper of gargantuan proportions. Hitting just .258 with 10 homers in A ball is usually an indication a player is several years away. There are many reasons why assuming that with Brown may be a mistake. As his DT shows, his numbers were actually impressive. His 10 homers tied for the team lead on a squad that ran away with the Carolina League. He has an impressive pedigree: he was a first-round pick in 1996, and the MVP of the Northwest League in 1997. The Royals aggressively promoted him to high-A ball last year, and he started the year in a terrible funk, hitting .157 through the end of May, then hitting .298 the rest of the season. He may still be a few years away, but he might also be in the major leagues by August. Ignore him at your own risk.

Jeff Conine			LF/1B				Bats R		Age 33									
YEAR	TEAM	LGE	AB	H	DB	TP	HR	BB	R	RBI	SB	CS	OUT	BA	OBA	SA	EQA	EQR	DEFENSE
1996	Florida	NL	601	179	32	2	27	65	81	100	0	4	426	.298	.366	.493	.290	97	110-OF 96 34-1B 123
1997	Florida	NL	406	98	12	1	18	59	49	54	2	0	308	.241	.338	.409	.262	54	117-1B 115
1998	KansasCy	AL	303	74	18	0	10	27	33	34	3	0	229	.244	.306	.403	.246	34	73-OF 91
1999	KansasCy	AL	350	88	13	0	14	42	41	47	1	1	263	.251	.332	.409	.253	42	

From *The Herk Robinson Primer:* "If you make a mistake and allow a 26-year-old hitter to leave the organization, then watch that player blossom, the best way to correct your error is to re-acquire that player five years later, when he is 31 and his skills are in obvious decline." His return to KC is eerily similar to the acquisition of Kevin McReynolds six years before: a remarkably consistent left fielder in his early thirties, with a steady pattern of decline foreshadowing a steep drop-off. Little rebound potential.

Johnny Damon			CF/RF				Bats L		Age 25									
YEAR	TEAM	LGE	AB	H	DB	TP	HR	BB	R	RBI	SB	CS	OUT	BA	OBA	SA	EQA	EQR	DEFENSE
1996	KansasCy	AL	508	132	20	5	6	29	58	42	27	6	382	.260	.300	.354	.234	51	137-OF 104
1997	KansasCy	AL	462	123	11	8	8	43	55	48	16	10	349	.266	.329	.377	.247	53	128-OF 103
1998	KansasCy	AL	628	167	26	10	18	60	82	76	23	12	473	.266	.330	.425	.261	82	156-OF 103
1999	KansasCy	AL	538	149	23	7	12	48	73	65	21	10	399	.277	.336	.413	.257	67	

He's finally beginning to click. For two years Bob Boone jerked Damon up and down and in and out of the lineup, played him at all three outfield positions, and gave the impression that he had to hit .300 every week or lose his job. Damon has a history of not responding favorably to ridiculous expectations: as a senior in high school, he had a terrible season after he was touted as the best pre-season prep star in the nation. Muser left him alone, and the improvement in his numbers is only part of the story.

I saw him in September, and I couldn't believe he was the same player. Whereas before he would slap the ball to left field and ground out weakly, now he was driving the ball in the air to right field, fouling off the pitches he couldn't handle and hanging in against left-handed pitchers better than he ever has. He's only 25, and has the confidence that comes with a new history of success and a manager who believes in him. Last year I thought he could become the new Andy Van Slyke, and that seems more appropriate now. He may never hit left-handers, and his arm can be run on. What he can do will help put runs on the scoreboard.

Jermaine Dye			RF				Bats R		Age 25									
YEAR	TEAM	LGE	AB	H	DB	TP	HR	BB	R	RBI	SB	CS	OUT	BA	OBA	SA	EQA	EQR	DEFENSE
1996	Atlanta	NL	289	78	12	0	13	11	25	38	0	4	215	.270	.297	.446	.246	32	79-OF 96
1997	KansasCy	AL	259	59	11	0	8	17	21	24	2	1	201	.228	.275	.363	.218	22	64-OF 104
1997	Omaha	AA	140	38	4	0	8	9	14	21	0	1	104	.271	.315	.471	.262	18	27-OF 88
1998	Omaha	PCL	154	42	3	0	10	17	22	25	6	0	112	.273	.345	.487	.289	25	32-OF 112
1998	KansasCy	AL	210	46	4	1	5	12	13	16	2	2	166	.219	.261	.319	.194	14	59-OF 108
1999	KansasCy	AL	370	96	10	0	18	23	37	50	5	2	276	.259	.303	.432	.247	42	

What little he brings to a team (hitting left-handers and playing an adequate right field) is irrelevant in light of his inability to stay healthy. Muser was not impressed with him in spring training, and was frustrated with his fragility as the season wore on. His window of opportunity is just about closed.

Sal Fasano   **C**   **Bats R**   **Age 27**

YEAR	TEAM	LGE	AB	H	DB	TP	HR	BB	R	RBI	SB	CS	OUT	BA	OBA	SA	EQA	EQR	DEFENSE
1996	Omaha	AA	103	22	3	0	3	7	7	8	0	1	82	.214	.264	.330	.197	7	
1996	KansasCy	AL	141	27	1	0	6	13	9	12	1	1	115	.191	.260	.326	.198	10	
1997	Wichita	Tex	130	25	1	0	7	15	9	14	0	1	106	.192	.276	.362	.217	12	
1997	Omaha	AA	150	20	2	0	3	11	4	4	0	0	130	.133	.193	.207	.082	1	
1998	KansasCy	AL	212	45	8	0	8	11	14	19	1	0	167	.212	.251	.363	.207	16	67-C 107
1999	*KansasCy*	*AL*	*230*	*47*	*8*	*0*	*8*	*17*	*15*	*20*	*0*	*1*	*184*	*.204*	*.259*	*.343*	*.197*	*16*	

An excellent defensive catcher with some pop in his bat, and more than qualified as a backup. The Royals need to figure out that he's not a starter. Fasano's ability to get on-base is non-existent. He hit just .227 and walked 10 times in 216 at-bats, though he somehow tied for second in the AL with 16 hit-by-pitches in less than half a season. Toss in the fact that he's already 27, or two years older than Mike Sweeney, and what you have is a second-stringer. The new Mark Parent.

Carlos Febles   **2B**   **Bats R**   **Age 23**

YEAR	TEAM	LGE	AB	H	DB	TP	HR	BB	R	RBI	SB	CS	OUT	BA	OBA	SA	EQA	EQR	DEFENSE
1996	Lansing	Mid	364	89	14	3	5	49	48	32	15	8	283	.245	.334	.341	.242	41	91-2B 93
1997	Wilmngtn	Car	445	102	21	5	3	42	53	30	29	8	351	.229	.296	.319	.224	42	115-2B 94
1998	Wichita	Tex	416	109	17	3	11	65	71	46	30	11	318	.262	.362	.397	.272	62	115-2B 92
1998	KansasCy	AL	24	9	1	2	0	4	6	4	2	1	16	.375	.464	.583	.349	6	
1999	*KansasCy*	*AL*	*423*	*112*	*19*	*4*	*9*	*53*	*67*	*47*	*25*	*9*	*320*	*.265*	*.347*	*.392*	*.260*	*55*	

He's not an offensive juggernaut like Giambi and doesn't have Beltran's tools, but he may be the most enjoyable of the three to watch. He's a perfect leadoff hitter. He hits for average, draws an enormous number of walks, and steals bases with abandon—100 the last two seasons, with a success rate of 79%. He scored 110 runs in 126 games at Double-A. He's also an excellent defensive second baseman, which explains why the Royals are so nonchalant about losing Jose Offerman to free agency.

Jeremy Giambi   **LF**   **Bats L**   **Age 24**

YEAR	TEAM	LGE	AB	H	DB	TP	HR	BB	R	RBI	SB	CS	OUT	BA	OBA	SA	EQA	EQR	DEFENSE
1996	Spokane	Nwn	240	51	6	0	4	42	30	18	10	4	193	.213	.330	.287	.229	24	54-OF 86
1997	Lansing	Mid	116	33	4	0	4	17	17	16	3	1	84	.284	.376	.422	.283	18	
1997	Wichita	Tex	261	72	8	1	9	37	35	36	3	3	192	.276	.366	.418	.273	38	55-OF 102
1998	Omaha	PCL	316	110	16	1	17	52	61	65	7	4	210	.348	.440	.566	.339	70	62-OF 90
1998	KansasCy	AL	57	12	4	0	2	11	7	7	0	1	46	.211	.338	.386	.251	7	
1999	*KansasCy*	*AL*	*347*	*107*	*13*	*0*	*19*	*52*	*60*	*65*	*7*	*4*	*244*	*.308*	*.398*	*.510*	*.307*	*64*	

He's not particularly fast, and his defense won't make anyone stand up and cheer. But he has a clear idea of what he's doing at the plate. He has better plate discipline than all but a few players in baseball, very good power, and hit .372 at Triple-A. The Pacific Coast League is not what it used to be—Omaha used to be in the American Association—so Giambi's numbers are not solely a product of a good offensive environment. He should be a front-runner for Rookie of the Year in 1999. He only hit .224 in a short callup, but drew as many walks (11) in three weeks as Dye did all year. The Royals need his bat in the lineup from start to finish this year.

Raul Gonzalez   **OF**   **Bats R**   **Age 25**

YEAR	TEAM	LGE	AB	H	DB	TP	HR	BB	R	RBI	SB	CS	OUT	BA	OBA	SA	EQA	EQR	DEFENSE
1995	Wilmngtn	Car	317	96	15	2	12	13	36	46	4	3	224	.303	.330	.476	.272	43	68-OF 99
1995	Wichita	Tex	77	20	2	1	2	7	10	8	3	0	57	.260	.321	.390	.255	9	19-OF 98
1996	Wichita	Tex	83	21	2	1	1	4	6	7	1	1	63	.253	.287	.337	.213	7	16-OF 90
1997	Wichita	Tex	441	104	18	2	10	30	38	39	8	5	342	.236	.285	.354	.219	39	93-OF 91
1998	Wichita	Tex	439	105	11	1	10	43	41	40	6	5	339	.239	.307	.337	.225	41	100-OF 89
1999	*KansasCy*	*AL*	*399*	*103*	*15*	*1*	*11*	*32*	*42*	*45*	*6*	*4*	*300*	*.258*	*.313*	*.383*	*.237*	*41*	

He may have had his finest season in 1998. He's 25 and the development of Beltran probably dooms him to remain outside the Royals' plans for their outfield of the future.

Shane Halter   IF   Bats R   Age 29

YEAR	TEAM	LGE	AB	H	DB	TP	HR	BB	R	RBI	SB	CS	OUT	BA	OBA	SA	EQA	EQR	DEFENSE	
1996	Omaha	AA	299	65	10	0	4	28	24	20	6	2	236	.217	.284	.291	.202	22	49-OF 87	14-3B 81
1997	KansasCy	AL	121	32	5	1	2	10	13	12	4	3	92	.264	.321	.372	.240	13	23-OF 84	
1998	KansasCy	AL	200	41	8	0	3	13	11	11	2	5	164	.205	.254	.290	.175	11	47-SS 108	
1998	Omaha	PCL	95	24	4	0	1	5	9	7	3	1	72	.253	.290	.326	.216	8		
1999	KansasCy	AL	267	64	11	1	4	22	24	23	4	4	207	.240	.298	.333	.213	22		

He's been a utility player since he reached Triple-A, with his defensive versatility overshadowing his inability to hit. He started at shortstop after the Felix Martinez disaster, only to be demoted after botching a squeeze bunt in June. When you hit .221, you better have your fundamentals down. Returned late in the year and played well enough for the 25th spot. As long as the Royals understand his value is strictly on defense, he's not a liability.

Jed Hansen   2B   Bats R   Age 26

YEAR	TEAM	LGE	AB	H	DB	TP	HR	BB	R	RBI	SB	CS	OUT	BA	OBA	SA	EQA	EQR	DEFENSE	
1996	Wichita	Tex	398	98	16	1	10	26	39	37	11	5	305	.246	.292	.367	.229	38	96-2B 101	
1997	Omaha	AA	372	86	14	2	8	29	33	32	6	1	287	.231	.287	.344	.220	33	85-2B 100	24-SS 97
1997	KansasCy	AL	92	28	6	1	1	13	16	11	3	2	66	.304	.390	.424	.286	14	25-2B 98	
1998	Omaha	PCL	410	97	11	5	11	38	43	40	14	8	321	.237	.301	.368	.233	42	115-2B 98	
1999	KansasCy	AL	408	100	18	2	10	34	44	41	11	6	314	.245	.303	.373	.231	40		

His skills, varied as they are, fall just short of major-league caliber. He has B power, B- speed and C+ plate discipline. If he hit for a good average, he'd already have a job, but he hit .278 at Triple-A last year, and that's his career high. Offerman had a great year, Febles is ready to take over, and Hansen's caught in the middle. I still think he'll have a career, just elsewhere.

Chris Hatcher   OF   Bats R   Age 30

YEAR	TEAM	LGE	AB	H	DB	TP	HR	BB	R	RBI	SB	CS	OUT	BA	OBA	SA	EQA	EQR	DEFENSE
1996	Jackson	Tex	153	40	4	0	8	8	15	20	2	1	114	.261	.298	.444	.252	18	26-OF 93
1996	Tucson	PCL	337	84	11	2	12	12	28	35	8	6	259	.249	.275	.401	.228	32	70-OF 94
1997	Omaha	AA	218	40	5	0	7	15	10	14	0	1	179	.183	.236	.303	.174	11	37-OF 81
1998	Omaha	PCL	473	129	12	0	30	22	48	72	7	6	350	.273	.305	.488	.264	63	74-OF 92
1999	KansasCy	AL	435	115	12	0	25	24	45	64	5	3	323	.264	.303	.464	.255	53	

Can't play defense, has terrible plate discipline, and he's 29 years old. He also hit 46 homers last year, the highest minor league total in 15 years and the highest ever by any Royal, majors or minors. He's capable of helping a major league team in the right role, but the Royals have to adjust to the idea that a power hitter can thrive in Kauffman Stadium. There's talk he'll be in Japan.

Jeff King   1B   Bats R   Age 34

YEAR	TEAM	LGE	AB	H	DB	TP	HR	BB	R	RBI	SB	CS	OUT	BA	OBA	SA	EQA	EQR	DEFENSE	
1996	Pittsbrg	NL	588	155	32	4	30	73	85	91	13	1	434	.264	.345	.485	.285	94	74-1B 95	61-2B 91
1997	KansasCy	AL	532	122	27	1	28	89	79	73	16	5	415	.229	.340	.442	.272	80	150-1B 129	
1998	KansasCy	AL	476	120	16	1	23	44	54	63	9	2	358	.252	.315	.435	.259	61	109-1B 109	
1999	KansasCy	AL	480	115	17	1	26	63	63	70	8	2	367	.240	.328	.442	.262	65		

One of the biggest hurdles for the Royals to clear is the understanding that you can't afford mediocre production at the corners. King would make a fine hitter if he still played second base; at first, he's being pitted against Vaughn and Palmeiro and Delgado and Thome and even Tony Clark and Jason Giambi, and he's not better than any of them. King resisted a move across the diamond to third, leading to the Joe Randa trade. So much for the "team player" label fastened to his collar.

Mendy Lopez   SS   Bats R   Age 24

YEAR	TEAM	LGE	AB	H	DB	TP	HR	BB	R	RBI	SB	CS	OUT	BA	OBA	SA	EQA	EQR	DEFENSE
1996	Wichita	Tex	322	80	14	2	6	24	34	29	10	3	245	.248	.301	.360	.233	32	90-3B 116
1997	Wichita	Tex	351	66	10	2	4	31	21	17	5	3	288	.188	.254	.262	.172	18	100-SS 92
1998	Omaha	PCL	193	29	5	1	2	17	5	5	2	2	166	.150	.219	.218	.124	5	56-SS 105
1998	KansasCy	AL	202	46	9	2	1	13	16	13	4	2	158	.228	.274	.307	.200	14	64-SS 107
1999	KansasCy	AL	377	84	13	2	6	30	31	28	6	3	296	.223	.280	.316	.201	27	

He won the shortstop job by default. He hasn't shown he can hit Double-A pitching successfully, but he has little-ball skills. Lopez is a tiny bit better than Halter in every manner, and should have the upper hand fighting for the utility job this spring now that Rey Sanches will man short.

Shane Mack   OF   Bats R   Age 35

YEAR	TEAM	LGE	AB	H	DB	TP	HR	BB	R	RBI	SB	CS	OUT	BA	OBA	SA	EQA	EQR	DEFENSE	
1997	Boston	AL	128	40	4	0	4	9	16	18	2	1	89	.312	.358	.438	.276	18	33-OF 102	
1998	KansasCy	AL	202	54	14	1	6	16	27	24	7	2	150	.267	.321	.436	.262	26	29-OF 90	
1999	*KansasCy*	*AL*	*156*	*44*	*6*	*0*	*7*	*13*	*20*	*23*	*3*	*1*	*113*	*.282*	*.337*	*.455*	*.269*	*21*		

His once-diverse skills have deserted him, but what he does have left (gap power and relatively fleet in the outfield) was put to the good use on a team with converted first basemen all over the outfield and a shortage of bats on the bench. Ended the year on the DL; his career could end at any moment. Won't be back in Kansas City.

Felix Martinez   SS   Bats B   Age 25

YEAR	TEAM	LGE	AB	H	DB	TP	HR	BB	R	RBI	SB	CS	OUT	BA	OBA	SA	EQA	EQR	DEFENSE	
1996	Omaha	AA	394	85	11	1	5	45	39	25	17	9	318	.216	.296	.287	.209	32	116-SS 101	
1997	Omaha	AA	402	88	15	2	2	27	32	21	17	8	322	.219	.268	.281	.191	26	110-SS 91	
1998	KansasCy	AL	84	10	0	1	0	5	2	2	3	1	75	.119	.169	.143	—	-1	27-SS	99
1998	Omaha	PCL	161	35	5	2	2	14	14	11	5	2	128	.217	.280	.311	.207	13	41-SS 105	
1999	*KansasCy*	*AL*	*313*	*68*	*12*	*2*	*3*	*26*	*27*	*20*	*10*	*5*	*250*	*.217*	*.277*	*.297*	*.195*	*21*		

Last year we wrote that a player like Martinez "can get hundreds of at-bats in the big leagues before someone in power realizes how bad they are." Actually, it only took 85 at-bats, a .129 batting average, an EQA below zero, surprisingly bad defense, an "accidental" kick that broke Otis Nixon's jaw, a sucker punch to Phil Nevin during a Royals-Angels brawl, a suspension, and a psychiatric evaluation before the Royals realized how bad Felix Martinez is. He was released, and he won't be missed.

Hal Morris   1B/DH   Bats L   Age 34

YEAR	TEAM	LGE	AB	H	DB	TP	HR	BB	R	RBI	SB	CS	OUT	BA	OBA	SA	EQA	EQR	DEFENSE	
1996	Cincnnti	NL	526	161	32	4	16	53	74	80	5	5	370	.306	.370	.473	.288	82	136-1B 97	
1997	Cincnnti	NL	330	88	20	1	1	25	34	28	2	1	243	.267	.318	.342	.232	31	88-1B 91	
1998	KansasCy	AL	461	137	25	2	1	34	52	47	1	0	324	.297	.345	.367	.251	51	40-1B 110	32-OF 83
1999	*KansasCy*	*AL*	*399*	*112*	*21*	*1*	*5*	*36*	*47*	*45*	*2*	*1*	*288*	*.281*	*.340*	*.376*	*.248*	*44*		

Morris defines the Herk Robinson era in Kansas City. He had a terrible season by doing exactly what the Royals expected him to do. When Chili Davis left town, the Royals were down a DH. Rather than replace him from within or sign a Bob Hamelin-type on the cheap, Herk brought in Hal Morris to be "a line-drive hitter." He also hit one home run, or one fewer than Kerry Wood. The cost-cutting measures in Kansas City may be all that save the Royals from another year of the least-imposing DH in recent memory. A free agent at this writing; Boston is a rumored destination.

Rod Myers   OF   Bats L   Age 26

YEAR	TEAM	LGE	AB	H	DB	TP	HR	BB	R	RBI	SB	CS	OUT	BA	OBA	SA	EQA	EQR	DEFENSE
1996	Omaha	AA	410	113	21	1	14	50	72	49	35	8	305	.276	.354	.434	.282	64	111-OF 105
1997	Omaha	AA	139	29	6	0	2	14	12	9	5	3	113	.209	.281	.295	.202	10	37-OF 108
1997	KansasCy	AL	99	24	4	0	3	17	15	11	4	0	75	.242	.353	.374	.267	14	19-OF 108
1998	Omaha	PCL	100	16	2	1	0	10	4	3	3	3	87	.160	.236	.200	.132	3	25-OF 112
1999	*KansasCy*	*AL*	*281*	*65*	*8*	*0*	*9*	*32*	*33*	*28*	*12*	*5*	*221*	*.231*	*.310*	*.356*	*.233*	*29*	

Fragile. Last year, he was an early front-runner for an outfield spot before he tore up his shoulder diving for a ball, and was unimpressive when he did return. If his power returns he may yet have a career, but he's 26 and there's no guarantee that his career isn't at a construction site or in a valet parking lot.

Jose Offerman   2B   Bats B   Age 30

YEAR	TEAM	LGE	AB	H	DB	TP	HR	BB	R	RBI	SB	CS	OUT	BA	OBA	SA	EQA	EQR	DEFENSE
1996	KansasCy	AL	547	162	30	8	5	70	90	62	25	12	397	.296	.376	.408	.278	81	91-1B 107 28-2B 102
1997	KansasCy	AL	415	120	23	6	2	41	54	44	9	10	305	.289	.353	.388	.257	51	99-2B 89
1998	KansasCy	AL	591	180	25	13	7	89	114	71	40	12	423	.305	.396	.426	.295	100	153-2B 99
1999	Boston	AL	529	157	26	7	5	74	92	63	24	11	383	.297	.383	.401	.277	78	

Arguably the best second baseman in the AL last season. Like his expected replacement (Carlos Febles), he's a prototypical leadoff hitter. Batting second or third for the Royals was partly a concession to Damon's development, and partly a response to having guys like Hal Morris at the power positions. He still makes a number of errors, but his range has held up well at second base, and he ranked second in the AL in double plays turned. The Red Sox are being widely criticized for giving him four years and $26 million, but if they play him at second base he won't be as overpaid as everyone thinks. If Jeff Frye is healthy, he could see considerable time at first, and while he was an exceptional defensive first baseman in 1996, this is a terrible idea.

Dean Palmer   3B   Bats R   Age 30

YEAR	TEAM	LGE	AB	H	DB	TP	HR	BB	R	RBI	SB	CS	OUT	BA	OBA	SA	EQA	EQR	DEFENSE
1996	Texas	AL	564	147	24	2	34	55	68	90	2	0	417	.261	.326	.491	.276	83	144-3B 83
1997	Texas	AL	350	84	16	0	16	26	33	43	1	0	266	.240	.293	.423	.244	39	92-3B 88
1997	KansasCy	AL	183	49	10	1	9	16	22	27	1	2	136	.268	.327	.481	.270	26	41-3B 98
1998	KansasCy	AL	559	149	24	2	33	51	70	88	7	2	412	.267	.328	.494	.277	84	127-3B 75
1999	Detroit	AL	539	140	21	1	31	51	65	86	3	1	400	.260	.324	.475	.268	75	

A very good player, with as much power as any third baseman in baseball, but his one weakness is getting on base, and on a team with so many players with the same problem, his value to the Royals was limited. His homer total was just two away from the franchise record of 36; of course, McGwire hit 38 homers just at home last year. He's off to Detroit on a hefty five-year contract.

Kit Pellow   3B   Bats R   Age 25

YEAR	TEAM	LGE	AB	H	DB	TP	HR	BB	R	RBI	SB	CS	OUT	BA	OBA	SA	EQA	EQR	DEFENSE
1996	Spokane	Nwn	279	60	5	1	8	12	16	20	4	3	222	.215	.247	.326	.190	18	43-1B 92
1997	Lansing	Mid	254	57	5	1	6	15	16	20	1	0	197	.224	.268	.323	.200	18	49-3B 70
1997	Wichita	Tex	237	49	6	0	8	17	16	19	3	1	189	.207	.260	.333	.202	17	65-3B 99
1998	Wichita	Tex	364	76	11	1	16	20	25	34	3	2	290	.209	.250	.376	.210	29	87-3B 86
1999	KansasCy	AL	418	100	13	1	17	25	37	47	4	1	319	.239	.282	.397	.228	40	

He isn't ready for the job, and may never be. The acquisition of Randa means he won't be playing. Pellow is the third in a chain of Royals "prospects," beginning with Phil Hiatt and continuing with Craig Paquette, who play a passable third base and amaze everyone with their power in batting practice, but are so helpless against a major league curveball they can't hear "Tom Gordon" without breaking out in hives. Pellow has better power than the other two, and he can field reasonably well at third base after converting from the outfield just two years ago. He's an overrated prospect by virtue of his age, defense, and good hitter's parks.

Terry Pendleton   3B   Bats B   Age 38

YEAR	TEAM	LGE	AB	H	DB	TP	HR	BB	R	RBI	SB	CS	OUT	BA	OBA	SA	EQA	EQR	DEFENSE
1996	Atlanta	NL	161	31	3	0	5	16	11	12	2	1	131	.193	.266	.304	.196	11	39-3B 89
1996	Florida	NL	407	103	18	1	8	29	35	40	0	2	306	.253	.303	.361	.228	38	104-3B 95
1997	Cincnnti	NL	112	26	6	0	2	13	12	10	2	1	87	.232	.312	.339	.230	11	23-3B 87
1998	KansasCy	AL	232	57	6	0	4	16	17	20	1	0	175	.246	.294	.323	.214	19	
1999	KansasCy	AL	245	57	5	0	7	23	20	24	1	1	189	.233	.299	.339	.217	21	

Even Tony Muser makes mistakes. The Royals raved about that "clubhouse influence" and are making noises about bringing him back. This may be a situation where Pendleton may have to say, "I don't have anything left." He'll have no problem finding a coaching position; the Braves have made a standing offer.

Mark Quinn   OF   Bats R   Age 25

YEAR	TEAM	LGE	AB	H	DB	TP	HR	BB	R	RBI	SB	CS	OUT	BA	OBA	SA	EQA	EQR	DEFENSE
1996	Lansing	Mid	434	101	10	1	7	28	31	32	6	4	337	.233	.279	.309	.201	31	105-OF 82
1997	Wilmngtn	Car	304	85	13	1	12	32	38	44	2	1	220	.280	.348	.447	.274	43	58-OF 81
1997	Wichita	Tex	93	30	8	0	2	12	15	14	1	1	64	.323	.400	.473	.301	16	19-OF 92
1998	Wichita	Tex	356	95	12	3	9	33	39	42	2	1	262	.267	.329	.393	.252	42	87-OF 87
1999	*KansasCy*	*AL*	*365*	*101*	*15*	*1*	*11*	*33*	*44*	*48*	*3*	*1*	*265*	*.277*	*.337*	*.414*	*.257*	*45*	

He deserves a major league job, because bats like his make up for a lot of weaknesses. He used to have an unorthodox, awkward-looking swing, but he swings much more gracefully now without hurting the end result: he won the Texas League batting title. The Royals have too many roster spots tied up in outfielders to give him a job, and he doesn't fit their mold anyway.

Larry Sutton   OF/1B   Bats L   Age 29

YEAR	TEAM	LGE	AB	H	DB	TP	HR	BB	R	RBI	SB	CS	OUT	BA	OBA	SA	EQA	EQR	DEFENSE
1996	Wichita	Tex	460	108	9	1	13	59	46	48	2	1	353	.235	.322	.343	.236	48	123-1B 85
1997	Omaha	AA	372	91	14	1	12	50	42	45	0	0	281	.245	.334	.384	.253	45	101-1B 99
1997	KansasCy	AL	68	19	2	0	2	5	7	8	0	0	49	.279	.329	.397	.252	8	
1998	KansasCy	AL	304	70	12	2	5	30	27	26	3	3	237	.230	.299	.332	.219	27	73-OF 94
1999	*KansasCy*	*AL*	*342*	*84*	*13*	*1*	*10*	*40*	*38*	*40*	*1*	*1*	*259*	*.246*	*.325*	*.377*	*.242*	*37*	

After a tough rookie season in which he wasn't quite able to meet the demands placed on him, he goes into spring training as unsure of his role as anyone on the team. He doesn't hit well enough to start at first base, and his defense—and Giambi and Beltran—mean he's out of luck in the outfield. His best role would be as a left-handed pinch-hitter.

Mike Sweeney   C   Bats R   Age 25

YEAR	TEAM	LGE	AB	H	DB	TP	HR	BB	R	RBI	SB	CS	OUT	BA	OBA	SA	EQA	EQR	DEFENSE
1996	Wichita	Tex	231	67	10	1	11	29	33	38	2	1	165	.290	.369	.485	.292	38	
1996	Omaha	AA	100	24	6	0	3	7	9	10	0	0	76	.240	.290	.390	.232	10	
1996	KansasCy	AL	162	44	6	0	5	17	18	20	1	3	120	.272	.341	.401	.255	20	
1997	KansasCy	AL	236	55	5	0	8	17	19	23	3	2	183	.233	.285	.356	.220	21	
1997	Omaha	AA	141	29	7	1	7	17	14	17	0	1	114	.206	.291	.418	.239	16	
1998	KansasCy	AL	276	68	13	0	9	25	27	31	2	3	211	.246	.309	.391	.240	30	82-C 98
1999	*KansasCy*	*AL*	*329*	*85*	*13*	*0*	*14*	*29*	*36*	*44*	*2*	*2*	*246*	*.258*	*.318*	*.426*	*.251*	*39*	

His future as a catcher is no longer a sure thing. I have no doubt that if he had been handled better the last two seasons he would already be one of the better catchers in baseball. But his defense has been ripped so much by the team that he's lost confidence in himself, and last year he threw out just 30% of basestealers (down from 42%), while committing nine passed balls. More than any other player, Sweeney needs a whole-hearted commitment from the Royals in 1999. If they do, he may yet become the new Chris Hoiles. If not, he could find himself at third or on another team.

Joe Vitiello   1B   Bats R   Age 29

YEAR	TEAM	LGE	AB	H	DB	TP	HR	BB	R	RBI	SB	CS	OUT	BA	OBA	SA	EQA	EQR	DEFENSE
1996	Omaha	AA	132	33	4	0	6	15	15	17	1	0	99	.250	.327	.417	.259	17	36-1B 94
1996	KansasCy	AL	252	59	13	1	8	36	31	29	2	0	193	.234	.330	.389	.254	31	
1997	KansasCy	AL	128	29	6	0	5	14	12	15	0	0	99	.227	.303	.391	.239	14	20-OF 98
1998	Omaha	PCL	369	88	11	1	12	33	32	40	0	0	281	.238	.301	.371	.232	37	89-1B 89
1999	*KansasCy*	*AL*	*301*	*74*	*10*	*0*	*14*	*33*	*33*	*41*	*0*	*0*	*227*	*.246*	*.320*	*.419*	*.251*	*36*	

It's becoming irrelevant whether he can stay healthy long enough to contribute. His skills have atrophied to the point where he's just not a very good hitter anymore, certainly not good enough to contribute at first base.

Ernie Young   OF   Bats R   Age 29

YEAR	TEAM	LGE	AB	H	DB	TP	HR	BB	R	RBI	SB	CS	OUT	BA	OBA	SA	EQA	EQR	DEFENSE
1996	Oakland	AL	452	104	17	4	18	49	48	53	7	6	354	.230	.305	.405	.243	52	131-OF 109
1997	Oakland	AL	172	37	4	0	6	19	14	16	1	3	138	.215	.293	.343	.217	15	57-OF 105
1997	Edmonton	PCL	184	43	4	0	5	28	21	19	3	2	143	.234	.335	.337	.241	20	42-OF 101
1998	Omaha	PCL	290	81	8	1	14	24	34	42	5	3	212	.279	.334	.459	.270	40	72-OF 104
1999	*KansasCy*	*AL*	*340*	*86*	*14*	*1*	*13*	*36*	*40*	*44*	*4*	*4*	*258*	*.253*	*.324*	*.415*	*.250*	*40*	

If they ever form a Quadruple-A minor league, he could be one of its stars. Every time he's sent to Triple-A he mercilessly beats on the league. But he has yet to show that talent in any of his trials in the major leagues. He may get another chance. Maybe.

PITCHERS (Averages: 4.00 ERA, 9.00 H/9, 1.00 HR/9, 3.00 BB/9, 6.00 K/9, 1.00 KWH)

Kevin Appier   Throws R   Age 31

YEAR	TEAM	LGE	IP	H	ER	HR	BB	K	ERA	W	L	H/9	HR/9	BB/9	K/9	KWH	PERA
1996	KansasCy	AL	214.3	186	67	14	60	205	2.81	16	8	7.81	0.59	2.52	8.61	2.82	2.77
1997	KansasCy	AL	242.0	214	80	22	64	191	2.98	17	10	7.96	0.82	2.38	7.10	2.00	3.01
1998	Omaha	PCL	29.3	49	26	7	13	16	7.98	1	2	15.03	2.15	3.99	4.91	0.30	7.98
1998	KansasCy	AL	15.7	21	10	3	4	9	5.74	1	1	12.06	1.72	2.30	5.17	0.72	5.74

The world may never know what an outstanding pitcher Appier has been. A freak accident (he slipped and broke his collarbone carrying his sister's wedding presents) pushed a shoulder that was slowly weakening from overuse to the operating room. The surgery for a torn labrum was not reconstructive, but it could not have been more poorly timed, coming just a week before the season began. He endured a lengthy rehab, interrupted by a hospital stay for a bizarre colon infection, and was still gaining arm strength at year's end. He has more work to do; his fastball was consistently 87 mph and his slider topped out at 78 mph, which is about 4-5 mph shy of his pre-injury form. His success was not all about velocity, and he can survive at this level, but he may never again show his dominant form. Herk Robinson gave Jeff King a no-trade clause in his contract, so with the Royals in a cost-cutting mood Appier looks to be gone. For years, Appier was the only reason to watch a Royals game, and for him to be traded at the lowest point in his career would be the nadir of the organization's relationship with him.

Brian Barber   Throws R   Age 26

YEAR	TEAM	LGE	IP	H	ER	HR	BB	K	ERA	W	L	H/9	HR/9	BB/9	K/9	KWH	PERA
1996	Louisvil	AmA	50.0	56	36	12	28	29	6.48	2	4	10.08	2.16	5.04	5.22	0.40	5.58
1997	Louisvil	AmA	93.0	126	80	20	44	63	7.74	2	8	12.19	1.94	4.26	6.10	0.54	6.39
1998	Omaha	PCL	128.7	135	65	22	55	76	4.55	6	8	9.44	1.54	3.85	5.32	0.58	4.62
1998	KansasCy	AL	44.3	42	21	5	12	24	4.26	2	3	8.53	1.02	2.44	4.87	0.86	3.45

A former Cardinals farmhand with great talent, not much idea what to do with it, and constant injury problems; to watch him pitch, you'd think he was convinced he could throw a ball right through a hitter's bat. He calmed down his act a bit after the Royals claimed him off waivers. Got killed (8 ER, 1.1 IP) in his first start, but had a 4.43 ERA after that. He's an extreme flyball pitcher. He's still making the transformation from thrower to pitcher, and given his injury history, is much better suited to relief.

Tim Belcher   Throws R   Age 37

YEAR	TEAM	LGE	IP	H	ER	HR	BB	K	ERA	W	L	H/9	HR/9	BB/9	K/9	KWH	PERA
1996	KansasCy	AL	242.0	250	91	24	54	112	3.38	16	11	9.30	0.89	2.01	4.17	0.70	3.76
1997	KansasCy	AL	220.3	241	107	28	61	111	4.37	11	13	9.84	1.14	2.49	4.53	0.63	4.33
1998	KansasCy	AL	246.0	232	96	33	66	127	3.51	15	12	8.49	1.21	2.41	4.65	0.79	3.59

Robinson had every opportunity to trade him in July, when the Angels were desperate for another starter. He declined, stating in the press that he hoped the Royals could contend for second place and spur interest in the team. "Contending for second place" is a fitting epitaph for Herk's entire tenure. Belcher's always worked up in the strike zone, and if he signs with a team that plays in a spacious park—do any still exist?—he could still be effective.

Brian Bevil   Throws R   Age 27

YEAR	TEAM	LGE	IP	H	ER	HR	BB	K	ERA	W	L	H/9	HR/9	BB/9	K/9	KWH	PERA
1996	Wichita	Tex	71.3	70	26	5	29	60	3.28	5	3	8.83	0.63	3.66	7.57	1.33	3.66
1996	Omaha	AmA	68.3	70	36	10	21	62	4.74	3	5	9.22	1.32	2.77	8.17	1.96	4.08
1997	Omaha	AmA	40.7	38	21	8	24	39	4.65	2	3	8.41	1.77	5.31	8.63	1.25	4.43
1998	KansasCy	AL	43.0	45	22	4	20	46	4.60	2	3	9.42	0.84	4.19	9.63	1.76	4.19

He's got wicked stuff, but a combination of mechanical flaws, nagging injuries and wildness have kept him down. Another flyball pitcher struggling to understand that major league hitters can hit anyone's fastball if it's thrown down the middle. Dan Miceli was 27 a year ago. The Royals can only hope Bevil will make the same adjustments.

Jamie Bluma   Throws R   Age 27

YEAR	TEAM	LGE	IP	H	ER	HR	BB	K	ERA	W	L	H/9	HR/9	BB/9	K/9	KWH	PERA
1996	Omaha	AmA	58.3	65	22	7	22	34	3.39	3	3	10.03	1.08	3.39	5.25	0.61	4.47
1996	KansasCy	AL	20.3	17	7	2	3	14	3.10	1	1	7.52	0.89	1.33	6.20	2.88	2.66
1998	Wichita	Tex	58.7	80	50	9	41	27	7.67	1	6	12.27	1.38	6.29	4.14	0.17	6.29
1998	Omaha	PCL	13.3	22	13	4	8	6	8.78	0	1	14.85	2.70	5.40	4.05	0.15	8.77

Wichita State hurlers are risky. Tyler Green, Darren Dreifort, and Bluma have all had major arm surgery, while Mike Drumright has fought arm troubles and suffered through a miserable season. After missing all of 1997, Bluma showed nothing in his return. His velocity was almost back by August, but he had zero command and even less movement. Modern medicine has brought many pitchers back from their deathbeds, but Bluma looks like he's six feet under.

Ricky Bones   Throws R   Age 30

YEAR	TEAM	LGE	IP	H	ER	HR	BB	K	ERA	W	L	H/9	HR/9	BB/9	K/9	KWH	PERA
1996	Milwauke	AL	149.3	162	79	24	50	59	4.76	7	10	9.76	1.45	3.01	3.56	0.32	4.58
1997	Tucson	PCL	39.7	43	17	2	8	17	3.86	2	2	9.76	0.45	1.82	3.86	0.63	3.63
1997	KansasCy	AL	81.0	102	49	9	22	35	5.44	3	6	11.33	1.00	2.44	3.89	0.41	5.00
1998	SaltLake	PCL	47.3	44	18	5	21	31	3.42	3	2	8.37	0.95	3.99	5.89	0.78	3.61
1998	KansasCy	AL	55.7	47	14	4	22	37	2.26	5	1	7.60	0.65	3.56	5.98	0.99	2.91

Muser has done an impressive job of maximizing the ability of marginal relievers, but Bones's performance is more fluke than managing. His stuff kept getting him extra chances when he wasn't getting anyone out, so he's probably set for another five years of big league paychecks on the fringe.

Tim Byrdak   Throws L   Age 25

YEAR	TEAM	LGE	IP	H	ER	HR	BB	K	ERA	W	L	H/9	HR/9	BB/9	K/9	KWH	PERA
1996	Wichita	Tex	80.0	133	76	17	47	42	8.55	2	7	14.96	1.91	5.29	4.72	0.21	7.87
1997	Wilmngtn	Car	39.0	44	19	4	12	30	4.38	2	2	10.15	0.92	2.77	6.92	1.28	4.38
1998	Wichita	Tex	51.0	65	27	3	31	28	4.76	2	4	11.47	0.53	5.47	4.94	0.29	5.12
1998	Omaha	PCL	35.3	35	12	3	19	25	3.06	3	1	8.92	0.76	4.84	6.37	0.70	3.82

His career was at a crossroads after he ran head-first into Triple-A hitters and then into the injuries that all minor league pitchers seem to face at some point. He has vanquished both for the moment, so now he's a left-hander with the kind of mediocre stuff that major leaguers feast on.

Kiko Calero   Throws R   Age 24

YEAR	TEAM	LGE	IP	H	ER	HR	BB	K	ERA	W	L	H/9	HR/9	BB/9	K/9	KWH	PERA
1996	Spokane	Nwn	68.7	111	43	6	22	33	5.64	3	5	14.55	0.79	2.88	4.33	0.33	6.29
1997	Wichita	Tex	124.7	127	69	16	44	83	4.98	5	9	9.17	1.16	3.18	5.99	0.92	4.04
1998	Wilmngtn	Car	89.7	105	44	10	64	58	4.42	5	5	10.54	1.00	6.42	5.82	0.38	5.12

Enrique, or "Kiko" as he is sometimes known, was the Royals' best pitching prospect a year ago. He was out with an arm injury for the first half and spent the rest of the year rehabbing in Wilmington. Like Jose Rosado, Calero has a long history of pitching in the Puerto Rican winter league, and the year-round strain of throwing caught up with him. He's already been successful at Double-A, so the success this year isn't very meaningful. His long-term future is still bright.

Chad Durbin   Throws R   Age 21

YEAR	TEAM	LGE	IP	H	ER	HR	BB	K	ERA	W	L	H/9	HR/9	BB/9	K/9	KWH	PERA
1997	Lansing	Mid	139.7	199	91	19	56	79	5.86	5	11	12.82	1.22	3.61	5.09	0.42	6.06
1998	Wilmngtn	Car	140.0	165	68	14	69	112	4.37	7	9	10.61	0.90	4.44	7.20	0.83	4.82

Given his age, stuff (the best change-up in the system), lack of injury history and numbers, he's probably the Royals' best starting pitcher prospect. He took a huge step forward last year, in part because having such a pitcher-friendly park at high A-ball gives Royals' minor league pitchers a superficial statistical boost, which helps set up a cycle of success. If you look at the teams whose farm systems have been historically productive, I'm pretty sure you'd find that most of them have a good pitchers' park somewhere in the system, or like the Dodgers, play in one themselves.

Bart Evans   Throws R   Age 28

YEAR	TEAM	LGE	IP	H	ER	HR	BB	K	ERA	W	L	H/9	HR/9	BB/9	K/9	KWH	PERA
1996	Wichita	Tex	21.3	42	45	8	44	13	18.98	0	2	17.72	3.38	18.56	5.48	0.07	10.97
1997	Wichita	Tex	30.7	53	20	4	9	21	5.87	1	2	15.55	1.17	2.64	6.16	0.69	7.04
1998	Omaha	PCL	53.3	61	21	4	23	40	3.54	3	3	10.29	0.68	3.88	6.75	0.86	4.39

If you're in a rotisserie league and want the deep-down, nobody's-heard-of-him-but-he-might-get-saves tip, you're welcome. Evans was only famous for his wildness (125 walks in 93 innings at one point), before he finally admitted his elbow was bothering him in 1996. He throws in the mid-90s and looked like the cat's pajamas a few years ago. After never tasting success above A-ball, he was an effective closer for Omaha last year.

Greg Hansell   Throws R   Age 28

YEAR	TEAM	LGE	IP	H	ER	HR	BB	K	ERA	W	L	H/9	HR/9	BB/9	K/9	KWH	PERA
1996	Minnesot	AL	77.3	78	35	12	25	46	4.07	4	5	9.08	1.40	2.91	5.35	0.81	4.19
1997	Tucson	PCL	81.0	109	48	13	26	57	5.33	3	6	12.11	1.44	2.89	6.33	0.86	5.78
1998	Omaha	PCL	65.0	74	27	6	16	44	3.74	4	3	10.25	0.83	2.22	6.09	1.23	4.29

He's been capable of helping a major league team out of the bullpen for five years, and he's only 28. His handicap is that he doesn't light up the radar gun, and he doesn't have any one outstanding pitch or skill to attract notice. With the Giants now; Dusty Baker rides his pen hard, so there's opportunity there.

Allen McDill   Throws L   Age 27

YEAR	TEAM	LGE	IP	H	ER	HR	BB	K	ERA	W	L	H/9	HR/9	BB/9	K/9	KWH	PERA
1996	Wichita	Tex	60.0	99	49	11	24	51	7.35	2	5	14.85	1.65	3.60	7.65	0.82	7.35
1997	Omaha	AmA	68.3	85	38	9	29	42	5.00	3	5	11.20	1.19	3.82	5.53	0.54	5.27
1998	Omaha	PCL	57.0	64	24	3	25	46	3.79	3	3	10.11	0.47	3.95	7.26	0.99	4.26

A left-handed reliever with borderline credentials who helped himself with a strong 1998. He'll get cups of coffee from time to time because he's a southpaw, but if he's going to establish himself in the majors it will be as a one-out specialist. Last year left-handed batters hit .243/.293/.286 off him at Triple-A, which is good but not quite good enough.

Jeff Montgomery   Throws R   Age 37

YEAR	TEAM	LGE	IP	H	ER	HR	BB	K	ERA	W	L	H/9	HR/9	BB/9	K/9	KWH	PERA
1996	KansasCy	AL	64.3	56	24	13	15	44	3.36	4	3	7.83	1.82	2.10	6.16	1.73	3.50
1997	KansasCy	AL	60.7	53	20	8	15	47	2.97	5	2	7.86	1.19	2.23	6.97	2.08	3.12
1998	KansasCy	AL	58.7	56	27	7	20	53	4.14	3	4	8.59	1.07	3.07	8.13	1.88	3.68

For the second straight year, he was horrible in the first half and did a bang-up job in the second. His ERA through June last year was 6.91; from then on it was 3.25. He's 37 years old and his last good season was 1993. He'll be back in Kansas City in 1999, signed to a one-year deal for less than $3 million.

Orber Moreno   Throws R   Age 22

YEAR	TEAM	LGE	IP	H	ER	HR	BB	K	ERA	W	L	H/9	HR/9	BB/9	K/9	KWH	PERA
1997	Lansing	Mid	133.3	190	88	19	48	87	5.94	5	10	12.83	1.28	3.24	5.87	0.62	6.07
1998	Wilmngtn	Car	32.0	11	4	2	11	33	1.12	4	0	3.09	0.56	3.09	9.28	6.75	-0.28
1998	Wichita	Tex	34.7	29	11	1	12	32	2.86	3	1	7.53	0.26	3.12	8.31	2.21	2.60

I'm waiting for an episode of the Simpsons to start with Bart writing on the chalkboard, "Pitchers are unpredictable. Pitchers are unpredictable." Moreno was a starter in 1997 and not impressive. Moved to the bullpen, he fooled hitters all summer. The numbers he put up in Wilmington don't fit into any framework we can understand: eight hits in 33 innings with 50 strikeouts. He had a team-best 2.88 ERA after a promotion to the bandbox in Wichita. The Royals are keeping quiet about him, but he has a scary good upside.

Robbie Morrison — Throws R — Age 22

YEAR	TEAM	LGE	IP	H	ER	HR	BB	K	ERA	W	L	H/9	HR/9	BB/9	K/9	KWH	PERA
1998	Spokane	Nwn	23.7	23	9	3	19	20	3.42	2	1	8.75	1.14	7.23	7.61	0.69	4.56

The man who gave up the College World Series-winning homer to Warren Morris a few years ago. He actually had an outstanding college career at Florida State, has the classic closer makeup and arsenal, and was taken in the second round by the Royals in June. His pro debut was promising, if wild. He could come on fast, as the Royals don't exactly have the Nasty Boys in their pen.

Scott Mullen — Throws L — Age 24

YEAR	TEAM	LGE	IP	H	ER	HR	BB	K	ERA	W	L	H/9	HR/9	BB/9	K/9	KWH	PERA
1996	Spokane	Nwn	73.7	115	58	7	35	43	7.09	2	6	14.05	0.86	4.28	5.25	0.34	6.35
1997	Lansing	Mid	85.7	124	54	16	35	49	5.67	3	7	13.03	1.68	3.68	5.15	0.41	6.51
1997	Wilmngtn	Car	56.3	81	39	6	26	30	6.23	2	4	12.94	0.96	4.15	4.79	0.32	5.91
1998	Wilmngtn	Car	78.3	95	38	5	32	36	4.37	4	5	10.91	0.57	3.68	4.14	0.32	4.60
1998	Wichita	Tex	69.7	71	30	6	27	33	3.88	4	4	9.17	0.78	3.49	4.26	0.43	3.88

His season doesn't look impressive because it's divided by a mid-season promotion. All told, he went 16-6 with a 3.06 ERA. He's not 16-6 good, but he's a lefty with a good idea of what he's doing on the mound. Mullen should start the year in Triple-A, and I suspect he'll need a full year there to make adjustments. His star potential is limited, but he could be the new Terry Mulholland.

Hipolito Pichardo — Throws R — Age 29

YEAR	TEAM	LGE	IP	H	ER	HR	BB	K	ERA	W	L	H/9	HR/9	BB/9	K/9	KWH	PERA
1996	KansasCy	AL	69.3	71	32	4	21	43	4.15	4	4	9.22	0.52	2.73	5.58	0.93	3.50
1997	KansasCy	AL	51.0	51	20	7	22	33	3.53	3	3	9.00	1.24	3.88	5.82	0.73	4.06
1998	KansasCy	AL	118.3	120	57	10	39	54	4.34	6	7	9.13	0.76	2.97	4.11	0.47	3.73

He's thought of as some sort of everyman, super-versatile pitcher who can fill any role, which disguises the fact that he's just not very good. He hasn't had an ERA under 4.00 since his rookie season, and is under contract for another year at more than $2 million. He badly needs a change of scenery.

Jim Pittsley — Throws R — Age 25

YEAR	TEAM	LGE	IP	H	ER	HR	BB	K	ERA	W	L	H/9	HR/9	BB/9	K/9	KWH	PERA
1996	Wichita	Tex	21.0	11	1	0	5	6	0.43	2	0	4.71	0.00	2.14	2.57	0.49	0.43
1996	Omaha	AmA	72.0	83	33	8	43	47	4.12	4	4	10.38	1.00	5.38	5.88	0.46	4.87
1997	Omaha	AmA	41.7	35	17	3	20	26	3.67	3	2	7.56	0.65	4.32	5.62	0.72	3.02
1997	KansasCy	AL	116.0	121	60	14	47	51	4.66	6	7	9.39	1.09	3.65	3.96	0.34	4.19
1998	KansasCy	AL	73.0	85	44	12	34	43	5.42	3	5	10.48	1.48	4.19	5.30	0.48	5.18

Every time I watch him, I think about what might have been. He was one of the top ten prospects in all of baseball before his elbow caved in. It was not thought to be a career-threatening injury, but he's come back as the worst kind of pitcher, the kind that throws 90 mph but everything's straight and up in the zone. Hitters went .322/.401/.557 against him last year, which is like facing a league full of Edgar Martinezes. There isn't a single positive to be extracted from his record the last two years, and it's time to cut bait.

Stephen Prihoda — Throws L — Age 26

YEAR	TEAM	LGE	IP	H	ER	HR	BB	K	ERA	W	L	H/9	HR/9	BB/9	K/9	KWH	PERA
1995	Spokane	Nwn	60.7	110	56	9	23	34	8.31	1	6	16.32	1.34	3.41	5.04	0.34	7.71
1996	Wilmngtn	Car	74.0	70	25	2	25	60	3.04	5	3	8.51	0.24	3.04	7.30	1.54	3.04
1997	Wichita	Tex	84.7	98	32	3	43	52	3.40	5	4	10.42	0.32	4.57	5.53	0.48	4.36
1998	Wichita	Tex	116.3	166	77	17	26	60	5.96	4	9	12.84	1.32	2.01	4.64	0.63	5.96

(Stephen Prihoda *continued*)

I'm stubborn, so I still think he can be an effective major leaguer. Throws slop with a herky-jerky motion and from all sorts of angles, and a lefty can find a niche that way. He spent a second season in Double-A, throwing 122 innings in relief, and a late-season shellacking killed his overall numbers. If the Royals grudgingly give him a promotion to Omaha, they may be surprised.

Pat Rapp   Throws R   Age 31

YEAR	TEAM	LGE	IP	H	ER	HR	BB	K	ERA	W	L	H/9	HR/9	BB/9	K/9	KWH	PERA
1995	Florida	NL	172.0	160	61	10	72	94	3.19	12	7	8.37	0.52	3.77	4.92	0.58	3.30
1996	Florida	NL	164.7	195	86	12	87	78	4.70	8	10	10.66	0.66	4.76	4.26	0.27	4.70
1997	Florida	NL	110.7	125	52	11	47	57	4.23	6	6	10.17	0.89	3.82	4.64	0.41	4.47
1997	San Fran	NL	33.7	39	22	6	20	25	5.88	1	3	10.43	1.60	5.35	6.68	0.60	5.35
1998	KansasCy	AL	200.0	201	91	22	97	130	4.09	11	11	9.05	0.99	4.37	5.85	0.65	4.09

Rapp is a big guy and looks imposing on the mound—he reminds me of Joey Hamilton physically—but he's just not a very good pitcher. He holds runners well and gets a lot of double-play grounders with his sinker. The problem is that even at the top of his game he still puts on too many baserunners. The league hit .285 off of him, and he ranked third in the AL in walks allowed. He fit the Royals' needs when they signed him last year. That purpose has expired, and they should let him walk.

Dan Reichert   Throws R   Age 22

YEAR	TEAM	LGE	IP	H	ER	HR	BB	K	ERA	W	L	H/9	HR/9	BB/9	K/9	KWH	PERA
1997	Spokane	Nwn	35.0	55	29	3	17	21	7.46	1	3	14.14	0.77	4.37	5.40	0.35	6.43
1998	Wichita	Tex	36.7	56	35	7	30	20	8.59	1	3	13.75	1.72	7.36	4.91	0.18	7.36
1998	Lansing	Mid	33.7	36	20	0	23	23	5.35	1	3	9.62	0.00	6.15	6.15	0.48	4.01
1998	Omaha	PCL	16.7	15	9	2	2	9	4.86	1	1	8.10	1.08	1.08	4.86	2.02	3.24

The Royals' #1 pick in 1997, he's been more remarkable as a human interest story than as a pitcher. He was so impressive out of spring training that he was started at Double-A, where he was saluted with line drives everywhere. He lost 25 pounds off an already-skinny frame and looked terrible. He was finally diagnosed with diabetes, and it would have been understandable if he had been given the year off to regain strength and learn how to handle the disease. But two months later he was throwing short outings in the Midwest League, and he came on so fast that he touched down for two starts in Wilmington and then held his own in Triple-A for three starts. For any player to reach Triple-A the year after he's drafted is impressive; given what Reichert's gone through, it's a miracle. He threw well in the Arizona Fall League. Diabetes is a tough disease to control given the unpredictable day-to-day schedule of the pro athlete; as a starter he only needs to follow a strict timetable about 35 times a year. It won't be easy, but don't bet against him.

Jose Rosado   Throws L   Age 24

YEAR	TEAM	LGE	IP	H	ER	HR	BB	K	ERA	W	L	H/9	HR/9	BB/9	K/9	KWH	PERA
1996	Omaha	AmA	98.0	89	36	16	42	72	3.31	7	4	8.17	1.47	3.86	6.61	1.04	3.77
1996	KansasCy	AL	107.7	96	30	6	21	63	2.51	9	3	8.02	0.50	1.76	5.27	1.48	2.67
1997	KansasCy	AL	210.0	207	98	24	64	126	4.20	11	12	8.87	1.03	2.74	5.40	0.90	3.73
1998	KansasCy	AL	183.3	171	81	23	51	132	3.98	10	10	8.39	1.13	2.50	6.48	1.50	3.49

His career is at a crossroads. When his arm is 100%, he's a wonderful pitcher to watch. It looks like he's thinking three steps ahead of every hitter, and ties them up in knots by changing speeds, working away, away, away, then busting them in, all with an aura of complete calm about him. But he hasn't been right since Bob Boone slagged his arm in 1997, and last year he would be on his game one time in three, getting hammered in one of the other starts. If he's handled right and makes the tiny concessions that every young pitcher must make, he'll make a lot of money in this game. If not, he may end up lost for years, always smelling success but unable to taste it.

Glendon Rusch   Throws L   Age 24

YEAR	TEAM	LGE	IP	H	ER	HR	BB	K	ERA	W	L	H/9	HR/9	BB/9	K/9	KWH	PERA
1996	Omaha	AmA	173.0	195	84	14	43	103	4.37	9	10	10.14	0.73	2.24	5.36	0.95	4.11
1997	KansasCy	AL	176.3	205	93	26	45	114	4.75	8	12	10.46	1.33	2.30	5.82	1.06	4.75
1998	KansasCy	AL	163.7	182	81	20	45	92	4.45	8	10	10.01	1.10	2.47	5.06	0.78	4.40

He was tabbed the #3 starter out of spring training, which probably wasn't fair to him, and he didn't handle the pressure well. He had control problems early in the year, and he missed a month; it's an open question how long he pitched in pain, since he went 0-6 with a 9.96 ERA before hitting the DL. He returned in September and was used in long relief, with good results (eight hits, one walk in 14 IP). To be effective, he'll have to walk no more than two batters a start.

Jose Santiago   Throws R   Age 24

YEAR	TEAM	LGE	IP	H	ER	HR	BB	K	ERA	W	L	H/9	HR/9	BB/9	K/9	KWH	PERA
1996	Lansing	Mid	73.0	105	40	6	22	37	4.93	3	5	12.95	0.74	2.71	4.56	0.44	5.55
1997	Wichita	Tex	26.3	34	11	1	8	10	3.76	2	1	11.62	0.34	2.73	3.42	0.28	4.78
1998	Wichita	Tex	71.7	85	31	8	28	24	3.89	4	4	10.67	1.00	3.52	3.01	0.18	4.77

For the second straight season he got a brief mid-season call-up, and for the second straight year I have no idea what the Royals see in him. He has never pitched particularly well, he doesn't have impressive K/BB ratios, and while his stuff is okay, it's not good enough to justify a promotion on its own. He's had attitude problems—including an unprecedented lifetime ban from the Carolina League after pegging a fan. The Royals seem to put up with instability in their prospects. Look at Felix Martinez.

Scott Service   Throws R   Age 32

YEAR	TEAM	LGE	IP	H	ER	HR	BB	K	ERA	W	L	H/9	HR/9	BB/9	K/9	KWH	PERA
1996	Indianap	AmA	46.3	42	20	5	12	45	3.88	3	2	8.16	0.97	2.33	8.74	3.01	3.11
1996	Cincnnti	NL	49.3	54	19	8	17	42	3.47	3	2	9.85	1.46	3.10	7.66	1.44	4.56
1997	Indianap	AmA	32.7	37	16	5	13	41	4.41	2	2	10.19	1.38	3.58	11.30	2.62	4.96
1997	KansasCy	AL	17.7	17	7	1	4	19	3.57	1	1	8.66	0.51	2.04	9.68	3.98	3.06
1998	KansasCy	AL	86.7	66	26	6	31	93	2.70	7	3	6.85	0.62	3.22	9.66	3.17	2.39

Muser's greatest success with his pitching staff was a career minor leaguer whose ability to be a competent major league reliever should have been blindingly obvious. Service throws in the upper 80s and has a terrific slider that has helped him strike out over a man per inning throughout his career, and I think he'll build on the success he had last year. Capable of being the closer if Montgomery doesn't return; if Monty comes back, Service will be one of the best set-up men in the league.

Jeff Suppan   Throws R   Age 24

YEAR	TEAM	LGE	IP	H	ER	HR	BB	K	ERA	W	L	H/9	HR/9	BB/9	K/9	KWH	PERA
1996	Pawtuckt	Int	146.0	138	58	16	25	123	3.58	9	7	8.51	0.99	1.54	7.58	3.29	3.27
1996	Boston	AL	24.0	27	13	2	11	13	4.88	1	2	10.13	0.75	4.13	4.88	0.43	4.50
1997	Boston	AL	117.3	134	59	11	31	65	4.53	6	7	10.28	0.84	2.38	4.99	0.76	4.30
1997	Pawtuckt	Int	60.0	57	24	7	13	33	3.60	4	3	8.55	1.05	1.95	4.95	1.10	3.45
1998	Arizona	NL	67.7	86	50	12	19	36	6.65	2	6	11.44	1.60	2.53	4.79	0.59	5.59
1998	Tucson	PCL	70.0	71	21	3	17	52	2.70	5	3	9.13	0.39	2.19	6.69	1.68	3.34

This is what's so frustrating about Herk Robinson: occasionally the light bulb goes on and he makes a really shrewd move. After acquiring the useless Jermaine Allensworth from Pittsburgh, Herk dumped his mistake on the Mets and somehow received Jeff Suppan back in a three-way trade. Suppan has yet to convert his considerable promise into major league performance, but he's still just 24 and a year removed from being the Diamondbacks' second expansion pick. He's not a finesse pitcher or an overpowering strikeout artist. He's healthy, has excellent control, and the Royals have a pretty good track record of developing starting pitchers. He pitched extremely well in a 12-inning audition last September. If he gets a rotation spot this April, I think he'll have an ERA a run better than league average.

Jamie Walker   Throws L   Age 27

YEAR	TEAM	LGE	IP	H	ER	HR	BB	K	ERA	W	L	H/9	HR/9	BB/9	K/9	KWH	PERA
1996	Jackson	Tex	93.3	118	40	8	40	64	3.86	5	5	11.38	0.77	3.86	6.17	0.65	5.01
1997	KansasCy	AL	44.7	46	23	6	18	24	4.63	2	3	9.27	1.21	3.63	4.84	0.52	4.23
1998	Omaha	PCL	43.7	65	17	3	12	16	3.50	3	2	13.40	0.62	2.47	3.30	0.25	5.56
1998	KansasCy	AL	18.3	29	15	5	3	15	7.36	0	2	14.24	2.45	1.47	7.36	1.94	7.85

The residue of the Tucker-for-Dye trade, Walker is a left-handed control freak with underwhelming stuff and a bleak future. If the Royals have to use him for more than a token appearance, I'll bet dollars to doughnuts that they finish no higher than fourth in the division.

Matt Whisenant   Throws L   Age 28

YEAR	TEAM	LGE	IP	H	ER	HR	BB	K	ERA	W	L	H/9	HR/9	BB/9	K/9	KWH	PERA
1996	Charlott	Int	125.3	162	97	15	112	81	6.97	3	11	11.63	1.08	8.04	5.82	0.27	5.89
1997	Charlott	Int	15.3	19	12	0	12	14	7.04	0	2	11.15	0.00	7.04	8.22	0.64	4.70
1997	KansasCy	AL	19.7	15	6	0	11	16	2.75	1	1	6.86	0.00	5.03	7.32	1.16	2.29
1998	KansasCy	AL	64.0	59	29	3	30	44	4.08	3	4	8.30	0.42	4.22	6.19	0.82	3.23

He held left-handed hitters to a .194 average and just one extra-base hit, but righties poked him to the tune of .326/.411/.432. Muser didn't use him as a strict one-out left-hander; the Royals used a reliever to face only one hitter just 17 times last year, the fewest in baseball. That's a reasonable decision, because the Royals are in the business of trying to develop their players, not get favorable platoon advantages at any cost, and Whisenant had a better rookie season than most expected. He's a rare left-handed groundball reliever, and could be awesome if he finds control.

SNWL				KANSAS CITY ROYALS							Park Effect: +11.8%	
PITCHER	GS	IP	R	SNW	SNL	SNPCT	W	L	RA	APW	SNVA	SNWAR
Appier, K.	3	15.0	13	0.4	1.4	.227	1	2	7.80	-0.40	-0.46	-0.36
Barber, B.	8	42.0	28	2.7	3.0	.470	2	4	6.00	-0.33	-0.19	0.26
Belcher, T.	34	234.0	127	14.1	11.9	.543	14	14	4.88	0.85	0.81	3.07
Haney, C.	12	61.3	54	2.3	5.7	.284	4	6	7.92	-1.70	-1.62	-1.13
Pichardo, H.	18	102.7	57	5.9	5.5	.518	7	5	5.00	0.25	0.10	1.06
Pittsley, J.	2	8.3	6	0.7	0.8	.456	1	1	6.48	-0.11	-0.10	0.04
Rapp, P.	32	188.3	115	10.2	11.6	.468	12	13	5.50	-0.50	-0.58	0.94
Rosado, J.	25	152.0	94	8.8	9.5	.481	8	10	5.57	-0.52	-0.31	1.01
Rusch, G.	24	141.0	101	7.0	10.6	.399	6	15	6.45	-1.76	-1.69	-0.46
Suppan, J.	1	6.0	0	0.7	0.0	1.000	0	0	0.00	0.32	0.34	0.40
Walker, J.	2	10.3	10	0.4	1.1	.263	0	1	8.71	-0.37	-0.37	-0.23
TOTALS	161	961.0	605	53.1	60.9	.465	55	71	5.67	-4.25	-4.07	4.61

When you lose a starter the quality of Kevin Appier, you're going to take a hit. The Royals dropped from 16th in SNVA with 0.1 in 1997 to 22nd in SNVA with -4.1 in 1998. This from a team that two short years ago had the best rotation in the AL. Unfortunately, they also had Bob Boone as manager, and they're still seeing the consequences of his experiments in fatigue. Most of the staff decline from 1997 to 1998 can be attributed to Appier, who lost almost four games of SNVA by himself. Speaking of Boone, one of his favorite subjects, the young Jose Rosado, returned from off-season surgery to try to rediscover his 1996 form. Rosado gave Royals fans a glimmer of hope, going 4.2-3.1 (.574) before the All-Star break. But he dashed those hopes with his second straight late-season collapse, going 4.5-6.3 (.427) during the second half.

Pitcher Abuse Points

PITCHER	AGE	GS	PAP	PAP/S	AAW	MAX	115+	130+
Barber, Brian	25	8	8	1.00	2.17	105	0	0
Belcher, Tim	36	34	383	11.26	11.26	132	7	1
Haney, Chris	29	12	7	0.58	0.88	106	0	0
Pichardo, Hipolito	28	18	60	3.33	5.56	121	1	0
Rapp, Pat	30	32	394	12.31	16.42	132	6	1
Rosado, Jose	23	25	212	8.48	21.20	123	4	0
Rusch, Glendon	23	24	132	5.50	13.75	118	1	0
TOTAL		161	1201	7.46	11.82	132	19	2
RANKING (AL)			10	10	13		14	10

More praise for Tony Muser: he took care of his pitchers and he used common sense. He let his veterans, Tim Belcher and Pat Rapp, pick up the lion's share of the load, while babying Glendon Rusch and Brian Barber. The only guy caught in the middle is Jose Rosado, who may have been worked over his limit by Muser, putting up a 6.23 ERA from August 1 on. He may still be re-developing his stamina after getting overworked by Bob Boone, but Muser has to show him the same respect he showed the other members of the 25-and-under crowd. Rosado, Rusch, and Jeff Suppan need the best possible protection if they're going to reach the potential the Royals expect from them.

Minnesota Twins

You say you want a revolution? We've got one here. The 1999 Twins, in a best-case scenario, will start a full lineup of young, home-grown players who can put runs on the board. The lineup will be led by "veterans" Matt Lawton and Todd Walker, both among the best offensively at their positions, and include new blood like David Ortiz, Corey Koskie, Torii Hunter, and Doug Mientkiewicz. While none of these players—except Ortiz—are potential superstars, they are all young, cheap, and likely to be improvements over their predecessors.

It appears the Twins have finally gotten religion. After delaying the inevitable while wasting time and money on people like Orlando Merced, Terry Steinbach, Brent Gates, and Otis Nixon, the plan now is to pare the payroll down, let the kids play and see what happens. Now, this is in part motivated by the uncertainty surrounding the franchise's future, but is a great idea regardless. The only position the Twins might not be able to fill with a reasonable internal solution is shortstop. The incumbent, Pat Meares, is arbitration-eligible and may be non-tendered. But there's likely to be sufficient bargain-basement solutions that he won't be missed. There's even a chance they could just hand Christian Guzman the job; he wouldn't be the worst shortstop in the league, and could pull a Mike Caruso.

The really fun part about this plan is how successful it could be. Fairly or not, younger teams are perceived differently by both the fans and media. They benefit from the backlash against—and this is a media creation—"greedy players" and tend to be more popular, and make for more positive coverage, than comparable teams with more veterans and a higher payroll. If this happens in Minneapolis, even a small uptick in attendance will make it easy to make money with such a small payroll.

Additionally, very young teams are volatile. Because all of the players are still developing, the potential is there for dramatic collective improvement. If some of the second-tier guys, like Koskie or Hunter, have years at the top of their range, the team could score 825 runs. It's not the Yankees, but

combined with some improvements in the pitching staff, it could be...

I think I see the problem. The Twins have had a terrible time developing pitchers since their 1991 World Series title. Despite breaking in a number of young starting pitchers, including Willie Banks, Pat Mahomes, Eddie Guardado, Carlos Pulido, Mike Trombley, and LaTroy Hawkins, only one of these, Radke, has ever posted an ERA under 4.00 as a starter for Minnesota. Trombley and Guardado have developed into effective relievers. The constant bombardment of young pitchers, along with the loss of what passed for reliable veteran starters (Kevin Tapani and Scott Erickson) and the franchise's increasing reluctance to spend for top-tier free agents, have left the Twins incapable of establishing a regular five-man rotation for much of the decade.

Nineteen ninety-eight may have been the beginning of a change. Brad Radke came off a strong 1997, but was worked hard early and went through a terrible stretch in July and August. Eric Milton and LaTroy Hawkins stayed in the rotation all year, flitting between average and poor, but established themselves as starters. After that, the Twins had bargain-basement free agents Mike Morgan and Bob Tewksbury, both of whom spent time on the disabled list. But unlike past years, Minnesota managed to keep from using a dozen starting pitchers and running four-month tryout camps for the last two spots. When Morgan and Tewksbury were hurt, and after Morgan was traded, Frankie Rodriguez and Dan Serafini got the bulk of their starts, with mixed results.

The Twins go into 1999 with three rotation spots set, and Serafini a good bet for the #4 slot. They may yet try and sign a veteran innings muncher. Given how low their payroll will be, it could be a good investment. The Twins had success with Bob Tewksbury the past two years in that role. As with the lineup, the rotation is young enough that we could see dramatic improvements.

Milton, in particular, could develop rapidly. Acquired in the Chuck Knoblauch trade, he had some very good starts this year and was not abused. A look at his Support-Neutral

---

Twins Prospectus

1998 record: 70-92; Fifth place, AL Central

Pythagorean W/L: 72-90

Runs scored: 734 (11th in AL)

Runs allowed: 818 (8th in AL)

Team EQA: .247 (12th in AL)

Park: Metrodome (moderate hitters')

1998: Changing of the guard; young players were allowed to make an impact.

1999: Influx of youth and development of best players could have Twins sneaking up on Cleveland.

---

data shows that his year did have value, and his SNWA was better than his real-life won-loss record. In my opinion, SN stats are particularly revealing for young pitchers, who are more prone to the disastrous outings that inflate ERA and opponents' OBP and SLG, but are only a bit more costly to a team than a "normal" bad start.

Milton was the jewel of the Knoblauch trade, which looks even better for the Twins now that it appears Knoblauch's peak as a dominant player is past. They got out from under a burdensome contract; cleared the way for their best offensive prospect, Todd Walker, to move back to his natural position; acquired a potential #1 starter who hadn't been abused; added a young shortstop prospect with great physical tools and the potential for explosive growth (Guzman); and even got a couple of C prospects, in Brian Buchanan and Chris Cumberland, to prop up the upper levels of the system.

It's rare that a team trading a superstar for a package of young players does even this well. If only Milton develops into a contributor, they're ahead of the game because of the benefit to Walker and the $20 million they can now spend elsewhere. Despite Terry Ryan's indiscriminate signing of mediocre veterans, he deserves a lot of credit for turning Knoblauch, Merced, and Morgan into Milton, Guzman, right-hander Matt Kinney, and a collection of second-tier prospects.

So what happens now? Well, as I mentioned, young teams have the potential to outstrip expectations if things break right. There are a couple of other markers pointing the Twins' way; they weren't as bad as their record indicated last year, with a Pythagorean projection of 72-90, two games better than they actually did. They carried a lot of dead weight last year offensively, with Terry Steinbach, Pat Meares, Ron Coomer, Alex Ochoa, and others. All of these players will see less playing time, and most will be replaced by better players. The pitching should be better, particularly the front-line starters. And it wouldn't surprise me to see a defensive improvement as well, especially at shortstop.

How much better can they be? Well, if the Indians insist on leaving the AL Central up for grabs by not winning 90 games, The Twins could give them a run. Whether they can be a wild-card contender depends not so much on what they do but what the Red Sox, Blue Jays, A's, and Mariners do. If it's

going to take 95 wins, I doubt they can get there; if it only takes 87, I like their chances.

A pennant race, or at least a wild-card chase, would complicate an already ugly mess. The Twins have threatened, cajoled, begged, pleaded, and wheedled, and they still can't get the state to build them a new stadium. Now, Governor-Elect Jesse "The Mind" Ventura (that had to make the book somehow) insists he will not support using taxpayer funds to build a playpen for the Twins. And their embarrassing flirtation with North Carolina left everybody unhappy.

However... ballot measures in San Diego and Denver rode the success of the Padres and Broncos to victories that will provide each of those teams a publically funded stadium. Despite the rejection of similar proposals in statehouses and general elections around the country, the pro-stadia forces always seem to keep coming back until they get what they want.

If the Twins can get Minneapolis excited next year, the drums will start beating again for a new stadium. A young, exciting, successful team could reignite the city's affection for the team. For all the bleating about how badly the Twins need a park to survive, the Twins drew enormous, raucous, handkerchief-waving mobs during their 1987 and 1991 championship seasons.

Minneapolis, like any city, will support a successful team that tries to win. No team can get support, nor should they expect it, when they are so obviously unwilling to make investments in winning. This is part of the problem in so-called "small markets." Organizations run down their chances and destroy any hope of developing an excitement about the team. Seattle and San Diego are just two places where it was said that the fans would not support a team in the current environment, that the market was too small. Anyone who watched the 1995, 1997, or 1998 postseasons would, I'd imagine, disagree.

Here's hoping the Twins can get people excited again, and that they don't hide behind their perceived disadvantages (isn't it funny how the Metrodome, their biggest advantage in 1987 and 1991, is now supposed to be their albatross?) to avoid making investments in winning. They're close to being a wild-card contender, closer than almost anyone thinks. The Twins will be a great story in about mid-August.

HITTERS (Averages: BA .260/ OBA .330/ SA .420, EQA .260)

Chad Allen   OF   Bats R   Age 24

YEAR	TEAM	LGE	AB	H	DB	TP	HR	BB	R	RBI	SB	CS	OUT	BA	OBA	SA	EQA	EQR	DEFENSE
1997	Ft Myers	Fla	405	113	12	2	4	35	47	38	13	8	300	.279	.336	.348	.242	43	103-OF 94
1997	New Brit	Eas	115	28	7	1	3	7	11	12	2	0	87	.243	.287	.400	.238	12	27-OF 80
1998	New Brit	Eas	508	128	25	5	8	45	58	48	16	7	387	.252	.313	.368	.239	54	132-OF 87
1999	*Minnesot*	*AL*	*465*	*122*	*21*	*2*	*7*	*37*	*52*	*45*	*11*	*6*	*349*	*.262*	*.317*	*.361*	*.233*	*46*	

One of a handful of similar Twins outfield prospects at New Britain and Salt Lake City. Allen seems to have established his level of play, and it's inadequate for a regular outfielder. Scouts are high on him, as befits a tools prospect, but he needs to step it up to stand out from John Barnes, Marc Lewis, and Jacque Jones. With the Twins in a state of flux, any young player who can get hot at the right time is in line for significant major league playing time. Keep that in mind as you read these evaluations.

John Barnes   OF   Bats L   Age 23

YEAR	TEAM	LGE	AB	H	DB	TP	HR	BB	R	RBI	SB	CS	OUT	BA	OBA	SA	EQA	EQR	DEFENSE
1997	Michigan	Mid	495	131	11	2	6	50	53	46	9	3	367	.265	.332	.331	.238	50	110-OF 98
1998	Trenton	Eas	380	99	10	0	14	36	39	46	3	6	287	.261	.325	.397	.247	44	92-OF 85
1998	New Brit	Eas	72	19	3	1	0	8	9	6	1	1	54	.264	.338	.333	.238	7	
1999	*Minnesot*	*AL*	*432*	*119*	*15*	*1*	*11*	*40*	*50*	*53*	*5*	*4*	*317*	*.275*	*.337*	*.391*	*.250*	*49*	

Part of the booty for Greg Swindell and Orlando Merced, Barnes looks a little like Merced as a hitter; a little average, a little plate discipline, some pop. It's unlikely that he'll play center field, so like Merced, he won't be very valuable as an everyday player. He could help a team as a fourth outfielder.

Papo Bolivar   OF   Bats R   Age 20

YEAR	TEAM	LGE	AB	H	DB	TP	HR	BB	R	RBI	SB	CS	OUT	BA	OBA	SA	EQA	EQR	DEFENSE
1997	Ft Wayne	Mid	324	76	8	2	7	7	21	24	10	6	254	.235	.251	.336	.197	22	88-OF 85
1998	Ft Myers	Fla	487	111	8	1	5	26	27	29	6	6	382	.228	.267	.279	.182	27	122-OF 87
1999	*Minnesot*	*AL*	*396*	*98*	*9*	*1*	*7*	*15*	*28*	*31*	*7*	*6*	*304*	*.247*	*.275*	*.328*	*.199*	*27*	

Continues to climb the charts as a teenager. He hasn't played well yet, so he's a bit of a stealth prospect. Bolivar didn't embarrass himself as a teenager in the Florida State League; continued physical development, coupled with gains in his plate discipline, will have him showing up on radar screens this summer. I like his chances, because youth is a tremendous advantage.

Brian Buchanan   OF   Bats R   Age 25

YEAR	TEAM	LGE	AB	H	DB	TP	HR	BB	R	RBI	SB	CS	OUT	BA	OBA	SA	EQA	EQR	DEFENSE
1996	Tampa	Fla	531	129	14	1	12	32	45	45	13	5	408	.243	.286	.341	.218	45	96-OF 94
1997	Norwich	Eas	467	129	19	2	7	24	45	46	8	6	344	.276	.312	.370	.235	46	111-OF 92
1998	SaltLake	PCL	481	106	17	2	12	33	39	39	11	2	377	.220	.270	.339	.212	39	120-OF 100
1999	*Minnesot*	*AL*	*479*	*124*	*17*	*1*	*13*	*31*	*49*	*51*	*10*	*3*	*358*	*.259*	*.304*	*.380*	*.234*	*48*	

Tools prospect who can't hit; ever get the feeling there's a factory somewhere in Myanmar where they make these guys for about eight cents a day? Buchanan has the advantage of being part of the Knoblauch trade: the organization would like him to succeed. He's not as good as the guys he's competing with, and in a fair fight would spend another year in Utah. There's a motivational tool.

Dan Cey   2B   Bats R   Age 23

YEAR	TEAM	LGE	AB	H	DB	TP	HR	BB	R	RBI	SB	CS	OUT	BA	OBA	SA	EQA	EQR	DEFENSE
1996	Ft Wayne	Mid	86	20	3	0	0	6	5	5	1	1	67	.233	.283	.267	.186	5	23-SS 88
1997	Ft Myers	Fla	524	139	26	2	8	31	54	49	12	5	390	.265	.306	.368	.235	52	63-SS 89
1998	New Brit	Eas	571	141	23	2	8	37	54	46	18	6	436	.247	.293	.336	.221	50	135-2B 98
1999	*Minnesot*	*AL*	*513*	*136*	*24*	*2*	*8*	*32*	*55*	*50*	*13*	*5*	*382*	*.265*	*.308*	*.366*	*.232*	*49*	

Not that he had a choice, but do you think Cey was all that happy about the position change? Ahead of him at shortstop in Minnesota was Pat Meares, a mediocrity; at Salt Lake City, Esteban Beltre. Sure, Luis Rivas was charging up from behind, but Cey had a two-level lead. Plenty of time to get some pension time in. Then he was moved to second base, and blocked at the major league level by the best player on the Twins. In fairness, he's probably a better second baseman than shortstop, but the move damaged his chances at a career.

Ron Coomer   3B/1B   Bats R   Age 32

YEAR	TEAM	LGE	AB	H	DB	TP	HR	BB	R	RBI	SB	CS	OUT	BA	OBA	SA	EQA	EQR	DEFENSE	
1996	Minnesot	AL	227	64	11	1	11	15	28	34	3	0	163	.282	.326	.485	.276	33	35-1B 140	15-OF 85
1997	Minnesot	AL	515	152	31	2	13	23	56	66	4	3	366	.295	.325	.439	.261	63	110-3B 101	
1998	Minnesot	AL	521	140	18	1	16	21	44	59	2	2	383	.269	.297	.399	.237	52	72-3B 97	44-1B 109
1999	*Minnesot*	*AL*	*446*	*123*	*22*	*1*	*14*	*20*	*45*	*56*	*3*	*2*	*325*	*.276*	*.307*	*.424*	*.245*	*48*		

An excellent example of a player who would be an excellent spare part, a real contributor to a championship team, but whose value disappears as a regular. Coomer hits left-handers very well and plays an acceptable third base. At 250 at-bats and $1,000,000, he's a good player. At 500 at-bats and more money, he's not. He could fall off a cliff any minute now; until he does, a great platoon partner for Koskie at third base or Mientkiewicz at DH.

Marty Cordova   LF   Bats R   Age 29

YEAR	TEAM	LGE	AB	H	DB	TP	HR	BB	R	RBI	SB	CS	OUT	BA	OBA	SA	EQA	EQR	DEFENSE
1996	Minnesot	AL	551	161	36	2	16	50	75	75	11	6	396	.292	.351	.452	.276	79	137-OF 99
1997	Minnesot	AL	372	90	18	4	15	31	40	46	5	3	285	.242	.300	.433	.249	44	91-OF 102
1998	Minnesot	AL	431	107	19	2	10	52	47	47	2	6	330	.248	.329	.371	.243	48	111-OF 95
1999	*Minnesot*	*AL*	*425*	*111*	*21*	*2*	*13*	*46*	*53*	*54*	*5*	*4*	*318*	*.261*	*.333*	*.412*	*.254*	*52*	

The problem with old rookies is that they're peaking even as you get to know them. Cordova hasn't been the same player since his plantar fascia injury in 1997. The Twins are trying to dump him, so pay close attention: if he ends up in the right situation, he could return to his 1995 level. He'd make a good Cub.

Michael Cuddyer   SS   Bats R   Age 20

YEAR	TEAM	LGE	AB	H	DB	TP	HR	BB	R	RBI	SB	CS	OUT	BA	OBA	SA	EQA	EQR	DEFENSE
1998	Ft Wayne	Mid	506	129	22	3	13	51	57	56	8	4	381	.255	.323	.387	.248	58	
1999	*Minnesot*	*AL*	*409*	*122*	*22*	*2*	*13*	*42*	*59*	*62*	*6*	*3*	*290*	*.298*	*.364*	*.457*	*.280*	*60*	

The Twins' 1997 first-round pick made a splash and ended up as Baseball America's #5 prospect in the Midwest League. It seems to be understood that he'll move to third base eventually, probably as soon as he catches up to Luis Rivas. He has a broad base of skills, and the plate discipline is nice to see in a teenager. The Twins' best prospect. ETA: late 2000.

Anthony Felston   OF   Bats L   Age 24

YEAR	TEAM	LGE	AB	H	DB	TP	HR	BB	R	RBI	SB	CS	OUT	BA	OBA	SA	EQA	EQR	DEFENSE
1996	Ft Wayne	Mid	206	57	3	1	0	33	33	16	11	3	152	.277	.377	.301	.257	25	56-OF 98
1997	Ft Wayne	Mid	343	77	5	1	2	41	37	19	20	9	275	.224	.307	.262	.209	28	89-OF 95
1998	Ft Myers	Fla	434	100	5	0	0	65	58	20	35	15	349	.230	.331	.242	.219	39	113-OF 96
1999	*Minnesot*	*AL*	*391*	*101*	*4*	*0*	*2*	*52*	*54*	*27*	*25*	*11*	*301*	*.258*	*.345*	*.284*	*.230*	*38*	

Felston is a bundle of extremes; a bit old for the Florida State League, he scorched it with 83 walks and 86 stolen bases in just 114 games. But he poked just eight doubles and had no other extra-base hits in 427 at-bats. I love OBP as much as the next guy, but you have to slug .350 or so to have value. The steals will get him noticed, though I doubt he'll be able to sustain his value even in Double-A. Pinch-runner prospect.

Brent Gates   3B/2B   Bats B   Age 29

YEAR	TEAM	LGE	AB	H	DB	TP	HR	BB	R	RBI	SB	CS	OUT	BA	OBA	SA	EQA	EQR	DEFENSE
1996	Oakland	AL	242	60	17	2	2	17	23	21	1	1	183	.248	.297	.360	.226	22	59-2B 97
1997	Seattle	AL	149	35	5	0	4	14	13	14	0	0	114	.235	.301	.349	.226	14	23-3B 105
1998	Minnesot	AL	328	80	8	0	5	37	32	28	3	3	251	.244	.321	.314	.224	30	70-3B 96
1999	*Minnesot*	*AL*	*259*	*68*	*9*	*0*	*5*	*25*	*28*	*27*	*2*	*1*	*192*	*.263*	*.327*	*.355*	*.237*	*26*	

Gates can't play shortstop, which limits his value as a utility infielder. He doesn't hit enough or run well or have a platoon split you can take advantage of. He's a failed second baseman, just clinging to the $150,000 a year and adding time to the pension. The Twins will improve when they clear guys like this from the roster.

Cristian Guzman   SS   Bats B   Age 21

YEAR	TEAM	LGE	AB	H	DB	TP	HR	BB	R	RBI	SB	CS	OUT	BA	OBA	SA	EQA	EQR	DEFENSE
1997	Greensbr	SAL	497	122	16	2	4	19	35	33	10	7	382	.245	.273	.310	.197	33	119-SS 99
1998	New Brit	Eas	567	153	27	4	1	19	50	43	17	11	425	.270	.294	.337	.217	47	139-SS 103
1999	Minnesot	AL	499	144	22	3	2	15	49	45	14	8	363	.289	.309	.357	.227	44	

Like Buchanan, Guzman came over in the Knoblauch trade, and will probably be given every chance to succeed. One thing to consider is that he is a late comer to the game, only having started playing about five years ago. By all accounts, he has the physical tools to play well, especially on defense. If someone can get through to him about patience, he will make a big leap forward. I like him, possibly as soon as this spring, if the Twins dump Meares in a cost-cutting move.

Denny Hocking   UT   Bats B   Age 29

YEAR	TEAM	LGE	AB	H	DB	TP	HR	BB	R	RBI	SB	CS	OUT	BA	OBA	SA	EQA	EQR	DEFENSE	
1996	SaltLake	PCL	126	27	3	1	2	9	9	8	2	1	100	.214	.267	.302	.194	8	18-SS 101	
1996	Minnesot	AL	125	22	2	0	2	7	4	4	3	4	106	.176	.220	.240	.134	3	25-OF 101	
1997	Minnesot	AL	249	63	11	4	2	19	24	22	3	5	191	.253	.306	.353	.225	23	33-SS 99	21-3B 91
1998	Minnesot	AL	195	38	5	1	3	17	12	11	2	1	158	.195	.259	.277	.181	11	17-SS 92	
1999	Minnesot	AL	210	47	8	1	3	17	16	16	2	3	166	.224	.282	.314	.198	14		

One of the Kelly Boys, that group of benign, amiable white guys who can't play baseball real well but, gosh darn it, they sure try hard. See Gates, Brent; Meares, Pat; Stahoviak, Scott. Hocking is better than Brent Gates because he can play shortstop, and would have much more value in the National League, where a player who can play six positions can have tactical value four days a week. He'll hit an empty .320 one of these years.

Torii Hunter   CF   Bats R   Age 23

YEAR	TEAM	LGE	AB	H	DB	TP	HR	BB	R	RBI	SB	CS	OUT	BA	OBA	SA	EQA	EQR	DEFENSE
1996	New Brit	Eas	346	89	16	2	7	24	35	34	6	5	262	.257	.305	.376	.234	35	95-OF 101
1997	New Brit	Eas	474	101	17	2	6	38	34	30	6	5	378	.213	.271	.295	.193	31	123-OF 99
1998	New Brit	Eas	309	85	22	2	6	17	36	33	9	7	231	.275	.313	.417	.248	36	81-OF 106
1998	SaltLake	PCL	88	24	4	0	3	1	7	10	2	2	66	.273	.281	.420	.233	9	22-OF 113
1999	Minnesot	AL	393	104	22	1	9	25	42	43	8	7	296	.265	.309	.394	.236	40	

Name sounds like the star of a movie Chris Kahrl might rent: "I Know Who You Did Last Summer, Starring Torii Hunter as Herself." When not acting as the setup for cheap jokes, Hunter likes to show people around beautiful downtown New Britain, a place he knows inside out after spending 2½ years there. Hunter's a good defensive outfielder with a strong arm, and should be the starting center fielder for the Twins this year. He's not a great player; if everything broke right for him he could be Devon White who, if you think about it, could co-star with Torii . . .

Jacque Jones   RF   Bats L   Age 24

YEAR	TEAM	LGE	AB	H	DB	TP	HR	BB	R	RBI	SB	CS	OUT	BA	OBA	SA	EQA	EQR	DEFENSE
1997	Ft Myers	Fla	541	147	21	3	14	30	55	60	12	7	401	.272	.310	.399	.244	59	129-OF 103
1998	New Brit	Eas	520	150	29	1	20	33	64	71	14	9	379	.288	.331	.463	.269	71	128-OF 108
1999	Minnesot	AL	497	143	25	2	17	28	62	67	14	7	361	.288	.326	.449	.261	63	

The best of the assorted Twins outfielders, Jones improved across the board while making the jump to Double-A and learning a new position. Broad-based improvement is a good sign; Jones still needs to be more patient and continue to improve offensively. He should start the year at Salt Lake City, a great hitting environment, which will raise his profile. I'm apparently writing about all the Trojan prospects this year. Fight on!

Corey Koskie   3B   Bats L   Age 26

YEAR	TEAM	LGE	AB	H	DB	TP	HR	BB	R	RBI	SB	CS	OUT	BA	OBA	SA	EQA	EQR	DEFENSE
1996	Ft Myers	Fla	343	80	9	1	9	32	29	33	1	1	264	.233	.299	.344	.223	31	86-3B 88
1997	New Brit	Eas	442	114	17	3	16	71	63	60	7	4	332	.258	.361	.419	.273	65	124-3B 81
1998	SaltLake	PCL	484	113	18	2	16	43	48	50	11	6	377	.233	.296	.378	.233	50	131-3B 81
1999	Minnesot	AL	444	110	17	1	15	48	51	53	7	4	338	.248	.321	.392	.244	50	

Koskie will outperform that projection in less playing time, because it's likely that Tom Kelly will platoon him. His defense is just passable and he has shown a platoon split, so it's not a terrible idea. Koskie isn't as good a third-base prospect as Glaus or Chavez, but he's probably a safe bet for 1999.

Chris Latham   OF   Bats B   Age 26

YEAR	TEAM	LGE	AB	H	DB	TP	HR	BB	R	RBI	SB	CS	OUT	BA	OBA	SA	EQA	EQR	DEFENSE
1996	SaltLake	PCL	365	86	11	2	9	33	41	32	21	7	286	.236	.299	.351	.232	37	108-OF 102
1997	SaltLake	PCL	468	111	13	2	6	48	46	36	16	14	371	.237	.308	.312	.217	41	116-OF 104
1998	SaltLake	PCL	360	88	11	2	7	46	50	32	20	4	276	.244	.330	.344	.247	42	92-OF 102
1998	Minnesot	AL	93	14	1	0	1	13	5	3	3	2	81	.151	.255	.194	.150	4	26-OF 101
1999	*Minnesot*	*AL*	*450*	*109*	*14*	*2*	*10*	*47*	*53*	*42*	*18*	*8*	*349*	*.242*	*.314*	*.349*	*.231*	*45*	

An interesting test of Tom Kelly's aptitude. Latham is qualified to be major league bench player, with speed, good range, and some hitting ability. He's not good enough to play every day ahead of Hunter, Lawton, or the better prospects, though his broad base of skills would make him an excellent reserve. I think Latham could turn into Stan Javier for a few years. That's a compliment.

Matt Lawton   RF/CF   Bats L   Age 27

YEAR	TEAM	LGE	AB	H	DB	TP	HR	BB	R	RBI	SB	CS	OUT	BA	OBA	SA	EQA	EQR	DEFENSE
1996	SaltLake	PCL	205	52	8	1	6	23	23	24	2	3	156	.254	.329	.390	.248	24	39-OF 99
1996	Minnesot	AL	245	58	8	1	5	27	24	22	4	5	192	.237	.312	.339	.226	23	69-OF 107
1997	Minnesot	AL	452	110	30	3	14	76	67	57	7	4	346	.243	.352	.416	.269	65	128-OF 97
1998	Minnesot	AL	547	150	35	6	21	87	91	82	14	8	405	.274	.374	.475	.291	93	151-OF 102
1999	*Minnesot*	*AL*	*503*	*135*	*31*	*3*	*17*	*75*	*80*	*72*	*10*	*6*	*374*	*.268*	*.363*	*.443*	*.276*	*75*	

Good hitter who has made dramatic gains the past two years with almost no one noticing. Lawton has excellent secondary skills—he helps you if he hits .260—and is just now reaching his peak. That projection is low; if he hits .260, his OPS will be around .875. If the singles drop in, he could put up a bad Manny Ramirez year, say .300/.400/.520. Playing in Minnesota means he'll be undervalued in most roto/fantasy/Strat leagues, so take advantage.

Matthew LeCroy   C   Bats R   Age 23

YEAR	TEAM	LGE	AB	H	DB	TP	HR	BB	R	RBI	SB	CS	OUT	BA	OBA	SA	EQA	EQR	DEFENSE
1998	Ft Wayne	Mid	230	55	7	1	7	27	23	26	0	0	175	.239	.319	.370	.241	25	46-C 93
1998	Ft Myers	Fla	200	55	4	1	9	18	22	29	1	1	146	.275	.335	.440	.266	27	42-C 94
1999	*Minnesot*	*AL*	*349*	*96*	*12*	*0*	*15*	*32*	*41*	*51*	*1*	*1*	*254*	*.275*	*.336*	*.438*	*.263*	*45*	

The player the Twins picked as compensation for the loss of Travis Lee. LeCroy hasn't yet endured the sniping about his defense that generally accompanies offense like this. With Terry Steinbach a free agent, and Javier Valentin a disappointment, the Twins are left with three young catchers (A.J. Pierzynski and Chad Moeller are the other two). LeCroy is the best of the bunch and has a path to a job. Call him the early front-runner for 2000 AL Rookie of the Year.

Marc Lewis   OF   Bats L   Age 24

YEAR	TEAM	LGE	AB	H	DB	TP	HR	BB	R	RBI	SB	CS	OUT	BA	OBA	SA	EQA	EQR	DEFENSE
1996	Macon	SAL	244	65	7	2	4	15	26	23	10	4	183	.266	.309	.361	.236	25	61-OF 90
1996	Durham	Car	260	65	6	1	5	19	26	22	11	5	200	.250	.301	.338	.226	24	62-OF 98
1997	Greenvil	Sou	497	106	8	2	12	18	29	31	14	9	400	.213	.241	.310	.182	28	126-OF 99
1998	SaltLake	PCL	426	102	18	1	11	22	34	38	8	8	332	.239	.277	.364	.216	36	110-OF 90
1999	*Minnesot*	*AL*	*448*	*113*	*15*	*1*	*14*	*23*	*40*	*47*	*10*	*8*	*343*	*.252*	*.289*	*.384*	*.225*	*41*	

Garret Anderson Lite. Lewis hits line drives, enough of them to hit .280-.300 if he got a job. He wouldn't be better than a fourth outfielder, if that. Stretched as a center fielder, he could platoon with Jacque Jones in left. It would certainly be a better solution than paying Luis Gonzalez or some other "proven" player.

Pat Meares — SS — Bats R — Age 30

YEAR	TEAM	LGE	AB	H	DB	TP	HR	BB	R	RBI	SB	CS	OUT	BA	OBA	SA	EQA	EQR	DEFENSE
1996	Minnesot	AL	507	127	24	7	7	14	41	43	9	5	385	.250	.271	.367	.216	42	138-SS 85
1997	Minnesot	AL	433	118	23	3	10	19	42	48	7	7	322	.273	.303	.409	.241	46	128-SS 105
1998	Minnesot	AL	535	136	24	3	9	27	45	49	6	4	403	.254	.290	.361	.223	47	145-SS 97
1999	Minnesot	AL	481	123	24	3	9	21	43	46	6	4	362	.256	.287	.374	.221	42	

About to become too expensive for his own good. Meares is a below-average shortstop, exactly the type of player the Twins collected in the post-1991 decline. He's arbitration-eligible, and a good bet to be non-tendered as the Twins get the payroll down under $20 million. I doubt he'll ever get 500 plate appearances again. I'm sure riots will ensue.

Doug Mientkiewicz — 1B — Bats L — Age 25

YEAR	TEAM	LGE	AB	H	DB	TP	HR	BB	R	RBI	SB	CS	OUT	BA	OBA	SA	EQA	EQR	DEFENSE
1996	Ft Myers	Fla	500	134	26	2	7	55	62	52	7	2	368	.268	.341	.370	.252	59	124-1B 93
1997	New Brit	Eas	473	111	21	2	11	81	68	48	15	6	368	.235	.347	.357	.254	60	106-1B 87
1998	New Brit	Eas	510	153	23	0	16	81	83	75	8	3	360	.300	.396	.439	.295	85	136-1B 96
1999	Minnesot	AL	488	139	26	1	14	71	79	69	10	3	352	.285	.376	.428	.280	73	

Mientkiewicz is blocked at the major league level by a younger, better version of himself, David Ortiz. He is good defensively (a converted third baseman), and would make a good bench player. I expect him to start the year at Salt Lake City, but make a few trips to Minnesota, possibly settling in as part of a cheap DH platoon. He'll eventually have a few Dave Magadan years.

Chad Moeller — C — Bats R — Age 24

YEAR	TEAM	LGE	AB	H	DB	TP	HR	BB	R	RBI	SB	CS	OUT	BA	OBA	SA	EQA	EQR	DEFENSE
1996	Elizbthn	App	61	15	0	0	2	11	7	7	0	1	47	.246	.361	.344	.251	7	
1997	Ft Wayne	Mid	388	91	8	1	7	35	32	32	5	4	301	.235	.298	.314	.213	32	
1998	Ft Myers	Fla	254	69	11	1	5	25	28	29	1	2	187	.272	.337	.382	.250	29	56-C 86
1998	New Brit	Eas	189	43	6	0	6	21	18	19	2	1	147	.228	.305	.354	.231	19	55-C 97
1999	Minnesot	AL	372	97	13	1	9	35	39	42	2	2	277	.261	.324	.374	.239	39	

Moeller continued to develop, but at the end of the year, it was LeCroy who got a week in Salt Lake City. His time is now, because LeCroy is a much better hitter and has a bit of an organizational halo. If he doesn't establish himself in 1999, he's marking time until he's a six-year free agent.

Paul Molitor — DH — Bats R — Age 42

YEAR	TEAM	LGE	AB	H	DB	TP	HR	BB	R	RBI	SB	CS	OUT	BA	OBA	SA	EQA	EQR	DEFENSE
1996	Minnesot	AL	637	206	38	8	8	52	96	84	18	7	438	.323	.374	.446	.286	96	
1997	Minnesot	AL	528	159	33	4	10	46	73	68	11	4	373	.301	.357	.436	.276	75	
1998	Minnesot	AL	493	135	28	5	4	48	62	50	8	2	360	.274	.338	.375	.253	58	
1999	Minnesot	AL	504	132	28	3	5	51	60	50	6	3	375	.262	.330	.359	.239	52	

Retired. Perceived as a very intelligent player and person, he was involved in the labor negotiations in 1990 and 1994-95. For most, it's a foregone conclusion he'll be successful as an executive. Should be interesting.

Otis Nixon — CF — Bats B — Age 40

YEAR	TEAM	LGE	AB	H	DB	TP	HR	BB	R	RBI	SB	CS	OUT	BA	OBA	SA	EQA	EQR	DEFENSE
1996	Toronto	AL	482	130	14	1	1	67	87	31	56	15	367	.270	.359	.309	.257	61	120-OF 114
1997	Toronto	AL	396	105	12	1	1	53	71	25	49	11	301	.265	.352	.308	.256	50	101-OF 107
1997	LosAngls	NL	176	50	7	2	1	14	25	16	11	2	128	.284	.337	.364	.255	21	32-OF 117
1998	Minnesot	AL	440	129	6	6	1	46	70	37	34	7	318	.293	.360	.341	.262	56	105-OF 102
1999	Atlanta	NL	446	107	10	3	1	55	58	28	32	9	348	.240	.323	.283	.232	45	

Against all odds, he's simply not declining as a player. Last year, he posted the highest batting average, second-highest slugging percentage (OK, .344, but still...), and highest stolen base percentage of his career. He is becoming useless from the right side, but as a platoon outfielder, pinch-runner, and defensive replacement, he can help a good team. The Braves have signed him to be the fourth outfielder.

Alex Ochoa   RF/LF   Bats R   Age 27

YEAR	TEAM	LGE	AB	H	DB	TP	HR	BB	R	RBI	SB	CS	OUT	BA	OBA	SA	EQA	EQR	DEFENSE
1996	Norfolk	Int	232	73	9	2	7	30	34	36	4	8	167	.315	.393	.461	.288	37	58-OF 97
1996	NY Mets	NL	284	86	20	2	5	19	36	36	3	3	201	.303	.347	.440	.269	38	61-OF 100
1997	NY Mets	NL	237	57	15	1	3	20	23	20	2	4	184	.241	.300	.350	.222	21	71-OF 86
1998	Minnesot	AL	245	61	14	2	2	12	22	19	5	3	187	.249	.284	.347	.217	20	61-OF 88
1999	*Minnesot*	*AL*	*257*	*71*	*14*	*1*	*4*	*18*	*28*	*28*	*4*	*4*	*190*	*.276*	*.324*	*.385*	*.240*	*27*	

Ochoa is a poor-hit, poor-field player who parlayed physical tools, including a strong arm, into prospect status. Tools are overrated. Strike zone judgment isn't. Ochoa brings nothing to the table you can't find in better players, and should be sent back to Triple-A.

David Ortiz   1B   Bats L   Age 23

YEAR	TEAM	LGE	AB	H	DB	TP	HR	BB	R	RBI	SB	CS	OUT	BA	OBA	SA	EQA	EQR	DEFENSE
1996	Wisconsn	Mid	488	140	16	0	17	37	52	66	2	2	350	.287	.337	.424	.262	62	122-1B 106
1997	Ft Myers	Fla	241	76	8	0	12	20	31	41	1	1	166	.315	.368	.498	.294	39	58-1B 93
1997	New Brit	Eas	258	79	17	2	11	16	33	42	2	4	183	.306	.347	.516	.285	40	32-1B 84
1997	Minnesot	AL	48	15	1	0	2	2	5	7	0	0	33	.312	.340	.458	.273	6	
1998	Minnesot	AL	273	74	13	0	11	40	38	40	1	0	199	.271	.364	.440	.281	41	67-1B 103
1999	*Minnesot*	*AL*	*443*	*130*	*18*	*0*	*22*	*40*	*57*	*75*	*1*	*2*	*315*	*.293*	*.352*	*.483*	*.280*	*65*	

Ortiz took a big leap forward last year in his plate discipline. A broken bone in his right wrist took cost him time and appeared to curtail his power when he returned. Don't worry about it. Ortiz could take another big step forward this year; 23 is an age at which many players boost their power. Get him.

A.J. Pierzynski   C   Bats L   Age 22

YEAR	TEAM	LGE	AB	H	DB	TP	HR	BB	R	RBI	SB	CS	OUT	BA	OBA	SA	EQA	EQR	DEFENSE
1996	Ft Wayne	Mid	434	106	20	1	7	14	28	35	0	2	330	.244	.268	.343	.204	31	
1997	Ft Myers	Fla	412	107	13	1	9	16	31	39	1	1	306	.260	.287	.362	.221	35	
1998	New Brit	Eas	212	61	6	0	4	10	18	23	0	2	153	.288	.320	.373	.237	21	56-C 103
1998	SaltLake	PCL	201	41	5	0	6	9	10	14	2	1	161	.204	.238	.318	.183	12	66-C 100
1999	*Minnesot*	*AL*	*401*	*106*	*13*	*1*	*10*	*17*	*33*	*43*	*1*	*1*	*296*	*.264*	*.294*	*.377*	*.225*	*35*	

Big guy who hits like Joel Skinner. Pierzynski could be the Twins' starting catcher on Opening Day, but he's just keeping the seat warm for Matt LeCroy. If it were up to me, I'd push Chad Moeller to the majors, get a veteran caddy for him, keep Pierzynski at Triple-A to back up LeCroy, and plan for LeCroy to be my catcher in 2000.

Michael Restovich   OF   Bats R   Age 20

YEAR	TEAM	LGE	AB	H	DB	TP	HR	BB	R	RBI	SB	CS	OUT	BA	OBA	SA	EQA	EQR	DEFENSE
1998	Elizbthn	App	240	65	8	1	7	37	33	32	2	1	176	.271	.368	.400	.272	34	59-OF 88
1999	*Minnesot*	*AL*	*233*	*81*	*13*	*1*	*7*	*31*	*42*	*43*	*1*	*1*	*153*	*.348*	*.424*	*.502*	*.317*	*43*	

MVP of the Appy League; we normally wouldn't cover guys this far down in the system, but Restovich has exceptional plate discipline and showed good power in his first pro season. He scuffled a bit with the transition to the outfield from his high school position (third base), but they seem to think he'll be adequate outfielder. He could leap three levels in one year, so pay attention.

Luis Rivas   SS   Bats R   Age 19

YEAR	TEAM	LGE	AB	H	DB	TP	HR	BB	R	RBI	SB	CS	OUT	BA	OBA	SA	EQA	EQR	DEFENSE
1997	Ft Wayne	Mid	421	87	16	3	1	26	26	19	14	10	344	.207	.253	.266	.173	21	120-SS 90
1998	Ft Myers	Fla	459	115	17	2	4	13	37	31	16	5	349	.251	.271	.322	.206	33	124-SS 93
1999	*Minnesot*	*AL*	*400*	*104*	*16*	*2*	*3*	*15*	*36*	*30*	*13*	*7*	*303*	*.260*	*.287*	*.333*	*.209*	*30*	

Just 18 years old, and held his own in the Florida State League. He regressed a bit by becoming too aggressive at the plate, but countered that by improving his glovework and, as we can expect him to do for awhile, hitting for more power. Scouts think he's the best prospect in the system; while he has a tremendous upside, I think Cuddyer and LeCroy are better prospects. Rivas is #3, however, and would be number one in many systems.

Terry Steinbach   C   Bats R   Age 37

YEAR	TEAM	LGE	AB	H	DB	TP	HR	BB	R	RBI	SB	CS	OUT	BA	OBA	SA	EQA	EQR	DEFENSE
1996	Oakland	AL	502	131	23	1	33	46	59	83	0	1	372	.261	.323	.508	.277	75	
1997	Minnesot	AL	440	107	25	1	13	36	46	47	6	1	334	.243	.300	.393	.241	47	
1998	Minnesot	AL	416	98	23	2	14	39	42	47	0	1	319	.236	.301	.401	.241	45	114-C 103
1999	*Minnesot*	*AL*	*417*	*97*	*21*	*1*	*15*	*39*	*42*	*48*	*1*	*1*	*321*	*.233*	*.298*	*.396*	*.234*	*43*	

He's slowly fading away, and if he wants to keep playing, he'll do so for much less money. Steinbach would make an effective backup catcher, and come in about $2 million cheaper than Joe Girardi. Whether he's willing to be a backup is an open question at this point.

Javier Valentin   C   Bats B   Age 23

YEAR	TEAM	LGE	AB	H	DB	TP	HR	BB	R	RBI	SB	CS	OUT	BA	OBA	SA	EQA	EQR	DEFENSE
1995	Ft Wayne	Mid	388	113	14	2	16	36	46	59	0	3	278	.291	.351	.461	.276	56	
1996	Ft Myers	Fla	341	85	13	1	9	28	32	36	1	0	256	.249	.306	.372	.236	34	
1996	New Brit	Eas	167	38	6	0	3	14	12	13	0	2	131	.228	.287	.317	.205	12	
1997	New Brit	Eas	371	83	8	0	8	24	24	27	2	2	290	.224	.271	.310	.196	25	
1998	Minnesot	AL	160	30	7	1	3	12	9	10	0	0	130	.188	.244	.300	.180	9	45-C 93
1999	*Minnesot*	*AL*	*268*	*66*	*8*	*0*	*7*	*20*	*23*	*27*	*1*	*1*	*203*	*.246*	*.299*	*.354*	*.221*	*23*	

For the most part, we're not running 1995 lines this year, but I've left Valentin's in to illustrate a point: past minor league performance, properly translated, predicts future major league performance as well as past major league performance. And like major league performance, sometimes there's an outlier. Valentin's 1995 had the analyst community drooling, but it's apparent that it was a favorite restaurant in Fort Wayne, or his girlfriend that year, or an alien taking over his body. It happens, in the majors and minors, more often than you'd think.

Todd Walker   2B   Bats L   Age 26

YEAR	TEAM	LGE	AB	H	DB	TP	HR	BB	R	RBI	SB	CS	OUT	BA	OBA	SA	EQA	EQR	DEFENSE	
1996	SaltLake	PCL	530	161	26	5	25	51	77	89	11	6	375	.304	.365	.513	.296	89	85-3B 97	34-2B 93
1996	Minnesot	AL	80	19	5	0	0	4	6	5	2	0	61	.237	.274	.300	.201	6	15-3B 118	
1997	Minnesot	AL	154	36	7	1	3	11	16	13	7	0	118	.234	.285	.351	.229	15	31-3B 110	
1997	SaltLake	PCL	303	84	10	1	8	38	38	38	4	4	223	.277	.358	.396	.264	40	73-3B 96	
1998	Minnesot	AL	518	162	39	3	12	49	82	72	17	7	363	.313	.372	.469	.290	82	133-2B 101	
1999	*Minnesot*	*AL*	*479*	*144*	*31*	*2*	*14*	*48*	*77*	*69*	*16*	*6*	*341*	*.301*	*.364*	*.461*	*.283*	*72*		

After a year as a victim of Tom Kelly, Walker got his position and his stroke back. He had a better year than Knoblauch, a trend you can expect to continue. Walker's defense was better at second base than third base, which isn't meant as damning with faint praise. He'll play in three to five All-Star Games; if he has the mid-career romance with walks that some late bloomers do, he'll be an MVP candidate once or twice. He's that good.

PITCHERS (Averages: 4.00 ERA, 9.00 H/9, 1.00 HR/9, 3.00 BB/9, 6.00 K/9, 1.00 KWH)

Rick Aguilera   Throws R   Age 37

YEAR	TEAM	LGE	IP	H	ER	HR	BB	K	ERA	W	L	H/9	HR/9	BB/9	K/9	KWH	PERA
1996	Minnesot	AL	114.7	116	52	17	22	83	4.08	6	7	9.10	1.33	1.73	6.51	2.02	3.92
1997	Minnesot	AL	70.3	64	24	8	19	66	3.07	5	3	8.19	1.02	2.43	8.45	2.69	3.33
1998	Minnesot	AL	76.7	72	28	7	13	55	3.29	5	4	8.45	0.82	1.53	6.46	2.42	3.17

Interchangeable with a couple dozen other relievers, if you don't mind paying $2 million less and getting a lot more upside. Aguilera has profited greatly from the closer myth, without being a good pitcher since 1995. Back with the Twins in 1999, he's best used as trade bait.

Travis Baptist Throws L Age 27

YEAR	TEAM	LGE	IP	H	ER	HR	BB	K	ERA	W	L	H/9	HR/9	BB/9	K/9	KWH	PERA
1996	Syracuse	Int	138.3	204	84	15	50	65	5.47	5	10	13.27	0.98	3.25	4.23	0.31	5.99
1997	New Brit	Eas	54.7	67	33	5	27	34	5.43	2	4	11.03	0.82	4.45	5.60	0.48	4.94
1997	SaltLake	PCL	46.0	48	14	3	9	22	2.74	3	2	9.39	0.59	1.76	4.30	0.84	3.52
1998	SaltLake	PCL	135.7	137	48	10	45	74	3.18	9	6	9.09	0.66	2.99	4.91	0.67	3.65
1998	Minnesot	AL	28.0	34	15	5	9	11	4.82	1	2	10.93	1.61	2.89	3.54	0.30	5.46

Soft-tosser who has chewed up the Pacific Coast League the last two years. It's unlikely that he'd be successful in the majors without an adjustment period, which hurts his chances. He needs to find a manager or a pitching coach who's willing to put up with his 1999-2000, so he can be Jamie Moyer in 2001-2004. I don't see Tom Kelly, with his notorious impatience with young players, as his hero.

Shane Bowers Throws R Age 27

YEAR	TEAM	LGE	IP	H	ER	HR	BB	K	ERA	W	L	H/9	HR/9	BB/9	K/9	KWH	PERA
1996	New Brit	Eas	120.3	173	85	16	44	70	6.36	4	9	12.94	1.20	3.29	5.24	0.48	6.06
1997	New Brit	Eas	63.3	89	37	5	23	40	5.26	3	4	12.65	0.71	3.27	5.68	0.59	5.54
1997	SaltLake	PCL	54.0	67	30	10	14	36	5.00	2	4	11.17	1.67	2.33	6.00	1.04	5.50
1998	SaltLake	PCL	110.7	149	69	16	44	77	5.61	4	8	12.12	1.30	3.58	6.26	0.68	5.77

Replacement-level pitcher who had his turn as the Twins' Next Big Thing in 1997 and pitched horribly. Now on the Scott Klingenbeck career track, he'll sign a lot of autographs in places like Omaha and Tacoma, waiting for a meteor to land in somebody's bullpen. Check back in 2002.

Hector Carrasco Throws R Age 29

YEAR	TEAM	LGE	IP	H	ER	HR	BB	K	ERA	W	L	H/9	HR/9	BB/9	K/9	KWH	PERA
1996	Cincnnti	NL	76.3	62	33	6	43	53	3.89	4	4	7.31	0.71	5.07	6.25	0.79	3.07
1997	Cincnnti	NL	53.3	52	21	3	23	42	3.54	3	3	8.78	0.51	3.88	7.09	1.11	3.54
1997	KansasCy	AL	35.7	29	17	4	14	29	4.29	2	2	7.32	1.01	3.53	7.32	1.55	3.03
1998	Minnesot	AL	64.7	73	24	4	28	45	3.34	4	3	10.16	0.56	3.90	6.26	0.74	4.31

Carrasco was dumped on the Twins at the end of spring training and had his most effective year since 1994. I don't like his chances to repeat, since he actually pitched pretty poorly; it just didn't show up on the scoreboard. Bad risk.

Chris Cumberland Throws L Age 26

YEAR	TEAM	LGE	IP	H	ER	HR	BB	K	ERA	W	L	H/9	HR/9	BB/9	K/9	KWH	PERA
1996	Columbus	Int	58.7	95	41	9	23	31	6.29	2	5	14.57	1.38	3.53	4.76	0.33	7.06
1996	Norwich	Eas	92.0	131	76	14	37	34	7.43	2	8	12.82	1.37	3.62	3.33	0.18	6.16
1997	Norwich	Eas	143.0	228	107	11	58	58	6.73	4	12	14.35	0.69	3.65	3.65	0.19	6.23
1998	New Brit	Eas	50.3	58	31	1	19	33	5.54	2	4	10.37	0.18	3.40	5.90	0.74	3.93
1998	SaltLake	PCL	31.0	39	19	2	19	15	5.52	1	2	11.32	0.58	5.52	4.35	0.23	4.94

Another part of the Knoblauch trade, the Twins re-established him by moving him to the bullpen. He's no different than a couple of dozen other guys, but has the advantages of being a player the organization has an investment in and that also isn't flush with relievers.

Eddie Guardado Throws L Age 28

YEAR	TEAM	LGE	IP	H	ER	HR	BB	K	ERA	W	L	H/9	HR/9	BB/9	K/9	KWH	PERA
1996	Minnesot	AL	75.7	59	33	10	27	74	3.93	4	4	7.02	1.19	3.21	8.80	2.58	2.85
1997	Minnesot	AL	47.3	45	18	6	15	53	3.42	3	2	8.56	1.14	2.85	10.08	3.12	3.61
1998	Minnesot	AL	68.0	64	27	9	26	52	3.57	4	4	8.47	1.19	3.44	6.88	1.22	3.71

Serviceable left-handed reliever who can be used as either a one-batter guy or as a long man, depending on your other personnel. Valuable to his manager, he has very little value in fantasy games. He doesn't get saves for roto, and he gives up too much power to be useful in Strat or Scoresheet. The sharp decline in his strikeout rate is ominous.

Jeff Harris			Throws R			Age 24										
YEAR	TEAM	LGE	IP	H	ER	HR	BB	K	ERA	W	L	H/9	HR/9	BB/9	K/9	KWH	PERA
1996	Ft Wayne	Mid	82.0	125	43	6	34	57	4.72	4	5	13.72	0.66	3.73	6.26	0.57	5.93
1997	Ft Myers	Fla	38.3	44	16	6	17	23	3.76	2	2	10.33	1.41	3.99	5.40	0.53	4.93
1997	New Brit	Eas	40.0	38	16	2	14	34	3.60	2	2	8.55	0.45	3.15	7.65	1.63	3.15
1998	New Brit	Eas	36.3	26	8	4	5	30	1.98	3	1	6.44	0.99	1.24	7.43	5.19	1.98
1998	SaltLake	PCL	33.7	37	19	4	19	20	5.08	2	2	9.89	1.07	5.08	5.35	0.43	4.81

Control pitcher who had a superficially big year at two levels (9-0, 8 saves). He's not much more than middle relief material, but in that class, anything that makes you stand out is a good thing. I think Harris's skill set is conducive to success as a setup man, and would love to see him get a clean shot.

LaTroy Hawkins			Throws R			Age 26										
YEAR	TEAM	LGE	IP	H	ER	HR	BB	K	ERA	W	L	H/9	HR/9	BB/9	K/9	KWH	PERA
1996	SaltLake	PCL	136.7	143	58	12	30	85	3.82	8	7	9.42	0.79	1.98	5.60	1.26	3.75
1996	Minnesot	AL	27.3	40	18	7	8	24	5.93	1	2	13.17	2.30	2.63	7.90	1.35	7.24
1997	SaltLake	PCL	74.7	98	43	4	14	43	5.18	3	5	11.81	0.48	1.69	5.18	1.01	4.70
1997	Minnesot	AL	107.7	133	59	18	41	57	4.93	5	7	11.12	1.50	3.43	4.76	0.45	5.43
1998	Minnesot	AL	197.7	220	101	25	55	103	4.60	9	13	10.02	1.14	2.50	4.69	0.66	4.42

There was a lot to like in Hawkins's performance last season. For one, he stayed healthy and in the rotation all year, which isn't as easy as it sounds. He's improved over his two previous stints in the rotation, displaying better command. While he's in a pretty bad environment for a flyball pitcher, I think 1999 will continue the improvement curve. In my opinion, Hawkins is one of the AL's biggest sleepers.

Matt Kinney			Throws R			Age 22										
YEAR	TEAM	LGE	IP	H	ER	HR	BB	K	ERA	W	L	H/9	HR/9	BB/9	K/9	KWH	PERA
1996	Lowell	NYP	87.7	85	53	1	49	45	5.44	4	6	8.73	0.10	5.03	4.62	0.36	3.39
1997	Michigan	Mid	111.0	126	66	6	81	82	5.35	4	8	10.22	0.49	6.57	6.65	0.49	4.62
1998	Sarasota	Fla	117.7	134	73	6	84	72	5.58	4	9	10.25	0.46	6.42	5.51	0.35	4.59
1998	Ft Myers	Fla	35.3	39	20	0	20	29	5.09	2	2	9.93	0.00	5.09	7.39	0.81	3.82

Getting this kid for two months of Greg Swindell and Orlando Merced is criminal. Kinney is a tall drink of water with a four-pitch arsenal. Upon arrival, he became the second-best pitching prospect in the organization, and just needs more physical maturity and innings to become the next big thing. Capable of explosive development, and also capable of going Millitello.

Mike Lincoln			Throws R			Age 24										
YEAR	TEAM	LGE	IP	H	ER	HR	BB	K	ERA	W	L	H/9	HR/9	BB/9	K/9	KWH	PERA
1996	Ft Myers	Fla	54.7	88	40	8	27	19	6.59	2	4	14.49	1.32	4.45	3.13	0.11	6.91
1997	Ft Myers	Fla	121.0	182	59	6	29	55	4.39	6	7	13.54	0.45	2.16	4.09	0.43	5.50
1998	New Brit	Eas	163.3	217	90	14	34	82	4.96	7	11	11.96	0.77	1.87	4.52	0.68	5.01

His command is among the best in the minor leagues, but there are real concerns about his ability to succeed without a plus fastball. The best pitching prospect in the organization, so I think you have to look at the performance and give him a shot. Short-term outlook isn't good; long-term is very good. Be patient.

Joe Mays			Throws R			Age 23										
YEAR	TEAM	LGE	IP	H	ER	HR	BB	K	ERA	W	L	H/9	HR/9	BB/9	K/9	KWH	PERA
1996	Everett	Nwn	63.0	71	36	4	25	32	5.14	3	4	10.14	0.57	3.57	4.57	0.43	4.29
1997	Wisconsn	Mid	76.3	86	26	4	25	51	3.07	5	3	10.14	0.47	2.95	6.01	0.91	4.01
1997	Lancastr	Cal	95.7	122	50	9	33	57	4.70	5	6	11.48	0.85	3.10	5.36	0.61	4.99
1998	Ft Myers	Fla	87.7	129	52	9	26	60	5.34	4	6	13.24	0.92	2.67	6.16	0.80	5.85
1998	New Brit	Eas	55.3	74	42	4	20	35	6.83	2	4	12.04	0.65	3.25	5.69	0.62	5.20

Mays is an unknown, despite displaying many of the same traits as Lincoln: good command, keeps the ball in the park; he even has a fastball. Struggled a bit after the promotion to New Britain, although the peripherals were still there. I'd like to have him in my organization.

Travis Miller   Throws L   Age 26

YEAR	TEAM	LGE	IP	H	ER	HR	BB	K	ERA	W	L	H/9	HR/9	BB/9	K/9	KWH	PERA
1996	SaltLake	PCL	159.7	195	85	18	56	124	4.79	7	11	10.99	1.01	3.16	6.99	1.06	4.90
1996	Minnesot	AL	27.3	44	22	6	7	15	7.24	1	2	14.49	1.98	2.30	4.94	0.55	7.24
1997	SaltLake	PCL	123.3	139	60	10	52	70	4.38	6	8	10.14	0.73	3.79	5.11	0.51	4.38
1997	Minnesot	AL	50.3	64	41	7	20	25	7.33	1	5	11.44	1.25	3.58	4.47	0.37	5.36
1998	SaltLake	PCL	59.0	63	29	3	33	51	4.42	3	4	9.61	0.46	5.03	7.78	0.94	4.12
1998	Minnesot	AL	24.3	25	8	0	9	22	2.96	2	1	9.25	0.00	3.33	8.14	1.61	3.33

A conversion to relief agreed with him at both Triple-A and in a brief stint with the Twins. Will battle for jobs in spring training for the next few years, winning more than losing, and make enough dough to put the kids through college. It's the American Dream. Unlikely to have much fantasy value.

Ryan Mills   Throws L   Age 21

YEAR	TEAM	LGE	IP	H	ER	HR	BB	K	ERA	W	L	H/9	HR/9	BB/9	K/9	KWH	PERA
1998	Ft Myers	Fla	4.7	3	5	0	1	2	9.64	0	1	5.79	0.00	1.93	3.86	1.00	1.93

The Twins' 1998 #1 strained his shoulder after two professional outings, which really has to make the player development staff reach for the Maalox. As with anyone taken in the top ten of the draft, he's expected to be a #1 starter. He's a pitching prospect; the only thing I expect him to be is hurt.

Eric Milton   Throws L   Age 23

YEAR	TEAM	LGE	IP	H	ER	HR	BB	K	ERA	W	L	H/9	HR/9	BB/9	K/9	KWH	PERA
1997	Tampa	Fla	90.0	98	40	10	16	71	4.00	5	5	9.80	1.00	1.60	7.10	2.41	4.00
1997	Norwich	Eas	75.7	68	28	2	33	51	3.33	5	3	8.09	0.24	3.93	6.07	0.87	2.97
1998	Minnesot	AL	179.3	190	91	23	63	104	4.57	9	11	9.54	1.15	3.16	5.22	0.68	4.27

Good and getting better. Milton got a year's experience under his belt without being abused; his overall numbers weren't exciting, but his performance was. Left-handers with fastballs like this make a lot of money playing baseball. He'll be to the next Minnesota championship what Frank Viola was for the 1987 Twins.

Dan Naulty   Throws R   Age 29

YEAR	TEAM	LGE	IP	H	ER	HR	BB	K	ERA	W	L	H/9	HR/9	BB/9	K/9	KWH	PERA
1996	Minnesot	AL	59.3	42	19	5	28	56	2.88	5	2	6.37	0.76	4.25	8.49	2.00	2.43
1997	Minnesot	AL	31.7	28	16	8	9	22	4.55	2	2	7.96	2.27	2.56	6.25	1.44	3.98
1998	Minnesot	AL	24.3	25	13	3	9	15	4.81	1	2	9.25	1.11	3.33	5.55	0.75	4.07

Naulty hasn't been healthy for more than three weeks at a time since the strong 1996. He's eminently replaceable, and rather than waste time with someone whose best season they've already seen, the Twins would be better off using his roster spot to bring along a Lincoln or Mays in a low-pressure role. Traded to the Yankees.

Dan Perkins   Throws R   Age 24

YEAR	TEAM	LGE	IP	H	ER	HR	BB	K	ERA	W	L	H/9	HR/9	BB/9	K/9	KWH	PERA
1996	Ft Myers	Fla	127.3	168	67	9	40	87	4.74	6	8	11.87	0.64	2.83	6.15	0.84	5.02
1997	New Brit	Eas	134.0	192	98	16	49	88	6.58	4	11	12.90	1.07	3.29	5.91	0.62	5.91
1998	New Brit	Eas	111.0	168	72	9	31	60	5.84	4	8	13.62	0.73	2.51	4.86	0.52	5.84
1998	SaltLake	PCL	48.3	47	23	7	20	28	4.28	2	3	8.75	1.30	3.72	5.21	0.63	4.10

Another Twins pitching prospect with Tim Belcher's strikeout rates. Perkins improved in his second tour of the Eastern League, enough to raise some eyebrows with his newfound commitment to the strike zone. It's OK to get people out without a great strikeout rate; it would just be nice to see someone in this organization breathe fire. Perkins is behind Lincoln, and I'd rather have Mays. One will pitch well enough at Salt Lake City to visit the state "The Body" conquered.

Brad Radke   Throws R   Age 26

YEAR	TEAM	LGE	IP	H	ER	HR	BB	K	ERA	W	L	H/9	HR/9	BB/9	K/9	KWH	PERA
1996	Minnesot	AL	238.0	217	94	34	46	147	3.55	15	11	8.21	1.29	1.74	5.56	1.62	3.33
1997	Minnesot	AL	245.3	231	93	26	41	169	3.41	16	11	8.47	0.95	1.50	6.20	2.26	3.23
1998	Minnesot	AL	220.3	229	87	21	38	142	3.55	13	11	9.35	0.86	1.55	5.80	1.74	3.68

(Brad Radke *continued*)

Averaged 7⅓ IP/start through June 15, when he was 8-5, 2.68. Collapsed after that, going 4-9, 5.73. Overall, however, he pitched at his established level. If he's handled more reasonably, he can have a few more Cy Young-type seasons. He's thrown a lot of pitches in four years; watch him carefully.

Mark Redman			**Throws L**		**Age 25**

YEAR	TEAM	LGE	IP	H	ER	HR	BB	K	ERA	W	L	H/9	HR/9	BB/9	K/9	KWH	PERA
1996	Ft Myers	Fla	77.3	88	32	2	37	57	3.72	5	4	10.24	0.23	4.31	6.63	0.75	4.07
1996	New Brit	Eas	102.0	122	54	6	48	75	4.76	5	6	10.76	0.53	4.24	6.62	0.72	4.59
1997	SaltLake	PCL	157.0	198	96	17	71	104	5.50	6	11	11.35	0.97	4.07	5.96	0.58	5.22
1998	New Brit	Eas	44.3	51	13	4	18	37	2.64	3	2	10.35	0.81	3.65	7.51	1.12	4.47
1998	SaltLake	PCL	102.7	112	61	11	42	72	5.35	4	7	9.82	0.96	3.68	6.31	0.83	4.38

Sometimes life isn't terribly fair. Redman is a 1995 #1 draft pick who cruised through the Twins system in 1995 and 1996. Then, instead of pitching in someplace nice, like Columbus or Rochester, he was sentenced to Salt Lake City and the hell that is the Pacific Coast League. Park and league adjustments to performance are nice, but I think that the experience of pitching in an environment like that absolutely ruins some pitchers for no good reason. There has to be a mental toll to giving up four runs in six innings every time out, whether or not people tell you it's OK. Not to mention the inevitable adjustments in an effort to improve on a performance that isn't bad to begin with, tinkering that can move a pitcher further from success. I don't get to make these decisions, but if you gave me an organization I'd do everything in my power to keep my affiliates out of the "old" PCL and Texas League. Redman can obviously pitch; either bring him to the majors or let him keep plugging away at New Britain, but keep him the heck away from Salt Lake. If given a job, I think he'll grow into a #3 starter.

Frankie Rodriguez		**Throws R**		**Age 26**

YEAR	TEAM	LGE	IP	H	ER	HR	BB	K	ERA	W	L	H/9	HR/9	BB/9	K/9	KWH	PERA
1996	Minnesot	AL	213.3	207	97	23	63	110	4.09	12	12	8.73	0.97	2.66	4.64	0.70	3.59
1997	Minnesot	AL	146.7	146	68	11	52	63	4.17	8	8	8.96	0.67	3.19	3.87	0.39	3.62
1998	Minnesot	AL	73.3	86	47	6	27	61	5.77	3	5	10.55	0.74	3.31	7.49	1.20	4.54
1998	SaltLake	PCL	97.7	102	46	8	37	61	4.24	5	6	9.40	0.74	3.41	5.62	0.74	3.96

Gets groundballs and strikeouts, and as long as he does, I'll believe. Rodriguez needs to get out of Minnesota, get somewhere with grass and people like Deivi Cruz behind him. Then we'd see the pitcher we've been waiting for. Kelly is obviously frustrated with him, and he's arbitration-eligible, so a new address could be coming. Will be good at his next stop, unless it's Coors.

Benj Sampson		**Throws L**		**Age 24**

YEAR	TEAM	LGE	IP	H	ER	HR	BB	K	ERA	W	L	H/9	HR/9	BB/9	K/9	KWH	PERA
1995	Ft Myers	Fla	138.3	223	108	19	55	72	7.03	4	11	14.51	1.24	3.58	4.68	0.32	6.83
1996	Ft Myers	Fla	65.3	76	36	8	28	51	4.96	3	4	10.47	1.10	3.86	7.03	0.92	4.82
1996	New Brit	Eas	71.0	128	58	9	24	40	7.35	2	6	16.23	1.14	3.04	5.07	0.39	7.35
1997	New Brit	Eas	110.0	138	60	12	45	71	4.91	5	7	11.29	0.98	3.68	5.81	0.61	5.15
1998	SaltLake	PCL	168.3	195	78	21	51	111	4.17	9	10	10.43	1.12	2.73	5.93	0.93	4.65
1998	Minnesot	AL	17.7	10	2	0	5	15	1.02	2	0	5.09	0.00	2.55	7.64	3.37	1.02

Scuffled until the last two years, when he got more serious about the strike zone. Sampson can throw 90, so he's not another Twin soft-tosser, and he did pitch well in his September callup. I think there's an adjustment period ahead of him; if it doesn't happen in March, he could be the #5 starter. A bad risk in 1999.

Dan Serafini		**Throws L**		**Age 25**

YEAR	TEAM	LGE	IP	H	ER	HR	BB	K	ERA	W	L	H/9	HR/9	BB/9	K/9	KWH	PERA
1996	SaltLake	PCL	130.7	171	74	22	57	95	5.10	6	9	11.78	1.52	3.93	6.54	0.69	5.85
1997	SaltLake	PCL	150.3	161	68	16	49	98	4.07	8	9	9.64	0.96	2.93	5.87	0.91	4.13
1997	Minnesot	AL	27.0	27	9	1	10	15	3.00	2	1	9.00	0.33	3.33	5.00	0.62	3.33
1998	SaltLake	PCL	55.0	56	24	4	21	32	3.93	3	3	9.16	0.65	3.44	5.24	0.65	3.76
1998	Minnesot	AL	78.0	93	47	9	26	45	5.42	3	6	10.73	1.04	3.00	5.19	0.63	4.85

The Twins' probable #4 starter in 1999, although a veteran signing would push him back to #5, possibly into a battle with Sampson. Scouts like him, and he supposedly throws 90, but I haven't been impressed with what I've seen; he doesn't seem to throw hard or aggressively. I did like his breaking ball, so it wasn't all bad. I'd rather see Lincoln or Redman get a shot.

Brent Stentz   Throws R   Age 23

Year	Team	Lge	IP	H	ER	HR	BB	K	ERA	W	L	H/9	HR/9	BB/9	K/9	KWH	PERA
1996	Fayettvl	SAL	89.0	135	70	6	30	55	7.08	2	8	13.65	0.61	3.03	5.56	0.56	5.76
1997	Ft Myers	Fla	64.3	74	27	5	27	52	3.78	4	3	10.35	0.70	3.78	7.27	1.01	4.48
1998	New Brit	Eas	56.7	55	14	3	27	50	2.22	5	1	8.74	0.48	4.29	7.94	1.26	3.49

A closer prospect, throws hard and had a nice year at New Britain, leading the minors in saves; he followed that up with a good Arizona Fall League appearance. Could easily make the Twins out of spring training, serving an apprenticeship under Rick Aguilera and taking over as the closer in July after Aggy is dealt to a contender. As a potential closer, the hype will be stifling, so remember: relievers are interchangeable.

Bob Tewksbury   Throws R   Age 38

YEAR	TEAM	LGE	IP	H	ER	HR	BB	K	ERA	W	L	H/9	HR/9	BB/9	K/9	KWH	PERA
1996	San Dieg	NL	203.0	249	115	17	41	113	5.10	9	14	11.04	0.75	1.82	5.01	0.94	4.52
1997	Minnesot	AL	172.7	196	68	10	26	89	3.54	11	8	10.22	0.52	1.36	4.64	1.17	3.86
1998	Minnesot	AL	152.7	167	65	17	18	58	3.83	9	8	9.84	1.00	1.06	3.42	0.84	3.95

Still effective, but can't make 32 starts a year. At this writing, he's supposed to be headed to Boston as the Sox #5 starter. I don't think that's a particularly good park for him, but it would give him a chance at the postseason, a nice change of pace. If you missed him pitching to McGwire, find a buddy with a tape.

Joe Thomas   Throws R   Age 24

YEAR	TEAM	LGE	IP	H	ER	HR	BB	K	ERA	W	L	H/9	HR/9	BB/9	K/9	KWH	PERA
1997	Lowell	NYP	64.0	117	70	5	29	32	9.84	1	6	16.45	0.70	4.08	4.50	0.23	7.17
1998	Michigan	Mid	112.7	194	79	9	47	57	6.31	4	9	15.50	0.72	3.75	4.55	0.27	6.71
1998	Ft Wayne	Mid	32.0	47	24	3	5	18	6.75	1	3	13.22	0.84	1.41	5.06	1.03	5.62

Trinket #3 in the Swindell swindle. Thomas is old for his league but gets high marks for "knowing how to pitch." It's hard not to look impressive being compared to 18- and 19-year-olds. Thomas needs a big leap fast, or risks becoming an organizational soldier. By June, we'll know.

Mike Trombley   Throws R   Age 32

YEAR	TEAM	LGE	IP	H	ER	HR	BB	K	ERA	W	L	H/9	HR/9	BB/9	K/9	KWH	PERA
1996	SaltLake	PCL	35.3	28	12	3	11	30	3.06	3	1	7.13	0.76	2.80	7.64	2.19	2.55
1996	Minnesot	AL	70.3	58	18	2	21	57	2.30	6	2	7.42	0.26	2.69	7.29	2.00	2.43
1997	Minnesot	AL	84.7	76	35	6	27	72	3.72	5	4	8.08	0.64	2.87	7.65	1.89	3.08
1998	Minnesot	AL	100.3	87	32	15	37	87	2.87	7	4	7.80	1.35	3.32	7.80	1.76	3.41

Valuable, effective, and resilient, Trombley has been one of the better relievers in the league for three years, after being mismanaged as a starter. The kind of pitcher, like Steve Reed, who will never quite get the credit he deserves because he's not used in the glamour role. Trombley was ridden hard last year, so I'm a little wary of him going into 1999.

SNWL							MINNESOTA TWINS					Park Effect: -3.0%
PITCHER	GS	IP	R	SNW	SNL	SNPCT	W	L	RA	APW	SNVA	SNWAR
Hawkins, L.	33	190.3	126	8.4	13.9	.377	7	14	5.96	-2.23	-2.54	-1.08
Milton, E.	32	172.3	112	9.3	12.2	.432	8	14	5.85	-1.82	-1.47	0.14
Morgan, M.	17	95.0	41	6.3	4.4	.587	4	2	3.88	0.99	0.94	1.72
Radke, B.	32	213.7	109	13.0	11.4	.532	12	14	4.59	0.62	0.74	2.61
Rodriguez, Frankie	11	60.3	45	2.9	5.2	.355	4	6	6.71	-1.19	-1.12	-0.57
Sampson, B.	2	13.0	3	1.1	0.3	.783	1	0	2.08	0.39	0.37	0.50
Serafini, D.	9	46.0	33	2.3	3.4	.400	3	4	6.46	-0.78	-0.50	-0.14
Tewksbury, B.	25	147.3	82	8.4	9.1	.480	7	13	5.01	-0.23	-0.49	0.95
Trombley, M.	1	4.7	3	0.2	0.3	.432	0	0	5.79	-0.05	-0.04	0.00
TOTALS	162	942.7	554	51.7	60.2	.462	46	67	5.29	-4.30	-4.11	4.15

Those numbers aren't all that special, but they do represent a step in the right direction for the Twins. The Twins' SNVA improved by 3 games, from -7.1 in 1997 to -4.1 last year, despite suffering a decline in the performances of their two best starters, Radke and Tewksbury. The biggest difference in 1998 was durability. The individual Twins starters weren't anything special, but they did make their starts every week, and that allowed the team to avoid the spot starts and minor league callups that in 1997 resulted in Travis Miller (.256 SNPct in 7 starts), Shane Bowers (.229 SNPct in 5 starts), and Kevin Jarvis (.026 SNPct in 2 starts).

Pitcher Abuse Points

PITCHER	AGE	GS	PAP	PAP/S	AAW	MAX	115+	130+
Hawkins, LaTroy	25	33	135	4.09	8.86	123	2	0
Milton, Eric	22	32	99	3.09	8.25	119	2	0
Morgan, Mike	38	17	13	0.76	0.76	111	0	0
Radke, Brad	25	32	554	17.31	37.51	134	13	1
Rodriguez, Frankie	25	11	82	7.45	16.15	122	2	0
Serafini, Dan	24	9	26	2.89	6.74	116	1	0
Tewksbury, Bob	37	25	13	0.52	0.52	106	0	0
TOTAL		162	938	5.79	12.72	134	20	1
RANKING (AL)			13	13	12		12-T	11-T

Tom Kelly usually does a good job with his pitchers, even if he (and Dick Such) never get them to develop. The one exception is Brad Radke, who like a lot of young aces established himself as a major league starter at such a young age (22) that three years later his manager looks at him and thinks, "he's got a lot of experience . . . I think he can handle being the #1 guy in our rotation." Presto—you've got a young pitcher's arm handling the expectations of a veteran. Radke went 3-8, 6.27 ERA after the Break, and you have to be a little concerned. Eric Milton, the staff's prized rookie, was handled well, but the results weren't what the Twins hoped.

Anaheim Angels

For the third time in four years, the Angels came up on the losing end of a September race, being eliminated on the last weekend of the season by the Texas Rangers. In what is becoming a disturbing pattern, Anaheim Sports Enterprises made a lot of noise about putting a winner on the field, then backed up their words by shopping at the bargain bin for talent and doing nothing about the logjam at the corner outfield and first base slots.

Entering the off-season ASE, the Disney subsidiary that administers the Angels and the NHL's Mighty Ducks of Anaheim, has established a pattern of unwillingness to make the expenditures necessary to acquire top-tier talent. They have excelled at the low-risk, low-budget signings and trades that so-called "small-market" teams are fond of making. After the ill-advised signing of Ken Hill to a three-year, $15 million contract last winter, their next-most-significant moves were signing Cecil Fielder and Jack McDowell, both of whom were really good as recently as 1991. In the trade market, while the Rangers were grabbing Todd Stottlemyre, Royce Clayton, and Todd Zeile, the Angels settled for Jeff Juden, Charlie O'Brien, and Gregg Jefferies.

Tony Tavares, the Angel president, had been adamant in his stance that no player is worth $10 million a year. This viewpoint caused the Angels to drop out of the bidding for Mark McGwire in mid-1997, for fear they would not be able to sign the first baseman after the season. Tavares's statements showed him to be someone who did not view player salaries as an investment, one on which a profit can be made. Ask the Cardinals if McGwire earned his $9 million this year.

The reality of the current market is that the stars are the only ones who you can expect to make money on. It's the middle class, the Ken Hills and Willie Blairs, who end up being a terrible return on the investment because the risk is high and the realistic expectation so low. It's unlikely that Ken Hill is going to either draw enough fans or create enough wins to justify his mid-tier contract. The Angels would probably be better off in the pocketbook and on the field if they gave nothing to Ken Hill, Gary DiSarcina, and Garret Anderson, and instead spent that money on Kevin Brown.

So from an economic standpoint, I would turn Tavares's argument on its head. Some players are worth $10 million per year. But very few players are a good investment at $4 million to $8 million per year. That's where you have most of your bad risks; it's better to have a $60 million payroll if that means three guys combining for $30 million, and 22 splitting the other $30 million, than five or six guys at $6 million each and the rest splitting that same $30 million.

For example, let's look at the Angels' moves in the winter of 1997-98. They signed Ken Hill for three years at $5 million per. They brought in Cecil Fielder for one year and $2.7 million and Jack McDowell for an incentive-laden deal that ended up costing about $1 million. For the $8.7 million, plus an additional investment of $2 million/year for two more years, they could have signed Darryl Kile, who went to Colorado for three years, $21 million. Kile had an off-year, but his peripheral stats and age indicated he would be a much better risk than the declining Hill. They also could have entered the bidding for Andy Benes, who signed a five-year deal for comparable money. Benes looked like an even better risk than Hill or Kile; signing Hill kept them from being involved when he became a free agent.

Even better, avoid the B-class of pitchers entirely, take the $6 million you've saved, and pour in into international scouting and development. That dough can go a long way in the Dominican, Antigua, or Korea. That's a talent pipeline that keeps on giving, and the presents aren't 32-year-old "aces" who are 30 innings away from Dr. Jobe's Christmas card list; foreign development provides young, cheap talent that your organization controls for eight to ten years.

While you're planning that scouting trip to Bermuda, recognize that the talent in major league baseball is not evenly distributed. There are very few great players, and those players are inordinately valuable. But the values of the players below them do not follow linearly. There is only one Mike Piazza, and he will make $13 million because he is a

---

Angels Prospectus

1998 record: 85-77; Second place, AL West

Pythagorean W/L: 81-81

Runs scored: 787 (10th in AL)

Runs allowed: 783 (6th in AL)

Team EQA: .263 (t-9th in AL)

Park: Edison Field (moderate pitchers')

1998: Once again fell short after not making a significant expenditure on talent.

1999: Depends on which of Edmonds or Anderson is traded; the four-win gap could make the difference.

scarce resource. But there are lots of players half as good as Mike Piazza; they should not make $6.5 million, because they are not scarce. If you can't sign Terry Steinbach cheaply, go get Kelly Stinnett. Can't get Stinnett? Build a platoon of Carlos Hernandez and Greg Myers. Below a certain level, most players are interchangeable, a view that most organizations are slow to recognize.

A winning strategy involves paying top dollar for the most scarce resources, and as little as possible for the common ones. Ken Hill is and was a fairly commmon resource, and was paid as if he was scarce.

Of course, this philosophy requires a willingness to stay out of the bidding for non-star free agents, and to avoid the temptation to "just do something" to satiate fans and beat writers and talk-radio callers. It requires the courage to make bold decisions in assembling a roster. Rather than sign middle-market free agents and trade for veterans with little or no upside, you have to have the confidence in so-called "unproven" players, and in your ability to evaluate talent. You have to get off the "proven veteran" treadmill and give chances to players who can play championship-caliber baseball for a small cost.

There are plenty of these players available. In the Angel system alone, they have a perfectly good right-handed setup man named Anthony Chavez, who will be just as good as, and much cheaper than, Rich DeLucia. They can assemble a catching platoon of Bret Hemphill and Ben Molina for about $400,000, and give up nothing in production compared to Matt Walbeck. Go outside the organization and you can pick up a second baseman like Frankie Menechino or Mark Bellhorn for nothing. With the money you've saved by not bringing in a veteran middle reliever, or giving $2 million to Walbeck or Charlie O'Brien, or signing an obvious mistake like Carlos Baerga, you're in a better position to afford Kevin Brown or Bernie Williams.

Or Mo Vaughn, who will be wearing periwinkle in 1999. The Angels finally broke out of their Ken Hill cycle and invested in a top-tier free agent, signing the first baseman to a six-year, $80 million contract. Was Vaughn the best fit for the Angels? Probably not, since his signing will likely cause them to trade Jim Edmonds, their second-best player, and doesn't address their lack of rotation depth. Vaughn is 31, and his weight has already caused him some knee problems that age won't make better. However, he is one of the best hitters in the game, a reasonable bet for a series of .290/.380/.560 seasons. Add in that the redesigned ballpark is a solid moneymaker, that they're owned by one of the most profitable corporations on Earth, and they have the marketing strength, headed by Director Michelle Kahler, to maximize any investment through the kind of cross-promotion that corporation is famous for. You can expect Disney and

ASE to promote the heck out of Vaughn, his fondness for kids, and his history of helping out in the community.

It appears the Angels have learned a valuable lesson: doing something is not enough. The Angels had been in a never-ending spasm of reflexive hole-filling, with no vision of what kind of club they want to be, and no plan for how to get there. As long as players like Garrett Anderson and Gary Disarcina are soaking up Disney's money, the Angels will continue to wonder why they haven't won. Vaughn is a step in the right direction; trading Anderson and keeping Edmonds would be another one.

It will be interesting to see if, now that they are off the Ken Hill treadmill, there's a follow-through. By June, there will be a new crop of players available from teams looking to 2000 for their pennant push. Will the Angels add an Edgar Martinez, a Larry Walker, or a Curt Schilling—players who actually can make a difference over 80 games, who can actually push a team towards a championship? The Angels have not acquired that type of player, either in mid-winter or at the trade deadline, in some time. If they stop fiddling around with people like Ken Hill and Chad Kreuter, they will give themselves the opportunity to really improve.

The perception that the Angels are a young team has got to go. Of the players you can expect to make positive contributions in 1999, only Garret Anderson, Darin Erstad, and Troy Glaus are 27 or under (and whether Anderson and Glaus will be assets this year is open to debate). Core players Jim Edmonds and Tim Salmon are 29 and 30, and both have had injury problems. The pitching staff is led by Chuck Finley and Hill, who are 36 and 33, respectively. Perecption does not match reality: this is just not a notably young team

Why are they perceived as such? In recent years the Angels have emphasized drafting college players. This can pay off big, when players like Erstad and Glaus fly through the system and quickly establish themselves as potential stars. But even then, these players reach the major leagues at 22 or 23.

The practice of drafting collegians isn't a bad one. You get more mature players who are closer to being ready for the major leagues. On this score, avoiding high school players does have benefits; but there is another route to getting players through your system at a younger age: international development. Players like Andruw Jones, Aramis Ramirez, and Adrian Beltre were all major leaguers by 20, and all were non-drafted free agents. Scouting and development overseas, particularly for a team with the resources of Anaheim, can provide a pipeline to exceptionally talented 16- and 17-year-olds who can become franchise players in just a few years.

The Angels have historically struggled to develop these players, but took a big step forward this summer with the reopening of their complex in the Dominican Republic, closed since 1995. While it will take a few years to reap the benefits of the reopening, this is exactly the kind of move that helps a team find great young players. If the worldwide draft continues to be more plan than execution, Disney can use its vast resources to funnel players from the Dominican into their system, while continuing to draft more mature college players who can contribute soon after being drafted.

The final piece to this puzzle is to recognize that by the time the college players reach free agency, you've gotten their best value: their lowest-paid years, and their most explosive growth. Most of these players will hit the market at ages 28-30, toward the end of their peak. If you're lucky, you can buy out a year of free agency for the good ones, putting them on the market at 29-31, let someone else pay for their good years with you, and funnel the money back into your system and bonuses for top draftees.

Judicious use of free agency, meaning only signing the best players, and only when those players are young enough to be a good risk; finding low-cost solutions to problems, either internally or externally, rather than paying for a high-risk, low-reward solution; a willingness to make the correct decision, even in the face of fan and media criticism; putting money into international development; and following an amateur drafting strategy that gives you access to a player's best years at below-market cost. Put it together, and in the hands of a machine like Disney, it's the blueprint for years of success. If Anaheim Sports Enterprises wants to run a dynasty, they have everything they need.

HITTERS (Averages: BA .260/ OBA .330/ SA .420, EQA .260)

Garrett Anderson — RF/LF — Bats L — Age 27

YEAR	TEAM	LGE	AB	H	DB	TP	HR	BB	R	RBI	SB	CS	OUT	BA	OBA	SA	EQA	EQR	DEFENSE
1996	Calfrnia	AL	597	165	31	2	12	24	55	63	7	11	443	.276	.304	.395	.236	60	140-OF 100
1997	Anaheim	AL	613	183	36	3	8	31	70	69	10	4	434	.299	.332	.406	.257	72	142-OF 103
1998	Anaheim	AL	615	182	39	7	16	32	73	83	7	3	436	.296	.331	.460	.270	82	154-OF 98
1999	Anaheim	AL	565	161	38	3	13	30	66	71	6	4	408	.285	.321	.432	.257	68	

I've said enough bad things about Anderson to last the rest of the millennium, so I'll point out here that he did change his approach in 1998, driving the ball more, resulting in more power. But that was the only change in his game. He's a .300 hitter who doesn't put enough runs on the board, and doesn't have the defense to carry his production. I think he'll have his best year in 1998, hitting around .330 with 20 or so home runs, which should make him a bit above average.

Justin Baughman — 2B — Bats R — Age 24

YEAR	TEAM	LGE	AB	H	DB	TP	HR	BB	R	RBI	SB	CS	OUT	BA	OBA	SA	EQA	EQR	DEFENSE
1996	CedarRpd	Mid	465	96	10	4	5	31	35	24	24	10	379	.206	.256	.277	.186	28	127-SS 88
1997	Lk Elsin	Cal	476	113	9	2	2	31	48	25	35	9	372	.237	.284	.277	.206	36	129-SS 102
1998	Vancouvr	PCL	220	62	9	3	0	13	32	16	23	7	165	.282	.322	.350	.247	25	46-2B 107
1998	Anaheim	AL	194	50	9	1	1	7	19	13	9	4	148	.258	.284	.330	.214	16	54-2B 105
1999	Anaheim	AL	428	110	16	3	2	24	49	30	29	10	328	.257	.296	.322	.222	38	

The presence of Gary Disarcina and a lack of better options induced the Angels to move Baughman to second base. He handled the move reasonably well, but struggled turning the deuce, which is to be expected. The bigger problem is that he can't hit, and there's no expectation that he will. If he improves as a second baseman, his speed and glove will make him a good fifth infielder. A broken leg suffered in the Mexican League should keep him out of action for much of the season.

Danny Buxbaum — 1B — Bats R — Age 26

YEAR	TEAM	LGE	AB	H	DB	TP	HR	BB	R	RBI	SB	CS	OUT	BA	OBA	SA	EQA	EQR	DEFENSE
1996	Lk Elsin	Cal	293	67	8	1	8	20	21	26	0	0	226	.229	.278	.345	.213	24	73-1B 92
1997	Midland	Tex	495	101	18	1	7	39	30	30	1	1	395	.204	.262	.287	.184	29	118-1B 101
1998	Midland	Tex	286	70	8	0	9	20	24	29	1	1	217	.245	.294	.367	.227	27	54-1B 106
1998	Vancouvr	PCL	98	27	1	0	2	2	6	9	0	1	72	.276	.290	.347	.213	8	22-1B 95
1999	Anaheim	AL	372	89	8	0	10	23	27	35	1	1	284	.239	.284	.341	.213	30	

(Danny Buxbaum *continued*)

Buxbaum got caught in a numbers game in the spring and was returned to Midland, where he continued to hit well. He might have received an earlier callup, but an injury sidelined him in May and he wasn't brought up to Vancouver until August. Past the point of prospect status, he now joins the ranks of Triple-A hitters waiting for a shot at glory. I think he could contribute.

Mike Colangelo   OF   Bats R   Age 22

YEAR	TEAM	LGE	AB	H	DB	TP	HR	BB	R	RBI	SB	CS	OUT	BA	OBA	SA	EQA	EQR	DEFENSE
1998	CedarRpd	Mid	84	20	4	0	3	10	10	9	2	1	65	.238	.319	.393	.249	10	
1998	Lk Elsin	Cal	143	48	7	0	5	11	19	23	1	4	99	.336	.383	.490	.290	22	
1999	*Anaheim*	*AL*	*178*	*58*	*6*	*1*	*9*	*16*	*27*	*33*	*3*	*3*	*123*	*.326*	*.381*	*.522*	*.303*	*31*	

1997 draftee who didn't sign in time to play that year, but jumped in with both feet in 1998, beating up two leagues and showing impressive plate discipline. He is exactly the kind of player the Angels could use at the top of their lineup. If he can scale the Double-A wall this year, he'll add to the depth Anaheim has in the outfield.

Jason Dewey   C   Bats R   Age 22

YEAR	TEAM	LGE	AB	H	DB	TP	HR	BB	R	RBI	SB	CS	OUT	BA	OBA	SA	EQA	EQR	DEFENSE
1997	Boise	Nwn	268	62	5	1	7	25	22	25	2	1	207	.231	.297	.336	.220	24	
1998	Lk Elsin	Cal	393	102	15	1	13	53	49	50	5	5	296	.260	.348	.402	.261	52	84-C 86
1999	*Anaheim*	*AL*	*316*	*85*	*9*	*0*	*12*	*37*	*39*	*44*	*3*	*2*	*233*	*.269*	*.346*	*.411*	*.264*	*42*	

Todd Greene's continuing shoulder woes have opened the door for other catchers in the organization. Dewey is the best of the bunch at the lower levels, and that rare Angel prospect with plate discipline. I wouldn't be surprised to see him advance all the way to Triple-A this year. He's a sleeper with a very high upside.

Gary Disarcina   SS   Bats R   Age 31

YEAR	TEAM	LGE	AB	H	DB	TP	HR	BB	R	RBI	SB	CS	OUT	BA	OBA	SA	EQA	EQR	DEFENSE
1996	Calfrnia	AL	528	129	24	4	5	19	36	40	2	1	400	.244	.271	.333	.204	37	146-SS 106
1997	Anaheim	AL	541	130	27	2	4	19	36	36	7	8	419	.240	.266	.320	.195	35	149-SS 105
1998	Anaheim	AL	545	157	39	3	3	24	59	53	10	7	395	.288	.318	.387	.243	58	156-SS 97
1999	*Anaheim*	*AL*	*480*	*122*	*28*	*2*	*4*	*20*	*40*	*39*	*5*	*5*	*363*	*.254*	*.284*	*.346*	*.213*	*38*	

Next time you see Gary Disarcina on one of those experts' polls of "good players," consider this. In the last week of April, Gary had yet to draw a walk; when asked about this, he replied his goal was to not walk all season. He felt that he was a better hitter when he wasn't walking. No word on whether Gary thinks he's faster when he wears lead shoes. Disarcina is below average in most years, and approaches average in a year like 1998. He's 31; the end could come quickly.

Jim Edmonds   CF   Bats L   Age 29

YEAR	TEAM	LGE	AB	H	DB	TP	HR	BB	R	RBI	SB	CS	OUT	BA	OBA	SA	EQA	EQR	DEFENSE
1996	Calfrnia	AL	421	125	28	3	26	43	64	79	4	0	296	.297	.362	.563	.308	78	109-OF 109
1997	Anaheim	AL	492	141	21	0	28	60	67	84	5	7	358	.287	.364	.500	.290	81	111-OF 111
1998	Anaheim	AL	592	183	36	2	27	60	86	101	6	5	414	.309	.373	.514	.299	101	151-OF 109
1999	*Anaheim*	*AL*	*538*	*160*	*25*	*1*	*31*	*61*	*80*	*100*	*4*	*3*	*381*	*.297*	*.369*	*.520*	*.300*	*94*	

Very good, very consistent player who added durability to the mix last year, playing through some nagging hurts during the summer and maintaining his production. I still think it's a good idea to move him to left field. At the least, get him 20 starts a year as a DH; some players can really be helped by the rest, and I think Edmonds is one of them. Likely to be elsewhere in 1999.

Darin Erstad   1B/LF   Bats L   Age 25

YEAR	TEAM	LGE	AB	H	DB	TP	HR	BB	R	RBI	SB	CS	OUT	BA	OBA	SA	EQA	EQR	DEFENSE	
1996	Vancouvr	PCL	351	106	19	3	7	41	54	46	10	5	250	.302	.375	.433	.283	53	82-OF 96	
1996	Calfrnia	AL	204	56	5	1	4	16	20	22	3	4	152	.275	.327	.368	.240	21	44-OF 111	
1997	Anaheim	AL	528	155	33	4	16	52	82	71	23	8	381	.294	.357	.462	.284	82	122-1B 92	
1998	Anaheim	AL	531	159	38	3	20	45	81	79	19	6	378	.299	.354	.495	.290	86	68-OF 90	57-1B 104
1999	*Anaheim*	*AL*	*564*	*168*	*41*	*3*	*19*	*53*	*90*	*84*	*19*	*8*	*404*	*.298*	*.358*	*.482*	*.288*	*90*		

His strained hamstring on August 3 did to the Angels what Tony Phillips's arrest for crack cocaine possession did in 1997: it effectively ended their run as a good team. Erstad had played in every game up to that point and hit .303/.361/.513. He played in just 22 of 51 games afterwards, hitting .253/.300/.320, and the Angels, 59-52 when he pulled up lame, limped home at 26-25. A small difference, but enough to cost them the AL West. Erstad should be back in the outfield in 1999.

Troy Glaus — 3B — Bats R — Age 22

YEAR	TEAM	LGE	AB	H	DB	TP	HR	BB	R	RBI	SB	CS	OUT	BA	OBA	SA	EQA	EQR	DEFENSE
1998	Midland	Tex	182	48	6	0	13	32	29	33	3	1	135	.264	.374	.511	.301	33	48-3B 98
1998	Vancouvr	PCL	217	65	9	0	15	20	30	41	3	2	154	.300	.359	.548	.301	38	58-3B 105
1998	Anaheim	AL	163	35	6	0	2	16	12	11	1	0	128	.215	.285	.288	.200	11	46-3B 99
1999	*Anaheim*	*AL*	*450*	*137*	*23*	*1*	*32*	*52*	*73*	*94*	*4*	*2*	*315*	*.304*	*.376*	*.573*	*.315*	*88*	

Glaus might have been rushed to the majors, despite his manhandling of two leagues. It will be interesting to see how the Angels handle him in 1999, particularly if his performance in the majors is comparable to 1998. I think he'll develop the power more than the other skills, becoming a Matt Williams-type hitter. Great prospect, but behind Chavez and Beltre.

Todd Greene — C?/LF — Bats R — Age 28

YEAR	TEAM	LGE	AB	H	DB	TP	HR	BB	R	RBI	SB	CS	OUT	BA	OBA	SA	EQA	EQR	DEFENSE
1996	Vancouvr	PCL	222	62	8	0	6	14	21	26	0	2	162	.279	.322	.396	.245	24	
1997	Vancouvr	PCL	250	78	9	0	17	15	34	46	5	1	173	.312	.351	.552	.301	43	
1997	Anaheim	AL	122	35	6	0	9	7	16	22	2	0	87	.287	.326	.557	.293	20	
1998	Vancouvr	PCL	108	28	4	0	6	10	12	16	1	0	80	.259	.322	.463	.268	15	
1998	Anaheim	AL	70	18	3	0	1	3	5	6	0	0	52	.257	.288	.343	.215	6	
1999	*Anaheim*	*AL*	*285*	*76*	*11*	*0*	*15*	*19*	*33*	*42*	*3*	*0*	*209*	*.267*	*.312*	*.463*	*.264*	*38*	

The shoulder injuries have probably ended his career as a catcher, and with it what was left of his chance at stardom. Greene has tremendous power, and if he can become a passable defensive left fielder he can help a team win a championship. More likely, he'll carve out a role as a platoon DH/first baseman and have a few good years in his thirties, like Geronimo Berroa.

Bret Hemphill — C — Bats B — Age 27

YEAR	TEAM	LGE	AB	H	DB	TP	HR	BB	R	RBI	SB	CS	OUT	BA	OBA	SA	EQA	EQR	DEFENSE
1996	Lk Elsin	Cal	395	72	7	1	8	32	19	20	2	2	325	.182	.244	.266	.165	18	
1997	Midland	Tex	256	53	6	1	5	34	22	20	0	1	204	.207	.300	.297	.210	21	
1998	Vancouvr	PCL	154	34	6	1	3	10	10	12	0	1	121	.221	.268	.331	.201	11	
1999	*Anaheim*	*AL*	*216*	*49*	*7*	*0*	*6*	*20*	*18*	*21*	*0*	*1*	*168*	*.227*	*.292*	*.343*	*.217*	*19*	

Hemphill missed most of the year after surgery on his right shoulder, so take his 1998 performance with a grain of salt. A switch-hitting catcher who can contribute offensively and is good behind the plate makes an excellent backup. Don't put too much weight on his poor Arizona Fall League stint; he'll go into camp with a shot at a major league job.

Dave Hollins — 3B — Bats B — Age 33

YEAR	TEAM	LGE	AB	H	DB	TP	HR	BB	R	RBI	SB	CS	OUT	BA	OBA	SA	EQA	EQR	DEFENSE
1996	Minnesot	AL	410	92	17	0	14	67	51	45	6	5	323	.224	.333	.368	.248	49	113-3B 107
1996	Seattle	AL	91	31	3	0	3	13	14	16	0	2	62	.341	.423	.473	.306	16	26-3B 111
1997	Anaheim	AL	561	159	29	2	16	62	79	72	16	6	408	.283	.355	.428	.274	80	129-3B 96
1998	Anaheim	AL	359	87	16	2	11	46	46	40	10	3	275	.242	.328	.390	.254	45	86-3B 93
1999	*Anaheim*	*AL*	*441*	*112*	*19*	*1*	*15*	*59*	*60*	*56*	*9*	*4*	*333*	*.254*	*.342*	*.404*	*.262*	*58*	

His decline last year was typical for a player of his age and skill set, and he's unlikely to ever again be as good as he was in 1997. He's signed cheaply, and worth keeping on the roster as insurance for Glaus and to play against people like Orlando Hernandez. His erratic arm makes him a defensive liability at third base.

Norm Hutchins — OF — Bats L — Age 23

YEAR	TEAM	LGE	AB	H	DB	TP	HR	BB	R	RBI	SB	CS	OUT	BA	OBA	SA	EQA	EQR	DEFENSE
1996	CedarRpd	Mid	467	90	11	8	3	18	21	19	11	5	382	.193	.223	.270	.156	18	124-OF 102
1997	Lk Elsin	Cal	559	145	20	5	14	17	53	54	23	10	424	.259	.281	.388	.230	54	130-OF 101
1998	Midland	Tex	381	97	14	4	8	11	37	33	19	7	291	.255	.276	.375	.226	35	88-OF 100
1999	*Anaheim*	*AL*	*448*	*113*	*16*	*4*	*10*	*15*	*41*	*41*	*16*	*8*	*343*	*.252*	*.276*	*.373*	*.222*	*40*	

(Norm Hutchins *continued*)

Everything you need to be an overrated prospect: high batting averages, good hitters' parks in good hitters' leagues, and speed. Hutchins isn't a bad player, but he walks less than Larry Flynt. It's hard to be a great player when your batting average is your OBP. Hutchins, like Hemphill, had a poor AFL; unlike Hemphill, he's blocked at the major league level. He would make a good fourth outfielder, and could have a nice little career in that role.

Gregg Jefferies   LF   Bats B   Age 31

YEAR	TEAM	LGE	AB	H	DB	TP	HR	BB	R	RBI	SB	CS	OUT	BA	OBA	SA	EQA	EQR	DEFENSE	
1996	Philadel	NL	405	120	17	2	8	38	58	47	17	7	292	.296	.357	.407	.270	55	53-1B 100	44-OF 105
1997	Philadel	NL	476	122	24	3	12	55	59	54	10	6	360	.256	.333	.395	.254	59	110-OF 94	
1998	Philadel	NL	479	138	21	2	9	32	56	54	12	3	344	.288	.333	.397	.256	57	107-OF 93	
1998	Anaheim	AL	71	25	5	0	1	1	9	10	1	0	46	.352	.361	.465	.286	10		
1999	*Anaheim*	*AL*	*513*	*146*	*24*	*2*	*9*	*43*	*64*	*60*	*10*	*5*	*372*	*.285*	*.340*	*.392*	*.256*	*62*		

There's not much left to say about Jefferies, who has only been a good player twice in his major league career. He does serve as an illustration of the value of reaching the majors at a young age. His first full season was at 22, and he's been a regular ever since. A regular despite never reaching the greatness some thought he would, despite not being a real contributor since 1994, and despite having little offensive or defensive value. Jefferies has an 8% chance at 3,000 hits in his career, as measured by Bill James's "Favorite Toy." That, ladies and gentlemen, is the value of reaching the majors at 22 instead of 25.

Chad Kreuter   C   Bats B   Age 34

YEAR	TEAM	LGE	AB	H	DB	TP	HR	BB	R	RBI	SB	CS	OUT	BA	OBA	SA	EQA	EQR	DEFENSE
1996	ChiSox	AL	113	25	7	0	3	12	11	11	0	0	88	.221	.296	.363	.228	11	
1997	Anaheim	AL	215	49	7	1	4	21	18	18	0	2	168	.228	.297	.326	.214	18	
1998	ChiSox	AL	241	60	9	1	2	33	27	22	1	0	181	.249	.339	.320	.238	25	73-C 101
1999	*Anaheim*	*AL*	*232*	*52*	*8*	*1*	*4*	*31*	*23*	*21*	*0*	*1*	*181*	*.224*	*.316*	*.319*	*.223*	*21*	

Approaching Rick Cerone's mark for most years milked out of a fluke season, in this case his .371OBA/.484 SA 1993. By most accounts, he's a good defensive catcher; as backups go, I'd rather have him than the Girardi/Manwaring class.

Adam Leggett   2B   Bats B   Age 23

YEAR	TEAM	LGE	AB	H	DB	TP	HR	BB	R	RBI	SB	CS	OUT	BA	OBA	SA	EQA	EQR	DEFENSE
1997	Boise	Nwn	220	27	6	0	1	21	5	5	2	1	194	.123	.199	.164	.034	0	57-2B 88
1998	CedarRpd	Mid	451	100	11	1	9	62	47	37	10	8	358	.222	.316	.310	.223	42	122-2B 102
1999	*Anaheim*	*AL*	*353*	*79*	*9*	*0*	*8*	*42*	*34*	*31*	*6*	*4*	*278*	*.224*	*.306*	*.317*	*.219*	*31*	

If Keith Luuloa comes back to earth—and he should—I like Leggett's chance to show up in Anaheim. He's not a great prospect; he's just a player with a well-rounded game, including very good secondary skills. The players in front of him, Baughman and Durrington, are nothing special. Leggett doesn't have a high profile, which will hurt him. Check back in August.

Keith Luuloa   IF   Bats R   Age 24

YEAR	TEAM	LGE	AB	H	DB	TP	HR	BB	R	RBI	SB	CS	OUT	BA	OBA	SA	EQA	EQR	DEFENSE	
1996	Midland	Tex	517	105	14	0	6	42	30	27	3	3	415	.203	.263	.265	.176	27	100-2B 97	37-SS 96
1997	Midland	Tex	406	86	18	2	7	30	29	29	5	3	323	.212	.266	.318	.199	28	92-2B 85	27-SS 88
1998	Midland	Tex	462	124	24	4	12	60	62	59	4	3	341	.268	.352	.416	.268	63	57-2B 94	30-3B 109
1999	*Anaheim*	*AL*	*476*	*123*	*19*	*2*	*12*	*49*	*54*	*55*	*4*	*3*	*356*	*.258*	*.328*	*.382*	*.247*	*54*		

The Angels were more convinced than I was and gave Luuloa a ticket to Arizona, where he continued to play well. I don't buy it; 23 is an age where players often make big leaps, particularly in power, but when a guy does it in his third year at Midland, it's better to be skeptical. Continued to hit in the AFL, so watch him in the spring. Luuloa could make a good utility infielder.

Norberto Martin   2B   Bats R   Age 32

YEAR	TEAM	LGE	AB	H	DB	TP	HR	BB	R	RBI	SB	CS	OUT	BA	OBA	SA	EQA	EQR	DEFENSE
1996	ChiSox	AL	138	49	3	0	2	5	22	16	12	3	92	.355	.378	.420	.287	20	17-SS 91
1997	ChiSox	AL	211	64	7	1	2	6	18	22	1	4	151	.303	.323	.374	.236	20	19-SS 95
1998	Anaheim	AL	193	41	2	0	1	7	8	8	3	1	153	.212	.240	.238	.148	6	45-2B 110
1999	*Anaheim*	*AL*	*183*	*46*	*3*	*0*	*2*	*7*	*12*	*13*	*3*	*2*	*139*	*.251*	*.279*	*.301*	*.195*	*12*	

I can't say he'd be my first choice as a backup infielder, but I will say this: Martin can play defense. He showed excellent range in limited duty, turned the double play as well as anyone, and has a good arm. Unfortunately, this was pretty much all he brought to the table. Linked in my mind, for some reason, with Esteban Beltre; Beltre spent the year as the starting shortstop for the Salt Lake City Buzz. They could easily exchange roles this season.

Ben Molina   C/DH   Bats R   Age 24

YEAR	TEAM	LGE	AB	H	DB	TP	HR	BB	R	RBI	SB	CS	OUT	BA	OBA	SA	EQA	EQR	DEFENSE
1996	Midland	Tex	354	78	13	1	6	23	23	25	0	1	277	.220	.268	.314	.196	23	
1997	Lk Elsin	Cal	148	37	6	1	3	5	11	13	0	1	112	.250	.275	.365	.214	12	
1997	Midland	Tex	101	28	5	0	4	8	11	14	0	0	73	.277	.330	.446	.266	13	
1998	Midland	Tex	148	43	3	0	6	11	15	21	0	1	106	.291	.340	.432	.264	19	33-C 92
1998	Vancouvr	PCL	182	50	7	1	1	5	14	15	1	1	133	.275	.294	.341	.216	14	
1999	Anaheim	AL	299	84	10	1	8	14	27	37	0	1	216	.281	.313	.401	.244	32	

If the Angels pay more than about $400,000 for their catchers this year, it's a mistake. Hemphill and Molina could step in and be an effective, cheap platoon until Dewey is ready. You hear a lot of nonsense about the "veteran presence" a warmed-over out like Matt Walbeck supposedly provides, but when your rotation is older than dirt (Chuck Finley, Ken Hill), how much presence do you need? Ask Finley, who got horrible run support, what he'd rather have: presence or runs. Molina was removed from the 40-man roster in December.

Phil Nevin   C   Bats R   Age 28

YEAR	TEAM	LGE	AB	H	DB	TP	HR	BB	R	RBI	SB	CS	OUT	BA	OBA	SA	EQA	EQR	DEFENSE
1996	Jacksnvl	Sou	345	87	7	1	15	44	40	46	4	1	259	.252	.337	.409	.261	45	
1996	Detroit	AL	118	34	4	0	8	7	14	20	1	0	84	.288	.328	.525	.286	18	
1997	Detroit	AL	247	57	16	1	9	26	26	29	0	1	191	.231	.304	.413	.245	28	31-OF 98
1998	Anaheim	AL	235	53	9	1	8	18	19	24	0	0	182	.226	.281	.374	.224	22	62-C 93
1999	Anaheim	AL	278	68	11	1	12	26	29	37	1	0	210	.245	.309	.421	.251	33	

As mid-career transitions go, this one looks pretty good. Give credit to Nevin for his willingness to go behind the plate in an effort to have a career, and to the Tigers for trying something different. Nevin was pressed into an almost-everyday role in July, and wore down badly. If kept within his limits, he'll be a good role player for years to come, and could have a few seasons like 1996.

Charlie O'Brien   C   Bats R   Age 38

YEAR	TEAM	LGE	AB	H	DB	TP	HR	BB	R	RBI	SB	CS	OUT	BA	OBA	SA	EQA	EQR	DEFENSE
1996	Toronto	AL	318	71	14	0	13	27	28	34	0	1	248	.223	.284	.390	.229	31	
1997	Toronto	AL	223	49	16	1	4	22	21	19	0	2	176	.220	.290	.354	.220	20	
1998	ChiSox	AL	162	42	5	0	5	10	14	18	0	0	120	.259	.302	.383	.236	16	52-C 101
1999	Anaheim	AL	203	44	7	0	5	19	16	17	0	1	160	.217	.284	.325	.207	16	

A life-threatening broken thumb limited him to just 11 at-bats after the Angels acquired him in July. O'Brien was "due back soon" for most of the second half, not that it would have mattered much. O'Brien is a decent backup catcher who has happened to be in the right place at the right time much of his career. Think of him as Forrest Gump with shinguards.

Orlando Palmeiro   OF   Bats L   Age 30

YEAR	TEAM	LGE	AB	H	DB	TP	HR	BB	R	RBI	SB	CS	OUT	BA	OBA	SA	EQA	EQR	DEFENSE
1996	Vancouvr	PCL	246	67	8	2	1	25	29	22	6	2	181	.272	.339	.333	.242	26	63-OF 89
1996	Calfrnia	AL	85	23	6	1	0	8	10	8	0	1	63	.271	.333	.365	.242	9	25-OF 81
1997	Anaheim	AL	132	28	2	2	0	17	11	8	2	2	106	.212	.302	.258	.198	9	45-OF 87
1998	Vancouvr	PCL	139	36	9	1	1	14	16	13	2	1	104	.259	.327	.360	.242	15	37-OF 97
1998	Anaheim	AL	163	53	7	2	0	21	26	19	4	4	114	.325	.402	.393	.281	24	39-OF 103
1999	Anaheim	AL	262	73	13	2	1	31	36	26	5	4	193	.279	.355	.355	.252	31	

I'm not just an analyst, I'm a fan. Palmeiro's performance made me unnaturally happy this year. As someone who's been pushing him as a fourth outfielder for a while, it was good to see him establish himself. He will have similar years to this for a while.

Tim Salmon — DH/RF — Bats R — Age 30

YEAR	TEAM	LGE	AB	H	DB	TP	HR	BB	R	RBI	SB	CS	OUT	BA	OBA	SA	EQA	EQR	DEFENSE	
1996	Calfrnia	AL	566	157	28	4	28	89	87	95	4	2	411	.277	.376	.489	.296	98	147-OF	97
1997	Anaheim	AL	569	165	24	1	34	95	92	103	9	12	416	.290	.392	.515	.304	106	147-OF	102
1998	Anaheim	AL	457	139	26	1	27	91	84	92	0	1	319	.304	.420	.543	.326	97		
1999	Anaheim	AL	501	144	23	1	30	88	85	97	2	4	361	.287	.394	.517	.308	95		

The injury that limited him to designated hitter, a tear of the plantar fascia in his left foot, is similar to the one that cost Marty Cordova 1997 and caused the break in Mark McGwire's career. He absolutely could not run, and didn't play in the field after April, but put up an excellent year anyway. Be impressed: it's a very painful injury.

Craig Shipley — IF — Bats R — Age 36

YEAR	TEAM	LGE	AB	H	DB	TP	HR	BB	R	RBI	SB	CS	OUT	BA	OBA	SA	EQA	EQR	DEFENSE
1996	San Dieg	NL	92	29	2	0	2	3	13	10	7	0	63	.315	.337	.402	.271	12	
1997	San Dieg	NL	139	39	6	0	6	8	15	19	1	1	101	.281	.320	.453	.262	18	11-SS 94
1998	Anaheim	AL	145	37	7	1	2	6	10	13	0	4	112	.255	.285	.359	.210	11	23-3B 93
1999	Anaheim	AL	134	34	3	0	4	5	10	13	2	2	102	.254	.281	.366	.217	11	

Once-useful utility infielder now running out of usefulness. The Angels have better, cheaper candidates for the job, so the only reason to keep Shipley around is a fear of the unknown. Shipley appeared to be noticeably slower running the bases last season; has maybe one year left as major leaguer, so don't miss the farewell tour.

Randy Velarde — 2B — Bats R — Age 36

YEAR	TEAM	LGE	AB	H	DB	TP	HR	BB	R	RBI	SB	CS	OUT	BA	OBA	SA	EQA	EQR	DEFENSE	
1995	NY Yanks	AL	360	99	19	1	7	53	53	43	5	1	262	.275	.368	.392	.272	50	52-2B 98	25-SS 110
1996	Calfrnia	AL	518	144	26	3	13	66	70	66	7	8	382	.278	.360	.415	.269	72	108-2B 79	19-3B 120
1998	Anaheim	AL	186	49	14	1	4	34	32	23	6	2	139	.263	.377	.414	.282	29	49-2B 103	
1999	Anaheim	AL	188	50	10	1	4	28	28	23	3	3	141	.266	.361	.394	.265	25		

When bad things happen to good people. Velarde had finally gotten the regular job he craved when he blew out his elbow. He tried to come back this year with mixed results; offensively, he was the same player, but he had one setback in May, reinjuring the elbow, and when he returned from that he was not the second baseman he had been. Re-signed by the Angels.

Matt Walbeck — C — Bats B — Age 29

YEAR	TEAM	LGE	AB	H	DB	TP	HR	BB	R	RBI	SB	CS	OUT	BA	OBA	SA	EQA	EQR	DEFENSE
1996	Minnesot	AL	211	43	5	0	3	8	9	10	3	1	169	.204	.233	.270	.160	9	
1997	Toledo	Int	59	16	0	1	1	3	5	6	0	0	43	.271	.306	.356	.229	5	
1997	Detroit	AL	135	37	3	0	3	12	14	14	3	3	101	.274	.333	.363	.242	15	
1998	Anaheim	AL	334	86	15	2	6	32	35	35	1	1	249	.257	.322	.368	.241	36	96-C 98
1999	Anaheim	AL	266	67	10	1	6	22	26	28	2	2	201	.252	.309	.365	.233	26	

The following is not intended as sarcasm: Walbeck has improved as a hitter. He's been the brunt of jokes in almost every edition of BP, but there are a lot of catchers who don't manage a .240 EQA in consecutive years. He still plays far too much, but as a switch-hitter with some defensive value, he's not much different than Chad Kreuter, and would be a serviceable backup.

PITCHERS (Averages: 4.00 ERA, 9.00 H/9, 1.00 HR/9, 3.00 BB/9, 6.00 K/9, 1.00 KWH)

Anthony Chavez — Throws R — Age 28

YEAR	TEAM	LGE	IP	H	ER	HR	BB	K	ERA	W	L	H/9	HR/9	BB/9	K/9	KWH	PERA
1996	Midland	Tex	71.3	94	41	4	29	44	5.17	3	5	11.86	0.50	3.66	5.55	0.53	5.05
1997	Midland	Tex	45.3	61	23	1	18	26	4.57	2	3	12.11	0.20	3.57	5.16	0.46	4.76
1997	Vancouvr	PCL	25.7	25	9	2	6	16	3.16	2	1	8.77	0.70	2.10	5.61	1.28	3.51
1998	Vancouvr	PCL	47.0	54	23	5	18	31	4.40	2	3	10.34	0.96	3.45	5.94	0.74	4.60

The price you pay for not throwing hard: Chavez has thrown 80 innings of 2.60 ball in the Pacific Coast League the past two years, and was rewarded by being taken off the 40-man roster in September. If he finds a manager who will look past the radar gun, he's not too old to make some real money in this game. A sleeper.

Brian Cooper   Throws R   Age 24

YEAR	TEAM	LGE	IP	H	ER	HR	BB	K	ERA	W	L	H/9	HR/9	BB/9	K/9	KWH	PERA
1996	Lk Elsin	Cal	153.3	203	94	18	35	105	5.52	6	11	11.92	1.06	2.05	6.16	1.16	5.28
1997	Lk Elsin	Cal	111.0	132	58	8	27	69	4.70	5	7	10.70	0.65	2.19	5.59	1.00	4.38
1998	Midland	Tex	158.3	240	126	33	62	111	7.16	4	14	13.64	1.88	3.52	6.31	0.62	7.05

The enthusiasm his successful return from surgery stirred in 1997 was short-lived. Cooper was beaten like a drum this year. That ERA above isn't just the result of a translation: it was 7.13 in real life. He pitched a little better in the second half; I wouldn't give up on him yet, and I'm not just saying that because he's a Trojan. Stands to benefit as much as anyone from the move to Erie.

Rich DeLucia   Throws R   Age 34

YEAR	TEAM	LGE	IP	H	ER	HR	BB	K	ERA	W	L	H/9	HR/9	BB/9	K/9	KWH	PERA
1996	San Fran	NL	64.0	64	38	8	29	50	5.34	3	4	9.00	1.12	4.08	7.03	1.01	4.08
1997	Anaheim	AL	43.7	30	15	5	23	41	3.09	3	2	6.18	1.03	4.74	8.45	1.83	2.47
1998	Anaheim	AL	73.3	57	30	10	41	71	3.68	4	4	7.00	1.23	5.03	8.71	1.62	3.19

Another data point in the case that relievers are interchangeable. There's no real difference between DeLucia and 50 other guys; DeLucia just happened to get a shot as a reliever after he bombed as a starter, and has parlayed his one effective pitch (a slider) into a nice little career. If teams would recognize that there are plenty of guys like this, it would go a long way towards improving player personnel management. DeLucia can be replaced by Chavez at 10% of the cost and no loss in effectiveness.

Jason Dickson   Throws R   Age 26

YEAR	TEAM	LGE	IP	H	ER	HR	BB	K	ERA	W	L	H/9	HR/9	BB/9	K/9	KWH	PERA
1996	Midland	Tex	56.3	57	23	3	11	35	3.67	3	3	9.11	0.48	1.76	5.59	1.47	3.36
1996	Vancouvr	PCL	118.7	154	77	10	38	59	5.84	4	9	11.68	0.76	2.88	4.47	0.45	5.01
1996	Calfrnia	AL	44.3	49	17	6	15	20	3.45	3	2	9.95	1.22	3.05	4.06	0.41	4.47
1997	Anaheim	AL	210.3	230	91	29	49	112	3.89	12	11	9.84	1.24	2.10	4.79	0.83	4.32
1998	Anaheim	AL	124.0	147	75	16	37	59	5.44	5	9	10.67	1.16	2.69	4.28	0.48	4.79

In case you missed it, Dickson has been pretty ineffective since making the 1997 AL All-Star team. He did pitch well out of the bullpen last year (0.77 ERA in 20.1 IP), but since his strikeout rate was identical as both a starter and reliever, I wouldn't put too much stock in that. Like most pitchers with his skill set, he'll never be someone you can count on, but will have occasional good years.

Bo Donaldson   Throws R   Age 25

YEAR	TEAM	LGE	IP	H	ER	HR	BB	K	ERA	W	L	H/9	HR/9	BB/9	K/9	KWH	PERA
1997	Boise	Nwn	46.3	50	16	0	26	39	3.11	3	2	9.71	0.00	5.05	7.58	0.88	3.88
1998	Lk Elsin	Cal	66.7	98	54	9	50	56	7.29	2	5	13.23	1.22	6.75	7.56	0.48	6.61

Closer prospect, no visible scars or contusions, but he's not getting any notice. Despite pitching well in both 1997 and 1998, he hasn't been moved up at midseason. He's another one of the Angels' college draftees who doesn't really have the luxury of moving up one level at a time. As with Chavez, I like him more than the Angels seem to, and would like to see him at least get a chance to be a prospect. Performance counts.

Geoff Edsell   Throws R   Age 27

YEAR	TEAM	LGE	IP	H	ER	HR	BB	K	ERA	W	L	H/9	HR/9	BB/9	K/9	KWH	PERA
1996	Midland	Tex	88.0	93	51	10	55	50	5.22	4	6	9.51	1.02	5.63	5.11	0.37	4.50
1996	Vancouvr	PCL	95.0	111	50	8	44	39	4.74	5	6	10.52	0.76	4.17	3.69	0.23	4.64
1997	Vancouvr	PCL	165.3	219	121	11	91	72	6.59	5	13	11.92	0.60	4.95	3.92	0.20	5.28
1998	Vancouvr	PCL	62.7	78	50	7	35	47	7.18	2	5	11.20	1.01	5.03	6.75	0.61	5.31

Good relievers emerging from the carcasses of mediocre-to-failed starters happens quite frequently. Edsell was bumped from the Vancouver rotation by Scot Schoeneweis and Jarrod Washburn, and immediately improved his strikeout rate by 75%. Edsell is a replacement-level relief pitcher who deserves a chance to come back to the United States and play.

Seth Etherton   Throws R   Age 22

YEAR	TEAM	LGE	IP	H	ER	HR	BB	K	ERA	W	L	H/9	HR/9	BB/9	K/9	KWH	PERA
1998	Midland	Tex	47.3	63	33	9	12	28	6.27	1	4	11.98	1.71	2.28	5.32	0.78	5.89

The Angels' 1998 #1 pick out of USC. Give them credit for skipping the formalities and sending him straight to Midland. He got hit pretty hard, but so what? He's not going to develop anything coming out of college and going to the Midwest League to abuse high school kids. He already changes speeds off his 88-91 mph fastball with a palmball. Here's hoping the Angels give him 350 innings to develop before bringing him to Anaheim in late 2000.

Mike Fetters   Throws R   Age 34

YEAR	TEAM	LGE	IP	H	ER	HR	BB	K	ERA	W	L	H/9	HR/9	BB/9	K/9	KWH	PERA
1996	Milwauke	AL	63.0	62	21	3	21	53	3.00	4	3	8.86	0.43	3.00	7.57	1.62	3.43
1997	Milwauke	AL	72.7	61	24	4	29	60	2.97	5	3	7.56	0.50	3.59	7.43	1.53	2.85
1998	Oakland	AL	48.0	48	21	3	19	33	3.94	3	2	9.00	0.56	3.56	6.19	0.90	3.56
1998	Anaheim	AL	11.3	14	7	2	4	9	5.56	0	1	11.12	1.59	3.18	7.15	1.08	5.56

Another "We're serious about this" acquisition by the Angels, Fetters had about as much effect on the AL West race as your kid sister. Fetters has a "closer" label for some reason, and should latch on with a bad team somewhere and throw 60 innings of 3.75 ball, pick up 15 saves, and make two trips to the disabled list for a pulled eyelid. Now ask me where I think the sun is going to come up.

Chuck Finley   Throws L   Age 36

YEAR	TEAM	LGE	IP	H	ER	HR	BB	K	ERA	W	L	H/9	HR/9	BB/9	K/9	KWH	PERA
1996	Calfrnia	AL	243.7	229	94	23	76	213	3.47	15	12	8.46	0.85	2.81	7.87	1.95	3.40
1997	Anaheim	AL	170.3	148	63	18	56	151	3.33	11	8	7.82	0.95	2.96	7.98	2.06	3.12
1998	Anaheim	AL	227.7	212	82	19	98	205	3.24	15	10	8.38	0.75	3.87	8.10	1.52	3.48

Dammit, THIS is the year he falls apart! I swear he's lost it...really.... Having underrated Finley ever since the strike ended, I have to admit he's been consistent at a level I didn't think he could maintain. He's stayed healthy—his shortened 1997 was the result of a fluke injury—and given the Angels quality innings every year for the last ten. Sometimes, being wrong doesn't feel bad at all. Collins rode him very hard last year, and he wore down in September, so keep an eye on him: if he ever does lose it, I don't think it will be a long, slow decline.

Erik Hanson   Throws R   Age 34

YEAR	TEAM	LGE	IP	H	ER	HR	BB	K	ERA	W	L	H/9	HR/9	BB/9	K/9	KWH	PERA
1995	Boston	AL	192.3	180	73	16	47	142	3.42	12	9	8.42	0.75	2.20	6.64	1.79	3.18
1996	Toronto	AL	222.3	231	108	22	82	155	4.37	11	14	9.35	0.89	3.32	6.27	0.95	4.01
1998	Toronto	AL	51.7	72	28	9	26	21	4.88	2	4	12.54	1.57	4.53	3.66	0.18	6.27
1998	Vancouvr	PCL	74.3	99	49	7	38	44	5.93	3	5	11.99	0.85	4.60	5.33	0.39	5.45

Hanson pitched effectively at Vancouver after his release by the Blue Jays in May. If I had to pick one pitcher to be 1999's Pete Harnisch, it would be Hanson. He's already come back from one major injury (a torn ACL in 1994), and it often takes a lost season to come back from shoulder surgery. His problem last year was a loss of velocity. If he can adjust to that, he still has the nasty curveball. He needs a team that will baby him, the way the Red Sox did with Bret Saberhagen.

Mark Harriger   Throws R   Age 24

YEAR	TEAM	LGE	IP	H	ER	HR	BB	K	ERA	W	L	H/9	HR/9	BB/9	K/9	KWH	PERA
1997	Boise	Nwn	42.0	82	75	3	44	20	16.07	0	5	17.57	0.64	9.43	4.29	0.08	7.93
1997	CedarRpd	Mid	46.0	99	62	5	39	32	12.13	0	5	19.37	0.98	7.63	6.26	0.20	8.61
1998	CedarRpd	Mid	106.0	131	55	5	50	60	4.67	5	7	11.12	0.42	4.25	5.09	0.41	4.67
1998	Lk Elsin	Cal	73.0	118	54	6	27	41	6.66	2	6	14.55	0.74	3.33	5.05	0.40	6.29

Harriger found the strike zone in 1998, and with it a trip for one to beautiful Peoria, Ariz. His AFL stint went well, so look for him to join the ranks of the wildly overrated this winter. Harriger is a mediocre pitching prospect in a thin organization. Remember: opportunity counts, so watch him.

Pep Harris — Throws R — Age 26

YEAR	TEAM	LGE	IP	H	ER	HR	BB	K	ERA	W	L	H/9	HR/9	BB/9	K/9	KWH	PERA
1996	Midland	Tex	39.7	50	24	2	10	24	5.45	1	3	11.34	0.45	2.27	5.45	0.86	4.54
1996	Vancouvr	PCL	107.3	154	71	14	44	51	5.95	4	8	12.91	1.17	3.69	4.28	0.29	6.04
1996	Calfrnia	AL	33.0	30	12	4	14	20	3.27	2	2	8.18	1.09	3.82	5.45	0.71	3.55
1997	Anaheim	AL	83.0	81	27	6	33	55	2.93	6	3	8.78	0.65	3.58	5.96	0.85	3.58
1998	Anaheim	AL	60.7	55	27	7	21	33	4.01	3	4	8.16	1.04	3.12	4.90	0.71	3.41

Out for 1999 after reconstructive elbow surgery. When healthy, very valuable to a real-life team with a poor back of the rotation, like the Angels. Harris is unlikely to graduate to a larger role than middle relief, but in that role he's effective. He can pitch a lot, shuts down the running game and doesn't get torched by left-handed batters.

Shigetoshi Hasegawa — Throws R — Age 30

YEAR	TEAM	LGE	IP	H	ER	HR	BB	K	ERA	W	L	H/9	HR/9	BB/9	K/9	KWH	PERA
1997	Anaheim	AL	121.0	115	48	13	40	81	3.57	7	6	8.55	0.97	2.98	6.02	1.07	3.57
1998	Anaheim	AL	98.3	86	31	13	29	71	2.84	7	4	7.87	1.19	2.65	6.50	1.52	3.20

I'm not convinced he wasn't the team MVP. Those 90-odd innings were very high-leverage. His usage patterns changed as the year progressed: eight of his nine three-inning outings came before August. After that time, Collins began to use him more with a lead, and more often; this caught up to him in September. I think he's more effective as a long man, because he has the repertoire to go around the lineup more than once. He can probably throw 120 innings, but I doubt he can make 80 appearances. The best Japanese pitcher in baseball.

Ken Hill — Throws R — Age 33

YEAR	TEAM	LGE	IP	H	ER	HR	BB	K	ERA	W	L	H/9	HR/9	BB/9	K/9	KWH	PERA
1996	Texas	AL	262.3	230	79	16	77	170	2.71	20	9	7.89	0.55	2.64	5.83	1.22	2.85
1997	Texas	AL	117.3	123	54	10	49	66	4.14	6	7	9.43	0.77	3.76	5.06	0.54	4.07
1997	Anaheim	AL	81.3	64	28	7	35	37	3.10	6	3	7.08	0.77	3.87	4.09	0.46	2.77
1998	Anaheim	AL	105.0	124	51	6	42	55	4.37	5	7	10.63	0.51	3.60	4.71	0.44	4.46

A galactically stupid signing. The Angels got to see him for two months at the end of 1997; did they notice the change from power pitcher to nibbler? The declining strikeout rate? The control problems? No. Three years, $15 million for an obviously burnt-out pitcher. But it gets better: Hill started 1998 with 14 shutout innings, and entered May with a 2.50 ERA before running into trouble. By May 20, his ERA was 4.42. That night, he allowed seven hits and six walks to the A's in eight innings, throwing almost 130 pitches, and was sent out to the mound to start the ninth! Only after after getting two outs, allowing a hit and a walk, and reaching 146 pitches did Terry Collins come and get him. What kind of sick joke is this? He was obviously ineffective, but somehow scuffled through eight innings. You have $13.5 million more invested in him for the next two years and four months. You have a strong bullpen, including a top closer. And Hill had been ineffective in his most recent outings. What could possibly have been gained by having him finish this game that would justify risking the investment in him? If there was a way to make the signing worse, Collins found it. This got my vote for Idiot Move of the Year, so apologies to Mike Hargrove supporters. Hill would eventually land on the disabled list for 2½ months, having bone spurs cleaned out of his pitching elbow.

Mike Holtz — Throws L — Age 26

YEAR	TEAM	LGE	IP	H	ER	HR	BB	K	ERA	W	L	H/9	HR/9	BB/9	K/9	KWH	PERA
1996	Midland	Tex	41.7	56	31	6	10	36	6.70	1	4	12.10	1.30	2.16	7.78	1.74	5.62
1996	Calfrnia	AL	30.0	21	8	1	15	31	2.40	2	1	6.30	0.30	4.50	9.30	2.29	2.10
1997	Anaheim	AL	44.7	37	17	7	13	39	3.43	3	2	7.46	1.41	2.62	7.86	2.37	3.02
1998	Anaheim	AL	31.0	39	14	0	13	28	4.06	1	2	11.32	0.00	3.77	8.13	1.16	4.35

The funny thing about his midseason demotion was that it came after he got his act together. He was brutal through June, but pitched well in July; a couple of bad days against the Yankees and Red Sox got him sent down for a month. Holtz didn't seem to have the same fastball he did in 1997, which left him with just the big-breaking curveball. It's a nice pitch, but any pitcher needs more than that. His strong September makes me think he's OK.

Mike James   Throws R   Age 31

YEAR	TEAM	LGE	IP	H	ER	HR	BB	K	ERA	W	L	H/9	HR/9	BB/9	K/9	KWH	PERA
1996	Calfrnia	AL	82.7	60	20	6	34	64	2.18	7	2	6.53	0.65	3.70	6.97	1.51	2.29
1997	Anaheim	AL	65.3	68	26	3	25	56	3.58	4	3	9.37	0.41	3.44	7.71	1.38	3.72
1998	Anaheim	AL	14.3	10	3	0	6	12	1.88	2	0	6.28	0.00	3.77	7.53	1.80	1.88

Suspended for ugly facial hair by Gene Budig, he vowed never to return. Attendance spiked up by 30% from that day forward, mostly from the return of women and children. Okay, it could have happened. James actually tore a muscle in his right forearm in May, which ended his season. Since it's not a joint injury, his prognosis is pretty good. When he's healthy, he's a top-tier setup man.

Jeff Juden   Throws R   Age 28

YEAR	TEAM	LGE	IP	H	ER	HR	BB	K	ERA	W	L	H/9	HR/9	BB/9	K/9	KWH	PERA
1996	San Fran	NL	42.7	41	20	8	19	32	4.22	2	3	8.65	1.69	4.01	6.75	0.99	4.22
1996	Montreal	NL	33.3	23	11	1	14	24	2.97	3	1	6.21	0.27	3.78	6.48	1.34	1.89
1997	Montreal	NL	133.3	131	57	18	52	96	3.85	8	7	8.84	1.22	3.51	6.48	1.01	3.98
1997	Clevelnd	AL	32.0	32	18	6	13	28	5.06	2	2	9.00	1.69	3.66	7.88	1.41	4.50
1998	Milwauke	NL	144.3	153	79	21	61	101	4.93	6	10	9.54	1.31	3.80	6.30	0.82	4.49
1998	Anaheim	AL	40.7	34	27	7	16	38	5.98	2	3	7.52	1.55	3.54	8.41	1.99	3.32

By all accounts an unpopular cuss. The Angels are his seventh organization in six years, and he will be with his eighth by the time you read this. Juden is hard to bet on because he seems incapable of gaining an organization's confidence. He has a good arm, he hasn't been worked overly hard, doesn't have an injury history, and except for last year, hasn't really been all that bad. (And he wasn't terrible in 1998; his peripheral numbers were considerably better than his ERA.) I'm convinced he's one pitching coach away from a good career. Think Eric Plunk, circa 1991, and get him.

Jack McDowell   Throws R   Age 33

YEAR	TEAM	LGE	IP	H	ER	HR	BB	K	ERA	W	L	H/9	HR/9	BB/9	K/9	KWH	PERA
1996	Clevelnd	AL	198.7	200	88	18	54	140	3.99	11	11	9.06	0.82	2.45	6.34	1.36	3.62
1997	Clevelnd	AL	41.7	44	21	6	15	37	4.54	2	3	9.50	1.30	3.24	7.99	1.56	4.32
1998	Anaheim	AL	77.0	96	38	10	17	44	4.44	4	5	11.22	1.17	1.99	5.14	0.89	5.03

The workload from 1991-1995 caught up to him, and while he was never the pitcher the media thought he was, he did have a fine six-year run. The White Sox cost him ten or twenty million dollars by keeping him in the minors in 1989. If he was a free agent after 1993, he probably signs a five-year deal for $25 million. Remember that when you're calling a player "greedy" and buying into anything an owner says. McDowell re-upped with Anaheim for 1999; he's probably not going to be very good.

Omar Olivares   Throws R   Age 31

YEAR	TEAM	LGE	IP	H	ER	HR	BB	K	ERA	W	L	H/9	HR/9	BB/9	K/9	KWH	PERA
1996	Detroit	AL	164.7	160	68	14	61	80	3.72	10	8	8.74	0.77	3.33	4.37	0.49	3.61
1997	Detroit	AL	117.0	114	59	7	46	72	4.54	6	7	8.77	0.54	3.54	5.54	0.74	3.46
1997	Seattle	AL	65.7	77	32	9	25	28	4.39	3	4	10.55	1.23	3.43	3.84	0.31	4.93
1998	Anaheim	AL	186.7	191	78	18	81	109	3.76	11	10	9.21	0.87	3.91	5.26	0.58	4.00

As with Jason Dickson in 1997, the Angels got a performance completely over a pitcher's head, then acted surprised when he reverted to form. (Olivares's ERA, by half: 3.39/4.78; strikeout rate, by half: 5.30/5.74). Terry Collins didn't help matters by treating Olivares like Nike treats a 8-year-old Filippino girl, working him into the ground during a seven-start stretch in May and June to set up his brutal July. 1998 is probably the top of Olivares's range; he can help a bad team, but is not a championship-caliber pitcher. He's back with the Angels in 1999.

Ramon Ortiz   Throws R   Age 23

YEAR	TEAM	LGE	IP	H	ER	HR	BB	K	ERA	W	L	H/9	HR/9	BB/9	K/9	KWH	PERA
1996	Boise	Nwn	18.3	30	12	4	7	11	5.89	1	1	14.73	1.96	3.44	5.40	0.43	7.85
1997	CedarRpd	Mid	170.0	214	93	26	58	148	4.92	8	11	11.33	1.38	3.07	7.84	1.32	5.40
1998	Midland	Tex	46.0	56	28	10	16	42	5.48	2	3	10.96	1.96	3.13	8.22	1.48	5.67

Probably one of the better candidates for a workman's compensation lawsuit following his injury-plagued 1998. A broken elbow and bone chips were the damage after he was abused in 1997, throwing seven complete games in the second half of the year. He avoided surgery, and was reportedly throwing well in instructional league, which is really beside the point. I see no evidence that the Angels have connected his workload in 1997 to the injury in 1998. I'm rooting for Ortiz; he doesn't deserve to be cheated out of fame and a large amount of money because the people he entrusted his future to are incompetent.

Troy Percival   Throws R   Age 29

YEAR	TEAM	LGE	IP	H	ER	HR	BB	K	ERA	W	L	H/9	HR/9	BB/9	K/9	KWH	PERA
1996	Calfrnia	AL	75.0	38	15	7	25	99	1.80	7	1	4.56	0.84	3.00	11.88	7.74	0.96
1997	Anaheim	AL	54.0	39	16	6	19	70	2.67	4	2	6.50	1.00	3.17	11.67	4.96	2.33
1998	Anaheim	AL	68.0	46	26	5	34	84	3.44	5	3	6.09	0.66	4.50	11.12	3.38	2.25

The spiritual successor to Al Hrabosky. Percival is terribly nearsighted and squints like Mr. Magoo on the mound. He enters the game to bad 70s rock (Deep Purple), missed time this year due to complications stemming from caffeine addiction, and was called for a delay-of-game balk while psyching himself up to pitch. His perceived value is about a quarter of his actual value. I'd rather have him than Mariano Rivera, but I'm certain he would make better trade bait than anything else. Relievers are interchangeable; "closers" are a myth. Have we learned nothing from Jeff Shaw? Mike Jackson? Kerry Ligtenberg?

Rich Robertson   Throws L   Age 30

YEAR	TEAM	LGE	IP	H	ER	HR	BB	K	ERA	W	L	H/9	HR/9	BB/9	K/9	KWH	PERA
1996	Minnesot	AL	194.3	190	86	19	95	114	3.98	11	11	8.80	0.88	4.40	5.28	0.54	3.89
1997	Minnesot	AL	152.3	168	87	18	61	67	5.14	6	11	9.93	1.06	3.60	3.96	0.33	4.49
1998	Vancouvr	PCL	158.7	208	96	13	71	90	5.45	6	12	11.80	0.74	4.03	5.11	0.41	5.22

Replacement-level pitcher who can succeed with the right defense behind him. I don't think there's as much difference between him and Brian Bohanon as 1998 would make you think. Robertson would be a good tenth pitcher on a staff that had a mostly right-handed rotation, with a manager who is willing to live with the walks.

Scot Schoeneweis   Throws L   Age 25

YEAR	TEAM	LGE	IP	H	ER	HR	BB	K	ERA	W	L	H/9	HR/9	BB/9	K/9	KWH	PERA
1996	Lk Elsin	Cal	87.7	103	47	6	25	55	4.83	4	6	10.57	0.62	2.57	5.65	0.88	4.31
1997	Midland	Tex	113.0	156	74	7	41	78	5.89	4	9	12.42	0.56	3.27	6.21	0.71	5.26
1998	Vancouvr	PCL	168.3	212	103	17	58	105	5.51	7	12	11.33	0.91	3.10	5.61	0.67	5.03

The best prospect in the system. Schoeneweis has advanced steadily, fighting off a minor arm injury in 1997 and coming back to post a strong season at Vancouver. He'll enter spring training with a shot to win a starting job, with his chance hinging on whether the Angels sign or trade for any starting pitchers. For my money, he's a better pitcher than Washburn; less inclined to nibble, more of a fastball/slider pitcher. I'd love to see him get 90 innings or so in low-leverage relief, kind of the way the Astros broke in Scott Elarton last year.

Steve Sparks   Throws R   Age 33

YEAR	TEAM	LGE	IP	H	ER	HR	BB	K	ERA	W	L	H/9	HR/9	BB/9	K/9	KWH	PERA
1995	Milwauke	AL	212.0	205	87	16	71	100	3.69	13	11	8.70	0.68	3.01	4.25	0.52	3.44
1996	Milwauke	AL	92.0	99	51	17	42	21	4.99	4	6	9.68	1.66	4.11	2.05	0.08	4.89
1996	New Orln	AmA	56.3	79	50	8	43	22	7.99	1	5	12.62	1.28	6.87	3.51	0.11	6.39
1998	Midland	Tex	38.3	59	41	3	17	24	9.63	1	3	13.85	0.70	3.99	5.63	0.43	6.10
1998	Vancouvr	PCL	25.7	28	13	2	6	14	4.56	1	2	9.82	0.70	2.10	4.91	0.87	3.86
1998	Anaheim	AL	131.0	131	56	13	52	87	3.85	8	7	9.00	0.89	3.57	5.98	0.83	3.85

Came back from the dead to pitch as well as he did in 1995. In between, he had his elbow taken apart and put back together. I liked him after 1995 and I like him now. Baseball can never have too many knuckleball pitchers.

Jarrod Washburn   Throws L   Age 24

YEAR	TEAM	LGE	IP	H	ER	HR	BB	K	ERA	W	L	H/9	HR/9	BB/9	K/9	KWH	PERA
1996	Lk Elsin	Cal	88.0	94	37	5	30	63	3.78	5	5	9.61	0.51	3.07	6.44	1.06	3.78
1996	Midland	Tex	89.7	79	37	11	27	52	3.71	5	5	7.93	1.10	2.71	5.22	0.95	3.21
1997	Midland	Tex	190.0	222	97	24	66	123	4.59	9	12	10.52	1.14	3.13	5.83	0.77	4.78
1998	Vancouvr	PCL	86.7	101	43	7	41	53	4.47	4	6	10.49	0.73	4.26	5.50	0.51	4.57
1998	Anaheim	AL	75.0	71	34	10	24	47	4.08	4	4	8.52	1.20	2.88	5.64	0.97	3.72

(Jarrod Washburn *continued*)

Washburn went at least five innings in each of his ten starts after a June callup, posting a 4.38 ERA, and was sent down at the end of July anyway. I know it was a numbers thing, but as much trouble as the Angels had with their rotation, you'd think they would have found a way to keep him around. He should open the year as the Angels' fourth or fifth starter, and is going to make a nice chunk of change in this game.

Allen Watson   Throws L   Age 28

YEAR	TEAM	LGE	IP	H	ER	HR	BB	K	ERA	W	L	H/9	HR/9	BB/9	K/9	KWH	PERA
1996	San Fran	NL	191.0	194	91	28	65	116	4.29	10	11	9.14	1.32	3.06	5.47	0.80	4.15
1997	Anaheim	AL	207.0	213	97	34	64	138	4.22	11	12	9.26	1.48	2.78	6.00	1.05	4.26
1998	Anaheim	AL	94.3	122	57	11	30	62	5.44	4	6	11.64	1.05	2.86	5.92	0.79	5.25

Watson's carping about his role was part of the reason for Washburn's exile, which means Watson was both ineffective and an off-field problem. But hey, he wasn't gunning down the fans behind the third-base dugout or slipping Rohypnol into Tim Salmon's java, so maybe he wasn't all that bad. Will be elsewhere in 1999. The skills are there, so if he ends up in some place like Houston or San Diego, he'll have a few good years. If he ends up in Colorado, somebody's gonna get hurt.

Matt Wise   Throws R   Age 23

YEAR	TEAM	LGE	IP	H	ER	HR	BB	K	ERA	W	L	H/9	HR/9	BB/9	K/9	KWH	PERA
1997	Boise	Nwn	74.3	95	48	6	38	43	5.81	3	5	11.50	0.73	4.60	5.21	0.38	5.09
1998	Midland	Tex	166.3	210	98	22	47	105	5.30	7	11	11.36	1.19	2.54	5.68	0.84	5.19

I was impressed by the Angels' handling of Wise. After giving him a taste of pro ball in 1997, they jumped him to Midland this year and left him alone; no up-and-down, no bullpen/rotation shuffle, just let him get 27 starts under his belt. He has wonderful command, and I think he's going to be a very good pitcher. The Angels' second-best prospect.

SNWL												ANAHEIM ANGELS		Park Effect: 0.0%

PITCHER	GS	IP	R	SNW	SNL	SNPCT	W	L	RA	APW	SNVA	SNWAR
Dickson, J.	18	101.3	87	3.6	9.8	.267	7	10	7.73	-3.00	-2.96	-2.11
Finley, C.	34	223.3	97	14.1	10.4	.575	11	9	3.91	2.44	1.92	3.69
Hill, K.	19	103.0	60	6.5	6.7	.494	9	6	5.24	-0.33	0.07	0.91
Juden, J.	6	35.3	29	1.2	3.1	.286	1	3	7.39	-0.92	-0.95	-0.60
Mcdowell, J.	14	76.0	45	4.2	5.3	.444	5	3	5.33	-0.31	-0.48	0.18
Olivares, O.	26	160.0	86	9.6	8.7	.524	7	9	4.84	0.17	0.39	1.81
Sparks, S.	20	121.7	60	7.3	6.6	.528	9	4	4.44	0.65	0.36	1.42
Washburn, J.	11	68.3	34	3.7	3.4	.519	6	2	4.48	0.33	0.11	0.66
Watson, A.	14	71.3	60	2.8	6.8	.295	5	7	7.57	-1.99	-1.92	-1.25
TOTALS	162	960.3	558	53.0	60.6	.467	60	53	5.23	-2.97	-3.45	4.72

The Angels' rotation ranked 21st in 1998 and 20th in 1997. The main difference in 1998 is that the Angels had a more extreme starting staff, better on top but worse on the bottom. At the top, Chuck Finley was putting together his best season since 1993. A number of other pitchers like scrap heap pickups Omar Olivares and Steve Sparks produced quality innings at various points in the season. Unfortunately, the Angels had the worst starter in the majors in Jason Dickson, and another of the ten worst in Allen Watson. Because of the duo's perceived history of success, they were given a large number of starts to work through their problems. Neither ever righted himself, and both did a lot of damage to the rotation's overall numbers. If you replaced Dickson and Watson with replacement-level pitching (as I'm defining it—pitchers with a .425 SNPct), the Angels' ranking would have risen from 21st to 13th.

Pitcher Abuse Points

PITCHER	AGE	GS	PAP	PAP/S	AAW	MAX	115+	130+
Dickson, Jason	25	18	120	6.67	14.44	122	4	0
Finley, Chuck	35	34	907	26.68	26.68	147	16	3
Hill, Ken	32	19	185	9.74	9.74	146	2	1
Juden, Jeff	27	6	84	14.00	25.67	128	2	0
McDowell, Jack	32	14	32	2.29	2.29	111	0	0
Olivares, Omar	30	26	357	13.73	18.31	130	7	1
Sparks, Steve	32	20	470	23.50	23.50	142	7	3
Washburn, Jarrod	23	11	93	8.45	21.14	121	3	0
Watson, Allen	27	14	27	1.93	3.54	113	0	0
TOTAL		162	2275	14.04	17.07	147	41	8
RANKING (AL)			3	3	6		8-T	3

Terry Collins has long had a reputation as a manager who likes to leave his starters in, and he did nothing to dispel that notion last year. He did have a largely veteran staff and used a little more caution with youngsters like Dickson and Washburn. Ken Hill went straight to the disabled list after a 146-pitch flogging, while Finley, possibly showing the effects of his high workload, had a 5.52 ERA in September and gave up 54 baserunners in just 31 innings. The Angels' big pennant race acquisition, Jeff Juden, was already the Brewers' most overworked starter. Collins certainly didn't bother to take care of him, so perhaps it's not surprising he bombed (1-3, 6.75 ERA).

Oakland Athletics

By the time you read this, you will have spent a considerable portion of the winter listening to comments about how the current state of the game is enough to make fans in most markets weep. Economic disparity is supposedly going to prevent at least 20 teams from being seriously competitive, a circumstance which is going to only get worse and worse, until finally the owners either decide to blame this circumstance on the players' union or come to their senses and create a working revenue-sharing plan.

What if none of this is really the case? What if teams do not have to spend at least $50 million to have a serious crack at winning the World Series? Perhaps even more dangerous to the assumption of the necessity of revenue sharing, what if teams that aren't the Yankees or the Braves or the Indians don't need revenue-sharing to build contending teams?

One of the teams that's positioning itself to make nonsense of the arguments that big payrolls buy playoff spots and that revenue sharing is an inevitable part to baseball's future is the Oakland A's.

Say what?

The A's claim that they're one of the game's "small market" teams. That argument is based on what passes for poor ticket sales these days (1.2 million per year), limited television revenues, few other potential revenue streams, the pain of learning to live with Al Davis, and jealous glances across the Bay to where PacBell Park will rise on the shoreline to house the unneighborly Giants. The expectation is that life will get better for the franchise once it gets a new stadium, probably in a different location. So from an organizational point of view, the A's have two challenges: the annual pursuit of trying to build a better baseball team, and the long-term plan of how to get a new stadium.

Pending that stadium, the A's expect that they can only raise their salary budget to a certain point. That means they're going to have to make sacrifices. That does not mean levelling the franchise in a Finleyesque way, or being Huizenganated. Having to control costs isn't the end of the

> ## Athletics Prospectus
>
> **1998 record:** 74-88; Fourth place, AL West
> **Pythagorean W/L:** 75-87
> **Runs scored:** 804 (9th in AL)
> **Runs allowed:** 866 (11th in AL)
> **Team EQA:** .263 (t-9th in AL)
> **Park:** Oakland Alameda County Stadium (moderate pitchers')
> **1998:** Better than many expected as veteran arms stabilized the rotation.
> **1999:** One pitcher short of winning the division; can Billy Beane find him?

world, nor does it eliminate the opportunity to build a competitive team.

The current financial structure of the game is haphazard in the way it distributes wealth to the players. While the MLB Players' Association has focused on the high end of the pay scale, trying to make certain that star players make continuous gains through arbitration and free agency, it's arguable that they've neglected the majority of their membership and the mechanisms that make the little guys wealthier. Taking advantage of that, organizations have employed variations on what's now popularly called the "Cleveland strategy," the art of signing young players to multi-year deals before they reach arbitration eligibility. The tradeoff on such deals is that the teams offer players security and higher initial salaries in exchange for security and relatively lower salaries at the back end of these deals (lower relative to what they'd expect to pay through arbitration). For teams, the gamble is that the players are worth it over the length of the contract.

The Indians didn't invent the idea—the White Sox were among the first to try to bridge the years where players would be eligible for arbitration to the years they're eligible for free agency by offering multi-year deals. It didn't work for the Sox; in their inimitable way, they were cheap about it, and still ended up having the player-management confrontations they were supposed to be avoiding. What set the Indians apart is that they were successful with it, and success breeds imitation. When this approach was employed by the Indians, it was to lock in young star players with futures, notably Jim Thome and Manny Ramirez. Later, as the team got successful and Jacobs Field turned the franchise into a money machine, the definitions got blurred, and now almost everybody employed by the Indians gets multi-year deals, regardless of age or talent, and regardless of whether or not it's reasonable to expect to get value in terms of player performance over the life of the contract.

What does that have to do with the A's? Like the Indians of the early '90s, the A's have some outstanding young hitters, and it will be in the organization's interest to lock them up for several years as soon as possible. They've already signed Matt Stairs and Jason Giambi to multi-year deals. Ben Grieve and Eric Chavez are the most important players for Billy Beane to focus on getting signed, and up to a point you could extend this argument to A.J. Hinch or Ryan Christenson or Miguel Tejada, and eventually Mario Encarnacion.

The problem comes if the A's really are limited in the resources they're willing to commit to their salary structure. In terms of available talent, guys like Grieve or Chavez or Ramirez or Thome aren't ones you can get cheaply, except at the point that your organization controls their future: the first six years of their major league careers. No competitive organization can skimp on the cost of having great talent on the roster. Generally, the only ways you get players of this caliber is through player development or the tremendous expense of signing them as free agents. Because most players become free agents at the tail end of the most productive years of their careers, playing the free agent market consistently disappoints organizations. Player development, by contrast, not only gives the poorer organizations their only crack at having players of this calibre in the first place, it puts them in a position to make the "Cleveland strategy" pitch to those players, offering security and wealth in exchange for avoiding salary arbitration, and sometimes getting them to put off free agency for a year or two.

So how do you keep costs down if you've committed yourself to spending money up front that you didn't have to spend? You stop paying top dollar for marginal talent. What does that mean? Whether you're trying to control costs or not, it means that you don't shell out big money for Mike Blowers or Bip Roberts. It means you play hardball with Scott Spiezio, and cut him loose the minute he's eligible for arbitration and makes it clear he wants big money. It isn't that any of these players are bad, or that any player who isn't a superstar is undesirable. It's that the overwhelming majority of these players don't have skills significantly better than the

many major leaguers scrambling for non-roster invitations year after year, or any number of minor league veterans trapped at Triple-A. It means that under the game's current financial setup, you take advantage of the fact that the union hasn't done a great job fighting for better compensation or job security for the bottom end of the pay scale.

In the past, we've written quite a bit about what the A's organization is doing well. They have a unique player development program that emphasizes offensive skills of value: patience and power. Their drafts have recently combined selecting top-grade high school players with relatively polished college pitchers, and they reinforce those drafts with a good Latin American scouting and player development network. The jury is still out on the college pitchers; some, like Eric Dubose or Chad Harville, are looking pretty good. Some, like Chris Enochs or Marcus Jones or Brad Rigby or Bill King, aren't panning out too well yet. Throw that together with a small group of veterans (Tony Phillips, Giambi, Stairs, Kenny Rogers, and Tom Candiotti), and you have a team that's going to be cheap and competitive in a division with two poorly-run organizations and an old Rangers team. Continuing along the path they're currently following should have them well-situated to take a shot at the division title in '99, and competitive for years.

The big question for them whether they'll play for higher stakes; the core talent is in place, and all they really need is experience, some luck and one starting pitcher. If the A's manage to add an ace starter, they could win the division handily. Don't think that Billy Beane and his staff don't know this. We'll have to see whether they take advantage of the opportunity; certainly a winning season won't hurt in their drive to convince San Jose or Sacramento or Dublin or Moraga or Yuba City to build them a stadium. The bigger question for all of baseball is if the A's manage to win with a payroll well under $30 million, will revenue-sharing initiatives never get off the ground?

HITTERS (Averages: BA .260/ OBA .330/ SA .420, EQA .260)

Danny Ardoin — C — Bats R — Age 24

YEAR	TEAM	LGE	AB	H	DB	TP	HR	BB	R	RBI	SB	CS	OUT	BA	OBA	SA	EQA	EQR	DEFENSE
1996	Modesto	Cal	313	65	8	2	4	35	23	21	2	4	252	.208	.287	.284	.197	22	
1997	Visalia	Cal	144	26	5	0	2	17	9	8	0	0	118	.181	.267	.257	.178	8	
1997	Huntsvil	Sou	206	39	6	1	3	13	9	10	2	2	169	.189	.237	.272	.163	9	
1998	Huntsvil	Sou	364	83	12	0	14	48	40	41	5	3	284	.228	.318	.376	.243	41	84-C 100
1999	Oakland	AL	365	83	9	0	12	42	36	38	4	3	285	.227	.307	.351	.230	36	

Untranslated, we're talking about a catcher with a good throwing arm who drew 62 walks and hit 16 home runs. In most organizations, that's somebody with a future; with the A's, it's a Cajun sideshow from the main events, A.J. Hinch and Ramon Hernandez. His hope is that he can claim the backup role; the A's don't want to simultaneously carry both of the big prospects, and they may not sign a veteran caddy.

Mark Bellhorn　　2B/3B　　Bats B　Age 24

YEAR	TEAM	LGE	AB	H	DB	TP	HR	BB	R	RBI	SB	CS	OUT	BA	OBA	SA	EQA	EQR	DEFENSE	
1996	Huntsvil	Sou	467	107	17	2	10	59	54	42	12	2	362	.229	.316	.338	.235	49	57-2B 88	54-SS 94
1997	Edmonton	PCL	225	60	10	2	8	53	42	33	5	5	170	.267	.406	.436	.295	40	40-2B 100	22-SS 97
1997	Oakland	AL	220	49	9	1	6	32	28	21	7	1	172	.223	.321	.355	.244	25	28-3B 110	
1998	Edmonton	PCL	303	67	14	3	8	57	42	33	5	2	238	.221	.344	.366	.255	39	44-3B 94	33-2B 107
1999	*Oakland*	*AL*	*365*	*87*	*16*	*2*	*11*	*60*	*52*	*44*	*8*	*3*	*281*	*.238*	*.346*	*.384*	*.261*	*49*		

It was a very bad year for Bellhorn. First, he scuffled in the 1997 Arizona Fall League. Then he lost out on a major league job because of decisions like bringing in Mike Blowers, and had to watch as the A's acquired Bip Roberts to do things he could do better. He deserves a crack at the second base job, because Spiezio hasn't earned the right to go unchallenged, Bellhorn's a much better defensive player and potentially the better hitter.

Mike Blowers　　3B　　Bats R　Age 34

YEAR	TEAM	LGE	AB	H	DB	TP	HR	BB	R	RBI	SB	CS	OUT	BA	OBA	SA	EQA	EQR	DEFENSE
1996	LosAngls	NL	320	87	19	2	7	39	41	40	0	0	233	.272	.351	.409	.266	43	80-3B 78
1997	Seattle	AL	147	43	5	0	5	21	20	22	0	0	104	.293	.381	.429	.285	23	30-1B 123
1998	Oakland	AL	406	97	23	2	12	41	43	45	1	0	309	.239	.309	.394	.243	45	103-3B 96
1999	*Oakland*	*AL*	*289*	*69*	*15*	*1*	*9*	*35*	*33*	*35*	*0*	*0*	*220*	*.239*	*.321*	*.391*	*.249*	*34*	

His arm is still getting rave reviews, which is just indolence on the part of the people asked to evaluate this sort of thing if you ask me. Mike Blowers is a great non-roster invitee for a team that could use some right-handed sock, and a lousy guy to give a guaranteed contract or 300 plate appearances. Part of that was beyond the A's control, in that he was signed to share the job with Dave Magadan and Magadan got hurt. It was unfortunate and inflexible of them to just hand the extra playing time to Blowers.

Rafael Bournigal　　SS/2B　　Bats R　Age 33

YEAR	TEAM	LGE	AB	H	DB	TP	HR	BB	R	RBI	SB	CS	OUT	BA	OBA	SA	EQA	EQR	DEFENSE	
1996	Oakland	AL	248	57	12	2	0	14	18	14	4	4	195	.230	.271	.294	.190	15	56-2B 100	10-SS 101
1997	Oakland	AL	218	60	5	0	2	16	20	20	2	1	159	.275	.325	.326	.230	20	61-SS 100	
1998	Oakland	AL	207	46	6	0	3	12	15	13	6	1	162	.222	.265	.295	.195	14	30-SS 102	30-2B 98
1999	*Oakland*	*AL*	*212*	*50*	*4*	*0*	*3*	*14*	*16*	*15*	*4*	*1*	*163*	*.236*	*.283*	*.297*	*.202*	*15*		

If you're the Braves and you win every year, Bobby Cox gets to keep a Raffy Belliard around because that's what he wants. If you're the A's, and you haven't won anything since Clinton was elected, you shouldn't get too attached to your defensive replacements. Bournigal is handy enough, but when Spiezio went down, handing the defensive replacement the playing time was the worst thing they could have done. Released.

Justin Bowles　　LF　　Bats L　Age 25

YEAR	TEAM	LGE	AB	H	DB	TP	HR	BB	R	RBI	SB	CS	OUT	BA	OBA	SA	EQA	EQR	DEFENSE
1996	So Oregn	Nwn	217	45	5	1	5	20	17	16	4	2	174	.207	.274	.309	.202	16	51-OF 85
1997	Modesto	Cal	392	108	25	3	6	42	50	45	3	2	286	.276	.346	.401	.261	50	88-OF 96
1998	Huntsvil	Sou	274	67	10	1	8	26	26	30	1	1	208	.245	.310	.376	.238	29	62-OF 94
1999	*Oakland*	*AL*	*312*	*81*	*14*	*1*	*8*	*29*	*35*	*36*	*2*	*1*	*232*	*.260*	*.323*	*.388*	*.248*	*36*	

A member of the '96 LSU Tigers, Bowles has already turned out better than expected. Unfortunately, the A's think he can only handle left field. Even with a solid set of hitting skills, at best he's looking at a career as a platoon player.

Eric Chavez　　3B　　Bats L　Age 21

YEAR	TEAM	LGE	AB	H	DB	TP	HR	BB	R	RBI	SB	CS	OUT	BA	OBA	SA	EQA	EQR	DEFENSE
1997	Visalia	Cal	512	118	17	1	14	29	39	44	7	4	398	.230	.272	.350	.212	41	119-3B 103
1998	Huntsvil	Sou	332	105	15	1	20	32	52	61	9	3	230	.316	.376	.548	.310	62	77-3B 95
1998	Edmonton	PCL	188	56	9	0	10	12	23	30	2	3	135	.298	.340	.505	.281	28	46-3B 82
1998	Oakland	AL	45	14	5	1	0	3	7	5	1	1	32	.311	.354	.467	.277	6	
1999	*Oakland*	*AL*	*509*	*155*	*28*	*1*	*24*	*35*	*70*	*85*	*9*	*5*	*359*	*.305*	*.349*	*.505*	*.289*	*81*	

Baseball America's Player of the Year for '98, an early favorite for the '99 AL Rookie of the Year, and somebody you should have heard plenty about by now. He's a better offensive prospect than Grieve, who isn't exactly a slouch. Hard work has led to improvement in the field, but he still bounces some throws over to first.

Ryan Christenson CF   Bats R   Age 25

YEAR	TEAM	LGE	AB	H	DB	TP	HR	BB	R	RBI	SB	CS	OUT	BA	OBA	SA	EQA	EQR	DEFENSE
1996	So Oregn	Nwn	138	27	1	0	3	12	7	8	3	4	115	.196	.260	.268	.174	7	34-OF 94
1996	W Michgn	Mid	123	31	1	0	2	9	9	10	1	2	94	.252	.303	.309	.210	9	30-OF 104
1997	Visalia	Cal	305	70	9	2	9	53	41	33	10	6	241	.230	.344	.361	.252	38	80-OF 104
1997	Huntsvil	Sou	117	37	7	1	2	19	22	16	4	3	83	.316	.412	.444	.299	20	28-OF 117
1998	Edmonton	PCL	86	19	3	1	1	14	11	7	3	1	68	.221	.330	.314	.236	9	20-OF 122
1998	Oakland	AL	367	96	23	2	5	38	42	38	4	6	277	.262	.331	.376	.245	41	104-OF 107
1999	*Oakland*	*AL*	*409*	*106*	*19*	*2*	*10*	*50*	*54*	*48*	*10*	*7*	*310*	*.259*	*.340*	*.389*	*.256*	*51*	

Maybe we're overly proud of him, because we were talking about Christenson before anyone else was. Even with the cheesy Bradyburns, he's mind-altering in the field because few center fielders are as good as he is at racing in to spear dying quails and bloop singles before they drop. In a fan's life, those have been dropping in for hits since the days of Dwayne Murphy. Don't be surprised if Christenson outperforms that projection; he's shown a marked tendency to improve as a season progresses, which given his rapid advancement could be a learning curve at work.

D.T. Cromer 1B   Bats L   Age 28

YEAR	TEAM	LGE	AB	H	DB	TP	HR	BB	R	RBI	SB	CS	OUT	BA	OBA	SA	EQA	EQR	DEFENSE	
1996	Modesto	Cal	490	123	17	3	15	17	41	49	10	5	372	.251	.276	.390	.227	45	58-1B 111	43-OF 84
1997	Huntsvil	Sou	533	132	20	2	9	42	50	47	8	5	406	.248	.303	.343	.225	49	131-1B 94	
1998	Edmonton	PCL	491	117	17	2	10	27	39	41	9	5	379	.238	.278	.342	.213	39	116-1B 97	
1999	*Oakland*	*AL*	*472*	*119*	*21*	*2*	*12*	*30*	*48*	*49*	*10*	*5*	*358*	*.252*	*.297*	*.381*	*.235*	*48*		

Next time you hear somebody talk about the good old days, when players spent a whole year at a single level, and "learned how to play the game," keep in mind what that means for somebody like Cromer. He's a decent but hardly great hitter, and he's 28 going on 40 or accounting or real estate sales. He needs to go to Japan, and was an unsigned minor league free agent as of late November.

Mario Encarnacion OF   Bats R   Age 21

YEAR	TEAM	LGE	AB	H	DB	TP	HR	BB	R	RBI	SB	CS	OUT	BA	OBA	SA	EQA	EQR	DEFENSE
1996	W Michgn	Mid	409	85	8	2	7	36	31	26	12	5	329	.208	.272	.289	.196	28	107-OF 99
1997	Modesto	Cal	362	97	11	4	15	34	44	49	9	6	271	.268	.331	.445	.265	49	79-OF 98
1998	Huntsvil	Sou	357	91	9	1	14	47	43	46	7	5	271	.255	.342	.403	.260	47	90-OF 99
1999	*Oakland*	*AL*	*354*	*89*	*7*	*1*	*14*	*38*	*41*	*44*	*10*	*6*	*271*	*.251*	*.324*	*.395*	*.251*	*43*	

One of the youngest players in Double-A in '98, Encarnacion is a good bet to be starting in one of the outfield corners by Opening Day 2000. He's still raw in the field, but flashes a great throwing arm. Encarnacion is still figuring out what to do at the plate, but Dominicans who've figured out that walks are good are about as numerous as power-hitting badgers, so he's someone to pay attention to.

Jason Giambi 1B   Bats L   Age 28

YEAR	TEAM	LGE	AB	H	DB	TP	HR	BB	R	RBI	SB	CS	OUT	BA	OBA	SA	EQA	EQR	DEFENSE	
1996	Oakland	AL	522	145	34	1	20	48	64	75	0	1	378	.278	.339	.462	.273	73	38-1B 99	33-3B 114
1997	Oakland	AL	508	146	38	2	21	56	71	81	0	1	363	.287	.358	.494	.289	81	55-OF 92	42-1B 109
1998	Oakland	AL	557	168	23	0	30	84	86	101	2	2	391	.302	.393	.504	.307	102	142-1B 84	
1999	*Oakland*	*AL*	*540*	*151*	*24*	*0*	*28*	*69*	*76*	*92*	*1*	*1*	*390*	*.280*	*.361*	*.480*	*.289*	*87*		

His career's showing a nice, normal progression, but keep in mind that players with Giambi's skills don't have long, illustrious careers. He's a DH in the making with two or three good years to look forward to on a team where Ben Grieve isn't looking like someone who'll be in the outfield forever.

Ben Grieve   RF   Bats L   Age 23

YEAR	TEAM	LGE	AB	H	DB	TP	HR	BB	R	RBI	SB	CS	OUT	BA	OBA	SA	EQA	EQR	DEFENSE
1996	Modesto	Cal	273	82	11	1	8	27	35	38	4	4	195	.300	.363	.436	.275	39	66-OF 96
1996	Huntsvil	Sou	232	49	4	1	7	28	19	21	0	2	185	.211	.296	.328	.215	20	57-OF 85
1997	Huntsvil	Sou	364	108	17	1	19	66	63	66	4	1	257	.297	.405	.505	.313	71	96-OF 97
1997	Oakland	AL	91	28	3	0	4	13	13	16	0	0	63	.308	.394	.473	.301	16	18-OF 100
1998	Oakland	AL	578	170	39	2	20	88	92	91	2	2	410	.294	.387	.472	.297	99	146-OF 87
1999	*Oakland*	*AL*	*576*	*172*	*33*	*1*	*25*	*83*	*93*	*101*	*3*	*2*	*406*	*.299*	*.387*	*.490*	*.302*	*102*	

Probably the signature player for the A's new player development scheme, in the way Jose Canseco was for the LaRussa pygmy dynasty. Just as Canseco was the front man for a team built around power, Grieve is representative of an offensive strategy focused on getting on base; he may never turn into the same sort of power hitter, but that's what Eric Chavez is for. Grieve can frustrate you when he chooses to jump on a pitch when he's ahead in the count, only to hit a 4-6-3 dribbler. He could be the slowest man under 25 in professional baseball. One scout referred to him as "the new Johnny Grubb...a stylish hitter with average power who plays without a pulse." Scouts don't exactly get evaluated very often, but either this is the same guy who says Terry Pendleton still has something left, or there's more than one lousy scout. If the A's are lucky, it's the same guy with who sings Garret Anderson's praises down in Anaheim.

Nathan Haynes   OF   Bats L   Age 19

YEAR	TEAM	LGE	AB	H	DB	TP	HR	BB	R	RBI	SB	CS	OUT	BA	OBA	SA	EQA	EQR	DEFENSE
1997	So Oregn	Nwn	82	15	2	0	0	18	12	3	6	2	69	.183	.330	.207	.214	7	21-OF 97
1998	Modesto	Cal	508	109	11	4	1	44	41	24	22	11	410	.215	.277	.258	.188	31	119-OF 90
1999	*Oakland*	*AL*	*349*	*82*	*6*	*2*	*1*	*32*	*34*	*21*	*16*	*8*	*275*	*.235*	*.299*	*.272*	*.205*	*26*	

The fastest player in the '97 draft, Haynes is still extremely raw. Although he was named the #4 prospect in the California League, he needs to develop real power and improve his strike zone judgment to come even close to living up to what scouts are predicting for him.

Rickey Henderson   OF   Bats R   Age 40

YEAR	TEAM	LGE	AB	H	DB	TP	HR	BB	R	RBI	SB	CS	OUT	BA	OBA	SA	EQA	EQR	DEFENSE
1996	San Dieg	NL	470	117	18	2	10	126	98	50	31	16	369	.249	.408	.360	.283	79	121-OF 94
1997	San Dieg	NL	292	83	7	0	8	73	68	35	26	4	213	.284	.427	.390	.308	56	66-OF 107
1997	Anaheim	AL	113	20	2	0	2	26	21	5	17	4	97	.177	.331	.248	.238	13	
1998	Oakland	AL	538	131	16	1	15	120	115	51	62	13	420	.243	.381	.361	.282	88	142-OF 97
1999	*Oakland*	*AL*	*470*	*108*	*14*	*1*	*11*	*122*	*96*	*47*	*31*	*10*	*372*	*.230*	*.389*	*.334*	*.274*	*73*	

Had an outstanding season by his own lights and by anyone's expectations. Rickey still has the eye at the plate, the speed on the bases, and a great glove in left. What he could use is two days off per week to keep his chronically cranky hammies healthy. He was signed by the Mets, and is expected to be the everyday left fielder and leadoff hitter. Henderson's lack of power in 1998 was a big part of the case for not re-signing him. The problem with the A's letting him leave is that it's a case of robbing Peter to pay Paul: what's the bigger problem, the need for a slugger, or having a good leadoff hitter? The A's problem isn't positional in nature. The don't need a power-hitting left fielder any more than anybody else wouldn't mind having one. The A's need to build a stronger, more balanced lineup, and that means not playing Mike Blowers regularly and not being satisfied with Scott Spiezio. It means getting good production out of Hinch and Tejada and Christenson, rather than having to worry that other teams can have guys like Scott Eyre make spot starts to shut down a lineup that's heavily dependent on left-handed power.

Ramon Hernandez   C   Bats R   Age 23

YEAR	TEAM	LGE	AB	H	DB	TP	HR	BB	R	RBI	SB	CS	OUT	BA	OBA	SA	EQA	EQR	DEFENSE	
1996	W Michgn	Mid	457	106	14	0	12	52	43	44	1	2	353	.232	.310	.341	.228	44		
1997	Visalia	Cal	323	102	11	1	12	28	41	51	1	2	223	.316	.370	.467	.287	49		
1997	Huntsvil	Sou	160	24	1	0	3	15	4	4	0	0	136	.150	.223	.213	.123	4		
1998	Huntsvil	Sou	477	132	15	1	14	43	52	59	3	3	348	.277	.337	.400	.256	58	50-C 95	19-1B 74
1999	*Oakland*	*AL*	*470*	*129*	*15*	*1*	*16*	*44*	*53*	*64*	*1*	*2*	*343*	*.274*	*.337*	*.413*	*.260*	*59*		

His glovework behind the plate angers some people because he moves around too much. He spent much of the year DHing and getting spot starts at first base to rest a sore shoulder. That has healed up, and the A's can afford to let him go to Triple-A, to wait and see if Hinch makes progress while Hernandez polishes his catching.

A.J. Hinch   C   Bats R   Age 25

YEAR	TEAM	LGE	AB	H	DB	TP	HR	BB	R	RBI	SB	CS	OUT	BA	OBA	SA	EQA	EQR	DEFENSE	
1997	Modesto	Cal	331	89	13	0	14	32	39	45	5	2	244	.269	.333	.435	.265	44		
1997	Edmonton	PCL	116	36	4	0	3	17	18	17	2	0	80	.310	.398	.422	.294	19		
1998	Oakland	AL	334	78	8	0	10	32	30	33	3	0	256	.234	.301	.347	.227	32	107-C 102	
1999	Oakland	AL	330	88	9	0	13	34	39	45	3	1	243	.267	.335	.412	.261	42		

A smooth defensive catcher with a compact swing at the plate, Hinch was something of a disappointment even if he was essentially rocketing up from the California League. Tendinitis in his elbow created concerns about his ability to catch every day in '98, but those worries lessened as the season progressed. There's still a lot here to like, and should the A's avoid keeping a veteran to leech too much playing time away from Hinch, he should have a much better sophomore season.

Brian Lesher   1B/OF   Bats R   Age 28

YEAR	TEAM	LGE	AB	H	DB	TP	HR	BB	R	RBI	SB	CS	OUT	BA	OBA	SA	EQA	EQR	DEFENSE	
1996	Edmonton	PCL	405	99	15	1	14	30	38	44	5	4	310	.244	.297	.390	.235	42	70-1B 84	41-OF 84
1997	Edmonton	PCL	393	95	13	2	12	48	47	43	10	3	301	.242	.324	.377	.248	46	96-OF 89	
1997	Oakland	AL	129	29	3	1	4	9	11	12	4	1	101	.225	.275	.357	.221	12	26-OF 107	
1998	Edmonton	PCL	352	85	15	1	8	38	36	35	2	3	270	.241	.315	.358	.234	36	69-OF 87	
1999	Oakland	AL	395	99	17	1	15	42	48	50	6	3	299	.251	.323	.413	.256	49		

In the past two years the A's have brought in Pat Lennon, Kevin Mitchell, Shane Mack, and Jack Voigt, so to say that they don't have a lot of confidence in Lesher as a platoon partner for any of the troika of Grieve, Stairs, or Giambi would belabor the obvious.

Mike Macfarlane   C   Bats R   Age 35

YEAR	TEAM	LGE	AB	H	DB	TP	HR	BB	R	RBI	SB	CS	OUT	BA	OBA	SA	EQA	EQR	DEFENSE
1996	KansasCy	AL	372	100	24	2	18	29	45	55	3	4	276	.269	.322	.489	.271	53	
1997	KansasCy	AL	252	57	12	2	8	25	23	27	0	2	197	.226	.296	.385	.232	26	
1998	Oakland	AL	205	52	10	0	8	13	19	25	1	0	153	.254	.298	.420	.245	23	55-C 99
1999	Oakland	AL	222	52	11	1	8	16	21	25	1	1	171	.234	.286	.401	.234	23	

Let's hope his caretaker role with the team is over and done with. There's nothing wrong with having an ex-Royal in green and gold; it's just sort of like naming Ronald Reagan a Hero of the Soviet People or something. Mac was another member of the A's "second cadre" of coaches, along with Magadan and Henderson, who were supposed to help shepherd the various younger players this year.

Dave Magadan   3B/1B   Bats L   Age 36

YEAR	TEAM	LGE	AB	H	DB	TP	HR	BB	R	RBI	SB	CS	OUT	BA	OBA	SA	EQA	EQR	DEFENSE	
1996	ChiCubs	NL	168	41	7	0	4	30	21	19	0	2	129	.244	.359	.357	.254	21	30-3B 98	
1997	Oakland	AL	264	78	10	1	4	50	44	34	1	0	186	.295	.408	.386	.289	42	28-3B 99	17-1B 102
1998	Oakland	AL	108	35	6	0	2	14	16	16	0	1	74	.324	.402	.435	.292	17	23-3B 110	
1999	Oakland	AL	152	41	3	0	4	28	22	20	0	1	112	.270	.383	.368	.271	21		

Magadan is given a healthy amount of credit for his elder statesman act for the A's younger left-handed hitters. He's probably closing in on lifetime employment, starting out as a minor league hitting instructor. If you can afford roster space for a pinch-hitter, Magadan is a fine guy to keep around. Asking for much more than that, as the A's did entering '98, can leave you flat-footed when he goes down with yet another injury.

T.R. Marcinczyk   1B   Bats R   Age 25

YEAR	TEAM	LGE	AB	H	DB	TP	HR	BB	R	RBI	SB	CS	OUT	BA	OBA	SA	EQA	EQR	DEFENSE	
1996	So Oregn	Nwn	219	33	3	1	3	13	6	6	1	2	188	.151	.198	.215	.093	2	41-1B 126	
1997	Modesto	Cal	464	109	19	1	16	54	48	53	2	2	357	.235	.315	.384	.243	52	94-1B 102	17-3B 99
1998	Huntsvil	Sou	501	119	14	1	19	34	39	54	1	4	386	.238	.286	.383	.226	47	109-1B 84	
1999	Oakland	AL	432	103	10	0	17	34	37	49	1	2	331	.238	.294	.380	.231	42		

(T.R. Marcinczyk *continued*)

Drafted out of the University of Miami, Marcinczyk isn't a great prospect. He can pound an extra-base hit, and the A's have continued to use him in a few games at third base. He's effectively chased D.T. Cromer out of the organization, which sounds about right in that first base prospects who don't absolutely kill their leagues will get plenty of time figuring out where the nice places to eat are all around the Pacific Coast League.

Jason McDonald · OF · Bats B · Age 27

YEAR	TEAM	LGE	AB	H	DB	TP	HR	BB	R	RBI	SB	CS	OUT	BA	OBA	SA	EQA	EQR	DEFENSE
1996	Edmonton	PCL	471	95	6	2	7	56	45	27	26	9	385	.202	.287	.268	.202	35	121-2B 89
1997	Edmonton	PCL	264	47	7	2	3	58	40	14	21	7	224	.178	.326	.254	.226	27	76-OF 103
1997	Oakland	AL	231	59	11	4	4	36	37	24	13	8	180	.255	.356	.390	.263	32	63-OF 101
1998	Oakland	AL	174	45	7	0	2	27	27	15	9	4	133	.259	.358	.333	.253	22	48-OF 103
1999	*Oakland*	*AL*	*359*	*82*	*12*	*2*	*7*	*59*	*54*	*32*	*21*	*8*	*285*	*.228*	*.337*	*.331*	*.246*	*43*	

After an especially grisly collision in the outfield, he spent most of the season recovering from the concussion it gave him. Right now, there's some consideration being given to letting him play left field and lead off. McDonald hasn't been worth much so far against left-handers, so using him as a spot starter and defensive replacement in conjunction with Tony Phillips would probably help both players.

Frank Menechino · 2B · Bats R · Age 28

YEAR	TEAM	LGE	AB	H	DB	TP	HR	BB	R	RBI	SB	CS	OUT	BA	OBA	SA	EQA	EQR	DEFENSE
1996	Birmnghm	Sou	418	101	13	2	8	46	41	39	4	5	322	.242	.317	.340	.230	41	123-2B 88
1997	Nashvill	AA	114	21	1	0	3	22	12	9	2	1	95	.184	.316	.272	.215	10	28-2B 91
1997	Birmnghm	Sou	318	76	14	2	7	58	45	35	5	2	244	.239	.356	.362	.259	42	77-2B 94
1998	Edmonton	PCL	372	81	6	3	7	57	38	32	7	7	298	.218	.322	.306	.224	35	73-2B 91
1999	*Oakland*	*AL*	*388*	*93*	*12*	*2*	*9*	*59*	*49*	*42*	*6*	*5*	*300*	*.240*	*.340*	*.351*	*.246*	*45*	

Drafted from the White Sox in the minor league portion of the Rule V draft, Menechino isn't a great bet to ever get an opportunity. However, the A's second base situation should be considered up for grabs, and Menechino can toss in a few walks. If they suffer an injury or two, Menechino is a far better choice than letting Bournigal start.

Mike Neill · OF · Bats L · Age 29

YEAR	TEAM	LGE	AB	H	DB	TP	HR	BB	R	RBI	SB	CS	OUT	BA	OBA	SA	EQA	EQR	DEFENSE
1996	Modesto	Cal	431	105	7	2	10	43	44	40	11	4	330	.244	.312	.339	.231	42	95-OF 89
1997	Huntsvil	Sou	475	123	14	1	8	51	52	46	10	5	357	.259	.331	.343	.240	50	117-OF 91
1998	Edmonton	PCL	363	88	10	3	6	54	42	36	4	4	279	.242	.341	.336	.242	40	93-OF 93
1999	*Oakland*	*AL*	*412*	*106*	*12*	*1*	*9*	*52*	*50*	*45*	*6*	*4*	*310*	*.257*	*.341*	*.357*	*.248*	*48*	

A bum shoulder long ago ruined his chances of having a real career, costing him time in '93, '94, and '95, and a bad shoulder is what ended his season this year. He could still end up being a huge asset as a pinch-hitter and bench player, sort of how they initially envisioned Matt Stairs, but not as good.

Santos Ortiz · 2B/SS · Bats R · Age 22

YEAR	TEAM	LGE	AB	H	DB	TP	HR	BB	R	RBI	SB	CS	OUT	BA	OBA	SA	EQA	EQR	DEFENSE	
1997	Modesto	Cal	497	108	16	2	14	49	46	43	13	8	397	.217	.288	.342	.219	45	114-SS 99	
1998	Huntsvil	Sou	353	92	18	1	6	37	46	34	15	6	267	.261	.331	.368	.249	41	58-2B 95	31-SS 94
1999	*Oakland*	*AL*	*388*	*102*	*17*	*1*	*11*	*39*	*51*	*45*	*15*	*6*	*292*	*.263*	*.330*	*.397*	*.257*	*49*		

Ortiz was a bit too error-prone at shortstop for the organization's taste, so with Miguel Tejada and Scott Spiezio, the A's played a hunch about the future and moved him to second base. The A's could make things interesting and let him take a crack at snagging Spiezio's job as soon as this spring, but for now they have him penciled in as the starting shortstop at Vancouver.

Adam Piatt · 3B · Bats R · Age 23

YEAR	TEAM	LGE	AB	H	DB	TP	HR	BB	R	RBI	SB	CS	OUT	BA	OBA	SA	EQA	EQR	DEFENSE
1997	So Oregn	Nwn	214	42	2	0	6	20	15	14	6	3	175	.196	.265	.290	.192	14	50-3B 87
1998	Modesto	Cal	503	127	18	2	16	63	63	59	12	4	380	.252	.336	.392	.257	64	121-3B 76
1999	*Oakland*	*AL*	*366*	*94*	*9*	*0*	*14*	*42*	*45*	*46*	*8*	*4*	*276*	*.257*	*.333*	*.396*	*.256*	*46*	

A teammate of Eric DuBose's at Mississippi State, Piatt was dominating in the California League during the second half, building modest credentials as a power-hitting prospect. Has a Chavez-sized roadblock in front of him at the major league level, and although the A's think he's a better fielder at third base than Spiezio was at the same point, they don't envision him being able to move to another position.

Bip Roberts   UT   Bats B   Age 35

YEAR	TEAM	LGE	AB	H	DB	TP	HR	BB	R	RBI	SB	CS	OUT	BA	OBA	SA	EQA	EQR	DEFENSE
1996	KansasCy	AL	333	92	15	3	1	23	37	28	13	11	252	.276	.323	.348	.233	33	50-2B 115
1997	KansasCy	AL	339	102	17	2	1	21	45	32	15	3	240	.301	.342	.372	.256	40	72-OF 93
1997	Clevelnd	AL	84	23	4	0	3	7	12	10	3	0	61	.274	.330	.429	.268	11	
1998	Detroit	AL	111	27	5	0	0	16	16	7	6	1	85	.243	.339	.288	.237	12	
1998	Oakland	AL	180	51	6	0	3	16	24	18	10	3	132	.283	.342	.367	.256	22	21-2B 96
1999	*Oakland*	*AL*	*339*	*89*	*15*	*1*	*3*	*32*	*41*	*30*	*10*	*5*	*255*	*.263*	*.326*	*.339*	*.237*	*35*	

The Loathesome One, working his way towards being almost universally despised, derided, and insulted by managers, GMs, and ex-teammates. The baseball equivalent of using bags of cement as life preservers. Expensive cement.

Scott Spiezio   2B   Bats B   Age 26

YEAR	TEAM	LGE	AB	H	DB	TP	HR	BB	R	RBI	SB	CS	OUT	BA	OBA	SA	EQA	EQR	DEFENSE
1996	Edmonton	PCL	513	122	20	1	19	51	52	58	6	4	395	.238	.307	.392	.241	56	129-3B 114
1997	Oakland	AL	529	125	28	4	14	45	54	54	9	3	407	.236	.296	.384	.236	55	143-2B 95
1998	Oakland	AL	403	106	17	1	10	46	45	47	1	3	300	.263	.339	.385	.252	48	110-2B 99
1999	*Oakland*	*AL*	*461*	*118*	*20*	*1*	*15*	*47*	*52*	*58*	*3*	*2*	*345*	*.256*	*.325*	*.401*	*.253*	*55*	

A tribute to A's infield coach Ron Washington, the guy who had to turn Spiezio into a second baseman in mid-March of '97. It's worked: Spiezio isn't too shabby in the field. He needs to become significantly better player in all phases of the game if he's going to deserve to play regularly. Injuries tend to sap the life out of the careers of second basemen, and Spiezio's had a few already.

Ed Sprague   3B   Bats R   Age 31

YEAR	TEAM	LGE	AB	H	DB	TP	HR	BB	R	RBI	SB	CS	OUT	BA	OBA	SA	EQA	EQR	DEFENSE	
1996	Toronto	AL	579	136	33	2	34	56	64	84	0	0	443	.235	.302	.475	.261	77	144-3B 87	
1997	Toronto	AL	499	115	28	4	15	52	51	55	0	1	385	.230	.303	.393	.239	54	126-3B 88	
1998	Toronto	AL	376	87	16	0	18	26	32	44	0	2	291	.231	.281	.418	.235	39	104-3B	88
1998	Oakland	AL	86	13	4	0	3	3	3	4	1	0	73	.151	.180	.302	.145	3	22-3B 96	
1999	*Oakland*	*AL*	*499*	*112*	*24*	*1*	*23*	*43*	*47*	*61*	*0*	*1*	*388*	*.224*	*.286*	*.415*	*.238*	*54*		

When even the absurdly loyal Toronto media noted that he'd lost it in the field—as if he ever really had it—it was clear he needed to go back to his roots: pinch-hitter, backup corner infielder, and part-time DH. Like Jeff Manto, just without the cool Crash Davis rep. And wealthier.

Matt Stairs   DH   Bats L   Age 30

YEAR	TEAM	LGE	AB	H	DB	TP	HR	BB	R	RBI	SB	CS	OUT	BA	OBA	SA	EQA	EQR	DEFENSE
1996	Edmonton	PCL	175	51	7	1	6	17	21	26	0	0	124	.291	.354	.446	.276	25	
1996	Oakland	AL	133	35	6	1	9	18	19	24	1	1	99	.263	.351	.526	.292	23	32-OF 94
1997	Oakland	AL	344	101	15	0	28	50	55	72	3	2	245	.294	.383	.581	.318	70	76-OF 87
1998	Oakland	AL	518	155	30	1	28	62	80	91	7	3	366	.299	.374	.523	.303	92	
1999	*Oakland*	*AL*	*438*	*127*	*19*	*1*	*28*	*56*	*67*	*84*	*3*	*2*	*313*	*.290*	*.370*	*.530*	*.304*	*80*	

We should all appreciate the beauty of Matt Stairs's batting stance. No, it isn't a Ted Williams "works every time" smoothie. It's an upright, plate-crowding, Sadaharu Oh leg-kick beer-league stance, and it's one of those things that make an afternoon at the ballpark a great way to spend the day. There's more than a little Fred Lynn in him, in that when asked to play the field, he charges all over the place, takes chances, makes a surprisingly good play once in a while, and leaves you convinced he'd kill himself trying to do it over a full season. Someone stuck him with the nickname "Wonder Hamster," which besides sounding like a straight line for a DOA *Saturday Night Live* sketch, just isn't the sort of thing you'd want to be called as a grown man.

Miguel Tejada   SS   Bats R   Age 23

YEAR	TEAM	LGE	AB	H	DB	TP	HR	BB	R	RBI	SB	CS	OUT	BA	OBA	SA	EQA	EQR	DEFENSE
1996	Modesto	Cal	451	104	8	2	14	36	40	41	13	9	356	.231	.287	.350	.220	40	109-SS 89
1997	Huntsvil	Sou	494	117	13	2	16	40	46	49	11	7	384	.237	.294	.368	.229	48	128-SS 97
1997	Oakland	AL	98	19	3	2	2	2	5	6	2	0	79	.194	.210	.327	.176	5	23-SS 95
1998	Oakland	AL	362	85	19	1	12	30	34	38	4	6	283	.235	.293	.392	.232	37	105-SS 100
1999	*Oakland*	*AL*	*469*	*120*	*19*	*2*	*16*	*36*	*51*	*56*	*10*	*7*	*356*	*.256*	*.309*	*.407*	*.246*	*54*	

Is everything peachy in Tejada's march to prominence as one of the American League's ubiquitous supershortstops? He was younger than Nomar Garciaparra was when he became a regular, about the same age as Derek Jeter, and older than Alex Rodriguez. As a player, he isn't similar to any of them. The guys Tejada is similar to, by offensive profile and being a starting shortstop at 22, are a rogue's gallery: the Dodgers' Mariano Duncan put up a .234 EQA in his rookie year; Shawon Dunston .252 in '85 for the Cubs; Alex Gonzalez, .247 for the Jays in '95; Benji Gil, .196 for the Rangers in '95; Mark Lewis, .232 for the Indians in '91. I don't have the data handy for Rey Quinones and Andres Thomas, but you get the idea. The recent shortstops who turned out to have great careers starting out at this age? From the last fifteen years or so, we've got Jeter and Cal Ripken, and as a hitter, Tejada doesn't have anything in common with either one of them. Duncan and Spike Owen (Mariners, '83) wound up with long and productive careers, but Tejada will be written off as a disappointment if he ends up being the new Mariano Duncan.

Roberto Vaz   OF   Bats L   Age 24

YEAR	TEAM	LGE	AB	H	DB	TP	HR	BB	R	RBI	SB	CS	OUT	BA	OBA	SA	EQA	EQR	DEFENSE
1998	Huntsvil	Sou	455	121	13	3	7	41	51	43	15	10	344	.266	.327	.354	.239	48	118-OF 93
1999	*Oakland*	*AL*	*294*	*78*	*7*	*1*	*5*	*24*	*30*	*29*	*7*	*6*	*222*	*.265*	*.321*	*.347*	*.233*	*29*	

He's been compared to Tony Gwynn for his line-drive stroke as well as his girth. Although the A's are pretty high on him, he's looking like a platoon hitter without the power you want from a corner outfielder. The A's have this problem already, and have better fielders than Vaz available.

Jorge Velandia   SS   Bats R   Age 24

YEAR	TEAM	LGE	AB	H	DB	TP	HR	BB	R	RBI	SB	CS	OUT	BA	OBA	SA	EQA	EQR	DEFENSE
1996	Memphis	Sou	392	86	10	0	9	24	25	28	3	4	310	.219	.264	.314	.194	26	120-SS 108
1997	LasVegas	PCL	389	81	8	1	3	24	23	18	10	2	310	.208	.254	.257	.173	19	114-SS 98
1998	Edmonton	PCL	476	120	23	1	6	35	45	41	7	5	361	.252	.303	.342	.224	43	127-SS 114
1999	*Oakland*	*AL*	*448*	*105*	*11*	*0*	*9*	*30*	*35*	*36*	*6*	*3*	*346*	*.234*	*.282*	*.319*	*.207*	*34*	

Almost enough of a hitter to run Raffy Bournigal out of town, but by any other yardstick, not a prospect. If Tejada falls flat on his face in a ugly run of E-6s and nightly sombreros at the plate, don't be surprised if Velandia gets a peek at major league playing time.

George Williams   C   Bats B   Age 30

YEAR	TEAM	LGE	AB	H	DB	TP	HR	BB	R	RBI	SB	CS	OUT	BA	OBA	SA	EQA	EQR	DEFENSE
1995	Edmonton	PCL	281	71	7	0	10	41	32	36	0	3	213	.253	.348	.384	.256	35	
1996	Oakland	AL	129	17	4	0	3	27	10	7	0	0	112	.132	.282	.233	.184	8	
1997	Oakland	AL	196	55	8	1	3	35	30	24	0	1	142	.281	.390	.378	.276	28	
1999	*Oakland*	*AL*	*87*	*21*	*1*	*0*	*3*	*14*	*10*	*11*	*0*	*0*	*66*	*.241*	*.347*	*.356*	*.252*	*11*	

Williams missed all of '98 after surgery on his throwing shoulder and was outrighted to Edmonton prior to the Rule V draft. If he's healthy, he could end up being a noticeable improvement for teams goofing off with the Matheny or Servais types; if he isn't healthy and can't catch, he'll end up like Eric Wedge or Matt Stark, a nice Triple-A DH.

PITCHERS (Averages: 4.00 ERA, 9.00 H/9, 3.00 BB/9, 1.00 HR/9, 6.00 K/9, 1.00 KWH)

Willie Adams　　　　Throws R　　　Age 26

YEAR	TEAM	LGE	IP	H	ER	HR	BB	K	ERA	W	L	H/9	HR/9	BB/9	K/9	KWH	PERA
1996	Edmonton	PCL	108.0	105	47	13	38	69	3.92	6	6	8.75	1.08	3.17	5.75	0.89	3.75
1996	Oakland	AL	77.7	73	30	9	19	68	3.48	5	4	8.46	1.04	2.20	7.88	2.50	3.36
1997	Edmonton	PCL	74.0	104	46	11	18	47	5.59	3	5	12.65	1.34	2.19	5.72	0.88	5.96
1997	Oakland	AL	62.3	69	41	8	28	36	5.92	2	5	9.96	1.16	4.04	5.20	0.50	4.62

Adams spent most of '98 recuperating from shoulder surgery, but at year's end he was throwing 90 mph again. Just a body to mention in the race for the rotation, since Jimmy Haynes was brutal down the stretch, and neither Blake Stein or Mike Oquist did enough that they can stop renting.

Jason Anderson　　　Throws L　　　Age 23

YEAR	TEAM	LGE	IP	H	ER	HR	BB	K	ERA	W	L	H/9	HR/9	BB/9	K/9	KWH	PERA
1997	So Oregn	Nwn	45.3	91	47	5	22	19	9.33	1	4	18.07	0.99	4.37	3.77	0.14	7.94
1998	Modesto	Cal	137.0	184	73	7	58	70	4.80	6	9	12.09	0.46	3.81	4.60	0.34	5.06
1998	Huntsvil	Sou	16.3	19	14	3	9	11	7.71	0	2	10.47	1.65	4.96	6.06	0.53	5.51

Formed a one-two punch with Tim Manwiller at Radford in the Big South Conference, after which both were drafted by the A's in '97. Throws hard for a left-hander and has a full complement of pitches. He will probably spend 1999 at Double-A.

Tom Candiotti　　　Throws R　　　Age 41

YEAR	TEAM	LGE	IP	H	ER	HR	BB	K	ERA	W	L	H/9	HR/9	BB/9	K/9	KWH	PERA
1996	LosAngls	NL	150.0	187	88	19	40	71	5.28	6	11	11.22	1.14	2.40	4.26	0.51	5.04
1997	LosAngls	NL	132.3	140	59	23	35	79	4.01	7	8	9.52	1.56	2.38	5.37	0.96	4.42
1998	Oakland	AL	204.7	216	101	28	56	95	4.44	10	13	9.50	1.23	2.46	4.18	0.56	4.18

Star of a little-known play of manners, "The Importance of Not Being Don Wengert." Candiotti gave his team what it needed, which was regular starts and lots of innings. He was much better in the second half, so he's looking pretty good going into the last year of his contract with the A's. Could be leading a double life: you never see him and jazz great Paolo Conte in the same place, now do you? How many stubbly gray Italians are there, anyhow?

Steve Connelly　　　Throws R　　　Age 25

YEAR	TEAM	LGE	IP	H	ER	HR	BB	K	ERA	W	L	H/9	HR/9	BB/9	K/9	KWH	PERA
1996	Modesto	Cal	62.0	67	30	5	30	43	4.35	3	4	9.73	0.73	4.35	6.24	0.69	4.21
1997	Huntsvil	Sou	67.3	83	31	3	19	38	4.14	3	4	11.09	0.40	2.54	5.08	0.69	4.41
1998	Edmonton	PCL	73.7	71	32	6	23	50	3.91	4	4	8.67	0.73	2.81	6.11	1.15	3.42

Control fiend who gets a good number of ground balls, and a good bet to see plenty of time with the A's in one way or another. Spent his college career at Oklahoma being a bad news mop-up man on some good teams, so I'll tip my cap to the scout who saw enough to have the A's pick him at all.

Carl Dale　　　Throws R　　　Age 26

YEAR	TEAM	LGE	IP	H	ER	HR	BB	K	ERA	W	L	H/9	HR/9	BB/9	K/9	KWH	PERA
1996	Modesto	Cal	119.0	152	80	12	71	64	6.05	4	9	11.50	0.91	5.37	4.84	0.28	5.37
1997	Huntsvil	Sou	80.3	113	61	10	44	42	6.83	2	7	12.66	1.12	4.93	4.71	0.27	6.05
1998	Modesto	Cal	17.3	20	8	2	3	8	4.15	1	1	10.38	1.04	1.56	4.15	0.80	4.15
1998	Edmonton	PCL	60.3	75	32	11	27	31	4.77	3	4	11.19	1.64	4.03	4.62	0.36	5.67

One of the numerous ex-Cardinal prospects the A's received in exchange for all of Tony LaRussa's favorite A's, Dale has had problems staying healthy his entire career. He had a good run in the Arizona Fall League, but he hasn't been that good even when he's healthy. Will have to improve to build on the legacy of Joe Slusarski.

Eric DuBose

YEAR	TEAM	LGE	IP	H	ER	HR	BB	K	ERA	W	L	H/9	HR/9	BB/9	K/9	KWH	PERA
1997	Visalia	Cal	38.0	51	34	4	27	27	8.05	1	3	12.08	0.95	6.39	6.39	0.40	5.92
1998	Visalia	Cal	70.0	70	36	6	39	54	4.63	3	5	9.00	0.77	5.01	6.94	0.80	3.99
1998	Huntsvil	Sou	79.7	98	35	3	28	52	3.95	5	4	11.07	0.34	3.16	5.87	0.74	4.41

Throws L   Age 23

The big left-hander out of Mississippi State was selected with the compensation pick for Mike Bordick, so let's give Peter Angelos a big round of applause, A's fans. He's now a good bet to end up spending time in the major league rotation in '99. Dubose improved dramatically in '98 by smoothing out his mechanics and slowing down his delivery; he has good heat and breaking stuff.

Chris Enochs

YEAR	TEAM	LGE	IP	H	ER	HR	BB	K	ERA	W	L	H/9	HR/9	BB/9	K/9	KWH	PERA
1997	So Oregn	Nwn	9.0	17	5	0	2	5	5.00	0	1	17.00	0.00	2.00	5.00	0.55	6.00
1997	Modesto	Cal	43.7	58	19	0	11	31	3.92	3	2	11.95	0.00	2.27	6.39	1.13	4.33
1998	Huntsvil	Sou	141.0	182	95	14	52	79	6.06	5	11	11.62	0.89	3.32	5.04	0.49	5.17

Throws R   Age 23

Enochs is a reflection of the organization's player development strategy: in the early rounds of the draft, they go for college pitching or high-end high school hitters. Right now, Enochs is frustrating the bejeezuz out of the A's because of his tendency to fall in love with his curve, only to see it get hammered. He's got a good fastball/curve/change mix and a developing slider, but his control took a step backwards in '98.

Kevin Gregg

YEAR	TEAM	LGE	IP	H	ER	HR	BB	K	ERA	W	L	H/9	HR/9	BB/9	K/9	KWH	PERA
1997	Visalia	Cal	115.7	132	73	8	73	95	5.68	4	9	10.27	0.62	5.68	7.39	0.70	4.67
1998	Modesto	Cal	136.7	173	76	10	81	92	5.00	6	9	11.39	0.66	5.33	6.06	0.45	5.14

Throws R   Age 21

A huge flamethrowing Oregon kid drafted out of high school. He wasn't as good in his second spin through the California League, although he did still manage to keep the ball down.

Buddy Groom

YEAR	TEAM	LGE	IP	H	ER	HR	BB	K	ERA	W	L	H/9	HR/9	BB/9	K/9	KWH	PERA
1996	Oakland	AL	79.3	82	29	7	28	57	3.29	5	4	9.30	0.79	3.18	6.47	1.06	3.86
1997	Oakland	AL	68.3	70	29	8	21	44	3.82	4	4	9.22	1.05	2.77	5.80	0.99	3.95
1998	Oakland	AL	58.7	60	24	4	18	35	3.68	4	3	9.20	0.61	2.76	5.37	0.85	3.68

Throws L   Age 33

Groom has been adequate for a left-handed setup man, which is more than they could have wished for when they got him off the scrap heap. He's another example of what you can get if you just stick with any reliever for more than a week or two. Hopefully he's been on the vine long enough to be offered around to some team hunting for veteran moxie and that always-critical second or third left-hander in the pen to intensify their wild-card fantasies.

Chad Harville

YEAR	TEAM	LGE	IP	H	ER	HR	BB	K	ERA	W	L	H/9	HR/9	BB/9	K/9	KWH	PERA
1997	Visalia	Cal	18.3	30	14	3	13	17	6.87	1	1	14.73	1.47	6.38	8.35	0.56	7.36
1998	Visalia	Cal	67.7	71	25	1	33	50	3.33	5	3	9.44	0.13	4.39	6.65	0.80	3.72
1998	Huntsvil	Sou	14.3	8	4	0	11	19	2.51	1	1	5.02	0.00	6.91	11.93	3.08	1.88

Throws R   Age 22

A second-round pick in the great '97 draft. Nagging shoulder woes kept cropping up, so the A's moved the short (5'9") right-hander to the pen. Harville can get his fastball up to 97 mph, and he put the fear of God into some people in the Arizona Fall League. He has an excellent chance to end up in the A's pen in '99.

Jimmy Haynes   Throws R   Age 26

YEAR	TEAM	LGE	IP	H	ER	HR	BB	K	ERA	W	L	H/9	HR/9	BB/9	K/9	KWH	PERA
1996	Rochestr	Int	29.0	33	16	5	19	21	4.97	1	2	10.24	1.55	5.90	6.52	0.53	5.28
1996	Baltimor	AL	90.0	122	68	12	46	64	6.80	3	7	12.20	1.20	4.60	6.40	0.55	5.90
1997	Rochestr	Int	102.3	101	46	9	51	91	4.05	5	6	8.88	0.79	4.49	8.00	1.21	3.87
1997	Edmonton	PCL	29.3	36	18	3	10	20	5.52	1	2	11.05	0.92	3.07	6.14	0.83	4.91
1997	Oakland	AL	77.3	71	29	6	35	64	3.38	5	4	8.26	0.70	4.07	7.45	1.24	3.37
1998	Oakland	AL	199.3	225	102	24	79	130	4.61	9	13	10.16	1.08	3.57	5.87	0.71	4.61

Haynes can be frustrating to watch, which may be the point. He has a good fastball, but from what I've seen he uses it as a waste pitch to set up his over-the-top change-up and a good curve. When he does show you the fastball, he aims it at the catcher's right knee, and more often than not it has guys fishing. He was absolutely awful in the second half, which should be a good warning sign that the A's can't take him for granted going into '99.

Gil Heredia   Throws R   Age 33

YEAR	TEAM	LGE	IP	H	ER	HR	BB	K	ERA	W	L	H/9	HR/9	BB/9	K/9	KWH	PERA
1996	Texas	AL	76.3	83	36	10	12	43	4.24	4	4	9.79	1.18	1.41	5.07	1.39	4.13
1997	Iowa	AmA	43.7	68	27	6	9	23	5.56	2	3	14.02	1.24	1.85	4.74	0.65	6.39
1997	Ottawa	Int	42.3	58	30	5	9	30	6.38	1	4	12.33	1.06	1.91	6.38	1.29	5.53
1998	Edmonton	PCL	136.3	180	73	12	19	74	4.82	6	9	11.88	0.79	1.25	4.89	1.20	4.89
1998	Oakland	AL	43.3	41	11	4	3	26	2.28	4	1	8.52	0.83	0.62	5.40	4.12	2.91

He hasn't really gotten that much better or worse than when he was having his good years for Felipe Alou. He's a poor man's Bob Tewksbury, working fast and keeping his infielders busy. If the A's have to carry a Telgheder or Oquist at the bottom of the rotation, then my pick for the job in '99 would be Heredia.

Tim Hudson   Throws R   Age 23

YEAR	TEAM	LGE	IP	H	ER	HR	BB	K	ERA	W	L	H/9	HR/9	BB/9	K/9	KWH	PERA
1997	So Oregn	Nwn	26.7	20	10	0	16	18	3.38	2	1	6.75	0.00	5.40	6.08	0.76	2.36
1998	Modesto	Cal	36.3	24	11	0	20	30	2.72	3	1	5.94	0.00	4.95	7.43	1.41	1.98
1998	Huntsvil	Sou	128.7	158	79	15	59	82	5.53	5	9	11.05	1.05	4.13	5.74	0.54	5.11

A '97 pick out of Auburn after tying for the NCAA lead in wins and finishing third in strikeouts, Hudson opened people's eyes in camp when he pitched batting practice to the major league squad. Rick Peterson got him away from the "maximum effort" delivery he used to have, so now his mechanics are cleaner and he isn't doing cartwheels on his follow-through. Has command of four pitches, but an especially good fastball and splitter. A sleeper, and someone to watch. Why'd he fall to the fifth round? At six feet, he's probably considered short.

Bill King   Throws R   Age 26

YEAR	TEAM	LGE	IP	H	ER	HR	BB	K	ERA	W	L	H/9	HR/9	BB/9	K/9	KWH	PERA
1996	Modesto	Cal	150.3	228	102	11	39	63	6.11	5	12	13.65	0.66	2.33	3.77	0.33	5.75
1997	Huntsvil	Sou	165.0	253	101	17	29	75	5.51	6	12	13.80	0.93	1.58	4.09	0.57	6.00
1998	Edmonton	PCL	113.7	186	95	18	44	44	7.52	3	10	14.73	1.43	3.48	3.48	0.18	7.13

A soft-tossing control artist, King's shot at a major league rotation is sort of like Don Wengert's: if everything else goes wrong, somebody has to pitch. It's the rules, you know.

Tim Kubinski   Throws L   Age 27

YEAR	TEAM	LGE	IP	H	ER	HR	BB	K	ERA	W	L	H/9	HR/9	BB/9	K/9	KWH	PERA
1996	Huntsvil	Sou	99.7	98	41	8	36	56	3.70	6	5	8.85	0.72	3.25	5.06	0.67	3.61
1997	Edmonton	PCL	73.7	67	34	7	33	41	4.15	4	4	8.19	0.86	4.03	5.01	0.57	3.42
1997	Oakland	AL	13.3	12	7	2	5	10	4.72	0	1	8.10	1.35	3.38	6.75	1.25	3.37
1998	Edmonton	PCL	70.7	91	42	7	23	40	5.35	3	5	11.59	0.89	2.93	5.09	0.57	5.09

Was throwing with much more velocity in '98, nudging some of his pitches over 90 mph for the first time. There's no reason whatsoever to prefer Buddy Groom to Kubinski other than name recognition with the doorman at Tippy Martinez's gentleman's club for left-handed men or something.

Brett Laxton   **Throws R**   **Age 25**

YEAR	TEAM	LGE	IP	H	ER	HR	BB	K	ERA	W	L	H/9	HR/9	BB/9	K/9	KWH	PERA
1997	Visalia	Cal	134.0	168	62	8	53	78	4.16	7	8	11.28	0.54	3.56	5.24	0.51	4.77
1998	Huntsvil	Sou	120.3	139	68	5	71	60	5.09	5	8	10.40	0.37	5.31	4.49	0.27	4.49
1998	Edmonton	PCL	44.7	50	33	6	24	17	6.65	1	4	10.07	1.21	4.84	3.43	0.18	4.84

Injuries after his freshman year at LSU wiped out his draft value, but Laxton has been a pleasant surprise for a 24th-rounder. He finished third in the Southern League in ERA, but he's been a bit too wild to expect him to succeed at the major league level. He hit 15 batters last season, so you might wonder how much of his wildness is intentional.

Tim Manwiller   **Throws R**   **Age 24**

YEAR	TEAM	LGE	IP	H	ER	HR	BB	K	ERA	W	L	H/9	HR/9	BB/9	K/9	KWH	PERA
1997	So Oregn	Nwn	26.3	29	12	0	13	14	4.10	1	2	9.91	0.00	4.44	4.78	0.39	3.76
1997	Modesto	Cal	19.7	25	8	1	7	12	3.66	1	1	11.44	0.46	3.20	5.49	0.62	4.58
1998	Modesto	Cal	144.3	195	81	11	53	78	5.05	6	10	12.16	0.69	3.30	4.86	0.44	5.24
1998	Edmonton	PCL	10.7	9	1	0	1	8	0.84	1	0	7.59	0.00	0.84	6.75	5.33	1.69

A California League All-Star in his first full season, and one of the Radford twins along with Jason Anderson. He doesn't throw hard, just with precision. Ticketed for Double-A in '99.

T.J. Mathews   **Throws R**   **Age 29**

YEAR	TEAM	LGE	IP	H	ER	HR	BB	K	ERA	W	L	H/9	HR/9	BB/9	K/9	KWH	PERA
1996	St Louis	NL	83.7	69	31	8	30	72	3.33	5	4	7.42	0.86	3.23	7.75	1.88	2.90
1997	St Louis	NL	46.3	43	13	5	16	41	2.53	4	1	8.35	0.97	3.11	7.96	1.83	3.50
1997	Oakland	AL	30.3	33	14	5	10	23	4.15	1	2	9.79	1.48	2.97	6.82	1.20	4.75
1998	Oakland	AL	74.3	69	36	6	26	51	4.36	4	4	8.35	0.73	3.15	6.17	1.09	3.27

Mathews has the makings of the next Jeff Nelson: he hides the ball well in a springy, coiled delivery, and he has a nice change-up. None of it helps him much against left-handers, so he runs out a cheesy slider that gets pasted to the gaps. Not many relievers are still screwing around with their assortments in major league games, and Mathews pays for it.

Mike Mohler   **Throws L**   **Age 30**

YEAR	TEAM	LGE	IP	H	ER	HR	BB	K	ERA	W	L	H/9	HR/9	BB/9	K/9	KWH	PERA
1996	Oakland	AL	83.0	77	28	8	34	64	3.04	6	3	8.35	0.87	3.69	6.94	1.17	3.47
1997	Oakland	AL	108.3	109	49	10	47	65	4.07	6	6	9.06	0.83	3.90	5.40	0.62	3.90
1998	Oakland	AL	62.3	69	31	6	23	41	4.48	3	4	9.96	0.87	3.32	5.92	0.79	4.33

Time for the A's patience to wear thin. Has flopped as a setup man, and never should have been used as a starter. Mohler's value, such as it is, is as a long reliever. He's too hittable to be useful in any other role, but he's tantalizingly good enough to be a good tenth or 11th man on a staff.

Mark Mulder   **Throws L**   **Age 22**

The A's top pick from Michigan State in '98, Mulder is already being considered for the major league rotation in '99. He had a good pro debut in the '98 Arizona Fall League. In college, he flashed smooth mechanics and good velocity and control. We're just putting him here to let you know to stay on your toes and see what happens in camp.

Mike Oquist   **Throws R**   **Age 31**

YEAR	TEAM	LGE	IP	H	ER	HR	BB	K	ERA	W	L	H/9	HR/9	BB/9	K/9	KWH	PERA
1996	LasVegas	PCL	135.7	153	55	13	47	86	3.65	8	7	10.15	0.86	3.12	5.71	0.77	4.38
1997	Edmonton	PCL	50.7	60	21	3	16	28	3.73	3	3	10.66	0.53	2.84	4.97	0.61	4.26
1997	Oakland	AL	113.3	104	47	14	37	70	3.73	7	6	8.26	1.11	2.94	5.56	0.95	3.49
1998	Oakland	AL	178.7	205	103	26	51	108	5.19	7	13	10.33	1.31	2.57	5.44	0.84	4.74

"Congratulations, Mr. Oquist! You're this year's winner of Oakland's annual Rotation Spot Giveaway! Your lovely prize is good for at least 25 single-seat seatless tickets, where you'll be required to be on the field and do some moderate exercise every half-inning. You'll also receive a personalized uniform, as many free caps as you can wear, an invitation to the postgame spread, and the opportunity to hang out with players most folks just get to read about in the papers! Athletic supporter—or support—not included."

Juan Perez   Throws L   Age 26

YEAR	TEAM	LGE	IP	H	ER	HR	BB	K	ERA	W	L	H/9	HR/9	BB/9	K/9	KWH	PERA
1996	Modesto	Cal	91.7	141	66	12	34	56	6.48	3	7	13.84	1.18	3.34	5.50	0.49	6.48
1997	Visalia	Cal	61.0	61	33	6	27	39	4.87	3	4	9.00	0.89	3.98	5.75	0.69	3.98
1998	Huntsvil	Sou	33.0	40	16	4	15	26	4.36	2	2	10.91	1.09	4.09	7.09	0.84	5.18
1998	Edmonton	PCL	38.7	40	17	3	19	28	3.96	2	2	9.31	0.70	4.42	6.52	0.77	3.96

A slow-ripening left-hander from the A's Dominican program, he's been pitching in the States for six years. Perez did the Dana Allison-style belly flop as a starter, so he was moved to the pen and pitched well enough to get added to the 40-man roster. Will get a look-see for left-handed setup duties in camp; he's probably already passed Kubinski.

Ariel Prieto   Throws R   Age 32

YEAR	TEAM	LGE	IP	H	ER	HR	BB	K	ERA	W	L	H/9	HR/9	BB/9	K/9	KWH	PERA
1996	Oakland	AL	129.0	125	50	8	43	74	3.49	8	6	8.72	0.56	3.00	5.16	0.76	3.35
1997	Oakland	AL	133.3	147	65	15	62	88	4.39	7	8	9.92	1.01	4.19	5.94	0.64	4.52
1998	Edmonton	PCL	50.3	54	21	3	13	37	3.75	3	3	9.66	0.54	2.32	6.62	1.46	3.75
1998	Oakland	AL	8.7	17	9	2	4	8	9.35	0	1	17.65	2.08	4.15	8.31	0.71	9.35

Battling both shoulder and elbow woes, and it looks like he won't pitch for the entire season. Basically, Cuban boondoggle #1.

Brad Rigby   Throws R   Age 26

YEAR	TEAM	LGE	IP	H	ER	HR	BB	K	ERA	W	L	H/9	HR/9	BB/9	K/9	KWH	PERA
1996	Huntsvil	Sou	158.3	181	83	15	55	96	4.72	8	10	10.29	0.85	3.13	5.46	0.69	4.43
1997	Edmonton	PCL	81.0	94	39	9	23	40	4.33	4	5	10.44	1.00	2.56	4.44	0.55	4.56
1997	Oakland	AL	82.0	85	33	13	19	33	3.62	5	4	9.33	1.43	2.09	3.62	0.51	4.17
1998	Edmonton	PCL	65.7	98	52	4	18	26	7.13	2	5	13.43	0.55	2.47	3.56	0.29	5.62

After flubbing his shot at the fifth starter slot in camp, Rigby's '98 season was ruined by a herniated disk and a few bulging disks. He's resting through the winter, and at best is on the fringe of the fight for a rotation spot.

Kenny Rogers   Throws L   Age 34

YEAR	TEAM	LGE	IP	H	ER	HR	BB	K	ERA	W	L	H/9	HR/9	BB/9	K/9	KWH	PERA
1996	NY Yanks	AL	185.3	166	71	14	68	91	3.45	12	9	8.06	0.68	3.30	4.42	0.55	3.16
1997	NY Yanks	AL	148.0	159	84	17	53	75	5.11	6	10	9.67	1.03	3.22	4.56	0.50	4.26
1998	Oakland	AL	242.7	208	77	18	59	133	2.86	18	9	7.71	0.67	2.19	4.93	1.08	2.71

When he's on, his stuff is wicked to the point that he's playing patty-cake with the batter, flipping two-hoppers to Giambi all day long. Where the flaky reputation comes from baffles me; it may just as well be one of those self-fulfilling prophecies. He's great at holding and/or picking off baserunners, a heady fielder, and can pitch a little.

Blake Stein   Throws R   Age 25

YEAR	TEAM	LGE	IP	H	ER	HR	BB	K	ERA	W	L	H/9	HR/9	BB/9	K/9	KWH	PERA
1996	St Pete	Fla	154.7	179	70	8	58	119	4.07	8	9	10.42	0.47	3.38	6.92	1.02	4.25
1997	Arkansas	Tex	124.0	154	69	18	50	92	5.01	5	9	11.18	1.31	3.63	6.68	0.82	5.30
1997	Huntsvil	Sou	33.0	42	24	4	20	19	6.55	1	3	11.45	1.09	5.45	5.18	0.32	5.45
1998	Edmonton	PCL	22.7	24	12	1	11	25	4.76	1	2	9.53	0.40	4.37	9.93	1.78	3.97
1998	Oakland	AL	120.3	116	77	21	64	86	5.76	4	9	8.68	1.57	4.79	6.43	0.75	4.34

Stepped to the forefront with a good 1997 Arizona Fall League season, including 48 strikeouts in 39.1 IP. He tried to get by with just a four-seam fastball and a sinker. He's junked the forkball he used to throw, and his breaking stuff needs a lot of work. Basically, a big guy who made an impression early, and who still has a lot to learn. Would have been much better off in the old Coliseum.

Billy Taylor — Throws R — Age 37

YEAR	TEAM	LGE	IP	H	ER	HR	BB	K	ERA	W	L	H/9	HR/9	BB/9	K/9	KWH	PERA
1996	Edmonton	PCL	10.7	12	1	0	3	10	0.84	1	0	10.13	0.00	2.53	8.44	2.08	3.37
1996	Oakland	AL	62.0	50	22	4	20	66	3.19	4	3	7.26	0.58	2.90	9.58	3.27	2.47
1997	Oakland	AL	77.0	66	24	3	31	64	2.81	6	3	7.71	0.35	3.62	7.48	1.50	2.81
1998	Oakland	AL	74.3	69	30	7	19	56	3.63	4	4	8.35	0.85	2.30	6.78	1.79	3.27

One of my favorites, in that he used to have these streaks where right-handed batters could only hunker down, call for air support, and pray. Those didn't come as often this year. If the A's fade early, cashing Taylor in for prospects from a contender has to be considered.

Luis Vizcaino — Throws R — Age 22

YEAR	TEAM	LGE	IP	H	ER	HR	BB	K	ERA	W	L	H/9	HR/9	BB/9	K/9	KWH	PERA
1997	So Oregn	Nwn	42.3	87	58	6	30	23	12.33	0	5	18.50	1.28	6.38	4.89	0.15	8.72
1998	Modesto	Cal	98.0	90	42	7	45	70	3.86	6	5	8.27	0.64	4.13	6.43	0.91	3.40
1998	Huntsvil	Sou	36.7	50	26	9	19	20	6.38	1	3	12.27	2.21	4.66	4.91	0.32	6.87

A slender Dominican, and the best pitcher in years to come out of the A's program down there, Vizcaino has a good fastball and slider, but he's still learning how to change speeds and throw a change-up. He'll need to refine his stuff, but is somebody to keep an eye on.

Jay Witasick — Throws R — Age 26

YEAR	TEAM	LGE	IP	H	ER	HR	BB	K	ERA	W	L	H/9	HR/9	BB/9	K/9	KWH	PERA
1996	Huntsvil	Sou	66.7	52	19	4	24	47	2.57	5	2	7.02	0.54	3.24	6.35	1.33	2.43
1997	Edmonton	PCL	27.0	25	11	3	14	14	3.67	2	1	8.33	1.00	4.67	4.67	0.42	3.67
1997	Oakland	AL	12.0	13	5	2	5	8	3.75	1	0	9.75	1.50	3.75	6.00	0.74	4.50
1998	Edmonton	PCL	142.7	146	74	17	51	118	4.67	7	9	9.21	1.07	3.22	7.44	1.40	4.04
1998	Oakland	AL	27.7	36	20	9	14	28	6.51	1	2	11.71	2.93	4.55	9.11	1.17	7.16

Witasick had been getting by almost entirely on power, but he has made improvements with his change-up and curve, which has been enough to keep him a starting pitcher for the time being. The A's are still wrestling with what to do with him. At this stage he could fit the bill either in the rotation or the pen as a long reliever.

Tim Worrell — Throws R — Age 31

YEAR	TEAM	LGE	IP	H	ER	HR	BB	K	ERA	W	L	H/9	HR/9	BB/9	K/9	KWH	PERA
1996	San Dieg	NL	119.3	123	46	9	37	89	3.47	7	6	9.28	0.68	2.79	6.71	1.31	3.70
1997	San Dieg	NL	107.0	123	62	15	45	72	5.21	4	8	10.35	1.26	3.79	6.06	0.70	4.88
1998	Detroit	AL	63.7	65	34	10	17	46	4.81	3	4	9.19	1.41	2.40	6.50	1.44	4.10
1998	Oakland	AL	36.3	33	14	5	8	32	3.47	2	2	8.17	1.24	1.98	7.93	2.91	3.22

I've always liked Worrell, so I'm a bit biased when I say that he could end up being an extremely effective setup man. He throws hard and he throws strikes, and his mediocre breaking stuff isn't as much of a glaring weakness in the bullpen. He's griped about wanting to start in the past, but this year's miseries in Motor City ought to have laid that to rest.

SNWL	OAKLAND ATHLETICS										Park Effect: +8.4%	
PITCHER	GS	IP	R	SNW	SNL	SNPCT	W	L	RA	APW	SNVA	SNWAR
Candiotti	33	201.0	124	10.5	12.7	.453	11	16	5.55	-0.84	-1.02	0.64
Haynes	33	194.3	124	10.2	12.9	.441	11	9	5.74	-1.19	-1.31	0.37
Heredia	6	40.0	14	2.8	1.2	.703	2	3	3.15	0.83	0.84	1.10
Oquist	29	170.0	122	8.5	11.5	.425	7	11	6.46	-2.31	-1.47	0.01
Prieto	2	8.3	11	0.1	1.4	.043	0	1	11.88	-0.58	-0.63	-0.56
Rogers	34	238.7	96	16.6	8.5	.662	16	8	3.62	3.79	3.83	5.95
Stein	20	109.0	86	5.4	9.0	.373	5	8	7.10	-2.21	-1.82	-0.75
Telgheder	2	9.3	7	0.3	0.8	.317	0	1	6.75	-0.16	-0.19	-0.12
Witasick	3	15.7	17	0.3	2.0	.114	0	3	9.77	-0.75	-0.81	-0.70
TOTALS	162	986.3	601	54.6	60.0	.477	52	60	5.48	-3.41	-2.58	5.94

It's easy to look at last year and be optimistic about the A's starting pitching. After all, they have a lot of young starters and they got a lot better in 1998, going from an unspeakably bad -11.9 SNVA (last in the majors) to a not-bad -2.58 (16th in the majors). But it wasn't their young guys who were the source of the improvement. It was replacing some of their truly embarrassing performances of 1997—Wengert, Adams, Mohler—with 40-year-old Tom Candiotti and 33-year-old Kenny Rogers. Replace Rogers with a league-average pitcher, and the A's would have had a -6.41 SNVA, 26th in the league. That was easily the best performance by an A's starter since 1991. In contrast to that pleasant surprise, the A's youngsters did not progress as hoped. Both Jimmy Haynes and Mike Oquist went from .500+ SNPcts in 1997 to below .450 in 1998. Blake Stein had a rookie season that would have looked right in place in that 1997 staff. Would you believe that this was the best A's starting staff in the past seven years? I know A's fans would believe it, but I think the rest of us are only vaguely aware of how consistently bad the A's pitching has been, and for how long.

Pitcher Abuse Points

PITCHER	AGE	GS	PAP	PAP/S	AAW	MAX	115+	130+
Candiotti, Tom	40	33	442	13.39	13.39	147	5	2
Haynes, Jimmy	25	33	371	11.24	24.36	131	8	1
Heredia, Gil	32	6	3	0.50	0.50	103	0	0
Oquist, Mike	30	29	101	3.48	4.64	120	2	0
Rogers, Kenny	33	34	417	12.26	12.26	138	8	1
Stein, Blake	24	20	218	10.90	25.43	130	4	1
TOTAL		162	1573	9.71	14.54	147	27	5
RANKING (AL)			7	7	8		8	6-T

Art Howe has a tenuous grip on his job, and while his players support him and the A's are beginning to put together a championship offense again, I worry about his use of his starters. The A's were right in the middle of the AL overall, but while most of the PAPs were sucked up by veterans Tom Candiotti and Kenny Rogers, young Jimmy Haynes had nearly the same workload, as did rookie Blake Stein once he was called up. Both Haynes and Stein have control problems that need to be ironed out, and if that happens the problems, their pitch counts may follow suit. If not, Howe needs to be more realistic with his expectations, because the A's have few talented young pitchers as it is.

Seattle Mariners

The end of the world was heralded with a phone call and a tap on the shoulder. When Randy Johnson was summoned by Lou Piniella to walk back into the Mariners' clubhouse during a July 31st game against the Yankees, the entire city of Seattle went on suicide watch. In a season when the team had regularly and openly proclaimed its intention to make one last grab for a World Championship, the front office had betrayed everyone by folding up the tent and trading the team's disgruntled ace.

At the time, the Mariners were 48-59, closer to last place—one game ahead of Oakland—than to first place—10 games behind Anaheim—and in a state of total disarray. Right fielder Jay Buhner was battling an elbow injury that ruined his production and shortened his season to 72 games. Johnson was griping and whining his way through a subpar contract year with an ERA over 5.00 at the All-Star break. Left field was a revolving door for the umpteenth consecutive year. Sophomore Ken Cloude, counted on to provide innings in the #4 spot, was awful, while receiving the usual support from his manager ("The kid's not ready, guys."). And has always been the case with Lou Piniella in Seattle, the bullpen was a pile of gasoline-soaked timber.

Yet the city remained in denial. Newspapers and commentators screamed that Woodward had pulled the plug on a team that was well within striking distance of the division title. Indeed, the '95 team had overcome a larger deficit with fewer games to play, they said. All that he got in return was a couple of minor leaguers, they said, as if "minor leaguer" was some sort of ethnic slur. David Segui delivered a soliloquy that would make Andrew "Dice" Clay blush. Ken Griffey Jr. voiced his disappointment as well. No one pointed to the inadequacy of the pre-trade roster for a playoff run, or to the daily damage done by Lou Piniella to the team's chances of current and future contention.

Whether Woodward received full value—or even fair value—for Johnson will not be clear for several years. Less emotional observers rightly pointed out that he received two very good prospects in middle infielder Carlos Guillen and

starting pitcher Freddy Garcia, both of whom were very close to being ready for the majors. The player to be named later was John Halama, a pitcher who could step in as the Mariners' #5 starter. However, Woodward failed to land any of the Astros' top four upper-level prospects: Scott Elarton, Lance Berkman, Richard Hidalgo, or Darryl Ward. How the actual package and other, seemingly better packages will pan out isn't certain.

Whether he did the right thing by dumping, or whether he should have dumped other players, is a more interesting debate. The team had already labelled '98 a last-gasp grasp for a ring; if the ring was truly out of reach, shouldn't the team begin the rebuilding process early? Was the ring truly out of reach, or was this squad likely enough to catch the division leaders to make the status quo the best option? Given the imminent opening (July '99) of Safeco Field, the Mariners' new taxpayer-funded stadium, what was the team's best strategy?

Our answer: he should have gone farther. Woodward may have netted himself some good prospects by dealing Johnson, but the Mariners are ill-positioned to compete in the first years of Safeco Field. At this point, the team bears a striking resemblance to many of the losing Mariners' teams of the 1980s: a handful of very good or great players surrounded by a lot of chaff. The team is old, the farm system is barren, the manager has a poor track record at breaking in young players, and the team's two top talents are nearing $100-million paydays. Half-hearted attempts to rebuild while remaining semi-competitive will yield teams that struggle to reach .500 for a decade, occasionally breaking through but never sustaining any sort of success. These Mariners are already moving down that path.

The local backlash against the mere concept of folding the tent stopped Woodward from going further, and created dissension among the ownership committee about when or whether to dump Johnson right up until the deadline. Acting in that environment would be difficult for even the most skilled trader, and Woodward's track record is spotty at best.

No one on this team should be untouchable. David

Mariners Prospectus

1998 record: 76-85; Third place, AL West

Pythagorean W/L: 81-81

Runs scored: 859 (5th in AL)

Runs allowed: 855 (9th in AL)

Team EQA: .277 (2nd in AL)

Park: Kingdome (until June; slight pitchers')

1998: Bullpen woes took them out of the race; they haven't filled in a team around the two legends.

1999: Some recovery, but they still have questionable pitching and at least two lineup holes.

Segui is coming off his two best offensive seasons, his defensive prowess has received increased attention, and he's entering the last year of his contract. Jeff Fassero is an effective 200-inning left-hander who suffered a bout of arm soreness last spring, and is entering the last year of his contract. Jamie Moyer is coming off his best season and has established himself as an inning-eating left-hander, and is entering the last year of his contract. Without Johnson, the Mariners clearly aren't headed to the playoffs even if all three manage to repeat their 1998 performances. These players should be moved immediately for prospects or underutilized young players who will lead the team to contention in the years after Safeco Field opens.

The situation is exacerbated by the dearth of talent in the farm system. The player supply has dried up in parallel with the graying of the major-league roster. The top three teams are heavily populated with journeymen, ex-prospects, or, in the case of the Double-A team, loaners from the Devil Rays. Many major-league organizations have Triple-A and Double-A affiliates that aren't producing the necessary talent to fill the parent club's needs; the Mariners might be the only one whose A-ball affiliates can't produce the talent to fill the Double-A club's needs.

The blame for this situation lies mostly at the feet of Woodward and his front-office staff. The club has a well-known history of trading away just about any prospect by the time he reaches the upper levels. Everyone knows the Mariners acquired Mike Timlin, now gone to Baltimore, and Paul Spoljaric, traded for Mark Leiter, in exchange for Jose Cruz, who could easily have ended their revolving-door in left field. They've traded Arqui Pozo, Derek Lowe, Jason Varitek—all of whom would have helped the 1998 Mariners better than Rico Rossy—Steve Gajkowski, and any of the backup catchers the team has used. The problem that receives somewhat less attention is that few top prospects even reach the upper levels of Seattle's system. The team's international scouting record is dismal, and their draft record is spotty at best, with only three major draft products since 1993 showing any impact in the majors: Alex Rodriguez, Ken Cloude, and Cruz.

However, a large chunk of the blame lies with Piniella. The Cult of Lou in Seattle is mindboggling to any outside observer. In the eyes of many Mariners fans and the Seattle media, Piniella is the hapless victim of outside circumstances. They claim that the front office is meddling and incompetent, so Piniella doesn't get the players he needs, such as decent relievers, even though the Mariners have plenty of relievers who are adequate when handled correctly. It doesn't help that he goes through at least one pitching coach every season.

In some sense, he is the victim of missteps by his superiors in the team's front office. However, he has mishandled or even damaged much of the young talent handed him. He doggedly avoided playing Alex Rodriguez in 1995 when the kid was clearly ready, instead going with proven commodities like Luis Sojo. He was a driving force in returning Jose Cruz to the minors in 1997, even though he appeared ready and the team had no better alternatives in the majors. He refused to play Darren Bragg as his starting left fielder for years. Now he has brought his magic talents with pitchers to bear on Ken Cloude, who had his confidence shattered by Piniella's public tirades and erratic hook. Based on his history, I'd sooner trust Piniella with my lungs than with a 21-year-old pitching prospect.

The Mariners must acknowledge the need for a rebuilding process, and that Piniella is not the manager for that job. He has never gone through a true rebuilding, instead taking on established teams in New York and Cincinnati, squeezing short-term success out of older squads without replenishing the talent pool. The Yankees went into a protracted down period during and after Piniella's tenure because the system wasn't producing talent to replace the team's veterans, and Lou mismanaged the veterans. Piniella's best trick in Cincinnati was simply not putting himself in the lineup (unlike Pete Rose) for a team that had finished second four of the five years before Lou arrived. Piniella has shown neither the acumen nor the patience to go through an extensive slash-and-burn rebuilding; the first step for the M's is to remove any obstacles to that process, and Piniella is at the top of that list.

So while Mariners fans may believe that the Johnson deal represented treason of the highest order, and that the team's inevitable struggles will somehow stem from their 1998 disappointments, the anger is misdirected. Few teams have managed to win without some help from their minor-league affiliates and a major-league staff able to develop talent; none have achieved protracted success under those conditions. Until the Mariners acknowledge their situation and the inadequacy of their current personnel for it, they will continue to flounder and rely on poor showings by division-mates to make themselves seem competitive.

HITTERS (Averages: BA .260/ OBA .330/ SA .420, EQA .260)

Rich Amaral — OF — Bats R — Age 37

YEAR	TEAM	LGE	AB	H	DB	TP	HR	BB	R	RBI	SB	CS	OUT	BA	OBA	SA	EQA	EQR	DEFENSE	
1996	Seattle	AL	305	87	10	3	1	44	55	26	27	7	225	.285	.375	.348	.271	43	81-OF 94	
1997	Seattle	AL	187	52	2	0	2	11	20	14	13	9	143	.278	.318	.321	.225	17	40-OF 88	
1998	Seattle	AL	132	36	3	0	2	13	20	11	10	1	97	.273	.338	.341	.254	16	29-OF 95	
1999	Baltimor	AL	154	39	1	0	2	18	19	12	9	4	119	.253	.331	.299	.233	16		

Leyland : Wehner :: Piniella : _____. His late-starting career may be reaching an end following Seattle's declining to offer him arbitration. Past the point of contributing, but laughably added to the Orioles for his skill as a pinch-runner.

David Bell — 2B/3B — Bats R — Age 26

YEAR	TEAM	LGE	AB	H	DB	TP	HR	BB	R	RBI	SB	CS	OUT	BA	OBA	SA	EQA	EQR	DEFENSE	
1996	Louisvil	AA	136	23	3	1	0	8	4	4	1	2	115	.169	.215	.206	.102	2	30-2B 102	
1996	St Louis	NL	145	30	4	0	2	11	9	8	1	1	116	.207	.263	.276	.180	8	31-3B 101	13-2B 125
1997	St Louis	NL	142	30	7	2	1	11	11	9	1	0	112	.211	.268	.310	.198	10	18-3B 97	14-2B 90
1998	Clevelnd	AL	332	81	18	2	10	24	30	36	0	4	255	.244	.295	.401	.234	34	93-2B 101	
1998	Seattle	AL	79	25	9	0	0	5	11	9	0	0	54	.316	.357	.430	.273	11		
1999	Seattle	AL	310	73	17	1	7	20	27	29	1	2	239	.235	.282	.365	.218	27		

Bell finally got his chance, in Cleveland three years after he was first ready for a major league role. He's great insurance for Carlos Guillen, and can easily put in some time at third base. Not suited for a full-time job at the corner.

Jay Buhner — OF — Bats R — Age 34

YEAR	TEAM	LGE	AB	H	DB	TP	HR	BB	R	RBI	SB	CS	OUT	BA	OBA	SA	EQA	EQR	DEFENSE
1996	Seattle	AL	552	147	24	0	44	80	80	107	0	1	406	.266	.359	.549	.301	101	133-OF 91
1997	Seattle	AL	530	127	18	2	40	119	86	100	0	0	403	.240	.379	.508	.302	101	142-OF 101
1998	Seattle	AL	240	57	7	1	15	39	31	38	0	0	183	.237	.344	.463	.277	37	65-OF 94
1999	Seattle	AL	369	87	14	0	26	70	56	66	0	0	282	.236	.358	.485	.288	63	

Major elbow problems may have ended his tenure as a right fielder. Here's Seattle thinking for you: if Bone has to DH, let's move Edgar Martinez to first base (which he plays poorly), and move David Segui (an incredible fielder at first) to right field, so we have two hitters out of position. Yes, that's much more sensible than finding another right fielder and trading the 35-year-old Buhner.

Raul Chavez — C — Bats R — Age 26

YEAR	TEAM	LGE	AB	H	DB	TP	HR	BB	R	RBI	SB	CS	OUT	BA	OBA	SA	EQA	EQR	DEFENSE
1996	Ottawa	Int	197	45	4	0	3	11	11	13	0	1	153	.228	.269	.294	.187	12	
1997	Ottawa	Int	309	69	9	0	5	15	17	20	1	2	242	.223	.259	.301	.185	18	
1998	Tacoma	PCL	230	40	2	0	3	20	8	8	1	1	191	.174	.240	.222	.141	7	84-C 112
1999	Seattle	AL	271	60	3	0	5	18	16	18	1	1	212	.221	.270	.288	.186	16	

Hits like a great defender. One of many possibilities for the job Wilson's caddy, but he's probably behind Tom Lampkin for the #2 job.

Jermaine Clark — 2B — Bats L — Age 22

YEAR	TEAM	LGE	AB	H	DB	TP	HR	BB	R	RBI	SB	CS	OUT	BA	OBA	SA	EQA	EQR	DEFENSE
1998	Wisconsn	Mid	453	129	17	6	7	46	62	51	18	8	332	.285	.351	.395	.264	59	114-2B 93
1999	Seattle	AL	363	113	16	4	6	33	57	47	16	7	257	.311	.369	.427	.279	53	

Hit well in his first full pro season after demolishing Everett in '97. He has great speed and a good eye, so naturally he's seen as a future leadoff hitter. His defense has been suspect, but he improved his work on double plays this year and now projects to be average or slightly below. If he keeps improving his hitting like this, it won't matter much anyway. Clark could step into the majors tomorrow and outproduce Tony Womack.

Russ Davis				3B			Bats R		Age 29								
YEAR TEAM	LGE	AB	H	DB	TP	HR	BB	R	RBI	SB	CS	OUT	BA	OBA	SA	EQA EQR	DEFENSE
1996 Seattle	AL	164	37	5	0	6	16	15	17	2	0	127	.226	.294	.366	.231 16	44-3B 92
1997 Seattle	AL	414	111	27	1	21	28	50	61	6	2	305	.268	.314	.490	.271 58	115-3B 98
1998 Seattle	AL	495	126	27	1	21	36	51	64	4	3	372	.255	.305	.440	.253 60	132-3B 94
1999 Seattle	*AL*	*446*	*114*	*24*	*1*	*19*	*33*	*49*	*60*	*4*	*2*	*334*	*.256*	*.307*	*.442*	*.254 55*	

So he's a subpar fielder. If he can hit, so what? The problem is that Piniella's games—head games, benching Davis, moving him to left field—have obviously carried over to Davis's bat. He is not as bad with the glove as Piniella or Lou's toadies in the local media have made him out to be, and if they'd leave Davis alone, he'd give them a good offensive year or two.

Rob Ducey				OF			Bats L		Age 34								
YEAR TEAM	LGE	AB	H	DB	TP	HR	BB	R	RBI	SB	CS	OUT	BA	OBA	SA	EQA EQR	DEFENSE
1997 Tacoma	PCL	72	19	4	0	0	6	7	6	0	0	53	.264	.321	.319	.225 6	21-OF 99
1997 Seattle	AL	141	40	15	2	5	6	19	20	3	3	104	.284	.313	.525	.274 20	57-OF 80
1998 Seattle	AL	214	50	17	2	5	24	26	23	4	3	167	.234	.311	.402	.246 25	59-OF 97
1999 Seattle	*AL*	*187*	*48*	*19*	*1*	*5*	*17*	*24*	*24*	*2*	*3*	*142*	*.257*	*.319*	*.449*	*.258 24*	

Another of Piniella's sick fascinations: the ex-Blue Jay outfield prospect. He's better than "prospect" Ricky Cradle, but that's about it.

Charles Gipson				UT			Bats R		Age 26									
YEAR TEAM	LGE	AB	H	DB	TP	HR	BB	R	RBI	SB	CS	OUT	BA	OBA	SA	EQA EQR	DEFENSE	
1996 PortCity	Sou	409	99	10	2	1	32	37	25	17	9	319	.242	.297	.284	.206 31	70-OF 99	38-SS 112
1997 Memphis	Sou	317	60	5	2	1	25	21	12	19	5	261	.189	.249	.227	.167 15	30-3B 95	29-SS 103
1998 Tacoma	PCL	275	53	8	2	0	23	17	10	11	9	231	.193	.255	.236	.163 12	38-OF 100	
1998 Seattle	AL	50	11	1	0	0	6	5	2	2	1	40	.220	.304	.240	.197 3		
1999 Seattle	*AL*	*341*	*75*	*9*	*3*	*0*	*27*	*29*	*17*	*16*	*8*	*274*	*.220*	*.277*	*.264*	*.189 21*		

There are better fifth outfielders on waivers. If Gipson stumbled into an organization willing to make him into F.P. Santangelo, he might be able to salvage a career. Players who can play the infield and outfield passably are pretty valuable, even with poor offensive skills. Maybe not this poor.

Ken Griffey Jr				CF			Bats L		Age 29								
YEAR TEAM	LGE	AB	H	DB	TP	HR	BB	R	RBI	SB	CS	OUT	BA	OBA	SA	EQA EQR	DEFENSE
1996 Seattle	AL	532	159	26	2	47	74	96	116	17	1	374	.299	.384	.620	.330 117	135-OF 109
1997 Seattle	AL	597	180	32	3	57	76	105	136	15	4	421	.302	.380	.652	.332 134	150-OF 113
1998 Seattle	AL	623	176	32	3	56	78	104	130	18	5	452	.283	.362	.613	.317 128	156-OF 109
1999 Seattle	*AL*	*595*	*168*	*33*	*2*	*50*	*75*	*101*	*127*	*13*	*3*	*430*	*.282*	*.363*	*.597*	*.315 120*	

If I were he, I'd be on the first Alaska Airlines flight out as soon as my contract was up, and would leave in search of a championship ring. Griffey has the best shot of any current major leaguer at Aaron's career record, and should become one of the youngest players to reach 400 in his career, probably in September.

Carlos Guillen				2B			Bats B		Age 23								
YEAR TEAM	LGE	AB	H	DB	TP	HR	BB	R	RBI	SB	CS	OUT	BA	OBA	SA	EQA EQR	DEFENSE
1996 Quad Cit	Mid	113	33	3	1	3	12	16	14	7	4	84	.292	.360	.416	.271 16	30-SS 82
1997 Jackson	Tex	385	84	10	1	8	33	29	29	4	3	304	.218	.280	.312	.203 28	109-SS 93
1998 New Orln	PCL	372	105	14	3	11	30	41	49	3	4	271	.282	.336	.425	.261 47	98-SS 96
1998 Tacoma	PCL	91	18	0	1	1	8	4	5	1	2	75	.198	.263	.253	.168 4	23-2B 98
1998 Seattle	AL	38	13	0	1	0	3	6	4	2	0	25	.342	.390	.395	.289 6	
1999 Seattle	*AL*	*413*	*109*	*12*	*2*	*11*	*33*	*42*	*48*	*5*	*4*	*308*	*.264*	*.318*	*.383*	*.242 44*	

Finally stayed healthy long enough to fulfill the expectations that dogged him for years. Guillen will provide the Mariners with two things they haven't had in eons: a second baseman who can hit and a second baseman who can field. He should be an All-Star someday, but Piniella will probably screw him up.

Adonis Harrison   2B   Bats L   Age 22

YEAR	TEAM	LGE	AB	H	DB	TP	HR	BB	R	RBI	SB	CS	OUT	BA	OBA	SA	EQA	EQR	DEFENSE
1996	Wisconsn	Mid	198	46	11	0	2	13	16	14	3	2	154	.232	.280	.318	.205	15	51-2B 82
1997	Wisconsn	Mid	413	113	17	2	7	43	52	43	13	10	310	.274	.342	.375	.251	49	114-2B 89
1998	Lancastr	Cal	254	70	13	2	2	38	40	25	12	8	192	.276	.370	.366	.263	34	66-2B 93
1998	Orlando	Sou	189	35	3	1	3	24	14	11	4	2	156	.185	.277	.259	.188	12	56-2B 95
1999	*Seattle*	*AL*	*407*	*111*	*18*	*1*	*8*	*50*	*57*	*46*	*14*	*10*	*306*	*.273*	*.352*	*.381*	*.258*	*52*	

Built on his 1997 gains, then skidded out at Double-A. He's left-handed, has a good eye, and a great name, so he'll get his chance.

Raul Ibanez   LF   Bats L   Age 27

YEAR	TEAM	LGE	AB	H	DB	TP	HR	BB	R	RBI	SB	CS	OUT	BA	OBA	SA	EQA	EQR	DEFENSE
1996	PortCity	Sou	76	25	4	1	1	6	11	10	2	1	52	.329	.378	.447	.287	11	
1996	Tacoma	PCL	402	106	15	2	10	40	45	45	6	5	301	.264	.330	.386	.249	47	105-OF 94
1997	Tacoma	PCL	425	108	17	2	11	25	39	43	6	4	321	.254	.296	.381	.232	42	108-OF 94
1998	Tacoma	PCL	189	32	3	1	4	20	9	10	1	1	158	.169	.249	.259	.168	9	40-OF 96
1998	Seattle	AL	97	24	8	1	2	5	9	10	0	0	73	.247	.284	.412	.236	10	
1999	*Seattle*	*AL*	*313*	*77*	*12*	*1*	*8*	*24*	*30*	*32*	*4*	*2*	*238*	*.246*	*.300*	*.367*	*.230*	*30*	

Ibanez probably would have been their left fielder to start the year were it not for an injury, and he's certainly no worse than any of the other options the M's have. Unfortunately, his entire career comprises hitting for power in good power parks, and being mediocre in every other phase of the game. There are better options available on waivers.

Craig Kuzmic   3B   Bats B   Age 22

YEAR	TEAM	LGE	AB	H	DB	TP	HR	BB	R	RBI	SB	CS	OUT	BA	OBA	SA	EQA	EQR	DEFENSE	
1998	Everett	Nwn	185	37	5	0	5	21	15	14	1	1	149	.200	.282	.308	.204	14	25-3B	94
1999	*Seattle*	*AL*	*150*	*38*	*4*	*0*	*5*	*16*	*16*	*18*	*1*	*1*	*113*	*.253*	*.325*	*.380*	*.245*	*17*		

Eighth-rounder out of Texas A&M who had a promising debut in Everett, hitting for good power, drawing some walks, and playing an adequate third base. He needs to be more aggressive at the plate—how often do we say that?—particularly as he faces tougher competition.

Edgar Martinez   DH   Bats R   Age 36

YEAR	TEAM	LGE	AB	H	DB	TP	HR	BB	R	RBI	SB	CS	OUT	BA	OBA	SA	EQA	EQR	DEFENSE
1996	Seattle	AL	482	156	47	2	26	117	110	103	3	4	330	.324	.456	.591	.350	120	
1997	Seattle	AL	529	174	30	1	30	118	108	112	2	4	359	.329	.451	.560	.342	123	
1998	Seattle	AL	545	174	38	2	31	107	106	113	1	1	372	.319	.431	.567	.336	122	
1999	*Seattle*	*AL*	*510*	*151*	*31*	*1*	*28*	*115*	*103*	*103*	*1*	*2*	*361*	*.296*	*.426*	*.525*	*.326*	*109*	

Consistently great, but gradually fading. If he can continue to DH, he has at least four more good years in him, but they will be very expensive, and teams can get good offense out of all sorts of players. Paying a huge chunk of change for an old DH is fine if you have a great young lineup, but that isn't the Mariners.

Victor Martinez 2B/OF Bats R   Age 21

YEAR	TEAM	LGE	AB	H	DB	TP	HR	BB	R	RBI	SB	CS	OUT	BA	OBA	SA	EQA	EQR	DEFENSE	
1997	Everett	Nwn	58	8	2	0	0	5	1	1	0	0	50	.138	.206	.172	.057	0		
1998	Everett	Nwn	281	71	6	1	3	17	23	21	7	5	215	.253	.295	.313	.211	22	26-2B 103	21-OF 102
1999	*Seattle*	*AL*	*205*	*55*	*3*	*0*	*3*	*10*	*17*	*18*	*4*	*3*	*153*	*.268*	*.302*	*.327*	*.216*	*17*		

Martinez joined the organization in 1995, and finally escaped short-season ball with a breakout season. He's still just 21 this year, but he needs to keep the performance up at Wisconsin to establish himself as a prospect. The M's also need to settle on a position for him; while he's most comfortable at third, he may not hit enough for the hot corner.

John Marzano   **C**   **Bats R   Age 36**

YEAR	TEAM	LGE	AB	H	DB	TP	HR	BB	R	RBI	SB	CS	OUT	BA	OBA	SA	EQA	EQR	DEFENSE	
1996	Seattle	AL	105	25	6	0	0	6	8	6	0	0	80	.238	.279	.295	.195	7		
1997	Seattle	AL	86	24	1	0	2	7	8	10	0	0	62	.279	.333	.360	.244	9		
1998	Seattle	AL	131	30	6	1	4	10	12	13	0	0	101	.229	.284	.382	.227	12	42-C	99
1999	*Seattle*	*AL*	*105*	*22*	*1*	*0*	*3*	*8*	*6*	*8*	*0*	*0*	*83*	*.210*	*.265*	*.305*	*.191*	*7*		

Embarrassed the organization by outhitting their better-paid starting catcher. As a reward, the M's declined to offer him arbitration and let him walk, signing Tom Lampkin in his place. Marzano should be darkening someone's doorstep this spring.

Dave McCarty   **1B**   **Bats R   Age 29**

YEAR	TEAM	LGE	AB	H	DB	TP	HR	BB	R	RBI	SB	CS	OUT	BA	OBA	SA	EQA	EQR	DEFENSE	
1996	San Fran	NL	174	37	2	0	6	19	14	16	2	1	138	.213	.290	.328	.216	15	35-1B 85	13-OF 90
1997	Phoenix	PCL	410	112	13	1	14	37	47	52	7	3	301	.273	.333	.412	.259	52	70-1B 96	
1998	Tacoma	PCL	391	103	17	1	8	49	49	43	7	5	293	.263	.345	.373	.254	48	60-OF 101	36-1B 104
1999	*Seattle*	*AL*	*382*	*103*	*14*	*1*	*12*	*46*	*50*	*50*	*6*	*3*	*282*	*.270*	*.348*	*.406*	*.264*	*51*		

If Dave McCarty didn't exist, would the pundits just invent him? McCarty has now become the comparison every writer makes when speaking of a prospect who didn't break through in his first call-up. Todd Walker was going to be the next David McCarty. Now it's Paul Konerko. Anyway, McCarty could still help a lot of teams as a backup left fielder/first baseman and right-handed bat off the bench.

Shane Monahan   **OF**   **Bats L   Age 24**

YEAR	TEAM	LGE	AB	H	DB	TP	HR	BB	R	RBI	SB	CS	OUT	BA	OBA	SA	EQA	EQR	DEFENSE
1996	Lancastr	Cal	566	121	17	5	10	18	32	35	9	3	448	.214	.238	.314	.183	32	127-OF 101
1997	Memphis	Sou	393	103	16	3	10	24	41	42	11	5	295	.262	.305	.394	.242	42	91-OF 90
1997	Tacoma	PCL	83	22	2	0	2	4	8	8	4	1	62	.265	.299	.361	.234	8	20-OF 109
1998	Tacoma	PCL	273	61	6	4	3	18	19	19	5	3	215	.223	.271	.308	.198	19	63-OF 105
1998	Seattle	AL	208	49	8	1	4	9	14	17	1	2	161	.236	.267	.341	.203	15	58-OF 96
1999	*Seattle*	*AL*	*488*	*123*	*18*	*4*	*10*	*23*	*44*	*46*	*10*	*5*	*370*	*.252*	*.286*	*.367*	*.223*	*44*	

Scouts love Monahan's swing and aggressiveness; I see a guy whose lack of plate discipline is going to stunt his development. The Butch Huskey acquistion means he'll struggle to play even as much as he did in 1998, and that isn't a bad thing. The Mariners need good young players, not just any young player.

Joe Oliver   **C**   **Bats R   Age 33**

YEAR	TEAM	LGE	AB	H	DB	TP	HR	BB	R	RBI	SB	CS	OUT	BA	OBA	SA	EQA	EQR	DEFENSE
1996	Cincnnti	NL	288	68	11	1	11	29	30	33	2	0	220	.236	.306	.396	.244	32	
1997	Cincnnti	NL	346	86	10	0	15	27	31	42	0	3	263	.249	.303	.408	.241	37	
1998	Detroit	AL	153	33	4	0	5	8	9	12	0	1	121	.216	.255	.340	.197	10	43-C 103
1998	Seattle	AL	84	19	2	0	2	10	9	7	1	0	65	.226	.309	.321	.225	8	24-C 95
1999	*Seattle*	*AL*	*249*	*57*	*7*	*0*	*11*	*22*	*23*	*29*	*1*	*1*	*193*	*.229*	*.292*	*.390*	*.233*	*25*	

No better than Marzano, but he was an ex-Red, another Piniella fetish. Now an ex-Mariner, he'll go trawling through his little black book, hoping for one more $200,000 payday.

Ryan Radmanovich   **OF**   **Bats L   Age 27**

YEAR	TEAM	LGE	AB	H	DB	TP	HR	BB	R	RBI	SB	CS	OUT	BA	OBA	SA	EQA	EQR	DEFENSE
1996	New Brit	Eas	460	120	18	1	19	39	49	59	5	7	347	.261	.319	.428	.253	56	117-OF 95
1997	SaltLake	PCL	467	94	11	2	17	53	41	43	8	4	377	.201	.283	.343	.218	42	127-OF 92
1998	Tacoma	PCL	390	98	20	1	10	39	41	43	2	3	295	.251	.319	.385	.244	43	94-OF 90
1998	Seattle	AL	68	15	3	0	2	4	5	6	1	1	54	.221	.264	.353	.207	5	
1999	*Seattle*	*AL*	*449*	*110*	*19*	*1*	*16*	*46*	*50*	*54*	*5*	*5*	*344*	*.245*	*.315*	*.399*	*.245*	*51*	

One of those "better options" for left field mentioned above, Radmanovich never got much of a chance. He can help someone. Designated for assignment in November.

Jason Regan — 3B — Bats R — Age 23

YEAR	TEAM	LGE	AB	H	DB	TP	HR	BB	R	RBI	SB	CS	OUT	BA	OBA	SA	EQA	EQR	DEFENSE	
1996	Everett	Nwn	127	19	4	0	2	19	8	5	1	2	110	.150	.260	.228	.163	6	25-3B 80	
1997	Wisconsn	Mid	178	40	5	1	7	18	16	20	1	0	138	.225	.296	.382	.235	18		
1997	Lancastr	Cal	256	64	10	1	16	36	33	42	1	1	193	.250	.342	.484	.280	40	40-2B 109	19-3B 72
1998	Lancastr	Cal	414	100	11	2	14	82	60	52	5	2	316	.242	.367	.379	.268	59	116-3B 100	
1999	*Seattle*	*AL*	*370*	*92*	*13*	*2*	*14*	*52*	*48*	*50*	*2*	*1*	*279*	*.249*	*.341*	*.408*	*.262*	*49*		

It was ridiculous that the Mariners had him repeat Lancaster despite a .281/.399/.627 performance there in '97, and they didn't promote him when he continued to hit this year. Why? Because they're concerned that his swing is too long. He led all minor leaguers in walks with 106, so what exactly is the problem? Switched back to third base this year; the M's need to stop screwing around and just push Regan up the ladder at one position.

Alex Rodriguez — SS — Bats R — Age 23

YEAR	TEAM	LGE	AB	H	DB	TP	HR	BB	R	RBI	SB	CS	OUT	BA	OBA	SA	EQA	EQR	DEFENSE
1996	Seattle	AL	585	207	45	2	37	55	107	125	16	5	383	.354	.409	.627	.340	129	144-SS 105
1997	Seattle	AL	577	171	38	3	24	42	89	84	29	6	412	.296	.344	.497	.289	92	139-SS 99
1998	Seattle	AL	675	209	34	5	42	48	111	117	42	13	479	.310	.355	.561	.306	124	159-SS 94
1999	*Seattle*	*AL*	*622*	*203*	*38*	*3*	*41*	*47*	*111*	*124*	*31*	*10*	*429*	*.326*	*.374*	*.595*	*.320*	*124*	

A fantastic hitter, in case you didn't already know. Rodriguez shouldn't be hitting ahead of Griffey; his .360 OBP was good, but you want better in the two-spot ahead of a 50-home-run hitter. The other concern with Rodriguez is defense, as he continued to lose ground at shortstop, and will probably wind up the solution to the third base problem. All that said, what he has done with the bat at his age is remarkable.

Rico Rossy — 3B — Bats R — Age 35

YEAR	TEAM	LGE	AB	H	DB	TP	HR	BB	R	RBI	SB	CS	OUT	BA	OBA	SA	EQA	EQR	DEFENSE	
1996	LasVegas	PCL	405	75	11	1	3	56	30	20	4	4	334	.185	.284	.240	.182	24	128-SS 98	
1997	Ottawa	Int	375	82	10	0	9	29	28	29	4	0	293	.219	.275	.317	.205	28	85-SS 90	22-2B 75
1998	Tacoma	PCL	207	50	8	0	6	22	21	22	1	1	158	.242	.314	.367	.237	22	50-SS 90	
1998	Seattle	AL	80	16	5	0	1	6	5	5	0	0	64	.200	.256	.300	.186	5	20-3B 108	
1999	*Seattle*	*AL*	*320*	*69*	*9*	*0*	*8*	*34*	*28*	*27*	*2*	*1*	*252*	*.216*	*.291*	*.319*	*.212*	*26*		

Just to get back to Russ Davis: his defense was nowhere nearly bad enough to justify digging up Rico Rossy and starting him at third. Nuclear holocausts, biblical floods, or a plague of locusts eating Davis alive wouldn't have justified it.

David Segui — 1B — Bats B — Age 32

YEAR	TEAM	LGE	AB	H	DB	TP	HR	BB	R	RBI	SB	CS	OUT	BA	OBA	SA	EQA	EQR	DEFENSE
1996	Montreal	NL	412	113	25	1	12	62	60	56	3	4	303	.274	.369	.427	.277	61	113-1B 104
1997	Montreal	NL	456	136	21	2	22	60	67	79	1	0	320	.298	.380	.498	.300	79	122-1B 101
1998	Seattle	AL	513	155	33	1	20	51	72	81	3	1	359	.302	.365	.487	.291	82	133-1B 129
1999	*Seattle*	*AL*	*437*	*122*	*21*	*1*	*17*	*55*	*61*	*67*	*2*	*1*	*316*	*.279*	*.360*	*.449*	*.280*	*65*	

Segui makes you appreciate that first base, while at the right end of the defensive spectrum, is still a tough job. Very agile, great hands, good instincts. He belongs at first base, not in right field. Likely to start to return to earth this year offensively, although he should still earn his keep.

Jake Weber — OF — Bats L — Age 23

YEAR	TEAM	LGE	AB	H	DB	TP	HR	BB	R	RBI	SB	CS	OUT	BA	OBA	SA	EQA	EQR	DEFENSE
1998	Everett	Nwn	272	58	6	0	5	40	26	21	4	4	218	.213	.314	.290	.216	24	73-OF 88
1999	*Seattle*	*AL*	*215*	*59*	*7*	*1*	*6*	*31*	*29*	*29*	*2*	*3*	*159*	*.274*	*.366*	*.400*	*.268*	*30*	

A sixth-round selection out of UNC-Charlotte, Weber was old for the Northwest League. At least he did what he had to do: he ripped it up, earning recognition as the best player in the circuit. Solid defense in right field, with an arm that should suffice in the majors. Don't read anything into the fact that he wasn't promoted; the M's wanted to let him chase the league batting title and runs-scored record.

Dan Wilson   C   Bats R   Age 30

YEAR	TEAM	LGE	AB	H	DB	TP	HR	BB	R	RBI	SB	CS	OUT	BA	OBA	SA	EQA	EQR	DEFENSE	
1996	Seattle	AL	482	134	18	0	19	30	49	64	1	2	350	.278	.320	.434	.257	59		
1997	Seattle	AL	500	133	29	1	16	40	58	61	7	2	369	.266	.320	.424	.257	62		
1998	Seattle	AL	320	79	16	1	9	26	32	34	2	1	242	.247	.303	.387	.238	34	92-C 99	
1999	*Seattle*	*AL*	*388*	*104*	*15*	*1*	*14*	*32*	*44*	*51*	*3*	*1*	*285*	*.268*	*.324*	*.420*	*.257*	*48*		

A year wrecked by injuries and a substantial drop in offense. Might be the beginning of the end; he wasn't all that special to begin with. His underachieving was a popular excuse for the Mariners' woes this year, which means expectations for Wilson border on the extravagant.

Mattson Woodward   1B   Bats R   Age 23

YEAR	TEAM	LGE	AB	H	DB	TP	HR	BB	R	RBI	SB	CS	OUT	BA	OBA	SA	EQA	EQR	DEFENSE	
1998	Everett	Nwn	111	6	1	0	0	4	1	1	0	0	105	.054	.087	.063	—	-8	31-1B	67
1999	*Seattle*	*AL*	*83*	*8*	*0*	*0*	*0*	*2*	*1*	*1*	*0*	*0*	*75*	*.096*	*.118*	*.096*	*—*	*-5*		

"Dad, can I get a summer job with your company?"
"Sure thing, son—but remember, don't try too hard. After all, they won't fire you."
"Gee, thanks, Pops! You're the greatest!"

PITCHERS (Averages: 4.00 ERA, 9.00 H/9, 1.00 HR/9, 3.00 BB/9, 6.00 K/9, 1.00 KWH)

Ryan Anderson   Throws L   Age 19

YEAR	TEAM	LGE	IP	H	ER	HR	BB	K	ERA	W	L	H/9	HR/9	BB/9	K/9	KWH	PERA
1998	Wisconsn	Mid	108.7	111	50	7	75	102	4.14	6	6	9.19	0.58	6.21	8.45	0.94	4.14

After all the hype, he started his career in a Johnsonesque way: lots of strikeouts, a low opponents' BA (.220), and too many walks. He missed a little time with arm soreness, but came back strong. If that's behind him, his performance in A-ball at age 17 is nothing short of outstanding. Injuries are the only thing that can hold him back, but he's a pitcher, so you knew that.

Bobby Ayala   Throws R   Age 29

YEAR	TEAM	LGE	IP	H	ER	HR	BB	K	ERA	W	L	H/9	HR/9	BB/9	K/9	KWH	PERA
1996	Seattle	AL	69.0	61	33	9	20	60	4.30	4	4	7.96	1.17	2.61	7.83	2.21	3.26
1997	Seattle	AL	101.0	87	35	13	35	89	3.12	7	4	7.75	1.16	3.12	7.93	1.95	3.21
1998	Seattle	AL	79.0	95	52	8	24	66	5.92	3	6	10.82	0.91	2.73	7.52	1.43	4.67

Piniella's bizarre usage patterns and regular berating finally blew Ayala out. He tried to be too fine and got away from his game of trying to gas people, so people started crushing his stuff, even as his control improved a little. He needs a change of scenery, and will be effective if he gets it.

Rafael Carmona   Throws R   Age 26

YEAR	TEAM	LGE	IP	H	ER	HR	BB	K	ERA	W	L	H/9	HR/9	BB/9	K/9	KWH	PERA
1996	Seattle	AL	93.3	90	35	10	45	61	3.38	6	4	8.68	0.96	4.34	5.88	0.69	3.86
1997	Tacoma	PCL	56.0	56	28	7	31	45	4.50	3	3	9.00	1.12	4.98	7.23	0.87	4.18
1998	Lancastr	Cal	12.0	17	12	1	6	6	9.00	0	1	12.75	0.75	4.50	4.50	0.26	6.00
1998	Orlando	Sou	10.0	23	18	4	6	8	16.20	0	1	20.70	3.60	5.40	7.20	0.35	11.70

Recovering from a massive offseason car wreck; he was definitely in their plans for '98, and I'd guess they'll give him an opportunity to mount a comeback in '99.

Ken Cloude   Throws R   Age 24

YEAR	TEAM	LGE	IP	H	ER	HR	BB	K	ERA	W	L	H/9	HR/9	BB/9	K/9	KWH	PERA
1996	Lancastr	Cal	168.7	179	77	15	56	110	4.11	9	10	9.55	0.80	2.99	5.87	0.91	4.00
1997	Memphis	Sou	127.7	151	59	15	45	97	4.16	7	7	10.64	1.06	3.17	6.84	1.04	4.79
1997	Seattle	AL	53.0	39	25	8	23	45	4.25	3	3	6.62	1.36	3.91	7.64	1.69	2.72
1998	Seattle	AL	163.3	180	92	27	72	111	5.07	7	11	9.92	1.49	3.97	6.12	0.71	4.85

(Ken Cloude *continued*)

The tremendous pitching prospect whose confidence was shredded early on by Piniella's handling, sometimes yanking him at the first sign of trouble, sometimes hanging him out to dry. Like most young Mariner pitchers, his outlook improves if he moves to another team. That tells you a lot about this organization's problems.

Jeff Fassero   Throws L   Age 36

YEAR	TEAM	LGE	IP	H	ER	HR	BB	K	ERA	W	L	H/9	HR/9	BB/9	K/9	KWH	PERA
1996	Montreal	NL	237.3	226	84	20	53	201	3.19	16	10	8.57	0.76	2.01	7.62	2.53	3.26
1997	Seattle	AL	243.7	214	84	19	73	183	3.10	17	10	7.90	0.70	2.70	6.76	1.61	2.95
1998	Seattle	AL	233.0	211	89	31	59	171	3.44	15	11	8.15	1.20	2.28	6.61	1.76	3.32

Fassero shook off arm soreness in the spring to post a pretty good season. I still worry that the workload will catch up to him someday, even if he spent most of his 20s as a reliever. If he stays healthy into July, he'll be excellent trade bait.

Steve Gajkowski   Throws R Age 29

YEAR	TEAM	LGE	IP	H	ER	HR	BB	K	ERA	W	L	H/9	HR/9	BB/9	K/9	KWH	PERA
1996	Nashvill	AmA	101.0	146	75	11	49	37	6.68	3	8	13.01	0.98	4.37	3.30	0.14	5.97
1997	Tacoma	PCL	84.3	112	43	10	23	36	4.59	4	5	11.95	1.07	2.45	3.84	0.38	5.34
1998	Tacoma	PCL	70.0	69	24	2	21	45	3.09	5	3	8.87	0.26	2.70	5.79	1.05	3.21
1998	Seattle	AL	9.0	14	6	3	3	3	6.00	0	1	14.00	3.00	3.00	3.00	0.16	8.00

Called up to be Seattle's closer in June. Even if you're awesome, that is still a tremendous amount of pressure to put on a rookie. Gajkowski is not awesome.

Freddy Garcia   Throws R   Age 22

YEAR	TEAM	LGE	IP	H	ER	HR	BB	K	ERA	W	L	H/9	HR/9	BB/9	K/9	KWH	PERA
1996	Quad Cit	Mid	56.0	79	32	4	28	35	5.14	2	4	12.70	0.64	4.50	5.62	0.42	5.62
1997	Kissimme	Fla	167.7	217	78	9	55	98	4.19	9	10	11.65	0.48	2.95	5.26	0.60	4.78
1998	Jackson	Tex	115.0	107	46	8	58	91	3.60	7	6	8.37	0.63	4.54	7.12	1.00	3.52
1998	New Orln	PCL	13.3	16	5	2	1	10	3.38	1	0	10.80	1.35	0.68	6.75	4.69	4.72
1998	Tacoma	PCL	32.0	32	12	6	12	24	3.38	2	2	9.00	1.69	3.38	6.75	1.12	4.50

Bears the unfortunate label of being the primary pitcher acquired for Randy Johnson. Garcia is a tremendous prospect, with a good fastball and a plus curve. He did suffer some arm soreness in August, which isn't the first time that's happened; if it prevented a call-up, it saved his workload from approaching the danger zone. The Piniella factor makes him a bad bet.

David Holdridge   Throws R Age 30

YEAR	TEAM	LGE	IP	H	ER	HR	BB	K	ERA	W	L	H/9	HR/9	BB/9	K/9	KWH	PERA
1996	Vancouvr	PCL	30.0	49	23	5	25	20	6.90	1	2	14.70	1.50	7.50	6.00	0.24	7.50
1997	Memphis	Sou	32.0	41	16	2	18	26	4.50	2	2	11.53	0.56	5.06	7.31	0.69	5.06
1997	Tacoma	PCL	22.7	23	9	0	13	18	3.57	2	1	9.13	0.00	5.16	7.15	0.81	3.57
1998	Tacoma	PCL	67.7	63	29	2	36	54	3.86	4	4	8.38	0.27	4.79	7.18	0.96	3.33

Eleven years in the minors, and he finally got his first cup of coffee. Next thing you know, he'll be anointed closer, banished to mop-up when he blows his first save, and released.

Felipe Lira   Throws R   Age 27

YEAR	TEAM	LGE	IP	H	ER	HR	BB	K	ERA	W	L	H/9	HR/9	BB/9	K/9	KWH	PERA
1996	Detroit	AL	199.7	191	92	26	53	112	4.15	11	11	8.61	1.17	2.39	5.05	0.93	3.61
1997	Detroit	AL	94.3	104	53	14	39	62	5.06	4	6	9.92	1.34	3.72	5.92	0.71	4.67
1997	Tacoma	PCL	19.3	23	8	1	5	13	3.72	1	1	10.71	0.47	2.33	6.05	1.10	4.19
1998	Tacoma	PCL	121.0	163	72	9	45	65	5.36	5	8	12.12	0.67	3.35	4.83	0.43	5.21

Many good pitchers have gone to Seattle, tried to be too fine to avoid walking people—a capital offense on Planet Piniella—and gotten pasted. Like nearly everyone else on the staff, Lira's best shot is with another organization, so he's off to Detroit as an NRI.

Damaso Marte — Throws L — Age 25

YEAR	TEAM	LGE	IP	H	ER	HR	BB	K	ERA	W	L	H/9	HR/9	BB/9	K/9	KWH	PERA
1996	Wisconsn	Mid	130.0	192	104	12	83	74	7.20	3	11	13.29	0.83	5.75	5.12	0.26	6.16
1997	Lancastr	Cal	134.3	175	76	16	66	82	5.09	6	9	11.72	1.07	4.42	5.49	0.44	5.49
1998	Orlando	Sou	115.3	163	82	15	42	73	6.40	4	9	12.72	1.17	3.28	5.70	0.58	5.93

Poor results will eventually negate the halo created by good stuff. Marte has good stuff, but he also has problems with consistency, mental lapses, and control. His fastball runs up to 92 mph on a good day, but the standard deviation there is pretty high. He could be masking an injury. As a left-hander, Marte will get roughly two million more opportunities to prove himself than he would if he were born normal.

Greg McCarthy — Throws L — Age 30

YEAR	TEAM	LGE	IP	H	ER	HR	BB	K	ERA	W	L	H/9	HR/9	BB/9	K/9	KWH	PERA
1996	Tacoma	PCL	61.3	73	36	2	56	69	5.28	3	4	10.71	0.29	8.22	10.12	0.87	4.99
1997	Tacoma	PCL	20.3	24	8	3	15	25	3.54	1	1	10.62	1.33	6.64	11.07	1.30	5.31
1997	Seattle	AL	30.7	26	16	4	14	33	4.70	1	2	7.63	1.17	4.11	9.68	2.24	3.23
1998	Tacoma	PCL	18.3	18	14	2	23	18	6.87	1	1	8.84	0.98	11.29	8.84	0.59	4.91
1998	Seattle	AL	24.3	18	10	6	15	24	3.70	2	1	6.66	2.22	5.55	8.88	1.60	3.70

Soft-tossing left-hander with a penchant for walking people, especially in succession. At least it seemed that way. Lou lost confidence in McCarthy after about two days, which is fast even for him.

Gilbert Meche — Throws R — Age 20

YEAR	TEAM	LGE	IP	H	ER	HR	BB	K	ERA	W	L	H/9	HR/9	BB/9	K/9	KWH	PERA
1997	Everett	Nwn	71.3	95	40	9	25	34	5.05	3	5	11.99	1.14	3.15	4.29	0.37	5.55
1997	Wisconsn	Mid	11.0	16	5	1	5	9	4.09	0	1	13.09	0.82	4.09	7.36	0.76	5.73
1998	Wisconsn	Mid	145.0	171	82	13	71	112	5.09	6	10	10.61	0.81	4.41	6.95	0.77	4.78

1996 first-rounder (#22 overall) who pitched adequately, but not remarkably, at Wisconsin this year. Meche throws a fastball around 90 with some movement, but his out pitch is a curveball that some scouts say is "too good"—in other words, they claim that minor-league umpires don't realize it's a strike. That pile of garbage belongs on a barge headed out from Nassau County. Meche, on the other hand, belongs in Lancaster this year, but is at least three years away from the majors.

Jamie Moyer — Throws L — Age 36

YEAR	TEAM	LGE	IP	H	ER	HR	BB	K	ERA	W	L	H/9	HR/9	BB/9	K/9	KWH	PERA
1996	Boston	AL	95.3	99	35	12	22	50	3.30	7	4	9.35	1.13	2.08	4.72	0.86	3.97
1996	Seattle	AL	72.0	61	26	8	15	29	3.25	5	3	7.63	1.00	1.88	3.62	0.69	2.75
1997	Seattle	AL	195.0	176	63	19	37	110	2.91	14	8	8.12	0.88	1.71	5.08	1.39	3.00
1998	Seattle	AL	241.7	220	76	21	37	153	2.83	18	9	8.19	0.78	1.38	5.70	2.16	2.90

The Doug Jones of starting pitchers. He doesn't just survive on an assortment of offspeed pitches and other junk—he thrives. Posted career bests in innings and strikeouts, nearly posted career bests in wins and ERA. Topped it off with three shutouts. As long as he keeps his control, he could pitch another three or four years at this level.

Jose Paniagua — Throws R — Age 25

YEAR	TEAM	LGE	IP	H	ER	HR	BB	K	ERA	W	L	H/9	HR/9	BB/9	K/9	KWH	PERA
1996	Ottawa	Int	83.3	79	37	7	23	52	4.00	5	4	8.53	0.76	2.48	5.62	1.12	3.35
1996	Montreal	NL	52.7	58	21	7	22	25	3.59	3	3	9.91	1.20	3.76	4.27	0.37	4.61
1997	Ottawa	Int	138.0	175	71	13	39	71	4.63	6	9	11.41	0.85	2.54	4.63	0.55	4.89
1998	Tacoma	PCL	66.3	71	23	2	21	48	3.12	4	3	9.63	0.27	2.85	6.51	1.16	3.66
1998	Seattle	AL	22.7	14	4	3	4	15	1.59	3	0	5.56	1.19	1.59	5.96	3.01	1.59

Paniagua has always been able to pitch, and he certainly showed it with Tacoma this year, pitching extremely well in the always-tough PCL, including just two homers allowed in 68.1 innings. Still, he's a groundballer who will have to deal with Seattle's turf and porous infield defense. Caution is recommended.

Brandon Parker   Throws R   Age 23

YEAR	TEAM	LGE	IP	H	ER	HR	BB	K	ERA	W	L	H/9	HR/9	BB/9	K/9	KWH	PERA
1998	Wisconsn	Mid	119.7	165	99	12	96	95	7.45	3	10	12.41	0.90	7.22	7.14	0.43	6.02

Cut him some slack: his college coaches at Southern Mississippi used him as a closer, so this season had to be a severe adjustment. The Mariners' #2 pick behind Anderson in '97, Parker throws a fastball up to 95 with a plus curve; he'll need to develop a good offspeed pitch to make it as a starter. This is a crucial year for him, but I expect to see a big step forward now that he's used to starting again.

Joel Pineiro   Throws R   Age 20

YEAR	TEAM	LGE	IP	H	ER	HR	BB	K	ERA	W	L	H/9	HR/9	BB/9	K/9	KWH	PERA
1997	Everett	Nwn	46.7	68	34	3	20	32	6.56	1	4	13.11	0.58	3.86	6.17	0.56	5.59
1998	Wisconsn	Mid	93.7	112	40	11	32	56	3.84	5	5	10.76	1.06	3.07	5.38	0.66	4.80
1998	Lancastr	Cal	44.7	70	40	7	24	32	8.06	1	4	14.10	1.41	4.84	6.45	0.46	6.85

Throws three pitches for strikes, with a solid curve as his out pitch, but showed signs of fatigue and overthrowing at Lancaster. He finished the year extremely poorly, with an ERA near 12.00 in his last seven starts.

Chris Seelbach   Throws R   Age 26

YEAR	TEAM	LGE	IP	H	ER	HR	BB	K	ERA	W	L	H/9	HR/9	BB/9	K/9	KWH	PERA
1996	Charlott	Int	146.3	168	99	25	78	87	6.09	5	11	10.33	1.54	4.80	5.35	0.43	5.23
1997	Charlott	Int	51.7	64	32	7	32	41	5.57	2	4	11.15	1.22	5.57	7.14	0.62	5.57
1998	Orlando	Sou	109.3	131	68	5	49	75	5.60	4	8	10.78	0.41	4.03	6.17	0.66	4.45
1998	Tacoma	PCL	11.0	15	9	5	2	8	7.36	0	1	12.27	4.09	1.64	6.55	1.60	8.18

Ex-Braves prospect who had his best showing in three years. The arm strength is still there, but his control is subpar and he was big-fly Ackeresque in a brief stint at Tacoma. Signed to a minor-league deal by Atlanta; if anyone can fix him, they can.

Heathclif Slocumb   Throws R   Age 33

YEAR	TEAM	LGE	IP	H	ER	HR	BB	K	ERA	W	L	H/9	HR/9	BB/9	K/9	KWH	PERA
1996	Boston	AL	88.3	63	21	2	45	88	2.14	8	2	6.42	0.20	4.58	8.97	2.05	2.14
1997	Boston	AL	49.3	57	26	4	30	35	4.74	2	3	10.40	0.73	5.47	6.39	0.54	4.74
1997	Seattle	AL	29.3	25	10	2	14	27	3.07	2	1	7.67	0.61	4.30	8.28	1.56	3.07
1998	Seattle	AL	71.0	70	32	5	40	50	4.06	4	4	8.87	0.63	5.07	6.34	0.67	3.80

Seattle hates this guy more than it hates George Karl, but no one exactly forced the Mariners to pick up his $3 million option for '98. Slocumb was awful, thrown completely off his wormkilling power/groundball ways by repeated dressings-down from Piniella and some protracted problems with control. Like a lot of Mariner pitchers, he could be very valuable to a team with patience, good infield defense, and a decent pitching coach.

Sean Spencer   Throws L   Age 24

YEAR	TEAM	LGE	IP	H	ER	HR	BB	K	ERA	W	L	H/9	HR/9	BB/9	K/9	KWH	PERA
1997	Lancastr	Cal	59.7	47	11	4	14	48	1.66	6	1	7.09	0.60	2.11	7.24	2.63	2.26
1998	Orlando	Sou	41.7	39	17	4	15	33	3.67	3	2	8.42	0.86	3.24	7.13	1.40	3.46
1998	Tacoma	PCL	12.7	11	6	0	6	13	4.26	0	1	7.82	0.00	4.26	9.24	1.92	2.84

Outstanding left-handed relief prospect who has exceeded all expectations. He slipped into the 31st round after a college injury, so the M's got lucky. In addition to throwing three pitches for strikes (fastball, curve, change-up), Spencer has a deceptive delivery that fools hitters on both sides of the plate. Tremendous confidence and presence on the mound. The Mariners have claimed for years that they needed bullpen help; this should get them started.

Paul Spoljaric   Throws L   Age 28

YEAR	TEAM	LGE	IP	H	ER	HR	BB	K	ERA	W	L	H/9	HR/9	BB/9	K/9	KWH	PERA
1996	Syracuse	Int	21.3	22	9	2	7	19	3.80	1	1	9.28	0.84	2.95	8.02	1.76	3.80
1996	Toronto	AL	38.7	30	12	5	15	38	2.79	3	1	6.98	1.16	3.49	8.84	2.41	2.79
1997	Toronto	AL	48.7	38	14	3	18	41	2.59	4	1	7.03	0.55	3.33	7.58	1.84	2.40
1997	Seattle	AL	23.7	24	10	1	13	26	3.80	2	1	9.13	0.38	4.94	9.89	1.62	3.80
1998	Seattle	AL	87.3	83	53	13	50	87	5.46	3	7	8.55	1.34	5.15	8.97	1.37	4.12

Spoljaric sputtered as a minor-league starter, which prompted a move to the pen, so Piniella, the Master Handler of Pitchers, decided that he knew best and moved Spoljaric back into the rotation. He was awful there. Now a Phillie, he'll likely return to form as a good, but not outstanding, left-handed setup man if they don't get all silly and try to start him. The Phillies are talking about giving him the opportunity to win a job in the rotation.

Mac Suzuki — Throws R — Age 24

YEAR	TEAM	LGE	IP	H	ER	HR	BB	K	ERA	W	L	H/9	HR/9	BB/9	K/9	KWH	PERA
1996	PortCity	Sou	70.0	87	44	11	29	51	5.66	3	5	11.19	1.41	3.73	6.56	0.77	5.40
1996	Tacoma	PCL	20.7	34	19	4	12	12	8.27	0	2	14.81	1.74	5.23	5.23	0.26	7.40
1997	Tacoma	PCL	78.7	83	52	13	56	51	5.95	3	6	9.50	1.49	6.41	5.83	0.42	4.92
1998	Tacoma	PCL	129.0	139	63	18	67	96	4.40	6	8	9.70	1.26	4.67	6.70	0.74	4.67
1998	Seattle	AL	27.3	34	18	3	13	19	5.93	1	2	11.20	0.99	4.28	6.26	0.61	5.27

He learned a splitter. You could almost guess it from the stat lines. In addition, his velocity inched back to near its pre-1995 level. He still has plenty of work to do on his control, but a good arm with a good new pitch is worth watching. Should not be entrusted to Piniella yet.

Bill Swift — Throws R — Age 37

YEAR	TEAM	LGE	IP	H	ER	HR	BB	K	ERA	W	L	H/9	HR/9	BB/9	K/9	KWH	PERA
1996	Colorado	NL	21.0	20	8	1	5	5	3.43	1	1	8.57	0.43	2.14	2.14	0.19	3.00
1997	Colorado	NL	71.7	80	44	11	24	27	5.53	3	5	10.05	1.38	3.01	3.39	0.28	4.65
1998	Seattle	AL	151.3	175	82	20	46	75	4.88	7	10	10.41	1.19	2.74	4.46	0.52	4.70

Kept pulling things from his bag of tricks until the All-Star break, after which he got lit up (7.42 ERA) like Barney Gumbel at 99¢ Duff Night. Someone will give him a chance, but his arm is about out of comebacks at this point.

Mike Timlin — Throws R — Age 33

YEAR	TEAM	LGE	IP	H	ER	HR	BB	K	ERA	W	L	H/9	HR/9	BB/9	K/9	KWH	PERA
1996	Toronto	AL	58.0	45	18	3	14	52	2.79	4	2	6.98	0.47	2.17	8.07	3.22	2.17
1997	Toronto	AL	47.7	41	14	6	13	35	2.64	3	2	7.74	1.13	2.45	6.61	1.72	3.02
1997	Seattle	AL	26.7	26	10	2	4	9	3.38	2	1	8.78	0.68	1.35	3.04	0.58	3.04
1998	Seattle	AL	82.0	73	20	5	14	58	2.20	7	2	8.01	0.55	1.54	6.37	2.47	2.74

Had a great second half, which he parlayed into a new four-year deal with Baltimore. Rob Neyer pointed out to me this summer that Timlin falls apart with men on, which is not a desirable trait in an expensive "closer."

Bob Wells — Throws R — Age 33

YEAR	TEAM	LGE	IP	H	ER	HR	BB	K	ERA	W	L	H/9	HR/9	BB/9	K/9	KWH	PERA
1996	Seattle	AL	134.7	130	57	22	37	93	3.81	8	7	8.69	1.47	2.47	6.22	1.35	3.88
1997	Seattle	AL	70.7	83	38	10	16	50	4.84	3	5	10.57	1.27	2.04	6.37	1.41	4.71
1998	Seattle	AL	53.3	52	30	11	14	28	5.06	2	4	8.78	1.86	2.36	4.72	0.81	4.22

Control pitcher whose extreme flyball tendencies did not mesh well with the Kingdome, not to mention with having Buhner in right. Released; could be an adequate 11th man for a team in a big ballpark.

SNWL — SEATTLE MARINERS — Park Effect: +4.0%

PITCHER	GS	IP	R	SNW	SNL	SNPCT	W	L	RA	APW	SNVA	SNWAR
Abbott, P.	4	24.7	11	1.4	1.1	.559	3	1	4.01	0.27	0.15	0.34
Bullinger, J.	1	3.3	10	0.0	0.9	.001	0	1	27.00	-0.77	-0.46	-0.40
Cloude, K.	30	155.3	116	7.4	12.9	.363	8	10	6.72	-2.74	-2.56	-1.26
Fassero, J.	32	224.7	115	12.8	11.7	.522	13	12	4.61	1.02	0.33	2.37
Johnson, R.	23	160.0	90	9.1	9.0	.502	9	10	5.06	-0.04	-0.02	1.40
Moyer, J.	34	234.3	99	16.1	9.5	.627	15	9	3.80	3.04	3.08	5.18
Spoljaric, P.	6	26.7	28	1.0	3.0	.259	1	3	9.45	-1.23	-0.84	-0.67
Suzuki, M.	5	24.7	19	1.2	2.2	.351	1	2	6.93	-0.49	-0.50	-0.25
Swift, B.	26	140.3	96	6.4	10.6	.378	10	8	6.16	-1.65	-2.03	-0.80
TOTALS	161	994.0	584	55.4	61.0	.476	60	56	5.29	-2.59	-2.85	5.93

The Mariners' rotation dropped off a little, ranking 18th in the league with a -2.9 SNVA compared to ranking 12th with a 0.9 in 1997. All of the dropoff can be attributed to Randy Johnson's average pitching (and subsequent trade) in 1998. Among pitchers with 25 or more starts, Ken Cloude and Billy Swift ranked third from last and sixth from last, respectively, in SNPct. The 25+ game starters who had SNPcts less than .400, worst-to-"best": Vazquez, Navarro, Cloude, Hawkins, Darwin, Swift, Astacio. When you play for the hit-happy Mariners, though, it's often possible to hide your poor pitching behind a decent W/L record, as both Cloude and Swift did. Normally I'd look at two awful starters' seasons like that and actually see it as reason for optimism for the next year, the reasoning being that teams don't usually get two seasons that bad and they're not likely to get them again next year. Not the Mariners: the last three years, they just haven't been able to get any respectable seasons from starters except the ones from their big three. Since 1996, the best SNPct they've gotten in 15+ starts from someone not named Johnson, Moyer, or Fassero is .428, from Sterling Hitchcock in 1996.

Pitcher Abuse Points

PITCHER	AGE	GS	PAP	PAP/S	AAW	MAX	115+	130+
Cloude, Kenny	23	30	172	5.73	14.33	121	3	0
Fassero, Jeff	35	32	787	24.59	24.59	141	15	4
Johnson, Randy	34	23	1215	52.83	52.83	144	16	11
Moyer, Jamie	35	34	465	13.68	13.68	131	9	1
Spoljaric, Paul	27	6	1	0.17	0.31	101	0	0
Suzuki, Mac	23	5	11	2.20	5.50	107	0	0
Swift, Billy	36	26	30	1.15	1.15	111	0	0
TOTAL		161	2699	16.76	18.51	144	44	16
RANKING (AL)			2	2	4		2	2

Lou Piniella believes in letting a starter put out his own fires to begin with; what did you think would happen when his bullpen (with Lou's help) imploded? Randy Johnson is a big part of the story, but Jeff Fassero, not exactly Mr. Workhorse, helped give the Mariners the only teammates in baseball to each record at least 700 PAPs. To his credit, Piniella handled Jamie Moyer very well, while Moyer set a career-high in innings. Ken Cloude certainly can't complain about getting left out there. Of course, it's hard to leave a pitcher out there very long when he's given up seven runs by the fifth inning. The always-fragile Billy Swift was treated with dexterity, but three years in Colorado was too much to overcome.

Texas Rangers

Last year at this time, with the Rangers coming off a .475 season and a third-place finish in a weak division, we heard a lot about what they were doing wrong. Everyone from the Dallas sports barfly to the serious analyst laid in to the Rangers' front office for mismanaging their huge payroll by signing overpriced free agents, trading decent talent for mediocrities like Tom Goodwin and Jim Leyritz, and failing to act quickly to repair the disintegrating pitching staff. Most important, the criticism was right on target.

But as Johnnie Cochran would be happy to tell you, there are two sides to every story. This year, as Ranger fans bask in the glory of a division title, they can look at the organization with pride and celebration. After all, they've earned the right to be thrashed by the Yankees in two of the last three years; they must be doing something right. What accounts for the Rangers' success these last few years, and are they on the right track for more?

Let's talk about player acquisition, particularly high-priced free agent signings, since that's where the Rangers take and deserve the most heat. In BP '98, we argued that the Rangers' two high-profile free agent signings of recent years, Will Clark and John Wetteland, were paid money that could have been better spent elsewhere. Especially Clark, because he just hasn't been that special since 1991. Certainly both players played a positive role in last year's division championship; the only question is whether the money spent on them could have been used to get someone who would have played an even bigger role, like a front-line starter or two. The second-tier free agents signed by the Rangers in recent years have also been unspectacular, ranging from qualified success (Ken Hill) to unmitigated disaster (Mike Henneman).

So the Rangers could have done better at acquiring free agents. But keep in mind that signing other teams' players is only part of the free agency game. An equally important part is signing your own players, and keeping your own superstars from ever filing, if possible. On that front, the Rangers have been near-perfect, keeping their two biggest superstars in the fold with contract extensions. The team has contract options on Juan Gonzalez until after the 2000 season, and

Rangers Prospectus

1998 record: 88-74; First place, AL West; Lost to New York Yankees in Division Series, 3-0

Pythagorean W/L: 87-75

Runs scored: 940 (2nd in AL)

Runs allowed: 871 (12th in AL)

Team EQA: .271 (5th in AL)

Park: The Ballpark at Arlington (good hitters')

1998: Bludgeoned their way to the division title; deep bench and stable rotation helped.

1999: It's a weak division; they could win it again.

Ivan Rodriguez is locked up until after 2002. What clubs can boast three home-grown veterans the quality of Gonzalez, Rodriguez, and Rusty Greer? Just two—Seattle with Ken Griffey, Alex Rodriguez, and Edgar Martinez; and Atlanta with Tom Glavine, Chipper Jones, and Javy Lopez. The Rangers' decision to keep Gonzalez and Rodriguez played at least a small role in winning the division.

Another cog in the Rangers' 1998 success was their intelligent selection and use of "fill-in-the-blank players." That's what I call the players you dig up to fill your holes after you've exhausted your own organizational options and the supply of big-name free agents. The Rangers, like any team, had their share of journeymen getting significant playing time during 1998. What set the Rangers apart from a lot of other teams was that their journeymen were strong contributors. Luis Alicea, Roberto Kelly, Bill Haselman, Mike Simms, and Lee Stevens comprised the strongest bench in the league. Some of these players were platooned effectively, particularly Kelly with Tom Goodwin and Simms with Stevens. While not all of the above group had career years, some did, and none of them were big disappointments.

How well are the Rangers set up to win in the future? Even in the day and age of free agency and salary-dump trades, player development is still the primary job of an organization. The Rangers had a good record on this front in the late '80s and early '90s, with Rodriguez, Gonzalez, Greer, and Sammy Sosa emerging from the farm system. The system has hit a drought for the last few years, but GM Bob Melvin has taken steps toward rebuilding it. Exactly how far he's gotten is a point of some contention: many serious analysts disparage the Ranger organization, calling it one of the worst in baseball. On the other hand, Howe Sportsdata named Texas their Organization of the Year, and the mainstream baseball media has been raving as well. I think the truth lies somewhere in between.

There's no question the system has been improved. While Triple-A Oklahoma was nothing to write home about, there was a fair amount of talent at Double-A and below in 1998. Two Ranger minor league teams, the Tulsa Drillers

(Texas League) and the Gulf Coast Rangers (Gulf Coast League), won their league championships. The aggregate farm team winning percentage was .526, up from .486 in 1997. The system's strength is not in its blue-chippers, but in the volume of potential future major leaguers. For example, the starting rotation in Oklahoma in 1999 may consist entirely of guys under 25 who each have a fighting chance at a five-year major league career. That may sound like it ought to be the norm for a Triple-A club, but it isn't. Melvin has also restored and revamped the once-proud Latin American scouting effort that produced Gonzalez, Rodriguez, and Sosa. The Rangers' Latin pipeline is now on par with the Dodgers' and the Astros', and it is starting to pay dividends with prospects like Ruben Mateo, Cesar King, and Joaquin Benoit.

With all that good news, some of the superlatives that are being thrown around go a bit too far. For one thing, the Rangers system is lacking in blue-chippers, guys who look like they'll not only make the majors, but be All-Stars when they get there. At the moment, Mateo is the only Ranger farmhand who fits that description, and even he has some big holes in his game. Another problem, and one that's contributed to the excessive hype, is that some of the so-called "emerging" prospects are actually guys who are old for their level. They're getting lots of attention for great years when they're actually moving slowly through the system and having those years by beating up younger competition. I'm thinking specifically of Kelly Dransfeldt and Mike Zywica. Their play last year is encouraging, but it needs to be viewed skeptically until they they show something comparable at higher levels.

Another problem with the farm system is Melvin's eagerness to plunder it. You'd think that in 1998 of all years, the Rangers of all organizations would question the wisdom of trading promising young players for a couple of months of declining old ones. While watching one of the approximately 12 billion Sammy Sosa replays, the Rangers' brass could have taken a few moments to reflect on the trade that sent Sosa and Wilson Alvarez to the White Sox for a 30-year-old Harold Baines during an ill-fated run at the 1989 pennant. The lesson must have been lost on Melvin. In three separate trades down the stretch, he gave up Fernando Tatis, Jose Santos, and Warren Morris in return for veterans, none of whom were stars. All three of the prospects have the potential to become major league regulars or better, and all three play positions at which the Rangers are weak. Whether trading them bought the West title for the Rangers last year or not—and I'd say probably not—they were way too high a price to pay in terms of possible future titles.

So the Rangers' long-term picture is reasonably bright, albeit dimmed by their own actions. But what about the short term? You may have noticed that in the discussion of the Rangers' 1998 success, there is almost no mention of the pitching staff. I could discuss the Rangers' starting pitchers in depth, but then we'd have to put a parental advisory label on the book and we'd lose the lucrative age 9-to-14 market. The 1998 Rangers were an example of a team that suceeded despite their pitching rather than because of it. The offense was good to an even greater extent than the pitching was bad.

Can the 1999 Rangers repeat this feat, with the offense carrying the load of a below-average pitching staff? It's unlikely that the Rangers can stand still and expect to win the division again. They seem to recognize this, signing solid #3 starter Mark Clark to a two-year deal and throwing their hat in the ring for Roger Clemens. One newly acquired front-line starter like Clemens could drop the team's runs allowed total by 70 or more. If Melvin can use his persuasive powers, not to mention new owner Thomas Hicks's sizable checkbook, to bring a quality starter or two to Arlington, the 1999 Rangers could easily repeat. If not, look for another "What They're Doing Wrong" article in this space next year.

BATTERS (Averages: BA .260/ OBA .330/ SA .420, EQA .260)

Luis Alicea — IF — Bats B — Age 33

YEAR	TEAM	LGE	AB	H	DB	TP	HR	BB	R	RBI	SB	CS	OUT	BA	OBA	SA	EQA	EQR	DEFENSE
1996	St Louis	NL	381	98	26	2	6	53	55	40	9	3	286	.257	.348	.383	.260	50	116-2B 92
1997	Anaheim	AL	380	94	16	7	5	69	65	37	22	8	294	.247	.363	.366	.266	54	103-2B 98
1998	Texas	AL	252	65	13	3	6	37	34	31	3	3	190	.258	.353	.405	.265	34	39-2B 95
1999	Texas	AL	283	72	15	3	5	48	44	33	7	4	215	.254	.363	.382	.260	37	

His defensive skills are on the wane, but his flexibility is valuable and he continues to get on base at a respectable rate. He showed a bit more pop than he has in the past. Contrary to the projection above, I wouldn't be surprised to see the power continue to increase next year.

Andy Barkett   1B   Bats L   Age 24

YEAR	TEAM	LGE	AB	H	DB	TP	HR	BB	R	RBI	SB	CS	OUT	BA	OBA	SA	EQA	EQR	DEFENSE
1996	Charlott	Fla	401	110	15	1	9	49	49	48	2	1	292	.274	.353	.384	.261	51	97-1B 96
1997	Tulsa	Tex	461	119	23	5	7	53	53	50	1	2	344	.258	.335	.375	.249	53	129-1B 90
1998	Tulsa	Tex	156	34	7	0	2	22	16	12	0	0	122	.218	.315	.301	.220	14	42-1B 95
1998	Oklahoma	PCL	251	73	14	3	4	32	36	32	3	3	181	.291	.371	.418	.276	36	69-1B 87
1999	*Texas*	*AL*	*417*	*115*	*19*	*2*	*8*	*54*	*56*	*52*	*2*	*2*	*304*	*.276*	*.359*	*.388*	*.258*	*51*	

Barkett had an impressive debut at Triple-A, combining his usual good eye with a career-best EQA. The organization's efforts to get him to develop some power still haven't shown any results, though. If he learns how to reach the fences with regularity, he might end up being an average major league first baseman. If not, he might still find a part-time major league role during his peak years as Mark Grace Lite.

Domingo Cedeno   IF   Bats B   Age 30

YEAR	TEAM	LGE	AB	H	DB	TP	HR	BB	R	RBI	SB	CS	OUT	BA	OBA	SA	EQA	EQR	DEFENSE	
1996	Toronto	AL	276	73	9	2	2	14	24	23	5	3	207	.264	.300	.333	.219	23	59-2B 100	
1997	Texas	AL	359	100	19	6	4	27	40	40	3	3	262	.279	.329	.398	.251	41	56-2B 101	29-SS 104
1998	Texas	AL	138	34	8	1	2	10	14	12	2	1	105	.246	.297	.362	.228	13	25-SS 95	
1999	*Texas*	*AL*	*215*	*58*	*13*	*2*	*3*	*15*	*24*	*23*	*2*	*2*	*159*	*.270*	*.317*	*.391*	*.238*	*22*		

Like many Rangers, Cedeno started off '98 hitting relatively well: .292/.339/.425 before the break. But he was awful in the second half, and he didn't see much action after Clayton arrived. He may never again reach the offensive "peak" he had in 1997, but his glovework is steady enough that at his '98 or projected '99 levels of offensive performance, he's worth having around as a backup.

Will Clark   1B   Bats L   Age 35

YEAR	TEAM	LGE	AB	H	DB	TP	HR	BB	R	RBI	SB	CS	OUT	BA	OBA	SA	EQA	EQR	DEFENSE
1996	Texas	AL	420	110	20	1	12	60	55	53	2	1	311	.262	.354	.400	.266	57	112-1B 98
1997	Texas	AL	384	123	26	1	13	50	61	65	0	0	261	.320	.399	.495	.308	69	98-1B 101
1998	Texas	AL	538	156	31	1	24	73	79	89	1	0	382	.290	.375	.485	.295	90	131-1B 88
1999	*Baltimor*	*AL*	*446*	*120*	*20*	*0*	*19*	*63*	*61*	*69*	*0*	*0*	*326*	*.269*	*.360*	*.442*	*.281*	*68*	

Not much of an argument for the Hall of Fame right now (campaign slogan: "Keith Hernandez without the glove"), but Clark still has time to pad his résumé. He played his heart out with a broken toe down the stretch, and demonstrated that his power resurgence of '97 was no fluke. He may have a case if his body will allow him to play at this level for a few more years, but don't bet on it. He's a bargain for the Orioles at two years, $11 million, and could have a nice power year in that park. That projection is low.

Royce Clayton   SS   Bats R   Age 29

YEAR	TEAM	LGE	AB	H	DB	TP	HR	BB	R	RBI	SB	CS	OUT	BA	OBA	SA	EQA	EQR	DEFENSE
1996	St Louis	NL	490	136	21	4	6	37	62	46	27	16	370	.278	.328	.373	.246	55	111-SS 108
1997	St Louis	NL	575	154	40	4	10	37	72	58	26	11	432	.268	.312	.403	.249	67	145-SS 106
1998	St Louis	NL	353	82	17	1	5	42	45	27	20	7	278	.232	.314	.329	.233	37	88-SS 108
1998	Texas	AL	181	49	10	1	5	14	21	21	4	5	137	.271	.323	.420	.251	22	51-SS 101
1999	*Texas*	*AL*	*550*	*150*	*33*	*3*	*11*	*46*	*73*	*61*	*21*	*12*	*412*	*.273*	*.329*	*.404*	*.248*	*63*	

One of the top fielding shortstops in the game, by reputation and by numbers. The only questions are the bat and the price tag. Is the difference between him and Elster (or him and Sheldon) worth Tatis? At $5 million a year? My answers: no, no, and no. Re-signed with the Rangers for four years.

Kelly Dransfeldt   SS   Bats R   Age 24

YEAR	TEAM	LGE	AB	H	DB	TP	HR	BB	R	RBI	SB	CS	OUT	BA	OBA	SA	EQA	EQR	DEFENSE
1996	HudsnVal	NYP	291	60	5	1	6	19	18	18	6	3	234	.206	.255	.292	.185	17	72-SS 106
1997	Charlott	Fla	471	98	13	3	7	36	33	29	13	9	382	.208	.264	.293	.190	30	130-SS 88
1998	Charlott	Fla	245	70	8	0	12	23	30	38	3	1	176	.286	.347	.465	.279	36	65-SS 103
1998	Tulsa	Tex	224	49	8	2	7	14	19	20	5	1	176	.219	.265	.366	.217	19	57-SS 110
1999	*Texas*	*AL*	*447*	*108*	*13*	*1*	*13*	*34*	*43*	*44*	*10*	*4*	*343*	*.242*	*.295*	*.362*	*.223*	*40*	

(Kelly Dransfeldt *continued*)

A lot of fans are excited about Dransfeldt based on that '98 Charlotte line. Let me throw some cold water on them: he was old for his level, and that great half-season came in his second year at A-ball, making it of dubious predictive value. That said, he hit well in the Arizona Fall League, and a defensive whiz shortstop doesn't have to hit much better than that '99 projection to be a major league contributor, especially on the Rangers. The signing of Clayton damages his chances at shortstop in this organization, but there's no one in front of him if he moves to second base.

Kevin Elster   SS   Bats R   Age 34

YEAR	TEAM	LGE	AB	H	DB	TP	HR	BB	R	RBI	SB	CS	OUT	BA	OBA	SA	EQA	EQR	DEFENSE
1996	Texas	AL	501	116	31	2	21	48	54	61	4	1	386	.232	.299	.427	.248	59	150-SS 103
1997	Pittsbrg	NL	137	30	5	2	7	22	17	19	0	2	109	.219	.327	.438	.259	19	32-SS 112
1998	Texas	AL	290	63	7	1	8	34	24	27	0	2	229	.217	.299	.331	.218	26	84-SS 102
1999	*Texas*	*AL*	*257*	*58*	*11*	*1*	*9*	*30*	*27*	*29*	*1*	*1*	*200*	*.226*	*.307*	*.381*	*.232*	*26*	

Released by the Rangers after acquiring Clayton, Elster couldn't find a team to latch on to during the stretch drive. I suspect somebody will give him a chance in 1999, just to see if he still has some of that 1996-97 offense left in him.

Shawn Gallagher   1B   Bats R   Age 22

YEAR	TEAM	LGE	AB	H	DB	TP	HR	BB	R	RBI	SB	CS	OUT	BA	OBA	SA	EQA	EQR	DEFENSE	
1996	HudsnVal	NYP	178	44	5	1	4	6	13	15	4	3	137	.247	.272	.354	.212	14	41-1B	66
1996	Charl-SC	SAL	310	65	7	1	7	14	16	20	3	1	246	.210	.244	.306	.182	17	87-1B	63
1997	Pulaski	App	194	44	3	1	6	6	11	16	1	0	150	.227	.250	.345	.199	13	49-1B	62
1997	Charlott	Fla	99	12	4	0	0	5	2	2	0	0	87	.121	.163	.162	—	-2	26-1B	87
1998	Charlott	Fla	522	148	22	2	22	56	70	77	9	4	378	.284	.353	.460	.280	78	128-1B	65
1999	*Texas*	*AL*	*454*	*122*	*17*	*1*	*18*	*33*	*50*	*61*	*6*	*3*	*335*	*.269*	*.318*	*.430*	*.251*	*53*		

Developed both power and some plate discipline at 21, a very nice combination. Gallagher was named the "Tom Grieve Minor League Player of the Year" for the organization, and a second-team selection to *Baseball America*'s minor league All-Star team. His future with the Rangers is as a DH, because of his defensive ineptitude and Carlos Pena.

Juan Gonzalez   RF   Bats R   Age 29

YEAR	TEAM	LGE	AB	H	DB	TP	HR	BB	R	RBI	SB	CS	OUT	BA	OBA	SA	EQA	EQR	DEFENSE
1996	Texas	AL	523	155	30	2	43	41	74	108	2	0	368	.296	.348	.608	.311	99	88-OF 90
1997	Texas	AL	524	153	24	3	42	34	67	104	0	0	371	.292	.335	.590	.301	93	55-OF 100
1998	Texas	AL	589	179	42	1	45	48	86	121	2	1	411	.304	.356	.608	.314	113	115-OF 89
1999	*Texas*	*AL*	*547*	*167*	*29*	*1*	*42*	*42*	*80*	*117*	*1*	*0*	*380*	*.305*	*.355*	*.592*	*.305*	*98*	

Tremendously consistent production over the past four years, and that consistency is a little surprising coming from a player who doesn't walk much. If he ever leaves the Rangers, look for his numbers, even the park-adjusted ones, to drop. He gets more of a boost from The Ballpark than the typical Ranger—more than 100 points of OPS since it opened—despite the longer dimensions and higher wall in left field.

Tom Goodwin   CF   Bats L   Age 30

YEAR	TEAM	LGE	AB	H	DB	TP	HR	BB	R	RBI	SB	CS	OUT	BA	OBA	SA	EQA	EQR	DEFENSE
1996	KansasCy	AL	514	141	13	4	1	36	79	31	70	26	399	.274	.322	.321	.240	56	126-OF 102
1997	KansasCy	AL	360	95	12	4	2	20	47	25	34	10	275	.264	.303	.336	.234	36	88-OF 106
1997	Texas	AL	204	47	13	2	0	25	28	13	16	6	163	.230	.314	.314	.231	21	46-OF 113
1998	Texas	AL	505	138	11	3	2	74	76	41	32	19	386	.273	.366	.319	.251	61	132-OF 109
1999	*Texas*	*AL*	*523*	*140*	*20*	*3*	*2*	*57*	*76*	*41*	*35*	*16*	*399*	*.268*	*.340*	*.329*	*.237*	*54*	

His most important role on this team is to cover the outfield ground that his two range-challenged colleagues can't, and he did that quite nicely. He also discovered an obscure baseball rule . . . something called the "base on balls." All in all, a surprising season by Goodwin, but I'm still looking forward to the day I see "Mateo CF" in the morning box score.

Rusty Greer   LF   Bats L   Age 30

YEAR	TEAM	LGE	AB	H	DB	TP	HR	BB	R	RBI	SB	CS	OUT	BA	OBA	SA	EQA	EQR	DEFENSE
1995	Texas	AL	407	106	20	2	13	53	52	53	3	1	302	.260	.346	.415	.266	55	112-OF 93
1996	Texas	AL	520	161	37	6	16	58	84	82	9	0	359	.310	.379	.496	.302	90	123-OF 102
1997	Texas	AL	588	186	42	3	26	83	103	105	9	5	407	.316	.401	.531	.315	114	144-OF 96
1998	Texas	AL	580	169	29	5	15	81	84	83	2	4	415	.291	.378	.436	.283	89	151-OF 92
1999	*Texas*	*AL*	*578*	*174*	*37*	*3*	*20*	*81*	*96*	*96*	*5*	*3*	*407*	*.301*	*.387*	*.479*	*.293*	*95*	

The only Ranger position player to play significantly below expectations. Accordingly, he's the only Ranger position player that can reasonably be expected to boost his performance in 1999. There are plenty of reasons to expect him to be back to his usual .300+ EQA self this year. For one, there's the way he came on during the last half of 1998. Last year's pre-break OPS: .786; post-break: .903.

Bill Haselman   C   Bats R   Age 33

YEAR	TEAM	LGE	AB	H	DB	TP	HR	BB	R	RBI	SB	CS	OUT	BA	OBA	SA	EQA	EQR	DEFENSE
1996	Boston	AL	231	59	13	1	7	17	25	26	4	2	174	.255	.306	.411	.247	26	
1997	Boston	AL	209	48	12	0	7	16	17	22	0	2	163	.230	.284	.388	.226	20	
1998	Texas	AL	102	30	4	0	6	4	11	17	0	0	72	.294	.321	.510	.277	15	26-C 93
1999	*Texas*	*AL*	*157*	*39*	*6*	*0*	*8*	*9*	*15*	*21*	*1*	*1*	*119*	*.248*	*.289*	*.439*	*.239*	*17*	

The second nicest surprise in the Aaron Sele trade. Even with Pudge having his best season at the plate, Haselman hit just as well in his limited at-bats. He's never met a pitch he didn't like, though: against left-handers, he achieved the rarely met "Guillen standard"—a higher BA (.405) than OBP (.400). A free agent, the Rangers' acquisition of Gregg Zaun will end his stay in Arlington.

Roberto Kelly   OF   Bats R   Age 34

YEAR	TEAM	LGE	AB	H	DB	TP	HR	BB	R	RBI	SB	CS	OUT	BA	OBA	SA	EQA	EQR	DEFENSE
1996	Minnesot	AL	312	95	17	4	5	21	43	38	10	2	219	.304	.348	.433	.274	43	85-OF 98
1997	Minnesot	AL	243	69	19	2	5	17	32	29	7	4	178	.284	.331	.440	.264	32	49-OF 97
1997	Seattle	AL	119	35	7	0	7	5	15	19	2	1	85	.294	.323	.529	.283	18	20-OF 108
1998	Texas	AL	250	77	6	3	15	10	27	45	0	2	175	.308	.335	.536	.287	38	57-OF 107
1999	*Texas*	*AL*	*300*	*86*	*14*	*2*	*14*	*17*	*36*	*47*	*3*	*2*	*216*	*.287*	*.325*	*.487*	*.267*	*40*	

Kelly hit like he always has in 1998—he was just used effectively. The Rangers exploited Kelly's huge platoon split by giving him more than half of his at-bats against left-handers. The strategy paid big dividends, both for Kelly and for Goodwin, who saw his playing time against left-handers drop. I expect this year to be more of the same for Kelly, assuming he's used in the same way.

Cesar King   C   Bats R   Age 21

YEAR	TEAM	LGE	AB	H	DB	TP	HR	BB	R	RBI	SB	CS	OUT	BA	OBA	SA	EQA	EQR	DEFENSE
1996	Charl-SC	SAL	284	66	4	1	6	16	19	22	4	3	221	.232	.273	.317	.201	20	
1997	Charlott	Fla	311	86	9	3	6	31	36	36	4	3	228	.277	.342	.383	.254	37	
1997	Tulsa	Tex	44	14	0	0	1	4	4	6	0	1	31	.318	.375	.386	.262	5	
1998	Tulsa	Tex	314	56	9	1	3	25	13	12	1	1	259	.178	.239	.242	.150	11	86-C 101
1999	*Texas*	*AL*	*323*	*83*	*8*	*0*	*8*	*26*	*30*	*34*	*2*	*2*	*242*	*.257*	*.312*	*.356*	*.226*	*29*	

King is still may be one of the crown jewels of the Rangers system, but last year he took a big step in the direction of cubic zirconium. He was awful out of the gate in '98. In July, just when he seemed to be getting his '97 swing back, he fractured his wrist and missed the rest of the season. At his age, playing in Ivan Rodriguez's organization, he'll have plenty of time to recover.

Ruben Mateo   OF   Bats R   Age 21

YEAR	TEAM	LGE	AB	H	DB	TP	HR	BB	R	RBI	SB	CS	OUT	BA	OBA	SA	EQA	EQR	DEFENSE	
1996	Charl-SC	SAL	508	124	20	4	8	19	42	40	14	5	389	.244	.271	.346	.213	41	125-OF	93
1997	Charlott	Fla	387	116	15	4	13	20	48	53	11	3	274	.300	.334	.460	.273	53	88-OF	96
1998	Tulsa	Tex	425	116	20	1	14	25	47	51	12	6	315	.273	.313	.424	.253	51	106-OF	106
1999	*Texas*	*AL*	*454*	*133*	*20*	*2*	*15*	*23*	*55*	*62*	*12*	*5*	*326*	*.293*	*.327*	*.445*	*.259*	*56*		

(Ruben Mateo *continued*)

I'm not concerned about the drop in his numbers. He was bothered by a shoulder injury in the first half, when he hit .223 with six home runs. In the second half he was healthy, and he hit .354 with 12 bombs. He's still the Rangers' top prospect, and still on track to become the next "next Roberto Clemente."

Mark McLemore   2B   Bats B   Age 34

YEAR	TEAM	LGE	AB	H	DB	TP	HR	BB	R	RBI	SB	CS	OUT	BA	OBA	SA	EQA	EQR	DEFENSE
1996	Texas	AL	497	131	21	4	4	82	82	45	27	11	377	.264	.368	.346	.262	66	146-2B 112
1997	Texas	AL	343	88	17	2	1	40	41	28	7	5	260	.257	.334	.327	.236	35	84-2B 105
1998	Texas	AL	448	103	13	1	5	89	63	37	10	4	349	.230	.358	.297	.244	51	121-2B 93
1999	*Texas*	*AL*	*422*	*102*	*18*	*1*	*4*	*74*	*62*	*37*	*11*	*5*	*325*	*.242*	*.355*	*.318*	*.241*	*46*	

He's gotten great at drawing walks, but his power continues to plummet. Almost all of the Ranger infielders took big hits in their defensive ratings between 1997 and 1998. I think there might be a pitching staff effect at work. My own evaluation is that McLemore's still average defensively, but even so he's one of the poorest second basemen in the league.

Chad Mottola   OF   Bats R   Age 27

YEAR	TEAM	LGE	AB	H	DB	TP	HR	BB	R	RBI	SB	CS	OUT	BA	OBA	SA	EQA	EQR	DEFENSE
1996	Indianap	AA	362	91	20	1	8	23	36	35	9	6	277	.251	.296	.378	.232	36	92-OF 95
1996	Cincnnti	NL	79	17	2	0	3	6	6	7	2	2	64	.215	.271	.354	.211	7	23-OF 98
1997	Chattang	Sou	167	46	5	1	3	11	18	17	4	1	122	.275	.320	.371	.244	18	42-OF 87
1997	Indianap	AA	284	75	7	4	6	14	29	28	10	3	212	.264	.299	.380	.237	29	70-OF 93
1998	Oklahoma	PCL	253	53	8	1	1	16	15	12	6	2	202	.209	.257	.261	.174	13	66-OF 92
1999	*Texas*	*AL*	*344*	*88*	*13*	*1*	*8*	*26*	*37*	*35*	*9*	*4*	*260*	*.256*	*.308*	*.369*	*.230*	*33*	

Acquired from the Reds for a PTBNL, Mottola will someday teach a seminar called "How To Convince Your New Team You're Not A Prospect in 300 At-Bats or Less!". Step 1: As a 26-year-old outfielder, hit like Rey Ordonez swinging a broom handle. Step 2: Miss 41 games after breaking your thumb horsing around with Rick Wrona.

Warren Newson   OF   Bats L   Age 34

YEAR	TEAM	LGE	AB	H	DB	TP	HR	BB	R	RBI	SB	CS	OUT	BA	OBA	SA	EQA	EQR	DEFENSE
1996	Texas	AL	227	53	12	1	9	35	30	29	3	0	174	.233	.336	.414	.264	31	52-OF 101
1997	Texas	AL	166	35	9	1	10	31	25	24	3	0	131	.211	.335	.458	.275	26	49-OF 89
1998	Oklahoma	PCL	393	104	12	1	14	55	51	52	6	4	293	.265	.355	.407	.267	54	68-OF 86
1999	*Texas*	*AL*	*333*	*82*	*14*	*2*	*14*	*54*	*48*	*48*	*3*	*1*	*252*	*.246*	*.351*	*.426*	*.266*	*46*	

A long-time favorite of analysts and a lifetime member of the Ken Phelps All-Star Team. He's the antithesis of a tools player: not fast, poor fielder, doesn't hit for average, only a little power. He's still useful, but his shot at Phelps-like greatness is gone.

Carlos Pena   1B   Bats L   Age 21

YEAR	TEAM	LGE	AB	H	DB	TP	HR	BB	R	RBI	SB	CS	OUT	BA	OBA	SA	EQA	EQR	DEFENSE
1998	Savannah	SAL	113	34	5	0	5	7	14	17	2	1	80	.301	.342	.478	.278	16	26-1B 89
1999	*Texas*	*AL*	*108*	*37*	*6*	*0*	*5*	*5*	*15*	*20*	*1*	*1*	*72*	*.343*	*.372*	*.537*	*.298*	*17*	

The consensus best first baseman taken in the 1998 amateur draft did not disappoint during his first professional half-season at low-A. The Rafael Palmeiro signing will affect his future in very bad ways, and is downright silly given how soon Pena will be ready for a major league job.

Juan Piniella   OF   Bats R   Age 21

YEAR	TEAM	LGE	AB	H	DB	TP	HR	BB	R	RBI	SB	CS	OUT	BA	OBA	SA	EQA	EQR	DEFENSE
1997	Pulaski	App	124	20	0	1	1	5	4	4	3	2	106	.161	.194	.202	.083	1	31-OF 99
1998	Savannah	SAL	258	78	10	3	3	25	38	29	13	7	187	.302	.364	.399	.269	35	69-OF 95
1998	Charlott	Fla	222	61	6	2	2	22	29	20	11	4	165	.275	.340	.347	.248	25	50-OF 97
1999	*Texas*	*AL*	*328*	*97*	*11*	*2*	*3*	*26*	*43*	*34*	*14*	*7*	*238*	*.296*	*.347*	*.369*	*.248*	*37*	

Opened some eyes at low-A Savannah and kept them open at high-A Charlotte. Piniella hit for average to all fields and showed great plate discipline for a 20-year-old. He plays a capable corner outfield. The only thing missing is the power, which he's still young enough to develop.

Ivan Rodriguez   C   Bats R   Age 27

YEAR	TEAM	LGE	AB	H	DB	TP	HR	BB	R	RBI	SB	CS	OUT	BA	OBA	SA	EQA	EQR	DEFENSE
1996	Texas	AL	620	173	43	3	17	34	69	78	5	0	447	.279	.317	.440	.260	77	
1997	Texas	AL	586	181	34	4	20	39	76	89	7	3	408	.309	.352	.483	.284	88	
1998	Texas	AL	563	172	37	4	20	35	76	85	8	0	391	.306	.346	.492	.286	86	136-C 111
1999	*Texas*	*AL*	*557*	*165*	*39*	*2*	*19*	*33*	*74*	*83*	*8*	*1*	*393*	*.296*	*.336*	*.476*	*.272*	*76*	

The 1998 team MVP, hands down. Everybody knows about his rifle arm, but I'm not sure everybody grasps just how valuable it is. Last year he threw out 42 of 80 would-be basestealers, and picked off another seven. I won't show my work, but that means Pudge's arm saved around 25 runs compared to an average catcher. Very few pitchers, let alone catchers, save 25 runs above average in a season. That, and he can hit a little.

Marc Sagmoen   OF   Bats L   Age 28

YEAR	TEAM	LGE	AB	H	DB	TP	HR	BB	R	RBI	SB	CS	OUT	BA	OBA	SA	EQA	EQR	DEFENSE	
1996	Tulsa	Tex	382	83	12	2	6	26	25	26	4	5	304	.217	.267	.306	.193	25	93-OF 90	
1996	Oklahoma	AA	115	30	3	0	4	5	9	13	1	0	85	.261	.292	.391	.235	11	25-OF 99	
1997	Oklahoma	AA	413	91	22	4	3	22	29	26	3	2	324	.220	.260	.315	.193	26	95-OF 95	
1998	Oklahoma	PCL	398	91	15	3	10	29	34	36	5	2	309	.229	.281	.357	.220	35	86-OF 100	14-1B 79
1999	*Texas*	*AL*	*414*	*103*	*21*	*2*	*9*	*31*	*41*	*42*	*4*	*2*	*313*	*.249*	*.301*	*.374*	*.227*	*39*		

His first major league hit, in 1997, was an inside-the-park homer. Sagmoen won't be in professional baseball for too many more years, but with a memory like that he won't walk away empty-handed.

Rob Sasser   3B   Bats R   Age 24

YEAR	TEAM	LGE	AB	H	DB	TP	HR	BB	R	RBI	SB	CS	OUT	BA	OBA	SA	EQA	EQR	DEFENSE	
1996	Macon	SAL	476	107	20	1	7	48	48	35	15	5	374	.225	.296	.315	.218	41	108-3B 94	21-1B 116
1997	CedarRpd	Mid	499	109	12	1	12	50	47	39	17	8	398	.218	.290	.319	.215	43	130-3B 112	
1998	Tulsa	Tex	413	95	14	1	6	49	43	32	11	8	326	.230	.312	.312	.221	37	110-3B 103	
1999	*Texas*	*AL*	*465*	*116*	*18*	*1*	*10*	*47*	*54*	*46*	*14*	*7*	*356*	*.249*	*.318*	*.357*	*.232*	*46*		

Sasser is arguably the Rangers' best third base prospect, which shows just how barren the organization has become at the position. It makes the trades of Tatis and Santos that much more questionable.

Tom Sergio   2B   Bats L   Age 24

YEAR	TEAM	LGE	AB	H	DB	TP	HR	BB	R	RBI	SB	CS	OUT	BA	OBA	SA	EQA	EQR	DEFENSE
1997	Pulaski	App	225	37	3	0	3	20	9	7	6	3	191	.164	.233	.218	.142	7	55-2B 95
1998	Charlott	Fla	453	111	19	3	4	37	46	35	14	6	348	.245	.302	.327	.222	40	108-2B 89
1998	Tulsa	Tex	39	8	2	0	0	3	2	2	0	0	31	.205	.262	.256	.171	2	
1999	*Texas*	*AL*	*370*	*93*	*16*	*2*	*3*	*28*	*38*	*30*	*11*	*4*	*281*	*.251*	*.304*	*.330*	*.218*	*31*	

Sergio is arguably the Rangers' best second base prospect, which just shows how barren the organization has become at that position. It makes the trade of Morris that much more questionable. Actually, the situation is not quite as dire at second base as it is at third, but that's only because '97 first-round pick Jason Romano has been moved from there from third base.

Scott Sheldon   SS   Bats R   Age 30

YEAR	TEAM	LGE	AB	H	DB	TP	HR	BB	R	RBI	SB	CS	OUT	BA	OBA	SA	EQA	EQR	DEFENSE	
1996	Edmonton	PCL	342	84	14	1	8	35	35	35	4	2	260	.246	.316	.363	.238	36	65-SS 95	
1997	Edmonton	PCL	400	94	18	3	11	45	43	43	4	2	308	.235	.312	.377	.241	44	79-SS 99	28-2B 101
1998	Oklahoma	PCL	489	109	19	2	19	52	47	54	2	2	382	.223	.298	.387	.235	51	122-SS 96	
1999	*Texas*	*AL*	*424*	*102*	*19*	*1*	*17*	*47*	*49*	*54*	*3*	*1*	*323*	*.241*	*.316*	*.410*	*.246*	*48*		

Let me get this straight. The Rangers mortgage the future to get two months of Royce Clayton at the same time they're sitting on a shortstop who hits 29 homers and draws 62 walks at Triple-A? It's not like Sheldon can't handle the position; he's not at Clayton's level defensively, but he has a reputable glove. As good as his 1998 numbers were, they could have been better. He collapsed during the last month of the season, right after the Clayton trade. In the best possible scenario for Sheldon this year, he'll be given a chance to prove he belongs on a major league roster during spring training. He shouldn't have to. The last three years are proof enough.

Mike Simms — DH — Bats R — Age 32

YEAR	TEAM	LGE	AB	H	DB	TP	HR	BB	R	RBI	SB	CS	OUT	BA	OBA	SA	EQA	EQR	DEFENSE
1996	Tucson	PCL	63	16	0	0	5	7	6	11	0	2	49	.254	.329	.492	.266	9	
1996	Houston	NL	68	12	3	1	1	4	4	3	1	0	56	.176	.222	.294	.169	3	
1997	Texas	AL	109	27	4	0	6	9	11	15	0	1	83	.248	.305	.450	.253	13	
1998	Texas	AL	181	51	8	0	16	24	27	38	0	1	131	.282	.366	.591	.311	35	26-OF 87
1999	Texas	AL	171	45	7	0	12	20	23	31	0	1	127	.263	.340	.515	.279	26	

Definite Ken Phelps All-Star Team material. Simms tied the 33-year-old record for most home runs in fewer than 200 at-bats, but the national sports media ignored his quest and gave all the attention to those McGwire and Sosa characters. Must be another case of East Coast media bias.

Lee Stevens — DH — Bats L — Age 32

YEAR	TEAM	LGE	AB	H	DB	TP	HR	BB	R	RBI	SB	CS	OUT	BA	OBA	SA	EQA	EQR	DEFENSE	
1996	Oklahoma	AA	433	128	23	2	22	52	64	75	3	0	305	.296	.371	.510	.300	75	34-1B 91	19-OF 92
1996	Texas	AL	76	16	2	2	3	6	7	8	0	0	60	.211	.268	.408	.228	7		
1997	Texas	AL	419	124	24	2	21	23	49	68	1	3	298	.296	.333	.513	.281	62	51-1B 100	16-OF 90
1998	Texas	AL	336	84	15	4	19	32	38	52	0	2	254	.250	.315	.488	.268	47	22-1B 94	
1999	Texas	AL	389	107	19	2	20	37	51	64	1	1	283	.275	.338	.488	.274	55		

The combined 1998 numbers of the Simms/Stevens DH platoon: 530 AB, 36 HR, 55 BB, .344 OBA, and slugged .547. Not bad, and I think that can stay more or less the same in '99. I agree with the projections—Simms will come down to earth, but Stevens can improve, especially given the way he ripped the ball in the second half (.954 OPS).

Andrew Vessel — OF — Bats R — Age 24

YEAR	TEAM	LGE	AB	H	DB	TP	HR	BB	R	RBI	SB	CS	OUT	BA	OBA	SA	EQA	EQR	DEFENSE
1995	Charlott	Fla	506	127	17	1	11	27	38	46	3	10	389	.251	.289	.354	.215	42	111-OF 90
1996	Charlott	Fla	491	107	22	3	5	39	35	33	1	4	388	.218	.275	.305	.196	33	116-OF 93
1997	Tulsa	Tex	507	113	18	1	11	35	36	40	2	1	395	.223	.273	.327	.205	37	132-OF 88
1998	Tulsa	Tex	403	77	8	0	7	18	15	17	3	3	329	.191	.226	.263	.149	14	90-OF 107
1999	Texas	AL	440	100	18	1	9	26	31	35	2	2	342	.227	.270	.334	.197	30	

Once a highly regarded prize in the Rangers' system, he's had one disappointing year after another. It's the same story you've probably read a hundred times in these pages: skills trump "tools" every time.

Corey Wright — OF — Bats L — Age 19

YEAR	TEAM	LGE	AB	H	DB	TP	HR	BB	R	RBI	SB	CS	OUT	BA	OBA	SA	EQA	EQR	DEFENSE
1998	Pulaski	App	135	27	2	1	2	33	21	10	5	2	110	.200	.357	.274	.241	16	39-OF 104
1999	Texas	AL	106	27	3	1	2	26	21	12	4	2	81	.255	.402	.358	.274	16	

Unheralded 12th-round draft pick out of a California high school. Why is he here, instead of the back of the book with the other one-liners? Only because I was awed by his walk totals and translated OBP. Yeah, it's 178 plate appearances in rookie ball, and it doesn't mean anything. But if he goes on to become the next Ted Williams, or even the next Warren Newson, remember you read about him here first.

Todd Zeile — 3B — Bats R — Age 33

YEAR	TEAM	LGE	AB	H	DB	TP	HR	BB	R	RBI	SB	CS	OUT	BA	OBA	SA	EQA	EQR	DEFENSE	
1996	Philadel	NL	502	135	20	0	22	69	66	74	1	1	368	.269	.357	.440	.277	74	106-3B 88	26-1B 88
1996	Baltimor	AL	115	27	7	0	5	15	14	15	0	0	88	.235	.323	.426	.258	15	27-3B 101	
1997	LosAngls	NL	581	160	15	1	33	88	82	97	6	7	428	.275	.371	.475	.288	96	157-3B 92	
1998	LosAngls	NL	159	42	6	1	8	11	17	23	1	1	118	.264	.312	.465	.262	21	39-3B 74	
1998	Florida	NL	235	70	12	1	7	33	35	35	2	3	168	.298	.384	.447	.287	37	64-3B 97	
1998	Texas	AL	175	43	12	1	6	28	25	23	1	0	132	.246	.350	.429	.272	25	51-3B 102	
1999	Texas	AL	566	149	19	1	26	78	76	86	3	3	420	.263	.352	.438	.268	78		

Yet another reason the late-season Ranger prospect purge was lunacy: Tatis played much better down the stretch for St. Louis than Zeile did for Texas. Zeile is an OK player for a guy who bounces around as much as he does; Texas is his seventh team in four years. He declined his right to demand a trade, so he'll be back in a Rangers uniform in '99. It's a good thing, given the aforementioned dearth of third base prospects in the organization.

Michael Zywica   OF   Bats R   Age 23

YEAR	TEAM	LGE	AB	H	DB	TP	HR	BB	R	RBI	SB	CS	OUT	BA	OBA	SA	EQA	EQR	DEFENSE
1996	Charl-SC	SAL	69	10	1	0	2	5	2	2	1	1	60	.145	.203	.246	.129	2	19-OF 99
1997	Charlott	Fla	468	112	17	2	12	44	46	45	10	10	366	.239	.305	.361	.229	46	110-OF 93
1998	Charlott	Fla	252	87	14	1	9	28	44	43	8	3	168	.345	.411	.516	.318	48	61-OF 90
1998	Tulsa	Tex	211	51	10	2	4	16	22	19	5	2	162	.242	.295	.365	.230	21	50-OF 102
1999	*Texas*	*AL*	*409*	*114*	*18*	*1*	*12*	*37*	*52*	*52*	*9*	*6*	*301*	*.279*	*.339*	*.416*	*.255*	*49*	

Sing along with me: one of these lines is not like the others.... As with Dransfeldt, I'd caution against reading too much into Zywica's tearing up A-ball in his second year there. However, also as with Dransfeldt, Zywica ripped the ball in the Arizona Fall League.

PITCHERS (Averages: 4.00 ERA, 9.00 H/9, 1.00 HR/9, 3.00 BB/9, 6.00 K/9, 1.00 KWH)

Scott Bailes   Throws L   Age 36

YEAR	TEAM	LGE	IP	H	ER	HR	BB	K	ERA	W	L	H/9	HR/9	BB/9	K/9	KWH	PERA
1997	Oklahoma	AmA	42.3	55	24	5	14	29	5.10	2	3	11.69	1.06	2.98	6.17	0.82	5.31
1997	Texas	AL	22.7	18	7	2	8	14	2.78	2	1	7.15	0.79	3.18	5.56	1.02	2.78
1998	Texas	AL	43.3	58	25	5	10	30	5.19	2	3	12.05	1.04	2.08	6.23	1.16	5.40

Bailes actually pitched quite well through the middle of June, but after that he was a disaster (10.00 ERA). Right-handed batters hit .400 off of him, and even left-handed hitters hit .300. Even with all that bad news, I know better than to pronounce a left-handed reliever's career to be over.

Joaquin Benoit   Throws R   Age 19

YEAR	TEAM	LGE	IP	H	ER	HR	BB	K	ERA	W	L	H/9	HR/9	BB/9	K/9	KWH	PERA
1998	Savannah	SAL	74.3	104	49	10	22	42	5.93	3	5	12.59	1.21	2.66	5.09	0.58	5.81

Recruited by the Rangers' Latin network, Benoit attracted attention by rolling through the Dominican Summer League and the Gulf Coast League during '96 and '97. His first full season of pro ball was cut short by a shoulder injury, but the strikeout and walk rates he had pre-injury were promising. Worth watching next year.

John Burkett   Throws R   Age 34

YEAR	TEAM	LGE	IP	H	ER	HR	BB	K	ERA	W	L	H/9	HR/9	BB/9	K/9	KWH	PERA
1996	Florida	NL	155.0	160	75	15	40	97	4.35	8	9	9.29	0.87	2.32	5.63	1.10	3.77
1996	Texas	AL	71.7	68	23	3	13	47	2.89	5	3	8.54	0.38	1.63	5.90	1.87	2.89
1997	Texas	AL	198.0	225	82	18	25	135	3.73	12	10	10.23	0.82	1.14	6.14	2.43	4.05
1998	Texas	AL	207.0	215	99	17	41	129	4.30	11	12	9.35	0.74	1.78	5.61	1.42	3.61

Prior to '98, could have been nicknamed "Mr. Average." From 1993 to 1997, Burkett made at least 30 starts each year, and his Support Neutral Winning Percentage ranged from a low of .504 to a high of .559. Last year all that changed, as he gave up the most earned runs in the league and had the highest ERA in Ranger history. What happened? I don't know. But here are a couple of reasons why I think he'll bounce back this year: his ERA was much higher than you'd expect from his peripheral stats, and he was a lot better after the All-Star break.

Tim Crabtree   Throws R   Age 29

YEAR	TEAM	LGE	IP	H	ER	HR	BB	K	ERA	W	L	H/9	HR/9	BB/9	K/9	KWH	PERA
1996	Toronto	AL	69.0	55	19	3	18	57	2.48	6	2	7.17	0.39	2.35	7.43	2.46	2.22
1997	Toronto	AL	42.3	64	27	7	15	25	5.74	2	3	13.61	1.49	3.19	5.31	0.49	6.59
1998	Texas	AL	90.7	81	30	3	31	59	2.98	6	4	8.04	0.30	3.08	5.86	1.04	2.88

Brought over from the Blue Jays in exchange for adequate catching prospect Kevin Brown. That's looking like a great deal for the Rangers. After a one-year detour due to elbow problems, Crabtree not only bounced back to his previous effectiveness, but he did it while handling a heavy workload. Health is still a concern for him; he's been on the disabled list three times over his last 365 professional innings.

Douglas Davis   Throws L   Age 23

YEAR	TEAM	LGE	IP	H	ER	HR	BB	K	ERA	W	L	H/9	HR/9	BB/9	K/9	KWH	PERA
1997	Charlott	Fla	46.0	42	23	3	36	39	4.50	2	3	8.22	0.59	7.04	7.63	0.75	3.91
1998	Charlott	Fla	144.3	171	82	10	83	124	5.11	6	10	10.66	0.62	5.18	7.73	0.81	4.74

Davis moved up the list of Ranger pitching prospects with his first full year at high A-ball. He led the Florida State League in strikeouts and was seventh in ERA. Unfortunately, he was also fourth in walks. If he can continue improving that control this year at Double-A, the pitching-starved Rangers will start salivating.

R.A. Dickey   Throws R   Age 24

YEAR	TEAM	LGE	IP	H	ER	HR	BB	K	ERA	W	L	H/9	HR/9	BB/9	K/9	KWH	PERA
1997	Charlott	Fla	31.7	68	38	10	14	24	10.80	0	4	19.33	2.84	3.98	6.82	0.45	10.52
1998	Charlott	Fla	53.3	82	40	11	26	36	6.75	2	4	13.84	1.86	4.39	6.08	0.46	7.26

A 1996 first-round draft pick, Dickey couldn't stay healthy in two years as a pro starter, so they converted him to closer for '98. The result? Not only did Dickey stay healthy, but he tied the Florida State League record for saves in a season with 38. The above translations reflect that Dickey was too old to still be at A-ball, but he did have a good season. If his serious injuries are behind him, he still has a shot of working his way up to the bigs.

Tony Fossas   Throws L   Age 41

YEAR	TEAM	LGE	IP	H	ER	HR	BB	K	ERA	W	L	H/9	HR/9	BB/9	K/9	KWH	PERA
1996	St Louis	NL	47.0	48	19	8	20	32	3.64	3	2	9.19	1.53	3.83	6.13	0.80	4.40
1997	St Louis	NL	52.7	66	30	8	23	37	5.13	2	4	11.28	1.37	3.93	6.32	0.68	5.47
1998	Seattle	AL	12.0	18	9	1	6	10	6.75	0	1	13.50	0.75	4.50	7.50	0.69	6.00
1998	ChiCubs	NL	4.0	10	4	0	6	6	9.00	0	0	22.50	0.00	13.50	13.50	0.45	9.00
1998	Texas	AL	7.7	3	0	0	3	7	0.00	1	0	3.52	0.00	3.52	8.22	4.08	0.00

Released by two teams, and still came back for more. Fossas walked 22 batters in 34.1 professional innings, at age 40, and still might find work in '99. Memo to U.S. policymakers: the surest route to full employment in this country is to teach our children to throw left-handed.

Ryan Glynn   Throws R   Age 24

YEAR	TEAM	LGE	IP	H	ER	HR	BB	K	ERA	W	L	H/9	HR/9	BB/9	K/9	KWH	PERA
1996	Charl-SC	SAL	107.3	183	98	15	70	43	8.22	2	10	15.34	1.26	5.87	3.61	0.11	7.38
1997	Charlott	Fla	122.3	199	101	17	51	71	7.43	3	11	14.64	1.25	3.75	5.22	0.37	6.92
1998	Tulsa	Tex	144.0	176	75	13	65	85	4.69	7	9	11.00	0.81	4.06	5.31	0.47	4.87

His stock rose more than any other pitcher in the Ranger farm system last year. Glynn added a slider to complete a four-pitch repertoire, and the new pitch made him much more effective at getting groundballs and dramatically lowered his hit and home run rates. He finished third in the Texas League in ERA and was a league All-Star. He's still not a stellar prospect to be sure, but last year moves him even with or ahead of Lee, Knight, and Kolb.

Eric Gunderson   Throws L   Age 33

YEAR	TEAM	LGE	IP	H	ER	HR	BB	K	ERA	W	L	H/9	HR/9	BB/9	K/9	KWH	PERA
1996	Pawtuckt	Int	33.0	44	15	2	10	27	4.09	2	2	12.00	0.55	2.73	7.36	1.24	4.91
1996	Boston	AL	18.7	19	12	5	6	7	5.79	1	1	9.16	2.41	2.89	3.38	0.32	4.82
1997	Texas	AL	51.7	42	14	5	13	30	2.44	4	2	7.32	0.87	2.26	5.23	1.24	2.61
1998	Texas	AL	72.3	83	33	12	17	40	4.11	4	4	10.33	1.49	2.12	4.98	0.85	4.85

Another year, another late season collapse. Gunderson's career ERA from Opening Day through July: 3.31; August through October: 9.29. He's up to 212 career innings now, so it's getting less and less likely that the split is a small sample-size fluke. Last year's split was 2.91/10.98. Does he lack the stamina to throw a full season?

Rick Helling   Throws R   Age 28

YEAR	TEAM	LGE	IP	H	ER	HR	BB	K	ERA	W	L	H/9	HR/9	BB/9	K/9	KWH	PERA
1996	Oklahoma	AmA	138.0	148	59	9	45	127	3.85	8	7	9.65	0.59	2.93	8.28	1.82	3.85
1996	Texas	AL	21.3	22	12	6	7	16	5.06	1	1	9.28	2.53	2.95	6.75	1.25	5.06
1996	Florida	NL	27.3	15	5	2	7	23	1.65	3	0	4.94	0.66	2.30	7.57	3.78	0.99
1997	Florida	NL	77.3	64	34	13	44	47	3.96	5	4	7.45	1.51	5.12	5.47	0.59	3.61
1997	Texas	AL	57.0	45	22	5	18	45	3.47	3	3	7.11	0.79	2.84	7.11	1.87	2.53
1998	Texas	AL	228.7	195	81	24	71	161	3.19	15	10	7.67	0.94	2.79	6.34	1.40	2.99

It'd be nice to think that the Rangers knew exactly what they were doing when they reacquired Helling in 1997, getting a better-than-average workhorse who could rack up the wins with a powerhouse offense behind him. It would also be nice to think a pint of Haagen-Dazs a day isn't bad for you. In truth, the Rangers left Helling exposed in the first round of the Expansion Draft. The Diamondbacks took Edwin Diaz, and the Rangers got a 20-game winner. You don't always have to be smart to look good next to some management teams.

Xavier Hernandez   Throws R   Age 33

YEAR	TEAM	LGE	IP	H	ER	HR	BB	K	ERA	W	L	H/9	HR/9	BB/9	K/9	KWH	PERA
1996	Houston	NL	75.3	73	35	11	24	70	4.18	4	4	8.72	1.31	2.87	8.36	2.10	3.82
1997	Texas	AL	52.0	48	21	7	19	35	3.63	3	3	8.31	1.21	3.29	6.06	1.01	3.63
1998	Texas	AL	61.3	40	20	5	27	40	2.93	5	2	5.87	0.73	3.96	5.87	1.11	2.05

Last year we called him "a complete question mark at this point." That question has been answered. He came back from 1997's season-ending shoulder surgery and had his best season since his first stint with the Astros. The new question is how long that shoulder, and the rest of his injury-prone body, will allow him to keep pitching like this.

Jonathan Johnson   Throws R   Age 24

YEAR	TEAM	LGE	IP	H	ER	HR	BB	K	ERA	W	L	H/9	HR/9	BB/9	K/9	KWH	PERA
1996	Tulsa	Tex	165.7	207	92	17	43	85	5.00	7	11	11.25	0.92	2.34	4.62	0.61	4.84
1997	Tulsa	Tex	69.0	76	32	3	14	39	4.17	4	4	9.91	0.39	1.83	5.09	1.07	3.65
1997	Oklahoma	AmA	60.0	92	52	6	29	29	7.80	1	6	13.80	0.90	4.35	4.35	0.24	6.30
1998	Oklahoma	PCL	108.3	118	61	14	30	77	5.07	5	7	9.80	1.16	2.49	6.40	1.26	4.32

The second time was the charm for Johnson at Triple-A. After bombing with the 89ers in '97, Johnson returned to the newly renamed Oklahoma Redhawks in '98 and pitched moderately well. He even improved the strikeout rate that we complained about last year. He should compete with Perisho for a rotation spot, but his chances of major league success in 1999 are slim.

Brandon Knight   Throws R   Age 23

YEAR	TEAM	LGE	IP	H	ER	HR	BB	K	ERA	W	L	H/9	HR/9	BB/9	K/9	KWH	PERA
1996	HudsnVal	NYP	47.7	88	39	2	24	32	7.36	1	4	16.62	0.38	4.53	6.04	0.36	6.80
1996	Charlott	Fla	91.0	167	87	15	50	59	8.60	2	8	16.52	1.48	4.95	5.84	0.31	8.01
1997	Charlott	Fla	86.3	109	41	12	24	68	4.27	5	5	11.36	1.25	2.50	7.09	1.33	5.21
1997	Tulsa	Tex	86.3	92	48	13	35	70	5.00	4	6	9.59	1.36	3.65	7.30	1.14	4.48
1998	Tulsa	Tex	79.7	114	56	11	36	68	6.33	3	6	12.88	1.24	4.07	7.68	0.84	6.10
1998	Oklahoma	PCL	62.3	107	68	15	28	43	9.82	1	6	15.45	2.17	4.04	6.21	0.46	8.23

Prior to 1998, Knight was clearly the most highly regarded Ranger pitching prospect. He hit a big snag last year, was a complete bust at Triple-A, and even took a step backward at Double-A. He is still young and still has a rising strikeout rate. I expect him to conquer Double-A this year and continue his rise through the system.

Danny Kolb   Throws R   Age 24

YEAR	TEAM	LGE	IP	H	ER	HR	BB	K	ERA	W	L	H/9	HR/9	BB/9	K/9	KWH	PERA
1996	Charl-SC	SAL	115.7	128	71	8	69	75	5.52	4	9	9.96	0.62	5.37	5.84	0.48	4.44
1996	Charlott	Fla	34.0	54	25	2	15	22	6.62	1	3	14.29	0.53	3.97	5.82	0.45	6.09
1997	Charlott	Fla	121.3	198	114	14	71	61	8.46	2	11	14.69	1.04	5.27	4.52	0.20	6.90
1998	Tulsa	Tex	147.0	231	115	11	78	64	7.04	4	12	14.14	0.67	4.78	3.92	0.17	6.24

(Danny Kolb *continued*)

The organization's biggest flop in recent years. Two years ago he was the consensus best arm in the farm system, and a likely future major leaguer. But he stalled at high-A in '97, and fizzled further at Double-A last year. If that news wasn't bad enough, he threw an alarmingly high number of pitches for his age. A move to the bullpen could resurrect his career.

Corey Lee								**Throws L**		**Age 24**						
YEAR	TEAM	LGE	IP	H	ER	HR	BB	K	ERA	W	L	H/9	HR/9	BB/9	K/9	KWH	PERA
1996	HudsnVal	NYP	49.3	66	35	2	26	34	6.39	1	4	12.04	0.36	4.74	6.20	0.51	5.11
1997	Charlott	Fla	149.0	180	84	13	69	107	5.07	7	10	10.87	0.79	4.17	6.46	0.69	4.83
1998	Tulsa	Tex	132.3	137	88	17	104	101	5.98	5	10	9.32	1.16	7.07	6.87	0.54	4.76

Kind of an odd year for one of the Rangers' most highly regarded minor league pitchers. In most ways, he progressed nicely during his debut at Double-A. He was very tough to hit and his strikeout rate continued to rise. But his command of the strike zone suddenly went from mediocre to abysmal. Maybe it's just the Kerry Wood example overly fresh in my mind, but I'd rather have a prospect who gives up lots of walks and few hits than the other way around. If the control problems persist this year at Triple-A, it's time to worry.

Al Levine								**Throws R**		**Age 31**						
YEAR	TEAM	LGE	IP	H	ER	HR	BB	K	ERA	W	L	H/9	HR/9	BB/9	K/9	KWH	PERA
1996	Nashvill	AmA	58.7	74	33	4	29	36	5.06	3	4	11.35	0.61	4.45	5.52	0.45	4.91
1996	ChiSox	AL	18.3	21	11	1	6	12	5.40	1	1	10.31	0.49	2.95	5.89	0.86	3.93
1997	Nashvill	AmA	35.7	67	35	3	12	23	8.83	1	3	16.91	0.76	3.03	5.80	0.49	7.32
1997	ChiSox	AL	28.0	35	18	4	14	21	5.79	1	2	11.25	1.29	4.50	6.75	0.67	5.46
1998	Oklahoma	PCL	48.7	63	37	7	18	22	6.84	1	4	11.65	1.29	3.33	4.07	0.32	5.55
1998	Texas	AL	61.3	64	23	5	14	19	3.38	4	3	9.39	0.73	2.05	2.79	0.30	3.67

Acquired from the White Sox for Benji Gil, Levine bounced up and down between Arlington and Oklahoma City all year. He surprised the Rangers by giving them 60 quality innings, exceeding anything he had shown previously in the majors or the minors. He did it despite, or perhaps because of, a dramatic drop in strikeouts. Could be used similarly in 1999.

Esteban Loaiza								**Throws R**		**Age 27**						
YEAR	TEAM	LGE	IP	H	ER	HR	BB	K	ERA	W	L	H/9	HR/9	BB/9	K/9	KWH	PERA
1996	Calgary	PCL	68.0	64	30	5	25	32	3.97	4	4	8.47	0.66	3.31	4.24	0.48	3.31
1996	Pittsbrg	NL	54.3	68	28	11	18	29	4.64	3	3	11.26	1.82	2.98	4.80	0.52	5.63
1997	Pittsbrg	NL	205.3	204	76	17	50	109	3.33	14	9	8.94	0.75	2.19	4.78	0.87	3.46
1998	Pittsbrg	NL	94.0	99	44	13	28	49	4.21	5	5	9.48	1.24	2.68	4.69	0.65	4.21
1998	Texas	AL	84.7	97	43	14	20	54	4.57	4	5	10.31	1.49	2.13	5.74	1.13	4.78

After what appeared to be a breakthrough year in 1997, Loaiza once again couldn't produce results to match his stuff in 1998. When the Pirates saw what the desperate Rangers were willing to give for any pitcher with a pulse, they got rid of him in a heartbeat. It's conceivable he'll find the '97 magic and be next year's Aaron Sele, but the price for getting to find out (Warren Morris) was a little too high.

Eric Moody								**Throws R**		**Age 28**						
YEAR	TEAM	LGE	IP	H	ER	HR	BB	K	ERA	W	L	H/9	HR/9	BB/9	K/9	KWH	PERA
1996	Tulsa	Tex	87.3	120	52	5	28	62	5.36	4	6	12.37	0.52	2.89	6.39	0.86	5.15
1997	Oklahoma	AmA	109.7	135	53	12	23	56	4.35	5	7	11.08	0.98	1.89	4.60	0.76	4.76
1997	Texas	AL	20.0	24	8	4	2	12	3.60	1	1	10.80	1.80	0.90	5.40	2.25	4.95
1998	Oklahoma	PCL	94.3	131	55	8	24	54	5.25	4	6	12.50	0.76	2.29	5.15	0.70	5.34

Once again the Rangers jerked Moody back and forth between the bullpen and the rotation. He made six starts for the Redhawks, but also recorded a team-leading 12 saves. He's 28 and his numbers have flattened out, suggesting that this is as good as he's going to get.

Jimmy Myers — Throws R — Age 30

YEAR	TEAM	LGE	IP	H	ER	HR	BB	K	ERA	W	L	H/9	HR/9	BB/9	K/9	KWH	PERA
1996	Rochestr	Int	51.7	60	19	1	13	16	3.31	4	2	10.45	0.17	2.26	2.79	0.25	3.83
1996	Baltimor	AL	13.7	18	10	3	3	6	6.59	1	1	11.85	1.98	1.98	3.95	0.50	5.93
1997	Norfolk	Int	67.0	68	24	1	33	23	3.22	4	3	9.13	0.13	4.43	3.09	0.18	3.49
1998	Oklahoma	PCL	58.0	66	22	4	21	18	3.41	3	3	10.24	0.62	3.26	2.79	0.18	4.19

Pitched effectively at Triple-A for the fourth consecutive year. Scouts don't like him, and PERA doesn't either for the same reason: he throws junk and doesn't strike guys out, but he seems to know how to prevent runs. It's a shame that a guy like this can't get a shot.

Danny Patterson — Throws R — Age 28

YEAR	TEAM	LGE	IP	H	ER	HR	BB	K	ERA	W	L	H/9	HR/9	BB/9	K/9	KWH	PERA
1996	Oklahoma	AmA	79.0	94	24	5	18	43	2.73	6	3	10.71	0.57	2.05	4.90	0.82	4.22
1997	Texas	AL	74.3	66	22	3	20	67	2.66	6	2	7.99	0.36	2.42	8.11	2.55	2.78
1998	Texas	AL	64.3	60	23	10	17	32	3.22	4	3	8.39	1.40	2.38	4.48	0.75	3.64

A second straight solid year in the majors by Patterson, although his peripheral numbers were not nearly so good this time around. His strikeout rate was nothing special, but that shouldn't be surprising; the 1997 number was way out of line with anything he'd done previously. More troubling were the 11 home runs he gave up—not a good sign for an extreme ground-ball pitcher.

Roger Pavlik — Throws R — Age 31

YEAR	TEAM	LGE	IP	H	ER	HR	BB	K	ERA	W	L	H/9	HR/9	BB/9	K/9	KWH	PERA
1996	Texas	AL	211.0	200	86	23	66	127	3.67	12	11	8.53	0.98	2.82	5.42	0.92	3.50
1997	Texas	AL	60.7	56	22	7	27	34	3.26	4	3	8.31	1.04	4.01	5.04	0.57	3.71
1998	Texas	AL	14.7	16	6	2	4	8	3.68	1	1	9.82	1.23	2.45	4.91	0.75	4.30

Missed the bulk of the season for the second straight year, this time with a fractured finger and a shoulder tear. When healthy, he has always been a better-than-average starter. Now a free agent.

Matt Perisho — Throws L — Age 24

YEAR	TEAM	LGE	IP	H	ER	HR	BB	K	ERA	W	L	H/9	HR/9	BB/9	K/9	KWH	PERA
1996	Lk Elsin	Cal	121.0	155	69	10	53	66	5.13	5	8	11.53	0.74	3.94	4.91	0.40	5.06
1996	Midland	Tex	55.0	49	18	4	21	45	2.95	4	2	8.02	0.65	3.44	7.36	1.48	3.11
1997	Midland	Tex	73.0	63	22	5	26	52	2.71	5	3	7.77	0.62	3.21	6.41	1.24	2.96
1997	Vancouvr	PCL	48.7	71	37	3	25	38	6.84	1	4	13.13	0.55	4.62	7.03	0.61	5.73
1997	Anaheim	AL	47.3	59	28	6	25	34	5.32	2	3	11.22	1.14	4.75	6.46	0.59	5.32
1998	Oklahoma	PCL	87.3	98	38	6	41	49	3.92	5	5	10.10	0.62	4.23	5.05	0.45	4.33

Perisho bombed in his first two shots at the majors, giving up 51 runs in 50 innings. But he had a nice season at Triple-A, so he'll be back. He'll almost certainly compete for the fifth starter job in spring training. If he wins it, I suspect he'll struggle, at least at first. Two worrisome characteristics of his 1998: his walk rate stayed high, while his strikeout rate took a dive.

Aaron Sele — Throws R — Age 29

YEAR	TEAM	LGE	IP	H	ER	HR	BB	K	ERA	W	L	H/9	HR/9	BB/9	K/9	KWH	PERA
1996	Boston	AL	167.3	174	78	12	55	137	4.20	9	10	9.36	0.65	2.96	7.37	1.47	3.76
1997	Boston	AL	185.0	189	92	23	70	119	4.48	9	12	9.19	1.12	3.41	5.79	0.80	4.09
1998	Texas	AL	227.7	222	86	12	77	165	3.40	15	10	8.78	0.47	3.04	6.52	1.19	3.36

Sele finally rediscovered the form that made him such a promising pitcher in the early 90's. In fact, all of the '98 rate stats above are nearly identical to those from his last good year with Boston, 1994. Even with the good season, I'm not confident about his becoming/remaining a star. The curve is his bread-and-butter pitch, but he still can't throw it consistently for strikes.

Todd Stottlemyre   Throws R   Age 34

YEAR	TEAM	LGE	IP	H	ER	HR	BB	K	ERA	W	L	H/9	HR/9	BB/9	K/9	KWH	PERA
1996	St Louis	NL	223.3	212	97	31	89	175	3.91	13	12	8.54	1.25	3.59	7.05	1.22	3.83
1997	St Louis	NL	182.3	162	78	17	59	143	3.85	10	10	8.00	0.84	2.91	7.06	1.60	3.11
1998	St Louis	NL	166.7	147	63	20	46	135	3.40	11	8	7.94	1.08	2.48	7.29	2.02	3.19
1998	Texas	AL	65.0	64	25	5	27	56	3.46	4	3	8.86	0.69	3.74	7.75	1.36	3.60

Had his third straight year of effective, improved pitching under LaRussa. He endeared himself to Rangers fans in his brief time there, mostly because he managed to have his best Texas starts in some of the year's most critical games. Reaching the age where injuries and physical decline could start limiting his effectiveness, so he's too big a risk for a hefty multi-year contract, like the four-year deal the Diamondbacks have given him. For the short term, I wouldn't expect a big drop-off; it's hard to find rate stats more consistent than these.

John Wetteland   Throws R   Age 32

YEAR	TEAM	LGE	IP	H	ER	HR	BB	K	ERA	W	L	H/9	HR/9	BB/9	K/9	KWH	PERA
1995	NY Yanks	AL	61.3	41	18	6	11	67	2.64	5	2	6.02	0.88	1.61	9.83	7.46	1.61
1996	NY Yanks	AL	65.7	50	17	8	17	68	2.33	5	2	6.85	1.10	2.33	9.32	4.08	2.47
1997	Texas	AL	67.0	41	13	5	18	61	1.75	6	1	5.51	0.67	2.42	8.19	3.78	1.34
1998	Texas	AL	64.7	43	12	6	13	70	1.67	6	1	5.98	0.84	1.81	9.74	6.57	1.67

What can you say? Just when you thought he couldn't be more dominating, he goes out and strikes out more batters and lowers his already-minuscule ERA. Had off-season elbow surgery to remove a bone spur that bothered him during the season. If that's what he does with a bone spur, I can't wait to see what he does without it.

Jeff Zimmerman   Throws R   Age 26

YEAR	TEAM	LGE	IP	H	ER	HR	BB	K	ERA	W	L	H/9	HR/9	BB/9	K/9	KWH	PERA
1998	Charlott	Fla	13.0	15	3	1	1	9	2.08	1	0	10.38	0.69	0.69	6.23	4.05	4.15
1998	Tulsa	Tex	57.0	54	22	5	23	46	3.47	3	3	8.53	0.79	3.63	7.26	1.28	3.47

A great story, with a chance to get better. Not drafted after college, Zimmerman spent three years playing for the Canadian National Team. Then he spent a year in the independent Northern League, winning that league's top rookie pitching honor. He finally got a job in a major league system the same way the rest of us get our jobs—by sending out résumés all over North America. Absolutely dominated A ball and Double-A as a closer last year (the DTs damp his numbers a bit because of his age), and was the "Nolan Ryan Minor League Pitcher of the Year" for the Rangers organization. Once a million-to-one shot to ever make the majors, now better than even money.

SNWL				TEXAS RANGERS							Park Effect: +13.9%	
PITCHER	GS	IP	R	SNW	SNL	SNPCT	W	L	RA	APW	SNVA	SNWAR
Burkett, J.	32	195.0	131	10.8	12.5	.464	9	13	6.05	-1.51	-0.72	0.90
Gunderson, E.	1	1.7	4	0.1	0.3	.160	0	1	21.60	-0.28	-0.13	-0.11
Helling, R.	33	216.3	109	13.3	10.8	.553	20	7	4.53	1.67	1.24	3.07
Johnson, Jo	1	4.3	4	0.1	0.5	.155	0	0	8.31	-0.13	-0.22	-0.17
Loaiza, E.	14	79.3	57	4.1	6.1	.400	3	6	6.47	-0.96	-0.95	-0.25
Oliver, D.	19	103.3	84	4.4	8.6	.340	6	7	7.32	-2.15	-2.08	-1.11
Perisho, M.	2	5.0	17	0.0	1.7	.003	0	2	30.60	-1.30	-0.83	-0.73
Sele, A.	33	212.7	116	13.7	11.3	.547	19	11	4.91	0.83	1.24	3.04
Stottlemyre, T.	10	60.3	33	3.4	3.6	.484	5	4	4.92	0.23	-0.04	0.41
VanPoppel, T.	4	19.3	20	0.7	2.0	.260	1	2	9.31	-0.80	-0.67	-0.46
Witt, B.	13	68.3	62	2.7	6.5	.291	5	4	8.17	-2.01	-1.82	-1.24
TOTALS	162	965.7	637	53.3	64.1	.454	68	57	5.94	-6.40	-4.98	3.36

The 1998 Rangers earned the dubious distinction of having the worst starting pitching of any post-season qualifiers in the past seven years. The only other possible claim to that title would come from the 1994 Rangers, who were in first place when the season ended but were technically not playoff qualifiers because there were no actual playoffs. The 1998 staff was even worse than the disappointing 1997 group, dropping from 24th in the majors with a -3.9 SNVA to 26th with a -5.0 SNVA. Two big weights dragging the Rangers' numbers down were Bobby Witt and Darren Oliver. I don't know how the Rangers could have seen it coming, based on their SN numbers prior to 1998. Bobby Witt had been consistently mediocre; his SNPcts for 1993-1997 were .493, .450, .531, .473, .488. Darren Oliver did not have the long history of Witt, but he was clearly above average in each of his two full years in the majors: .556 and .521. In neither case did their run prevention performance show signs they'd be among the very worst starters in the league in 1998. Having said that, my I should mention that both pitchers were identified in BP '98 as having troubling drops in their strikeout rates. Aaron Sele was the flakiest starter in the majors last year, based on start-to-start variance of SNVA; i.e., on a given night, he was either very good or very bad. He had eight starts in which he allowed six or more runs, but he also had six starts in which he allowed no runs. As a result, he was substantially underrated by cumulative run prevention stats like ERA and Adjusted Pitching Wins. John Burkett was also one of the flakiest starters in the league, and he was similarly underrated by APW. In fact, the Rangers' staff as a whole was quite a bit better than their APW or RA suggested.

Pitcher Abuse Points

PITCHER	AGE	GS	PAP	PAP/S	AAW	MAX	115+	130+
Burkett, John	33	32	137	4.28	4.28	117	1	0
Helling, Rick	27	33	585	17.73	32.50	138	11	3
Loaiza, Esteban	26	14	100	7.14	14.29	119	2	0
Oliver, Darren	27	19	114	6.00	11.00	124	2	0
Sele, Aaron	28	33	426	12.91	21.52	126	11	0
Stottlemyre, Todd	33	10	148	14.80	14.80	129	4	0
Witt, Bobby	34	13	81	6.23	6.23	123	2	0
TOTAL		162	1592	9.83	15.80	138	33	3
RANKING (AL)			6	6	7		6	8-T

After jerking Rick Helling around for years and finally dumping him on the Marlins for almost nothing, it was almost inconceivable that the Rangers should be lucky enough to get him back for the steep price of Ed Vosberg. Thanks to those mistakes, by the time he got the opportunity to be an ace, he was old enough to handle the workload without breaking down. Helling was worked harder than I like to see, but I don't think it's terminal. Aaron Sele, despite facing an average of one more batter per start, and despite giving up more walks than Helling, had a significantly lower PAP score and appears to be only mild injury risk of. Todd Stottlemyre didn't work as hard as you would expect from a hired gun, but that's a reflection on how poorly he pitched, not how carefully Johnny Oates was looking out for his future.

Field General or Backstop?
Evaluating the Catcher's Influence on Pitcher Performance
By Keith Woolner

One of the great remaining unknowns in sabermetrics is the true defensive impact of the catcher. What few commonly available stats we do have deal with peripheral defensive responsibilities like passed balls and throwing out base stealers. Yet most knowledgeable observers believe that the aspect of the catcher's job that has the most impact is his game-calling: his ability to work with pitchers and help them throw more effectively. The cumulative effect of game-calling is potentially huge. For example, a catcher who catches 130 games a year and who may reduce the ERAs of his pitchers by just a quarter of a run (0.25) is worth 32.5 runs defensively—a figure that ranks up there with the top shortstops and outfielders in the league. Yet there have been no satisfyingly thorough attempts to quantify this presumably crucial aspect of run prevention.

Currently, the most common way to evaluate game-calling in the majors is expert evaluation—in other words, managers' and coaches' opinions and assessments. Ultimately, this approach is contrary to the spirit of sabermetric investigation, which is to find objective (not subjective) knowledge about baseball. What we'd like to discover is a sensible, objective measure that can be used to compare to expert evaluation.

The most comprehensive previously published sabermetric study on the topic is Craig Wright's "Catcher's ERA" (or CERA) in his fine book The Diamond Appraised. In it, he develops a process where catchers on the same team can be compared by how well a common set of pitchers perform with each catcher. Wright uses a technique called "matched innings" to control for the differences in how often a catcher worked with each pitcher. The results were labeled Catcher's ERA, and can be used to draw intrateam comparisons among catchers. STATS has gone on to publish CERA in their Major League Handbook, though it appears that they have not used the matched innings to normalize for opportunities, but rather produce a raw report of the team's ERA when that catcher is behind the plate. This makes it less useful for the kind of comparisons Wright investigated.

Unfortunately, CERA, even as envisioned by Wright, has several limitations. The first is a problem of sample size. In small numbers of innings, or particularly with backup catchers, wide fluctuations are expected. Wright himself admitted this. However, there's little attempt to quantify the amount of natural variation that would be present even if no true game-calling ability was present. Therefore, it's impossible to tell how much of the variation should be attributed to simple chance, and how much of it lies with a catcher's actual ability. The other problem is that Wright doesn't systematically check whether game-calling ability correlates from year to year (that is whether good/bad CERA tends to stick around from year to year, as opposed to being random). A true ability should manifest itself as good (or bad) players tending to stay good or bad from year to year. That's not to say that you won't see some players flip-flop, but overall the tendency should be that good catchers should be expected to continue being good the next season, and so on. Wright does use some anecdotal examples to show that Rick Demspey, Mike Macfarlane, and Doug Gwodsz were good defensive catchers, Geno Petralli and Jamie Quirk were poor defensive cathers, and so on. However, without a comprehensive analysis (which was not provided in The Diamond Appraised), it's impossible to tell whether these examples are selected because they serve to make CERA look good, or whether they are truly representative of a larger phenomenon.

Isolating Game-Calling

For the purposes of the following study, I was most interested in isolating a catcher's game-calling ability, separate from other parts of his defensive responsibilities. I wanted to determine whether a catcher influences the rates of hits, walks, and extra bases a pitcher surrenders to the opposition. This is more focused but more limited than CERA, which incorporates all factors that contribute to run scoring (since it directly measures runs). On the other hand, CERA suffers from the same discrepancies in separating earned runs from unearned runs as basic ERA does.

I'm not trying to measure his ability to control the running game, or throw out base stealers. Nor am I trying to quantify his ability to block the plate and prevent passed balls and wild pitches. By looking solely at the outcomes of batter plate appearances, we can see how well the catcher affected the batting performance of his opponents relative to the other catchers working with the same pitcher.

Once we've isolated game-calling, there are two main questions that we must answer before deciding whether we've discovered a measurable ability:

1. Do the differences in game-calling among catchers vary from what we'd expect solely from chance?
2. Do we see stability from year to year in game-calling. Do good catchers tend to stay good from one season to the next, and do bad catchers stay bad?

If neither of these conditions exist, then it's likely that any differences in CERA or game-calling are the result of random chance, and are not indicative of an actual skill possessed by the catcher.

Data Collection

For this study, I used data from the play-by-play database available from Retrosheet (for 1981-83), and licensed from the Baseball Workshop (now part of Total Sports) for the years 1984-97. This in-depth data includes the complete defensive roster on the field for every plate appearance in every game for the entire season, making it very easy to create aggregate splits for each battery. With 17 years of data collected, concerns about sample size or single-season flukes can be mitigated.

For each catcher, I looked at all pitchers with whom he caught at least 100 plate appearances, and generated totals for the pitcher both with and without the catcher. This gave me a sample set of 6347 battery-seasons spanning 17 years to work with, and included a broad and robust base of different kinds of pitchers and catchers. For example, see table 1.

"EstPA" refers to the number of plate appearances as estimated solely from at-bats, hits, and bases on balls. It does not include hit-by-pitches, sacrifices, catcher's interference, and so on. The significance of this figure will become relevant later on. After this section, I use PA and EstPA interchangeably to mean the total of hits, outs, and walks (excluding the minor events just mentioned).

To put that in more familiar statistical terms, Hentgen+ Santiago gave up an AVG/OBP/SLG of .246/.300/.378 over 621 batters faced. Hentgen with all other Blue Jay catchers combined to allow.266/.310/.440 over 445 batters. In this case Charlie O'Brien caught all the games with Hentgen that Santiago didn't, but generally speaking the "without" column includes totals from more than one catcher.

Is the difference between the 678 OPS (On-base Plus Slugging) and the 750 OPS with O'Brien enough to conclude that Santiago was the better game-caller for Hentgen? Or is it within the range of what you'd expect from chance when splitting Hentgen's 1066 total batters faced in these proportions?

Investigating the Differences

The details of the calculation are explained in the appendix, but I'll state it briefly here. For each set of data, I computed the average run value of each plate appearance using Thorn and Palmer's Linear Weights system. This yields a rate value I call Pitching Runs per Plate Appearances (PR/PA). The difference between the PR/PA in each subset of PAs yields a number called Run Prevention Rate or RPR, which represents how many fewer runs the pitcher yielded per batter faced with the catcher in question. Lower numbers are better, as with ERA.

Then, I converted RPR and the number of plate appearances into a statistical Z-value. A Z-value represents how likely such a difference would be over a sample size of the number of PA's if the difference were due strictly to chance. The value represents how many standard deviations away from the expected mean (of zero difference) that data point represents. The importance of the Z-value is that it inherently takes into account the effect of small sample size.

Like RPR, I designed game-calling Z-scores to follow the same rule as ERA or CERA. Good performance gets lower numbers. In particular, a negative Z-score indicates that the catcher did better than his counterparts with that pitcher. Conversely, a positive Z-score means that a catcher did worse handling a pitcher than the other catchers on the team.

Let's take a look at some of the best and worst performances in tables 2 and 3.

A few things jump out at you: on teams where two catchers work the bulk of the games, the rating of one moves in the opposite direction of the other. So while Kirt Manwaring shined when working with Mike DeJean, turning in a +3.38 Z score, Jeff Reed (who was the only other catcher to work with DeJean in 1997) came in at -3.38. Several other examples can be found on the list above.

Note that Chad Kreuter made the top 5 twice in '97, and Brad Ausmus made the top 5 three times in 1996. Quite impressive, and if there is a game-calling ability, we have a hint that these two might be the cream of the crop. But we're getting ahead of ourselves.

The next step was to evaluate the data against the null hypothesis that all observed differences between catchers are due to chance, and not to game-calling skills. This will address the first of the two questions posed earlier, and help us determine whether game-calling exists as a measurable ability.

In many statistical analyses, data points that are not more than two standard deviations away from the mean are considered to be consistent with the null hypothesis. In other words, Z-values less than two indicate that the difference isn't different from what you'd expect from random

Table 1.

1997	w/ Catcher Santiago									W/o Catcher Santiago								
Pitcher	PA	AB	1B	2B	3B	HR	BB	Outs	EstPA	PA	AB	1B	2B	3B	HR	BB	Outs	EstPA
Hentgen	627	577	98	25	6	13	44	435	621	449	418	75	17	1	18	27	307	445

Table 2. Top 5 Catcher Splits in Each Season, 1995–97

YEAR	Pitcher	Catcher	PA	Pitcher w/ Catcher				PA	Pitcher w/o Catcher				RPR	Z-SCORE
				AVG	OBP	SLG	PR/PA		AVG	OBP	SLG	PR/PA		
1997	DeJean, Mike	Manwaring, Kirt	128	.175	.227	.275	-0.067	160	.368	.431	.535	0.093	-0.160	-3.38
1997	Mercedes, Jose	Levis, Jesse	165	.182	.212	.296	-0.069	476	.273	.345	.469	0.039	-0.107	-2.77
1997	Smiley, John	Oliver, Joe	346	.266	.292	.404	-0.003	313	.335	.396	.570	0.089	-0.092	-2.67
1997	Hill, Ken	Kreuter, Chad	146	.176	.233	.316	-0.052	674	.289	.378	.440	0.046	-0.097	-2.59
1997	Watson, Allen	Kreuter, Chad	604	.253	.316	.427	0.015	257	.340	.397	.604	0.099	-0.083	-2.50
1996	Lima, Jose	Ausmus, Brad	157	.231	.280	.320	-0.031	159	.361	.409	.707	0.133	-0.165	-3.24
1996	Lira, Felipe	Ausmus, Brad	423	.222	.288	.341	-0.021	400	.319	.370	.541	0.069	-0.090	-3.00
1996	Tewksbury, Bob	Johnson, Brian	272	.214	.243	.305	-0.053	585	.304	.344	.447	0.031	-0.084	-2.84
1996	Thompson, Mark	Reed, Jeff	392	.250	.319	.404	0.010	345	.326	.400	.557	0.086	-0.076	-2.36
1996	Keagle, Greg	Ausmus, Brad	133	.218	.301	.437	0.012	284	.339	.465	.561	0.114	-0.101	-2.20
1995	Charlton, Norm	Wilson, Dan	151	.130	.205	.188	-0.098	123	.267	.374	.362	0.024	-0.122	-2.85
1995	Fernandez, Sid	Daulton, Darren	174	.170	.241	.296	-0.053	222	.286	.360	.578	0.076	-0.129	-2.83
1995	Fernandez, Alex	LaValliere, Mike	322	.207	.252	.316	-0.045	526	.286	.350	.438	0.032	-0.077	-2.69
1995	Cone, David	Knorr, Randy	130	.149	.208	.215	-0.091	813	.241	.315	.396	0.007	-0.098	-2.55
1995	Pettitte, Andy	Leyritz, Jim	349	.246	.281	.357	-0.021	386	.298	.383	.463	0.054	-0.075	-2.50

variation and no game-calling ability. However, even under the two standard deviation rule, you still expect that about 5% of the observations would exceed plus or minus two standard deviations. So, what we are really interested in is comparing the shape of the results to the normal distribution. If the shapes match well, then the data is consistent with the no-game-calling-skill hypothesis. So let's look at the distribution of Z-scores from all 6000+ data points in Figure 1.

As you can see, the shape of the curve is pretty close to the classic bell curve of the normal distribution. A tiny bit wider and shorter, but otherwise a very good fit. The normal curve is what we'd expect if there were no game-calling ability, and if all differences in splits were due to chance alone. This is pretty good evidence that the distribution of game-

calling splits are consistent with the no-game-calling-skill hypothesis.

Now this in and of itself doesn't prove that game-calling doesn't exist. For one thing, it's possible that game-calling ability is normally distributed among major league catchers. However, one thing that a true ability would show is a tendency to persist from one season to the next. For example, we believe that a batter's ability to hit HR's is a true ability, and therefore Mark McGwire is a better bet to hit 40 HR next year than Darren Lewis. Randy Johnson should strike out more batters than Bob Tewksbury. We should be able to look at game-calling ability and see the same tendency—namely, that good game-callers stay good over time, and vice versa. This is the second question posed back at the beginning.

Table 3. Worst 5 Catcher Splits in Each Season, 1995–97

YEAR	Pitcher	Catcher	PA	Pitcher w/ Catcher				PA	Pitcher w/o Catcher				RPR	Z-SCORE
				AVG	OBP	SLG	PR/PA		AVG	OBP	SLG	PR/PA		
1997	Burba, Dave	Taubensee, Eddie	193	.296	.383	.586	0.087	495	.240	.315	.370	-0.001	0.088	2.44
1997	Bergman, Sean	Flaherty, John	295	.357	.414	.576	0.097	142	.231	.296	.346	-0.016	0.114	2.56
1997	Burkett, John	Rodriguez, Ivan	714	.326	.350	.465	0.039	99	.168	.202	.253	-0.085	0.124	2.77
1997	Mercedes, Jose	Matheny, Mike	420	.284	.357	.488	0.050	221	.185	.222	.303	-0.062	0.111	3.13
1997	DeJean, Mike	Reed, Jeff	160	.368	.431	.535	0.093	128	.175	.227	.275	-0.067	0.160	3.38
1996	Paniagua, Jose	Fletcher, Darrin	107	.351	.430	.606	0.112	111	.218	.288	.287	-0.035	0.148	2.61
1996	Valdes, Ismael	Prince, Tom	111	.333	.369	.590	0.084	817	.239	.284	.343	-0.023	0.107	2.66
1996	Peters, Chris	Kendall, Jason	123	.389	.463	.611	0.127	153	.210	.261	.392	-0.018	0.145	2.74
1996	Hamilton, Joey	Flaherty, John	208	.319	.404	.500	0.072	680	.238	.301	.340	-0.016	0.088	2.80
1996	Grimsley, Jason	Slaught, Don	152	.381	.487	.603	0.134	446	.256	.336	.389	0.014	0.120	3.08
1995	Cone, David	Parrish, Lance	335	.282	.337	.460	0.033	608	.198	.280	.321	-0.029	0.062	2.24
1995	Bielecki, Mike	Fabregas, Jorge	185	.313	.384	.578	0.086	139	.220	.288	.315	-0.028	0.114	2.29
1995	Nitkowski, C. J.	Flaherty, John	138	.390	.457	.683	0.144	189	.272	.349	.426	0.029	0.115	2.31
1995	Pettitte, Andy	Stanley, Mike	386	.298	.383	.463	0.054	349	.246	.281	.357	-0.021	0.075	2.50
1995	Anderson, Brian	Myers, Greg	151	.345	.397	.813	0.158	269	.247	.297	.367	-0.011	0.169	3.54

Field General or Backstop?

Figure 1. Normalized Pitcher-Catcher Splits

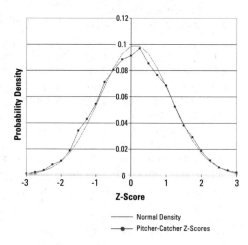

Figure 2. Year-to-Year Trends in SO Rates

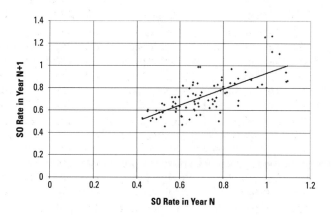

Figure 3. Year-to-Year Trend in HR Rate

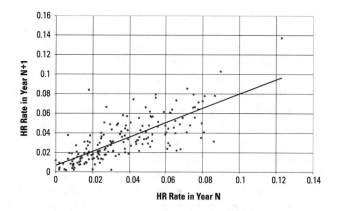

Do the Hot Stay Hot While the Cold Stay Cold?

One way to measure the tendency is to look at the correlation between one year's rate of production and the following year's. Correlation is a comparison between two sets of numbers, in our case game-calling Z-scores in a year (year 1, or N), and the following year (year 2, or N +1). Correlation values range from -1 to +1. A positive correlation means that a high value in one year tends to be followed by a similarly high value the next year. A negative value means that a high value in one year tends to be followed by a low value the following year. Values near zero indicate that there's no relationship between the value in one year and the value the following year. We expect that at true ability should have a significant positive correlation. Indeed, when we look at the correlation in year-to-year home run rates for players with more than 300 AB between 1996 and 1997, the correlation is +0.76. For pitchers with at least 100 IP, the correlation in year-to-year strikeout rates is +0.71.

However, when we look at the year-to-year correlation for catchers working with the same pitchers, the correlation is only +0.02. That's essentially zero, for all practical intents. How well a catcher worked with a pitcher this year tells you nothing about how they'll work together next year, relative to the other catchers on the club. Nothing. Never mind changes in pitching staff—a catcher doesn't even maintain a relative level of performance with the same pitchers.

A couple of charts may help illustrate the point of the preceding paragraphs more clearly. A geometric interpretation of correlation is the degree to which you can fit a straight line through the data points, if you plot them on a graph with X values coming from the first series, and the Y values coming from the other series, see figures 2 and 3.

The charts in figures 2 and 3, which represent year-to-

year trends in home run (HR) rate for hitters and strikeout (SO) rate for pitchers show a mostly linear trend. There's a lot of fluctuation around the line, but the general trend for low values in year N are matched with low values in year N+1, and vice versa.

Not so with Z-scores, see figure 4.

Contrast the shape of this chart with those for HR and SO, and notice how there's no implicit line that can be drawn through the Z-score graph. The dispersal of points is pretty much uniform in every direction, meaning that there's no tendency for good performances in one year to be followed by good performances in the next.

Now maybe the problem is that we're looking at all battery combinations. Surely, the batteries who were unusually good or bad together show some tendency to continue, right? We'll, let's find out.

We can separate the good from the bad using the Z score. As a first simple pass, let's use better or worse than average. I set up two groups: those with Z<0 (the good) and those with Z> or =0 (the bad). Within each group, I looked

Figure 4. Year-to-Year Trend in Battery Z-Scores

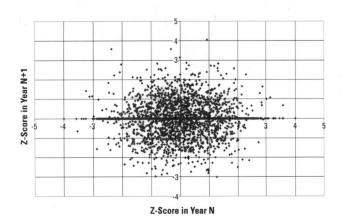

only at pitcher-catcher pairs that appeared on the list in consecutive seasons. There were 1832 such pairs. The median Z score in the following season for the good group was -0.015 (936 pairs, with median score in year 1 of +0.73), while the median score for the bad group was -0.003 (896 pairs, with median score in year 1 of -0.70). So all that tells us is that there's little to no evidence we can even differentiate game-calling into good and bad halves, let alone a finer granulation.

Maybe we have to give up on separating the mediocre from the slightly above average, but the standouts (in both directions) should surely continue to shine or bumble, right? I repeated the same process, comparing battery combos that were at least one standard deviation away from 0 in one year (that is, either Z>1 or Z<-1), and looked at their performance in the subsequent year. There were 637 battery combinations that met these criteria. The 313 members of the >1 group (especially bad combos) had a median Z score of 1.41 in the first year, then returned to average the next season with a median Z score of 0.028 in year 2, and a negligible correlation of +0.04. The 324 members of the <-1 group (especially good combos) had a median Z score of -1.421 in the first season, then also returned to almost exactly average with a Z score of -0.099 and a correlation of -0.10 in the follow-up season. Both groups, despite being selected for usually good or poor performances looked virtually indistinguishable just a year later.

What does that mean? We're still an order of magnitude away from even approaching the kind of demonstration of skill we see with other ordinary attributes like power and strikeouts. If home run power was as unreliable as game-calling is from year to year, you'd place even money on Jose Offerman topping Ken Griffey Jr. in the home run race next year.

This is an important result, and it's worth exploring why in a little more depth.

Go back to the example of home runs for hitters, and strikeouts for pitchers. In each case, we have an intuitive

understanding that the ability to do these things is a real skill, something physical or mental about the player that makes him more (or less) likely to hit a home run or strike out an opposing batter than the average player. Indeed, the entire purpose of player evaluation is to look at the past for information about what the future holds. This holds true for major league teams and rotisserie leagues alike. It's reasonable to ask how this game-calling result might look if there was a strong, demonstrable effect.

One way to do this is to construct similar charts for the more familiar HR rate and SO rate. I compared all batters with 300 or more at bats in 1996, and charted their home run rates in 1996. I split the groups into two equal halves—those with HR rates above the median, and those below the median. Then, I followed each group into 1997, and compared their HR rates again. The chart of their results looks like figure 5.

Figure 5. HR Rates for Good/Bad in Following Seasons

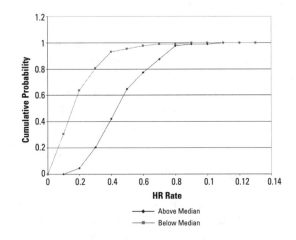

Each point represents the percentage of players in the group (the Y value) whose HR rate was below the number on the X-value. For example, about 80% of the players whose HR rates were below the median in 1996 had a HR/AB rate in 1997 below 0.03. On the other hand, only 20% of those who were above the median HR rate in '96 had a '97 HR rate below 0.03. The vertical gap between the two line represents the actual differences in ability between the two groups.

Now let's look at SO rate in figure 6.

Here, we see the same thing. For those who were below the median in '96, 90% of them turned in a '97 strikeout rate below 0.8 SO/IP, whereas only 45% of those who turned in high strikeout rates in '96 were under 0.8 the following season.

So to recap, if the above/below line have a large gap between them, then the attribute you are measuring tends to be preserved from year to year, which is characteristic of a real ability or skill. If the lines are close together, previous

Figure 6. Cumulative Probability for Above/Below Median in SO Rate

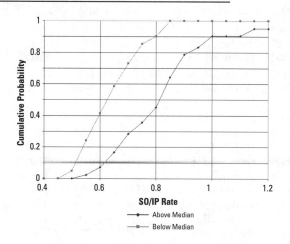

Figure 7. Comparison of Good/Bad Catchers with the Same Pitchers in Following Year

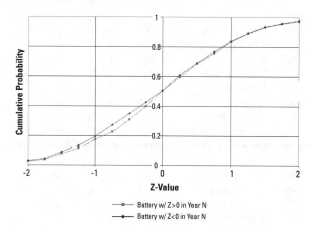

performance is not related to current or future performance, and thus there is less evidence that a real skill is at work.

Now, let's look at catcher's game-calling ability in figure 7.

In this case, the Z-score is the equivalent of HR rate, and Z>0 and Z<0 define our below/above median measurements. As you can see the graphs are very close together, indicating that last year's performance doesn't contribute information about this year's performance. Our suspicions are rising that we're not seeing a skill in action.

Seasons and Careers

Of course, one catcher and one pitcher don't work together very much, and the small number of plate appearances that work together creates a lot of statistical variance. Is it possible that looking at catchers' performance in the aggregate (across several pitchers) would overcome the problem? This is what Wright attempted to do with CERA, using "matched innings." We'll use a different statistical weighting procedure to address the same concern (details in the appendix). We'll weight the performance of each pitcher who worked with a catcher in such a way that they contribute equal amounts to the overall variance of the catcher's rating.

We'll also see a new figure in the tables below—Extra Runs Allowed (which we'll call XRA to distinguish it from ERA). XRA is simply the product of Run Prevention Rate (RPR) and plate appearances (PA), and thus represents the number of additional runs the opposition would be score if the catcher was used instead of a catcher who performs like the composite of all the other catchers on his team that season over the number of plate appearances the catcher actually caught. Negative numbers mean that the opposition scored fewer runs when the catcher in question would play. Positive numbers mean that the opposition would score more runs when the catcher was in the game.

So how do the catchers rank? The results in tables 4–7 may surprise you.

As with the battery combos, I looked at catchers' season RPR in consecutive seasons looking for some correlation. The conclusions were similar: of the 781 season pairs, the correlation in RPR from year N to N+1 was 0.01. Dividing the catchers into above/below average groups did not show any persistent trend to remain above/below average. The following-season median RPR of the above and below groups were -0.001 and -0.002 respectively. In other words, the two groups were again almost identical in the following year.

Conclusions

Looking at these results, though we would colloquially say that game-calling doesn't exist, it's more accurate to say that if there is a true game-calling ability, it lies below the threshold of detection. There is no statistical evidence for a large game-calling ability, but that doesn't preclude that a small ability exists that influences results on the field. For example, a genuine game-calling ability that reduces a pitcher's ERA by 0.01, resulting in a savings of about 1.6 runs per year for the entire team, could be masked by the statistical variance in the sample size we have to work with. Players would need to play thousands more games than they actually do to have enough data to successfully detect such a skill statistically.

There are other places to look for a catcher's influence beyond the game-calling ability looked for in this study. A catcher might be able to impact the "clutch" performance of the pitcher, helping him focus in high leverage situations. Such a pitcher would surrender fewer runs than expected from his hits and walks allowed. A catcher who senses what his pitcher is throwing well might be more efficient in calling pitches, reducing the pitch count per batter, and thus allowing

Table 4. Top 5 Catchers per Season by RPR, 1995–97 (min. 1,000 PA caught)

Year	Catcher	PA	RPR	XRA
1997	Lopez, Javier	2742	-0.0360	-98.7
1997	Kreuter, Chad	1902	-0.0304	-57.8
1997	Girardi, Joe	2615	-0.0287	-75.2
1997	Oliver, Joe	2897	-0.0231	-66.9
1997	Difelice, Mike	2161	-0.0208	-44.9
1996	Piazza, Mike	2724	-0.0392	-106.8
1996	Walbeck, Matt	1620	-0.0325	-52.6
1996	Leyritz, Jim	1091	-0.0280	-30.5
1996	Santiago, Benito	2382	-0.0217	-51.8
1996	Hundley, Todd	1143	-0.0215	-24.6
1995	Mayne, Brent	2068	-0.0252	-52.2
1995	Macfarlane, Mike	1786	-0.0245	-43.7
1995	Myers, Greg	1117	-0.0230	-25.7
1995	Daulton, Darren	2068	-0.0178	-36.9
1995	Knorr, Randy	1205	-0.0171	-20.6

Table 5. Worst 5 Catchers Each Season by RPR, 1995–97 (min. 1,000 PA caught)

Year	Catcher	PA	RPR	XRA
1997	Taubensee, Eddie	1251	0.0167	20.8
1997	Johnson, Charles	2667	0.0169	45.1
1997	Rodriguez, Ivan	3002	0.0265	79.6
1997	Posada, Jorge	1535	0.0276	42.4
1997	Wilson, Dan	1701	0.0410	69.7
1996	Pena, Tony	1359	0.0192	26.1
1996	Fletcher, Darrin	2504	0.0196	49.1
1996	Rodriguez, Ivan	3373	0.0234	79.0
1996	Girardi, Joe	1137	0.0292	33.2
1996	Servais, Scott	1670	0.0353	59.0
1995	Tingley, Ron	1144	0.0259	29.6
1995	Stanley, Mike	1443	0.0263	37.9
1995	Parrish, Lance	1405	0.0269	37.8
1995	Sheaffer, Danny	1271	0.0272	34.5
1995	Ausmus, Brad	1034	0.0319	33.0

Table 6. Top 10 Catcher Careers by RPR, 1981–97, (min. 10,000 PA caught)

Name	PA	RPR	XRA
Kreuter, Chad	10859	-0.0148	-160.5
Skinner, Joel	12265	-0.0115	-141.4
Berryhill, Damon	11391	-0.0088	-100.8
Surhoff, B. J.	16827	-0.0086	-145.5
Dempsey, Rick	23108	-0.0082	-189.9
Martinez, Buck	10467	-0.0080	-84.0
Fisk, Carlton	30402	-0.0075	-228.0
LaValliere, Mike	21126	-0.0073	-155.0
Harper, Brian	13527	-0.0068	-91.8
Hassey, Ron	18935	-0.0060	-114.3

Table 7. Worst 10 Catcher Careers by RPR, 1981–97 (min. 10,000 PA caught)

Name	PA	RPR	XRA
Steinbach, Terry	26575	0.0047	126.1
Cerone, Rick	22859	0.0053	120.4
Heath, Mike	25820	0.0053	136.3
Stanley, Mike	15058	0.0059	89.0
Ortiz, Junior	13599	0.0068	92.0
Bando, Chris	10202	0.0078	79.1
Flaherty, John	10253	0.0082	83.9
Petralli, Geno	10651	0.0089	95.1
Rodriguez, Ivan	16780	0.0103	173.3
Girardi, Joe	13675	0.0136	185.5

the starter to go deeper into the game and preserving the bullpen. Nothing in this study precludes any of these possibilities from being true, and this is a promising line for future investigation.

However, if we believe the results from this study, namely that catchers do not have significant differences among their game-calling abilities, the implications are staggering. First of all, the much-maligned stats we've been using for years to evaluate catchers—runners thrown out and passed balls—might actually quantify their defensive value. Furthermore, the relative unimportance of the running game could prompt teams to shift better offensive players to catcher without significantly hurting the team's defense. You could open up another position on the field besides first base for prospects who don't have the reflexes to play the infield, or the speed or instincts to play the outfield. The position is still the most physically demanding to play, but you could potential keep two dynamite offensive players in the lineup—say

Mike Piazza and Frank Thomas—but swapping them between catcher and first base so that neither gets overworked behind the plate. Far from being the position with the lowest expected offense, it could flip to the other side of the defensive spectrum entirely, and become a place to hide a slow-footed slugger.

Even though our foray into Z scores, RPR, and XRA have led us to conclude that catcher game-calling isn't a statisticaly significant skill, I'm well aware that many of you will want to see the results for your favorite catcher, or to review how other catchers measured up. I've calculated seasonal and career RPR and XRA for most catchers. These are Appendices B and C of this study, and you can find them on the Baseball Prospectus website (www.baseballprospectus.com). Just keep in mind that the results are almost certainly due to randomness rather than aptitude. 1998 figures will probably be posted on the BP web site as soon as the data are available.

Acknowledgments

This research would not have been possible without the generous assistance and contributions of several other people. Thanks to Tom Fontaine for his help is extracting the pitcher-catcher splits. Thanks to Phil Beineke of Stanford's Statistics Department for his consulting, advice, and patience, particularly with the computation and analysis of the weighted averages and Z-scores. Thanks to Baseball Workshop/Total Sports, and to Retrosheet for making the data available for this kind of work. And most of all, thanks to my wife, Kathy, who's been making do without a husband for most of the past two months.

References

Total Baseball, John Thorn, Pete Palmer, Michael Gershman, David Pietrusza

The Hidden Game of Baseball, John Thorn and Pete Palmer

The Diamond Appraised, Craig Wright and Tom House

Baseball by the Numbers: How Statistics are Collected, What They Mean, and How They Reveal The Game, Willie Runquist

Business Statistics, Meek, Taylor, Dunning and Klafehn

Major League Handbook, STATS Publishing (1998 and previous years)

Appendix A: Design of Analysis: How to Calculate PR/PA, RPR, and Z-Scores

An important step in the analysis was to identify a rate statistic that could be used as a basis of comparison between battery-season subsets. A key requirement for this rate of production was that it could be measured on a per-plate-appearance basis. That way, each PA could be treated as a separate trial or measurement. ERA failed this test, since its denominator is based on outs (innings pitched). Popular rate measurements such as On-base Plus Slugging (OPS) failed because they aren't true rate statistics (OPS combines rates with differing denominators; On-base Percentage, or OBP, uses plate appearances, while Slugging Average, or SLG, uses At-Bats). My approach was to turn to Thorn and Palmer's The Hidden Game of Baseball and Total Baseball. In these books, they describe their Linear Weights system, which assigns a value to each basic offensive event that reflects that events contribution to run scoring. Their table follows:

Event	Run Value
Single	0.47
Double	0.78
Triple	1.09
Home Run	1.40
Walk	0.33
Out	-0.25

Side note: Thorn and Palmer tweak the value of an out each year to make the entire performance of the league add up to zero. For this analysis, there is no need to balance league-wide offense to zero, so we use a constant average value for outs throughout.

In this model, I segregated each pitcher's performance with each catcher as a series of independent trials (one per batter faced). Each trial could end with one of several outcomes (single, double, triple, HR, walk, out) that carried a certain weight (taken from the table above). From this, you can compute an average value per trial, which is the expected number of Pitching Runs per Plate Appearance, which we abbreviate as PR/PA.

Let's use the Hentgen-Santiago example shown again in table 8.

We compute the PR/PA for Hentgen working with Santiago as:

$(0.47 \times 98 + 0.78 \times 25 + 1.09 \times 6 + 1.40 \times 13 + .33 \times 44 - 0.25 \times 435)/621 = -0.00633$ PR/PA

Similarly, we can compute the PR/PA for the Hentgen–Other Catcher subset:

$(0.47 \times 75 + 0.78 \times 17 + 1.09 \times 1 + 1.40 \times 18 + .33 \times 27 - 0.25 \times 307)/445 = 0.01564$ PR/PA

Run Prevention Rate, or RPR, is simply the difference between these two rates:

-0.00633 PR/PA (PR/PA w/ Santiago) $- 0.01564$ (PR/PA w/o Santiago) $= -0.02197$ RPR

Next, in order to determine whether the difference between two subsets of performance is significant, we need

Table 8.

1997	w/ Catcher Santiago									W/o Catcher Santiago								
Pitcher	PA	AB	1B	2B	3B	HR	BB	Outs	EstPA	PA	AB	1B	2B	3B	HR	BB	Outs	EstPA
Hentgen	627	577	98	25	6	13	44	435	621	449	418	75	17	1	18	27	307	445

to know the variance and standard deviation of a single plate appearance in our model. Variance is computed as $VAR(x) = E(x^2) — E(x)^2$, and is 0.163 for Hentgen-Santiago, and 0.192 for Hentgen-O'Brien.

Given a RPR and variance for each subset, we can move on to perform statistical tests to see if the null hypothesis (that there is no statistically significant difference between the performance with the catcher and without) could be rejected.

A Z-score is a representation of how likely you are to observe a given split between two samples of data under the assumption that they are drawn from the same distribution—that is, that the samples are statistically the same. The formula for computing a Z score is:

$$Z\left(\mu_1,\sigma_1,n_1,\mu_2,\sigma_2,n_2\right) = \frac{\mu_1 - \mu_2}{\sqrt{\frac{(n_1-1)\sigma_1^2 + (n_2-1)\sigma_2^2}{n1+n2-2}}\sqrt{\frac{1}{n_1}+\frac{1}{n_2}}}$$

where:

μ = PR/PA for a subset
σ = standard deviation of a subset
n = sample size of the subset

and the subscripts 1 and 2 refer to performance with and without the catcher, respectively.

Weightings for seasonal and career performances (big thanks to Phil Beineke of Stanford's Statistics Department for his invaluable advice in this section in particular): Basically, the idea here is that we want each pitcher who worked with a catcher to contribute an equal amount of variance to that catcher's rating. Thus, if the sample from one pitcher is highly variable due to small sample size, it will get a low weight, while less variable estimates (pitchers with larger sample sizes) will get higher weights. For each battery combo, we need to estimate the variance of each subset of PA (with and without) separately. This is different from the variance of the number of runs produced in a single plate appearance and is computed as follows:

$$\sigma^2\left(PRPA, PA, N_{OUT}, N_{1b}, N_{2b}, N_{3b}, N_{HR}, N_{BB}\right) = \frac{\sum_{Event=Out,1B,2B,3B,HR,BB}\left(PRPA - LW_{Event}\right)^2 \times N_{Event}}{(PA-1)^2}$$

where

$PRPA$ = PR/PA for that set of PA's (with or without the catcher in question)
NX = number of event X that occurred
PA = total number of plate appearances
LW_{Event} = linear weight of event X

Once we've computed the variance for the with-catcher and without-catcher subsets, we add them together to get the overall variance weight.

Given the above, we re-weight each RPR so that its variance equals one. We do this by dividing its variance. Then we take the sum of the weighted quantities, and divide by the sum of the weights to get the desired weighted average.

Top 40 Prospects

The lifeblood of any organization is its farm system. Teams have been trying to buy pennants since the dawn of free agency, and the last twenty years is littered with the ruins of desperate teams that took that course and collapsed under the weight of slow, aging hitters, injury-prone pitchers, and terrible defense. Teams that try a quick fix usually need to bring in several veterans, and rather than pay the steep price for a prime-of-career player, spread the wealth around to several 32-year-olds, and 18 months later that's a whole lot of money down the drain. Look at the Diamondbacks last year: they signed Jay Bell and Matt Williams, and now Bell's a ridiculously overpaid second baseman and Williams is a league-average hitter.

Most teams still haven't grasped this fundamental truth: you build a winning franchise in the minor leagues. But it's hard to look at the enormous payrolls of the top teams and not think they somehow spent their way to the top. The Yankees won 114 games with a number of imports—but their most valuable players were Bernie Williams and Derek Jeter, both homegrown products, and three-fifths of their rotation, their closer, and long man Ramiro Mendoza have only pitched for the Yankees. Even the 1997 Marlins—supposedly the shining example of a World Championship bought—developed their own catcher (Charles Johnson), shortstop (Edgar Renteria), and two of their starters (Livan Hernandez and Tony Saunders), traded for their rightfielder (Gary Sheffield) when he was just 24, picked up their second baseman (Craig Counsell) out of the Rockies' Triple-A team, and built their bullpen (Robb Nen, Jay Powell, Felix Heredia) out of their own system.

You can supplement a homegrown team by judiciously signing one or two players that fill specific needs, but throwing money at free agents indiscriminately to prove to your fan base that you're "committed to winning" is foolish and counterproductive. Winning teams have high payrolls because they spend money to keep the great players they develop, not because they buy them on the open market.

For your reading pleasure, we've provided our list of the 40 best prospects in the game. A "prospect" is simply any player who still has his rookie status (50 innings or 130 at-bats) intact, and includes everyone from the 24-year-old Triple-A hitter who's slated to win a major league job in spring training, to the teenage sensation in A-ball who has enormous potential but is still three years away. When deciding who makes the cut, there are two things to consider about every player: his upside and his risk. In general, the further down the minor league system you go, the higher the upsides and the higher the risk. A player's potential—what a scout might refer to as his projectability—is a product of his established ability and his age. A player who hits .250 in Double-A but is just 20 years old has yet to show the ability to play at a major league caliber, but is young enough that he can be expected to improve significantly. He may be a better prospect than his 23-year-old teammate who hit .300.

In general, when we rank players, we want to know who has the best upside—in other words, we want to rank the potential 40-HR hitter ahead of the guaranteed utility player. But ranking by potential has its limits. Almost anyone who has yet to reach Double-A is an enormous risk, because the jump A-ball to Double-A is probably more difficult than the jump to the major leagues for players who succeed at Double-A or Triple-A. Until we see how a player adjusts to that level of competition, it is difficult to project him with any degree of confidence.

We can't stress this point enough: other things being equal, pitchers have a much, much higher level of risk than hitters, for three main reasons. They get hurt a lot, they have trouble staying healthy, and above all, they get injured all the time. For every pitcher who makes the major leagues, a good four or five with the same level of ability will get hurt and lose their effectiveness before they make it, whether it happens in the minor leagues, college, or even high school. If you look back five or ten years and see who the best pitching prospects were and compare their accomplishments to those of the best hitting prospects of their time, almost without exception, you will find that the hitters have gone on to better careers.

This list is an excellent barometer of which teams are investing in their future wisely, and which teams are playing fast and loose with posterity. Here you can see why the Yankees and Braves are such great organizations—only the Cardinals have more prospects (four) on the list, and the Braves traded a potential fourth, Rob Bell, to Cincinnati. Listed with each prospect is his translated batting average, OBP, and slugging average for 1997 and 1998, as well as his overall EqA. For pitchers, you'll see hits/game, walks/game, and strikeouts/game, followed by his translated ERA. Any seasons with a small sample size (less than 300 ABs or 100 IP) are noted. All ages are as of July 1st, 1999.

The Baseball Prospectus Prospect of the Year is...

Eric Chavez or J.D. Drew...Chavez or Drew...Chavez or Drew. It's a nice dilemma to decide which of them you'd rather have. Do you gamble on taking the one who has farther to go on the learning curve, or do you go with the sure thing? The guy who embarrassed the minor leagues all year, or the one who was so impressive in his major league debut that he set the all-time record for slugging average (.972) for anyone with at least 20 at-bats? In the end, the decision came down to this: Chavez is two years younger than Drew. The single most important factor in evaluating a prospect—aside from his ability—is his age. Two years represents an enormous difference in potential. It's possible Chavez could struggle for two or more years before he establishes himself in the major leagues. But if he doesn't struggle—and we don't think he will—by the time Chavez is as old as Drew is right now, he'll already be the best third baseman in the American League. Drew is the significantly better bet to make a big impact this season. He's more likely to win the Rookie of the Year award. But Chavez is the one more likely to carve out a Hall of Fame career.

1. Eric Chavez, 3B, Oakland Athletics　　　　Age: 21

　　1997: .230/.272/.350　　　EqA: .212
　　1998: .310/.363/.527　　　EqA: .289

Chavez is the complete package at the plate, capable of hitting .300 right now, with 25-homer power, and his plate discipline is decent and rapidly improving. The A's organization does a good job of stressing that players work on taking walks walk as part of their offensive arsenal. In only his second pro season, Chavez increased his walk rate by nearly 50%. His season last year was eerily similar to that of his teammate, defending AL Rookie of the Year Ben Grieve, the year before. The only thing Grieve did better was control the strike zone, and Grieve was a year older than Chavez at that point. The only thing between Chavez and superstardom is his defense at third, which is raw but improving, and needs to be smoothed out.

2. J. D. Drew, OF, St. Louis Cardinals　　　　Age: 23

　　1997: .285/.372/.497　　　EqA: .294 (165 AB)
　　1998: .322/.422/.567　　　EqA: .336 (289 AB)

It sounds silly to call Drew the "sure thing" when he has fewer than 200 at-bats in organized baseball to his name (in case you're wondering, his DTs above include his playing time in the independent Northern League), but you have to appreciate how remarkable it is for a player to sign a pro contract, go straight to Double-A, and immediately become the best player in the league. The Cardinals think so highly of his defense that they're talking about moving Lankford to right. The odds-on favorite for NL Rookie of the Year.

3. Alex Escobar, CF, New York Mets　　　　Age: 20

　　1998: .282/.352/.467　　　EqA: .285

He's not very well known yet, but hey, that's why you bought the book. Escobar is a phenomenal talent, arguably the best package of tools (49 steals) and production (.310 average, 27 HRs) since Andruw Jones, and like Jones he could easily rip through four levels this year and make the major leagues by September. He hit just .229 with 1 homer in his pro debut in 1997, but that was blamed on an injured hamstring. He was healthy last year, and his work ethic is considered excellent. He may have to move to an outfield corner in the long run, but at the plate and on the basepaths, he doesn't need to change a thing.

4. Bruce Chen, LHP, Atlanta Braves　　　　Age: 22

　　1997: 9.80, 3.39, 7.53　　　ERA: 4.58
　　1998: 7.76, 3.27, 8.35　　　ERA: 2.98

He's young, he's left-handed, he throws hard, he hasn't been overworked, and he gets nothing but rave reviews for his pitching instincts. And he's a Brave with the #5 starter's job in his lap. He did nothing to disappoint in four major league starts in September, and he's a far better prospect now than Kevin Millwood was a year ago. Panama, the nation which gave us Juan Berenguer, may soon be toasting a more talented native son.

5. Pablo Ozuna, SS, St. Louis Cardinals　　　　Age: 20

　　1997: .221/.245/.283　　　EqA: .177 (226 AB)
　　1998: .320/.349/.428　　　EqA: .269

If you expect to be a Top 10 prospect without knowing the strike zone, you better do everything else really well. Fortunately, Ozuna does: he's a great defensive shortstop who won the Midwest League batting title and stole 62 bases as a 19 year-old. He's not a power hitter yet, but he's not Rey Ordonez either; he had 46 extra-base hits last season, and figures to be a 15-20 home run hitter as he develops. He's still raw, drawing only 29 walks and getting thrown out 26 times trying to steal, but his defense has already pushed aside fellow Cardinals prospect Brent Butler from the position. The shortstop job for the Cardinals will be in a holding pattern until Ozuna arrives.

6. Nick Johnson, 1B, New York Yankees　　　　Age: 20

　　1997: .257/.353/.386　　　EqA: .264
　　1998: .280/.393/.438　　　EqA: .291

Larry Bowa's nephew may be the best pure hitting prospect in the game. He picked apart the high-A-ball Florida State League as a teenager. He has incredible power potential, and already commands the strike zone with authority: 68 walks in just 92 games, and 19 hit-by-pitches to boot. By 2000 he'll just be wasting time if he's still in the minors. He has a chance to be the Yankees' best first baseman since Lou Gehrig. But keep in mind that he also hasn't reached Double-A and could prove to be no better than Ryan Klesko—which would still be a heck of a player.

7. Octavio Dotel, RHP, New York Mets   Age: 23

1997: 11.62, 5.68, 5.16	ERA: 5.94
1998: 7.56, 3.51, 8.48	ERA: 3.40

Dotel had a very promising 1996, when injuries and ineffectiveness almost threw him off the prospect radar entirely. He came back healthy and in a big way in 1998, with improved command of both his curve and slider. Given that his fastball was already in the mid-90s, it isn't surprising that he overmatched both the Eastern and International Leagues. He's a Met prospect, and thus contractually obligated to handle a high workload; he averaged around 26 batters a start, which is high but not egregiously so for a 22-year-old. He's ready for a major league job now, but hopefully it will be in middle relief as a rookie.

8. Jeremy Giambi, LF, Kansas City Royals   Age: 24

1997: .279/.369/.419	EqA: .276
1998: .327/.424/.539	EqA: .326

If Chavez doesn't have a smooth transition to the major leagues, Giambi may be the next best bet to win AL Rookie of the Year honors. He's a little old for a rookie, largely because the Royals had their heads buried in sand last year and didn't bring him up until September. But he was the first minor leaguer to clear an 1100 OPS since Billy Ashley in 1994, and Giambi wasn't playing in Albuquerque. He's not likely to have a fifteen- or twenty-year career, because he's getting a late start and has no defensive value. But for the next ten years, he could be as good a hitter as anyone.

9. Carlos Beltran, CF, Kansas City Royals   Age: 22

1997: .218/.281/.326	EqA: .211
1998: .280/.349/.459	EqA: .279

There hasn't been a great prospect to come out of Puerto Rico since it was made subject to the draft in 1990, but Beltran should change all that. A second-round pick in 1995 on the basis of his tools, he put it all together in 1998 and got better as the season went along. He played well in September and the Royals love their tools prospects even if they can't hit, so he should get every opportunity to succeed this year. He's not a threat for Rookie of the Year, but he's very young and should have an outstanding career.

10. Matt Clement, RHP, San Diego Padres   Age: 24

1997: 8.68, 2.97, 7.07	ERA: 3.02
1998: 8.02, 4.22, 6.83	ERA: 3.89

Clement is one of the few top prospects from a year ago who spent most of 1998 in the minor leagues, made some adjustments in Triple-A while trying to develop his control. He may come out of the adjustment period better than ever. He's got nasty stuff, with arguably the best slider in the minor leagues, and a great sinking fastball; he also hit 30—that's right, three-zero—batters last season. Ouch. All that intimidation makes him tough to hit, as he led Triple-A with 160 Ks, and opposing batters hit just .245 against him, an impressive mark in Las Vegas. He's thrown a ton of pitches the last two years: he faced over 28 batters per start last year, and even more in 1997. Despite a strong build, he has to be considered an injury risk, but if healthy, he should be one of the best rookie pitchers in baseball this year.

11. Rick Ankiel, LHP, St. Louis Cardinals   Age: 19

1998: 8.65, 3.41, 8.88	ERA: 4.12

The Cardinals must be the only team sending Scott Boras a Christmas card each year. Ankiel was considered the best high school lefty in years, but his contract demands scared everyone away—so the Cards took him in the second round, gave him $2.5 million, and now he looks like a bargain, giving the Cardinals three of the game's top 11 prospects. Ankiel throws in the low to mid 90s, but his best pitch is his curveball, which he used to lead the minors in strikeouts with 222. He only just turned 19, making him the youngest player on this list. If the Cardinals baby him for the next few years, he could be something special.

12. Ruben Mateo, CF, Texas Rangers   Age: 21

1997: .300/.334/.460	EqA: .273
1998: .270/.311/.420	EqA: .251

Another tools hitter who can actually hit, Mateo made a seamless jump to Double-A despite missing over a month with a dislocated shoulder, and actually hit better on his return to action. He's faster than Beltran but doesn't draw enough walks, though to his credit he doesn't strike out much either. He's not guaranteed a major league job this year, but if I were Tom Goodwin, I'd keep a suitcase handy.

13. Russ Branyan, 3B, Cleveland Indians   Age: 23

1997: .270/.366/.535	EqA: .302
1998: .277/.391/.596	EqA: .323

Just seven years after the Indians pumped out an outstanding left-handed power-hitting third baseman who draws a ton of walks, they're doing it again. Branyan may have even more power than Jim Thome. It's not a reach to project him as a 45-home run hitter—he holds the Sally record with 40 homers for Columbus in 1996. He missed most of last year with a wrist injury, but still hit 16 homers in just 43 games. Like Thome, there were early concerns that he'd never play third at the major league level, and like Thome, he's improved in the field as he got more experience. The Indians need to find a spot for him now, if he can avoid losing more time the wrist injury.

14. Brad Penny, RHP, Arizona Diamondbacks   Age: 21

1997: 9.40, 3.58, 6.13	ERA: 3.90
1998: 8.76, 2.08, 7.45	ERA: 3.34

Penny was the first pitcher to be named California League MVP in nearly 40 years, and with good reason. It's not just his numbers, although he did strike out 207 while walking just 35, a K/BB ratio Greg Maddux would be proud of. It's that he did it in a batting cage known as Mavericks Stadium. High Desert is just that: the air is thin and hot, and as a result you won't find a better park for hitters outside of Denver. On the road, Penny put up a 1.38 ERA and gave up just one home run all year.

15. Ben Davis, C, San Diego Padres   Age: 22
1997: .244/.278/.368   EqA: .219
1998: .260/.309/.400   EqA: .244

Taking a high school catcher in the first round of the draft has historically been about as shrewd as betting on the Washington Generals, and the Padres got roasted when Davis struggled mightily out of the gate. They now deserve credit, because Davis is turning into a gem. In 1997 he developed power, and in 1998 he did something even more significant: he learned the strike zone, improving his K/BB ratio from 107/28 to 60/42. He did that while making the jump to Double-A. He's 21 and his defense is spoken of with almost as much reverence as Charles Johnson's, and he threw out over half of attempted basestealers last year. He needs another year in the minors to consolidate his gains, but by 2000 you can add the Padres to the list of teams you just don't want to run on.

16. Chad Hermansen, OF, Pittsburgh Pirates   Age: 21
1997: .238/.319/.384   EqA: .248
1998: .243/.315/.460   EqA: .267

A year ago he was one of the top five prospects in the game, and he recovered from a terrible start to hit 28 homers, and he was the youngest player in Triple-A. So why has he slipped so much? Because he doesn't have a position, and the Pirates aren't helping. It's fairly clear now that he can't handle the middle infield, but it's still an open question whether he can handle center field or will remain in left. With the acquisition of Brian Giles, the big question is whether the Pirates have any intention of bringing Hermansen up at all this year. He needs to be put at a position he can handle and left there, but long-term we still like him a lot.

17. Lance Berkman, LF, Houston Astros   Age: 23
1997: .282/.386/.479   EqA: .298 (188 AB)
1998: .270/.377/.467   EqA: .291

Outstanding power, a ton of walks, and a good average add up to one terrific hitter, even if he is slow and doesn't play great defense. He's a switch-hitter, but is so far more proficient from the left side. The Astros have no room for him, and he may be stuck in Triple-A for a full year, which is a shame, because he doesn't need it. If some team puts together a package to relieve Houston of the responsibility of finding him playing time, they won't regret it.

18. Mitch Meluskey, C, Houston Astros   Age: 25
1997: .283/.361/.422   EqA: .272
1998: .343/.449/.536   EqA: .340

Another Astros' switch-hitter, and unlike Berkman, he should have a starting job sealed and delivered for him this year. Meluskey's defense has held him back before, which is why it has taken him this long to get to the major leagues. But his defense was much improved last year, and his bat is lethal. He was the MVP of the International League, and with a half dozen stars in the Astros' lineup to take the pressure off him, he should contribute from the get-go.

19. Marcus Giles, 2B, Atlanta Braves   Age: 21
1997: .240/.314/.324   EqA: .226 (204 AB)
1998: .287/.374/.483   EqA: .294

The rich get richer. Giles is just 5'8", but he generates amazing power, hitting 37 homers in his first full pro season. He was an outfielder in high school and only converted to second base in junior college, so he's still learning the position. If he masters it, he could end up somewhere between Jeff Kent and Ryne Sandberg on the continuum of slugging second basemen. If he has to move to the outfield, he loses a lot of his value, but even then he should be an everyday player. Keep in mind that Ron Gant started off as a second baseman, and Danny Tartabull was a shortstop all the way up to Triple-A.

20. D'Angelo Jimenez, SS, New York Yankees   Age: 21
1997: .246/.328/.343   EqA: .234
1998: .236/.321/.348   EqA: .234

The rich get richer, continued. A young switch-hitting shortstop with good defense, and he knows the strike zone? I'll take two, thank you. The Yankees don't need him, and Jimenez could certainly benefit from another year in the minors. Whether they have to move Jeter to third or trade Jimenez elsewhere, at some point the Yankees will have to let him play.

21. Michael Barrett, C/3B, Montreal Expos   Age: 22
1997: .257/.311/.361   EqA: .234
1998: .311/.349/.494   EqA: .284

Drafted as a shortstop, moved to catcher after just one season. As soon as he'd mastered the position, the Expos decided to try him at third base. Nobody, not even a lot of coaches in their organization, understands the move. Chris Widger isn't exactly Gary Carter behind the plate, and Barrett was getting rave reviews for his glovework. He hit for a good average and doubles power, but he needs work on his patience at the plate. At worst he's a right-handed B.J. Surhoff.

22. George Lombard, RF, Atlanta Braves   Age: 23
1997: .247/.325/.382   EqA: .252
1998: .278/.362/.467   EqA: .290

Lombard is a speed guy who developed power about the same time he learned the strike zone, and would not have been overmatched as the Braves' starting right fielder as early as this season. The signing of Brian Jordan quashes that, but his defense, power, and speed should find him a spot on the Braves' bench before long, and he has the ability to expand on that role before long.

23. Ben Petrick, C, Colorado Rockies　　Age: 22

1997: .233/.316/.372	EqA: .244	
1998: .236/.333/.438	EqA: .264	

Petrick hits for a low average but has good power and draws lots of walks. He's got more speed than you would expect from a backstop, although his steals dropped from 30 in 1997 to just 7 last year. Any hitter who gets drafted by the Rockies has won the lottery, and although he struggled to keep his average up in New Haven, once he reaches Colorado Springs and then Denver, he's going to have some fun. He's about a year away, and could win the Rookie of the Year award in 2000 if voters don't take the park into account, and we already know they don't.

24. Peter Bergeron, CF, Montreal Expos　　Age: 21

1997: .262/.339/.329	EqA: .238	
1998: .272/.350/.374	EqA: .261	

This is your Public Service Announcement: friends don't let friends hire Tommy Lasorda as a General Manager. Bergeron is not the only prospect heisted from the Dodgers, but he may be the best of them. He jumped two levels in 1998 while having his best season. He has a terrific on-base percentage, his range in center is good enough that the Expos are talking about trading or moving Rondell White, and he's an excellent base stealer and bunter. Naturally, he's being compared to Brett Butler, and that's not a bad comparison.

25. Ed Yarnall, LHP, Florida Marlins　　Age: 23

1997: 9.36, 3.18, 7.20	ERA: 3.31	
1998: 7.76, 3.85, 6.21	ERA: 4.05	

The big prize acquired from the Mets for Mike Piazza, Yarnall could be the Marlins' ace by the end of the year. He struggled to control his breaking ball when he got moved to Triple-A, and would probably be best suited with another three months in Charlotte. He has yet to throw more than 150 innings in a season, and if the Marlins bring him along gently he could be the #1 starter they re-build their staff around.

26. Carlos Febles, 2B, Kansas City Royals　　Age: 23

1997: .229/.296/.319	EqA: .224	
1998: .268/.367/.407	EqA: .277	

Here's the Royals' leadoff hitter for the new millennium. Febles is a table-setter of the highest order. He's developing power, and he plays a mean second base (Royals great Frank White raves about his defense). He hit .400 in a brief September audition, and the Royals didn't even pretend to be interested in re-signing Jose Offerman. The job is his to lose.

27. Scott Williamson, RHP, Cincinnati Reds　　Age: 23

1997: 12.12, 3.84, 6.00	ERA: 4.32 (75 IP)	
1998: 8.97, 3.47, 7.32	ERA: 4.00	

Williamson throws a deadly splitter and gave up just six home runs all year. He's pitched well enough to encourage the Reds to move him up quickly, reaching Triple-A in his first full season. The acquisition of Neagle gives the Reds the luxury of giving Williamson another full season in the minors if he needs it, but it wouldn't be a surprise if he surfaced by July.

28. Calvin Pickering, 1B, Baltimore Orioles　　Age: 22

1997: .291/.359/.470	EqA: .284	
1998: .289/.396/.506	EqA: .307	

For a first baseman, he makes a fine offensive lineman. He's listed at 6'5" and 283 pounds, and that's after losing some weight in an off-season training program last year. Still, a left-handed power hitter in Camden Yards who's just 22? Memo to Peter Angelos: there's a way to cut payroll and improve the team. The scouts say he moves well for a big guy, which is an awfully nice thing to say, but he could still achieve the highly-coveted "anvil" class of speed before he turns 30. As long as he hits, who cares?

29. Ronnie Belliard, 2B, Milwaukee Brewers　　Age: 24

1997: .234/.317/.326	EqA: .228	
1998: .304/.379/.458	EqA: .291	

Rafael's cousin, but don't be frightened: he's actually a very good hitter, and in fact a very similar player to Carlos Febles. Belliard walks a little less but has more power and may play even better defense, and the Brewers rave about his ability to move runners and play "team baseball," so in all likelihood he'll bat second. If they can trade Vina and get Belliard into the lineup, they'll improve the team.

30. Freddy Garcia, RHP, Seattle Mariners　　Age: 22

1997: 11.65, 2.95, 5.26	ERA: 4.19	
1998: 8.70, 3.99, 7.02	ERA: 3.54	

The most impressive of the three prospects acquired by the Mariners for Randy Johnson, Garcia is a Venezuelan right-hander with an excellent curveball and a fastball known to get up to 98. His control is good and getting better, and he's almost ready for the major leagues. In Seattle, pitchers get promoted before they're ready, so don't be surprised to find him in the rotation out of spring training. He's capable of handling the pressure, but if Piniella could derail Kenny Cloude's career, you have to worry about Garcia.

31. Dernell Stenson, RF, Boston Red Sox　　Age: 21

1997: .262/.342/.392	EqA: .258	
1998: .247/.345/.408	EqA: .264	

Your classic Red Sox outfielder prospect: a pretty swing, always reaching for the fences, and indifferent on defense. He impressed a lot of observers in the Eastern League with his power and knowledge of the strike zone, and he doesn't turn 21 until June. Trot Nixon, the former phenom who revived his prospect status with the Red Sox last year, is much the same player, but Stenson is four years younger. Stenson should be no worse than Mike Greenwell, and could be a lot better.

32. Rob Bell, RHP, Cincinnati Reds   Age: 22

1997:	11.86, 3.22, 5.87	ERA: 5.11
1998:	10.98, 2.81, 7.08	ERA: 4.63

Bret Boone hit .223 with 7 homers just a year ago, but now he can bring in Denny Neagle and this stud? Bell had the best curveball in the Carolina League and led the circuit with 197 Ks last year. The Braves will probably never even notice that he's gone, but between Bell and Scott Williamson, and the addition of Neagle as their best starter, the Reds are suddenly looking at having one of the best rotations in the division by 2000.

33. Gabe Kapler, OF, Detroit Tigers   Age: 23

1997:	.268/.329/.426	EqA: .259
1998:	.305/.361/.516	EqA: .296

Baseball Weekly's Minor League Player of the Year is the latest really low draft pick to emerge as a top prospect. The Tigers have to make room for him, and in that way he resembles Jeff Conine, who had to wait until he was 27 to catch a break. If the Tigers wake up and dump Brian Hunter, Kapler's a decent longshot for rookie honors.

34. Daryle Ward, 1B/LF, Houston Astros   Age: 24

1997:	.297/.358/.449	EqA: .279
1998:	.299/.354/.495	EqA: .289

Our tough luck listing. Ward's been ready to hit major league pitching for over a year, but the world is filled with first basemen who can hit, and Ward's in the same organization as Jeff Bagwell. Trying to broaden their options, the Astros moved Ward to left at New Orleans in 1998. He didn't embarrass himself, but if the way to a spot on the Astros' major league roster is blocked for Lance Berkman, you can bet it's even more blocked for Ward.

35. Joe Crede, 3B, Chicago White Sox   Age: 21

1997:	.242/.283/.319	EqA: .205
1998:	.297/.362/.457	EqA: .281

As good a prospect as Carlos Lee is, he's also probably not going to be a major league third baseman for the White Sox for very long. That doesn't have much to do with his limitations in the field as it does with the presence of mighty Joe Crede. A smooth defender and a hitter with power to all fields, Crede is adjusting quickly after nearly winning the triple crown in the Carolina League. If he succeeds in Birmingham early (and he's been red hot to open the last two seasons), he could be up by August.

36. Angel Pena, C, Los Angeles Dodgers   Age: 24

1997:	.236/.292/.396	EqA: .234
1998:	.296/.348/.439	EqA: .271

He's relatively unknown for a Dodger prospect, but he had an excellent season in the harsh environment of San Antonio, and he was considered to be the best defensive catcher in the Texas League. Imagine Terry Steinbach with more power, and you've got quite a player.

37. Roy Halladay, RHP, Toronto Blue Jays   Age: 22

1997:	10.70, 3.22, 4.21	ERA: 4.99
1998:	9.19, 3.44, 5.05	ERA: 3.79

Normally a pitcher with strikeout-to-walk ratios as bad as his would never make our list, but Halladay isn't your typical pitching prospect. He was rushed by the Blue Jays, reaching Triple-A at 20, and it's taken him nearly two years for him to get comfortable. He throws a dandy knuckle-curve and featured a new-and-improved slider last year, which supposedly helped him become more of a groundball pitcher. Probably needs a couple more months in Syracuse, because he needs it, and because of what Tim Johnson might do to him over a full season.

38. Tom Evans, 3B, Toronto Blue Jays   Age: 24

1997:	.256/.340/.407	EqA: .259
1998:	.272/.345/.433	EqA: .268

Evans isn't a newcomer to these lists; he's been one of the best third baseman in the minor leagues for three years now. Ed Sprague is finally gone, leaving Evans as the obvious alternative. He's what he was three years ago: a good glove man with excellent patience and solid power. While he doesn't have star potential, he can be an above-average third baseman for several years to come.

39. Luke Prokopec, RHP, Los Angeles Dodgers   Age: 21

1997:	11.77, 3.46, 6.69	ERA: 5.57 (39 IP)
1998:	9.87, 3.31, 8.08	ERA: 3.52

Rany got to see Prokopec on a minor league jaunt with John Sickels, and neither one of them knew too much about him going in, but afterwards they wanted to find out more. He was an Australian catcher who had a good arm but couldn't hit, but after switching to the mound in the middle of the 1997 season, he throws in the upper 80s, has an excellent curveball, and almost unbelievable mound instincts for someone with barely a year's experience under his belt. He's got a relatively fresh arm in an organization where good prospects move fast, so watch out for him.

40. Jackie Rexrode, 2B, Arizona Diamondbacks   Age: 20

1997:	.237/.337/.291	EqA: .232
1998:	.278/.393/.327	EqA: .273

Rexrode is one of the more unique talents in baseball. He's an on-base machine, posting a .430+ OBP at two levels last year, and he was only 19. He was 41-for-45 in stolen base attempts. His power is nonexistent, and even at his age you want to see a prospect hit some doubles now and then. He's similar to but significantly better than the Marlins' Luis Castillo as a prospect; Castillo's lack of power has really stunted his development. Rexrode doesn't play great defense and his on-base skill is his only ticket to the major leagues, but if he starts to drive the ball at all and survives the jump to Double-A, he could become one of the majors' premier leadoff hitters.

Honorable mentions

Mark Johnson, the White Sox' young catcher, gets attention for his defense but not for his ability to draw 100 walks a year and post a .420 OBP; Ryan Bradley, the Yankees' first round pick in 1997, was rushed to the major leagues last year, and may end up in the bullpen; Mario Encarnacion, a young, multitalented A's outfielder, held his own in Double-A at the age of 20; Rob Fick is a sleeper pick for Rookie of the Year in the AL if the Tigers don't give up on him as a catcher; Carlos Lee is the heir apparent to Robin Ventura in Chicago, with doubles power and improving defense; Odalis Perez is barely 21, yet may find himself in the Braves' bullpen this year; Jason LaRue, the Reds' catcher of the future, has a bat that could push Eddie Taubensee out of the way as soon as this year; Carlos Guillen, the Mariners' new second baseman, finally showed what he could do when healthy; John Patterson, the Diamondbacks' bonus baby, has an outstanding curveball and numbers almost as impressive as Brad Penny's were; and Pat Burrell, the first pick in the 1998 draft, switched over to wood bats and had an outstanding debut in the Florida State League.

Extra Players Section

This year, we've included an extra players section for players who didn't get commented on in team chapters. Here you'll find any major league player who had 50 plate appearances or any minor league player from the full-season minor leagues who had 300 or more plate appearances or 80 or more innings pitched.

Hitters (Averages: .260 BA/ .330 OBA/ .420 SA, .260 EQA)

PLAYER	AGE	AM	LGE	AB	H	DB	TP	HR	BB	R	RBI	SB	CS	OUT	BA	OBA	SA	EQA	EQR	DEFENSE
Andy Abad	26	Pawtuckt	Int	360	92	10	1	11	54	52	48	6	4	272	.256	.353	.381	.257	45	24-OF 91
John Adams	22	HighDes	Cal	297	65	11	4	9	19	29	32	5	2	234	.219	.266	.374	.220	27	31-OF 95
Carlos Adolfo	23	Jupiter	Fla	333	74	8	1	9	29	30	33	4	4	263	.222	.285	.333	.212	27	80-OF 91
Alejandro Ahumada	20	Michigan	Mid	393	94	14	2	1	21	31	29	2	4	303	.239	.278	.293	.194	25	20-2B 90
Kurt Airoso	24	Lakeland	Fla	387	88	9	0	10	49	42	40	3	2	301	.227	.314	.328	.224	36	65-OF 85
Efrain Alamo	22	Asheville	SAL	488	92	10	0	10	20	23	26	7	6	402	.189	.220	.270	.157	20	126-OF 87
Rashad Albert	23	Hickory	SAL	386	75	10	1	4	12	19	17	9	6	317	.194	.219	.256	.152	14	97-OF 95
Chad Alevras	24	Michigan	Mid	285	54	5	0	5	19	13	16	0	0	231	.189	.240	.260	.160	12	15-1B 65
Chad Alexander	25	Jackson	Tex	413	92	16	1	8	53	45	40	3	4	325	.223	.311	.324	.220	37	115-OF 95
Jeff Alfano	22	Stockton	Cal	392	82	12	1	4	29	28	25	4	2	312	.209	.264	.276	.182	22	107-C 95
Marlon Allen	26	Chattang	Sou	310	55	4	0	5	18	11	12	1	3	258	.177	.223	.239	.136	9	79-1B 99
Erick Almonte	21	Greensbr	SAL	451	77	6	0	5	25	15	15	3	1	375	.171	.214	.217	.120	9	119-SS 79
Jerome Alviso	23	Asheville	SAL	477	92	12	1	4	14	18	19	4	5	390	.193	.216	.247	.140	14	25-2B 80
Jesus Ametller	24	PrWillm	Car	357	93	10	0	4	5	26	33	2	3	267	.261	.271	.322	.204	25	79-2B 91
Mike Amrhein	24	Rockford	Mid	456	109	12	1	7	21	36	40	3	2	349	.239	.273	.316	.203	32	26-1B 108
Brian Anthony	25	SalemVA	Car	444	96	7	0	10	24	28	35	3	4	352	.216	.256	.300	.187	27	116-1B 94
Rogelio Arias	23	Asheville	SAL	312	60	7	1	3	11	12	13	0	1	253	.192	.220	.250	.142	10	73-C 92
Chris Ashby	24	Norwich	Eas	440	114	13	0	11	56	63	53	12	3	329	.259	.343	.364	.252	52	21-1B 104
Jesus Azuaje	26	inghmtn	Eas	385	88	13	1	5	40	43	32	9	1	298	.229	.301	.306	.216	32	36-SS 99
Lorenzo Bagley	23	Hagerstn	SAL	360	71	9	1	8	29	24	27	1	1	290	.197	.257	.294	.185	21	71-OF 89
Rod Bair	24	SalemVA	Car	426	108	24	2	7	22	46	46	6	3	321	.254	.290	.369	.229	40	111-OF 92
Jeff Ball	30	Fresno	PCL	445	108	13	0	15	45	50	56	4	2	339	.243	.312	.373	.238	47	110-1B 89
Bret Barberie	31	Oklahoma	PCL	494	126	23	3	4	48	57	51	2	2	370	.255	.321	.338	.231	47	109-2B 97
Glen Barker	28	Jacksnvl	Sou	453	106	19	2	5	37	52	38	17	5	352	.234	.292	.318	.217	39	108-OF 116
Tony Barron	32	Scran-WB	Int	374	90	14	1	13	32	42	47	5	3	287	.241	.300	.388	.238	39	54-OF 91
Jeff Barry	30	ColSprin	PCL	337	66	10	3	5	37	28	24	3	1	272	.196	.275	.288	.192	22	89-OF 95
Blake Barthol	26	SalemVA	Car	447	105	16	0	9	37	42	44	2	2	344	.235	.293	.331	.216	37	101-C 84
Jayson Bass	23	Lancastr	Cal	386	90	11	2	14	29	46	44	17	8	304	.233	.287	.381	.233	40	71-OF 83
Allen Battle	30	Ottawa	Int	446	113	20	1	8	57	71	47	21	5	338	.253	.338	.357	.250	53	123-OF 94
Howard Battle	27	Greenvil	Sou	283	74	12	1	7	23	34	36	2	1	210	.261	.317	.385	.245	31	64-3B 85
Jorge Bautista	22	KaneCnty	Mid	277	61	7	1	6	31	26	26	1	2	218	.220	.299	.318	.212	23	
Juan Bautista	24	Birmnghm	Sou	417	89	8	1	4	8	19	22	4	7	335	.213	.228	.266	.157	16	119-SS 94
Doug Bearden	23	Stockton	Cal	361	67	5	0	2	21	13	13	3	3	297	.186	.230	.216	.130	9	88-SS 72
Ramy Beatriz	20	Beloit	Mid	306	70	4	1	4	27	29	24	8	3	239	.229	.291	.288	.204	23	81-OF 89
Brian Becker	24	StPete	Fla	490	107	16	1	6	32	35	36	0	0	383	.218	.266	.292	.189	30	113-1B 127
Tim Belk	29	Toledo	Int	289	66	12	0	7	14	25	28	3	0	223	.228	.264	.343	.210	23	76-1B 71
Mike Bell	24	Binghmtn	Eas	275	66	8	1	11	30	32	37	2	4	213	.240	.315	.396	.242	31	50-2B 88
Clay Bellinger	30	Columbus	Int	393	72	13	1	6	27	21	21	3	2	323	.183	.236	.267	.162	17	19-3B 117
Esteban Beltre	31	SaltLake	PCL	491	100	13	2	2	32	35	24	17	8	399	.204	.252	.251	.171	24	121-SS 96
Gary Bennett	27	Scran-WB	Int	282	64	9	0	8	19	24	29	0	0	218	.227	.276	.344	.213	23	68-C 101
Jeff Berblinger	28	Tacoma	PCL	384	75	13	1	4	19	22	20	8	5	314	.195	.233	.266	.164	17	21-3B 74
Brandon Berger	24	Wilmngtn	Car	350	69	11	1	7	45	34	27	6	2	283	.197	.289	.294	.203	26	84-OF 92

PLAYER	AGE	AM	LGE	AB	H	DB	TP	HR	BB	R	RBI	SB	CS	OUT	BA	OBA	SA	EQA	EQR	DEFENSE
Matt Berger	24	Hickory	SAL	471	106	9	0	13	35	38	46	1	1	366	.225	.279	.327	.208	36	28-3B 97
Robert Berns	24	Charl-SC	SAL	478	90	7	0	7	39	23	25	0	1	389	.188	.250	.247	.158	19	128-1B 113
Mike Berry	28	Norwich	Eas	401	102	21	0	11	41	52	51	5	2	301	.254	.324	.389	.248	46	100-3B 81
Oscar Betancourt	23	CedarRpd	Mid	341	52	3	0	3	19	10	10	0	1	290	.152	.197	.188	.058	1	86-3B 94
Andy Bevins	23	Peoria	Mid	510	101	12	1	12	25	29	36	3	2	411	.198	.236	.296	.176	27	89-OF 92
Kurt Bierek	26	Norwich	Eas	348	70	8	1	9	39	29	30	0	1	279	.201	.282	.307	.200	25	94-1B 104
Mo Blakeney	26	CapeFear	SAL	308	49	7	1	1	19	9	9	3	5	264	.159	.208	.198	.093	3	32-1B 101
Greg Blosser	28	Durham	Int	371	82	12	1	17	59	51	51	7	4	293	.221	.328	.396	.250	46	88-OF 82
Derrick Bly	24	Rockford	Mid	496	109	20	2	4	41	42	36	4	3	390	.220	.279	.292	.196	33	19-1B 82
Ramon Borrego	21	FtWayne	Mid	431	100	11	1	6	48	45	38	8	6	337	.232	.309	.304	.214	36	20-3B 85
Terry Bradshaw	30	Omaha	PCL	292	64	6	0	9	42	36	30	9	5	233	.219	.317	.332	.228	29	86-OF 90
Danny Bravo	22	CapeFear	SAL	344	74	6	2	3	25	23	22	3	5	275	.215	.268	.270	.179	19	26-3B 96
Darryl Brinkley	30	Nashvill	PCL	363	109	15	2	6	23	50	49	8	6	260	.300	.342	.402	.260	45	81-OF 92
J. J. Brock	24	1SthBend	Mid	357	68	9	1	2	18	14	14	1	3	292	.190	.229	.238	.141	11	91-SS 88
Tarrik Brock	25	Orlando	Sou	367	83	14	3	11	41	45	42	10	6	290	.226	.304	.371	.234	38	94-OF 90
Anthony Brooks	22	Macon	SAL	496	97	12	1	9	20	25	29	7	8	407	.196	.227	.278	.163	22	132-OF 96
Ray Brown	26	Wichita	Tex	389	92	10	1	11	40	41	45	2	1	298	.237	.308	.352	.230	38	106-1B 78
Richard Brown	22	Tampa	Fla	282	72	9	1	9	37	39	38	4	3	213	.255	.342	.390	.254	35	53-OF 88
Vick Brown	26	Norwich	Eas	353	89	9	1	5	31	47	32	21	8	272	.252	.312	.326	.231	35	99-2B 91
Cliff Brumbaugh	25	Tulsa	Tex	479	98	13	1	10	40	35	37	1	2	383	.205	.266	.299	.190	30	23-3B 96
Chris Bryant	26	Frederck	Car	492	102	7	0	10	42	36	36	5	2	392	.207	.270	.283	.188	30	44-OF 83
Clint Bryant	25	SalemVA	Car	436	79	5	1	5	21	15	16	3	3	360	.181	.219	.232	.132	11	111-3B 86
Jim Buccheri	30	Durham	Int	346	89	11	2	4	19	43	31	22	10	267	.257	.296	.335	.226	33	68-OF 89
Mark Budzinski	25	Akron	Eas	475	102	14	2	8	41	41	38	7	5	378	.215	.277	.303	.199	33	126-OF 98
Shawn Buhner	26	Orlando	Sou	346	65	7	1	6	31	20	21	1	2	283	.188	.255	.266	.170	17	71-1B 81
Antuan Bunkley	23	WMichgn	Mid	500	121	12	0	8	35	43	47	2	1	380	.242	.292	.314	.210	39	124-1B 92
Kevin Burford	21	Clinton	Mid	454	103	17	2	7	50	50	41	7	2	353	.227	.304	.319	.219	40	109-OF 79
Gary Burnham	24	Clearwtr	Fla	510	117	18	4	6	47	50	45	4	2	395	.229	.294	.316	.212	41	113-1B 90
Kevin Burns	23	Kissimme	Fla	474	110	14	1	14	54	54	54	5	2	366	.232	.311	.354	.232	47	127-1B 97
Patrick Burns	21	Columbia	SAL	479	106	15	1	8	40	43	40	7	2	375	.221	.281	.307	.205	36	114-1B 98
Xavier Burns	24	Augusta	SAL	420	77	8	2	7	29	23	22	6	4	347	.183	.236	.262	.161	18	83-3B 83
Darren Burton	26	Scran-WB	Int	395	94	14	2	13	42	48	50	6	0	301	.238	.311	.382	.243	44	104-OF 90
Allen Butler	24	Greensbr	SAL	473	95	9	0	10	36	30	33	2	2	380	.201	.257	.283	.180	26	123-3B 92
Michael Byas	23	SanJose	Cal	528	105	6	1	1	61	39	23	14	12	435	.199	.282	.220	.168	25	133-OF 102
Wilmy Caceres	20	Charl-WV	SAL	393	85	9	3	1	16	25	21	10	8	316	.216	.247	.262	.169	19	104-SS 89
Nick Caiazzo	24	Beloit	Mid	503	106	8	1	5	16	23	27	1	1	398	.211	.235	.260	.159	20	32-1B 65
Troy Cameron	20	Macon	SAL	475	88	11	1	14	53	36	38	2	2	389	.185	.267	.301	.191	31	59-3B 70
Jose Camilo	22	Brevard	Fla	356	65	11	1	3	20	16	14	4	4	295	.183	.226	.244	.145	12	85-OF 87
Aaron Capista	20	Michigan	Mid	473	108	18	2	6	20	35	38	2	2	367	.228	.260	.313	.195	31	123-SS 94
Brett Caradonna	20	Hickory	SAL	449	98	11	1	3	37	34	29	6	6	357	.218	.278	.267	.185	26	97-OF 85
Cesarin Carmona	22	RCucmng	Cal	364	79	8	4	3	13	26	23	11	5	290	.217	.244	.286	.182	20	99-SS 102
Dustin Carr	24	StPete	Fla	519	102	11	2	5	53	36	30	4	2	419	.197	.271	.254	.176	27	135-2B 84
Joe Caruso	24	Lansing	Mid	422	84	8	2	7	42	34	29	9	5	343	.199	.272	.277	.188	26	44-2B 91
Jhonny Carvajal	24	Harrisbg	Eas	339	78	10	2	1	30	30	24	3	4	265	.230	.293	.280	.197	23	95-SS 99
Jovino Carvajal	30	Vancouvr	PCL	385	88	14	2	5	18	36	30	16	9	306	.229	.263	.314	.202	28	103-OF 100
Steve Carver	26	Reading	Eas	459	99	7	0	15	50	40	48	0	2	362	.216	.293	.329	.213	38	27-OF 82
Carlos Casimiro	22	Frederck	Car	480	106	14	5	15	27	42	51	6	4	378	.221	.262	.365	.214	40	114-2B 96
Joe Cathey	23	QuadCit	Mid	404	73	7	1	2	26	15	14	7	7	338	.181	.230	.218	.133	11	
Jesus Cedeno	23	Lakeland	Fla	284	53	7	1	4	17	13	14	0	2	233	.187	.233	.261	.154	11	80-OF 95
Jose Cepeda	24	Wilmngtn	Car	400	99	14	3	1	31	42	33	8	2	303	.248	.302	.305	.215	33	26-2B 101
Dionys Cesar	22	Visalia	Cal	497	116	22	3	7	43	57	45	16	7	388	.233	.294	.332	.221	44	20-2B 94
Frank Charles	30	Shrevprt	Tex	404	92	15	1	8	13	28	36	0	1	313	.228	.252	.329	.197	27	40-1B 86
Virgil Chevalier	25	Sarasota	Fla	321	77	11	1	5	19	30	30	5	2	246	.240	.282	.327	.213	26	
Paul Chiaffredo	23	Dunedin	Fla	286	52	7	0	4	14	10	12	0	2	236	.182	.220	.248	.139	9	81-C 91
Dan Cholowsky	28	ColSprin	PCL	331	59	8	1	5	23	16	16	3	1	273	.178	.232	.254	.154	13	74-C 90
Eddie Christian	27	Midland	Tex	386	91	18	2	3	34	39	33	6	6	301	.236	.298	.316	.212	31	50-OF 82

Extra Players

PLAYER	AGE	AM	LGE	AB	H	DB	TP	HR	BB	R	RBI	SB	CS	OUT	BA	OBA	SA	EQA	EQR	DEFENSE
Kevin Clark	26	HighDes	Cal	488	90	9	1	10	23	20	26	0	0	398	.184	.221	.268	.154	18	95-1B 92
Kirby Clark	25	Piedmont	SAL	321	66	12	1	3	18	19	20	1	0	255	.206	.248	.277	.174	16	27-3B 87
Rodney Clifton	22	Modesto	Cal	434	102	18	3	8	41	47	45	6	3	335	.235	.301	.346	.225	40	104-OF 92
Gary Coffee	24	Lansing	Mid	291	63	8	2	6	38	31	28	2	1	229	.216	.307	.320	.218	25	45-1B 86
Eric Cole	23	QuadCit	Mid	500	114	14	2	9	18	39	41	13	9	395	.228	.255	.318	.197	34	125-OF 97
Bobo Colina	28	StPete	Fla	360	79	10	1	4	31	28	27	1	1	282	.219	.281	.286	.194	23	
Francis Collins	25	Piedmont	SAL	309	65	3	1	0	28	20	15	4	2	246	.210	.276	.227	.168	14	78-OF 76
Mike Coolbaugh	27	ColSprin	PCL	371	79	18	1	10	26	31	36	0	2	294	.213	.264	.348	.207	29	18-1B 101
Brandon Copeland	22	Columbia	SAL	350	69	10	0	9	40	33	28	7	3	284	.197	.279	.303	.201	26	100-OF 82
Willy Cordero	20	Savannah	SAL	379	76	8	1	1	18	20	15	9	6	309	.201	.237	.235	.151	14	92-SS 95
Erick Corps	24	StPete	Fla	305	58	6	1	2	31	17	15	1	3	250	.190	.265	.236	.160	13	29-SS 83
Miguel Correa	27	ElPaso	Tex	516	98	11	1	7	18	21	23	5	4	422	.190	.217	.256	.147	17	129-OF 84
Caonabo Cosme	20	Modesto	Cal	412	96	17	2	2	21	35	30	8	4	320	.233	.270	.299	.197	28	60-SS 86
Tim Costo	30	Syracuse	Int	359	89	11	1	10	20	33	42	1	1	271	.248	.288	.368	.226	33	39-1B 97
John Cotton	28	WestTenn	Sou	313	73	7	2	8	10	25	31	5	2	242	.233	.257	.345	.208	24	25-3B 83
Rickey Cradle	26	Tacoma	PCL	291	71	13	1	9	21	34	35	7	4	224	.244	.295	.388	.236	30	71-OF 98
Benny Craig	24	Burlingt	Mid	341	59	5	0	9	32	19	20	1	1	283	.173	.244	.267	.165	16	19-OF 71
Todd Crane	25	Clearwtr	Fla	442	88	9	2	6	51	40	29	12	5	359	.199	.282	.269	.192	29	118-OF 94
Cesar Crespo	20	Columbia	SAL	430	92	12	2	5	36	43	29	20	8	346	.214	.275	.286	.199	30	109-2B 84
Mark Cridland	24	Beloit	Mid	295	57	6	1	4	10	12	14	0	0	238	.193	.220	.261	.149	10	75-OF 81
Shane Cronin	23	Clinton	Mid	382	74	4	0	4	21	15	17	2	1	309	.194	.236	.236	.146	13	113-1B 89
Cirilo Cruz	24	Lancastr	Cal	536	121	15	0	6	38	39	41	1	1	416	.226	.277	.287	.193	34	83-1B 86
Fausto Cruz	27	Vancouvr	PCL	417	94	18	4	3	24	36	32	6	3	326	.225	.268	.309	.199	29	84-SS 90
Trent Cuevas	22	VeroBch	Fla	320	69	14	0	5	19	23	25	1	0	251	.216	.260	.306	.192	20	36-3B 99
John Curl	26	Mobile	Sou	360	82	10	1	11	25	32	39	3	1	279	.228	.278	.353	.218	31	15-1B 100
Matt Curtis	24	Midland	Tex	420	84	10	2	7	26	25	28	1	1	337	.200	.247	.283	.175	22	28-C 90
Patrick Cutshall	24	QuadCit	Mid	426	78	8	1	4	23	17	16	5	5	353	.183	.225	.235	.139	13	
Tony Darden	25	Binghmtn	Eas	318	76	13	2	3	20	28	28	3	4	246	.239	.284	.321	.208	24	48-3B 90
David Davalillo	24	LkElsin	Cal	491	96	15	1	1	28	23	20	2	1	396	.196	.239	.236	.148	17	123-2B 100
Jeff Davanon	25	Modesto	Cal	304	77	6	1	4	40	44	29	14	6	233	.253	.340	.319	.238	32	67-OF 82
Cleatus Davidson	22	FtMyers	Fla	528	112	9	4	3	38	43	30	20	10	426	.212	.265	.261	.182	30	124-2B 97
Travis Dawkins	20	Burlingt	Mid	368	84	5	3	2	30	37	24	16	6	290	.228	.286	.274	.200	26	101-SS 92
Jeff Deardorff	20	Beloit	Mid	329	75	8	0	10	22	28	34	1	1	255	.228	.276	.343	.213	27	87-3B 92
Rob Deboer	28	Visalia	Cal	413	82	7	1	8	66	40	33	3	3	334	.199	.309	.278	.203	31	61-C 85
Billy Deck	22	PrWillm	Car	362	80	10	1	5	38	33	30	3	3	285	.221	.295	.296	.204	27	108-1B 102
Steve Decker	33	Norfolk	Int	348	90	11	0	9	43	43	45	0	1	259	.259	.340	.368	.247	39	21-C 87
Tomas Delarosa	21	Jupiter	Fla	389	84	14	1	3	31	36	25	12	4	309	.216	.274	.280	.194	26	
Alex Delgado	28	Syracuse	Int	284	55	7	0	5	19	16	17	1	0	229	.194	.244	.271	.169	13	81-C 99
Ariel Delgado	22	CedarRpd	Mid	511	96	16	1	5	31	27	24	10	7	422	.188	.234	.252	.157	21	125-1B 80
Jose Delgado	24	DanvillC	Car	305	60	5	0	3	18	15	14	4	3	248	.197	.241	.243	.155	12	32-SS 73
Eddy Delossantos	24	StPete	Fla	389	69	5	1	0	14	13	13	2	2	322	.177	.206	.195	.091	4	
Darrell Dent	25	Frederck	Car	463	88	8	1	1	35	26	17	13	7	382	.190	.247	.218	.150	17	129-OF 95
Juan Dilone	26	SanJose	Cal	315	80	7	1	10	21	36	38	10	6	241	.254	.301	.378	.236	33	62-OF 85
Bo Dodson	28	Rochestr	Int	387	92	18	1	6	50	47	40	3	2	297	.238	.325	.336	.232	38	111-1B 92
Rhodney Donaldson	25	KaneCnty	Mid	344	52	4	0	1	37	10	10	7	5	297	.151	.234	.172	.103	5	81-OF 87
John Dorman	25	Kinston	Car	325	57	7	2	2	28	19	12	10	5	273	.175	.241	.228	.151	12	98-SS 97
David Doster	28	Scran-WB	Int	577	140	27	2	12	40	66	60	15	5	442	.243	.292	.359	.229	55	134-3B 102
Jeb Dougherty	23	CedarRpd	Mid	425	84	6	1	2	19	23	16	15	5	346	.198	.232	.231	.152	16	103-OF 95
Brian Downs	24	Hickory	SAL	328	64	5	0	5	13	13	16	1	2	266	.195	.226	.256	.150	12	59-C 88
Chad Durham	21	Hickory	SAL	480	92	5	2	2	25	21	18	13	9	397	.192	.232	.223	.142	15	118-2B 98
Trent Durrington	23	Midland	Tex	345	60	7	0	1	41	22	12	13	7	292	.174	.262	.203	.153	13	25-OF 92
Mike Eaglin	26	Greenvil	Sou	486	95	11	1	6	32	31	26	15	11	402	.195	.245	.259	.168	23	123-2B 98
Michael Edwards	22	Columbus	SAL	498	114	20	1	6	50	50	43	6	3	387	.229	.299	.309	.212	40	115-3B 92
Robert Eenhoorn	31	Norfolk	Int	326	62	6	2	5	17	14	18	0	3	267	.190	.230	.267	.155	13	93-SS 92
David Elliott	25	Stockton	Cal	318	68	9	0	6	20	24	24	6	5	255	.214	.260	.299	.190	20	86-OF 89
Chad Epperson	27	Trenton	Eas	384	83	15	0	11	30	32	38	2	5	306	.216	.273	.341	.207	30	

Extra Players

PLAYER	AGE	AM	LGE	AB	H	DB	TP	HR	BB	R	RBI	SB	CS	OUT	BA	OBA	SA	EQA	EQR	DEFENSE
Corey Erickson	22	StLucie	Fla	342	65	15	2	5	14	19	20	2	1	278	.190	.222	.289	.166	16	40-2B 96
Emiliano Escandon	24	Wilmngtn	Car	371	83	13	1	5	61	44	34	2	4	292	.224	.333	.305	.223	34	66-2B 82
Juan Espinal	24	Sarasota	Fla	501	107	11	1	11	28	33	40	1	1	395	.214	.255	.305	.189	31	126-3B 82
Johnny Estrada	23	Piedmont	SAL	298	70	6	1	4	6	17	24	0	0	228	.235	.250	.302	.187	17	73-C 99
Jason Evans	28	Calgary	PCL	413	79	17	3	2	40	32	22	7	3	337	.191	.263	.262	.177	22	117-OF 85
Lee Evans	21	Augusta	SAL	340	64	12	1	4	24	20	18	3	2	278	.188	.242	.265	.165	15	87-C 89
Alex Fajardo	23	Piedmont	SAL	459	99	10	1	4	32	38	28	14	3	363	.216	.267	.268	.187	28	113-OF 102
Paul Faries	34	Toledo	Int	453	111	14	3	1	37	54	33	20	6	348	.245	.302	.296	.216	38	28-SS 94
Cordell Farley	26	PrWillm	Car	549	133	16	4	9	25	56	50	22	10	426	.242	.275	.335	.215	46	128-OF 91
Mark Farris	24	Carolina	Sou	367	82	10	1	5	26	28	29	2	2	287	.223	.275	.297	.195	24	22-1B 83
Josh Fauske	25	Hickory	SAL	377	72	4	0	8	24	18	22	1	1	306	.191	.239	.265	.163	16	29-C 88
Pedro Felix	22	Shrevprt	Tex	359	84	13	1	10	7	26	37	0	1	276	.234	.249	.359	.207	27	96-3B 97
Dave Feuerstein	25	NewHavn	Eas	502	118	9	3	5	19	37	38	11	7	391	.235	.263	.295	.192	32	125-OF 90
Franky Figueroa	22	Delmarva	SAL	510	114	17	1	9	12	33	40	3	0	396	.224	.241	.314	.189	31	133-1B 87
Luis Figueroa	22	Wisconsn	Mid	311	75	5	0	3	32	30	26	3	1	237	.241	.312	.286	.211	24	87-3B 80
Mark Fischer	23	Michigan	Mid	384	78	8	1	6	27	25	25	4	3	309	.203	.255	.276	.178	21	92-OF 92
Tony Fisher	24	Savannah	SAL	464	93	9	2	7	37	35	29	13	9	380	.200	.259	.274	.181	26	114-OF 99
Jason Fitzgerald	23	Columbus	SAL	487	101	13	1	9	28	34	35	8	4	390	.207	.250	.294	.185	29	126-OF 95
Tim Flaherty	22	Bakrsfld	Cal	477	97	12	0	18	32	34	47	0	0	380	.203	.253	.342	.201	34	78-C 89
Jose Flores	26	Scran-WB	Int	345	91	11	1	5	39	45	38	7	5	259	.264	.339	.345	.241	37	82-SS 92
Quincy Foster	24	KaneCnty	Mid	551	107	10	3	1	35	36	21	25	11	455	.194	.242	.229	.158	23	131-OF 97
Lou Frazier	34	Calgary	PCL	386	81	13	2	9	46	55	32	30	7	312	.210	.294	.324	.226	38	71-OF 95
Ricky Freeman	27	WestTenn	Sou	366	79	9	1	10	29	31	34	4	3	290	.216	.273	.328	.206	28	83-1B 87
Terrance Freeman	24	Augusta	SAL	414	75	7	1	1	58	32	16	15	11	350	.181	.282	.210	.165	19	116-2B 95
Alejandro Freire	24	Jacksnvl	Sou	492	121	14	0	15	20	42	56	2	1	372	.246	.275	.366	.221	43	124-1B 117
Anton French	23	Lancastr	Cal	375	78	5	3	5	24	33	24	19	5	302	.208	.256	.277	.190	24	90-OF 96
Aaron Fuller	27	Daytona	Fla	292	61	8	2	3	44	33	22	6	2	233	.209	.312	.281	.210	24	56-OF 81
Joe Funaro	26	Portland	Eas	338	78	5	2	4	25	28	27	5	4	264	.231	.284	.293	.199	23	57-SS 87
Bryon Gainey	23	StLucie	Fla	330	77	7	2	12	13	25	39	0	2	255	.233	.262	.376	.216	28	71-1B 75
Guillermo Garcia	27	Indianap	Int	331	73	10	0	14	17	27	38	0	1	259	.221	.259	.378	.216	28	89-C 101
Luis Garcia	23	WnstnSlm	Car	388	91	13	1	10	15	32	39	4	3	300	.235	.263	.351	.211	31	98-OF 93
Neil Garcia	26	StPete	Fla	327	77	5	0	5	28	27	29	1	2	252	.235	.296	.297	.204	24	58-C 88
Sandro Garcia	21	Charl-WV	SAL	367	65	9	0	4	20	14	13	4	3	305	.177	.220	.234	.135	10	27-2B 95
Vicente Garcia	24	NewHavn	Eas	429	85	12	0	11	58	41	37	5	4	348	.198	.294	.303	.205	33	121-2B 93
Webster Garrison	33	Huntsvil	Sou	296	66	7	0	8	35	28	31	1	2	232	.223	.305	.328	.218	26	19-OF 74
Aaron Gentry	24	Peoria	Mid	283	49	4	1	2	20	11	9	5	2	236	.173	.228	.216	.133	8	72-3B 88
Chip Glass	28	Norwich	Eas	424	99	6	1	3	31	36	30	9	4	329	.233	.286	.274	.195	28	105-OF 95
Ross Gload	23	KaneCnty	Mid	507	128	19	1	10	42	54	57	3	3	382	.252	.310	.353	.231	49	128-1B 86
Manny Gonzalez	23	Birmnghm	Sou	366	98	20	1	2	14	39	35	6	4	272	.268	.295	.344	.224	32	93-OF 94
Wikleman Gonzalez	25	RCucmng	Cal	289	62	7	1	6	17	19	24	0	0	227	.215	.258	.308	.191	18	
Brian Gordon	20	SthBend	Mid	469	116	15	2	9	12	37	47	3	2	355	.247	.266	.345	.211	36	113-OF 81
Jason Grabowski	23	Savannah	SAL	360	78	5	2	9	42	35	34	6	5	287	.217	.299	.317	.213	30	60-C 89
Jess Graham	23	Michigan	Mid	422	89	10	2	7	37	33	33	4	2	335	.211	.275	.294	.195	28	105-OF 88
Pedro Grifol	29	Binghmtn	Eas	393	70	8	0	3	22	14	14	1	1	324	.178	.222	.221	.126	9	110-C 102
Ryan Grimmett	24	WMichgn	Mid	424	77	7	5	1	38	28	17	17	8	355	.182	.249	.229	.160	18	110-OF 99
Mike Groppuso	29	ElPaso	Tex	420	90	14	2	12	46	41	44	1	1	331	.214	.292	.343	.218	37	50-1B 100
Jeff Guiel	25	LkElsin	Cal	324	69	9	1	10	57	44	35	9	6	261	.213	.331	.340	.234	35	89-OF 87
Matt Guiliano	27	Reading	Eas	439	80	9	1	8	36	24	24	1	2	361	.182	.244	.262	.162	19	32-2B 92
Mark Gulseth	27	SanJose	Cal	468	99	15	1	6	34	33	33	1	1	370	.212	.265	.286	.186	28	71-1B 83
Victor Gutierrez	21	Augusta	SAL	467	101	16	2	1	45	51	26	26	11	377	.216	.285	.266	.197	33	123-SS 77
Edwards Guzman	22	Fresno	PCL	316	85	9	0	9	22	34	42	1	0	231	.269	.317	.383	.244	34	74-3B 89
Danny Haas	23	Michigan	Mid	302	55	7	0	3	16	11	11	0	1	248	.182	.223	.235	.135	8	67-OF 85
Travis Hafner	22	Savannah	SAL	415	83	8	1	11	53	38	36	3	2	334	.200	.291	.304	.204	32	21-3B 87
Steve Hagins	24	LkElsin	Cal	357	80	9	1	11	19	29	36	3	3	280	.224	.263	.347	.208	28	47-C 78
Jason Hairston	23	Macon	SAL	411	75	8	1	11	24	21	26	4	4	340	.182	.228	.287	.167	19	62-OF 64
Dave Hajek	31	LasVegas	PCL	519	136	27	2	3	20	54	48	10	5	388	.262	.289	.339	.221	44	124-2B 89

PLAYER	AGE	AM	LGE	AB	H	DB	TP	HR	BB	R	RBI	SB	CS	OUT	BA	OBA	SA	EQA	EQR	DEFENSE
Chip Hale	34	Memphis	PCL	408	90	10	0	7	51	38	36	1	2	320	.221	.307	.297	.209	32	30-1B 106
Noah Hall	22	CapeFear	SAL	449	117	12	3	8	41	57	50	14	6	338	.261	.322	.354	.240	48	104-OF 88
Toby Hall	23	Charl-SC	SAL	378	91	11	1	4	28	32	33	1	3	290	.241	.293	.307	.206	28	102-C 88
Patrick Hallmark	25	Wilmngtn	Car	375	83	9	1	4	38	38	27	14	9	301	.221	.293	.283	.202	27	22-C 92
Garrick Haltiwanger	24	StLucie	Fla	344	48	6	0	6	26	9	9	3	3	299	.140	.200	.209	.097	4	91-OF 86
Kevin Ham	24	LkElsin	Cal	355	58	8	2	3	27	11	11	1	2	299	.163	.223	.223	.125	8	98-OF 93
Jon Hamilton	21	Columbus	SAL	491	107	13	4	12	63	55	50	9	5	389	.218	.307	.334	.223	46	131-OF 99
Todd Haney	33	Norfolk	Int	430	123	22	3	2	43	62	50	6	2	309	.286	.351	.365	.255	51	23-OF 87
Mike Hardge	27	Arkansas	Tex	349	76	9	1	5	31	28	27	4	5	278	.218	.282	.292	.195	23	15-3B 87
Jason Hardtke	27	Iowa	PCL	327	77	10	1	8	29	34	34	5	5	255	.235	.298	.346	.222	30	65-3B 86
Harvey Hargrove	23	Wisconsn	Mid	454	90	12	2	11	33	35	35	9	4	368	.198	.253	.306	.191	29	116-OF 89
Brian Harris	24	Clearwtr	Fla	435	91	9	2	4	35	31	27	7	7	351	.209	.268	.267	.179	24	116-2B 99
Jamal Harrison	21	FtWayne	Mid	395	98	15	1	9	32	42	45	3	3	300	.248	.304	.359	.230	38	49-1B 101
Ron Hartman	24	Tucson	PCL	424	96	10	0	9	21	29	37	1	2	330	.226	.263	.314	.196	28	102-3B 86
Heath Hayes	27	Akron	Eas	328	55	7	1	7	19	12	15	1	2	275	.168	.213	.259	.142	10	85-C 91
Jon Heinrichs	24	Brevard	Fla	469	105	9	1	8	38	41	38	8	4	368	.224	.282	.299	.202	34	106-OF 85
Chris Heintz	24	WnstnSlm	Car	509	120	13	1	7	29	40	43	4	4	393	.236	.277	.306	.200	35	28-C 89
Dan Held	28	Scran-WB	Int	397	94	17	2	11	27	38	46	1	2	305	.237	.285	.373	.226	37	107-1B 88
Juan Hernaiz	24	Jacksnvl	Sou	381	86	14	1	9	8	28	34	5	2	297	.226	.242	.339	.199	26	78-OF 86
Mike Hessman	21	DanvillC	Car	448	85	11	0	18	30	30	40	2	2	365	.190	.241	.335	.192	30	112-3B 94
Jeremy Hill	21	Lansing	Mid	287	57	6	1	4	13	15	16	2	1	231	.199	.233	.268	.163	12	80-C 99
Shea Hillenbrand	23	Michigan	Mid	496	144	15	1	14	14	54	70	6	4	356	.290	.310	.409	.250	56	84-C 87
Rich Hills	25	Orlando	Sou	437	79	6	0	4	38	19	17	1	1	359	.181	.246	.222	.143	14	48-SS 90
Todd Hogan	23	PrWillm	Car	488	119	17	2	2	21	43	36	13	9	378	.244	.275	.299	.199	34	122-OF 112
Daren Hooper	22	Delmarva	SAL	321	53	5	1	5	20	10	11	0	1	269	.165	.214	.234	.126	8	21-OF 75
Kyle Houser	24	NewHavn	Eas	312	64	2	0	1	18	14	13	3	2	250	.205	.248	.221	.148	10	91-SS 91
Matt Howard	31	Fresno	PCL	397	86	8	0	3	34	31	24	7	5	316	.217	.278	.259	.184	23	24-2B 101
Mike Huelsmann	24	Kinston	Car	443	109	12	2	5	59	56	42	10	8	342	.246	.335	.316	.230	43	112-OF 98
Brent Huff	23	StLucie	Fla	445	91	13	1	8	20	25	30	3	5	359	.204	.239	.292	.174	23	102-OF 92
Johnny Hunter	24	Clinton	Mid	422	75	8	1	7	57	36	24	13	5	353	.178	.276	.251	.181	25	106-OF 89
Bernard Hutchison	25	SalemVA	Car	300	48	5	0	2	31	16	9	14	6	258	.160	.239	.197	.139	9	99-OF 92
Tim Hyers	27	Charlott	Int	295	68	14	1	5	21	26	28	0	2	229	.231	.282	.336	.210	23	38-OF 86
Darron Ingram	23	Chattang	Sou	463	96	15	4	16	30	38	48	3	2	369	.207	.256	.361	.209	37	113-OF 89
Garey Ingram	28	Albuquer	PCL	363	85	15	2	6	25	40	33	14	5	283	.234	.284	.336	.219	32	18-3B 98
Johnny Isom	25	Bowie	Eas	323	65	7	0	9	24	22	26	1	2	260	.201	.256	.307	.188	20	89-OF 91
Cesar Izturis	19	Hagerstn	SAL	409	85	8	1	1	18	21	18	8	5	329	.208	.241	.240	.156	16	125-SS 100
Jeremy Jackson	23	Ashevlle	SAL	356	73	6	1	6	18	20	23	5	5	288	.205	.243	.278	.172	18	89-OF 85
Mandy Jacomino	25	WMichgn	Mid	282	44	3	0	4	28	9	8	1	1	239	.156	.232	.209	.124	7	
Kenny James	22	CapeFear	SAL	449	91	7	2	1	17	25	18	16	4	362	.203	.232	.234	.155	17	94-OF 105
Frank Jaramillo	24	Savannah	SAL	320	60	6	2	5	26	18	19	3	3	263	.188	.249	.266	.168	15	24-1B 74
Link Jarrett	27	NewHavn	Eas	325	62	6	1	0	18	12	12	3	6	269	.191	.233	.215	.129	8	27-3B 106
Felipe Jimenez	22	Rockford	Mid	370	69	8	2	1	22	21	13	15	6	307	.186	.232	.227	.151	14	113-OF 100
Anthony Johnson	26	RCucmng	Cal	528	122	12	1	13	19	39	49	7	6	412	.231	.258	.331	.201	37	128-OF 95
Damon Johnson	23	Dunedin	Fla	332	72	10	0	4	14	22	21	6	5	265	.217	.249	.283	.178	18	89-OF 93
Earl Johnson	27	Toledo	Int	358	76	6	5	1	15	25	19	12	5	287	.212	.244	.265	.174	18	104-OF 101
Gary Johnson	22	Daytona	Fla	409	76	4	0	10	44	28	27	4	1	334	.186	.265	.269	.180	23	111-OF 96
J. J. Johnson	25	NewBrit	Eas	372	85	11	2	10	21	32	38	4	4	291	.228	.270	.349	.212	30	45-OF 87
Jason Johnson	21	Piedmont	SAL	447	99	10	2	1	30	35	26	13	7	355	.221	.270	.260	.183	25	104-OF 98
Mark Johnson	31	Indianap	Int	355	94	18	1	16	54	56	61	1	2	263	.265	.362	.456	.279	54	22-OF 86
Ric Johnson	25	Kissimme	Fla	381	77	7	1	4	24	23	21	7	4	308	.202	.249	.257	.168	18	102-OF 96
Rontrez Johnson	22	Michigan	Mid	317	75	10	2	5	51	45	32	10	5	247	.237	.342	.328	.239	34	81-OF 100
Thomas Johnson	23	Columbia	SAL	307	54	9	2	3	20	16	13	8	4	257	.176	.226	.248	.152	12	83-OF 100
Ryan Jones	24	Knoxvill	Sou	403	83	10	0	9	30	28	31	2	2	322	.206	.261	.298	.188	25	65-1B 97
Jeff Keaveney	23	Michigan	Mid	385	81	8	0	11	48	35	38	0	1	305	.210	.298	.317	.211	31	24-1B 94
Gus Kennedy	25	RCucmng	Cal	434	85	10	2	10	54	39	35	7	5	354	.196	.285	.297	.200	32	107-OF 94
Robbie Kent	25	RCucmng	Cal	452	85	9	0	5	22	17	19	1	1	368	.188	.226	.241	.142	14	92-3B 80

Extra Players

PLAYER	AGE	AM	LGE	AB	H	DB	TP	HR	BB	R	RBI	SB	CS	OUT	BA	OBA	SA	EQA	EQR	DEFENSE
Troy Kent	25	Kinston	Car	334	65	9	1	4	20	18	18	1	1	270	.195	.240	.263	.162	14	22-3B 84
Scott Kidd	25	Greensbr	SAL	471	93	9	0	9	30	26	30	3	3	381	.197	.246	.274	.170	23	122-2B 92
Joe Kilburg	23	Columbus	SAL	450	81	9	1	5	49	29	21	8	5	374	.180	.261	.238	.164	20	118-2B 88
David Kim	23	Peoria	Mid	469	116	15	0	11	38	45	53	1	3	356	.247	.304	.350	.226	43	109-OF 85
Brendan Kingman	26	Lancastr	Cal	444	107	9	1	9	26	37	43	3	3	340	.241	.283	.327	.210	34	21-3B 111
Scott Kirby	21	Beloit	Mid	365	65	11	0	8	39	24	23	2	2	302	.178	.257	.274	.175	19	16-OF 75
Stacy Kleiner	24	Arkansas	Tex	328	67	13	1	5	26	24	24	1	1	262	.204	.263	.296	.188	20	86-C 99
Larry Kleinz	25	Brevard	Fla	322	69	8	1	5	32	26	26	0	0	253	.214	.285	.292	.198	22	73-3B 102
Eric Knowles	25	Tampa	Fla	357	70	8	2	1	22	17	15	1	3	290	.196	.243	.238	.149	12	73-SS 89
Mike Koerner	23	Visalia	Cal	358	66	8	1	9	22	19	23	3	5	297	.184	.232	.288	.167	17	99-OF 93
Eric Kofler	23	Tampa	Fla	332	84	14	1	8	16	31	39	0	1	249	.253	.287	.373	.228	31	55-OF 88
Dennis Konrady	24	Kinston	Car	436	90	9	2	9	58	41	38	3	2	348	.206	.300	.298	.207	34	38-C 85
Jake Kraus	25	Beloit	Mid	277	64	6	1	4	31	27	25	0	0	213	.231	.308	.303	.213	22	79-1B 76
Steve Lackey	24	Lakeland	Fla	410	87	8	2	2	23	26	22	7	4	327	.212	.254	.256	.170	20	95-SS 96
Michael Lamb	23	Charlott	Fla	535	135	22	1	8	36	57	54	8	4	404	.252	.299	.342	.225	48	133-3B 108
Jacques Landry	25	Lakeland	Fla	392	71	6	1	6	19	14	17	3	3	324	.181	.219	.247	.142	12	98-3B 83
Todd Landry	26	Binghmtn	Eas	428	97	13	1	7	29	34	37	2	1	332	.227	.276	.311	.202	30	88-1B 97
Selwyn Langaigne	23	Dunedin	Fla	469	92	5	0	0	30	19	18	8	8	385	.196	.244	.207	.136	13	126-OF 105
Derrick Lankford	24	Augusta	SAL	465	100	10	1	12	42	39	43	3	3	368	.215	.280	.318	.205	35	56-1B 101
Eddie Lara	23	Visalia	Cal	440	98	9	2	5	21	29	31	6	6	348	.223	.258	.286	.183	25	52-3B 118
Jason Lariviere	25	Arkansas	Tex	430	84	15	2	5	37	33	26	8	4	350	.195	.259	.274	.181	24	122-OF 94
Greg Larocca	26	LasVegas	PCL	294	73	12	3	6	16	30	33	5	3	224	.248	.287	.371	.228	28	17-SS 84
Dan Lauterhahn	23	WMichgn	Mid	309	54	11	0	1	18	11	10	3	1	256	.175	.220	.220	.128	7	92-SS 94
Tony Lawrence	24	Clinton	Mid	301	53	5	1	5	25	14	15	2	2	250	.176	.239	.249	.154	12	24-C 92
Jason Layne	26	Wilmngtn	Car	368	87	15	3	8	36	39	42	0	0	281	.236	.304	.359	.230	36	93-1B 97
Nick Leach	21	SanBern	Cal	468	90	15	1	6	34	27	26	3	6	384	.192	.247	.267	.166	21	117-1B 101
Juan Lebron	22	Lansing	Mid	446	94	11	3	14	44	43	45	8	6	358	.211	.282	.343	.214	38	109-OF 91
Derek Lee	32	Rochestr	Int	363	90	10	2	13	39	43	50	3	4	277	.248	.321	.394	.246	41	51-OF 91
Jason Lee	22	Peoria	Mid	387	83	9	2	5	33	29	29	4	5	309	.214	.276	.287	.191	25	108-OF 95
Ryan Lehr	20	Macon	SAL	398	92	12	1	10	35	37	42	0	2	308	.231	.293	.342	.218	34	39-3B 66
Chris Lemonis	26	Lakeland	Fla	323	63	7	1	2	19	14	15	0	0	260	.195	.240	.241	.151	11	23-1B 84
Carlos Leon	19	Michigan	Mid	380	83	4	2	3	41	31	26	4	5	302	.218	.295	.263	.191	24	104-2B 91
Donny Leon	23	Tampa	Fla	380	90	11	1	8	19	30	37	0	0	290	.237	.273	.334	.209	29	98-3B 77
John Lindsey	22	Ashevlle	SAL	465	97	10	1	9	19	25	33	1	2	370	.209	.240	.292	.175	24	112-1B 95
David Lindstrom	24	Lakeland	Fla	338	61	11	0	4	37	21	17	0	1	278	.180	.261	.249	.165	15	97-C 93
Nelson Liriano	35	ColSprin	PCL	273	63	9	2	4	31	30	25	6	7	217	.231	.309	.322	.218	24	14-3B 90
Claudio Liverziani	24	Wisconsn	Mid	358	66	10	1	3	20	17	15	6	2	294	.184	.228	.243	.149	13	94-1B 97
Doug Livingston	25	SalemVA	Car	520	110	15	1	2	41	40	29	11	3	413	.212	.269	.256	.181	29	130-2B 92
Kyle Logan	23	QuadCit	Mid	357	75	11	1	4	26	27	23	8	7	289	.210	.264	.280	.184	21	100-OF 89
Tony Longueira	24	Lansing	Mid	355	74	8	1	4	17	19	21	2	3	284	.208	.245	.270	.168	16	32-2B 97
Jose Lopez	23	Binghmtn	Eas	325	83	16	1	10	16	37	41	5	2	244	.255	.290	.403	.240	35	77-3B 98
Manny Lopez	21	FtWayne	Mid	400	96	12	1	8	31	38	41	3	2	306	.240	.295	.335	.219	34	108-OF 94
Mickey Lopez	25	ElPaso	Tex	443	82	13	2	2	33	23	18	6	5	366	.185	.242	.237	.151	16	115-2B 91
Jamie Lopiccolo	26	Lakeland	Fla	432	93	14	1	7	17	27	32	3	2	341	.215	.245	.301	.183	25	22-OF 88
Luis Lorenzana	20	Lynchbrg	Car	288	62	4	1	3	33	23	21	1	1	227	.215	.296	.267	.194	19	87-2B 105
Torey Lovullo	33	Buffalo	Int	325	92	12	2	12	43	50	55	2	2	235	.283	.367	.443	.279	48	73-3B 81
Brian Loyd	25	1RCucmng	Cal	316	67	7	0	3	29	21	21	0	2	251	.212	.278	.263	.181	17	72-C 91
Lou Lucca	28	Charlott	Int	389	93	14	0	10	9	28	39	1	4	300	.239	.256	.352	.206	29	29-OF 90
Jon Macalutas	24	Stockton	Cal	527	116	11	0	6	28	33	35	3	4	415	.220	.259	.275	.178	28	112-1B 84
Rob Mackowiak	23	Lynchbrg	Car	294	72	17	4	3	17	31	30	3	2	224	.245	.286	.361	.224	27	79-3B 83
Rob MacRory	24	Peoria	Mid	491	104	7	1	1	33	32	23	13	8	394	.212	.261	.236	.167	22	122-2B 95
Taber Maier	24	Peoria	Mid	277	54	5	0	2	32	19	14	2	2	225	.195	.278	.235	.170	13	52-3B 103
Jeff Maloney	22	Dunedin	Fla	298	45	4	1	7	20	10	10	3	2	255	.151	.204	.242	.128	8	44-OF 95
Dwight Maness	25	Trenton	Eas	314	68	7	2	9	30	32	31	10	5	250	.217	.285	.338	.217	28	83-OF 109
Nate Manning	25	Daytona	Fla	418	79	7	0	9	19	18	23	1	2	341	.189	.224	.270	.156	16	22-1B 75
Mike Marchiano	24	Wisconsn	Mid	448	99	11	0	10	33	37	39	5	3	352	.221	.274	.312	.202	32	100-OF 77

PLAYER	AGE	AM	LGE	AB	H	DB	TP	HR	BB	R	RBI	SB	CS	OUT	BA	OBA	SA	EQA	EQR	DEFENSE
Kevin Marn	25	Charl-WV	SAL	345	61	8	1	2	20	13	12	5	3	287	.177	.222	.223	.132	9	67-OF 81
Roy Marsh	25	Sarasota	Fla	355	70	7	3	1	30	24	17	9	5	290	.197	.260	.242	.168	17	106-OF 96
Casey Martin	23	CedarRpd	Mid	339	66	5	1	7	26	20	23	1	1	274	.195	.252	.277	.175	17	38-C 90
Chris Martin	31	Durham	Int	446	97	17	1	6	50	47	35	11	8	357	.217	.296	.300	.207	35	125-SS 88
Chris Martine	23	PrWillm	Car	286	46	6	0	3	33	11	10	1	3	243	.161	.248	.213	.136	8	92-C 92
Hipolito Martinez	22	Modesto	Cal	342	67	11	1	8	32	28	26	6	6	281	.196	.265	.304	.192	23	88-OF 90
Rafael Martinez	23	Sarasota	Fla	328	68	4	1	4	39	26	23	2	2	262	.207	.292	.262	.189	20	99-1B 99
Raul Marval	23	Shrevprt	Tex	293	59	3	1	1	11	11	11	1	1	235	.201	.230	.229	.138	8	84-SS 99
Henry Mateo	22	CapeFear	SAL	418	91	12	2	3	31	33	27	9	8	335	.218	.272	.278	.187	25	108-2B 83
Joe Mathis	24	Orlando	Sou	391	81	12	2	4	16	24	23	7	6	316	.207	.238	.279	.171	19	94-OF 101
Francisco Matos	29	Columbus	Int	285	79	10	1	2	15	30	30	2	1	207	.277	.313	.340	.231	26	62-2B 92
Julius Matos	24	HighDes	Cal	426	90	12	1	3	16	24	23	8	7	343	.211	.240	.265	.166	19	110-SS 90
Freddy May	23	Lynchbrg	Car	475	122	15	3	5	46	58	47	12	8	361	.257	.322	.333	.231	46	119-OF 84
Brian McClure	25	RCucmng	Cal	493	94	11	3	6	44	30	29	2	2	401	.191	.257	.262	.170	24	123-2B 87
Jason McConnell	23	FtWayne	Mid	321	67	7	1	2	22	22	17	7	5	259	.209	.259	.255	.173	16	29-2B 87
Will McCrotty	20	SanBern	Cal	341	61	7	0	4	8	12	12	1	1	281	.179	.198	.235	.118	7	102-C 93
Cody McKay	25	Modesto	Cal	402	83	8	1	4	26	22	24	1	2	321	.206	.255	.261	.169	19	92-C 96
Dan McKinley	23	Bakrsfld	Cal	375	91	9	1	5	22	35	32	9	4	288	.243	.285	.312	.210	29	93-OF 101
Buck McNabb	26	WestTenn	Sou	379	86	11	2	5	33	37	31	11	8	301	.227	.289	.306	.207	29	98-OF 88
Sean McNally	26	Wichita	Tex	312	57	9	0	4	28	17	16	1	2	257	.183	.250	.250	.160	13	27-1B 98
Rusty McNamara	24	Clearwtr	Fla	519	115	15	1	7	18	33	37	6	4	408	.222	.248	.295	.183	29	120-3B 76
Aaron McNeal	21	QuadCit	Mid	374	95	7	1	12	25	35	48	1	2	281	.254	.301	.374	.233	37	101-1B 101
Ryan Medrano	25	Charl-WV	SAL	369	57	7	0	4	34	11	11	2	1	313	.154	.226	.206	.118	8	21-SS 81
Steve Medrano	21	Lansing	Mid	341	75	11	2	1	28	29	22	6	2	268	.220	.279	.273	.191	21	103-SS 107
Tony Medrano	24	Wichita	Tex	291	68	8	1	6	21	26	28	2	2	225	.234	.285	.330	.212	23	20-3B 83
Max Mejia	21	VeroBch	Fla	285	62	10	1	5	16	24	22	7	5	228	.218	.259	.312	.196	19	69-OF 91
Alex Melconian	24	KaneCnty	Mid	460	77	4	0	4	35	15	15	7	2	385	.167	.226	.202	.122	10	19-C 93
Carlos Mendoza	19	SanJose	Cal	365	65	5	1	1	15	13	13	6	4	304	.178	.211	.205	.111	6	109-SS 101
Todd Mensik	24	Modesto	Cal	383	83	10	0	10	45	37	37	1	2	302	.217	.299	.321	.213	32	60-1B 91
Rod Metzler	24	Lansing	Mid	326	59	8	1	2	24	17	12	6	3	270	.181	.237	.230	.147	11	18-OF 99
Aaron Miles	22	QuadCit	Mid	372	77	16	3	2	19	29	21	12	7	302	.207	.246	.282	.180	21	99-2B 95
Marc Mirizzi	24	Greensbr	SAL	374	77	10	1	6	22	23	25	1	2	299	.206	.250	.286	.177	20	19-2B 96
Andres Mitchell	23	Ashevlle	SAL	447	79	9	2	5	40	25	20	9	6	374	.177	.244	.239	.156	18	136-OF 100
Derek Mitchell	24	Jacksnvl	Sou	424	82	15	1	2	51	33	23	4	2	344	.193	.280	.248	.178	23	127-SS 99
Mike Mitchell	26	Mobile	Sou	501	129	15	1	11	39	52	59	0	0	372	.257	.311	.357	.233	49	120-1B 100
Chris Miyake	25	Lynchbrg	Car	416	82	11	1	2	27	22	19	2	1	335	.197	.246	.243	.156	16	23-3B 95
Dustan Mohr	23	Kinston	Car	500	114	13	5	17	37	49	59	4	2	388	.228	.281	.376	.226	47	116-OF 91
Izzy Molina	28	Edmonton	PCL	297	58	8	1	6	15	18	19	2	0	239	.195	.234	.290	.174	15	88-C 97
Jose Molina	24	WestTenn	Sou	319	58	7	0	2	21	11	11	1	3	264	.182	.232	.223	.132	8	96-C 105
Wonderful Monds	26	NewHavn	Eas	453	109	20	2	7	26	54	40	26	10	354	.241	.282	.340	.222	41	115-OF 102
Craig Monroe	22	Charlott	Fla	476	106	17	3	15	55	65	51	25	9	379	.223	.303	.366	.236	52	119-OF 91
Brian Moon	21	Beloit	Mid	443	96	14	0	2	38	32	28	0	0	347	.217	.279	.262	.183	25	95-C 104
Kenderick Moore	26	Wilmngtn	Car	398	87	9	2	4	37	35	28	9	9	320	.219	.285	.281	.194	26	45-2B 89
Kerwin Moore	28	Huntsvil	Sou	347	60	8	2	1	64	40	14	23	9	296	.173	.302	.216	.188	23	97-OF 93
Juan Mora	21	WMichgn	Mid	310	64	11	2	4	12	19	20	3	2	248	.206	.236	.294	.176	16	65-OF 100
Francisco Morales	26	Harrisbg	Eas	313	57	7	1	6	24	17	18	1	1	257	.182	.240	.268	.164	14	61-C 95
Juan Moreno	23	Columbia	SAL	434	94	10	1	6	27	35	30	12	5	345	.217	.262	.286	.190	27	100-OF 75
Shea Morenz	25	Norwich	Eas	409	90	12	1	11	25	33	39	5	4	323	.220	.265	.335	.205	31	79-OF 89
Russ Morman	37	Durham	Int	363	87	14	1	8	25	33	39	0	1	277	.240	.289	.350	.220	31	21-1B 107
Greg Morrison	23	Hagerstn	SAL	430	88	8	1	8	22	23	29	1	3	345	.205	.243	.284	.172	21	103-1B 90
Mark Mortimer	23	DanvillC	Car	345	71	5	1	6	36	25	26	0	2	276	.206	.281	.278	.188	21	20-OF 71
Billy Munoz	24	Columbus	SAL	422	78	8	1	6	47	27	24	1	1	345	.185	.267	.251	.170	21	116-1B 91
Adrian Myers	24	Charlott	Fla	457	98	12	3	5	41	45	31	20	13	372	.214	.279	.287	.197	32	97-OF 102
Mike Neal	27	Jackson	Tex	334	86	11	1	10	28	37	44	2	3	251	.257	.315	.386	.242	36	27-SS 81
Garrett Neubart	25	Binghmtn	Eas	360	83	8	2	2	27	37	24	17	6	283	.231	.284	.281	.203	26	90-OF 96
Scott Neuberger	21	Charl-SC	SAL	477	93	10	0	4	34	23	23	2	3	387	.195	.249	.241	.155	18	130-OF 98

Extra Players

PLAYER	AGE	AM	LGE	AB	H	DB	TP	HR	BB	R	RBI	SB	CS	OUT	BA	OBA	SA	EQA	EQR	DEFENSE
David Newhan	25	Mobile	Sou	489	105	14	2	9	46	48	40	15	6	390	.215	.282	.307	.207	38	111-2B 93
Doug Newstrom	27	NewHavn	Eas	333	79	13	1	4	33	36	30	4	3	257	.237	.306	.318	.218	28	25-1B 88
Wilbert Nieves	21	Clinton	Mid	386	85	9	0	5	38	32	29	3	5	306	.220	.290	.282	.195	26	91-C 97
Les Norman	30	Oklahoma	PCL	372	96	19	1	8	15	39	43	5	2	278	.258	.287	.379	.232	36	74-OF 99
Sergio Nunez	24	Birmnghm	Sou	433	90	2	0	2	24	26	18	15	5	348	.208	.249	.226	.160	18	114-2B 100
Brandon O'Ghearn	24	Charl-WV	SAL	392	65	9	0	4	22	13	13	1	2	329	.166	.210	.219	.114	7	93-OF 81
John Oliver	21	Charl-WV	SAL	416	79	11	0	9	19	22	24	5	5	342	.190	.225	.281	.163	18	103-OF 78
Jose Olmeda	21	Sarasota	Fla	356	61	11	2	5	16	14	14	4	3	298	.171	.207	.256	.140	11	111-SS 83
Jose Olmeda	31	Richmond	Int	366	79	12	1	3	22	25	24	4	5	292	.216	.260	.279	.180	20	75-SS 97
Dan Olson	24	WnstnSlm	Car	409	92	15	2	14	35	41	48	3	3	320	.225	.286	.374	.226	39	79-OF 80
Dave Orndorff	21	FtWayne	Mid	388	91	14	1	7	36	45	36	14	7	304	.235	.300	.330	.222	35	16-OF 81
Bill Ortega	23	Peoria	Mid	401	85	11	1	2	29	25	23	1	4	320	.212	.265	.259	.172	20	45-OF 90
Garrett Osilka	21	Beloit	Mid	500	113	17	1	8	53	51	44	8	6	393	.226	.300	.312	.213	41	01-33 95
Ricky Otero	27	Rochestr	Int	350	87	17	4	3	17	36	33	6	4	267	.249	.283	.346	.219	30	86-OF 103
Richard Ozarowski	24	WMichgn	Mid	305	61	10	1	2	22	19	16	2	2	246	.200	.254	.259	.168	14	22-2B 101
John Pachot	24	Ottawa	Int	340	69	14	1	2	12	17	17	1	1	272	.203	.230	.268	.160	14	78-C 103
Pete Paciorek	23	RCucmng	Cal	480	108	13	1	13	47	46	50	4	4	376	.225	.294	.338	.218	42	135-1B 93
Roy Padilla	23	Sarasota	Fla	361	72	10	1	3	23	22	19	5	1	290	.199	.247	.258	.168	17	107-OF 95
Jarrod Patterson	25	HighDes	Cal	479	114	13	2	10	43	48	50	4	1	366	.238	.301	.336	.223	43	40-1B 96
Eddie Pearson	25	Calgary	PCL	342	81	13	1	5	19	29	31	1	1	262	.237	.277	.325	.207	26	
Alex Pena	21	Augusta	SAL	294	63	9	1	4	21	22	22	3	3	234	.214	.267	.293	.189	18	86-OF 95
Jose Pena	22	Savannah	SAL	467	116	13	2	5	15	43	39	17	9	360	.248	.272	.317	.207	35	106-OF 85
Jersen Perez	23	Columbia	SAL	482	100	9	4	5	15	25	28	5	2	384	.207	.231	.274	.166	22	100-SS 87
Tony Peters	24	Hagerstn	SAL	324	69	3	1	5	18	21	21	5	4	258	.213	.254	.275	.178	17	78-OF 89
Chris Petersen	28	Iowa	PCL	382	72	10	0	6	19	17	19	2	3	313	.188	.227	.262	.153	14	111-SS 111
Charles Peterson	25	Carolina	Sou	292	62	7	1	6	14	22	22	9	6	236	.212	.248	.305	.189	18	72-OF 87
Josh Phelps	21	Hagerstn	SAL	385	83	13	1	6	33	31	31	1	0	302	.216	.278	.301	.198	26	82-C 94
Wynter Phoenix	24	SanBern	Cal	318	59	7	1	5	25	21	17	9	6	265	.186	.245	.261	.168	15	77-OF 79
Rene Pinto	21	Greensbr	SAL	367	68	12	2	1	27	17	15	1	3	302	.185	.241	.237	.147	13	106-C 95
Scott Podsednik	23	Charlott	Fla	305	74	7	2	4	34	38	28	11	5	236	.243	.319	.318	.227	29	62-OF 104
Charles Poe	27	LasVegas	PCL	382	84	14	1	6	22	30	30	4	2	300	.220	.262	.309	.196	25	96-OF 93
Joe Pomierski	25	StPete	Fla	391	70	10	1	7	29	19	21	1	1	322	.179	.236	.263	.159	16	94-OF 83
Simon Pond	22	Jupiter	Fla	342	67	10	1	1	20	15	15	0	2	277	.196	.240	.240	.148	12	71-3B 80
Scott Pose	32	Columbus	Int	480	117	15	5	3	41	63	38	28	11	374	.244	.303	.315	.223	44	99-OF 89
Dave Post	25	Ottawa	Int	324	83	17	1	5	23	36	35	4	5	246	.256	.305	.361	.230	31	28-OF 78
John Powers	25	Mobile	Sou	471	117	16	2	9	52	56	52	5	4	358	.248	.323	.348	.235	48	110-3B 102
Nick Presto	24	Chattang	Sou	477	97	10	0	5	54	40	28	12	11	391	.203	.284	.256	.184	28	129-2B 93
Alejandro Prieto	23	Wichita	Tex	374	77	12	3	2	25	23	22	2	4	301	.206	.256	.270	.172	19	105-SS 91
Chris Prieto	26	LasVegas	PCL	342	81	10	3	2	33	39	27	14	8	269	.237	.304	.301	.214	29	90-OF 101
Chris Pritchett	29	Vancouvr	PCL	372	83	11	1	6	32	31	32	2	2	291	.223	.285	.306	.203	27	88-1B 95
Luke Quaccia	24	Peoria	Mid	441	93	9	1	8	32	31	33	2	1	349	.211	.264	.290	.188	27	125-1B 98
Tom Quinlan	31	Oklahoma	PCL	531	125	21	1	12	36	50	55	3	0	406	.235	.284	.347	.219	46	124-3B 100
Danny Ramirez	25	StLucie	Fla	462	87	7	1	3	23	19	17	9	9	384	.188	.227	.227	.137	13	119-OF 99
Jaisen Randolph	20	Rockford	Mid	494	123	15	5	2	33	51	41	14	11	382	.249	.296	.312	.212	40	119-OF 100
Mark Raynor	26	Reading	Eas	377	88	5	2	1	30	30	26	4	1	290	.233	.290	.265	.193	24	42-2B 91
Julian Redman	22	Lynchbrg	Car	529	127	19	6	8	33	58	50	19	9	411	.240	.285	.344	.221	47	130-OF 100
Scott Richardson	28	Albuquer	PCL	336	77	11	1	7	21	35	30	13	4	263	.229	.275	.330	.214	28	73-OF 82
Diego Rico	23	Daytona	Fla	362	78	12	3	6	39	37	31	7	4	288	.215	.292	.315	.211	29	95-OF 89
Cash Riley	22	VeroBch	Fla	430	80	9	1	7	27	22	22	5	5	355	.186	.234	.260	.158	18	95-OF 86
Brian Rios	24	WMichgn	Mid	346	69	8	0	3	16	16	16	2	2	279	.199	.235	.249	.152	13	64-3B 87
Fernando Rios	20	Burlingt	Mid	409	86	6	1	5	34	30	26	7	5	328	.210	.271	.267	.182	23	116-OF 101
Carlos Rivera	21	Augusta	SAL	315	76	10	1	4	11	23	27	1	3	242	.241	.267	.317	.198	21	65-1B 96
Michael Rivera	22	WMichgn	Mid	405	97	19	1	8	12	32	40	0	1	309	.240	.261	.351	.209	31	104-C 96
Roberto Rivera	22	Delmarva	SAL	390	75	13	2	5	20	23	22	7	3	318	.192	.232	.274	.167	18	100-OF 89
Jonathan Rivers	24	Knoxvill	Sou	297	65	12	2	7	34	36	29	12	8	240	.219	.299	.343	.223	28	83-OF 91
Jason Roach	23	Columbia	SAL	374	82	10	1	10	23	29	35	1	1	293	.219	.264	.332	.203	27	24-1B 103

PLAYER	AGE	AM	LGE	AB	H	DB	TP	HR	BB	R	RBI	SB	CS	OUT	BA	OBA	SA	EQA	EQR	DEFENSE
J.P. Roberge	26	Albuquer	PCL	457	107	15	1	7	26	45	38	15	5	355	.234	.275	.317	.209	36	33-2B 78
Kevin Roberson	31	Calgary	PCL	418	92	16	0	18	31	41	51	4	1	327	.220	.274	.388	.227	40	114-OF 95
Mike Robertson	28	Tucson	PCL	397	83	7	2	8	28	27	31	1	0	314	.209	.261	.297	.189	24	104-1B 84
Ryan Robertson	26	Portland	Eas	309	65	5	0	6	34	24	25	0	1	245	.210	.289	.285	.195	21	86-C 96
Adam Robinson	24	Visalia	Cal	297	49	6	1	1	31	14	9	6	2	250	.165	.244	.202	.137	9	80-SS 92
Kerry Robinson	25	Orlando	Sou	305	65	3	3	2	16	24	17	15	6	246	.213	.252	.262	.180	17	62-OF 97
John Rodriguez	23	Greensbr	SAL	417	82	10	1	6	47	34	27	5	2	337	.197	.278	.269	.187	25	99-OF 80
Miguel Rodriguez	24	Stockton	Cal	291	58	5	0	4	15	15	15	4	3	236	.199	.239	.258	.161	12	35-OF 80
Serafin Rodriguez	20	Charl-WV	SAL	323	78	6	0	5	15	29	27	11	4	249	.241	.275	.307	.206	24	83-OF 95
Dan Rohrmeier	33	Tacoma	PCL	499	123	26	2	18	50	60	70	0	3	379	.246	.315	.415	.249	59	38-OF 84
Jason Romano	20	Savannah	SAL	528	123	13	2	6	38	51	41	17	10	415	.233	.284	.299	.204	39	132-2B 88
Willie Romero	24	Albuquer	PCL	389	93	16	2	8	24	45	37	18	11	307	.239	.283	.352	.222	36	104-SS 94
Mike Rose	22	QuadCit	Mid	275	71	7	1	6	40	37	34	4	4	208	.258	.352	.356	.248	32	75-C 93
Jason Ross	25	DanvillC	Car	378	62	6	1	5	15	12	12	5	3	319	.164	.196	.225	.113	7	114-OF 92
Aaron Royster	26	Reading	Eas	431	90	18	2	5	45	38	33	2	1	342	.209	.284	.295	.198	30	99-OF 82
Toby Rumfield	26	Greenvil	Sou	453	102	13	0	8	26	35	37	5	3	354	.225	.267	.307	.197	30	112-1B 90
Jacob Ruotsinoja	22	Clinton	Mid	347	62	7	1	6	34	20	19	1	1	286	.179	.252	.256	.165	16	80-OF 79
Chad Rupp	27	SaltLake	PCL	397	89	12	2	12	49	46	45	6	2	310	.224	.309	.355	.232	40	58-1B 97
Tom Russin	25	Visalia	Cal	382	82	7	1	8	22	24	31	0	1	301	.215	.257	.301	.187	23	29-OF 90
Mike Ryan	22	FtWayne	Mid	418	114	14	2	9	34	50	54	3	2	306	.273	.327	.380	.247	47	108-3B 84
Matt Sachse	23	Lancastr	Cal	283	58	8	1	6	30	24	24	2	2	227	.205	.281	.304	.200	20	76-OF 97
Juan Salazar	21	Rockford	Mid	327	73	12	0	5	36	33	28	3	2	256	.223	.300	.306	.211	26	16-C 88
Jerry Salzano	24	Greenvil	Sou	318	80	11	2	6	32	40	35	8	5	243	.252	.320	.355	.237	33	24-3B 84
Nelson Samboy	22	Kissimme	Fla	525	131	23	3	3	31	58	44	18	9	403	.250	.291	.322	.217	44	54-OF 92
Toby Sanchez	24	Charl-WV	SAL	418	73	8	1	6	45	23	20	1	3	348	.175	.255	.242	.157	17	121-1B 70
Victor Sanchez	27	Jackson	Tex	430	94	10	1	13	15	29	40	2	2	338	.219	.245	.337	.197	29	103-1B 96
Yuri Sanchez	25	Binghmtn	Eas	316	69	9	4	3	28	30	24	7	5	252	.218	.282	.301	.201	23	85-SS 89
Tracy Sanders	29	Carolina	Sou	341	63	7	1	13	70	41	36	2	2	280	.185	.324	.326	.225	34	78-1B 78
Danny Sandoval	20	Hickory	SAL	430	79	6	1	1	25	15	15	5	7	358	.184	.229	.209	.123	10	126-SS 94
Brian Sankey	25	VeroBch	Fla	306	56	5	0	5	17	12	14	0	0	250	.183	.226	.248	.145	10	51-1B 92
Pedro Santana	22	WMichgn	Mid	443	105	15	3	5	22	53	34	29	6	344	.237	.273	.318	.217	38	114-2B 97
Jose Santos	21	Savannah	SAL	387	105	9	3	16	42	58	60	12	5	287	.271	.343	.434	.269	54	103-3B 99
Chris Saunders	28	Ottawa	Int	471	105	17	0	7	36	38	39	1	1	367	.223	.278	.304	.199	32	39-1B 105
Steve Scarsone	33	Vancouvr	PCL	404	98	15	3	14	29	43	53	3	2	308	.243	.293	.399	.238	42	42-3B 100
Jake Schaffer	24	Lakeland	Fla	392	74	9	1	7	23	20	22	2	2	320	.189	.234	.270	.162	17	84-2B 91
Gene Schall	29	Richmond	Int	332	83	11	0	15	29	37	49	1	2	251	.250	.310	.419	.249	39	24-1B 103
Jim Scharrer	22	DanvillC	Car	410	71	10	0	8	19	14	17	1	3	342	.173	.210	.256	.138	12	95-1B 91
Greg Schaub	22	Stockton	Cal	475	109	14	1	4	2	26	31	5	3	369	.229	.233	.288	.174	23	125-OF 94
Heath Schesser	23	WMichgn	Mid	330	53	7	0	1	24	10	10	0	0	277	.161	.218	.191	.095	4	72-3B 88
Tony Schifano	24	Brevard	Fla	301	53	1	2	1	12	10	10	3	1	249	.176	.208	.203	.104	4	63-3B 108
Brian Schneider	22	Jupiter	Fla	300	68	7	1	3	18	22	22	2	2	234	.227	.270	.287	.189	18	76-C 103
Chris Schwab	24	Jupiter	Fla	433	75	7	0	14	30	22	27	3	3	361	.173	.227	.286	.165	20	47-OF 90
Brad Schwartzbauer	22	Ashevlle	SAL	347	71	9	1	7	43	31	29	2	1	277	.205	.292	.297	.203	26	26-3B 98
Damian Scioneaux	24	Charl-SC	SAL	275	47	5	1	2	30	15	10	5	4	232	.171	.252	.218	.148	10	70-OF 95
Scott Seal	24	RCucmng	Cal	427	77	11	1	4	34	21	18	4	3	353	.180	.241	.239	.151	16	113-OF 85
Brad Seitzer	29	Tacoma	PCL	467	117	18	1	11	56	58	57	3	2	352	.251	.331	.364	.243	51	114-3B 92
Bill Selby	29	Buffalo	Int	333	74	11	0	11	30	32	37	2	0	259	.222	.287	.354	.222	30	25-3B 100
Chris Sexton	27	ColSprin	PCL	444	91	12	2	2	58	40	27	5	2	355	.205	.297	.255	.191	28	122-SS 89
Jon Shave	31	SaltLake	PCL	301	75	9	1	3	28	32	28	6	6	232	.249	.313	.316	.219	26	55-2B 94
Chris Sheff	28	Edmonton	PCL	394	95	14	3	7	55	56	42	12	4	303	.241	.334	.345	.242	44	117-OF 106
Juan Silvestre	21	Wisconsn	Mid	402	91	11	2	13	18	33	43	3	1	312	.226	.260	.361	.213	33	67-OF 90
Benji Simonton	27	SanJose	Cal	303	78	11	1	9	37	40	41	2	1	226	.257	.338	.389	.254	37	26-1B 81
Chris Singleton	26	Columbus	Int	407	85	12	6	4	20	28	28	5	2	324	.209	.246	.297	.184	23	116-OF 102
Steve Sisco	29	Omaha	PCL	364	86	10	0	14	22	33	44	3	5	283	.236	.280	.379	.224	34	19-SS 103
Jason Smith	28	Rockford	Mid	466	82	6	2	6	21	16	17	8	4	388	.176	.211	.236	.134	13	111-SS 98
Nester Smith	21	FtWayne	Mid	419	95	10	3	9	32	36	40	3	4	328	.227	.282	.329	.209	33	109-OF 94

Extra Players

PLAYER	AGE	AM	LGE	AB	H	DB	TP	HR	BB	R	RBI	SB	CS	OUT	BA	OBA	SA	EQA	EQR	DEFENSE
Rod Smith	23	Tampa	Fla	327	66	8	1	5	31	32	21	17	8	269	.202	.271	.278	.194	22	83-2B 90
Stewart Smothers	23	Macon	SAL	507	73	8	1	5	34	14	14	6	6	440	.144	.198	.193	.078	4	138-OF 95
Clay Snellgrove	24	1Clinton	Mid	370	63	5	1	2	19	12	12	4	4	311	.170	.211	.205	.107	6	71-2B 93
Casey Snow	24	SanBern	Cal	333	69	11	1	3	24	22	21	2	3	267	.207	.261	.273	.177	18	28-C 80
Danny Solano	20	Charlott	Fla	265	59	6	0	3	35	27	21	4	3	209	.223	.313	.279	.207	20	68-SS 107
Fausto Solano	25	1Knoxvill	Sou	285	55	10	1	7	22	20	22	2	3	232	.193	.251	.309	.186	17	59-SS 97
Scott Sollmann	24	Lakeland	Fla	402	77	8	1	2	47	37	18	22	10	335	.192	.276	.231	.179	23	96-OF 106
Jose Soriano	25	Visalia	Cal	287	60	6	1	3	23	23	17	11	9	236	.209	.268	.268	.183	17	74-OF 96
Nicolas Sosa	21	Visalia	Cal	354	79	9	0	4	32	29	27	1	0	275	.223	.288	.282	.196	24	76-1B 89
Ryan Soules	23	Greensbr	SAL	340	74	6	1	10	42	33	36	1	1	267	.218	.304	.329	.219	30	75-1B 89
Jeff Spencer	22	Macon	SAL	437	93	8	1	17	36	38	47	5	3	347	.213	.273	.352	.214	37	89-OF 80
Scott Stahoviak	29	SaltLake	PCL	381	94	19	3	11	37	47	50	4	2	289	.247	.313	.399	.246	44	66-1B 112
Alex Steele	23	WMichgn	Mid	437	86	10	1	5	45	28	27	0	3	354	.197	.272	.259	.175	23	119-OF 97
Wyley Steelmon	23	SthBend	Mid	316	72	6	1	7	37	31	32	0	0	244	.228	.309	.320	.219	27	62-1B 93
Andy Stewart	28	Wichita	Tex	292	72	9	0	7	13	24	31	0	1	221	.247	.279	.349	.216	24	78-C 94
Craig Stone	23	Dunedin	Fla	351	76	12	1	9	16	25	31	1	3	278	.217	.251	.333	.196	24	55-1B 120
Chris Stowers	24	Harrisbg	Eas	511	127	22	3	15	36	63	62	17	6	390	.249	.298	.391	.241	56	127-OF 99
Darren Stumberger	26	Akron	Eas	540	132	21	1	8	43	52	54	1	1	409	.244	.300	.331	.220	46	136-1B 105
Pedro Swann	28	Toledo	Int	415	104	17	1	11	32	46	50	4	2	313	.251	.304	.376	.236	43	74-OF 86
Kevin Sweeney	25	HighDes	Cal	331	60	8	1	5	40	24	19	3	2	273	.181	.270	.257	.175	18	52-OF 81
E.J. TGhoen	23	CedarRpd	Mid	446	78	7	0	12	37	24	27	4	3	371	.175	.238	.271	.165	20	125-SS 86
Brett Taft	26	Wilmngtn	Car	414	87	9	0	4	30	30	24	8	3	330	.210	.264	.261	.179	22	117-SS 92
John Tamargo	23	StLucie	Fla	346	65	12	1	1	32	22	15	6	4	285	.188	.257	.237	.161	15	46-SS 85
Jesus Tavarez	28	Rochestr	Int	361	87	12	4	1	21	39	27	14	3	277	.241	.283	.305	.211	28	97-OF 94
Jamie Taylor	28	NewHavn	Eas	306	89	10	0	9	32	42	47	1	1	218	.291	.358	.412	.269	41	69-3B 103
Nathan Tebbs	26	Trenton	Eas	394	81	13	1	2	29	28	21	9	8	321	.206	.260	.259	.173	20	28-SS 99
Mike Terhune	23	DanvillC	Car	369	69	2	0	4	18	13	13	4	2	302	.187	.225	.225	.135	10	25-3B 86
Jeff Terrell	24	Piedmont	SAL	398	81	6	2	1	43	30	20	6	4	321	.204	.281	.236	.175	20	118-2B 88
Tim Tessmar	25	StLucie	Fla	373	71	9	1	3	23	18	17	4	2	304	.190	.237	.244	.153	14	63-1B 77
Marcus Thames	22	Tampa	Fla	452	109	11	1	10	21	38	45	6	3	346	.241	.275	.336	.212	36	119-OF 103
James Thomas	23	QuadCit	Mid	352	78	5	0	14	42	36	42	3	2	276	.222	.305	.355	.228	34	25-1B 93
Karl Thompson	25	Lancastr	Cal	310	56	5	1	4	17	11	13	1	2	256	.181	.223	.242	.139	9	89-C 94
A.D. Thorpe	22	Macon	SAL	516	102	13	1	2	34	28	23	8	7	421	.198	.247	.238	.156	20	36-3B 74
Ozzie Timmons	28	Indianap	Int	324	73	14	1	9	23	30	34	1	2	253	.225	.277	.358	.217	28	91-OF 86
Luis Tinoco	24	Lancastr	Cal	405	83	9	3	4	27	25	25	2	1	323	.205	.255	.272	.175	21	93-OF 83
Juan Tolentino	23	CedarRpd	Mid	499	103	12	1	9	37	42	34	20	14	410	.206	.261	.289	.189	32	131-OF 97
Goefrey Tomlinson	22	Lansing	Mid	277	67	8	2	7	29	35	31	9	4	214	.242	.314	.361	.237	29	59-OF 110
Paul Torres	28	Orlando	Sou	451	96	8	1	8	45	36	36	2	2	357	.213	.284	.288	.196	30	41-1B 75
Mike Trahan	24	Charl-SC	SAL	320	55	5	0	5	25	13	13	2	2	267	.172	.232	.234	.141	10	80-2B 85
Gary Trammell	26	Jackson	Tex	311	57	6	1	2	16	11	11	2	3	257	.183	.223	.228	.132	8	61-OF 90
Brad Tyler	30	Edmonton	PCL	423	94	14	2	12	51	49	46	7	1	330	.222	.306	.350	.230	42	98-OF 97
Victor Valencia	22	Tampa	Fla	409	79	9	0	13	22	23	32	0	1	331	.193	.234	.311	.179	23	115-C 96
Jon Valenti	25	Bakrsfld	Cal	374	64	7	1	4	39	18	15	1	1	311	.171	.249	.227	.148	13	22-1B 94
Ramon Valera	23	Wisconsn	Mid	427	101	10	1	4	34	46	32	20	10	336	.237	.293	.293	.208	33	22-2B 92
Yohanny Valera	22	StLucie	Fla	295	53	10	0	11	18	18	23	1	1	243	.180	.227	.325	.182	17	79-C 102
Bob Van	21	Piedmont	SAL	465	99	12	1	3	43	33	30	0	0	366	.213	.280	.262	.183	26	107-1B 92
Ramon Vazquez	22	Lancastr	Cal	464	100	17	2	2	64	49	32	7	6	370	.216	.311	.274	.204	35	121-SS 92
Jose Velazquez	23	Charl-SC	SAL	417	97	9	1	7	40	37	39	0	1	321	.233	.300	.309	.211	33	
Jose Velez	26	Kissimme	Fla	326	65	6	1	2	13	13	14	2	3	264	.199	.230	.242	.145	11	92-OF 84
Jeff Venghaus	24	Brevard	Fla	380	51	6	1	2	39	10	10	4	4	333	.134	.215	.171	.070	2	112-2B 90
Chris Wakeland	25	Lakeland	Fla	484	108	10	2	10	47	45	44	7	7	383	.223	.292	.314	.209	38	121-OF 84
Morgan Walker	24	Lynchbrg	Car	376	97	11	0	11	20	35	47	0	0	279	.258	.295	.375	.233	36	22-1B 108
Chris Walther	22	Stockton	Cal	418	100	15	2	3	17	31	34	1	1	319	.239	.269	.306	.197	27	23-1B 102
Jeremy Ware	23	Jupiter	Fla	487	99	20	1	8	19	33	32	10	3	392	.203	.233	.298	.180	27	111-OF 99
Bryan Warner	24	SalemVA	Car	426	82	7	1	8	32	24	26	2	2	346	.192	.249	.270	.170	21	98-OF 80
Mike Warner	28	Richmond	Int	319	56	10	3	4	38	23	18	4	4	267	.176	.263	.263	.174	17	87-OF 104

Player	Age	Team	Lge																		
Ron Warner	30	Memphis	PCL	366	82	15	1	6	35	35	33	3	4	288	.224	.292	.320	.210	29	35-OF 92
Eric Welsh	22	Burlingt	Mid	523	108	17	2	6	21	29	32	3	3	418	.207	.237	.281	.170	25	124-1B 82
Barry Wesson	22	QuadCit	Mid	496	104	10	1	7	25	31	31	9	7	399	.210	.248	.276	.175	26	137-OF 109
Gabe Whatley	27	Richmond	Int	467	100	23	2	7	42	45	38	7	3	370	.214	.279	.317	.206	36	102-OF 96
Chad Whitaker	22	Kinston	Car	462	95	13	0	12	34	36	38	9	6	373	.206	.260	.312	.195	31	116-OF 93
Braxton Whitehead	23	Charl-WV	SAL	410	75	8	0	4	24	16	15	2	2	337	.183	.228	.232	.138	12	76-C 95
Darrell Whitmore	30	Nashvill	PCL	306	82	11	1	14	30	41	50	3	3	227	.268	.333	.448	.266	42	65-OF 80
Luke Wilcox	25	Orlando	Sou	326	78	11	2	11	25	33	41	1	2	250	.239	.293	.387	.233	33	69-OF 95
Paul Wilder	21	Charl-SC	SAL	269	46	4	0	9	35	19	20	1	2	225	.171	.266	.286	.183	16	66-OF 77
Eddie Williams	34	LasVegas	PCL	296	83	10	0	14	27	40	51	1	1	214	.280	.341	.456	.273	42	44-1B 90
Jewell Williams	22	Columbus	SAL	351	68	8	1	6	22	22	21	8	4	287	.194	.241	.274	.172	18	91-OF 85
Keith Williams	27	Fresno	PCL	343	84	14	1	12	15	32	43	0	1	260	.245	.277	.397	.230	33	28-1B 82
Reggie Williams	33	Vancouvr	PCL	372	90	17	3	4	45	47	36	10	10	292	.242	.324	.336	.229	37	95-OF 107
Dave Willis	24	Lansing	Mid	370	78	13	1	6	12	23	26	4	1	293	.211	.236	.300	.180	20	33-3B 80
Brandon Wilson	30	Buffalo	Int	334	78	13	1	5	26	35	29	9	4	260	.234	.289	.323	.215	28	19-3B 85
Thomas Wilson	28	Tucson	PCL	356	83	8	2	8	34	35	37	2	1	274	.233	.300	.334	.221	31	
Mike Wolff	26	Modesto	Cal	320	69	7	1	4	23	22	23	1	1	252	.216	.268	.281	.186	19	76-1B 96
Jerrod Wong	25	DanvillC	Car	297	56	4	2	4	10	11	14	2	1	242	.189	.215	.256	.146	10	57-OF 84
Ken Woods	28	Shrevprt	Tex	330	77	11	1	2	20	26	24	4	5	258	.233	.277	.291	.193	21	27-3B 96
Shawn Wooten	26	LkElsin	Cal	393	88	7	0	10	26	28	37	0	1	306	.224	.272	.318	.201	28	77-1B 90
Rick Wrona	35	Oklahoma	PCL	295	68	10	1	3	13	20	23	1	2	229	.231	.263	.302	.191	18	84-C 90
Mike Young	22	Hagerstn	SAL	522	117	15	2	11	42	48	48	7	4	409	.224	.282	.324	.210	41	13-SS 99
Travis Young	24	SanJose	Cal	522	98	10	1	3	43	30	21	12	7	431	.188	.250	.228	.155	20	133-2B 93
Junior Zamora	23	StLucie	Fla	363	83	9	1	8	20	28	34	2	2	282	.229	.269	.325	.203	26	80-3B 111
Alexis Zapata	22	WMichgn	Mid	382	100	10	1	10	28	45	46	9	5	287	.262	.312	.372	.239	40	77-OF 92
Scott Zech	25	CapeFear	SAL	308	60	8	1	2	29	20	16	4	4	252	.195	.264	.247	.168	15	89-3B 101
Jesse Zepeda	25	Hagerstn	SAL	297	42	1	0	2	39	8	8	1	1	256	.141	.241	.165	.095	4	14-2B 95
Jon Zuber	29	Scran-WB	Int	280	80	17	2	3	36	43	38	0	0	200	.286	.367	.393	.268	37	28-1B 98
Tony Zuniga	24	SanJose	Cal	399	76	9	1	6	28	21	22	1	1	324	.190	.244	.263	.164	18	103-3B 95

PITCHERS (Averages: 4.00 ERA, 9.00 H/9, 1.00 HR/9, 3.00 BB/9, 6.00 K/9, 1.00 KWH)

PLAYER	AGE	TEAM	LGE	IP	H	ER	HR	BB	K	ERA	W	L	H/9	HR/9	BB/9	K/9	KWH	PERA
Jose Acevedo	20	Charl-WV	SAL	151.3	210	78	11	47	82	4.64	7	10	12.49	0.65	2.80	4.88	0.51	5.47
Matt Achilles	21	Delmarva	SAL	138.3	197	86	17	86	76	5.60	5	10	12.82	1.11	5.60	4.94	0.26	7.29
Stevenson Agosto	22	RCucmng	Cal	100.3	172	92	18	76	59	8.25	2	9	15.43	1.61	6.82	5.29	0.20	10.14
Jordy Alexander	21	Lansing	Mid	85.7	137	69	15	36	46	7.25	2	8	14.39	1.58	3.78	4.83	0.32	8.09
Gene Altman	19	Burlingt	Mid	126.0	168	82	16	54	73	5.86	4	10	12.00	1.14	3.86	5.21	0.44	6.14
John Ambrose	23	Birmnghm	Sou	135.3	181	84	20	59	80	5.59	5	10	12.04	1.33	3.92	5.32	0.45	6.38
Jeffrey Andrews	23	SthBend	Mid	110.0	184	84	6	37	39	6.87	3	9	15.05	0.49	3.03	3.19	0.17	6.87
Rafael Arias	21	Michigan	Mid	99.7	179	86	12	36	45	7.77	2	9	16.16	1.08	3.25	4.06	0.24	8.40
Neal Arnold	23	Peoria	Mid	134.3	254	151	12	72	66	10.12	2	13	17.02	0.80	4.82	4.42	0.18	9.25
Julio Ayala	23	Lancastr	Cal	131.0	217	104	17	52	80	7.15	4	11	14.91	1.17	3.57	5.50	0.43	7.83
Benito Baez	21	Huntsvil	Sou	116.3	184	86	14	52	65	6.65	3	10	14.23	1.08	4.02	5.03	0.33	7.50
Jason Baker	23	Harrisbg	Eas	98.0	123	78	20	71	67	7.16	3	8	11.30	1.84	6.52	6.15	0.39	7.62
Jim Baron	24	Norwich	Eas	93.0	117	37	2	21	50	3.58	6	4	11.32	0.19	2.03	4.84	0.76	4.06
Mike Bauder	23	FtMyers	Fla	88.3	145	76	8	55	54	7.74	2	8	14.77	0.82	5.60	5.50	0.27	8.15
Richard Bauer	21	Delmarva	SAL	108.0	174	84	13	54	50	7.00	3	9	14.50	1.08	4.50	4.17	0.20	7.83
Andrew Bausher	21	Augusta	SAL	101.3	149	83	6	44	72	7.37	3	8	13.23	0.53	3.91	6.39	0.59	6.22
Greg Beck	25	ElPaso	Tex	98.0	150	73	13	28	56	6.70	3	8	13.78	1.19	2.57	5.14	0.56	6.70
Ryan Becks	22	CapeFear	SAL	107.7	203	114	15	71	42	9.53	2	10	16.97	1.25	5.93	3.51	0.09	10.28
Todd Belitz	22	Charl-SC	SAL	117.7	146	60	10	61	71	4.59	6	7	11.17	0.76	4.67	5.43	0.42	5.58
Jason Bell	23	NewBrit	Eas	161.3	183	100	23	60	125	5.58	6	12	10.21	1.28	3.35	6.97	1.07	5.08
Manuel Bermudez	21	SanJose	Cal	126.3	212	97	13	47	57	6.91	4	10	15.10	0.93	3.35	4.06	0.24	7.55
Justin Bettencourt	24	Lakeland	Fla	93.7	148	74	7	81	56	7.11	2	8	14.22	0.67	7.78	5.38	0.20	8.55

Extra Players

PLAYER	AGE	TEAM	LGE	IP	H	ER	HR	BB	K	ERA	W	L	H/9	HR/9	BB/9	K/9	KWH	PERA
Bobby Bevel	24	SalemVA	Car	85.7	100	35	5	33	55	3.68	5	5	10.51	0.53	3.47	5.78	0.69	4.52
Jeremy Blevins	20	Greensbr	SAL	112.7	158	90	6	78	69	7.19	3	10	12.62	0.48	6.23	5.51	0.29	6.71
Rod Bolton	29	Indianap	Int	172.0	189	81	14	61	94	4.24	9	10	9.89	0.73	3.19	4.92	0.57	4.29
Rob Bonanno	27	Midland	Tex	94.0	130	48	18	18	40	4.60	4	6	12.45	1.72	1.72	3.83	0.51	6.22
Aaron Bond	21	Savannah	SAL	152.7	247	115	13	50	72	6.78	4	13	14.56	0.77	2.95	4.24	0.31	6.84
Shawn Boskie	31	Ottawa	Int	86.7	108	45	6	20	41	4.67	4	6	11.22	0.62	2.08	4.26	0.58	4.47
Steve Bourgeois	25	ColSprin	PCL	120.7	156	67	12	65	70	5.00	5	8	11.64	0.90	4.85	5.22	0.36	6.04
Mike Bovee	24	Vancouvr	PCL	87.3	126	64	6	49	60	6.60	3	7	12.98	0.62	5.05	6.18	0.44	6.60
Bryan Braswell	23	Kissimme	Fla	142.7	240	115	26	57	81	7.25	4	12	15.14	1.64	3.60	5.11	0.36	8.58
Anthony Briggs	24	Richmond	Int	122.7	137	74	15	54	76	5.43	5	9	10.05	1.10	3.96	5.58	0.59	4.99
Elliot Brown	23	Charl-SC	SAL	90.3	189	104	11	56	32	10.36	1	9	18.83	1.10	5.58	3.19	0.07	11.16
Jim Bullinger	32	Tacoma	PCL	97.3	118	62	12	59	57	5.73	4	7	10.91	1.11	5.46	5.27	0.35	6.10
Terry Burrows	29	Rochestr	Int	127.0	123	52	8	39	90	3.69	8	6	8.72	0.57	2.76	6.38	1.27	3.40
Ken Carlyle	28	Richmond	Int	155.3	229	98	20	44	62	5.68	6	11	13.27	1.16	2.55	3.59	0.29	6.37
Matt Carnes	22	FtWayne	Mid	94.3	165	95	8	43	57	9.06	2	8	15.74	0.76	4.10	5.44	0.34	8.11
Marcos Castillo	19	VeroBch	Fla	134.3	171	100	17	52	57	6.70	4	11	11.46	1.14	3.48	3.82	0.27	5.69
Carlos Chantres	22	WnstnSlm	Car	85.3	92	50	12	50	59	5.27	3	6	9.70	1.27	5.27	6.22	0.57	5.48
Jake Chapman	24	Wilmngtn	Car	144.0	230	107	6	51	67	6.69	4	12	14.38	0.38	3.19	4.19	0.29	6.44
Carlos Chavez	25	ElPaso	Tex	89.3	113	67	5	52	61	6.75	3	7	11.38	0.50	5.24	6.15	0.47	5.64
Jason Childers	23	Beloit	Mid	106.0	151	66	11	29	63	5.60	4	8	12.82	0.93	2.46	5.35	0.68	5.86
Terry Clark	37	Oklahoma	PCL	157.0	175	73	8	35	74	4.18	8	9	10.03	0.46	2.01	4.24	0.67	3.67
Trevor Cobb	24	NewBrit	Eas	122.7	203	96	19	51	63	7.04	3	11	14.89	1.39	3.74	4.62	0.29	8.14
Luis Colmenares	21	SalemVA	Car	156.7	235	107	22	76	83	6.15	5	12	13.50	1.26	4.37	4.77	0.29	7.41
Derrick Cook	22	Charlott	Fla	152.7	225	98	16	73	80	5.78	6	11	13.26	0.94	4.30	4.72	0.29	6.84
Mark Corey	23	Burlingt	Mid	127.3	183	76	13	47	63	5.37	5	9	12.93	0.92	3.32	4.45	0.35	6.22
Reid Cornelius	28	Tucson	PCL	96.3	108	57	14	26	51	5.33	4	7	10.09	1.31	2.43	4.76	0.69	4.67
Danny Crawford	23	Augusta	SAL	94.7	177	95	10	21	38	9.03	2	9	16.83	0.95	2.00	3.61	0.29	8.08
Jack Cressend	23	Trenton	Eas	145.0	198	90	14	55	99	5.59	5	11	12.29	0.87	3.41	6.14	0.67	5.83
Nelson Cruz	25	Calgary	PCL	128.3	165	73	16	41	80	5.12	5	9	11.57	1.12	2.88	5.61	0.71	5.47
John Curtice	18	Michigan	Mid	125.3	137	75	11	88	97	5.39	5	9	9.84	0.79	6.32	6.97	0.59	5.46
Todd Cutchins	22	Columbia	SAL	114.3	154	59	6	60	59	4.64	6	7	12.12	0.47	4.72	4.64	0.28	5.83
Tommy Darrell	21	LkElsin	Cal	89.7	155	86	9	48	37	8.63	2	8	15.56	0.90	4.82	3.71	0.14	8.43
David Darwin	24	Jacksnvl	Sou	123.0	200	107	23	47	56	7.83	3	11	14.63	1.68	3.44	4.10	0.25	8.20
Robert Davies	22	FtWayne	Mid	116.0	169	79	9	63	70	6.13	4	9	13.11	0.70	4.89	5.43	0.35	6.67
Jason Davis	23	Reading	Eas	104.7	132	68	9	56	62	5.85	4	8	11.35	0.77	4.82	5.33	0.39	5.76
Zach Day	20	Tampa	Fla	96.3	169	92	6	35	52	8.60	2	9	15.79	0.56	3.27	4.86	0.34	7.47
Ernie Delgado	22	Dunedin	Fla	113.0	153	64	6	67	71	5.10	5	8	12.19	0.48	5.34	5.65	0.37	6.13
Kris Detmers	24	Arkansas	Tex	139.7	218	111	14	85	65	7.15	4	12	14.05	0.90	5.48	4.19	0.17	7.73
Matt Dewitt	20	PrWillm	Car	137.3	182	87	18	21	81	5.70	5	10	11.93	1.18	1.38	5.31	1.29	5.18
Dan DeYoung	22	Charlott	Fla	108.0	150	74	14	44	44	6.17	4	8	12.50	1.17	3.67	3.67	0.22	6.42
Roland DeLaMaza	26	Omaha	PCL	124.3	189	81	20	38	64	5.86	4	10	13.68	1.45	2.75	4.63	0.43	7.02
Dwayne Dobson	22	CedarRpd	Mid	92.3	126	56	12	36	42	5.46	3	7	12.28	1.17	3.51	4.09	0.29	6.24
Kevin Dougherty	20	Columbia	SAL	128.3	144	56	10	60	66	3.93	7	7	10.10	0.70	4.21	4.63	0.38	4.77
Scott Downs	22	Daytona	Fla	160.7	209	81	14	63	86	4.54	8	10	11.71	0.78	3.53	4.82	0.42	5.43
Al Drumheller	26	Mobile	Sou	91.7	97	47	6	45	84	4.61	4	6	9.52	0.59	4.42	8.25	1.21	4.42
Renny Duarte	19	LkElsin	Cal	116.7	191	95	18	52	49	7.33	3	10	14.73	1.39	4.01	3.78	0.18	8.18
Justin Duchscherer	20	Michigan	Mid	131.3	225	106	14	53	71	7.26	3	12	15.42	0.96	3.63	4.87	0.32	7.88
Brandon Duckworth	22	Piedmont	SAL	135.0	166	78	12	31	68	5.20	6	9	11.07	0.80	2.07	4.53	0.67	4.53
Pat Dunham	22	Lancastr	Cal	100.0	123	52	10	45	57	4.68	5	6	11.07	0.90	4.05	5.13	0.44	5.40
Adam Eaton	20	Clearwtr	Fla	125.7	188	74	12	52	66	5.30	5	9	13.46	0.86	3.72	4.73	0.33	6.66
Robert Ellis	27	Louisvil	Int	144.7	198	103	20	74	64	6.41	4	12	12.32	1.24	4.60	3.98	0.21	6.72
Jose Espinal	21	Daytona	Fla	144.7	190	91	19	57	88	5.66	5	11	11.82	1.18	3.55	5.47	0.54	5.97
Leoncio Estrella	23	Columbia	SAL	106.3	174	90	11	33	52	7.62	3	9	14.73	0.93	2.79	4.40	0.35	7.11
Keith Evans	22	Harrisbg	Eas	118.3	158	64	14	29	59	4.87	5	8	12.02	1.06	2.21	4.49	0.57	5.40
Bill Everly	23	VeroBch	Fla	99.0	141	76	14	37	41	6.91	3	8	12.82	1.27	3.36	3.73	0.24	6.55
Steve Falteisek	26	Ottawa	Int	161.0	203	102	16	57	68	5.70	6	12	11.35	0.89	3.19	3.80	0.30	5.25

PLAYER	AGE	TEAM	LGE	IP	H	ER	HR	BB	K	ERA	W	L	H/9	HR/9	BB/9	K/9	KWH	PERA
Joe Farley	23	WnstnSlm	Car	111.0	172	93	18	72	46	7.54	3	9	13.95	1.46	5.84	3.73	0.13	8.51
Mike Farmer	29	ColSprin	PCL	131.7	177	89	17	59	60	6.08	5	10	12.10	1.16	4.03	4.10	0.26	6.29
Jim Farrell	24	Pawtuckt	Int	163.0	190	95	29	48	118	5.25	7	11	10.49	1.60	2.65	6.52	1.14	5.30
Miguel Felix	21	Hickory	SAL	89.0	153	106	15	79	53	10.72	1	9	15.47	1.52	7.99	5.36	0.17	10.52
Justin Fenus	23	Piedmont	SAL	114.7	255	128	16	64	44	10.05	2	11	20.01	1.26	5.02	3.45	0.09	11.93
Mick Fieldbinder	24	FtMyers	Fla	117.0	242	135	17	58	41	10.38	2	11	18.62	1.31	4.46	3.15	0.09	10.77
Tony Fiore	26	Scran-WB	Int	90.7	108	55	4	49	57	5.46	3	7	10.72	0.40	4.86	5.66	0.46	5.06
Jason Flach	24	DanvillC	Car	96.3	156	59	7	43	65	5.51	4	7	14.57	0.65	4.02	6.07	0.47	7.19
Emar Fleming	21	Savannah	SAL	126.3	200	105	22	74	81	7.48	3	11	14.25	1.57	5.27	5.77	0.33	8.62
Aaron France	24	Lynchbrg	Car	117.0	145	74	12	61	65	5.69	4	9	11.15	0.92	4.69	5.00	0.36	5.77
Ryan Franklin	25	Tacoma	PCL	122.0	163	73	17	32	70	5.39	5	9	12.02	1.25	2.36	5.16	0.70	5.68
Brian Fuentes	22	Lancastr	Cal	115.0	155	78	10	91	90	6.10	4	9	12.13	0.78	7.12	7.04	0.43	7.12
Mike Fyhrie	28	Norfolk	Int	100.7	124	76	11	43	49	6.79	3	8	11.09	0.98	3.84	4.38	0.34	5.45
Josh Gandy	22	FtWayne	Mid	92.0	156	75	6	40	47	7.34	2	8	15.26	0.59	3.91	4.60	0.27	7.43
Apostol Garcia	21	Lakeland	Fla	114.3	189	94	17	59	42	7.40	3	10	14.88	1.34	4.64	3.31	0.12	8.42
Gabe Garcia	21	Kissimme	Fla	131.0	224	109	19	69	69	7.49	3	12	15.39	1.31	4.74	4.74	0.23	8.79
Mike Gardiner	32	Charlott	Int	88.0	116	58	16	33	43	5.93	3	7	11.86	1.64	3.38	4.40	0.36	6.44
Hal Garrett	23	VeroBch	Fla	105.0	145	87	13	69	60	7.46	3	9	12.43	1.11	5.91	5.14	0.27	7.20
Joshua Garrett	20	Sarasota	Fla	149.7	219	112	20	45	51	6.73	4	13	13.17	1.20	2.71	3.07	0.20	6.43
George Glinatsis	29	ColSprin	PCL	95.0	110	61	16	50	68	5.78	4	7	10.42	1.52	4.74	6.44	0.63	5.97
Edwin Gonzalez	20	Lansing	Mid	121.0	162	69	8	44	71	5.13	5	8	12.05	0.60	3.27	5.28	0.53	5.36
Gabe Gonzalez	26	Charlott	Int	88.0	109	62	3	51	33	6.34	3	7	11.15	0.31	5.22	3.38	0.15	5.32
Jason Gooding	23	Wichita	Tex	128.3	185	82	14	45	53	5.75	5	9	12.97	0.98	3.16	3.72	0.25	6.24
Mike Gordon	25	Knoxvill	Sou	109.3	147	79	14	60	69	6.50	3	9	12.10	1.15	4.94	5.68	0.40	6.67
Jeff Granger	26	Oklahoma	PCL	122.0	178	79	10	38	73	5.83	4	10	13.13	0.74	2.80	5.39	0.59	5.90
Jason Grimsley	30	Buffalo	Int	87.3	86	38	10	54	55	3.92	5	5	8.86	1.03	5.56	5.67	0.49	4.95
Abraham Hacen	22	Frederck	Car	138.0	181	99	20	91	64	6.46	4	11	11.80	1.30	5.93	4.17	0.19	7.04
Luther Hackman	23	NewHavn	Eas	133.3	200	109	20	54	69	7.36	3	12	13.50	1.35	3.65	4.66	0.33	7.15
Tim Harikkala	26	Orlando	Sou	97.0	133	58	10	13	40	5.38	4	7	12.34	0.93	1.21	3.71	0.69	5.01
Brett Haring	23	Charl-WV	SAL	96.3	173	62	7	36	49	5.79	4	7	16.16	0.65	3.36	4.58	0.29	7.85
Brian Harrison	29	Omaha	PCL	143.0	217	114	21	43	57	7.17	4	12	13.66	1.32	2.71	3.59	0.26	6.86
Scott Harrison	20	Columbus	SAL	124.3	211	111	16	65	75	8.03	3	11	15.27	1.16	4.71	5.43	0.31	8.54
Ryan Hawblitzel	27	Charlott	Int	103.0	141	61	19	13	58	5.33	4	7	12.32	1.66	1.14	5.07	1.38	5.77
Al Hawkins	20	Beloit	Mid	85.0	117	56	6	22	43	5.93	3	6	12.39	0.64	2.33	4.55	0.54	5.19
Woody Heath	21	Hagerstn	SAL	87.7	111	53	5	33	50	5.44	4	6	11.40	0.51	3.39	5.13	0.51	4.93
Brett Herbison	21	StLucie	Fla	139.7	207	102	12	58	70	6.57	4	12	13.34	0.77	3.74	4.51	0.31	6.44
Wilson Heredia	26	Columbus	Int	88.0	126	74	20	47	57	7.57	2	8	12.89	2.05	4.81	5.83	0.41	8.18
Matt Herges	28	Albuquer	PCL	90.7	117	54	8	38	60	5.36	4	6	11.61	0.79	3.77	5.96	0.61	5.46
Elvin Hernandez	20	Carolina	Sou	102.3	134	61	15	25	53	5.36	4	7	11.79	1.32	2.20	4.66	0.63	5.54
Livan Hernandez	23	Florida	NL	239.3	277	120	38	95	149	4.51	12	15	10.42	1.43	3.57	5.60	0.63	5.42
Brett Hinchliffe	23	Tacoma	PCL	156.0	141	71	21	85	82	4.10	8	9	8.13	1.21	4.90	4.73	0.42	4.44
Kevin Hodges	25	Jackson	Tex	98.7	132	60	8	41	50	5.47	4	7	12.04	0.73	3.74	4.56	0.35	5.66
Mike Holmes	22	Visalia	Cal	144.7	235	92	18	23	63	5.72	5	11	14.62	1.12	1.43	3.92	0.55	6.66
David Hooten	23	FtMyers	Fla	142.3	246	116	9	69	93	7.33	4	12	15.56	0.57	4.36	5.88	0.38	7.84
Brandon Huntsman	22	Delmarva	SAL	87.3	163	77	6	68	42	7.94	2	8	16.80	0.62	7.01	4.33	0.12	9.79
Doug Hurst	22	Chattang	Sou	86.7	97	38	10	31	29	3.95	5	5	10.07	1.04	3.22	3.01	0.21	4.67
Victor Hurtado	21	Brevard	Fla	93.7	132	64	15	26	44	6.15	3	7	12.68	1.44	2.50	4.23	0.42	6.34
Brent Iddon	22	RCucmng	Cal	129.7	192	77	13	44	70	5.34	5	9	13.33	0.90	3.05	4.86	0.43	6.32
Todd Incantalupo	22	Beloit	Mid	91.7	177	85	11	57	37	8.35	2	8	17.38	1.08	5.60	3.63	0.10	10.21
Hansel Izquierdo	21	Hickory	SAL	162.3	218	125	17	92	113	6.93	4	14	12.09	0.94	5.10	6.26	0.48	6.49
Dwayne Jacobs	21	DanvillC	Car	106.7	120	82	14	106	79	6.92	3	9	10.13	1.18	8.94	6.67	0.37	7.09
Ryan Jacobs	24	Greenvil	Sou	97.7	126	70	15	66	55	6.45	3	8	11.61	1.38	6.08	5.07	0.27	7.10
Jason Jacome	27	Buffalo	Int	152.3	173	57	12	36	88	3.37	10	7	10.22	0.71	2.13	5.20	0.93	4.02
Thomas Jacquez	22	Clearwtr	Fla	159.7	269	114	15	36	79	6.43	5	13	15.16	0.85	2.03	4.45	0.48	6.93
Jared Jensen	24	Visalia	Cal	133.7	224	110	19	50	64	7.41	3	12	15.08	1.28	3.37	4.31	0.27	7.95
Jason Jensen	22	SthBend	Mid	140.0	236	112	12	72	71	7.20	4	12	15.17	0.77	4.63	4.56	0.22	7.97

Extra Players

PLAYER	AGE	TEAM	LGE	IP	H	ER	HR	BB	K	ERA	W	L	H/9	HR/9	BB/9	K/9	KWH	PERA
Ryan Jensen	22	Bakrsfld	Cal	159.3	205	98	18	67	105	5.54	6	12	11.58	1.02	3.78	5.93	0.60	5.71
Craig Johnson	22	WMichgn	Mid	145.7	218	97	20	27	71	5.99	5	11	13.47	1.24	1.67	4.39	0.64	6.24
Marcus Jones	23	Visalia	Cal	122.3	200	91	10	53	69	6.69	4	10	14.71	0.74	3.90	5.08	0.34	7.28
Jarod Juelsgaard	30	Tacoma	PCL	119.7	147	88	12	74	69	6.62	3	10	11.06	0.90	5.57	5.19	0.33	6.02
Jason Karnuth	22	PrWillm	Car	99.3	120	39	4	17	35	3.53	6	5	10.87	0.36	1.54	3.17	0.45	3.81
Bra Kaufman	26	LasVegas	PCL	119.0	153	78	11	67	66	5.90	4	9	11.57	0.83	5.07	4.99	0.32	6.05
John Kaufman	23	StPete	Fla	95.0	119	46	7	40	64	4.36	5	6	11.27	0.66	3.79	6.06	0.65	5.21
Phil Kendall	20	Beloit	Mid	145.0	213	105	23	61	73	6.52	4	12	13.22	1.43	3.79	4.53	0.31	7.14
Calvin Key	23	Piedmont	SAL	102.0	235	121	9	49	40	10.68	1	10	20.74	0.79	4.32	3.53	0.10	11.47
Scott Key	21	Lansing	Mid	87.0	96	46	6	46	48	4.76	4	6	9.93	0.62	4.76	4.97	0.39	4.76
Brian Keyser	31	Indianap	Int	113.3	150	68	12	54	53	5.40	5	8	11.91	0.95	4.29	4.21	0.26	6.04
Andrew Kimball	22	Modesto	Cal	91.0	142	68	9	31	61	6.73	3	7	14.04	0.89	3.07	6.03	0.63	6.73
Brian Knoll	24	SanJose	Cal	98.0	197	70	6	26	61	6.43	3	8	18.09	0.55	2.39	5.60	0.54	8.54
Eric Knott	23	HighDes	Cal	137.7	220	90	19	33	60	5.88	5	10	14.38	1.24	2.16	3.92	0.37	7.00
Gary Knotts	21	KaneCnty	Mid	147.7	199	103	16	76	96	6.28	5	11	12.13	0.98	4.63	5.85	0.46	6.34
Jake Kringen	22	Ashevlle	SAL	135.7	253	106	23	38	70	7.03	4	11	16.78	1.53	2.52	4.64	0.38	9.02
Kris Lambert	24	Lynchbrg	Car	144.3	234	113	18	61	87	7.05	4	12	14.59	1.12	3.80	5.42	0.40	7.67
Frank Lankford	27	Columbus	Int	93.0	122	57	11	31	47	5.52	3	7	11.81	1.06	3.00	4.55	0.44	5.61
Derek Lee	23	Stockton	Cal	124.7	175	83	12	55	85	5.99	4	10	12.63	0.87	3.97	6.14	0.56	6.28
Brandon Leese	22	Portland	Eas	128.0	146	63	17	36	73	4.43	6	8	10.27	1.20	2.53	5.13	0.76	4.71
Derrick Lewis	22	Macon	SAL	107.7	140	72	8	72	59	6.02	4	8	11.70	0.67	6.02	4.93	0.26	6.27
Richie Lewis	32	Rochestr	Int	119.0	126	78	16	40	105	5.90	4	9	9.53	1.21	3.03	7.94	1.64	4.46
Julian Leyva	20	Modesto	Cal	130.0	189	75	12	27	60	5.19	5	9	13.08	0.83	1.87	4.15	0.53	5.61
Aaron Lineweaver	24	Wilmngtn	Car	149.7	200	93	7	73	69	5.59	6	11	12.03	0.42	4.39	4.15	0.24	5.59
Marcus Logan	26	Arkansas	Tex	112.0	205	103	14	63	48	8.28	2	10	16.47	1.12	5.06	3.86	0.13	9.40
Kyle Lohse	19	Rockford	Mid	158.3	220	97	12	50	81	5.51	6	12	12.51	0.68	2.84	4.60	0.45	5.51
Kevin Lomon	26	LasVegas	PCL	124.0	134	69	12	63	93	5.01	5	9	9.73	0.87	4.57	6.75	0.77	4.86
Brian Looney	28	Columbus	Int	92.0	110	49	12	50	51	4.79	4	6	10.76	1.17	4.89	4.99	0.35	5.87
Shane Loux	18	WMichgn	Mid	140.3	258	124	20	58	59	7.95	3	13	16.55	1.28	3.72	3.78	0.17	9.04
Rob Luce	23	Orlando	Sou	161.3	246	97	22	42	57	5.41	6	12	13.72	1.23	2.34	3.18	0.24	6.64
Larry Luebbers	28	Memphis	PCL	164.3	204	88	22	48	85	4.82	7	11	11.17	1.20	2.63	4.66	0.55	5.26
Jim Lynch	22	QuadCit	Mid	89.7	126	67	6	70	60	6.72	3	7	12.65	0.60	7.03	6.02	0.31	7.23
Macrae	23	Chattang	Sou	110.0	123	66	6	48	52	5.40	4	8	10.06	0.49	3.93	4.25	0.34	4.42
Bill Malloy	23	1SanJose	Cal	110.3	186	105	13	48	62	8.56	2	10	15.17	1.06	3.92	5.06	0.32	7.99
James Manias	23	1StPete	Fla	124.3	218	114	30	45	54	8.25	3	11	15.78	2.17	3.26	3.91	0.22	9.48
Barry Markey	21	Daytona	Fla	106.7	135	59	8	35	44	4.98	5	7	11.39	0.68	2.95	3.71	0.31	4.98
Lee Marshall	21	FtWayne	Mid	96.0	176	88	8	38	46	8.25	2	9	16.50	0.75	3.56	4.31	0.24	8.25
Chandler Martin	24	SalemVA	Car	147.3	191	74	12	60	62	4.52	7	9	11.67	0.73	3.67	3.79	0.25	5.44
Jesus Martinez	24	Indianap	Int	91.3	132	75	10	39	32	7.39	2	8	13.01	0.99	3.84	3.15	0.15	6.50
Jose Martinez	23	Charlott	Fla	110.7	166	72	14	34	59	5.86	4	8	13.50	1.14	2.77	4.80	0.46	6.59
Steven Matcuk	22	SalemVA	Car	95.3	136	68	15	23	47	6.42	3	8	12.84	1.42	2.17	4.44	0.53	6.23
Brian Matz	23	CapeFear	SAL	86.3	117	54	6	39	33	5.63	3	7	12.20	0.63	4.07	3.44	0.18	5.73
Chris McBride	24	Knoxvill	Sou	149.3	212	98	19	34	67	5.91	5	12	12.78	1.15	2.05	4.04	0.47	5.85
Matt McClellan	21	Hagerstn	SAL	130.0	155	82	9	71	77	5.68	5	9	10.73	0.62	4.92	5.33	0.40	5.26
Jason McCommon	26	Bowie	Eas	118.3	143	72	18	45	52	5.48	5	8	10.88	1.37	3.42	3.95	0.32	5.55
Sam McConnell	22	Lynchbrg	Car	115.0	152	58	6	24	54	4.54	6	7	11.90	0.47	1.88	4.23	0.60	4.62
Neal McDade	22	Lynchbrg	Car	85.3	113	42	9	24	50	4.43	4	5	11.92	0.95	2.53	5.27	0.69	5.38
Tony McKnight	21	Kissimme	Fla	143.3	239	113	15	56	77	7.10	4	12	15.01	0.94	3.52	4.83	0.33	7.60
Josh McNatt	20	Frederck	Car	151.7	179	89	14	83	82	5.28	6	11	10.62	0.83	4.93	4.87	0.34	5.40
Doug Meiners	24	Knoxvill	Sou	106.3	155	65	7	41	43	5.50	4	8	13.12	0.59	3.47	3.64	0.22	6.01
David Melendez	22	Jacksnvl	Sou	139.7	205	108	18	50	65	6.96	4	12	13.21	1.16	3.22	4.19	0.31	6.64
Reynol Mendoza	27	Charlott	Int	125.0	177	93	17	55	48	6.70	4	10	12.74	1.22	3.96	3.46	0.18	6.70
Carlos Mercedes	22	QuadCit	Mid	129.7	223	125	20	64	62	8.68	2	12	15.48	1.39	4.44	4.30	0.20	8.81
Phil Merrell	20	Charl-WV	SAL	141.7	211	98	13	51	73	6.23	5	11	13.40	0.83	3.24	4.64	0.37	6.35
Bob Milacki	33	1NewOrln	PCL	174.0	230	102	18	51	80	5.28	7	12	11.90	0.93	2.64	4.14	0.41	5.38
Justin Miller	20	Ashevlle	SAL	158.7	224	95	16	48	89	5.39	6	12	12.71	0.91	2.72	5.05	0.55	5.84

PLAYER	AGE	TEAM	LGE	IP	H	ER	HR	BB	K	ERA	W	L	H/9	HR/9	BB/9	K/9	KWH	PERA
Scott Mitchell	25	Harrisbg	Eas	123.3	179	74	14	40	57	5.40	5	9	13.06	1.02	2.92	4.16	0.34	6.28
Francisco Montero	22	Piedmont	SAL	106.3	206	89	15	20	39	7.53	3	9	17.44	1.27	1.69	3.30	0.28	8.72
Paul Morse	25	SanBern	Cal	134.0	233	148	16	97	66	9.94	2	13	15.65	1.07	6.51	4.43	0.14	9.40
Henry Mota	20	Charlott	Fla	87.3	128	64	14	44	44	6.60	3	7	13.19	1.44	4.53	4.53	0.26	7.52
Joe Nathan	23	SanJose	Cal	108.7	145	67	16	55	71	5.55	4	8	12.01	1.33	4.56	5.88	0.47	6.63
Joe Nation	19	Macon	SAL	140.0	220	105	17	47	89	6.75	4	12	14.14	1.09	3.02	5.72	0.57	7.01
Jason Navarro	22	PrWillm	Car	124.3	203	106	17	82	72	7.67	3	11	14.69	1.23	5.94	5.21	0.23	8.76
Joe Nelson	23	Greenvil	Sou	107.0	141	68	10	59	58	5.72	4	8	11.86	0.84	4.96	4.88	0.30	6.14
Eric Newman	25	Mobile	Sou	128.3	194	108	15	66	86	7.57	3	11	13.61	1.05	4.63	6.03	0.43	7.29
Chris Nichting	32	Buffalo	Int	95.0	113	51	9	36	78	4.83	4	7	10.71	0.85	3.41	7.39	1.12	4.93
Randy Niles	22	Visalia	Cal	142.0	180	99	15	59	66	6.27	5	11	11.41	0.95	3.74	4.18	0.31	5.51
Elvin Nina	22	Visalia	Cal	125.0	169	83	12	69	85	5.98	4	10	12.17	0.86	4.97	6.12	0.46	6.34
Steve Norris	22	Peoria	Mid	129.7	221	138	16	107	60	9.58	2	12	15.34	1.11	7.43	4.16	0.11	9.65
Paul O'Malley	25	Jackson	Tex	138.0	201	122	21	77	64	7.96	3	12	13.11	1.37	5.02	4.17	0.20	7.57
John O'Reilly	23	Stockton	Cal	87.7	134	76	9	65	57	7.80	2	8	13.76	0.92	6.67	5.85	0.28	8.11
Jay O'Shaughnessy	23	VeroBch	Fla	94.3	118	76	10	100	81	7.25	2	8	11.26	0.95	9.54	7.73	0.42	7.82
Shawn Onley	23	DanvillC	Car	87.7	119	60	6	60	50	6.16	3	7	12.22	0.62	6.16	5.13	0.26	6.57
Pablo Ortega	21	StPete	Fla	148.0	225	110	16	44	82	6.69	4	12	13.68	0.97	2.68	4.99	0.51	6.45
Ricardo Palma	18	Rockford	Mid	94.7	158	74	9	41	44	7.04	3	8	15.02	0.86	3.90	4.18	0.22	7.61
Brian Paluk	22	VeroBch	Fla	93.3	150	86	22	49	43	8.29	2	8	14.46	2.12	4.73	4.15	0.19	9.26
Christian Parker	22	Harrisbg	Eas	120.7	152	73	10	45	57	5.44	5	8	11.34	0.75	3.36	4.25	0.36	5.15
Chad Paronto	22	Frederck	Car	99.3	150	52	6	47	60	4.71	5	6	13.59	0.54	4.26	5.44	0.38	6.52
Justin Pederson	23	Lansing	Mid	137.3	205	98	13	82	69	6.42	4	11	13.43	0.85	5.37	4.52	0.21	7.27
Trey Poland	23	Charlott	Fla	133.0	207	105	18	72	95	7.11	4	11	14.01	1.22	4.87	6.43	0.45	7.85
Lou Pote	26	Midland	Tex	146.7	229	111	17	60	85	6.81	4	12	14.05	1.04	3.68	5.22	0.39	7.18
Rich Pratt	27	Calgary	PCL	134.3	200	96	26	46	61	6.43	4	11	13.40	1.74	3.08	4.09	0.30	7.37
Ryan Price	20	Ashevlle	SAL	162.3	229	100	25	50	91	5.54	6	12	12.70	1.39	2.77	5.05	0.54	6.38
Kenny Pumphrey	21	StLucie	Fla	136.0	159	73	8	64	74	4.83	6	9	10.52	0.53	4.24	4.90	0.40	4.83
Edward Quezada	23	CapeFear	SAL	118.0	211	107	14	71	44	8.16	3	10	16.09	1.07	5.42	3.36	0.10	9.23
Craig Quintal	23	Lakeland	Fla	117.7	219	107	16	28	41	8.18	3	10	16.75	1.22	2.14	3.14	0.21	8.41
Rob Radlosky	24	NewBrit	Eas	122.7	162	73	17	40	84	5.36	5	9	11.89	1.25	2.93	6.16	0.82	5.80
Hector Ramirez	26	Charlott	Int	86.7	114	62	14	29	41	6.44	3	7	11.84	1.45	3.01	4.26	0.38	6.02
Ken Ray	23	Wichita	Tex	117.3	160	70	7	49	56	5.37	5	8	12.27	0.54	3.76	4.30	0.30	5.60
Steve Reed	22	Arkansas	Tex	109.0	187	90	18	31	42	7.43	3	9	15.44	1.49	2.56	3.47	0.23	8.09
Nathan Rice	24	Bakrsfld	Cal	105.7	187	124	10	98	50	10.56	2	10	15.93	0.85	8.35	4.26	0.10	10.14
John Riedling	22	Chattang	Sou	100.7	129	64	11	50	68	5.72	4	7	11.53	0.98	4.47	6.08	0.54	5.90
Paul Rigdon	22	Kinston	Car	118.0	168	82	13	42	65	6.25	4	9	12.81	0.99	3.20	4.96	0.45	6.18
Mike Riley	23	Bakrsfld	Cal	118.3	172	86	10	67	67	6.54	4	9	13.08	0.76	5.10	5.10	0.29	6.85
Juan Rincon	19	FtWayne	Mid	91.0	112	58	9	60	49	5.74	3	7	11.08	0.89	5.93	4.85	0.27	6.13
Dan Rios	25	Omaha	PCL	116.3	178	89	13	42	40	6.89	3	10	13.77	1.01	3.25	3.09	0.16	6.81
Luis Rivera	20	Macon	SAL	91.3	96	55	9	49	74	5.42	4	6	9.46	0.89	4.83	7.29	0.87	4.83
Jake Robbins	22	Tampa	Fla	145.0	204	88	7	82	63	5.46	6	10	12.66	0.43	5.09	3.91	0.18	6.21
Jeromie Robertson	21	Kissimme	Fla	164.0	232	93	16	59	97	5.10	7	11	12.73	0.88	3.24	5.32	0.52	6.04
Dustin Robinson	22	Charl-WV	SAL	129.0	204	101	15	57	53	7.05	3	11	14.23	1.05	3.98	3.70	0.18	7.40
Michae Romano	26	Syracuse	Int	112.3	155	68	12	51	56	5.45	4	8	12.42	0.96	4.09	4.49	0.30	6.25
Mike Rooney	22	SthBend	Mid	96.7	165	93	9	42	45	8.66	2	9	15.36	0.84	3.91	4.19	0.22	7.82
Matt Ruebel	28	Durham	Int	126.0	157	70	16	43	70	5.00	5	9	11.21	1.14	3.07	5.00	0.54	5.36
Matthew Saier	25	Wichita	Tex	99.7	146	67	13	31	58	6.05	3	8	13.18	1.17	2.80	5.24	0.56	6.41
Scott Sauerbeck	26	Norfolk	Int	161.0	191	74	8	65	97	4.14	9	9	10.68	0.45	3.63	5.42	0.57	4.58
Brett Schlomann	23	Norwich	Eas	119.0	171	94	22	53	53	7.11	3	10	12.93	1.66	4.01	4.01	0.23	7.34
Brian Scott	22	WnstnSlm	Car	96.7	150	83	12	54	53	7.73	2	9	13.97	1.12	5.03	4.93	0.26	7.82
Tom Shearn	20	QuadCit	Mid	110.7	129	51	12	58	62	4.15	6	6	10.49	0.98	4.72	5.04	0.39	5.45
Kevin Shipp	23	Piedmont	SAL	159.0	319	143	23	36	76	8.09	4	14	18.06	1.30	2.04	4.30	0.38	9.34
Allan Simpson	20	Wisconsn	Mid	90.7	114	56	8	69	58	5.56	3	7	11.32	0.79	6.85	5.76	0.32	6.55
Dan Smith	22	Tulsa	Tex	140.7	198	106	27	58	83	6.78	4	12	12.67	1.73	3.71	5.31	0.45	7.17
Russell Spear	20	Lakeland	Fla	93.3	124	72	11	49	58	6.94	2	8	11.96	1.06	4.73	5.59	0.42	6.36

Extra Players

PLAYER	AGE	TEAM	LGE	IP	H	ER	HR	BB	K	ERA	W	L	H/9	HR/9	BB/9	K/9	KWH	PERA
Corey Spiers	23	FtMyers	Fla	136.7	228	87	9	45	67	5.73	5	10	15.01	0.59	2.96	4.41	0.33	6.91
Jay Spurgeon	21	Delmarva	SAL	126.7	153	60	10	58	62	4.26	7	7	10.87	0.71	4.12	4.41	0.32	5.12
Paul Stabile	22	Augusta	SAL	116.7	158	106	18	65	75	8.18	3	10	12.19	1.39	5.01	5.79	0.41	7.02
Jason Stephens	22	LkElsin	Cal	112.0	171	86	9	52	57	6.91	3	9	13.74	0.72	4.18	4.58	0.27	6.83
Kris Stevens	20	1Reading	Eas	148.7	179	94	10	69	89	5.69	6	11	10.84	0.61	4.18	5.39	0.48	5.02
Jason Stevenson	24	Knoxvill	Sou	129.7	185	84	17	46	73	5.83	4	10	12.84	1.18	3.19	5.07	0.47	6.39
Paul Stewart	19	Beloit	Mid	135.7	212	110	29	51	76	7.30	3	12	14.06	1.92	3.38	5.04	0.40	8.09
Jason Stockstill	21	LkElsin	Cal	92.0	145	73	13	48	51	7.14	2	8	14.18	1.27	4.70	4.99	0.28	7.92
Dave Swartzbaugh	30	Iowa	PCL	131.7	130	61	15	51	85	4.17	7	8	8.89	1.03	3.49	5.81	0.82	4.17
Craig Taczy	21	SanBern	Cal	117.0	198	112	11	71	55	8.62	2	11	15.23	0.85	5.46	4.23	0.16	8.38
Kerry Taylor	27	Toledo	Int	109.3	159	81	17	57	75	6.67	3	9	13.09	1.40	4.69	6.17	0.47	7.41
Nathan Teut	22	Rockford	Mid	92.3	147	69	13	28	42	6.73	3	7	14.33	1.27	2.73	4.09	0.32	7.21
Travis Thompson	23	Ashevlle	SAL	134.3	222	93	12	51	61	6.23	4	11	14.87	0.80	3.42	4.09	0.25	7.30
Todd Thorn	21	Wilmngtn	Car	140.7	165	72	16	33	70	4.61	7	9	10.56	1.02	2.11	4.48	0.67	4.54
Brian Tokarse	23	LkElsin	Cal	111.3	205	117	9	49	59	9.46	2	10	16.57	0.73	3.96	4.77	0.26	8.49
Brian Tollberg	25	LasVegas	PCL	110.0	143	73	19	28	86	5.97	4	8	11.70	1.55	2.29	7.04	1.39	5.81
Ben Tucker	24	SanJose	Cal	96.3	149	80	12	41	39	7.47	2	9	13.92	1.12	3.83	3.64	0.19	7.29
Jimmy Turman	22	1CapeFear	SAL	98.3	182	92	13	39	44	8.42	2	9	16.66	1.19	3.57	4.03	0.20	8.97
Mark Turnbow	19	Columbus	SAL	86.0	124	53	10	31	46	5.55	3	7	12.98	1.05	3.24	4.81	0.41	6.38
Chris Tynan	19	Savannah	SAL	106.7	155	82	13	88	59	6.92	3	9	13.08	1.10	7.43	4.98	0.19	8.18
Tomoyuki Uchiyama	29	Reading	Eas	114.7	156	59	13	53	68	4.63	6	7	12.24	1.02	4.16	5.34	0.42	6.28
Tim Vanegmond	29	Louisvil	Int	126.7	152	72	22	43	80	5.12	5	9	10.80	1.56	3.06	5.68	0.73	5.61
Mike Vavrek	24	NewHavn	Eas	106.3	179	95	26	52	51	8.04	2	10	15.15	2.20	4.40	4.32	0.21	9.65
Dustin Viator	22	Clinton	Mid	85.0	152	82	6	41	42	8.68	2	7	16.09	0.64	4.34	4.45	0.21	8.26
Ismael Villegas	21	Greenvil	Sou	124.3	149	67	12	59	96	4.85	6	8	10.79	0.87	4.27	6.95	0.79	5.28
Adam Virchis	24	WnstnSlm	Car	94.3	149	76	12	28	44	7.25	2	8	14.22	1.14	2.67	4.20	0.35	6.96
Mike Walker	31	Indianap	Int	100.0	98	48	6	46	51	4.32	5	6	8.82	0.54	4.14	4.59	0.43	3.87
Tyler Walker	22	Columbia	SAL	106.0	168	77	10	49	64	6.54	3	9	14.26	0.85	4.16	5.43	0.37	7.30
Clint Weibl	23	Arkansas	Tex	129.3	192	88	21	55	66	6.12	4	10	13.36	1.46	3.83	4.59	0.31	7.31
Matt Wells	23	Bakrsfld	Cal	95.7	141	74	12	53	43	6.96	3	8	13.26	1.13	4.99	4.05	0.19	7.34
Marty Weymouth	20	Hickory	SAL	104.7	165	85	8	38	62	7.31	3	9	14.19	0.69	3.27	5.33	0.46	6.71
Dan Wheeler	20	Charl-SC	SAL	167.0	277	116	19	34	85	6.25	6	13	14.93	1.02	1.83	4.58	0.58	6.90
Curtis Whitley	24	Hickory	SAL	94.3	174	106	8	84	45	10.11	1	9	16.60	0.76	8.01	4.29	0.10	10.30
Jeff Williams	29	Albuquer	PCL	124.0	163	73	12	50	74	5.30	5	9	11.83	0.87	3.63	5.37	0.50	5.66
Matt Williams	27	Norwich	Eas	152.0	228	105	15	72	79	6.22	5	12	13.50	0.89	4.26	4.68	0.29	6.93
Kris Wilson	21	Lansing	Mid	109.7	162	63	10	18	48	5.17	4	8	13.29	0.82	1.48	3.94	0.59	5.58
Trevor Wilson	32	Vancouvr	PCL	131.0	153	70	13	59	72	4.81	6	9	10.51	0.89	4.05	4.95	0.43	5.08
Shannon Withem	25	Syracuse	Int	181.7	209	77	13	55	91	3.81	10	10	10.35	0.64	2.72	4.51	0.54	4.26
Kerry Woodson	29	ColSprin	PCL	98.7	109	60	4	68	41	5.47	4	7	9.94	0.36	6.20	3.74	0.17	5.11
Finley Woodward	22	Peoria	Mid	122.3	230	122	19	78	56	8.98	2	12	16.92	1.40	5.74	4.12	0.13	10.37
Widd Workman	24	RCucmng	Cal	95.3	156	111	9	65	40	10.48	1	10	14.73	0.85	6.14	3.78	0.12	8.40
Jeff Yoder	22	Daytona	Fla	141.7	186	97	19	54	94	6.16	5	11	11.82	1.21	3.43	5.97	0.66	5.91

Index

About the Authors

Clay Davenport got hooked on baseball analysis in the mid-1980s by Bill James's *Baseball Abstracts* and Pete Palmer's *Hidden Game of Baseball*. Since then he's spent too much time, in the opinion of his family and friends, doing just that instead of real work. He currently resides in Washington, D.C., and writes computer routines for weather forecasting at NOAA.

Rany Jazayerli is completing his final year of medical school at the University of Michigan, and is currently trying to squeeze his way into the ridiculously competitive field of dermatology. (If you happen to be on faculty in a dermatology department, I've got a strong work ethic and establish a good rapport with patients. And I make a really good cup of coffee.) When he's not on the interview trail, he lives in Ann Arbor with his ever-patient wife, Belsam.

Chris Kahrl works in publishing, running the business end of an academic press in Chicago. He's finishing up his master's degree in public history at Loyola University. When not finding ways to amuse his wife, he spends his time loathing the minivan menace that blights America's suburbs. He remains convinced that everything you need to know about life beyond baseball is best figured out on horseback.

Keith Law will receive his MBA from Carnegie Mellon University in May. He lives in Pittsburgh with his wife, Christa.

Dave Pease attends school and works for a wireless communications company in San Diego. He's also working on a pilot for an animated series, and enjoys working on his darts game with his limited edition Rupert Murdoch dartboard in his free time.

Steven Rubio is a lecturer in American studies and English at the University of California at Berkeley. A Giants fan since 1958, he will miss Candlestick Park when it's gone.

Joseph S. Sheehan is an analyst and freelance writer. He lives in Huntington Beach, California, with his wife Sophia, a marriage and family therapist. She's the smart one.

Michael Wolverton has been interested in baseball analysis ever since he learned what they meant by "ERA" on the back of his baseball cards. Between baseball projects in recent years, he's found time to get a Ph.D. in computer science, become a Grammy-winning recording artist, and enjoy the relative success of the two teams from his native Texas. He works as a research scientist in the San Francisco Bay Area, where he lives with his wife, Cindy, and son, Scott.

Keith Woolner works as a product manager in Silicon Valley, mostly for money to feed his baseball book fetish. He also maintains Stathead.com, a website dedicated to baseball research, moderates rec.sport.baseball.analysis, manages the Boston Red Sox mailing list, and travels the world smiting "intangibles" heretics wherever they may be found. He double-majored at MIT, earned a master's degree from Stanford University.